Encyclopedia of
Modern Asia

Editorial
Board

Encyclopedia of
Modern Asia

Volume 1
Abacus to China

A Berkshire Reference Work
David Levinson · Karen Christensen, Editors

CHARLES SCRIBNER'S SONS®

New York • Detroit • San Diego • San Francisco • Cleveland • New Haven, Conn. • Waterville, Maine • London • Munich

Encyclopedia of Modern Asia

David Levinson and Karen Christensen, Editors

Copyright © 2002 Berkshire Publishing Group

Charles Scribner's Sons
An imprint of The Gale Group
300 Park Avenue South
New York, NY 10010

Gale and Design™ and Thomson Learning™ are trademark s used herein under license.

For more information, contact
The Gale Group, Inc.
27500 Drake Rd.
Farmington Hills, MI 48331–3535
Or you can visit our Internet site at
http://www.gale.com

LIBRARY OF CONGRESS CATALOGING-IN-PUBLICATION DATA

Levinson, David, 1947-
  Encyclopedia of modern Asia : / David Levinson, Karen Christensen,
    p. cm.
Includes bibliographical references and index.
  ISBN 0-684-80617-7 (set hardcover : alk. paper)
  1. Asia—Encyclopedias. I. Christensen, Karen, 1957- II. Title.
  DS4 .L48 2002
  950'.03—dc21

                                                                      2002008712

Printed in United States of America
3 5 7 9 11 13 15 17 19 20 18 16 14 12 10 8 6 4 2

Editorial and Production Staff

Contents

Volume 1

List of Maps ix
Preface xi
Acknowledgments xxi
Survey of Asia's Regions and Nations xxv
Regional Maps xxxiii
Reader's Guide xxxix
Abacus to *China*

Volume 2

List of Maps vii
Survey of Asia's Regions and Nations ix
Regional Maps xvii
Reader's Guide xxiii
China-India Relations to *Hyogo*

Volume 3

List of Maps vii
Survey of Asia's Regions and Nations ix
Regional Maps xvii
Reader's Guide xxiii
Iaido to *Malay-Indonesian Language*

Volume 4

List of Maps vii
Survey of Asia's Regions and Nations ix
Regional Maps xvii
Reader's Guide xxiii
Malaysia to *Portuguese in Southeast Asia*

Volume 5

List of Maps vii
Survey of Asia's Regions and Nations ix
Regional Maps xvii
Reader's Guide xxiii
Possession to *Turkey*

Volume 6

List of Maps vii
Survey of Asia's Regions and Nations ix
Regional Maps xvii
Reader's Guide xxiii
Turkic Languages to *Zuo Zongtang*
Directory of Contributors 225
Index 271

List of Maps

Front Matter of All Volumes
Central Asia
China and East Asia
South Asia
Southeast Asia—Insular
Southeast Asia—Mainland
West and Southwest Asia

Volume 1
Afghanistan 21
Altay Mountains 89
Amu Dar'ya 94
Andaman and Nicobar Islands 101
Aral Sea 122
Armenia 159
Azerbaijan 205
Bangladesh 237
Bay of Bengal 269
Bhutan 287
Borneo 308
Brahmaputra River 317
Brunei 329
Cambodia 408
Caucasus 449
Chang River 488
China 504

Volume 2
East Timor 314
Euphrates and Tigris .352
Fergana Valley 375
Ganges River 423
Gobi Desert 438
Great Wall 449
Gulf of Thailand 461
Himalayas 513

Hong Kong 548
Huang River 558

Volume 3
India 9
Indonesia 53
Indus River 77
Iran 96
Iraq 123
Irian Jaya 144
Irrawaddy River 147
Jammu and Kashmir .203
Japan 207
Java and Bali 267
Kalimantan 302
Karakoram Highway .317
Kara-Kum Canal 319
Kara-Kum Desert 320
Kazakhstan 337
Killing Fields—Cambodia (1999) 369
Kyrgyzstan 424
Laos 443
Luzon 530
Macao 532

Volume 4
Malaysia 3
Maldives 22
Mauritius 86
Mekong River and Delta 136
Mindanao 148
Mongolia 165
Myanmar (Burma) 245
Nepal 307
North Korea 348
Pakistan 424

Pamir Range 457
Persian Gulf 480
Philippines 492

Volume 5
Red River and Delta 60
Réunion 82
Sarawak 130
Siberia 195
Silk Road 208
Singapore 212
South Korea 270
Spratly Islands 314
Sri Lanka 317
Strait of Malacca 339

Sumatra 354
Syr Dar'ya 362
Taiwan 380
Tajikistan 394
Taklimakan Desert 406
Thailand 452
Tian Shan 481
Tibet (Xizang) 484
Tonle Sap 513
Turkey 540

Volume 6
Turkmenistan 7
Uzbekistan 43
Vietnam 60

Preface

The *Encyclopedia of Modern Asia* is an unprecedented effort at global understanding. With a readership of students and nonspecialists in mind, a team of more than eight hundred scholars and other experts from around the world has compiled this six-volume, 2.2-million-word publication. In it, we explore economics, religion, technology, politics, education, the family, the arts, environmental issues, international relations, scientific advances, and other vital aspects of the Asian experience that will shape the twenty-first century. The Encyclopedia explains the relationship of Asia to the rest of the world through its extensive coverage of the historical exchange of ideas and inventions. Most important, it provides a variety of perspectives on issues and events, and encompasses the past and the present of Asia in an authoritative and fully cross-disciplinary work.

To provide the comprehensive view needed by students and scholars in our global age, the Encyclopedia takes the broad and dynamic view of Asian history and culture that does not make false assumptions about Asian unity or uniformity, but allows us to look for continuity and diversity, change and variation, across and beyond this vast territory.

The Encyclopedia contains over 2,600 entries, which range from 200 to 4,000 words. The text is supplemented by 1,300 illustrations, tables, and sidebars of mainly primary-source materials; 90 maps; topical and regional outlines; and an extensive index. Articles have been written by experts from more than a dozen scholarly disciplines, from fields including banking, economic development, law, and human rights, and from more than sixty nations.

Our goal when we began this project with Charles Scribner's Sons in 1998 was to make the *Encyclopedia of Modern Asia* the standard reference work on Asia. Much has happened in Asia since then—the Asian economic crisis of 1997–1998 (the effects of which remain), the September 11th terrorist attack on the United States in 2001 and subsequent invasion of Afghanistan and war on terrorism, and increased fighting in the Middle East—to name just a few.

After September 11, 2001, people were fascinated by the fact that three years earlier we came up with the idea for this project, complete with coverage of the Central Asian republics, the Taliban, and many articles on Islam. "Were you smart or lucky?" someone asked. Our small publishing company's mission is to focus on the "global experience and contemporary issues." Our first publication after September 11 was the *Encyclopedia of Fundamentalism*, followed by the *Encyclopedia of Crime and Punishment*, and now the *Encyclopedia of Modern Asia*.

Four years ago we had no idea that terrible, dramatic events would have Americans riveted by information on the religion and culture of Islam, or that bookstores would be selling Afghanistan maps by their cash registers. We did know that Asia was important and not well understood. We found its diversity and complexity absorbing. It's been thrilling to work with Asia scholars all over the world, even though we've dealt with threats that e-mail service in Turkmenistan would be stopped by the government, contributors' worries about political repercussions, and a variety of linguistic and cultural barriers.

As new political and economic conflicts—and opportunities—develop worldwide, and international trade barriers come down, and as there is an increasing migration and exchange of people and ideas, the *Encyclopedia of Modern Asia* will be a vital source of reliable and accessible information on the events, ideas, and issues that are shaping our future. The readership we have in mind is not just scholars and students but also journalists, businesspeople, governmental officials, and tourists.

Our essential purpose has been, since the first time we discussed this ambitious and sometimes nearly overwhelming project, to provide readers with information and knowledge about modern Asia from an Asian perspective. This immediately raises several questions about what readers will find in the *Encyclopedia of Modern Asia*. What is information? What is knowledge? What is Asia? What is modern Asia? What is an Asian perspective?

What Are Information and Knowledge?

In the age of rapid information availability via the Internet, understanding and appreciating the distinction between information and knowledge is crucial to making our way in the global community. Information and knowledge are both valuable, but they are not the same thing, and in the end only knowledge will enable the citizens of the twenty-first century to work together to create a better world.

By information we mean facts—dates, places, people, events, statistics—about who, what, where, and when. In the Encyclopedia you will find tens of thousands of facts, as our goal is always to provide information about the who, what, where, and when of modern Asia. Some of these facts stand alone, others paint a broad picture when combined with other facts, and still others provide context for deeper analysis and discussion.

By knowledge we mean information that has been organized, combined, studied, analyzed, and synthesized to answer questions about how and why. Here, you will find much knowledge, primarily in the form of articles by hundreds of international experts. These articles provide comprehensive, up-to-date, and authoritative discussions of the key elements of the history and culture of modern Asia.

What Is Asia?

By Asia we mean the thirty-three nations that comprise the subregions of East Asia, Southeast Asia, South Asia, Central Asia, and West-Southwest Asia. Geographically, these nations range from Japan in the east to Turkey in the west and from Kazakhstan in the north to Indonesia in the south. Temporally, Asia includes nations and civilizations that are several thousand years old, such as China, Japan, and Iran (ancient Persia); nations that came into being as nation-states only in the twentieth century, such as Turkey and Singapore, and one nation—East Timor—that is brand new.

The use of the label Asia in this work is not meant to imply that there is one Asia nor to mask the significant variations that exist both across the region and between and even within nations. In fact, quite the opposite is the case. The Encyclopedia emphasizes diversity, with attention given to each region and each nation.

One cannot exaggerate just how diverse Asia is in language, religion, economy, form of government, history, and culture. It is more diverse and has less political and economic unity than any other region in the world today. There is no single historical or modern feature that defines or unites all of Asia.

In Asia, there is no religion like Christianity, which has long provided unity across Europe and the New World. Islam is the most widespread religion in the region, but is a minority religion in several large nations such as Japan, India, China, and the Philippines, and the majority of people in Asia are not Muslims. Buddhism is the major religion in East and mainland Southeast Asia but is no longer prominent in Central Asia and never was in West Asia. Western colonialism also did not produce regional unity as it has in parts of Africa. Asia was never colonized by one nation, although British influence was the broadest and in places the deepest. China has had much influence in East and northern Southeast Asia, but little in Central and West Asia. Asian colonization by the Mongols moving south and west, Hindu Indians moving east, and the Chinese moving south and east has had subregional rather than regional influence.

Every form of government has been found, and many still can be found, across Asia—theocracies, monarchies, constitutional monarchies, stable democracies, emerging democracies, communist states, and military dictatorships. Although Asian nations are members of the United Nations, there is no pan-regional body that is the equivalent of NATO, the European Union, the Organization of American States, or the Organization of African Unity. In fact, it is subregional associations like NATO for Turkey, ASEAN for Southeast Asian nations, and CIS for Central Asian nations which are especially important today.

The economy is also diverse, often within nations and across the region. In much of southern Asia and the east, wet-rice agriculture and village and family life based on it have been a powerful unifying force. But elsewhere, in rural areas, we find other primary subsistence methods including nomadic pastoralism, the farming of wheat and barley, horticulture, hunting, and fishing. In modern times, Asian nations have experienced very different patterns of economic development, with some relying on a single resource, such as oil, natural gas, or timber. Others rely on industrialized farming, while still others reply on manufacturing and others on a service-based economy. Asia houses the poorest nation in the world (Afghanistan), the second-leading economy (Japan), and the fastest-growing economy (China). Within nations, there is much difference in wealth between rural and urban areas and also in many nations with an emerging and increasingly influential middle class.

Culturally and linguistically, the region is again the most complex in the world. As the dozens of articles on languages show, there are thousands of languages spoken across Asia and within several nations (for example, India, China, Indonesia) people speak many different languages. Asia is also home to at least a thousand different cultural groups, some of whom have never been studied closely. India and Indonesia have several hundred each, China has at least fifty-five, and even ethnically homogeneous nations such as Japan and Iran have visible ethnic minorities.

The nations of Asia also vary in the amount of freedom of expression they afford their citizens. Some nations—Iran, Iraq, China, Vietnam—are considered to be quite restrictive in this regard. This had important implications, as it limited the number of experts from these nations who would agree to write for the project. Several authors made it clear that their contributions were for scholarly purposes only, and one asked that his article be published without attribution.

Perhaps the one factor common to all of Asia in 2002 is contact with the West and reactions to Westernization. The different regions of Asia feel the effects of Westernization differently and respond to it differently, but it is an issue all of Asia faces. And, to a significant degree, how it is dealt with will have much to do with the nature of Asia in the twenty-first century.

It must be noted that there are several nations and regions not covered here in detail that some experts might classify as belonging in Asia: the Caucasus or Caucasia, Siberia, and Australia. Caucasia and Siberia are covered in several articles, but not in the same detail as other regions, mainly because most experts agree that from a cultural and political perspective they are better classified as being in Europe. Australia, too, though it now has close ties to several Asian nations and a growing Asian population, is politically, linguistically, and culturally European. Thus, it is not covered in detail although its relations with Asian nations are well covered. Also not covered in detail are several West Asian nations—Lebanon, Syria, Jordan, Israel and the nations of the Arabian peninsula—which are geographically part of Asia. They are not covered in detail for both conceptual and practical reasons. Conceptually, they form much of a separate region known as the Middle East, a region defined by Arab culture and Islam. The three nations of the Middle East covered here—Turkey, Iran, and Iraq—are part of what used to be called the Near East and in several ways are tied to Asia to the east. And from a practical standpoint, we realized early on that six volumes is still very little space to cover all of Asia and so we restricted breadth of coverage so as not to compromise depth of coverage.

One factor in choosing not to include the other Middle Eastern nations was the point made by expert advisers that we would also have to cover North Africa, which is culturally and politically part of the Middle East. A second consideration was the availability of reference material on these nations. In 1996 Macmillan published its four-volume *Encyclopedia of the Modern Middle East*, which provides excellent coverage of these nations.

Because we take a dynamic, international relations perspective, the Encyclopedia also covers many nations outside Asia. For example, the many articles about relations between Asian nations and the United States and about Asian nations and Europe or European nations, tell us much about the United States and Europe today. Similarly, the many articles on economics and commerce emphasize both the international and regional dimensions, a significant consideration in this time of rapid globalization.

What Is Modern Asia?
Now that we have defined Asia, what do we mean by modern Asia? Not surprisingly, there is no single date that marks the transition to modern—if such a date actually exists at all—that applies to all nations. Early on in the project, the year 1850 was suggested by historians as a reasonable date, but we do not apply it systematically across Asia. From a temporal point of view, we have focused on Asia in the twentieth century and on those earlier events that have continuing impact today. Because Asian nations have rich and deep histories and much cultural continuity over time, many articles cover people, places, events, developments, trends, and ideas of the past.

Our conceptualization of modern Asia is dynamic and interactional and stresses those points in recent Asian history when Asian nations became more open to contact with other nations both in the region and beyond. This, of course, varies widely from nation to nation, and in fact some nations, such as Iran and Afghanistan, have in recent times moved to restrict contact with the outside world. Nonetheless, this emphasis on interactions and relationships is an important defining feature of our meaning of "modern" and also a defining and unique focus of this work. It is the reason that there are over one hundred articles on relationships between nations (such as China—India Relations and Japan—United States Relations), dozens of articles on trade, articles on environmental issues across the continent, surveys of human rights, and articles on the media, tourism, and Asian communities outside Asia.

Conceptually, this encyclopedia takes a modern world systems view of Asia, with Asian nations and the institutions in them seen as increasingly significant participants in regional and international economic, political, and cultural networks. This approach allows us to extensively cover topics ignored or given less attention in earlier reference works on Asia: contemporary political and business dynasties, international business networks, economic development, the changing roles of women, human rights, migration, regional and subregional alliances, and ethnic relations.

What Is an Asian Perspective?

When we first began discussing this project with scholars, several told us that they were concerned that other works took a Western perspective and they wanted this work to be different—to describe and explain Asia as Asians see and experience it. We knew that this was what we wanted to do: provide a fresh view of a vital part of the world, a view that would enable students to travel, intellectually and imaginatively, to the heart of Asia.

Our determination to provide an Asian perspective—in addition to explaining the Western perspective—influenced the project's development on a practical level. First, we included many articles on topics that do not translate neatly into English. This is why there are several dozen articles with Asian terms as their titles, such as *chaebol*, *juche*, *bedaya*, and *kyoiku mama*.

Second, it meant that we had to cover the diversity of Asia. We did this in several ways, by, for example, including separate articles on the same phenomenon in different places or forms. The dozens of articles on Islam, Buddhism, and Christianity across Asia reflect this diversity. We also included general survey articles on several topics—history, politics, economy, human rights, women, marriage and family, education—for each nation or subregion. These articles highlight both similarities and differences and make cross-nation and -region comparisons easy and quick. By including hundreds of articles on specific topics such as puppetry, sumo, haiku, and batik, we are able to highlight unique cultural, political, and economic features of all the nations. Finally, we ensured diversity by recruiting an international team of editors and authors—nearly nine hundred in all from more than sixty nations.

All of the above decisions were "field-tested" in April 2001 by we two editors and our two children, aged twelve and fifteen, on a month-long trip to Japan, China, and Kazakhstan. Through contacts made during the project, we knew people in all three nations and through their hospitality we were able to sample life in these nations in a way not possible for many travelers.

Our trip began during the week in 2001 when the United States and China were acrimoniously negotiating over a grounded U.S. spy plane and its twenty-four-member crew. It was soon after the sinking of the Ehime Maru, a Japanese fishing boat, by a U.S. nuclear submarine. As we drove to the airport, it occurred to us that the destination we were on best terms with was Kazakhstan.

In Beijing we had meetings with contributors to the encyclopedia, executives at an Internet company, and an editor at the *People's Daily*, which is based in grounds guarded by soldiers. We spoke to the Rotary Club in Almaty, Kazakhstan. Our final few days were spent in Kyoto, Japan, in the tranquil setting of Amherst House, on the Doshisha University campus. "I might want to be an expat," said our daughter Rachel reflectively.

We managed without tour guides and were the only westerners on most of our flights (some of which were delayed—we were glad we brought a spare suitcase of paperback books). We still talk about the day we got a taxi to take us to Heaven Lake, in the mountains north of Urumqi in the far west of China. Negotiation with the driver centered around a tiny map in my guidebook and my memory of the Chinese name for the mountains. He and the hotel doorman seemed to know where we wanted to go, but as we left the doorman waved and said politely, "Hoping to see you again some day."

In China and Japan we sampled the traditional and the modern, although the modern was far more ubiquitous in Japan. The mix of old and new is perhaps most striking in Beijing where broad shopping streets lined with modern department stores and shops are just around the corner from traditional courtyards (hutong) fronted by tiny food stalls with dirt floors. It is also apparent in comparing rural and urban life and life in the rapidly developing Beijing region and in the less-developed Xinjiang province in the far west. In Kyoto, Japan, the old and new is more neatly structured with steel and glass office complexes standing alongside ancient Shinto shrines and Buddhist temples. In Kazakhstan we witnessed the issues involved in making the transition from a state to a private economy with dramatic inequalities of wealth, deteriorating public services, and a grab-it-while-you-can attitude. We also learned of the work of Western medical missionaries trying to fill a health care gap so wide that the rural poor often die from serious, but treatable, illnesses.

In all three nations we were continually aware of the Western and especially, the American, presence, and often had to consciously act so as to avoid it. In Almaty, Kazakhstan, there is the TexasKazakh Bank, an "Outback" steakhouse, and three luxurious and brand new hotels serving the international business community. In Beijing, major street signs are in English and Chinese and throughout the nation much is done to make travel easy for tourists. In China we talked with several young men who spoke a bit of English and were eager to learn more. One of these young men guided an English couple and us through the intricacies of changing money at a bank in return for the opportunity to speak English for an hour. And in Kyoto, it was hard not to feel that one was in a smaller, neater, more polite United States.

By talking to people in all three nations we also learned the deep mistrust that pervades much of foreign relations in Asia. Some Japanese seem to view the Chinese as backward and uncultured, and also as a threat to Japanese economic dominance in East Asia. The Chinese have yet to forget their treatment at the hands of the Japanese before and during World War II. And, the Kazakhs worry at any moment the Chinese will invade to obtain Kazakhstan's mineral riches.

At the same time, there are friendly exchanges among the nations. We saw many Japanese tourists in China and Chinese students in Japan. And the planes from Urumqi, China, to Almaty, Kazkahstan, were filled with Russian Kazakhs on shopping trips to China, where goods are much cheaper.

The contradictions and complexities we experienced gave us new enthusiasm for the coverage we were providing in the Encyclopedia of Modern Asia and a fresh appreciation for the challenges faced by scholars trying to explain in clear, accessible English the sheer variety, volatility, and vitality of the Asia of the twenty-first century.

Content and Types of Articles

The *Encyclopedia of Modern Asia* provides coverage of the following general topics:

Arts, Literature, and Recreation

Clothing

Cuisine

Economics, Commerce, and Transportation

Education

Ethnicity

Geography and the Natural World

Government, Politics, and Law

History and Profile

Human Rights

International Relations

Language and Communication

Marriage and Family

Media

People, Cultures, and Society

Provinces and Cities

Regional and International Relations

Religion and Philosophy

Science, Technology, and Health

Significant People

For all of these topics there are both long and short articles, articles that focus on unique elements of a single nation or region, and general articles that allow comparisons across nations and regions. There are also several dozen pan-Asia articles, such as those on environmental issues, on organizations (United Nations, IMF) whose actions affect all of Asia, on events that impacted the entire continent (such as World War II), on relations between Asia and other parts of the world, and on pan-Asian trends concerning issues such as fertility and AIDS. In order to facilitate both understanding of each nation and comparisons across nations, we have included a standard list of articles for each nation or each region. For each nation or each subregion you will find articles on the political system, economic system, history, education system, human rights, cuisine, clothing, literature, arts, music, religion, marriage and family, international relations, marriage and family, media, women, and Westernization.

Additional Content

The Encyclopedia is enriched by maps, photos, and sidebars, which provide information not included in the articles themselves.

The maps are meant to help the reader locate places mentioned in the entries. There are a general map of Asia and maps of each region in the front matter of each volume. Each nation—profile article (such as Bangladesh—Profile) includes a political map of the nation showing cities, natural features, and provinces as required. Other maps show the location of particular places, such as major rivers or lakes and accompany the entries on those topics.

The photographs provide images of places, peoples, events mentioned in the text, and examples of important features of Asian life. They are meant to provide readers with another form of information about Asia and were carefully selected from the vast Corbis collection and from the private collection of Stephen G. Donaldson, who spent eighteen months photographing Asia from 1996 to 1998.

The sidebars are an especially important part of the Encyclopedia. The content in the sidebars is meant to supplement the articles and provide readers with additional resources on Asia. The sidebars are of ten different types:

1. Extracts of text from historical documents, such as agreements, treaties, and conventions that provide readers with primary source documentation for significant events in the history, politics, and international relations of Asian nations.

2. Extracts of text from ethnography that provide readers with first-hand accounts of daily life and the cultures and customs of Asian peoples.

3. Extracts from the literature, poetry, drama, and religious texts of Asia that allow readers to experience the broad and deep literary traditions of Asia.

4. Recipes for dishes for all major Asian cuisines that enable readers to enjoy the riches and variety of Asian life by cooking Asian dishes themselves.

5. Up-to-date statistical profiles of each nation that provide readers with a snapshot of the nation and allow easy comparisons across nations.

6. The preambles to national constitutions, which accompany the Nation—Political System articles. These allow readers to experience the philosophy that forms the ideological basis for the nation.

7. Timelines that trace the history of nations and major eras and historical periods and that allow readers to quickly place events in their historical context.

8. Accounts by early travelers and settlers (mainly European) of life in Asia that provide readers with insights into how and why the European or Western image of Asia developed as it did.

9. Notations for the approximately one hundred places described in the encyclopedia that are designated by the United Nations as World Heritage Sites. These notations assist tourists in selecting sites to visit and in learning more about them.

10. Text written for the encyclopedia that highlights especially significant or interesting facts or that provides additional information.

Using the *Encyclopedia of Modern Asia*

The Encyclopedia is a complex work, and to help readers make most effective use of it, we have provided several user aids. Perhaps most important are the comprehensive index in Volume 6 and the Reader's Guide at the front of each volume. The index helps readers find articles on related topics across the encyclopedia, while the Reader's Guide helps readers find articles on related topics for each nation and region. In addition, there are more than one-hundred blind entries that direct readers to relevant articles as well as cross-references at the end of many articles.

We have also tried to help readers in the manner in which we have organized the articles. The basic organization is A to Z from Volume 1 through Volume 6. Within this structure we have tried to group related articles together. For example, all basic survey articles on each nation are found under the nation's name (for example, Pakistan—Profile, Pakistan—Economic System, Pakistan—Political System, and so forth). Also all major articles on a topic are placed together (for example, Islam—Myanmar, Islam—South Asia; Islam—Southeast Asia, and so forth).

Finally, we have considered the needs of readers in the editorial and style decisions we made. Most importantly, we have made considerable effort to standardize spelling of places and names despite the considerable diversity of such spellings in the literature. Nonetheless, standardization is not complete as some contributors insisted that particular spellings be used. Also of much importance was our decision after much discussion and consultation with experts to not include diacritics except for the ayn and hamza used in Arabic, Persian, and related languages. (Our language articles are exceptions to this rule, as to express linguistic points it is often absolutely essential to use diacritics.) Our decision was based in part on the needs of general users who, we learned, are intimidated by diacritics which they do not understand. Our hope is that by letting general readers experience the richness of the Asian experience without the barrier of diacritics, we may draw people to further study—at which point they will be able to learn the complexities of the many often conflicting methods of representing Asian languages in English.

Another issue was how to order the names of people covered or mentioned in the Encyclopedia. Our first principle in listing people was to list them by the significant identifying portion of their name. For most nationalities and ethnic groups, this is the family name. Because European and American family names come after the personal name, this means that European and American people are listed in the traditional inverted fashion familiar to users of catalogues and reference materials (for example, John Smith becomes Smith, John). Because Chinese, Japanese, and Korean family names come before the personal name, on the other hand, most entries for Chinese, Japanese, or Korean figures are listed in their traditional order, with no comma, as no inversion has occurred (so Mao Zedong is listed as Mao Zedong, not Mao, Zedong). In Thailand it is customary to identify people by their personal name rather than their family name, therefore Thai figures can be found under their personal name, with their family name coming second and no intervening comma.

In the case of certain very well-known figures, however, a second principle came into play; namely, that we wanted to list people in the way that most readers would think to search for them. In some cases this second principle has led to deviations from the first principle. In all cases where there is ambiguity about a name or multiple well-known spellings of a name (for instance, Genghis Khan versus Chinggis Khan), we have included blind entries to direct the reader to our listing of the figure in question.

Final Thoughts

Massive as this publication is, it is by no means the last word on Asia. We have felt constrained by space limitations as we learned more about the intricacies of regional relations in Asia and beyond and about the ever-present links between the past and the present and the future. In addition, as more nations, such as those in Central Asia, open up to more outside study, our knowledge of Asia will grow and change. For example, more and more Central Asian scholars are studying their nations, and their work is replacing that of previous generations of Russian scholars.

Although this is a work produced by scholars and experts, it is intended for a broad audience. We hope that journalists, tourists, government officials, writers, teachers, and the general reading public will find something of interest and use. We welcome suggestions and corrections, and further information about modern Asia. Please write to us at asiainfo@berkshirepublishing.com.

David Levinson and Karen Christensen
Berkshire Publishing Group
http://www.Berkshirepublishing.com

Acknowledgments

T he purpose of this section is to explain the division of labor for the project and to publicly acknowledge and thank the many people who contributed to the project.

The *Encyclopedia of Modern Asia* took nearly four years to organize and produce and involved the efforts of more than eight hundred people around the world. The first acknowledgment must go to editor Karen Christensen, CEO of Berkshire Publishing Group, who conceived the idea of a general encyclopedia on modern Asia and has served as a steadying influence and the project's senior diplomat throughout its development. Her childhood passion for everything Japanese led to her trying to persuade her Minnesotan father to move the family to Japan instead of the Silicon Valley in 1968, so the encyclopedia has become the culmination of lifelong interest.

I served as senior project director and took primary responsibility for shaping the scope of the work, creating consistency across countries and regions, stepping in to deal with certain articles, reviewing articles as necessary, and managing the sidebar, photo, and map research. As a cultural anthropologist and editor, I welcomed the opportunity to work again with some of the contributors to the *Encyclopedia of World Cultures* and *Encyclopedia of Cultural Anthropology*, as well as with scholars from a wide variety of fields.

In the early discussion stages of the project, several people were especially helpful, not all of whom became involved with or remained with the project. They are Virginia Aksan (McMaster University), Doris G. Bargen (University of Massachusetts, Amherst), Thomas Headland (Summer Institute of Linguistics), Paul Hockings (University of Illinois, Chicago), Jennifer Jay (University of Alberta), Anatoly Khazanov (University of Wisconsin), Uli Schamiloglu (University of Wisconsin), Caroline Herrick (editor of *Persimmon: Asian Literature, Arts, and Culture*), Jonathan Benthall (Royal Anthropological Institute, London), the late Douglas Pike (Texas Tech University), and William McNeill (Emeritus, University of Chicago).

The editors and associate editors played a major role in selecting topics for coverage, recommending contributors, and reviewing articles. Editors are Virginia Aksan (McMaster University), Edward Beauchamp (University of Hawaii, Honolulu), Anthony and Rebecca Bichel (Central Michigan University and Pennsylvania State University), Linsun Cheng (University of Massachusetts, Dartmouth), Gerald Fry (University of Minnesota), Bruce Fulton (University of British Columbia), Paul Hockings (University of Illinois, Chicago), and Robert LaPorte, Jr. (Pennsylvania State

University). The associate editors are Linda Arthur (University of Hawaii, Manoa), Jamal Elias (Amherst College), Allen Guttmann (Amherst College), Josie Hernandez de Leon (Laurentian University), Gustaaf Houtman (Royal Anthropological Institute, London), Bruce Lockhart (Singapore National University), Patit Mishra (Sambalpur University), and Anthony Smith (Institute of Southeast Asian Studies).

Editorial board members also advised on numerous editorial issues, and Bruce Fulton, Gerald Fry, and Josie Hernandez de Leon must be thanked for their wise counsel and timely help on these matters. In addition, Stephen Forrest (University of Massachusetts, Amherst) was a ready source of counsel.

The work on the Encyclopedia is perhaps best described as evolutionary, with the list of articles and contributors not completely finalized until the last few months of the project. At various stages, several experts provided timely and very helpful assistance in recommending changes to the article list and suggesting contributors: David Buck (University of Wisconsin), Marta Simidchieva (York University), Thomas Dolan (Colombus State Universirty), Vincent Kelly Pollard (University of Hawaii, Manoa), Kevin Alan Brook, Paul Kratoska (National University of Singapore), and Kirk Denton (Ohio State University).

We also want to acknowledge and thank publicly our hosts in Asia who opened many doors that would not otherwise been available to us: Dr. Marty Barrett and the Rotary Club in Almaty, Wu Shao Ping and Dr. Chen Bao-xing in Beijing, and Fusako and Hideo Higuchi in Japan.

The Encyclopedia was developed and managed from our offices in Great Barrington, Massachusetts, a small New England town with a population of 7,700, only a few miles from Stockbridge where Norman Rockwell painted some of the most well-known images of an idealized American way of life. The languages spoken by staffers over the course of the project include Korean, Turkish, Japanese, Persian, Hindi, and Mandarin.

Junhee (June) Kim, Project Editor, managed the project and deserves unbounded praise for so smoothly coordinating the work of some eight hundred editors, authors, and copy editors and managing the flow of more than twenty-six hundred manuscripts. For her, dealing with hundreds of e-mails a day was routine. June was born in Korea, moved to Thailand at age six with her family, then to Turkey for high school and to the United States for college—experiences that left her uniquely qualified to carry out the responsibilities of Project Editor.

Senior Editor Francesca Forrest did an incredible job managing the enormously complex editorial side of the project. With many years specializing in editing resources on Asia and several years' residence in Japan, she was just the right person to develop the editorial guidelines and manage the copyediting and fact-checking processes. The consistency one sees across articles—and the sensible editorial decisions behind this consistency—is largely due to her efforts. She was ably aided by Associate Editor Marcy Ross who also smoothly handled a good bit of the fact-checking and updating of the articles.

Debbie Dillon and Trevor Young deserve special mention for so cheerfully meeting our programming needs to provide the complex database system needed to manage the project. Other members of the Berkshire staff who cheerfully pitched in when needed were Ben Manning, Shana Stalker, Robin O'Sullivan, Poyan Lofti, George Woodward, and Liz Eno. Interns Shannon Bell and James McGirk relieved us of many of the clerical tasks; James also gathered information for a number of the sidebars. We also want to thank Paul Exner at Exner Productions for producing the maps and Steve Donaldson for supplying a portion of the photos and the stories of his travels that went with them.

At Scribners, we want to thank Karen Day for signing the project four years ago and Frank Menchaca and Tim DeWerff for their strong support. John Fitzpatrick and Sarah Feehan made coordination and delivery of the manuscript smooth and easy, and their timely responses to our questions helped move the project along.

Finally, our thanks go to Encyclopedia editors Gerald Fry and Linsun Cheng, Robert Baensch of the New York University Center for Publishing, Kalai Huang of the Massachusetts College of Liberal Arts, friend and author Simon Winchester, and Hahm Chaibong of Yonsei University for the contacts they provided when Karen Christensen again visited China in August 2002, as the final typesetting for the *Encyclopedia of Modern Asia* was taking place. Our effort to bring information about Asia to students in the U.S. is welcomed in Asia itself, and the networks developed through our work with hundreds of scholars around the globe continue to expand and provide inspiration for further research and publishing efforts.

David Levinson
Berkshire Publishing Group
Great Barrington, Massachusetts

Survey of Asia's Regions and Nations

The *Encyclopedia of Modern Asia* covers thirty-three nations in depth and also the Caucasus and Siberia. We have divided Asia into five major subregions and assigned the thirty-three nations to each.

West and Southwest Asia

The West Asian nations covered in detail here are Turkey, Iran, and Iraq. Afghanistan and Pakistan form Southwest Asia, although in some classifications they are placed in Central and South Asia, respectively. Afghanistan, on the crossroads of civilizations for thousands of years, is especially difficult to classify and displays features typical of Central, West, and South Asia.

Despite diversity in language (Persian in Iran, Arabic in Iraq, Turkish in Turkey) form of government (theocracy in Iran, dictatorship in Iraq, and unstable democracy in Turkey) and international ties (Iran to the Islamic world, Iraq to the Arab Middle East, Turkey to the West), there are several sources of unity across West Asia. Perhaps the oldest is geographical location as the site of transportation routes between Europe and Central, East, and South Asia. Since ancient times, people, goods, wealth, and ideas have flowed across the region. In 2002 the flow of oil was most important, from the wells of Iran and Iraq through the pipelines of Turkey. Another source of unity is Sunni Islam, a major feature of life since the seventh century, although Iran is mainly the minority Shi'a tradition and there have long been Zoroastrian, Jewish, Christian, and Baha'i minorities in the region. Diversity is also evident in the fact that Turkey is a "secular" state while Iran is a theocracy, and in the conflict between fundamentalist and mainstream Islam in all the nations.

Another important common thread is the shared historical experience of being part of the Ottoman Empire and having to cope with British and Russian designs on their territory and, more recently, American influence. And, in the twentieth century, all three nations have sought to deal with the Kurdish minority and its demands for a Kurdish state to be established on land taken from all three nations.

Unity across Afghanistan and Pakistan is created by adherence to Sunni Islam (although there is a Shi'ite minority in Afghanistan) and the prominence of the Pashtun ethnic group in each nation. Both nations also experienced British colonialism, although the long-term British influence is more notable in Pakistan, which had been tied to India under British rule. West Asia is the only region in the world never colonized by Britain, although some experts argue that it did experience significant British cultural influence. In all nations resistance to external control—British, Russian, or United States—is another common historical experience.

Across the region (although less so in Afghanistan) is the stark contrast between the traditional culture and the modernity of liberation from imperial rule, still not complete across the region. This contrast is apparent in clothing styles, manners, architecture, recreation, marriage practices, and many elements of daily life.

In 2002 all the nations faced a water crisis of both too little water and water pollution. They all also faced issues of economic and social development, including reducing external debt, controlling inflation, reducing unemployment, improving education and health care, and continually reacting to the ongoing Arab-Israeli conflict, which exacerbates many of these problems. The governments also faced the difficult task of solving these problems while resisting Americanization and also while controlling internal political unrest. Political unrest is often tied to efforts at creating democratic governments and the persistence of elite collaboration with tyrannical governments.

Central Asia

Central Asia is known by many names, including Eurasia, Middle Asia, and Inner Asia. At its core, the region is composed of five states that became independent nations following the collapse of the Soviet Union in 1991: Kazakhstan, Kyrgyzstan, Tajikistan, Turkmenistan, and Uzbekistan. Scholars sometimes include Afghanistan, Mongolia and the Xinjiang province of China within the label Central Asia. For this project, Central Asia is restricted to the five former Soviet countries, while Afghanistan is classified in Southwest Asia, and Mongolia and Xinjiang as part of East Asia. These states have a shared landmass of 1.5 million square miles, about one-half the size of the United States.

The region's unity comes from a shared history and religion. Central Asia saw two cultural and economic traditions blossom and intermix along the famed Silk Road: nomadic and sedentary. Nomadic herdsmen, organized into kinship groupings of clans, lived beside sedentary farmers and oasis city dwellers. Four of the countries share Turkic roots, while the Tajiks are of Indo-European descent, linguistically related to the Iranians. While still recognizable today, this shared heritage has developed into distinct ethnic communities.

The peoples of Central Asia have seen centuries of invasion, notably the legendary Mongol leader Genghis Khan in the thirteenth century, the Russians in the nineteenth and the Soviets in the twentieth century. For better or worse, each invader left behind markers of their presence: the Arabs introduced Islam in the seventh century. Today Islam is the predominant religion in the region, and most Central Asians are Sunni Muslims. The Russians brought the mixed legacy of modernism, including an educated populace, alarming infant mortality rates, strong economic and political participation by women, high agricultural development, and environmental disasters such as the shrinking of the Aral Sea. It was under Russian colonialism that distinct ethno-national boundaries were created to divide the people of the region. These divisions largely shape the contemporary Central Asian landscape.

Today the five Central Asian nations face similar challenges: building robust economies, developing stable, democratic governments, and integrating themselves into the regional and international communities as independent states. They come to these challenges with varied resources: Kazakhstan and Turkmenistan have rich oil reserves; several countries have extensive mineral deposits; and the Fergana Valley is but one example of the region's rich agricultural regions.

Finally, the tragic events of September 11, 2001, cast world attention on Afghanistan's neighbors in Central Asia. The "war on terrorism" forged new alliances and offered a mix of political pressure and economic support for the nations' leaders to suppress their countries' internal fundamentalist Muslim movements.

Southeast Asia

Southeast Asia is conventionally defined as that subregion of Asia consisting of the eleven nation-states of Brunei, Cambodia, East Timor, Indonesia, Laos, Malaysia, Myanmar, Philippines, Singapore, Thailand, and Vietnam. Myanmar is sometimes alternatively classified as part of South Asia and Vietnam as in East Asia. The region may be subdivided into Mainland Southeast Asia (Cambodia, Laos, Myanmar, Thailand, and Vietnam) and Insular Southeast Asia (Brunei, East Timor, Indonesia, Philippines, and Singapore). Malaysia is the one nation in the region that is located both on the mainland and islands, though ethnically it is more linked to the island nations of Indonesia, Brunei, and the Philippines.

Perhaps the key defining features for the region and those that are most widespread are the tropical monsoon climate, rich natural resources, and a way of life in rural areas based on cooperative wet-rice agriculture that goes back several thousand years. In the past unity was also created in various places by major civilizations, including those of Funan, Angkor, Pagan, Sukhothai, Majapahit, Srivijaya, Champa, Ayutthaya, and Melaka. Monarchies continue to be significant in several nation—Brunei, Cambodia, Malaysia, and Thailand—today. Subregional unity has also been created since ancient times by the continued use of written languages, including Vietnamese, Thai, Lao, Khmer and the rich literary traditions associated with those languages.

The region can also be defined as being located between China and India and has been influenced by both, with Indian influence generally broader, deeper, and longer lasting, especially on the mainland, except for Vietnam and Singapore, where influences from China have been more important. Islamic influence is also present in all eleven of the Southeast Asian nations. Culturally, Southeast Asia is notable for the central importance of the family, religion (mainly Buddhism and Islam), and aesthetics in daily life and national consciousness.

In the post–World War II Cold War era, there was a lack of regional unity. Some nations, such as Indonesia under Sukarno, were leaders of the nonaligned nations. Countries such as Thailand and the Philippines joined the U.S. side in the Cold War by being part of the Southeast Asia Treaty Organization (SEATO). A move toward greater unity was achieved with the establishment of the Association of Southeast Asian Nations (ASEAN) in 1967, with the founding members being Indonesia, Malaysia, the Philippines, Singapore, and Thailand. Subsequently other Southeast Asian nations joined ASEAN (Brunei, 1984; Laos, Myanmar, and Vietnam 1997; Cambodia 1999). As of 2002, communism was still the system in Laos and Vietnam and capitalism in Brunei, Cambodia, East Timor, the Philippines Thailand, Indonesia, Malaysia and Singapore. Political, economic, and cultural cooperation is fostered by the Association of Southeast Asian Nations (ASEAN), with headquarters in Jakarta, Indonesia. Economically, all the nations have attempted to move, although at different speeds and with different results, from a reliance on agriculture to an industrial or service-based economy. All nations also suffered in the Asian economic crisis beginning in July 1997.

Alongside these sources of similarity or unity that allow us to speak of Southeast Asia as a region is also considerable diversity. In the past religion, ethnicity, and diverse colonial experience (British, Dutch, French, American) were major sources of diversity. Today, the three major sources of diversity are religion, form of government, and level of economic development. Three nations (Indonesia, Malaysia,

Brunei) are predominately Islamic, five are mainly Buddhist (Vietnam, Laos, Cambodia, Thailand, Myanmar), two are mainly Christian (Philippines and East Timor), and Singapore is religiously heterogeneous. In addition, there is religious diversity within nations, as all these nations have sizeable and visible religious minorities and indigenous religions, in both traditional and syncretic forms, also remain important.

In terms of government, there is considerable variation: communism in Vietnam and Laos; state socialism in Myanmar; absolute monarchy in Brunei; evolving democracy in the Philippines, Thailand, Cambodia, and Indonesia; and authoritarian democracy in Malaysia and Singapore. The economic variation that exists among the nations and also across regions within nations is reflected in different levels of urbanization and economic development, with Singapore and Malaysia at one end of the spectrum and Laos and Cambodia at the other. Myanmar is economically underdeveloped, although it is urbanized, while Brunei is one of the wealthiest nations in the world but not very urbanized.

In 2002, Southeast Asia faced major environmental, political, economic, and health issues. All Southeast Asian nations suffer from serious environmental degradation, including water pollution, soil erosion, air pollution in and around cities, traffic congestion, and species extinctions. To a significant extent all these problems are the result of rapid industrial expansion and overexploitation of natural resources for international trade. The economic crisis has hampered efforts to address these issues and has threatened the economies of some nations, making them more dependent on international loans and assistance from nations such as Japan, Australia, and China. The persisting economic disparities between the rich and the poor are actually exacerbated by rapid economic growth. Related to poverty is the AIDS epidemic, which is especially serious in Cambodia, Myanmar, and Thailand and becoming more serious in Vietnam; in all these nations it associated with the commercial sex industry.

Politically, many Southeast Asian nations faced one or more threats to their stability. Political corruption, lack of transparency, and weak civic institutions are a problem to varying degrees in all the nations but are most severe in Indonesia, which faces threats to its sovereignty. Cambodia and Thailand face problems involving monarch succession, and several nations have had difficulty finding effective leaders. Myanmar's authoritarian rulers face a continual threat from the political opposition and from ethnic and religious separatists.

In addition, several nations faced continuing religious or ethnic-based conflicts that disrupt political stability and economic growth in some provinces. The major conflicts involve Muslim separatists in the southern Philippines, Muslims and Christians in some Indonesian islands and Aceh separatists in northern Sumatra, and Muslims and the Karen and other ethnic groups against the Burman government in Myanmar. Since the economic crisis of 1997, ethnic and religion-based conflict has intensified, as wealthier ethnic or religious minorities have increasingly been attacked by members of the dominant ethnic group. A related issue is the cultural and political future of indigenous peoples, including the so-called hill tribes of the mainland and horticulturalists and former hunter-gatherers of the islands.

In looking to the future, among the region's positive features are the following. First, there is Southeast Asia's strategic location between India and China, between Japan and Europe, and between Europe and Oceania. It stands in close proximity to the world's two most populous countries, China and India. Singapore, the centrally located port in Southeast Asia, is one of two major gateways to the dynamic Pacific Basin (the other is the Panama Canal). Second, there is the region's huge population and related economic market, with a total population approaching that of one half of China's. Indonesia is the world's fourth most populous nation. Third, there is enormous tourist potential in sites and recreational locales such as Angkor Wat, Bali, Borobudur, Phuket, and Ha Long Bay. Fourth, there is the region's notable eclecticism in borrowing from the outside and resiliency in transcending tragedies such as experienced by Cambodia and Vietnam. Fifth, there is the region's significant economic potential: Southeast Asia may well have the world's highest-quality labor force relative to cost. And, sixth, there is the region's openness to new technologies and ideas, an important feature in the modern global community.

South Asia

South Asia is the easiest region to demarcate, as it is bounded by the Hindu Kush and Himalayan ranges to the north and the Bay of Bengal and Arabian Sea to the south. It contains the nation-states of Bangladesh, Bhutan, India, Nepal, and Sri Lanka and the more distant island nations of the Maldives and Mauritius. Myanmar and Pakistan, which are considered part of South Asia in some schemes, are here classified in Southeast Asia and Southwest Asia, respectively.

While the region is diverse economically, culturally, linguistically, and religiously, there is unity that, in some form, has existed for several thousand years. One source of unity is the historical influence of two major civilizations (Indus and Dravidian) and three major religions (Hinduism, Buddhism, and Islam). Regionally, Sikhism and Jainism have been of great importance. There is also considerable economic unity, as the majority of people continue to live by farming, with rice and especially wet-rice the primary crop. In addition, three-quarters of the people continue to live in rural, agricultural villages, although this has now become an important source of diversity, with clear distinctions between urban and rural life. A third source of unity is the caste system, which continues to define life for most people in the three mainland nations. Another source of unity is the nature and structure of society, which was heavily influenced by the several centuries of British rule. A final source of political unity in the twentieth century—although sometimes weakened by ethnic and religious differences—has been nationalism in each nation.

South Asia is diverse linguistically, ethnically, religiously, and economically. This diversity is most obvious in India, but exists in various forms in other nations, except for the isolated Maldives, which is the home of one ethnic group, the Divehi, who are Muslims and who have an economy based largely on tourism and fishing.

The dozens of languages of South Asia fall into four major families: Indo-European, Austroasiatic, Dravidian, and Tibeto-Burman and several cannot be classified at all. Because of its linguistic diversity, India is divided into "linguistic" states with Hindi and English serving as the national languages.

Hinduism is the dominant religion in South Asia, but India is the home also to Buddhism, Jainism, and Sikhism. India also has over 120 million Muslims and the world's largest Zoroastrian population (known in India as Parsis) and Bangladesh is a predominately Muslim nation. India also has about twenty-five million Christians and until recently India had several small but thriving Jewish communities. Nepal is mainly Hindu with a Buddhist minority, and Bhutan the reverse. Sri Lanka is mainly Theravada Buddhist with Hindu, Muslim, and Christian minorities. Mauritius, which has no indigenous population, is about 50 percent Hindu, with a large Christian and smaller Muslim and Buddhist minorities.

Linguistic and religious diversity is more than matched by social diversity. One classification suggests that the sociocultural groups of South Asia can be divided into four general and several subcategories: (1) castes (Hindu and Muslim); (2) modern urban classes (including laborers, non-Hindus, and the Westernized elite); (3) hill tribes of at least six types; and (4) peripatetics.

Economically, there are major distinctions between the rural poor and the urban middle class and elite, and also between the urban poor and urban middle class and elite. There are also significant wealth distinctions based on caste and gender, and a sizeable and wealthy Indian diaspora. There is political diversity as well, with India and Sri Lanka being democracies, Bangladesh shifting back and forth between Islamic democracy and military rule, the Maldives being an Islamic state, and Nepal and Bhutan being constitutional monarchies.

In 2002, South Asia faced several categories of issues. Among the most serious are the ongoing ethnic and religious conflicts between Muslims and Hindus in India, the conflict between the nations of Pakistan and India; the ethnic conflict between the Sinhalese and Sri Lankan Tamils in Sri Lanka; and the conflict between the Nepalese and Bhutanese in both nations. There are also various ethnic separatists movements in the region, as involving some Sikhs in India. The most threatening to order in the region and beyond is the conflict between India and Pakistan over the Kashmir region, as both have nuclear weapons and armies gathered at their respective borders.

A second serious issue is the host of related environmental problems, including pollution; limited water resources; overexploitation of natural resources; destruction and death caused by typhoons, flooding, and earthquakes; famine (less of a problem today), and epidemics of tropical and other diseases. The Maldives faces the unique problem of disappearing into the sea as global warming melts glaciers and raises the sea level. Coastal regions of Bangladesh could also suffer from this.

There are pressing social, economic, and political issues as well. Socially, there are wide and growing gaps between the rich and middle classes and the poor, who are disproportionately women and children and rural. Tribal peoples and untouchables still do not enjoy full civil rights, and women are often discriminated against, although India, Sri Lanka, and Bangladesh have all had women prime ministers. Economically, all the nations continue to wrestle with the issues involved in transforming themselves from mainly rural, agricultural nations to ones with strong industrial and service sectors. Politically, all still also struggle with the task of establishing strong, central governments that can control ethnic, religious, and region variation and provide services to the entire population. Despite these difficulties, there are also positive developments. India continues to benefit from the inflow of wealth earned by Indians outside India and is emerging as a major technological center. And, in Sri Lanka, an early 2002 cease-fire has led to the prospect of a series of peace negotiations in the near future.

East Asia

East Asia is defined here as the nations of Japan, South Korea, North Korea, China, Taiwan, and Mongolia. It should be noted that Taiwan is part of China although the People's Republic of China and the Republic of China (Taiwan) differ over whether it is a province or not. The inclusion of China in East Asia is not entirely geographically and culturally valid, as parts of southern China could be classified as Southeast Asian from a geographical and cultural standpoint, while western China could be classified as Central Asian. However, there is a long tradition of classifying China as part of East Asia, and that is the approach taken here. Likewise, Mongolia is sometimes classified in Central Asia. As noted above, Siberia can be considered as forming North and Northeast Asia.

Economic, political, ideological, and social similarity across China, Korea (North and South), and Japan is the result of several thousand years of Chinese influence (at times strong, at other times weak), which has created considerable similarity on a base of pre-existing Japanese and Korean cultures and civilizations. China's influence was greatest before the modern period and Chinese culture thus in some ways forms the core of East Asian culture and society. At the same time, it must be stressed that Chinese cultural elements merged with existing and new Korean and Japanese ones in ways that produced the unique Japanese and Korean cultures and civilizations, which deserve consideration in their own right.

Among the major cultural elements brought from China were Buddhism and Confucianism, the written language, government bureaucracy, various techniques of rice agriculture, and a patrilineal kinship system based on male dominance and male control of family resources. All of these were shaped over the centuries to fit with existing or developing forms in Korea and Japan. For example, Buddhism coexists with Shinto in Japan. In Korea, it coexists with the indigenous shamanistic religion. In China and Korea traditional folk religion remains strong, while Japan has been the home to dozens of new indigenous religions over the past 150 years.

Diversity in the region has been largely a product of continuing efforts by the Japanese and Koreans to resist Chinese influence and develop and stress Japanese and Korean culture and civilization. In the twentieth century diversity was mainly political and economic. Japanese invasions and conquests of parts of China and all of Korea beginning in the late nineteenth century led to hostile relations that had not been completely overcome in 2002.

In the post–World War II era and after, Taiwan, Japan, and South Korea have been closely allied with the United States and the West; they have all developed powerful industrial and postindustrial economies. During the same period, China became a Communist state; significant ties to the West and economic development did not begin until the late 1980s. North Korea is also a Communist state; it lags behind the other nations in economic development and in recent years has not been able to produce enough food to feed its population. In 2002 China was the emerging economic power in the region, while Taiwan and South Korea held on and Japan showed signs of serious and long-term economic decline, although it remained the second-largest (after the United States) economy in the world. Mongolia, freed from Soviet rule, is attempting to build its economy following a capitalist model.

Politically, China remains a Communist state despite significant moves toward market capitalism, North Korea is a Communist dictatorship, Japan a democracy, and South Korea and Taiwan in 1990s seem to have become relatively stable democracies following periods of authoritarian rule. Significant contact among the nations is mainly economic, as efforts at forging closer political ties remain stalled over past grievances. For example, in 2001, people in China and South Korea protested publicly about a new Japanese high school history textbook that they believed did not fully describe Japanese atrocities committed toward Chinese and Koreans before and during World War II. Japan has refused to revise the textbook. Similarly, tension remains between Mongolia and China over Mongolian fears about Chinese designs on Mongolian territory. Inner Mongolia is a province of China.

Major issues with regional and broader implications are the reunification of Taiwan and China and North and South Korea, and threat of war should reunification efforts go awry. Other major regional issues include environmental pollution, including air pollution from China that spreads east, and pollution of the Yellow Sea, Taiwan Strait, and South China Sea. A third issue is economic development and stability, and the role of each nation, and the region as a unit, in the growing global economy. A final major issue is the emergence of China as a major world political, economic, and military power at the expense of Taiwan, South Korea, and Japan, and the consequences for regional political relations and stability.

Overview

As the above survey indicates, Asia is a varied and dynamic construct. To some extent the notion of Asia, as well as regions within Asia, are artificial constructs imposed by outside observers to provide some structure to a place and subject matter that might otherwise be incomprehensible. The nations of Asia have rich and deep pasts that continue to inform and shape the present—and that play a significant role in relations with other nations and regions. The nations of Asia also face considerable issues—some unique to the region, others shared by nations around the world—as well as enormous potential for future growth and development. We expect that the next edition of this encyclopedia will portray a very different Asia than does this one, but still an Asia that is in many ways in harmony with its pasts.

David Levinson (with contributions from Virginia Aksan, Edward Beauchamp, Anthony and Rebecca Bichel, Linsun Cheng, Gerald Fry, Bruce Fulton, and Paul Hockings)

Regional Maps

0 250 500 Miles
0 250 500 Kilometers

RUSSIA

⊛Astana   •Semey

KAZAKHSTAN

Lake Balkhash

Aral Sea   *Syr Dar'ya*

•Almaty

⊛Bishkek

Caspian Sea   UZBEKISTAN   KYRGYZSTAN

Tashkent⊛   •Osh   CHINA

TURKMENISTAN   •Samarqand

•Bukhara   TAJIKISTAN

⊛Ashgabat   *Amu Dar'ya*   ⊛Dushanbe

•Mary

PAKISTAN

CENTRAL ASIA   IRAN   AFGHANISTAN   INDIA

N

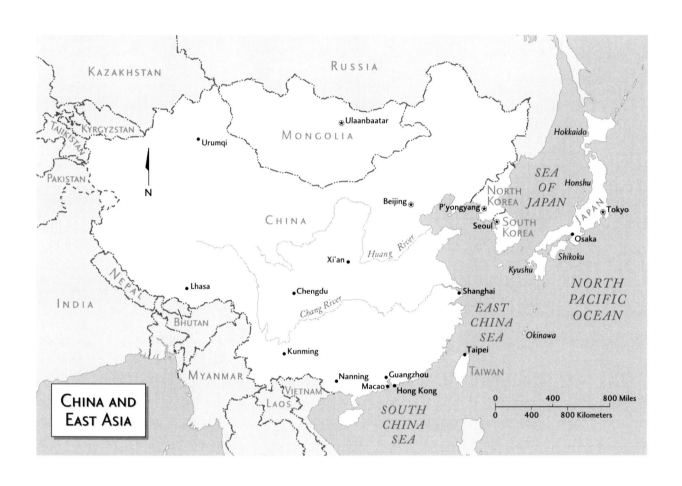

CHINA AND
EAST ASIA

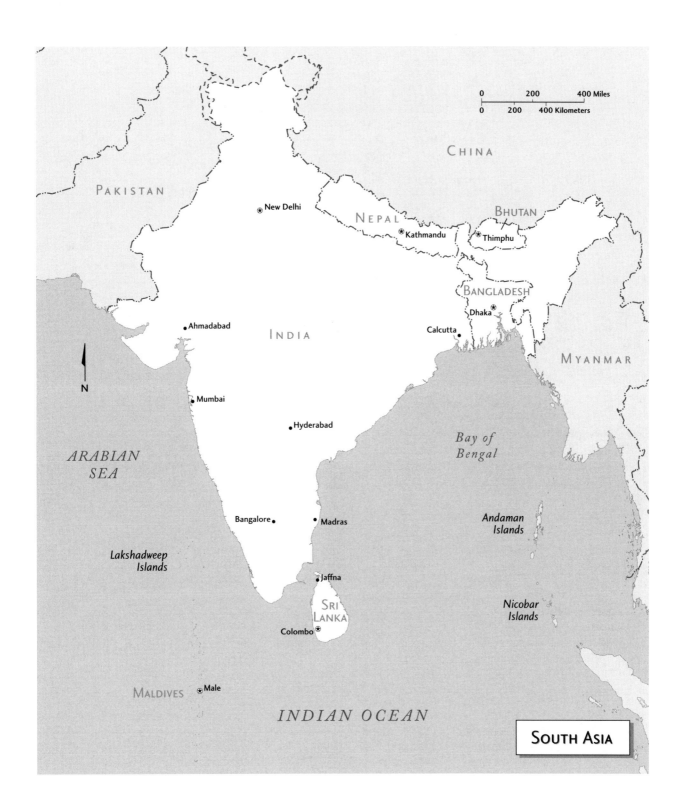

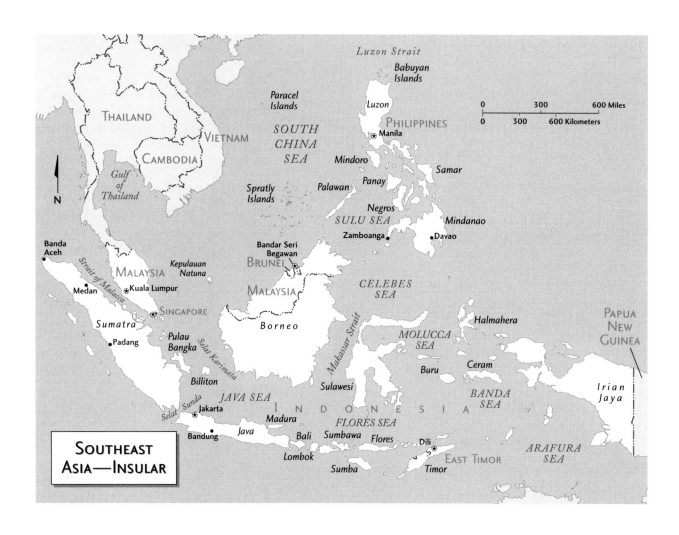

THAILAND

VIETNAM

CAMBODIA

Gulf of Thailand

N

Banda Aceh

Strait of Malacca

Medan

MALAYSIA

Kuala Lumpur

Kepulauan Natuna

SINGAPORE

Sumatra

Padang

Pulau Bangka

Selat Karimata

Billiton

Selat Sunda

Jakarta

Bandung

Java

JAVA SEA

Madura

Bali

Lombok

Sumbawa

Sumba

Paracel Islands

SOUTH CHINA SEA

Spratly Islands

Palawan

Bandar Seri Begawan

BRUNEI

MALAYSIA

Borneo

Makassar Strait

Sulawesi

FLORES SEA

Flores

Luzon Strait

Babuyan Islands

Luzon

PHILIPPINES

Manila

Mindoro

Panay

Negros

SULU SEA

Zamboanga

Samar

Mindanao

Davao

CELEBES SEA

MOLUCCA SEA

Buru

Ceram

Halmahera

BANDA SEA

I N D O N E S I A

Dili

East Timor

Timor

ARAFURA SEA

PAPUA NEW GUINEA

Irian Jaya

0   300   600 Miles
0   300   600 Kilometers

SOUTHEAST
ASIA—INSULAR

INDIA

CHINA

0   200   400 Miles
0   200   400 Kilometers

MYANMAR

Irrawaddy River

● Mandalay

VIETNAM

Hanoi ⊛   ● Haiphong

LAOS

Gulf of
Tonkin

Chiang ●   Vientiane
Mai   ⊛

Mekong River

N

THAILAND

SOUTH
CHINA
SEA

Yangon ⊛

● Bangkok

CAMBODIA

ANDAMAN
SEA

Phnom
Penh ⊛

● Ho Chi
Minh City

Gulf of
Thailand

**SOUTHEAST
ASIA—MAINLAND**

Phuket ●

MALAYSIA

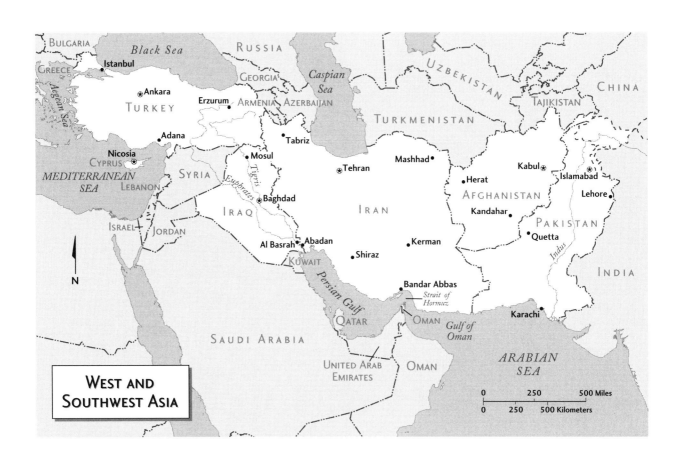

BULGARIA

Black Sea

RUSSIA

GREECE

Istanbul

⊛ Ankara

Aegean Sea

TURKEY

Erzurum

GEORGIA

Caspian Sea

UZBEKISTAN

CHINA

ARMENIA AZERBAIJAN

TAJIKISTAN

TURKMENISTAN

Adana

Tabriz

Nicosia

Mosul

CYPRUS ⊛

Euphrates

Tigris

Mashhad

Kabul ⊛

Islamabad ⊛

MEDITERRANEAN SEA

SYRIA

⊛ Tehran

Herat

Lehore

LEBANON

Baghdad ⊛

IRAN

AFGHANISTAN

PAKISTAN

IRAQ

Kandahar

ISRAEL

JORDAN

Kerman

Quetta

Indus

N

Al Basrah

Abadan

INDIA

Shiraz

KUWAIT

Bandar Abbas

Persian Gulf

Strait of Hormuz

OMAN

Gulf of Oman

Karachi

QATAR

SAUDI ARABIA

ARABIAN SEA

WEST AND SOUTHWEST ASIA

UNITED ARAB EMIRATES

OMAN

0	250	500 Miles
0	250	500 Kilometers

Reader's Guide

ASIA

Arts, Literature, and Recreation
Asian Games
Board Games
Chinese New Year
Jade
Kabaddi
Kites and Kite Flying
Mountaineering
Olympics
Storytelling

Economics, Commerce, and Transportation
Asian Development Bank
Asian Economic Crisis of 1997
Asia-Pacific Economic Cooperation Forum
Automobile Industry
Bogor Declaration
Drug Trade
Export-Led Development
Golden Crescent
High-Technology Industry
Information Technology Industry
Intellectual Property
Islamic Banking
Manila Action Plan
Measurement Systems
Osaka Action Plan
Shanghai Cooperation Organization
Silk Road
Spice Trade
Sustainability
Tin Industry
Tourism
World Bank in Asia

Geography and the Natural World
Air Pollution
Bamboo
Buffalo, Water
Camel, Bactrian
Caspian Sea
Chicken
Cormorant
Deforestation
Duck and Goose, Domesticated
Earthquakes
Endangered Species
Goat
Mangroves
Monsoons
Opium
Pacific Ocean
Pacific Rim
Pig
Rhinocerous, Asiatic
Rice and Rice Agriculture
Soil Loss
South China Sea
Surkhob River
Tiger
Toxic-Waste Disposal
Typhoons
Volcanoes
Water Issues

Government, Politics, and Law
Corruption

International Relations
Africa-Asia Relations
Australia-Asia Relations

ASIA *(continued)*
   International Relations *(continued)*
Europe-Asia Relations
International Monetary Fund
Land Mines
New Zealand-Asia Relations
Nuclear Arms
United Nations
World War I
World War II
   Language and Communication
Altaic Languages
Austroasiatic Languages
English in Asia
Hmong-Mien Languages
Indo-European Languages
Language Purification
Media
Self-Censorship
Sinitic Languages
Tibeto-Burman Languages
Turkic Languages
Uralic Languages
   Peoples, Cultures, and Society
Fertility
Homosexuality
New Rich
Orientalism
   Religion and Philosophy
Asian-Christian Religious Dialogue
Baraka
Muslim Saints
Religious Self-Mortification
Shamanism
Shari'a
Zoroastrianism
   Science, Technology, and Health
AIDS
Disease, Tropical
Terrace Irrigation

CENTRAL ASIA
   Arts, Literature, and Recreation
Alpamish
Architectural Decoration—Central Asia
Architecture—Central Asia
Buzkashi
Carpets—Central Asia
Chagatay
Cuisine—Central Asia
Dance—Central Asia
Dastan, Turkic
Dombra
Edige

Felting—Central Asia
Fine Arts—Central Asia
Folklore—Central Asia
Gorkut Ata
Koroghli
Literature—Central Asia
Minaret
Music—Central Asia
Nava'i, Mir' Ali Shir
Tile Work—Central Asia
Woodworking—Central Asia
   Kazakhstan
Auezov, Mukhtar
Daulpaz
Dulatov, Mirzhaqyp
Kalmakanov, Bukharzhrau
Kobyz
Kunanbaev, Abai
Mailin, Beiimbet
Makhambet Utemisov
Seifullin, Saduakas
Taimanov, Isatai
Valikhanov, Chokan
Aitmatov, Chingis
Manas Epic
   Tajikistan
Bun Bang Fai
   Turkmenistan
Kuli, Maktum
   Uzbekistan
Abdalrauf Fitrat
Abdullah Quaisi
Mamadali Mahmudov
   Economics, Commerce, and Transportation
Agriculture—Central Asia
Caravans
Energy—Central Asia
Oil and Mineral Industries—Central Asia
   Kazakhstan
Kazakhstan—Economic System
   Kyrgyzstan
Kyrgyzstan—Economic System
   Tajikistan
Tajikistan—Economic System
   Turkmenistan
Turkmenistan—Economic System
   Uzbekistan
Uzbekistan—Economic System
   Education
Madrasahs
   Kazakhstan
Altynsarin, Ibrahim
Kazakhstan—Education System

Kyrgyzstan
Kyrgyzstan—Education System
Tajikistan
Tajikistan—Education System
Turkmenistan
Turkmenistan—Education System
Uzbekistan
Alisher Navoiy Samarkand State University
Uzbekistan—Education System
Geography and the Natural World
Altay Mountains
Aral Sea
Bactria
Balkhash, Lake
Camel, Arvana Dromedary
Fergana Valley
Horse, Akhal-teke
Horse, Karabair
Horse, Lokai
Kara-Kum Desert
Khwarizm
Leopard, Snow
Murgab River
Pamir Range
Paracel Islands
Radioactive Waste and Contamination—
    Central Asia
Sheep, Karakul
Sheep, Marco Polo
Syr Dar'ya
Tedzhen River
Tobol River
Trans Alai
Tura Lowland
Turugart Pass
Ustyurt Plateau
Zerafshan River
Kazakhstan
Irtysh River
Ishim River
Kazakh Uplands
Mangyshlak Peninsula
Turgay Plateau
Tajikistan
Kafirnigan River
Sarez Lake
Turkmenistan
Garabil Plateau
Government, Politics, and Law
Basmachi Movement
Communism—Central Asia
Great Game
Russification and Sovietization—Central Asia
Timur

Tribes and Tribal Federations—Central Asia
Urgench
Kazakhstan
Almaty
Astana
Bokeikhanov, Alikhan
Kazakhstan—Political System
Kunaev, Dinmukhamed
Nazarbaev, Nursultan
Oral
Petropavlovsk
Saryshaghan
Semipalatinsk Movement
Seralin, Mukhammedzhan
Suleimenov, Olzhas
Kyrgyzstan
Akaev, Askar
Aksakal
Bishkek
Kurmanjan Datka
Kyrgyzstan—Political System
Osh
Usubaliev, Turdakun Usubalievich
Tajikistan
Dushanbe
Gafurov, Bobojan Gafurovich
Islamic Renaissance Party—Tajikistan
Khorog
Khujand
Kulob
Nabiev, Rakhmon
Qurghonteppa
Rakhmonov, Imomali
Tajikistan—Political System
Tajikistan Civil War
Turkmenistan
Ashgabat
Mary
Niyazov, Saparmurat
Turkmenabat
Turkmenistan—Political System
Uzbekistan
Bukhara
Guliston
Karakalpakstan
Karimov, Islam
Karshi
Mahalla
Nukus
Rashidov, Sharof Rashidovich
Samarqand
Tashkent
Termez
Uzbekistan—Political System

CENTRAL ASIA (*continued*)
   History and Profile
Bukhara, Khanate of
Central Asia—Early Medieval Period
Central Asia—Late Medieval and Early Modern
Central Asia—Modern
Khiva, Khanate of
Paleoanthropology—Central Asia
Quqon, Khanate of
   Kazakhstan
Kazakhstan—History
Kazakhstan—Profile
   Kyrgyzstan
Kyrgyzstan—History
Kyrgyzstan—Profile
   Tajikistan
Tajikistan—History
Tajikistan—Profile
   Turkmenistan
Turkmenistan—History
Turkmenistan—Profile
   Uzbekistan
Uzbekistan—History
Uzbekistan—Profile
   International Relations
Central Asia—Human Rights
Central Asia-China Relations
Central Asian Regionalism
Central Asia-Russia Relations
   Language and Communication
Central Asian Languages
Farsi-Tajiki
Media—Central Asia
   Kazakhstan
Ai Qap
Baitursynov, Akhmet
Kazak
Leninshil Zhas
   Peoples, Cultures, and Society
Dungans
Germans in Central Asia
Kalym
Kishlak
Koreans in Central Asia
Marriage and Family—Central Asia
Nomadic Pastoralism—Central Asia
Pamir Peoples
Russians in Central Asia
Westernization—Central Asia
Women in Central Asia
Yurt
   Kazakhstan
Kazakhs

   Kyrgyzstan
Clothing, Traditional—Kyrgyzstan
Kyrgyz
   Tajikistan
Clothing, Traditional—Tajikistan
Tajiks
   Turkmenistan
Clothing, Traditional—Turkmenistan
Turkmen
   Uzbekistan
Clothing, Traditional—Uzbekistan
Karakalpaks
Uzbeks
   Religion and Philosophy
Buddhism—Central Asia
Bukharian Jews
Christianity—Central Asia
Islam—Central Asia
Ismaili Sects—Central Asia
Jadidism
Minaret
Muslim Religious Board of Central Asia
Naqshbandiya
   Science, Technology, and Health
Ariq Water System
Ibn Sina
Kara-Kum Canal
Kariz Irrigation System
Medicine, Traditional—Central Asia

EAST ASIA
   Arts, Literature, and Recreation
   China
Ang Lee
Architecture—China
Architecture, Vernacular—China
Ba Jin
Beijing Opera
Birds and Bird Cages
Calligraphy—China
Cao Xueqin
Chen Kaige
Chuci
Ci
Cinema—China
Cloisonne
Cui Jian
Cuisine—China
Dazu Rock Carvings
Ding Ling
Dragon Boat Festival
Drama—China
Du Fu
Five Classics

Fu Baoshi
Gao Xingjian
Gardening—China
Ginseng
Gong Li
Guo Moruo
Hong lou meng
Hong Shen
Humor in Chinese History
Hungry Ghost Festival
Imperial Palace
International Labor Day—China
Jin ping mei
Lao She
Li Bai
Literature—China
Longmen Grottoes
Lu Xun
Mei Lanfang
Mid-Autumn Festival
Mogao Caves
Music—China
National Day—China
Nu Shooting
Painting—China
Poetry—China
Qi Baishi
Qigong
Qin Tomb
Qingming
Qiu Jin
Quan Tangshi
Shadow Plays and Puppetry
Shen Congwen
Shi
Shijing
Social Realism—China
Sports—China
Spring Festival—China
Summer Palace
Tai Chi
Tea—China
Temple of Heaven
Thirteen Ming Tombs
Tian Han
Tofu
Twelve Muqam
Wang Yiting
Wu Changshi
Wushu
Xiqu
Xu Beihong
Xu Zhimo
Zhang Yimou

Dance, Modern— East Asia
Lacquerware
Masks—East Asia
Porcelain—East Asia
   Japan
Aikido
Ando Tadao
Anime
Aoi Matsuri
Arata Isozaki
Architecture—Japan
Architecture—Modern Japan
Baseball—Japan
Basho
Bento
Biwa
Bon Matsuri
Bonsai
Bunjinga
Bunraku
Calligraphy—Japan
Ceramics—Japan
Children's Day—Japan
Chugen
Cinema—Japan
Cinema, Contemporary—Japan
Cuisine—Japan
Dazai Osamu
Drama—Japan
Edogawa Rampo
Emakimono
Enchi Fumiko
Endo Shusaku
Eto Jun
Fugu
Fujieda Shizuo
Fujisawa Takeo
Fujita Tsuguhara
Fukuchi Gen'ichiro
Fukuzawa Yukichi
Funakoshi Gichin
Futabatei, Shimei
Geisha
Gion Matsuri
Haiku
Hakata Matsuri
Hayashi
Hina Matsuri
Hiratsuka Raicho
Iaido
Ito Noe
Judo
Jujutsu
Kabuki

EAST ASIA (continued)

Arts, Literature, and Recreation (continued)

Japan (continued)

Karaoke
Karate
Kawabata Yasunari
Kendo
Koto
Kouta
Kurokawa Kisho
Literature—Japan
Manga
Mori Ogai
Murasaki Shikibu
Music—Japan
Music, Ryukyuan
Naguata
Natsume Soseki
Nihonga
Noh-Kyogen
Oe Kenzaburo
Oh Sadaharu
Origami
Pachinko
Painting—Japan
Poetry—Japan
Shakuhachi
Shamisen
Shimazaki Toson
Sports—Japan
Tange Kenzo
Tanizaki Jun'ichiro
Tatsuno Kingo
Tea Ceremony
Teahouses
Three Imperial Regalia—Japan
Utai
Yoga

Koreas

Architecture—Korea
Calligraphy—Korea
Ceramics—Korea
Chajon Nori
Ch'oe Nam-son
Ch'usok
Cuisine—Korea
Dance—Korea
Dance Drama, Mask—Korea
Drama—Korea
Hanshik
Hwang Sun-won
Kim Myong-sun
Kim Sowol
Literature—Korea

Music—Korea
Paik, Nam June
Painting—Korea
Pak Kyung-ri
P'ansori
Paper Crafts and Arts—Korea
Poetry—Korea
Pojagi
Shin Saimdang
So Chongju
Sol
Sottal
Sports—Korea
Ssirum
Tae Kwon Do
Tanch'ong
Tano
Yi Kyu-bo
Yi Mun-yol
Yun Sun-do

Mongolia

Buh
Cuisine—Mongolia
Damdinsuren, Tsendiyn
Geser Khan
Khararkhi
Natsagdori, Dashdorjiyn

Economics, Commerce, and Transportation

China

Agriculture—China
Agricultural Collectivization—China
China—Economic System
Defense Industry—China
Development Zones—China
Energy Industry—China
Fishing Industry—China
Household Responsibility System—China
Machinery and Equipment Industry—China
Privatization—China
Rural Workers, Surplus—China
Salt Tax
Shanghai Pudong New Area
Shenzhen Special Economic Zone
South Manchuria Railway
Special Economic Zones—China
Taiwan Economic Miracle
Taiwan Investment in Asia
Toy Industry—China
Transportation System—China
Department Stores—East Asia
Textile and Clothing Industry—East Asia

Japan

Danchi
Denki Roren

Economic Planning Agency
Economic Stabilization Program
Electronics Industry—Japan
Farmer's Movement
Financial Crisis of 1927
Fishing Industry—Japan
Furukawa Ichibei
Japan—Economic System
Japan—Money
Japanese Firms Abroad
Japanese Foreign Investments
Japanese International Cooperation Agency
Kawasaki
Nikkyoso
Overseas Economic Cooperation Fund
Quality Circles
Ringi System
Settai
Shibusawa Eiichi
Shunto
Whaling—Japan
  Koreas
Chaebol
Fishing Industry—Korea
Food Crisis—North Korea
North and South Korean Economic Ventures
North Korea—Economic System
South Korea—Economic System
Steel Industry—Korea
  Mongolia
Cashmere Industry
Forest Industry—Mongolia
Mongolia—Economic System
Trans-Mongolian Railway
  Education
  China
Academia Sinica
China—Education System
Hu Shi
National Taiwan University
Peking University
Taiwan—Education System
  Japan
Asiatic Society of Japan
Cram Schools
Daigaku
Ebina Danjo
Gakureki Shakai
Ienaga Saburo
Imperial Rescript on Education
Japan—Education System
Kyoiku Mama
Nitobe Inazo
Shiga Shigetaka

  Koreas
Korea Institute of Science and Technology
North Korea—Education System
Seoul National University
South Korea—Education System
  Mongolia
Mongolia—Education System
  Geography and the Natural World
Siberia
Yellow Sea
  China
Bramaputra River
Cathaya Tree
Chang River
East China Sea
Emei, Mount
Famine—China
Greater Xing'an Range
Hengduan Ranges
Huang River
Huang Shan
Huanglongsi
Jiuzhaigou
Kunlun Mountains
Lu, Mount
Panda
Qinling Range
Tai Shan
Taiwan Strait
Taklimakan Desert
Tarim Basin
Tian Shan
Wudang Shan
Wulingyuan
Wuyi, Mount
Yak
  Japan
Amami Islands
Chrysanthemum
Chubu
Chugoku
Etorofu Island
Fuji, Mount
Hokkaido
Honshu
Iriomotejima Island
Kansai Region
Kanto Region
Kinki Region
Kunashiro Island
Kyushu
Sado Island
Setouchi Region
Shikoku

EAST ASIA *(continued)*
   Geography and the Natural World *(continued)*
      Japan (continued)
Tohoku Region
Tokaimura Nuclear Disaster
Tsushima Island
Yakushima Island
      Koreas
Amnok River
Han River
Kaema Plateau
Keumkang, Mount
Korea Bay
Korea Strait
Kum River
Naktong River and Delta
Nangnim Range
T'aebaek Mountains
Taedong River
Tumen River
      Mongolia
Gobi Desert
Hangai Mountains
Hentii Mountains
Horse, Przewalski's
   Government, Politics, and Law
      China
Anhui
Beijing
Cadre System—China
Chen Duxiu
Chen Shui-bian
Chen Yun
Chengde
Chengdu
Chiang Kai-shek
Chilung
China—Political System
Chinese Civil War of 1945–1949
Chinese Communist Party
Chongqing
Ci Xi, Empress Dowager
Civil-Service Examination System—China
Communism—China
Corruption—China
Cultural Revolution—China
Deng Xiaoping
Fujian
Gang of Four
Gansu
Great Leap Forward
Guangdong
Guangxi
Guangzhou

Guizhou
Guomindang
Hainan
Hangzhou
Harbin
Hebei
Heilongjiang
Henan
Hong Kong
Hu Jintao
Hu Yaobang
Hubei
Hunan
Hundred Days Reform
Hundred Flowers Campaign
Jiang Zemin
Jiangsu
Jiangxi
Jilin
Kang Youwei
Kao-hsiung
Kong Xiangxi
Lee Teng-hui
Lhasa
Li Hongzhang
Li Peng
Liang Qichao
Liaoning
Lin Biao
Liu Shaoqi
Long March
Macao
Manchuria
Manchurian Incident
Mao Zedong
May Fourth Movement
Nanjing
Nei Monggol
Ningxia
Northern Expedition
People's Liberation Army
Political Participation, Unofficial—China
Qinghai
Quemoy and Matsu
Red Guard Organizations
Republican Revolution of 1911
Self-Strengthening Movement
Shaanxi
Shandong
Shanghai
Shanxi
Sichuan
Socialist Spiritual Civilization—China
Song Ziwen

Sun Yat-sen
Suzhou
Tainan
Taipei
Taiping Rebellion
Taiwan—Political System
Thought Work—China
Three and Five Antis Campaigns
Tiananmen Square
Tianjin
Tibet
Tibetan Uprising
Wang Jingwei
White Terror
Wu Zetian
Xi'an
Xi'an Incident
Xinjiang
Yen, Y.C. James
Yuan Shikai
Yunnan
Zeng Guofan
Zhang Zhidong
Zhao Ziyang
Zhejiang
Zhou Enlai
Zhu De
Zhu Rongji
Zuo Zongtang

Government, Politics, and Law
Japan
Abe Iso
Aichi
Akita
Aomori
Araki Sadao
Aum Shinrikyo Scandal
Baba Tatsui
Buraku Liberation League
Chiba
Citizen's Movement
Constitution, Postwar—Japan
Constitutional Crisis of 1881
Democratic Socialist Party—Japan
Eda Saburo
Ehime
Enomoto Takeaki
Fukuda Hideko
Fukuda Takeo
Fukui
Fukumoto Kazuo
Fukuoka
Fukushima
Gifu

Goto Shinpei
Gumma
Hara Takashi
Hatoyama Ichiro
Higashikuni Naruhiko
Hirohito
Hiroshima
Hyogo
Ibaraki
Ichikawa Fusae
Ikeda Hayato
Ishihara Shintaro
Ishikawa
Iwate
Japan—Political System
Japan Communist Party
Japan Socialist Party
Kagawa
Kagoshima
Kanagawa
Kanno Suga
Kato Takaaki
Kishi Nobusuke
Kochi
Kodama Yoshio
Komeito
Konoe Fumimaro
Kumamoto
Kyoto
Liberal Democratic Party—Japan
Lockheed Scandal
Maruyama Masao
Mie
Minobe Tatsukichi
Miyagi
Miyazaki
Mori Arinori
Nagano
Nagasaki
Nakasone Yasuhiro
Nara
Niigata
Ogasawara
Oita
Okayama
Okinawa
Osaka
Recruit Scandal
Saga
Saionji Kinmochi
Saitama
Sapporo
Sasagawa Ryoichi
Sato Eisaku

EAST ASIA (*continued*)
  Government, Politics, and Law (*continued*)
    Japan (*continued*)
Sendai
Shiga
Shimane
Shipbuilding Scandal
Shizuoka
Showa Denko Scandal
Siemens Incident
Tanaka Giichi
Textbook Scandal
Tochigi
Tojo Hideki
Tokushima
Tokyo
Tottori
Toyama
Wakayama
Yamagata
Yamagata Aritomo
Yamaguchi
Yamamoto Isoroku
Yamanashi
Yoshida Shigeru
Yoshida Shoin
    Koreas
April 19 Revolution—Korea
Chagang Province
Cheju Province
Ch'ongjin
Chun Doo Hwan
Communism—North Korea
Corruption—Korea
Democratization—South Korea
Haeju
Hamhung
Han Yong-un
Inchon
Juche
Kaesong
Kangwon Province
Kim Dae Jung
Kim Il Sung
Kim Jong Il
Kim Pu-shik
Kim Young-sam
Kim Yu-sin
Kwangju
Kwangju Uprising
Kyonggi Province
March First Independence Movement
Namp'o
North Cholla Province

North Ch'ungch'ong Province
North Hamgyong Province
North Hwanghae Province
North Korea—Political System
North Kyongsang Province
North P'yongan Province
Park Chung Hee
Pusan
Pyongyang
Rhee, Syngman
Roh Tae Woo
Sadaejuui
Sejong, King
Seoul
Sinuiju
South Cholla Province
South Ch'ungch'ong Province
South Hamgyong Province
South Hwanghae Province
South Korea—Political System
South Kyongsang Province
South P'yongan Province
Taegu
Taejon
Three Revolutions Movement
Ulchi Mundok
Wang Kon
Yanggang Province
Yi Ha-ung
Yi Song-gye
Yi T'ae-yong
Yu Kwan Sun
Yushin
    Mongolia
Aimag
Batmonkh, Jambyn
Choybalsan, Horloogiyn
Chormaqan, Noyan
Darhan
Erdenet
Genghis Khan
Golden Horde
Gurragchaa, Jugderdemidiyn
Karakorum
Khubilai Khan
Mongolia—Political System
Mongolian Social Democratic Party
Narantsatsralt, Janlavyn
Ochirbat, Punsalmaagiyn
Sukhbaatar, Damdiny
Tsedenbel, Yumjaagiyn
Ulaanbaatar
United Party of Mongolia

History and Profile
East Asia
Paleoanthropology—East Asia
   China
China—Profile
Han Dynasty
Hongcun and Xidi
Jurchen Jin Dynasty
Lijiang, Old Town of
Ming Dynasty
Pingyao, Ancient City of
Qin Dynasty
Qing Dynasty
Republican China
Shang Dynasty
Sixteen Kingdoms
Song Dynasty
Sui Dynasty
Taiwan—Profile
Taiwan, Modern
Tang Dynasty
Warring States Period—China
Yuan Dynasty
Zhou Dynasty
   Japan
Choshu Expeditions
Heian Period
Heisei Period
Japan—Profile
Jomon Period
Kamakura Period
Meiji Period
Muromachi Period
Nara Period
Showa Period
Taisho Period
Tokugawa Period
Yayoi Period
   Koreas
Choson Kingdom
Korea—History
Koryo Kingdom
North Korea—Profile
Parhae Kingdom
South Korea—Profile
Three Kingdoms Period
Unified Shilla Kingdom
   Mongolia
Mongol Empire
Mongolia—History
Mongolia—Profile
International Relations
Chinese Influence in East Asia
United Front Strategy

China
Boxer Rebellion
Central Asia-China Relations
China—Human Rights
China-India Relations
China-Japan Peace and Friendship Treaty
China-Japan Relations
China-Korea Relations
China-Russia Relations
China-Taiwan Relations
China-United States Relations
China-Vietnam Relations
Chinese Influence in East Asia
Chinese Influence in Southeast Asia
Hart, Robert
Japan-Taiwan Relations
Mongolia-China-Russia Relations
Nanjing Massacre
Open Door Policy
Opium War
Sino-French War
Spratly Islands Dispute
Taiwan—Human Rights
Taiwan-United States Relations
Tibet—Image in the Modern West
   Japan
China-Japan Peace and Friendship Treaty
China-Japan Relations
Comfort Women
Japan—Human Rights
Japan-Africa Relations
Japan-France Relations
Japan-Germany Relations
Japan-Korea Relations
Japan-Latin America Relations
Japan-Pacific Islands Relations
Japan-Philippines Relations
Japan-Russia Relations
Japan-Taiwan Relations
Japan–United Kingdom Relations
Japan–United States Relations
Japanese Expansion
Nixon Shock
Northern Territories
Nuclear Allergy
Plaza Accord
Russo-Japanese War
San Francisco Peace Treaty
Sino-Japanese Conflict, Second
Sino-Japanese War
Status of Forces Agreement
United States Military Bases—Japan
United States-Japan Security Treaty
Yasukuni Shrine Controversy

EAST ASIA *(continued)*
  History and Profile *(continued)*
  Koreas
China-Korea Relations
Japan-Korea Relations
Korea-Japan Treaty of 1965
Korean War
North Korea—Human Rights
North Korea-South Korea Relations
North Korea-United States Relations
South Korea—Human Rights
South Korea-European Union Relations
South Korea-United States Relations
  Mongolia
Mongolia—Human Rights
Mongolia-China-Russia Relations
Mongolia-Soviet Union Relations
Polo, Marco
  Language and Communication
  China
Chinese, Classical
Dai Qing
Hakka Languages
Mandarin
Media—China
Min
Romanization Systems, Chinese
Sino-Tibetan Languages
Wu
Xiang
Yue
  Japan
Feminine Language
Japanese Language
Matsumoto Shigeharu
Media—Japan
  Koreas
Hangul Script
Korean Language
Media—South Korea
Romanization Systems, Korean
  Mongolia
Khalkha
Mongolian Languages
Tungus Languages
  Peoples, Cultures, and Society
Marriage and Family—East Asia
Westernization—East Asia
  China
Aboriginal Peoples—Taiwan
China—Internal Migration
China—Population Resettlement
Chinese, Overseas
Clothing, Traditional—China

Clothing, Traditional—Hong Kong
Clothing, Traditional—Taiwan
Clothing, Traditional—Tibet
Courtyards
Foot Binding
Guanxi
Hakka
Han
Hmong
Hui
Manchu
Marriage and Family—China
Miao—China
Moso
Muslim Peoples in China
National Minorities—China
Qingke
Single-Child Phenomenon—China
Social Associations—China
Social Stratification—China
Tibetans
Tujia
Uighurs
Women in China
Yao
Yi
Zhuang
  Japan
Aging Population—Japan
Ainu
Burakumin
Chinese in Japan
Clothing, Traditional—Japan
Ijime
Koreans in Japan
Social Relations—Japan
Women in Japan
  Koreas
Ch'onmin
Clothing, Traditional—Korea
Koreans
Koreans, Overseas
Kye
Nobi
Women in Korea
Yangban
  Mongolia
Clothing, Traditional—Mongolia
Mongols
Russians in Mongolia
  Religion and Philosophy
Ancestor Worship—East Asia
Zodiac System—East Asia

China
Analects
Atheism, Official—China
Buddhism—China
Buddhism, Chan
Buddhism—Tibet
Buddhism, Pure Land
Bureau of Religious Affairs
Christianity—China
Confucian Ethics
Confucianism—China
Confucius
Cult of Maitreya
Dalai Lama
Falun Gong
Feng Shui
Five Phases
Four Books
Judaism—China
Laozi
Marxism-Leninism-Mao Zedong Thought
Mencius
Mozi
Neo-Confucianism
Potala Palace
Religion, Folk—China
Ricci, Matteo
Taoism
Xunzi
Zhu Xi
    Japan
Atsuta Shrine
Buddhism—Japan
Christianity—Japan
Confucianism—Japan
Hayashi Razan
Honen
Ikkyu
Ise Shrine
Iwashimizu Hachiman Shrine
Izumo Shrine
Kukai
Motoori Norinaga
Nichiren
Nishida Kitaro
Religion, Folk—Japan
Religions, New—Japan
Saicho
Shinran
Shinto
Suzuki Daisetsu Teitaro
Twenty-Six Martyrs
Uchimura Kanzo
Yamato Damashii

Yasukuni Shrine
    Koreas
Buddhism—Korea
Ch'ondogyo
Christianity—Korea
Confucianism—Korea
Religions, New—Korea
Seshi Customs
Taejonggyo
Tan'gun Myth
Taoism—Korea
Tonghak
Unification Church
Yi I
    Mongolia
Bogdo Khan
Buddhism—Mongolia
Gandan Lamasery
Islam—Mongolia
Shamanism—Mongolia
  Science, Technology, and Health
Calendars—East Asia
    China
Abacus
Acupuncture
Dujiangyan
Grand Canal
Great Wall
Gunpowder and Rocketry
Junk
Li Shizhen
Magnetism
Massage—China
Medicine, Traditional—China
Moxibustion
Needham, Joseph
Printing and Papermaking
Science, Traditional—China
Sericulture—China
Three Gorges Dam Project
Xu Guangqi
    Koreas
Science Towns—Korea

SOUTH ASIA
  Arts, Literature, and Recreation
Chitra/Ardhachitra/Chitrabhasha
Conveyance Arts
Cricket
Cuisine—South Asia
Drama—South Asia
Farid, Khwaja Ghulam
Indigo
Islam, Kazi Nazrul

SOUTH ASIA (*continued*)
  Arts, Literature, and Recreation (*continued*)
Jatra
Kama Sutra
Kipling, Joseph Rudyard
Literature, Bengali
Literature, Sanskrit
Literature, Tamil
Mahabharata
Manto, Sadaat Hasan
Nur Jehan
Painting—South Asia
Persian Miniature Painting
Raga
Ramayana
Rubab
Sarangi
Sarod
Sculpture—South Asia
Shah, Lalon
Shehnai
Veena
    Bangladesh
Dance—Bangladesh
Music—Bangladesh
    Bhutan
Textiles—Bhutan
    India
Anand, Mulk Raj
Architecture—India
Bachchan, Amitabh
Chatterjee, Bankim Chandra
Chaudhuri, Nirad Chandra
Chughtai, Ismat
Cinema—India
Dance—India
Diwali
Drama—India
Forster, E. M.
Ghalib, Mirza Asadullah Khan
Holi
Kalidasa
Khan, Vilayat
Khusrau, Amir
Kumar, Dilip
Literature—India
Mangeshkar, Lata
Music—India
Music, Devotional—India
Narayan, R.K.
Nataka
Poetry—India
Prakarana
Premchand

Rahman, A.R.
Rao, Raja
Rasa
Ray, Satyajit
Sports—India
Taj Mahal
    Sri Lanka
Coomaraswamy, Ananda Kentish
Dance, Kandyan
Literature, Sinhalese
  Economics, Commerce, and Transportation
Agriculture—South Asia
British East India Company
French East India Company
Hawkins, William
Nomadic Pastoralism—South Asia
Tea—South Asia
    Bangladesh
Bangladesh—Economic System
Grameen Bank
    India
Agriculture—South Asia
British East India Company
French East India Company
Hawkins, William
India—Economic System
Nomadic Pastoralism—South Asia
Remittances
Salt Tax
Tea—South Asia
    Nepal
Nepal—Economic System
    Sri Lanka
Sri Lanka—Economic System
  Education
Panini
Sayyid, Ahmad Khan
    Bangladesh
Bangladesh—Education System
    India
India—Education System
    Nepal
Nepal—Education System
    Sri Lanka
Sri Lanka—Education System
  Geography and the Natural World
Andaman Sea
Bay of Bengal
Bramaputra River
Bustard, Hubara
Chagos Archipelago
Elephant, Asian
Green Revolution—South Asia
Himalaya Range

Indian Ocean
Indian Subcontinent
Indo-Gangetic Plain
Jhelum River
Jute
K2, Mount
Kangchenjunga, Mount
Kaveri River
Kistna River
Mongoose
Punjab
Reunion Island
Sundarbhans
Tarai
  India
Abu, Mount
Andaman and Nicobar Islands
Bhopal
Chenab River
Dekkan
Eastern Ghats
Ganges River
Godavari River
Hindu Kush
Jumna River
Lion, Asiatic
Mahanadi River
Narmada Dam Controversy
Narmada River
Rann of Kachchh
Satpura Range
Sutlej River
Thar Desert
Tungabhadra River
Vindhya Mountains
Western Ghats
Zebu
  Nepal
Everest, Mount
Kathmandu Valley
  Government, Politics, and Law
Bahadur Shah
Birla Family
Colombo Plan
Hastings, Warren
Humayun
Ibn al-Qasim, Muhammad
Jahangir
Marxism—South Asia
Poros
Raziya
Roy, Rammohan
Shah Jahan
Singh, Jai

Tata Family
Tipu Sultan
  Bangladesh
Awami League
Bangladesh—Political System
Bangladesh Nationalist Party
Chittagong
Dhaka
Ershad, H.M.
Hasina Wajid, Sheikh
Jatiya Party
Rahman, Mujibur
Rahman, Ziaur
Zia, Khaleda
  Bhutan
Thimphu
Wangchuck, King Jigme Singye
  India
Afzal Khan
Agartala
Agra
Ahmadabad
Ajanta
Ajodhya
Akbar
Ali Janhar, Mohamed
Allahabad
Ambedkar, B.R.
Amritsar
Andhra Pradesh
Arunachal Pradesh
Asoka
Assam
Aurangabad
Aurangzeb
Awadh
Azad, Abu'l-Kalam
Babur
Bangalore
Bengal, West
Bentinck, William Cavendish
Bhosle, Shivaji
Bhubaneshwar
Bihar
Bodh Gaya
Bose, Subhas Chandra
Calcutta
Calicut
Canning, Charles John
Chandigarh
Chhattisgarh
Coimbatore
Constitution—India

SOUTH ASIA *(continued)*
  Government, Politics, and Law *(continued)*
   India (continued)
Cranganur
Curzon, George Nathaniel
Dadra and Nagar Haveli Union Territory
Daman and Diu Union Territory
Darjeeling
Dehra Dun
Delhi Union Territory
Devi, Phoolan
Fazl, Abu'l
Gandhi, Indira
Gandhi, Mohandas K.
Gangtok
Goa
Godse, Nathuram Vinayak
Gujarat
Guwahati
Haidar, Ali Khan
Harsa
Haryana
Himachal Pradesh
Hindu Law
Hindu Nationalism
Hyderabad
Imphal
India—Political System
Indore
Jaipur
Jammu and Kashmir
Jharkhand
Jodhpur
Kanpur
Karnataka
Kautilya
Kerala
Khilafat Movement
Kohima
Ladakh
Lakshadweep
Laxmibai
Leh
Lucknow
Macaulay, Thomas B.
Madhya Pradesh
Madras
Madurai
Maharashtra
Mangalore
Manipur
Mathura
Meghalaya
Mizoram

Montagu-Chelmsford Reforms
Morley-Minto Reforms
Mumbai
Muslim League
Mysore
Nagaland
Nehru, Jawaharlal
Nehru, Motilal
Nilgiri District
Ootacamund
Orissa
Patna
Pondicherry
Pune
Puri
Raipur
Rajagopalachari, Chakravarti
Rajasthan
Rajkot
Ramachandran, Marudur Gopalamenon
Sarnath
Satyagraha
Shillong
Sikkim
Simla
Sindhia Family
Srinagar
Tamil Nadu
Thanjavur
Tripura
Trivandrum
Uttar Pradesh
Uttaranchal
Varanasi
Vishakapatnam
   Nepal
Kathmandu
Nepal—Political System
Rana
   Sri Lanka
Bandaranaike, Sirimavo Ratwatte Dias
Bandaranaike, Solomon West Ridgeway Diaz
Colombo
Jaffna
Kandy
Polonnaruva
Sri Lanka—Political System
Trincomalee
  History and Profile
British Indian Empire
Chera
Chola
Dogra Dynasty
Gupta Empire

Harappa
Holkars
Mauryan Empire
Mughal Empire
Paleoanthropology—South Asia
Pandya
South Asia—History
Vijayanagara Empire
  Bangladesh
Bangladesh—History
Bangladesh—Profile
  Bhutan
Bhutan—History
Bhutan—Profile
  India
Anglo-Mysore Wars
India—Medieval Period
India—Profile
Mutiny, Indian
Quit India Movement
  Maldives
Maldives—History
Maldives—Profile
  Mauritius
Mauritius—Profile
  Nepal
Nepal—History
Nepal—Profile
  Sri Lanka
Sri Lanka—History
Sri Lanka—Profile
  International Relations
  Bangladesh
Bangladesh-India Relations
Bangladesh-Pakistan Relations
  India
Bangladesh-India Relations
China-India Relations
India—Human Rights
India-Myanmar Relations
India-Pakistan Relations
India-Southeast Asia Relations
India-Sri Lanka Relations
India-United Kingdom Relations
India-United States Relations
  Sri Lanka
India-Sri Lanka Relations
Sri Lanka—Human Rights
  Language and Communication
Bengali Language
Dravidian Languages
Indo-Aryan Languages
Media—South Asia
Munda Languages

India
Hindi-Urdu
Sanskrit
Tamil Language
  Sri Lanka
Sinhala
  Peoples, Cultures, and Society
Bengalis
Ethnic Conflict—South Asia
Gama, Vasco da
Ismaili Sects—South Asia
Marriage and Family—South Asia
Nagas
Panjabi
Refugees—South Asia
South Asians, Overseas
Westernization—South Asia
Women in South Asia
  Bhutan
Bhutanese
Clothing, Traditional—Bhutan
  India
Anglo-Indians
Aryan
Assamese
Bhil
Brahman
Caste
Clothing, Traditional—India
Garo
Gond
Gujarati
Hill Tribes of India
Khasi
Oriyas
Pahari
Pandit
Parsi
Peripatetics
Rajput
Sanskritization
Santal
Sati
Tamils
Telugu
Untouchability
  Sri Lanka
Sinhalese
Vedda
  Religion and Philosophy
Buddhism—South Asia
Chishtiya
Christianity—South Asia

SOUTH ASIA (continued)
   Religion and Philosophy (continued)
Islam—South Asia
Jones, William
Judaism—South Asia
Khwaja Mu'in al-Din Chishti
Nurbakhshiya
Pilgrimage—South Asia
Sankara
Siddhartha Gautama
Sufism—South Asia
Vivekananda, Swami
Wali Allah, Shah
   Bhutan
Bhutan—Religion
   India
Blavatsky, Helena Petrovna
Bhakti
Dev, Nanak Guru
Hindu Philosophy
Hindu Values
Hinduism—India
Jainism
Jesuits— India
Lingayat
Nagarjuna
Nizam ad-din Awliya
Possession
Ramakrishna
Ramanuja
Sai Baba, Satya
Sikhism
Tagore, Rabindranath
Teresa, Mother
Upanishads
   Science, Technology, and Health
Calendars—South Asia
Climatology—South Asia
   India
Medicine, Ayurvedic
Medicine, Unani

SOUTHEAST ASIA
   Arts, Literature, and Recreation
Architecture—Southeast Asia
Batik
Cockfighting
Drama—Southeast Asia
Hari Raya Puasa
Kain Batik
Kain Songket
Mendu
Sepak Takraw
Thaipusam

   Cambodia
Angkor Wat
Literature, Khmer
   Indonesia
Arja
Bali Barong-Rangda
Balinese Sanghyang
Bedaya
Borobudur
Cuisine—Indonesia
Dance—Bali
Gambang Kromong
Gambuh
Gamelan
Hikayat Amir Hamza
Ludruk
Masks, Javanese
Music—Indonesia
Noer, Arifin C.
Pramoedya Ananta Toer
Puisi
Randai
Rendra, W.S.
Riantiarno, Nano
Sandiwara
Wayang Beber
Wayang Golek
Wayang Kulit
Wayang Topeng
Wayang Wong
Wijaya, Putu
   Laos
Ikat Dyeing
Luang Prabang
Music, Folk—Laos
Palm-Leaf Manuscripts
Textiles—Laos
That Luang Festival
Wat Xieng Khouan
   Malaysia
Bangsawan
Chang Fee Ming
Chuah Thean Teng
Cuisine—Malaysia
Dance—Malaysia
Dikir Barat
Gawai Dayak
Jikey
Jit, Krishen
Labu Sayong
Lim, Shirley
Mak Yong
Maniam, K.S.
Manora

Pesta Menuai
Petronas Towers
Songket
Tarian Asyik
Tarian Portugis
Tay Hooi Keat
   Myanmar
Burmese Arts
Literature—Myanmar
Mandalay Palace
Pagodas, Burmese
   Philippines
Arnis
Bagonbanta, Fernando
Balisong
Baltazar, Francisco
Bulosan, Carlos
Cuisine—Philippines
Guerrero, Fernando M.
Literature—Philippines
Luna Y Novicio, Juan
Poetry—Philippines
   Thailand
Bidyalankarana
Cuisine—Thailand
Damkoeng, Akat
Dokmai Sot
Drama—Thailand
Emerald Buddha
Fish Fighting
Khun Chang, Khun Phaen
Literature—Thailand
Longboat Racing
Muay Thai
Nirat
Phumisak, Chit
Ramakien
Siburapha
Sot Kuramarohit
   Vietnam
Ao Dai
Cuisine—Vietnam
Dai Viet Su Ky
Doan Thi Diem
Ho Xuan Huong
Hoang Ngoc Phach
Hoat, Doan Viet
Khai Hung
Linh Nhat
Literature—Vietnam
Nguyen Du
Nguyen Thieu Gia
Opera—Vietnam
Plowing Ritual—Vietnam

Poetry—Vietnam
Puppetry, Water
Tet
Tran Do
Truong Vinh Ky
Tu Luc Van Doan
Wandering Souls

Economics, Commerce, and Transportation

Agriculture—Southeast Asia
Burma-Thailand Railway
Fishing Industry—Southeast Asia
Forest Industry—Southeast Asia
Golden Triangle
Ho Chi Minh Trail
Rubber Industry
   Cambodia
Cambodia—Economic System
   Indonesia
Indonesia—Economic System
Manufacturing Industry—Indonesia
Repelita
   Laos
Chintanakan mai
Laos—Economic System
Mittaphap Bridge
   Malaysia
Malaysia—Economic System
Manufacturing Industry—Malaysia
Mineral Industry—Malaysia
New Economic Policy—Malaysia
Rubber Industry—Malaysia
Timber Industry—Malaysia
   Myanmar
Burma Road
Myanmar—Economic System
   Philippines
Manufacturing Industry—Philippines
Pan-Philippine Highway
Philippines—Economic System
Suki
   Singapore
Banking and Finance Industry—Singapore
Singapore—Economic System
   Thailand
Thailand—Economic System
Thompson, Jim
   Vietnam
Doi Moi
Ho Chi Minh Trail
Mekong Project
New Economic Zones
Vietnam—Economic System

SOUTHEAST ASIA *(continued)*
  Education
    Brunei
Universiti Brunei Darussalam
    Cambodia
Cambodia—Education System
Royal University of Phnom Penh
    Indonesia
Bandung Institute of Technology
Gadjah Mada University
Indonesia—Education System
University of Indonesia
    Laos
Laos—Education System
Sisavangvong University
    Malaysia
Malaysia—Education System
Universiti Sains Malaysia
University of Malaya
    Myanmar
Myanmar—Education System
    Philippines
Philippines—Education System
    Singapore
Nanyang Technological University
National University of Singapore
Singapore—Education System
    Thailand
Chulalongkorn University
Thailand—Education System
    Vietnam
Vietnam—Education System
  Geography and the Natural World
Andaman Sea
Banteng
Borneo
Dangrek Range
Green Revolution—Southeast Asia
Leopard, Clouded
Mongoose
Orangutan
Sun Bear
    Cambodia
Cardamon Mountains
Elephant Range
Kompong Som Bay
Tonle Sap
    Indonesia
Babirusa
Bali
Banda Sea
Flores Sea
Java Sea
Komodo Dragon

Maluku
Nusa Tenggara
Timor Sea
    Laos
Bolovens Plateau
Plain of Jars
    Malaysia
Cameron Highlands
Kinabalu, Mount
Strait of Malacca
    Myanmar
Arakan Yoma Mountains
Inle Lake Region
Irrawaddy River and Delta
Salween River
Sittang River
    Philippines
Agno River
Cagayan River
Caraballo Mountains
Celebes Sea
Cordillera Central
Luzon Group
Maguey
Mindanao
Philippine Sea
Sierra Madre
Sulu Archipelago
Visayan Islands
Zambales Mountains
    Thailand
Chao Phraya River and Delta
Doi Inthanon
Gulf of Thailand
Khon Kaen
Nakhon Ratchasima
Peninsular Thailand
Three Pagodas Pass
    Vietnam
Cam Ranh Bay
Central Highlands of Vietnam
Con Dao Islands
Ha Long Bay
Ho Dynasty Citadel
Hoan Kiem Lake
Karun River and Shatt al Arab River
Mekong River and Delta
Red River and Delta
Tonkin Gulf
  Government, Politics, and Law
Albuquerque, Afonso de
British Military Administration
Doumer, Paul
Dutch East India Company

Romusha
Weld, Frederick
  Brunei
Azahari, A.M.
Bandar Seri Begawan
Brooke, James
Hassanal Bolkaih
Parti Rakyat Brunei
  Cambodia
Buddhist Liberal Democratic Party—Cambodia
Cambodia—Civil War of 1970-1975
Cambodia—Political System
Cambodian People's Party
Fa Ngoum
FUNCINPEC
Heng Samrin
Hun Sen
Jayavarman II
Jayavarman VII
Khieu Samphan
Khmer Rouge
Killing Fields
Lon Nol
Phnom Penh
Phnom Penh Evacuation
Pol Pot
Ranariddh, Norodom
Sam Rainsy
Sihanouk, Norodom
  East Timor
Belo, Bishop Carlos
Dili
Dili Massacre
Fretilin
Gusmao, Xanana
Ramos-Horta, José
  Indonesia
Airlangga
Amboina Massacre
Bandung
Batavia
Bosch, Johannes van den
Budi Utomo
Coen, Jan Pieterszoon
Cukong
Daendels, Herman
Darul Islam
Ethnic Colonial Policy—Indonesia
Gajah Mada
Gerindo
Gestapu Affair
Golkar
Habibie, B.J.
Hamengku Buwono IX, Sri Sultan

Hatta, Mohammad
Hizbullah
Indonesia—Political Parties
Indonesia—Political System
Indonesian Democratic Party
Indonesian Revolution
Irian Jaya
Jakarta
Jakarta Riots of May 1998
Java
Kalimantan
Malik, Adam
Medan
Megawati Sukarnoputri
Military, Indonesia
Moerdani, Leonardus Benjamin
New Order
Old Order
Pancasila
Partai Kebangkitan Bangsa
Partai Persatuan Pembangunan
Rais, Muhammad Amien
Sarekat Islam
Solo
Speelman, Cornelius
Suharto
Sukarno
Sulawesi
Sumatra
Surabaya
Taman Siswa
Treaty of Giyanti
Umar, Teuku
Wahid, Abdurrahman
Yogyakarta
  Laos
Bokeo
Chao Anou
Civil War of 1956–1975—Laos
Kaysone Phomvihan
Lao People's Revolutionary Party
Laos—Political System
Louangnamtha
Pathet Lao
Setthathirat
Souphanuvong, Prince
Souvanna Phouma, Prince
Vientiane
Xayabury
  Malaysia
Abdul Razak
Abu Bakar
Anwar, Ibrahim
Badawi, Abdullah Ahmed

SOUTHEAST ASIA *(continued)*
  Government, Politics, and Law *(continued)*
  Malaysia (continued)
Bendahara
Birch, James W. W.
Bumiputra
Clifford, Hugh
Federal Territories—Malaysia
Federation of Malaysia
Haji, Raja
Hussein Onn
Iskandar Muda
Johor
Kapitan Cina
Kedah
Kelantan
Kota Kinabalu
Kuala Lumpur
Kuching
Laksamana
Light, Francis
Lim Chong Eu
Mahathir Mohamad
Mahmud Shah
Malay States, Unfederated
Malayan People's Anti-Japanese Army
Malayan Union
Malaysia—Political System
Malaysian Chinese Association
Mansur Shah
Mat Salleh Rebellion
May 13 Ethnic Riots— Malaysia
Melaka
Negeri Sembilan
Ningkan, Stephen Kalong
Onn Bin Jaafar
Pahang
Pangkor Treaty
Penang
Perak
Perlis
Raffles, Thomas Stamford
Resident System
Rukunegara
Sabah
Sarawak
Straits Settlements
Swettenham, Frank
Tan Siew Sin
Temenggong
Templer, Gerald
Trengganu
Wan Ahmad
Yap Ah Loy

  Myanmar
All Burma Students Democratic Front
Anawratha
Anti-Fascist People's Freedom League—Myanmar
Aung San
Aung San Suu Kyi
Bassein
Burma Independence Army
Chin State
Communist Party of Burma
Irrawaddy Division
Kachin Independence Organization
Kachin State
Karen National Union
Karen State
Kayah State
Magwe Division
Mandalay
Mandalay Division
Mon State
Mong Tai Army
Moulmein
Myanmar—Political System
National League for Democracy—Myanmar
National Unity Party—Myanmar
Ne Win, U
Nu, U
Palaung State Liberation Party
Pao National Organization
Pegu
Rakhine State
Sagaing Division
Shan State
Shan State Army
State Law and Order Restoration Council—Myanmar
Tenasserim Division
Thakins
Than Shwe
Thant, U
Union Solidarity and Development Association—Mya
United Wa State Party
Yangon
Yangon Division
  Philippines
Aquino, Benigno
Aquino, Corazon
Autonomous Region of Muslim Mindanao
Baguio
Cebu
Davao
Estrada, Joseph
Garcia, Carlos P.

Huk Rebellion
Macapagal, Diosdado
MacArthur, Douglas
Magsaysay, Ramon
Manila
Marcos, Ferdinand
Marcos, Imelda
Moro Islamic Liberation Front
Moro National Liberation Front
Nur Misuari
People Power Movement
Philippines—Political System
Ramos, Fidel
Rizal, José
Romulo, Carlos Peña
Urdaneta, Andres de
Zamboanga
    Singapore
Barisan Sosialis
Goh Chok Tong
Goh Keng Swee
Jeyaretnam, Joshua Benjamin
Lee Kuan Yew
Lim Chin Siong
Marshall, David
Singapore—Political System
Singapore Democratic Party
Workers' Party—Singapore
    Thailand
Anand Panyarachun
Bangkok
Bhumipol Adulyadej
Chart Thai
Chavalit, Yongchaiyudh
Chiang Mai
Chuan Leekpai
Chulalongkorn, King
Ekaphap
Manhattan Incident
Mongkut
National Peacekeeping Council—Thailand
Nation-Religion-Monarch
October 6 Crisis—Thailand
Phalang Dharma Party
Phuket
Phya Taksin
Pibul Songgram
Pridi Banomyong
Rama Khamheng
Rama Tibodi I
Sarit Thanarat
Student Uprising of 1973—Thailand
Sulak Sivaraksa
Thai Revolution of 1932

Thailand—Political Parties
Thailand—Political System
Thaksin Shinawatra
Thanom Kittikachorn
Trailok
Ungphakorn Puey
    Vietnam
An Duong Vuong
Anh Dao Duy
Army of the Republic of Vietnam
August Revolution
Ba Trieu
Bac Son Uprising
Bao Dai
Co Loa Thanh
Communism—Vietnam
Da Nang
Dalat
Duong Van Minh
Haiphong
Hanoi
Ho Chi Minh
Ho Chi Minh City
Ho Tung Mau
Hoi An
Hue
Huynh Tan Phat
Iron Triangle
Lac Long Quan
Le Duan
Le Duc Anh
Le Duc Tho
National Front for the Liberation of South Vietnam
Ngo Dinh Diem
Ngo Dinh Nhu
Nguyen Cao Ky
Nguyen Thi Minh Khai
Nguyen Van Thieu
Nhu, Madame Ngo Dinh
People's Army of Vietnam
Phan Boi Chau
Phieu Le Kha
Revolt of the Short Hair
Revolutionary Youth League of Vietnam
Tay Son Rebellion
Tran Van Giau
Trung Sisters
Vietnam—Political System
Vietnam Communist Party
Vo Nguyen Giap
Vo Van Kiet

    History and Profile
British in Southeast Asia
Dutch in Southeast Asia

SOUTHEAST ASIA (*continued*)
  History and Profile (*continued*)
Paleoanthropology—Southeast Asia
Portuguese in Southeast Asia
Srivijaya
  Brunei
Brunei—Political System
Brunei—Profile
  Cambodia
Cambodia—History
Cambodia—Profile
Khmer Empire
  East Timor
East Timor—Profile
  Indonesia
Aceh Rebellion
Amangkurat
British-Dutch Wars
Candi of Java
Indonesia—History
Indonesia—Profile
Java War
Konfrontasi
Majapahit
Mataram
Netherlands East Indies
Padri War
Pakualaman
Sailendra
  Laos
Laos—History
Laos—Profile
  Malaysia
Anglo-Dutch Treaty
Federated Malay States
Malaysia—History
Malaysia—Profile
Melaka Sultanate
White Rajas
  Myanmar
Myanmar—History
Myanmar—Profile
Pagan
  Philippines
Philippines—History
Philippines—Profile
  Singapore
Singapore—History
Singapore—Profile
  Thailand
Ayutthaya, Kingdom of
Ban Chiang
Sukhothai
Thailand—History

Thailand—Profile
  Vietnam
Vietnam—History
Vietnam—Profile
  International Relations
Association of South-East Asian Nations
Bali Summit
Bandung Conference
Bangkok Declaration
Chinese Influence in Southeast Asia
Five Power Defence Arrangements
India-Southeast Asia Relations
Indochina War of 1940–1941
Piracy—Southeast Asia
Southeast Asia—Human Rights
Southeast Asia Treaty Organization
Treaty of Amity and Co-operation of 1976
ZOPFAN
  Cambodia
Cambodia-Laos Relations
Cambodia-Vietnam Relations
United Nations Transitional Authority in Cambodia
  East Timor
United Nations in East Timor
  Indonesia
Indonesia-Malaysia Relations
Indonesia–United States Relations
Irian Jaya Conquest
Volksraad
  Laos
Cambodia-Laos Relations
Laos-Thailand Relations
Laos-Vietnam Relations
  Malaysia
Indonesia-Malaysia Relations
Malayan Emergency
Malaysia-Europe Relations
Sabah Dispute
  Myanmar
India-Myanmar Relations
Myanmar—Foreign Relations
Myanmar—Human Rights
  Philippines
Japan-Philippines Relations
Philippines—Human Rights
Philippines–United States Relations
  Thailand
Laos-Thailand Relations
  Vietnam
Cambodia-Vietnam Relations
China-Vietnam Relations
Franco-Viet Minh War
Laos-Vietnam Relations
Soviet-Vietnamese TFOC

Vietnam War
Vietnam–United States Relations
Language and Communication
Austronesian Languages
Malay-Indonesian Languages
Media—Insular Southeast Asia
Media—Mainland Southeast Asia
Mon-Khmer Languages
Tai-Kadai Languages
Indonesia
Bahasa Indonesia
Javanese
Mohamad, Goenawan
Tempo
Laos
Lao-Tai Languages
Myanmar
Burmese
Philippines
Philippine Languages
Singapore
Chinese-Language Newspapers—Singapore
Straits Times, The
Thailand
Saek
Vietnam
Chu Nom
Vietnamese Language
Peoples, Cultures, and Society
Adat
Akha
Borneo Peoples
Chinese in Southeast Asia
Clothing, Traditional—Tribal Southeast Asia
Ethnic Relations—Southeast Asia
Hmong
Khmu
Marriage and Family—Insular Southeast Asia
Marriage and Family—Mainland Southeast Asia
Refugees—Southeast Asia
Westernization—Southeast Asia
Women in Southeast Asia
Cambodia
Clothing, Traditional—Cambodia
Indonesia
Acehnese
Balinese
Clothing, Traditional—Indonesia
Coastal Malays
Madurese
Peranakan
Pribumi
Priyayi
South Asians in Southeast Asia

Sundanese
Laos
Clothing, Traditional—Laos
Khmer
Malaysia
Clothing, Traditional—Malaysia
Orang Asli
Myanmar
Burmans
Chin
Chinese in Myanmar
Ethnic Conflict—Myanmar
Kachin
Karen
Mon
Rohingya
Shan
Philippines
Godparenthood—Philippines
Thailand
Clothing, Traditional—Thailand
Mechai Viravaidya
Thai
Vietnam
Boat People
Chinese in Vietnam
Clothing, Traditional—Vietnam
Sino-Vietnamese Culture
Vietnam—Internal Migration
Vietnamese
Vietnamese, Overseas
Religion and Philosophy
Basi
Buddhism, Theravada—Southeast Asia
Christianity—Southeast Asia
Islam—Mainland Southeast Asia
Muang
Pali Canon
Protestant Fundamentalism—Southeast Asia
Zikir
Brunei
Islam—Brunei
Indonesia
Abangan
Hosen, Ibrahim
Islam—Indonesia
Muhammadiyah
Nahdlatul Ulama
Prambanan Hindu
Santri
Laos
Prabang
That Luang

SOUTHEAST ASIA (*continued*)
  Religion and Philosophy (*continued*)
    Malaysia
Angkatan Belia Islam Malaysia
Islam—Malaysia
    Myanmar
Christianity—Myanmar
Islam—Myanmar
Spirit Cults
    Philippines
Catholicism, Roman—Philippines
Iglesia ni Christo
Islam—Philippines
Philippine Independent Church
Ruiz, Saint Lorenzo
Sin, Jaime
    Thailand
Buddhadasa, Bhikku
Dhammayut Sect
Hinduism—Thailand
Phra Pathom Chedi
    Vietnam
Buddhism—Vietnam
Cao Dai
Catholicism, Roman—Vietnam
Hoa Hao
Thich Nhat Hanh
  Science, Technology, and Health
Bedil
Calendars—Southeast Asia
Gunpowder and Rocketry

SOUTHWEST ASIA
  Arts, Literature, and Recreation
Alghoza
Bhitai, Shah Abdul Latif
Jami, 'Abdurrahman
Khushal Khan Khatak
Shah, Waris
    Afghanistan
Cuisine—Afghanistan
    Pakistan
Ali Khan, Bade Ghulam
Bhit Shah
Faiz Ahmed Faiz
Gulgee
Hir Ranjha Story
Iqbal, Muhammad
Makli Hill
Naqsh, Jamil
Nusrat Fateh Ali Khan
Sabri Brothers
Sadequain

  Economics, Commerce, and Transportation
    Afghanistan
Afghanistan—Economic System
    Pakistan
Karakoram Highway
Pakistan—Economic System
  Education
    Pakistan
Pakistan—Education System
  Geography and the Natural World
Badakhshan
Kabul River
Karakoram Mountains
Khyber Pass
Ravi River
    Afghanistan
Afghan Hound
Dasht-e Margo
Hunza
Wakhan
    Pakistan
Azad Kashmir
Baltistan
Bolan Pass
Indus River
Indus River Dolphin
Khunjerab Pass
Sutlej River
  Government, Politics, and Law
Afghani, Jamal ad-din
Baluchistan
Dost Muhammad
Taxila
    Afghanistan
Afghanistan—Political System
Amanollah
Bagram
Bamian
Bin Laden, Osama
Daud, Muhammad
Dawai, Abdul Hadi
Din Mohammad, Mushk-e Alam
Ghazna
Herat
Kabul
Mahmud of Ghazna
Mazar-e Sharif
Mujahideen
Omar, Mullah Muhammad
Taliban
Zahir Shah
    Pakistan
Abdullah, Muhammad
Anarkali

Ayub Khan
Bhutto, Benazir
Bhutto, Zulfiqar Ali
David, Collin
Hadood
Islamabad
Jamaʿat-e-Islami
Jinnah, Mohammed Ali
Karachi
Khan, Abdul Ghaffar
Lahore
Mohenjo Daro
Muhajir Qawmi Movement
Multan
Musharraf, Pervez
North-West Frontier Province Sarhad
Pakistan—Political System
Pakistan People's Party
Peshawar
Rahmat Ali, Chauduri
Rohtas Fort
Sehwan
Sind
Zia-ul-Haq, Mohammad
History and Profile
Afghanistan
Afghanistan—History
Afghanistan—Profile
Durrani
Pakistan
Federally Administered Tribal Areas—Pakistan
Pakistan—History
Pakistan—Profile
International Relations
Afghanistan
Afghanistan—Human Rights
Treaty of Gandomak
Pakistan
Bangladesh-Pakistan Relations
India-Pakistan Relations
Pakistan—Human Rights
Language and Communication
Pashto
Afghanistan
Dari
Peoples, Cultures, and Society
Afridi
Baluchi
Brahui
Pashtun
Pashtunwali
Waziri
Clothing, Traditional—Afghanistan
Ethnic Conflict—Afghanistan

Hazara
Pakistan
Sindhi
Siraiki
Women in Pakistan
Religion and Philosophy
Bakhsh, Data Ganj
Islam—Southwest Asia
Shah, Mihr Ali
Shahbaz Qalandar Lal
Sufism—Southwest Asia
Afghanistan
Ansari, Abdullah
Bitab, Sufi
Pakistan
Mawdudi, Abu'l-A'la
Muhajir

WEST ASIA
Arts, Literature, and Recreation
Architecture—West Asia
Architecture, Islamic—West Asia
Cinema—West Asia
Music—West Asia
Rudaki
Shahnameh Epic
Sports—Islamic Asia
Twelver Shiʿism
Iran
Cuisine—Iran
No-ruz
Literature, Persian
Iraq
Cuisine—Iraq
Poetry—Iraq
Turkey
Children's Day—Turkey
Cuisine—Turkey
Guney, Yilmaz
Literature—Turkey
Music—Turkey
Nesin, Aziz
Pamuk, Orhan
Economics, Commerce, and Transportation
Agriculture—West Asia
Industry—West Asia
Oil Industry—West Asia
Organization of Petroleum Exporting Countries
Iran
Iran—Economic System
Iraq
Iraq—Economic System
Turkey
Etatism—Turkey

WEST ASIA (*continued*)
  Economics, Commerce, and Transportation
    (*continued*)
Turkey—Economic System
  Education
    Iran
Iran—Education System
    Iraq
Iraq—Education System
    Turkey
Turkey—Education System
  Geography and the Natural World
Caucasia
Euphrates River
Sistan
Tigris River
    Iran
Abkhazia
Amu Dar'ya
Dagestan
Elburz
Gulf of Oman
Persian Gulf
Zagros Mountains
    Turkey
Aegean Sea
Anti-Taurus
Ararat, Mount
Black Sea
Bosporus
Cappadocia
Cilician Gates
Dardanelles
Gaziantep
Izmir
Kizel Irmak River
Marmara, Sea of
Tarsus
Taurus Mountains
Yesilirmak River
  Government, Politics, and Law
Aleppo
Karabag
Yerevan
    Iran
Abadan
Ardabil
Azerbaijan
Bakhtaran
Bandar Abbas
Bazargan, Mehdi
Constitution, Islamic—Iran
Esfahan
Fars

Hamadan
Iran—Political System
Islamic Revolution—Iran
Kandahar
Kerman
Khomeini, Ayatollah
Khurasan
Khuzestan
Mashhad
Qom
Sana'i
Shariati, Ali
Shiraz
Tabriz
Tehran
Veleyet-e Faqih
    Iraq
Al-Najaf
Baghdad
Basra
Hussein, Saddam
Iraq—Political System
Karbala
Kirkuk
Mosul
Sulaymaniya
    Turkey
Adalet Partisi
Adana
Afyon
Amasya
Anatolia
Ankara
Antakya
Antalya
Ataturk
Bayar, Mahmut Celal
Bodrum
Bursa
Constitution—Turkey
Demirel, Suleyman
Democrat Party—Turkey
Diyarbakir
Edirne
Erzurum
Halide Edib Adivar
Hikmet, Nazim
Inonu, Mustafa Ismet
Istanbul
Iznik
Kars
Kas
Kemal, Yasar
Konya

Kutahya
Menderes, Adnan
Mersin
North Cyprus, Turkish Republic of
Ozal, Turgut
Pergamon
Refah and Fazilet Parties
Republican People's Party—Turkey
Rize
Samsun
Sardis
Sinop
Sivas
Tanzimat
Trabzon
Turkey—Political System
Urfa
Van
Zonguldak
   History and Profile
   Iran
Iran—History
Iran—Profile
Pahlavi Dynasty
Qajar Dynasty
   Iraq
Iraq—History
Iraq—Profile
   Turkey
Archaeology—Turkey
Byzantines
Hittites
Ottoman Empire
Turkey—Profile
Turkey, Republic of
   International Relations
Ibn Battutah
   Iran
Iran—Human Rights
Iran-Iraq Relations
Iran-Russia Relations
Iran–United States Hostage Crisis
Iran–United States Relations
   Iraq
Iran-Iraq Relations
Iraq—Human Rights
Iraq-Turkey Relations
Persian Gulf War
   Turkey
European Union and Turkey
Iraq-Turkey Relations

North Atlantic Treaty Organization and Turkey
Turkey—Human Rights
Turkey-Russia Relations
Turkey–United States Relations
   Language and Communication
Arabic
Media—West Asia
Persian
   Peoples, Cultures, and Society
Arabs
Armenians
Kurds
Marriage and Family—West Asia
Turks—West Asia
Westernization—West Asia
Women in West Asia
   Iran
Azerbaijanis
Bakhtiari
Persepolis
Persians
   Iraq
Clothing, Traditional—Iraq
Marsh Arabs
   Turkey
Albanians
Bulgarians
Circassians
Clothing, Traditional—Turkey
Greeks in Turkey
Miletus
Tatars
   Religion and Philosophy
Alevi Muslims
Baha'i
Islam—West Asia
Judaism—West Asia
Muslims, Shi'ite
Muslims, Sunni
Oriental Orthodox Church
Qadiriya
Saint Paul
   Iran
Babism
   Turkey
Eastern Orthodox Church
   Science, Technology, and Health
Calendars—West Asia
Kariz Irrigation System
Medicine, Traditional—West Asia

Encyclopedia of
Modern Asia

ABACUS A manual computing device used in ancient China, the abacus (*suan pan*, or "counting plate") was probably invented there in ancient times. The word "abacus" has its roots in the Phoenician term for a flat surface, and its Greek and Roman forms used flat surfaces with grooves for beads.

The Chinese abacus has a frame of thirteen wires holding seven beads on each wire; a horizontal divider separates the top two beads from the bottom five, sometimes referred to as the "heaven" and the "earth" beads, respectively. Chinese sources show wide use of the device by 190 CE, popularization during the Song dynasty (960–1279), and printed instructions appearing in the 1300s during the Yuan (1279–1368). By the Ming dynasty (1368–1644), the Chinese abacus had taken on its modern form and had become an integral part of business and financial accounting. This basic counting machine spread by the 1600s to Japan and then to eastern Russia, with small modifications in the number of beads above and below the divider.

In China, the abacus replaced paper-and-pencil mathematical calculations; the beads served as markers representing quantity, and the beads' position on the vertical wires represented value. A skilled user of an abacus performed addition, subtraction, multiplication, and division quickly and easily, with the additional advantage of requiring no electricity to produce a readout that cannot be lost or erased without being manually changed. Because of the traditional Chinese use of 16 as an important standard weight, the Chinese abacus is particularly useful for calculations using a base number system of 2 and 16.

Among storekeepers and small businesses in China, an abacus remained a standard piece of office equipment until the 1980s. Even today, shopkeepers in Russia sometimes use abaci to calculate customers' purchases. A good-quality abacus is generally about two feet wide by one foot tall and made of sturdy brass with hardwood beads.

Margaret Sankey

Further Reading
Dilson, Jesse. (1968) *The Abacus: A Pocket Computer*. New York: St. Martin's Press.
Menninger, Karl. (1992) *Number Words and Number Symbols: A Cultural History of Numbers*. Trans. by Paul Broneer. New York: Dover.
Pullan, J. M. (1968) *The History of the Abacus*. London: Hutchinson and Company.

ABADAN (1997 est. pop. 308,000). The Iranian city of Abadan is located in the southeast corner of the country along the east bank of the Shatt al Arab River, 55 kilometers from the Persian Gulf. Its population is mainly Persian, though with a considerable Arab minority. According to popular belief the city was founded by a mystic named 'Abbad in the eighth or ninth century CE. Its proximity to the port of Basra allowed it to develop quickly into a prosperous town, but it was reduced to an impoverished village after the Mongol conquests of the thirteenth century. The establishment of the Safavid dynasty in 1501 promised to bring stability but the Ottoman conquest of Iraq in 1534 and the ensuing Ottoman-Safavid conflict prevented any renewed prosperity. It was not until 1847 that the Ottomans finally recognized Persian sovereignty over Abadan. In 1909, following the discovery

The Abadan Refinery burns following an attack at the start of the Iran-Iraq War in 1980. (FRANCOISE DE MULDER/CORBIS)

of oil in the area, the Anglo-Persian Oil Company chose Abadan as its main refinery site. By 1956 Abadan had become one of Iran's major cities, boasting the world's largest oil refinery and a busy maritime port. During the Iran-Iraq War (1980–1988) the city, along with its industrial infrastructure, was completely destroyed. Reconstruction started immediately after the war and some oil exports have resumed.

Thabit Abdullah

ABANGAN *Abangan* (Javanese "red") is a term popularized by the anthropologist Clifford Geertz (b. 1926) to describe the rural Javanese Muslims whose Islam is blended syncretistically with older animist and Hindu-Buddhist beliefs. The term has entered Indonesian usage and is now considered pejorative, implying laxness in belief. The complex of beliefs that Geertz described are now more commonly called Kejawen ("Javanism"). *Abangan* belief centers on spirits, magic, and the ceremonial feast or *slametan*. Most spirits are malicious beings who intervene in human affairs on their own initiative, whereas magic involves the direct control of supernatural forces by a sorcerer or *dukun*. The skills of a *dukun* include treating disease, preventing accidents or injury, controlling natural phenomena, and both casting and lifting spells. The *slametan* is a feast offered to the immediate (male) community and accompanied by incense and prayer to mark a special occasion, to placate the spirits, and to confer on participants and their families a state of being *slamet*, or healthy and calm. Geertz distinguished

abangan beliefs from the similarly syncretistic Javanese aristocratic *priyayi* tradition, but most observers now use the term *priyayi* to indicate aristocratic status and culture in general and regard it as part of the broader *abangan* or Kejawen category.

The *abangan* stand in contrast to the *santri*, considered more pious Muslims, and both are referred to as *aliran* (streams) in Javanese society. They became one of the bases for political organization after Indonesian independence, the Partai Nasional Indonesia initially having a strong *abangan* base. During the 1950s, the Partai Komunis Indonesia won increasing *abangan* support, because the party espoused the interests of the rural poor. Many *abangan* were therefore among the victims of the anti-Communist massacres of 1965–1966, in which perhaps half a million people died. Ironically, however, President Suharto (b. 1921, reigned 1967–1998) was *abangan* in upbringing and strongly supported *abangan* beliefs in his early years in office. *Abangan* belief was the responsibility of the powerful Department of Education and Culture and in the early 1980s came close to receiving recognition as "belief" distinct from "religion."

Since 1950, the Indonesian state had provided massive support for religion by constructing places of worship, maintaining Islamic universities, and paying the salaries of religious officials. The Department of Religion was generally dominated by orthodox Muslims who regarded *abangan* belief as heterodox and lax and therefore ensured that no funds went to *abangan* purposes. A passage in the Indonesian constitution, which refers to religion and belief as if they were separate phenomena, however, gave the government a legal basis for regarding belief as part of culture and therefore for supporting it through the Department of Education and Culture, in which *abangan* Javanese tended to be more influential. Nevertheless, from the late 1980s, official support for *abangan* practice weakened as Suharto's New Order began to cultivate orthodox Islam.

Traditionally, *abangan* belief was not at all organized, but from the late colonial period formal organizations began to emerge, generally centered on mystical practice (*kebatinan*, "innerness"). The largest of these, including Pangestu and Subud, also have a following outside Java.

Robert Cribb

See also: **Islam—Indonesia**

Further Reading
Beatty, Andrew. (1999) *Varieties of Javanese Religion: An Anthropological Account.* Cambridge, U.K.: Cambridge University Press.
Geertz, Clifford. (1960) *The Religion of Java.* Glencoe, NY: Free Press.

ABDALRAUF FITRAT (1886–1938), Bukharan writer, educator, social activist. Abdalrauf Fitrat was born in 1886 in the emirate of Bukhara to a merchant family, and little is known of his early years. As a young student he attended the Mir-I Arab *madrasah* (Islamic school) until 1909, when he received a scholarship to continue his education in Constantinople. He spent five years there and traveled broadly throughout the Ottoman empire, Iran, and Xinjiang, China. In 1911, he published his well-known and popular *Bayanat-I sayyah-I hindi* (Tales of an Indian Traveler) in Persian. It was published in Samarqand in Russian in 1914. The novel denounces Bukhara's poverty-ridden conditions and the corrupt practices of many Islamic clerics and teachers. It challenges the emirate's social order, which was a common theme in his professional and social activities. In 1917, Fitrat was elected secretary of the *jadidist-* (new method) influenced Young Bukharan Party, which seized power in Bukhara during the Russian Civil War. Following the Bolshevik victory, he became the minister for education in the newly established Soviet republic. He is credited with revising the educational system and helping to establish a European-style university in Tashkent, Uzbekistan. In 1923, he was removed from office after being accused of bourgeois nationalism. He was arrested in 1938 and executed during the Stalinist party purges.

Steven Sabol

Further Reading
Allworth, Edward. (1990) *The Modern Uzbeks from the Fourteenth Century to the Present: A Cultural History.* Stanford, CA: Hoover Institution.
Carrere d'Encausse, Helene. (1988) *Islam and the Russian Empire: Reform and Revolution in Central Asia.* Berkeley and Los Angeles: University of California Press.
Khalid, Adeeb. (1998) *The Politics of Muslim Cultural Reform: Jadidism in Central Asia.* Berkeley and Los Angeles: University of California Press.

ABDUL RAZAK (1922–1976), Second prime minister of Malaysia. Abdul Razak bin Dato' Hussein, second prime minister of Malaysia (1970–1976), effected major policy changes with long-term implications for the multiethnic population and the nation. Born on 11 March 1922 in Pekan, Pahang, he was educated at the Malay College, Kuala Kangsar, and Raffles College, Singapore. During the Japanese occupation (1941–1945), he joined the Anti-Japanese Malay Resistance Movement (Wataniah). On a scholarship, he read law at Lincoln's Inn, England, and was called to the bar in 1950. He married Hajah Rahah on 4 September 1952 in Johor.

Abdul Razak believed that poverty and socioeconomic imbalances among Malaysia's multiethnic population could be alleviated through rural development and education. He was instrumental in establishing such agencies as the Federal Land Development Authority (FELDA), Malayan Industrial Development Finance (MIDF), and Council of Indigenous People's Trust (Majlis Amanah Rakyat, MARA). In 1956 he chaired a committee whose recommendations (Razak Report) formed the basis of Malaysia's education policy. During his premiership, he reshaped Malaysia's socioeconomic landscape through the New Economic Policy (NEP) aimed at eradicating poverty and restructuring society by focusing on rural development and education.

He played a pivotal role in reestablishing public order and the resumption of parliamentary rule (1971) in the aftermath of the 13 May 1969 racial troubles. He expanded the Alliance Party to form a larger coalition, the National Front (Barisan Nasional). During the mid-1970s, he faced a resurgence of Communist activities on the peninsula and secessionist tendencies in Sabah.

Prime Minister Abdul Razak in Kuala Lumpur in 1968. (BETTMANN/CORBIS)

Abdul Razak was closely involved in the formation of Malaysia (1963) and in the reconciliation with Indonesia following Konfrantasi (the Confrontation, 1966). He argued for regional economic cooperation that subsequently led to the formation of the Association of Southeast Asian Nations (ASEAN) in 1967. He proposed the concept for a Zone of Peace, Freedom, and Neutrality (ZOPFAN) in Southeast Asia (adopted in 1971) and advocated a nonaligned stance for Malaysia and established relations with socialist countries.

Ooi Keat Gin

Further Reading
Means, Gordon P. (1976) *Malaysian Politics*. 2d ed. London: Hodder & Stoughton.
Paridah Abd, Samad. (1998) *Tun Abdul Razak. A Phenomenon in Malaysian Politics: A Political Biography*. Kuala Lumpur, Malaysia: Affluent Master.
Shaw, William. (1976) *Tun Abdul Razak: His Life and Times*. Kuala Lumpur, Malaysia: Longman Malaysia.

Wan Hashim. (1983) *Race Relations in Malaysia*. Kuala Lumpur, Malaysia: Heinemann Educational Books (Asia).

ABDULLAH, MUHAMMAD

(1905–1982), Kashmiri nationalist leader and statesman. Born in Soura, Srinagar District, Kashmir, in a family of shawl merchants, Sheikh Muhammad Abdullah was educated in Lahore and Aligarh and earned a Master's degree in physics in 1930. He became a central figure in Kashmiri politics, even though for much of his political life he was in prison or under house arrest in Ootacamund, in south India. In 1931 he was arrested for the first time for his role in the Indian independence movement.

After the 15 August 1947 partition establishing the separate states of India and Pakistan, the Hindu maharaja of Kashmir wanted his kingdom to remain autonomous of both nations, but on 20 October 1947 Pakistani militia, with government backing, occupied a western sector of Kashmir that has been known ever since as Azad Kashmir (Free Kashmir). In response, the maharaja urgently requested support from India, acting on the advice of Sheikh Abdullah.

Sheik Muhammad Abdullah in Kashmir, c. 1950. (BRADLEY SMITH/CORBIS)

The maharaja executed the Instrument of Accession to the Indian Union, and thereupon, India rushed airborne troops to secure Srinagar, Kashmir's capital. Sheikh Abdullah was a signatory to the Indian constitution and never advocated the secession of Kashmir to Pakistan. In January 1948 the U.N. Security Council, convened at the request of India, imposed a cease-fire in the region. Thus, Kashmir became a pawn in regional power politics. Soon Abdullah was leading a struggle to oust the maharaja of Kashmir who, unlike the majority of Kashmiris, was not a Muslim. But in 1953, he was dismissed as prime minister because of Pandit Nehru's suspicion that Abdullah wanted independence for Kashmir. He was kept under house arrest in India, but was finally released in 1964. Abdullah, called the Lion of Kashmir by Muslims and others, became chief minister of the Indian state of Jammu and Kashmir in 1975 and held that position until his death.

Paul Hockings

Further Reading
Bazaz, Prem Nath. (1954) *History of the Struggle for Freedom in Kashmir: Cultural and Political, from the Earliest Times to the Present Day.* New Delhi: Pamposh Publications.

ABDULLAH QUAISI (1894–1938), Master of Uzbek literature. Abdullah Quaisi produced many of the first modern indigenous plays, stories, and novels of Central Asia and had a major role in establishing the genre of the novel in modern Uzbek literature. His works, published between 1913 and 1923, reflect the changing circumstances of Uzbek life under the late czarist and early Soviet regimes.

Initially attracted to the Turan society (a chauvinistic idea of a superpolitical unity of the Turkic language–speaking nations) as a reformer, he later became involved in promoting the revolutionary cause of the Bolsheviks, as reflected in his story *Atam va Bolshevik* (My Father and the Bolshevik, 1922). Quaisi came to prominence with the publication of *Otgan Kunlar* (Past Days, 1923), credited as the first Uzbek historical novel, as a nationalist work, and as an attack on traditional Uzbek attitudes. His second novel, *Mehradban Chayan* (The Scorpion from the Mihrab), also received acclaim. Quaisi died in Stalin's purges of the 1930s, but gained posthumous recognition in 1956, and since Uzbek independence he has been recognized as a martyred nationalist.

Leonard A. Stone

Further Reading
Murphy, Christopher. (1992) "Abdullah Qadiriy and the Bolsheviks: From Reform to Revolution." In *Muslims in Central Asia*, edited by Jo-Ann Gross. Durham, NC: Duke University Press, 269–270.

ABE ISO (1865–1949), Father of Japanese socialism. A native of Fukuoka Prefecture and graduate of Japan's first important Christian university, Doshisha, Abe Iso spent his career advocating pacifism, Christianity, and labor rights. Following an early stint as a minister and a time of study at Hartford School of Theology in Connecticut, Abe joined the Waseda University faculty in 1899, a post he would hold for most of his remaining life.

A moderate socialist, Abe helped launch Japan's most important socialist parties and organizations. In 1901, he was a creator of Japan's first socialist party, the short-lived Socialist Democrats; in later years, he helped found the Socialist People's Party (1928), the Socialist Masses Party (1932), and the Nationalist Labor Party (1940). He was elected to the Diet in 1928 and continued to win in successive elections, until he resigned in 1940, in opposition to Japan's growing militarism.

Though lacking a brilliant personality (he called himself a "utility man," drawing on the language of baseball, which he loved passionately), Abe was admired by supporters for the dogged consistency of his ideals and damned by more radical leftists as too moderate and pragmatic. His insistent antimilitarist stance made him a target of the right wing, and in 1938, he was nearly assassinated. After World War II, he served as an advisor to the Japan Socialist Party.

James L. Huffman

Further Reading
Powles, Cyril. (1978) "Abe Isoo: The Utility Man." In *Pacifism in Japan*. Kyoto, Japan: Minerva Press.

ABIM. See **Angkatan Belia Islam Malaysia.**

ABKHAZIA A semiautonomous republic in northwestern Georgia, Abkhazia borders Russia to the north, along a ridge of peaks in the Caucasus Mountains; the northeastern coast of the Black Sea defines its southern boundary. With some river valleys and a few lakes breaking the terrain, its steep northern slopes run from glaciers to pastures, to mixed forests, and eventually to a long, narrow strip of fertile coastland. Because Abkhazia has a subtropical climate along its coastal slopes and lowlands, its farms have long been known for their abundant yields of tea, citrus fruit, tobacco, grapes, and other crops. The capital is the port of Sukhum, erected on the grounds of a former Greek colony.

The Abkhaz region has been the site of human settlement since prehistoric times. Some of the first recorded histories of the region involve the Colchis state of the first millennium BCE; Greece conquered it in approximately 100 BCE. In later periods, both the Romans and Byzantines supported trading posts and garrisons in Abkhazia in order to maintain control over the Black Sea. The first Abkhaz kingdom was established in the eighth century CE; a later manifestation of this state merged with a Georgian kingdom in the eleventh century. The region fell to Mongol-Turkic invasions in the thirteenth century, and the Ottoman Turks claimed Abkhazia in the sixteenth century. The Russians seized it in the early nineteenth century. With the rise of the Soviet Union, and throughout most of the Soviet period, Abkhazia was designated an Autonomous Soviet Socialist Republic within the republic of Georgia. The consolidation of Russian—and later Soviet and Georgian—control over the region led to the migration of ethnic Abkhazians, mostly to Turkey. Soviet restrictions on Abkhaz ethnolinguistic expression and institutions were particularly severe under Stalin and the Communist Party.

Ethnic Abkhaz—often referring to themselves as Apsua, or variations thereof—are generally regarded as descendents of those peoples who had entered the region by the first century CE. Images of traditional Abkhazians depict a people with great longevity who are associated with cattle husbandry along the slopes and agriculture in the lowlands. About half are Orthodox Christians; Sunni Muslims comprise the other half. The Abkhaz language is part of the Northwest group of Caucasian languages and, despite periods of severe suppression under the Soviets, maintains both written and literary traditions. According to the 1990 census, Abkhazia had a population of almost 550,000; of these fewer than 20 percent were ethnic Abkhaz. The majority were Georgian—almost 50 percent—with Armenians, Russians and Ukrainians, and some smaller groups constituting the remaining 30 percent. In the mid-1990s, however, large numbers of non-Abkhaz peoples left amid armed conflict.

Despite their minority status, Abkhazians were particularly active in promoting their ethnolinguistic and political rights in the later years of the Soviet Union,

and since its collapse. In 1978, the Abkhazians proposed a petition for secession, and in 1990 the Abkhazian Supreme Soviet declared independence—envisioning a federation with Georgia rather than a subordinate state in a larger Georgian republic. In 1992, military conflicts between the Abkhaz and Georgia ensued. Since 1994, a relative peace has been imposed by Russia, according to terms that critics view as favoring Russia, Georgia, and the Commonwealth of Independent States (CIS). However, having been forced to accept peace under the threat of Russian force and trade sanctions imposed by the CIS, the resolution to the problem of Abkhaz autonomy and sovereignty are far from resolved.

Kyle T. Evered

Further Reading
Benet, Sula. (1974) *Abkhasians: The Long-Living People of the Caucasus.* New York: Holt, Rinehart, and Winston.
Hewitt, B. George. (1993) "Abkhazia: A Problem of Identity and Ownership." *Central Asian Survey* 12, 3: 267–323.
Slider, Darrell. (1985) "Crisis and Response in Soviet Nationality Policy: The Case of Abkhazia." *Central Asian Survey* 4, 4: 51–68.

ABORIGINAL PEOPLES—TAIWAN The aboriginal people of Taiwan are the island's non-Chinese indigenous inhabitants. Their cultures and languages are Austronesian and include the oldest languages of the Austronesian family. Archaeological evidence suggests that their ancestors came from the Asian mainland at least 6,000 years ago and then became the source of the migrations south into the Pacific and insular Southeast Asia. It appears that later migration northward from the Philippines brought new groups back to southern Taiwan. The twenty-two aboriginal languages and cultures in Taiwan, of which ten are still living, are a major anthropological source for research into Austronesian origins.

History

Aboriginal peoples were the only inhabitants of Taiwan until 1624, when the Dutch established a colony and Chinese migration began. Today, the remaining ten aboriginal "tribes" number some 400,000 people, or 1.8 percent of Taiwan's population. By the early twentieth century, almost all the plains aborigines (Pingpuzu) were sinicized and had intermarried into Chinese settler society. While there is a Pingpu ethnic revival today, their real descendents are the Hokkien-speaking Taiwanese, most of whom have Pingpu as well as Chinese ancestors. The ten groups inhabiting the mountains and eastern coast survived in part because of geograph, and in part because they were feared as "savages" and headhunters. Aboriginal people were called Mountain People (Shandiren, Shanbao) until the "Return our Name" movement resulted in the official adoption of the term "Taiwan Aboriginal People" (Yuanzhuminzu) in 1994.

Relations between the settler society and mountain aborigines were shaped by trade and a Chinese defensive line along the mountain fringe until the 1860s, when export demand for tea and camphor led the settlers to push into the mountains, especially in northern Taiwan. Aboriginal resistance and settler reprisals characterized a generation of sporadic warfare in the north, which ended only with the imposition after 1895 of a strong defense line by the new Japanese rulers of Taiwan. They separated mountain aboriginal areas from the rest of Taiwan, forbidding Chinese settlement and any non-Japanese cultural influence on them. Ultimately, this colonial control strategy contributed to the preservation of aboriginal territory and culture. The imposition of harsh Japanese police administration was resisted most strongly by the Tayal tribe. It took a five-year military campaign (1910–1914) in which thousands of lives were lost before the Tayal were conquered. In 1930 there was a final uprising, the Wushe Incident, in central Taiwan. The Japanese moved villages out of the deep mountains, introduced rice agriculture and cash economy, and educated a generation of aboriginal elite, while destroying much traditional aboriginal social structure. Aboriginal culture today is deeply marked by Japanese custom and language.

Importance of Churches in Modern Period

After 1945, the Republic of Taiwan (under the Chinese Nationalists) continued most Japanese policies, but the government opened the mountains to Chinese settlement and Christian evangelism. Policies of agricultural development, enforcement of Mandarin Chinese education, suppression of aboriginal languages, and politicized sinicization in the 1950s were aimed at assimilating the aboriginal people. Attempts by some among the aboriginal elite to oppose these policies were quickly crushed, notably with the execution of several leaders of the "Formosan National Salvation Alliance" in 1954. Most local leaders joined the Guomindang Nationalist Party (GMD) and learned how to win elections in the thirty Mountain Townships, low-level units of self-government that serve as conduits for patronage and corruption. Much aboriginal reserve land, held in trust since Japanese days by the state for aboriginal users, fell into Chinese hands. Aboriginal so-

ciety became tormented by poverty, alcoholism, suicide, and family breakdown. The aboriginal people became sources of cheap labor in construction, mining, factories, and fishing. These problems persist despite improvements in the aboriginal people's situation.

The churches became the basis of aboriginal cultural persistence and ethnic revival. Presbyterian and Catholic evangelism resulted in about 70 percent of the aboriginal people becoming Christian by 1960. Christianity is often seen in Taiwan as a mark of aboriginal identity. Especially among Presbyterians, leadership by aboriginal clergy, use of aboriginal language in worship, and inclusion of traditional forms of social cooperation in church organization meant that the churches became the only autonomous aboriginal people's organizations outside state control that affirmed and perpetuated aboriginal identity.

From the mid-1970s on, a charismatic movement revitalized the aboriginal Presbyterian churches, and human-rights ideas combined with biblical images of the chosen people and the promised land, bringing elements of aboriginal nationalism into everyday religious practice. Politically, most aboriginal politicians remained loyal members of the Guomindang. In the early 1980s, widespread opposition to authoritarian GMD rule began to gather strength in Taiwan. A few educated youths began to challenge GMD control of the aboriginal people and in 1984 founded the Alliance of Taiwan Aborigines (ATA), with support from the Presbyterian Church. Aboriginal churches were already engaged in a campaign to gain land rights from the state, and, with the ATA, began to be overtly critical of state policies. In 1987 several highly publicized local protests ensued over land issues, in which Presbyterian clergy played leading roles. In 1988 these coalesced into the "Return our Land" movement and a mass aboriginal demonstration in Taipei on 25 August 1988.

Aboriginal Rights Movements and Contemporary Policies

The Return our Land movement resulted in only about 13,000 hectares of land being released, but it raised the profile of aboriginal issues in the media and among Taiwan's political elite. Aboriginal politicians, formerly GMD party hacks, sought to outdo one another in fighting for long-denied rights. Native language and self-government became popular social causes. These were enshrined in constitutional revisions between 1992 and 1997:

> The State affirms cultural pluralism and shall actively preserve and foster the development of aboriginal languages and culture.

The state shall, in accordance with the will of the ethnic groups, safeguard the status and political participation of the aborigines. The state shall also guarantee and provide assistance and encouragement for aboriginal education, culture, medical care, economic activity, land and social welfare, measures for which . . . shall be established by law.

(Republic of China Constitution, Additional Article 10)

A cabinet-level Council of Aboriginal Affairs was established in 1996, but it has no administrative authority. Nonetheless, the large funding and policy consultation role it has been given has contributed to an aboriginal renaissance as well as to the development of many local and national nongovernmental initiatives. In the 1990s aboriginal peoples became key symbols of the new multicultural Taiwan, symbolized by the major role they played in the inauguration of President Chen Shuibian (b. 1950) in May 2000. Chen appointed one of the leaders of the aboriginal rights movement, a Presbyterian minister, to head the Council of Aboriginal Affairs and made classes in native languages part of the regular school curriculum. If proposals to establish aboriginal autonomous areas are realized, Taiwan's aboriginal peoples will not only be the most economically and socially advantaged in Asia (notwithstanding many continuing social problems), but will also be a political model for transition from the ethnic margins to the political center.

Michael Stainton

Further Reading

Bellwood, Peter. (1991) "The Austronesian Dispersal and the Origin of Languages," *Scientific American* 191 (July): 88–93.

Chen, Chi-lu. (1968) *Material Culture of the Formosan Aborigines.* Taipei, Taiwan: Taiwan Provincial Museum.

Li Kuang-chou, Chang Kwang-chih, Arthur P. Wolf, and Alexander Chien-chun Yin, eds.(1989) *Anthropological Studies of the Taiwan Area: Accomplishments and Prospects.* Taipei, Taiwan: National Taiwan University.

Republic of China Government Information Office. (2000) "Taiwan's Indigenous Peoples," *Republic of China Yearbook 2000.* Taipei, Taiwan: 29–36.

Rubinstein, Murray, ed. (1999) *Taiwan: A New History.* Armonk, NY: M. E. Sharpe.

Shepherd, John Robert. (1993) *Statecraft and Political Economy on the Taiwan Frontier 1600–1800.* Stanford, CA: Stanford UP.

Stainton, Michael. (1995) "Return Our Land: Counterhegemonic Presbyterian Aboriginality in Taiwan." M.A. thesis. York University, Toronto, Canada.

———. (1995) "Taiwan Aborigines in the UN: International and Domestic Implications," *East Asia Forum* 4 (Fall): 63–79.

ABU BAKAR (1843?–1895), sultan of Johor. Regarded as the father of modern Johor, Abu Bakar (reigned 1862–1895) presided over the emergence of a fairly prosperous bureaucratic state in Malay with a vibrant commercial agricultural sector. During the last quarter of the nineteenth century, Johor was the only independent peninsular Malay state; all the others were dominated by foreign powers, including the British. Abu Bakar cultivated close ties with the British. Through his influence, the British were able to impose indirect rule on the Sri Menanti Confederacy (present-day Negeri Semblian, a state in the Federation of Malaysia) and Pahang (also a state in the Federation of Malaysia) in the late 1880s. The British sanctioned his annexation of Muar, a Malay principality nominally under the kingdom of Johor, following the death of Sultan Ali Iskandar Shah of Muar (reigned 1855–1877).

Abu Bakar outmaneuvered the governor of the Straits Settlements, Sir Frederick Weld (governed 1880–1887), by signing a treaty in 1885 with Britain, bypassing Weld and the British Colonial Office. Thereby Abu Bakar was recognized as sultan and an independent ruler. He established the Johor Advisory Board, a quasi-diplomatic representation, in London.

Abu Baker promulgated a written constitution in 1894, a code of laws, and a bureaucratic form of administration. Roads, schools, and hospitals were built. Europeans were engaged as legal and technical advisers to the government. The economy was developed in partnership with Chinese and European entrepreneurs and financiers. Having led an extravagant lifestyle with expensive Anglophile tastes and habits, he died in 1895, bequeathing to his son and successor Ibrahim his kingdom, an empty royal purse, and a hefty debt.

Ooi Keat Gin

Further Reading

Gullick, J. M. (1992) *Rulers and Residents: Influence and Power in the Malay States, 1870–1920.* Kuala Lumpur, Malaysia: Oxford University Press.

Thio, Eunice. (1969) *British Policy in the Malay Peninsula, 1880–1910, Vol. I: The Southern and Central States.* Kuala Lumpur, Malaysia: University of Malaya Press.

Trocki, C. (1978) *Prince of Pirates: The Temenggongs and the Development of Johor and Singapore, 1784–1885.* Singapore: Singapore University Press.

ABU, MOUNT Mount Abu (1,722 meters) forms an isolated spur of the Aravalli Range, in southern

Rajasthan State of northwest India. It rises like a precipitous granite island from the surrounding plains. The mountain is sacred to the Jains who call the place Dilwara; several of its peaks are covered with a multitude of architecturally superb Jain temples dating from the eleventh through thirteenth centuries as well as other shrines and tombs. The structures are the best examples of Jain religious architecture and stand out because they are built of white marble. To the Jains, Dilwara is an important pilgrimage destination. A fort five kilometers from Dilwara served as headquarters of the local Paramara chiefs (ninth to eleventh centuries), and contains two Jain temples of the same period.

Among the most important temples on Mount Abu are one built during 1197–1247 and remarkable for the delicacy of its marble carvings; and another, built circa 1032 CE, is one of the oldest known Jain buildings and is devoted to the god Parsvanath.

There is also a hill-station or sanitarium on the mountain, at about 1,200 meters elevation. Called Mount Abu (1991 population 15,547), it was originally constructed for the convenience of Europeans seeking to escape the hot summer weather. The temperature ranges from 70 to 90° F, never hotter; annual rainfall is about 68 inches. The town has a church, club, hospital, a small artificial lake, and a school originally built for the children of British soldiers, as well as scenic roadways and bridle paths.

Paul Hockings

Further Reading
Davies, Philip, and George Michell. (1989). "Mount Abu." In *The Penguin Guide to the Monuments of India: Buddhist, Jain, Hindu.* 2 vols. New York: Viking Penguin, 273–276.

ACADEMIA SINICA

Academia Sinica, founded in Nanjing in 1928, is the most prominent academic institution in the Republic of China (ROC). Although it is affiliated directly to the ROC Presidential Office, Academia Sinica, which is located in Taipei, enjoys independence and autonomy in formulating its own research agenda. Its major tasks are to conduct academic research in sciences, humanities, and social sciences, as well as to provide guidance, coordination, and incentives to raising academic standards in Taiwan. An international graduate school to train future scholars is currently under preparation; it will recruit five to ten graduate students every year from 2002 for each of its eleven Ph.D. programs.

Academia Sinica has made tremendous progress in recent years. An increasing number of research papers written by its faculty, which numbered 1,150 in 2001, are appearing in well-known international journals. Some journals, published by Academia Sinica itself, such as *Zoological Studies* and *Statistical Sinica*, have received international recognition. Academia Sinica plays a major role in the field of Chinese studies. For example, the archaeological findings by researchers at the Institute of History and Philology have, in combination with written documents, led to a virtual rewriting of ancient Chinese history, pushing back the span of Chinese history by many centuries.

The current president of Academia Sinica is Dr. Yuan-tseh Lee, a 1986 Nobel laureate in chemistry. The convocation currently consists of 199 members (academicians), which includes five ethnic Chinese Nobel laureates.

Chang Jui-te

ACEH REBELLION

(1873–1903). Despite the Dutch arrival in Indonesia in the seventeenth century, expansion into Aceh did not occur until the end of the nineteenth century. The people of Aceh fiercely resisted Dutch encroachment on their territory in northern Sumatra. While Aceh's independence was guaranteed by the 1824 Anglo-Dutch Treaty of London, in 1858 the Dutch gained access to east coast ports in an agreement with the sultan of Siak. The sultan of Aceh saw this as a threat and sought to forge alliances with external powers, particularly Turkey. In turn the Dutch and the British forged an alliance under a treaty in 1871, which allowed the Netherlands to launch their 1873 invasion. After a disastrous initial foray in 1873, the Dutch eventually captured the sultan's palace in Banda Aceh in 1874, but this failed to end resistance. Traditional village rulers organized a sustained rebellion in which a purist strain of Islam, notable among Acehnese, was used as a rallying point to oppose the Dutch *kafir* ("nonbelievers"). The destruction of the Aceh sultanate saw Islamic leaders assume control of the resistance, the most prominent of whom was Teungku Cik di Tiro (1836–1891). The Dutch were able to break the resistance through the use of local sympathizers, and troops from cooperative Indonesian ethnic groups. The fighting, which lasted until around 1903, proved costly to the Netherlands. But resistance continued throughout Dutch rule in what was the most troublesome part of Indonesia, even after the official end of the conflict. This resistance continued into the establishment of the

An Indonesian woman protests the government repression of the Aceh rebellion outside the United Nations office in Jakarata on 7 August 2001. (REUTERS NEWMEDIA INC./CORBIS)

Republic of Indonesia, when guerrilla elements continued to push their demands for independence.

Anthony L. Smith

Further Reading
Ricklefs, M. C. (1993) *A History of Modern Indonesia Since c.1300*. London: The MacMillan Press Ltd.
Tarling, Nicholas. (1966) *A Concise History of Southeast Asia*. Singapore: Donald Moore Press Ltd.
Tate, D. J. M. (1971) *The Making of Modern South-East Asia: The European Conquest*. London: Oxford University Press.

ACEHNESE Four million people live in Aceh (pronounced ah-chay) in northwestern Sumatra, Indonesia, and consider themselves distinct from other peoples of Indonesia. Ninety percent of them are ethnically Acehnese and live in the lowlands, while the minority Gajo live in the highlands..

In 500 CE, the Acehnese were Buddhist, but when Marco Polo visited in the thirteenth century they had already converted to Islam. The 1824 Anglo-Dutch agreement placed them under the Dutch sphere of influence, but they resisted and were never completely subjugated. Consequently, many Acehnese reject Indonesia's claim to sovereignty over the territory.

Given the status of an autonomous Indonesian province in 1949, Aceh's amalgamation with North Sumatra province in 1950 provoked a brief rebellion in 1953. In 1956, Aceh was made a special province, administratively equal with other provinces, to quiet discontent, though this action implied reneging on the promise of autonomy.

Aceh's natural gas, petroleum, and other natural resources exploited by foreign and Indonesian companies appear not to benefit the Acehnese, who are poorer than residents of resource-poor Java, where the Indonesian government is centered. Awareness of economic exploitation feeds support for independence among the Acehnese, who are such devout Muslims that they want the Islamic legal code applied in the province.

In the late 1970s, when support for the Free Aceh Movement (GAM) was centered in only one district, Indonesia tried to suppress dissent, and some Acehnese were deported. Resistance subsided until 1989, when some Libyan-trained guerrillas returned to Aceh and began attacking Indonesian soldiers and non-Acehnese migrants, provoking military overreaction. From 1990 to 1998, Indonesian counterinsurgency operations virtually placed the province under martial law.

After Suharto (b. 1921) resigned as Indonesian president in 1998, many Acehnese returned from Malaysia and some from Libya. Partial withdrawal of the military was ordered, but troops were stoned as they paraded during a 31 August ceremony marking the withdrawal, provoking brutal military retaliation.

In January 1999, an Aceh student congress proposed a referendum on independence. Abdurrahman Wahid (b. 1940), elected Indonesian president in October 1999, at first indicated approval. When the Indonesian government later declared opposition to a referendum, GAM organized support and attacked symbols of Indonesian authority. Security forces, ordered to arrest ringleaders, instead perpetrated widespread atrocities, prompting moderate Acehnese to support independence. The outcome of the struggle remains uncertain.

Michael Haas

Further Reading
Human Rights Watch. (1999) *Indonesia: Why Aceh Is Exploding*. New York: Human Rights Watch Press.

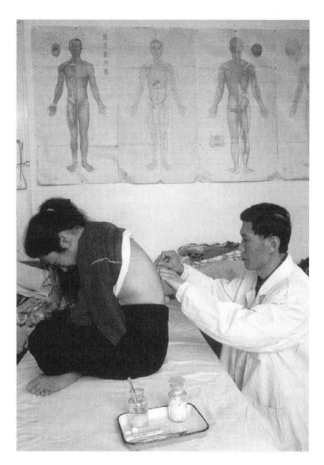

Smith, Holly S. (1998) *Aceh: Art and Culture.* New York: Oxford University Press.

ACUPUNCTURE   Acupuncture is an ancient treatment technique still routinely used in traditional Chinese medicine and also in Western medicine. The *Huangdi Nei Jing* (Canon of Medicine), compiled between 475 BCE and 23 CE, is the earliest extant medical book in which acupuncture is described. One of its components, *Ling Shu* (Canon of Acupuncture), describes nine instruments, some of which are still in use. Techniques for making bamboo needles and for casting bronze needles developed during the Shang dynasty (1766–1045 BCE). During the Song dynasty (960–1267 CE), the Jurchen Jin dynasty (1126–1234 CE), and the Yuan dynasty (1267–1368 CE), acupuncture developed widely in China. However, during the Qing dynasty (1644–1912) the practice was banned from general use by decree because it was perceived as suitable for application to the emperor. Although banned, acupuncture continued to flourish in local use. Although acupuncture had been popular among the Chinese-American community for over one hundred years, non-Chinese Americans became more aware of acupuncture after President Richard Nixon's 1972 visit to China.

An understanding of the healing art of acupuncture requires familiarity with the concepts of channels and collaterals. In Chinese medicine, channels are the main trunks running lengthwise through the body, and collaterals are their connecting branches. Together they connect the superficial, interior, upper, and lower portions of the human body. *Qi* (life energy) flows through the channels. The twelve regular channels include the three yin channels of each hand and foot and the three yang channels of each hand and foot. Yin and yang are the two basic, complementary principles of which all phenomena partake: wetness, introversion, and coldness are yin characteristics, for example, and dryness, extroversion, and heat are yang characteristics. The eight extra channels are the *du* channel, the *ren* channel, the *chong* channel, the *dai* channel, the *yinqiao* channel, the *yangqiao* channel, the *yinwei* channel, and the *yangwei* channel.

The acupuncture points or acupoints are distributed along the channels and collaterals. The 361 channel points and 231 common points are named in Chinese and also are named using the Roman alphabetical and Western numerical system. For example, the often-used acupoint *zusanli*, which is along the channel connecting the stomach to the foot, is internationally named "S-36." Acupuncture needles are in-

A woman receives acupuncture treatment from a Chinese physician at a hospital in Beijing in 1989. (DAVID & PETER TURNLEY/CORBIS)

serted at the points, and their stimulation releases blocked *qi*, which in turn leads to healing.

In China acupuncture is used to treat diseases in nearly every branch of medicine, whether it is cardiology or dentistry, infectious diseases, or obstetrics. Responding to research, acupuncture techniques have embraced such new technologies as laser and electrical stimulation. In Chinese hospitals that provide acupuncture services, the acupuncture section is always called the department of acupuncture and moxibustion (moxibustion is the burning of medicinal substances, usually herbs, on the acupoints for therapeutic effect). Although the predominant treatment in the department is acupuncture, moxibustion plays an important role. Even as Western medicine becomes more common in China in the twenty-first century, acupuncture continues to be used, especially in hospitals that rely on traditional medicine and also those that combine traditional and Western approaches.

Bao-xing Chen and Garé Lecompte

Further Reading

Academy of Traditional Chinese Medicine. (1978) *An Outline of Chinese Acupuncture*. Monterey Park, CA: Chan's Corporation.

Cooperative Group of Shandong Medical College and Shandong College of Traditional Chinese Medicine. (1982) *Anatomical Atlas of Chinese Acupuncture Points*. Jinan, China: Shandong Science and Technology Press.

Geng Junying and Su Zhihong. (1991) *Practical Traditional Chinese Medicine and Pharmacology: Acupuncture and Moxibustion*. Beijing: New World Press.

Zhang Enqin. (1990) *Chinese Acupuncture and Moxibustion*. Shanghai, China: Publishing House of the Shanghai College of Traditional Chinese Medicine.

ADALET PARTISI   The Adalet Partisi, or Justice Party (JP; 1961–1980), was a political party founded in 1961 in Turkey by the lower echelons of the Democrat Parti (Democrat Party [DP]). The DP had been dissolved by the military junta that staged the 1960 coup. The JP's first leader, Ragip Gumuspala (1897–1964), was chief of the General Staff and was among the 5,000 officers involuntarily retired by the junta to rejuvenate the armed forces in August 1960 (the "Eminsu" case). In 1964, following the death of Gumuspala, Suleyman Demirel (1924–) was elected the second leader of the party and occupied this position until the 1980 military junta banned the party.

The JP's ideology accorded the private sector an important role in economic development and emphasized social justice, rapid economic development, and religious tolerance. The party represented the newly emerging political elite made up of industrialists, small entrepreneurs, artisans, merchants, and professionals who had not been given enough representation by the central organization of the old DP.

The JP was not a uniform body. The party's caucus included, in addition to liberal elements, religious groups, extreme rightists, and devout supporters of the former DP. The mixed composition led to two major splits. The first ended with the dismissal of the nationalist-fundamentalist group from the party in 1967. The second came in December 1970, when seventy-two members of parliament and senators resigned from the party and founded the Democratik Party (Democratic Party).

The party's adoption of an import-substitution policy accelerated the expansion of a capitalist economy at the expense of small merchants and artisans, who withdrew support and moved toward small right-wing parties promising a more nationalist economy. Slowing economic growth, inflation, and labor-related conflicts cooled relations between the party and the private sector. The party's relationship with the military and bureaucrats, on the other hand, was always troublesome.

The JP was in government for half of its twenty years of existence, serving as a coalition partner (November 1961–June 1962, February–October 1965, March 1975–June 1977 [I. Nationalist Front], July 1977–January 1978 [II. Nationalist Front]), as the majority government (October 1965–October 1969, November 1969–February 1970, March 1970–March 1971), and as a minority government (October 1979–September 1980). After the 1980 military intervention, it was dissolved, and its leaders were banned from political activities.

Ayla H. Kilic

Further Reading

Heper, Metin, and Jacob M. Landau, eds. (1991) *Political Parties and Democracy in Turkey*. London: Tauris.

ADANA   (2000 est. pop. 1.1 million). The fifth-largest city of Turkey, Adana is located at the confluence of the Seyhan and Ceyhan Rivers in the rich agricultural plain of Cukurova in southeastern Anatolia. Adana has changed hands often. In 1516 the Ottoman sultan Selim I (1468–1520) took possession of the city during his campaign against the Mamluks. The Ottomans left the administration of this newly conquered territory to local vassals for some years, but in 1608 the territory became a province of the Ottoman empire. In 1833 Adana was ceded in the Treaty of Kutahya to Muhammad Ali Pasha (or Mehmet Ali Pasa, 1769–1849), a rebel Ottoman officer who had succeeded in creating a more or less independent dynasty in Egypt.

The Ottoman empire recovered Adana with the London Convention of 1840, and the city again became a provincial capital in 1867. The city's importance as an agricultural trading center dramatically increased during the American Civil War (1861–1865), when Adana benefited from the sudden shortage of cotton on the international market. As a measure of this increasing importance, a railroad connecting Adana to the Mediterranean port of Mersin was built in 1886, and this line was later included in the Baghdad Railway.

In 1909, Adana was the site of a short-lived Armenian uprising that was brutally suppressed. The French occupied the city in 1919, following the 1918 defeat of the Ottoman empire in World War I. Unwilling to invest the men and moneys necessary to maintain this occupation, however, France ceded the territory to the Turkish Nationalist forces in 1922 at the Treaty of Ankara.

Adana maintains its importance as an agricultural center, and cotton continues to be a significant local crop. Other important crops include oranges, lemons, rice, and sesame. During the Turkish Republic, agriculturally related industries such as textile and vegetable oil production also assumed increasing importance. Adana is home to Cukurova University, founded in 1973. Yasar Kemal (b. 1922), arguably the most famous author of Republican Turkey, was born here and based many of his works on the Turkish and Kurdish folktales of the surrounding countryside.

Howard Eissenstat

Further Reading
Cross, Toni M., and Gary Leiser. (2000) *A Brief History of Ankara.* Vacaville, CA: Indian Ford Press.

ADAT   *Adat* refers to the wide range of local customary regimes characterizing the diversity of ethnic groupings and local communities across the Malay-Indonesian archipelago. Variously translated as "custom," "tradition," "practice," and "rule," the concept conveys a sense of the local order of things—bequeathed and validated by ancestors, maintained and adapted by their descendants. *Adat* typically orders property rights, marriage and inheritance practices, resource access, and local governance. Transgressions of *adat* prescriptions or prohibitions may result in social or supernatural retribution; hence the regulatory aspect of *adat* goes beyond tradition or convention and invokes a legal dimension. But *adat* has broader connotations than Western concepts of either custom or law convey: it also implicates propriety and commonality and appeals to particular moral styles and models of social consensus. *Adat* relationships typically encompass social behavior, ritual responsibilities, reciprocal relations, and collective obligations, as well as other duties and privileges of membership in a community or kinship group. Critically important are the ancestral and communal sanctions that make law and custom living religious and social practices.

Of Arabic derivation, the term *adat* entered Malay, the trading language of the region, and came to encompass numerous analogous concepts in indigenous languages: *dresta* (ancient custom) in Balinese, *ada ntotua* (the customs of the elders) among Kaili speakers in Sulawesi, and *adat perpatih* (matrilineal customary law) for the Minangkabau peoples of Sumatra (In-

donesia) and Negeri Sembilan (Malaysia), for example. The long history of contact with external religious and legal systems—Indic since the fourth century, Islamic since the fourteenth century, and European since the sixteenth century—through trade and colonization resulted in a fusion of *adat* with compatible aspects of these imported traditions. But as the Dutch *adat* scholar Cornelis Van Vollenhoven (1874–1933) argued, it is the indigenous system that prevails in the popular legal consciousness.

While in no sense representing a homogeneous set of principles, the concept of *adat* nevertheless evokes the disparate meanings and significant identities associated with "the local" across Indonesia. Stretching from very specific ethnic, community, or kin group referents—for example, *adat* Minangkabau (an ethnic group), or *adat* Desa Tenganan (a particular village)—to a broad, generic notion of a pan–Malay-Indonesian cultural substratum that predated and fused with the religious traditions of Hinduism and Islam, the notion of *adat* is fundamentally concerned with the reciprocal rights of individuals and their responsibilities to their community and the ancestors that ensure the community's collective well-being.

The Leiden Adatrecht School
Adat law became a major discipline of Dutch colonial legal studies. Building on the earlier writings of G. A. Wilken, William Marsden, and Stamford Raffles, the Adatrecht (literally *"Adat* Law") School was pioneered by Cornelis Van Vollenhoven after his 1901 appointment to the professorship of Constitutional Law and Administration at the University of Leiden.

Van Vollenhoven understood *adat* to be founded on more or less autonomous "jural communities" organized along kinship or territorial lines. But *adat* authority could also be vested in voluntary associations that might be subsets of communities at one end of the spectrum or, at the other end, claimed by hierarchically structured principalities that incorporated *adat* communities or kin groups, which retained various degrees of autonomy.

Van Vollenhoven argued that it was inappropriate to divorce legal institutions from other elements of popular culture. The embeddedness of *adat* in local institutions and beliefs made it impossible to draw a clear distinction between *adat* as either custom or law. Rules or customs that might otherwise be regarded merely as etiquette represent a sensibility to community harmony and ancestral obligation that integrates social, religious, and legal dimensions of everyday life. One codification of customary law, the Ninety-Nine Laws of Perak (translated in Hooker 1978), for example, includes sections on abusive language, ceremonial bathing, payments to the caretaker of village spirits, and the keeping of elephants.

Customary sanctions may be applied because of the failure to perform communal obligations or carry out village cleansing rituals, the omission of compulsory contributions to a feast, the felling of trees without permission, or the transgression of rules on prohibited marriages. Sanctions might require formal expulsion from the *adat* community, or they remain implicit in common understandings that the failure to observe proper social relationships, conduct rituals, or reciprocate appropriately would bring ancestral disfavor and misfortune. Van Vollenhoven and his students recognized these culturally defined norms and rules that regulate everyday life as legitimate forms of law, which exist alongside codified regulations imposed by formal institutions of authority.

The Dutch authorities published volumes of *adat* law documents as part of their colonizing project. These *Adatrechtbundels* (*Adat* Law Collections), including inventories of local *adat* practices, codifications of rules and penalties, and records of disputes and court cases, were collected annually from different parts of the archipelago between 1911 and 1955. For the Leiden School, these voluminous materials demonstrated the importance of indigenous customary law and the potential for codifying it. The highly localized and heterogeneous sources for interpreting *adat*, however, make generalization difficult.

Adat may apply primarily to groups organized by kinship or to a territorial community in which kinship is not important. It may privilege inheritance through male (as among the Balinese and Batak) or female lines (as among the Minangkabau), or it may stipulate equal inheritance from both parents, as in the most prevalent bilateral kinship arrangement in Southeast Asia.

Insofar as the diversity of *adat* regimes can be said to share underlying patterns or principles, a pragmatic tolerance for—or at least a recognition of—local variation is perhaps foremost among them. Different beliefs, prohibitions, obligations, prerogatives, ritual practices, and clothing and housing styles may be prescribed or justified as local *adat*. Certain aspects of *adat* practice may be privileged as central to group identity—for instance, matrilineal descent among the Minangkabau, ritual service obligation *(ayahan)* among the Balinese, or the *runggun* decision-making forum among the Karo Batak—in a certain period, locale, or context and remain without emphasis in another. As the Balinese adage *Desa kala patra* (according to "place,

time, and circumstance") indicates, *adat* is open to situational interpretation and revision.

Van Vollenhoven likened variation in local *adat* to dialects of a common language, in which an underlying grammar could be revealed by scholarly analysis. The studies carried out by the Leiden School assert that common underlying features could be identified beneath the surface diversity. *Adat* stresses local autonomy, recognizing and legitimizing variation from one social group to the other, and exhibits flexibility over time. *Adat* is geared toward maintaining harmonious relations; because local constructions of *adat* are acutely attuned to reciprocal relations in pursuit of social consonance, balance and equivalence have great resonance in its rhetorical and ritual expression. Nevertheless, in most of the cultures of the archipelago, *adat* also accommodates hierarchic social structures that grant degrees of precedence and prerogative to founding ancestors or aristocratic lineages. Communal interest theoretically takes priority over individual interest; consequently the *adat* ethos is geared toward consensual deliberation and mutual aid. Local *adat* is more often than not uncodified, taking its social force from the collective memory and ancestral bonds of community members, as interpreted through the wisdom and spiritual powers of *adat* specialists. *Adat* authority tends to be diffuse, vested variously in corporate membership, village elders, and rulers, but it is subject to the intervention of supernatural forces—auspicious or ominous events signifying the favor or dissatisfaction of ancestors and local guardian spirits. The power and knowledge of the spirit domain are often exercised by inspired or charismatic practitioners operating outside formal lines of authority.

Controversies: Of Rights and Identities

Most of the controversies surrounding *adat* in academic literature, political circles, and popular debates among the regional cultures of Indonesia center on its relevance to modernity, its relationship to orthodox religions, and its implications for property, status, and gender.

Gender, Religion, and Modernity Conflicts and accommodations among *adat*, capitalist modernity, and Islamic revival movements have been of special interest to scholars of gender and religion. *Adat* typically recognizes women's right to initiate divorce and, in the predominantly bilateral kinship systems of the archipelago, to equal inheritance rights and an equal share in property acquired during marriage.

Matrilineal customary law *(adat perpatih)* among the Minangkabau people of West Sumatra in Indonesia and Negeri Sembilan in West Malaysia has received considerable attention because of the long-standing accommodation of Islam to women's customary inheritance rights. Under matrilineal *adat*, ancestral property passes through the female line, whereas Islamic law formally gives women the right to a one-third share of family property, compared to two-thirds for male descendants. The difference between Minangkabau *adat* and Islamic law was traditionally resolved through a distinction between ancestral property *(harta pusako)*, transmitted from mothers to daughters, and individually acquired property *(harta pencarian)*, which may be disposed of according to the wishes of the owner.

Although the Minangkabau generally regard Islam and *adat* as mutually reinforcing aspects of their identity, modernist political movements in West Sumatra challenged *adat*-based relations, particularly women's property rights under *adat*, without substantively altering *adat* inheritance practice. In Malaya, during what became known as the *Adat* crisis of 1951, when a branch of the United Malay National Organization mooted a proposal to abolish matrilineal inheritance in Negeri Sembilan, women mounted a successful campaign threatening proponents with divorce.

Individually acquired property still tends to be converted over generations to ancestral property. The continuity of this practice, despite the individualization and commercialization of property and other aspects of social life, attests to the resilience of Minangkabau *adat* and the continued significance of the cultural identities and social ties it underpins. Nevertheless, wider social change through urbanization, industrialization, and the commercialization of agriculture (which accompanied the green-revolution intensification of rice production) has altered the complex constellation of social relations and cultural beliefs that connected land, ancestors, and female mediation in ritual and family affairs. These forces have tended to marginalize the cultural values and social relations of these once predominantly agrarian societies, with consequences for the position of women.

While the *adat* arrangements of the predominantly bilateral or matrilineal cultures of the archipelago support relatively egalitarian gender relations, for women in patrilineal systems, such as the Balinese and Batak, the opposite is true. For example, Bali Hindu authorities obtained exemption from divorce and inheritance provisions of the 1974 Marriage Law that stipulate equal division of property on the grounds of patrilineal *adat*. Nevertheless, anthropologists find underlying bilateral principles across the cultures of Southeast Asia that moderate formally lineal practices.

Property Rights and Modernity Since the colonial period, the question of official recognition of *adat* property rights has been among the most vexing of political and economic issues. With respect to land and resources, *adat* is tied to concepts of territoriality and community rights of allocation, generally referred to as *hak ulayat* ("territorial right"). These include communal access or customarily allocated rights to residential lands, cultivated fields, uncultivated forests, and grazing and fallow areas.

The religious, social, and economic dimensions of *adat* make property rights and resource access more complex than individual private-property rights under Western law. Since the individual's rights to land and resources are in varying degrees defined and validated by community or group membership, it is impossible to draw clear distinctions between private and common property. Migration or expulsion from the community could mean the loss of rights to corporately held land. In Bali, for example, some of the oldest communities retain strict regulations on land alienation. Tenganan village does not permit the purchase or sale of village land, most of which is communally owned, and serious transgressions of *adat* rules, or marriage to someone from outside the village, result in loss of rights to communal property.

Under *adat* regulations, outside groups require permission and usually pay "recognition fees" for resource access rights to *adat* community territory. Smaller-scale payments may also be required of members themselves in acknowledgment of overarching group rights. *Adat* typically limits individual property rights to land that can be effectively worked by member households. Communities, custodians, or individual holders of *adat* land traditionally have ritual obligations to ancestors and guardian spirits that validate their property rights.

With cultural, social, and economic links so intimately connected, *adat* land has been widely regarded as inalienable from the community or descent group. This aspect of *adat* has not sat comfortably with national land laws, which in both Malaysia and Indonesia give great weight to forms of private-property rights inherited from the Western legal tradition. Land not officially registered under formal law was subject to appropriation by the state.

The Dutch colonial Domain Declaration arrogated to the state all land for which legally recognized property rights could not be proved. This principle became the subject of scholarly controversy between the Leiden School, which sought to defend *adat* rights as legal rights to land, and the competing School of Law and

Administration at Utrecht. The latter refused *adat* the status of law, arguing that *adat*-based rights were an impediment to modernization and development. The premise of the Domain Declaration was later incorporated into the Indonesian constitution and subsequent national land and resource laws, marginalizing the token acknowledgments of *adat* in the same legislation.

In practice, local claims to uncultivated areas under *hak ulayat* were disregarded or granted only residual recognition under colonial and postcolonial regimes. Land and resource rights asserted under *adat* were overridden by the state whenever they competed with alternative land uses. Widespread expropriation of *adat* domains for industry, resettlement, and other development projects set the stage for later, sometimes violent struggles over land, resources, and cultural rights.

Myths and Reformations

For its critics, the *adat* law project of the Leiden School was an idealist construction, which exaggerated the internal coherence and underlying commonality of *adat* regimes. Joel Kahn (1993) and Peter Burns (1989) critiqued the neotraditional romanticism of Dutch scholars and administrators who sought a pristine indigenous legal archetype. Clifford Geertz argued that the Dutch *adat* law framework reified a living, culturally defined legal sensibility, misrepresenting "an indigenous sense of what justice is, social consonance, in terms of an imported one of what order is, a *Rechtsstaat* [state law]" (Geertz 1983: 209).

Debate among contemporary scholars continues to reflect the earlier conflict between the Leiden and Utrecht schools, the former supporting the practical and ethical grounds for the recognition of *adat* as law and the case for legal pluralism, the latter regarding it as an artificial and inappropriate application of the concept of law, which hindered the development of a modern codified legal system. Parallel positions idealizing and contesting the character and role of *adat* regimes continue among indigenous writers confronting questions of equality, sustainability, nationalism, and modernity. As environmental concerns became linked to indigenous-rights issues, *adat* regulation of natural resources has become the focus of similar debate.

Controversies about the place of *adat* in the lives of the peoples of the archipelago and its legal viability in Malaysia and Indonesia have not abated. Indeed, the localization processes accompanying globalization place *adat* at the center of much of the discourse associated with issues of indigenous rights, local management of resources, and decentralized governance. In Indonesia,

the reform movement that ended the Suharto regime in 1998 spawned an alliance of *adat* communities supported by nongovernmental organizations and aimed at reasserting the rights of local indigenous minorities. The Alliance of *Adat* Communities of the Archipelago was formed in 1999 to press for revision of land, resource, and governance legislation and to gain full recognition of *adat* institutions, property, and cultural rights. Regional-autonomy policies have been developed in response to self-determination demands and to the interethnic conflicts partly generated by decades of marginalization of *adat* regimes under the auspices of government development policies.

While debate over the contemporary relevance of *adat* continues in scholarly and policy-making circles, evidence of the continuity of *adat* practices reveals an inner dynamic of meanings and values that demand recognition. These meanings and values take new forms as local regimes become linked to global movements focused on the rights of indigenous minorities. The politicization of *adat* has led to more crystallized and sometimes more rigidly defined conceptions of *adat*, reformed and reconstituted as a focus of political demands. As Maila Stivens (1996) says of matriliny in Negeri Sembilan, *adat*, for significant numbers among the populations of Malaysia and Indonesia, is no "traditional relic." Across the Malay-Indonesian archipelago, *adat* remains a vital force, a sometimes diffuse, sometimes explicit sociolegal sensibility, and a ground for contestation and for defining common identity and interest.

Carol Warren

Further Reading

Acciaioli, Greg. (2002) "Re-empowering the 'Art of the Elders': The Revitalization of *Adat* among the To Lindu of Central Sulawesi and throughout Contemporary Indonesia." In *Beyond Jakarta: Regional Autonomy and Local Societies in Indonesia*, edited by Minako Sakai. Adelaide, Australia: Crawford House.

Adatrechtbundels. (1910–1955) Vols. 1–45. The Hague, Netherlands: Martinus Nijhoff.

Benda-Beckman, Franz von. (1979) *Property in Social Continuity*. The Hague, Netherlands: Martinus Nijhoff.

———, Keebet von Benda-Beckman, and J. Hoekma, eds. (1997) *Natural Resources, Environment, and Legal Pluralism*. The Hague, Netherlands: Martinus Nijhoff.

Benda-Beckman, Keebet von. (1984) *The Broken Stairways to Consensus: Village Justice and State Courts in Minangkabau*. Dordrecht, Netherlands: Foris.

Burns, Peter. (1989) "The Myth of *Adat*." *Journal of Legal Pluralism* 28: 1–127.

Geertz, Clifford. (1983) "Local Knowledge: Fact and Law in Comparative Perspective." In *Local Knowledge*, by Clifford Geertz. New York: Basic Books, 167–234.

Holleman, Johan Frederick, ed. (1981) *Van Vollenhoven on Indonesian Adat Law*. The Hague, Netherlands: Martinus Nijhoff.

Hooker, Michael. (1978) *Adat Laws in Modern Indonesia*. Kuala Lumpur, Malaysia: Oxford University Press.

———. (1970) *Readings in Malay Adat Laws*. Singapore: Singapore University Press.

Josselin de Jong, Jan Petrus Benjamin. (1948) *Customary Law, A Confusing Fiction*. Koninklijk Instituut voor de Tropen, 80; Mededeling Afdeling Volkenkunde, 29. Amsterdam: Indisch Instituut.

Kahn, Joel. (1993) *Constituting the Minangkabau: Peasants, Culture, and Modernity in Colonial Indonesia*. Oxford: Berg.

Koesnoe, Mohammed. (1971) *Introduction into Indonesian Adat Law*. Nijmegen, Netherlands: Katholieke Universiteit.

Li, Tania Murray. (2000) "Articulating Indigenous Identity in Indonesia: Resource Politics and the Tribal Slot." *Comparative Studies in Society and History* 42, 1: 149–179.

Pannell, Sandra. (1997) "Managing the Discourse of Resource Management: the Case of *Sasi* from 'Southeast' Maluku, Indonesia." *Oceania* 67: 289–307.

Slaats, Herman, and Karen Portier. (1992) *Traditional Decision-Making and Law*. Yogyakarta, Indonesia: Gadjah Mada University Press.

Stivens, Maila. (1996) *Sexual Politics and Social Change in Rural Malaysia*. Saint Leonards, Australia: Allen and Unwin.

Ter Haar, Bernard. (1948) *Adat Law in Indonesia*. New York: Institute of Pacific Relations.

Warren, Carol. (1993) *Adat and Dinas: Balinese Communities in the Indonesian State*. Kuala Lumpur, Malaysia: Oxford University Press.

———, and John McCarthy. (2002) "Customary Regimes and Collective Goods in the Changing Political Constellation of Indonesia." In *Shaping Common Futures*, edited by Sally Sargeson. London: Routledge, 75–101.

Zerner, Charles. (1994) "Through a Green Lens: The Construction of Customary Environmental Law and Community in Indonesia's Maluku Islands." *Law & Society Review* 28, 5: 1079–1122.

AEGEAN SEA The Aegean Sea is located between the coasts of Greece and Turkey and the islands of Crete and Rhodes. Its covers an area of 210 square kilometers; its maximum depth is 3,543 meters, found to the east of Crete. More than two thousand islands of varying sizes, most of which belong to Greece, are scattered throughout the Aegean. Some, such as Lesbos, Chios, Rhodes, and Crete, are of substantial size and sustain significant populations. Many islands and islets, however, are too small and barren to sustain human habitation.

The prevailing winds in the Aegean Sea are northerly, dry, and relatively cold. During the mild winter season, these alternate with milder northwesterly winds. As with much of the Mediterranean, the Aegean is considered to be poor in resources. The flow of colder and less saline water from the Black Sea

Sailboats in the harbor of Bodrum, Turkey, on the Aegean Sea. (NIK WHEELER/CORBIS)

through the Turkish straits (the Bosporus and the Dardanelles) and the Sea of Marmara tends to cool the water temperatures and reduce the high salinity of the Aegean Sea. This flow of water and the fish that migrate from the Black Sea through the Turkish straits have had a positive effect on the fish resources of the Aegean. On the other hand, the Aegean has been adversely affected by the increasing levels of pollution in the Black Sea as well as in other adjoining seas. In the Aegean, illegal dumping of waste materials by both Greek and Turkish industries has contributed to the pollution, with harmful effects on marine resources.

Increased shipping from ports in the Black Sea and the prospect of considerably higher tanker traffic carrying Caspian and Central Asian oil through the Aegean have generated fears in Greece and Turkey, as well as among environmentalists, of still more acute threats to the ecosystem and cleanliness of the Aegean.

Modest deposits of petroleum have been discovered and exploited off the coast of the island of Thassos, and some experts have predicted more extensive discoveries elsewhere in the Aegean. However, disputes between Greece and Turkey over the limits of territorial seas and sovereign rights over the continental shelf have prevented explorations for oil and gas in much of the sea that remains outside the six-mile territorial seas that both countries maintain in the Aegean. The settlement of disputed maritime issues related to the continental shelf and territorial sea entitlement of the two neighbors will open the door to greater exploration activity for oil and gas in the Aegean. No less important, improved relations between Greece and Turkey will yield greater cooperation to help resolve the increasingly serious threats to the environment of the Aegean.

Tozun Bahcheli

Further Reading
Kariotis, Theodore C., ed. (1997) *Greece and the Law of the Sea*. The Hague, Netherlands: Kluwer Law International.
Ozturk, Bayram, ed. (2000) *The Aegean Sea: Proceedings of the International Symposium on the Aegean Sea*. Istanbul, Turkey: Turkish Marine Research Foundation.

AFGHAN HOUND The Afghan hound is a tall, slender hunting dog (*Canis familiaris*) with long, strong legs, a heavy, silky coat (although there are short-haired varieties of Afghans), and typically long ears. An adult stands about 70 centimeters at shoulders and weighs about 27 kilograms. Belonging to the hound group, Afghan hounds are supposedly related to greyhounds.

Afghan hounds originated in the Middle East and were used for hunting in mountainous regions of northern Afghanistan. Some have suggested that the breed was known in ancient Egypt as early as the third millennium BCE; the Egyptians certainly had some sort of hound at an early date. Afghans came to England with British soldiers who brought them back from the Indo-Afghanistan area in the late nineteenth century; the breed reached the United States in the early 1930s.

The Afghan dog's agility in covering difficult terrain made it a suitable companion for mountain-dwelling hunters mounted on horseback. An Afghan's long legs allow it to move with great speed in a characteristic, racehorse-like gallop. Like all sight hounds, such as the Borzoi or Russian wolfhound, the whippet, and the greyhound, the Afghan courses by sight rather than by smell; thus its swiftness lets it keep pace with and run down fast-moving game, and its agility enables it to follow its prey's evasive actions. Today Afghans are primarily companion dogs and show dogs rather than hunters, esteemed for their stylish lines and beautiful, tireless movement in all Western countries, where Afghan puppies command a high price.

Paul Hockings

Further Reading
Fogle, Bruce (1995) *Encyclopedia of the Dog*. New York: DK Publishing.

AFGHANI, JAMAL AD-DIN (1838/39–1896/ 97), Islamic theorist and activist. Jamal ad-din al-Afghani (the "al" is often dropped) was a controversial and significant influence in the Islamic world during the last half of the nineteenth century. His influence continues through his writings, which stress anti-imperialism, nationalism, and Pan-Islamism.

Although he claimed that he was born in Afghanistan, several documents indicate that he was actually born in Iran and raised as a Shi'ite Muslim. His assertion of Afghan and Sunni Islam birth was probably made to avoid discrimination by, and lower status among, Sunni Muslims, who constitute about 90 percent of the world's Muslims. Evidence suggests that he received early education in Iran and higher education at Shi'ite shrine cities in Iraq. His papers indicate that he studied with great interest the innovative school of Shi'a Islam called Shaikhi, which was founded on the writings of Shaikh Ahmad al-Asa'i (1752–1826). He then settled in India where he apparently developed his lifelong hatred of the British and their colonial system. From India he traveled to Mecca and eventually arrived in Afghanistan via Iran.

In Afghanistan, he served as a counsel to the emir until his anti-British opinions cost him his position and led to his expulsion when a pro-British emir came to power in 1868. He eventually settled in Istanbul and became active in educational circles. In a series of controversial university lectures, he argued that philosophy and prophecies were crafts, skills that could be developed and learned. This view was seen as heretical by the religious authorities and led to his expulsion from Istanbul. He lived and taught in Cairo until 1879, where he encouraged his followers to replace the Egyptian leader Isma'il with his candidate, Tawfiq. Tawfiq did come to power, but only with British and French support, and Jamal ad-din Afghani's anti-British rhetoric again led to his expulsion. He moved back to India and settled in the Muslim state of Hyderabad, where he wrote his most influential work on nationalism, *The Refutation of the Materialists*. In 1883 he moved to Paris, where he was joined by a disciple from Cairo, Muhammad Abduh. Together they put out a free Muslim newspaper, *Al-Urwa Al-Wuthqa* (The Firmest Bond), which took strong Pan-Islamist and anti-British positions. It was short-lived but very influential.

After the closing of the newspaper, Jamal ad-din Afghani was on the move again. In Britain he was involved in a plot to end British influence in Egypt; in Iran and Russia he tried to no avail to start a war between Russia and Britain. In Iran he spoke out against the shah's economic concessions to Europe, which caused him to be exiled to Iraq. On an invitation from the Ottoman sultan, he moved to Istanbul, where he was eventually banned from lecturing and publishing. It is believed that he encouraged one of his disciples to assassinate the shah of Iran, Naser al-Din Shah. He died of cancer in 1897, although a rumor persists that the sultan had him poisoned.

Houman A. Sadri

Further Reading

Adamec, Ludwig W. (1997) *Historical Dictionary of Afghanistan.* 2d ed. Lanham, MD: Scarecrow Press.

Edwards, David B. (1996) *Heroes of the Age: Moral Fault Lines on the Afghan Frontier.* Berkeley and Los Angeles: University of California Press.

Haynes, Jeff, ed. (1999) *Religion, Globalization, and Political Culture in the Third World.* New York: St. Martin's Press.

Mawsilili, Ahmad. (1999) *Historical Dictionary of Islamic Fundamentalist Movements in the Arab World, Iran, and Turkey.* Lanham, MD: Scarecrow Press.

AFGHANISTAN—PROFILE

(2001 est. pop. 26.8 million). Afghanistan (Land of the Afghans), formerly the Republic of Afghanistan (called Jomhuri-ye Afghanistan in Dari Persian, Da Afghanistan Jamhawriyat in Pashto), has undergone dramatic sociopolitical changes during the past 150 years and particularly since 1989. As a crossroads of Eurasian commerce for nearly four millennia, it has been a conduit for invaders from east and west and a recipient of major religious ideologies, including Buddhism and Islam. Hence, Afghanistan is ethnically and linguistically diverse, a mosaic of cultures and languages, especially in the north. In 2001, the self-proclaimed Taliban government, which at one time controlled 90 percent of the nation, referred to the country as the Islamic Emirate of Afghanistan, whereas the Northern Alliance, the umbrella grouping of anti-Taliban forces, fought for the Islamic State of Afghanistan (Dowlat-e Eslami-ye Afghanestan in Dari Persian).

Location, Geography, and Ecology

Afghanistan is a landlocked Central Asian nation bounded on the north by three former Soviet republics—now members of the Commonwealth of Independent States (Turkmenistan, Uzbekistan, and Tajikistan)—on the northeast by the People's Republic of China, on the east and south by Pakistan, and on the west by Iran. Afghanistan's current boundaries were established during the late nineteenth century in the context of the "Great Game," a rivalry between the British then occupying India on the Asian subcontinent

After more than twenty years of war and civil disorder, much of Afghanistan in 2002 is in ruins. These damaged buildings line a main street in the capital city of Kabul. (BACI/CORBIS)

AFGHANISTAN

Country name: Islamic State of Afghanistan, Islamic Emirate of Afghanistan
Area: 647,500 sq km
Population: 26,813,057 (July 2001 est.)
Population growth rate: 3.48% (2001 est.)
Birth rate: 41.42 births/1,000 population (2001 est.)
Death rate: 17.72 deaths/1,000 population (2001 est.)
Net migration rate: 11.11 migrant(s)/1,000 population (2001 est.)
Sex ratio—total population: 1.06 male(s)/female (2001 est.)
Infant mortality rate: 147.02 deaths/1,000 live births (2001 est.)
Life expectancy at birth—total population: 46.24 years, male: 46.97 years, female: 45.47 years (2001 est.)
Major religions: Sunni Islam, Shiʿa Islam
Major languages: Pashtu, Dari, Turkic languages
Literacy—total population: 31.5%, male: 47.2%, female: 15% (1999 est.)
Government type: no functioning central government, administered by factions
Capital: Kabul
Administrative divisions: 32 provinces
Independence: 19 August 1919 (from U.K. control over Afghan foreign affairs)
National holiday: Independence Day, 19 August (1919)
Suffrage: no information
GDP—real growth rate: no information
GDP—per capita (purchasing power parity): $800 (2000 est.)
Population below poverty line: no information
Exports: $80 million (1996 est.)
Imports: $150 million (1996 est.)
Currency: afghani (AFA)

Source: Central Intelligence Agency. (2001) *The World Factbook* 2001. Retrieved 18 October 2001 from: http://www.cia.gov/cia/publications/factbook. "Administrative Divisions of Countries." (2001) In *Administrative Subdivisions of Countries*, edited by Gwillim Law. Jefferson, NC: McFarland & Company. Retrieved 17 February 2002, from: http://www.mindspring.com/~gwil/statoids.html.

and the Russians in Central Asia; Afghanistan was called the "Northwest Frontier" by the British. The borders of Afghanistan with its six neighbors cover 6,529 kilometers.

The nation covers 647,500 square kilometers—approximately the size of Texas or the United Kingdom—and has a shape similar to a clenched right fist with the thumb extended to the northeast, the narrow Wakhan Corridor leading to China. Major physical features include the Amu Dar'ya (the ancient Oxus) River, forming much of the northern international border; the steppes, the Turkistan Plains in the north; a mountainous center and northeast dominated by the Hindu Kush mountain range (the western extension of the Himalayas) and the Pamirs; the Sistan Basin with plains in the southwest, through which flows the Helmand River; and deserts (Dasht-i Margo) to the far west and south (Rigestan). Except for the Amu Dar'ya, which flows westward into the Caspian Sea, and the Kabul River, which flows eastward and joins the Indus, the other rivers end in inland seas, swamps, or salt flats.

The northern plains are a major agricultural region, accounting for 80 percent of the grain crops;

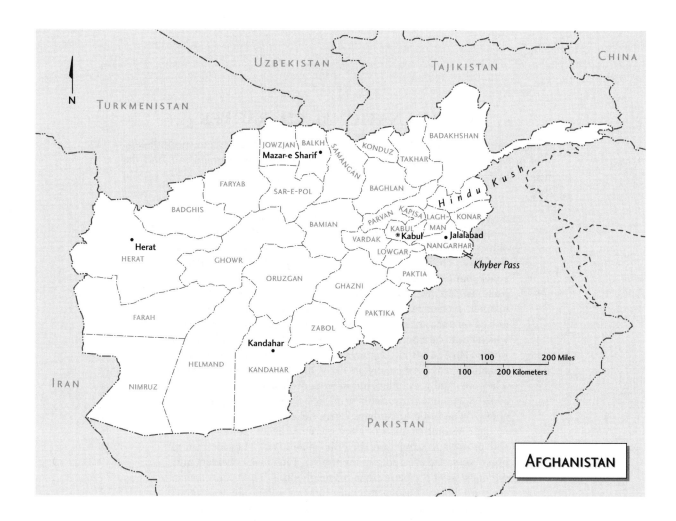

the southwestern plateau is a desert and semidesert except for the irrigation agriculture associated with the Helmand River; the central highlands are dominated by the Hindu Kush, which is traversed by only a few high mountain passes. Nearly half of the total land area lies above 2,000 meters; thus, much of Afghanistan has a subarctic mountain climate with dry, cold winters and short, cool summers, whereas the semiarid steppe lowlands have cold winters and hot summers, and the southwest has a hot, arid, desert climate. Annual precipitation varies from 75 millimeters in the desert to 1,280 millimeters in the Hindu Kush. The elevation extremes are on the Amu Dar'ya (258 meters) and at Noeshak (7,485 meters). Climate, flora, and fauna vary with elevation, and temperatures range greatly. Agricultural products include wheat, rice, fruits, nuts, and vegetables, although only 12 percent of the land is arable, whereas 46 percent consists of permanent pastures, 37 percent deserts, and only 3 percent forests. A four-year drought (1998–2001) has decimated the agricultural lands and pastures.

Many species of the indigenous animal population are endangered due to heavy exploitation and the ravages of twenty-three years of international (Soviet-Afghan) and civil wars.

Sociopolitical Characteristics

Administratively, the nation has thirty-two *velayat* (provinces): Badakhshan, Badghis, Baghlan, Balkh, Bamian, Farah, Faryab, Ghazni, Ghowr, Helmand, Herat, Jowzjan, Kabul, Kandahar, Kapisa, Khowst, Konar, Kunduz, Laghman, Lowhar, Nangarhar, Nimruz, Nuristan, Oruzgan, Paktia, Paktika, Parvan, Samangan, Sar-e Pol, Takhar, Vardak, and Zabul (Zabol). The two newest are Khowst and Nuristan. There has never been an official, comprehensive census, but the population in 1998 was estimated by the United Nations at 21.5 million, including 2.5 million nomads, whereas the U.S. Central Intelligence Agency (CIA) in 2001 projected 26.8 million, including 3.2 million refugees in Pakistan, 1.9 million in Iran, 300,000 in Turkmenistan,

AFGHAN NATIONAL CHARACTER

While extreme and stereotypical, this 1908 profile of the Afghan, nonetheless, does provide some insight into the nature of relations in Afghanistan, and the difficulties faced by any government in creating national unity—a key task in 2002.

As a race the Afghans are handsome and athletic, often with a fair complexion, the features highly aquiline. Their step is full of resolution, their bearing proud and apt to be rough. Inured to bloodshed from childhood, they are familiar with death, audacious in attack, but easily discouraged by failure. They are treacherous and passionate in revenge, which they will satisfy in the most cruel manner, even at a cost of their own lives. Nowhere is crime committed on such trifling grounds, in spite of the severe manner in which crimes are punished when brought home to offenders. The women have handsome features of a Jewish cast, fair complexions, sometimes rosy, especially in early life, though usually sallow. They are rigidly secluded; but in spite of this, and of the fact that adultery is almost invariably punished by death, intrigue is frequent. "The pride of Afghans," says Bellew, "is a marked feature of their natural character. They eternally boast of their descent and prowess in arms and their independence. They despise all other races; and even among themselves, each man considers himself equal to, if not better than his neighbour." They enjoy a character for liberal hospitality; guest and strangers are fed free of charge in the village guest houses; and by the law of honor known as *nanawatai*, the Afghan is expected, at the sacrifice of his own life and property if necessary, to shelter and protect anyone, even an enemy, who in extremity may seek an asylum under his roof. This protection, however, only extends to the limits of the premises; and once beyond this, the host may be the first to injure his late protégé. *Badal*, or retaliation, must be exacted for the slightest personal injury or insult, or for damage to property. Where the avenger takes the life of his victim in retaliation for the murder of one of his relatives, the act is termed *kisas*.

Source: Imperial Gazetteer of India: Afghanistan and Nepal. (1908) Calcutta, India: Superintendent of Government Printing, 26–27.

Uzbekistan, and Tajikistan, and 150,000 residing elsewhere. The largest city is the capital, Kabul (Kabul *velayat)*, with 1.4 million inhabitants, located in the eastcentral region; next are Kandahar (Kandahar *velayat)*, with 225,500, located in the southwest; Mazar-i Sharif (Balkh *velayat)*, with 185,000, located in the northcentral region; Herat (Herat *velayat)*, with 175,000, located in the upper northwest; and Jalalabad (Nangarhar *velayat)*, with 120,000, located east of Kabul.

U.N. data list the major ethnic groups as Pashtuns (54 percent of the population), Tajiks (concentrated in the north, 27 percent), Uzbeks (8 percent), and Hazara (7 percent). Others include Kyrgyz, Arabs, Baluchis, Turkmen, Nuristani, Chahar Aimak, Brahui, Sikhs, and Jews. CIA data list Pashtuns (38 percent), Tajiks (25 percent), Hazara (19 percent), and Uzbeks (6 percent). The Pashtun tribes, both sedentary farmers and nomadic pastoralists, inhabit principally the southern and eastern parts of Afghanistan. Tajik farmers and village craftspeople live in Kabul and Badakhshan *velayat* to the northeast and in Herat to the far west.

Languages

The official languages of Afghanistan include Pashto (more precisely, Southern Pashto) and the Dari dialect of Persian (Eastern Farsi or Dari). The 2001 CIA data list Pashto (35 percent); Afghan Persian or Dari (50 percent); Turkic languages, primarily Turkmen and Uzbek (11 percent); and thirty minor languages. Summer Institute of Linguistics data in 1996 listed the number of languages at forty-seven, then all "living" (spoken) languages. Many individuals, especially men, are bilingual and trilingual, although the effects of warfare have undoubtedly altered the numbers of multilingual males. Thirty of the forty-seven languages are indigenous to Afghanistan; five derive from Pakistan and four from Tajikistan.

Approximately 85 percent of the population are Sunni Muslim (Hanafi school), and 14 percent are Shi'ite (primarily in the north), with the remainder Ismaili Muslims, Hindus, Sikhs, and others. By 2001, the Sikh population of Afghanistan was estimated at about five thousand, and the number of Jews had shrunk from forty thousand in 1989 to fewer than seven hundred.

Charles C. Kolb

Further Reading

Allchin, F. Raymond, and Norman Hammond, eds. (1978) *The Archaeology of Afghanistan: From Earliest Times to the Timurid Period*. London: Academic Press.

Asimov, Mukhammed S., and Clifford E. Bosworth, eds. (1998) *The Age of Achievement, A.D. 750 to the End of the Fifteenth Century*, Pt. 1: *The Historical, Social, and Economic Setting*. Vol. 4 of *History of Civilizations of Central Asia*. Paris: UNESCO Publications.

Bradsher, Henry S. (1999) *Afghan Communism and Soviet Intervention*. New York: Oxford University Press.

Central Intelligence Agency. (2001) "Afghanistan." In *The CIA World Factbook 2001*. Washington, DC: Central Intelligence Agency. Retrieved 18 January 2002, from: http://www.odci.gov/cia/publications/factbook.af.html

CountryWatch.com. (2001) *Country Review: Afghanistan, 2001–2002*. Retrieved 18 January 2002, from: http://www.countrywatch.com

Dani, Ahmad Hasan, and Vadim Mikhailovich Masson, eds. (1992) *History of Civilizations of Central Asia*, Vol. 1: *The Dawn of Civilization: Earliest Times to 700 B.C.* Paris: UNESCO Publications.

Dupree, Louis. (1980) *Afghanistan*. Rev. ed. Princeton, NJ: Princeton University Press.

Gregorian, Vartan. (1969) *The Emergence of Modern Afghanistan: Politics of Reform and Modernization, 1880–1946*. Stanford, CA: Stanford University Press.

Harmatta, Janos, Basant J. Puri, and Ghulam F. Etemandi, eds. (1994) *History of Civilizations of Central Asia*, Vol. 2: *The Development of Sedentary and Nomadic Civilizations, 700 B.C. to A.D. 250*. Paris: UNESCO Publications.

Meyer, Karl E., and Shareen Blair Brysac. (1999) *Tournament of Shadows: The Great Game and the Race for Empire in Central Asia*. Washington, DC: Counterpoint.

Nytrop, Richard F., and Donald M. Seekins, eds. (1986) *Afghanistan: A Country Study*. 5th ed. Washington, DC: U.S. Government Printing Office.

Summer Institute of Linguistics. (2001) *Ethnologue Report for Afghanistan, 2001*. Dallas, TX: SIL International. Retrieved 18 January 2002, from: http://www.ethnologue.com/show_country.asp?name=Afghanistan

AFGHANISTAN—ECONOMIC SYSTEM

As of 2002, Afghanistan does not have a viable economic system. The traditional economy, which was based mainly on subsistence agriculture and animal husbandry and which usually provided enough food for the Afghan population plus a surplus for trade, was essentially destroyed beginning in 1979 with the Soviet invasion and war, which lasted until 1989. The economy suffered further during the civil unrest of the first half of the 1990s and then recovered in some regions during Taliban rule from 1995 to 2001. The U.S.-led invasion of 2001–2002 damaged much of what was left of the economy and infrastructure, and the World Bank concluded that Afghanistan had become the poorest nation in the world. The situation was made worse by a drought that began in 1999 and limited crop production and livestock herding. It is also important to note that statistics regarding the Afghanistan economy for the last twenty or so years are untrustworthy.

The year 2002 marked the beginning of a large-scale international effort to rebuild the Afghanistan economy and infrastructure through billions of dollars of financial, material, and managerial support. The first major event was the Tokyo Conference on 21–22 January, convened to address the problems of Afghanistan's devastated economy.

Afghanistan has a relatively small (estimated at 18–20 million) rural population, most of whom live in small villages. The traditional economy is in accord with this population pattern and is based on a mix of farming (wheat, barley, corn, and fruits are the main crops) and herding (mainly sheep and goats and also cattle, camels, donkeys, and horses). Farming and herding are limited by the rough terrain and dry climate, and agriculture typically requires irrigation.

The Afghanistan economy is based primarily on subsistence agriculture. Here, a farmer plows a field with a team of oxen. (CAROLINE PENN/CORBIS)

Farming and herding are done mainly to support the family, but in good years prior to 1979 a surplus was sometimes produced and exported. These major subsistence activities are supported by village-level weaving, blacksmithing, and goldsmithing and cottage industries such as carpet weaving. Prior to 1979, other economic activities included a small manufacturing sector (cement, carpets, textiles) and foreign aid, which supported government programs and the development of a technology and communication infrastructure that mainly served the cities. From 1979 on, millions of Afghans fled to Pakistan and other nations, and remittances they sent to relatives back home provided another source of revenue.

The ten-year war with the Soviets destroyed many roads and irrigation systems and government programs and services, rendered land useless because of land mines, and caused several million to flee. The civil war following the Soviet withdrawal caused additional damage, and it was not until the Taliban took control and eventually ruled 90 percent of the nation that the economy begin to recover. Especially in the south and east, farming and herding improved to a limited extent, trade with Pakistan increased, and natural resources such as timber, precious stones, and marble and granite were harvested and traded. Opium farming also expanded rapidly, and Afghanistan became the largest supplier of illicit opium until the Taliban banned opium production in July 2000. Opium production continued, however, in the north, where it was an important source of income for the Northern Alliance, the major rival of the Taliban. The drought that began in 1999 and continued into 2002 undid the agricultural and herding gains and made a significant portion of the population dependent on international aid for food, shelter, and health care.

In 2002, as the international community plans for the development of the Afghan economy, it faces a challenging task. Among the major obstacles are the absence of political stability; weak or nonfunctioning economic institutions such as banks, a state treasury, and civil-service system; corruption in the distribution of international aid; an environment unsuited to farming in many regions; few passable roads; no railroad; and no access to the sea. On the positive side are a long tradition of self-sufficiency, natural gas and oil resources, and the sizable international effort.

David Levinson

Further Reading

Ahmed, Akbar S. (1980) *Pukhtun Economy and Society: Traditional Structure and Economic Development in a Tribal Society.* London: Routledge and Kegan Paul.
Dupree, Louis. (1980) *Afghanistan.* Princeton, NJ: Princeton University Press.

AFGHANISTAN—HISTORY   Archaeologically, Afghanistan's prehistory dates to fifty thousand years ago and includes Middle and Upper Paleolithic sites (particularly in the northern foothills of the Hindu Kush) and abundant Bronze and Iron Age sites in the north, south, and east. Modern Afghanistan, located at the crossroads of Central, West, and South Asia, incorporates partially or wholly the ancient regions of Aria, Bactria, Sogdiana, Arachosia, and Drangiana—part of the Achaemenid empire (559–330 BCE) and more recently the empire of Alexander of Macedon and his Hellenic successors (c. 330 BCE–150 CE). The territory was also a part of the Parthian, Yueh-chih/Tokharian, Saka, and Kushana polities and the Sasanid empire (c. 224/228–651 CE) and was incorporated into the lands conquered by the Arab Muslims about 700 CE. Portions of Afghanistan remained under the Abbasid caliphate into the ninth century and then under the temporary control of a series of polities: the Samanids, Kerts, Ghaznavids, Ghurids, Mongols, and the Timurids and successor states.

In the sixteenth century, the Mughal empire of India and the Safavids (Persians) were political rivals with Afghanistan as a frontier until the emergence of the native Afghan Durrani dynasty. This dynasty began rule in 1747 and continued nominally under Pashtun Abdali ethnic-group rulers until the Communist coup in 1978. Afshar Persian sociopolitical influence began in the 1720s and remained into the nineteenth century, when Afghanistan was thrust into the geopolitical arena of Britain versus Russia (initially through the British East India Company) in the Great Game. Three Anglo-Afghan wars (1838–1842, 1878–1879, and 1919) served to help establish Afghan independence in the twentieth century under a succession of rulers: Abdur Rahman Khan (1880–1901), Habibullah (1901–1919), King Amanullah (1919–1929), Muhammad Nadir Shah (1929–1933), and Muhammad Zahir Shah (1933–1973), with a republic being established by Muhammad Daoud (1973–1978).

The 1978 leftist coup led to a Soviet military presence until 1989, when the Afghan Islamic resistance movement (with U.S. and Pakistani aid) caused the Soviets to abandon the conflict and withdraw 100,000 troops. The mujahideen (Afghan guerrillas who fought against the Soviets) were composed of many ethnic Afghans and foreign warriors from throughout the Islamic world (particularly Saudi Arabia, Yemen, and Pakistan), who began to fall out with one another, precipitating internecine rebellions and attacks on Kabul. Beginning in 1990, a violent civil conflict raged. On one side was the Pashtun fundamentalist Taliban militia, with seventy thousand soldiers, politically led by Mullah Muhammad Omar since 1993,

who had supported the international terrorist Osama bin Laden since 1995. On the other side was the anti-Taliban Northern Alliance. The fragile Northern Alliance, whose fifteen thousand soldiers had been led by the charismatic Ahmad Shah Masood (an ethnic Tajik who assembled Tajik, Uzbek, and Shi'ite Muslim Hazara support), survived Masood's assassination in September 2001. The war precipitated a critical refugee problem—perhaps one-third of Afghan inhabitants had been displaced by the autumn of 2001—as the Taliban, who had once controlled 90 percent of the nation, faced a reinvigorated Northern Alliance aided by Western powers seeking to bring bin Laden to justice for the terrorist attacks of 11 September 2001. The drought, a decimated sociopolitical infrastructure, the destruction of cultural patrimony (library and museum collections and archaeological treasures, such as the Buddhas of Bamian), and health and human rights issues (particularly concerning women and minority groups) exacerbated the military and political scene.

Charles C. Kolb

Further Reading

Asimov, Mukhammed S., and Clifford E. Bosworth, eds. (1998) *The Age of Achievement, A.D. 750 to the End of the Fifteenth Century*, Pt. 1: *The Historical, Social, and Economic Setting*. Vol. 4 of *History of Civilizations of Central Asia*. Paris: UNESCO Publications.

Bradsher, Henry S. (1999) *Afghan Communism and Soviet Intervention*. New York: Oxford University Press.

Dani, Ahmad Hasan, and Vadim Mikhailovich Masson, eds. (1992) *The Dawn of Civilization: Earliest Times to 700 B.C.* Vol. 1 of *History of Civilizations of Central Asia*. Paris: UNESCO Publications.

Dupree, Louis. (1980) *Afghanistan*. Rev. ed. Princeton, NJ: Princeton University Press.

Harmatta, Janos, Basant J. Puri, and Ghulam F. Etemandi, eds. (1994) *The Development of Sedentary and Nomadic Civilizations, 700 B.C. to A.D. 250*. Vol. 2 of *History of Civilizations of Central Asia*. Paris: UNESCO Publications.

AFGHANISTAN—HUMAN RIGHTS

The chaos of over two decades of warfare has left Afghanistan without an infrastructure of any kind and without human rights. Human rights suffered especially after 1996, when the Taliban, a group of Islamic fundamentalists, captured Kabul and resolved to make Afghanistan accord with their vision of a pure Islamic state. The most flagrant departures from international standards of human rights were in the Taliban's treatment of women and the severity with which the Taliban punished crimes.

WOMEN'S RIGHTS IN AFGHANISTAN

Women's rights were a major human rights issue in Afghanistan during the years of Taliban rule. The following text is from a flyer produced by the Afghanistan Is Everywhere movement for the 8 March 2002 International Women's Day.

In Afghanistan women risked their lives to attain basic human rights. Many women's organizations worked publicly and privately, secretly educating thousands of girls and securing healthcare under the brutal Taliban regime. They developed educational opportunities, conducted courses and vocational training, and opened hospitals for refugee Afghan women and children. The female spirit was strong and fearless during these horrific times.

The Taliban's Treatment of Women

After consolidating power, one of the first things that the Taliban saw to was the removal of women from all social and public life. Thus, women and girls were not allowed to work outside the home or even to venture out unless in the company of a close male relative and they were prohibited from attending schools or universities. All women were forced to wear the *burka*, an all-enveloping garment that completely hides the body, with a mesh in front of the eyes to allow for seeing and breathing. Male doctors could not examine female patients and female doctors could not practice, which meant that women were essentially denied access to modern health care. Proscriptions for women reached absurd levels, with women and girls being forbidden to wear white socks or shoes that made any noise when they walked. In short, women had to become invisible, and were virtually under house arrest.

The punishments meted out on women for transgressing these laws were severe and harsh. A large number of women were stoned to death for walking with a man who was not a husband. Thousands of women were beaten for not wearing proper clothing. Many women were publicly executed for alleged sexual improprieties. A large percentage of Afghanistan's female population is war widows; these women were forced to beg in order to subsist, since all work was denied them. Women were shot at or beaten if they ventured out of the house alone.

Before the Taliban took control, women in Afghanistan were a very progressive group. In Kabul, prior to 1996, 60 percent of the teachers and 50 percent of the students at Kabul University were women; 70 percent of the schoolteachers, 50 percent of the government workers, and 40 percent of the doctors were women. Thus, the Taliban suddenly disenfranchised a large segment of the workforce and the intelligentsia.

The Taliban's Treatment of Men

Men were also subjected to brutal treatment. Every male was forced to grow a beard, wear a turban, and never show his arms or his legs. Flouting these laws meant public flogging or even summary execution. Most males of fifteen years and older were forced to join the Taliban army; those who refused were shot, along with their families; there were reports of entire villages being murdered in this fashion.

Punishment of Crimes

Severe punishment was meted out to those whom the Taliban saw as hindering their progress toward a perfect Islamic state. Thus, those convicted of stealing (most of these people stole food) had their right hands cut off; these events were held at the Kabul soccer stadium, and drew huge crowds. This stadium was also used for public executions. The relatives of victims publicly executed convicted killers; the method of dispatching the criminal was by cutting of the throat. Those convicted of homosexuality were placed against a brick wall, which was then knocked down by a tank; after thirty minutes, the rubble was cleared; those that could be pulled out alive were exonerated. For adultery, men were given a hundred lashes in a public place, while women were stoned to death.

Human-Rights Problems in the Post-Taliban Era

With the toppling of the Taliban in 2001, a new set of human-rights problems emerged. Women still do not have free access to health, education, and personal safety; lifting of the veil has not bettered their lot. Post-Taliban Kabul has seen an influx of orphans, who have flocked to the capital in search of food, clothing, and some form of security. In the Taliban era, street children in Kabul were estimated at 25,000; currently, there are over 70,000, and this figure is increasing daily, since people keep flocking to the capital, all of them driven from their villages by extreme poverty and drought. In fact, many parents abandon their children at the city's two orphanages in the hope that these fledgling institutions will be better able to look after their children, which sadly is not the case. As well, female street children are routinely beaten and abused, because the larger society cannot accept a female wandering on her own.

Adding to this catalog of human misery are two additional factors: ethnic turmoil and avaricious warlords. Afghanistan is a land of many people. The largest and most powerful group is the Pashtuns, who populate the southern portions of the country. The Taliban were ethnically Pashtun, and they systematically sought to destroy their traditional enemies, such as the Persian-speaking Tajiks. The Taliban undertook an ethnic cleansing of sorts, and there is much evidence of mass murder, especially in the Shomali Valley, in the north of the country, which is the traditional Tajik homeland. The transitional government of Hamid Karzai has said that it will establish a tribunal to try individuals for war crimes and create a system of compensation for the victims. However, such a procedure will take many long years, and the transitional government will be gone before the tribunal can be securely established.

Warlords too have become a severe handicap for the country, in that they often hamper the movement of relief supplies from one area to the next. This is an acute problem when food and medical supplies need to be delivered to remote villages. It is often the case that entire truckloads of aid material simply disappear. The food and supplies given in aid by foreign countries is often stolen by these warlords and sold at a profit on the black market. Thus, the general population is still suffering because of widespread theft by those in power.

Extreme poverty and hunger still rule Afghanistan. Life expectancy is forty-six; one out of four children dies before reaching the age of five; almost 80 percent of the population is illiterate; and all rural areas (a large portion of the country) have no access to health care, safe drinking water, or electricity. A large percentage of the farmland has been sowed with land mines, so farmers are afraid to venture out into their fields. As well, years of drought have turned farming villages into dried, deserted ruins; urban warfare has destroyed factories, dams, and roads; there are no banks, no commercial infrastructure, and therefore no foreign investment. The only viable cash crop available to many farmers is the poppy, which is cultivated for opium. The land is still unstable and there are continued fears that powerful warlords, military commanders, or Muslim extremists may topple the present government. In such an atmosphere, human rights are of little concern in Afghanistan. The situation will only change when a measure of stability is established in the land.

Nirmal Dass

Further Reading
Ellis, Deborah. (2000) *Women of the Afghan War.* Westport, CT, and London: Praeger.
Goodson, Larry P. (2001) *Afghanistan's Endless War: State Failure, Regional Politics and the Rise of the Taliban.* Seattle, WA: University of Washington Press.
Griffin, Michael. (2001) *Reaping the Whirlwind: The Taliban Movement in Afghanistan.* London and Sterling, VA: Pluto Press.
Maley, William, ed. (1998) *Fundamentalism Reborn? Afghanistan and the Taliban.* New York: New York University Press.
Rashid, Ahmed. (2000) *Taliban: Militant Islam, Oil, and Fundamentalism in Central Asia.* New Haven, CT: Yale University Press.
Skane, Rosemary. (2002) *The Women of Afghanistan Under the Taliban.* Jefferson, NC: McFarland.

AFGHANISTAN—POLITICAL SYSTEM

The political history of Afghanistan has been a continuous competition for power and privilege between central and local leaders, with central leaders using a carrot, stick, or combination thereof in attempts to gain control of the rebellious provinces.

Monarchic and Local Institutions

Afghanistan has been a monarchy throughout most its history, from 1747 to the 1973 coup. The kings, who have almost exclusively been of Pashtun origin, traditionally based their rule on fragile tribal confederations and were heavily dependent on cultivating the goodwill of their supporters. Abdur Rahman Khan (reigned 1880–1901) was the first ruler to address this vulnerability actively, by building an independent military and establishing strong administrative and judicial control throughout the country. Centrally this system had no cabinet, only an auditing department with a mandate to control the bureaucracy and expand the tax base. Because the tax base was not expanded, Abdur Rahman Khan's regime depended on subsidies from the British, who controlled neighboring India. With the Russians to its immediate north, Afghanistan's current borders were established in the 1890s to make the country a buffer between the British and Russian empires. At the local level the regime used a system of middlemen appointed by their communities and recognized by the state; they

THE PREAMBLE TO THE CONSTITUTION OF AFGHANISTAN, 1990

Adopted 28–29 May 1990

In the name of Allah, the Beneficent, the Merciful

The prideful history of our beloved homeland, Afghanistan, is enriched, with the heroic struggle of our brave people for independence, national unity, democracy and social progress. At the present stage the state of the republic of Afghanistan is actively carrying on the policy of national reconciliation relying on the support of national, political and patriotic forces.

Therefore, keeping in mind the historic changes that have taken shape in our homeland and in our contemporary world, adhering to the principles of the sacred religion of Islam, abiding by the accepted afghan traditions and rituals, relying upon the realities of the country's history and culture, respecting the valuable heritages of the constitutionalist movement and in conformity with the charter of the United Nations and the universal declaration of human rights, and for the purpose of: preserving the independence, defending the territorial integrity and strengthening the national sovereignty; achieving countrywide peace and deepening national unity; securing justice and democracy; socioeconomic reconstruction and balanced growth and enhancing the people's living standards; promoting the role and prestige of the count[r]y in the international arena; creating favourable conditions for determining the legal status of permanent neutrality of Afghanistan and its demilitarization; we, the representatives of the people of Afghanistan to the *loya jirga*, of twenty eight and twenty ninth of May, one thousand nine hundred and ninety amended as follows the constitution ratified by the *loya jirga* of November thirty, one thousand nine hundred and eighty seven which comprised thirteen chapters and one hundred and forty nine articles.

Source: Afghan-web.com. Retrieved 8 March 2002, from: http://www.afghan-web.com/history/const/const1990.html.

are called *arbab* and sometimes *malik* (both mean "village headman" in both Pashtu and Dari languages). The *arbab* represented the state vis-à-vis his community and vice versa, and had considerable freedom of maneuver in relation to both.

Constitutions and Government Reforms

The country got its first constitution in 1922, under King Amanullah (reigned 1919–1929). It provided for a council of state, including both elected and appointed officials, and a president who was also to be a member of the council. There was no parliament, but there was a formalized role for the traditional *loya jirga*, a council of local leaders, convened to approve major reforms.

Habibullah (reigned 1901–1919) had previously established the first educational institutions, and Amanullah went on to institute an extensive network of primary schools in the 1920s. The basic philosophy of government, inspired by developments in the West, was that modernization had to be spearheaded by the elite and that education was the principal instrument. The results were an educated class, largely based in the capital Kabul, whose fortune was wholly tied to the state and a deepening split between state and society.

Nader Shah (reigned 1929–1933) introduced a new political arrangement with a bicameral system: an elected council and a council of notables. Practically, parliaments remained the loyal backers of their government until 1964, when Zahir Shah (b. 1914, reigned 1933–1973) initiated his experiments in "new democracy" and promulgated a new constitution, which suggested new political freedoms including a free press and the right to form political parties. The king never signed the bill on political parties into law. Nonetheless, a range of political parties emerged, rooted in the city-based educated strata.

Zahir Shah was overthrown in 1973 by Daud Khan, who established a republic and ruled by revolutionary council until 1977, when he created a constitution that legitimized his presidency. Daud was removed by the Communist coup in April 1978.

The Era of Civil War

The People's Democratic Party of Afghanistan (PDPA), a relatively marginal group on the eve of the coup, set out to implement dramatic reforms. The *arbabs* were thought to constitute a feudal class that had to be removed. PDPA failed both to realize that it did not have the resources to establish an alternative system at the local level, and that the existing intermediaries often enjoyed strong support in their communities. Therefore spontaneous resistance emerged throughout Afghanistan as the PDPA moved to implement its reforms, often with violent means. During the rule of the Communists (1978–1992), Afghanistan was plagued by civil war, internationalized by the direct involvement of the Soviet Union. In this period, there was no significant move toward a representative political system, although the "reconciliation policy" from 1986 onward implied certain moves to accommodate larger groups of the population.

In the same period various political arrangements developed in regions of the country not controlled by the government. At the local level the *arbabs* either developed into military figures or were replaced by religious figures or by young Islamic radicals, who not only enjoyed religious legitimacy, but were also preferred by Pakistan, which effectively controlled the distribution of external support to the resistance. Like the traditional *arbabs*, the resistance leaders maintained a delicate balance between their local supporters and the political parties, the latter being their primary source of money and arms.

Hamid Karzai, who was appointed interim leader of Afghanistan on 5 December 2001. (AFP/CORBIS)

Soon after the Soviet invasion (December 1979), Pakistan had selected seven parties that were to represent Afghan resistance, also known as the *mujahedin* (Islamic freedom fighters). All had a foundation in either radical or traditional Islam. Local resistance leaders depended on relations with the resistance parties for survival. Several *mujahedin* parties established close links to radical Islamic groups outside the country, and from the early 1980s, young men from other Muslim nations came to Afghanistan for military training and combat exercise. One of several key persons was Osama bin Laden, who apart from taking part in combat served as an intermediary for both money and new recruits.

In many cases, councils (Arabic, *shura*, or Pashtu, *jirga*) were established both at the community level and at higher levels, largely to coordinate the military effort and at times also to deal with the welfare of the population. The *shura* institution took on new functions throughout the civil war. The *shuras* were increasingly seen by foreign aid agencies as representatives of the local communities; they also maintained an important coordinating role at various levels within the *mujahedin* during the war and after these parties took control in Kabul in 1992. The resistance parties established various governments, in exile as well as in post-1992 Kabul, none of which really functioned. To

AFGHANISTAN'S INTERIM GOVERNMENT

As of March 2002, the key figures in Afghanistan's government are:

Hamid Karzai, Chairman—A Pashtun and former deputy defense minister and leader of the resistance to the Taliban in the south.

Yunas Qanooni, Interior Minister—A Tajik and close ally of assassinated Northern Alliance leader Ahmed Shah Massoud.

Muhammad Fahim, Defense Minister—A Tajik and former aide to assassinated Northern Alliance leader Ahmed Shah Massoud.

Abdullah Abdullah, Foreign Minister—A Tajik and Pashtun ophthalmologist and public spokesman for the Northern Alliance.

Other leading figures without official positions in the new government are Abdul Rashid Dostrum, the Uzbek leader in the north; Ismail Khan, the Tajik leader in the west, Hajji Abdul Qadir, the Pashtun governor of the Jalalabad region; and Abdul Rasul Sayyaf, the Pashtun leader of a fundamentalist faction.

Source: The New York Times
(24 December 2001), B4.

establish a representative government, some parties suggested mechanisms ranging from elections to *loya jirga*, while others argued against any such mechanism.

The Taliban Era

The *mujahedin* government, in power in Kabul from 1992 to 1996, was divided by war between its constituent parties. Key players in the government were of Tajik, Uzbek, and Hazara origin, whereas there was scant representation of the Pashtun, the largest ethnic group. From 1994, the Taliban ("religious students") movement emerged as a new political actor, rooted in traditional religious networks that had been greatly expanded in both Afghanistan and Pakistan throughout the war of the 1980s, recruiting mainly among the Pashtuns. Many of the leaders had a *mujahedin* background; otherwise, the recruits were largely men who had grown up during the war. Public disappointment with the existing government and large-scale support from Pakistan were key factors in the Taliban's success. After the capture of Kabul in 1996, the Taliban instituted its own inflexible interpretation of *shari'a* (Islamic law), and ten-

sions with the international community intensified. Gradually, the Taliban government built relations with Osama bin Laden and his al-Qaeda organization, as well as with armed opposition movements in places such as Chechnya, China, and Uzbekistan.

The movement gradually reestablished an administrative system modeled on prewar arrangements. At the village level, the role of the *arbab* was revitalized at the cost of the *shura*. Also the village mullahs related to the Taliban regime, which was strongly integrated with the religious networks. Hence, the Taliban were often well informed about local events and became adept at tax collection. At the central level, the Taliban administration gradually evolved from being broadly consultative to being increasingly dominated by a small group of men, and ultimately by one individual, Mullah Mohammad Omar. By 1996, the Taliban made it clear that it considered itself representative of all groups in the country, that Mullah Omar constituted the ultimate authority, and that the concept of general elections was against Islam and thus to be rejected.

The Collapse of the Taliban

Upon linking Osama bin Laden to the attack on the U.S. Pentagon and the World Trade Center towers in New York City on 11 September 2001, the United States repeated its demand for the government to hand over bin Laden unconditionally, which the Taliban refused. The United States launched attacks on the Taliban in collaboration with groups from the *mujahedin*, still internationally acknowledged as Afghanistan's legitimate government. The Taliban regime fell in December 2001, and representatives of different opposition groups met in Bonn to establish a transition plan. The Bonn agreement resulted in an Interim Authority with a six-month mandate, within which a *loya jirga*, for the first time in history, is to appoint a new government.

Kristian Berg Harpviken

Further Reading

Dupree, Louis. (1980) *Afghanistan.* 2d ed. Princeton, NJ: Princeton University Press.
Ghani, Ashraf. (1985) "Afghanistan: Administration." In *Encyclopedia Iranica* 1, edited by Ehsan Yarshater. London: Routledge and Kegan Paul, 558–564.
Olesen, Asta. (1995) *Islam and Politics in Afghanistan.* Richmond, U.K.: Curzon Press.
Rashid, Ahmed. (2000) *Taliban: Islam, Oil, and the New Great Game in Central Asia.* London: I. B. Tauris.
Roy, Olivier. (1986) *Islam and Resistance in Afghanistan.* Cambridge, U.K.: Cambridge University Press.

AFRICA–ASIA RELATIONS

Africa is the world's second largest continent (after Asia); it includes a continental mass of 29.94 million square kilometers and the great oceanic island of Madagascar, which covers a further 594,180 square kilometers in the western Indian Ocean. Africa is attached to Asia by a thin strip of land forming the western border of the Sinai Peninsula in Egypt. This corridor is only 130 kilometers in width, and is marked today by the Suez Canal. The Cape of Good Hope lies some eight thousand kilometers to the south of it.

Prehistory

The importance of Africa for Asian prehistory cannot be exaggerated, for it was from this continent that early hominids spread northwards and eastwards to populate the Asian continent some 1 million years ago. By approximately 600,000 BCE hominids were living in the caves of Zhoukoudian, just outside the modern city of Beijing. These hominids were of the species *Homo erectus* ("Peking Man"). They used irregularly shaped stone tools, but also had control of fire. Until about ten thousand years ago, they and their descendants across Asia were without exception hunters and gatherers. By about 120,000 years BCE a transitional form of *Homo sapiens* was living at Ngandong, in Java, however, and by approximately 30,000 years BCE the inhabitants of the same Zhoukoudian cave were *Homo sapiens*.

The earliest hominids, and the earliest toolmakers, all evolved in Africa. The continent is thus the cradle of humanity. It was only the extremely slow spread of culture-bearers across Asia that ensured that, being totally cut off from their most ancient roots, they would evolve distinctively Asian cultures over time.

The earliest fully modern humans, *Homo sapiens*, evolved in Africa, most anthropologists believe, and may be represented by fossil material at Klasies River mouth, on the south coast of South Africa. Its caves and rock shelters were occupied intermittently from about 125,000 to 70,000 BCE. In due course the species spread throughout Asia and Europe too.

Early Civilization

One of the world's earliest and greatest high civilizations, a political state, arose on the African continent: this was Egypt. Only Mesopotamia had an earlier claim to the title of a civilization. Although some recent African historians object to characterizing it as such, Egypt was essentially a Near Eastern civilization. Undoubtedly the main influence on the people of the Nile Valley, which led to the development of this civilization in the fourth millennium BCE, was not the for-

aging cultures of East or Central Africa but urbanized Mesopotamia and the Levant. Nubia, lying just to the south of Egypt, was a source only of gold, wood, and slaves. Wheat and barley, introduced from the Near East, were being grown in the Faiyum (near Cairo) by 5000 BCE. Cattle, domesticated over two thousand years earlier in the Near East, also began to be herded around this time. In this early period, too, cotton spread from India to Egypt, while finger millet spread from the Ethiopian region to India. A state arose in Egypt by about 3100 BCE, but it had derived its basic ideas about divine kingship, bureaucracy, and urban organization from the city-states of Mesopotamia (from about 3500 BCE there). Nonetheless, one should not exaggerate the debt of the ancient Egyptians to their Near Eastern neighbors, for they did develop their own written script, one that was in no way borrowed from contemporary Mesopotamian scripts. In art and architecture, too, the Egyptians quickly developed a distinctive national style that had nothing to do with Near Eastern prototypes. Around 2650 BCE Egypt became the first country in the world to raise monumental pyramids to commemorate their dead rulers.

Iron Age

Egypt had begun a long, slow decline by the time Solomon was ruling in Jerusalem in the mid-tenth century BCE, and it never recovered its early grandeur. Although the ancient religion, language, and writing continued in use until the Roman period, the great civilizations of the world were now to be found in Greece and Asia: in Persia, Assyria, China, and Mauryan India.

Meanwhile in the rest of Africa south of the Sahara things were much as they had been before, the desert conditions having isolated them from influences of other civilizations. Eventually an Iron Age succeeded the Late Stone Age, and with none of the intervening phases of Mesolithic, Neolithic, and Bronze Age that had preceded the Iron Age elsewhere in the Old World. Shortly after 2000 BCE the Hittites of Anatolia began the dangerous process of smelting iron, and long kept it a state secret. Eventually it reached Egypt, but the first evidence of iron smelting in sub-Saharan Africa dates to about 480 BCE (at Taruga, Nigeria).

Religions

The interaction between Asia and Africa has been a religious as well as a mercantile and military one. Neither Hinduism nor Buddhism, two of the great Asian religions, reached Southern Africa until very recent times, but other faiths had a much earlier impact. Judaism came to the cities of North Africa some two

CIVIL DISOBEDIENCE FROM SOUTH AFRICA TO INDIA

Mohandas Gandi's campaign for Indian independence from Great Britain actually began in South Africa, where he organized civil disobedience protests to end discrimination against Indians in South Africa. The following extract describes his first civil disobedience campaign in South Africa from 1906 to 1914, which helped reduce discrimination and served as a model for his subsequent campaigns in India.

The first mass *Satyagraha* [civil disobedience movement] and the most important, in historical perspective was launched by Gandhiji [Mohandas Gandhi] in South Africa in 1906, to fight the organized discrimination of the South African Whites against Indians who had settled there. Refusal to register, to give finger-prints and to receive permits which Gandhiji claimed would stigmatize the Indian community in South Africa as criminal was followed by wholesale arrests. In January, 1908, General Smuts promised to repeal the Ordinance and validate registration if the Indians would register voluntarily. An agreement was reached, and Gandhiji and others were released from jail. But when General Smuts did not carry out his agreement, when the ordinance was not repealed, and when new legislation was introduced barring all further Indian immigration, the resumption of the struggle became inevitable.

On September 16, 1908, two thousand registration certificates were burned in Johannesburg on a public bonfire. The fight was on. Fines, imprisonments, floggings and firing were followed in 1913 by a High Court Judgment invalidating all Indian marriages as not in accordance with the local law. The agitation finally culminated in the classic invasion of the Transvaal on the morning of November 6, 1913. The position of the Union Government became intolerable, and by the end of July, 1914, the Indian Relief Bill was passed, repealing the three pound poll tax, validating Hindu and Muslim [acceptance of] the domicile certificate as conclusive evidence of citizenship. An eight-year struggle, unique in the history of world, ended with justice. It provided the experience and techniques for Gandhiji's subsequent campaigns in India.

Source: R. R. Satyagraha Diwakar. (1948) *The Power of Truth*.
Hinsdale, IL: Henry Regnery Co., 71–72.

thousand years ago, and Christianity reached Egypt during the first century CE, soon spreading to Ethiopia. Islam spread westward along the Mediterranean coast as far as Rabat, and then south to such sub-Saharan cities as Tombouctou (Timbuktu) and Gao in present-day Mali. A second route for the spreading new faith was down the East African coast as far as Kilwa (in present-day Tanzania). But there is at least a possibility that Africa also influenced Asian religions, and in very ancient times. The most influential monotheisms—Christianity, Judaism, Islam, Sikhism, Zoroastrianism, and Bahaism—all originated in Asia, yet the world's oldest monotheism was African. This was the Atenism of the Pharoah Akhenaten

(Amenhotep IV, reigned 1379–1362 BCE), which seemingly disappeared in Egypt after his death. This however was the period when the Hebrews were captive in Egypt, thus raising the distinct possibility that the severe monotheism of Moses (whose very name, Ahmose, is Egyptian) had grown out of the Atenism of the preceding century.

Ancient Voyagers

From the first millennium BCE the Arabian Sea became a Phoenician lake. King Solomon's famed temple on the Mount in Jerusalem was built with a large number of imported materials, including some from South India and some from Nubia. The latter land was the source of wood and gold, but an even longer sea journey brought sandalwood for the temple columns, huge amounts of gold, ivory, peacocks, monkeys, silver, ebony, precious stones, and harps from South India. (In the Hebrew Bible we find that these items all have Dravidian, not Semitic, names: the harp, for example, is *kinnor* in Hebrew, from Tamil *kinnari*.)

The source for these materials was Ernad Taluk in Malabar and its immediate hinterland, an area anciently known as Abita ("cowherd place"), which was rendered as Ophir in the Bible. In later centuries, seafarers on the Egyptian coast or based near Aden (Dedenites in the Old Testament) spread out across the western part of the Indian Ocean, probably discovering how to make use of the monsoon winds in different seasons, and traded regularly with western India; but they also pushed further and further down the east coast of Africa. Numerous Dravidian place-names in the interior of southern Africa suggest these ancient mariners penetrated far inland in search of slaves and raw materials—going, for example, to the copper mines of Zimbabwe.

Eventually, some two thousand years ago, the island of Madagascar acquired a human population, not from the neighboring African coast nor yet from the wandering Phoenician traders, but from a far more distant and unlikely source: Sumatra. It is a well-documented fact that Malagasy is the only African language in the Austronesian language family. Language affiliation is a sure sign of cultural affiliation, and in this case helps to identify with some precision the original homeland of the Malagasy people. Theirs does not appear to have been an intentional voyage of exploration, like Vasco da Gama's (c. 1460–1524), but rather an accident that had been waiting to happen. The prevailing winds and currents at a certain time of the year flow and blow westward right across the Indian Ocean toward the great island. Occasionally Indonesian fishermen lost their sails and, unable to return to port,

were blown off course until, with good fortune, they made a landfall in Madagascar, bringing bananas, rice, taro, and poultry with them.

Archaeological research shows that the first Indonesian occupants were there by about the first century CE. A return to Indonesia was out of the question, but the land of Madagascar was rich, and settled farming proved to be easy. Malagasy myth actually refers to the Indian city of Mangalore, no doubt a stopover port for some of the hapless migrants. A few Indian place-names are found in Madagascar, definitely predating colonial times (such as Mahajanga, from the Marathi *maha + jangal*, "great forest"); so we must presume that occasionally Indian fishermen suffered the same fate when the northeasterly monsoon was blowing.

By the eighth century CE a new force was sweeping down the east coast of Africa and into Madagascar too: this was seaborne Islam. The successors of the ancient Phoenician merchant-sailors were now Arabs, usually Muslims. Their influence even reached as far as Mozambique, and inland to Zimbabwe. The great city of Kilwa was a Muslim city, with mosques and slave quarters, on the African coast opposite the northern tip of Madagascar. Persian, Indian, and even Chinese trade goods have been found yet further south, on the Limpopo River, which borders South Africa. Chinese and Islamic pottery were the luxury goods these traders brought; but their commonest "gift" in these nonmonetary economies was beads, which found their way deep into Africa. In return, gold, copper, ivory, and slaves were brought out. One even reads of a gift of African pygmies and a zebra to a Chinese emperor. Equally surprising, medieval India began to import ivory from Africa, because of the ritual requirement that every Hindu widow break her ivory bangles during her husband's funeral. The Indian supply was consequently becoming too diminished. From the eleventh century Kilwa became the most important East African port, and its Shirazi dynasty (of Persian origin) began to mint the first coins in sub-Saharan Africa.

The gold and copper mines of Zimbabwe were already well known to Indian mining entrepreneurs in this period, six centuries before the first European explorer set foot in the area. (It was the time of the Chola, Hoysala, and Vijayanagar empires in southern India.) Although there is no historical documentation of this phase of Indian overseas expansion, the archaeological evidence of ancient mines is there for anyone to see, and the place-name evidence is quite compelling. Well over a hundred Dravidian place-names can be identified in southern Africa.

CREATING ASIA—AFRICA UNITY

In April, 1955, delegates from 29 Asian and African nations meet at Bandung, Indonesia, to discuss common concerns and the role of developing nations in the post–World War II Cold War world. The following extract is their agreement on economic cooperation.

1. The Asian-African Conference recognized the urgency of promoting economic development in the Asian-African region. There was general desire for economic cooperation among the participating countries on the basis of mutual interest and respect for national sovereignty. The proposals with regard to the economic cooperation within the participating countries do not preclude either the desirability or the need for cooperation with countries outside the region, including the investment of foreign capital. It was further recognized that the assistance being received by certain participating countries from outside the region, through international or under bilateral agreements, had made a valuable contribution to the implementation of their development programmes.

Source: George M. Kahin. (1955) *The Asian-African Conference, Bandung, Indonesia, April, 1955.* Ithaca: Cornell University Press, 76.

The Colonial Phase

After a thousand years of Islamic influence, Africa was colonized, mainly during the nineteenth century, by a variety of Western European powers: the Dutch in South Africa, the Portuguese and Belgians in Central Africa, the French in North and West Africa and Madagascar, the Germans in East Africa, the Spanish in the Western Sahara, the Italians in North and East Africa, and the British in West Africa and a broad swath of lands running from Egypt more or less continuously to South Africa. In a sense they were the successor occupiers to the Asian miners, traders, and slave dealers who had come there some six centuries before them, sometimes even reopening the same old mines. They established colonial states, usually with unrealistic straight-line boundaries, and governed through an elite European civil service. They established roads, railroads, cities, schools, and industries, often built with indentured Indian labor. But when most of them left the continent in the 1950s and 1960s, they also left behind a tradition of racism and attitudes of European cultural superiority that lived on in South Africa.

While the number of Europeans in any African country was always a tiny percentage of the total population, the British had an unexpected demographic impact on the continent by importing indentured labor from South Asia. During the latter part of the nineteenth century and the early twentieth, thousands of Indians were brought to South and East Africa to work on building railroads (especially the Uganda railway, which opened up the interior), on harbors and other modern installations, or to labor in the mines, factories, and plantations. In Uganda, Tanzania, and Kenya these were mainly Gujarati and Kachchi speakers, though some were Punjabi Sikhs. Parsis were sometimes brought in from Bombay as supervisors and clerks on these projects. Lawyers such as M. K. Gandhi (1869–1948) appeared to champion Indian interests, and many Gujarati traders also arrived from that same port to open small businesses in the African countries, often in competition with Lebanese. In South Africa too laborers were brought in from the ports of Bombay, Madras, and Calcutta, which caused them to be labeled respectively Bombayis, Madrasis, and Bengalis, regardless of their actual place of origin. The three categories tended to form endogamous, caste-like communities.

After independence came to some East African countries such as Somalia, Communist Chinese or Korean labor gangs could be seen helping to develop the local infrastructure, notably by building new railroad tracks. Recently, however, an intractable economic decline in numerous regions of East Africa has induced the local Indian traders and professional families to leave for other continents. The English-speaking countries, mainly Canada, Australia, the United States, and Britain, with their stable economies and good schools, have been the prime targets for these economic refugees, although some have returned to India or Pakistan. In South Africa the many middle-class Indians have retained their position; whereas in East Africa most have not been so fortunate.

In the Uganda census of 1969 "Asians" (primarily from South Asia) numbered about seventy thousand. Though many of them were born in Uganda, they were officially considered foreigners. In that same year the government of Milton Obote threatened to nationalize many industries, causing the wealthy Asians to export their assets and then move elsewhere. Then in 1972 President Idi Amin deported nearly seventy thousand Asians, leaving only a tiny minority behind. A decade later a few returned to claim their expropriated property, including factories and estates. By the end of the century only about ten thousand Asians were to be found in Uganda, and fewer still in other East African countries. Universally they have seen better opportunities for their families overseas.

Paul Hockings

See also: **Bandung Conference; Japan-Africa Relations**

Further Reading

Bharati, Agehananda. (1972) *The Asians in East Africa: Jayhind and Uhuru.* Chicago: Nelson-Hall Company.
Devisse, J., and S. Labib. (1984) "Africa in Inter-Continental Relations." In *General History of Africa.* Vol. 4: *Africa from the Twelfth to the Sixteenth Century.* London: Heinemann Educational Books, 635–672.
Domenichini-Ramiaramanana, B. (1988) "Madagascar." In *General History of Africa.* Vol. 3: *Africa from the Seventh to the Eleventh Century.* London: Heinemann Educational Books, 681–703.
Kuper, Hilda. (1960) *Indian People in Natal.* Durban, South Africa: Natal University Press.
Mangat, J. S. (1969). *A History of the Asians in East Africa, c. 1896–1965.* Oxford: Clarendon Press.
Sheriff, A. M. H. (1981) "The East African Coast and Its Role in Maritime Trade." In *General History of Africa.* Vol. 2: *Ancient Civilizations of Africa.* London: Heinemann Educational Books, 551–567.
Talib, Y. (1988) "The African Diaspora in Asia." In *General History of Africa.* Vol. 3: *Africa from the Seventh to the Eleventh Century.* London: Heinemann Educational Books, 704–733.

AFRIDI Through the centuries the Afridis, a Pakistani ethnic group among the Pashtun people inhabiting parts of Afghanistan and Pakistan, battled various powers. Afridi territory extends from the eastern Safid range to northern Pakistan, including the Khyber Pass.

In the eighteenth century the Afridis fought with the army of the Afghan ruler Ahmad Shah Durrani and later offered sanctuary to his grandson, Shah Shoja (reigned 1803–1809). From 1839 to 1842 the Afridis clashed with the British during the first Anglo-Afghan War, when they joined the resistance to General George Pollock's march on Kabul. After the British had annexed the Punjab in 1849, further clashes occurred because of British efforts to keep the Khyber Pass open.

The Afridis eventually joined the Red Shirt Movement, which sought independence from the British. When Pakistan achieved independence, the northwest province of Afridi territory was included in its borders. This led to a new movement for a Pashtun state uniting all Afridi lands, including those in Afghanistan.

The ethnic communities in Pakistan and Afghanistan were underrepresented in their respective governments until 1997, when Pakistan's president Farooq Leghari lifted voting restrictions to allow them all to vote. Previously, only eight ethnic people had represented more than four million in the National Assembly.

Houman A. Sadri

Further Reading

Adamec, Ludwig W. (1997) *Historical Dictionary of Afghanistan.* 2d ed. Lanham, MD: Scarecrow Press.
Cleveland, William L. (1994) *A History of the Modern Middle East.* Boulder, CO: Westview Press.
Gilzad, Salmay. (1994) *External Influences and the Development of the Afghan State in the Nineteenth Century.* New York: P. Lang.
Norton, Augustus Richard, ed. (1996) *Civil Society in the Middle East.* Leiden, Netherlands: Brill.

AFYON (2000 est. pop.124,000). Located in western-central Turkey, Afyon has depended on agriculture since the Hittite era (1900–1300 BCE). Like most of Anatolia, Afyon survived centuries of invading or occupying civilizations and rulers right up to the Ottoman demise in the mid-twentieth century. A large proportion of the economy depended on feeding armies. The city's chief enterprises are still farm- or rural-based.

Poppies are an important crop. A local, state-run alkaloid factory refines poppy straw into opiates, supplying close to one-third of pharmaceutical opium to world markets. The city is also famous for a rich, clotted cream produced as a regional specialty.

Twenty-first-century Afyon is a conservative city with many devout Muslims. The towering black citadel that overlooks the town is believed to have been a refuge for Byzantines during the first few centuries CE. The Greek invading army occupied Afyon, but were driven out in 1921 by Mustafa Kermal (1881–1938; later known as Ataturk, "Father of Turkey"), the future founder of modern Turkey. The rout of the Greeks at Afyon made possible the goal of an independent Turkish state.

Suzanne Swan

Further Reading

Lewis, Bernard. (1975) *The Emergence of Modern Turkey.* Oxford: Oxford University Press.
Mitchell, Stephen. (1993) *Anatolia, Land, Men and Gods in Asia Minor.* Vol. 1. Oxford: Oxford University Press.

AFZAL KHAN (d. 1659), Bijapur general. Afzal Khan was a brilliant seventeenth-century general in Bijapur (in the Indian state of Maharashtra). Afzal was sent by the sultan of Bijapur with an army of ten thousand men in 1659 to suppress the rising Maratha warlord Shivaji, who had conquered Bijapur lands in the Konkan and neighboring areas between 1646 and 1655. Within two weeks, Afzal had reached Wai, driving all resistance aside; but meanwhile Shivaji was safely within the fort of Pratapgarh. As Afzal could not tempt him forth, he engaged in negotiations with Shivaji, calling for a conference between the two leaders. Shivaji went to this ostensibly unarmed but, fearing treachery from the Muslim general, he carried arms hidden on him. As the two men embraced, the stalwart general tried to throttle Shivaji; but Shivaji immediately killed Afzal by ripping his stomach open with the metal "tiger's claws" (*baghnakh*) Shivaji was carrying. The Marathas went on to defeat the Bijapur forces in battle, and this ended Bijapur's hostilities.

Paul Hockings

AGARTALA (2002 pop. 193,000). Since 1850 the capital of tiny Tripura state in northeastern India, picturesque Agartala lies near the Bangladesh border on the Haroa River in an intensively cultivated plain. It is dominated by the Ujjayanta Palace. Built by Maharaja Radha Krishna Kishore Manikya Bahadur in 1901 in a mixed European-Mughal style, the gleaming white palace now houses the state legislative assembly. Its grounds extend over seventy acres of parkland, including formal gardens, artificial lakes, and the Ummaneshwar and Jagannath Temples, both in a striking yellow-orange hue. Nearby are the Gedu Mian

A family wades through flood waters near Agartala in September 2001. (AFP/CORBIS)

Mosque, encrusted with an unusual mosaic of broken crockery pieces, and the Buddhist Venuban Vihar.

The city features the State Museum, a tribal museum, busy bazaars, and colleges affiliated with the University of Calcutta. The principal languages are Bengali, Kokbarak, and Manipuri; English is not widely spoken. The population is largely Bengali but includes members of the nineteen "scheduled" tribes. (Such scheduled tribes have special protections under the Indian Constitution.) These people, with a rich and varied culture, belong mainly to the Tripuris, Reang, Chakma, Halam, and Usai communities and live in elevated houses of bamboo called *tong*. Old Agartala, the former capital, is five kilometers to the east. The Temple of Fourteen Deities there draws thousands of Hindu devotees each July for Kharchi Puja, a festival celebrating worship of the earth.

C. Roger Davis

Further Reading

Tripura University. (1992) *Seminar on Autonomy Movements in Tripura since Independence.* Agartala, India: Tripura University.

AGING POPULATION—JAPAN

Perhaps the most significant challenge facing Japan over the coming decades is its aging population. By the middle of the twenty-first century, Japan will have the most aged society in the world, with approximately one in three Japanese being 65 years of age or more. The population by then will have shrunk to about 100 million. As early as 2010, more than 21 percent of the Japanese population will be aged 65 years or more (compared with, for example, 13 percent in the United States), an increase of 6 percent since 1998. By 2025, Japan is projected to have the highest average age in the world. This has been the result of several factors, the first being the rapid rise in birthrates following the end of World War II until 1947. The second factor is the falling birthrate, which dropped steeply through the 1950s, stabilizing around 1960 and declining slowly thereafter. At present, the birthrate is less than 1.4 children per Japanese woman (of childbearing age), while replacement is about 2.1. The birthrate is expected to fall to about 1.1 by 2020. The third factor is the longevity of the Japanese, who live longer than anyone else in the world—approximately 77 years for men and 84 for women. Japan has a massive change looming that will affect virtually every aspect of its social, political, and economic organization. Some have called the problem Japan's "demographic time bomb."

The Cost of Caring for Elderly People

In the coming decades, one of Japan's major difficulties will be to deal with the costs of supporting an aging population. Funding of basic pensions is the most immediate problem, and pressure will increase steadily. By 2020, the Organization of Economic Cooperation and Development has estimated, the cost of providing pensions will amount to 14 percent of Japan's gross domestic product (GDP), about three times that of the United States. At present, Japan spends only about 7 percent of GDP on pensions, and the Japanese government has recently introduced nursing-care insurance to commit the population to support of the aged. Fundamentally, such schemes are designed to make people responsible for their own financial security in old age rather than dependent on state support. At the same time, it is clear that the Japanese government will have to play a more significant role, and the so-called Golden Plan of 1989 and the 1994 New Golden Plan are examples of the state's attempt to play a role in the provision of pensions for the elderly. The overriding concern of these new measures is to avoid a financial crisis in the coming decades.

Other costs will also rise. Outlays for medical care will go up given that, with people living longer, elderly people will need more intensive medical care and over a longer time. In 1993, the number of Japanese over the age of 80 was only 3 million, but this is expected to jump to 9.5 million by 2025.

A related problem is providing adequate housing for the elderly. Most Japanese are urbanites, and there is a concentration of population in the Tokyo-Nagoya-Osaka belt. Indeed, today more than 20 percent of Japanese over the age of 60 are living alone in Tokyo, while approximately 78 percent of this age group is classified as urban. To a significant extent, this is a result of postwar industrialization and rural-urban migration, so that there is some conflict between earlier, rural-based values and the reality of contemporary high-density living. Housing pressures are a well-known phenomenon, and one of the limitations for extended family support is simply the lack of space, specifically affordable space, in the urban areas (where most elderly Japanese live, in spite of a disproportionate number of elderly in rural areas). There is additional pressure on the state to provide specialized facilities for the care of the elderly, alternative home-care models, special nursing homes, facilities for physically disabled persons, and so on. Given the pressures of modern urban living, men are often too preoccupied with work commitments and the required commuting to have time to look after elderly parents; if care is undertaken at home, the burden falls on women.

Labor Shortages

A fundamental problem in Japan is that there are fewer and fewer younger people to support the elderly. At present there are about 5 people working per retiree, but this will be reduced to about 2.5 workers by 2010, according to Japanese government projections. According to a different temporal comparison, in 1980 there were 12 people contributing to employee pension funds for every one pensioner, while the ratio by 2025 will be 2:1. That is, the number of people aged 65 or over per 100 people aged 20 to 64 in 2010 will be 37 and in 2025, 49. In short, the working population in Japan will peak in 2005 and thereafter decline, producing a substantial labor shortage.

This labor shortage means that labor costs will rise, and Japan will become less competitive as the cost of production increases; this process has already been underway for some time, and the situation is getting worse. Higher costs also mean that there is pressure to increases taxes, and the Ministry of Health and Welfare projects the social security tax to rise from 14.5 percent in 1994 to 34.8 percent in 2025. These factors, taken together, will drive more and more industry offshore, to lower-wage countries, especially those in Asia. Also, as more funding goes into this sector, there will be less available for investment in the economy; with fewer people working, there will be less savings available for investment. Ultimately this means a reduction in Japan's external trade surplus, which will have a profound effect on the global economy.

Alternative Sources of Labor

One response of Japan's policy makers has been to keep older Japanese working longer. It may be that the retirement age will simply be steadily increased, with older Japanese being asked to work to, say, the age of 70. Already the age of eligibility for the national pension is going up, from 60 years to 65 by 2013 (though the Employees Pension Insurance scheme still allows benefits from age 60). At the same time, there is a well-established (at least in the postwar period) tradition in Japan of having people continue to work after retirement in a company affiliated with their main place of employment. In 1993, for example, the proportion of Japanese who remained economically active after the age of 65 was 24.9 percent, as opposed to 6.6 percent in Sweden and 12.2 percent in Singapore.

If one assumes, however, that the number of Japanese workers will decline (and this will happen eventually as a substantial portion of the workforce enters very old age), the question of labor shortages arises. A common policy option in the West is to encourage immigration. The problem in Japan's case is that it is not an immigrant country but, on the contrary, has had a tendency to be exclusionist. Only about 2 percent of Japan's population are migrants. So much of Japanese culture has revolved around being isolationist and resistant to having large numbers of foreigners in the land that people often find it difficult to interact with those from different cultural backgrounds. One compromise has been to facilitate the entry of Brazilians of Japanese descent, and there are now about 270,000 of them in Japan. However, many more migrants are required. The U.N. estimates a need for as many as 600,000 immigrants per year on a continuing basis to sustain the country's economic growth. If such a recommendation is followed (and there is overwhelming resistance to it in Japan), it would put pressure on the Japanese government to treat immigrants more equitably. The Japanese government may compromise further on this issue and allow more foreigners into the country on temporary work permits.

A third option in dealing with an aging population is to change the way in which Japanese women are treated in the workplace. To date, their labor is not utilized effectively. Many are well educated but not supported by society or the state to the point that they can rise to the level of their abilities. The aging population, however, will force changes in the area of women's employment. The demand for labor will provide women with a greater range of employment opportunities. Also, the present trend toward career interruptions for the purpose of raising children will have to change as labor becomes scarce. One indication that the Japanese government is taking this issue seriously is the 1999 modification of the 1986 Equal Employment Opportunity Law, which removed many of the barriers to female employment in Japan.

Impact on Global Trade and Investment

With the growth in the global economy, particularly the high level of interconnectedness between the major economies, events in one country are quickly felt in others. This is particularly the case with Japan. Despite its continuing recession, Japan is the second-largest economy in the world and enjoys one of the world's largest per capita incomes. Its products are used in virtually every country in the world, and brands such as Sony, Panasonic, and Mitsubishi are household names. Japanese companies also are increasingly manufacturing their products in other countries, either to avoid protective tariffs, penetrate local markets, or enjoy the benefits of low-cost labor. Japanese investors are also heavily involved in other countries, especially the United States. In spite of Japan's economic slowdown through the 1990s, it remains crucial to global trade, manufacturing, and investment. Therefore, substantial socioeconomic change in Japan will have profound effects, directly and indirectly, and both positively and negatively, on the rest of the world.

Curtis Andressen

Further Reading

Ezrati, Milton. (1997) "Japan's Aging Economics." *Foreign Affairs* 76, 3 (May–June): 96–104.

Kono, Makoto. (2000) "The Impact of Modernisation and Social Policy on Family Care for Older People in Japan." *Journal of Social Policy* 29, 2 (April): 181–203.

Kuroda, Toshio. (1994) "The Nature and Policies of Population Aging in Japan." In *The Ageing of Asian Populations: Proceedings of the United Nations Round Table on the Ageing of Asian Populations, Bangkok, 4–6 May, 1992.* Bangkok, Thailand: United Nations, 92–95.

McCune, Jenny. (1990) "Japan Says Sayonara to Womb-to-Tomb Management." *Management Review* 79, 11 (November): 12–17.

Miyakoshi, Tatsuyoshi. (1999) "Trade-off between Pensions and Jobs for the Elderly: Theoretical and Empirical Observations from Japan." *Asian Economic Journal* 13, 11: 93–107.

Peterson, Peter. (1999) "Gray Dawn: The Global Aging Crisis." *Foreign Affairs* 78, 1 (January–February): 42–52.

Schultz, James, Allan Borowski, and William Crown. (1991) *Economics of Population Aging.* New York: Auburn House.

Skeldon, Ronald. (1999) *Aging of Rural Populations in South-East and East Asia, Part 1.* Bangkok, Thailand: SD Dimensions.

Sokdovsky, Jay. (1990) *The Cultural Context of Aging: Worldwide Perspectives.* New York: Bergin and Garvey.

Watanabe, Mieko. (1992) "Employment of Older Persons and Need for Support System." *Japan Labor Bulletin* (Japan Institute of Labour, no. 31): 1–6.

AGNO RIVER The Agno River is one of the main rivers in Luzon Province, Philippines. It is almost 150 kilometers long, originating at Binga Lake in Benguet Province, running down its deep valleys, and turning westward in the lowlands of Pangasinan Province before draining into the Lingayen Gulf.

The Ibaloi people of Benguet regard the river as sacred because it gives life. But its "life-giving" properties extend beyond Benguet because it also irrigates the lowlands of Pangasinan, which are part of the "rice bowl" of the Philippines. With its connection to Binga Lake, the Agno River is harnessed to power hydroelectric plants of the Binga and Ambuklao Dams, providing electricity to the Cagayan Valley region.

Another dam, the San Roque, is under construction along the Agno River. This project has been met with stiff resistance by the people of Benguet because the dam will inundate towns and threaten the environment.

Aaron Ronquillo

Further Reading

Department of Tourism. (1994) *The Philippines: Spirit of Place.* Manila, Philippines: Department of Tourism.

Lancion, Conrado Jr. (1995) *Fast Facts about Philippine Provinces.* Manila, Philippines: Tahanan Books.

Parkes, Carl. (1999) *Philippines Handbook.* Emeryville, CA: Moon Travel Handbooks.

Salita, Domingo. (1974) *Geographic and Natural Resources of the Philippines.* Quezon City, Philippines: College of Arts and Sciences, University of the Philippines.

AGRA (2001 est. pop. 1.3 million). Agra, located in the state of Uttar Pradesh in northwest India, is renowned for its ancient architecture. The city developed by virtue of its location on major trade routes and waterways.

The first settlement is thought to have been established here in 2 BCE. The sultan of Delhi settled in Agra in 1492, making it his capital, renovating its ancient fort, and ruling the city until the Mughal dynasty came to power in 1526. The Mughals then made Agra the seat of their empire's government for a time and constructed the great Friday mosques (built specially for Friday worship) during their reigns

The city's most famous landmark is the Taj Mahal (built c. 1632–1652), the white marble mausoleum

AGRA FORT—WORLD HERITAGE SITE

Designated a World Heritage Site in 1983, Agra Fort is a huge brick red seventeenth-century Mughal fortress that protects the Mughal imperial city of Agra within its 2.5 kilometers of walls. A stone's throw away from the Taj Mahal, Agra Fort contains many Mughal architectural masterpieces.

Sikandra, the tomb of Emperor Akbar in Agra. (WILD-COUNTRY/CORBIS)

commissioned by Shah Jahan for his wife Mumtaz Mahal considered a masterpiece of that period's architecture. Legend says that Shah Jahan maimed and blinded the architect to prevent him from ever constructing a building of similar beauty. Unfortunately the Taj Mahal and other monuments in Agra are threatened by the modern city's pollution.

The first European visitors compared Agra to London and Paris. After the British annexed Agra in 1803, the city became the headquarters for the presidency in the northwest provinces.

Modern Agra is composed of the ancient city and the nineteenth-century British cantonment. Today Agra is a center for commerce, higher education, and tourism. Despite its modernity, traditional crafts such as marble carving, stone setting, and carpet manufacture are still practiced.

Linda Dailey Paulson

Further Reading

Carroll, David. (1972) *The Taj Mahal.* New York: Newsweek.
Davies, Philip, ed. (1989) "Agra." In *The Penguin Guide to Monuments of India.* Vol. 2. London: Viking, 189–199.

AGRICULTURAL COLLECTIVIZATION —CHINA

Private land ownership and the one-family farm were the basis of Chinese agriculture for more than two thousand years before the establishment of the People's Republic of China in 1949. Until the early 1950s, the Chinese Communist Party (CCP) claimed that it would first improve, rather than eliminate, the system of private family farms. The land reform of the CCP during the 1940s and early 1950s won great support of the majority of Chinese peasants because it actually allowed more peasants to own their own lands and thus to create their own family farms. However, CCP leaders, particularly Mao Zedong (1893–1976), shared Marxists' goal of eventually eliminating private ownership of land and achieving socialist collectivization. As early as 1943, Mao had proclaimed that agricultural collectivization would be the only way for Chinese peasants to escape poverty and would be the CCP's long-range goal. Before land reform was completely accomplished, the CCP was prepared to begin the gradual introduction of agricultural collectivization.

China's agricultural collectivization was carried out in three stages. The first stage was to promote mutual aid teams (MATs). MATs were small scale, usually with five or six households joining to work cooperatively during busy times (such as sowing and harvesting). Each family retained ownership of its own land, and the crops grown on that land basically belonged to that family. The move toward MATs was relatively successful. By 1952, 40 percent of China's rural households joined a mutual aid team.

During the same period, a small number of peasants were starting to move to the next stage of collectivization: the "lower" or "semisocialist" agricultural producers' cooperative (APC). An APC usually encompassed a small village or section of a village (twenty to forty households on average). Members of the APC pooled their lands and large agricultural tools and draft animals and worked the land together. A management committee kept records, usually measuring in daily "work points," of the amount of labor done by each family. At the end of a year, the crop and other income (after taxes had been paid and reserve funds had been subtracted) would be divided among the members of the APC according to the accumulated work points of each family and the land and tools they had contributed. Fifteen thousand APCs were established when the CCP began to encourage peasants to replace MATs with APCs at the end of 1953.

From APCs to Full Collectivization

The third stage was the fully socialist collectives, or "higher" APCs. Most higher APCs contained 150 to 200 households. Unlike in the semisocialist APC, in which an individual family still retained nominal ownership of its lands and derived its income partially from these lands, the lands now were legally the property of the APC. The amounts of land and capital contributed by each family were no longer taken into account in determining how much each family would receive at the end of a year. The APC would distribute crops solely on the basis of each family's labor contributions: to each according to his deeds.

Originally, China's agricultural collectivization was planned quite cautiously. The CCP leaders who were in charge of this work knew that this transformation would have to be managed carefully to avoid the bloodshed and catastrophic results that had accompanied the rapid collectivization initiated by Joseph Stalin (1879–1953) in the Soviet Union. The CCP Central Committee predicted that the transition to socialist collectivization would be accomplished in fifteen years from 1953. The committee disbanded tens of thousands of APCs in 1953 and 1955 on the grounds that these APCs were premature and were organized against peasants' own will.

However, Mao was unsatisfied with the cautious approach to collectivization. According to Mao, China would suffer both economic and social problems unless the transition to collectivization speeded up. Mao believed that a socialist system of agriculture would bolster agricultural productivity, stimulate rural markets for industrial products, and divert sufficient workers and funds to accelerate China's industrialization. In the meantime, a fully socialist agriculture system would end the division between the haves and have-nots in China's countryside.

Despite the opposition of many key figures within the CCP and many peasants, Mao's view prevailed finally. The CCP launched a drive to organize more higher APCs in the autumn of 1955. After it started, the campaign moved much faster than even Mao had initially proposed. Provincial and lower-level cadres implemented the collectivization drive with such enthusiasm that China's agricultural socialization was completed in less than a year. In 1954, there were 114,000 APCs nationwide, 200 of them higher APCs. By 1956, 120 million agricultural households, or 96.3 percent of China's rural families, were organized in 750,000 collectives, of which 88 percent were the fully socialist higher APCs.

Endorsed by Mao, "people's communes" were organized in the countryside in 1958 on the basis of higher APCs. Each commune amalgamated dozens of higher APCs and had twenty-five thousand people on average. By the end of 1958, there were twenty-six thousand communes, in which 98 percent of China's rural population lived. The commune became a new organizational form for the countryside, combining political, administrative, and military functions in one organization. Economically, however, the principal internal unit in each commune was the production brigade, which often corresponded to a higher APC.

Results of Collectivization

Agricultural collectivization had profound influence in China. It gave the CCP greater power to exert its authority over Chinese peasants and to more effectively extract a large portion of agricultural income from the countryside to fund China's industrialization. In the meantime, collectivization was pushed too soon and too hard after 1955, resulting in inefficiencies in agricultural productivity, dissatisfaction among peasants, and mismanagement in China's rural areas. Peasants were deprived of their land and other private property and lost the incentive to work harder. China's agricultural productivity stagnated until 1979, when Deng Xiaoping (1904–1997) launched economic reform. With the dismemberment of the people's communes in 1982, China's agricultural collectivization collapsed. Family farms again became the basis of Chinese agriculture; more than 97 percent of peasants ran their own farms under the household responsibility system (which turned responsibility for production back over to individual households) by 1983.

Ju Wang and Elizabeth D. Schafer

See also: **Household Responsibility System—China**

Further Reading

Francisco, Ronald A., Betty A. Laird, and Roy D. Laird, eds. (1979) *The Political Economy of Collectivized Agriculture: A Comparative Study of Communist and Non-Communist Systems.* New York: Pergamon Press.

Hinton, William. (1997) *Fanshen: A Documentary of Revolution in a Chinese Village.* Berkeley and Los Angeles: University of California Press.

Lin, Justin Yifu. (1990) "Collectivization and China's Agricultural Crisis in 1959–1961." *Journal of Political Economy* 6, 98 (December): 1228–1252.

Meurs, Mieke. (1999) *Many Shades of Red: State Policy and Collective Agriculture.* Lanham, MD: Rowman & Littlefield.

Nee, Victor, and Su Sijin. (1990) "Institutional Change and Economic Growth in China: The View from the Villages." *Journal of Asian Studies* 1, 49 (February): 3–25.

Nolan, Peter. (1988) *The Political Economy of Collective Farms: An Analysis of China's Post-Mao Rural Reforms.* Oxford: Polity Press.

AGRICULTURE—CENTRAL ASIA

The five Central Asian republics (CARs: Kazakhstan, Uzbekistan, Tajikistan, Kyrgyzstan, and Turkmenistan) were prime suppliers of agricultural products, metals, and minerals to population centers in the Soviet Union. After independence in 1991, farm production fell during the efforts to restructure the inefficient and highly subsidized agricultural sector.

Monoculture Farming

Before independence the CARs provided the Soviet Union with 90 percent of its cotton needs, 15 percent of its vegetable oils, nearly 50 percent of its rice, and 35 percent of its fruits and vegetables. In turn the CARs imported grain, meat, dairy products, and sugar from the Soviet Union. Then and now the CARs depend on their agriculture sectors, which are prime employers and contributors to economic growth. (See Table 1.)

Since the breakup of the Soviet Union in 1991, farm production and overall economic growth in Central Asia have dropped precipitously. (See Table 2.) This terrible economic performance has increased the level of poverty in the CARs, and the productivity of labor in farming has declined.

In the context of the Soviet Union, the CARs were never meant to be integrated, stand-alone economies. Rather, they were set up to be primary product producers for the more industrialized republics. Farm economies in Uzbekistan, Turkmenistan, and Tajikistan specialized in cotton; Kyrgyzstan specialized in wool and mutton; Kazakhstan in grain.

Second-stage processing for these raw materials was discouraged in Central Asia, so that the CARs did not benefit from the jobs and economic activity that processing, milling, and manufacturing would have afforded. Links with non-USSR markets were discouraged or prohibited. The structural dependence that developed between the "center" and "periphery" of the Soviet Union was broken with its dissolution. When the USSR collapsed, the economy of the Russian Federation also plunged, greatly debilitating the markets it once offered to the CARs.

Other Economic Problems in Agriculture

Soviet planners, in an effort to expand production, brought land that was marginal for agriculture into cultivation and employed excessive chemical inputs to maximize production. With the exception of Kyrgyzstan, which exports water, the CARs suffer from severe droughts and a shortage of irrigation. Existing irrigation systems have fallen into disrepair during the years of independence. The issue of water is also a problem for ecological reasons. Monocrop farming has ravaged natural resources, as evidenced by the despoliation of the Aral Sea. As rivers that drained into the Aral were diverted to provide irrigation water for cotton, new deserts were created, and much of the Aral Sea dried up. Now the wind blows salt and pesticide residue across an increasingly barren landscape.

Another factor accounting for the decline in production in the CARs is the withdrawal of agricultural subsidies. During the time of the Soviet Union and especially in the Gorbachev era (1985–1991), the CARs benefited from the All-Union budget transfers that provided investment resources for agriculture and other sectors of the economy. Physical inputs were also subsidized. These transfers tended to hide inefficiencies in agriculture while increasing production.

When exposed to the world markets, the agricultural products grown in the CARs suffered from substantial price fluctuations. Cotton prices were relatively high early in the 1990s but fell substantially later in the decade. At the same time imported inputs (like fertilizers and seeds) rose in price, imperiling the profitability of the agricultural sector and causing a cost-price squeeze.

Although some of the CARs' agricultural trade is still with other countries of the former Soviet Union for historical or physical reasons, that trade is declining. Other economically challenged former Soviet states may delay paying hard currency or may want to barter instead, while the CARs need hard currency to purchase inputs. By 1996 fifty percent of the total trade of the CARs was with countries that had not been part

TABLE 1

Central Asia's dependence on the agricultural sector for contributions to GDP and employment in 1999

	Percent of GDP in agricultural sector	Percent of total labor force in agricultural sector
Kazakhstan	10	23
Uzbekistan	31	44
Kyrgyzstan	44	42
Tajikistan	25	52
Turkmenistan	25	44

SOURCES: Data for this table from World Bank (2000: Table 12) and Turner (1999, 2000, 2001).

TABLE 2

Percentage of economic growth and growth of agriculture sector, annual data for 1990–1999

	GDP	Value added by agriculture
Kazakhstan	−5.9	−12.2
Uzbekistan	−2.0	−1.0
Kyrgyzstan	−7.4	−1.5
Tajikistan	−9.8	−12.2
Turkmenistan	−3.5	No data

SOURCE: World Bank (2000: Table 11).

During Russian and Soviet rule, cotton became the primary agricultural product in Central Asia. Here, a woman picks cotton in Muynak in 1989. (DAVID & PETER TURNLEY/CORBIS)

of the former Soviet Union. The CARs need new markets, and as physical links with southern and eastern neighbors are developed and access to the Mediterranean Sea and to Indian and Pacific Ocean ports increases, trade with other former Soviet states can be expected to decline further.

In an effort to cultivate new markets, the CARs turned south to Turkey, Pakistan, and Iran, which had formed the Economic Cooperation Organization (ECO) in 1985. Central Asian countries were admitted to ECO in 1992, along with Afghanistan and Azerbaijan. These additions gave the ECO cultural cohesion as it included all of the non-Arab Islamic countries of West Asia and Central Asia. While the ECO has not significantly increased the CARs' trade, it has provided a forum for discussion of regional trade disagreements and a forum for future peaceful settlement of conflicts. Similarity in resource endowments and overlapping commodity composition limit trade options between the three original ECO members and the CARs. For example, cotton, an important CARs export, is also important to both Turkey and Pakistan.

The CARs are aiming to build more diversity into their economies. For example, to substitute for imported grain, Tajikistan reduced its cotton acreage by 25 percent between 1990 and 1996 and planted wheat. Tajikistan's efforts to develop were impaired by civil war. While a peace agreement has been signed, there is still unrest in the country.

Restructuring Agriculture

The CARs are struggling to reform the archaic system of farm possession and management through privatization or land reform. Farming in the Soviet Union took place on state land or state farms (*sovkhozy*) and collective farms (*kolkhozy*). Theoretically state farms were "factories in the field," paying a wage to workers, whereas capital and land belonged to the state. Any profit at the end of the year entered the government's coffers.

On the collective farms, also called cooperatives, buildings and machinery belonged to a group of worker members. Theoretically a profit at the end of the year was divided among the members according to some predefined plan. But since so many state and collective farms showed a loss as the Soviet Union came to an end, wages were often paid to collective farm members, but there were infrequent profits to divide.

Although there are some country differences, the state and collective farms of the Soviet Union shared some common characteristics:

1. The farms were large in average number of workers. A farm with 1,500 irrigated hectares and 1,500 workers was not unusual.
2. Laborers on these farms accomplished work communally. A farm's labor force was divided into brigades of, say, a dozen people, with the brigade leader responsible to the chairperson of the *kolkhoz* or the director of the *sovkhoz*. One brigade might be responsible for 200 hectares of cotton on the farm, tending it from planting to harvest.
3. Each farm received state orders each year stipulating the production targets and the price to be paid for each commercial commodity. If the farm exceeded its targets, the extra amount could be sold through nongovernmental channels for, presumably, a higher price.
4. The properties received from the state the inputs and credit deemed necessary to fulfill the production targets, automatically and often at a subsidized price.
5. The personnel on the farms were chastised in various ways if targets were not met, but bankrupt farms continued to be given subsidies and did not go "out of business."
6. The state and collective farms provided medical and other social and educational services to their members and workers.
7. The farming system, while dominated by large farms, provided workers' and members' families with small auxiliary parcels of about a quarter of a hectare each. On these small parcels farm families grew vegetables

or fruits for their own consumption, occasionally selling some of this produce. Some of these plots were very productive, and if the worker-members remained on good terms with the large farm's administrators, they were sometimes given inputs.

Many of these large centrally directed farms became a serious financial burden for the state well before independence. Subsidies were generous, production targets were infrequently met, productivity was low, incentives to work to capacity did not exist, and expenses for social infrastructure were high.

After independence the CARs enacted land reforms in an effort to reinvigorate agriculture. But such profound changes require years to institute completely. Land reforms included reorganizing the farms to make them smaller, placing them in the hands of former members and workers, and semiprivatizing them. International authorities argued that family farms would be the best alternative to state and collective farms, whereas local specialists believed that there were economies of scale that would be destroyed in the conversion to family farms. Some felt that land should be turned over to the owners so they could buy, sell, and inherit land; eventually, it was thought, the market would dictate its efficient allocation. Others argued that complete privatization would result in a reconcentration of land, and they wanted the land to remain state property while giving long-term leases to former members and workers.

Group Farming Still Prevails

Some members and workers opted for private individual farms, but most decided on some variant of cooperative farming with related families or with families who had worked together for a long time under the old system. Joint-stock companies gave negotiable paper shares to members or to production cooperatives or other associative organizational forms. With the exception of the private individual farm (sometimes called a *dekhan* farm) the other farm organizations were not a great deal different from the old *sovkhoz* or *kolkhoz*, though they were usually smaller in acreage and membership. The auxiliary parcels were often granted to those who held them before independence.

There were sound reasons that associative organizations were preferred to family farms. Workers and members were used to this team effort. Group farming meant that farming risk was minimized, and an eight-hour day could usually be observed. Most of those who worked in the former system considered themselves to be laborers and not farmers; they felt that they simply did not have the management and financial experience that farmers needed. Furthermore the machinery from the old state or collective farm could be used if it was in good repair (although much was not), and it was impractical to use this heavy equipment on small farms. The barns and other outbuildings were large and all but useless for family farms. Moreover to obtain inputs a special relationship with a neighboring large farm had to be established; there was no system enabling individual farmers to buy fertilizer, seeds, and farm chemicals or even to obtain credit.

Those who criticize the associative structure of reorganization feel that the old authoritative structure is simply duplicated in the new system. Often the old presidents or directors of the collective or state farms became administrative heads of the new entities. Nor is the incentive issue solved. There is the continuing problem of so-called free riders. With group rather than individual effort, it is easier to slack off and let someone else do the hard work. Also it is difficult for members to change their minds about the structure they prefer. For instance in most of the associative forms it is difficult to break away and become a family farmer once one has opted for an associative choice. Few mechanisms exist for selling one's shares unless one goes through an authority figure, who is usually anxious that members not leave the organization. The right to sell shares may exist, but it is usually difficult to exercise this right.

Land reform is further along in Kazakstan and Kyrgyzstan than in the other CARs. In Kazakstan, however, only 4 to 5 percent of agricultural production comes from private individual farms; in Kyrgyzstan half of the farmland in the country was transferred to private individual farmers on the basis of 99-year leases, and these farms provide about half of the country's agricultural produce. If the goal of the CARs is to reorganize into a system of private individual farms (and it is not completely clear that this is the case), it has a long distance to travel.

Future Implications

The CARs face a myriad of problems in reshaping their agriculture sectors. These countries have shown large drops in gross domestic product and agricultural-sector growth since independence. To get agriculture moving, the CARs must develop reliable sources of credit and inputs, find new markets, diversify their farm economies, fix their irrigation systems and create new ones, let market prices prevail, and develop institutional forms conducive to agricultural development.

William C. Thiesenhusen

See also: **Aral Sea**

Further Reading

"The Aral Sea: Saving the Last Drop." (1 July 2000) *The Economist* 356, 8177: 42.

Auty, Richard M. (1998) "Sustainable Mineral-Driven Development in Turkmenistan." In *Sustainable Development in Central Asia*, edited by Shirin Akiner, Sander Tideman, and John Hay. Richmond, U.K.: Curzon Press, 167–185.

Beisenova, Aliia S. (1998) "Environmental Problems in Kazakhstan." In *Sustainable Development in Central Asia*, edited by Shirin Akiner, Sander Tideman, and John Hay. Richmond, England: Curzon Press, 159–166.

Bloch, Peter, James M. Delehanty, and Michael J. Roth. (1996) *Land and Agrarian Reform in the Kyrgyz Republic.* LTC Research Paper 128. Madison, WI, and Bishkek, Kyrgyzstan: Land Tenure Center.

Economist Intelligence Unit. (1996) *Country Report: Kyrgyz Republic, Tajikistan, Turkmenistan, Uzbekistan.* London: EIU.

Pomfret, Richard. (1999) *Central Asia Turns South: Trade Relations in Transition.* London: Royal Institute of International Affairs (Russia and Eurasia Programme).

Rumer, Boris. (2000) "Economic Crisis and Growing Intraregional Tensions." In *Central Asia and the New Global Economy*, edited by Boris Rumer. Armonk, NY: M. E. Sharpe, 3–56.

Spoor, Max. (1997) *Agrarian Transition in the Former Soviet Union: Central Asia, Stagnation and Progress.* Working Paper No. 243. The Hague, Netherlands: Institute of Social Studies.

Thiesenhusen, William. (1998) *Agriculture and Land Reform in Tajikistan.* Dushanbe, Tajikistan, and Madison, WI: Land Tenure Center.

Trushin, Eskender, and Eshref Trushin. (2000) "Problems of Market Transition." In *Central Asia and the New Global Economy*, edited by Boris Rumer. Armonk, NY: M. E. Sharpe, 86–148.

Turner, Barry. (1999 and 2000) *The Statesman's Yearbook: The Politics, Cultures, and Economies of the World.* New York: Macmillan.

———. (2000) *World Development Report 2000/2001.* New York: Oxford University Press.

———, ed. (2000, 2001, 2002) *The Statesman's Yearbook: The Politics, Cultures, and Economics of the World, 2000, 2001, 2002.* New York: St. Martin's Press.

World Bank. (1993) *Kazakhstan: The Transition to a Market Economy.* Washington, DC: International Bank for Reconstruction and Development, 130–143.

———. (2000) *World Development Report 2000/2001.* New York: Oxford University Press.

AGRICULTURE—CHINA Today Chinese agriculture sustains 22 percent of the world's popula-

tion, with less than 8 percent of the world's arable land. The pattern of intensive agriculture varies in accordance with regional differences in environmental conditions: double or even triple cropping in the southern coastal regions; double cropping with a summer rice crop in the Chang (Yangtze) River basin of central and eastern China; winter wheat–summer crop cycles on the North China plains; single-crop, spring-grown cereals in the Northeast.

Chinese Agriculture in the Early Twentieth Century

Historically China has long been plagued by an unfavorable human-to-land ratio. As economic conditions worsened in the countryside by the early twentieth century, some observers argued that poor peasants were exploited by parasitic landowners through exorbitant rents, and their plight was exacerbated by usurious interest rates, high taxes, and recurrent warfare and natural disasters. Therefore, only a radical restructuring of rural society and redistribution of wealth could alleviate endemic poverty. Others contended that technological backwardness was the root of impoverishment. In this case, the introduction of modern farming techniques and inputs and the availability of low-cost credit were the proper prescriptions.

The Communist Policy of Land Reform

Whatever the correct diagnosis of China's agricultural ills, the Communist victory in the Chinese civil war of 1946–1949 succeeded in large part because the Communists used a land-reform campaign to mobilize the impoverished and discontented peasants by appealing to their hunger for land. The land reform started in Communist-occupied areas of China in the late 1920s. It was temporarily suspended after the Chinese Communist Party (CCP) formed an alliance with the Nationalist government to oppose the Japanese invasion of China in 1936. After Japan surrendered in 1945, the CCP resumed the land-reform campaign to win the support of peasants during the period of civil war. When the People's Republic of China (PRC) was established in 1949, land reform spread throughout the country.

Agricultural Policies between 1950 and 1958

In this bloody land-reform campaign (1950–1953), the CCP destroyed the wealth and power base of the rural elite, redistributed land among the peasant class on an egalitarian basis, and elevated local leaders from the poor peasant stratum. Between the land-reform

MOUNT QINCHENG—WORLD HERITAGE SITE

The birthplace of Taoism and home to dozens of ancient temples, Mount Qincheng was designated a World Heritage site in 2000. Mount Qincheng is also home to the Dujiangyan Irrigation System, an engineering project that continues to irrigate the Chengdu plains after more than two thousand years of operation.

campaign and the beginning of economic reform in 1978, agricultural policies were based primarily on centralized planning and collectivization of agriculture, despite various changes in direction. In fall 1953, the government introduced compulsory procurement of farm products, whereby peasants were obligated to sell fixed quotas of their produce (including grain, cotton, and edible oils) to the state at government-set prices. Private markets were increasingly restricted.

Agriculture supported the state's focus on heavy industrial development by providing cheap food and by earning foreign exchange to import capital goods. To raise agricultural production without diverting resources from industry, the government adopted a strategy that involved the mass mobilization of rural labor to work on labor-intensive infrastructure projects (including irrigation, flood control, and land reclamation) and by raising agricultural productivity through more intensive application of traditional methods and inputs (for example, closer planting, more careful weeding, and more use of organic fertilizers). Collectivization was seen as the institutional means to implement that strategy.

To make the transition from a small-holder rural economy at the completion of land reform to a collectivized system, the Communists first promoted the creation of mutual-aid teams composed of five to fifteen households that exchanged labor and shared the use of tools and draft animals rented from owner-participants. Next the mutual-aid teams were consolidated into primary agricultural-producer cooperatives of approximately twenty to twenty-five households, which pooled land resources and paid participants according to the amount of labor, land, and tools contributed. The third stage in socialist development was the creation of advanced agricultural-producer cooperatives made up of 150 to 200 households and combining the principles of collective farming and payment according to labor only. Most peasants had joined advanced cooperatives by the end of 1956.

The Great Leap Forward and Its Aftermath

Mao Zedong's Great Leap Forward (1958–1960) was intended to catapult China into the front ranks of industrial nations, making China a Communist paradise in a short time. Some 740,000 advanced cooperatives were consolidated into 26,500 communes, self-sufficient communities averaging five thousand households each, which merged the functions of agriculture, industry, and trade and assumed responsibilities for administration, education, and defense. The production brigade, equivalent to one or more natural villages, constituted a middle tier in the commune structure. In turn, a brigade was composed of a number of production teams, each composed of tens of families drawn from one neighborhood.

Communal kitchens, mess halls, and nurseries both promoted collective living and released labor that was mobilized in large teams in massive water-conservancy and irrigation projects intended to raise agricultural productivity dramatically. In place of economic incentives, ideological exhortations inspired the people to work hard for the common good. Reports of bountiful harvests prompted the partial implementation of the Communist principle, to each according to his needs. Net income was distributed primarily on a per capita basis and only partially on the basis of individual labor contributions.

This utopian movement ended in disaster. Local cadres claimed fantastic productivity gains, leading higher authorities to harbor unrealistic expectations and to make escalating grain-procurement demands on peasants. Peasants, in turn, were left with little or nothing to eat and were physically exhausted by the relentless labor demand. Construction and industrial projects diverted rural labor needed for grain harvesting. Programs to promote rural industrialization, based on the transformation of local materials, most notably backyard furnaces to make steel out of iron reclaimed from utensils and tools, wasted resources but manufactured few usable products. Difficulties were further compounded by bad weather and the withdrawal of Soviet aid. Some 30 million people perished in the resultant famine from 1959 to 1961.

The original communes were reorganized into smaller and more manageable units with the tripling of their numbers to 74,000 in 1961 and 1962, and the small production team was reestablished as the basic unit of planning and accounting. Rural markets and the right to cultivate small private plots were restored. Improved economic incentives paved the way for recovery of grain production by 1963.

Mao's Cultural Revolution of 1966–1976

Mao, disturbed by the reforms of the early 1960s, which he considered steps toward the restoration of capitalism, launched the Cultural Revolution in 1966. In the ten years of turmoil that ensued, not only was Chinese society violently traumatized by political persecutions and internal disorder, but agriculture suffered from the discontinuation of technical development; discouragement or even elimination of private plots, sideline activities, and rural markets; and primacy of political criteria over technical or economic considerations in economic policy making and in determination of individual earnings.

Despite the disruptions of the Great Leap Forward and the Cultural Revolution, China's total grain output increased at an average annual growth of 3.5 percent, or from 113.2 million metric tons to 304.8 million metric tons between 1949 and 1978. Agriculture was the primary foreign-exchange earner, accounting for more than 60 percent. Much new land was opened in the Northeast, extensive flood control and irrigation systems were constructed, and a number of improved crop varieties (including dwarf and semidwarf fertilizer-responsive varieties of rice and cold-tolerant, quick-maturing wheats) were developed and propagated. However, reflecting state policies that squeezed agriculture to promote industrial development, even as real per capita income increased almost threefold from 1952 to 1978, per capita peasant income stagnated. Agriculture grew at an average annual rate of 1.9 percent, compared with 10.8 percent for industry and 6.0 percent for total national income.

Agricultural Policies of Deng Xiaoping from 1978 to the Mid-1980s

After Deng Xiaoping became the leader of China in 1978, the government focused on the Four Modernizations: industry, agriculture, national defense, and science and technology. The state sought to stimulate agricultural production by reintroducing private economic incentives into peasant production decisions in the early 1980s: Crop- and animal-purchase prices were raised, and, most important, collective farming was replaced by household-based farming.

The latter was achieved largely through the household-responsibility system, which was originally an unauthorized local initiative by some poor rural communities in the late 1970s and sanctioned by the state

only in 1981 as it proved successful in raising peasant incomes. Each household contracted with the state for the management of a fixed amount of land for from one to three years, thereby assuming responsibility to pay certain specified quotas and taxes to the state or collective, but also gaining the right to make its own economic decisions on such matters as the allocation of production inputs or the disposal of any surplus output. By the end of 1983, more than fifty thousand communes were dismantled as 200 million farm families joined the household-responsibility system. In 1984, the duration of contracts was extended to fifteen or more years, and in 1993, it was extended an additional thirty years. The government also gave permission to farm households to exchange and employ labor in 1983 and to sublease land to other households in 1984.

Agriculture from the Mid-1980s to the Present

From the mid-1980s, rural reform was gradually extended from production to liberalization of marketing, distribution, and trade of farm products, first for fruits and vegetables, then fishery products, livestock products, and oilseeds. Wholesale markets were legalized, free-market trade permitted, and the number of items covered by procurement quotas reduced by the government. Private marketing enterprises, which bought from traders in local markets or directly from farmers, multiplied. Even the marketing of the most heavily regulated products has been partially liberalized since the mid-1980s: The government reduced quotas for grain purchased at state-set prices, while purchasing additional quantities above the quota at negotiated prices and allowing peasants to sell the remainder in the open market at higher prices.

With the dissolution of the communes, the government permitted townships to take over their administrative functions and property, while villages appropriated the functions and property of the production brigades. Many townships and villages formed collective industrial and commercial enterprises (TVEs) providing a variety of goods and services. Private enterprises also grew rapidly. Rural industries helped to absorb surplus labor and boost household income. By 1987, the gross product of rural industry had surpassed that of all agricultural production. Between 1978 and 1993, the number of TVEs expanded from 1.5 million to 20.8 million, with their output at the annual rate of 21 percent and employment at 12 percent, thereby creating nearly 80 million jobs.

The expansion of food supplies has exceeded the growth of domestic demand. Between 1991 and 1999, yield for wheat increased from 3.2 to 3.9 metric tons

COOPERATIVES IN THE PEOPLE'S REPUBLIC OF CHINA

The formation of agricultural cooperatives was major change effected by the new communist government in China in the 1950s. The following text setting forth government policy states the general principles for collectives and also membership criteria.

Model Regulations for Advanced Agricultural Producers' Cooperatives
(Adopted on June 30th, 1956 by the First National People's Congress of the People's Republic of China at its third session)

General Principles
Article 1. An agricultural producers' cooperative (the term as used in this document means the agricultural producers' cooperative of advanced type) is a socialist, collective economic organization formed on a voluntary and mutually beneficial basis, with the guidance and help of the Communist Party and the People's Government.

Article 2. The agricultural producers' cooperative, in accordance with socialist principles, converts the chief means of production owned privately by its members into the collective property of the cooperative. The members are organized for collective work, and the cooperative applies the principle of "from each according to his ability, to each according to his work," giving equal pay for equal work, irrespective of sex or age."

Membership
Article 7. All working peasants who have reached the age of 16 and other working people able to take part in the work of the cooperative may be admitted as members. Applications for membership must be voluntary and approved by a general meeting of members' delegates.

The cooperative shall make every effort to take in as members the dependents of revolutionary martyrs, of soldiers and government workers, and disabled as well as demobilized servicemen (including the military personnel who came over from the Kuomintang armed forces and those who accepted the peaceful liberation of the regions under their control but who have since been demobilized and returned to the countryside). The aged, the weak, the orphaned, the widowed and the disabled should also be admitted as members. New settlers should also be drawn into the cooperative.

Source: W. R. Geddes. (1963). *Peasant Life in Communist China: Monograph #6.* Ithaca, New York: Society for Applied Anthropology, 56.

per hectare, yield for rice from 5.6 to 6.3, yield for corn from 4.6 to 4.9, while yields for sorghum and millet remained steady at 3.5 and 1.6, respectively. Between 1979 and 1984, total grain output expanded by 4.9 percent per annum to reach the level of 407.3 million metric tons. Growth was much more modest from 1985 to 2000 at 1.3 percent per annum. Between 1978 and 2000, rice production rose from 136.9 to 187.9 million metric tons (with a high of 200.7 in 1997), wheat production from 53.8 to 99.6 (with a high of 113.9 in 1999), and corn production from 56.0 to 106.0 (with a high of 133.0 in 1998).

The quality and varieties of food have significantly improved as consumer demand for better quality food increased with rising incomes. Between 1983 and 1999, urban per capita consumption of poultry meat rose from 2.6 to 4.9 kilograms, while consumption of seafood grew from 8.1 to 10.3 kilograms; corresponding figures for rural residents were 0.8 to 2.5 kilograms and 1.6 to 3.8 kilograms, respectively. To meet expanding domestic and foreign demand, China's animal output increased even more rapidly than grain production in the 1990s: from 25.1 to 47.6 million metric tons for red meat and 4.0 to 11.2 million metric tons for poultry. Aquatic production more than tripled in that decade, reaching 39.0 million metric tons in 1998.

Between 1978 and 1991, cotton production grew about two and one-half times, from 2.2 to 5.7 million metric tons, but hovered around 4.5 million metric tons thereafter. Production of oilseeds, on the other hand, continually expanded throughout the reform period, from 5.2 in 1978 to 16.4 in 1991 to 26.0 million metric tons in 1999.

China has become a significant participant in the global market for agricultural commodities. It exported as much as 10 percent of the world's traded corn while importing as much as 17 percent of the world's traded wheat, 25 percent of fertilizer, and 28 percent of soybean oil. Leading agricultural exports in 2000 were cotton yarn and fabric ($3.73 billion), fish and seafood ($2.27 billion), prepared meat and fish ($1.88 billion), and cereals ($1.64 billion). Oilseeds and miscellaneous grains ($3.07 billion), hides and skins ($2.95 billion), and cotton yarn and fabric ($2.79 billion) headed the list of major agricultural imports.

The expansion of economic opportunities from improved incentives and particularly from rural industries has contributed significantly to the rise in rural income. Per capita annual net income of rural households in yuan rose from 133.6 in 1978 to 397.6 in 1985 to 686.3

in 1990 to 2162 in 1998. More than 210 million peasants were raised from extreme poverty, though 50 million still remained in that state as of 1997.

Despite the fundamental shift from collective socialism to an increasingly market-oriented and privatized economy since 1978, self-sufficiency in food as a matter of national security and the provision of stable and cheap grain supplies for urban residents remained constant concerns in Communist economic policy.

Alarmists in 1994 even voiced the fear that China might be unable in the future to produce enough food grain for an increasing population and enough feed grain for a rapidly growing livestock industry, thereby driving up international grain prices and leading to starvation in poor countries that will be unable to compete with China to import grain. Such scenarios have been taken by the Chinese government as an attack on its ability to provide for the needs of the people. Moreover, questions were raised by Chinese officials concerning the reliability of foreign food-grain suppliers. Such considerations reinforced the long-standing policy of food sufficiency.

The marketing of most agricultural commodities has become commercialized and marketized. Since 1999, even cotton procurement and prices are no longer mandated by the state; a cotton exchange was established, and the state's purchase monopoly over cotton was ended. Grain remains the sole agricultural product whose marketing is still largely controlled by the state. Under the governor's responsibility system, or grain-bag policy, introduced in 1995, responsibility for stabilizing grain supplies and prices was shifted to provincial leaders. In a major reform initiative in 1998, quota procurement grain prices were to be determined by the prevailing market price. But mounting deficits prompted the state to reclaim monopoly control over grain distribution and to permit private grain dealers to sell only grain purchased from government grain-marketing enterprises. Limited private grain marketing was allowed again only in 2000.

This emphasis on food security has resulted in devoting unnecessarily large efforts to the cultivation of relatively low-value basic crops, including grain and cotton, and has prevented peasants from increasing their production of high value-added agricultural commodities.

The land market itself has been incompletely reformed. Ownership of land has remained with the collective, and peasants have remained concerned about the long-term stability of land tenure. Consequently they have been reluctant to invest for the long term.

Agriculture's share of gross domestic product and trade has fallen from about 30 percent in 1980 to about 20 percent and 10 percent, respectively, by 1997. By the 1990s, rural industry suffered from a declining capacity to create additional employment. Income gaps between cities and rural areas had been closing between 1978 and 1985, after which they grew again until the mid-1990s, when per capita income for urban residents remained at around two and one-half times that for rural residents, about the same as in 1978.

Future Prospects for Chinese Agriculture

Further expansion of agricultural production faces a number of constraints. Official data indicate a loss of arable land since 1978: from 99 to 95 million hectares. While other independent estimates based on Landsat (satellite photography) data have yielded much higher figures for China's land under cultivation, ranging from 125 to 140 million hectares, there is little doubt that much arable land has been damaged by soil erosion, desertification, salinization, and alkalization. The 80,000 dams built since the 1950s have, ironically, contributed to the problem. Intended to control flooding, improve irrigation, raise farm yields, and free peasants to engage in industrial labor, many dams caused the waterlogging of upstream farmland; others became clogged with silt and caused severe flooding; and thousands of dams collapsed.

Aside from environmental problems, an unknown quantity of land has been left uncultivated or under-cultivated by farmers who grew one crop for subsistence needs while household members worked in local industrial enterprises. In other cases, farmers wanting to keep their claims to the land as security leased their land-use rights to households not engaged in rural enterprises; the latter were typically too poor in resources to make good use of the land. In many households, married women, in addition to housekeeping and child rearing, were forced to assume responsibility for tilling the fields while their men worked outside agriculture or even remained idle and spent their time gambling.

By 1997 administrative responsibilities for rural areas were shared by 2,100 counties and county-level cities, 44,700 townships and towns, and 740,000 village residents' committees. Increasingly, local governments have devoted more of their budgets to the salaries of the rapidly growing numbers of officials, to the detriment of social services (including health and education) and agricultural investment. In recent years many local governments have levied a plethora of special taxes on farmers; these eat up 20 percent or more of rural household income. They have often issued IOUs in lieu of payments for grain procurements. Ensuing peasant anger has erupted in a number of protests and demonstrations.

Government policy makers have become increasingly concerned about raising farm incomes since the early 1990s, and they have introduced a number of policy innovations to address these problems. One innovation attempted to introduce economies of scale by concentrating farm management on a large scale in certain regions. In another innovation, user rights for the development of certain types of wastelands were extended for longer periods, along with inheritance, transfer, leasing, and mortgage rights. Premier Zhu Rongji (b. 1928) proposed for the ninth Five-Year Plan (2001–2005) the promotion of downstream efficiency of agriculture, or the processing of produce after it leaves the farm, with the idea that added value would boost the incomes of farmers.

Further challenges to Chinese agriculture come with China's accession to the World Trade Organization (WTO) in 2001. China is obligated to lower tariffs on agricultural imports from an average of 22 to 15 percent and to end government grain quotas and food-distribution monopolies. The resultant flood of food imports may throw out of work 13 million farmers, mainly producers of wheat, corn, rice, and cotton. On the other hand, fruit, vegetable, and meat producers will gain more open access to overseas markets and add 2 million jobs. As of 2001 some 330 million people or 70 percent of the rural labor force still worked in agriculture.

Chinese agriculture in the twenty-first century faces the prospect of considerable restructuring to deal with environmental degradation, peasant discontent, and problems and opportunities stemming from greater economic globalization.

Robert Y. Eng

Further Reading

Hsu, Hsin-hui, and Fred Gale, eds. (2001) *China: Agriculture in Transition.* Agriculture and Trade Reports, no. WRS-01-2. Washington, DC: U.S. Department of Agriculture.

Kang Chao. (1970) *Agricultural Production in Communist China, 1949–1965.* Madison, WI: University of Wisconsin Press.

Nyberg, Albert, and Scott Rozelle. (1999) *Accelerating China's Rural Transformation.* Washington, DC: World Bank.

Oi, Jean C. (1999) "Two Decades of Rural Reform in China: An Overview and Assessment." *China Quarterly* 159: 616–628.

Perkins, Dwight, ed. (1977) *Rural Small-Scale Industry in the People's Republic of China.* Berkeley and Los Angeles: University of California Press.

Yang, Yongzheng, and Weiming Tian, eds. (2000) *China's Agriculture at the Crossroads.* New York: St. Martin's Press.

AGRICULTURE—SOUTH ASIA

The patterns of South Asian agriculture are discernible as far back as the Indus Valley civilization (c. 2300–1750 BCE). Traditional agricultural systems include shifting cultivation and settled cultivation. Shifting agriculture is substantially the same worldwide. Settled agriculture, however, separates into New World and Old World patterns.

Shifting agriculture is still practiced in certain mountainous areas in Assam, India, which receive large amounts of rain; in the adjacent hilly areas of eastern Bangladesh bordering Burma; in the Western Ghats in Karnataka, India; and in some remote parts of Madhya Pradesh and Orissa, India. In this system farmers clear a patch of bamboo jungle using slash and burn techniques, then sow a mixture of crops in the ashes. The crops include indigenous upland rice, maize, millet, cotton, vegetables, and bananas.

Whereas shifting cultivation brings the crops to the accumulated biochemical energy, settled cultivation requires that energy be brought to the crops. In South Asia, as was the case in the Old World in general, farm animals play an essential part in this process. In addition to supplying draft power and useful products in their own right, farm animals serve as energy gatherers when they browse beyond the cultivated fields and bring back the material they collect in the form of manure. In addition they act as energy recyclers when they consume what would otherwise be agricultural waste. South Asian farmers apply this general strategy with a mixture of crops, animals, and institutional traditions closely adapted to the area's physiography and climate.

Physiography

South Asia is divided into three major zones. Proceeding from north to south, they are a great arch of mountains on the edge of the Asian continental plate; the subduction zone between the Asian and South Asian plates, which is filled by the alluvium of the Indo-Gangetic Plain; and the old continental mass of peninsular India with its highest elevations on its western side running down to its southern tip, the Western Ghats.

Climate

The South Asian landforms interact with the prevailing winds to produce the distinctive pattern of a monsoon climate. The climate dictates cropping seasons and often sharp cropping gradients over small ge-

Farmers in the Tamil Nadu region of South India work in a rice field. (ARVIND GARG/CORBIS)

ographical distances, which in turn shape intervillage and interregional trade.

The climate involves a regular succession of wet and dry periods. The South Asian new year, beginning in mid-April, marks the onset of a hot, dry season during which the preceding winter's crops are harvested. From June through July, the summer monsoon season begins, as moisture-bearing winds proceed across the region from the southwest. Another hot, dry season begins in late September, when the summer's crops are harvested, followed by the development and retreat of winter and the northeast monsoon. In April the cycle starts again.

Local patterns of rainfall depend on an area's exposure to the prevailing winds and its proximity to the sea. In areas with a dominant southwest exposure, the summer rainy season is the heaviest. Where the exposure is north and east, as on the east side of the Western Ghats in southern India, the summer is the dry season, and the main rainy season is October through January. Where exposure is more balanced, both seasons provide useful rain, and in areas with no strong exposure at all, as in the Indus Valley from Lahore eastward, one finds a desert climate.

Cropping

After climate and soil, the most immediate constraint on cropping is the need to produce fodder. Since fodder has a low cash value, farmers rarely grow more than they need and therefore have little to sell to those who might not grow enough. The human diet imposes less of a constraint because farmers produce more food than fodder for sale. The South Asian diet usually involves two main meals a day, each consisting of one grain accompanied by one or at most two vegetables or pulses prepared as a soup or stew with

AGRICULTURE—SOUTH ASIA

This extract of a government report in India shows how village farmers combine traditional and modern farming methods.

Villagers keep seeds for the next harvest. Poor families borrow seeds from the better off farmers and return these to them after the harvest. It is very rare that a farmer goes to a *bania* for borrowing seeds because *bania* charges high rate of interest.

Villagers cared little about improved seeds in the past. Now they are gradually developing interest for such seeds. Improved seeds of wheat and better sugarcane are becoming popular among farmers. Wheat seeds are given to villagers on return basis. The Gram Sewak gives villagers certain quantity of wheat seed for sowing and takes back the same quantity out of the produce of improved seed. This is given to another villager on the same terms and conditions. The sugarcane seed has been distributed against cash payment. Most people prefer their own seeds. If improved types of seeds are provided at cheaper rates, these could be more popular.

Cowdung is the common manure that the farmers use. This is used after mixing with dry and rotten leaves. In the earlier days, compost pits for depositing cow-dung were not common and the manure was directly transferred to the fields or dumped in front of the houses. But now things are changing a little. Pits are dug for storing cowdung in the fields. In these, compost is prepared. Manure is carried to the fields in baskets or *kiltas*.

Chemical fertilizers are also being used. A depot has been opened in the village and Nirmal Das, a local shopkeeper, sells these. There are a few farmers who use these manures. One theory put forward by them is that chemical fertilizers harden the soil which means more labour while ploughing the fields for the next sowing. Rates for the fertilizer are nominal.

Source: R. C. Pal Singh. (1961) *Himachal Pradesh: A Village Survey of Moginand (Nahan Tehsil, Sirmur District)*. Census of India 1961, vol. 20, part 4, no. 8, 33–34.

onions, chilies, and local spices. Tea, introduced into India in 1839, is the most common beverage after water and is usually served with substantial amounts of milk and brown sugar. Sugarcane is both an important cash crop and an important food. Since it mainly is consumed in unrefined forms, it is higher than any other foods in available energy and iron. Pickles made of unripe fruits and chilies preserved in oil are common accompaniments to a meal.

In each season, farmers plant approximately three to six crops along with a small kitchen garden. Each array must provide vegetables for consumption in the current season, at least one grain or pulse to store for the next season, fresh fodder for consumption in the current season, and fodder for storage for future use. If possible, farmers plant more than one crop for each purpose (1) to reduce the risk of a total failure in any one category, (2) to level out labor requirements and thereby maximize the utilization of family labor, (3) to provide a better mixture of desirable qualities, (4) to balance more desirable crops with those that are more reliable or cheaper to produce, and (5) to provide better crop rotations.

The most abundantly produced grains are rice, several kinds of millet, wheat, and barley. Millet is the most widely planted grain. Rice is the preferred grain in the south and the east, and wheat is preferred in the north. The most popular pulses are chickpeas, lentils, pigeon peas, beans, and mash. Common vegetables are squashes, greens, onions, garlic, and chilies. Oilseeds and milk provide dietary fats except along the coasts and in Bangladesh, where fish largely replace pulses. South Asians eat meat, primarily goat and sometimes chicken, only occasionally.

Multicropping commonly involves both irrigated and rain-fed land. Most villages own both types of land, and farmers try to have plots in each area. Wheat and rice are usually irrigated, millets and barley are rain-fed. Likewise the other major crop categories include varieties that produce better on irrigation as well as some that can survive drought.

Animals

The animal complex includes eleven principal species. These stand in the same functional relation to each other across the region despite local preferences regarding varieties. The eleven species are single-humped Indian camel or dromedary, humped oxen or zebu (*Bos indicus*), buffalo, goat, sheep, horse, ass, mule, pig, dog, and cat. Some families also keep chickens and ducks.

Camels, oxen, and buffalo are the most important animals to farmers. Horses, asses, and mules generally are owned by artisans, who use them to carry heavy goods in packs. Dogs, which live in village packs rather than in individual households, hunt rats and similar pests in the fields. Cats are rare but are treated similarly to dogs.

Camels are prominent on the northwestern Indo-Gangetic Plain. In desert areas along the border of India and Pakistan, nomadic pastoralists still raise camels to sell in the surrounding farming communities. Important for their hair, hides, milk, and for use as beasts of burden in the desert climate, camels are particularly favored for operating Persian wheels (a Persian wheel is a mechanism for lifting water from a well by means of a chain of pots or buckets, operated by animal power).

The main draft animal is the bullock, a castrated male *Bos indicus*. Bullocks vary greatly in size according to the terrain and the food supply. The largest bullocks, raised in the semidesert plains of Haryana, India, between the Ganges and Indus drainages, reach nearly two meters at the shoulders. In the mountains, where fields are small and slopes are steep, bullocks are less

than waist high. In other areas, like Bangladesh and Tamil Nadu, India, where holdings are small and fodder is scarce and poor, bullocks reach a size between those extremes. The females of *Bos indicus*, the stereotypical Indian sacred cows, are usually kept only in sufficient numbers to provide the needed bullocks.

The buffalo, originally domesticated in Sind, Pakistan, from the wild river buffalo, is the primary milk-giving animal. Buffalo milk has about twice the butterfat content of cows' milk, and the lactation period is about nine months in contrast with six months in cows. However, in hot weather buffalo need access to water to bathe once or twice a day. Male buffalo are rare in hot, dry areas, but in wetter areas they are sometimes kept for plowing or water lifting. Like *Bos indicus* they vary in size. The largest varieties live on the plains, where moisture and fodder are abundant; the smallest varieties live in the mountains; and the mid-sized varieties live where fodder is scarce. Several Indian states have developed artificial insemination programs to improve the quality of the buffalo herd.

Both farmers and the landless keep goats, which provide milk and the most widely accepted meat. Goats of the region also give cashmere wool. Most sheep are kept for wool by specialized herders.

Because fodder shortages are endemic, animals are usually fed individually and according to need. Working animals, those plowing or lactating, are fed more than animals that are not working.

The common Western pig (*Sus scrofa*) was originally domesticated in India and eastern Turkistan. In villages, pigs normally are kept by those people who sweep out the barns and streets, and the pigs eat what they find. Pigs produce bristles, meat, and leather. Although the meat frequently is infected with parasites, it is sold at a low price in markets and is consumed by the poor. The British established sanitary piggeries, which have persisted long after British rule, to raise local varieties for urban markets.

Organization of South Asian Agriculture

South Asian agriculture is peasant agriculture organized and carried out by independent households with smallholdings, generally between 0.2 and 4.0 hectares. Although kings and great landlords have been prominent in South Asian history and large landlords persist in Pakistan and a few Indian states, they exercise little or no managerial control, simply drawing a share of the production.

Within the Household The division of labor within the household is based on sex and generation. In

AGRICULTURE AND AGRARIAN REFORM

Since independence India has been a mainly rural and agricultural society and the government has been concerned with making farming more efficient and productive. The resolution below from the April 1950 Indian National Congress Economic Planning Conference sets forth five measures to improve agriculture.

India's economic and social progress will in large measure be conditioned by the extent to which her land and water resources are developed. On the efficiency of the country's agricultural production will depend not only the satisfaction of the basic need of an adequate balanced diet for its growing population but also the supply of raw materials for some of her major industries.

The immediate object in agriculture that the country has set before itself is self-sufficiency in food to be attained by the end of 1951 as well as in cotton and jute; and concerted measures to this end are already under way. These consist of reclamation of land, offerings of incentives and assistance for the diversion of land from other crops to the cultivation of cotton and jute and improving the yield and quality of agricultural products. What is needed for the purposes of the immediate programme is an intensification of some of these measures as well as the creation of conditions conducive to better farming. Increased efficiency of agriculture postulates more than improvement in facilities organisation and techniques; the maintenance and restoration of soil fertility; and the provision of irrigation. All this will fail to confer full or lasting benefit unless the tiller of the soil is given a sense of security and self-respect and the economic and social condition of the agricultural labour.

The specific measures which have to be planned for the improvement of agriculture as part of the immediate programme will comprise the following:

(1) The provision of irrigation facilities by way of reconditioning old and constructing new tanks and wells including tube wells. Such minor works will appeal most readily to the rural population and secure their active co-operation. They will supplement the irrigation that will be provided by the river valley projects which should be completed as early as possible as part of the long-term plans of the Central and State Governments.

(2) The rapid multiplication of better seed. A well regulated procedure is required in all the States for the production of nuclear seed, its multiplication under carefully controlled conditions and its testing before final distribution to the cultivator.

(3) The stimulation of compost-making if necessary by legislation and the full utilisation of the various other forms of organic manures available in the country. Definite planning is required for the conservation and use of waste material, human and animal excreta and residual matter from the carcasses of animals and for maintaining soil fertility.

(4) The reclamation and conservation of the soil. There are still large areas in most states which could be brought under cultivation with the help of tractors and other machines. New areas brought under cultivation could assist materially in the settlement of displaced population and works undertaken to prevent soil erosion will provide employment very appropriate to the agricultural worker.

(5) The development of an effective and widespread agricultural extension service. Such a service will act as a two-way link between the cultivator and the scientific departments of the State, so that the cultivator's practical difficulties are solved in the laboratories and the results are conveyed to him convincingly. It should be the special concern of the services to bring about an improvement in the arrangement for the designing, production and maintenance of better implements. (The quotas for the supply of iron and steel required for agricultural implements must be raised for a significant improvement in this direction to be possible.)

CONTINUED ON NEXT PAGE

CONTINUED FROM PREVIOUS PAGE

Agriculture will remain in a state of flux so long as the structure and pattern of rural economy does not become clear and definite. It is, therefore, necessary to shorten the period of transition by expediting the abolition of *zamindari* and *malguzari* by paying compensation if necessary in bonds. Provision should be made for fixity of tenure to the tiller, subletting even if allowed should be for a period of just less than five years and for regulated rates of rent.

Co-operative Better Farming Societies should be organised in every region in a planner manner with fixed targets. Experiments in co-operative joint farming may also be made in selected areas. Both to multipurpose co-operatives and co-operative joint farms special facility should be granted by the State and they should receive priority in all matters of State assistance. In areas where fragmentation is intense, consolidation of holdings should be undertaken in a determined manner. Special efforts should be made to organise co-operatives for uneconomic holdings.

Special attention should be given to the organisation of agricultural labour for the betterment of their condition. Agrestic serfdom should be made a cognizable offence and the President of the Union Board of the village *panchayat* might be empowered to enforce the law. Debts of agricultural labourers should be selected down and wherever found inequitable wiped out. High priority should be given to provision of house sites for agricultural labourers and to the removal of the disabilities attached to the present house-sites.

The problem connected with the development of India's agriculture offers a challenge to the planner and an immense scope for purposeful co-operation between the Government and the people; and success or failure in solution of these problems will make all the difference between growing prosperity and continuing poverty in the land.

Source: Indian National Congress. (1954) *Resolutions on Economic Policy and Programme.* New Delhi: A.I.C.C., 52–53.

general, men are concerned with what goes on outside the house, and women are responsible for what occurs within it. Men deal with the production and disposal of crops and animals in the fields; women deal with food storage and preparation, with fodder and seed storage, with servants and those who provide services for the household, and with the household budget. The principal woman is usually the wife of the household head and the mother of the active sons. The head man is the senior male and the father of the working sons or someone of his level, depending on competence. Since property rights are generally acquired by birth rather than by succession, the household acts much more as a partnership than as an autocracy.

Among Households The division of labor among households involves three main occupational groups that are substantially uniform across the region except in remote areas, where tribal customs prevail. The most populous group, about half the population, is the farmers, who usually share membership in one or a small number of local clans (*got* or *gotra*). About one-third of the families are agricultural laborers, and the remainder are specialized artisans, such as shopkeepers, potters, masons, carpenters, blacksmiths, tailors, cotton ginners, and weavers.

Village occupational specializations cannot be accurately characterized as based on caste. Although villagers recognize an idea of caste, in the sense of a stereotypical family occupation based on a distinctive inherited property, as a part of their ideas of kinship relations, they recognize the occupational division of labor as a separate matter that follows different rules. People are hired according to need, competence, and return. Wages are set by bargaining. Nevertheless, all arrangements must contain certain components, and a definite sense of a fair wage dominates as opposed to simply what the market will bear. While sweeper, blacksmith, mason, and carpenter are recognized castes, agricultural laborer and landowner are not. It is impossible to predict with confidence the caste of any household from its occupation. The work of masons, carpenters, and blacksmiths, for example, is commonly done by men who answer to any of the labels, and a village usually includes more families who do not perform their stereotypical caste occupations than those who do.

Labor usually is hired under one of three arrangements: a partnership, an annual contract, or a daily wage. In a partnership, an employee works with a landowner for a year or a season and receives a share of the crop. Under an annual contract, an employee works for a farmer for a full year and receives a fixed annual fee, or an employee provides a specified service for the household for a year in return for a fixed payment in cash, in kind, or both. An example of the latter would be a potter supplying pots to a household in exchange for foodstuffs, cash, or both. Under the third arrangement, a daily wage, a farmer makes an agreement with a worker or a group of workers, who agree to perform a certain operation on a specific field in return for payment in cash or in kind calculated daily.

Payments for labor normally involve money and maintenance. Under an annual contract the maintenance component might be food, clothing, and medical expenses for the year. For the worker receiving daily wages, maintenance would include a specific understanding about meals and teas that the farmer provides for the laborer to eat in the field.

Village Organizations Villagers commonly make collective arrangements that affect agriculture by (1) differentiating between land that will be used for house sites and land that will be used as agricultural fields; (2) maintaining village roads, work areas, and public areas, such as cremation grounds or burial grounds; and (3) constructing village irrigation tanks and wells. Villages are usually strongly nucleated with agricultural fields laid out around the centers. In areas prone to flooding, the populated areas are on the high elevations, and the fields are on lower ground. Some roads radiate out from the populated center to the main fields, but they do not reach every field. Accordingly fields are unfenced except for those devoted to permanent orchards. Security most of the year is based on mutual assistance, and when crops are particularly vulnerable family members stand watch day and night.

Village irrigation tanks, filled by rainfall, from a local stream, or from a canal, are particularly common in peninsular India and in Sri Lanka. Usually the village land watered by irrigation tanks is reserved for rice, and the rain-fed land is devoted to millets and other dryland crops. Historically irrigation tanks were managed by a hereditary village water tender, who was paid a set share of the crops he tended. Villages arranged to share the trapped fish at the end of the irrigation season and to share collective maintenance responsibilities. Management arrangements coped with low-water years by reducing the area irrigated. Each farmer was allowed a share of the reduced area proportional to his or her share in the entire area. After Indian independence, state or national governments took control of irrigation tanks. The traditional arrangements were disrupted, and irrigation performance has declined.

Organizations beyond the Village Beyond the village, the principal organizations that influence agriculture are the government, cooperatives, and private firms. The government, over most of history, has provided economic markets, collected taxes, and introduced new crops and products for trade, and sometimes it has built canals and reservoirs. During the colonial period, tax collection was institutionalized in revenue departments, and irrigation departments had oversight of irrigation construction. Agriculture departments, marketing boards, and a few specialized research institutes were established to stimulate the adoption of productive technologies and crops deemed especially important either as strategic commodities or for international trade, including the rice, wheat, jute, cotton, indigo, tea, coffee, sugar, rubber, spices, and oilseeds not readily grown in Europe. The first agricultural colleges were founded in 1886, but these institutions only trained prospective government officers and did not conduct research.

After independence, beginning in the mid-1960s, Pakistan, Bangladesh, and India developed agricultural universities patterned on the American land-grant system. The principle aims were to stimulate the spread of scientific farming technologies among the farm population and to undertake extensive basic agricultural research, including but not limited to research supporting the introduction of Green-Revolution crops and technologies. The effectiveness of the institutions varies greatly by country. The American program stands on the three equal and interdependent legs of research, teaching, and extension. In Pakistan, Bangladesh, and most Indian states, however, the extension programs are either limited or nonexistent; consequently research is driven by government priorities, as was typical in the colonial-era agriculture departments, rather than by farm problems.

The lack of credit continues to constrain agricultural growth in the region. No significant commercial credit is available to small farmers. Only India has a nationally supported system of cooperative credit. Even there, government appointees dominate the management in most states, and a majority of the farmers are not members of cooperatives.

Private firms have become increasingly important. Large industrial firms produce a full range of modern agricultural chemicals and farm equipment, such as well pumps and tractors. Smaller manufacturers produce simpler tools, like plows and fodder choppers, of-

TABLE 1

Increases in paddy and wheat production from 1965 to 1995		
	Paddy	Wheat
All South Asia	193%	258%
Bangladesh	143%	not significant
India	209%	260%
Nepal	127%	349%
Pakistan	222%	237%
Sri Lanka	348%	not grown

SOURCE: Food and Agriculture Organization of the United Nations (2000).

ten of improved designs originating in the agricultural universities.

Prospects

In the 1950s it was widely believed that South Asia's population growth would soon outpace its food production, and in the mid-1960s widespread famine was averted only by massive imports. Subsequently governments and international agencies have placed a higher priority on agricultural development, encouraging efforts such as the Green Revolution between about 1965 and 1978. Steady growth continues, and with the exception of Bangladesh, the region became self-sufficient in about 1980. Table 1 gives the increases in paddy (unmilled rice) and wheat production from 1965 to 1995 for the region as a whole and for each major producing country. All production figures are from the statistical service of the Food and Agriculture Organization (FAO) of the United Nations. The FAO in turn receives data from the statistical services of the respective countries; therefore quality varies widely.

Despite the gains, yields do not approach those attained in developed countries. Table 2 gives some comparisons for 1998.

The differences indicate the force of existing institutional and financial constraints and suggest a scope for improvement.

Murray J. Leaf

See also: **Green Revolution—South Asia; Rice and Rice Agriculture; Water Issues**

Further Reading

Food and Agriculture Organization of the United Nations. (2000) FAOStat. Retrieved August 2000, from: http://apps.fao.org/cgi-bin/nph-db.pl?subset=agriculture.

Gill, Manohar Singh. (1983) *Agriculture Cooperatives.* New Delhi: Vikas Publishing House.

Johnson, B. L. C. (1969) *South Asia: Selective Studies of the Essential Geography of India, Pakistan, and Ceylon.* London: Heinemann Educational Books.

Leaf, Murray J. (1998) *Pragmatism and Development: The Prospect for Pluralist Transformation in the Third World.* Westport, CT, and London: Bergin and Garvey.

———. (1984) *Song of Hope: The Green Revolution in a Punjab Village.* New Brunswick, NJ: Rutgers University Press.

Randhawa, M. S. (1980–1986) *A History of Agriculture in India.* 4 vols. New Delhi: Indian Council of Agricultural Research.

Singh, Baljit, and Shirdhar Misra. (1965) *A Study of Land Reforms in Uttar Pradesh.* Honolulu, HI: East-West Center Press.

AGRICULTURE—SOUTHEAST ASIA

Southeast Asia, as a whole, is richly endowed with natural resources. Expansive river valleys and deltas, generally rich soils, and a humid tropical climate ensure that the constraints to agricultural development have historically been more economic and institutional than environmental. Agriculture was the primary source of income, employer of labor, and contributor to export revenues in the precolonial and colonial eras (until about 1950). Agricultural output, value, and trade volumes have continued to grow in the past half century.

TABLE 2

Yields in South Asia and in developed countries in 1998					
(in kilograms per hectare)					
	Cereals, total	Wheat	Paddy	Sorghum	Pulses, total
South Asia	22,479	23,735	28,344	8,239	6,160
France	74,084	76,028	58,252	55,573	52,445
Italy	50,643	35,785	58,333	55,584	15,777
United States	56,799	29,034	63,542	42,262	18,489

SOURCE: Food and Agriculture Organization of the United Nations (2000).

However, the character of Southeast Asian agriculture has changed dramatically, and its relative importance, as measured by its shares of national income, employment, and trade, has diminished tremendously as other sectors have expanded. Whereas in 1965, agriculture accounted for between one-fourth and one-half of GDP in the market economies of Southeast Asia, by the late 1990s its share had fallen to 20 percent in the Philippines, 16 percent in Indonesia, and even less in Malaysia and Thailand, according to the World Bank. In today's Southeast Asia, the only countries in which agricultural activities still dominate national income are those, such as Laos, Cambodia, and Myanmar (Burma), that have failed to grow in other ways. Within the market economies of the region, with the exception of plantation sectors producing specialized export crops and remote, poor areas with little or no complementary infrastructure, other forms of economic activity now dominate the lives of most households.

Agriculture remains important in terms of land area, even though cropped area per person averages only 1/5 hectare, or about half an acre, and is growing at an average rate of less than 2 percent per year. Temporary crops, of which rice is the single largest by area, are the dominant agricultural land use in all countries except Malaysia. About a quarter of temporary crop area is irrigated.

Overview and History

Southeast Asian agriculture has always been centered on rice, the staple cereal and the major crop grown in the large, fertile, and densely populated river deltas. Two countries, Thailand and Vietnam, are among the world's top three exporters of this crop (along with the United States), but most other countries are net importers. In the poorer countries of the region, rice provides more than two-thirds of daily calorie intake, a figure that falls to about one-third in the region's wealthier countries. Because of its importance as a foodstuff and income source, rice has been, and remains, a crop with powerful cultural and political significance. Throughout the region, seasonal festivals are keyed to rice planting and harvesting dates. The success of the rice crop and the provision of adequate food for the population remain major responsibilities for Southeast Asian governments. Historically, this was reflected in religious rites requesting divine intercession to ensure a good crop; the turning of the first sod for rice planting is an annual ceremony still presided over by the monarchy in Thailand and Cambodia. In modern times, achieving and maintaining national self-sufficiency in rice has persisted as a policy goal, and even as a measure of the competence and credibility of political regimes.

While rice is grown primarily for domestic consumption, a number of crops of global economic and/or culinary importance are native to Southeast Asia, and in modern times the region has become a leading world producer of several others. Early trade between West and Northeast Asia and the "Spice Islands" located in what is now eastern Indonesia consisted of the exchange of silver, ceramics and other manufactures, and silk for nutmeg, mace, cloves, and pepper. The earliest European contacts with the region (and, indeed, virtually all the great early European voyages of discovery, by Vasco da Gama, Magellan, and others) were motivated by the trade in these highly prized and very expensive foodstuffs. So lucrative was the global spice trade that in the early seventeenth century the Dutch, seeking to establish monopoly control, traded Manhattan to Britain in exchange for the tiny nutmeg-growing island of Run in the Banda archipelago, Indonesia.

Trade with early Europeans also led to the introduction of some other plant species that have since become important in Southeast Asian diet and economy. These include maize, peanuts, and chilies (dubbed "red peppers" by Columbus), all of which are native to the Americas but are now grown widely in the region.

During the colonial period entrepreneurs introduced commercial cultivation of several export-oriented plantation crops including sugarcane, coffee, oil palm, rubber, and coconut. For the latter three crops, Southeast Asian supply now dominates the world market. Indonesia, Malaysia, and Thailand account for 81 percent of world oil palm production, and the region as a whole produces 74 percent of the world's natural rubber. More than one-half of world coconut production (54 percent) comes from Southeast Asia, one-third of it from Indonesia alone. In addition, regional coffee production has risen from 12 percent of the world total in 1990 to 20 percent in 2000, with Vietnam's share rising from 1.5 percent to 11.5 percent in just a decade. The spread of these plantation crops has been an important factor driving land colonization since the late nineteenth century, especially in Malaysia, southern Thailand, and the islands of the Indonesian archipelago.

The fortunes of other major Southeast Asian crops have fluctuated over time. Tropical fruits—bananas, mangoes, pineapples, and many others—and other horticultural crops have become significant export earners, especially for Thailand and the Philippines. Livestock raising, in the sense of large commercial herds, has never been a major feature of the Southeast Asian rural economy, although of course animals raised in small-scale and backyard operations provide a significant source of protein and rural income. Fiber crops such as abaca and kenaf have declined in importance, especially with the development of cheaper synthetic fibers.

Population Growth, Land Scarcity, and Food Policy 1950–1965

Whereas Southeast Asia was historically a region of food surplus and labor scarcity, rapid population growth beginning in the late nineteenth century soon began to apply pressure to the agricultural land base. In the two decades after World War II, a period during which the region's population grew very rapidly, the "land frontier" (the geographic limit of productive arable land) was reached or neared in several countries. With static technologies, domestic food production per capita began to decline, and the share of food in the value of imports to rise. Ultimately, pressure on land was alleviated by a combination of technical progress, investments in infrastructure, industrialization, and increasing openness to trade. However, the period from the 1950s to the 1970s was formative in Southeast Asian history, and agricultural development was at the center of the picture.

First, food security—and more specifically, national self-sufficiency—became a highly sensitive political goal and inspired a great deal of policy. Initially, the governments of the region played a dominant role, controlling trade, distribution, prices, and even (in some countries) production, through state agencies. These entities, most notably Bulog in Indonesia, developed into large and highly diversified commercial enterprises and, with liberal budgetary support, featured prominently in efforts to promote rural development. High levels of state intervention in food markets were apparent even in Thailand, whose natural resources make it one of the developing world's least import-dependent food producers. Second, in spite of these investments, increasingly intense competition for land spawned or encouraged rural-based antigovernment insurgencies, some Communist and others based on ethnic or cultural divisions. Some of these insurgencies degenerated into armed conflict and even civil war. Thus the increasing shortage of land spilled over into national politics with calls for land tenure reform as a measure to redress income inequity, poverty, and the spread of Communism.

Many regional governments attempted to overcome domestic food shortages and to alleviate civil unrest in the 1950s and 1960s by investing in irrigation, land development, and productivity-improving infrastructure. They also supported internal migration. In Malaysia and Indonesia, federal agencies cleared forests, built roads, houses, and schools, and sponsored resettlement in frontier areas by rural households from more densely populated regions. In the Philippines, the National Irrigation Authority (NIA) was formed to undertake major investments in the construction and operation of dams, canal systems, and drainage in agricultural lowlands. As with state grain-trading corporations, these investments seldom recouped even a fraction of their costs—indeed it is unlikely that they were ever intended to do so. As such, they constituted a means of redistributing income to rural areas through government expenditures.

Other economic policies were also deployed as tools of agricultural development. In the immediate postwar decades, all food-importing Southeast Asian countries made strenuous attempts to control prices received by farmers and paid by consumers. While the intent of such policies was to promote development, they often backfired. In exporting countries such as Burma and Thailand, export taxes and quotas diminished farmers' incentives to produce and export rice, and promoted smuggling. In Indonesia and the Philippines, the loss-making state trading agencies displaced private grain trade and storage. By the mid-1970s, the NIA and the National Grains Authority, the state rice-and-corn trading corporation, were the two most heavily indebted government corporations in the Philippines. In spite of this, frequent rice price "crises" (most notably in 1972, but as recently as August 1996 in the Philippines) testify to the incapacity of state agencies to maintain effective price controls and adequate domestic supplies during droughts and other periods of unexpectedly low domestic production.

Agricultural Technology and Resource Use since 1966

Massive public investments in agricultural development helped somewhat to mitigate, but not forestall, a crisis of agricultural development in Southeast Asia. Indonesia in particular was widely identified as a country where population growth was expected to outstrip productive capacity; one writer observed that as the result of population growth Java, the main island, was "asphyxiating for want of land" (Keyfitz 1965:503). In the early 1970s, a series of crop failures caused by drought and disease left the region critically short of rice. Food availability in the largest importing countries (Indonesia and the Philippines) was maintained only by massive imports and infusions of foreign aid, and most food prices rose sharply.

Workers harvest rice in a field near Mount Agung, the most sacred mountain in Bali, Indonesia. (LINDSAY HEBBERD/CORBIS)

In the long run, the solution to food security in the largest food importers came through technical progress. Research directed at producing high-yielding rice varieties, especially that carried out at the International Rice Research Institute, an international agricultural research center based in the Philippines, led to the release of new plant types with properties that greatly enhanced the productive capacity of irrigated rice land. The "modern varieties," first released in 1966, were stiff-strawed and of short stature, to increase light-use efficiency and reduce grain losses when plants bend (or "lodge") under the weight of their grain during monsoonal rain and winds. They were also rapid-maturing and non-photoperiod sensitive, meaning that plant growth and grain maturity occurred in a fixed number of days rather than in response to seasonal changes in day length and climate. These properties made it possible to grow rice at all times of year, and more than once per year on a single plot of land. Finally, the new rice varieties were highly responsive to nitrogen. The "Green Revolution" technological package of modern rice varieties, irrigation, and fertilizer proved capable of yielding double or even triple the quantity of grain produced per crop by traditional cultivars.

The technology of the Green Revolution spread quickly through Southeast Asia. In countries and subnational regions with adequate irrigation, and where fertilizer and other complementary inputs were available to farmers, rice yields increased rapidly. Higher yields and correspondingly greater demand for labor both helped transform these regions' agricultural economies. In the two decades following the release of the modern varieties, rice production in Southeast Asia's rapidly developing economies grew rapidly, while the total harvested area grew by much less, or even declined. In Indonesia, per-capita rice availability rose from 83 kilograms of milled rice in 1962–1964 to 140 kilograms in 1986–1988. Once the world's largest rice importer, Indonesia achieved the politically significant goal of self-sufficiency in 1985.

In many areas, the adoption of modern rice varieties was accompanied or shortly followed by mechanization. In most countries the adoption of mechanical technologies was motivated by the desire to reduce costs in economies experiencing rapid growth of labor demand. In Thailand, for example, the adoption rate of farm tractors accelerated rapidly as wages began rising in the late 1980s, reflecting the increasingly rapid transfer of labor to nonagricultural sectors.

Gains in rice production were generally achieved at some cost to other agricultural sectors. In most countries of the region nonfood crops, and even corn and other grains grown mainly for feed, received relatively low allocations of public spending and research effort. Until the 1980s, production and yields of these crops typically grew much less quickly than for rice. As agricultural diversification became the watchword toward the end of the decade, nonrice agricultural production and research began to receive a larger share of public resources and policy attention.

Modern agricultural development in Southeast Asia has been associated with tremendous stress on natural resource stocks and environmental quality. The expansion of cultivated area has been achieved at the expense of forest resources, and intensification (the shortening of fallow periods, and land-use changes from perennial to annual crops) has resulted in increased land degradation and soil erosion in many areas. In the 1970s, large areas of northeastern Thailand were deforested during an export boom in cassava, a crop that was sold to the European Union as an ingredient in animal feed. In the late 1990s, fires used to clear forests for agriculture (especially oil palm plantations) contributed to an annual "haze" that blanketed the Indonesian islands, Singapore, and large parts of the Malay Peninsula. The spread of irrigation has raised demands for water at the same time that deforestation has reduced the natural capacity of watersheds to store this precious resource during monsoon rains and to release it gradually throughout the year. Chemical residues and suspended solids from soil erosion have contributed to the degradation of drinking-water supplies, silting of dams and irrigation canals, and damage to estuarine and coastal ecosystems. Although "environment friendly" pest-management techniques such as Integrated Pest Management (IPM) are increasingly popular, chemical control remains the norm. Uncontrolled pesticide use and inappropriate application methods account for many ailments and deaths among farmers and their families. There is growing concern over biodiversity losses in areas where monoculture and plantation crops such as oil palm have experienced rapid growth.

All of these resource and environmental costs have become pressing policy concerns, and occasionally the subjects of heated public debate, in the region. The Green Revolution may have also brought some indirect environmental benefits, however. Productivity gains and increased rice supplies in irrigated lowlands, where they occurred, helped to alleviate pressures for forest conversion and agricultural intensification at the land frontier in uplands and watersheds. In this way, increases in lowland employment and incomes helped compensate upland farmers who, lacking irrigation and often facing difficulties obtaining credit and agricultural inputs, had generally derived little direct benefit from Green Revolution technologies.

Globalization, Trade-Policy Reform, and Agricultural Trends

In the final two decades of the twentieth century, trade and agricultural policy liberalization again helped transform the economic scene for Southeast Asian agriculture. Some policy reforms were undertaken as the result of regional trade agreements (such as AFTA, the ASEAN Free Trade Agreement), in response to bilateral trade opportunities, or as conditions for accession to international trading institutions such as the World Trade Organization (WTO). Others were forced upon countries by economic and political crises. Whatever their motivation, the effects of trade and price policy liberalization have been profound.

Liberalized rules governing domestic and international trade in cereals, and a lessening of the earlier emphasis on self-sufficiency in rice, have in general been associated with greater stability in food supply and food prices. At the household level, trade reforms have helped improve incomes, and not only through their direct effects on agriculture. Policy reforms that reduced discrimination against labor-intensive manufacturing sectors such as garments, consumer appliances, computer parts, and semiconductors have promoted employment growth and wages in nonagricultural sectors. Export crops such as pineapple, mango, and other fruits have benefited from easier access to foreign markets, and area planted has grown accordingly. These trends have reduced the reliance of Southeast Asian rural households on the vicissitudes of weather and agricultural prices.

Ian Coxhead

See also: **Forest Industry—Southeast Asia; Green Revolution—Southeast Asia; Rice and Rice Agriculture; Terrace Irrigation**

Further Reading
Coxhead, Ian. (2000) "The Consequences of Philippine Food Self-Sufficiency Policies for Economic Welfare and Agricultural Land Degradation." *World Development* 28, 1 (January): 111–128.

Coxhead, Ian, and Jiraporn Plangpraphan. (1999) "Economic Boom, Financial Bust, and the Decline of Thai Agriculture: Was Growth in the 1990s Too Fast?" *Chulalongkorn Journal of Economics* 11, 1 (January): 76–96.

David, Cristina C., and Keijiro Otsuka, eds. (1994) *Modern Rice Technology and Income Distribution in Asia.* Boulder, CO and London: Lynne Reinner Publishers; Los Baños, Philippines: International Rice Research Institute.

Dawe, David. (2001) "How Far Down the Path to Free Trade? The Importance of Rice Price Stabilization in Developing Asia." *Food Policy* 26: 163–175.

Food and Agriculture Organization of the United Nations (FAO). (2001)"FAO Statistical Databases." Retrieved 2 May 2001, from : http://apps.fao.org/.

International Rice Research Institute (IRRI). (1991) *World Rice Statistics 1990.* Los Baños, Philippines: IRRI.

———. (2001) "Rice Facts." Retrieved 2 May 2001, from: http://www.cgiar.org/irri/Facts.htm.

Keyfitz, Nathan. (1965) "Indonesian Population and the European Industrial Revolution." *Asian Survey* 10: 503–514.

Reid, Anthony. (1988–1993) *Southeast Asia in the Age of Commerce, 1450–1680.* New Haven, CT: Yale University Press.

Rola, Agnes C., and Prabhu L. Pingali. (1993) *Pesticides, Rice Productivity, and Farmers' Health: An Economic Assessment.* Los Baños, Philippines, and Washington, DC: International Rice Research Institute and World Resources Institute.

"A Taste for Adventure." (2000) *Economist* (19 December).

World Bank. (various years) *World Development Report.* Washington, DC: Oxford University Press for the World Bank.

World Resources Institute (WRI). (2000) *World Resources 1998–99.* Washington, DC: WRI.

Wheat fields along the road between Shahrud and Shahpasand, Iran. (ROGER WOOD/CORBIS)

AGRICULTURE—WEST ASIA

Although industry is advancing more rapidly than agriculture, the latter is of considerable importance in the economies of West Asian nations. Local farming produces much of the food consumed in the region and employs a large part of the workforce. The value added by agriculture to the gross national product (GNP), as well as the number of people employed in agriculture, has shown great variability. This variability is due to the economic and political crises experienced in the region and to agriculture's vulnerability to the vagaries of the weather. In Turkey, agriculture usually contributes about 16 percent of the GNP, in Iran about 20 percent, and in Iraq about 40 percent. In the 1990s, agriculture employed approximately 40 percent of the workforce in Turkey and about 30 percent in Iran and Iraq.

Natural Conditions

Natural conditions play an important role in agriculture in West Asia. Climate, for example, is especially significant for agriculture and varies greatly from one subregion of West Asia to another. Both the growing season and the range of crops are limited by the amount of precipitation, which, in general, is insufficient in West Asia. Average annual precipitation ranges from 5 centimeters in the Iranian deserts to more than 254 centimeters near the Black Sea in Turkey. Only about one-fourth of the land in Iran can be farmed because of a severe water shortage.

The most productive farmlands in Turkey are Thrace, the Mesopotamian lowlands, and the coastal

TABLE 1

Land use and irrigation in 1998

(in thousands of hectares)

Country	Total area	Land area	Arable land	Permanent crops	Permanent pasture (1994 data)	Forest and woodland (1994 data)	Other land (1994 data)	Irrigated land	As % of land area
Iran	163,319	162,200	16,837	1,966	44,000	11,400	87,841	7,562	4.66
Iraq	43,832	43,737	5,200	340	4,000	192	33,765	3,525	8.06
Turkey	77,482	76,963	24,438	2,530	12,378	20,199	16,615	4,200	5.46
Total	284,633	282,900	46,475	4,836	60,378	31,791	138,221	15,287	5.40

SOURCE: Data for this table from *European Marketing Data and Statistics 2001* (2001) and *International Marketing Data and Statistics 2001* (2001).

THE ANNUAL CYCLE

This extract of text from an ethnographic study of a farming village in central Turkey summarizes the annual farming cycle and also provides some insight into the Turk view of manual labor.

As soon as the spring comes, the men get busy. The oxen weakened by the long winter must be got into training work, and spring ploughing and sowing must be done. The ox-herds and shepherds take charge of the animals. The sheep are lambing and in each household a woman must be ready at midday to milk the ewes. Ploughing and sowing of spring wheat and barley is immediately followed by the ploughing of the year's fallow, which goes on perhaps into May, even until June, depending on individual circumstances. Meanwhile the vineyards must be dug over, and potatoes and other vegetables sown. Most of this later work is done by women.

In June, all grasses and weeds growing in odd places among the crops are cut for hay, again mostly by women. During late May and June the men are comparatively idle. In July the harvest begins, first with vetch and lentils, then with the main crops of rye and wheat. Threshing follows the reaping; reaping, threshing, and storing together last about two months of ceaseless activity for everyone; a whole household frequently works right through a moonlit night.

In September the pressure eases. As soon as rain falls on the hard baked ground—even before, if the rains are late—the men must plough again and sow their winter rye and wheat. By November there remains for the men only a visit to town to lay in supplies of coffee, paraffin, salt and so on, and perhaps cheap vegetables for the months of winter isolation, and then idleness again until the spring. He was overstating his case and, as someone commented, in two months harvesting they do four months' work; but the idea of having, like an English agricultural labourer, to work for wages day in and day out all year round was greeted with horror.

Source: Paul Sterling. (1965) *The Village Economy;* London: Charles Birchall & Sons, 47.

regions; in Iran, the most productive farmlands are the Caspian Sea coast and the fertile valleys in the northern and central parts of the Zagros Mountains; in Iraq, the southern plain, which begins near Samarra and extends southeast to the Arabian-Persian Gulf. More than half of West Asia's arable land is in Turkey, and half of the irrigated land in the region is in Iran. (See Table 1.)

Contemporary Status

On the basis of the methods used, the agrarian sector of West Asia must be defined as highly dualistic. Generally, in the most productive subregions, agriculture has a high level of mechanization, uses modern irrigation schemes, and has considerable export potential. In contrast, in the remote mountain subregions, the wooden plow and hoe are still the most

TABLE 2

Production of cereals in 1999

(in thousands of metric tons)

Country	Wheat	Barley	Maize	Rice	Total
Iran	8,687	1,919	941	2,300	13,847
Iraq	800	500	100	240	1,640
Turkey	18,000	9,000	2,400	317	29,717
Total	27,487	11,419	3,441	2,857	45,204

SOURCE: Data for this table from *European Marketing Data and Statistics 2001* (2001) and *International Marketing Data and Statistics 2001* (2001).

commonly used agricultural implements. In the Anatolian plateau and eastern Turkey, as well as in the northern plain in Iraq and in the central plateau of Iran, modern agricultural machinery is used on only a limited scale.

There are big differences among the nations in agricultural production. Turkey has a strong agricultural base. It is self-sufficient in cereals and exports much of its agrarian production. Turkish farms are predominantly family businesses with small landholdings. One of the main problems in Turkish agriculture is that the average size of farms is declining because of the inheritance custom of dividing land equally among sons. Large estates do still exist, mainly in the south, but about 70 percent of farmers cultivate holdings of just 1.5 hectares.

Iran must import much of its food. Before 1970, Iran was self-sufficient in agricultural production and exported many crops. However, contemporary Iran faces many problems because successive governments have neglected agriculture, the population has increased rapidly, and the productivity of farms is low.

In the 1990s, Iraq's agriculture experienced serious problems. Some of these problems were due to scarceness of agricultural inputs (that is, fertilizer and pesticides) caused by U.N. sanctions since 1990. Even with good rainfall, contemporary Iraq usually has low crop production, which is attributed to inadequate use of fertilizer and herbicides; poor land preparation due to lack of machinery; deteriorated farm and irrigation infrastructure; increased infestation by insects, pests, and weeds; and continuous use of land without crop rotation.

Agricultural Structure

In West Asia, farming and animal husbandry are equally developed. About 50 percent of the cropland is used to grow grains. Wheat is the chief grain, followed by barley and maize. Turkey is the main producer of cereals in the region. (See Table 2.) Central Anatolia accounts for nearly 40 percent of Turkish wheat production. However, this subregion often has long droughts that cause serious losses of crops.

West Asia is a major producer of sugar beets, potatoes, fruits, and vegetables. (See Table 3.) Large quantities of cotton are grown for both fiber and cottonseed oil. Turkey produces and exports large quantities of tobacco, which is grown along the Black and Aegean Seas, as well as eggplants, grapes and raisins, hazel-

TABLE 3

Production of selected crops in 1999

(in thousands of metric tons)

Country	Sugar beet	Tomatoes	Potatoes	Grapes	Apples
Iran	4,987	3,204	3,430	2,315	1,944
Iraq	8	800	380	290	80
Turkey	20,000	6,600	5,315	3,650	2,500
Total	24,995	10,604	9,125	6,255	4,524

SOURCE: Data for this table from *European Marketing Data and Statistics 2001* (2001) and *International Marketing Data and Statistics 2001* (2001).

TABLE 4

Circulation of livestock in 1999				
(in thousands)				
Country	Horses	Cattle	Sheep	Goats
Iran	250	8,047	53,900	25,757
Iraq	46	1,100	6,000	1,300
Turkey	391	11,185	30,238	8,376
Total	687	20,332	90,138	35,433

SOURCE: Data for this table from *European Marketing Data and Statistics 2001* (2001) and *International Marketing Data and Statistics 2001* (2001).

A woman carrying a load on her head in the market in Ahmadabad in c. 1982. (ADAM WOOLFITT/CORBIS)

nuts, melons, and oranges. Iran exports dried fruits and nuts.

The mainstays of West Asia's stockbreeding are sheep and goats. (See Table 4.) Nomadic stockbreeding still exists in some areas, especially in western and southwestern Iran. Turkey raises half of the world's Angora goats. Wool is Turkey's most valuable livestock product. Iran is among the world's largest exporters of karakul lamb. Turkey and Iran supply the world with large quantities of hides and skins.

Turkey is the main producer and exporter of agricultural products in West Asia. About half of Turkish agricultural exports are shipped to the European Union. Other main markets include the Middle East and North Africa, which absorb about half the exports of fruits and vegetables and virtually all the exports of livestock and meat.

Dimitar L. Dimitrov

Further Reading

Ayalon, Ami, ed. (1996) *Middle East Contemporary Survey 17: 1993.* Boulder, CO: Westview Press.
Bates, Daniel, and Amal Rassam. (1983) *Peoples and Cultures of the Middle East.* Englewood Cliffs, NJ: Prentice Hall.
European Marketing Data and Statistics 2001. (2001) London: Euromonitor Plc.
International Marketing Data and Statistics 2001. (2001) London: Euromonitor Plc.
Issawi, Charles. (1995) *Selected Essays.* Princeton, NJ: Markus Wiener Publishing.

AHMADABAD (2001 est. pop. 3.5 million). Ahmadabad, the gateway to Gujarat state in western India and its principal city, sprawls on the Sabarmati River about 450 kilometers (280 miles) north of Bombay. It is one of the busiest industrial centers in India, with cotton milling predominant. Ahmadabad was founded in 1411 by the Muslim ruler Sultan Ahmad Shah; it thrived in the fifteenth and sixteenth centuries under the early Mughal kings and prospered again since the British annexation in 1818. Of particular interest are compact housing clusters of families linked by caste, profession, or religion, dating to 1714.

Many monuments of Hindu, Muslim, and Jain architecture in the walled city testify to its past glory and present prosperity. Kankaria Lake, built in 1451, offers promenades, boating, an aquarium, and a museum designed by Charles-Édouard Jeanneret (called Le Corbusier; 1887–1965). The Sidi Bashir Mosque features the mysterious "shaking minarets." From the Satyagraha Ashram, in 1930, Mohandas K. Gandhi (called Mahatma; 1869–1948) began his march to the sea to protest the British salt tax. A memorial center and sound-and-light show highlight his life and the Indian Freedom Movement.

C. Roger Davis

Further Reading
Gillion, Kenneth L. (1968) *Ahmedabad: A Study in Indian Urban History.* Berkeley and Los Angeles: University of California Press.
Patel, B. B. (1989) *Workers of Closed Textile Mills: Patterns and Problems of Their Absorption in a Metropolitan Labour Market.* Columbia, MO: South Asia Books.
Mehta, Meera, and Dinesh Mehta. (1990) *Metropolitan Housing Market: A Study of Ahmedabad.* Newbury Park, CA: Sage.

AI QAP *Ai Qap* was a Kazakh journal published in Troitsk by Energiia Press from January 1911 until September 1915. Starting as a monthly, by the end of 1912 it appeared twice a month until it ceased publication. Edited by Mukhammedzhan Seralin, *Ai Qap* was the first successful independent Kazakh-language periodical published before World War I. It became a vital forum in which Kazakh intellectuals could collectively articulate their growing social concerns and discuss the various issues confronting the Kazakh economy, culture, language, and national future. In addition, the journal devoted attention to a myriad of other subjects. Education and land redistribution dominated, but other issues graced its pages, including Russia's role in the war. Many notable Kazakhs published articles in *Ai Qap*, including Alikhan Bokeikhanov, Akhmet Baitursynov, Mirzhaqyp Dulatov, Sultanmakhmut Toraighyrov, and Saken (Sadvakos) Seifullin. The journal also published translated works by Lermontov, Krylov, Tolstoy, and Pushkin. In its four-and-a-half-year existence *Ai Qap* published a total of eighty-eight issues. Never sufficiently capitalized, the journal finally succumbed to the material and economic pressures brought on by World War I. *Ai Qap*'s success was clearly due to Seralin, who gathered reformists and nationalists together, as well as a host of diverse scholars, educators, politicians, and writers.

Steven Sabol

Further Reading
Bennigsen, Alexandre, and Chantal Lemercier-Quelquejay. (1964) *Le Presse et le Mouvement National chez les Musulmans de Russie Avant 1920.* Paris: Mouton & Co.
Subkhanberdina, Ushkultai. (1961) *Aiqap betindegi maqalalar men khat-khabarlar* (An Index of Articles and News Stories). Almaty, Kazakhstan: Kazak Memleket Baspasy.
Subkhanberdina, Ushkultai, and S. Dautova, eds. (1995) *Aiqap.* Almaty, Kazakhstan: Kazak Enstiklopediiasy.

AICHI (2002 est. pop. 7.1 million). Aichi Prefecture is situated in the central region of Japan's largest island, Honshu. A leading industrial area, it occupies an area of 5,139 square kilometers. Its primary geographical features are the Mikawa Highland in the east and the Nobi Plain in the west, with the Kisogawa and the Yahagigawa as the main rivers. Aichi is bordered by the Pacific Ocean and by Mie, Gifu, Nagano, and Shizuoka Prefectures.

The prefectural capital is Nagoya, which grew around the castle erected in 1614 by Tokugawa Ieyasu (1542–1616), the first of the Tokugawa shoguns; it was controlled by his descendants until the 1868 Meiji Restoration. Rebuilt following bombing damage sustained in World War II, Nagoya at the dawn of the twenty-first century is Japan's third-largest city. It is a leading commercial and industrial center with a busy port. It is home to Nagoya University and to Atsuta, the imperial shrine second in importance only to Ise. The prefecture's other important cities are Toyohashi, Toyota, Ichinomiya, and Okazaki.

During Japan's medieval period (1185–1573), the prefecture was divided into Mikawa and Owari Provinces. Beginning in 1573 three warlords from this region, Oda Nobunaga (1534–1582), Toyotomi Hideyoshi (1536–1598), and Tokugawa Ieyasu, completed the unification of Japan. In 1872, following the Meiji Restoration, the prefecture assumed its present name and borders.

During the twentieth century, the prefecture developed into an important industrial area, anchoring the Chukyo Industrial Zone (the region between Tokyo and Kyoto) and leading all other prefectures in industrial production. The main industries are steel, chemicals, automobiles, ceramics, and textiles. Agricultural products include rice, vegetables, and chickens. Lumber processing also is a major economic activity.

E. L. S. Weber

Further Reading
"Aichi Prefecture." (1993) *Japan: An Illustrated Encyclopedia.* Tokyo: Kodansha Ltd.

AIDS Asia contains 60 percent of the world's population and almost 20 percent of the adults with HIV infections—some 6 million of the estimated 34.4 million worldwide at the end of the twentieth century. But the epidemic is relatively new to the region. It was first detected in the early to mid-1980s, the earliest cases of infection reflecting sexual contacts with infected persons from outside the region. By 2000, there were an estimated 6 million infections; national experiences were diverse as to sources, levels, and prospects.

Estimated HIV prevalences ranged from near zero in the Democratic People's Republic of (North) Korea to one per several thousand in most countries and as high as 2–3 percent in Cambodia, Myanmar (Burma), Thailand, and some states of India.

Today, all the governments of the region have HIV/AIDS task forces and action plans to deal with the threat, though these commitments are relatively recent and the translation into real programs remains variable. In Thailand, action by both the Thai government and the private sector has been aggressive and notably effective since 1987. Other governments generally have expended less in resources and have less to show for their efforts.

Drivers of the Asian Epidemic

Across much of the region, the spread of HIV is driven by sex work and associated sexual networking and by patterns of use of injected drugs. There are external, visitor-driven, and internal dimensions to each of these. The initial patterns were focal epidemics of some intensity involving men having sex with men (MSM) and intravenous drug users (IDU). Rates of infection due to MSM have since declined, while rates of infection due to IDU have not. Whether in each national population there is breakout to the general population is mainly a function of patterns of heterosexual sex in sexual networks. The pattern and magnitude of the heterosexual epidemic in each society reflect the social structures and behaviors characteristic of each, particularly the prevalence of men having multiple partners, including sex workers.

Demographic and Social Impacts

In Eastern and Southern Africa, AIDS is among the top ten causes of death, and AIDS deaths have substantially diminished the rate of population growth. The demographic impacts are much weaker thus far in Asia, though population growth rates have already been reduced slightly in Myanmar, Cambodia, and Thailand, and it is estimated that those three countries have each lost three years of life expectancy. One key to understanding the social impact is the fact that HIV infection disproportionately strikes the adult population rather than children or elderly people, resulting in the loss of economically productive members of households and of society as a whole. The repercussion is a dramatic loss of quality of life or even of life chances among infants and children, due to orphanhood and diminished household incomes. A full accounting of impacts must consider lost productivity and economic progress, the private (that is, family) and

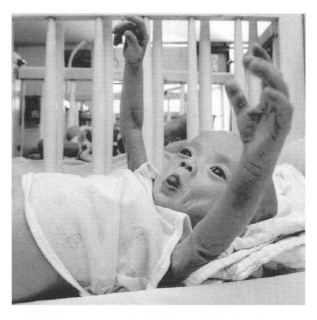

In Asia, many women and children are HIV-infected. Here, a one-year-old HIV-infected girl plays in her bed at Phaya Thai Baby's Home, a facility for HIV-infected children in Bangkok, Thailand. (AFP/CORBIS)

public costs of medicines and care, and the social costs of weakened families and other institutions.

Prospects for Behavior Change and Control

Projections of the spread of HIV infections and cases of AIDS vary dramatically by country and with what is assumed about the national epidemic patterns. The future of HIV in Asia hinges on what occurs in certain critical countries, among them China, India, Thailand, Myanmar, and Cambodia. The Monitoring the AIDS Pandemic or MAP network lists five countries in which HIV prevalence is increasing and another ten in which it is slowly increasing. This leaves only two countries in decline (Australia and New Zealand), and one, Thailand, which is tending to stabilize.

The case of Thailand is illuminating. In the mid-1980s, there was worrying evidence from IDU data and data on sex work, and by 1993 the HIV rate among army recruits (virtually a representative sample of young adult males) was at 4 percent (much higher in the north, due both to the greater poverty there as well as the prevailing sexual behaviors, which encourage the spread of infection). Infection levels then peaked and have been declining as a direct consequence of imaginative programs. Some of these have brought messages about the dangers of infection and the protection afforded by condoms directly into the brothels. Levels of condom use in brothels have risen dramatically. Similarly, HIV prevalence among pregnant women peaked at about 2 percent in 1995. Whether the same positive experience can be shared by other Asian countries depends on their government and private-sector efforts and policies.

Myanmar, Cambodia, and Vietnam are showing the patterns and levels once witnessed in Thailand. Their epidemics have thus far been driven by intravenous drug use and sex work, though Cambodia has high infection levels among pregnant women as well. These countries illustrate the potential for HIV to spread quickly. In China, Malaysia, and Nepal, HIV has spread among IDU populations but apparently not yet outside those groups. Cambodia has begun to show hopeful signs. Government and nongovernmental institutions are in place, and campaigns are underway. Condom use in brothels rose between 1997 and 1999, as did HIV prevalence among young sex workers.

China is viewed as a potential focus of rapid epidemic spread. There is now in place an extensive sentinel or monitoring system, by 1999 covering nearly a hundred sites in thirty provinces and focused on female sex workers, intravenous drug users, long-distance truck drivers, blood donors, and antenatal women. Recent returns from this system indicate rising infection rates for IDU and female sex workers. Overall, reported sexually transmitted infections reached 836 thousand in 1999. The government estimates that there are 3 million drug users in China and that needle sharing is common. There are a similar number of sex workers, half of whom report never using condoms. The working estimates of HIV infections in China were 400,000 at the end of 1998, 600,000 in 2000, and probably over 1 million by late 2001. There is enormous potential for pandemic and massive numbers of infections.

India displays a diverse set of experiences across its states and metropolitan areas, from very low HIV prevalences to as high as 2 percent of adults in the state of Tamil Nadu and the city of Mumbai (Bombay), from epidemics driven by heterosexual transmission (Tamil Nadu, Maharashtra) to epidemics driven by intravenous drug users (Maniput). A surveillance system was put in place only recently, and the 1999 estimate of 3.5 million HIV infections certainly will be revised as new data are examined.

Considering the diversity of national patterns and mixture of experiences for subgroups within countries, overall projections are difficult. The United Nations' AIDS coordinating agency or UNAIDS produces such projections, and these were incorporated into the United Nations' 1998 round of population projections. Among the twenty-nine largest countries with

HIV prevalences of 2 percent or greater, three are in Asia: India, Thailand, and Cambodia.

Observations

Unlike many other diseases, with HIV/AIDS, behavioral knowledge and behavioral change are intimately connected. The HIV/AIDS epidemic is behaviorally driven and linked to intimate areas of personal life. The knowledge-gathering needed to deal with HIV/AIDS is akin to an X ray of the social corpus, with the HIV virus taking the role of radioisotopes, revealing aspects not usually seen. There is revealing new knowledge of marriage, family, and sexual systems, and even national polities are being placed under a scrutiny that exposes political interests and underlying values.

The attention now being given throughout Asia to heretofore off-limits behavior is generating pressure for change. Before the HIV/AIDS pandemic has become history, it is likely that important social changes will occur or will be accelerated because of it: in gender relations (such as wives' changed expectations of their husbands, and more openness within unions about marital and sexual relationships), in family-based care and in the role of governments and private agencies in supplementing it, in the relationships between parents and their young adult children, in the role of public or private reproductive health services to young unmarried people, and in the status of marginalized population groups such as sex workers and drug users.

Peter Xenos

Further Reading

Brown, Tim, Roy Chan, Doris Mugrditchian, Brian Mulhall, Rabin Sarda, and Werasit Sittitrai. (1998) *Sexually Transmitted Diseases in Asia and the Pacific.* Armidale, Australia: Venereology Publishing.

MAP. (2000) "Monitoring the AIDS Pandemic: The Status and Trends of the HIV/AIDS Epidemics in the World: Provisional Report, July 5–7, 2000." Durban, South Africa: MAP. Retrieved 31 January 2002, from: http://www.unaids.org/hivaidsinfo/statistics/MAP.

———. (2001) "Monitoring the AIDS Pandemic: The Status and Trends of the HIV/AIDS/STI Epidemics in Asia and the Pacific, 2001." Melbourne, Australia: MAP. Retrieved 31 January 2002, from: http://www.unaids.org/hivaidsinfo/statistics/MAP.

UNAIDS. (2001) "AIDS Epidemic Update." Retrieved 30 January 2002, from: http://www.unaids.org/epidemic_update/report_dec01/index.html.

World Heath Organization. (2001) "HIV/AIDS in Asia and the Pacific Region." New Delhi: Regional Office for South-East Asia; Manila: Regional Office for the West-

ern Pacific. Retrieved 31 January 2002, from: http://www
.wpro.who.int/pdf/sti/aids2001/complete.pdf.

AIKIDO Aikido is a Japanese martial art that takes
several different modern forms. The sport was
founded by Ueshiba Morihei (1883–1969) who in the
1920s and 1930s combined techniques from Daito-ryu
jujutsu with ancient Japanese philosophical beliefs
to create a new martial art form that stressed defense
and the use of one's opponent's strength and aggression. In general, aikido is less aggressive than other
martial arts and is characterized by grabbing, joint-
twisting, balance-breaking, and pinning. The popularity of aikido outside Japan is due largely to the work
of Ueshiba's students and the Aiki-kai association he
founded. Modern forms of aikido are associated with
particular schools and associations, including the Japan
Aikido Association (Tomiki Aikido), Yoshin-kan, Ki
no Kenkyu-kai (Ki Society), and Yosei-kan. Each
school promotes somewhat different techniques and
philosophy and they also differ in their support of
competitions as opposed to training sessions for personal growth. Because of the emphases on training and
the performance of choreographed routines called
kata, aikido is popular as a form of exercise with
women and the elderly.

Fumiaki Shishida

Further Reading
Pranin, Stanley. (1991) *The Aiki News Encyclopedia of Aikido.*
Tokyo: Aiki News.
Shishida, Fumiaki, and Tetsuro Nariyama. (1985) *Aikido
Kyoshitsu (Aikido Course).* Tokyo: Taishukan Shoten.

AIMAG The Mongolian People's Republic is divided into eighteen *aimag*s, or provinces—Bayan Olgii,
Hovd, Uvs, Zavhan, Gov'altay, Bayanhongor, Arhangai,
Bulgan, Hovsgol, Selenge, Tov, Ovorhangai, Dundgov', Omnogov', Dornogov', Hentii, Suhbaatar, and
Dornod. In 1994, the regions around three prominent
cities (Erdenet, Darhan, and Choir) were also declared
aimags with largely urban populations (respectively,
Orhon Aimag, 2000 population 72,000; Darhan-Uul,
2000 population 83,000; Gobi-sumber, 2000 population 12,000). Mongolia's national capital, Ulaanbaatar,
is its own administrative unit with a population of
760,000.

The Eastern Provinces
Mongolia's eastern provinces of Dornod, Suhbaatar, and Hentii are dominated by grassy steppe, a

geography that suits the region's major economy—
sheep, cattle, and horse breeding. Although several minority peoples make these provinces their home, the
population consists primarily of the Khalkha majority.
Dornod is the farthest east of Mongolia's provinces
(2000 population 75,000, area 123,000 square kilometers), famous for free-ranging herds of antelope that
often number in the thousands. The province's Hal-
hyn Gol region became noteworthy in 1939 when
Mongolian troops and the assisting Soviet Red Army
routed a large force of invading Japanese soldiers. Suhbaatar Aimag (2000 population 65,000, area 82,000
square kilometers) in the southeast was named after
Damdiny Suhbaatar, the founder of the Mongolian
People's Republic and one of the region's native sons.
The Dariganga volcanic plateau, a region with dozens
of extinct volcanoes, interrupts the province's undu-
lating plains. Hentii Aimag (2000 population 71,000,
area 82,000 square kilometers) in northeast Mongolia
is considered by many to be the native home of
Genghis Khan. Mountains of the Hentii range cover
the province's northern region and gradually slope
into a hilly steppe in the south. Mineral springs are
found throughout the province.

The Gobi Provinces
The three Gobi provinces of Dornogov', Omnogov', and Dundgov' have some of the smallest population densities in Mongolia and are almost exclusively
populated by the Khalkha ethnic majority. Mining and
camel or sheep breeding contribute most to these regions' economies. Dornogov' (2000 population
51,000, area 110,000 square kilometers) is in the
southeastern part of the country, dominated by rolling
plains and semidesert. An ancient caravan route from
Russia to China, which has now been subsumed by the
Trans-Mongolian Railroad, once passed through this
area. Fluorite mining has made important contributions to the region's economy. Omnogov' (2000 population 47,000, area 165,000 square kilometers)
occupies the extreme south of the country and is the
aimag with both the largest area and the smallest population. The great massifs of the eastern Gov'altay
range and the Gobi Tian Shan dominate the province.
The wealth of prehistoric fossils in this region makes
it a popular spot for paleontological research. Directly
north of the other two Gobi provinces, Dundgov'
(2000 population 52,000, 78,000 square kilometers)
consists more of rich grassy steppes than of desert.

The Central Provinces
The five central provinces of Tov, Selenge, Bulgan, Ovorhangai, and Arhangai occupy a region of

well-watered mountains and rich, fertile valleys. Drawing water from two mountain ranges, this lush, arable region supports a large population, the majority being Khalkha speakers. Tov Aimag (2000 population 99,000, area 81,000 square kilometers) is the site of Mongolia's capital, Ulaanbaatar. The province's economy reflects its unique location, with most activity geared towards supplying the capital city and servicing the Trans-Mongolian railway. Directly north of Tov Aimag, Selenge Aimag (2000 population 100,000, area 65,000 square kilometers) occupies the fertile basin of the Selenge River and serves as Mongolia's breadbasket. In 1990, 40 percent of the country's cereal crop production came from this region alone. The region also served as the cradle of the Mongolian People's Revolution when Damdiny Suhbaatar recruited the first units of volunteer militias here in the early twentieth century. The province's Amarbaysgalant monastery stands as one of the few prominent monasteries that the revolution left untouched. To the west of Selenge, Bulgan Aimag (2000 population 62,000, area 49,000 square kilometers) occupies a portion of the Selenge River basin and the northern Hentii Mountains. The 70 percent of land that is not covered by forest is used for farming and livestock breeding. West of Bulgan, Arhangai (2000 population 97,000, area 55,000 square kilometers) lies in the basins of the Selenge River's tributaries and rises to the high parts of the Hangay highlands. The province is famous for the state-protected Terhiin Tsagaan Lake, formed when volcanic lava dammed up the Sumangiin Gol River. Livestock breeding is the primary economic activity, with yak and yak hybrid comprising 40 percent of the province's herds. To the south of Arhangai, Ovorhangai (2000 population 91,000, area 64,000 square kilometers) lies between the fertile regions of the north and the semideserts of the Gobi. The province attracts many with its natural wonders, most notably its 24-meter-high waterfall, Ulaan Tsutgalan. It is also the site of Karakorum, the ancient Mongolian capital, and one of Mongolia's largest Buddhist monasteries, Erdene Zuu. Livestock breeding concentrates on sheep and horses.

The Northwestern Provinces

The three northwestern provinces of Hovsgol, Uvs, and Zavkhan cover a rugged mountainous region. Hovsgol Aimag (2000 population 119,000, area 102,000 square kilometers) is named after the enormous freshwater lake for which the province is famous. The forested mountains that surround the lake have led some to call Hovsgol Aimag "Mongolia's Switzerland." Most livestock breeding focuses on cattle, yaks, and yak hybrids. Near Lake Hovsgol, the Tsataan ethnic group

has become famous for its reindeer herding. West of Hovsgol, Zavhan (2000 population 90,000, area 82,000 square kilometers) is the home of Otgon Tenger, the highest peak of the Hangay Mountains and a sacred spot for many Mongolians. From the high peaks of the Hangay range the province descends westward into semidesert and desert expanses. The intermediate region is suited to sheep breeding, and the province boasts the largest sheep population in the country. Farther west, Uvs (2000 population 90,000, area 84,000 square kilometers) has a majority of Dorvod speakers. The province's many rivers and lakes are frequented by several species of waterfowl, including the rare pink pelican. Besides being a major supplier of coal fuel to the country, the province specializes in sheep, cattle, and horse breeding.

The Southwestern Provinces

The four southwestern provinces of Bayanhongor, Gov'altay, Hovd, and Bayan-Olgii cover arid regions of high mountains and wide deserts. Despite their barren appearance, they are home to rare Mongolian wildlife—the wild camel, Gobi bear, and steppe antelope. Bayanhongor (2000 population 85,000, area 116,000 square kilometers) descends from the South Hangay plateau to the Gobi Desert. The province is famous for its mineral springs, and specializes in goat breeding. Gov'altay (2000 population 87,000, 142,000 square kilometers) is at the easternmost tail of the Altay mountain range. The province's great Gobi Reserve is Mongolia's largest protected area and a habitat for rare Mongolian wildlife—the mountain sheep, wild goat, snow leopard, steppe antelope, and reed boar. West of Gov'altay, the Altay Mountains of Hovd (2000 population 64,000, area 76,000 square kilometers) are home to a wide variety of ethnic groups. The farthest west of Mongolia's provinces, Bayan Olgii (2000 population 91,000, area 46,000 square kilometers) is unique among the Mongolian *aimag*s in that the majority of its inhabitants are a non-Mongolian speaking ethnic group—the Kazakhs. Much of the province's official and cultural business takes place in Kazakh.

Daniel Hruschka

Further Reading

Bawden, Charles R. (1968) *The Modern History of Mongolia.* London: Weidenfeld & Nicolson.

Mongolian People's Republic Academy of Sciences. (1990) *Information Mongolia.* Oxford: Pergamon Press.

AINU   In the Ainu language the word *ainu* means "human being." For the rest of the world, the word

A SHIP'S CAPTAIN REFLECTS ON THE AINU

In *A Voyage of Discovery to the North Pacific Ocean*, William R. Broughton, captain of the HMS *Providence*, presented his analysis of the Ainu in the late eighteenth century:

This people appear to have intelligence. Their beards are long, black, and strong. They have brown skin and their heads are shaved with the exception of a tusk of hair the size of two fingers, which rests at the front of the head. They put their hands together below their heads as a greeting. They are dressed in bear skins and armed with bow and arrow. . . . The people seem to have no religion. They eat like barbarians, without any sort of ceremony. . . . They seem to have no government, no writing or books, and no one seems able to read or write.

Source: W. R. Broughton. (1804) *A Voyage of Discovery to the North Pacific Ocean* 1804, 89ff.

designates the small indigenous population that lives in the northern part of Japan. Although Japan has several minority groups (Burakumin, Koreans, Chinese), only the Ainu are both ethnically distinct from the Japanese and have lived in the Japanese islands from long before written history.

In prehistoric times, the Ainu could be found on the islands of Honshu, Hokkaido, Sakhalin, and the Kurile Archipelago; in modern times, they mainly inhabit Hokkaido. Their number at present is estimated to be around twenty-five thousand, but after decades of intermarriage with the Japanese it is now rare to encounter a person purely of Ainu blood. The population estimate thus represents those people who think of themselves as being both Ainu and Japanese.

Origins

The origins of the Ainu people and their language are unknown. Many different theories have been proposed, but none has managed to gain general acceptance among scholars. For a long time, Western scholars believed that the Ainu were of Caucasian descent, which greatly stimulated research and resulted in a large body of literature on all aspects of Ainu culture. The theory was never widely accepted by Japanese scholars and has been thoroughly discredited by newer research. A consensus gradually emerged that the ethnic origins of the Ainu must be sought in Japan's prehistoric Jomon culture (10,000–300 BCE).

The Ainu language has no writing system. Traditions, beliefs, and tales about the past were orally transmitted through epics, songs, and stories memorized and told by the old to the young. There were originally three distinct dialects of Ainu—Sakhalin, Kurile, and Hokkaido. However, there is no longer anyone who speaks the Ainu language as a mother tongue.

The traditional lifestyle of the Ainu was based on hunting, fishing, and gathering edible plants. Society centered on villages (*kotan*) of five to twenty families under the leadership of a male chief (*otona*). Villages were usually placed near a river to ensure access to water and fish. Deer and fox were hunted near the villages, and brown bear were hunted in the mountains—all with bow and arrow.

Customs

The Ainu are famous for their skilled woodwork. Formerly, the products were bowls and utensils, decorated wooden prayer sticks, and whittled sticks offered to the gods. In modern times, most woodcraft is aimed at the tourist trade. Clothes were woven from the shredded bark of the elm tree and decorated with dyed patterns or cotton appliqué. Men and women wore coat-like dresses fastened with a belt. Accessories such as headgear, earrings, and necklaces were used for festive occasions. Shoes were made from fish skin.

A NINETEENTH-CENTURY VIEW
OF THE AINU PEOPLE

Isabella Bird, an adventurous traveler to Japan in the late 1800s, recorded her impressions of the Ainu in *Unbeaten Tracks in Japan*:

They have no history, their traditions are scarcely worth the name, they claim descent from a dog, their houses and persons swarm with vermin, they are sunk in the grossest ignorance, they have no letters, or any numbers above a thousand, they are clothed in the bark of trees and the untanned skins of beasts, they worship the bear, the sun, moon, fire, water, and I know not what, they are uncivilisable and altogether irreclaimable savages, yet they are attractive, and in some ways fascinating, and I hope I shall never forget the music of their low sweet voices, the soft light of their mild brown eyes and the wonderful sweetness of their smile (Bird 1881: 75).

Source: Isabella Bird. (1881) *Unbeaten Tracks in Japan: An Account of Travels in the Interior Including Visits to the Aborigines of the Yezo and the Shrines of Nikko and Ise.* London: Murray.

Male and female lineages were kept separate. The men's lineage was shown by their totem animal *(itokpa)* on various utensils, whereas the women's lineage in the form of patterns on a belt *(upsor)* was worn under the clothes. Women also wore tattoos around the mouth and on their forearms and hands. These were produced by making small incisions with sharp stones and rubbing soot into the open wounds.

The Ainu gods are called *kamuy* and are believed to be present as spirits everywhere in nature, as well as in a spirit world of their own. Everything in the human world is seen as a visitor from the spirit world. The most important *kamuy* was the brown bear. Every year, all over Hokkaido, bear cubs were caught and kept in cages in villages. When a cub reached young adulthood, a ceremony was held to send its spirit back to its ancestors in the spirit world. By providing an elaborate ceremony and honoring the bear, it was hoped that it would speak well of human beings to the other bear spirits. If this happened, many bear spirits would venture into the land of the humans, ensuring a steady supply of bears for hunting. After the bear was ceremoniously killed, its meat was eaten by the villagers and its head was placed on an altar outside the chief's house.

The Ainu and the Japanese

The Japanese knew of the Ainu as far back as the tenth century, when Ainu were still present on the main island of Honshu. By the fifteenth century the Japanese had managed to establish several strongholds in southern Hokkaido from which they traded metal and rice to the Ainu for fur, fish, and other natural products. By the beginning of the Edo period (1600/1603–1868), Matsumae, a Japanese warrior clan, gained authority over the Japanese-dominated parts of the island and established a trade monopoly. Trade came to be conducted through Japanese merchants who traveled to specified trading posts on the island under the control of the Matsumae clan. Deceiving the Ainu in trade transactions was common, and a number of Ainu were forced into slave-like labor for the Japanese. This situation gave rise to several Ainu rebellions, but eventually the Ainu succumbed to the Japanese.

After the Meiji Restoration in 1868, the Ainu came to be considered as Japanese citizens and were forced to adopt Japanese names. They were, however, still considered second-class citizens and were greatly disadvantaged in terms of education, health, and employment. The Meiji government started a large-scale colonization of Hokkaido that led to mass immigration from other parts of Japan, and eventually the Ainu were reduced to only a small percentage of the total population on Hokkaido. Deprived of their lifestyle as hunters and fishermen, they quickly sank into poverty and apathy. To ameliorate this situation, the Hokkaido

Former Aborigines Protection Act was enacted in 1899, granting education and small plots of land to the Ainu.

In the late twentieth century, a new pride in being Ainu emerged. Cultural events, language classes, and study groups attempted to revive the Ainu culture. Bowing to pressure from Ainu organizations that saw the protection law as discriminatory, in 1997 the government repealed the Protection Act and replaced it with a new law to promote Ainu culture and facilitate public understanding of Ainu tradition.

Kirsten Refsing

Further Reading

Fitzhugh, William, and Chisato Dubreil, eds. (1999) *Ainu, Spirit of a Northern People*. Washington, DC: Arctic Studies Center, National Museum of Natural History in association with University of Washington Press.

Kayano Shigeru. (1994) *Our Land Was a Forest*. Boulder, CO: Westview Press.

Kreiner, Josef, ed. (1993) *European Images of Ainu and Ainu Studies in Europe*. Munich, Germany: Iudicium Verlag.

Refsing, Kirsten. (1986) *The Ainu Language*. Aarhus, Denmark: Aarhus University Press.

Refsing, Kirsten. (1996–2000) *The Ainu Library*. 20 vols. Richmond, U.K.: Curzon Press.

Siddle, Richard. (1996) *Race, Resistance and the Ainu of Japan*. New York: Routledge.

AIR POLLUTION   Throughout Asia air pollution is a significant threat to human health and the environment. Industrial emissions from fossil fuel use constitute the bulk of the pollutants released into the atmosphere, but forest fires and the combustion of biomass fuels also add pollutants. Combating air pollution is difficult because it requires action on many different levels, from upgrading household stoves to reducing regional emissions to battling global climate change internationally. Scientists warn that, if current trends continue, by 2025 three times as many people in Asia will suffer poor health due to air pollution as did in 1990.

Industrial Pollution

Industrial development in the past century was powered largely by fossil fuels like coal, oil, and natural gas. Used to generate electricity, drive industrial processes, and send automobiles down the road, fossil fuels release sulfur dioxides, nitrogen oxides, and tiny particulates of partially combusted fuel into the atmosphere. Even the cleanest fossil fuels produce carbon dioxide emissions, formed when carbon in the fuel combines with atmospheric oxygen. Industrial air pollution is a global problem but is nowhere more serious than in Asia, where fossil fuel consumption has risen by a factor of 20 in the past half-century.

The local effects of air pollution have been most severe in cities undergoing rapid industrialization and population growth. Of the fifteen cities worldwide suffering from the worst concentrations of air pollutants, twelve are in the Asia-Pacific region. Beijing, Chongqing, and other Chinese cities have the highest concentrations of sulfur dioxide, joined by Jakarta, Manila, and Seoul on the list of those with high levels of particulate matter. High levels of air pollution have meant increased rates of bronchitis, asthma, lung cancer, and infant mortality. A World Bank study attributes some 67,200 premature deaths and over a half-million cases of chronic bronchitis in Asia to urban air pollution.

Industrial air pollution also takes a toll on the environment. The area around Guilin, China, famous for its mountain scenery, has been especially hard hit. Not only has pollution from Guilin's factories obscured the mountain in haze, but the region's limestone geological formations are being eroded by the acidic sulfur dioxide. Acid rain, another by-product of atmospheric sulfur dioxide, damages forests and aquatic life far from the source of the pollution. While Japan has made significant progress in reducing its own air pollution, it now contends with acid rain originating in China and Korea. Japan, southern China, mountainous areas of Southeast Asia, and southwestern India all have soils and vegetation particularly sensitive to acidification.

Globally the most significant environmental changes may be due to emissions of so-called greenhouse gasses, which trap heat inside the atmosphere. Trace amounts occur naturally in the atmosphere, but their concentrations have risen exponentially since the Industrial Revolution. The increase of carbon dioxide, the most significant greenhouse gas, has been linked directly to increased use of fossil fuels and the loss of forests, whose trees and other flora absorb carbon dioxide. In 1990 international scientists predicted that an overall rise in temperatures, sea levels, and severe weather could be expected if greenhouse-gas emissions were not curbed. The consequences could be especially severe for Asia if climatic changes lead to reduced crop yields or the inundation of heavily populated coastal areas.

Pollution from Biomass Fuels and Forest Fires

In the developing countries of Asia the highest levels of air pollution occur inside homes where biomass fuels like wood, grasses, or animal dung are used for cooking and heating. Three-quarters of India's households rely on biomass fuels. Smoke from these fuels contains many harmful chemicals and compounds. Women and children, who are in the home the most, have the greatest exposure; they risk developing respiratory infections, lung cancer, and eye damage. Half of India's cases of tuberculosis may be attributed to respiratory damage from cooking smoke.

Forest fires were the source of the air pollution that blanketed much of Indonesia and its neighbors in 1997 and 1998. An unprecedented number of fires decimated tropical forests on the island of Kalimantan (Borneo) during a two-year drought linked to the El Niño southern oscillation, a periodic shift in global weather systems. The disaster was exacerbated by the expansion of fire-prone oil-palm plantations. Some 12.5 million people in the surrounding region were exposed to hazardous air pollution levels, forcing the Indonesian president to apologize officially to Malaysia, Singapore, the Philippines, and Thailand. The fires released as much carbon into the atmosphere as a year of fossil fuel use by Western Europe. As with other major forest fires, such as the giant blaze on the Chinese-Siberian border a decade earlier, the severest impacts were on the health and livelihood of the local community and surrounding natural environment.

Combating Air Pollution

Action to reduce air pollution is underway at many levels in Asia. While much attention has been given to international assistance programs promoting the use of expensive new technologies to remove pollutants from atmospheric emissions, the most successful strategies call for substituting cleaner fuel sources and using fuels more efficiently. China has long supported a program to popularize the use of biogas digesters; biomass fuels processed in these devices are converted to cleaner-burning methane gas, leaving a rich mixture of compounds useful as fertilizer. Elsewhere, biomass fuels are being replaced in the home by coal briquettes, natural gas, or electricity from power plants. For national power generation, China and India are taking steps to limit the use of coal high in sulfur, substituting other energy sources such as hydroelectric power, though these have their own environmental and social consequences.

The efficiency with which fossil fuels are used in Asia varies widely. Japan's fuel use is now among the most efficient in the world, but elsewhere in the region outdated technologies in factories and vehicles burn fuels less efficiently and pollute more. Modernization may help reduce pollution levels, an outcome especially critical in the area of greenhouse gasses.

Coal-dependent China and India are among the world's biggest sources of carbon dioxide, but, pointing to their low per-capita emissions compared with Japan, Korea, or other more developed countries, they argue that it would be unfair for international treaties to cap their emissions at current levels.

The Future

Air pollution poses ongoing challenges to human health and environmental quality in Asia, especially with Asia's growing economic development and increased fossil fuel consumption. The effects of air pollution are felt in the home, in rapidly developing urban areas, and across national boundaries. Current trends are alarming, but concerted efforts may reduce the damage air pollution causes to the people and environment of Asia.

Mark G. Henderson

See also: **Bhopal; Forest Industry—Southeast Asia**

Further Reading
Harwell, Emily E. (2000) "Remote Sensibilities: Discourses of Technology and the Making of Indonesia's Natural Disaster." *Development and Change* 31, 1: 307–340.

Hughes, G. (1997) *Can the Environment Wait? Priority Issues for East Asia*. Washington, DC: The World Bank.

Marland, G., T. A. Boden, and R. J. Andres. (2000) "Global, Regional, and National CO$_2$ Emissions." Retrieved 21 September 2001 from: http://cdiac.esd.ornl.gov/ndps/ndp030.html.

Smith, Kirk R. (1987) *Biofuels, Air Pollution, and Health*. New York: Plenum Press.

AIRLANGGA (991–1049?), Hindu-Javanese king. Airlangga lived when eastern Java had become a rival in the international spice trade of the maritime empire of Sriwijaya in Sumatra. According to the Calcutta stone inscription of 1041 CE, Airlangga was born to Balinese King Udayana and his wife, Queen Mahendradatta, daughter of the King Dharmawangsa Teguh of eastern Java. The latter kingdom was destroyed in 1017, either by Srivijayan attack or due to internal friction. After two years in a hermitage, Airlangga set out in 1019 to restore the kingdom of King Dharmawangsa. By 1035 he succeeded in subjugating all of Dharmawangsa's former vassals through military and political prowess. His kingdom became an international trade center and he himself a promoter of old-Javanese literature. Toward the end of his life, he retreated into the forest to become a hermit again. To forestall succession disputes between his two sons, he divided his kingdom into Kadiri and Janggala around

1049. After his death, he was revered as an incarnation of the Hindu god Vishnu.

Martin Ramstedt

Further Reading
Coedès, Georges. (1964) *Les États Hindouisés d'Indochine et d'Indonésie.* Paris: Éditions E. de Boccard.
Kempers, A. J. Bernet. (1991) *Monumental Bali: Introduction to Balinese Archaeology and Guide to the Monuments.* Singapore: Periplus Editions.
Vlekke, Bernard H. M. (1959) *Nusantara: A History of Indonesia.* The Hague, Netherlands: W. van Hoeve.
Zoetmulder, P. J. (1974) *Kalangwan: A Survey of Old Javanese Literature* (Translation Series 16). Leiden, Netherlands: KITLV (Royal Institute of Linguistics and Anthropology).

AITMATOV, CHINGIS (b. 1928), Kyrgyz writer. Chingis Torekulovitch Aitmatov is probably the best-known non-Russian author of the former Soviet Union. Aitmatov was born in the village of Sheker in Kyrgyzstan on 12 December 1928. His mother and father saw to it that he was exposed to Russian literature and language, while his maternal grandmother and aunt exposed him to the language, songs, epics, and folk tales of traditional Kyrgyz culture. Aitmatov experienced tragedy early in his life, as his father was killed in the Stalinist purges of 1937.

Aitmatov began writing in the late 1940s, contributing articles and sketches to local newspapers in Kyrgyzstan. He went on to train as a veterinarian but continued writing. The publication of several short stories while he was working as a livestock specialist in Kyrgyzstan earned him the right to join the writers' union and admission to the prestigious Gorky Literary Institute. He completed his studies at the institute in 1958.

Aitmatov's works were often pessimistic in tone and were openly critical of the Soviet system. His novels addressed such issues as the passing of traditional ways of life (*The White Steamship*, 1970) and the Stalinist terror (*The Day Lasts Longer than 100 years*, 1981).

Andre Sharp

Further Reading
Mozur, Joseph P., Jr. (1988) "Chingiz Torekulovich Aitmatov" In *Reference Guide to Russian Literature*, edited by Neil Cornwell. London and Chicago: Fitzroy Dearborn Publishers.

AJANTA (1991 pop. 600,000). Ajanta, a village located in the state of Maharashtra in the Sahyadri Hills near the Waghora River in India, is the site of approximately 30 Hindu and Buddhist cave temples and monasteries first created between the second century BCE and the late fifth century CE, and expanded and lavishly decorated again during the Gupta period (c. 230–c. 500 CE).

The caves were carved from the granite walls of a ravine, and are approximately 80 meters high and 380 meters long. Their interiors are covered with vibrant frescos and relief sculptures. Some of the caves are lit by natural light at certain times of day, enhancing the artistic effect. The majority of the caves are Buddhist, the art is inspired by legends, Jataka stories (ancient Pali fables), and real life; both mythological figures and ordinary people engaged in everyday tasks are depicted.

In 1819 British officers in the Madras army rediscovered the caves. Some historic accounts state the group was on a military expedition; according to other accounts the British were hunting in the area. Zealous archaeologists and local officials damaged the paintings to allow the findings to be displayed in museums. Public fervor destroyed early preservation efforts, which began about 1839. To prevent further debasement of the monuments, wire screens were placed over the art in all the major caves in 1903; today, however, the paintings remain at risk of deterioration. Various methods of preservation, including sealing them behind fiberglass, have been proposed. Because the frescoes represent a major example of Buddhist painting and because of their extraordinary quality, the caves of Ajanta were designated a UNESCO World Heritage site.

Linda Dailey Paulson

Further Reading
Michell, George, ed. (1989) "Ajanta." In *The Penguin Guide to the Monuments of India*, 1. London: Viking, 335–343.

AJANTA CAVES—WORLD HERITAGE SITE

A treasure trove of ancient Buddhist art and sculpture, the Ajanta Caves were first constructed more than two thousand years ago. These caves were added to the UNESCO list of World Heritage Sites in 1983.

AJODHYA (2002 pop. 51,000). An ancient city also called Ayodhya, Oudh, or Awadh, Ajodhya, now part of the city of Faizabad, lies on the Ghaghara River in the eastern Uttar Pradesh state of northern India. Ajodhya is one of seven holy places for Hindus, revered as the legendary birthplace of Rama, hero of the *Ramayana* epic. It was the capital of the Ikshvaku dynasty's Kosala kingdom (sixth century BCE) and a center of Gupta power (third–fifth centuries CE). By the fifth century CE the Chinese Buddhist monk Fa-hsien reported one hundred monasteries there. In the eleventh and twelfth centuries, Ajodhya became part of the Kanauj kingdom, then the Delhi sultanate, the Jaunpur kingdom, and, in the sixteenth century, the Mughal empire. It came under the control of the East India Company in 1764.

In 1856 Ajodhya was annexed by the British; loss of hereditary rights helped spark the 1857 Indian Mutiny. Oudh joined the Agra Presidency in 1877 to form the North-West Provinces and later the United Provinces of Agra and Oudh. On 6 December 1992, the sixteenth-century Mosque of Babur, built on a site sacred to Hindus and Muslims, was demolished by Hindu fundamentalists; over one thousand died in the ensuing riots.

C. Roger Davis

Further Reading
Chanchreek, K. L., and Saroj Prasad, eds. (1993) *Crisis in India*. Columbia, MO: South Asia Books
Jindal, T. P. (1995) *Ayodhya Imbroglio*. Columbia, MO: South Asia Books.

Hindus lay the foundation stones at the temple in Ajodhya that had been the source of conflict between Hindus and Muslims. (ZEN ICKNOW/CORBIS)

AKAEV, ASKAR (b. 1944), President of Kyrgyzstan. Askar Akaev was born in 1944 in the village of Kyzyl-Bairak, located in the Chon-Kemin region of Kyrgyzstan. He is not, by profession, a politician. Prior to holding the office of president of Kyrgyzstan he had never held a public political office. Akaev began his adult life as a professor of engineering and computers. From 1962 to 1972 he obtained his education at the Leningrad Institute of Precise Optics and Mechanics. Upon returning from Russia to Kyrgyzstan, he moved steadily up the academic ladder to become president of the Academy of Sciences in 1988. Two years later, on 27 October 1990, Akaev was appointed by the parliament as president of Kyrgyzstan. Early Western euphoria over Akaev's commitment to authentic democracy and economic reform has significantly diminished due to increasing repression and corruption.

The first serious repression began in 1994 when Akaev, disillusioned with the democratic constraints on his executive power, launched an authoritarian offensive that has increasingly strangled democratic culture. First, Akaev formed the Committee to Defend the Honor and Dignity of the President. Next, Akaev began building a power base to support him as a permanent president. In February 1996 President Akaev held a referendum that greatly extended his powers. This referendum violated both the constitution and the Law on Referendums. Voter apathy was high, turnout was low, and ballot stuffing was rampant, yielding results "reminiscent of the Soviet era" (U.S. Department of State 2000: 11).

Akaev's power was thus consolidated, and he became the dominant political force in Kyrgyzstan—not so much "the head of the executive branch but a kind of republican monarch who serves as the guarantor of the constitutions . . . operating at the pinnacle of state power" (Huskey 1997: 17). He has the power to nominate the prime minister and appoint government ministry heads and the director of the state bank. Akaev also controls the courts and has taken serious measures (mainly via the courts) to silence and subjugate the media. The culmination of these controls was evident in the February–March 2000 parliamentary elections, where blatant governmental manipulation resulted in spontaneous countrywide protests, including demonstrations, hunger strikes, and even a suicide, by citizens frustrated with the overt corruption and their inability to elect their own representatives.

L. M. Handrahan

Further Reading
Eshimkanov, Melis. (1995) *A. Akayev: The First President of Independent Kyrghyzstan*. Bishkek, Kyrgyzstan: ASABA.

Huskey, Eugene. (1997). "Kyrgyzstan: The Fate of Political Liberalization." In *Conflict, Cleavage, and Change in Central Asia and the Caucasus*, edited by Karen Dawisha and Bruce Parrott. Cambridge, U.K.: Cambridge University Press, 254–268.

———. (1995) "The Rise of Contested Politics in Central Asia: Elections in Kyrgyzstan, 1989–1990." *Europe-Asia Studies* 47, 5: 813–833.

U.S. Department of State. (2000) *U.S. Department of State Country Reports on Human Rights Practices: Kyrgyz Republic, 1999*. Washington, DC: U.S. Department of State.

AKBAR (1542–1605), Mughal emperor. The greatest emperor of the Mughal dynasty in India, Akbar, the eldest son of Humayun, ruled from 1556 to 1605, initially with the help of the regent Bairam Khan. An ambitious man, a superb strategist, and a diplomat, Akbar conquered Gujarat in 1573 and took control of Bengal in 1576. Kashmir came under his control in 1586, and by the time Asirgarh was conquered in 1601, he ruled over most of north, west, and east India, and his suzerainty was acknowledged by kingdoms in central India as well.

Akbar's conquests were accompanied by political consolidation and administrative reorganization. His administrative changes included reforming the *Mansabdari* rank system in the military to root out corruption, introducing a uniform, high-quality coinage and mint, and improving revenue assessment and collection. Akbar sought to reduce the authority of individual revenue holders by converting lands into crown holdings and distributing territory under the direct administration of salaried officers.

The tomb of Akbar in Sikandra, India, in 1975. (CORBIS)

Akbar's belief in universal toleration and the political need to unite Hindus under the Muslim Mughals found expression in his marrying two Hindu princesses; one, Jodha Bai, was mother of the heir to the throne. Akbar also appointed Hindus (particularly Rajput kings) to important state positions, abolished religious taxation, and even founded his own religion, the *Din-i-Ilahi* ("divine religion"), an eclectic mix of different faiths, including Brahmanism, Christianity, and Zoroastrianism. Though illiterate and lacking a formal education, Akbar was a cultured sovereign and a generous patron of the arts.

Chandrika Kaul

Further Reading
Habib, Irfan, et al. (1997) *Akbar and His India*. New Delhi: Oxford University Press.

AKBAR ON EUROPEANS AND ALCOHOL

"[The Emperor] Akbar published a decree permitting intoxicating spirits to be sold to Europeans, because, he said, 'they are born in the element of wine, as fish are produced in that of water, and to prohibit them the use of it is to deprive them of life.'"

Source: Philip Anderson: *The English in Western India* (1856)

AKHA The Akha are a highland people inhabiting parts of eastern and southern Shan State in Myanmar

An Akha girl in traditional costume in northern Thailand in 1986. (CHRISTINE KOLISCH/CORBIS)

tions along nationality lines, unlike the Shan, Wa, and other ethnic neighbors.

The Akha population of Myanmar is estimated at around 100,000. In 1995, there were an estimated 500,000 Akha in Yunnan, China, 40,000 in northern Thailand, and 66,108 in Laos. They represent 50 percent of the Tibeto-Burmese family in Laos. The highest concentrations of Akha in Myanmar are in rural districts around Kengtung. Many Akha communities can be recognized by the wooden gateways at the entrance to each village. Generally, Akha villages are situated in higher mountain areas, where many communities still practice swidden (slash-and-burn) agriculture. Their principal crops include maize, tobacco, sugar cane, and opium, although in the 1990s a number of crop-substitution schemes were introduced after cease-fires were agreed to by local armed opposition groups.

The Akha subgroups are most often distinguished by the distinctive headdresses of their women, many of whom wear a traditional costume of black clothes and embroidered jackets. According to Akha legend, there are seven families or clans, who represent the seven brothers from whom all Akha people descend. Other names for the Akha are Iko, Ikor, Kho, Kha Ko, and Ekow. They call themselves Akha.

During the twentieth century, both Christianity and Buddhism had increasing impact on Akha communities. Nevertheless, Akha history and myths continue to be preserved by a strong oral tradition of storytelling. There are, however, growing concerns among Akha elders about the social effects of armed conflict, internal displacement, narcotics abuse and, more recently, the spread of HIV/AIDS, all of which threaten the traditional fabric of Akha society.

Martin Smith

Further Reading

Chazee, Laurent. (1999) *The Peoples of Laos: Rural and Ethnic Diversities.* Bangkok, Thailand: White Lotus Press.

Hanks, Lucien, and Jane Hanks. (1975) "Reflections on Ban Akha Mae Salong." *Journal of Siam Society* 63, 1: 72–83.

Lebar, Frank, Gerald Hickey, and John Musgrave. (1964) *Ethnic Groups of Mainland Southeast Asia.* New Haven, CT: Human Relations Area Files.

Lewis, Paul, and Elaine Lewis. (1984) *Peoples of the Golden Triangle: Six Tribes in Thailand.* London: Thames & Hudson.

(Burma) as well as adjoining border regions in China, Thailand, and Laos. They speak a Tibeto-Burmese language that is related to that of the Lahu people who inhabit many of the same mountain areas. Reputedly descended from the ancient Lolo peoples, the Akha are believed to have migrated into Shan State from China's Yunnan Province in a centuries-long process of migration into Southeast Asia that continued into the twentieth century.

Few academic studies have been completed on the Akha in Myanmar. Under British rule (1886–1948), they were indirectly governed under the Frontier Areas Administration. Subsequently, many Akha-inhabited areas were badly disrupted by the Chinese Guomindang invasion and insurgencies that began in the late 1940s after Myanmar's independence. As a result, over the years Akha villagers have sometimes crossed as refugees into Thailand. However, despite the degree of political violence within Myanmar, the Akha have never formed armed opposition organiza-

AKITA (2002 est. pop. 1.2 million). Akita Prefecture is situated in the northern region of Japan's island of Honshu. Known for its mountainous terrain and heavy snowfalls, it occupies an area of 11,613 square kilometers. Its primary geographical features are the Oga Peninsula and the Ou and Dewa Mountains. The main bodies of water are the rivers Omonogawa and Yoneshirogawa, along with Lake Tazawa and part of Lake Towada. Akita is bordered by the Sea of Japan and by Aomori, Iwate, Miyagi, and Yamagata Prefectures. In ancient times Akita Prefecture was part of the Ugo section of Dewa Province; the prefecture assumed its present name and borders in 1871.

The capital of the prefecture is Akita city, situated at the mouth of the river Omonogawa. Akita is home to five universities, including Akita University, and it is the site of the famous Kanto lantern festival (4–7 August), associated with welcoming and seeing off the spirits of one's ancestors. A distribution center for agricultural goods, it also is a manufacturing center for petrochemicals, fertilizer, machinery, wood pulp, and zinc. Akita originated from a military fort (Akitajo) built in 733 CE to pacify the indigenous Ezo people. It prospered in the 1600s as the castle town of the Satake family. In the Akita Incident of 1881, a cabal of farmers and former samurai attempted to overthrow the government. The other important cities of Akita Prefecture are Noshiro, Yokote, Odate, and Kazuno.

The coastal alluvial Akita Plain in the central area is cultivated in rice, and the large crop supplies an active sake-brewing industry. Forestry supports pulp and plywood production, and the area's mines yield copper, gold, silver, and zinc. The west coast Akita oil fields, at their maximum output in 1959, pumped over two-thirds of Japan's crude oil production. An offshore oil field started in 1960 continues to supply the prefecture's petroleum industry. The major tourist attractions include hot spring resorts, Towada-Hachimantai National Park, and the Kurikomayama peak (1,628 meters).

E. L. S. Weber

Further Reading
"Akita Prefecture." (1993) *Japan: An illustrated Encyclopedia.* Tokyo: Kodansha.

AKSAKAL In the former Soviet Central Asia country of Kyrgyzstan, renewed tribalism since the collapse of Soviet rule has resulted in practices such as the revived Aksakal courts. These courts, the name of which is literally translated as "white beard courts," consists of the oldest men in the village who make all moral and family decisions. The Aksakals are not elected, but their powers of judgment and punishment are sup-

ported by the police force of Kyrgyzstan's President Akayev.

The Aksakals were reorganized following a call reportedly make by President Akayev at a January 1995 national congress. He is alleged to have encouraged the creation of a network of autonomous and active civil institutions, independent of state and political structures. The 1995 congress reportedly adopted a provisional status regulating the activities of Aksakal courts, whereby Aksakals were given responsibility for examining cases of administrative violations; property, family, and other disputes; and minor crimes passed to them by state procurators. The president is reported to have signed a decree approving this statue on 25 January 1995.

President Akayev has publicly supported the role of Aksakal courts and has reinforced and revived their importance in Kyrgyz society despite reported cases of medieval punishment, such as public stoning by the Aksakals as punishment for violating local custom and rules. Allegations of human rights abuses by the Aksakals, including illegal detention, whippings, and stonings, have been brought to the attention of human rights groups. The U.S. State Department Report for 1996 charged these local elders with abuses, including torture. Militias, known as *choro* and operating under the authority of the Aksakal, have little restriction placed on their activities by regular law enforcement bodies. In some villages, *azindans*, or places of illegal detention, have even been established. Corporal and capital punishment by the Aksakal and *choro* have also been reported.

L. M. Handrahan

Further Reading
Amnesty International. (1996) *Kyrgyzstan: A Tarnished Human Rights Record.* London: Amnesty International.
U.S. Department of State. (1997) *U.S. Department of State: Kyrgyz Republic Country Report on Human Rights Practices for 1996.* Washington, DC: U.S. Department of State.
———. (2000) *U.S. Department of State Country Reports on Human Rights Practices: Kyrgyz Republic, 1999.* Washington, DC: U.S. Department of State.

ALBANIANS In Asia, Albanian settlements exist throughout Turkey, especially in Istanbul and Bursa, and in Damascus, Syria. The large Albanian colony in Egypt, dating from the nineteenth century, has all but disappeared. Albanians first arrived in Turkey as conscripts for the Turkish janissary forces (the janissaries were established in the fourteenth century) and subsequently for the Ottoman forces in the eighteenth and nineteenth centuries. A second wave of Albanians,

Albanian soldiers serving the Ottoman Empire pose in distinctive uniforms, c. 1900. (MICHAEL MASLAN HISTORIC PHOTOGRAPHS/CORBIS)

from Kosovo and southern Serbia, arrived from the 1930s through the 1960s. The Serbs deported several hundred thousand of these Kosovo Albanians from Yugoslavia against their will under the absurd pretence that, as Muslims, they were Turks.

In Albania, the Albanians form two cultural groups separated by the Shkumbin River: the northern Albanians or Ghegs, sometimes spelled Gegs, and the southern Albanians or Tosks. Though dialect and cultural differences between the Ghegs and Tosks can be substantial, both sides strongly identify with their common national and ethnic culture, and both speak dialects of Albanian, an Indo-European language.

In Europe, in addition to the Republic of Albania with its centrally located capital city of Tirana, Albanians live in ethnically compact settlements in other large areas of the southwest Balkan Peninsula. The Republic of Albania, which includes only about 60 percent of all Albanians in the Balkans, is a mountainous country along the southern Adriatic coast across from the heel of Italy. An approximately 10 percent Albanian minority population lives north of Albania in Montenegro, in regions along the Albanian-Montenegrin border. Northeast of Albania is the United Nations–administered territory of (the self-proclaimed Republic of) Kosova, also known as Kosovo, techni-

cally a part of the Federal Republic of Yugoslavia. Kosovo's population is about 90 percent Albanian speakers. East of the Republic of Albania is the former Yugoslav Republic of Macedonia, about one-third of which, along the Albanian border, has an Albanian majority.

There are no reliable figures for the (largely assimilated) Albanian population living in Asia (mainly Turkey), but there are an estimated six million Albanians in Europe. Of these, about three and a half million live in the Republic of Albania, about two million in Kosovo, about half a million in the Republic of Macedonia, and about 100,000 in Montenegro. There are also large Albanian minorities in Italy and Greece.

Albania is on the border dividing three great religions: Islam, Greek Orthodoxy, and Roman Catholicism. Approximately 70 percent of Albanians in the Republic of Albania are Muslim. Among them are the Bektashi, a Muslim sect closely linked to the Albanian nationalist movement of the late nineteenth century. About 20 percent of Albanians, mostly in the south, are of Orthodox background, and about 10 percent, mostly in the north, are of Catholic background. Albanian history is intertwined with that of the Ottoman empire. Albanians were the backbone of much of the Ottoman military and administrative system. Many Albanians rose from the ranks of the janissaries to high offices in the Ottoman empire; some even became ministers and prime ministers of the imperial court.

Robert Elsie

Further Reading
Hall, Derek. (1994) *Albania and the Albanians.* London: Pinter.
Jacques, Edwin E. *The Albanians: An Ethnic History from Prehistoric Times to the Present.* Jefferson, NC: McFarland & Co.
Vickers, Miranda. (1994) *Albania: A Modern History.* London and New York: I. B. Tauris.

ALBUQUERQUE, AFONSO DE (1453–1515),
Portuguese viceroy. Born in Alhandra, south of Lisbon, Afonso de Albuquerque was the architect of the Portuguese maritime empire in the Indian Ocean. His strategy of securing key points along major trade routes and establishing fortresses with permanent settlers achieved the dual objective of carrying the crusade against the Muslims in Asia and capturing the lucrative spice trade, then under the control of Arab and Indian Muslims in the Arabian Sea, Indian Ocean region, and Southeast Asia. Albuquerque himself gained his early military experience in North Africa fighting the Berbers or Moors, before traveling to the East in 1503.

Following Vasco da Gama's pioneering voyage in 1498 around the Cape of Good Hope and to India, Cochin was captured by the Portuguese in 1503. Dom Francisco de Almeida, the first viceroy of Portuguese India (1505–1509), defeated a confederation of Muslim powers (Egypt, ruled by a Mameluke sultan; Gujerat, ruled by Bahadur Shah; Calicut, ruled by Samorin [Zamorin]) at the Battle of Diu off the northwest coast of India in 1509.

Albuquerque succeeded as viceroy in 1509 and set out to conquer the Gulf of Aden, for control of the Red Sea; Ormuz (today's Hormuz) Strait on the Persian Gulf; Goa state in India; and Melaka, the spice-trade emporium on the Malay Peninsula. Attempts to capture Aden failed, but Albuquerque conquered Socotra Island in 1507, before becoming the second viceroy of Portuguese India. He seized Goa in 1510 and Melaka in 1511. At Melaka, Albuquerque constructed an imposing fortress, A Famosa, which withstood all attacks for 130 years. Ormuz fell to the Portuguese in 1515. Following the Ormuz campaign, Albuquerque was taken ill and died en route to Goa.

Keat Gin Ooi

Further Reading
Birch, W. de G. ([1875–1884] 1970) *The Commentaries of the Great Afonso Dalboquerque.* 4 vols. Reprint ed. London: Hakluyt Society.
Boxer, C. R. (1969) *The Portuguese Seaborne Empire, 1415–1825.* London: Hutchinson.
Cortesao, A., ed. (1944) *The 'suma Oriental' of Tome Pires.* 2 vols. London: Hakluyt Society.
Meilink-Roelofsz, M. A. P. (1962) *Asian Trade and European Influence in the Indonesian Archipelago between 1500 and About 1630.* The Hague, Netherlands: Nijhoff.

ALEPPO (2001 est. pop. 2 million). Aleppo, the
second city of modern Syria and one of the oldest continuously inhabited cities in the world, is 110 kilometers inland from the Mediterranean and 30 kilometers south of the Syrian-Turkish frontier. Until the mid-nineteenth century, Aleppo was the western terminus of the Silk Road, ensuring its long-lasting prosperity.

Aleppo passed under several occupiers until the Arab conquest in 636 CE. Many of its best-known buildings (including the imposing Citadel and the Great Mosque) were restored or constructed under the Zangids and their successor Saladin (1137/38–1193) in the twelfth century. Under the Ottomans (1516–1918), the city prospered and grew, becoming one of the leading commercial centers of the eastern Mediterranean. Evidence of this prosperity can still be seen in the souks (marketplaces) and caravansaries (inns) dating from Ottoman times. The presence of foreign traders and diplomats also benefited their local intermediaries, often members of the Christian and Jewish minorities, who accounted for some 35 percent of the population in 1900.

After the creation of Syria in 1920, Aleppo suffered from the loss of its traditional markets in Anatolia and northern Iraq and for the first time became administratively subordinate to Damascus, the new capital. It gradually recovered its commercial and industrial vigor, partly as a result of the expansion of the cultivation of cash crops to the east of the city and also through large-scale migration from the countryside.

Peter Sluglett

Further Reading
Marcus, Abraham. (1989) *The Middle East on the Eve of Modernity: Aleppo in the Eighteenth Century.* New York: Columbia University Press.
Meriwether, Margaret L. (1999) *The Kin Who Count: Family and Society in Ottoman Aleppo, 1770–1840.* Austin, TX: University of Texas Press.
Raymond, André. (1984) *Great Arab Cities in the 16th–18th Centuries: An Introduction.* New York: New York University Press.

ALEVI MUSLIMS The Alevi Muslims, also known as Alavis, Alawis, Alawites, or Alouites, form a distinct branch of the twelve-imam Shi'ite tradition (Twelvers). Their interpretation of Islam and Shi'ism is known as Alevism or the Alevi faith. Various Alevi sects differ in some aspects of their faith, but they all subscribe to an unorthodox interpretation of Islam, which makes them distinct from all other Muslims whether Shi'ite or Sunni. The Alevis, who live mainly in Turkey, are estimated to be between 12 and 20 million in number, with much smaller communities in Syria, Iraq, and Iran.

Like other Muslims, the Alevis recognize the prophet of Islam, Muhammad, as the last prophet. Like Shi'ite Muslims, they believe that Imam Ali, the cousin and son-in-law of Muhammad, is his true successor and rightful imam. They also believe that the other eleven Shi'ite imams, who were all descended from Ali, were Imam Ali's true successors. Their heavy emphasis on Imam Ali as the perfect human plays a key role in their faith. This is reflected in their name, Alevi: "of Ali" or "follower of Ali." The latter emphasis is one of the factors making them distinct from other Shi'ites.

Certain characteristics also distinguish the Alevis from other Muslims, both Shi'ite and Sunni. While believing in the Qur'an, they do not follow it as the guide to their faith. Rather, they consider it a holy book along with those of the Jews and Christians, and all the holy books, according to them, are all the same in essence. The Alevis have no mosques or formal clergy, and they do not observe daily Islamic prayers. They do not fast in the month of Ramadan like other Muslims, but in the month of Muharam and for a period shorter than a month. For the Alevis, making a pilgrimage to Mecca is not a religious necessity. Unlike other Muslims, their religious ceremonies include men and women praying together through speeches, poetry, and dance. The drinking of alcohol is not forbidden among most Alevi sects. The Alevis forbid polygamy and generally advocate equality of all people regardless of gender. For this reason most Alevis are against Islamic restrictions on women, including veiling. Most favor the separation of religion and state and advocate secularity.

These distinctive characteristics of the Alevis have provided grounds for the persecution of their main community in Turkey. The Sunni clergy of Turkey consider them non-Muslim. This has created a justification for their persecution by Sunni extremists in that country, including attacks on their lives and property.

Hooman Peimani

Further Reading
Olsson, Tord, Elisabeth Özdalga, and Catharina Raudvere. (1998) *Alevi Identity.* Istanbul, Turkey: Swedish Research Institute in Istanbul.

ALGHOZA *Alghoza* is a generic term for various types of twin-fluted wind instruments originating in Sindh, the southeastern province of Pakistan, and in northern India. The musician plays both flutes vertically at the same time, producing the two sounds simultaneously.

The lengths of the wooden flutes vary from region to region but are commonly around 48 centimeters (19 inches). Each flute has six finger holes on the lower end. Continuous sound is achieved through the technique of circular breathing. The melody is produced on both flutes. A variation is the smaller (27 centimeters [11 inches]) double-fluted *pawo*, made from bamboo, which has one melody flute and one flute sounding the drone. It is thought that the *alghoza* and its variations are over two thousand years old. The sweet melodies played on the *alghoza* are reminiscent of the Western recorder. Traditional *alghoza* music revolves around the themes of love, separation, and sorrow. Renowned contemporary players of the *alghoza* include Khamiso Khan and Misri Khan Jamali.

Daniel Oakman

Further Reading
Deva, B. Chaitanya. (1978) *Musical Instruments of India: Their History and Development.* New Delhi: Munshiram Manoharal.
Yusuf, Zohra. (1988) *Rhythms of the Lower Indus: Perspectives of the Music of Sindh.* Karachi, Pakistan: Government of Sindh, Department of Culture and Tourism.

ALI JANHAR, MOHAMED (1878–1931), prominent figure of India's independence movement. The Ali brothers, Mohamed and Shaukat, were born in Najibabad, Bijnor District, Uttar Pradesh. Both were good orators and well-educated Muslims. Mohamed Ali became an established scholar who produced one of the most authoritative translations of the Qur'an into English.

In 1912, Mohamed Ali and M. A. Ansari led a Red Cross mission to Turkey during the Balkan Wars. Mohamed and Shaukat Ali later became leaders of the Khilafat movement, which arose in reaction to the humiliating terms imposed on Turkey at the Versailles Conference in 1919. This movement soon collapsed, however, because Kemal Ataturk (1881–1938) dramatically revived Turkey; the caliphate there was abolished in 1924; and despite its Muslim majority, Turkey declared itself a secular state. Mohamed Ali then joined with Mohandas Gandhi (1869–1948) in leading the Non-Cooperation Movement during the 1920–1924 period and, in so doing, for the first time united Indian Hindus and Muslims in a political endeavor. In 1923 Mohamed Ali became president of the Indian National Congress. Later he broke with Gandhi when the latter founded the Civil Disobedience Movement in 1930. Nonetheless Mohamed Ali remained an influential Muslim and nationalist leader for the final year of his life. He died in London in 1931 while attending the First Round-Table Conference between British authorities and representatives of the Indian National Congress.

Paul Hockings

Further Reading
Ali, Mohamed. (1942) *My Life, a Fragment: An Autobiographical Sketch of Maulana Mohamed Ali*, Afzal Iqbal, ed. Lahore, Pakistan: Sh. Muhammad Ashraf.

Iqbal, Afzal. (1979) *Life and Times of Mohamed Ali: An Analysis of the Hopes, Fears, and Aspirations of Muslim India from 1878–1931*. Lahore, Pakistan: Institute of Islamic Culture.

ALI KHAN, BADE GHULAM
(1902–1968), Hindustani vocalist. Bade ("The Great") Ghulam Ali Khan was one of the finest Hindustani vocalists of the twentieth century, one whose style and standing reflect a unique historical setting. Bridging the gap between royal cultivation and public appreciation, his was a generation of musicians whose artistry linked nineteenth century restraint to twentieth century romanticism.

Ghulam Ali was trained by his uncle, Kale Khan, and his father, Ali Baksh Khan, the latter a court musician to the Maharaja of Kashmir. As royal patrons were often musically erudite, Ghulam Ali's years of discipleship were spent in a musical ethos that was unhurried, rigorous, and majestic. Yet, his own career grew in an age of radical social transformation—bringing new patronage (the state), a changed economy (capitalism) and a new sovereign (independent India). Ghulam Ali consequently became the first of a new generation of musicians who was sensitive to a new "public" audience: one that was increasingly large, varied, and anonymous.

Ghulam Ali was born and musically groomed in Kasur, just outside of Lahore, Pakistan. From his debut in Calcutta in 1939, he toured throughout India, becoming widely known. After Partition, he made Pak-

istan his "home." While the government of India granted him visas for short concert tours, it prohibited radio broadcast of his recitals, even forbidding mention of his name. A decade later he became a citizen of India.

Ghulam Ali's *khayal* style of singing was so dominant that two generations of musicians continue to emulate it. What endeared him to the masses, however, were his renditions of *bhajan-s* (devotional songs) and his incorporation of folk tunes. He became, as such, India's first classical celebrity, a musician whose reputation lay in its circulation between the radio broadcast, the commercial recording, and the public concert.

Dard Neuman

ALISHER NAVOIY SAMARQAND STATE UNIVERSITY
The Alisher Navoiy Samarqand State University is one of the oldest institutions of modern higher education in Central Asia. It was established in 1927 as the Uzbek Higher Pedagogical Institute, with sixty-five students and ten faculty members. Samarqand was then the capital of Uzbekistan and the Higher Pedagogical Institute was part of the Soviet regime's efforts to train teachers as part of its program of eliminating illiteracy and establishing a system of universal education. Postgraduate classes began in 1931, and in 1933, the pedagogical institute was turned into the Uzbek State University. During World War II, the university briefly became a satellite campus of the Central Asian State University in Tashkent. In 1960, it acquired its present name.

The Soviet regime's efforts to fight illiteracy and establish universal education have succeeded, and the university has grown over the decades. In the early 2000s, its has an enrolment of nearly ten thousand students who attend classes in a modern skyscraper not far from the city's historic center.

Adeeb Khalid

ALL BURMA STUDENTS DEMOCRATIC FRONT
The All Burma Students Democratic Front (ABSDF) is an armed student group that became prominent in the decade following the assumption of power by the military State Law and Order Restoration Council in 1988. Students have stood in the forefront of political protest in Burma (now Myanmar) since the 1930s, when student leaders such as Aung San (1915–1947) and U Nu (1907–1995) led the opposition to British colonial rule.

The decision to take up arms was made by student leaders after the Burmese army's suppression of pro-democracy demonstrations in 1988. A three-prong strategy was implemented: the mainstream All Burma Federation of Students Unions remained the above-ground face of student politics; a new organization, the Democratic Party for New Society, was established to pursue legal party politics; and the ABSDF was formed in October that year among the thousands of students who had fled into territory controlled by armed ethnic opposition forces. At one stage, eighteen student battalions were organized in Myanmar's borderlands.

The ABSDF, however, was badly weakened during the 1990s by a factional split into two wings, headed by Dr. Naing Aung and Moe Thee Zun, respectively. The ABSDF was also hampered by logistical difficulties and strained relations with several of its ethnic minority hosts. As a result, the number of armed ABSDF members dwindled steadily. Instead, many students took political asylum abroad, where ABSDF exiles became active voices in the international campaign for democratic transition in Myanmar.

Martin Smith

Further Reading

Smith, Martin. (1999) *Burma: Insurgency and the Politics of Ethnicity*. 2d ed. London: Zed Books.

Thaung Htun. (1995) "Student Activism in Burma: A Historical Perspective." *Burma Debate* 2, 2 (April): 4–10.

NIGHT LIFE IN COLONIAL ALLAHABAD

"Allahabad is now one of the gayest, and is, as it always has been, one of the prettiest stations in India. We have dinner-parties more than enough, balls occasionally; a book society; some five or six billiard-tables; a pack of dogs; some amongst them hounds, and (how could I have forgotten!) fourteen spinsters!"

Source: Fanny Parks (1832) *Wanderings of a Pilgrim in Search of the Picturesque During Four and Twenty Years in the East with Revelations of Life in the Zenana/Fanny Parks*. London: Pelham Richardson.

Hindus taking a ritual cleansing bath in the Ganges River in Allahabad during the Khumb Mela festival in 1988. (JANEZ SKOK/CORBIS)

ALLAHABAD (2001 pop. 990,000). Allahabad is a holy city in India, whose name means "City of God." Located in the northern state of Uttar Pradesh, it is at the junction of the Ganges and Jumna Rivers, which Hindus consider sacred places of spiritual cleansing. In addition to attracting many religious pilgrims, Allahabad is an important historic and cultural site. In 2001 it was the location of the world's largest religious gathering, when perhaps 70 million devotees coming to participate in the Maha Kumbh Mela, or Grand Pitcher Festival, a Hindu festival which is held about once every 12 years. Founded in about 200 CE, ancient Allahabad's structures remain partly intact today. Major architectural sites include a monument from the reign of Ashoka, a third-century-BCE king famed for his benevolence; the Jama Musjid or Great Mosque; and the palace and fort constructed in 1583 by Akbar, the Mughul emperor who gave the city its present name. Allahabad was ruled by the Marathas, an ethnic group in India, the Pashtuns, an ethnic group in modern Pakistan and Afghanistan, and the British. The city was the capital of the United Provinces of Agra and Oudh, now Uttar Pradesh state, between 1901 and 1949.

Two of India's most famous modern politicians were born in Allahabad: Jawaharlal Nehru, the first Indian prime minister, in 1889, and Indira Gandhi, his daughter and also a prime minister, in 1917. The Nehru family estate now houses a museum. The ashes of Mohandas K. Gandhi, assassinated in 1948, were consigned to the Ganges at Allahabad. Today Allahabad is an important commercial center with exchanges for cotton, sugar, and other agricultural products.

Linda Dailey Paulson

Further Reading
Michell, George, and Philip Davies, eds. (1989) "Allahabad." In *The Penguin Guide to the Monuments of India*, 1 and 2. London: Viking, 1:152–153; 2:200–203.

ALMATY (1999 est. pop. 1,129,400). Almaty is a former capital and the largest city in the Republic of Kazakhstan, a Central Asian state. Situated in the southeastern part of the country, Almaty sits on the banks of the Bolshaia (Greater) Almatinka and Malaia (Lesser) Almatinka Rivers, at the foot of the Zailiysky Alatau mountains, and in a seven-river valley known as Jetysu in Kazak, or Semirechie in Russian. The city was founded as a Russian fortress named Vernoe (Loyal) at the ancient site of Almatu in 1854. In 1867, Vernoe was recognized as a town and received the slightly different name of Verniy. It was the main stronghold during Russia's further invasions in Central Asia.

In the late nineteenth through the twentieth centuries, Verniy was a place of exile for Russian revolutionaries. In 1916, it was the center of the major anti-Russian Jetysu Rebellion, which was crudely suppressed. After the Bolshevik Revolution in Russia (1917), Verniy became the headquarters of the anti-Bolshevik Beloe Dvizhenie (White Movement) in Semirechie (1918–1920), which eventually was defeated by the Red Army. In 1921, the city was renamed Alma-Ata (Father of Apples) after its remarkable apple orchards.

From 1929 to 1991, Alma-Ata was the capital of the Kazakh Soviet Socialist Republic, a constituent part of the Union of Soviet Socialist Republics (USSR). In December 1986, the city was the site of a massive student uprising to protest against Moscow's decision to replace Dinmukhamed Kunaev (1912–1993), the first secretary of the Communist Party of Kazakhstan, with Gennady Kolbin (b. 1927), a native Russian. After the dissolution of the USSR in 1991, the city received its original name of Almaty in 1994 and remained the capital of the Republic of Kazakhstan until 1997. In January 1998, the capital of Kazakhstan was transferred to Aqmola, subsequently renamed Astana, in northern Kazakhstan.

Present-day Almaty remains the country's most important business and cultural center, with 7.5 percent of the entire population of Kazakhstan. Almaty survived two major earthquakes, in 1887 and 1911, and a massive mud slide in 1921. The famous highland ice rink Medeu (inaugurated in 1951), with an area of 10,500 square meters, is situated 15 kilometers southeast of Almaty, at an attitude of 1,700 meters above sea level. The historical declaration on the dissolution of the Soviet Union, the Alma-Ata Declaration, was signed by the leaders of twelve Soviet republics in Almaty on 21 December 1991.

Natalya Yu. Khan

Further Reading
Maliar, Iosif Iserovich. (1983) *Alma-Ata: A Guide.* Moscow: Raduga.
Soucek, Svat. (2000) A *History of Inner Asia.* Cambridge, U.K.: Cambridge University Press.

AL-NAJAF (2002 est. pop. 563,000). Also known as Mashhad 'Ali, al-Najaf is one of the holiest cities of Shi'a Islam. It is located in Central Iraq, a few kilometers west of the Euphrates River near Kufa. Prior to their expulsion during the Iran-Iraq War, nearly one-quarter of the city's population was of Iranian descent.

According to tradition, the city contains the burial site of 'Ali ibn Abi Talib (c. 600–661 CE), cousin and son-in-law of the Prophet Muhammad, fourth caliph, and the spiritual founder of Shi'a Islam. A shrine was built over 'Ali's presumed tomb in the early tenth century after it had already become a center of pilgrimage. The shrine was destroyed and rebuilt several times, and today it constitutes a sanctuary with a large mosque and an adjoining Shi'a college. The old city is still encircled by a wall that dates back to Ottoman times, and the outskirts contain a number of Shi'a cemeteries. Also nearby are the remains of several early Christian monasteries. The city contains a series of mazelike cellars that was constructed to provide shelter from the desert heat and has been used as a hiding place for political opposition groups. Due to its religious status al-Najaf developed a strong tradition of political autonomy, which often led to resistance and rebellion against the central authorities in Baghdad.

Thabit Abdullah

ALPAMISH Alpamish is an oral epic found among the Turkic peoples of Central Asia, in particular the Uzbeks, Kazakhs, and Karakalpaks. Versions of the epic are also found among the Tatars, Bashkirs, and Altaians. The best-known version of Alpamish is the epic written down from the Uzbek singer Fazil Yoldash-oghli in 1928. The earliest version of the Alpamish story is found in the tale of Bamsi Beyrek in the Oghuz epic of *Gorkut Ata* (Grandfather Korkut). The story is in two parts: the winning of the bride and the return of the hero. In the first part, Alpamish wins the hand of the beautiful Barchin in a suitor contest involving a horse race, bow shooting, and a wrestling match. In the second part, Alpamish becomes a captive in the land of the Kalmucks, but is finally rescued from the dungeon with the help of his horse. On his return home, his wife is about to be remarried to the usurper of his realm. Alpamish tests his wife's fidelity in a song contest and overcomes his rival in a bowshooting contest. The epic is also important in offering a close parallel to the return of Odysseus.

Karl Reichl

Further Reading

Abdurakhimov, M., and Tora Mirzaev. (1999) *Alpamysh: Uzbekskijiy narodny geroicheskiy epos* (Alpamysh: An Uzbek Heroic Folk Epic). Tashkent, Uzbekistan: Fan.

Chadwick, Nora K., and Viktor Zhirmunsky. (1969) *Oral Epics of Central Asia*. Cambridge, U.K.: Cambridge University Press.

Reichl, Karl. (1992) *Turkic Oral Epic Poetry: Traditions, Forms, Poetic Structure*. Albert Bates Lord Studies in Oral Tradition 7. New York: Garland.

Zhirmunsky, Viktor M. (1960) *Skazanie ob Alpamyshe i bogatyrskaya skazka* (The Tale of Alpamysh and the Heroic Tale). Moscow: Izd. Vostochnoy Literatury.

ALTAIC LANGUAGES The Altaic languages are a group of languages and language families, widespread in and dominating parts of Central and Northern Asia. The name *Altaic* alludes to the Altai mountain range in southern Siberia, where nineteenth-century scholars located the original habitat of the speakers of these languages.

Linguists usually consider the Turkic, Mongolian, and Tungusic languages, often referred to as micro-Altaic, as the principal members of this group; some scholars also include Korean and Japanese, referred to as macro-Altaic. While linguists agree that all these languages show a high degree of structural uniformity and many shared lexical (word-related) and, to a lesser degree, morphological (form-related) materials, the "Al-

taic theory" continues to be one of the most controversial issues in contemporary comparative linguistics.

The gist of this debate is the question of whether these language families—or a subset of them—are to be viewed as members of a higher-level family of languages (often called a macrofamily), for which a common linguistic ancestor (a protolanguage) can be reconstructed and from which the languages diverged, or whether the common traits and elements found in these languages arose during millennia-long processes of "areal convergence," or large-scale language contact, of originally unrelated languages.

The Altaic Debate

Scholars noticed the high degree of structural similarity shared by the Altaic languages as early as the late eighteenth century and thus assumed that the languages were genetically related. One salient typological feature is vowel harmony: words may contain only vowels belonging to one of two or more mutually exclusive classes, such as front versus back or rounded versus unrounded vowels. The principal morphological technique in Altaic languages is that of agglutination: largely monofunctional affixes (almost exclusively suffixes) added to the roots they modify, in a fixed order, and without the high degree of fusion common, for instance, in Indo-European languages (as in the Latin word *librorum* ["of the books"], where the ending *-rum* simultaneously carries the functions of plural and genitive). The basic word order in ordinary sentences in Altaic languages is generally subject—object—verb; modifying constituents, like adjectives, always precede the constituent they modify; postpositions rather than prepositions are found.

Modern linguists, however, no longer view such typological similarities as indicative of genetic relations, mostly because the similarities can change (especially in situations of intensive language contact), and because these and other phenomena once viewed as "typically Altaic" traits occur on a global scale unknown when the Altaic theory was first developed.

Furthermore, critics of the Altaic hypothesis often point to the fact that some typological hallmarks of Altaic languages are historical innovations. For instance, the earliest Mongolian texts (thirteenth century CE) have elements atypical for Altaic (when compared with Old Turkic, for instance), including grammatical gender, no rigid verb–final word order, and adjectives following rather than preceding nouns. Mongolian later developed into a "typical" Altaic language. Somewhat similarly, in Tungusic, the Evenki and Even languages, spoken on the northern and western fringes of the language family's territory in central Siberia and Mongolia, are typologically much more divergent from the Altaic archetype than those spoken in the center, where they have been in contact with Mongolian for centuries.

Proponents of the genetic relations theory usually maintain that the Altaic languages share many lexical items from all semantic spheres, including basic vocabulary. These lexical commonalities are characterized by highly regular phonological correspondences, the most important criterion for genetic relationship. A considerable number of shared morphological elements (affixes) have been identified, and all these observations imply that these languages share a common origin.

Critics of the genetic approach to Altaic linguistics often argue that while the great number of lexical commonalities cannot be denied, most if not all can be explained as early borrowings. In micro-Altaic, the most readily identifiable layers of borrowings are Turkic loans in proto-Mongolian and Mongolian loans in proto-Tungusic. From the time of Ghengis Khan (c. 1162–1227) on, Mongolian elements begin to abound in Turkic languages, and a thin layer of Tungusic loans in early Mongolian is sometimes acknowledged. In particular, the fact that many words common to Turkic and Mongolian show, in Mongolian, traits of one of the subgroups of Turkic, namely the Bolgharic branch (of which modern Chuvash is the sole survivor), leads to the hypothesis that a strong proto-Bolgharic influence on proto-Mongolian is responsible for most commonalities in the two language families. The borrowing hypothesis is further strengthened by the fact that the Altaic languages share few lexical items that belong to those semantic areas that are generally thought to be stable over time and least amenable to linguistic borrowing. Altaicists claim that phonological correspondences between the languages are highly regular, which presupposes the acceptance of many etymologies; these are problematical for numerous reasons, including philological problems of determining the earliest Turkic, Mongolian, and other forms that alone should enter any external comparison; problems of inexact or vague semantic mapping in forms and words compared; and so on. The systems of correspondences proposed by Altaicists contain gaps, as well. Morphological elements compared by Altaicists are mostly confined to derivational morphology and usually involve very short morphemes, often consisting of merely one phoneme, the functions of which may be vague.

Some critics of the Altaic theory maintain that, once all comparisons for which these and similar objections

ALTAIC LANGUAGES

"The Altaic languages share almost no basic vocabulary, nor do they possess any uncontroversial material parallels in their morphological systems. The only logical conclusion is that the Altaic entities were both genetically and geographically clearly separate from each other, until . . . intensive contacts arose between Pre-Proto-Bulgharic and Pre-Proto-Mongolic."

Source: Juha Janhunen. (1996) *Manchuria: An Ethnic History.* Helsinki, Finland: Finno-Ugrian Society, 241–242.

may be brought forward are removed, the remaining potentially comparable items are so few that they could all be explained as chance similarities. Others do not completely reject the Altaic theory, believing that the evidence, when sifted through, will justify a leaner version of the theory.

All these points have been and continue to be addressed by proponents of the theory; both the methodological principles (such as insisting on allowing internal reconstruction of proto-Mongolian, proto-Turkic, and so on always to precede external Altaic-level comparisons) and the factual claims (for example, the acceptability of individual etymologies and sound-correspondences based on them) of their critics have been challenged. Thus, the Altaic debate still continues and has developed into an ideal testing ground for the methodology of assessing (or rejecting) the genetic relations of languages in general.

Stefan Georg

Further Reading
Doerfer, Gerhard. (1963) *Türkische und mongolische Elemente im Neupersischen*, Band I: *Mongolische Elemente im Neupersischen*. Wiesbaden, Germany: Harrassowitz, esp. 51–106.

Georg, Stefan, Peter Michalove, Alexis Manaster Ramer, and Paul J. Sidwell. (1998) "Telling General Linguists about Altaic." *Journal of Linguistics* 35: 65–98.

Janhunen, Juha. (1996) *Manchuria: An Ethnic History.* Helsinki, Finland: Finno-Ugrian Society.

Martin, Samuel Elmo. (1996) *Consonant Lenition in Korean and the Macro-Altaic Question.* Honolulu, HI: Center for Korean Studies.

Miller, Roy Andrew. (1996) *Languages and History: Japanese, Korean, and Altaic.* Bangkok, Thailand: White Orchid Press.

Poppe, Nicholas. (1965) *Introduction to Altaic Linguistics.* Wiesbaden, Germany: Harrassowitz.

ALTAY MOUNTAINS The Altay Mountains are a complex and multifrontier chain with three distinctive spurs: the Altay proper (Russia and Kazakhstan), Mongolian Altay (Mongolia and China), and Gobi Altay (China). The assemblage stretches 2,000 kilometers (1,250 miles) in a southeast to northwest direction from the Gobi Desert to the West Siberian Plain and reaches an elevation of 4,506 meters (14,783 feet) on Belukha. In the Turkic-Mongolian language, *altan* means "golden," reflecting the belief of early inhabitants that the mountains were rich in precious metals. Sediments dating from 500 to 300 million years ago were uplifted during the recent Quaternary period (1.6 million years ago) and have since been sculpted by glacial and river erosion into an alpine appearance. There are 1,500 active glaciers, 3,500 lakes, and 4 distinct mountain vegetation zones (subdesert, steppe, forest, and alpine). Animal life is of Mongolian (e.g., marmot, antelope) or Siberian (e.g., bears, lynx, musk deer) origin. The extreme continental climate results in long and very cold winters and short, warm summers. Average annual precipitation varies with elevation, from 500–1,000 millimeters (20–40 inches), and is highest on the windward western slopes. Altay ridgelines divide the Arctic-bound Ob/Irtysh River from the interior and often saline basins of Central Asia.

Indigenous Altaic peoples, Russians, and Kazakhs share the Altay proper. Khalkha Mongols and Kazakhs predominate in the Mongolian and Gobi Altay. Livestock (cattle, sheep, and horses), agriculture, mining, forest products, and food processing are the most

ALTAY MOUNTAINS— WORLD HERITAGE SITE

The Altay Mountains in western Siberia are a wonder of ecological abundance. The more than 1.6 million hectares of mountain, lake and alpine plain are home to snow leopards and two major rivers. The mountains were designated as a World Heritage Site in 1998.

important economic pursuits. Since the 1940s, Soviet and Chinese government policies have opened this once remote region to logging, mining, and hydroelectric development.

Stephen F. Cunha

Further Reading
Campbell, Matthew. (1994) "Ice Maiden of the Steppes." *World Press Review* 41, 6: 40–41.
Natural History Museum of Los Angeles County. (1989) *Nomads of Eurasia.* Seattle, WA: University of Washington Press.
Polosmak, Natalia. (1994) "A Mummy Unearthed from the Pastures of Heaven." *National Geographic* 186, 4 (October): 80–103.
Rerikh, Nikolai K. (1996) *Altai-Himalaya: A Travel Diary.* Delhi: Book Faith, India.

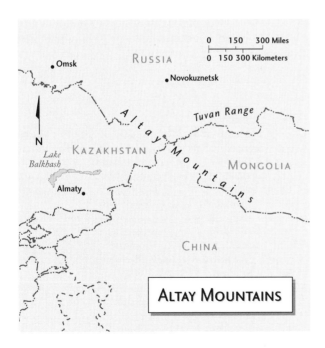

ALTAY MOUNTAINS

ALTYNSARIN, IBRAHIM (1841–1889), Kazakh educator, social activist, author. Altynsarin is considered by many scholars to be one of the first Kazakh intellectuals whose principal professional activity was to create greater educational opportunities for Kazakh children. In 1850 he entered the Orenburg School for Kazakhs, where he was educated in Russian classics, such as by Alexander Pushkin and Mikhail Lermontov. In addition, he was trained in mathematics and the natural sciences. In 1864 he opened a school for Kazakh children in Turgai. He was a supporter of the Nikolai Il'minskii's educational system for Russia's national minorities. The Russian government, concerned that Tatar religious views were having a potentially negative influence on young Kazakhs, supported steps to introduce lessons in the Kazakh vernacular. Altynsarin was assigned the task of compiling the lessons used in the textbook. In 1879 Altynsarin's most significant work, *Nachal'noe rukovodstvo k obucheniiu kirgiz russkomu iazyku* (Beginning Handbook for Teaching a Kazakh the Russian Language), was published with the twin goals of educating Kazakh youth in the Russian language and eliminating illiteracy among the Kazakh population. He was also a leader in the effort to publish a newspaper in the Kazakh language; however, the authorities always denied his requests. In addition, Altynsarin worked tirelessly to educate Kazakh girls. In 1891, two years after his death, the first school for girls was opened in Turgai.

Steven Sabol

Further Reading
Kreindler, Isabelle. (1983) "Ibrahim Altynsarin, Nikolai Il'minskii, and the Kazakh National Awakening." *Central Asian Survey* 2: 99–116.

AMAMI ISLANDS (2000 est. pop. 150,000). The Amami Islands, or Amami Gunto, form the northern half of the Nansei Island chain, south of Kyushu, Japan, and are located between 29° and 27° north latitude. The islands include Amami Oshima, Kikaishima, Tokunoshima, Okinoerabu, and Yoronjima, as well as several smaller islands, eight of which are populated. Amami Oshima is the largest of the Amami Islands, with an area of 720 square kilometers and a population of about 74,000; it ranks third in size among Japan's offshore islands (after Okinawa and Sado). The main city is Naze, located in Amami Oshima, and serves as the business, political, and administrative center of the islands. The semitropical islands, while hilly, are chiefly agricultural, with sugarcane, sweet potatoes, and fruits being the main products.

The Amami Islands are administered as part of Kagoshima Prefecture. Prior to becoming an administrative part of Kagoshima in 1871, they were controlled by the Satsuma domain in Kyushu, which took over the islands in 1609. Before that, the islands had belonged to the Ryukyu Kingdom (1429–1879) in Okinawa. After World War II, the United States occupied the islands from 1946 to 1953, when they were returned to Japanese control, following a reversion movement led by local education and political leaders and those from Amami living in Tokyo and other parts of mainland Japan.

Robert D. Eldridge

Further Reading
Eldridge, Robert D. (forthcoming) *The Political and Diplomatic History of the Return of the Amami Islands.* Lexington, MA: Lexington Books.

AMANGKURAT Amangkurat (to have the world on one's lap) is a Javanese royal title. The rule of the four Amangkurats in Javanese history was dominated by bloody crises and repeated interventions of the Dutch East India Company (VOC). Sultan Agung (reigned 1613–1646) had established the greatest Javanese realm since the time of Hindu-Buddhist Majapahit. With the rule of his son and successor Amangkurat I (reigned 1646–1677), however, the hegemony of the Mataram dynasty in central and east Java came to an end. Amangkurat I's tyrannical rule, alienating him from powerful court allies and regional vassals, isolated the monarchy and weakened its military might. The empire disintegrated, and in 1677 the court of Mataram fell to rebel armies. Only with the help of the VOC was his son and successor Amangkurat II (reigned 1677–1703) restored to the throne, founding the new court of Kartasura. During the First Javanese War of Succession (1704–1708), the VOC supported Amangkurat II's brother, the future Pakubuwana I (reigned 1704–1719), against Amangkurat III (reigned 1703–1708). Pakubuwana I's death in 1719 initiated the Second Javanese War of Succession (1719–1723). Amangkurat IV (reigned 1719–1726) succeeded him upon the throne but also needed the VOC to fight for him.

Edwin Wieringa

Further Reading
Ricklefs, M. C. (1993) *War, Culture, and Economy in Java, 1677–1726: Asian and European Imperialism in the Early Kartasura Period.* Sydney: Asian Studies Association of Australia; Allen & Unwin.

AMANOLLAH (1892–1960), King of Afghanistan. Amanollah Khan, also known as Amanullah Barakzai, was the king of Afghanistan from 1919 to 1929. He was responsible for leading Afghanistan to independence from Britain in 1919 as well as instituting major economic, political, and social reforms to modernize Afghanistan.

Born the third son of Habibollah Khan, who ruled in Afghanistan from 1901 to 1919, Amanollah served as the governor of Kabul. When his father was assassinated, Amanollah used his political shrewdness to gain the throne over the claims of his brothers and uncle. He soon initiated war against the British rule in his country and, within one month, had secured independence for his people. The Soviet Union quickly embraced the newly independent administration, and Amanollah went on to establish relations with France, Germany, Italy, Japan, and the Ottoman empire.

During his reign, Amanollah instituted some far-reaching changes, some of which have prevailed to the present. He reorganized the administrative divisions within the country, declared a constitution, instituted a new tax system, and allowed a free press to operate. However, he also instituted some cultural changes toward a more secular way of life, such as removing the requirement for women to wear veils, which created a backlash of opposition. In addition, he alienated his army through changes in compensation, which left him without military support when several revolts took place in 1928. These pressures ultimately led Amanollah to relinquish his throne in May of 1929. He tried to regain his throne through a military campaign toward Kabul, but it failed. He ultimately left the country to live in Italy in exile.

Houman A. Sadri

Further Reading
Adamec, Ludwig W. (1996) *Dictionary of Afghan Wars, Revolution, and Insurgencies*. Lanham, MD: Scarecrow Press.
———. (1997) *Historical Dictionary of Afghanistan*. 2d ed. Lanham, MD: Scarecrow Press.
Nyrop, Richard F., and Donald M. Seekins. (1986) *Afghanistan: A Country Study*. Foreign Area Studies. Washington, DC: The American University.

AMASYA (2002 est. pop. 78,000). Amasya, known historically as Amaseia, is the capital city of the province of Amasya (population 346,191) in Turkey. The city straddles the Yesilirmak River in central Anatolia.

The city was under the rule of nine different civilizations, beginning with the Hittites (second millennium BCE) and ending with the Ottomans (1453–1922), before it became part of the Turkish Republic. The town most likely began as a Hittite settlement, falling to Alexander of Macedon in the fourth century BCE. Under King Mithridates II (123–88 BCE; ruler of the Pontic kingdom that flourished from the fourth century to 66 BCE), Amasya flourished as the Roman royal capital of the kingdom of Pontus. Much of its wealth and power derived from its strategic location on the Roman road system. In about 47 BCE, as Roman influence in Anatolia declined, the city fell under Byzantine (330 CE) and then Seljuk (1075) rule.

The Mongols under Genghis Khan routed the city in the thirteenth century. The town was finally lost to the Ottoman army, led by the sultan Bayezid I (c. 1360–1403). Under Ottoman rule, Amasya flourished as one of the training and education centers for crown princes who often served as governors. During the fif-

teenth century, it was a center for calligraphic monograms (*tuora*), and during the nineteenth century it became a major center of Islamic education.

The city also played a major role in Turkish independence when, on 12 June 1919, Mustafa Kemal Ataturk (1881–1938), the founder of the Turkish Republic, came to Amasya. There he met secretly with associates to plan the war of independence to drive out the victorious Allies and Greeks and make Turkey an independent nation. The city suffered a devastating fire in 1915, which destroyed many of its buildings and monuments, as well as earthquakes in 1734, 1825, and 1939.

Amasya is known for its orchards of apples, cherries, and peaches; as well as the rock tombs of the rulers of Pontus, Ottoman buildings, and nineteenth-century wooden homes. Economic activity centers on agriculture, textiles, and mining. It is also known as the birthplace of the Greek geographer and historian Strabo (64 or 63 BCE–after 23 CE).

T. Isikozlu-E.F. Isikozlu

Further Reading
Statistical Yearbook of Turkey, 1998. (1998) Ankara, Turkey: Devlet Ystatistik Enstitusu.

AMBEDKAR, B. R. (1891–1956), Indian reformer and statesman. Dr. Bhimrao Ramji (Babasaheb) Ambedkar has two claims to fame. He was India's undisputed untouchable leader of the untouchables, creating a movement that has brought much progress to that religiously, socially, and economically oppressed group. He was also a statesman who often testified to government commissions and served as labor minister in the preindependence cabinet of India and as law minister in the first cabinet after 1947. His work as chair of the drafting committee for India's new constitution is honored today. His statue or portrait is visible in untouchabale homes and neighbors and in city centers all over India.

Born to an army schoolteacher, Ambedkar was one of the first untouchables to graduate from college. Aided by non-Brahman reformist princes, he then secured an M.A. and Ph.D. in economics from Columbia University in New York and a D.Sc. from the London School of Economics. He became a barrister from Grey's Inn. Returning to India, he immediately began newspapers, organized conferences for "The Depressed Classes," began work in education, pressed for the political rights of untouchables, taught at Government Law College, began a political party and a

to cooperate with its British counterpart, the East India Company. Although there was little or no commercial cooperation, the VOC was forced to permit British traders to work from Ambon and other centers.

Relations between the two nationalities were difficult, and in 1623 the Dutch governor of Ambon arrested eight British traders and some Japanese mercenaries on charges of plotting to seize the island's fortress. After they were tortured, the accused were summarily tried, found guilty, and executed. The executions became a cause célèbre in Britain and contributed to mounting hostility between Britain and the Netherlands. The main effect, however, was to convince the British to withdraw from the Indies and to concentrate their commercial and imperial efforts in India.

Robert Cribb

See also: **Dutch East India Company; Dutch in Southeast Asia**

Further Reading
Milton, Giles. (1999) *Nathaniel's Nutmeg: How One Man's Courage Changed the Course of History.* London: Hodder and Stoughton.
Vlekke, Bernard H. M. (1943) *Nusantara: A History of the East Indian Archipelago.* Cambridge, MA: Harvard University Press.

AMNOK RIVER The Amnok River (in Korean, Amnokkgang), known in Chinese as the Yalu River, is the longest river in Korea and is one of two rivers that form the border between North Korea and China. (The name Yalu is supposedly derived from the green color of the ducks' heads, which match the green colored river waters.) It begins on the slopes of Mount Paektu and flows southwest in a deeply entrenched course for 790 kilometers until it passes through an industrial area to its mouth at two cities on the East China Sea (Yellow Sea)—Sinuiju, North Korea, and Dandong, China. In its middle reaches it is up to 160 meters wide, although the flow varies from season to season. It has a drainage basin of 38,700 square kilometers, half of which is in the Chinese provinces of Jilin (Kirin) and Liaoning. In the early1900s, the Amnok was navigable for 672 kilometers by 1,000-ton ships, but due to sedimentation, only 500-ton ships can navigate the river at present.

The Amnok River has been the tentative northwest border of Korea since the end of the fourteenth century. Under King Sejong of Korea (reigned 1419–1450) four outposts were created along the upper Amnok River, making the river the de facto northern border.

B. R. Ambedkar in 1950. (BETTMANN/CORBIS)

labor union, and, at first, conducted temple entry campaigns.

By the time of his death, he had established his third political party; converted to Buddhism along with millions of his followers; and created a network of educational institutions run by his People's Education Society, which in turn produced more innovations, including a new literary movement called Dalit (oppressed) sahitya.

Eleanor Zelliot

Further Reading
Moon, Vasant, ed. (1979) *Dr. Babasaheb Ambedkar: Writings and Speeches.* Bombay, India: Education Department, Government of Maharashtra.
Zelliot, Eleanor. (1996) *From Untouchable to Dalit: Essays on the Ambedkar Movement.* New Delhi: Manohar Publishers and Distributors.

AMBOINA MASSACRE In 1605 the Dutch East India Company (Verenigde Oostindische Compagnie, VOC) seized the island of Ambon (Amboina) in the Moluccas or Spice Islands as a military base and center for clove production. An important element in VOC policy was to exclude Western trading rivals from the Indies (today's Indonesia), but in 1619 a treaty between Britain and the new Dutch Republic required the VOC

In 1875 it became the legal international border. During the Korean War (1950–1953), the Chinese army crossed the Yalu River to fight the United Nations forces.

The Japanese colonial rule (1910–1945) built a series of dams along the Yalu River in order to harvest hydroelectric power for Korea and Manchukuo. The Yalu River remains an important source of hydroelectric power for both North Korea and China.

Brandon Palmer

Further Reading
Korean Overseas Information Service. (1993) *A Handbook of Korea*. Seoul: Korean Overseas Information Service.

AMRITSAR   (1991 est. pop. 709,500). Well situated on a southern extension of the Silk Route, Amritsar ("a pool of nectar") is a vibrant commercial, cultural, and transportation center in India's Punjab state. An important center of the Sikh faith, Amritsar was founded around a sacred pool in 1577 by Ram Das, the fourth guru of the Sikhs. The city's the Golden Temple or Hari Mandir houses the *Granth Sahib*, a sacred scripture compiled by the fifth Sikh guru, Arjun in 1604. Amitsar is also believed to be where the sage Valmiki wrote the Hindu epic *Ramayana*. Sacked by Afghans in 1761, the temple was rebuilt in 1803 and its dome covered in gold foil, by

Ranjit Singh, the maharaja of Punjab and ruler of the sovereign Sikh commonwealth until 1849 when Amritsar was annexed by the British.

Amritsar was the site of two violent political clashes. During the Jallianwala Bagh Massacre, 13 April 1919, British troops fired on a crowd of Indian protesters, killing at least 400 to 2,000 by some accounts and wounding hundreds more. On 6 June 1984, Indian Army troops killed hundreds of Sikh separatists—again causalities numbering 2,000 in some reports—at the Golden Temple where arms were being stored for attacks on the government of Indira Gandhi. In an act of retaliation Prime Minister Indira Gandhi was assassinated in 1984.

C. Roger Davis

Further Reading
Alter, Stephen. (2001) *Amritsar to Lahore: A Journey Across the India-Pakistan Border*. Philadelphia: University of Pennsylvania Press.
Dhanjal, Beryl. (1994) *Amritsar*. New York: Dillon Press.

AMU DAR'YA   The longest river in Central Asia (length measurements vary between 2,200 and 2,500 kilometers), the Amu Dar'ya (Oxus) has two annual floods: in the spring, from precipitation, and in the summer, from the Pamir Mountains' melting glaciers and snows. On contemporary political maps, the Amu

Sikh pilgrims at the Golden Temple in Amritsar in July 1996. (STEPHEN G. DONALDSON PHOTOGRAPHY)

Dar'ya begins with two streams rising in the Pamirs plateau in northwestern Afghanistan, continues northwest through the Hindu Kush, forming the boundary between Tajikistan and northeastern Afghanistan, then flows west and northwest through Turkmenistan and Uzbekistan, into the marshes on the south shore of the Aral Sea in the Karakalpak Autonomous Republic. Its delta at the mouth is about 161 kilometers long, and the river basin is some 466,000 square kilometers.

The river's lower extent and associated oases divide the Kara-Kum and Kyzyl Kum Deserts and have been critical to the cultural ecologies of Central Asia throughout the history of human occupation. Beginning with early hunter-gatherers, societies arose in the river's proximity and developed complex economies based on systems of agriculture, pastoralism, or both. Bronze Age irrigation projects allowed the region's first urban civilizations to emerge; ancient *qalas* (fortified cities) became local political and commercial centers. Collectively these civilizations' early city-states became the basis of wider regional and extraregional trade networks, such as those from as early as the third and second centuries BCE making up the Silk Road through Central Asia. While societies rose and declined along the Amu Dar'ya throughout the Bronze and Iron Ages and afterward, effective irrigation was a constant concern for the region's aristocratic and commercial elite; some speculate, for instance, that Khworezm's shift of capitals to Khiva was due largely to natural alterations of the Amu Dar'ya.

Beyond the origins of societies and urbanization, the Amu Dar'ya was also a symbolic frontier in Central Asian history. For the Achaemenid rulers of Persia (c. 553–331 BCE) the river bounded the region they controlled or sought to advance beyond; cities were founded along its course in Alexander of Macedon's pacification campaign of the fourth century BCE; it marked a limit to the subsequent Chinese advance into Central Asia (second century BCE); and since medieval times it constituted a powerful psychological (and often geopolitical) boundary separating Turkic and Iranic peoples and states. Its seventh-century crossing by Arab armies represented the advance of Islam. Over the following centuries, enabled by an increased construction of irrigation works known as *qanats* or *kariz* and by the investments of new regional leaders and states during and after Islamicization, urban centers grew both in terms of their populations and infrastructure. This was a period of cultural (e.g., architectural, literary, artistic, and so forth) florescence due to the patronage of local and regional elites.

In the early eighteenth century Peter the Great commissioned the Amu Dar'ya's exploration with the

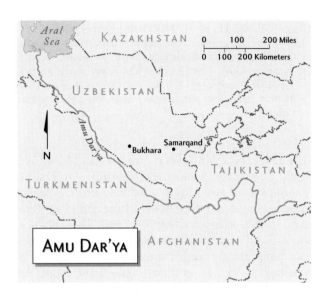

AMU DAR'YA

hope of securing a route to India, though the region was not fully under Russian control until the twentieth century. Associated with cotton production for centuries, this part of Central Asia was the core region in Leninist plans for the Soviets to attain self-sufficiency in this commodity. A water-intensive crop, cotton cultivated at this scale in this environment required massive irrigation projects (e.g., Turkmenistan's Kara-Kum Canal, the largest in Central Asia). The consequence of these projects was environmental degradation of catastrophic proportions, with destruction of the river's deltas, desiccation of the Aral Sea, associated climatic changes, exhaustion and salinization of once productive lands, and declines in local food production.

Though cotton production peaked in 1977 at more than 5.5 million metric tons, construction of manmade diversions continued into the post-Soviet era. By the mid-1990s more than seventy thousand irrigation canals were in operation, and their collective inefficiency is considerable; most waters diverted are actually lost to seepage and evaporation. Alleviation of this worsening crisis is not likely, due to the increasing development demands of the states and societies in question (primarily Turkmenistan, Uzbekistan, and Kazakhstan), their perceived lack of alternatives, barriers to the scale of multinational cooperation critical to its resolution, and the ongoing and cumulative degradation of local and regional ecosystems.

Kyle T. Evered

Further Reading

Bernard, Paul. (1994) "An Ancient Greek City in Central Asia." *Scientific American* 5, 1: 66–75.

Glantz, Michael H., ed. (1999) *Creeping Environmental Problems and Sustainable Development in the Aral Sea Basin.* Cambridge, U.K.: Cambridge University Press.

Le Strange, Guy. ([1905] 1966) *The Lands of the Eastern Caliphate: Mesopotamia, Persia, and Central Asia from the Moslem Conquest to the Time of Timur.* Reprint. London: Frank Cass.

AN DUONG VUONG (reigned c. 257–c. 208 BCE), Legendary founder of Vietnam. An Duong Vuong, whose given name was Thuc Phan, is traditionally considered the founder of the nation of Vietnam. In 258 BCE, according to legend, Thuc Phan, a warlord and ruler of neighboring lands, conquered the Van Lang, the territory of modern-day Vietnam. He renamed it Au Lac and gave himself the name An Duong Vuong (King An Duong).

Related legends hold that while building his capital city, Co Loa, An Duong Vuong saw all the work accomplished during the daytime crumble each night. After a couple of weeks, he learned in a dream that the site of his city was located on the back of a turtle god. The king changed the location of his capital, and a large city in the form of a conch shell was constructed in no time at all. As a token of thanks, the turtle deity offered the king one of its claws, which, when used as a trigger on a bow, multiplied its arrow by the thousands. As a result, Zhao To, a Chinese general, failed time and again in his attempts to subjugate Au Lac, until Zhao To married his son to An Duong Vuong's daughter and the son stole the magic weapon. Zhao To finally succeeded in annexing Au Lac to his own Chinese territory and founded the kingdom of Nan Yueh (Nam Viet) in 207 BCE.

Truong Buu Lam

Further Reading
Taylor, Keith W. (1983) *The Birth of Vietnam.* Berkeley and Los Angeles: University of California Press.

ANALECTS The *Analects* (Chinese *Lunyu*) is one of the most influential texts in Chinese philosophy. It was compiled by the disciples of Confucius (551–479 BCE) and their followers, though scholars argue over exactly when. D. C. Lau holds the traditional view that the first fifteen books were written shortly after Confucius' death and the remaining five by the second generation of disciples. John Makeham argues that the changing textual material was not settled into its present form until 150 BCE. E. Bruce and Taeko Brooks propose that books four through eleven are the old-

est, that nine through eleven were written by second-generation disciples, while what remains was written at different times.

It is known that the *Analects* was basically in its present form by 55 BCE based on the fragments excavated at Dingzhou. The *Analects* is first among the so-called Four Books, the Confucian texts whose mastery was required for the imperial civil-service examination system up to 1905.

The *Analects* is composed of brief statements mostly attributed to Confucius; some are ascribed to his disciples or rulers. The modern reader is generally struck by the brevity of the statements and the apparent lack of sustained prose or argument, which may very well have been Confucius' method of pedagogy. He expected his students to be eager to learn: He only gave them one corner, and if they did not return with the other three, he would not review the lesson (*Analects* 7:8).

The general thrust of the text is to assist the reader in self-cultivation so that the reader might become a moral example for others. One might find the proper way to live and behave by practicing various virtues (*de*), thereby becoming a humane person (*ren zhe*) or a prince of virtue (*junzi*, usually rendered "gentleman"). Humanity or benevolence (*ren*) is the most important virtue in the *Analects*; it is mentioned more than one hundred times. *Ren* is an achievement concept; one is not born humane, but one must learn to become so. *Ren* means to love others (*Analects* 12:22). The practice of ritual action (*li*) is the best way to express one's human kindness. Ritual action is not limited to state and religious functions, but covers the spectrum of human behavior. Speaking pragmatically, first a child must learn filial piety (*xiao*) and brotherly love (*di*); then, as one grows one can extend one's family love to others in the form of *ren*.

Confucius emphasized literacy, study, and learning to develop the practice of moral wisdom. Rote memorization is not sufficient; one must be thoughtful. Confucius also expected his disciples to be loyal and to do what was proper, especially in government service. When Zigong asked if there was a single word that one could use as guidance, Confucius replied (*Analects* 15:24, 12:2) that perhaps it would be empathy (*shu*): to "never do to another what you do not desire."

James D. Sellmann

Further Reading
Ames, Roger T., and Henry Rosemont, Jr., trans. (1998) *The Analects of Confucius: A Philosophical Translation.* New York: Ballantine Books.

Brooke, E. Bruce, and Taeko Brooks. (1998) *The Original Analects*. New York: Columbia University Press.

Chan, Wing-tsit. (1963) *A Source Book in Chinese Philosophy*. Princeton, NJ: Princeton University Press.

Dawson, Raymond, trans. (1993) *Confucius: The Analects*. Oxford: Oxford University Press.

Graham, Angus C. (1989) *Disputers of the Tao*. La Salle, IL: Open Court.

Hsiao, Kung-chuan. (1979) *A History of Chinese Political Thought*. Trans. By F. Mote. Princeton, NJ: Princeton University Press.

Jensen, Lionel M. (1997) *Manufacturing Confucianism: Chinese Traditions and Universal Civilization*. Durham, NC, and London: Duke University Press.

Lau, D. C., trans. (1979). *The Analects (Lun Yü)*. London.: Penguin Books.

Leys, Simon, trans. (1997) *The Analects of Confucius*. New York: Norton.

Makeham, John. (1996) "The Formation of *Lunyu* as a Book," *Monumenta Serica*, 44: 1–24.

Munro, Donald J. (1969) *Concept of Man in Early China*. Stanford, CA: Stanford University Press.

ANAND, MULK RAJ (b. 1905), Indian writer.

An influential Indian novelist and short story writer in the mid-twentieth century, Mulk Raj Anand was born in 1905 in Peshawar, now in western Pakistan, and as a young man was active in literary circles in England until 1939. His first novels formed a trio: *Untouchable* (1935), *Coolie* (1936), and *Two Leaves and a Bud* (1937). Written in English, such books struck a chord with a somewhat leftist readership both in Britain and in India. They offered a rather superficial political and psychological analysis of India's "downtrodden masses" that drew its inspiration from D. H. Lawrence, E. M. Forster, Emile Zola, Charles Dickens, various Russian novelists, Marxism, and Gandhian nationalism. But Anand was able to contribute something new to Indian writing by showing how a novelist can make use of the drama of revolutionary nationalism. Tellingly, he wrote little of any note after India gained independence in 1947. Like his contemporaries Raja Rao and R. K. Narayan, Anand was concerned with exploring the importance of Indian society for humanity at large.

Paul Hockings

Further Reading

Verma, K. D. (2000) *The Indian Imagination: Critical Essays on Indian Writing in English*. New York: St. Martin's Press.

Williams, H. M. (1977) *Indo-Anglian Literature 1800–1970: A Survey*. Columbia, MO: South Asia Books.

ANAND PANYARACHUN (b. 1932), Thai political leader.

Anand Panyarachun is one of Thailand's

Former Prime Minister Anand Panyarachun (L) in November 2000 at a meeting of the Association of Southeast Asian Nations. (AFP/CORBIS)

most prominent political figures. In 1952, Anand graduated from Cambridge University in law. He joined the Thai Ministry of Foreign Affairs in 1955, eventually becoming a top diplomat. In the 1960s, Anand served as Thailand's representative to the United Nations before being named ambassador to Canada and, later, the United States. In 1976, he was appointed deputy foreign minister before serving as ambassador to West Germany in 1977. In 1979, Anand left public office for the business world, serving as president of Saha-Union and chairman of the Thai Industrial Federation.

However, his renowned integrity and leadership drew Anand back to politics. Between 1980 and 1988, Thailand was led by Prem Tinsulanond, the former Thai army chief, who managed the nation with a series of coalition governments through a considerable economic boom, as well as two failed military coups. However, having never actually joined a political party, and never standing for an election as a member of Parliament, Prem was not seen as "democratic." Amid pressure to push further economic and political reforms in Thailand, Prem was defeated in the 1988 election by another former general, Chatichai Choonhavan. Although Chatichai presided over continued economic prosperity, his coalition government was notoriously corrupt. Following a bloodless military coup in February 1991, Anand emerged as a reform-minded consensus leader. He reluctantly accepted an appointment as interim prime minister, widely seen as the only politician capable of steering Thailand toward democracy.

After national elections in March 1992 produced a shaky five-party coalition, the military effectively seized power by positioning former strongman Suchinda Kraprayoon as prime minister. Opposition to the move mounted dramatically between March and May, when the military was called in to Bangkok to replace police dealing with protesters. Between 17 May and 20 May 1992, violence broke out between the army and thousands of protesters, leading to one of the darkest episodes in Thai political history. Although official statistics listed fifty-two killed, other reasonable estimates were over two hundred killed. Only the personal intervention of King Bhumipol Adulyadej prevented an even bloodier conflict. Still widely popular with the Thai people, on the king's advice Anand was again chosen to lead the government.

In his second term as prime minister (June–September 1992), Anand boldly tackled the military's political power in hopes of distancing it from government. He also set in place numerous other political and economic reforms that helped stabilize the nation and stimulate its financial boom. In recognition of his distinguished career, in 1997, Anand won the highest award for government service. Although officially retired from politics, Anand remains one of the most important and respected public figures in Thailand.

Arne Kislenko

Further Reading
Anand Panyarachun. (1992) *Management, Reform, and Visions: A Selection of Speeches by Prime Minister Anand Panyarachun.* Bangkok, Thailand: Secretariat of the Prime Minister, Government House.
Murray, David. (1996) *Angels and Devils: Thai Politics from February 1991 to September 1992—A Struggle for Democracy.* Bangkok, Thailand: White Orchid Press.
Prasan Marukkhaphitak. (1998) *Anan Panyarachun, Chiwit, Khwamkit, lae Kanngan khong Adit Nayokratthamontri Song Samai* (Anand Panyarachun, Life, Thoughts, and Work of the Former Two-Time Prime Minister). Bangkok, Thailand: Ammarin Publishing.

ANARKALI Anarkali is a commercial district in inner-city Lahore, Pakistan, famous for its retail shops and colorful atmosphere. The area derives its name from a mausoleum dated 1615, purportedly that of a slave girl named Anarkali ("pomegranate blossom"), buried alive in a wall by order of the Mughal emperor Akbar (d. 1605) in 1599. As William Finch, an Englishman visiting Lahore, first reported in 1611, Akbar allegedly suspected Anarkali of an illicit relationship with his son Prince Salim (later crowned emperor Jahangir, d. 1628). Because the legend is not mentioned in Indian sources until the nineteenth century, most commentators believe that the story is either false or heavily embellished. Nevertheless it inspired writers

(e.g., the Urdu drama *Anarkali* by Imtiyaz Ali Taj) and filmmakers.

Archeological research showed that Anarkali's tomb does contain human remains, though these may belong to a wife of Jahangir who died in Lahore around this time. The tomb was originally surrounded by extensive gardens. After the British annexation of Lahore in 1849, the tomb served as a Protestant church from 1851 to 1891 and then as a government records office. The present Anarkali bazaar, which evolved gradually over the past 150 years, is particularly well known for women's apparel.

Shahzad Bashir

Further Reading
Baqir, Muhammad. (1952) *Lahore, Past and Present.* Lahore, Pakistan: Panjab University Press.
Foster, William, ed. (1921) *Early Travels in India, 1583–1619.* London: Oxford University Press.
Latif, Syad Muhammad. (1892) *Lahore: Its History, Architectural Remains, and Antiquities.* Lahore, India: New Imperial Press.

ANATOLIA (1997 est. pop. 54 million). Anatolia, also called Anadolu or Asia Minor, is Turkey's Asiatic region, a mountainous peninsula surrounded by the Black Sea on the north and the Mediterranean and Aegean Seas on the south and west. To the northwest are the Bosporus Strait, Sea of Marmara, and Dardanelles. Anatolia encompasses 743, 634 square kilometers—about three-fifths of the area of Turkey.

The Pontic and Taurus (Toros) Mountains border the flat, central Anatolian plateau on the north and south. Mount Ararat is Anatolia's highest peak (5,172 meters). The region is prone to earthquakes. Major rivers are the Euphrates and Tigris. Of the three hundred lakes that enrich the land, Lake Van in the east is the largest. Anatolia's climate ranges from cold winters in the central plateau to sweltering heat in the Mediterranean region. Its crops include grain, tobacco, olives, figs, and cotton; animal life includes the Angora goat.

Anatolia, considered the cradle of many cultures and civilizations, was inhabited at least as early as the eighth millennium BCE and served as a bridge between Europe and Asia; it is rich in architectural and archaeological remains, rock reliefs, burials, pottery, and stone implements. Ancient inhabitants included the Hatti, Hittites, Trojans, Urartians (kingdom of Urartu, later, Armenia), Phrygians (led by King Midas), Lycians, and Lydians.

The Persians invaded Anatolia in 546 BCE, Alexander of Macedon in 334 BCE. By the end of the second century BCE, Anatolia was under Roman rule. Following a civil war in the early fourth century, the victor, Constantine, established the capital at Byzantium and renamed it Constantinople. After his death, the new empire was divided. The eastern half, centered in Constantinople, came to be known as the Byzantine empire. By 711, all Anatolia was under Byzantine rule.

Early in the eleventh century, the Seljuk victory at the battle of Manzikert (1071; modern Malazgirt) opened Anatolia to further Turkish invasions. The territory gradually became Turkicized after the rise of the Ottoman Turks around the thirteenth century. Anatolia came under Muslim Ottoman rule when Mehmet II (reigned 1432–1481) captured Constantinople in 1453. In 1923, Mustafa Kemal Ataturk (1881–1938), a nationalist general, established the new Turkish Republic.

Anatolia has seventy-four provinces, grouped into seven regions: Black Sea coast; Marmara and Aegean coasts; Mediterranean coast; western Anatolia; central Anatolia; southeastern Anatolia; eastern Anatolia. Ninety percent of Anatolia's population is Turkish, and 99 percent is Muslim. Non-Turkish elements are mostly Greeks, Jews, Armenians, Kurds, and Arabs.

T. Isikozlu–E.F. Isikozlu

Further Reading
Izbırak, Resat. (1976) *Geography of Turkey*. Ankara, Turkey: Directorate of Press and Information.

ANAWRATHA

(d. 1077), King of Burma. Anawratha (also Aniruddha, reigned 1044–1077) was the first great king of the classical Burmese kingdom of Pagan as well as an important figure in the early history of Theravada Buddhism in Burma. A number of significant historical developments are attributed to Anawratha, although the historicity of these attributions is open to question. Under Anawratha, Pagan's rulers are believed to have undergone a transition from chieftains to kings. But he is chiefly remembered in Burmese history because of his perceived role in the early development of Theravada Buddhism in Burma. He himself is said to have been converted to orthodox Theravada Buddhism by the Mon monk Shin Arahan. In 1057, Anawratha captured Thaton, the Theravada center of southeastern Burma. According to the fifteenth-century Kalyani inscription, Anawratha brought Theravada Buddhist monks back to Pagan with thirty copies of the Tipitaka, the orthodox Theravada Buddhist scriptures.

Anawratha is also credited with purging Pagan's Buddhist monkhood of the "heretical" Ari sect. Today, Anawratha is considered one of Burma's greatest kings. The achievements of his rule were carried by a later successor, Kyanzittha (reigned 1084–1112).

Michael Walter Charney

Further Reading
Harvey, G. E. ([1925] 1967) *History of Burma: From the Earliest Times to 10 March 1824, the Beginning of the English Conquest*. Reprint ed. London: Frank Cass.
Taw Sein Ko, ed. and trans. (1892) *The Kalyani Inscriptions: Erected by King Dhammaceti at Pegu in 1476 a.d.* Rangoon, Myanmar: Supt. of Govt. Printing.

ANAYASA. See **Constitution—Turkey.**

ANCESTOR WORSHIP—EAST ASIA

Asia's widespread tradition of venerating ancestors has been shaped by indigenous folk beliefs and major religious traditions. Depending on the local culture, this worship or veneration may combine elements of filial piety, agricultural traditions and seasonal observances, lineage patterns, animistic concepts of the actions of spirits in the world of the living, an emphasis on obligations to superiors, and the idea that human beings become deities at death. Confucian ancestral rites and the fundamental concept of filial piety and the Buddhist tenet of transmigration of souls are common ancestral beliefs throughout Asia, but the relative importance of these two organized religions vis-à-vis local folk beliefs makes for diversity. Scholars debate, for example, whether ancestor worship in Japan primarily sprang from indigenous beliefs or was imported from China. Before the introduction of Buddhism, the Japanese had already incorporated Confucian ancestral rites and the concept of filial piety. Buddhism certainly made a major contribution to the development of the ancestral cult in Japan, but the Japanese practice that evolved is unlike that of other Buddhist cultures of Asia.

Characteristics

The basic premise of ancestor worship is that the world of the living and the spirit world of the dead are interdependent. What happens in this world is, to use Mark Mullins's term, "causally influenced" by the world of the spirits. While all the spirits command a certain amount of respect, one should show particular devotion to one's ancestors. Some scholars interpret this devotion not as worship, but as an expression of

THE CHANGING SIGNIFICANCE OF ANCESTOR WORSHIP

Ancestor worship is a key element of traditional religion in East Asia. It has survived and even influenced the spread of major religions in the region. However, in the last half of the twentieth century it did decline in importance, for some of the reasons mentioned in the discussion about rural China that follows.

Today the ancestral cult is very largely in eclipse. The social changes sponsored by the government—especially the equality of status of males and females, the new marriage practices, and the greater emphasis on the importance of the younger generation—have undermined the cult. Directly, the validity of the old supernatural belief was contradicted by the orthodox Marxist doctrine of atheism which informs the whole school curriculum and is propagated in the speeches of government leaders and all lesser officials. The process is a cumulative one. The village has been going through a period of rising material welfare. Success, not failure, has followed the desertion of old practices and beliefs for new. The prestige of the new doctrine and of the teachers of it is therefore high amongst a people in whom part of the motive for cultivating their ancestors was the search for material benefits.

Source: W. R. Geddes. (1963) *Peasant Life in Communist China: Monograph #6.* Ithaca, NY: Society for Applied Anthropology, 48.

gratitude and respect toward those to whom one is indebted.

The ancestral cult is essentially a patrilineal phenomenon. As Janelli and Janelli noted about Korean practice, commemorating ancestors was the obligation of the oldest son, and women were normally excluded from officiating at veneration rites. These scholars saw a correspondence between property inheritance or household succession and the degree of obligation to carry out rituals:

In China, where all sons normally inherit equal shares of property, and none succeed to the headship of their parents' household, each descendant is equally obligated to his forebears. . . . In Japan, by contrast, ritual obligations are vested in corporate households, not descent lines. Whoever succeeds to the headship of the household inherits all of its property; and only members of a household worship its preceding heads, their spouses, and its deceased dependents. . . . The Korean pattern for allocating ritual obligations has similarities to both the Chinese and Japanese systems. Each son receives a share of his parents' property and is obligated to participate in their rites. Yet the eldest son receives the largest share of their ancestors' property and succeeds to the headship of their household, and in return he is expected to bear most of the costs of the rituals and to offer these rites at his home.

(Janelli and Janelli 1982: 179–180)

Actual hereditary lineage is not an essential condition for ancestor worship. Robert J. Smith points out that in Japan "ancestors" are foremost a category of the dead who exercise powers over a group to whom they are considered ancestors. In other words, blood ties are not as essential as the sense of a shared heredity, but in this framework there is a commonly recognized order of ascendance. The descendant group may be a household, some linkage of families, a village, a guild, or even the entire nation. Freedman points to similar elements in China: "In a very general sense the ancestors collectively embody the dignity and authority of the groups over which they preside. Their due is gratitude and praise. And in paying them their due, the living are made conscious of their membership of the groups within which they worship" (Freedman 1979: 297).

THE STORY OF THE ANCESTOR TABLETS

A common feature of the rural Chinese home is the ancestor tablet. This folktale provides one version of how such tablets came to be.

I once asked a Chinese schoolboy about the origin of the ancestral tablet, and he told me the following story:

Once upon a time there was a very cruel and bad man who did not love his mother. He did nothing she wanted him to do, but only scolded her. Whenever he came home he immediately wanted a meal. But who can make a whole meal in a minute? So he beat her and scolded her. But the softhearted woman did not complain. One day, when working in the fields, the son heard the cawing of crows in the air and saw a crow with food in its mouth, coming from a far away place to a tree at the corner of the field, to feed its young. He was moved and thought, 'These crows are birds but even they collect food from their relatives and care for them. This means that I am not even as good as a bird. I am acting ungratefully towards my mother. My father died long ago, and even if I were to behave as well as I could, I still could not make her forget his death. Shame upon me.' He decided to be nice to his mother from then on.

Just at this time, his mother came to bring him his lunch. As soon as he saw her, he started running toward her to take lunch so that she wouldn't have to walk so far. It was his first good deed for the old lady. But how could she know about his sudden change of heart? She thought he would beat her as usual. So she hurriedly put down the basket with the lunch and started running away. It happened that she hit a small tree, fell down, and died. The son was deeply disturbed, and in order to keep his mother and this unhappy event in mind forever, he cut down the tree and made a small tablet which he preserved. Thus the ancestral tablet came into being.

Source: Wolfram Eberhard. (1952) *Chinese Festivals.* New York, NY: Henry Schuman, 43–44.

In this worldview it is only natural that the living perform rituals and make offerings to their ancestors, if they appropriately recognize their indebtedness to them. The living honor this debt through memorial services, on the assumption that success and prosperity in this life partly depend on the beneficent protection of the ancestors. The spirits of the ancestors are believed to be pleased by any positive accomplishment by a descendant, and announcements of such achievements before the memorial tablets on the altar or at the grave are considered important. In contrast, health problems, failures in enterprise, and problems in social relationships may be attributed to the failure of descendants to properly venerate the ancestors. The unpacified spirit may then exact retribution from the ungrateful descendants.

Ancestor Worship and Earthly Authority

Ancestor worship in Japan, for example, was affected by political and administrative factors, according to Smith. Smith convincingly argues that the veneration of ancestors alternately served the purposes of various religious bodies, the national government, and reformers throughout Japan's history. In the sixth and seventh centuries, ancestor worship was first employed in the promotion of Buddhism, and the two were linked for the next thousand years. In the early Tokugawa period, however, that relationship changed when the government used Buddhism to suppress Christianity by requiring every household in Japan to establish a formal registration with a Buddhist temple. Until that time, ancestor worship had been centered in the home and practiced without priests. As a consequence of the decree, ancestor worship became another ritual requiring the services of the Buddhist clergy and temples. In the twentieth century, worship of one's own ancestors was co-opted to support veneration of the imperial line and political actions.

Everyday Practice

In daily observance, veneration of ancestors may take the form of making offerings such as cooked rice, water or tea, flowers, incense, and other cooked foods at a Buddhist altar in the home or at the family grave. Annual observances involving ancestors often include families' visiting the household grave at the beginning of the new year and around the spring and fall equinoxes; during the visits families clean the grave and offer prayers and incense. At the beginning of the period of the Buddhist Festival of the Dead, also known as the Feast of Lanterns and the Feast of All Souls, the family greets the returning spirits with lanterns to ensure that they can find the way back.

Memorial services in the Buddhist tradition are held for individual ancestors, beginning with services every seventh day until the forty-ninth day following death. These ceremonies are of paramount importance in Buddhist belief, because after a person dies, he or she is thought to wander between this world and the next. The rites held for the benefit of the dead conduct the soul safely to the next world. Should the rites not be performed, the spirit of the deceased may wander, causing misfortune and calamity.

Demographic changes including the shift of population toward cities, declining birth rates, and the increasing ratios of nuclear families as well as changes in the legal systems regarding inheritance of property seem to have been accompanied by a steady decrease in the significance of ancestor veneration. While annual observances continue to be observed, dependence on the other world for support in this world seems to be on the decline. Current indications are that the traditional sense of gratitude and respect to previous generations will continue to decrease, the primary question being at what pace within each of Asia's cultures.

James M. Vardaman, Jr.

Further Reading

Freedman, Maurice. (1979) *The Study of Chinese Society.* Stanford, CA: Stanford University Press.

Hori, Ichiro. (1968) *Folk Religion in Japan: Continuity and Change.* Tokyo: University of Tokyo Press.

Janelli, Roger L., and Dawnhee Yim Janelli. (1982) *Ancestor Worship and Korean Society.* Stanford, CA: Stanford University Press.

Mullins, Mark R. (1998) *Christianity Made in Japan.* Honolulu, HI: University of Hawaii Press.

Smith, Robert J. (1974) *Ancestor Worship in Contemporary Japan.* Stanford, CA: Stanford University Press.

ANDAMAN AND NICOBAR ISLANDS

(2001 est. pop. 356,000). The Andaman and Nicobar Islands, a territory of the Indian Union, form a narrow chain running mostly north-south and stretching over 1,000 kilometers. The Andaman Islands (6475 square kilometers) to the north have four main and 200 small, mostly uninhabited islands. Divided by the Ten Degree Channel, the Nicobar Islands (1852 square kilometers) consist of three groups of nineteen islands. Part of a submarine Tertiary-period-fold mountain, the Andaman and Nicobar Islands are generally hilly, with Saddle Peak (738 meters above sea level) and Mount Thullier (614 meters) the two highest peaks on North Andaman and Great Nicobar, respectively. Because monsoons bring ample rainfall and temperatures are high, lush tropical forests with great biodiversity (including 242 bird and 78 reptile species) cover around 90 percent of the land. Such forests, partly still virgin, have great commercial value and represent the main source of income. Agriculture is only sparsely developed, with cultivation of rice, coconuts, and fruit trees. Foreigners are banned from the Nicobar Islands, but tourists are welcomed at the capital of Port Blair on Andaman and from there can visit other islands via day cruises.

Four different groups inhabit the Andaman and Nicobar Islands: Andamanese aborigines, Andaman Indians (descendants of an Indian penal colony functioning from 1848 to 1945), neosettlers who migrated from the mainland after Indian independence, and Nicobarese aborigines. The majority are Andaman Indians and neosettlers. The aborigine groups are each distinctive. With a total population of a few thousand, the Nicobarese aborigines are Indo-Chinese who are either animists or converted Christians and who still practice shifting cultivation. The Andamanese aborigines are pygmies and Negritos who hunt and fish. Though the Andaman and Nicobar Islands are sparsely and unevenly populated, around one-third of the inhabitants live in Port Blair, the only town and the business and commercial center. Elsewhere peo-

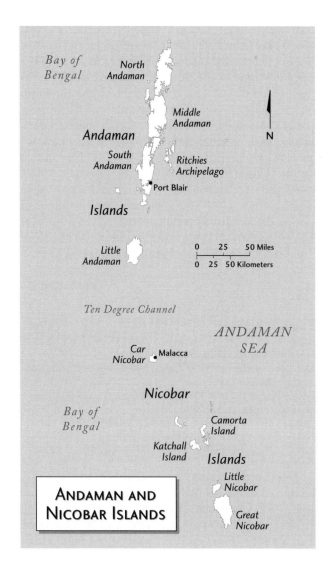

ANDAMAN AND NICOBAR ISLANDS

ple live in clusters of small villages. The only (domestic) airport for regular flights to Calcutta and Madras is at Port Blair, which is also the most important seaport, connecting all other major islands by regular boat service.

Manfred Domroes

Further Reading

Justin, Anstice. (1990) *The Nicobarese.* Calcutta, India: Seagull Books.

Radcliffe-Brown, A. R. (1948) *The Andaman Islanders.* Glencoe, IL: Free Press.

ANDAMAN SEA The Andaman Sea is located east of the main body of the Bay of Bengal and is bounded by Myanmar (Burma) to the north, southeastern Myanmar and southwestern Thailand to the east, the Andaman and Nicobar Islands (which belong to India) and the main body of the Bay of Bengal to the west, and the Strait of Malacca and Sumatra to the south. The Andaman Islands and the Nicobar Islands are divided into two groups: the Great Andaman (North, Middle, and South Andaman Islands) and the Little Andaman. The chief town and port is Port Blair (founded 1868), located on South Andaman Island. The Nicobar Islands are located 120 kilometers south of South Andaman Island and include Car Nicobar and Great Nicobar.

The Andaman Sea's strategic position just north of the Strait of Malacca (and thus between the Indian Ocean and the South China Sea) has made it a historically important site of Asian interaction. In the nineteenth century, the British attempted to colonize the Andaman Islands. In recent decades, India has also attempted to promote settlement of the islands.

Michael W. Charney

Further Reading

Ivanoff, Jacques. (1997) *Moken: Sea Gypsies of the Andaman Sea.* Bangkok, Thailand: White Lotus.

Sen, Satadru. (1999) "Policing the Savage: Segregation, Labor and State Medicine in the Andamans." *Journal of Asian Studies* 58, 3: 753–773.

ANDHRA PRADESH (2001 pop. 75.7 million). Andhra Pradesh is the fourth-largest state in India, having a population of 75.7 million and covering 275,068 square kilometers in the southeastern part of India. It has the longest coastline of all Indian states—970 kilometers along the Bay of Bengal. It is flanked by the states of Tamil Nadu, Karnataka, Maharashtra, Chhattisgarh, and Orissa on three sides apart from the long eastern coastline. Andhra Pradesh was the first state in India to be formed on a purely linguistic basis in 1953 with the merger of Telugu-speaking areas of the Nizam's Dominions and Madras State, subsequently expanded to include more such territory in the aftermath of the States Reorganization Act of 1956.

Andhra Pradesh has twenty-three administrative districts, which can be divided into three distinct regions: Andhra, incorporating nine coastal districts; Rayalaseema, incorporating four districts in the interior; and Telengana, incorporating ten districts, including the capital, Hyderabad. Because of its heterogeneous composition, Andhra Pradesh has grappled with the problem of regional imbalance in different forms. The state has a unicameral legislature with 295 seats. It has a representation of eighteen seats in the Rajya Sabha (Upper House) and forty-two seats in the Lok Sabha (Lower House) of the Indian Parliament. Historically, Andhra Pradesh has been associated with the reign of successive Indian dynasties, beginning with the Mauryas in the fourth century BCE and continuing, most notably, with the Kakatiyas in the thirteenth century and the Vijayanagar kings in the next two centuries. Later, it came under the rule of the Qutb Shahis and the Asaf Jahis, Muslim rulers of the Deccan who created the modern city of Hyderabad and struck an alliance with the advancing British colonial power. Traces of this legacy still exist in the form of monuments and architectural ruins.

A key feature of the state's terrain is the fertile coastal plain in the east. The two major rivers of the state, Godavari and Krishna, flow from the west to the east into the Bay of Bengal and form deltas. This fertile delta region supports extensive rice cultivation, which is the main crop, along with millet, groundnuts, chili, turmeric, tobacco, and sugarcane. Agriculture is the main occupation of the people, although a few major industries like machine tools, shipping, fertilizers, and electronics supplement income and employment. In recent times, Hyderabad has turned into a hub of economic activities, with particular emphasis on the growth of software technology. The state was the first to float the idea of e-governance in India through the use of computers in day-to-day administration. Among the main tourist attractions, the Golconda fort at Hyderabad, the Venkataswara temple at Tirupati, and the Nagarjuna Sagar dam are prominent.

Ram Shankar Nanda

Further Reading
Robinson, Marguerite S. (1988) *Local Politics: The Law of Sishes: Development through Political Change in Medak District, Andhra Pradesh (South India).* New Delhi: Oxford University Press.
Tapper, Bruce E. (1987) *Rivalry and Tribute: Society and Ritual in a Telugu Village in South India.* Delhi: Hindustan Publishing.

ANDO TADAO
(b. 1941), Japanese architect. Ando Tadao was born in Osaka on 13 September 1941. Unlike most contemporary architects, Ando did not receive any formal architectural training but was a carpenter's apprentice for a short time, during which he learned traditional Japanese wood construction. He taught himself architecture by visiting temples, shrines, and teahouses in Kyoto, Nara, and various other parts of Japan and through travels in the United States, Europe, and Asia, where he made a number of his detailed sketchbooks. In 1969, Ando established his own architectural firm in Osaka. He received his first award, the Architectural Institute of Japan's annual prize of 1979, for his row house in Sumiyoshi. He has designed some of the simplest and most lyrical buildings, especially houses, churches, temples, museums, and art galleries. By the manipulation of massive exposed concrete structures, Ando has produced a minimalist type of architecture. Among his well-known projects are the Rokko Housing I (1978); the Church on the Water (1985); the Church of the Light (1987); the Japanese Pavilion for International Expo 92 in Seville, Spain (1989); the Museum of Literature II (1993); the Suntory Museum in Osaka (1995); the UNESCO Mediation Space in Paris (1994); and the Modern Art Museum of Fort Worth, Texas (1997).

Nathalie Cavasin

Further Reading
Ando Tadao, and Richard Pare, eds. (1996) *The Colours of Light.* London: Phaidon.
Dal Co, Francesco. (1995) *Tadao Ando: Complete Works.* London: Phaidon.
Drew, Philip. (1996) *Church on the Water, Church of the Light: Tadao Ando.* London: Phaidon.

ANG LEE
(b. 1954), Chinese film director. Ang Lee was born in Taiwan on 23 October 1954. In 1978, he moved to the United States where he studied theater at the University of Illinois and film production at New York University. Lee directed his first feature film, *Pushing Hands*, in 1992, a tale of a Chinese family struggling to adapt to life in the United States, which in Taiwan won him three Golden Horse awards and a special jury prize for direction. *Pushing Hands* was followed in 1993 by *The Wedding Banquet*, a comedy about a gay Chinese man living in New York City, which received the Golden Bear award in Berlin. These films led to increased funding for *Eat, Drink, Man, Woman* (1994) and *Sense and Sensibility* (1995), both of which earned Academy Award nominations for Lee. In his next films, *Ice Storm* (1997) and *Ride with the Devil* (1999), Lee focused on American subjects. In a return to Chinese-language films, the martial arts adventure *Crouching Tiger, Hidden Dragon* (2000) won four Academy Awards including best foreign language film.

Bent Nielsen

Further Reading
Ang Lee, et al. (1994) *Two Films by Ang Lee.* Woodstock, NY: Overlook Press.

Ang Lee holds his Oscar for the best foreign language film at the 25 March 2001 Academy Awards in Los Angeles. (AFP/ CORBIS)

ANGKATAN BELIA ISLAM MALAYSIA

Angkatan Belia Islam Malaysia (Malaysian Islamic Youth Movement, or ABIM) was established in 1971 by Anwar Ibrahim, among others. The movement was officially registered by the Malaysian government on 17 August 1972. Among ABIM's objectives are Islamic training, defense, and propagation *(dakwah)* through mobilizing Muslim youths both in and out of school. Although not affiliated with any political party, the movement addresses sociopolitical issues and trains future politicians. For this reason, in particular, it is closely monitored by the authorities.

The first president of ABIM, Razali Mawawi, was replaced by Anwar Ibrahim in 1974. Upon his resignation as president of ABIM in 1982, Anwar was replaced by Siddiq Fadil. Siddiq was succeeded by Muhammad Nur Manuty in 1991. Ahmad Azam Abdul Rahman was elected as ABIM's fifth president in September 1997.

Although the ideology or mission of ABIM remains to foster the development of Islam and to voice Islamic aspirations, as expressed by the Malaysian Muslim community, its theme has evolved over the decades. In the 1970s, ABIM was more aggressive toward and critical of the government, an attitude that meshed with the general political climate of that decade. For example, while he was the ABIM secretary-general and president, Anwar defended impoverished Malay farmers from alleged government abuses. He was arrested in 1974 and then jailed without trial for twenty months under the Internal Security Act. ABIM regarded this Act as un-Islamic and accused the government of being secular-nationalist and arbitrary. In the 1980s, ABIM softened its attacks but remained critical of the ruling regime, as shown by its inclination toward problem solving by adopting the "working in the light of wisdom" approach. In the 1990s, the movement adopted a proactive approach and became a government partner in nation building. Since the leadership of Ahmad, ABIM has fostered the theme: "Revitalizing ABIM's ideals and extolling the movement's dynamism and struggle."

ABIM has long been the voice of the Islamic community, leading Muslims toward a more modern, nonconservative approach to religion and toward eventual leadership positions in all sectors. Despite his political contribution to these achievements, Mahathir Mohamad, the prime minister of the country since 1981, has dropped from his administration many of ABIM's most prominent leaders linked to Anwar, who served as deputy prime minister until 1998. This was particularly the case after the sack of Anwar and his imprisonment as a result of a power struggle between Anwar and Mahathir. Today, although ABIM is still recognized by the government as an Islamic organization, its influence is limited to the socioreligious and cultural spheres. ABIM, along with other Islamic organizations, has raised the idea of *reformasi* (a reform movement), continuing its criticism of the government, while the government uses all the powers at its disposal to keep ABIM under surveillance.

Andi Faisal Bakti

Further Reading

Chandra Muzaffar. (1987) *Islamic Resurgence in Malaysia.* Petaling Jaya, Malaysia: Fajar Bakti.
Gill, Ranjit. (1998) *Anwar Ibrahim Mahathir's Dilemma.* Singapore: Epic Management Services, Pte Ltd.
Hussin Mutalib. (1995) "ABIM." In *The Oxford Encyclopedia of Modern Islamic World*, vol. 1, edited by John Esposito. New York: Oxford University Press, 15–17.

Milne, R. Stephen, and Diane Mauzy. (1999) *Malaysian Politics under Mahathir.* London: Routledge.

Mohd Anuar Tahir. (1993) *Pendirian Politik ABIM* (ABIM's Political Principles). Petaling Jaya and Selangor, Malaysia: Angkatan Belia Islam Malaysia, Budaya Ilmu Sdn Bhd.

Muhammad Kamal Hassan. "Malaysia." In *The Oxford Encyclopedia of Modern Islamic World*, vol. 3, edited by John Esposito. New York: Oxford University Press, 36–38.

Siddiq Fadil. (1989) *Koleksi Ucapan Dasar Muktamar Sanawi ABIM: Mengangkat Martabat Umat* (A Collection of Main Talks during the Annual Meetings of ABIM: Elevating the Dignity of the Community). Kuala Lumpur, Malaysia: Dewan Pustaka Islam.

Zainah Anwar. (1987) *Islamic Revivalism in Malaysia: Dakwah among the Students.* Petaling Jaya and Selangor, Malaysia: Pelanduk Publications.

ANGKOR WAT   While more than one hundred major temple sites are found in and around the town of Siem Reap and Tonle Sap ("Great Lake") in northwest Cambodia, Angkor Wat is unique among them. An early capital of the Khmer empire, which flourished in classical Southeast Asia from the sixth to the mid-fifteenth century, Angkor Wat is the largest temple complex in the entire Angkor plain (other famous sites on the plain include Bayon and Ta Prom) and the largest religious monument in the world. Reputedly constructed as a funerary temple and mausoleum from sandstone at Phnom Kulen by Suryavarman II (1113–1150 CE), the ruins encompass an area of approximately 104 square kilometers and took more than thirty years to build. It was named a UNESCO World Heritage Site in 1992.

Architecture

Angkor Wat was dedicated to the Hindu god Vishnu, but its impeccably crafted and detailed ornamental architecture and bas reliefs depict all manner of Khmer legends and history of Angkor Wat. Measuring 1.5 by 1.3 kilometers in size, the complex is distinguished by its westward orientation, as well as by the wall and moat (measuring 190 meters wide) that surround it. These features not only delineate the temple boundaries but also represent other mountain ranges and oceans. A central avenue, 475 meters in length, connects the main entrance—accessed via a causeway across the moat—to the central temple, passing between two libraries and reflecting pools. The central temple consists of three stories, each of laterite, with five towers. The central tower, rising 55 meters above the ground, stands for Mount Meru, in Hindu mythology the center of the universe and home of the gods. The towers also serve as the current symbol of the Kingdom of Cambodia.

History

Established by Yasovarman I (reigned 889–900/ 910), Angkor achieved its zenith in the twelfth century, when the Khmer empire ruled over an area that stretched from Vietnam to China and India. However,

Monks at the ruins of the Bayon Temple, Angkor Wat, Cambodia, in 1996. (KEREN SU/CORBIS)

ANGKOR WAT— WORLD HERITAGE SITE

Angkor Wat was designated a UNESCO World Heritage Site in 1992 because it is the most important archaeological site in Southeast Asia. Special measures have been taken to protect the site and the surrounding area.

the city was sacked by the Chams of southern Vietnam in 1177, and Angkor Wat was converted into a Buddhist temple prior to the Siamese conquest of 1431. Jayavarman VII (c.1120–c.1215; reigned 1181–c.1215) subsequently established a new capital, Angkor Thom, which was abandoned in 1434. Overgrown by jungle, the ruins of both were rediscovered by the French in 1861, although their existence was well known to local Khmer residents and early European explorers.

Warfare in Cambodia in the 1970s and 1980s prevented tourists from visiting the site, a threat that persisted in remote parts of the complex through 1999, when guerilla soldiers of the Khmer Rouge even occupied Angkor Wat itself for a brief period. In the first years of the twenty-first century, tourist visits to Angkor Wat are again on the increase, and tourism has become a major source of foreign exchange for the Cambodian government. Land mines continue to be a threat in rural areas surrounding the complex, however, while theft and vandalism are the most serious physical threat to the monuments themselves. In order to prevent statues and carvings that give vitality to the temples and their histories from being stolen for private collectors, many have been removed for safekeeping and restoration.

Greg Ringer

Further Reading
Chandler, David P. (2000). *A History of Cambodia*. 3d ed. Boulder, CO: Westview Press.
Cook, Ian G., Marcus A. Doel, and L. I. Rex. (1996). *Fragmented Asia: Regional Integration and National Disintegration in Pacific Asia*. Aldershot, U.K.: Ashgate.
Dutt, Ashok, ed.(1985). *Southeast Asia: Realm of Contrasts*. Boulder, CO: Westview Press.
Higham, Charles. (2002) *The Civilization of Angkor*. Berkeley and Los Angeles: University of California Press.
Ringer, Greg, (2000). "Tourism in Cambodia, Laos and Myanmar: From Terrorism to Tourism?" In *Tourism in South and Southeast Asia: Issues and Cases*, edited by C. Michael Hall and Stephen Page. Oxford: Butterworth-Heinemann, 178–194.

ANGLO-DUTCH TREATY   The Anglo-Dutch Treaty (1824) aimed to terminate Anglo-Dutch rivalry in the Malay Archipelago and East Indies. It attempted to end clashes and disputes between British and Dutch merchants by dividing the Malay Peninsula and the East Indies into British and Dutch spheres of influence. The treaty was signed in London by British and Dutch officials without consulting the local rulers concerned.

The line demarking British and Dutch spheres of influence was south of the Straits of Singapore. The Netherlands transferred to Britain her factories in India, relinquished Malacca and its dependencies, and accepted British occupation of Singapore; Britain surrendered its dependencies south of the Straits and Bencoolen on the southwest coast of Sumatra. The Dutch agreed to terminate tin monopoly treaties with Perak and Selangor in the Malay Peninsula. Both parties agreed not to conclude treaties with local leaders or form new settlements on islands in each other's spheres of influence.

The treaty did not fully end Anglo-Dutch rivalry. The British claimed Dutch agents still occasionally penetrated their territory. The Dutch protested in the 1840s and 1870s, when James Brooke and Dent and Overbeck took control over what are now parts of Sarawak and Sabah. Since the treaty failed to define the position of the island of Borneo, the British claimed Borneo was not covered by it.

The treaty broke up the Malay empire of Johore. The British and Dutch effectively excluded other powers from the region, using the treaty as a means of controlling what became British Malaya and the Netherlands East Indies.

Geetha Govindasamy

Further Reading
Andaya, Barbara Watson. (1982) *A History of Malaysia*. London: The Macmillan Press Limited.
Baker, Jim. (1999) *A Popular History of Singapore and Malaysia*. Kuala Lumpur, Malaysia: Times Books International.
Mills, L. A. (1971) *British in Malaya: 1824–1867*. New York: AMS Press.

ANGLO-INDIANS   Although "Anglo-Indian" originally meant someone of British descent who was born and lived permanently in India, after about 1900 the term came to mean a person of mixed European and Indian ancestry, a Eurasian.

THE MAKING OF ANGLO-INDIANS

"I had often admired a lovely Hindostanee girl who sometimes visited Carter at my house, who was very lively and clever. Upon Carter's leaving Bengal I invited her to become an inmate with me, which she considered to do, and from that time to the day of her death Jemdannee, which was her name, lived with me, respected and admired by all my friends by her extraordinary sprightliness and good humour. Unlike the women in general in Asia she never secluded herself from the sight of strangers; on the contrary, she delighted in joining in male parties, cordially joining in the mirth which prevailed, though she never touched wine or spirits of any kind."

Source: Alfred Spencer, ed. ([1787] 1913) *Memoirs of William Hickey.* London: Hurst & Blackett, Ltd.

Until the opening of the Suez Canal in 1869, British men vastly outnumbered European women in India, and these male residents commonly took Indian women as mistresses or housekeepers. After the canal opened, women could more easily travel from England, and the Anglo-Indian community then became a stable and largely endogamous unit.

Only a few thousand Anglo-Indians remain in India, since most emigrated to Britain, Australia, or Canada during the past half-century. The last census to enumerate them, taken in 1951 while their exodus was in progress, recorded 11,637 Anglo-Indians.

The main characteristics of the Anglo-Indians are Christian religion; English as mother tongue; European lifestyle and home décor; Western dress for children and adults; and employment in particular administrative and service professions (typically requiring fluency in English and a high-school education), such as the post office, railways, police work, teaching, and nursing.

Paul Hockings

Further Reading

Gaikwad, Vijay Singh R. R. (1967) *The Anglo-Indians: A Study in the Problems and Processes Involved in Emotional and Cultural Integration.* Bombay, India: Asia Publishing House.

Gist, Noel P., and Roy D. Wright. (1973) *Marginality and Identity: Anglo-Indians as a Racially Mixed Minority in India.* Leiden, Netherlands: E. J. Brill.

ANGLO-MYSORE WARS   The Anglo-Mysore wars were four wars conducted by British forces against Hyder Ali (1722–1782) and his son Tipu Sultan (1749–1799), the rulers of the kingdom of Mysore (now Karnataka), in southern India, during 1767–1769, 1780–1784, 1790–1792, and March–May 1799. The final conflict ended with the death of Tipu Sultan during his defense of Seringapatam, Tipu's capital.

Mysore was a rich agricultural territory with many superbly built hill forts, and it was a prize that the British East India Company saw as holding the key to a large conquest of southern India and to blocking French aspirations in the region. The wars began when Hyder Ali was fighting the Marathas to the north, and the British lent support to the nizam (ruler) of Hyderabad, who then invaded Mysore territory with a British detachment. Hyder got the Marathas on his side, won over the nizam, and then vented his fury on the British, who were based in Madras and outlying towns. Hyder reached the walls of Madras City, where he dictated a treaty to the panic-stricken residents.

His exasperation with the British flared anew in the Second Anglo-Mysore War, caused by the British failure to honor the treaty and render him assistance in his renewed struggle with the Marathas. Again Hyder marched on Madras, this time hoping to get assistance from the French based in Pondicherry. It failed to materialize. During this war Hyder Ali died of cancer, but his son Tipu Sultan took up the crusade against the British, who made peace with him in 1784 (the Treaty of Mangalore).

The next war began because the British in Madras wrote to the nizam of Hyderabad that they would help him regain territories lost to Tipu's forces. Anticipating further hostilities, Tipu attacked Travancore and thereabouts in 1789–1790. The British then entered into league with the nizam and also with the peshwa, the chief minister of the Marathas. In 1790 the British moved into southern Mysore, but Tipu denied them any clear victories. Lord Charles Cornwallis (1738–1805), the governor-general of India, then assumed command himself. He captured Bangalore and moved toward Seringapatam (or Sri Ranga Pattana), just outside Mysore City. Now Tipu's scorched earth policy brought famine into the British camp and obliged Cornwallis to retreat. He had more success in a subsequent campaign, and in 1792 besieged Seringapatam. This led to Tipu's submission, and another treaty was concluded in March. Tipu was obliged to surrender two of his sons as hostages, pay a massive indemnity, and cede up half of his dominions, which were then incorporated into the British East India Company territories as the "Ceded Districts". Tipu also was forced to cede territory to the Marathas and the nizam.

The Fourth Mysore War, a three-month engagement, was caused by Tipu's refusal to accept an alliance with the British. The new governor-general, Lord Richard Wellesley (1760–1842), suspected Tipu's intentions because following the previous treaty Tipu had tried to form alliances with France, Istanbul, and the shah of Afghanistan, hoping to drive the British out of India altogether. Three armies, one led by Arthur Wellesley (1769–1852), the future Duke of Wellington, converged on Seringapatam and with two fierce attacks brought the war to an end. Tipu's dead body was found, sword in hand, among those of his soldiers at a north gate, on 4 May 1799. The nizam was given some of the captured territory, but much of it was restored as the Kingdom of Mysore under Krishnaraja, the maharaja of Mysore, and remained with Mysore until 1947. The alliance with the British was finally signed.

Paul Hockings

Further Reading
Forrest, Denys. (1970) *Tiger of Mysore: The Life and Death of Tipu Sultan.* London: Chatto & Windus.

Wilks, Mark. ([1810] 1930) *Historical Sketches of the South of India, in an Attempt to Trace the History of Mysoor: from the Origin of the Hindoo Government of that State, to the Extinction of the Mohammedan Dynasty in 1799.* Reprint ed. Mysore, India: Government Branch Press.

ANH DAO DUY (1904–1988), Vietnamese journalist, historian, leader in anticolonial struggle. Highly critical of Confucian culture that he believed bound the country to feudalism and colonialism, Anh Dao Duy established a Hue-based study group and began to publish books in *quoc ngu*—the Vietnamese vernacular—that introduced the Vietnamese public to Western social sciences in the 1920s. He was arrested by French authorities in 1929 for organizing the New Vietnam Revolutionary Party. Imprisoned for one year, he was given a three-year suspended sentence that led him to abandon politics and pursue scholarship. In 1938, he published the seminal *An Outline History of Vietnamese Culture.* Following the 1954 Geneva Accords, Anh joined a large number of North Vietnamese artists and writers who began to demand intellectual and literary freedoms, which the Lao Dong Party had stripped in its attempt to impose the rigid tenets of socialist realism on arts and letters; an event that became known as the Nhan Van–Giai Pham Affair. Anh asserted that the party's rigid adherence to Marxist ideology constrained social science research. Anh also attacked the cult of personality surrounding Ho Chi Minh and the monopoly of power held by the Lao Dong Party. In an April 1958 crackdown on the dissident intellectuals, Anh was forced to write a self-criticism. Effectively silenced, Anh died in 1988.

Zachary Abuza

Further Reading
Abuza, Zachary. (2001) *Renovating Vietnamese Politics in Contemporary Vietnam.* Boulder, CO: Lynne Rienner Publishers.

ANHUI (1995 est. pop. 59.6 million). The central eastern Chinese province of Anhui (Anhwei) is bordered by Hubei and Henan on the west, Shandong and Jiangsu on the north, Jiangsu and Zhejiang on the east, and Jiangxi on the south. The province, where agriculture is the principal occupation, covers an area of 139,000 square kilometers, making it one of China's smallest. It is traversed by the Chang (Yangtze) River from west to east. The capital Hefei (1993 population 1.1 million) is situated in the center of Anhui, north of Lake Chao, and the province is divided into nine regions and seventy counties.

Anhui is separated into two distinct regions by mountain ranges running northeast-southwest, with peaks in the western part reaching to 1,751 meters. The northern region, which has been densely popu-

ANHUI—WORLD HERITAGE SITE

Designated by UNESCO as a World Heritage Site in 2000, the Xidi and Hongcun villages in southern Anhui are uniquely preserved examples of rural trade posts from China's feudal period. Somehow the two villages have survived almost intact, down to the original decorations and water systems.

lated since the Han dynasty (206 BCE–220 CE), has a temperate monsoon climate, while the south, which was settled by Han Chinese from the seventh century on, has subtropical monsoon climate with a growing season of eight to nine months. The mountainous areas are mainly concentrated in the southern and western parts of the province; the rest is mostly fertile plains. Major crops in the north are wheat, soybeans, and cotton, while the southern region crops are dominated by rice and tea.

Bent Nielsen

ANIME

ANIME *Anime*, the Japanese term for animated films, refers to Japanese animation. Since the early 1950s, when the father of *anime*, Tezuka Osamu (1928–1989), created such famous series as *Jungle taitei* (known in the United States as "Kimba the White Lion") and *Tetsuon atomu* (known in the United States as "Astro Boy"), Japan has produced a stream of innovative and original animated films. Artistically, *anime* are known for their use of color, their textured and detailed backgrounds and foregrounds, and their complex camera points of view, which approximate those of acted films. Sympathetic characters are often depicted with enormous eyes, oddly colored hair, and childlike features. Story lines tend to be complex, and many *anime* appear as long series of episodes, with a multitude of characters and subplots.

Anime often have their roots in *manga* (comic books, or graphic novels), though not always; in recent times computer games have also inspired *anime*, as in the case of *Pokemon*. Other children's *anime* that have crossed the Pacific to intrigue U.S. audiences include *Mach Go! Go! Go!* (U.S. "Speed Racer"), *Uchu senkan Yamato* (U.S. "Starblazers"), *Dragonball Z*, and *Sailor Moon*. There are also many *anime* aimed at an older audience, which feature graphic sex and violence. Some *anime* are serious films; *Princess Mononoke*, the 1999 U.S. version of a full-length animated film by Japan's premier *anime* director, Miyazaki Hayao, received critical acclaim in the United States.

Michael Ashkenazi and Francesca Forrest

See also: **Cinema—Japan**

Further Reading
"A Brief History of Anime." Retrieved 20 July 2001, from: http://gwis2.circ.gwu.edu/~koulikom/history.html.
Napier, Susan J. (2000) *Anime from Akira to Princess Mononoke: Experiencing Contemporary Japanese Animation.* New York: Palgrave.

Schodt, Frederick L. (1983) *Manga! Manga! The World of Japanese Comics.* Tokyo, New York, and San Francisco: Kodansha International.

ANKARA

ANKARA (1997 pop. 3.7 million). Ankara (formerly Angora) is the capital and second-largest city of the Republic of Turkey. Located on the Central Anatolian plateau, Ankara is approximately 355 kilometers southeast of Istanbul, Turkey's largest city.

History
Ankara has been the site of continuous settlement since at least the Neolithic era (c. 10,300/10,000–3500 BCE) and was a sizable town throughout most of antiquity. Its situation along major caravan routes and its ample supplies of freshwater and easily defensible position were ideal for a trading town. Ankara was incorporated into the Roman empire in 25 BCE and was controlled at various times by the Persians, Arabs, Seljuks, and Byzantines.

The city was conquered in 1354 (some sources say 1356) by the second Ottoman sultan, Orhan I (c. 1281–1360). Orhan's son Murad I (1326–1389) incorporated Ankara into the Ottoman empire in 1360 or 1361. In 1402 the Mongols under Timur (Tamerlane, Timur-Lang; c. 1360–1403) defeated the Ottoman sultan Bayezid I (c. 1360–1403) in a battle just outside Ankara. Despite the ensuing civil war, Ankara remained under Ottoman control and served for some time as the regional capital of the province of Anatolia (Anadolu). Kuthaya eventually replaced it as regional capital, but Ankara was restored as a provincial center in the nineteenth century.

Throughout this period Ankara was a center of grain production. During the nineteenth century a luxury trade based on mohair, a particularly warm and soft fabric made from the hair of the local Angora goats, increased in importance, as did carpet production for the European market. A railway between Ankara and Izmit, financed by the Deutsche Bank and begun in 1889, increased Ankara's commercial importance as well as its ties to broader economic trends.

The Twentieth Century
Ankara's significance increased markedly during the Turkish War for Independence from 1919 to 1923. The British occupied the Ottoman capital of Istanbul, and Sivas, the initial center of nationalist resistance, was too far from the front. Consequently the nationalist forces chose Ankara as a new base of operations. On 27 December 1919 the nationalist government,

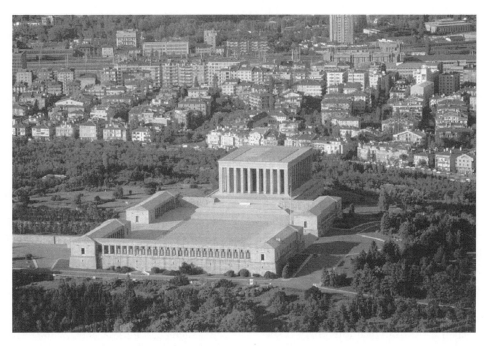

An aerial view of the mausoleum of Kemal Ataturk, the founder of the Republic of Turkey, in Ankara. (YANN ARTHUS-BERTRAND/CORBIS)

under the leadership of Mustafa Kemal (later Ataturk) (1881–1938), arrived in Ankara and began the workings of government in the town's agricultural school. The nationalist parliament (Buyuk Millet Meclisi) convened on 23 April 1920.

Such was the power and prestige of Istanbul, however, that the decision to make Ankara the capital in October 1923 was met with considerable surprise and not a little dismay. Compared to cosmopolitan Istanbul, Ankara was distinctly unglamorous, a sleepy town, dusty in summer and muddy in winter. However, this shift involved important symbolism. The move to Ankara underlined the republic's break from its Ottoman legacy and the foundation of a distinctly Turkish and Anatolian nation.

Ankara's new status as the Turkish Republic's capital brought dramatic growth and development to the city. In the first years of the republic a large number of important buildings were constructed in or near what is referred to as the Old City, principally around the Ulus district. After 1930 a broader plan for the city developed, and major institutions were constructed in districts southeast of the original town center. Planning could not control the effects of explosive population growth, however, and many districts were made up of unlicensed housing of varying quality, locally called *gecekondu* (literally, constructed at night). Although Ankara developed no actual "downtown," the district of Kizilay generally has been considered the city's hub. The wealthier district of Cankaya also has been an important center of trade and government.

Ankara Today

Ankara houses the parliament, presidential palace, and governmental ministries, and the city has become a cultural center of Turkey. Ankara University, Haceteppe University, Middle East Technical University, and Bilkent University, a private university, are important institutions for learning and research. Ankara is also home to the Ethnographic Museum and a world-class archaeological museum called the Museum of Anatolian Civilizations. The Haci Bayram Mosque (1429), dedicated to an important Muslim saint, is a point of local pilgrimage, and the Mausoleum of Mustafa Kemal Ataturk (Anit Kabir), designed by Emin Onat and Orhan Arda, is an example of republican-era architecture and a testament to Ataturk's place in the republic's national consciousness.

Despite its role as the seat of government, Ankara remains, culturally, economically, and demographically, Turkey's "second city" after Istanbul. Nevertheless, while Istanbul's palaces and mosques are a constant reminder of an Ottoman past, Ankara embodies the future, both as the capital of the Turkish Republic and as the urban embodiment of the republic's modernizing mission.

Howard Eissenstat

Further Reading

Cross, Toni M., and Gary Leiser (2000) *A Brief History of Ankara*. Vacaville, CA: Indian Ford Press.

ANSARI, ABDULLAH (1005–1089), Sufi religious figure. Khwaja Abdullah Ansari was a Sufi sheikh from Heart, Afghanistan, and a Hanbali traditionist, renowned for his sermons in rhymed prose and for his polemics against rationalist theology *(kalam)*. Ansari, a descendant of a Medinan companion of the Prophet Muhammad, was an exceptionally gifted child who composed poetry in Persian and Arabic and learned the Qur'an and the Prophetic traditions *(hadith)* before the age of nine. He embarked on the Sufi path under the guidance of his father, but his mysticism was tempered by rigorous scholastic training, and he shunned practices that sought to induce ecstatic states. He was also a renowned teacher of the Qur'an and the *hadith*, who castigated the influential Ash'arite theologians for subjecting the revealed word to logical inferences.

Ansari was primarily an orator, not a writer, and his works abound with assonances and rhythmic patterns that aid memorization. Most were either compiled from disciples' notes or dictated to scribes in his old age. Among his famous works are *Manazil al-Sa'irin* (The Stages of the Pilgrims), a Sufi spiritual guide in Arabic analyzing the psychological states and stations of the Sufi path; *Tabaqat al-Sufiyya* (Biographies of Sufis), an expanded translation of the Arabic work of the great Sufi master Sulami (c. tenth–eleventh centuries) into the ancient dialect of Herat; and *Kashf al-Asrar* (Unveiling of the Secrets), the first systematic commentary on the Qur'an written in a non-Arabic

language. His popular appeal rests primarily on his quatrains and on the *Munajat* (Intimate Conversations)—mystical invocations to God abstracted from his other works. Ansari is one of the most influential early Sufi authors whose rhymed prose, interspersed with parables and verses, was emulated by Sa'di, Jami and influenced other Persian classics.

Marta Simidchieva

Further Reading

Ansari, Abdullah. (1978) "Intimate Conversations." In *The Book of Wisdom*, edited by Ibn 'Ata' Allah and translated by Wheeler M. Thackston. New York: Paulist Press, 163–233.

Beaurecueil, Serge de. (1985) "Abdallah al-Ansari." In *Encyclopaedia Iranica*, Vol. 1, edited by E.Yarshater. London: Routledge and Kegan Paul, 187–190.

Ravan Farhadi, A. G. (1996) *Abdullah Ansari of Herat (1006–1089 CE): An Early Sufi Master*. Richmond, U.K.: Curzon Press.

Rypka, Jan. (1968) "History of Persian Literature up to the Beginning of the 20th Century." In *History of Iranian Literature*, edited by K. Jahn. Dordrecht, Netherlands: Reidel, 234–235.

ANTAKYA (1994 pop. 137,200). Antakya, the capital of Hatay (a province of approximately 1.2 million people) in southeastern Turkey, on the eastern bank of the Asi (Orontes) River, was an important city of the Roman empire. The Macedonian Seleucus I founded the city about 300 BCE and named it Antiochus (later Antioch). The city served as a central station for Roman commercial and military routes between Asia Minor and Mesopotamia and as a Roman army base for campaigns against the Persians. Although famous as a nucleus of Christianity, its original settlers were of many races and religions. The prosperity of Antioch diminished after a major earthquake in 526 and destruction by the Sasanid ruler Khosrow I in 540. The Arabs took Antioch in 638 CE.

After a brief Byzantine occupation Antioch fell to the Muslim Seljuk Turks in 1084. In 1098 the city was raided during the First Crusades and raided again in 1268 by Baybars I , Mamluk sultan of Egypt. When the Ottoman sultan Selim I (reigned 1512–) captured Antioch in 1516, the city was peopled primarily by Muslim Turkmen and Arabs and had long lost its importance as a Christian center. Antioch remained part of the Ottoman empire until after World War I. The city was occupied by French troops in 1919 and placed under French mandate by the League of Nations. An independent regime known as the Republic of Hatay was established in 1938 with Antioch as its capital. After a referendum the whole territory officially became

A QUATRAIN BY ABDULLAH ANSARI

Great shame it is to deem of high degree
Thyself, or over others recon thee:
Strive to be like the pupil of thine eye—
To see all else, but not thyself to see.

Source: Edward Browne. (1964)
A Literary History of Persia. Vol.
2. Cambridge, U.K.: Cambridge
University Press, 270.

part of the Turkish Republic (founded by Mustafa Kemal Ataturk, 1881–1938) on 23 June 1939. Since then the city has been officially called Antakya.

Surrounded by rich orchards, Antakya stands at the junction of important roads between Anatolia and other Middle Eastern countries. Its climate is mild, and its economy is based mainly on agriculture. The chief crops are cotton, grapes, wheat, rice, olives, vegetables, and fruits. Industries include olive-oil and soap factories, as well as cotton ginning and silk and shoe manufacturing. The Archaeological Museum of Antakya contains magnificent Roman mosaics and coins dating from the second and third centuries CE. A popular resort and tourist attraction is the site of ancient Daphne near Harbiye, perhaps the place where Antony married Cleopatra in 40 BCE. Another monument in the area is the Church of Saint Peter, where the apostle supposedly preached the first Christian sermons.

T. Isikozlu-E.F. Isikozlu

Further Reading
Statistical Yearbook of Turkey, 1998. (1998) Ankara, Turkey: Devlet Istatistik Enstitusu.

ANTALYA (2002 pop. 571,000). Antalya, capital of the province of Antalya (population 1 million; known in ancient Greece as Attalia) in southwestern Turkey, was founded in the second century BCE by Attalus II, king of Pergamum. Antalya is a Mediterranean port on the Gulf of Antalya, otherwise known as the Turquoise Coast. Due to its strategic location, it was once a seaport used by Crusaders to avoid Seljuk territory on their way to Palestine. Among many monuments from Antalya's past is the Hadrian Gate, a splendid structure consisting of three identical arches, built in CE 130 to commemorate Roman emperor Hadrian's visit. Saints Paul and Barnabas also visited the city on their way to Antioch. After the Seljuks captured Attalia in 1207, it became Antalya. Although Antalya was first occupied by Sultan Bayezud I (reigned 1389–1402) in 1391, it was not incorporated into the Ottoman empire until the late fifteenth century. Italian troops occupied Antalya after World War I until Turkish nationalist forces expelled them in 1921. Its ideal climate, beautiful natural setting, and proximity to ancient sites make Antalya a tourist resort. One of Turkey's fastest-growing cities, it is a center of art and culture. Natural vegetation includes bananas, citrus fruits, pine forests, and palm trees. The regional economy is largely supported by tourism and cotton production.

T. Isikozlu-E.F. Isikozlu

Further Reading
Statistical Yearbook of Turkey, 1998. (1998) Ankara, Turkey: Devlet Istatistik Enstitusu.

ANTI-FASCIST PEOPLE'S FREEDOM LEAGUE—MYANMAR The Anti-Fascist People's Freedom League (AFPFL) started out during World War II as an underground resistance movement against fascist occupation of Burma (now Myanmar) but was transformed into the dominant political party in postindependence electoral politics between 1948 and 1962. Originally founded as the Anti-Fascist Organization (AFO) in August 1944, its early leadership included Aung San (president), Than Tun (secretary general), and Thakin Soe. At various times, the AFO included the Burma Communist Party (BCP), the People's Revolutionary Party, Maha Bama, the Fabian Party, Myo Chit, the Shan Association, and the Youth League. Initially it declared its aim as resisting Japanese occupation.

The AFO was renamed the Anti-Fascist People's Freedom League at a mass meeting on 19 August 1945; organizers added the goal of securing national independence. When British colonial government returned to Burma in October 1945, the AFPFL demanded majority representation in it. When the British ignored this demand, fierce competition took place among different factions for influence. After a period of resistance and strikes against the colonial government, and after two changes in governor, the AFPFL finally emerged under Aung San as the force with which the British came to terms in September 1946. After a period of internal strife within the AFPFL, Aung San negotiated national independence from the British with the signing of the Attlee–Aung San agreement in January 1947.

In July 1947 Aung San was assassinated along with other cabinet ministers. After Aung San's assassination, U Nu took over the leadership of the AFPFL. Under U Nu's leadership, the AFPFL became the dominant parliamentary party until the coup by General Ne Win in 1962. During its years in power, the AFPFL was gradually weakened by four splits. The first of these splits occurred when Aung San expelled the BCP in November 1946. This was followed by the defection of the Peoples' Volunteer Army to the BCP in July 1948, the expulsion of the Burma Workers and Peasants Party in 1951, and the split in leadership between the Nu-Tin "Clean" and the Swe-Nyein "Stable" factions in 1958. The dominant role of the AFPFL ended when the Revolutionary Council under General Ne Win abolished all political parties on 23 March 1964 when it promulgated the Law Protecting National Unity.

Gustaaf Houtman

Further Reading

Sein Win. (1959) *The Split Story: An Account of Recent Political Upheaval in Burma with Emphasis on AFPFL.* Rangoon, Burma: The Guardian.

Tinker, Hugh. (1967) *The Union of Burma.* London: Oxford University Press.

ANTI-TAURUS The Anti-Taurus or southeastern Taurus (Guney Dogu Toros) Mountains are a folded limestone range lying between the Iranian border in southeast Turkey and the Seyhan River, at longitude 35° 30′ east. The range forms an arch. The western end merges with the Nur Mountains and the eastern with the Zagros Mountains of Iraq. Inside the arch is a plateau averaging 600 meters high, sloping gently down to the north Syrian plain. North of the Anti-Taurus is Turkey's largest lake, Lake Van. The Anti-Taurus range is up to 170 kilometers wide from north to south and includes (from west to east) the Tahtali (maximum height 3075 meters) and the Cilo-Sat (maximum height 4170 meters) Mountains.

Rainfall is generally around 500 millimeters, rising to over 1000 millimeters at the west and east extremities; in the Cilo-Sat Mountains, with ten permanent glaciers, rain falls mainly as snow. Most of the region has hot, dry summers and some snowfall in winter, melting quickly; tree cover has been removed by indiscriminate felling.

The range is dissected by three major rivers—the Ceyhan, Euphrates (Firat), and Tigris (Dicle); the last two supply irrigation and drinking water for Turkey, Syria, and Iraq as far south as the Persian Gulf. On the Euphrates are the Keban Dam (Baraj) and the Ataturk Dam and their lakes; they supply 26 billion kilowatt-hours per year of electricity and irrigate well over one million hectares. The road hub is Diyarbakir, from which passes run to Bitlis, Bingol, Elazig, and Gaziantep, with roads to Malatya-Kayseri and Adana.

The practice of transhumance, moving flocks in season to high summer pastures, is now less profitable than the cultivation of orchard trees, cotton, and vegetables on irrigated lands. The population, historically Turkish, Kurdish, and Armenian, and now mainly Kurdish, has been reduced by the military policy of evacuating villages believed to help the Kurdistan Workers Party or PKK, a Marxist terrorist organization. A small amount of petrol comes from the Batman area; copper mines at Ergani and chrome deposits at Guleman are exploited by Etibank, the State mining concern. The most popular tourist destination is Nemrut Mountain, near Adiyaman, where a Roman client king erected a tomb and statues on an isolated summit.

Kate Clow

Further Reading

Darke, Diana. (1990) *Discovery Guide to Eastern Turkey and the Black Sea Coast.* The Hague, Netherlands, and London: Michael Haag.

ANWAR, IBRAHIM (b. 1948), Malaysian politician. Ibrahim Anwar is the popular former Malaysian deputy premier who was ousted in 1998. Born in 1948 in Penang, Anwar was a youth leader and vocal critic of the government in the 1970s. In 1972 he founded the Angkatan Belia Islam Malaysia (Islamic Youth Movement, or ABIM), which grew to some 100,000 members. He was courted by the United Malay National Organization (UMNO) party leaders, and he joined the ruling party in 1982. He won a seat in parliament that year and also narrowly won the UMNO Youth leadership, putting him in touch with the party's grass roots. In 1987 Anwar became one of UMNO's three vice presidents. In 1991 he became the power-

Former deputy premier Anwar Ibrahim arriving at court in Kuala Lumpur on 5 October 1999. (AFP/CORBIS)

ful minister of finance, a post he held until 1998. In 1993 he became UMNO deputy president, the country's deputy premier, and a member of UMNO's 35-person supreme council.

Anwar was arguably the country's most popular politician, especially among the youth and indigenous Malays. His popularity was in part due to his stature as a student activist who challenged the political status quo and later became a youth leader for UNMO, but more so because he had become a model of a devout Muslim who was still committed to modernism and economic development. Although he was Prime Minister Muhammad Mahathir's hand-chosen successor, relations between the two began to sour in 1994. Anwar never challenged Mahathir in a leadership contest, though many within UMNO encouraged him to do so, and Mahathir saw Anwar as a threat and sacked him in 1998. Mahathir argued that Anwar was unfit to rule owing to corruption and sodomy allegations, but he was actually ousted over economic policies after the 1997 Asian economic crisis, which discredited Mahathir. Anwar was arrested and sentenced in a highly politicized trial to six years' imprisonment for corruption; he was later tried and sentenced to nine years' imprisonment for sodomy. Despite his arrest and imprisonment, Anwar remains a very popular politician. His supporters have rallied behind his wife, Wan Aziz, who founded the opposition Justice Party.

Zachary Abuza

Further Reading
Andaya, Barbara Watson, and Leonard Y. Andaya. (2001) *A History of Malaysia*. 2d ed. Honolulu, HI: University of Hawaii Press.
Crouch, Harold. (1996) *Government and Society in Malaysia*. Ithaca, NY: Cornell University Press.

AO DAI The *ao dai* (pronounced "ow zai" in the north and "ow yai" in the south and literally meaning "long dress") is the traditional dress of the Vietnamese people. The *ao dai* is a contoured, full-length dress worn over black or white loose-fitting trousers that brush the floor. The dress's body-hugging top splits into a front and back panel from above the waist and runs to just below the knee. The *ao dai* was originally designed for both genders, but the dress is more common today among women. Early versions of the *ao dai* date back to 1744, when Lord Vu Vong of the Nguyen dynasty (1802–1955) decreed that both women and men should wear an ensemble of a short gown that buttoned down the front and loose-fitting trousers. It

was not until 1932 that the modern-style *ao dai* appeared. Vietnamese designer Cat Tuong fitted the bodice to the curves of the body, moved the buttons from the front position to closer along the shoulder and side seam, and lengthened the top so that it reached the floor. During the 1950s, two tailors in Saigon, Tran Kim and Dung, started producing the dress with raglan sleeves that created a diagonal seam running from the collar to the underarm. The color of the top is traditionally indicative of the wearer's age and status in society. Young girls and students wear white, older but unmarried women wear soft pastels, married women wear rich, strong colors, and red is worn at weddings.

Traditionally the *ao dai* is custom made, accounting for the flattering fit that highlights the figure of the wearer, but today the popularity of the dress outside of Vietnam has dictated that it be mass produced to make it more available and affordable.

Richard B. Verrone

Further Reading
Lieu, N. T. (2000) "Remembering 'the Nation' through Pageantry: Femininity and the Politics of Vietnamese Womanhood in the Ha Hau Ao Dai Contest." *Frontiers* 21: 127–151.
"Style-Designer Minh Hanh Brings the Ao Dai, Vietnam's Traditional Costume, Back into Fashion." (2001) *People Weekly* (1 May): 66–72.

AOI MATSURI The Aoi Matsuri, held in Kyoto on 15 May, is the oldest festival in Japan and possibly in the world. It was first held in the mid-sixth century as a petition to the goddess of rain and the god of thunder for relief from the terrible storms and floods that were battering the country and destroying the harvest. The plea was successful, for the storms and floods soon abated; the ceremonies have been reenacted ever since in gratitude and to ensure a bountiful harvest.

The grand procession, shrine offerings, and rituals are the culmination of a series of purification rites that take place during the first half of the month. The day's events occur in three parts: *kyuchu* (at the palace), *rochu* (on the road), and *shachu* (at the shrine). Traditionally, a messenger from the emperor, together with an entourage of around five hundred nobles and courtiers, performed sacred rituals at Kyoto Imperial Palace, early in the morning. The participants then left the palace grounds and proceeded to Shimogamo Shrine and then Kamigamo Shrine in the stately procession that formed the highlight of the festival. Those events are now recreated by actors; the gorgeous costumes are authentic recreations of the sumptuous court dress of the Heian period (794–1185). The mounted imperial messenger and two ox-drawn lacquered carts, decorated with wisteria flowers and fine bamboo blinds, lead the procession, followed by a retinue of officials and attendants. Then comes the *saio-dai*, an unmarried princess-priestess wearing the elaborate twelve-layer silk robes of a Heian noblewoman and riding on a palanquin, attended by court ladies, dancers, and mounted guards.

When the entourage has arrived at Shimogamo Shrine, prayers and offerings are presented to the deities and ceremonies and ancient court music and dances are performed. The procession then continues to nearby Kamigamo Shrine, where prayers and dances are again offered and the final ceremonies are performed.

Often translated as "hollyhock" the name *aoi* actually refers to the *futaba aoi* wild ginger plant (*Asarum caulescens*), whose evergreen leaves are considered sacred and a powerful charm against thunderstorms. These leaves are used to decorate the festival costumes and carriages and the eaves of houses along the processional route, in addition to being offered to the deities at the two shrines. Today the Aoi Matsuri continues to be one of the greatest events in Japan's festival calendar, counting among Kyoto's three foremost festivals and attracting hundreds of thousands of spectators.

Lucy D. Moss

Further Reading
Haga, Hideo. (1970) *Japanese Folk Festivals Illustrated*. Trans. by Fanny Mayer. Tokyo: Miura Printing Company.
Vilhar, Gorazd, and Charlotte Anderson. (1994) *Matsuri: World of Japanese Festivals*. Tokyo: Shufunotomo.

AOMORI (2002 est. pop. 1.5 million). Aomori Prefecture is situated in the north of Japan's island of Honshu. A prime agricultural and fishing area, its Seikan Tunnel links Honshu with the island of Hokkaido to the north. It occupies an area of 9,619 square kilometers. Aomori's main geographical features are the Dewa and Ou Mountains, and the largest rivers are the Iwakigawa and the Oirasegawa. Two peninsulas, the Tsugaru on the west and the Shimokita on the east, form Mutsu Bay. Aomori is bordered by the Pacific Ocean, Tsugaru Strait, and the Sea of Japan and by Iwate and Akita Prefectures. In ancient times, Aomori was known as Tsugaru and Nambu districts,

which were combined in 1871 as Hirosaki Prefecture, later renamed Aomori Prefecture.

The capital of the prefecture is Aomori city, situated on Aomori Bay. It long has been a center for shipping and fishing since its harbor was constructed in 1624. Until the 1988 opening of the Seikan Tunnel, it also was the terminal for ferry service to Hokkaido. Aomori is famous for its Nebuta Festival, celebrating the ancient victory of the Tsugaru clan with a nighttime parade of illuminated floats. The prefecture's other important cities are Hachinohe, Hirosaki, Misawa, and Towada.

The economy is dominated by agriculture, forestry, and fishing, which permits a large catch of mackerel, pollack, and squid. While the cities of Aomori and Hirosaki continue the production of traditional lacquerware, some modern industry has clustered around Hachinoe. Tourists are drawn to the region by its many hot spring resorts, by Towada-Hachimantai National Park, and by the Shimokita Peninsula volcano of Osorezan, which has a temple featuring traditional shamanism.

E. L. S. Weber

Further Reading
"Aomori Prefecture." (1993) *Japan: An Illustrated Encyclopedia*. Tokyo: Kodansha Ltd.

APRIL 19 REVOLUTION—KOREA The April 19 Revolution refers to the 1960 collapse of the government of Syngman Rhee (1875–1965), the newly reelected president of the Republic of Korea (South Korea). On 15 March of that year, Rhee, the leader of the Liberal Party, had again won the office of president, but his success came amid widespread electoral fraud. A month later, on 19 April, massive student demonstrations rocked Korea, and Rhee was forced to resign and flee into exile.

Rhee was a complex figure. An aristocrat, a Methodist, and a proponent of republicanism, he had struggled to replace Korea's monarchic system with a modern government and in 1948 became the first president of the newly founded Republic of Korea. But his authoritarian manner—including his willingness to use the military and civil police to suppress any democratic dissent threatening his power—was apparent long before the 1960 election. When police killed a secondary student in a town outside the southern city of Pusan, anti-Rhee sentiments soon spread to Korea's capital, Seoul. In the following days, the violence continued, but the students, now joined by their teachers, succeeded in forcing Rhee's resignation.

Although the expulsion of Syngman Rhee reveals the importance of popular protest in the history of modern Korea, Rhee's ouster came in the aftermath of World War II, amid a much broader, fiercely fought struggle between the United States and its then rival, the Soviet Union. The Cold War (as this struggle became known) affected many other nations besides the two opponents. For instance, after World War II, Korea had been abruptly divided into two mutually hostile regions: a Communist north and a democratic south. Yet even today, the precise nature and extent of democracy in South Korea from 1945 and 1987 are widely debated.

In 1949, Kim Ku (b. 1876), the only figure capable of challenging Rhee's political legitimacy, had been assassinated. Rhee, who enjoyed the support of the U.S. military government in Korea from 1945 until his election as president in 1948, may have known about the assassination plan in advance. In 2001, documents resurfaced suggesting a possible connection between Ku's assassination and the Central Intelligence Agency (CIA) of the United States.

Michael Goodwin

See also: **Rhee, Syngman**

Further Reading

Hoare, James, and Susan Pares. (1999) *Conflict in Korea: An Encyclopedia*. Santa Barbara, CA: ABC-CLIO.

Lee, Ki-Baik. (1984) *A New History of Korea*. Cambridge, MA: Harvard University Press.

Oh, John Kie-chang. (2001) "The Student Uprising." *Korea Times* Retrieved 18 April 2001, from: www.hankooki.com/kt_op/200104/t2001041816442848110.htm.

AQUINO, BENIGNO (1932–1983), political leader in the Philippines. Born in Concepcion, Tarlac, as the son of a politician of national fame, Benigno ("Ninoy") Aquino, Jr. became a journalist and came to national prominence when he negotiated the surrender of the Huk rebel leader Luis Taruc in 1954. A reporter for the Manila *Daily Mirror*, Aquino had been secretly appointed by President Ramon Magsaysay to negotiate with Taruc.

Aquino entered politics and in 1956 was elected mayor of his home town, Concepcion, at the age of twenty-four. He became governor of Tarlac in 1961 and senator in 1967. His marriage to Corazon Cojuangco in 1954 produced five children.

Benigno Aquino in San Francisco in July 1983, just weeks before he returned to the Philippines, where he was assassinated on his arrival in Manila. (BETTMANN/CORBIS)

The leader of the political opposition, Aquino was arrested one day after President Ferdinand Marcos declared martial law on 22 September 1972. Kept in solitary confinement for eight years, he was put on trial in August 1973 on charges of murder, subversion, and illegal possession of weapons. The trial was off and on for four years, and the sentence of death by firing squad was not carried out.

In March 1980, Aquino suffered a heart attack and was allowed to travel to the United States for medical treatment. After bypass surgery, he accepted a fellowship at Harvard University and became an outspoken critic of the Marcos regime.

When Aquino returned three years later, he was assassinated in Manila as he left the plane. The Agrava Commission that convened to investigate the murder concluded it was the work of a conspiracy of army and air force officers, including General Fabian Ver, Marcos's cousin and chief of staff. Aquino's body lay in state for ten days, in the bloodstained clothes he was wearing when martyred. Millions lined the 30-kilometer route to the cemetery through metropolitan Manila. The procession took eleven hours. His death is seen as the catalyst to the events that led to the ouster of Ferdinand Marcos.

Damon L. Woods

Further Reading
Hill, Gerald N., and Kathleen Thompson Hill. (1984) *The True Story and Analysis of the Aquino Assassination.* Sonoma, CA: Hilltop Publishing Company.
Joaquin, Nick. (1983) *The Aquinos of Tarlac.* Manila, Philippines: Cacho Hnos.

AQUINO, CORAZON (b. 1933), seventh president of the Third Philippine Republic. Corazon ("Cory") Cojuangco Aquino was born 25 January 1933 in Tarlac, Philippines, and served as president of the Third Philippine Republic from 1986 to 1992. Born into one of the wealthiest families in the Philippines, she was educated in the Philippines and the United States. After she married Benigno ("Ninoy") Aquino, Jr. on 11 October 1954, she remained in the

Former president Corazon Aquino hangs yellow ribbons in February 2000 to mark the anniversary of the overthrow of Ferdinand Marcos in February 1986. (AFP/CORBIS)

background and stayed at home to raise their five children while her husband successfully pursued a political career.

After her husband's assassination on 21 August 1983, the devout Catholic housewife came to symbolize and represent the moral opposition to the regime of Ferdinand Marcos (1917–1989), who ruled the Philippines from 1966 to 1986. Although reluctant at first, she became the united opposition's candidate for the presidency in the "snap election" called by Marcos for 6 February 1986. Both Aquino and Marcos claimed victory. A military revolt led to the famous EDSA (Epifanio de los Santos, for the street where much of the action occurred) revolution and the victory of People Power. (People Power refers to the nonviolent gathering of hundreds of thousands of Filipinos in protest and to reject the Marcos regime. They gathered at the urging of Cardinal Jaime Sin to protect a group of military officials whose arrest had been ordered by Marcos.) Although not a participant in the EDSA revolution, Aquino benefited from it as Marcos, under strong pressure from Washington, left the country and she assumed the presidency on 25 February 1986. She issued a presidential proclamation on 25 March 1986 that based her government's legitimacy on the EDSA revolution rather than the election. Aquino promulgated a provisional constitution and appointed a commission to write a new constitution. This new constitution was ratified by popular vote in February 1987.

The question has been asked: Did the events of EDSA represent a revolution or a restoration? Aquino's government marked the return to power of the oligarchy that had controlled much of Philippine politics and the economy before the declaration of martial law by President Marcos on 22 September 1972. Her presidency was threatened by various coup attempts, but she survived to the end of her term in 1992. As of 2001, Aquino continues to be active in Philippine politics as a leader in People Power II, which led to the ouster of President Joseph Estrada (b. 1937) amid allegations of corruption on 20 January 2001.

Damon L. Woods

Further Reading
Komisar, Lucy. (1987) *Corazon Aquino: The Story of a Revolution.* New York: George Braziller.
Reid, Robert H., and Eileen Guerrero. (1995) *Corazon Aquino and the Brushfire Revolution.* Baton Rouge, LA: Louisiana State University Press.
Steinberg, David Joel. (2000) *The Philippines: A Singular and a Plural Place.* Boulder, CO: Westview Press.

ARABIC

ARABIC Arabic, *al-ʿArabiyya*, or *lisan al-ʿArab*, is the language spoken by 200 million people in twenty-one countries from the Arabian Gulf to the Atlantic. As the liturgical language of Muslims, it is the medium for a billion people all over the globe. It is a Semitic language, and its early extant script dates back to about 300 CE at Temple of Ramm in Sinai and about 328 CE at Nemara, in the Syrian desert. Early Arabic evolved from a number of dialects between the third and the sixth centuries, leading to the classical language, which received its full expansion between 632 and 710, when the message of Islam reached many lands east and west.

As the language of the Qur'an, the revealed word of God to all Muslims, it is inimitable. Taken as the standard for excellence, classical Arabic, the written language, has survived the ravages of time. Codification and standardization of Arabic began in the eighth century, following early Islamic expansion and the growth of urban centers, especially in Basrah, Baghdad, and Damascus. It was carried out not only to counteract solecism and corruption concomitant with intercultural and ethnic mixing but also to sustain its lexical and grammatical models, taking the Qur'an, pre-Islamic poetry, the Prophet's sayings, and early Islamic orations, poems, and speeches as the standard. The effort between the eighth and tenth centuries to collect and verify poetry, speech, and proverbs as carried out by Arab and non-Arab scholars proved to be of great value, both in explaining Qur'anic word usages and meanings, and in ensuring the survival of Islamic and Arabic tradition and culture.

The written grammatical standards as set by al-Khalil (d. 791) and carried out by his student Sibawayhi (d. 804) made use both of attested data, such as the Qur'an, poetry, and elicited material from the Prophet's tribe (Quraysh), and of analogy, or the use of explanation to rationalize speech that deviated from the norm.

Morphology and Syntax in Classical Arabic

The basis for Arabic morphology lies in the distinction between aplastic, or simple and unanalyzable words, and the complex, analyzable ones. Complex or analyzable words build on a trilateral root for further enriching the derivative process that gives Arabic its distinguishable life and richness.

Syntax, in Arabic grammar, is governed by the two formidable notions of ellipsis and conjecture, or paraphrase, which simultaneously sustain compression and enforce attention. Arabic rhetoric grew out of the study of the stylistic inimitable Qur'an, burgeoning

into treatises on linguistics, literature, law, jurisprudence, philology, theology, and the art of prose. Of relevance in this context is Arabic lexicography, beginning with al-Khalil's lexicon *al-ʿAyn* with its phonetic and phonological ordering, to be followed by the works of Ibn Duraid (d. 933), al-Jawhari (d. 1003), Ibn Sidah (d. 1066), and many others before reaching Dawud al-Antaki (d. 1405) and al-Bustani (d. 1883).

Spoken Arabic

While the term classical Arabic applies to writing at large, based on standardized norms since the classical period (that is, from the eighth to the thirteenth centuries), we must understand it in relation to its descendants, early Middle Arabic and Modern Standard Arabic (MSA). Insofar as MSA is concerned, the syntactic and morphological standards are there, largely sustained through education and cultivated media programs. Despite geographical and cultural obstacles and barriers among Arab lands, the classical norm in writing and public speeches is respected. It is a sign of cultivation and genuine belonging and is sought after by politicians and public figures. Spoken Arabic, on the other hand, varies, and vernaculars abound.

Dialects remain outside the domain of the classical. Islamic expansion since 632 CE entailed the leveling of dialects, but it also brought some interdialectal habits and forms. A makeshift practice could easily emerge among newly converted people, freedmen, and indigenous non-Muslim tribes and inhabitants. Although aspirants to high position needed a polished style and lucid expression to fit into the ruling discourse, artisans, laborers, and businessmen could survive with this or that Arabic dialect or with the remnants of indigenous languages and dialects.

The Decline of Classical Arabic

From the start of the decline of the Abbasid caliphate in the late tenth century, and well before the fall of Baghdad in 1258, there was a decline in the use of classical Arabic outside formal or solemn occasions. Arabic language of the Seljuk period (1038–1157), for instance, demonstrates a mixture of the classical and the colloquial. Aside from the Andalusian practice of using local dialects in strophic street songs (*zajal*) like Ibn Quzman's (d. 1160), writers like Ibn Danyal (d. 1294) show a similar bent. Conversely, epistolographers since the fifteenth century insisted on writing in a polished style. The fact remains, however, that historians, scientists, and philosophers since the fifteenth century have resorted to the use of Middle Arabic, which largely kept to standards without meticulously following classical expression and usage. The descendant of this Middle Arabic can be traced in the present-day language of the media and official reports.

Arab philologists of the nineteenth century were aware of the increasing impact of the media, and the Lebanese Ibrahim al-Jazidji (1847–1906) wrote his book *Lughat al-Sahafah* (The Language of Dailies) to draw attention to faultiness and deviations from classical norms. Many royal academies were established to curb the impact of the media on Arabic classical usage. Purists like the Iraqi Christian cleric P. Anstanse al-Karmali issued in 1911–1931 *Lughat al-Arab* (The Language of the Arabs), to consolidate the classical against both the media Middle Arabic and the vernaculars that were beginning to appear in writing. While the purists put up a fight, they recognized the need to cope with modernization processes through appropriation of scientific words, adaptation of others, and expansion of vocabulary through derivation. At present, the classical in its middle usage is largely used in writing, ceremonies, and solemn occasions. In its standard form it provides the written medium throughout the Arab world, and among devout Muslims. Vernaculars and dialects are there in spoken Arabic, oral communications, and daily transactions.

Muhsin J. al-Musawi

Further Reading

Al-Musawi, Muhsin J. (2001) "Arabic Rhetoric." In the *Encyclopedia of Rhetoric*, ed. by Thomas O. Sloane. Oxford: Oxford University Press, 29–33.

Cowan, Milton J. A. (1979) *Dictionary of Modern Written Arabic*. Wiesbaden, Germany: O.Harrassowitz.

Stetkevych, Yaroslav. (1970) *The Modern Arabic Literary Language: Lexical and Stylistic Developments*. Chicago: Chicago University Press.

Versteegh, Kees. (1997) *The Arabic Language*. New York: Columbia University Press.

ARABS Although there are references to Arabs in ancient Assyrian and Babylonian inscriptions, which use the names *Aribi* or *Arabu* to identify the nomadic people living in northern Arabia, today the term identifies the Arabic-speaking peoples who inhabit the countries of North Africa and western Asia. The Arabs of western Asia inhabit modern-day Jordan, Syria, Lebanon, Iraq, Saudi Arabia, the Gulf States, Yemen, and former Palestine, today comprising Israel and the Occupied Territories of East Jerusalem, the West Bank, and Gaza.

Though the Arabic language is the most obvious trait Arabs share, all the Arabs of western Asia—the Muslim majority and the Christian and Jewish minorities—are also bound by a culture that expresses itself through social, religious, and political institutions. The main institutions of the Islamic societies of western Asia emerged between the eighth and sixteenth centuries, centered on Islam as the basis of all thought and organization, and Arabic as the medium of expression. This Arabic-Islamic culture defined the structure of social classes, the status of women and non-Muslim minorities, the content and transmission of knowledge, and the formation of cities.

The Pre-Islamic Period

In the period before Islam was founded in 622 CE, Arabic-speaking people lived as nomads organized in tribes or clans in the Arabian and Jordanian deserts, engaging in desert produce (camel raising). For these Bedouin, poetry emerged as the pinnacle of cultural expression: poets praised the virtues of loyalty to the tribe, bravery in battle, and hospitality to guests. Other Arabs established advanced urban settlements, such as the second- and third-century Nabataean centers in Petra (southern Jordan) and Palmyra (central Syria) that serviced trade along the caravan routes.

Arab-Islamic Culture

These examples of ancient Arab culture and language remained confined to Arabia, Jordan, and the Levant until Muhammad Ibn Abdallah (c. 570–632), a merchant from Mecca, southern Arabia, founded a new religion—Islam—based on what Muslims believe were divine revelations communicated to Muhammad in Arabic, which were later collected to form the Qur'an. Arab-Islamic culture emerged in this desert region and extended throughout the Middle East.

The culture that developed in the subsequent centuries stressed Islam as a guiding principle in thought and social organization, and Arabic as the main idiom of expression. Two successive Arab-Islamic dynasties, the Umayyads (661–749/750 CE), based in Damascus, and the Abbasids (749/750–1258 CE), who ruled from Baghdad, contributed to the formation of this Arab-Islamic culture, with Islamic law, theology, and philosophy based on belief in Muhammad's divine revelation. Those who possessed and controlled knowledge of this language and religion, known collectively as the *ulama*, wielded great authority and status in society, acting as its judges, lawyers, teachers, and religious leaders.

By the eleventh century, Arab-Islamic culture had appeared in the main social and religious institutions of Western-Asian Arab cities. Most of these urban centers included ornate congregational mosques, such as

FASTING AND RAMADAN

Adherence to Islam is an important element of Arab cultural identity, even though not all Arabs are Muslims. Among the central tenets of Islam is fasting during the month of Ramadan.

Next to prayer the most important religious observance in Arabia is fasting. Every Mohammedan must fast one lunar month out of the twelve. The month called Ramadhan is set apart for this observance. By fasting the Arab means abstinence from all food, drink, and tobacco from early morning to sunset. From the time in the morning when a black thread can be distinguished from a white one until sundown, he may taste nothing. During the night, however, men may eat and drink, and thus it happens that the fast month by day is a feast month by night. It is the season *par excellence* for indigestible pastries and impossible candies. The bazaar is frequently open and brilliantly illuminated the whole night. More cases of acute indigestion come to the hospital during this month than in any other two . . .

But violations of the spirit and letter of this law are rare among the Arabs. The month is a time of great hardship for cultivators and other working men. Since the Mohammedan year of twelve lunar months is about ten days shorter than a solar year, the different months move gradually around the circle of the four seasons. The fast month works less hardship in winter than when it comes to summer. A pious Arab considers it next to infidelity to complain of any hardship caused by the fast, and the men who do the heavy work of the cities are frequently the most scrupulous of all in its observance. Their constancy reflects no small credit on their religious devotion, especially in summer when the days are long and hot. From the beginning of the fast at early dawn till sunset may be sixteen hours or even more, and heavy work under an almost tropical sun for that period of time without food or drink is an indication of real religious zeal. There is no difference between Sunni and Shiah here. All are examples of faithfulness.

Source: Paul W. Harrison. (1924) *The Arab at Home*. New York: Crowell, 238–239.

the Umayyad Mosque in Damascus; theological colleges (*madrasaha*) to teach religion, law, and philosophy; and shrines, such as the Dome of the Rock in Jerusalem.

Non-Muslims and Women

Christians and Jews were seen by the Muslim majority as "People of the Book," that is, communities that were linked to Islam by being recipients of God's earlier revealed books—Torah, Psalms, and Gospels—of which the Qur'an was the final revelation. These groups were tolerated but were required to observe limitations in dress and to pay poll taxes; nonetheless, many flourished in crafts, in trade with East Asia, or as high-ranking administrators in the service of Muslim rulers. Though women in Arab-Islamic society rarely engaged in production or trade, many pursued education privately, possessed property, and regularly sought redress in Islamic courts concerning personal and financial disputes.

The strength of Arab-Islamic culture is attested to by its persistence in western Asia despite invasions by Christian, Turkic, and Mongol armies between the eleventh and fifteenth centuries.

The Encounter with the West

By the nineteenth century, the increasing influence of European culture and politics in the Middle East challenged the beliefs and institutions of this traditional Arab-Islamic culture. The advent of modern methods of industrial production and more efficient means of transportation (steamships, railroads) led to an expansion of Middle Eastern trade with Europe. Concurrent with these technological advances were improvements in the art of war and weaponry that allowed European armies to conquer Arab lands, beginning with Napoleon's invasion of Egypt in 1798.

In the face of these military and political threats, many of the Arab political and intellectual elite in western Asia maintained that Islamic societies needed to adopt modern European methods of government, thought, and technology to limit the European commercial, cultural, and military incursions in the Middle East. For a society traditionally based on the knowledge of Islam and the Qur'an, this acceptance of non-Islamic ideas articulated through European languages signaled a profound cultural shift and an undermining of the traditional Arabic-Islamic culture.

European military penetration into the Middle East continued after World War I, as the British and French imposed League of Nations Mandates on Syria, Lebanon, Palestine, and Iraq. Britain's promise to secure a homeland for the Jewish people in Palestine led to the declaration of the state of Israel by Palestine's Jewish community in 1948 and a war between the Arab states and Israel in that year, the first of five (1956, 1967, 1973, 1982).

The Challenge to Arab-Islamic Culture

The upheavals in Palestine after World War II and the continued influence of Britain and France over Arab countries inspired the political movement known as Pan-Arabism, which called for greater unity among Arab countries, independence from Western powers, and secular reforms in law and government. But in the last quarter of the twentieth century, the disparity in wealth among Arab countries has inspired many poorer Arabs to abandon secularist ideals and to support Islamic political movements that address their grievances: poverty, the Palestinian issue, and the increasing influence of Western culture. Clearly, the growing support for an indigenous source of identity in politics (Islam) signals the failure of foreign political ideals (Western secular nationalism) to mobilize Arabs and confront issues important to them. For Arab women, such factors as class, state legal systems, and differences between rural and urban lifestyles determine how extensively they can participate in the most important institutions in society, such as government, education, and the workforce.

Though the Arabic-Islamic culture continues to be an important source of identity for the Arabs of western Asia, modern technologies, changes in law and education, and exposure to various cultural influences have challenged how this Arab-Islamic culture is received and interpreted by Arabs.

Awad Eddie Halabi

See also: **Islam—West Asia**

Further Reading
Boullata, Issa. (1990) *Trends and Issues in Contemporary Arab Thought*. Albany, NY: State University of New York Press.

Esposito, John. (1996) *Islam and Democracy*. New York: Oxford University Press.

Hourani, Albert. (1991) *A History of the Arab Peoples*. Cambridge, MA: Belknap Press.

Mansfield, P. (1992) *The Arabs*. New York: Rev. ed. Penguin Press.

Musallam, Basim. (1983) *The Arabs: A Living History*. London: Collins.

Smith, Charles. (2001) *Palestine and the Arab-Israeli Conflict*. Rev. ed. Boston: Bedford/St. Martin's Press.

ARAKAN YOMA MOUNTAINS The Arakan Yoma Mountains are a range stretching 650 kilometers from north to south in Myanmar (Burma). The range divides Myanmar into the Irrawaddy Valley to the west and a thin strip of coastal land known as Arakan to the east. The average altitude is between fifteen hundred and two thousand meters, with the highest point being Mount Victoria at 3,010 meters. The Arakan Yoma range is traversable via three major passes: the An, the Gwa, and the Taungup.

The Arakan Yoma range is sparsely populated. Chins, Nagas, and other groups populate its numerous valleys and slopes. Prior to British rule, these groups were not brought under the control of any of the precolonial lowland kingdoms of either Arakan or the Irrawaddy Valley.

The Arakan Yoma range is important to Myanmar history chiefly for two reasons. First, the Arakan Yoma is a "rain barrier" to dry middle Myanmar, blocking monsoonal rains coming from the southwest off of the Bay of Bengal. Second, the Arakan Yoma range has historically split the Burmans into two branches: the Burmans of the Irrawaddy Valley and the Arakanese, the latter living along the thin coastal strip of land on the western slope of the mountain range.

Michael Walter Charney

Further Reading

Charney, Michael W. (2000) "A Reinvestigation of Kon-baung-Era Burman Historiography on the Relationship between Arakan and Ava (Upper Burma)." *Journal of Asian History* 34, 1: 53–68.

ARAKI SADAO (1877–1966), Japanese general and politician. Araki Sadao was a general, politician, and leader of the Imperial Way faction (Kodoha, an ultra-nationalist group during the 1930s). A native of Tokyo and a graduate of the Japanese Military Academy and the Army War College, Araki served in the Russo-Japanese War in 1904 and with the Japanese forces in Siberia in 1918. Before he served as principal of the war college, he was promoted to lieutenant general in 1927. In 1931 he briefly served as inspector general of the Army Educational Administration. The same year he became army minister in the Inukai Tsuyoshi (1855–1932) and Saito Makoto (1858–1936) cabinets, retaining the position until he resigned in 1934.

A failed coup d'état plan against the government in October 1931 sought to overthrow the cabinet and install Araki as prime minister. In February 1936 a group of junior-ranking army officers rose up in insurrection, assassinating Saito Makoto and other cabinet members. As Araki had tacitly supported the insurrectionists, he was forced to quit his position. Appointed minister of education in 1938, Araki reinforced military instruction at the schools. After World War II, he was convicted of class-A war crimes and sentenced to life imprisonment, but he was released in 1955 due to ill health.

Nathalie Cavasin

Further Reading

Bix, Herbert P. (2000) *Hirohito and the Making of Modern Japan.* New York: HarperCollins Publishers.
Shillony, Ben-Ami. (1973) *Revolt in Japan: The Young Officers and the February 26, 1936 Incident.* Princeton, NJ: Princeton University Press.

ARAL SEA The Aral Sea is the world's fourth-largest lake, but because of human influence, it has been shrinking since the 1960s at a pace that is unique in modern times. Desiccation has caused a spectrum of severe environmental and human problems. National and international efforts are underway to cope with them, but they will be enormously costly and require many years to deal with.

The Aral Sea is a terminal lake, that is, a lake without surface outflow, in the deserts of Central Asia. Its level is mainly determined by the balance between surface inflow from two large rivers (the Amu Dar'ya and Syr Dar'ya) and net evaporation (evaporation minus precipitation). Most of the sea's drainage basin is located in the territory of Uzbekistan, Kazakhstan, Tajikistan, Kyrgyzstan, and Turkmenistan, newly independent states that were part of the former Soviet Union until the end of 1991.

For the first six decades of the twentieth century, the Aral's water balance was in equilibrium and level fluctuations minor. In 1960 the Aral had a level 53 meters above sea level and an area of 67,381 square kilometers. It had an average salinity of around 10 grams/liter, and its twenty indigenous species of fish supported a major fishery. The Aral also served as a key regional transportation route. The deltas of the Syr Dar'ya and Amu Dar'ya rivers sustained a diversity of natural flora and fauna as well as having major economic importance for agriculture, animal husbandry, and fishing.

Changes in the Aral Sea Region since the 1960s

Over the past four decades, the Aral Sea has steadily shrunk as expanding irrigation diminished inflow to it

A boat grounded in a receded area of the the Aral Sea in Uzbekistan in 1992. (SHEPARD SHERBELL/CORBIS)

from the Amu Dar'ya and Syr Dar'ya. In 1987, the sea split into two bodies of water. During the 1990s, average annual inflow was only 27 percent of the 1911–1960 figure.

The Aral's drying up has caused severe harm. The sea's native fishes disappeared by the early 1980s as salinity rose beyond their ability to adapt. This ended commercial fishing and threw tens of thousands of people out of work. Areas well beyond the sea and its immediate shoreline suffered as well. A 400,000-square-kilometer region around the sea, with a population of 3–4 million, has been designated an "ecological disaster zone" by the Central Asian governments.

The rich ecosystems of the Amu Dar'ya and Syr Dar'ya deltas have been particularly hard hit. Desertification has severely affected both deltas, as native plant communities are displaced by others, more tolerant of saline soil and dry climatic conditions. The extent of unique *tugai* forests, primarily composed of water-consuming trees and shrubs that once stretched along the main rivers and delta channels, has substantially diminished, as has the diversity of animals inhabiting the forests. Lakes and wetlands, which provide prime habitat for a variety of permanent and migratory waterfowl, have diminished significantly, along with aquatic bird populations.

Because irrigation now uses reduced and salinized river flow from upstream, crop yields have fallen. Declining productivity of pastures has harmed animal husbandry. Salt and dust blown from the former sea bottom carries far downwind and settles over a considerable area. This has substantially slowed plant growth and depressed crop yields. Even the climate in a 100-kilometer-wide band around the sea's former coastline has changed, with a steady trend toward warmer summers and cooler winters. The growing

season has shortened, forcing a switch from cotton to rice in the northern part of the Amu Dar'ya delta.

The population living near the Aral Sea suffers acute health problems directly related to the sea's recession. These include respiratory and digestive afflictions, possibly cancer from inhalation and ingestion of blowing salt and dust, and poorer diets from the loss of Aral fish. Bacterial contamination of drinking water is pervasive, leading to very high rates of waterborne disease.

Rehabilitation Efforts

In the late 1980s, the Soviet Union initiated programs to deal with the Aral Sea problem, but they stopped with the collapse and dissolution of the USSR in 1991. Responsibility for dealing with Aral issues fell on the five newly independent nations of the Aral Sea basin. The states signed a water-sharing measure in 1992 that guaranteed a certain share of the flow of the Amu Dar'ya and Syr Dar'ya to the Aral Sea and the river deltas. Subsequently, they signed an agreement that created an Interstate Council on the Aral Sea (ICAS) and the Interstate Fund for the Aral Sea (IFAS). The former was charged with developing and implementing a program for dealing with the Aral crisis in coordination with foreign donors. The latter's responsibility was to raise money from the five member countries for carrying out the program. The two entities merged in 1997 under the IFAS name.

International help began in 1990, but only became significant after 1991. Through its Aral Sea Basin Program, the World Bank has been coordinating the most ambitious efforts. Other key players have been the European Union, United Nations (through UNEP and UNESCO), the United States, and the Asian Development Bank.

Partial restoration of the separated northern part of the Aral Sea is feasible. This would cut salinity to levels tolerable by indigenous fishes and allow commercial fishing to resume. But restoring the much larger southern part would be much more difficult. It would require a substantial increase in water inflow from the Amu Dar'ya, which in turn would require major improvements and reductions in irrigation. Neither is likely in the foreseeable future.

Philip Micklin

Further Reading
Glantz, Michael H., ed. (1999) *Creeping Environmental Problems and Sustainable Development in the Aral Sea Basin.* Cambridge, UK: Cambridge University Press.

Micklin, Philip P. (1988) "Desiccation of the Aral Sea: A Water Management Disaster in the Soviet Union." *Science* 241, 4870 (2 September): 1170–1176.

———. (1991) *The Water Management Crisis in Soviet Central Asia*, Carl Beck Papers in Russian and East European Studies, no. 905. Pittsburgh, PA: Center for Russian and East European Studies.

———. (1994) "The Aral Sea Problem." *Civil Engineering, Proceedings of the Institution of Civil Engineers* August: 114–121.

———. (2000) *Managing Water in the Aral Sea Basin*. Central Asian and Caucasian Prospects. London: Royal Institute of International Affairs, Russia and Eurasia Programme.

———, ed. (1992) "Special Issue on the Aral Sea Crisis." *Post-Soviet Geography* 33 (May): 5.

Micklin, Philip P., and William D. Williams, eds. (1996) *The Aral Sea Basin*. Proceedings of an Advanced Research Workshop, May 2–5, 1994, Tashkent, Uzbekistan. NATO ASI series, vol. 12. Heidelberg, Germany: Springer-Verlag.

World Bank. (1993) *The Aral Sea Crisis: Proposed Framework of Activities*. Washington, DC: World Bank.

———. (1996) *Aral Sea Basin Program, Phase 1, Progress Report No. 3*. Washington, DC: World Bank.

———. (1998) *Aral Sea Basin Program (Kazakhstan, Kyrgyz Republic, Tajikistan, Turkmenistan and Uzbekistan): Water and Environmental Management Project*. Washington, DC: World Bank.

ARARAT, MOUNT

Mount Ararat (Agri Dagi), positioned at latitude 44°20' east, longitude 39°20' north, is the highest mountain in Turkey at 5137 meters. From the main peak, Buyuk Agri, it is less than 20 kilometers southeast to the Iranian frontier and 30 kilometers northeast to the Russian frontier. Great Ararat is an extinct volcanic cone, accompanied by a secondary cone, Little Ararat (Kucuk Agri), which rises to 3885 meters just 12 kilometers southeast of its larger brother. Together they encompass about 250 square kilometers and rise spectacularly 4250 meters above the surrounding plain at Dogubeyazit. Ararat is the final volcano in a fault-line chain that includes Mounts Erciyes, Suphan, and Nemrut, and that crosses Turkey from the southwest.

Ararat includes basalt and andesite and is a major source of obsidian, used by early humans for the manufacture of tools. Fresh lava flows date from the last eruption on 2 June 1840, when Ahora town and a monastery on the northeast slopes were buried. The summit is permanently glaciated; the longest glacier descends to an altitude of 2500 meters and is reputed to contain the remains of Noah's Ark.

Josephus, in 70 CE, mentioned the existence of the Ark. Dr. Nouri, archdeacon of Babylon and Jerusalem, claimed to have located it in 1893. Russian expeditions during the two world wars took photographs (subsequently lost), and a sighting was claimed by an American researcher in 1987. Ararat was once the focus of the Urartean and later the Armenian civilizations. The area is now occupied by Kurds and features songs and legends documented by Yasar Kemal.

Mount Ararat with the village of Dogubayazit at its base. (ADAM WOOLFITT/CORBIS)

MARCO POLO DESCRIBES MOUNT ARARAT, c. 1295

"In the heart of Greater Armenia is a very high mountain, on which Noah's Ark is said to have rested. It is so broad and long that it takes more than two days to go round it. On the summit the snow lies so deep all the year that no one can ever climb it. But on the lower slopes the herbage is so lush and luxurious that, in summer, all the beasts from far and near resort here and yet the supply never fails."

Source: James Bryce (1996) *Transcaucasia and Ararat.* London: Macmillan and Co.

Confounding Marco Polo (c. 1295), who thought that the snow on the summit was so deep that no one could climb it, Ararat was first climbed by Professor Parrot, a German, in 1829. With military permission, a guide, and two overnight camps en route, it presents no technical problems, and mountaineering tourism is becoming an important source of local income.

Kate Clow

Further Reading

Bryce, James. (1996) *Transcaucasia and Ararat.* London: Macmillan and Co.

Kemal, Yasar. (1990) *Agridagi Efsanesi* (Legend of Mount Ararat). Istanbul: Toros Yayinlari.

Smith, Karl. (1994) *The Mountains of Turkey.* Cumbria, U.K.: Cicerone.

ARATA ISOZAKI

(b. 1931), Japanese architect. Born in Oita City, Japan, Arata Isozaki took an approach to architecture that was rooted in postwar art movements. His work has been described as "conceptual architecture" (Drew 1982: 18). Isozaki often used quotation to establish a certain sense of displacement; many of these references were obscure and personal, including distorted abstractions referring to Mickey Mouse and Marilyn Monroe, but a number also drew from the Western architectural canon.

In the 1960s Isozaki was best known for his drawings of dystopian structures rising from ruins. Isozaki's concurrent buildings reflected a fascination with technology, but were deliberately cold and abstract, rejecting their surroundings. In the 1970s, this abstraction grew pronounced; Isozaki developed a series that toyed with cubic volumes and barrel vaults to achieve a neutral emptiness. Inevitably, the emergence of postmodern architecture in the West during the1980s created many opportunities for Isozaki to work abroad, particularly in Spain and the United States, but his biting approach was frequently lost in the translation.

The 1990s and beyond saw Isozaki return to a criticism of technology, often juxtaposed with fragments from Western architecture. Throughout his career, Isozaki was a prolific essayist, and his writings offer a remarkable commentary, not only on his own work, but also on the trends influencing architects both in Japan and abroad.

Dana Buntrock

Further Reading

Arata Isozaki. (1991) *Arata Isozaki: Architecture 1960–1990.* New York: Rizzoli.

———. (1998) *Arata Isozaki: Four Decades of Architecture.* Los Angeles: The Museum of Contemporary Art.

Drew, Phillip. (1982) *The Architecture of Arata Isozaki.* New York: Harper & Row.

Stewart, David, ed. (1991) *Arata Isozaki, 1960/1990.* Tokyo: Executive Committee for Arata Isozaki, Architecture, 1960/1990.

ARCHAEOLOGY—TURKEY

Archaeology began in Turkey with Heinrich Schliemann's (1822–1890) dramatic discovery and excavation of ancient Troy, where he worked from 1870 on, and has continued to be dominated by foreigners who, in conjunction with Turkey's own archaeologists, use more and more sophisticated methods to unravel the history of this key land mass. Turkey's Cultural Ministry attracts some 0.02 percent of the state budget, only a fraction of which goes to the Museums and Sites Directorate for the preservation of huge concentrations of prehistoric and historic sites along Turkey's trade routes, coasts, and river valleys. Turkey has the greatest cultural variety of archeological remains of any country in the world.

One of the world's oldest towns has been discovered in Turkey—Catalhuyuk (dating from 6500 to 5500 BCE), and the supposed resting place of Noah's Ark, Mount Ararat, lies in Turkey, as do Van, capital of the ancient Urartean kingdom (which flourished from about the thirteenth to about the seventh century BCE), and Bogazkoy, capital of the mighty Hittite empire, which flourished from about 1700 to 1380 BCE. Other historic sites include Urfa, the birthplace of Abraham; Miletus, a colonizing Greek city-state;

Remains of the Library of Celsus in Ephesus, Turkey, in 1997. (STEPHEN G. DONALDSON PHOTOGRAPHY)

the seven churches of Asia originally founded by Saint Paul; Constantinople, the capital of the Eastern Roman empire; Hagia Sophia, the world's largest church; the medieval Armenian kingdom of Cilicia; a sprinkling of Crusader castles; and Trabzon, the last surviving outpost of Byzantium. The uniquely Turkish Seljuk and Ottoman empires are also represented almost exclusively in present-day Turkey.

Since the fashion for the grand tour began in Europe in the nineteenth century, this cultural storehouse has been raided by western collectors and museums; authorized exports include the Pergamon Zeus Altar, which has its own museum in Berlin; the tombs of Xanthos, in their own room in the British Museum; and the Heroon from Myra, on display in Vienna. Other collectors took advantage of a country of uneducated peasants, who, until only fifty years ago, filled the time between sowing and harvest by tomb raiding and treasure seeking. The treasures of Troy adorned Schliemann's wife and now reside in Russia; as recently as 1962, Dumbarton Oaks acquired early Byzantine silver artifacts that had been smuggled out of Turkey illegally, and the Getty Museum has recently returned portions of a Greek sarcophagus. Not surprisingly, to prevent a recurrence of art theft, all excavations in Turkey are now supervised by Cultural Ministry staff.

The first famous Turkish archaeologist was Osman Hamdi (1842–1910), who excavated the Royal Cemetery at Sidon and brought the sarcophagi back to the new Istanbul Museum. The Ankara Museum (established in 1921) resulted from Ataturk's interest in the Hittites. Together these institutions sparked a change in the perception of the educated public. Foreign organizations, in particular the British Institute of Archaeology in Ankara; the Spanish Archaeological Mission; the Middle Eastern Culture Center, Tokyo; the German Archaeological Institute; the Institute for Aegean Pre-History; the Institute for Classical Archaeology, Vienna, as well as universities in the United States, France, Belgium, Italy, and elsewhere have participated in investigations and excavations in Turkey. The drowning of many important prehistoric, Roman, and early Turkish sites by the construction of twenty-two dams on the Euphrates and the plan for a similar sequence of dams on the Tigris have made rescue archaeology an important part of the Turkish scene.

Prehistoric Period

The excavation of Upper Palaeolithic cave settlements near Antalya demonstrated early hominid occupation there. The Neolithic site of Catalhuyuk, near Konya, represents one of the world's first permanent settlements; it was discovered in 1958 by James Mellaart. Excavation continues, and this town, with houses and shrines decorated with relief sculptures and wall paintings, is now a World Heritage Site.

Bronze Age

Central Anatolia was ruled by the Hatti (early Bronze age indigenous inhabitants of the region, up until about 1800 BCE), whose royal tombs at Alacahoyuk were excavated from 1940 on by the Turkish archaeologists Remzi Oguz Arik and Hamit Kosay. They discovered bronze, silver, and gold objects of extraordinary beauty, including the famous deer standard now used as a symbol of Ankara. The excavation of the Assyrian trade colony at Kanesh (which dates from 1950 BCE) by Tahsin Ozguc and Nimet Ozguc yielded thousands of clay tablets inscribed with trade records in cuneiform script, as well as traces of early Hittite occupation. Levels contemporary with the Kanesh excavation at Troy held bronze weapons, silver objects, and Schliemann's treasure; sophisticated wheel-made pottery was also found.

Early Civilizations

Excavations at Bogazkoy, the capital of the Hittite civilization, whose physical remains were previously unknown, were begun by Hugo Winckler in 1906, suspended during World War I, and recommenced from 1931. The magnificent ruins of the site were uncovered, and a huge stock of cuneiform tablets was gradually deciphered to reveal a rich code of laws, legends, and customs; a contemporary fort at Ortakoy (Corum) is under excavation. Neo-Hittite sites under investigation include Arslantepe, Sirkeli Hoyuk, and Carchemish (Karkamis, which is to be submerged under a new dam on the Syrian border).

Farther east the Urartean site at Toprakkale, Van, was wrecked in the nineteenth century by Austin Henry Layard's hasty unprofessional excavation; Altintepe, near Erzurum, was excavated by Turkish archaeologists and yielded impressive graves; Oktay Belli is currently excavating a pair of Urartean fortresses near Van.

Four contemporaneous west Anatolian cultures (c. 700–300 BCE), the Phrygian, Lydian, Carian, and Lycian, have yielded important sites. Gordion, capital city of King Midas, was excavated first by German then by American teams; ornate grave goods, including inlaid tables, are now in the Ankara Museum. Sardis, the capital of Croesus's Lydian kingdom (c. seventh century–546 BCE), is currently under American excavation. Site of the world's first minted coins, it has yielded smelting furnaces. Lycian Xanthos has been excavated by the French since 1958, and Turkish excavations at nearby Patara have shown that the site was occupied as early as the eighth century BCE.

TROY—WORLD HERITAGE SITE

Troy was designated a UNESCO World Heritage site in 1992. Immortalized in Homer's *Iliad*, Troy is considered one of the world's most important archeological sites for its contribution to the understanding of early European culture.

Greek and Roman Periods

The first Greek colonies were founded on Turkey's western seaboard from 1000 BCE and began to expand in the seventh century BCE; most of these cities continued in occupation through the period of conquest by Alexander of Macedon (356–323 BCE) and the Roman annexation; by the first century CE the Romans had absorbed the independent states of the interior as far as the Euphrates. Development of the cities of Asia Minor accelerated progressively after Alexander until Marcus Aurelius (176 CE). The slow decline that followed was interrupted by periods of Byzantine revival, until many sites were abandoned in the face of the advance of Islam (eighth century). These glorious cities are currently being excavated and restored as tourism showcases and provide a source of revenue for the Culture Ministry. The most magnificent examples are Pergamon and Didyma, both currently being restored by German teams; Ephesus, with its huge, nearly intact theater, and a villa suburb where members of the Austrian Archaeological Institute are at work; the *colonia* of Sagalassos, where a systematic and thorough investigation and excavation under Marc Waelkens is supported by Belgian funds; and Aphrodisias, where conservation and a new museum mark considerable progress under the Americans. In comparison, the Turkish excavation of Saint Paul's city of Antioch in Pisidia is underfunded and poorly exhibited.

Rescue Archaeology

At a Roman villa suburb at Zeugma on the Euphrates, excavators fought against time to save mosaics from drowning beneath the Birecik dam in 2000. Some of the rescued mosaics are now on exhibition in Gaziantep museum; a new annex is being built to accommodate more. But frescoes at the site were lost and much of the site lies unexcavated beneath the water. The Chalcolithic-Bronze Age-Urak sites of Hainebi, Tilbes, and Horum Hoyuk are due to disappear beneath the same lake. Roman Samosata and several medieval churches were submerged under the Ataturk Dam. Museums in the area have participated in excavations of prehistoric sites and have excellent displays. Throughout Turkey individual museum directors are empowered to conduct salvage operations during local construction projects, but the loss of Turkey's, and particularly Istanbul's, Byzantine and Seljuk historic buildings is the most tragic aspect of Turkish archaeology today.

Later Periods

Since most Byzantine monuments were built over Roman sites, they must be excavated to get at the Greek and Roman remains beneath; only one or two churches have been excavated for their own merits. Seljuk and Ottoman sites are similarly neglected, although recent research projects have documented sites at Artvin, Ardahan, Harput, Binbir Kilise, and Aya Tekla, as well as the Georgian churches in the area between Bayburt and Artvin and churches at Nigde and Akhisar.

Prospects

At present, unless tourism promises a profit, Turkey's government will not prioritize archaeology; thus projects often depend on outside pressure and funding. Further rescue archaeology is now required before the Tigris valley dams flood the glorious medieval cave city of Hasan Keyf and other sites. However fund-raising is nearly complete for excavations at the tourism destination of Nemrut Dagi, where the tomb of Antiochus Commagene lies under a mountaintop tumulus surrounded by a pantheon of stone gods.

Kate Clow

Further Reading
Akurgal, Ekrem. (1985) *Ancient Civilizations and Ruins of Turkey.* Istanbul, Turkey: Haset Kitabevi.
The Museum of Anatolian Civilisations Handbook. Ankara, Turkey: Cultural Ministry.
Stoneman, Richard. (1993) *A Traveller's History of Turkey.* Gloucestershire, U.K.: Windrush Press.

ARCHITECTURAL DECORATION— CENTRAL ASIA

Throughout Asia indigenous peoples use local resources in developing regional types of architecture. Desert regions use clay, adobe, and fired bricks. In Western Asia, parts of India, China, Japan, and Korea, builders used carved wood. Great stone temples were built in Vietnam, Thailand, and Cambodia.

In Asia there is a distinction between the private and the public sphere. Public architecture must conform to certain rules. Public decorative architecture relies heavily on symmetry, which helps place the building and its users in a societal hierarchy that defines the rank of building itself. In China it is the difference between Taoism and Confucianism. Taoism is private and Confucianism is public. In the private sphere the symmetry collapses, and naturalistic forms of flowers, plants, and representational art are used to decorate structures. Private homes in China have unpainted wood, and ink paintings on the rough plaster walls. In Mughal India, harem buildings have paintings of dancing girls that would be strictly forbidden for a throne room.

In China, dating back to the Shinju dynasty, the use of colors defined status. Yellow was reserved for the royal family and black was for peasants, according to societal laws that remained in force until the end of the nineteenth century. Tie beams were carved with motifs of stylized dragons, mythical animals, nine-tailed turtles, and lucky symbols (including the auspicious swastika, a symbol of the sun or the rolling of time). The glazing of roof tiles began in the Tang dynasty.

In Muslim countries, geometric patterns are used to conform to the nonrepresentational art of Qur'anic law, and colors create distinctions between ruling powers. During the classical phase of Islamic architecture, the use of *muqarnas* (stalactite or honeycomb vaulting) was introduced. In the mosques, the formal structure is organized with the orientation of the *mihrab*, the niche that indicates the direction of Mecca. In Bukhara the ninth- to tenth-century mausoleum of the Samanids exemplifies the use of patterned and carved brick in a jewel of geometric balance. In Samarqand, palaces, mosques, and mausoleums displayed faultless, exquisite blue tiles; color variation was not allowed. In China, all decorations on the Temple of Heaven are perfect and geometrically precise; the woodwork, beams, brackets, floor tiles, and cobalt-blue roof tiles are as close to perfection as humanly possible. By contrast, in Japan the height of style and elegance is a teahouse with thatched roof, unpainted posts and lintels, and a floor made of rough boards. Nowhere in Asia was the imperfect valued as highly as in Japan.

Marcia Selsor

Further Reading
Hoag, John D. (1977) *Islamic Architecture.* New York: Abrams.
Pulatov, T. and L. Y. Mankovskaja. (1991) *Bukhara: A Museum in the Open.* Tashkent, Uzbekistan: Gafur Gulyam.
Williams, C. A. S. (1974) *Chinese Symbols and Art Motifs.* Boston: Tuttle.

ARCHITECTURE—CENTRAL ASIA

Architecture in Central Asia has a very long history—the oldest evidence of human-made structures was discovered in early farming settlements dated around 7000 BCE. These sites lie in the oases north of the Kopet Dag Mountains that extend about 645 kilometers between present-day northeast Iran and Turkmenistan. Here in southern Turkmenistan, the Neolithic village of Djeitun had thirty one-room houses made of mud bricks, with plastered floors, hearths, and often wall paintings. In the same area, at the Early Chalcolithic site of Chagilli Tepe, dated around 5000 BCE, were multiroom houses that formed large complexes along streets and alleys.

Larger settlements arose in Central Asia during the Middle Chalcolithic Age (c. 4000–3500 BCE). In the Tedzhen River delta in present-day south Turkmenistan, fortified settlements arose; these had circular towers connected to thick walls, with a large rectangular house on a platform in the middle. Protourban settlements (Namazga Tepe and Altyn Tepe) arose in the Late Chalcolithic (c. 3500–3000 BCE) and expanded in the Early Bronze Age (3000–2500 BCE), reaching areas of fifty and twenty-five hectares, respectively. At Altyn Tepe, pilastered ramparts 2.3 meters thick were flanked by two rectangular towers in the north, while two rectangular towers protected the main entrance, flanking the 6-meter-thick wall in the south. There was also an elite quarter with richly decorated multiroom houses and wide streets, a crafts quarter with pottery kilns and copper-smelting furnaces, a priests' quarter with shrines, and a monumental towerlike structure on a stepped platform, resembling Mesopotamian ziggurats (temple towers).

Several large settlements with square-shaped fortresses appeared in the delta of the Murgab River that flows though northwestern Afghanistan and southeastern Turkmenistan. Large sites are also noted north and south of the Amu Dar'ya River that flows from the Pamirs to the Aral Sea. In this region, the fortified settlement of Sapalli Tepe consisted of several multiroom quarters with T-shaped corridors clustered along the streets. Smaller fortified settlements with citadels appeared in the Murgab delta during the Early Iron Age (1200–800 BCE). Iron Age (700–400 BCE) settlements in the Fergana Valley, in today's Uzbekistan, Tajikistan, and Kyrgyzstan, had defensive walls with towers and monumental buildings.

The Rise of Cities

Several urban-type settlements and fortresses arose in southern Turkmenistan when this area became in-cluded in the Parthian kingdom (c. 250 BCE–c. 226 CE). The largest settlement, New Nisa, had a palatial building and several temples.

Following the eastern campaigns of Alexander of Macedon (356–323 BCE), Central Asia became part of an independent Bactrian kingdom (250–130 BCE), greatly influenced by Greek culture. The city of Ai Khanum, located on the left bank of the Amu Dar'ya River and protected by thick mud-brick walls, possessed impressive public buildings, including a royal palace, gymnasium, theater, arsenal, and Greek-style residential houses.

Later, Bactria was incorporated into the powerful Kushan kingdom (78–200), whose rulers encouraged the spread of Buddhism. The city of Airtam, on the Amu Dar'ya, had a significant Buddhist temple with a sculptured frieze. The city of Khalchyan on the Surkhandarya River in today's Uzbekistan included a palace with a gallery of sculptures of local rulers. Dalverzin Tepe on the same river had a citadel, palace, and residential areas within the city walls.

As early as the eighth or seventh century BCE, Afrasitab (Samarqand before the time of Timur, the Turkic conqueror, 1336–1405) and Yerkurgan had developed as fortified settlements along the middle stretches of the Zeravshan River, which flows through today's Tajikistan and Uzbekistan. During the third through sixth centuries, Yerkurgan possessed a palatial building and at least two temples. At the same time, Toprak-Qala, north of the Amu Dar'ya and opposite the city of Urganch in western Uzbekistan, was protected by rectangular clay walls; it had three towered castles with a range of palatial halls. The so-called Hall of Kings had painted walls and housed a collection of clay statues of local rulers, their wives, and warriors, some of them of Indian ancestry. A different architectural design consisting of concentric circles was found at the nearby site of Koy-Kryglan-Qala.

The fourth and fifth centuries saw a decline in urban development in Central Asia following the collapse of the Kushan state in India and the conquest of the region by the Persian Sasanid dynasty (224/228–651). In the sixth through eighth centuries, the older cities such as Samarqand, Toprak-Qala, and Mary (in today's Turkmenistan) recovered, and new ones (Pendjikent and many others) were established. These included fortified sites (such as castles, *keshk*), palaces, ritual places, and dwelling houses. Pendjikent consisted of blocks of two-story houses with vaulted roofs and walls often covered with paintings and decorated with carving. In Uzbekistan, the cities of Afrasiab, Varakhsha, and Pendjikent had monumental palaces erected on elevated platforms, with several large halls adorned with wall paintings. Ritual places reflected a multitude of religious beliefs: Zoroastrianism, Buddhism, and Manichaeism.

Islamic Architecture

The spread of Islam following the Arab conquests in the seventh and eighth centuries led to the emergence of architecture that was typically Islamic. The oldest mosques in Samarqand (Afrasiab), Mary, and Bashan are dated to the ninth and tenth centuries. Early mausoleums or monumental tombs are known in the city of Bukhara in Uzbekistan and Samarqand, among others. During the Seljuk dynasty (1038–1157), stone-built caravansaries arose along the Central Asian trade routes.

Timurid Architecture

The Mongol invasion in 1220–1221 led to almost total destruction of urban life in Central Asia. Only mausoleums have survived from that period. Timur, however, who made Samarqand his base of power in 1370, contributed to a new rise in urban development with the erection of numerous monumental buildings. Architectural traditions were enhanced under the reign of Ulugh Beg (1394–1449), Timur's grandson, who made Samarqand a center of Muslim culture. Impressive monuments of the Timurid era (fourteenth to fifteenth centuries) included mausoleums, mosques, and *madrasah*s (religious colleges) in Samarqand, as well as libraries, hospitals, and water-supply facilities.

Traditional Central Asian architecture included several types of mosques: a dome over a square chamber, an open barrel-vaulted hall, a richly decorated portal (the *iwan*), and an open court surrounded by arcades; the minarets or prayer towers were circular or conical. Mausoleums usually had a domed structure raised over a square base. The *madrasah* consisted of an inner courtyard surrounded by one- or two-story buildings that included a mosque, lecture rooms, and living rooms.

Developments in the Sixteenth through Nineteenth Centuries

In the sixteenth and seventeenth centuries, urban development was restricted to larger cities such as Samarqand and Bukhara, where impressive architectural assemblages were erected. Large mosques had a main dome, typically onion shaped in Central Asia, and an impressive arched *iwan* along the central axis; smaller district mosques had open *iwan*s; *madrasah*s were designed with four *iwan*s, a central court, numerous cells, a monumental *pishtak* (portico), and corner minarets. Domed bazaars and water reservoirs also date from this period.

During the eighteenth and nineteenth centuries, impressive palatial buildings were erected, particularly in Khiva, in the oasis west of the lower Amu Dar'ya in Uzbekistan. After Central Asia became part of the Russian empire in 1860, European-type agglomerations developed alongside the older structures in major administrative centers such as Tashkent and Samarqand in Uzbekistan and Ashkhabad in southern Turkmenistan. Under Soviet rule (1920–1991) there was an intensive development of residential housing throughout Central Asia, along with public buildings (theaters, museums, educational and recreational facilities). After independence in 1991, new official buildings were constructed, particularly in Turkmenistan and Uzbekistan, with the intention of developing an infrastructure for tourism.

Pavel Dolukhanov

ITCHAN KALA—WORLD HERITAGE SITE

The last oasis before Iran for caravaners crossing the desert, Itchan Kala in Uzbekistan was designated a UNESCO World Heritage site in 1990. The site still contains a few superb examples of Central Asian architecture, including the Djuma Mosque and two magnificent nineteenth-century palaces.

Further Reading
Bernard, P. N. (1982) "An Ancient Greek City in Central Asia." *Scientific American* 246: 126–135.
Gippenreiter, Vadim Evgenevich, and Robin Magowan. (1989) *Fabled Cities of Central Asia: Samarkand, Bukhara, Khiva.* New York: Abbeville Press.
Golombek, Lisa, and Donald Wilber. (1988) *The Timurid Architecture of Iran and Turan.* Princeton, NJ: Princeton University Press.
Herder, Klaus. (1990) *Formal Structure in Islamic Architecture of Iran and Turkistan.* Pref. by Oleg Grabar. New York: Rizzoli.
Knobloch, Edgar. (1972) *Beyond the Oxus: Archaeology, Art, and Architecture of Central Asia.* London: Ernst Benn.

———. (2001) *Monuments of Central Asia: A Guide to the Archaeology, Art, and Architecture of Turkestan.* London and New York: I. B. Tauris.

Pugachenkova, Galina Anatolevna. (1983) *Srednyaya Aziya: Spravochnik-putevoditel'* (Middle Asia: Dictionary-Guide). Moscow: Iskusstvo.

Stavisskii, Boris Iakovlevich. (1974) *Iskusstvo Srednei Azii* (Art of Middle Asia). Moscow: Iskusstvo.

ARCHITECTURE—CHINA

Since earliest times, Chinese aboveground construction has been dominated by wood. The timber frame is China's major technological contribution to world architecture, and its wooden architectural design is unparalleled in its flexibility, adaptability, versatility, and ability to withstand earthquakes.

The wooden support system can be traced through more than four millennia of Chinese building history, from the Neolithic period in the fourth and third centuries BCE into the twenty-first century CE. Other features of Chinese architecture with a multimillennial history include the foundation platform and the decorative roof. The part of the Chinese wooden structure in which change can most readily be seen is the bracket set, the group of wooden interlocking components that attach to pillars to help support the roof without the use of abrasives or other aids in joinery.

Chinese building styles evolved over time, but the developments often do not correspond to the change in dynasties. The Chinese most often define their architectural tradition according to early, middle, and late periods. Early structures are those from the beginnings of the Chinese building system in Neolithic times through the Bronze Age (last two millennia BCE), the Han dynasty (206 BCE–220 CE), and the period of disunion known as the Three Kingdoms and Northern and Southern dynasties (220–589 CE). The middle period begins with reunification under the Sui dynasty (581–618 CE) in the 580s and continues through the Tang dynasty (618–907) and the Song period (960–1279). Architectural historians do not agree on the break between the middle and late periods. Most understand the period of Mongolian rule (the Yuan dynasty, 1267–1368) as transitional, with later, or premodern architecture, defined as the fourteenth through nineteenth centuries. In this evolution, the years 1103 and 1734 are benchmarks. Those are the dates of issue of the two complete and extant court-sponsored building manuals, the *Yingzao fashi* (Building Standards) and *Gongbu gongcheng zuofa zeli* (Engineering Manual for the Board of Works). From these writings, it is known that even though general principles of Chinese construction seem to change little over long periods of time, at any given time the differences between important, or high-ranking, architecture and more humble construction are always apparent.

Three other features distinguish the Chinese building tradition from those of most other parts of the world. First, to a Chinese, the word architecture means not only buildings such as pagodas or temples, but cities, gardens, and tombs. Second, a Chinese building is almost always part of a complex of structures, joined to one another and interrelated physically by covered walkways or spatially by construction around courtyards. Third, rarely is the name of an architect associated with a building in China. Designs for palaces and cities and for imperial monasteries and imperial gardens were produced at court, the pay scale and allotments of materials for building construction were standardized, builders were craftsmen, and an overriding modular system made it possible for a group of craftsman-builders to erect a timber frame based on proportional units.

Early Architecture

Most of our knowledge of Chinese architecture before the first millennium CE has come from excavation. Some of the sites such as the Shang (c. 1700–1100 BCE) capital at Anyang (c. 1300–1050 BCE) have been studied for nearly eighty years. Others have been discovered and opened within the last decade. Most impressive about the Neolithic sites such as Banpo in Shaanxi, Chengziyai in Shandong, Hemudu in Zhejiang, and Niuhuliang in Liaoning is that although a different Neolithic culture is represented at each of them, each had four-sided structures defined by exterior columns, each had a great hall or temple, each shows evidence of platforms or walls made by the terre-pise method (also known as the rammed-earth method), and probably each was enclosed by an outer wall.

Anyang was preceded by six Shang capitals, two others also in Henan. From the three sites, we know that Shang cities were enclosed by walls as long as seven kilometers in perimeter, that large structures may have been palaces, that residential architecture was raised on building foundations, and that tombs of immense proportions were dug underground and were faced with wooden walls. It is also known that buildings, presumably funerary shrines or temples, stood above ground on top of the burial chambers.

Our first evidence of gardens is from the Zhou dynasty (1045–256 BCE). So far, information about gardens and pleasure palaces is known only through literary sources. Zhou was an extremely important period in the history of Chinese urbanism. Each of the hundred-plus rulers of cities or states had a walled capital. Among them were many with a wall-enclosed palace-city inside the outer wall. This feature was to become a trademark of Chinese imperial planning, preserved even in the last great capital, Beijing, and its Forbidden City. Among the plans of Zhou cities were three distinct ones: the palace area could be near the center of the outer wall, in the north center, or it could be adjacent to the outer city. Sometimes this last type is known as a double-city and sometimes the two walls reflect more than one building period. Finally, from the Zhou we have texts that describe the ideal ruler's city and ritual halls. The earliest remains of imperial ritual halls, so far, are from the Han dynasty.

From the period of unification of the Chinese states by the man known as the First Emperor (Qin Shi Huangdi, c. 259–210 BCE) in 221 BCE until the fall of the subsequent dynasty, the Han, in 220 CE, we have both aboveground building remains and extensive information about funerary architecture. The most impressive architectural achievement of the age was the Great Wall, the idea for which was promulgated by the First Emperor and construction of which occurred off and on from the Qin dynasty up through the sixteenth century. Inside the walls of the Qin capital at Xianyang and the Han capitals at Chang'an and Luoyang, palace complexes extended for miles.

Most of the freestanding architecture of the Han period is of a form known as *que*, a gate tower. These multistory, narrow structures stood in pairs at the entrance to tombs and on either side of gateways to cities and palace complexes and were mimicked in structures atop the corners of walls that enclosed palaces and cities. Additional evidence for the *que* form is preserved in countless relief sculptures that once lined the walls of Han tombs, especially in the provinces of Sichuan, Henan, and Shandong and in murals in tombs from almost every part of China. The actual burial chambers of the First Emperor and emperors and empresses of the Han remain unopened, but hundreds of Han tombs have been excavated. From them, it is known that while common people were buried in simple pits, wealthy citizens, aristocrats, and members of the royal family built tombs with as many as nine or ten rooms, the large ones connected along a line and joined to smaller side chambers by corridors. Made of permanent materials, primarily brick and stone, for eternal residence in the afterlife, these underground palaces were believed to have followed the forms of residential architecture above ground that were built in perishable wood. From the tombs and replicas of architectural forms, it is known that by the Han pe-

riod, bracket sets, ceramic-tile roofs, and vaulted ceilings were in widespread use.

The last period that represents early architecture in China was one in which Buddhism, brought to China from India and other Western regions, was the main religion. A capital city like Luoyang had more than 1,300 Buddhist monasteries in the period of Northern Wei rule (493–534). Only foundations remain from any of those temple complexes. Buddhist architecture of the third through sixth centuries survives in the form of pagodas and in interior construction and decoration of worship caves.

The earliest dated pagoda in China, from 523, stands at Songyue Monastery on Mt. Song in Henan Province. Its dodecagonal shape and fifteen tiers of densely spaced eaves are unique. The single-story, four-sided pagoda at Shentong Monastery in Licheng, Sichuan, was built in 544. In general, Chinese pagodas were four-sided in plan through the early years of the Tang dynasty, but in profile they could be of uniform exterior dimension, such as was the case at Shentong Monastery, or they could diminish in perimeter from base to roof. Made of either brick or stone, the exteriors were decorated with columns, bracket sets, and roof eaves in imitation of wooden architecture. Pagodas of both shapes are found inside Buddhist caves known as central-pillar caves.

Middle Period

The oldest extant wooden architecture in China is a hall dated to 782 of the Tang dynasty (618–907) at the Nanchan Monastery on the sacred Buddhist peak Mt. Wutai in Shanxi. The other three extant wooden buildings from the Tang period are also in Shanxi, a second on Mt. Wutai and two in the southern part of the province. The timber frame had reached full maturity at this time.

No palace building survives from the Tang, but excavation at the capital city, Chang'an, largest city in the world in the eighth century, with a population of more than 1 million, has been so extensive and textual descriptions are so excellent, that the placement of every building in every Tang palace complex is known. Many have been reconstructed on paper. The sites of the tomb of each emperor and empress of the Tang period are also known, and the monumental sculptures that lined the approaches to those tombs survive at several of them. Scores of tombs of Tang princes and princesses have been excavated; many of these are satellites to the tombs of the emperors and empresses. Finally, the earliest open-spandrel bridge in the world, Anji Bridge in Zhao county, Hebei, survives from the first decade of the seventh century, just before the founding of the Tang empire.

About fifty wooden buildings survive from the two centuries following Tang, including several of the most extraordinary wooden structures ever built in China. In far North China, in Inner Mongolia, the non-Chinese Liao dynasty (947–1125) commissioned pavilions and pagodas in wood that used more varieties of bracket sets than ever before in a single structure. The 67.31-meter pagoda of Fogong Monastery in Ying county, Shanxi, tallest wooden structure in the world, has fifty-four different types of bracketing. It also exhibits a second feature characteristic of Liao wooden buildings, concealed interior stories that do not correspond to those visible outside. The pagoda has five exterior stories plus a sixth set of roof eaves, and four additional mezzanine levels inside. In masonry construction, the Liao built four varieties of pagodas, some with base, shaft, and densely placed eaves like the pagoda dated to 523 on Mt. Song and others with a shaft and roof for each story. Most pagodas of Liao and Northern Song (960–1126), the Chinese dynasty to Liao's south, were octagonal in plan. Octagons and hexagons also became widespread in the shapes of underground rooms of both Liao and Song tombs.

Later Architecture

The modern period of Chinese architecture was ushered in by Mongolian rule. In spite of the ethnic background of the imperial family, most construction during the period known as the Yuan dynasty (1267–1368) followed Chinese building standards. More than 250 wooden buildings remain from the Yuan period. Among the most famous are a gate and three halls at Yongle Daoist Monastery in southern Shanxi.

The Forbidden City is the architectural masterpiece of China's last great age, the Ming (1368–1644) and Qing (1644–1912) dynasties. First and foremost, the Forbidden City was the home of Chinese emperors and the center of their universe. Its plan embodies the 2,000 years of architectural history leading up to it. The focus of the Forbidden City is the Three Great Halls, elevated together on a triple-layer marble platform. The capital-I shape of the platform was reserved for China's most eminent architectural arrangements. It is replicated directly behind, in the Three Back Halls, where the emperor and empress slept and where the empress held audiences. Surrounding are an array of palaces, where every aspect of life from the education of the princes to preparation of food to intrigues was enacted. Today, most of the Forbidden City is used for public exhibition halls

for former imperial treasures and offices of the Palace Museum. Directly in front, on ground once restricted from public passage, is Tiananmen Square.

Many of China's other architectural masterpieces of the Ming and Qing dynasties are in Beijing or its suburbs. Most important are the Ming Tombs, where thirteen emperors and their empresses are buried underneath circular mounds with ceremonial halls in front of them. Some of the ceremonial halls are raised on three-tier marble platforms like the one under the Three Great Halls, and the individual halls follow the forms of the principal halls of the Forbidden City. Surrounding the Forbidden City were the suburban altars, epitomized by the Altar of Heaven complex. Its three main halls along a north-south line were the locus of annual imperial supplications to heaven on behalf of the Chinese state. Circular in plan but surrounded by a four-sided enclosure, the Hall for Prayer for a Prosperous Year is the only Chinese structure with a three-tier conical roof. Qing imperial architecture extended beyond Beijing to include five summer palaces north of the Forbidden City; The Eastern and Western Imperial Tombs in Hebei; a palace and tombs in Shenyang, Liaoning; and a Summer Palace in Chengde, Hebei.

The last periods of premodern Chinese history were also times of architectural accomplishment outside the imperial sphere. Private gardens of wealthy citizens, especially in southeastern cities like Suzhou and Yangzhou, have attracted international attention. Contrasting with the poetics of landscape architecture are the residential styles of China's populations on the fringes of the empire—flat-roofed houses designed for mountainous settings in Tibet, tents of the Mongolian grasslands, houses raised on stilts in the humid swamplands of the south, circular houses of the Hakka in Fujian, and two-story houses with skywells in the center in Anhui, for example. It was finally in the Qing period that ethnicity became apparent in Chinese architecture.

Until modern architecture was imposed by city ordinances or national laws in the last half of the twentieth century, Chinese architecture resisted modernization. Chinese-style roofs still cap schools, hospitals, and government offices otherwise made of reinforced concrete. Public buildings retain courtyards at their entrances. Hotels and restaurants relinquish precious space for miniature replicas of Ming gardens. And the Forbidden City has remained the immutable focus of Beijing and symbol of all of China.

Nancy S. Steinhardt

See also: **Architecture, Vernacular—China; Court-yards; Great Wall; Imperial Palace**

Further Reading
Liang Ssu-ch'eng. (1984) *A Pictorial History of Chinese Architecture.* Cambridge, MA: MIT Press.
Steinhardt, Nancy S. (1984) *Chinese Traditional Architecture.* New York: China Institute.
———. (1990) *Chinese Imperial City Planning.* Honolulu, HI: University of Hawaii Press.

ARCHITECTURE—INDIA The architecture of India, from all periods in its history, presents a complex picture for the casual observer for several reasons. First, the country's continuous tradition of settled culture, from the fourth century BCE until the early 2000s, is punctuated by numerous political, social, religious, and cultural changes, affecting its built environment in significant ways. Second, the immense variety of formal treatments and spatial arrangements within Indian architecture have made any straightforward categorization extremely difficult. Scholarly research has, therefore, concentrated on particular periods or phases, rather than attempting a holistic treatment. Third, variations in Indian architecture (at least in its ancient and medieval phases), and particularly those dealing with stylistic and iconographic issues, were neither culture-specific nor region-specific. In the Indian context, styles of architecture over history were not necessarily limited by geographical, cultural or political constraints. Therefore, not only were there large variations and similarities in the architecture of different regions within a larger empire, but also in the architecture of successive dynasties.

Architectural developments in India are classified into four chronological phases, which, while being stylistically distinct, incorporated several common formal, spatial, and compositional characteristics. The first extended from the fourth century BCE to the fifth century CE. The second spanned the fifth to the thirteenth centuries. Building activity between the thirteenth and eighteenth centuries constituted the third, while the fourth phase began with the colonial period and continues in the twenty-first century.

Fourth Century BCE through Fifth Century CE
Documented remains from the earliest period of Indian architecture were brought to light in 1920s, through the excavation of Mohenjo Daro and Harappa, two cities in the Indus plain. Although more than four hundred miles apart, both were apparently organized on a rectangular plan, and had largely identical urban layouts—evidence that they were part of an extensive culture that once flourished over a large region. That culture reached its peak in the first quarter of the second millennium BCE. Beyond this, glimpses of ancient Indian settlements and building types may be gained from the enormous corpus of ancient literature, including great epics such as the *Mahabharata* and *Ramayana*; collations of folk legends, such as the *Jataka*s; or the *shastras*—all of which contain descriptions of ancient cities and buildings. Corroborating relief and fresco cycles seen at Sanchi, Bharhut, Amaravati, and Ajanta describe a great deal more, showing exactly what kinds of buildings were constructed in this era, and how they varied in size, function, complexity, and context. Also apparent are conventions that defined the physical layouts of structures (mainly sacred sites), settlements, military camps, and large cities.

Within this vast gamut, two specific kinds of buildings still survive for us to examine in more detail. These are the stupa (burial mound), and the rock-cut sanctuary, both structures serving the needs of the two predominant religions of the time, Buddhism and Jainism. From early versions constructed from impacted mud and clay, and serving as a simple demarcation of the deceased's remains, the stupa developed its typical hemispherical form, fixed at the cardinal points by formal gates or *torana*s. At the Mahastupa at Sanchi, this mound was enlarged to nearly twice its original size over a high drum-like plinth and clad in brick and stone. A double-ramp led to a terrace that ran around the drum, and was itself contained within an elaborately carved railing. The Mahabodhi temple at Gaya followed similar principles, although the vertical attenuation of the temple-tower, unusual for a stupa, resembled a temple *shikhara*. The Sanchi complex also has substantial remains of sanctuaries or monasteries. Organized either as rooms around a building courtyard or around centralized, enclosed spaces such as those in rock-cut *chaitya* halls, they served as hostels for traveling monks. Within the architectural details of the stupa and sanctuary, possibly the most striking feature is the rendition of timber details in stone, strongly suggesting that similar structures had existed in the past, constructed of wood. In several examples, fake stone beams and overhanging eaves seemingly supported barrel-vaulted, rock-cut halls. The Lomas Rishi Hall, for instance, was given a facade representing a timber structure with inclined posts, purlins, rafters, friezes, and bowed roof and pot finial, all carved out of solid rock. Similar discoveries have been made at Bhaja, Nasik, Junnar, Bedsa, Karle, Kanheri, Kondane, Pitalkhora, Aurangabad, Ellora and Ajanta.

Fifth through Thirteenth Centuries

Historically one of the most complex for developments in Indian architecture, this period was characterized by the growing popularity of Hinduism in large parts of the Indian subcontinent. The expansion of Hinduism coincided with an elaboration of the physical structure of the temple itself, which began to be controlled by a system of proportions and metaphysical rhythms in plan and elevation contained within the science of Vastushastra.

Early freestanding structures, such as Temple Seventeen at Sanchi and the Mahadeva Temple at Udayapur, were relatively simple, consisting of a portico connected to a flat-roofed square cella. In later constructions, in addition to an elaborate, stepped plinth that served to position the building, an upper shrine chamber was introduced above the cella. At the Durga and Meguti Temples at Aihole, a further preoccupation with the apsidal form of temple buildings occurred, allowing for two separate zones of ambulation—one within the cella, and the other outside. Meanwhile, extensive experimentation had also modified the temple structure, as demonstrated in the richly decorated *shikhara* of the Lakshmana Temple at Sirpur.

Rock-cut sanctuaries of the earlier period were elaborated upon in a similar manner. The relatively simple, apsidal, primarily residential *chaitya-griha* was modified into an elaborate rectangular hall with surrounding cells and portico, based to some extent on the nine-square formula that was also adopted for the layouts of freestanding temples. This was to be the characteristic feature of most of the major constructions at Ajanta, Ellora, and Elephanta. Finally, there were also points when temple construction and rock-cut sanctuaries merged. Perhaps inspired by the elaborate, gigantic rock-excavated constructions, there was a significant move towards building colossal structures, which served as physical evocations of the omnipotent sublime. The *ratha*s, carved from solid rock at Mahabalipuram, the Virupaksha Temple at Pattadakal, and the Kailasa Temple at Ellora, are important in this respect. Equally awe-inspiring for their size and grandeur are the temple complexes at Tiruvarur, Chidambaram, Darasuram, and Tanjavur.

Thirteenth through Eighteenth Centuries

Spanning the thirteenth through the eighteenth centuries, the third phase of developments comprised two separate trends: the activities of the Delhi sultanate (1192–1526), and architectural patronage under the Mughal empire (1526–1857). For both trends, the city of Delhi (the capital of present-day India) was a primary center of activity and retained its status as the imperial capital, although the actual site of the city or settlement changed substantially, giving rise to the celebrated legend of seven cities comprising Delhi.

The Delhi sultanate began with the Ghurid and Ghaznavid invasions of northern India, especially Delhi, between 940 and 1150. Within the occupied city of Delhi, the general Qutb-ud-din Aibak built the Quwwat-ul-Islam Masjid (the Might of Islam Mosque) in 1192. Incorporated within its construction were large parts and remains of older Hindu and Jain buildings; at a deeper level, however, it expanded on the formal, spatial, and iconographic vocabulary prevalent in pre-Sultanate-period constructions. Consequently, local masons employed for its construction, and for the several other monuments completed in this early period, were able to recycle older building elements (columns, capitals, beams, corbeled brackets, and domes) to create new ensembles following their own decorative and structural traditions. In effect, monuments such as the Quwwat-ul-Islam Masjid and the Ahrai-din-ja Jhompra at Ajmer, while being improvised versions of the hypostyle prayer-hall (prayer halls whose roofs were supported by rows of columns) prototypes typical in Iran and Central Asia, were evidence of an emerging aesthetic in the making. Stucco and tile were replaced by extensive stone carvings of vegetal motifs. Experimentation with the indigenous system employing columns (posts), beams, and corbels replaced the shell and vault constructions prevalent in large parts of Iran and Central Asia. There was also a great deal of innovation, particularly as Islamic building conventions blended with Indian traditions. Significant examples include the facade of five-corbeled ogee arches screening the Quwwat-ul-Islam Masjid's prayer hall; the red sandstone, gray quartzite, and white-marbled circular and acute-angled projections on the Qutb Minar; Iltutmish's richly carved, domed mausoleum; and the Sultan Ghari monument—a novel combination of an octagonal, subterranean tomb and mosque.

In addition to buildings, several new urban foundations in and around Delhi were established in this period: Siri, with its legendary Hazar Sutun (thousand-pillared) palace, founded by Ala-ud-din Khalji (1296–1316); the impregnable city of Tughlaqabad, built for Ghiyas-ud-din Tughluq out of massive masonry; the royal seat of Muhammad Tughluq (1325–1351) at Jahanpanah with the Begumpuri Mosque; and Kotla Firoz Shah, the fort palace of Firoz Shah. Additionally, other areas of the Indian subcontinent came under Muslim (Arabo-Persian) influence. These included Gujarat, where a spectacular capital and necropolis were created at Ahmedabad (1411–1442) and Sarkhej (1442–1451) respectively, both arrayed with superb mosques, *wav*s (public wells), and *rauza*s (mortuary complexes). In Bengal, the city of Gaur was established at Lakhnauti. Architectural innovations introduced there included an enormous *iwan* (arch) at Adina Masjid, the mosque of Sikandar Shah (1358–1389) at Hazrat Pandua, and the doubly curved *bangaldar* (bow- or boat-shaped) roof in the Eklakhi Mausoleum—elements that would reoccur in Mughal architecture in the centuries to come. At Jaunpur, established by Malik Sarwar, the Tughlaq viceroy, the extraordinary Atala Masjid with its massive, pylonlike *iwan* frontispieces came closest to the architecture of Bibi-Khanum Mosque, completed in 1394 at Samarqand for Timur (1336–1405).

Some of the Hindu kingdoms that successfully halted the onslaught of the Muslims also produced important architecture. The kingdom of Vijaynagara (1397–1565) was first among these, and its capital city (Hampi) was embellished with a royal complex and four magnificent temples. Other examples were the Rajput capital at Chittor under Rana Kumbha (1433–1468), the ancient hill-fort of Gwalior, and the great palaces of Orcha and Datia built between 1501 and 1627.

Few trends in Sultanate-period architecture, however, prefigure the elaborate developments of the Mughal period. The empire's Turko-Mongol lineage from the Timurids of Central Asia provided a unique stylistic element to their experiments in architecture and urban planning. From the time of Babur (1483–1530), an evident obsession with elaborate gardens, running water, and impressive pavilions is observed. Babur's successor, Humayun (1508–1556), witnessed the first of the architectural hybrids created by this process. A huge Mughal citadel, with the octagonal Sher Mandal (a miniature derivative of the Persian *hasht behisht*), dominated his capital at Dinpanah, itself based on a nine-square, urban maxigrid scheme. The other important structure from this period, though Afghan and not Mughal in its patronage, was the mausoleum of Sher Shah at Sasaram (1545). An octagonal structure, it was positioned at the center of a square pool of water.

The hybrid style was furthered by Akbar (1556–1605), who provided a substantial degree of imperial patronage during his long reign. Consequently, urban foundations at Agra, Lahore, Fatehpur Sikri, and Burhanpur developed very much on the lines of the great Timurid capitals in Central Asia, while retaining a distinct local character in buildings and urban ensembles. The Jahangiri Mahal in the Agra Fort was exemplary in drawing its inspiration from the Man Mandir at Gwalior, Timur's Aq Saray at Sharisyabz, and the great caliphate tradition of palace planning. Experimentation with local building techniques, materials, and craftsmen was also demonstrated at the Fatehpur Sikri complex. Here a complex arrangement of courtyards, open and closed spaces, and service and private areas effectively intermeshed to produce an urban environment with new building prototypes, which were emulated over the next few centuries.

Akbar's grandson, Shah Jahan (1628–1658), improved on these achievements, creating some of the most important architectural masterpieces of the Mughal period. The planned city of Shahjahanabad, with its grand bazaars, urban squares, mosques, caravanserais, baths, and impressive citadel, was completed between 1639 and 1648. Substantial additions to the urban structures at Agra and Lahore followed. In addition to cities, Shah Jahan's reign was characterized by a great refinement in the design of several important buildings, particularly mosques and mausoleums. While the Jami Masjid (Friday Mosque) at Shahjahanabad (1650–1656) was grand and large, being an imperial institution meant to serve the urban population, those at Lahore and Agra—the Mothi and Nagina Masjids (1645 and 1654)—were small and gem-like and meant for private prayer. Among mausoleums, the Taj Mahal (1632–1643), built for Shah Jahan's wife, has achieved lasting worldwide renown.

In addition to building funded by royal patronage, in many parts of the empire ancient traditions of temple architecture still survived, as did regional vestiges of older Indo-Islamic styles. Curious hybrids, drawing on provincial Mughal, Indo-Muslim, and traditional forms flourished in areas away from the Mughal court, especially as the empire declined in the eighteenth century.

Colonial Period to the Early 2000s

The arrival of Europeans in the eighteenth century infused Indian architecture with fresh elements, although older practices and traditions were not entirely discarded. British colonial architecture created through this interaction was termed the Indo-Saracenic. It was either a random mix of elements, or a complex hybrid that effectively combined foreign and indigenous styles. While its evolution depended partially on the fancy of the individual architects, it embodied above all a vision the British had of themselves as the rulers of India, linked directly to the Mughals, and hence to India's glorious past. Within this process, the most significant colonial structures were built at Calcutta, Mumbai (Bombay), Madras, and Bangalore, and at the imperial capital at New Delhi. In addition to churches, numerous minor structures were built across the country in a blander, standardized style, termed the Public Works Department (PWD) style.

Two distinct phases have characterized modern Indian architecture since the country's independence in 1947. The first, between 1947 and the early 1980s, relied more on trends of the international style prevalent in Europe and the United States to meet the growing needs of building design and construction in the country. The government buildings built at Chandigarh by French architect Le Corbusier (1887–1965) exemplified this trend. The second stage, stretching between the 1980s and into the 2000s, evolved to include more complex issues such as modernity, tradition, the vernacular, and new interpretations of institutions. The growing demand for new architecture, and consequently more architects, is reflected by the proliferation of architectural schools across the country, with those at Ahmedabad, Delhi, and Mumbai earning international acclaim. Some of the most important Indian architects today include B. V. Doshi, Anant Raje, and Charles Correa.

Manu P. Sobti

See also: **Taj Mahal**

Further Reading

Batley, Claude. (1973) *The Design Development of Indian Architecture.* 3d ed. New York: St. Martin's.
Bhatt, Vikram, and Peter Scriver. (1990) *After the Masters.* Ahmedabad, India: Mapin.
Brown, Percy. (1942) *Indian Architecture: Buddhist and Hindu Periods, The Islamic Period.* 2 vols. Mumbai, India: D. B. Taraporevala.
Herdeg, Klaus Walter. (1967) *Formal Structure in Indian Architecture.* Ithaca, NY: Rizzoli.
Koch, Ebba. (1991) *Mughal Architecture.* Munich: Prestel.
Kramrisch, Stella. (1954) *The Art of India: Traditions of Indian Sculpture, Painting, and Architecture.* New York: Phaidon.
Metcalf, Thomas R. (1989) *An Imperial Vision: Indian Architecture and Britain's Raj.* Boston: Faber & Faber.
Michel, George, and Philip Davies (1989). *The Penguin Guide to the Monuments of India.* New York: Viking.
Tadgell, Christopher. (1994) *The History of Architecture in India.* London: Phaidon.
Tillotson, G. H. R. (1989) *The Tradition of Indian Architecture: Continuity, Controversy, and Change Since 1850.* New Haven, CT: Yale University Press.
Volwahsen, Andreas. (1969) *Living Architecture: Indian.* Trans. by Ann E. Keep. New York: Grosset & Dunlap.

ARCHITECTURE, ISLAMIC—WEST ASIA

To understand Islamic architecture in the region comprising present-day Iran, Iraq, and Turkey, one must first understand its roots. The builders of Islamic cities that arose in the desert where no city existed before used architectural styles that they knew from other places. Nevertheless, they adapted these older styles to express new ideas about the meaning of Islam, its values, and its power. Older cities enveloped into Islam contained older structures that were reused and readapted to suit the new rulers.

Symbolism in Islamic architecture is often conveyed by the use of simple everyday geometrical forms in special ways. The dome placed over a cubic space is sometimes simply a convenient means of roofing and sometimes an awe-inspiring symbol of the heavens above the earth, which carries the further message of the all-powerful oneness of God. The arch may be used to indicate the direction in which one is to pray, but it may also be used in colonnades at a palace or as windows in a city house. Vernacular architecture (the architecture of the common people as opposed to sacred or civic architecture) shared many of the architectural elements found in sacred buildings such as mosques and *madrasah*s (religious schools).

The Ka'ba

The first Islamic building was the Ka'ba, a sacred monument that was the center of pagan pilgrimage and worship in Mecca, the "House of God," that, according to Muhammad's revelations, was built by Abraham and Ishmael to demonstrate their faith in the One God. The Ka'ba is a rectangular stone building approximately 14 meters high. The sacred black stone built into one of the walls had been venerated by Arabs since before Islam and was a site for pilgrimage and worship. All Muslims face the black stone in the Ka'ba when they pray, and all mosques face the Ka'ba. The Grand Mosque of Mecca that surrounds the Ka'ba has been built and rebuilt many times over the centuries and is not in itself a notable example of Islamic architecture.

Development of the Mosque

Although the first mosque no longer stands, essentially it was simply an empty rectilinear enclosure of some fifty-six square meters. Nine small rooms along the outside of one of the walls served as humble quarters for Muhammad's family. A shaded space facing the black stone contained in the Ka'ba in Mecca was constructed of a double row of palm trunks covered with a roof of palm leaves plastered with mud, and another shaded space was constructed to protect the poor from the blazing sun of the Hijaz. Its size and flexible character indicates that the courtyard was meant for communal worship. In addition, the first mosque was used for public gatherings and as a place to make announcements, adjudicate legal cases, and lodge visitors, and served as the center of the emergent state.

At some point a *mihrab* (prayer niche) was added in the *qibla* (the wall indicating the direction of prayer) to mark the place where Muhammad had led prayers. In Islam, prayers are said five times a day, and the way that Muhammad conducted these prayers would set the pattern for Muslims throughout history. The architectural history of Islamic history has its roots in these patterns.

About a century following the death of Muhammad, two distinct types of mosque emerged. One, the *masjid*, was a place for worship, and often came to be constructed as part of a complex including fortified garrisons housing the soldiers of an expanding empire, and theological schools meant to train the faithful in the Islamic sciences. A second type of mosque, called the Congregational, Friday, or Cathedral Mosque (*jami*), was designed for large-scale public worship on Fridays. Rather than having enough space for hundreds of worshippers, it could contain thousands.

Sometime following the death of Muhammad, during the expansion of the Islamic empire, Muslims began to add minarets to their mosques. From this high point, the muezzin would chant the call to prayer. This combination of the human voice and the lofty position of the muezzin differentiated the Islamic call to prayer from the Christians, who used bells or wooden clappers, and Jews, who used the shofar (a ram's horn trumpet) in their worship.

The Dome of the Rock

The caliph (leader of the Islamic faithful) 'Abd al-Malik (646–705) ordered the construction of the Dome of the Rock on the Herodian platform of the Jewish Temple in Jerusalem, which was known to Muslims as the Haram al-Sharif, or Noble Sanctuary. It was completed in 691 CE, making it the earliest surviving Islamic monument. It was also the first major artistic achievement of the earliest of the Islamic empires, the Umayyad (661–750). The methods of design and decoration were drawn directly from the Sasanian and Byzantine traditions, but the architecture of the Dome of the Rock achieved a distinct expression of Islamic faith and triumph.

The Dome of the Rock was designed as a pilgrimage site and invites comparison to the Ka'ba, with its own sacred rock (from which Muhammad ascended into heaven, and which bears his footprint) and tradition of worship. With its doors opening to the four points of the compass, the idea of pilgrimage is strongly suggested. The decoration of the building's

interior with mosaics depicting Byzantine and Sasanian crowns and jewels, vegetal motifs suggestive of paradise, and Qur'anic inscriptions asserting the victory of Islam over Christianity and its completion of God's revelation to man emphasize the triumphant stance of the Umayyads in the former stronghold and birthplace of Christianity.

The unusual plan of the building makes it unique in world architecture. The octagonal form crowned by a dome was used in Byzantine architecture to indicate where a special event had occurred. The Dome of the Rock is not a mosque, but a *mashhad*, a place of witness, marking the site of Muhammad's ascension to heaven after his miraculous journey on al-Buraq. Its gilded central dome rests upon a drum pierced with sixteen windows, which in turn rest upon a circular arcade of four piers and sixteen marble columns. Around this is an octagonal arcade of eight piers and sixteen columns. The octagonal exterior was finished with marble, but during the Ottoman period this was replaced with magnificent ceramic tiles. The lavish mosaics depict no animals or human beings. One of the most striking aspects of the Dome of the Rock is that the diameter of its dome is equal to its height, making for a perfect interior space. Decorated in reds and golds, the Dome of the Rock glows with an atmosphere of sanctity.

Abbasid Architecture in Iraq

When the administrative center of the Islamic empire shifted from Damascus to Iraq, economic development and Islamic culture became extremely rich. The growth in trade and agriculture was sustained by the enormous geographical sweep of the Abbasid empire (749–1258).

Perhaps the most outstanding feature of Abbasid architecture was the city of Baghdad itself. Over the years its original plan has been obscured, but written descriptions give us a fairly detailed view of what the city may have looked like. Baghdad was founded in 762 by the caliph al-Mansur (reigned 754–775). It was built in the shape of a circle to symbolize the navel of the universe. The outer ring of the city was made up of shops and houses with stout walls made for defense. This circle was divided into quadrants by four long streets covered with barrel vaults. Each street opened to the outside with a magnificent two-story gate and a complex of vaults and bridges over moats. On the top story of each great gate was a domed reception hall where travelers could be met and interviewed before being allowed to pass into the city. These gates were more symbolic than military, however, reflecting the great sense of security felt by the early Abbasids.

The large central area of the city was mostly empty, focusing attention upon the mosque and palace at the very heart of the circle. The mosque was joined to the palace and large enough to contain all the inhabitants of the city.

The Great Mosque at Samarra (north central Iraq), built by al-Mutawakkil (reigned 847–861) is the largest known in the Muslim world. Its outstanding feature is the unusual spiral minaret outside its walls. A second Samarra mosque is Abu Dalaf, which resembles the Great Mosque but is not quite as large.

The Shi'ite tombs at Kufa, Najaf, and Karbala are original structures but they have generally been inaccessible for scholarly study. The Great Mosque of Mosul, built between 1120 and 1122, is a notable structure, as are the Congregational Mosque of Dunaysir and the Mosque of Diyarbakr, also built in the twelfth centuries.

Abbasid Architecture in Iran

The emigration of Turkic tribes from the east into the Islamic world had an enormous influence upon urban society. The architectural styles that they brought with them eventually melded with Islamic designs as the soldiers and tribespeople became Islamicized, leading to the construction of notable mosques and tombs decorated with ornately carved stucco applied to brick constructions and elaborate brick structures in which the design is integrated into the structure itself. One of the most striking of these mosques was at Nayin (east of Esfahan) and dates to the tenth century. A Samanid tomb built around 914 in Bukhara is another remarkable structure dating from this period; there brick is used in a most elaborate way, fulfilling both structural and ornamental functions simultaneously. The influence of Turkic brick towers and stucco ornamentation on the minarets of Damghan and Jam in Iraq, as well as in locations in Central Asia, is readily appreciated.

The Great Mosque (Masjid-i Jumah) of Esfahan is one of the most celebrated of Islamic monuments. Built by the famed Seljuk vizier Nizam al-Mulk (1018–1092) between 1072 and 1092, it is a vast complex of buildings with 476 vaults, most of them topped by domes, which has been altered and added on to many times through the centuries. It contains a large rectangular courtyard, but also features an important new design element: the *iwan*. The *iwan* is a vaulted or flat-roofed hall that is open at one end. This mosque has four *iwan*s facing the inner courtyard and the entire composition is formal and elegant. Each of the *iwan*s frames a *pishtaq*, a lofty arch which marks a monumental entrance.

Architecture in Iran after the Mongol Invasions

Following the Mongol invasions of 1253–1258, the architecture of Iran was enriched by vibrant tiles that were used to decorate the exterior surfaces of buildings. One of the earliest buildings to survive from the Il-Khanid period (1256–1355) in Iran is the Tomb of Uljaytu, an enormous octagon topped by a dome, which had been part of an large citadel complex housing many structures, including a mosque, *madrasah*, hospice, hospital, and guesthouse. At Natanz in central Iran, the shrine of 'Abd al-Samad (1307) has a magnificent brick dome that masterfully uses vaulting made up of individual cells or small niches to bridge the transition between dome and pedestal, a technique first used in Egypt and North Africa in the twelfth century.

When Timur destroyed Damascus in 1401, he deported many of the engineers and artisans of that city to his capital, Samarqand (in present-day Uzbekistan), where they would work on Timurid projects. Khorasan also became a center for architectural innovation, as evidenced by the renovation of the shrine of Imam Riza (1416–1418) at Mashhad. The architect Qavam al-Din Shirazi developed a new kind of interior vaulting known as squinch-net vaulting, which allowed the weight of the roof to be distributed onto intersecting points of the vaults themselves, allowing the piercing of the walls by windows to let in light. This kind of vaulting dispensed with the need for piers, opening the rooms up and allowing for other ways to divide interior spaces. The Complex of Gauhar Shad in Mashhad (1417–1438) is a good example of this kind of design. The color and technical proficiency of the superb turquoise blue tiles that decorate the Blue Mosque of Tabriz (1465) in northwestern Iran have never been surpassed. Although many Timurid buildings have been lost, their influence upon the later Islamic architecture was enormous. The Safavid, Ottoman, and Mughal dynasties all incorporated Timurid ideals into their art and architecture.

Islamic Architecture in Anatolia (Turkey)

The first Ottoman capital of Bursa boasts some of the finest early examples of Ottoman architecture. In 1339 Orhan Gazi (c. 1288–c. 1360), the second Ottoman emperor, built a palace in the citadel, a public soup kitchen, a bath, a caravansary (resting place for caravans), and several mosques. Like the Mamluks (who ruled Egypt and Syria from 1250 to 1517), Ottoman rulers built public works as both a service to their subjects and as a way to legitimize their authority.

Other Turkic principalities in Anatolia built notable structures during the fourteenth century. Among these were the Menteshids (ruled southwestern Anatolia from the eighth century to 1421, when they were conquered by the Ottomans), who built the Mosque of Firuz Beg at Milas in 1394 and the Mosque of Ilyas Beg in Balat in 1404. These buildings are noteworthy for their elaborate and fine stone carvings. The Qaramanids, a Turkish dynasty that ruled the area around Konya and Nigde from 1262 to 1475, built the Ak Madrasah at Nigde in 1409. This mosque was modeled after a Seljuk hospital built in the fourteenth century in Amasya: it had an open courtyard with two *iwan*s flanked by rooms on two stories. It also has beautiful masonry typical of the Qaramanids.

In contention with the Christian Byzantine Empire, the Ottoman sultans also had to demonstrate the vitality and superiority of Islam over the defeated Christian authorities. This desire found expression in their architecture. Following the plan of an early Ottoman building in Iznik (Nicaea), they created mosques with a central dome, a domed vestibule, and a five-bay porch. These buildings also featured *iwan*s, and the structure was designed to shelter the Muslim-warrior brotherhoods responsible for the expansion of the Ottoman state. The Ottoman ruler Bayezid I (c. 1360–1403) also built a large congregational mosque in Bursa's central commercial district in 1399–1400 with booty from one of his victories over the Hungarians. This mosque featured multiple domed bays, a characteristic that increasingly became a mark of Ottoman style.

In the fifteenth century the newly resurgent Ottoman state again built impressive monuments. One of the first of these, and certainly among the most important Ottoman buildings, was the Yeshil Jami, or Green Mosque, begun by Mehmed I (reigned 1412–1421) at Bursa in 1412 and completed in 1424. The complex included a *madrasah*, soup kitchen, baths, and tombs. This mosque also featured the beautiful tiles made in a process known as *cuerda seca*, or dry cord. This technique, revived by the Ottomans but developed earlier, allows for the firing of numerous glazes on one tile, separated by a thin line of greasy manganese that, when fired, leaves a matte black line, giving the tile an effect similar to stained glass.

Sultan Mehmed II (1432–1481) was known as the Conquerer for his conquest of the Byzantine capital of Constantinople (1453). In addition to his military successes, he is known for his patronage of the arts and his interest in learning from Turkish, Persian, and European scholars, artists, and writers who eagerly came to Istanbul to assist in his many building projects, perhaps the most famous of which is the Top-kapi Palace. This enormous complex overlooks two seas and two continents. It took over a decade to complete and has been repaired and remodeled many times. Its arrangement appears haphazard, with kiosks, pavilions, halls, gardens, kitchens, and stables arranged in no particular way, but in fact the buildings were placed to take advantage of the views and the breezes. The name of the palace, which means "cannon gate," and the symbolic location overlooking the Dardanelle Straits reflect the security and confidence of a world power at the height of its military successes.

Today, the palace is a treasure trove of great works of all periods of Islamic art. The beautiful tile work there—especially the famed Iznik tiles, with their deep red glaze, brilliant white slip, and glowing turquoise hues that have never been reproduced—is stunning. In this palace one can appreciate the enormity of the jobs undertaken by the sultan in providing food for his entourage and for the city of Istanbul: the massive kitchens and workrooms in the palace could provide food for thousands at a time. The palace had barracks and stables for a large military contingent, musical bands, and other officials responsible for the financial records and the massive reports written by palace bureaucrats concerning their far-flung empire. Within one of the palace buildings the sultan could sit unseen behind a wooden grate to hear the petitions of his subjects. Palace schools trained the sultan's servants in the ways of the bureaucracy, as well as in courtly manners, the Islamic sciences, history, literature, and art. This was the administrative and artistic center of one of the greatest empires in human history.

Another of Mehmed's great building projects was the Fatih (Conqueror's) Complex, erected between 1463 and 1471. It was built in accordance with the Ottoman imperial mosques in Bursa, and was influenced by the Hagia Sophia Church. A central mosque dominates the symmetrical complex, which unlike the Topkapi palace does not take the landscape or views into account at all. Here the focus is upon the mosque, surrounded by imperial tombs, a primary school, a library, *madrasah*s, baths, residences, latrines, a hospital, a hospice, a soup kitchen, a caravansary, military barracks, a covered market, and an open-air market for horses, stable workers, and equestrian trades.

It was during the reign of Suleyman the Magnificent (1494–1566) that Ottoman architecture reached its peak. The most important of all Suleyman's many buildings was the Suleymaniye Complex in Istanbul, built from 1550 to 1557 by the famous architect Sinan Pasha (1489–1588). The Suleymaniye Complex emulated the Mehmed Fatih Complex. It includes a great congregational mosque, two mausoleums, a hospital, six *madrasah*s, a children's school, a bath, a hospital, a hospice, a public kitchen, a caravansary, rows of small shops to provide rental income for the complex, and a small *zawiya* (warriors' lodge). In the endowment deed, Suleyman specified that this complex was to become the center for religious law in the Ottoman empire.

The entire complex seems to be a mountain, its summit an enormous dome. The enormous interior space of the mosque, uninterrupted by any columns or piers, is a truly awe-inspiring sight. The four slim minarets, with their strong Turkish character, are elegant counterpoints to the mass of domes ascending to the topmost dome. The calligraphic decorations are one of the most remarkable features of the mosque. Suleyman is buried behind the mosque in a tomb that was modeled after the Dome of the Rock.

Iranian Architecture in the Sixteenth and Seventeenth Centuries

In Iran the Safavid dynasty (1501–1722/36) regained its strength under Shah Abbas (1571–1629), who established a new capital in Esfahan in the 1590s, and in the process developed a new style of architecture. The new capital in Esfahan featured an enormous square *(maidan)* for sports, promenades, and processions. Four monumental entrances face the *maidan*, one leading to the bazaar, one leading to the Mosque of Shaykh Luftallah, one leading to the Masjid-i Shah (Mosque of the Shah), and one leading to the royal palace. A magnificent boulevard was built, lined with the fine mansions of Safavid notables. One section of the boulevard was reserved for animals and carts, while the other was reserved for pedestrians. Surrounding the *maidan*, and housed in the elegant arched facades, were the stalls and shops of skilled craftsmen and merchants of valuable commodities. A special caravansary for textile merchants, goldsmiths, jewelers, and engravers was housed close to the royal mint. The overall appearance of the ceremonial square surrounded by the hubbub of the market enchanted European visitors to the royal city. Fifty thousand ceramic lamps suspended from long wooden poles illuminated the square at night. There was a music pavilion where the royal band would play during the day.

Each of the individual buildings in this massive complex was richly ornamented with tiles, carved wooden screens, and all of the traditional elements of Islamic architecture: *iwan*s, *muqarna*s (the units used to create the typically Islamic honeycomb or stalactite vaulting), vaults, domes, and arches. In Esfahan these elements achieve a marvelous balance, so that the rich ornamentation creates an atmosphere of tranquility and repose.

Judith Mendelsohn Rood

Further Reading
Aslanapa, O. (1971) *Turkish Art and Architecture.* London: Faber & Faber.
Atil, Esin. (1987) *The Age of Suleyman the Magnificent.* Washington, DC: National Gallery of Art.
Blair, Shiela S., and Jonathan M. Bloom. (1995) *The Art and Architecture of Islam 1250–1800.* Yale University Pelican History of Art Series. New Haven, CT: Yale University Press.
Ettinghausen, Richard. (1972) *From Byzantium to Sasanian Iran and the Islamic World.* Leiden, Netherlands: Brill.
Ettinghausen, Richard, and Oleg Grabar. (1989) *The Art and Architecture of Islam: 650–1250.* Yale University Pelican History of Art Series. New Haven, CT: Yale University Press.
Golombek, Lisa, and Donald Wilbur. (1988) *The Timurid Architecture of Iran and Turan.* Princeton, NJ: Princeton University Press.
Goodwin, Godfrey. (1971) *A History of Ottoman Architecture.* London: Thames & Hudson.
Grabar, Oleg. (1990) *The Great Mosque of Isfahan.* New York: Cambridge University Press.
Hillenbrand, Richard. (1994) *The Art of the Seljuqs in Iran and Anatolia.* Costa Mesa, CA: Mazda.
———. (1994) *Islamic Architecture.* New York: Columbia University Press.
Hoag, John D. (1977) *Islamic Architecture.* New York: Abrams.
Kuran, Aptullah. (1968) *The Mosque in Early Ottoman Architecture.* Chicago: University of Chicago Press.
Michell, George, ed. (1978) *Architecture of the Islamic World.* London: Thames & Hudson.
Necipoglu, Gulru. (1991) *Architecture, Ceremonial, and Power: The Topkapi Palace in the Fifteenth and Sixteenth Centuries.* Cambridge, MA: Harvard University Press.
O'Kane, Bernard. (1987) *Timurid Architecture in Khurasan.* Costa Mesa, CA: Mazda.
Rosen-Ayalon, Myriam. (1996) "Art and Architecture in Jerusalem in the Early Islamic Period." In *The History of Jerusalem: The Early Islamic Period 638–1099,* edited by Joshua Prawer and Haggai Ben-Shammai. New York: New York University Press, 386–412.

ARCHITECTURE—JAPAN Japan's architectural achievements, both secular and sacred, reflect the foreign and native influences that shaped Japanese culture as a whole.

The Early Period

The Jomon culture (10,000–300 BCE) offers the first evidence of architecture in Japan. Archaeological remains tell of square pit-dwellings, so named because their floor was approximately a half meter below

THE VARIETY OF JAPANESE ARCHITECTURE

This late nineteenth century description of Japanese homes makes clear the considerable diversity that existed at the time while also noting that the untrained Westerner might easily miss the diversity.

> Whatever may be said regarding the architecture of Japan, the foreigner, at least, finds it difficult to recognize any distinct differences among the houses, or to distinguish any radical differences in the various types of dwellings he sees in his travels throughout the country. It may be possible that these exist, for one soon gets to recognize the differences between the ancient and modern house. There are also marked differences between the compact house of the merchant in the city and the country house; but as for special types of architecture that would parallel the different styles found in our country, there are none. Everywhere one notices minor details of finish and ornament which he sees more fully developed in the temple architecture, and which is evidently derived from this source; and if it can be shown, as it unquestionably can, that these features were brought into the country by the priests who brought one of the two great religions, then we can trace many features of architectural detail to their home, and to the avenues through which they came.
>
> *Source:* Edward S. Morse. ([1896] 1961) *Japanese Homes and Their Surroundings*; New York: Dover, 47.

ground level. A thatched roof supported by posts and beams leaned into the middle of the structure, with one post at the very center. The more advanced Yayoi culture (300 BCE–300 CE) saw the advent of rice cultivation, and new buildings were developed for grain storage. Constructed of wooden boards with a thatched roof, the rectangular granary was raised off the ground and had a stepped plank leading into it. This style of building would have an influence on the shrines of later periods.

Important early evidence concerning architecture in Japan, however, comes from earthenware figurines known as *haniwa* (literally, "clay cylinder") that were placed around tomb mounds in the Kofun period (300–710 CE). The *haniwa* depicted buildings of different types, including single-story homes and two-story granaries. They show a main home conjoined by smaller secondary structures with hipped roofs covered in thatch; some had ridge-crossing cylinders, likely used for holding the rafters in place. Whatever their function, these striking architectural elements

later became a mark of both imperial buildings and Shinto shrines.

Two examples of early Shinto architecture may be found at the Ise and Izumo shrines, which date to the third and fourth centuries. Their simple style and elevated floor recall the Yayoi granaries. The distinctive features are the extensions of the outermost rafters *(chigi)* that extend up like horns forming a large V, and the row of weight-blocks *(katsuogi)* set along the ridge at right angles to it.

Buddhist Influence

The arrival of Buddhism in the sixth century had a tremendous influence on Japanese architecture, particularly the building of temple complexes. Based on Chinese models, early temples consisted of an entrance gate *(chumon)* that was part of a roofed enclosure encircling the main precinct, the pagoda, and the golden hall *(kondo)*, as in the Horyuji temple near Nara, Japan's earliest surviving temple, which dates from the late seventh century. The buildings in Horyuji are the world's oldest wooden structures. The *kondo*, following Chinese precedents, is set on a platform and utilizes post-and-lintel construction whereby the roof is supported by a system of brackets. The mid-eighth-century Todaiji complex, also at Nara, reflects the grand style of Chinese Buddhist architecture of the Tang dynasty (618–907 CE). The magnificent Daibutsuden (Great Buddha Hall) is approximately 47 meters high, 87 meters long, and 47 meters deep, making it the world's largest wooden building. The grand style of the Nara period (710–794), however, is best seen at Toshodaiji. The building is low and long, imparting a feeling of stability; the hipped roof with its extended eaves is supported by a three-tiered set of wooden brackets.

With the importation of esoteric Buddhism from China in the Heian period (794–1185), temples were located in mountainous areas away from the main centers of Nara and Kyoto. The temple complex of Muroji, of the late eighth or early ninth centuries, exemplifies this mountain-temple architectural style. The buildings are scaled down and set into the terrain, and they make use of rustic materials such as cypress-bark for roofing (in contrast to the tiled roofs of the earlier temple buildings). This influence is also seen in *shinden zukuri*, the Heian-period secular mansion favored by court nobles, consisting of a complex of buildings within an expansive garden. The main hall, *shinden*, was the master's residence and was surrounded on three sides by secondary living quarters. The garden was located to the south and contained a

A Japanese man in his garden. (HORACE BRISTOL/CORBIS)

HIMEJI—WORLD HERITAGE SITE

A pristine sixteenth-century Japanese castle, Himeji's labyrinthine eighty-three buildings and defense architecture still evoke Japan's classic Shogun feudal period. Himeji-jo was designated by UNESCO as a World Heritage Site in 1993.

large artificial pond. Covered verandah corridors connected the buildings to the garden, emphasizing the importance of this natural setting.

The Kamakura period (1185–1333) is known for both old and new architectural styles. The rebuilding of the Daibutsuden of the Todaiji, which was destroyed by fire in 1180, was a major project in the early years. Ties with China at this time are evident in the style known as *daibutsuyo* (Great Buddha style), in which brackets project at right angles from the wall in six increasing levels, with two more levels to support the roof. The other main architectural style during this period, also imported from China, was that of the Zen temple, which followed conventions of strict symmetry on a central axis. This architectural style was known as *karayo* (Chinese style). By contrast, the older styles came to be known as *wayo* (Japanese style). *Karayo* used decorative details such as bell-shaped windows, wooden latticework on transom windows, and complicated patterns of brackets. The support columns tapered at the top and were set upon stone bases.

Momoyama and Tokugawa Periods

The next major architectural innovation occurred in the Momoyama period (1573–1600) and was influenced by the interests of the samurai class. One type of building to develop was a distinctly Japanese form of castle. Constructed in the first half of the sixteenth century, the Japanese castle reached the height of its form in the early seventeenth century. Designed as a place to live, conduct business, and enjoy cultural activities, it was a testimony to the superior status of its occupants. The most beautiful castle in Japan is Himeji, also known as the White Heron Castle (1601–1609). Because Himeji was added to by a series of successive owners, the complex consists of a number of interlocking buildings placed in a mazelike arrangement. These include the five-story main building, several three-story structures, and watchtowers. The white buildings and hip-gabled roofs with Chinese-style upturned eaves give the impression of a large and graceful white heron. The other innovation of this period was the *shoin zukuri*, a grand residence characterized by its asymmetry and use of sliding doors *(fusuma)* and folding screens *(byobu)* to delineate interior space. The main room consisted of two levels, the upper level reserved for the highest-ranking samurai. Attached to this room was a study *(shoin)* and a number of other rooms, depending on the needs of the owner.

During the Edo or Tokugawa period (1600/1603–1868), the new shogunate refurbished and rebuilt older structures and erected new ones. Among the types of buildings constructed at this time was the Confucian temple, the need for which was underscored by the growing emphasis of Tokugawa shogunate policy on the study and practice of Confucianism by the samurai class. However, the next major innovation in architecture occurred in the Meiji period (1868–1912), when Japan began to adopt Western architectural styles. Architects from abroad introduced new materials and techniques to the Japanese. The most influential architect in shaping Japan's vision of Western buildings was Josiah Conder (1852–1920), an Englishman responsible for such structures as the Ueno Imperial Museum and the Rokumeikan (Deer Cry Pavilion), neither of which is extant. Conder's chief legacy may be found in the work of his students, who continued Conder's vision into the early twentieth century.

Catherine Pagani

See also: **Architecture—Modern Japan**

Further Reading
Alex, William. (1963) *Japanese Architecture*. New York: George Braziller.
Hashimoto Fumio. (1981) *Architecture in the Shoin Style*. Trans. and adapted by H. Mack Horton. New York: Kodansha.
Kirby, John B. (1962) *From Castle to Teahouse*. Rutland, VT: Charles E. Tuttle.
Paine, Robert Treat, and Alexander Soper. (1981) *The Art and Architecture of Japan*. 3d ed. New Haven, CT and London: Yale University Press.
Watanabe Yasutada. (1974) *Shinto Art: Ise and Izumo Shrines*. Trans. by Robert Ricketts. New York: Weatherhill.

ARCHITECTURE—KOREA Early forms of construction in Korea, in the form of shelters made of animal hides strung from posts and covered by branches, go back to the Upper Paleolithic period (40,000–10,000 BCE). Although these constructions evolved in shape and materials during the Neolithic

period (6000–1000 BCE), it was not until the Bronze Age (1000–300 BCE), when inhabitants of the Korean Peninsula started to become sedentary, that significant signs of architecture appeared. The structured society of that time, with its dominant and dominated classes, gave birth to different types of houses and also to other constructions like dolmen (which needed a significant amount of labor) or ramparts to protect human settlements.

Early Sources of Characteristics

Apart from the few archeological traces of these remote periods, including remains of ancient Korea (also known as "Old Choson," or *Ko Choson*), the traditional Korean architecture that can be seen today dates mostly from the seventeenth and eighteenth centuries. There are two reasons for this: the fragility of the building material, wood, which needs frequent restoration and reconstruction because of natural alterations as well as accidental ones like fires; and the recurrent and devastating invasions, first by the Mongols, then by the Japanese, and last by the Manchu (the last not ending until 1636).

Despite these invasions and more benignly introduced influences (especially from China), Korean architecture has its own characteristics. Temples, civil buildings like academies, and even palaces are of small scale and sober in style compared with those of Korea's neighbors. With the flourishing of Buddhism on the Korean Peninsula, especially during the Unified

A Buddhist pagoda in Keosong, North Korea, dating back to the twelfth century. (WERNER FORMAN/CORBIS)

Shilla period (668–935 CE), architecture of great quality appeared, with religious constructions such as the Sokkuram grotto or the Pulguk temple in the Kyongju area. The first of these, the only existing Buddhist grotto in Korea, is artificially constructed of granite blocks and covered with an earthen mound, so as to look like a natural element in its environment. A statue of Buddha stands in the middle of the circular main hall, whose carved walls reproduce the figures of bodhisattvas and guardian deities. The Pulguk temple is famous for its elegant stone stairways leading to the terrace where the temple stands, as well as for its two stone pagodas symbolizing Buddhism's contemplation of and detachment from the world.

Later, when Confucianism became Korea's official doctrine (under the Choson dynasty, 1392–1910 CE), the construction of temples declined while the construction of Confucian shrines and academic buildings notably increased. The architecture of this period expressed the principles of Confucianism, with its rigor, symmetry, and hierarchy, well demonstrated in the Chongmyo Palace in Seoul. Geomancy (building structures in accordance with cosmological principles), which became popular in Korea through the monk Toson (early tenth century CE), led to a sound integration of constructions and landscape, as the relationship of the building to the site was guided by the idea of cosmological balance. Last but not least, the hypocaust, or floor heating system (*ondol*), found in housing is unique in Asia and goes back to the Iron Age (200 BCE–200 CE), with prototypes developed a couple of centuries earlier.

Construction Techniques

From a technical point of view, buildings are structured vertically and horizontally. A construction usually rises from a stone subfoundation to a curved roof covered with tiles, held by a console structure and supported on posts; walls are made of earth (adobe) or are sometimes totally composed of movable wooden doors. Architecture is built according to the *k'an* unit, the distance between two posts (about 3.7 meters), and is designed so that there is always a transitional space between the "inside" and the "outside."

The console, or bracket structure, is a specific architectonic element that has been designed in various ways through time. If the simple bracket system was already in use under the Koguryo kingdom (37 BCE–668 CE)—in palaces in P'yongyang, for instance—a curved version, with brackets placed only on the column heads of the building, was elaborated during the early Koryo dynasty (918–1392). The Amita Hall of the Pusok temple in Antong is a good example. Later

on (from the mid-Koryo period to the early Choson dynasty), a multiple-bracket system, or an inter-columnar-bracket set system, was developed under the influence of China's Yuan dynasty (1279–1368). In this system, the consoles were also placed on the transverse horizontal beams. Seoul's Namtaemun Gate—Korea's foremost national treasure—is perhaps the most symbolic example of this type of structure.

In the mid-Choson period, the winglike bracket form appeared (one example is the Yongnyongjon Hall of Chongmyo, Seoul), which, according to some authors, better suited the peninsula's poor economic situation that resulted from repetitive invasions. Only in buildings of importance like palaces or sometimes temples (Tongtosa, for instance) were the multicluster brackets still used. Confucianism also led to more sober and simple solutions.

Temple Styles

Different styles of temples also arose in each period or culture. During the Three Kingdom period (Koguryo, Paekche, and Shilla; 57 BCE–668 CE), the "one-pagoda" style prevailed, in which only one pagoda was erected in a temple's hall. Sometimes, however, variations occurred: the Koguryo kingdom is famous for its "three-hall, one-pagoda" style (that is, one pagoda standing in the central hall). Among the temples of the Paekche period (18 BCE–663 CE), Miruksa is well known for its arrangement of three pagodas, each in front of one hall, along an east-west axis, giving the impression of three separate temples. During the Unified Shilla period, the "two-pagodas" style was favored, while during the Koryo period, both the one- and two-pagoda styles almost disappeared as specific shrines were added to temples.

Other Construction

Korea also has a rich architectural heritage of tombs and town-wall construction. The brick tomb of King Muryong (501–523 CE) is remarkable for its vaulted ceiling and arch construction. The most famous town walls are those of Seoul and Suwon. The capital's stone wall, constructed in 1396 and rebuilt in 1422, was sixteen kilometers long (only traces remain today) and had eight gates (including Namtaemun, the South Gate); Suwon's town wall, completed in 1796, was a model of construction methods in Asia at that time, as it benefited from Western influence and techniques.

Modern Architecture

Modern architecture in Korea has been ruled by the political context until very recently. During Korea's

Houses on South Korea's Cheju-do Island in 1986 showing the distinctive house shape and roof style. (MICHAEL S. YAMASHITA/CORBIS)

colonization (1910–1945), the Japanese introduced Western-style architecture (mainly made of stone, bricks, and concrete). After the Korean War (1950–1953), North Korean architecture followed a monumental Stalinist style, whereas South Korean architecture has been influenced by the so-called (Western) International style. Nevertheless, following the examples of innovative local architects such as Kim Sugun (1931–1986), who was a student of the Japanese architect Kenzo Tange, and Kim Chung-op (1922–1988), a disciple of the modernist Swiss architect Le Corbusier, today's young South Korean architects are developing a language of their own, aware of worldwide theoretical and aesthetic architectural debates, and are attempting to construct a more specifically Korean contemporary architecture.

Marie-Hélène Fabre-Faustino

Further Reading

Clément, Sophie, Pierre Clement, and Yong-hak Shin. (1987) *Architecture du paysage en Extrême-Orient*. Paris: École nationale supérieure des Beaux-Arts.

Eckert, Carter, Ki-baik Lee, Young Ick Lee, Michael Robinson, and Edward W. Wagner. (1990) *Korea Old and New: A History*. Seoul: Ilchokak.

Fabre, André. (2000) *Histoire de la Corée*. Paris: L'Asiathèque.

Macouin, Francis. (1998) *Pavillons et monastères de la Corée ancienne*. Paris: Findakly.

Park, Tae-soon. (1991) *Ch'oga* (The Ch'oga, Straw-Roofed Korean Cottages). Seoul: Youl Hwa Dang.

ARCHITECTURE—MODERN JAPAN

In the mid-nineteenth century, the profession of architecture was introduced to Japan from abroad, and the first architects were trained to use Western historical styles in their work. At the beginning of the twentieth century, however, the architect and architectural historian Ito Chuta (1867–1954) undertook to develop a modern local architecture, defining Asian traditions stylistically and through proportion. Ito remained tied to historical eclecticism. He moved comfortably between quasi-Japanese forms, illustrated by his Earthquake Memorial Hall (1930), and European styles, exemplified by his neo-Renaissance Kanematsu Lecture Hall at Hitotsubashi University (1927). However, his greatest impact was in encouraging the architects who followed him to draw on Japan's traditions; the most successful invariably blended these with Western abstraction and technology.

Emerging Japanese Approaches to Architecture

It was particularly in the 1920s and the early half of the 1930s that Japan's architects struggled to build a local architecture while also engaging in discourse with their peers abroad. For some, the solution was to marry a heavy roof, inspired by Japanese temples, to buildings that were essentially contemporary in their structure and building materials. This "Imperial Roof Style" persisted until the end of World War II. By contrast, Japan's first intellectual movement, the 1920s Bunri-ha (Secessionist School), advocated an architecture based in personal expression, linked more to the fine arts than to history.

As architects attempted to develop more nuanced fusions of Japanese and Western architectural practices, many turned to the *sukiya* style, associated with Japanese teahouses, emphasizing rich materials within a simple, structured organization. Teahouses also drew on the rustic beauty of Japan's vernacular architecture, neatly coinciding with the Arts and Crafts influences in European modern movements. The remarkable promise of this period, however, was cut short by a series of historical events. By 1927, Japan was in a recession that was followed by the Great Depression. Subsequently, Japan initiated a war with China that led to World War II; construction materials, especially steel, were diverted for military use. Sutemi Horiguchi (1895–1984), arguably one of the most skilled designers of the prewar period, completed only eighteen buildings between 1920 and 1945, and most of these were houses. Junzo Sakakura (1901–1969) designed the Japan Pavilion for the 1937 Paris Exposition. It received international acclaim, but Sakakura had few other opportunities to build during the war.

The period from 1937 to 1947 saw little construction. The profession of architecture survived through the publication of competitions and the construction of institutional buildings in Japan's colonies. There

JAPANESE INFLUENCES IN THE WEST

The Museum of Modern Art (MOMA) in New York City is an unlikely setting for a house designed in the style of a sixteenth-century Japanese villa, but in 1954 and 1955, just such a house was exhibited in the MOMA courtyard.

Japan's influence on individual architects is often controversial, but most scholars agree that some effect can be seen in the work of designers as diverse as Charles Renee Mackintosh (1868–1928) and Margaret MacDonald (1865–1933), the Austrian émigré Rudolph Schindler (1887–1953), and the California residential designers Charles Greene (1868–1957) and Henry Greene (1870–1954). Particularly important, though, is the impact of Japan on Frank Lloyd Wright and its exploitation by Modernists.

Frank Lloyd Wright (1867–1959) minimized the effect of Japanese architecture in his work, in favor of his enthusiasm for Japanese woodblock prints. His exposure to both came quite early, with the Hooden and a smaller Japanese "teahouse" at the 1893 World's Colombian Exposition in Chicago. Historians relate Japanese architecture to Wright's heavy roofs, open planning, spatial horizontality, and even the colors used in his "Prairie School" architecture. Ultimately, his passion for woodblock prints and later opportunities for work resulted in Wright making four trips to Japan. During his last, longest trip, he designed the Imperial Hotel in Tokyo (1922) and several minor buildings.

Wright made no effort to influence the direction of Japanese architecture. By contrast, Bruno Taut (1880–1938) significantly affected which buildings Japanese and Western architects considered important while in Japan in the 1903s. Taut rejected the popularity of Nikko's Toshogu (1636) in favor of the understated character of Katsura Rikyu (1625), an unknown villa in Kyoto, and published his convictions in English, German, and Japanese.

It is not surprising that Taut favored Katsura's restraint. The German Modernists promoted standardization and modularity, simplicity, and the articulation of a clear structural frame; there were marked similarities between their work and Japan's *shoin*-inspired residences. However, there seems to have been no attempt to promote these connections until Walter Gropius (1883–1969), a former director of the German Bauhaus, emigrated to the United States.

Americans resisted the aridity of Modernism, and intellectuals countered by drawing attention to Modernism's resemblance to Japan's traditional homes. Gropius made a highly publicized trip to Japan in 1954. Writing about that trip in *Katsura: Tradition and Creation in Japanese Architecture* (a celebrated English-language book on Katsura published in 1960), Gropius noted, "I had found . . . that the old handmade Japanese house had all the essential features required today for a modern, prefabricated house." (This was hardly a discovery, as Gropius's first contact with Japanese architects occurred over thirty years earlier.)

It was at this time that the Japanese house was built in MOMA's courtyard. MOMA's curator Arthur Drexler (1925–1986) also published a book on Japan's architecture, arguing that the endurance of residential styles confirmed the timelessness of Modernist architecture. Ironically, just as the West set about idealizing traditional Japanese houses, the Japanese people were more and more likely to move into contemporary concrete apartment buildings, contradicting the similarities promoted by Western theorists.

Dana Buntrock

was a division between theory and building; virtually none of the competitions led to construction and little of the colonial work demanded sophistication. Consequently, few architects were able to nurture their ability to execute work that was both intellectu-ally refined and well crafted. Kunio Maekawa (1905–1986) was one exception.

The rupture caused by economic depression and the later collapse of construction destroyed the careers of many promising architects. Most had difficulty reviving their practices after the war. Even some of the notable landmarks of the immediate postwar period, such as Sakakura's Museum of Modern Art (1952) or Antonin Raymond's (1888–1976) Reader's Digest Building (1951), were isolated anomalies. Only Maekawa produced work appreciated for both its theoretical and commercial strengths. He received accolades around the world for his Harumi Apartments (1959) and the spatially complex Tokyo Metropolitan Festival Hall (1961). The Japan Industrial Bank of Tokyo (1974) demonstrates Maekawa's continued prowess.

Architects in Postwar Japan

Few architects were trained during World War II. Into the breach stepped Kenzo Tange (b. 1913). His compelling design for the Hiroshima Peace Memorial Park was completed in 1955, and he subsequently went on to produce virtually all of the major works symbolizing Japan's international hopes (the Olympic Stadium complex of 1964), technical optimism (the 1960 plan for 10 million people to be housed over Tokyo Bay), and a critical political shift to local governance (for example, the Kagawa Prefectural Offices of 1958). Tange also responded to the influence of pre-war theorists by developing a modern architecture that drew on specific Japanese icons, especially Ise Shrine and Katsura Imperial Villa.

Many of the leading architects of the next generation were Tange's students, including Fumihiko Maki (b. 1928), Kiyonori Kikutake (b. 1928), Arata Isozaki (b. 1931), and Kisho Kurokawa (b. 1934). They published a manifesto in 1960 calling for an entirely new movement to rise from the ashes of the war. Eschewing tradition, the "Metabolists," as they were known, proposed an architecture that celebrated the nation's new technological prowess. One of the best-known works of this period was the Nakagin Capsule Hotel (1972) by Kurokawa; with unusual precision, tiny sleeping units made from shipping containers were attached to the side of a concrete core holding vertical transportation and building services. Gloomier representations, such as Isozaki's drawing entitled "Destruction of the Future City" (1968), presaged the collapse of Metabolism following the critical failure of the Osaka Exposition (1970).

Isozaki and Kurokawa have stood as weathervanes of subsequent architectural trends. As Kurokawa moved to the simple graphic style of his Rikyu period, named for the sixteenth-century tea master Sen no Rikyu, Isozaki adopted pop abstraction and the iconography of Marilyn Monroe. These architects, distracted by their attempts to develop coherent theoretical constructs, are better known for shaping the

Tokyo City Hall in the Shinjuku District. It was designed by Kenzo Tange and is the tallest building in the city. (MICHAEL S. YAMASHITA/CORBIS)

practice of architecture than they are for their body of work. However, Isozaki produced the Gumma Prefectural Art Museum (1974), which ranks among the finest buildings of the period. By contrast, their colleague Fumihiko Maki concentrated on construction. His best works, such as the Hillside Terrace complex (1969–1992) and the Spiral Building (1985), demonstrate an interest in urban form, spatial experience, and materials, although he has sometimes been dismissed as too decorative in his approach.

Although architects in the 1950s and 1960s were expected to perform internationally, two leading designers, Kiyonori Kikutake (b. 1928) and Kazuo Shinohara (b. 1925), advocated a more individual approach. Their influence became clear as the architects they educated and trained emerged, including Toyo Ito (b. 1941) and Itsuko Hasegawa (b. 1941). The architect and critic Hajime Yatsuka (b. 1948) has referred to this group as the Superficial Generation; their early work, mostly residential, explored a detached architectural language unrelated to trends at home or abroad and intended to be derived from personal conceits rather than professional concerns. As these architects matured, however, they struggled to find a more public role for their buildings. Hasegawa's Shonandai Culture Center (1991) and Hara's Yamato Building (1987) both did so through explicit references to village life and nature.

As a foil to the personal disposition of most architects of his generation, the pugnacious Tadao Ando (b. 1941) developed an austere minimalist style utilizing an uncompromising concrete construction. Less well recognized is the way Ando defined carefully modulated spatial progressions and shifts from a human to monumental scale. His work was recognized internationally at an early stage, and along with Maki, Ando is one of the few Japanese architects to have received the prestigious Pritzker Prize, the equivalent of a Nobel Prize for architecture.

In the 1990s, as Japan's economy again entered a prolonged recession, architects returned to a dignified modernism. Yoshio Taniguchi (b. 1937, Yoshiro Taniguchi's son) and Riken Yamamoto (b. 1945) have surpassed their more flamboyant cohorts in this setting. Taniguchi's crisp exactitude is best seen in his Kasai Rinkai Park Visitor's Center (1996) and in the Gallery of Horyuji Treasures (1999). Yamamoto came into his own with his Saitama University campus (1999). Younger architects working in a similar vein include the partnership Kazuyo Sejima (b. 1956) and Ryue Nishizawa (b. 1966), and Kengo Kuma (b. 1954). While clearly designing in an international style, their attention to detail, sensitivity to the use of light and translucent materials, and overlapping spatial zones remain rooted in earlier efforts to draw upon Japanese traditions as well.

Dana Buntrock

See also: **Architecture—Japan**

Further Reading

Bognar, Botond. (1985) *Contemporary Japanese Architecture: Its Development and Challenge*. New York: Van Nostrand Reinhold.

Kultermann, Udo. (1960). *New Japanese Architecture*. New York: Praeger.

Reynolds, Jonathan. (2001) *Maekawa Kunio and the Emergence of a Japanese Modernist Architecture*. Berkeley and Los Angeles: University of California Press.

Stewart, David B. (1987) *The Making of a Modern Japanese Architecture: 1868 to the Present*. Tokyo and New York: Kodansha.

Suzuki Hiroyuki, et al. (1985) *Contemporary Architecture in Japan, 1958–1984*. New York: Rizzoli.

Tempel, Egon. (1969) *New Japanese Architecture*. New York and Washington, DC: Praeger.

ARCHITECTURE—SOUTHEAST ASIA

By nature the architecture of Southeast Asia is always hybrid and eclectic, as open as its geographical context, and as receptive as its people's way of life. Located at the crossroads of world trading routes, Southeast Asia has been very open toward various influences from outside: Indian, Arab, Chinese, European, Japanese, and from the rest of the world. All of those influences were absorbed and adopted into local culture, then expressed in unique architectural forms and styles. Diversity, eclecticism, fusion, acculturation, and adaptation can perhaps describe the nature of Southeast Asian architecture and urbanism.

Vernacular Tradition

Vernacular architecture in Southeast Asia is largely made of wood and other perishable building materials. Post-and-beam frames, raised living floors, and dominant and elaborate roof forms are identifying characteristics.

There is a strong indication that the vernacular stilt house in the Southeast Asia and Pacific regions, which has some basic similarities, developed out of the rice-growing culture in the tropics. It appears to have originated from granary architecture and developed into a dwelling place. The attic under the roof is the place for gods and valuables, the middle space is the living area, and the underneath space between the floor and the ground is for utilities. For symbolic protection the roof was decorated with sharp objects, horns, dragons, or other animals. The saddle roof type is often interpreted as an imitation of the ancestral boats.

Indian Legacy

Around the first century CE Indian cosmology began to influence the formal and spatial ordering principles of Southeast Asian architecture and settlements. Hinduism and Buddhism were spreading from India northeastward to Cambodia, Laos, and Vietnam and southeastward to Sumatra, Java, and Bali.

From the fertile Mekong delta region, the source of the rice culture of Southeast Asia, the first kingdom of Funan was established in the Mekong delta around 100–600 CE, followed by the Chenla (600–790 CE), Pagan (849–1287), and Khmer (790–1431) kingdoms. To the east and northeast, the Champa kingdom flourished from 192 to 1471. The wet-rice culture, river systems, and international trade links with India and China that these kingdoms maintained influenced the architecture and settlement patterns of the Chams, Khmer, and Siamese. There are still marvelous artifacts from this period in the stone temples of Angkor

ASIAN COSMOLOGY AND ORDERING PRINCIPLES

Humanity occupies the middle position between the two poles of the universal order (good and evil, upper and lower, mountain and sea, north and south; or between sunrise and sunset, east and west, and so forth). The hierarchy of these three cosmological divisions serves as a metaphor for parts of the human body: the head, the torso, and the feet. It is also the metaphor for elements of the universe: the sky, the surface of the earth, and the ground underneath.

Traditional settlements across Southeast Asia follow this cosmological pattern, by situating a village in between a mountain and the sea or a river. The most important building or site (temple of origin, chief's house, ancestor's grave) is placed on the highest point of the village or to the direction of the mountain. The objects or functions associated with death or impurity (temple of death, dirt, waste disposal) were placed down near the waterfront. In many cases the rice barns—essential in a rice-growing community—were situated on the east side of the village facing the sunrise.

This indigenous cosmology was then elaborated further by the Indian mandala principle. (A mandala is a graphic symbol of the universe.) In a geometrical sense, a mandala can be drawn as a square subdivided into nine subsquares. It can be perceived as two superimposed hierarchies of space (upper and lower) facing towards the North and the East (the two primary orientations). The middle space is the neutral, the navel, the womb, or the center. The upper-right corner space is the head, the inner sanctum, or the most respected place. The lower-left corner space is the feet, the lowest, the dirtiest, or the threshold to the impure outside world. A city, a village, a house, or a room can be arranged according to this hierarchy of values and meanings. This basic spatial pattern can be found in Indian cities and temples, Balinese villages and houses, Chinese courthouses, and even in Japanese tearooms.

Johannes Widodo

in Cambodia and the brick temples of Champa in southern and central Vietnam.

The decline of those inland rice-growing kingdoms was soon followed by the rise of the Srivijaya empire of the Malay archipelago (600–1290), which took effective control of the main trading routes of the Malacca Strait and the Java Sea. The physical remains of this great cultural, political, and military Buddhist kingdom have almost vanished, due to the use of nondurable clay brick and timber materials, except for some archaeological sites and several rounded temples, such as Muara Takus temple in southern Sumatra. In Java many Buddhist and Hindu stone temples from around the eighth century still survive. The Mandalay palace complex in Myanmar (Burma) and the Angkor temple complex near Siemreab in Cambodia exemplify the transformation of basic Hindu design principles in Buddhist architecture. The enormous Buddhist stupas of Borobudur and the articulated Hindu portion of the Prambanan temple in central Java are the best artifacts from this period.

Palaces and ordinary buildings from this period have not survived, but archaeological findings suggest that the layouts of the royal capitals from this period (such as Ayutthaya near Bangkok and Majapahit in eastern Java) clearly show the underlying ordering principle of the Indian mandala. The same clear and strong spatial hierarchy, axiality, and orientation of structures still characterize contemporary Balinese dwellings and village architecture; the shrines and temples of Myanmar, Thailand, and Cambodia; and Javanese houses and palaces. The vernacular tradition has internalized Indian cosmology.

Buddhism spread from India northeastward to Nepal, Bhutan, Tibet, China, Korea, and Japan, eastward to Myanmar, Siam, Sumatra, and Java, and southward to Ceylon, generating unique forms of stupa architecture (temples, monasteries, and palaces). The best examples of this kind of architecture in Southeast Asia can be found in Myanmar, Thailand, Cambodia, Laos, and Vietnam. The simple rounded dome shape of stupa architecture in India and Ceylon became highly elaborate and complex in Southeast Asia. The largest Buddhist stone architecture in the world is Borobudur temple in central Java, Indonesia. Even though Buddhist rituals and symbolism determined its shape, the temple incorporated various Hindu ornaments and spatial patterns as well.

Islamic Legacy

Islam entered and spread throughout Southeast Asia along two main routes. The first one was through China along the Silk Road, and then by the voyages of the Ming-dynasty admiral Zheng He (1371?–1435) from southern China to the northern coast of Java, then to Melaka and throughout the Indonesian archipelago. The second route was through India, and was taken by Gujarat and Tamil traders to the Malay peninsula, to the west coast of Sumatra, and finally to the northern coast of Java and the entire Indonesian archipelago. Arab and Persian traders also opened direct trading routes to Southeast Asia, connecting Europe with Asia.

Islam introduced a new orientation (the *qiblat* or praying orientation toward Mecca) and new typology in architecture and urban space (sultans' palaces, mosques, urban central open space) into the vocabulary of Southeast Asian architecture and urban planning. Again the fusion process is clearly evident. The transition and transformation processes took place peacefully and naturally at such sites as Demak (the first Islamic sultanate in Java and the primary Islamic mission in Southeast Asia), Kudus, and Cirebon (both early Islamic cities on the northern coast of Java). The Javanese mosque typology, with three layers of pyramid roof, also existed in Melaka on the Malay Peninsula, in old Singapore, and in different parts of the Indonesian archipelago. It represented a blend of Hindu-Javanese architecture with Indian, Chinese, Malay, and even Greek and Persian architectural elements.

In the British Straits Settlements of the Malay Peninsula, mosques erected by the Muslim commu-

nity from southern India—also in eclectic architectural style—can be found in Melaka and Singapore. Located in the middle of Chinatown, in the same row as other religious buildings (Chinese temples, Hindu shrines), these southern Indian mosques reflected the cosmopolitan and tolerant nature of Southeast Asian urban culture in embracing and incorporating new foreign elements. Craftspeople from different racial and cultural groups worked together and blended their artistry and skill to create a new and unique building tradition and architectural totality.

Chinese Legacy

The Chinese dominated northern Vietnam from the second century BCE to the tenth century CE. Thang Long (the origin of Hanoi) was built as a new capital in 1010, following the traditional Chinese model for a capital city. A Chinese spatial order was superimposed on the previous vernacular organic settlement structure. Thang Long was dominated by Buddhist, Taoist, and Confucian primary elements (temples, pagodas, monasteries, public buildings, palaces). This ancient urban tissue persists especially in the Thirty-Sixth Street district of Hanoi, around the Citadel, where several temples and pagodas can be found scattered around the old quarter.

The voyages of Zheng He left traces along the coastal regions of Southeast Asia in the form of early southern Chinese trading posts and colonies. Many of these colonies were situated near river estuaries beside the preexisting native villages. Some of these early settlements then grew into flourishing entrepots (for example, Pattani, Melaka, Palembang) because of international maritime trading activities. The main features from this period were the Chinese temple dedicated to Mazu (goddess of the sea, protector of sailors), the fish market in front of the temple near the harbor, and the early typology of shop houses.

The Chinese architectural elements blended with local vernacular design patterns and features and created numerous variations of fusion building styles. One good example is the typical trader's house in Palembang, south Sumatra. The building plan and some of its construction methods are those used for the southern Chinese courthouse, but the saddle roofs, open verandah, timber material, and raised floor are definitely local.

The waves of Chinese immigrants from southern China in the nineteenth and early twentieth centuries further enhanced the development of unique architecture and the particular pattern of the cities within this region. More temples with different functions and different gods were erected, along with the construction of new generations of shop houses, community halls, and clusters of urban row houses for clan members. During this time, the Chinese played a strategic economic role as middlemen between the European colonialists and the local populations, and became prosperous. Their prosperity was expressed in the adoption of European design features into their architecture. The kind of architecture developed by the Chinese in Southeast Asia diverged from architecture in mainland China, reflecting instead the architecture of their adopted places.

European Legacy

The Europeans implemented their hegemonic ambitions beginning in the late fifteenth century, starting with the Portuguese (in India, Melaka, Java, eastern Indonesia, the Philippines, Taiwan, and Japan), followed by the Dutch (in India, Melaka, Indonesia, Taiwan, and Japan), the British (in India, the Malaya peninsula, Bengkulu, Java, and China), the Spanish (in the Philippines), the French (in Indochina and China), and the Germans (in China). Although Thailand remained an independent kingdom, it too absorbed influences from Europe. The Europeans came first as traders and missionaries and stayed as colonizers supported by military power, gradually and effectively penetrating and dominating the whole of Southeast Asia for almost five centuries.

The Europeans introduced such new architectural elements as boulevards, streetscapes, and façades, along with new building techniques and new types of buildings (military establishments, public buildings, churches, urban squares and plazas, markets, railroads, stations, plantation houses, and many more). The image of Paris was transplanted to Indochina in such cities as Phnom Penh, Vientiane, Hanoi, Saigon, and Danang in the form of wide boulevards and urban parks, multistory apartment blocks, monumental public buildings, villas and bungalows, and so forth. The Dutch transplanted the canals of Amsterdam and its row houses and elite villas into the old city of Batavia (present-day Jakarta). The British built esplanades and cricket fields in the Straits Settlements (Malaysia, Singapore). The Portuguese and Spanish created plazas, churches, and cathedrals in eastern Timor and the Philippines.

At first European design was directly applied in tropical Southeast Asia with only minor modifications. But then more responsive design solutions were invented, to adapt building and urban design to local climatic, aesthetic, and social-cultural conditions. There are European-style buildings with deep verandas and ventilation holes, for example, and gradually Chinese,

Indian, Malay, Arab, and other influences made themselves felt. As had happened with earlier influences, the European influences were naturally and openly accepted into the vocabulary of Southeast Asian architecture and urbanism.

The Legacy of Modernism

The ideas of modernism were brought into Southeast Asia by European-educated architects in the early twentieth century. They developed a new generation of modern buildings in various architectural styles including Orientalism (a mixture of all stylistic elements of the East) and modern-European-indigenous eclectic styles. In the 1920s and 1930s garden-city concepts—modified to suit local climates and environments—were implemented in major cities in Java, Sumatra, the Malay peninsula, Thailand, Cambodia, Laos, and Vietnam.

To create order and healthier and safer cities, building codes and regulations were implemented. Jack roofs, light wells, and sufficient openings in buildings were required in order to provide enough ventilation. Service areas were located in the backyard, connected to the back alley. Party walls were built between dwelling units to prevent the spread of fire, and a 1.5-meter arcade, known as a five-foot way, was provided between rows of shops to protect pedestrians from tropical rain and heat, particularly in the Straits Settlements (Malaysia, Singapore) and some cities in Indonesia. Density and zoning regulations were implemented to control urban growth.

New modern regional styles adapted to local environmental and cultural contexts gave a strong sense of identity to Southeast Asian architecture and cities until the Great Depression of the 1930s and the outbreak of World War II. The Depression and the war destroyed many parts of Southeast Asia's cities and ended a creative period of unique modern architectural discourse.

Soon after the war, a totally new kind of modernism—the International Style—appeared everywhere. In Hanoi a strong and rigid Soviet socialist utopian model of urban planning and architectural style changed the cityscapes. A huge mausoleum and vast parade ground were erected in the civic center, eliminating the previous colonial palace axis. Standardized public housing replaced older styles of dwelling. In the newly independent nations of Indonesia, Malaysia, the Philippines, and Myanmar, the International Style was used as a symbol of departure from the past. Japanese war reparation money and aid played an important role in the implementation and realization of these nationalistic ambitions in some Southeast Asian countries.

In Search of Identity

In Southeast Asia, diversity and harmonious unity are traditions, passed from generation to generation. All sorts of outside cultural influences have been considered as positive inputs and have enriched individuals, families, tribes, clans, peoples, and even nations. This has been expressed clearly in all levels of architecture, from ornaments and furniture to buildings, settlements, and cities.

The immense economic growth in Southeast Asia within the last two decades has changed the course of its architecture and urbanism dramatically. The models developed in America and Europe have been broadly and carelessly applied to Southeast Asian countries, creating conflicts, tensions, confusion, and loss of identity. New architectural styles, used for corporate office towers, commercial superblocks, and housing clusters for the newly rich, stand beside vast slum areas and shantytowns.

Amid these contradictions, Southeast Asia's own architects are creating many excellent designs. New and unprecedented discourses on Southeast Asian architecture and urban studies are flourishing across the region in architectural schools and the architectural profession. With its long history of plurality and creativity, and its long experience of blending everything harmoniously, Southeast Asian architecture has very promising prospects of finding its own identity.

Johannes Widodo

See also: **Angkor Wat; Borobudur; Mandalay Palace**

Further Reading
Dumarcay, Jacques. (1991) *The Palaces of South-East Asia: Architecture and Customs*. Singapore: Oxford University Press.

Dumarcay, Jacques, and Michael Smithies. (1998) *Cultural Sites of Malaysia, Singapore, and Indonesia*. Kuala Lumpur, Malaysia: Oxford University Press.

Hall, Kenneth R. (1985) *Maritime Trade and State Development in Early Southeast Asia*. Honolulu, HI: University of Hawaii Press.

Khan, Hasan-Uddin. (1995) *Contemporary Asian Architects*. Cologne, Germany: Taschen.

Major, Andrew. (2000) *The Living Past: History of Ancient India, China, and Southeast Asia*. Singapore: MPH.

Smith, Bardwell, and Holly Baker Reynolds, eds. (1987) *The City as a Sacred Center: Essays on Six Asian Contexts*. Leiden, The Netherlands: E. J. Brill.

Waterson, Roxana. (1998). *The Architecture of South-East Asia through Travellers' Eyes*. Kuala Lumpur, Malaysia: Oxford University Press.

———. (1990) *The Living House: An Anthropology of Architecture in South-East Asia*. London: Thames & Hudson.

Widodo, Johannes. (1998) "The Urban History of the Southeast Asian Coastal Cities." Ph.D. diss. University of Tokyo.

ARCHITECTURE, VERNACULAR—CHINA

China has a variety of climates and landforms as well as fifty-six diverse ethnic groups in an area nearly equal to that of the United States. Consequently China's vernacular architecture appears at first glance bewildering in variety. However, a closer examination reveals remarkably similar elements in layout and materials across space and through time. The ubiquitous, simple I-shaped dwellings are complemented by strikingly distinctive buildings of great complexity. Structures include extraordinarily beautiful centuries-old dwelling complexes built for merchants, quadrangular residences in the Beijing area, massive multistoried fortresses in the hilly south, and unique below-ground cave-like dwellings in the north, as well as tents and pile dwellings occupied by minority populations in remote areas of the country.

Divisions of Space

Throughout China, houses exhibit a limited range of conventional spatial forms in their plan and general layout. These fundamental building elements are rooted deeply in Chinese building traditions, and they have influenced the spatial conceptualization and building traditions of Japan and Korea as well. Chinese builders are attentive not only to structures—that is, enclosures with a roof—but also to open spaces for living, working, and leisure activities. The common denominator of any Chinese building, whether opulent palace or humble home, is a modular unit known as *jian*, a fundamental measure of width, the span between two lateral columns that constitutes a bay. *Jian* also represent the two-dimensional floor space between four columns and the volumetric measure of the void defined by the floor and the walls. Sometimes *jian* form a room, although quite often a room is made up of several structural *jian*. As a modular form, *jian* can be created and linked relatively easily as a family's circumstances and resources change over several generations.

Most Chinese dwellings consist of at least three *jian* linked laterally along a transverse line to create horizontal, I-shaped structures. In northern China *jian* range between 3.3 and 3.6 meters in width, while in southern China they are typically between 3.6 and 3.9 meters. The bays are usually deeper in southern China, reaching as much as 6.6 meters, while those in the north rarely exceed 4.8 meters. *Jian* generally are clustered in odd multiples, such as three, five, or seven, since the Chinese believe that odd-numbered units provide balance and symmetry. The traditional Chinese sumptuary regulations contributed to the standardization and modularization of Chinese houses by dictating the dimensions of timber. Decorative details and colors along the roof ridge, under the eaves, and on the gate, which indicated positions in the social hierarchy, were also written into sumptuary regulations. The central *jian* of a three- or five-bay rectangular dwelling typically is wider than the flanking *jian*, since the central *jian* is usually the principal ceremonial or utility room in the dwelling. Symbolic of unity and continuity, this space often is accentuated by the traditional placement of a long, narrow table facing the door. That table holds ancestral tablets, images of gods and goddesses, family mementos, and ceremonial paraphernalia.

Uncovered open areas of various dimensions, often referred to as courtyards, are critical divisions of exterior space in any fully formed Chinese dwelling. While open spaces are axiomatic elements of Chinese domestic spaces, their scales differ to such a degree that neither the common term "courtyard" nor its Chinese-language equivalents describe them clearly. From northeast to southeast China, the proportion of open space to enclosed space diminishes significantly. While courtyards may be expansive in northern China, in southern China they are usually condensed, so the Chinese term *tianjing*, translated as "skywell," catches their essence.

The quintessential Chinese courtyard in the northeast is in the Beijing *siheyuan*, an open space and the surrounding quadrangle of low buildings, whose traditions go back to the eleventh century BCE. The courtyard of a *siheyuan* represents about 40 percent of the total area of the dwelling. The back walls of the *siheyuan* lack windows and doors, and they are oriented to the cardinal directions. Further common characteristics of *siheyuan* include axiality (balanced side-to-side symmetry), a hierarchical organization of space, and a south- or southeast-facing main hall (south is considered the most auspicious direction in geomancy [feng shui]). Skywells in southern China are rectangular open spaces or voids that are so small and compact that they do not qualify as true courtyards. Ingenious sunken interior cavities whose scale restricts their openness to the sky, skywells are well designed for the hot and humid conditions of southern China as they catch passing breezes and release interior heat. Southern dwellings often have multiple skywells, each an atrium-like enclosed vertical space. The size, shape, and number of skywells vary according to the scale of the residence. Although dwellings with skywells are found throughout southern China, perhaps the most distinctive are those in the multistoried dwellings that survive from the Ming dynasty (1368–1644) in Anhui, Jiangxi, and Zhejiang provinces. Unlike northern structures that emphasize horizontality and openness to the sky, these southern dwellings resemble squat boxes or elongated loaves with solid walls and limited windows. While their building materials appear modest from the outside, the brick walls and expensive woods on the inside are ornamental as well as structural.

The courtyard evolved over thousands of years to meet changing environmental and social conditions. In both its expansive and its condensed forms, it remains an adaptable component of the spatial composition of Chinese residences throughout the country.

Building Materials and Structural Systems

Chinese houses generally incorporate a conventional set of elementary building parts (foundations, walls, and roofs) and commonly available structural materials (wood, earth, and stone). The walls of Chinese dwellings sometimes do not directly support the weight of the roof above but rather serve as curtains between complicated wooden frameworks. These wooden frameworks lift the roof and are independent of the walls, creating a kind of osseous structure, which Liang Sicheng, China's preeminent architectural historian of the twentieth century, characterized as analogous to the human skeleton. Two basic types of timber framework are employed widely, heavy pillars and beams in the north and pillars and transverse tie beams involving mortise and tenon joinery in the south. The latter is important in areas where earthquakes are common.

Traditional Chinese dwellings are built directly on compacted earth or are raised slightly on a solid podium of earth, stone, or brick to carry the substantial weight of a building safely to the ground without allowing it to become deformed. Basements are extremely rare. Fully developed structures, whether dwellings or palaces, always include a wooden skeleton of structural pillars and beams to lift the roof rather than relying on the walls to perform this task. Some houses have a relatively simple framework, but others are elaborate structural ensembles. For any Chinese house, the framework is the most costly and difficult building component to replace, while walls are reconstructed fairly easily from inexpensive local materials. Because a wooden skeleton of structural pillars and beams lifts the roof, the surrounding walls provide only enclosure and are not load-bearing components. Many types of materials, including tamped earth, adobe brick, fired brick, stone, wooden logs or planks, bamboo, and wattle and daub, may be added to the timber framing to enclose and protect the interior space.

The profile of a house constructed with a pillar-and-beam framework appears roughly similar to that of a house in the West constructed with roof trusses. However, the cross section of a Chinese pillar-and-beam structure, unlike that of the rigid triangular roof truss system, allows a degree of functional and aesthetic curvature in the roofline. The southern framing system of pillars and transverse beams permits more curvature than the northern system of pillars and beams. Traditional wooden frameworks rarely are secured with metal fittings, such as nails and clamps, but use dowels and wedges to ensure a snug fit.

Walls that enclose and surround space also protect and divide it. Walls either encircle the wooden skeleton or simply fill the gaps between the pillars. In southern China non-load-bearing walls are often relatively weak, composed of grasses, grain stalks, and cob (sand mixed with straw) that cannot support more than their own weight. However, some walls include sawed timber and bamboo and are quite strong.

Sturdy, load-bearing walls, which are far more common in the construction of Chinese dwellings than is generally acknowledged, are made of a variety of natural materials that are tamped, formed, or hewn. Mixtures of clay-textured soils and amalgamations of other substances are tamped. Blocks of clay are molded into bricks that are either sun-dried or kiln-fired. Hewn stone or timber must be shaped with tools. Load-bearing walls often combine these formed materials with naturally occurring materials, such as rocks, which have not been altered.

Tamping or pounding clay soil or other materials into solid walls, called the *hangtu* method of construction, has been used for much of Chinese history to erect houses and other buildings, to enclose compounds and open areas, and to fortify villages and cities. In the third century BCE the Qin emperor supervised the construction of an immense tamped earthen wall, the precursor of China's legendary Great Wall. Firing bricks was common by the third century BCE but did not become economical and widely available for housing construction until the fourteenth century CE.

The Chinese invest much effort in technique and symbolism when devising the form of the roof, unlike Western builders, who usually stress a building's facade. Distinctive roof profiles exhibiting a powerful elegance in their curvatures and coverings are more common in the residences of people with means than in humble dwellings.

Unprecedented rural prosperity during the last twenty-five years of the twentieth century led to the indiscriminate destruction of much of China's architectural patrimony in spite of efforts to preserve the residences of important historical personages. New styles of vernacular architecture in rural, urban, and suburban areas use materials and plans that differ significantly from traditional patterns. Builders now accept the use of reinforced concrete columns and beams where wood once was used exclusively, a compelling need in a country still plagued by a shortage of timber. New rural dwellings are all too often relatively nondescript blockish structures that have imposed a monotonous rhythm to villages. Public apathy, lack of coordination of conservation energies, and inadequate financial incentives for conservation frustrate efforts to preserve China's vernacular architectural heritage.

Ronald G. Knapp

See also: **Architecture—China; Courtyards; Feng Shui; Great Wall**

Further Reading

Blaser, Werner. (1995) *Courtyard House in China: Tradition and Present/Hofhaus in China: Tradition und Gegenwart.* Bilingual ed. Basel, Switzerland, and Boston: Birkhäuser Verlag.

Bray, Francesca. (1997) *Technology and Gender: Fabrics of Power in Late Imperial China.* Berkeley and Los Angeles: University of California Press.

Ho Puay-peng. (1995) *The Living Building: Vernacular Environments of South China/Gucheng jinxi: Zhongguo minjian shenghuofangshi.* Bilingual ed. Hong Kong: Chinese University of Hong Kong, Department of Architecture.

Knapp, Ronald G. (1999) *China's Living Houses: Folk Beliefs, Symbols, and Household Ornamentation.* Honolulu, HI: University of Hawaii Press.

———. (2000) *China's Old Dwellings.* Honolulu, HI: University of Hawaii Press.

———. (1989) *China's Vernacular Architecture: House Form and Culture.* Honolulu, HI: University of Hawaii Press.

Lo Kai-Yin, and Ho Puay-peng, eds. (1999) *Living Heritage: Vernacular Environment in China.* Bilingual ed. Hong Kong: Yungmingtang.

Lung, David. (1991) *Chinese Traditional Vernacular Architecture.* Bilingual ed. Hong Kong: Regional Council.

Ruitenbeek, Klaas. (1993) *Building and Carpentry in Late Imperial China: A Study of the Fifteenth-Century Carpenter's Manual "Lu Ban Jing."* Leiden, Netherlands: E. J. Brill.

ARCHITECTURE—WEST ASIA The West Asian nations of Iran, Turkey, and Iraq have a rich and varied architectural heritage dating back thousands of years. Many civilizations have left their mark on this region, and architecture has always been important to this region. In fact, many buildings of West Asia have played an important role in the development of world architecture. The history of architecture in West Asia can be broadly divided into three periods: architecture produced before the introduction of Islam to the region in the mid-seventh century CE, architecture produced after the introduction of Islam, and modern architecture (produced after 1850). This article discusses modern architecture. Even though the architecture of these three nations does not have a prominent position internationally, in the past century many of their important structures have helped shape the identity of these countries throughout the modern period.

Iran

The beginning of modern architecture in Iran goes back to the period from 1921 to 1941, as exemplified in such works as the Museum of Ancient Iran, designed by foreign architects hired by the government. During this period many Iranian cities were transformed to include such new building types as office buildings, factories, banks, and railway stations. These buildings were originally designed by foreign architects, but eventually foreign-educated Iranians and then, with the establishment of the first school of architecture in Iran in the early 1940s, Iranian-educated architects joined this group. In most of the architecture of this period, elements taken mostly from buildings from pre-Islamic Iranian architecture were mixed with new European elements.

The second period in modern Iranian architecture was from 1941 to the late 1960s. During this period, most architectural projects were carried out by a few Iranian architects. In these projects, greater attention was paid to the past architecture of Iran, especially. the geometrical patterns that are characteristic of Islamic Iranian architecture. One of the most prominent works of this period is the mausoleum of the Islamic scientist and philosopher Ibn Sina (Avicenna, 980–1037) in Hamedaan, by Hooshang Seyhoon.

The third period was from the late 1960s until the early years after the Islamic Revolution of 1980. During this period, the trend of infusing modern concrete buildings with elements from pre-Islamic and Islamic Iran was continued. The 1970s were characterized by the works of such architects as Nader Ardalan and Kamran Diba, who sought to preserve Iranian architecture by restoring several projects throughout Iran.

The fourth period, which started just after the revolution and continues today, is characterized by such works as the National Museum of Water by Seyyed Haadi Mirmiran, the National Iranian Library by Kaamraan Safaabakhsh, and the Academies of the Islamic Republic of Iran. The architecture of this period relies heavily upon the inclusion of Islamic motifs, such as geometric patterns and arches, in its design and decoration.

Turkey

The beginning of modern architecture in Turkey can be traced to the nineteenth century when the Balyan family of architects introduced into the architecture of Istanbul (then the capital of the Ottoman empire) motifs inspired by contemporary European architecture. European architects were also commissioned. In the late nineteenth and early twentieth centuries, European architects were also recruited to teach architecture at the Academy of Fine Arts (founded in 1883) and the College of Civil Engineering (founded 1884). Late Ottoman architecture in Istanbul became dependent on Western funding, technology, and ideas. Most of the buildings that were built in the last decades of the nineteenth century combined elements of neo-classical European architecture with elements from Islamic architecture. This style of architecture continued in the early twentieth century with buildings designed by Turkish architects. This style became known as the First National architectural style.

From the late 1920s, under the Republican government, new styles emerged, inspired by European Modernism. A number of European architects worked in Ankara, the new capital of Turkey, and influenced its architectural appearance. In 1931 the first Turkish architectural journal, *Mimar*, was founded, and it described works in the modern style by Turkish architects. During the 1930s, with the encouragement of the Republican government, monumental buildings inspired by German and Italian architecture were commissioned.

From the late 1930s, however, there was a shift in emphasis, known as the Second National architectural style, in which architects began to express in their work an awareness of a vernacular Turkish architecture but without a total rejection of Modernism. One of the most influential architects of this movement was Sedad Eldem, who defended local styles over international ones and included local features in his architecture. The main building of this period, the mausoleum of the soldier and statesman Kemal Ataturk (1881–1938) in Ankara (1944), by the architects Emin Onat and Orhan Arda, also expressed the preoccupation with this new style.

In the 1950s American and European architectural influences became important in Turkey. The Hilton Hotel (1952) in Istanbul, by the American architectural firm Skidmore, Owings, and Merrill with the collaboration of Eldem, was influential as an example of the International style (a movement in modern European and American architecture, famous for its use of glass, steel, and reinforced concrete and for its preoccupation with unornamented plane surfaces). The 1950s also brought industrial development and urban growth, especially in the cities of Istanbul, Ankara, and Izmir. Skyscrapers were introduced into city centers, and unplanned neighborhoods grew around the various cities. From the 1960s onward, new materials, such as exposed concrete, and new construction techniques have become increasingly common in Turkish architecture. Other prevalent trends in modern Turkish architecture include the integration of older architectural forms into modern buildings, as well as renovation and restoration of older buildings, especially in Istanbul.

Iraq

The mid-twentieth century marks the beginning of modern architecture in Iraq. It was introduced by foreign architects and later taken up by Iraqi architects such as Mohamad Makiya, Mahmoud al-Ali, and Rifat Chaderji. In 1959, Mohamad Makiya (who designed many residential and commercial buildings in Iraq) founded the first department of architecture in Iraq at Baghdad University.

One of the first expressions of modern architecture in Iraq was manifested in urban renewal projects in the capital of Baghdad, where many traditional neighborhoods were destroyed to make way for new commercial buildings and a new civic center (completed in 1986). The civic center includes the Municipality Building by Hisham Munir, the Income Tax Building by Mahdi al-Hassani, and the Water Board Building by Mahmoud al-Ali. Until the 1970s, much of the modern architecture of Iraq relied heavily upon Western styles. However, some architects (most prominently Rifat Chaderji) became concerned with the disappearance of traditional Iraqi architecture and set out to combine principles of traditional architecture with modern technologies. This attempt to preserve traditional Iraqi architecture also led to a project (headed by Chaderji, the Iraqi firm Mahmoud al-Ali and Partners, and the Architecture and Planning Partnership) to conserve and restore some residential neighborhoods and important Islamic shrines around Baghdad (their work stopped in 1984, and the project was not completed).

Since the mid-1980s, the majority of Iraqi architecture has been state-sponsored monumental architecture aimed at promoting and validating the rule of Saddam Hussein (b. 1937), Iraq's current leader.

Lara G. Tohme

Further Reading
Beazley, Elisabeth, and Michael Harverson. (1982) *Living with the Desert: Working Buildings of the Iranian Plateau.* Warminster, UK: Aris & Phillips.
Bozdogan, Sibel. (2001) *Modernism and Nation Building: Turkish Architectural Culture in the Early Republic.* Seattle, WA: University of Washington Press.
Fethi, Ihsan, and John Warren. (1982) *Traditional Houses in Baghdad.* Horsham, UK: Coach.

ARDABIL   (2000 est. pop. 500,000). A city in Iran's mountainous northwest and a provincial capital since the 1993 formation of Ardabil Province, Ardabil (Ardebil) was previously the most northeastern city of Iran's East Azerbaijan province. The vast majority of the population are Azeri Turks. Since its genesis, estimated to be at least as early as the fifth century CE, the city has been an overland junction. This was especially true when the silk trade flourished, during several centuries when Ardabil was capital of the Azerbaijan region of Persia. Close today to Iran's Caspian province of Gilan and to the international border between Iran and Azerbaijan, Ardabil continues to be a significant overland point in the region.

In historic terms, Ardabil is known as the hearth of the Safavid dynasty. Its most significant landmark is a circular, domed tower known as the shrine and mausoleum of the Persian saint Safi-od-Din (1252–1334), for whom the dynasty is named. In addition to his tomb, this mausoleum is also the resting place of his sons and other notables, including Shah Ismail I. Nonetheless, by the early-sixteenth century, Tabriz had eclipsed Ardabil as the center of the Azerbaijan region. Yet Ardabil should also be noted for its capacity to resurrect itself. Razed by Mongol armies in 1220, the city has been devastated numerous times throughout its history by earthquakes. The late-ninth-century earthquake centered on Ardabil accounted for roughly 150,000 deaths, making it one of the top ten most destructive earthquakes in recorded history.

Kyle Evered

Further Reading
Chehabi, H. E. (1997) "Ardabil Becomes a Province: Center-Periphery Relations in Iran." *International Journal of Middle East Studies* 29, 2: 235–253.

Morton, A. H. (1974, 1975) "The Ardabil Shrine in the Reign of Shah Tahmasp I." *Iran* 12: 31–64; 13: 39–58.

Zarinebaf-Shahr, Fariba. (1998) "Economic Activities of Safavid Women in the Shrine-City of Ardabil." *Iranian Studies* 31, 2: 247–261.

ARIQ WATER SYSTEM

The traditional method of distributing irrigation water to fields in pre-Soviet Central Asia, *ariq* in Uzbek simply means irrigation canal. This distribution system was arranged around the Islamic premise that water, like other natural goods, was the gift of God and could not be owned. Equitable distribution of water to fields was therefore a communal responsibility, although one which in the Emirate of Bukhara was regulated by the state. Canals were constructed and maintained by hand as part of a communal enterprise, which it was incumbent on all men in a community to perform on pain of losing their field holdings. Before the Soviet takeover, Central Asians (in what would be the republics of Kazakhstan, Kyrgyzstan, Tajikistan, Turkmenistan, and Uzbekistan) held water as a common good to be distributed according to need, with water theoretically being supplied on an equitable basis according to size of holding, fertility, or other considerations.

The construction of canals was overseen by an *usta* (expert) who used no surveying equipment beyond eye, thumb (to estimate elevation), and toe (to mark eventual course). Consequently, canals were often needlessly long, and suffered from evaporation and leakage. Channels were also prone to silting. Twice a year (at the end of February for major canals, March for minor ones) they were cleaned communally and the silt used as fertilizer.

At the village level, water supply was controlled by a *mirab* (literally "water controller") who channeled water to each holding by turn, judging the quantity needed by eye. Channels to individual fields were maintained by the farmer, but the system as a whole was supervised by an *aqsaqal* (authority) responsible for cleaning and maintenance and elected by all the villages using a main canal. In theory this prevented upstream villages taking more than their share of water, but in practice the system was open to abuse at both *aqsaqal* and *mirab* level. By the time of the Soviet takeover this system had fallen into considerable infrastructural decay, and it was replaced by more modern techniques.

Will Myer

Further Reading
Rumer, B. (1989) *Soviet Central Asia*. Boston: Unwin-Hyman.

Prokhorov, A. M., ed. (1973–1983) *Great Soviet Encyclopedia*. Translation of *Bol'shaia sovetskaia entsiklopediia*. New York: Macmillan.

ARJA

Arja, which developed from *gambuh*, Balinese dance, is a form of Balinese musical comedy incorporating song, dance, drama, comedy, and pantomime. It is commonly accompanied by a gamelan (Indonesian percussion instrument) gong orchestra, although early versions apparently had all-male casts and no gamelan accompaniment. A version with all-women casts also apparently existed at one time, but modern casts are mixed, albeit with comic female roles often played by men. Over the years, the comic elements have grown considerably in proportion to the dramatic action.

The main difference between *gambuh* and *arja* is that the latter places a much greater emphasis on drama and song rather than on dance and music, and *arja's* representation of dramatic action is considerably more flexible than that of the older genre. The musical accompaniment of *arja* is not continuous, allowing long passages of dialogue, often comic. The plots tend to be stereotyped romantic or sentimental narratives but also include stories from the medieval Javanese Panji romances, the Mahabharata epic, and Chinese sources. As in other Balinese genres, the clown servants Punta and Wijil serve the function of interpreting the action from the speech forms of classical theater into the vernacular.

Tim Byard-Jones

Further Reading
Eiseman, Fred B., Jr. (1990) *Bali: Sekala and Niskala*, Vol. 1: *Essays on Religion, Ritual, and Art*. Hong Kong: Periplus.

Yousouf, Ghulam-Sarwar. (1994) *Dictionary of Traditional South-East Asian Theatre*. Kuala Lumpur, Malaysia: Oxford University Press.

ARMENIANS

The Armenians emerged as a people in about 600 BCE, occupying a rugged region in the Transcaucasus in western Asia. Although at various times the Armenians created an independent state, which under the ruler Tigranes the Great (c. 140–c. 55 BCE) extended from the Caspian to the Mediterranean, the strategic importance of the Transcaucasus and Caucasus ensured that foreign powers continually struggled to control the region. Thus the Achaemenid Persians, Romans, Byzantines, Arabs, Seljuk Turks, Mongols, Ottomans, and Russians, among others, successively controlled the Armenian peoples, and the

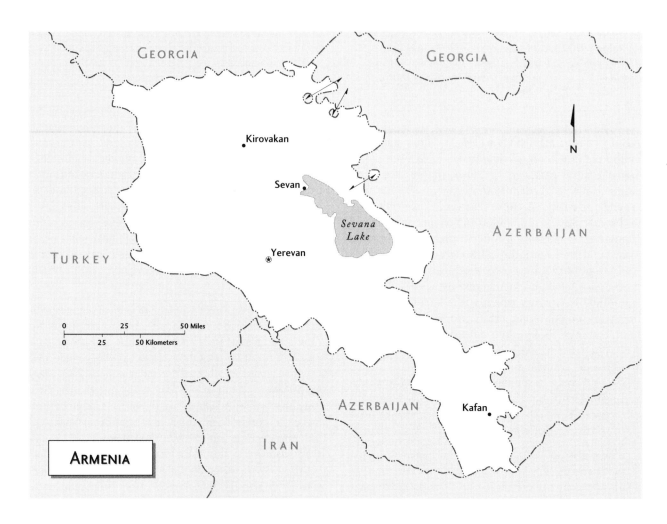

ARMENIA

Armenians, severely treated by the various foreign invaders, again and again emigrated to avoid persecution.

Although Armenians are thought to have descended from both native Transcaucasian populations and foreign invaders, the Armenian language is Indo-European, written with a unique thirty-eight-letter alphabet. The Armenian Apostolic (Orthodox) Church is one of the oldest Christian churches, having been established in the region two decades before Constantine made Christianity the official religion of the Roman empire (c. 313).

Early Armenia and Persian Dominance

Present-day Armenia, located in the Transcaucasus, occupies but a fraction of the territory of ancient Armenia, then known as eastern Armenia. Most of the land of the ancient kingdom (western Armenia) is now located in eastern Turkey. A small part of Georgia, another Transcaucasian country, falls within the region once occupied by ancient Armenia.

Of all the foreign powers that controlled the Armenians, the Persians were the most influential until the third century CE. Persian dominance was weakened, however, by the conversion of the Armenians to Christianity and the conquest of Persia (Iran) by the Arabs, Seljuk Turks, and Mongols. In the eleventh century, the Seljuk occupation of Armenia drove many Armenians into Iran.

Ottoman Rule

The Ottomans began their penetration into Armenia in the sixteenth century, about three centuries after the Ottoman empire was established, and during numerous wars in the sixteenth and seventeenth centuries, the Ottomans conquered and annexed parts of the Armenian land now located in eastern Turkey. These wars led to the forcible relocation of many Armenians, who moved to Iran; other areas of the Transcaucasus, including the current Armenia and Azerbaijan; and parts of the Ottoman empire. As the neighbor of Armenia, Iran became the home to the largest Armenian diaspora, concentrated in the current provinces of Isfahan, Tehran, and western and eastern Azerbaijan. Much smaller communities were

A tenth-century Armenian church in western Turkey. (O. ALAMANY & E. VICENS/CORBIS)

created in present-day Turkey, especially in the areas close to the Transcaucasus and in Istanbul. In 1639, the Treaty of Zuhab partitioned Armenia between the Ottomans and the Iranians. The former took western Armenia (now part of eastern Turkey), and the latter took eastern Armenia (present-day Armenia). Turkey has kept its part to this date. The persecution of the Armenians in the Ottoman empire and their forcible relocation in the nineteenth and early twentieth centuries led to the migration of many Armenians from western Armenia to Iran.

Struggles with Russia

The fall of the Iranian Safavid empire in the early eighteenth century allowed the Russian empire to extend its influence to the Caucasus. This also encouraged the Ottoman empire to conquer the entire region. Consequently, the Caucasus and Transcaucasus, including Armenia, became the scene of wars and rivalry between Russia, the Ottomans who wanted to expand their territories, and the Iranians who wanted to regain their lost lands. For most of a century until 1828, the Armenians were ruled by three empires whose territories in the region expanded and contracted several times.

Two long series of wars between Iran and Russia led to the Turkmenchai Treaty of 1828. This confirmed Russia's annexation of the Caucasus and Transcaucasus, including present-day Armenia. The

Bolshevik Revolution gave rise to a short period of independence for Armenia, which emerged in 1918 as the independent republic of Armenia.

After crushing the Armenian republican forces, the Soviet Union regained control over Armenia in November 1920 and incorporated the Armenians into the Soviet Union as part of the Transcaucasian federation, which also included the Azerbaijanis and the Georgians. In 1936, Armenia became a full republic of the Soviet Union. It regained full independence only after the collapse of the Soviet Union in 1991.

Armenians Today

At the present time, the Armenians live in Armenia and many other countries. Their voluntary and involuntary migrations have created large Armenian diasporas throughout the world. The population of Armenia is about 3.5 million, but between 800,000 and 1.5 million Armenians have migrated to other countries since independence in 1991 because of economic reasons, political instability, or both. About 1 million Armenians live in the countries of the former Soviet Union, and there are about 4 million Armenians in large communities in Iran, India, Lebanon, Syria, Turkey, the United States, Canada, Argentina, and Western Europe.

The relations between the Armenians and the Turks have been particularly hostile. The Ottomans' persecution and the forcible migration of the Armenians living in western Armenia have been two major factors in this hostility. The Armenian diaspora continues to press the Turkish republic to accept responsibility for the genocide of 1915, estimated at costing 500,000 to 1.5 million Armenian lives.

Hooman Peimani

Further Reading
Country Profile 2000: Georgia-Armenia. (2000) London: Economist Intelligence Unit.

Hovannisian, Richard G. (1997) *The Armenian People from Ancient to Modern Times.* 2 vols. New York: St. Martin's Press.

ARMY OF THE REPUBLIC OF VIETNAM

On 26 October 1955, when Ngo Dinh Diem proclaimed the Republic of Vietnam (RVN) with himself as president, all of the RVN's army units became known collectively as the Army of the Republic of Vietnam, or ARVN. The ARVN, successor to the French-led Vietnamese National Army of the First Indochina War, had an initial strength of 150,000 troops and eventually grew to almost one million at the time of its demise in 1975. Organized in the mid-1950s by Lieutenant-Generals John W. O'Daniel and Samuel T. Williams, successive heads of the U.S. Military Assistance Advisory Group, modeled after the U.S. Army, and designed to meet a People's Army of Vietnam (PAVN) attack across the demilitarized zone (the DMZ: established 22 July 1954 along the seventeenth parallel in Vietnam), the ARVN initially was made up of four field divisions and six light divisions with thirteen territorial regiments for regional security.

Growing as the U.S. military presence in South Vietnam grew, the ARVN was beset by multiple problems, such as corruption, low morale, and poor leadership, which severely limited its effectiveness as a fighting force. The ARVN lacked officers, especially in the higher ranks, and many officers were appointed according to social rank and political favor rather than ability and integrity. The result was an almost entirely Catholic officer corps that led a fighting force that was more than 60 percent Buddhist. Logistics and technical services were crippled by senior officers' corruption. Many officers operated their units for financial gain by overreporting personnel numbers and pocketing the surplus pay, sharing the unit's confiscated materials with others who often sold the goods on the black market, and smuggling drugs.

Perhaps the most serious problem with the ARVN was that it was modeled on the U.S. Army and, like the U.S. Army, gauged to fight a conventional war in an unconventional war milieu, largely ignoring the counterinsurgency nature of the conflict. In addition, the ARVN grew to depend on the American military's assistance in everything from command and control to logistics and material support. Such dependence weakened the ARVN to the point that it could not stand up to PAVN assault without substantial American assistance. In 1975, during the final operation to liberate South Vietnam, PAVN easily crushed the ARVN forces, with the exception of elite airborne and ranger units, and reunited the two Vietnams.

Richard B. Verrone

Further Reading
Spector, Ronald H. (1983) *Advice and Support: The Early Years, 1941–1960.* Washington, DC: U.S. Army Center of Military History.

Tucker, Spencer C. (1999) *Vietnam.* Lexington, KY: University Press of Kentucky.

———, ed. (1998) *Encyclopedia of the Vietnam War.* Oxford: Oxford University Press.

ARNIS Arnis is a Filipino martial art and the national sport of the Philippines. It is based on the ancient Filipino martial art of *kali*, the traditional martial art of *eskrima*, other Asian martial arts, and Western-style boxing. Arnis emerged after World War II as a distinctive Filipino martial art, with training and ritual requirements resembling other Asian martial arts and competitions similar to boxing matches. Arnis competitors use 76-centimeter-long rattan sticks and score points by cleanly striking or disarming the opponent. Competitors wear a helmet and body padding to minimize injury. Although the sport remains popular only in the Philippines, the International Arnis Federation promotes the sport in some thirty nations.

David Levinson

Further Reading
Wiley, Mark. (1998) *Martial Culture of the Philippines.* Tokyo: Tuttle.

ARUNACHAL PRADESH (2001 est. pop. 1.1 million). "The land of the dawn-lit mountains," Arunachal Pradesh became a state in northeastern India in 1987. From 1947 to 1972 it was known as the North East Frontier Agency (NEFA), then in 1972 it became a union territory. Arunachal Pradesh stretches north to the main crest of the eastern Himalayas and east to an irregular line that passes through a series of lofty peaks that were known as "the Hump" during

A narrow suspension foot bridge crosses over the forest in Arunachal Pradesh. (LINDSAY HEBBERD/CORBIS)

World War II, when supplies to China were airlifted over it. Arunachal Pradesh borders China and Tibet to the north and Bhutan to the west with verdant mountain ranges sloping down to the plains of Assam, India, to the south.

According to legend, Parasurama, the sixth of the ten incarnations of the Hindu god Vishnu, created a passage through the hills for the Brahmaputra River with a stroke of his axe at Brahma Kund (in eastern Arunachal Pradesh), now a popular pilgrimage destination. Arunachal Pradesh's recorded history dates only from the sixteenth century, when the Ahom kings began their rule in Assam. By 1826 the British had made Assam part of British India, and in 1882 a political adviser was appointed to bring the area under British administrative control. In general the indigenous peoples of the region, labeled "hill tribes," were left to themselves until World War II. After Independence, Prime Minister Jawaharlal Nehru (1889–1964) supported efforts to prepare the tribes for the impact of the modern world. Developments toward village democracy increased after China invaded Tawang (in western Arunachal Pradesh) in 1962. The river valleys, separated by forbidding north-south ridges, have enabled distinct microcultures to flourish in Arunachal Pradesh. The region has at least fifteen distinct tribal groups known collectively to outsiders as the Abor. Among the principal tribes, whose beliefs blend Buddhism and traditional religions, are the Apa Tanis, Aka, Dafla, and the Sherdukpen.

Arunachal Pradesh, one of the last wilderness areas in India, exhibits great biodiversity in flora and fauna, including over five hundred species of orchids, in settings ranging from glacial terrain to alpine meadows and subtropical rain forests. Namdapha National Park is home to the rare hoolock gibbon, the legendary snow leopard, tigers, bears, pandas, and elephants. The capital, Itanagar, features the Jawaharlal Nehru State Museum and a Buddhist temple consecrated by the Dalai Lama.

C. Roger Davis

Further Reading

Bhattacharjee, Tarun Kumar. (1992) *Enticing Frontiers*. New Delhi: Omsans.

Elwin, Verrier. (1965) *Democracy in NEFA*. Shillong, Meghalaya, India: North-East Frontier Agency.

Fürer-Haimendorf, Christoph von. (1962) *The Apa Tanis and Their Neighbours*. New York: Free Press of Glencoe.

Mishra, Kiran. (1992) *Women in a Tribal Community: A Study of Arunachal Pradesh*. New Delhi: Vikas.

ARYAN The Aryans, far from being a "race," were speakers of Vedic Sanskrit in India, the earliest form of that classical Indo-European language. These people entered India from the northwest about 1500 BCE, and their descendants today form most of the population of Pakistan, Bangladesh, Nepal, Sri Lanka, and northern India, although these people do not identify themselves primarily as Aryans.

The term *arya* in Sanskrit means "noble" and doubtless refers to these people's high position in the Iron Age society they established. This term has been used, and largely misused, by European writers since 1835 and has fallen into disfavor among scholars because of the Nazi propagandists' assumptions that a community of speakers was equivalent to a biological race and that the mixed populations of northern and central Europe were the purest representatives of an "Aryan race."

Aryan speakers were certainly a major civilizing force in India (as they were in Iran), though not the first. They built the cities of the north from about 700 BCE and laid the foundation for the liturgy and theology of Hinduism, the caste organization of Indian society, and the flowering of the first among many Indian literatures. Their mark has been indelible.

Paul Hockings

Further Reading
Burrow, Thomas. (1975) "The Early Aryans." In *A Cultural History of India*, edited by A. L. Basham. Oxford: Clarendon, 20–29.
Childe, Vere Gordon. ([1926] 1987) *The Aryans: A Study of Indo-European Origins*. Reprint ed. New York: Dorset.

ASHGABAT (1999 est. pop. 606,700). Ashgabat is the capital and largest city of the republic of Turkmenistan, a Central Asian state. It is situated at the northern foot of the Kopet-Dag mountains, on the edge of the Kara-Kum ("black sand") desert, only 19 kilometers from the country's southern border with Iran.

The city was founded in 1881 as a Russian military fort and was named Ashkabad after a nearby Turkmen settlement. It became the administrative center of Russia's Zakaspiiskaia oblast (Transcaspian province), formed in 1881. In 1919 when Soviet power was established in this province, the city was renamed Poltoratsk, after the Russian revolutionary Pavel Poltoratsky (1888–1918). In 1927 Poltoratsk was re-

named Ashkhabad. From 1924 to 1991 the city was the capital of the Turkmen Soviet Socialist Republic, part of the Union of Soviet Socialist Republics.

Since the dissolution of the Soviet Union in 1991, Ashgabat has been the capital of the republic of Turkmenistan. In October 1948 the city was leveled by a powerful earthquake, which killed 110,000 people (two-thirds of the population). Present-day Ashgabat is Turkmenistan's biggest industrial, administrative, and cultural center.

Natalya Yu. Khan

Further Reading
Roy, Oliver. (2000) *The New Central Asia: The Creation of Nations*. New York: New York University Press.

ASIAN DEVELOPMENT BANK The Asian Development Bank is a developmental financial institution that provides loans, equity investments, and technical assistance to its member owners. Those owners are various nation-states with commercial interests in Asia. They refer to themselves as Developing Member Countries (DMCs), although several, most prominently the United States and Japan, are among the world's most advanced economies.

The bank opened for business in 1966 and must be understood within the context of world politics at that time. The motivating force was the United States, deeply involved in Asia through various anti-Communist military alliances but also, and more importantly, through its military adventure in Vietnam. That conflict made Asia the major foreign-policy concern for the presidential administration of Lyndon Johnson. That administration was severely criticized, at home and abroad, for its determination to seek a military solution to the various armed conflicts then raging in Southeast Asia. There was especial concern that little was being done to improve the life of the then-impoverished masses of Asians and, furthermore, that this oversight could only strengthen the appeal of Communist ideology in East Asia.

A financial institution dedicated to Asian economic progress thus offered several advantages to U.S. policymakers. It would demonstrate that the administration had a positive policy toward Asia and did not just rely on military solutions. This might placate domestic criticism of U.S. policy, while it could also entice various Asian nations to throw their lot with the West in the Cold War. Real economic progress in Asia would, it was believed, make that region of the world resistant to Communist penetration. Finally, there was a component of humanitarianism, a longtime staple of U.S. foreign policy, which genuinely looked to improve the common lot in East Asia. This somewhat awkwardly mixed collection of motives often prompted the charge that the bank was founded merely as a cat's-paw for U.S. foreign policy or that it was implicitly designed to expedite U.S. commercial penetration in Asia.

History

Twenty-one countries, operating under auspices of the United Nations, founded the bank during a conference in Manila (where its headquarters remains to this day). It was initially capitalized at $1 billion, with the United States subscribing to some 20 percent of that amount. No Communist countries participated. The bank was to be autonomous in nature, with governance similar to that of the International Monetary Fund.

When the bank was established, Asia, with the sole exception of Japan, was mired in millennia-old poverty. When compared with European and North American countries, nations such as Thailand, Malaysia, Taiwan, and Korean were largely rural, technologically backward, undereducated, and unindustrialized. Little more than a generation later these same states counted among the most advanced economies on the planet, although many factors besides the bank brought this about.

As an institution dedicated to Asian development, the bank took a broad view of its mission and sought to provide financing for projects that might stimulate long-term economic growth. It was not established to provide humanitarian aid as such, this being the provenance of international aid organizations or other foreign aid. As one bank publication put it, "The sheer numbers of the poor in Asian countries is sufficient reason for believing that a program consisting of a few welfare projects would have no perceptible impact on poverty" (Asian Development Bank 1978: 215). The bank, therefore, directed its attention away from the ordinary credit ventures associated with private lending and toward underwriting those things that might fundamentally ameliorate the inequitable distribution of wealth or, even better, create new sources of wealth.

Agriculture, for instance, was a prime concern of the bank from its earliest days. The bank looked to encourage land reform in those societies where agricultural property was concentrated in a few, often inefficient, hands. Furthermore, it was especially interested in funding enterprises that would alter the traditional subsistence or local market economy farming of much of Asia. This included such areas as fer-

tilizer production and genetic research. Finally, the bank was attentive to the credit needs of small farmers who could likely greatly increase yield if modest capital was made available to secure even a low level of mechanization and other improvements. Thus, the bank's lending was in some instances directed toward a restructuring of traditional societies.

Role in the Asian Financial Crisis

The bank has also performed some of the functions of a central bank, either by itself or in conjunction with other lending institutions. This includes assisting in currency stabilization, debt management, and emergency loans to sovereign states. Its involvement in the severe Asian financial crisis of the late 1990s was a premier example of this. Working with the International Monetary Fund and various national banks, the bank underwrote loans to, among various countries, Indonesia, Korea, and Taiwan. These loans relieved the liquidity crisis and assisted in stemming the precipitous drop in value of certain Asian currencies. The bank also acted as a sometime "policeman" to monitor national compliance with bailout plans put together by various financial institutions acting in concert.

By the early twenty-first century, the bank has grown substantially from its modest beginnings to become a significant factor for economic advancement and stabilization in Asia. Its membership has grown to nearly sixty nations, and it maintains offices in fourteen countries. Its employees number more than two thousand, some of whom are distributed in local liaison offices that supplement the formal branch structure of the bank. Its annual loans approach $6 billion, most of which has been lent to public entities in Asia for various projects aimed at alleviating poverty or promoting sustainable growth in new or existing industries that might benefit large sectors of the population. This sum is relatively modest when compared with capital made available from private lenders but still far from insignificant. In addition, the bank acts as a resource for sociological and financial scholarship on problems and opportunities among member companies. Its publishing house is a prime source for information on contemporary trends in Asian economies.

Robert K. Whalen

Further Reading

Asian Development Bank. (1978) *Rural Asia: Challenge and Opportunity.* New York: Praeger.
Chow, C. Y., and Bates Gills, eds. (2000) *Weathering the Storm: Taiwan, Its Neighbors, and the Asian Financial Crisis.* Washington, DC: Brookings Institution Press.

Dutt, Nitish K. (1997) "The United States and the Asian Development Bank." *Journal of Contemporary Asia* 97: 71–84.

McLeod, Ross H., and Ross Garnaut, eds. (1998) *East Asia in Crisis: From Being a Miracle to Needing One?* London: Routledge.

ASIAN DIASPORA. See **Chinese, Overseas; Koreans, Overseas; Refugees—South Asia**

ASIAN ECONOMIC CRISIS OF 1997 By "Asian currencies" one normally means those of Japan and of the former Asian "tiger" countries—Korea (won), China (yuan), Hong Kong (dollar), Taiwan (dollar), the Philippines (peso), Thailand (baht), Malaysia (ringgit), Singapore (dollar), and Indonesia (rupiah)—all of which have been strongly impacted by the profound currency and banking crisis that has gripped Asia and much of the world since 1997. It began in the summer of that year with the decision of a desperate Thai government to float the baht after exhaustive efforts to support it in the face of a severe financial overextension that was in part real-estate driven. It sank like a rock and took Thailand with it. At the time Thailand had acquired a burden of foreign debt that made the country effectively bankrupt even before the collapse of its currency. The drastically reduced import earnings that resulted from the forced devaluation then made a quick or even medium-term recovery impossible without strenuous international intervention.

From Thailand, contagion quickly spread south, all but closing down the Indonesian economy and severely impacting the Malaysian. In Indonesia, which was particularly hard it, it resulted in the 1998 fall of Indonesia's Suharto, whose power had once seemed a permanent fixture. Also severely impacted, once the contagion turned north, was Korea, which suffered a financial meltdown comparable to those of Thailand and Indonesia. In Hong Kong, which had the dubious benefit of a stable currency pegged to the dollar and the support of China, the currency and banking system survived but at the cost of a major recession. In the Philippines growth dropped to virtually zero in 1998. Only Singapore and Taiwan proved relatively insulated from the shock, but both suffered serious hits in passing, the former more so due to its size and geographical location between Malaysia and Indonesia. Even before the crisis, Japan had been in a state of profound recession due to a highly inefficient banking system laboring under mountains of bad debt, much of which up to that point had been relatively invisible because of the established Japanese banking practice of hiding the losses of major customers. The ripple effect ultimately spread to Brazil and threatened to take Latin America down like a house of cards, too. If it had fallen, the United States might well have been pulled down as well.

Identifying the Causes

The causes of the debacle are many and disputed. Clearly Thailand was an economic catastrophe waiting to happen with an economy that was little more than a bubble fueled by "hot money," that is, short-term capital flow that is expensive and often highly conditioned (for quick profit), and with more and more required as the size of the bubble grew. Much the same can be said of Malaysia, although Malaysia had better political leadership, and Indonesia, with the added complication of what has been called "crony capitalism." Development money went in a largely uncontrolled manner to certain people only, not particularly the best suited or most efficient, but those closest to the centers of power. In Korea, in the haste to build great, Japanese-style conglomerates to take on the world, Koreans forgot that the purpose of capital investment in a business is ultimately to ensure a return and profitability. The great Korean conglomerates, more or less completely controlled by the government, simply absorbed more and more capital and never looked back.

Other factors were globalization, in this case, the spread of American- and European-style capitalism to the entire world after the end of the Cold War, whether the world was ready for it or not, and economic shifts that have made much of the traditional Asian approach to business obsolete. One such shift has been the move to merchandising in which the consumer, not the producer, determines the product, contrary to recent Japanese and Korean practice. Another longer-term influence has been the changing relationship between the United States and Japan, with the United States no longer openly supporting the highly artificial trade environment and exchange rates that governed economic relations between the two countries for almost four decades after World War II.

International Response

Such was the scope and the severity of the collapses involved that outside intervention, considered by the Malaysians, among others, as a new kind of colonialism, became urgently needed. Since the countries melting down were among not only the richest in their region, but in the world, and since hundreds of billions of dollars were at stake, any response to the crisis had to be cooperative and international, in this case through the International Monetary Fund (IMF). The IMF created a series of bailout packages for the most affected economies, tying the packages to reforms that were intended to make the restored Asian currency, banking, and financial systems as much like those of the United States and Europe as possible.

Above all, capital had to be administered democratically in the future, with no favored parties receiving funds by preference. There had to be adequate government controls set up to supervise all financial activities, ones that were to be independent, in theory, of private interest. Insolvent institutions had to be closed, and insolvency itself had to be clearly defined. In short, exactly the same kinds of financial institutions found in the United States and Europe had to be created in Indonesia, Korea, and elsewhere, as a price for IMF support. In addition, financial systems had to become "transparent," that is, provide the kind of reliable financial information used in the West to make sound financial decisions. No more massive losses under the table, as in Japan, or loans off the books.

Although such reforms were, in most cases, long needed, the countries most involved—Korea, Thailand, and Indonesia—have ended up undergoing an almost complete political and financial restructuring. They have suffered permanent currency devaluations, massive numbers of bankruptcies, collapses of whole sectors of once-booming economies, real estate busts, high unemployment, and social unrest. Even the Philippines, which came through the storm less damaged than other economies, has also had to suffer severe IMF intervention, while Malaysia has walled itself off from the world and gone its own way (only Singapore, with its rigid control system, and China and Hong Kong, isolated from the turmoil by the controls of the Chinese currency system, have come through the storm relatively unaffected). For most of the countries involved, IMF intervention has been a bitter pill for which the international agency has been roundly criticized and a bitter pill that may or may not result in the regional renewal the IMF expects.

Assessment

The story of Asian currencies recently has been the story of the decline and fall or near-fall of the Asian "tigers," but their problems are by no means unique to them, and the recent crisis may be just the first of many. The United States, for example, has had its own financial bubble fueled by consumer debt and over-priced stocks (although the rapid depreciation of many stock values recently has now reduced this danger), and a U.S. meltdown could involve many of the recovering Asian states (especially Korea) in a new round

of collapse, including, this time, some that were relatively spared by the last crisis. This specter was raised again after 11 September 2001, when the economic ripples of the shock and U.S. recession were felt as far afield as Mongolia.

China, which kept itself above the fray in 1997 and 1998, depends heavily on trade with the United States and suffers from enormous financial weaknesses, including a primitive and inefficient banking system with too many bad loans, leaving aside the issue of a public sector that is just too big and too inefficient. Another cause of contagion may be Russia, which has absorbed masses of aid funds, including gigantic IMF loans. Although economic growth has resumed again under Putin, the economy remains fragile, and a Russian meltdown would take much of Europe with it—and Europe, with the United States, is a major funder of the IMF. Deprived of most of its funds, the IMF would then be unable to intervene in even a minor Asian state with currency or other financial problems.

Paul D. Buell

Further Reading
International Monetary Fund. (2001) "The International Monetary Fund Homepage." Retrieved 17 December 2001, from: http://www.imf.org/external/index.htm.

Noland, Markus, Li-gang Liu, Sherman Robinson, and Zhi Wang. (1998) *Global Economic Effects of the Asian Currency Devaluations.* Policy Analyses in International Economics, no. 56. Washington, DC: Institute for International Economics.

Pempel, T. J. (1999) *The Politics of the Asian Economic Crisis.* Ithaca, NY: Cornell University Press.

Ries, Philippe. (2000) *The Asian Storm: Asia's Economic Crisis Examined.* Trans. by Peter Starr. Boston: Tuttle.

ASIAN GAMES The Asian Games are the major Pan-Asian sports festival in which athletes from nearly all Asian nations are allowed to compete. Beginning in 1954 with the second Games, the Games have been held every four years, in the year midway between the Summer Olympics. The Games were established at India's suggestion after World War II. The first Games were held in the Indian capital of New Delhi in 1951, with only eleven nations sending athletes and only six events (all Western in origin): Japan was the major contender. Since then, Western sports have dominated the program, although attempts have been made to add indigenous Asian sports including martial arts and the Indian pursuit sport of *kabbadi*. Japan won the most medals from the first festival, a success that continued until 1982 when China emerged as the major regional sports power. The Thirteenth Asian

Games were held from 6 to 20 December 1998 in Bangkok, Thailand. They were the largest Games to date, with 9,469 athletes and officials from over forty-one nations. Unlike many earlier Games, they were free of major political problems in the spirit of its motto: Friendship Beyond Frontiers. In their current form, the Asian Games are the major Olympic "tune-up" festival, with most world-class athletes competing in preparation for the Olympics.

A defining feature of the Games for much of their history has been the effect of political conflicts across and beyond the region that have often resulted in some nations being excluded or refusing to participate in the Games. For example, Israel has often been excluded because of its ties to the West; Taiwan suffered the same fate in 1962. Mainland Chinese athletes did not compete until 1974, and Iraq was barred in 1990. The Games have also been used by political leaders in the host nation to build national pride and to enhance their own and their nation's power in Asia and beyond. In 1962, President Sukarno of Indonesia used the Jakarta Games to assert Indonesian leadership in the

HOST CITIES OF THE ASIAN GAMES

1951—New Delhi (India)
1954—Manila (Philippines)
1958—Tokyo (Japan)
1962—Jakarta (Indonesia)
1966—Bangkok (Thailand)
1970—Bangkok (Thailand)
1974—Teheran (Iran)
1978—Bangkok (Thailand)
1982—New Delhi (India)
1986—Seoul (Korea)
1990—Beijing (China)
1994—Hiroshima (Japan)
1998—Bangkok (Thailand)
2002—Puson (South Korea)

Third World, and angered both rival India and the International Olympic Committee as a result. His response was to found "The Games of the Newly Emerging Forces," which foundered after his political demise in 1965. Similarly, for the 1982 Games, which India hosted, Indira Gandhi spent nearly $1 billion to construct new sports facilities, and the South Korean government created a government ministry for sports when it hosted the 1988 Games. That action helped to make South Korea a legitimate power in several sports. At the same time, Korea was criticized for its repression of student protestors during the Games.

In addition to the Asian Games, there are several other major regional sports festivals in Asia. The largest is the Southeast Asian Games, a biannual festival for the nations of Southeast Asia. The first eight festivals (up to and including 1975) were called the Southeast Asian Peninsula Games. Since 1977, nations from outside the peninsula have participated as well. Also important are the East Asian Games and the recently inaugurated West Asian Games, which were first held in Tehran, Iran, in November of 1997. As with the Asian Games, most sports are Western Olympic sports and the festivals are now more about preparing athletes for international competition than nation building.

David Levinson

Further Reading

Trevithick, Alan. (1996) "Asian Games." In *Encyclopedia of World Sport: From Ancient Times to the Present*, edited by David Levinson and Karen Christensen. Santa Barbara, CA: ABC-Clio, 56–59.

INDIGENOUS SPORTS AT THE ASIAN GAMES

Promoting Asian culture is one of the goals of the Asian Games and toward that end an effort is made to include indigenous sports. One such sport is sepak takraw (known as footbag in the west), described below as it was played in Burmese villages in the late 1800s.

A very common amusement amongst Burmans, rarer amongst Talaing and still rarer amongst Kareng, is a game of ball called *khyee-loon*. The ball is made of open wicker-work and is struck with the sole of the foot, the elbow or any part of the body except the toes and hands. There are no sides but half a dozen lads or men join and standing in a ring endeavor to keep the ball off the ground, any one near whom it descends striking it upwards.

Source: Gazetteer of Burma. (1983) New Delhi: Cultural Publishing House, 394.

Wagner, Eric A. (1989) *Sport in Asia and Africa: A Comparative Handbook*. New York: Greenwood.

ASIAN–CHRISTIAN RELIGIOUS DIALOGUE

For centuries Christianity and the religions of Asia existed with little or no mutual contact or genuine dialogue. There was not even a desire for dialogue, if by "dialogue" is meant a respectful, empathetic conversation aimed at understanding the other religion as it understands itself. Such dialogue would even permit participants to be changed by what they learned. Until recently contacts between religions were more monologic than dialogic, more aimed at conversion or debating than mutual understanding.

Some early contacts did take place. Jesuit missionaries from Europe, such as de Nobili, Ricci, and Francis Xavier, brought the Christian message to India, China, and Japan. They respected the traditional cultures they encountered and sought to interpret Christian theology through the lens of local religious traditions. More commonly, however, Christian missionaries dismissed the cultures and religions they encountered, proclaiming that Christian beliefs should be understood in the context of European culture—an approach inimical to authentic dialogue.

The Asian religions of Hinduism, Buddhism, and Taoism are inherently tolerant of a variety of religions, tending not to claim that any one is the sole path to truth, salvation, or liberation. Christianity is different; it is a religion of orthodoxy (right belief) emphasizing the precise propositional expression of theological truths. Islam, which is an Eastern religion in that most of its adherents live in the Middle East and Asia, is also a religion of orthodoxy, but Christian-Muslim dialogue will not be discussed in this article.

In East and South Asia, boundaries between religions could be crossed, allowing participation in the beliefs and practices of more than one religion. In the West, however, the boundaries around a particular religion tend to preclude participation in any other.

European proselytizing in Asia actually converted very few, and Christianity remains a statistically small presence there to this day. Asian religions are, however, growing rapidly in the West through immigration and conversion, although adherents of Asian religions still make up a small percentage of the population.

Prelude to Dialogue

Dialogue between East and South Asian religions and Christianity formally began at the 1893 World's Columbian Exposition in Chicago with the World's Parliament of Religion. While most participants were from the West, Asian religious traditions were represented. It was radical for the times and gave new social and intellectual respectability to all religions involved.

Many events and individuals in the nineteenth century made the Parliament intellectually possible. Western colonialism and the opening of Japan exposed the West to the histories, cultures, and religions of Asia. Faster travel and communication augmented East-West contacts, as did a certain amount of immigration, particularly from East to West, fueled by growing Western economies, especially that of the United States.

More fundamentally, the United States saw the emergence of religious and intellectual movements either influenced by or compatible with aspects of Asian thought. As disseminated by Ralph Waldo Emerson (1803–1882) and Henry David Thoreau (1817–1862), Transcendentalism claimed association with ancient ideas connected with Hinduism and Buddhism, ideas such as the divinity or infinitude of each person. Although primarily a philosophical and literary reaction to the perceived limitations of the Enlightenment with its rational and empirical bias, Transcendentalism was deeply influenced by newly translated Asian religious texts.

Other American movements also contributed to a climate favoring dialogue. Theosophy (divine wisdom)—associated with Helena Blavatsky (1831–1891), Henry Steel Olcott (1832–1907), and the founding of the Theosophical Society in New York City in 1875—taught that the divine must be directly experienced to be knowable. Behind Theosophy lay a range of historical, philosophical, mystical, and religious influences, at the heart of which was the spiritual heritage of India as found in the early Vedas, the Upanishads, and later writings. Buddhism and Taoism also contributed to the content of Theosophy. New Thought, proposed by Phineas Quimby (1802–1866), likewise taught the infinitude of the individual, but maintained that evil and illness were manifestations of wrong thinking and a lack of spiritual insight. While influenced by Platonism, Swedenborgianism, philosophical idealism, and American Transcendentalism, a main source of New Thought was ancient Hinduism, especially its monistic understanding of ultimate reality.

The new availability of Asian religious texts in translation allowed Asian religions to have an influence. A prime source of such texts was the work of the German Orientalist and philologist Max Müller (1823–1900). Müller published translations of important Vedic texts and between 1879 and 1904 edited a fifty-one-volume series entitled *The Sacred Books of the East*. The English scholar T. W. Rhys Davids (1843–1922) and his Pali Text Society made Theravada Buddhist texts available to complement available Mahayana Buddhist texts.

Two further scholarly developments were also vital: biblical criticism and the new field of comparative study of religion. Biblical criticism took various modern critical methodologies that were applied to ancient texts and used them in studying the Bible as historical and literary writing. This approach treated the Bible and Asian religious texts alike as objects of academic investigation, seeking similarities and differences between them in context, purpose, use, and meaning. The academic study of religion emerged in the nineteenth century as an interdisciplinary means for intercultural study of the intentions, meanings, structures, and ideas of religion. This included a search for the origins both of religion and of the range of myths found in all religions—starting points for discussion between Asian and Western religions.

The rapid and overwhelming success of science and technology in the nineteenth century was also a factor uniting different religions. All faiths were challenged by issues such as the nature of the cosmos, the source of knowledge and the means of knowing reality, human values and the significance of the individual, and the worth of ancient religious wisdom.

Toward the end of the century the ecumenical movement arose within Protestantism to attempt to reverse denominational splintering and seek cooperation and even reunification among different churches. In the twentieth century ecumenism expanded to involve Roman Catholicism and Eastern Orthodoxy. This ecumenical disposition affected how and why dialogue arose between Asian and Western religions.

Dialogue Begins

The 1893 World's Parliament of Religion—recognized as epochal at the time—was possible only because of earlier historical, cultural, and intellectual developments in the nineteenth century. At the opening, Swami Vivekananda (1863–1902), a Hindu from India, hailed the spirit of tolerance and pluralism embodied in the gathering. Rabbi Emil Hirsch of Sinai Temple, Chicago, and the high priest of the Shinto religion in Japan, the Rt. Rev. R. Shibata, both praised the results of the Parliament.

Professor Max Müller regretted missing the Parliament. Jabez Sunderland (1842–1936), a Unitarian Universalist who attended the Parliament, noted its significance. Twentieth-century commentators on the Parliament continued to see it as pivotal in East-West

dialogue. The Western scholar Carl Jackson said that after Emerson spoke highly of Eastern religions, a series of events and movements gave Asian religions a growing prominence in the West that reached a pinnacle at the 1893 Parliament.

World War I shattered the nineteenth-century belief in inevitable social evolution powered by scientific and technological progress. Just as the postwar vision of a League of Nations faltered, so did the call of the religion scholar Rudolph Otto (1869–1937) for an Inter-Religious League. Nevertheless, the World Congress of Faiths started in the 1930s, and there was a World Alliance of Religions in the 1950s. The genocide of European Jewry during World War II made it obvious that in spite of modern scientific advances, religious hatred could still be used to justify state-sanctioned murder. The ecumenical movement intensified, and the Roman Catholic Church's Vatican Council II expressed a positive attitude toward Asian religions and the need for dialogue and understanding between Western religions and those of the East.

Key individuals heightened the desire for interreligious dialogue. Mohandas (Mahatma) Gandhi (1869–1948), a devout Hindu who practiced nonviolent opposition to the British rule of India, was deeply drawn to elements of the Christian gospels, especially Jesus' Sermon on the Mount. He said that there would not really be peace in the world until there was peace among the religions. D. T. Suzuki (1870–1966), a Japanese Buddhist, worked for years to introduce Buddhism—particularly Zen—to the West. The faith of the American Christian monk Thomas Merton (1915–1968) was profoundly affected by his developing understanding of Asian religions, especially Buddhism. While on the trip to Asia during which he unexpectedly died, Merton had a transformative religious experience at a Buddhist shrine in Sri Lanka and had warm meetings with the Dalai Lama, the leader of Tibetan Buddhism. The Dalai Lama has advocated East–West dialogue for decades and is one of the few universal voices of compassion and moral vision listened to in both Asia and the West.

Main Topics of the Dialogue

A main purpose of the dialogue has been to find ways for religions collectively to promote peace, justice, and reduction of human suffering. The dialogue has also addressed intellectual and theological topics, from the meaning of the Ultimate/God, the true self, ethical values, and salvation/liberation, to mystical experience and the understanding of the sacred in a secular, scientific age.

While Hinduism's view of the Ultimate has been thought of as incorporating aspects of both polytheism and monotheism, it actually tends more toward monism, or belief in a singular, all-pervading reality called Brahma. Hinduism says that Brahma is really beyond all human categories of thought and is ineffable. The individual self, called atman, is seen as one with Brahma, and human life is the passage beyond ignorance of one's true identity as divine. The reincarnation cycle is based upon karma, or action—a universal moral law based upon one's quality of virtue and insight in seeking liberation from the cycle of birth and death. This cycle ends with the full realization of one's divinity (moksa).

Buddhism developed out of Hinduism and came to see that there is no enduring, separate self (teaching of the no-self, or anatta). Awareness of this, or awakening, frees one from the cycle of suffering that belief in a permanent self makes inevitable. This freedom is called nirvana or the extinguishing of cravings, especially the craving to be an autonomous self. As in Hinduism, religious experience and meditation are vital to spiritual growth, along with compassion and devotion to the sacredness of existence.

Taoism, with its emphasis upon the Way of nature (the Tao), simplicity, harmony with the natural world, nonactive action (wuwei), and spontaneity, has attracted the attention of the West, but has not explicitly participated in interreligious dialogue other than to give new perspectives upon wisdom for living.

The very different views of Hinduism, Buddhism, and Taoism on the one hand and Christianity on the other make for interesting dialogue. Christianity rejects the notion of reincarnation in favor of a theistic interpretation of the Ultimate as a creator God. While being the creative source of human life and the self, God and the human self remain distinct entities. A human self is thought to endure; salvation is the action of God in freeing people to be fully themselves in the divine presence.

More generally, the interreligious dialogue has had to grapple with the difference between the East and South Asian focus on nothingness and emptiness as significant aspects of reality and the Western focus on being and fullness as central. Are the differences real or apparent? Dialogue makes clear which differences cannot be glossed over and where there are commonalities.

Perspectives and Prospects

The Asian-Christian interreligious dialogue has highlighted various attitudes toward religion itself and its claims. Exclusivism holds that one's own religion, or only one religion, is valid and is the path to truth. Inclusivism tends to advocate syncretism—the development of a universal religion shaped by all individual religions—or to claim that one's own religion is expansive enough to assimilate or constructively accept other religious paths. A third perspective is religious pluralism, which maintains the value of other religions without diminishing either the centrality or historical, theological uniqueness of one's own. One respects other religions and seeks to learn from and understand them empathetically.

The centennial of the World's Parliament of Religion was observed in 1993, again in Chicago, to mark the sometimes-dramatic developments in Asian-Christian interreligious dialogue that took place during the twentieth century. As Hinduism, Buddhism, and Taoism gain influence in the West, the West will learn not only other ways of seeing, but new ways to understand itself. And Asian religions can learn from Christianity not only different understandings of the nature of the cosmos and time, but also how to reinterpret themselves in the contemporary world.

Alan Altany

Further Reading

Coward, Harold. (1990) *Hindu-Christian Dialogue: Perspectives and Encounters*. Maryknoll, NY: Orbis.

Kasimow, Harold, and Byron Sherwin, eds. (1999) *John Paul II and Interreligious Dialogue*. Maryknoll, NY: Orbis.

Kornfeld, Jack, et al., eds. (1998) *Buddhism in the West: Spiritual Wisdom for the Twenty-first* Century. Carlsbad, CA: Hay House.

Kung, Hans, and Karl-Josef Kuschel, eds. (1993) *A Global Ethic: The Declaration of the Parliament of the World's Religions*. New York: Continuum.

Kung, Hans, Heinz Bechert, Josef Van Ess, and Heinrich Von Stietencron, eds. (1993) *Christianity and World Religions: Paths of Dialogue with Islam, Hinduism, and Buddhism*. Maryknoll, NY: Orbis.

The Origin Web Network. (1996) "The Dialogue Decalogue." Retrieved 12 November 2001, from: http://www .silcom.com/~origin/sbcr/sbcr265.

Smart, Ninian, and B. Srinivasa Murthy, eds. (1996) *East-West Encounters in Philosophy and Religion*. Long Beach, CA: Long Beach Publications.

Unitarian Universalist Historical Society. (1999) "The World's Parliament of Religions." Retrieved 12 November 2001, from: http://www3.edgenet.net/fcarpenter/ parliam.html.

ASIA–PACIFIC ECONOMIC COOPERATION FORUM

Today, the Asia–Pacific Economic Cooperation (APEC) forum is commonly referred to pejoratively as "four adjectives in search of

Singapore Prime Minister Goh Chok Tong, Thailand Prime Minister Thaksin Shinawatra, and U. S. President George W. Bush at the APEC summit in October 2001 in Shanghai, China. The key issues were terrorism and trade. (REUTERS NEWMEDIA INC./CORBIS)

a noun." Historically, the APEC forum was founded as an informal ministerial meeting of twelve Pacific Rim economies (Australia, Brunei, Canada, Indonesia, Japan, Malaysia, New Zealand, the Philippines, Singapore, South Korea, Thailand, and the United States) meeting in Canberra, Australia, in November 1989. The Australian prime minister Bob Hawke initiated the call to create the framework for the APEC. In light of the increasing pace of regional economic interdependence, the ministers acknowledged a need for more consultations to help strengthen the multilateral trading system, to foster greater opportunities for regional trade and investment, and to identify common economic interests. The ministerial communiqué and the report of the chairman (Gareth Evans, Australian minister for foreign affairs and trade) have provided substantial scope for an ambitious program. Despite significant results in the early meetings of the APEC forum, the prospects for APEC are unclear. Nevertheless, two major developments have completely changed APEC.

One was that the former U.S. president Bill Clinton invited all APEC members to a summit in Seattle, Washington, in 1993 to discuss world economic issues, such as the reduction of trade and investment barriers, economic cooperation and interdependence, and the expansion of the world economy and support for an open international trading system. Since then, the APEC summit meeting has been held yearly. The other major development was economic. At the 1994 meeting in Bogor, Indonesia, APEC set itself the ambitious goal of achieving free and open trade and investment among APEC members by 2010 for developed economies and by 2020 for developing members.

By 2002, APEC membership had grown to twenty-one countries (Australia; Brunei Darussalam; Canada; Chile; People's Republic of China; Hong Kong, China; Indonesia; Japan; Republic of Korea; Malaysia; Mexico; New Zealand; Papua, New Guinea; Peru; Philippines; Russia; Singapore; Chinese Taipei; Thailand; United States; and Vietnam). By the end of the twentieth century, APEC economies had a combined gross domestic product of over $18 trillion, more than half of the total world economy. The APEC Secretariat is located in Singapore and has an official website (www.apecsec.org.sg/body.htm). A number of APEC members have created their own websites, including Canada (www.dfait-maeci.gc.ca/canada-apec), China (www.apec-china.org.cn), New Zealand (www.apec.govt.nz), and the United States (http://usinfo.state.gov/regional/ea/apec/).

Although the APEC summit meeting usually focuses on economic issues, at the 17–18 October 2001 meeting in Shanghai the global political agenda, including antiterrorist activities, was also addressed. Despite the events of 11 September 2001 in the United States, the U.S. president George W. Bush attended this summit. APEC's condemnation of terrorist acts was included in the communiqué of the summit.

APEC members, however, have their disagreements. Prime Minister Mahathir of Malaysia, for example, proposed that an East Asia Economic Caucus (EAEC) made up only of East Asian nations meet. The United States strongly objected to this proposal. Moreover, European countries considered their interests unrepresented by APEC. Competition between the two continents (North America and Western Europe) over Asia has escalated. In March 1996, Europe and East Asia inaugurated the ASEM (Asia–Europe Meeting) in Bangkok, Thailand. Both the APEC and the ASEM represent attempts by the state policy-making elites of East Asia to consolidate the channels of economic and political communication with the other two developed regions of the world.

Unryu Suganuma

Further Reading

Abegglen, James. (1994) *Sea Change: Pacific Asia as the New World Industrial Center*. New York: Free Press.

Aggarwal, Vinod K., and Charles Edward Morrison, eds. (1998) *Asia Pacific Crossroads: Regime Creation and the Future of APEC*. New York: Palgrave.

Asia-Pacific Economic Cooperation (APEC) Secretariat. (2000) *APEC Getting Results for Business*. Singapore: APEC.

Grant, Richard L., Amos A. Jordan, Ernest H. Preeg, and Jusuf Wanandi. (1990) *Asia Pacific Economic Cooperation: The Challenge Ahead*. Washington, DC: Center for Strategic and International Studies.

Higgott, Richard. (1998) "The Pacific and Beyond: APEC, ASEM, and Regional Economic Management." In *Economic Dynamism in the Asia-Pacific: The Growth of Integration and Competitiveness*, edited by Grahame Thompson. London: Routledge.

Lawrence, Robert, Albert Bressand, and Takatoshi Ito. (1996) *A Vision for the World Economy: Openness, Diversity, and Cohesion*. Washington, DC: Brookings Institution.

Ruland, Jurgen, ed. (2002) *Asia-Pacific Economic Cooperation (APEC): The Final Decade*. Richmond, U.K.: Curzon.

ASIATIC SOCIETY OF JAPAN

Among the various learned societies that sprang up in Asia at the end of the nineteenth and throughout the twentieth century, the most active and prestigious has been the Asiatic Society of Japan. The society was established in Yokohama in 1872 and has continued its work despite financial and other difficulties, overcoming even the ordeal of the Pacific War. In 1997, the society's 125th anniversary was celebrated in Tokyo in the presence of four princes of the Japanese imperial family.

The society was founded by a group of learned and dedicated foreigners, mainly British. In the course of time, however, membership expanded to include other foreigners as well as several Japanese. The society is now open to all people who are interested in studying and disseminating Japanese culture in connection with other Asian cultures.

The society has always had two main pillars of activity: monthly lectures by distinguished speakers followed by discussions, and the publication in English of a widely acclaimed academic journal, *Transactions of the Asiatic Society of Japan*.

A council, elected by the members every year, various specialized committees, and the board of editors of *Transactions* are the driving force of the society. A monthly bulletin helps to keep members in Japan and abroad in touch with one another and with the various events and publications.

The names of the society's past presidents read as a kind of who's who of early Western scholars of Japan: Robert Grant Watson, Jane C. Hepburn, William G. Aston, Basil Hall Chamberlain, Sir Ernest Satow, Sir Charles Eliot, George B. Sansom, Dr. Robert Haus van Gulik, and many others.

In the early 2000s, the society faced financial difficulties as donors became scarce; it had to rely on the modest membership fee as the basic source of revenue.

Nevertheless, it has survived and continues its dedication to academic work.

George A. Sioris

Further Reading
Kenrick, Douglas Moore. (1978) "A Century of Western Studies of Japan." In *Transactions of the Asiatic Society of Japan* 3,14: 101–105, 353, 359–361.

ASOKA (d. c. 232 BCE), Maurya emperor. Asoka, or Ashoka (in full, Asokavardhana), third emperor of the Maurya empire (c. 325–180 BCE), ruled in India from about 269 to 232 BCE. He was also the king of Magada. There is much fable about his life, in both Sanskrit and Pali sources, and the Buddhist texts in particular paint his life in glowing images. He was the grandson of the founder of the Mauryan empire, Chandragupta, and only came to the throne himself, it was told in Sri Lankan sources, by first killing off

A worshiper before the Asoka Stupa in Patan, Nepal in 1996. (MACDUFF EVERTON/CORBIS)

ninety-nine of his brothers and half-brothers in war. He had two or more queens and several sons.

His empire covered most of the Indian subcontinent, except the far south, and was marked archaeologically by the creation of several dozen edicts, written in Brahmi script, on rocks and pillars located all over the country, many of which still exist. Two found in Afghanistan are in another local script. These inscriptions give a picture of a caring ruler who wanted to extend the law and the sense of dharma to all his subjects. Although hundreds of thousands had been killed in his early wars with the Kalingas of eastern India, in later life he either became a Buddhist or at least supported their missionary efforts. He did so even to the extent, it is believed, of sending his daughter Sanghamitra and his son Mahendra to introduce Buddhism to Sri Lanka.

Asoka's edicts show much concern for his people, calling for religious tolerance and for respect toward parents, elders, priests, and monks. He established rest houses for travelers and clinics for sick people and animals and had roadways planted with shade trees. He is said to have gone on tours of his realm and to have sent missionaries to foreign lands, even to Syria and Egypt. He made donations not only to Buddhist sects but also to their religious rivals. Asoka is also said to have established the main features of Buddhist pilgrimage by having set up throughout his realm 84,000 stupas (reliquary mounds) in which relics of the Buddha were preserved, and by formulating the basic itinerary of pilgrimage sites.

Paul Hockings

Further Reading
Gokhale, B. G. (1966) *Asoka Maurya*. New York: Twayne.
Strong, John S. (1983) *The Legend of King Asoka: A Study and Translation of the Asokavadana*. Princeton, NJ: Princeton University Press.

ASSAM (2002 est. pop. 27.2 million). With an area of 478,524 square kilometers, Assam is the largest of India's northeastern states and produces 60 percent of India's tea. It is connected with the rest of the country by a narrow submountainous corridor between Bhutan and Bangladesh. Named from the Sanskrit *Asoma* (peerless), Assam offers beauty and a rich legacy of civilization. Home to several different peoples—Austroasiatic, Mongolian, Dravidian, and Aryan—Assam developed a composite culture. The state is dominated by the river Brahamputra, whose lush 700-kilometer valley is sandwiched between the Himalayan foothills to the north and the hills and plateau of Meghalaya to the south.

The early history of Assam is obscure. The *Mahabharata* and the Puranas refer to a great kingdom known as Kamarupa in this region, ruled by a legendary king Narakasura. The first reliable description of the kingdom was that of the Chinese pilgrim Xuanzang, who in 640 attended the court of Bhaskaravarman, an ally of the Gupta monarch Harsha and a patron of Hinduism. Stone and copperplate inscriptions indicate a succession of Hindu dynasties, but any centralized kingship had collapsed into loose confederacies of Hindu rajas by the early thirteenth century. The Ahom kings from Myanmar (Burma) adopted Hinduism and provided increasing power and prosperity, culminating under King Rudra Singh (1696–1714), the renowned military strategist and patron of the *buranji*, or Ahom chronicles, who established an extensive trade with Tibet, repulsed seventeen Mughal invasions, and built the great cities of Nowgong and Rangpur. A Hinduism rejecting the caste system and based on community prayer was spread in monasteries that became centers for dance, music, and manuscript painting. The British eventually drove out the Myanmar invaders and made the area part of British India in 1826.

Following Indian independence in 1947, Assam shrank through cessions to Pakistan and the creation of new states and territories—in 1963, Nagaland; in 1972, Meghalaya; in 1986, Arunachal Pradesh and Mizoram. From the 1960s to the 1990s, Assam was the scene of recurrent riots and violence by minority ethnic groups including the Bodo, Mizo, Nagas, and Tripuri, and by the Assamese against outsiders, such as immigrants from Bangladesh. The United Liberation Front pursues the independence of Assam, and several militant Bodo groups promote a separate state.

C. Roger Davis

Further Reading
Baruah, Sanjib. (1999) *India against Itself: Assam and the Politics of Nationality*. Philadelphia: University of Pennsylvania Press.
Mahanta, Prafulla Kumar. (1986) *The Tussle between the Citizens and Foreigners in Assam*. New Delhi: Vikas.

ASSAMESE Assamese is similar to the Bengali language and is one of the state languages of India. Assamese speakers occupy the present state of Assam, which lies in the middle valley of the Brahmaputra River in northeastern India. Before the Age of Exploration the Assamese were the most easterly-dwelling people who spoke an Indo-European language. The population of the state of Assam totals about 22 million; there are about 15 million Assamese (as of 1991), as well as numerous tribal groups and recent immigrants who speak other languages.

The original Assamese were Ahoms from the Shan states in eastern Burma who migrated from Myanmar/Burma in the thirteenth century, after which they began to rule over the Brahmaputra valley region. "Assam" and "Aham" are variant names for the country. The Ahoms maintained chronicles of the main events that occurred during the reign of each ruler. In 1822 the region came under British control and remained so until 1947.

The majority of Assamese are Hindus, who live in rural settings in multicaste villages. Assamese mostly engage in rice agriculture, although tea is the important crop in the neighboring hills. While polytheistic Hinduism is the dominant religion, there are also egalitarian Hindu sects that are monotheistic and in which membership is by invitation. Here, as in some Protestant churches, people engage in congregational worship, have direct access to scriptural revelation, and believe in salvation through faith and mystical union. Among the Assamese there are also many Muslims and some Buddhists and Christians.

Paul Hockings

Further Reading
Cantlie, Audrey. (1984) *The Assamese*. London: Curzon.

ASSOCIATION OF SOUTH-EAST ASIAN NATIONS
The Association of South-East Asian Nations (ASEAN) was established on 7 August 1967 by Indonesia, Malaysia, the Philippines, Singapore, and Thailand. The organization's goals are spelled out in the ASEAN Declaration, adopted on the same date. ASEAN was formed to promote regional collaboration in Southeast Asia and, in so doing, to contribute to peace, development, and prosperity in the region. The relations between the member states are governed by two fundamental documents adopted in 1976: the Treaty of Amity and Cooperation in Southeast Asia (TAC, also known as the Bali Treaty) and the Declaration of ASEAN Concord. The core element of the structure of formal collaboration in ASEAN is the annual ASEAN Ministerial Meeting, which has been organized by member-states on a rotation basis since the establishment of the Association. As collaboration in ASEAN has expanded, the number of meetings has

considerably increased, and now there are hundreds of meetings each year in various field of cooperation. In 1981, the ASEAN Secretariat was established, and it has assumed a coordinating role.

Formation
ASEAN was established in 1967, but it was not the first attempt to establish a subregional association in Southeast Asia. In 1961, the Association of Southeast Asia (ASA) was established, bringing together what was then Malaya, the Philippines, and Thailand. In 1963, Indonesia, Malaya, and the Philippines established MAPHILINDO (a term formed from the combined first letters of the member nations' names) in an attempt to promote cooperation among the three countries. Cooperation within both ASA and MAPHILINDO was seriously hampered by the conflicts between Malaysia and Indonesia and Malaysia and the Philippines, respectively, over the formation of Malaysia in 1963. The decision to create ASEAN grew from the necessity to manage the relations between the five founding members.

Development
In 1967, ASEAN's expressed goal was to promote social and economic cooperation among the member states of the association. However, it is generally recognized that ASEAN has achieved more in terms of cooperation in the political and security fields than in the economic field. Through a system of informal and formal meetings between leaders, ministers, and senior officials, the ASEAN states have managed to build confidence, familiarity, and understanding of the positions of one another on different issues. ASEAN is renowned for its decision-making process, which requires that all decisions be reached by consensus. Particular emphasis has been put on promoting and achieving regional resilience—based on the internal resilience of each of the member-states—through economic development. This should result in greater political support for the governments and lead to enhanced political stability.

Achieving a high level of interaction, cooperation, and understanding among the original member states of ASEAN was a gradual process influenced by both intra-ASEAN developments and developments in the broader Southeast Asian region. The conflicts in Vietnam, Laos, and Cambodia and the progress of the leftist forces in the early 1970s leading to total victory by 1975, couple with the gradually diminishing U.S. involvement and then total withdrawal, created a new situation in Southeast Asia, bringing the perceived threat of international Communism to the doorstep of

ASEAN members, particularly Thailand. The ASEAN countries responded to these developments by issuing the Kuala Lumpur Declaration on 27 November 1971, which called for the creation of a Zone of Peace, Freedom, and Neutrality (ZOPFAN) in Southeast Asia. The next step came on 24 February 1976 with the signing of the TAC (which had been formulated in response to developments in the region) and the Declaration of ASEAN Concord (which grew from the evolving intra-ASEAN collaboration during the so-called formative years of 1967 to 1976), in connection with the first ASEAN Summit in Bali.

ASEAN has also achieved a high degree of success in its relations with countries outside the association. The strength obtained from acting together as one political force stems from a collective stand on major foreign policy issues. The most obvious example is ASEAN's success in gaining widespread international support for its stand on the Cambodian conflict. ASEAN expressed open condemnation of Vietnam's military intervention in Cambodia, attempted to secure a total withdrawal of Vietnamese troops from that country, and supported Cambodian groups opposing the Vietnam presence. In the post-Cambodian-conflict era, ASEAN has initiated two major initiatives, one leading to the creation of the ASEAN Regional Forum (ARF) and the other to the expansion of membership in ASEAN within the Southeast Asian region.

The ARF grew out of an increased awareness among the ASEAN states that there was a need for a multilateral forum to discuss security issues within the broader Pacific Asian context as a result of the end of the Cold War and indications of a reduction in the U.S. military presence and of its commitment to East and Southeast Asia.

The expansion of membership in ASEAN in the 1990s (Brunei had already joined in 1984) grew out of the rapprochement between ASEAN and the three Indochinese states (Vietnam, Cambodia, and Laos) following the settlement of the Cambodian conflict in 1991 and the ASEAN policy of "constructive engagement" toward Myanmar (Burma). These two processes led to the accession to the Bali Treaty by the four states. This was followed by ASEAN observer status and membership in ARF for the four states. Finally, Vietnam (in 1995), Laos and Myanmar (in 1997), and Cambodia (in 1998) acceded to full membership in ASEAN. The integration of the new members is a challenge to ASEAN and is leading to the gradual emergence of a more heterogeneous association.

The early 1990s also witnessed a strengthening of economic cooperation within ASEAN through in-creased intra-ASEAN trade and investment. In 1992, an agreement was reached on the establishment of an ASEAN Free Trade Area (AFTA) within fifteen years. The member states also signed an agreement on the Common Effective Preferential Tariff, which is the key instrument in the process through which AFTA will be established. Beginning in 1997, the expansion of economic cooperation was considerably slowed down by what came to be called the Asian financial crisis of 1997, which caused a regionwide economic recession. Some ASEAN members have still not recovered from the crisis, which has been a major issue of concern for them.

Challenges

Some observers argue that ASEAN was a success story up to the mid-1990s but that thereafter its image was tarnished by the challenges brought about by its expanding membership, the impact of that expansion on the association's coherence, and the impact of the Asian financial crisis that began in 1997. A more balanced picture is that ASEAN was not such a success story by the mid-1990s and that cooperation within ASEAN has not been weakened to the extent argued by its critics. Nevertheless, ASEAN faces many challenges, both interstate (relations among the member states) and intrastate (problems within the member states).

Ramses Amer

Further Reading
Amer, Ramses. (1999) "Conflict Management and Constructive Engagement in ASEAN's Expansion." *Third World Quarterly*. Special Issue on New Regionalisms, 20, 5 (October): 1031–1048.

Amer, Ramses, and David Hughes. (1999) "The Asian Crisis and Economic Cooperation: Implications for an Expanded ASEAN." In *Southeast Asian-Centred Economies or Economics?* edited by Mason Hoadley. NIAS Report Series, no. 39. Copenhagen, Denmark: Nordic Institute of Asian Studies, 113–136.

Aranal-Sereno, Maria Lourdes, and Joseph Sedfrey S. Santiago, eds. (1997) *The ASEAN: Thirty Years and Beyond.* Quezon City, Philippines: Institute of International Legal Studies, University of the Philippines Law Center.

"Special Issue on ASEAN." (1997) *Asian Journal of Political Science* 5, 1 (June).

ASTANA (1999 pop. 319,300). Astana (Akmolinsk until 1961, Tselinograd from 1961 to 1992, and Aqmola from 1992 to 1998) is the capital of Kazakhstan and is located on the Ishim River in north-central Kazakhstan. It is an important transportation entrepot

The public square in Astana, the capital of Kazakhstan. (LIBA TAYLOR/CORBIS)

on the Trans-Kazakhstan and South Siberian Railways, and is Kazakhstan's sixth-largest industrial and commercial center.

Akmolinsk was founded in 1830 as a Russian military settlement after Russians acquired the land from local Kazakh tribes, and gradually it became an important entrepot for trade between Turkistan and Russia. In 1868 it became a provincial center. After the delimitation of borders between the Russian Federation and the Kazakh Autonomous Republic in 1925, the city became an administrative center of the Aqmola Province of Kazakhstan. In 1929 to 1931 the strategically important railways were built, connecting the city with Petropavlovsk and Karaganda. Akmolinsk's importance was enhanced during the Virgin Land Campaign, as it became a center of Tselinnyi Krai and was renamed Tselinograd. It became an industrial and cultural center, with the population growing from 31,000 in 1939 to 180,000 in 1970 and to 222,000 in 1977. After independence in 1991, the city was renamed Aqmola. In 1994 Kazakhstan's government decided to move the capital from Almaty to Aqmola, and in 1998 it changed the name of the city to Astana. According to various estimates, during the first five years the government invested approximately $2 billion to upgrade infrastructure and to build new government facilities in the city.

Rafis Abazov

Further Reading

Cummings, Sally. (2000) *Kazakhstan: Centre-Periphery Relations.* London: The Royal Institute of International Affairs.

Evrazia. (1998) *Perenos stolitsy Kazakhstana v zerkale pressy i kommentariakh analitikov. Sbornik statei* (The Transfer of the Capital in a Mirror of Mass-Media and Analytical Commentaries). Moscow: Evrazia.

ATATURK (1881–1938), founder of the Republic of Turkey. Kemal Ataturk, the father of modern Turkey, was born in Thessaloniki, modern Greece, the son of a minor government official. His given name was Mustafa; the nickname Kemal (perfection) was given him at school. In 1934 he took the epithet Ataturk (father of Turks).

Ataturk attended the Second Military School in Thessaloniki from 1893 and was a cadet at the Military Academy at Monastir (now Bitola, Former Yugoslav Republic (FYR) of Macedonia) from 1895 to 1899 before graduating from the Staff College, Istanbul, in 1905. Posted in Damascus, Syria, Ataturk supported the Young Turk revolution of 1908 but failed to make an impact as a politician and returned to the military. He saw action in the Turko-Italian War in 1911–1912, when the Dodecanese were ceded to Italy, and the Second Balkan War of 1913, when Turkey lost virtually all of its European territory, including Thessaloniki and Monastir.

Ataturk in his military uniform, c. 1900. (HULTON-DEUTSCH COLLECTION/CORBIS)

Ataturk rose to prominence during World War I, when he defended the Dardanelles (Gallipoli) from a combined Australian–British–New Zealand assault. For this action, he won the honorific Ghazi (Warrior of the Faith).

A general at the close of the war, Ataturk refused to accept the peace terms imposed on the Ottoman sultan and established a rival government, the Grand National Assembly of Turkey, in Ankara in 1920. After driving out an invading Greek force in 1922, Ataturk abolished the sultanate, although a Turkish Republic was not formally declared until October 1923.

In 1923, Ataturk negotiated the Treaty of Lausanne, guaranteeing Turkish integrity inside its present borders, and in 1925 he signed a Treaty of Friendship with the Soviet Union, protecting the nation from Soviet territorial claims on behalf of the Armenians. He was now free to pursue a domestic policy based on six principles, which were enshrined in the Constitution in 1937. These were republicanism, nationalism, secularism, statism, populism, and revolutionism.

Ataturk's aim was to create a European-style secular nation-state. To this end all traces of the past were attacked and expressions of non-Turkish identities suppressed. Ottoman political and religious institutions were abolished and replaced by Western models in law (the Swiss code adopted in 1926), literature (the Latin alphabet introduced in 1928), and dress (European clothing enforced in 1925). In particular, Islam as the basis of traditional Turkish society was attacked, with the abolition of the caliphate, religious courts, and Sufi orders and with the emancipation of women. Secularization in Turkey went further than anywhere outside the USSR. Ataturk's reforms remain the basis of the Turkish state.

Ataturk suffered from kidney disease from 1919. Famed for his love of women, opera, and alcohol, he died of cirrhosis. Described by Yapp as "ruthless, ambitious, ungenerous, intolerant, and given to impulsive rages," he was nevertheless a man of exceptional determination and intellectual abilities, who salvaged modern Turkey from the wreckage of the Ottoman empire.

Will Myer

Further Reading

Shaw, S., and E. Shaw. (1977) *History of the Ottoman Empire and Modern Turkey.* Cambridge, UK: Cambridge University Press.

Yapp, Malcome. (1991) *The Near East since the First World War.* London: Longman.

ATHEISM, OFFICIAL—CHINA Since religion has permeated the fabric of Chinese social life from time immemorial, the rise to power of modern political forces, especially the avowedly atheist Chinese Communist Party (CCP), in 1949 seemed likely to have a profound impact on the state and society. Would the Communist Party state pursue a policy of reckless suppression of religious life, or would it tolerate religion, at least temporarily? Except during the Cultural Revolution (1966–1976), the religious policy of the CCP has been guided by practical considerations rather than by its atheist ideology.

Atheism as a Modern Concept

In the context of this article, atheism will be understood as a concept that rejects any form of religious belief. This definition does not include certain strands of Confucianism and Buddhism that are sometimes labeled as atheist on the grounds that they are not based on the concept of a personal deity. In fact, there is no reason to assume that they are incompatible with other forms of religion, and by and large they did not interfere with sacrifices and other forms of worship. As far as religious policy was concerned, the imperial authorities tried hard to suppress "heterodox" teachings and practices that were regarded as a threat to the state; at the same time, they sought to promote as well as control "orthodox" forms of worship.

Atheism as herein defined is a modern concept based on a strictly secular worldview. It entered China around 1900, along with a number of other ideologies imported from the West. Foremost among these were Social Darwinism, nationalism, and socialism/communism. They were based on a specific notion of human progress and pursued a secular goal (a vigorous nation-state or a classless society) that served as a substitute for religious attitudes. Transmission of these ideas was intimately linked to the emergence of a modern Chinese intelligentsia. Young urban intellectuals who were attracted by the new ideological currents became hostile to any form of Chinese religion, including folk religion, Taoism, Buddhism, Islam, Christianity, and, though it is not a religion in the strict sense of the term, Confucianism, which came under fire for its association with the official cult of the state. Since these intellectuals formed the backbone of revolutionary movements and of the emerging political parties, atheism played an important role in the political transformation of China.

Atheism in the Republican Period

Chinese atheism was first and foremost directed against religion's most "superstitious" form: folk, or popular, religion, which also includes certain elements of Buddhism and Taoism. The Republican Revolution of 1911 witnessed the first large-scale campaign against popular religion, in which many temples and shrines were destroyed. Although the provisional constitution of the newly founded Republic of China guaranteed religious freedom, attempts to weaken the institutions associated with popular religion (temples, religious associations, etc.) continued until about 1915.

The May Fourth Movement of 1919, a pro-Western intellectual movement, gave rise to the next wave of antireligious activity. In addition to the general critique of religion (which was guided by a belief in modern science), two specific targets were singled out: Confucianism, regarded as the main cause of China's conservatism and stagnation, and Christianity, by then regarded as an ally of Western imperialism.

The Guomindang (GMD), which established a national government in 1925, to some extent succeeded the antireligious movements of the 1920s but was not clearly atheist. The GMD did claim the supremacy of its ideology, the "Three Principles of the People," over all forms of religion. However, some of its leading members (including Sun Yat-sen, Chiang Kai-shek, and their families) were Christians, and in the 1930s attempts were made to revive Confucian doctrines. This ambiguity notwithstanding, GMD governments at various levels campaigned against "superstition," though with limited success.

Atheism in the People's Republic of China

The CCP took the Marxist view that religion was the opiate of the masses, but that it would ultimately disappear in the process of transition to a classless society. However, the party dealt with religion within the framework of its united front policy, a strategy designed to incorporate noncommunist social forces into the process of revolution and state building. Within this framework, the party could form alliances with religious people despite its disapproval of religious doctrines.

The religious policy of the CCP was therefore guided by practical considerations rather than by a narrow ideological approach. Although the party was clearly atheist, the state that it monopolized was not. This is reflected in constitutional law, which binds the state organs, though not the party. The constitution of 1954 granted the citizens "freedom of religious belief" without being very specific about what this exactly meant. The emphasis on belief rather than religious practice gave state and party the opportunity to suppress popular religion. Institutional religions were tolerated but brought under the supervision of the state. For that purpose, a number of so-called patriotic reli-

CONSTITUTION OF THE PEOPLE'S REPUBLIC OF CHINA OF 1982

Article 36
Citizens of the People's Republic of China enjoy freedom of religious belief.

No state organ, public organization or individual may compel citizens to believe in, or not to believe in, any religion; nor may they discriminate against citizens who believe in, or do not believe in, any religion.

The state protects normal religious activities. No one may make use of religion to engage in activities that disrupt public order, impair the health of citizens or interfere with the educational system of the state.

Religious bodies and religious affairs are not subject to any foreign domination.

Source: Kenneth Lieberthal. (1995) *Governing China. From Revolution through Reform.* New York: Norton, 363.

gious associations were set up to represent the five officially recognized religions: Buddhism, Taoism, Islam, Catholicism, and Protestantism (the latter two being regarded as separate religions rather than as different branches of the same religion). The Bureau of Religious Affairs, founded in 1954, served as a link between the state and the patriotic religious associations but was also to guide and control the latter. In spite of the constitutional guarantees, all religious organizations were under heavy pressure from the authorities. This was especially true of those religions suspected of foreign domination, particularly the two Christian ones, even though all Western missionaries had been expelled from China during the Korean War (1950–1953).

During the Cultural Revolution, all religions suffered from persecution and destruction. Leaders and activists were determined to eradicate religion, which was viewed as part of the "Four Olds" (old culture, old thinking, old habits, and old customs) that were to be destroyed. At the same time, constitutional law moved into the direction of state atheism. The constitution of 1975 declared that citizens enjoyed "freedom to believe in religion and freedom not to believe in religion and to propagate atheism." In other words, atheist propaganda was constitutional, while religious propaganda was not.

In the course of the policy of opening and reform initiated in 1978, the CCP has reassessed its religious policy. Although the party remains convinced that religion will eventually disappear as the result of the transition from socialism to communism and hence forbids its members to have any religious affiliation, it acknowledges that religion will continue to exist for some time. The Constitution of 1982, therefore, not only confirms the right to freedom of religious belief, but also establishes a framework for religious practice. The state protects "normal" religious activities, but it is unconstitutional to use religion to disrupt public order. Of course this provision leaves ample room for the authorities to decide which religious activities are "normal" and which are unlawful. The harsh treatment of Protestant "house churches" and the persecution of Falun Gong (a social movement with Taoist and Buddhist overtones) and its adherents, for example, must be viewed as attempts to maintain control over religious affairs and to suppress religious groups regarded as a threat to Communist rule.

Historical Review

Ever since Western secular ideologies found their way to China around 1900, atheism has had an enormous impact on the religious policy of the Chinese state. However, although the political elites that ruled twentieth-century China were frequently influenced by atheism, they have rarely tried to implement a thoroughly atheist policy. They took measures to combat superstition in the form of popular religion, but for the most part did not attempt to eliminate religion in general. Rather, they sought to control religious activities by officially recognizing a number of religious organizations. This is true of the most explicitly atheist political party, the CCP. The Communists have tried to incorporate the major institutionalized religions into the state (the turmoil of the Cultural Revolution being the exception rather than the rule). In the 1980s and 1990s, not only the officially recognized religions, but even popular religion has experienced an astonishing revival, by and large tolerated by the authorities.

It is true that the Chinese state still has sufficient power to crack down on religious groups charged with threatening public order. If in the future it will tighten or loosen its grip on religion remains yet to be seen. That it will take steps to actively promote atheism, by force, if necessary, is far from likely.

Thoralf Klein

Further Reading

Ching, Julia. (1990) *Probing China's Soul. Religion, Politics, and Protest in the People's Republic.* San Francisco: Harper & Row.

Cohen, Myron. (1992) "Religion in a State Setting: China." In *Asia: Case Studies in the Social Sciences. A Guide for Teaching,* edited by Myron Cohen. Armonk, NY: M. E. Sharpe, 17–31.

Duara, Prasenjit. (1991) "Knowledge and Power in the Discourse of Modernity: The Campaigns against Popular Religion in Early Twentieth-Century China." *Journal of Asian Studies* 50, 1: 67–83.

He Guanghu. (1998) "Religion and Hope—A Perspective from Today's China." *Zeitschrift fuer Missionswissenschaft und Religionswissenschaft* 82, 4: 245–254.

Luo Zhufeng, ed. (1991) *Religion under Socialism in China.* Armonk, NY: M.E. Sharpe.

Macinnis, Donald, ed. (1989) *Religion in China Today: Policy and Practice.* Maryknoll, NY: Orbis.

Pas, Julian F., ed. (1989) *The Turning of the Tide: Religion in China Today.* Hong Kong: Hong Kong Branch, Royal Asiatic Society/Oxford University Press.

ATSUTA SHRINE Located in Nagoya, Japan (in Aichi Prefecture), Atsuta Jingu (Atsuta Shrine) is one of the fifteen prestigious shrines entitled to receive visits from imperial messengers at festivals. It purportedly enshrines Kusanagi no Tsurugi (Grass-Mowing Sword), one of the three imperial regalia. This sword is said to have been removed from the tail of a serpent by Amaterasu's brother (Susanoo no Mikoto) and dedicated to his sister as a sign of submission to her rule. The shrine enshrines Atsuta no kami, Amaterasu, Susanoo no Mikoto, and Yamatotakeru, the possessor of the sword who died in the area.

Situated on 200,000 square meters of land, with groves of thousand-year-old camphor trees, the shrine was originally built in the Taisha style, as was the Izumo Shrine, with a slightly concave thatched roof and steep wooden steps at the entrance. It was rebuilt in 1893 and again in 1935 in the Shinmei style, long in frontage and short in depth, with logs placed at intervals across the ridgepole. Partly damaged during World War II, it was repaired in 1955 and now is popular for first visits at the New Year.

James M. Vardaman, Jr.

Further Reading

Bocking, Brian. (1995) *A Popular Dictionary of Shinto.* Surrey, U.K.: Curzon.

Holtom, D. C. (1965) *The National Faith of Japan: A Study in Modern Shinto.* New York: Paragon.

Picken, Stuart D. B. (1994) *Essentials of Shinto: An Analytical Guide to Principal Teachings.* Westport, CT: Greenwood.

AUEZOV, MUKHTAR

AUEZOV, MUKHTAR (1897–1961), Kazakh writer, poet, dramatist, social activist, scholar. Born in 1897 in eastern Kazakhstan, Mukhtar Auezov received his early education at the local Islamic school. He graduated from the Russian Teachers' Seminary in Semipalatinsk in 1908. While completing his studies he became active in the Kazakh political movement Alash Orda (The Horde of Alash). Alash Orda was a Kazakh political party that proclaimed independence during the Russian Civil War. It fought against the Bolsheviks; however, in 1920 it was forced to negotiate, and eventually surrendered and disbanded. Most members joined the Bolsheviks, but were purged from the Communist Party in the 1920s for "nationalist tendencies." Auezov did not fight, but was politically active.

After the Russian Civil War, Auezov attended the Institute of Language and Material Culture at Leningrad University. He continued his education at the Central Asian State University in Tashkent, receiving his degree in Oriental languages. His literary career began in 1918 with the publication of the drama *Baibishe Toqal* (Respectable Second Wife). This work and others contain elements of Kazakh folklore and traditional themes. During the purges of the 1930s, Auezov avoided arrest by publicly admitting his mistakes and "nationalist tendencies." He continued to write, and in 1939 he published the serialized version of his greatest work, a two-part fictional biographical work of the well-known Kazakh poet Abai Kunanbayev, *Abai zholy* (The Path of Abai), which was published in Russian in 1958. During his life he received numerous honors from the Soviet government, including the Order of Lenin. He died in 1961.

Steven Sabol

Further Reading
Auezov, Mukhtar. (1989) *Abai zholy* (The Path of Abai). Almaty, Kazakhstan: Zhazushy.

———. (1960) *Put' Abai* (The Path of Abai). Almaty, Kazakhstan: Kazakhskoe Gosudarstvennoe Izdatel'stvo.

Kumisbaev, Otegen. (1997) *Mukhtar Auezov zhane adebiet alemi* (Mukhtar Auezov and the Literary World). Almaty, Kazakhstan: Kazak University.

Taizhanov, Altai. (1997) *Mirovozzrenie Mukhtara Auezova* (The Worldview of Mukhtar Auezov). Almaty, Kazakhstan: Gylym.

AUGUST REVOLUTION

AUGUST REVOLUTION In Vietnamese history, the August Revolution was the proclamation of a sovereign Vietnamese government in August 1945. The Japanese occupied Vietnam during World War II and allowed the French, who were the colonial power in Indochina (present-day Vietnam, Laos, and Cambodia), to continue to administer the region. In May 1941, at Pac Bo in northern Vietnam, the Vietnamese Communists, led by Ho Chi Minh (1890–1969), formed a national front organization, the League for Independence of Vietnam, to fight against both the French and the Japanese. The League, better known by its Vietnamese abbreviated name, the Viet Minh, sought to enlist any Vietnamese citizen who would fight for national liberation from the French and Japanese.

When Japan surrendered at the end of World War II in the wake of Allied victory, Ho stepped in on 16 August 1945 and proclaimed himself president of the provisional government of a "free Vietnam." The Allies had other plans: they had agreed that Britain would occupy the southern part of Vietnam and the Nationalist Chinese would occupy the northern portion of the country. Before the Chinese troops arrived, the Viet Minh marched in and seized power in Hanoi on 19 August. The emperor of Vietnam, Bao Dai (1913–1997), complied with Ho's demands and abdicated and left for exile in France. On 24 August in Saigon (present-day Ho Chi Minh City), Tran Van Giau declared insurrection underway in the south. On 27 August Ho convened his first cabinet meeting in Hanoi, at which it was agreed that 2 September would be set as National Independence Day. On that day Ho publicly announced the formation of the Provisional Government of the Democratic Republic of Vietnam (DRV) with its capitol at Hanoi. In subsequent negotiations with the French, who were allowed to reoccupy Vietnam, Ho agreed to the return of 25,000 French colonial troops in the north for a five-year period rather than face occupation by the Nationalist Chinese. Ho placated his disgruntled comrades with reassurances that colonialism was dying and that the

HO CHI MINH ON FOREIGN DOMINANCE

"He [Ho Chi Minh] bluntly stated, 'I prefer to sniff French shit for five years than eat Chinese shit the rest of my life.'"

Source: Stanley Karnow. (1991) *Vietnam: A History*. New York: Viking, 169.

French would have a difficult time reestablishing permanent rule, and reminded them that the Chinese had occupied Vietnam in the past for over a thousand years and were the greater threat. The DRV and the French soon clashed over administrative and military issues after the French returned to Vietnam, resulting in the eruption of the First Indochinese War.

Richard B. Verrone

See also: **Franco-Viet Minh War; Ho Chi Minh**

Further Reading
Karnow, Stanley. (1991) *Vietnam: A History*. New York: Viking.

Marr, David. (1981) *Vietnamese Tradition on Trial, 1920–1945*. Berkeley and Los Angeles: University of California Press.

———. (1996) *Vietnam, 1945: The Quest for Power*. Berkeley and Los Angeles: University of California Press.

Patti, Archimedes L. A. (1980) *Why Vietnam? Prelude to America's Albatross*. Berkeley and Los Angeles: University of California Press.

AUM SHINRIKYO SCANDAL   In March 1995, a nerve gas attack by devotees of the Japanese religion Aum Shinrikyo killed twelve and injured thousands of commuters on the Tokyo subway. Police investigations subsequently found that besides this attack, Aum had engaged in criminal activities since the 1980s, including a nerve gas attack in the town of Matsumoto in June 1994, murders of opponents and dissident members, and attempts to manufacture biological and chemical weapons.

Led by its founder, Asahara Shoko, a charismatic leader who claimed to possess psychic powers, Aum was a millennial movement that believed the world was evil; only through ascetic practice could one escape its negative influences and attain salvation. Asahara preached that catastrophe would engulf the world at the end of the twentieth century, resulting in a war between the forces of good and evil in which he and his disciples would lead the forces of good and crush evil materialism. This message, along with Aum's promises of enhanced spiritual powers, attracted ten thousand followers, the majority of whom were young, well educated, and idealistic. Around eleven hundred followers renounced the world and severed all ties with their families to live at Aum's communes.

Aum's zealous followers failed to persuade the wider public of the validity of their message of imminent catastrophe, and this failure, coupled with strong criticism from opponents, including parents of members, made the organization increasingly introverted and hostile to the outside world. It used violence against members suspected of lacking faith, attacked critics, and confronted local authorities that impeded the development of its communes. Asahara's teachings became more extreme, emphasizing that Aum alone taught the truth, which had to be defended at all costs; those who opposed this truth deserved to die and go to hell. Such doctrines eventually legitimated the murder of opponents, while the belief in the imminence of a final war, coupled with Asahara's paranoia in which he believed the world was conspiring to persecute and destroy his movement, fueled an escalating cycle of violence.

Aum attempted to establish a political party and campaigned in elections in 1990, but lost. After this, the group abandoned all hope of influencing the world, which it condemned as unworthy of salvation, and began to manufacture biological and chemical weapons for use in the inevitable final war that Asahara prophesied. By March 1995, police raids were planned against the movement. Learning of these, Asahara ordered a preemptive strike on the Tokyo subway to stall the police and strike a blow against the materialist society he hated.

Immediately afterward, the police moved on Aum, uncovering evidence of its extensive criminality. Nearly two hundred Aum devotees were charged with serious offenses, including murder. Some were imprisoned or sentenced to death, while others, including Asahara, still await trial. Punitive laws have been enacted against the organization, and the majority of followers have renounced their faith. Around one thousand devotees continue to proclaim their faith in Asahara and support Aum.

The Aum affair provoked debates in Japan about the nature of Japanese society. While public interpretations portrayed Asahara as a crazed manipulator who beguiled naive and idealistic people into sharing his paranoid visions, they also recognized that his criticisms of society had a particular resonance for many people. Thus, the Aum affair was seen not only as a product and expression of the problems and failures of Japanese society, but also as an expression of the need for reform.

Ian Reader

Further Reading
Kisala, Robert J., and Mark R. Mullins, eds. *Religion and Social Crisis in Japan: Understanding Japanese Society through the Aum Affair*. Basingstoke, U.K., and New York: Palgrave and St. Martin's.

Reader, Ian. (2000) *Religious Violence in Contemporary Ja-pan: The Case of Aum Shinrikyo.* Richmond, U.K., and Honolulu, HI: Curzon and University of Hawaii Press.

AUNG SAN (1915–1947), Burmese resistance leader. Aung San is popularly remembered in Burma as principal leader of the resistance against foreign occupation, as hero-martyr in the struggle for independence, and as unifier of modern Burma.

Educated at a monastic school and a national high school, he joined Rangoon University in 1932. By 1935, after being elected to the Students' Union executive committee and becoming editor of the union magazine, he was expelled from the university for not revealing the name of a contributor. He joined U Nu, who had also been dismissed, in leading the 1936 university strike. The same year, after getting his B.A., he left the university and joined the nationalist Thakin movement. He started a Marxist study group, then with Ba Maw, he cofounded the Freedom Bloc and became its general secretary, leading resistance against the British in 1939. He approached the Japanese and, as lead member of the Thirty Comrades trained in Japan, then became founder and first commander of the Burma Independence Army that spearheaded the Japanese invasion of Burma in 1941. Unhappy with Japanese intentions toward Burma, he cofounded the Anti-Fascist Peoples' Freedom League (AFPFL) in 1943 to resist the Japanese.

Aung San negotiated the 27 January 1947 Attlee–Aung San Agreement that was to secure Burma its national independence in 1948. However, he was assassinated on 13 July 1947 along with six other colleagues while in charge of the Constituent Assembly engaged in writing a constitution for independent Burma. His functions in the AFPFL were taken over by U Nu. As a hero and martyr, to whom postindependence civilian politicians and army chiefs alike look back for inspiration, Aung San provided the basis for U Nu's political path. His speeches and slogans also influenced the declared ideology of the Burma Socialist Programme Party after the 1962 coup. However, after 1988 his political legacy became problematic under the State Law and Restoration Council–State Peace and Development Council regimes, when Aung San Suu Kyi challenged military control over the country in the name of her father, claiming that he had stood for democracy and not for military control. Aung San continues to be an inspiration to generations of Burmese students and the Burmese in general.

Gustaaf Houtman

Further Reading
Aung San Suu Kyi. (1991) *Aung San of Burma : A Biographical Portrait.* 2d ed. Edinburgh: Kiscadale.
Aung San, U, and Silverstein, Josef. (1972) *The Political Legacy of Aung San.* Ithaca, NY: Southeast Asia Program, Cornell University.
Kin Oung. (1993) *Who Killed Aung San?* 1st ed. Bangkok, Thailand: White Lotus.
Maung Maung, U. (1962) *Aung San of Burma.* The Hague, Netherlands: Published for Yale University, Southeast Asia Studies by M. Nijhoff.
———. (1962) *A Trial in Burma: The Assassination of Aung San.* The Hague, Netherlands: M. Nijhoff.
Naw, Angeline. (1988) "Aung San and the Struggle for the Independence of Burma." Ph.D. diss. University of Hawaii.
Sutton, Walter D. (1948) "U Aung San of Burma." *South Atlantic Quarterly* 47, 1 (January): 1–16.

AUNG SAN SUU KYI (b. 1945), Burmese political leader and activist. Daughter of national hero and martyr Aung San (1915–1947), who was assassinated when she was only two years old, Aung San Suu Kyi was brought up in Myanmar (then Burma) until 1960, when her mother, Daw Khin Kyi, was appointed ambassador to India. In 1964 she started a B.A. degree in philosophy, politics, and economics at St. Hughes College, Oxford. After completion, she assisted Hugh Tinker in his research on Burma at the School of

Aung San Suu Kyi speaking at a press conference in Yangon in September 1996. (STEPHEN G. DONALDSON PHOTOGRAPHY)

Oriental and African Studies in London and then moved in 1969 to New York, where she worked at the United Nations Secretariat. In 1972 she married Michael Aris, joining him in Bhutan, where she worked for two years as research officer on United Nations affairs for the Bhutan foreign affairs ministry. After her return to England, she gave birth to two sons, Alexander, in 1973, and Kim, in 1977. She briefly catalogued Burmese books in the Bodleian Library at the University of Oxford and then joined Aris at the Advanced Research Institute in Simla, northern India. She took up a one-year visiting fellowship in Kyoto in 1985–1986 to research the Japanese dimension of her father's biography, after which she returned to Simla on a fellowship. Shortly after returning to Oxford in 1987, she enrolled at the School of Oriental and African Studies for an advanced degree.

Aung San Suu Kyi has been preoccupied with Myanmar throughout her life in terms of research interests and through family and social contacts. It was her mother's stroke in March 1988 that took Aung San Suu Kyi on a visit to Myanmar from which she did not return, not even for her husband's funeral in March 1999. In the wake of Ne Win's resignation, the pent-up desire for change within the country after three decades of military control thrust her into the role of a political leader bringing fresh ideas to a hitherto closed country. Her speech at the Shwedagon

Pagoda on 26 August 1988 marked her public acceptance in Myanmar as the most promising national leader, much as her father's Shwedagon speeches had done in the 1940s. She subsequently cofounded the National League for Democracy, which won the May 1990 elections by a landslide majority and for which her popularity had been instrumental. The regime ignored the election outcome and she and her party members were subject to harassment and house arrest. Aung San Suu Kyi was kept under house arrest by the military-appointed State Law and Order Restoration Council (SLORC) between 1989 and 1995 and has been prevented from traveling outside Yangon (Rangoon) for most of the time after that. She was awarded the Nobel Peace Prize in 1991 and continues to advocate nonviolence.

In September 2000, Aung San Suu Kyi and other leaders of the National League for Democracy were confined to their homes by military authorities. On 6 May 2002, the Myanmar government freed Aung San Suu Kyi from house arrest. The action was seen by democracy advocates in Myanmar and outside observers as evidence that Myanmar's repressive regime might be entering a new era, giving rise to expectations that at least some political prisoners might be freed and that restrictions on the press may be lifted.

Gustaaf Houtman

The Bibi-ka-Maqbara, modeled on the Taj Mahal and built as the mausoleom for Rabia Durtrani, the wife of Aurangzeb. (HULTON-DEUTSCH COLLECTION/CORBIS)

Further Reading

Aung San Suu Kyi. (1998) "Heavenly Abodes and Human Development." Eleventh Pope Paul VI Memorial Lecture (delivered by Michael Aris on 3 November 1997 at the Royal Institution of Great Britain, London). *Bangkok Post* (4 January).

———. (1997) *Letters from Burma*. London: Penguin.

Aung San Suu Kyi, Alan Clements, U Kyi Maung, and U Tin U. (1997) *The Voice of Hope: Conversations with Alan Clements with Contributions by U Kyi Maung and U Tin U.* London: Penguin.

Aung San Suu Kyi, and Michael Aris, eds. (1991) *Freedom from Fear and Other Writings*. New York: Viking.

Houtman, Gustaaf. (1999) *Mental Culture in Burmese Crisis Politics: Aung San Suu Kyi and the National League for Democracy*. Tokyo: University of Tokyo Foreign Studies Institute.

Victor, Barbara. (1998) *The Lady: Aung San Suu Kyi, Nobel Laureate and Burma's Prisoner*. Winchester, MA: Faber & Faber.

AURANGABAD (2001 pop. 828,000). Named after the Mughal emperor Aurangzeb (1659–1707), the Indian city of Aurangabad served as a vice regal capital of the Mughal empire (1526–1857) in the Deccan region of South India. Prior to the advent of the Mughals, it was known as Khadki ("rocky place") and later renamed Fateh Nagar. It is located in the Marathwada region of the state of Maharashtra. Modern Aurangabad is an active city and a noted tourist center, well connected with the state capital, Mumbai (Bombay), and the city of Pune.

The attractions in Aurangabad include the Bibi-ka-Maqbara and the Paani-chakki. The former is a tomb built by Aurangzeb's son in 1679 in memory of his mother, Rabia. The architect Ata Ullah modeled it on the Taj Mahal, but it is hardly comparable to the architectural splendor of the original. It is, however, the only example of Mughal architecture in the Deccan. The Paani-chakki (water mill) is used for grinding flour for the residents of a *madrasah* (seminary) built by a Sufi saint, Baba Shah Muzzafar, in 1624.

Aurangabad is famous for the production of *himroo*, a typical fabric of the region, which has an intricate pattern woven in cotton and silk and is used for drapery, tapestry, and other items.

Sanjukta Das Gupta

Further Reading

Berkson, Carmel. (1986) *The Caves at Aurangabad: Early Buddhist Tantric Art in India*. New York: Mapin.

Michell, George, and Philip Davies. (1989) "Aurangabad." In *Penguin Guide to the Monuments of India*. New York: Viking, 347–348, 420–423.

AURANGZEB (1618–1707), Mughal emperor. Aurangzeb was an unscrupulous seventeenth-century Indian prince who, as the third son of the Mughal emperor Shah Jahan (1592–1666), came to power by imprisoning his father and defeating and killing his brothers—including the heir apparent, Dara Shikoh.

Having spent many years in the Deccan, he became obsessed with extending the Mughal empire (1526–1857) southward. But in so doing, he overextended the military and political resources of the Mughal state. His long absences from the capital of Delhi encouraged internecine conflict and proved politically destabilizing. He founded a new city, Aurangabad, but overall these campaigns only served to undermine Mughal authority and deplete the royal coffers without providing long-lasting gains of territory or prestige. His other major nemesis was the Maratha kingdom in western India, where the Hindu

A portrait of Aurangzeb by Pierre Duflos in 1780. (STAPLETON COLLECTION/CORBIS)

king Shivaji successfully resisted subjugation through a sustained guerrilla campaign.

Though a cultivated and learned man, Aurangzeb's fanatical devotion to the Sunni Muslim faith led him to make political decisions based on religious prejudice. He reimposed the *jaziya*, or poll tax, on non-Muslims, enforced a strict orthodox Muslim political culture, sanctioned the destruction of Hindu and Sikh religious shrines and the erection of mosques instead, removed Hindus from key administrative posts, and alienated substantial segments of the population. He is generally recognized as the most intolerant of all the Mughal emperors.

Chandrika Kaul

Further Reading
Lal, Muni. (1988) *Aurangzeb.* New Delhi, India: Vikas.
Richards, John F. (1993) *The Mughal Empire.* Cambridge, U.K.: Cambridge University Press.

AUSTRALIA–ASIA RELATIONS   It is often said that culture and geography contradict each other with respect to Australia's place in the Asian region. A result of European, primarily British, settlement just to the south of the Asian landmass, the relationships between Australia and Asia are bound to be complex. The situation is also complicated by the variety of Asian countries to Australia's north, ranging from some of the poorest nations in the world to some of the richest, from Christian to Buddhist to Hindu, and from reasonably democratic to totalitarian. It is little wonder that there have been, and continue to be, frictions between Australia and Asia.

These relationships, however, have undergone dramatic changes in the latter half of the twentieth century. From being a country dominated by Britain and dealing with multiple European colonies within Asia, Australia—and its relationship to Asia—has matured significantly, with successive Australian governments having to come to terms with many newly independent Asian countries. Today the connections between Australia and Asia, while still often difficult, are in most cases steadily becoming more cohesive and durable.

Early Connections
When Europeans first settled in Australia some two hundred years ago, it was primarily for the purpose of ridding England of unwanted convicts. The goal was to move them as far away from England as possible, and Australia seemed an apt choice. Being located on the southern fringe of Asia, however, left the descen-

dants of the new arrivals with the long-term challenge of dealing with neighbors of very different cultural backgrounds.

In the early days, there was relatively little interaction with Asia. The original inhabitants of Australia were the aborigines. The groups of aborigines who lived in the northern parts of the country had, for hundreds of years, carried out low-level trade with the region that is now eastern Indonesia. Beyond some limited trade with the European colonies of Asia, Australia remained in relative isolation.

The gold rushes of the mid-1800s began to more clearly define the relationship between Australia and Asia. Along with prospectors from around the world came significant numbers of Chinese. They were both fleeing the poverty of their homeland and being attracted, like other newcomers, by prospects of striking it rich. Problems soon followed. The key consideration seems to have been one of competition. The Chinese were seen to be a threat by virtue of their hard work and ambition. This was complicated by cultural characteristics that were not shared by the dominant European inhabitants.

Competition between Asians and the European settlers was complicated by the question of labor. After the gold rushes had subsided, the economy in what is now Australia grew by fits and starts. Particularly when there were recessions, the frictions came to the fore. Australian workers resented being placed in competition with low-cost Asian labor, primarily from China, Java, and the Pacific Islands. This economic problem was exacerbated by intolerance and racism. This was a time when social Darwinism was on the ascent, and European treatment of nonwhite settlers as well as aborigines was, on the whole, deplorable. Racism was a broadly accepted attitude of the day. Indeed, one of the first acts of the new government of Australia in 1901 was the Immigration Restriction Act, which sought to close the country to nonwhite, particularly Asian, immigration.

At the same time, Asia offered alluring opportunities for trade. In the late 1800s and early 1900s, there were Australian trade commissioners stationed in Asia who spoke eloquently about the possible markets for Australian products, particularly wool. On the whole, however, these voices were rare, and Australia's economic, political, and social systems remained closely intertwined with those of Britain.

World War II and Its Aftermath
The event that dramatically changed Asia-Australia relations was World War II. Until that time, Aus-

tralians had rested, perhaps complacently, under the protection of the United Kingdom. The Japanese invasion of Southeast Asia, delivering the war right to Australia's doorstep (including repeated bombings of Darwin), brought home to Australians their vulnerability. They were a small, mostly white, relatively rich country sitting beside countries that were populous, nonwhite, and mostly poor. The image of the yellow peril took hold of the Australian imagination and was reinforced by the menace of Communism in the postwar period. Poverty and instability in much of Asia kept many Australians in fear of Asia.

This fear drove Australian governments to undertake a massive immigration program. "Populate or perish" was the slogan of the time, with migrants needed both for protection of Australian soil as well as labor to build up an industrial economy. Australian immigration officials went to Britain on a recruiting drive. Unfortunately for their goals, insufficient numbers of English people were interested in migrating to Australia, and the search area had to be expanded. Italy and Greece were subsequently targeted, and massive numbers of people from those countries arrived in Australia.

The new immigrants had a profound effect on Australian society, transforming it from an essentially English colonial backwater to a more cosmopolitan, multicultural society. At the same time, through the 1950s and 1960s, the dominant European powers gave up most of their colonial possessions, and attitudes of acceptance and tolerance toward Asians began to take root. The United States and Canada dismantled their restrictive immigration acts, and Australia was forced to follow suit, though belatedly. It was not until 1973 that the Immigration Restriction Act was finally repealed, making possible a rapid rise in immigration from Asia.

The postwar period was also a time of positive relationship-building in other areas. The Colombo Plan of 1950, an initiative of Australia that was carried out in partnership with half a dozen other former British colonies, brought students from the developing countries of Asia to Australian universities. While there was obvious self-interest in raising the standard of living in the poorer countries of Southeast Asia (especially with Communism taking hold), it also brought Australians into direct contact with Asians, helping to reduce cultural barriers and paving the way for changes in the immigration system.

A more common Australian response in the 1950s and 1960s was continued fear of Asia. Although Australia sent troops to the Korean War and was involved in a low-level war (entitled Confrontation) with Indonesia in the early 1960s, the best-known response

KEY EVENTS IN AUSTRALIA–ASIA RELATIONS

1800s In mid-century, Chinese immigrate to Australia to participate in gold rushes.

1901 Australia enacts the Immigration Restriction Act, which seeks to close the country to nonwhite, particularly Asian, immigration.

1940–1945 During World War II a strong fear of Asia emerges in Australia.

1950 The Colombo Plan brings students from the developing countries of Asia to Australian universities.

1960s Australia and Japan become trade partners and Japan becomes a major market for Australian raw materials.

1965 Australia sends troops to Vietnam as part of a strategy to keep Asian wars in Asia, not in Australia.

1973 The Immigration Restriction Act is repealed, making possible a rapid rise in immigration from Asia.

1989 Australia joins the Asia–Pacific Economic Cooperation grouping to ensure its continued access to Asian and North American markets.

1990s Immigrants from Asia account for 50 percent of all immigrants to Australia.

1999 Australian troops are stationed in East Timor to protect its independence from Indonesia.

was the decision in 1965 to send Australian troops to Vietnam. This was a period of what the Australian military termed "forward defense," with the idea being to fight wars in Asia before they could spill over to the Australian mainland. Australian troops were conscripted, and the reaction in Australia followed the American pattern—general acceptance followed by disillusionment and then widespread antiwar demonstrations as the conflict continued.

Economic Relationships

One could argue that Australian integration with Asia from the 1960s to the present has been driven by economic imperatives. Australia's economy then, as now, was dominated by primary production—agricultural products and mineral resources. The main markets for these materials were the rapidly growing Asian economies. Especially important here was the beginning of the Common Market in Europe. When the British joined this organization, with its system of preferential tariffs for European trade, Australia was forced to look elsewhere to find markets for its products. Japan, which experienced rapid economic growth starting in the 1950s and which lacked raw materials, was a logical partner. Indeed, the first trade agreement was made with Japan in the late 1950s, and Japan has been, for some years, Australia's largest market.

Trade with Japan exemplifies the complexities of Australia's engagement with Asia: cross-cultural difficulties and wariness on the one hand and economic need on the other. Of all Asian countries, antagonism toward Japan runs the deepest in Australia. This was a direct result of Japanese aggression in World War II, particularly its treatment of Australian prisoners of war (POWs). Many Australian soldiers were trapped in Southeast Asia, especially Singapore, with the rapid advance of Japanese troops down the Malay peninsula in late 1941. The maltreatment and deaths of Australian POWs in Changi prison in Singapore and while helping to build the Thai-Burma Railway (immortalized in the film *Bridge over the River Kwai)* continue to create anti-Japanese sentiment in Australia, particularly among the older generation.

Economic imperatives have taken precedence in the Australia–Japan relationship, however, and in the decades since the war the trade connection has become important to both countries. Japan is one of the largest investors in Australia, particularly in mineral-extraction industries, automobile manufacturing, and tourism, and Japan is Australia's largest trading partner (20 percent of exports and 13 percent of imports in 2000).

The relationship has not been an easy one, however. In addition to lingering wartime hostility, there has been the aggressive nature of Japanese trade and investment. Japanese companies, like other powerful multinational corporations, seek the best return for their shareholders. They are tough negotiators and play the world market for the best prices. Coal has been a particular point of contention here. Japanese companies will put, for example, Canadian coal companies in competition with those in Australia to secure the best export price. The result is charges of unfair trade practices from both Canada and Australia, though from the Japanese side this is simply good business practice.

Investment is a second area of friction. Japanese companies invest in the areas in which there is a demand in Japan, hence their interest in coal, pulp and paper products, and tourism. The response in Australia is that Australia has become a combination of Japan's quarry and playground. Australians complain that if Japanese tourists fly to Australia on Japanese airlines, stay in Japanese hotels, and visit Japanese-owned tourist facilities, then Australian companies are

not gaining substantially in this area of services trade. The charge on the Australian side is vertical integration in the tourism industry. Japanese involvement in this sector was particularly evident in the late 1980s when, in the wake of the strengthening of the Japanese currency, massive investments were made in Australian real estate in tourist areas. Those Australians who were selling land and buildings benefited, while Australians seeking real estate were priced out of the market by the inflated prices that the land speculation generated. On the other hand, the Japanese became the most numerous tourists in Australia (nearly three-quarters of a million visitors annually in 2000) and the biggest spenders on a daily basis, inevitably resulting in positive economic benefits for Australia in spite of Japanese investment in this area.

A fundamental problem in Asia–Australia trade is that Australia has remained a supplier of primary products while importing value-added products from Asia. In other words, Australia exports minerals and foodstuffs and imports cars and consumer electronics. One could argue that Asian investment in areas of primary production has skewed investment priorities so that manufacturing has fallen behind. Successive Australian governments could be charged with short-sighted economic policies. The result, however, is that Australia faces a significant problem today. While the U.S. economy did well in the late 1990s as a result of the growth in the computer and associated high-technology industries, Australia is being charged with having a primary-producer economy, with agricultural products and minerals still dominating exports. At the same time, Australian manufacturing industries cannot compete with the low-wage countries of Asia, and progressively more industries are going bankrupt or leaving the country. In recent years, this has been particularly evident in the clothing and textiles industries. The mathematics on production costs is simple: It may cost $25 to make a shirt in Australia, whereas the same company can ship its machinery to Indonesia or the Philippines and make the same shirt for $2. Of course, this problem is also faced by Japanese and American companies, and they too are responding by relocating their production systems offshore, but they have other industries to replace them, in the high-technology area. Australia is experiencing difficulties in making this next technological leap.

A second major fear on the part of Australian companies is that, as the world appears to be dividing into trading blocs, they will be left out. Australian companies learned a hard lesson when Britain joined what became the European Union, and the North American Free Trade Agreement is causing further anxiety.

The result was the Asia–Pacific Economic Cooperation grouping, an initiative of the Bob Hawke Labour government in 1989. Australia's agenda in supporting the development of this organization is to ensure its continued access to Asian and North American markets. The disadvantage, from the point of view of Australian corporations, is that they will have to learn to function in a low-tariff environment, whereas until recently Australian industry was highly protected. Globalization is, therefore, already having, and will continue to have, a profound effect on Australian business and community attitudes.

Political Relationships

While the 1950s and 1960s could be characterized by a fear of Asia, the following decades saw a maturing of the political relationships between Australia and Asia. By the mid-1970s, the Communist insurgency in Malaysia was at an end, as was the war in Vietnam. The isolation of China was also ending, and that nation was emerging as both a promising new market and a powerful new competitor. With an increase in Asian immigration (rising to half of all new immigrants by the early 1990s), Australians were becoming more comfortable in the region.

This is not to say that Australia's foreign relations are now either smooth or easy. Its difficulties are, in part, a result of the multiple types of political systems with which it has to deal. One point of contention here is the way in which Australia balances its position on human rights with trade considerations. Sometimes this is relatively straightforward, as in the case of Myanmar (Burma). As this country is not important to Australia in an economic sense, the high ground of human rights is clearly Australia's position. The complexities come to the fore in the case of China. With the rapid growth in China's economy and increasing interconnectedness with regional economies, Australia must tread a fine line between its political and economic goals. Given the delicate relationship between China and Taiwan, for example, or the Chinese government's sensitivity over Tibet, Australia has to be careful in its diplomatic position. It does not have the economic, political, or military power of the United States and therefore tends more to a middle road in diplomatic terms.

This is less the case with the important Australia–Indonesia relationship. Diplomatic relations between the two countries have been on a roller coaster since the 1940s, and a particularly difficult issue has been that of East Timor. A Portuguese colony that was annexed by Indonesia in 1975, East Timor has remained a sticking point in Australia-Indonesia relations (particularly in the area of human rights) since then. The issue was complicated by the alleged killing of six Australian journalists when Indonesian troops invaded the colony in 1975. The result has been a division within Australia, with diplomatic efforts at odds with the

An Indonesian soldier accompanies Australian soldiers arriving for peacekeeping duty in East Timor in September 1999. (AFP/CORBIS)

media's antagonism toward the Indonesian government. When the Suharto government fell in 1998 and East Timor obtained independence (1999), Australian troops were stationed in the country to protect its independence. The use of the Australian military on former Indonesian territory has caused a nationalistic backlash in Indonesia and a deterioration in Australia-Indonesia relations.

The Future

The future of Australia–Asia relations promises to be as difficult as its past. Of particular concern is the impact of globalization, which will bring Australian industry under further pressure to be competitive in a global environment. As a high-wage country that is still dominated by exports of primary products, Australia's standard of living is steadily falling in relative terms. The reaction in domestic politics has been the rise of right-wing parties and policies that mistakenly favor a return to relative isolation and the greater wealth of the immediate postwar period; an attempt to resurrect those times through actions such as high tariff barriers would lead to economic disaster for the country. Such isolationist policies, while erroneous in conception and not economically viable, find fertile ground among those people disadvantaged by global competition. Anti-Asian sentiment is one offshoot.

On the international scene, Australia will remain a middle-level power that must engage with the countries to the north to sustain its economy. Nearly two-thirds of Australia's merchandise exports go to Asia, and this is highly influential in Australia's foreign economic and political policies. Given the political, economic, and cultural variations within Asia, Australia faces significant challenges in the future.

Curtis Andressen

Further Reading

Byrnes, Michael. (1994) *Australia and the Asia Game.* Sydney: Allen and Unwin.

Edwards, Peter. (1992) *Crisis and Commitments: The Politics and Diplomacy of Australia's Involvement in Southeast Asian Conflicts, 1948–1965.* Sydney: Allen and Unwin.

Higgott, Richard, Richard Leaver, and John Ravenhill, eds. (1993) *Pacific Economic Relations in the 1990s: Cooperation or Conflict?* Sydney: Allen and Unwin.

Keating, Paul. (2000) *Engagement: Australia Faces the Asia-Pacific.* Sydney: Macmillan.

McGillivray, Mark, and Gary Smith, eds. (1997) *Australia and Asia.* Melbourne, Australia: Oxford University Press.

Mediansky, Fedor. (1997) *Australian Foreign Policy: Into the New Millennium.* Melbourne, Australia: Macmillan.

Trood, Russell, ed. (1993) *The Future Pacific Economic Order: Australia's Role.* Brisbane, Australia: Griffith University.

Walker, David. (1998) *Anxious Nation: Australia and the Rise of Asia, 1850–1939.* Brisbane, Australia: University of Queensland Press.

AUSTROASIATIC LANGUAGES

The Austroasiatic family, the principal linguistic substrate of mainland Southeast Asian languages, exists today as a patchwork of more than a hundred languages spread across an area that ranges from central India to Vietnam and from Yunnan in China to Malaysia and the Nicobar Islands of the Andaman Sea. In only two countries are Austroasiatic languages the official tongues: Cambodia (Khmer, or Cambodian) and Vietnam (Vietnamese). In all other cases they are minority languages, spoken in single villages by only a few hundred people as well as in communities of several million people. Long ago before the domination by groups such as Thais, Burmese, Malays, and Indo-Aryans, the Austroasiatic peoples were probably the main population in Southeast Asia, and their languages may have been spoken even more widely than today, particularly in Indonesia and China.

Evidence of Common Ancestry

The common ancestry of the Austroasiatic languages is shown by their retention of a distinctive basic vocabulary, which readily identifies that group.

Because it was a prehistoric culture, the location of the original Austroasiatic homeland is not known, but some linguists speculate that it was in the hills of southern Yunnan in China, between 4,000 and 6,000 years ago.

Despite their common origins, Austroasiatic languages are structurally diverse, principally because many of them have been influenced by other, very different, language families for a long time. In India the Munda languages, which are in contact with the Aryan and Dravidian languages, have a complicated word structure that permits two or more syllables per word and an extensive system of grammatical affixes for both nouns and verbs. At the other typological and geographical extreme is Vietnamese: its lexicon or vocabulary is basically monosyllabic, and it relies on word order and compounding to express grammatical functions. In this case the direct influence of Chinese is clearly responsible. The great bulk of Austroasiatic languages lie between these extremes, utilizing a combination of affixation and word order.

Common Features

Most Austroasiatic languages have a rather distinctive word structure. Words may have one or two syllables, but in the two-syllable type the first syllable is never stressed, and the vowel in this syllable is normally short and neutral in quality. Words may begin with clusters of three or even four consonants, but the set of possible final consonants is always restricted. The range of word shapes in a typical Austroasiatic language is illustrated with the following examples from Jruq (West Bahnaric, Laos):

simplest:	CV	*ka* fish
	CVC	*dak* water
	CCVC	*plǎj* fruit
	CCVC	*ptɛh* earth
most complex:	CCCVC	*kbreh* blink

C = consonant
V = vowel

By contrast Munda languages permit much more complicated word shapes because many affixes can be used to build a single word or even a sentence, for example (Mundari, India):

suku-le-n-a-ko   *reŋeʔ-ta-n-a-ɲ*
"They had been happy."   "I am poor."

The set of distinctive sounds (or phonemes) can be large and have some unusual articulations in comparison to other languages of the world (including imploded and/or glottalized consonants and voiceless nasal and lateral sounds), and there may be tones or so-called registers (distinguishing breathy or creaky vowels). The Austroasiatic languages have the largest inventories of vowels of any language in the world, with some having more than thirty or even forty!

In many Austroasiatic languages the grammar is largely expressed by word order, although there is normally a moderate to large inventory of prefixes and some infixes, which have functions such as word derivation (e.g., deriving nouns from verbs) and marking grammatical relations such as causative (e.g., "to fall" or "to make fall"), reciprocal (e.g., "to hit somebody" or "to hit each other"), or instrumental (e.g., "to hit

or "to hit with something"). The Munda languages go much further, adding affixes to verbs to mark such things as tense (past and present versus future), aspect (complete or incomplete action), and transitivity (whether the sentence has a grammatical object).

Word order in these languages tends to be "left-headed"—modifying words (for example, adjectives, verbs) occur to the right of the "head" word they modify. Sentence-level word order is usually Subject-Verb-Object, or less often Subject-Object-Verb.

Classifying Austroasiatic Languages

The classification of Austroasiatic languages is a difficult issue, particularly because many of the languages are not well known or studied, while the better-known ones have borrowed significant lexicon and even grammar from unrelated languages such as Chinese, Pali, and Malay. However, field linguists continue to publish new and more detailed descriptions, and progress is being made in historical reconstruction. Most published texts present a classification of Austroasiatic languages based on rather preliminary studies carried out in the 1960s and 1970s with simple statistical methods. Recent research has greatly improved scholars' understanding of the internal structure of the family.

For most of the twentieth century it was thought that the Austroasiatic family consisted of two fundamental divisions: Munda and all other Austroasiatic languages. However this view was based on typological considerations and has not been supported by historical reconstruction. Also, the placement of Vietnamese in the Austroasiatic family was disputed for a long time, with many scholars (even now) believing it to be derived from Chinese. However it has been convincingly shown that the Chinese lexicon in Vietnamese was borrowed during the Middle Chinese period, and the development of tones and monosyllabic structure are internal Vietnamese developments.

TABLE 1

Comparison of words in Austroasiatic languages

	Mundari	Khasi	Wa	Viet.	Semai	Khmer	Bahnar
Blood	majam	sna:m	nham	—	bhi:pᵐ	jha:m	pha:m
Bird	sim*	sim	sim	cim	cɛ:pᵐ	—	sɛm
Eye	med	khjmat	—	mát	mat	—	mat
Hand	ti	kti	tai?	taj	tək̚ᵑ	taj	ti:
Louse	siku	ksi	si?	cʌj	cɛ:?	caj	si:
Root	red	tjnrai	riah	rê	rʔe:s	rik	rə:h
Nose	mū	khmut	miih	mū	muh	crəmuh	mu:h

*chicken

Below is the classification of the Austroasiatic language family based on the most recent comparative historical work. There are eleven principal branches listed, but various poorly documented and isolated languages spoken in China may yet turn out to reflect branch-level groupings. Language names are given in italics—the list below is not exhaustive, merely representative.

1. **Aslian** (Malaysia, Thailand):
   a) Jahaic: *Batek, Chewong, Jehai, Tonga, Kinsiu, Semang*
   b) Senoic: *Temiar, Semai, Jah Hut*
   c) Semelaic: *Semelai, Temoq, Semaq Bri*

2. **Bahnaric** (Vietnam, Laos, Cambodia):
   a) North Bahnaric: *Sedang, Jeh/Halang, Rengao, Hre*
   b) Central Bahnaric
      Alak
      Kasseng/Taliang
      Cua
      Tampuon, Bahnar
      South Central: *Chrau, Koho, Ma', Mnong, Stieng*
   c) West Bahnaric: *Loven/Jruq, Nhaheun, Sapuar, Sok, Oi, Cheng, Suq, Brao/ Laveh, Lawi*

3. **Katuic** (Laos, Vietnam, Thailand, Cambodia):
   a) *Katu of Vietnam*
   b) *Katu of Laos*
   c) *Ngeq*
   d) *Pacoh*
   e) North Katuic: *So, Bru, Tri, Makong, Siliq, Katang*
   f) Central Katuic: *Ta-Oi, Ong, Ir*
   g) West Katuic: *Suei, Nheu, Kuy, Kuay*

4. **Khasic** (Assam [India]): *Standard Khasi, Lyngngam, Synteng, War*

5. **Khmeric** (Cambodia, Thailand): *Cambodian, Surin Khmer*

6. **Monic** (Myanmar, Thailand): *Mon, Nyahkur*

7. **Nicobaric** (Nicobar Islands [India]):
   a) North Nicobar: *Car, Chowra, Teressa*
   b) Central Nicobar: *Camorta, Nancowry, Trinkut, Katchall*
   c) South Nicobar: *Great Nicobar, Little Nicobar*

8. **Northern** (Myanmar, Laos, Thailand, China):
   a) Palaungic
      i) East Palaungic: *Danaw, Palaung, Riang, Yinchia*
      ii) WestPalaungic: *Bulang, Lamet, Lawa, Samtao, U, Wa*
   b) Khmuic
      i) *Khao*
      ii) *Khmu, Mal-Phrai*
      iii) *Ksinhmul*
      iv) *Mlabri*
   c) Mangic: *Mang*

9. **Pakanic** (China): *Bolyu/Lai*

10. **Pearic** (Cambodia, Thailand): *Chong, Pear, Suoi, Saoch, Samre*

11. **Vietic** (Vietnam, Laos, Cambodia):
    a) Viet-Muong: *Vietnamese, Muong*
    b) Pong-Chut: *Arem, Maleng, Pong, Sach, Thavung*

There have been various proposals to link Austroasiatic with other language families of Southeast Asia into an "Austric" macrofamily. The long history of contact between the language families of Southeast Asia has resulted in many areal similarities that make the task of determining wider genetic relations difficult or impossible.

Paul Sidwell and Pascale Jacq

Further Reading
Huffman, Franklin E. (1986) *Bibliography and Index of Mainland Southeast Asian Languages & Linguistics*. New Haven, CT: Yale University Press.
Jenner, Philip N., Laurence Thompson, and Stanley Starosta, eds. (1976) *Austroasiatic Studies* 1, 2. Honolulu, HI: University of Hawaii Press.
Parkin, Robert. (1991) *A Guide to Austroasiatic Speakers and Their Languages*. Honolulu, HI: University of Hawaii Press.
Peiros, Ilia. (1998) *Comparative Linguistics in Southeast Asia*. Canberra, Australia: Australian National University.

AUSTRONESIAN LANGUAGES The Austronesian language family is one of the largest recognized language families in the world, with close to one thousand members. About half the languages in this family, and the great majority of the speakers, are found in Southeast Asia. Several major languages of the region, as well as hundreds of smaller ones, belong to this family.

The Austronesian Family and Proto-Austronesian

Family resemblances among neighboring languages of the Southeast Asian island region must have been apparent for millennia. Awareness of the Austronesian family's full extent, however, dates from the 17th century, when comparison of the vocabulary of Malay with those of Polynesian languages, such as Futuna, and Malagasy, the language of Madagascar, showed clear similarities that implied a common ancestor. From this linking of distant points comes an earlier name of the family, "Malayo-Polynesian." It is now recognized that Austronesian speakers are to be found from Madagascar in the west to Easter Island in the east—more than half the distance around the world.

An example of the sort of resemblance that would have been noticed on even a casual comparison of these languages is the following:

	Two	Eye	Stone
Malay	dua	mata	batu
Malagasy	rua	masu	vatu
Futuna	lua	mata	fatu

Although this family thus extends beyond Asia into the African and Pacific regions, it is in Southeast Asia that the largest concentration of Austronesian speakers is to be found, and it was undoubtedly in this region that the original ancestral language (Proto-Austronesian) was spoken. Comparing some numerals from languages spoken in several Asian countries shows the same family resemblance:

	Two	Four	Five	Ten
Paiwan (Taiwan)	Dusa	sepach	Lima	puLuq
Ilokano (Philippines)	dua	uppat	lima	sangapulo
Jarai (Vietnam)	dua	pâ	rema	pluh
Tetun (Timor)	rúa	hāt	líma	sanúlu
Javanese	loro	papat	lima	sapuluh

Systematic description and comparison of a wide range of Austronesian languages by many scholars during the nineteenth century culminated in the work of the German physician Otto Dempwolff (1934–38), who demonstrated how various present-day languages had developed via regular sound changes from their common ancestor, Proto-Austronesian. The vocabulary items compared above, for example, are derived from hypothetical ancestral forms *duSa (two), *maCa (eye), *batu (stone), *Sepat (four), *lima (five), and *puluq (ten).

The establishment of historical relations of these many languages to their common ancestor makes possible a "family tree" showing closer and more distant relationships within the family. This linguistic evidence can be combined with evidence from archaeology and other disciplines to produce an outline of the origins and migrations of the peoples who spoke these languages.

The precise interrelations of the Austronesian languages of Southeast Asia have yet to be fully worked out. One point of widespread agreement, however, is that the languages of the aboriginal people of Taiwan divided from the rest of Austronesian at a very early date, and are thus of prime importance in understanding the history of the family. This primary division between Formosan languages and the rest suggests that Proto-Austronesian was spoken either in Taiwan or possibly on the nearby Chinese mainland. Beginning at least 5,000 years ago, Austronesian speakers would have migrated south into the Philippines, Indonesia, and New Guinea, and from there east into the Pacific (during the second millennium BCE) and eventually west to Madagascar (during the first millennium CE).

Although the Austronesian languages have been diversifying from their common ancestral form for thousands of years, and have spread over a vast geographical range and a wide variety of cultures, certain family traits have persisted, not only in basic vocabulary (as shown above), but in certain aspects of word structure and grammatical devices. One feature that differentiates Austronesian from other major language families of the region is a preference for two-syllable nouns and verbs, with consonants permitted at beginning, middle, and end, as in Tagalog: payat (thin), ngipin (tooth), gatas (milk). Possessive pronouns appear as suffixes on the possessed noun, as in Rampi (Sulawesi): umo'-ku (my father), umo'-mu (your father), umo'-ne (his or her father). Another very widespread Austronesian feature is the distinction of first-person plural pronouns into "inclusive"and "exclusive," depending on whether the person spoken to is included or not. So Tagalog kamí (exclusive) means "I and others," as contrasted with táyo (inclusive) "I, you and others."

Austronesian Languages Yesterday and Today

Both Javanese (Kavi) and Malay appear in inscriptions from the middle of the first millennium CE, written in scripts of Indian origin. A number of other languages of Indonesia, Malaysia, and the Philippines have had Indian-derived writing systems, and after the arrival of Islam the Arabic alphabet was used to write Malay and other Austronesian languages of the region. Although some of these scripts have continued to be used into the present, the trend of the last few centuries has been for them to be replaced by orthographies based on the Roman alphabet.

Throughout their history, these languages have continued to supplement their inherited Austronesian vocabulary with new words borrowed from a variety of sources. The strong influence of Indian culture at the period of earliest literacy is also reflected in numerous Sanskrit words adopted into the vocabulary, such as Malay *bahasa* (language), *warna* (color), and *jaya* (victory). Islamic culture brought with it words of Arabic origin such as *hukum* (law) and *waktu* (time). Additions to the vocabulary during the last few centuries have reflected differing colonial histories: Spanish words in the Philippines, Dutch in Indonesia, and English in Malaysia.

In 2002, Austronesian languages were spoken by more than 90 percent of the population in Indonesia, Malaysia, Brunei, and the Philippines; in Singapore, Malay speakers are a substantial minority (15 percent). Within this region, apart from modern-era immigrant languages such as Chinese and Chabacano (creole Spanish), the principal non-Austronesian language areas are those of the Orang Asli of the Malay Peninsula, and the various Papuan language groups in eastern Indonesia (Irian Jaya, Halmahera, Timor). Various Austronesian language groups form one or two percent of the population in Cambodia, Thailand, Vietnam, and Taiwan; while China and Myanmar have a single Austronesian community each (Tsat on Hainan Island in China, Moken in coastal Myanmar) with a few thousand speakers. At the opposite extreme from these tiny enclaves are some languages which number their speakers in tens of millions, including Javanese (75 million), Malay (35 million), Sundanese (27 million), Tagalog (17 million), and Cebuano (15 million). Some of these exercise an influence beyond their communities of native speakers through use as national languages. Tagalog forms the basis of Filipino, the national language of the Philippines, while Malay (which has been a regional lingua franca for centuries and developed many local varieties) has been made a national language of both Malaysia and Indonesia.

Ross Clark

Further Reading

Bellwood, Peter, James J. Fox, and Darrell Tryon, eds. (1995) *The Austronesians: Historical and Comparative Perspectives.* Canberra: Department of Anthropology, Research School of Pacific and Asian Studies, Australian National University.

Blust, Robert. (1995). "The Prehistory of the Austronesian-speaking Peoples: A View from Language." *Journal of World Prehistory* 9,4: 453–510.

Dempwolff, Otto. (1934–1938) *Vergleichende Lautlehre des austronesischen Wortschatzes.* 3 vols. Berlin: Dietrich Reimer.

Tryon, Darrell T., ed. (1995) *Comparative Austronesian Dictionary: An Introduction to Austronesian Studies.* Berlin: Mouton de Gruyter.

Wurm, Stephen A., and Shirô Hattori, eds. (1981–1984) *Language Atlas of the Pacific Area.* Canberra: Australian Academy of the Humanities.

AUTOMOBILE INDUSTRY In 2000, Asian factories assembled 18 million four-wheel vehicles, 30 percent of the world output of 58 million units; Asian firms also accounted for another 6 million units made outside their home market, primarily in the United States and England. Japan, with domestic output of 10 million units in 2000, was by far the largest producer, followed by South Korea and China, the only other Asian markets with domestic production or domestic sales over 1 million units. World automotive trade was also substantial, about $550 billion in 1999. However $207 billion of that trade was internal to Europe, and another $98 billion was inside NAFTA; intra-Asian trade was only $17 billion, an indicator of the different structure of Asian markets.

Almost all Asian nations produce some vehicles domestically, including Uzbekistan, Jordan, and Myanmar (Burma). Despite small markets, in most countries over a dozen manufacturers coexist behind trade barriers, each turning out 20,000 or fewer units at high cost. Even though their output is minuscule by world standards, these firms typically loom large on the local landscape. At one extreme there is Toyota, Japan's largest manufacturer and the core firm in the world's fourth-largest automotive group, turning out 6 million units a year. At the other extreme is Iran Khodro, with output under 200,000 units a year, the largest producer in the Middle East and Iran's largest manufacturer. Similarly in Malaysia, the state-owned firm Proton looms large both politically and in the local economy, and Asian producers in general have strong ties to local elites and interest groups.

Defining the auto industry is not easy. Japanese data provide one example. In its mature market, Japanese auto parts account for two-thirds of the industry—assembly in Japan employs 262,000 people, while parts manufacturing employs 626,000. Denso, the largest parts firm, has 85,000 employees worldwide and has a consolidated auto-sector revenue larger than Suzuki or Fuji Heavy Industries (Subaru). Ancillary sectors, such as dealerships and repair facilities (1.28 million), petrol stands and other services (1.1 million), or for that matter transportation workers (3 million), each employ far more workers than does manufacturing proper. Comprehensive data are lacking, but in most

Asian markets the parts sector, while limited in the components produced, still employs more workers than does vehicle assembly.

A second aspect is that in most of Asia, automobiles are not the dominant segment. In India in 2000, passenger-car output was 580,000 units, but commercial vehicle output totaled 700,000 units—300,000 trucks and jeeps, 200,000 three-wheel trucks, and 200,000 tractors. At a total of 1.3 million units, the three- and four-wheel vehicle market was still dwarfed by sales of 3 million mopeds, scooters, and motorcycles. The same was long true in Japan, where trucks dominated the market until 1968.

Despite this heterogeneity, Asian markets share many features. One is that throughout the region, the industry is viewed as a potential leading sector and has developed behind high trade barriers. But because markets are fragmented between cars and trucks and into additional segments within those two broad categories, production volumes of individual vehicles are small. In contrast, industry leaders in Japan, Europe, and North America perceive economies of scale to be increasing, due to the research and development (R & D) required to develop new technologies such as fuel-cell and hybrid vehicles and the investment needed to incorporate electronic and safety systems in new vehicles. For example, on top of $6 billion of investment in plant and equipment, Toyota will undertake R & D expenditures of $4 billion in 2001, and other major firms are spending comparable amounts. At the same time, the information-technology (IT) revolution makes it easier to coordinate vehicle development and engineering for individual markets off a common "platform."

As evidenced by a series of mergers, acquisitions, and alliances, industry executives apparently believe that a firm must produce five million units annually to be viable. With the exception of Honda and BMW, since 1997 the smaller firms in the European Union (EU), Japan, and the United States have been incorporated into one of six global groups: GM, Volkswagen, Toyota, Ford, DaimlerChrysler, and Renault. If alliances under negotiation in 2001 come to fruition, no sizable independent producers will remain in the United Kingdom, Scandinavia, Italy, or Korea. Similarly, major direct (Tier I) suppliers to car companies are now consolidating and reorganizing, with mergers and divestments—and bankruptcies. One motive is to be able to design, engineer, and assemble "modules" or "systems," such as an entire heating-cooling system, rather than individual components such as a fan, air ducts, or air conditioning compressor. In addition suppliers are

being asked to set up operations wherever their customers are located. Major suppliers are thus spinning off and acquiring units to match this new strategy, as well as investing in manufacturing capacity around the world, including Japan and elsewhere in Asia.

Domestic manufacturing is nevertheless expanding in most countries. The industry's long-term tendency is to build where vehicles are sold rather than rely on trade, due to logistics costs, the vagaries of foreign exchange rates, and the need to adapt products to match the idiosyncratic nature of local markets. In addition, analysts project that much of the growth in world demand during the first two decades of the twenty-first century will be in Asia. Producers with a low presence in the region are thus seeking a foothold, investing in new capacity at the same time that incumbents are upgrading existing facilities in advance of World Trade Organization (WTO)–mandated trade liberalization, which will be phased in by 2006. Indeed during the 1990s the automobile industry added 19 million units of global capacity in a slowly growing aggregate market, resulting in excess capacity of 20 million units; Asia has about 7 million units of excess capacity and an average utilization rate of under 70 percent. As a result auto assemblers are not very profitable; among major firms only Honda and BMW earned a reasonable return on assets in 2000. Nevertheless the industry is poised for significant expansion in many Asian markets, in vehicle assembly and in the parts sector. It will require a decade for this process to stabilize and for excess capacity to be trimmed.

Commonalties: Political Economy

The automotive sector is large—5 percent of the economy in countries with a substantial industry, from Turkey to Malaysia and Thailand to Korea and Japan—and as a consumer good, is visible to citizens. Geographic concentration and formal organization (industry associations, unions) add to its political saliency. Volkswagen's "People's Car" strategy was widely copied. While in the 1960s the Japanese bureaucracy repeatedly failed in its efforts to designate one or more "national champions," President Mahathir of Malaysia and the sons of Indira Gandhi in India and Suharto of Indonesia all sponsored such projects, and China has adopted a series of "Big Three" policies.

Even without a national champion, the automotive industry received favorable treatment in the Asian region—above all, protection from imports. As intended, such policies led to new entry, with one or two firms producing vehicles in each niche, turning out a few thousand or even just a few hundred vehicles a year.

AUTOMOBILE INDUSTRY GIANTS

Of the twenty largest automobile manufacturers in Asia, sixteen are in Japan, two in South Korea, and one each in China and Indonesia. On the basis of sales revenues as reported in *Asia Week* (9 November 2001), the five largest firms are Toyota, Honda, Nissan, Mitsubishi (all in Japan), and Hyundai in South Korea. In 2001 Nissan was by far the largest with gross sales of $124,565.5 million, over twice that of second place Honda.

At one extreme China, with a history of local autonomy, had 119 producers in 2000, of which 26 had output of under 100 units. But even Malaysia, despite its small market (300,000 units) and the favored position of the dominant firm, Proton, had 14 firms; in addition Honda will start production in 2003 with a factory geared to turn out 20,000 cars a year with output split among four dissimilar models. Efficient plants in the developed world, however, are designed to churn out 240,000 similar models a year, fifty times the volume Honda anticipates in Malaysia.

Such inherently high-cost production can prevail only in markets where competition is repressed. In the case of Malaysia, tariffs of up to 300 percent are required to enable Proton's survival; import charges are 100 percent in India and 80 percent in China, compared with 2.5 percent in the United States and 0 percent in Japan. Initially, imported parts faced lower rates, encouraging completely knocked-down kit assembly. That, however, generated little employment, and Asian governments therefore mandated increasing levels of local content over time. But parts production often has greater economies of scale than does assembly, and local content rules typically lead to higher overall costs.

In Japan a combination of economic growth and a large domestic market eventually engendered sufficient competition to drive costs down to the point where exports were feasible; China, India, and Indonesia have large enough populations that this might also eventually happen. These countries have also chosen to liberalize their domestic markets, in line with the WTO, to accelerate this process. For idiosyncratic reasons Turkey (as an EU hopeful) and Thailand (with hopes for trade within the Association of Southeast Asian Nations, or ASEAN) have done the same.

Reform is a difficult political challenge, and WTO membership is being wielded to inhibit backsliding. The WTO requires that automotive tariffs be lowered to 25 percent, quantitative import restrictions eliminated, and direct foreign investment freed from mandates to use local partners, achieve minimum levels of local content, or commit to minimum levels of exports.

In practice, liberalization in larger markets results in increased inward investment and heightened competition. This is true even in Turkey, with access to EU markets, and in Thailand, which has a critical mass of suppliers, despite repeated economic crises. In contrast, consumers in markets such as that of Malaysia continue to pay extraordinarily high prices, without attracting a commensurate amount of investment.

The Dominant Force in Asia: Japan

Japan has both the largest and the oldest auto industry in Asia; Japanese firms, through local partners and trade, also dominate Asian markets, with the exception of Turkey and China. Volume production dates to 1925–1927, when Ford and General Motors set up local assembly plants, though rising nationalism led to their shuttering in 1936, just when Ford was set to break ground on a large-scale, integrated operation as an export base for Asia. Protection thus delayed the industry's rise as a major exporter for thirty-five years, until around 1971.

Toyota and Nissan entered the market in 1937, while the forerunners of Daihatsu and Mazda made three-wheelers, and Isuzu expanded from contract truck assembly for the military. However, production ceased in 1942, and though these firms resumed operations after 1945, output was still minimal in 1950. But economic growth and import prohibitions after 1955—40 percent tariffs proved insufficient to keep foreign cars from dominating the market—stimulated additional entry, with a peak of thirteen or fourteen producers in the early 1960s, spread across multiple niches. In 1960 the largest segment was three-wheel trucks, in a total vehicle market of under a half-million units. By 1968 passenger car output hit 2 million units, finally exceeding that of trucks. Competition pressured firms to lower costs, and new factories built to handle higher sales facilitated introducing better designs and production methods. Prices fell steadily until the late 1960s, by which time small Japanese cars were comparable in cost to those made in Europe.

From the 1950s low volumes of trucks were exported throughout Asia. Then, in the late 1960s, the Volkswagen Beetle ignited a small-car boom in the United States, and General Motors, Ford, and

Chrysler turned to Japanese firms for imports to counter the German invasion. The 1973 and 1979 oil crises increased that segment from a single-digit niche to 30 percent of the market in 1981, and imports from Japan rose to over 2 million units. A "voluntary" export restraint (VER) to the United States imposed in 1981 capped Japanese imports at 1.68 million units, well below the level of demand for the small, fuel-efficient cars, effectively creating a cartel and allowing Japanese firms to raise prices dramatically. This tactic generated huge profits, which the car firms used to finance the development of larger cars and the construction of "transplant" assembly operations in the United States. (Several European nations negotiated similar VERs, and Japanese firms responded similarly by setting up factories in the United Kingdom and, more recently, France and Eastern Europe.) Exports peaked in 1985, when a strong yen and escalating labor costs cut into competitiveness. The transplant operations turned to new European- and Japanese-owned parts plants—three hundred firms from each area entered the market—to cut import costs and keep transplant assembly competitive. During the next two decades Honda, Toyota, and Nissan built stand-alone operations in North America, from dealership networks, market research organizations, and car design studios to transmission and engine manufacturing, which enabled them and several smaller producers to grab 26 percent of the U.S. market in 2001, almost all through local production. Operations in the EU were begun later, and Japanese producers hold a smaller share of the market, since unlike in the United States they faced stiff competition in small-car segments there.

With the bursting of Japan's "bubble" economy in 1991, domestic car sales dropped by 20 percent, and truck sales by more. Although Japanese production outpaced that in the United States and the United Kingdom during 1980–1991, output during 1998–2001 dropped by 30 percent from the peak to 10 million units or less, while the North American and European markets boomed to surpass 17 million units in 2000. Unfortunately the industry was busily expanding in 1991, adding 1.5 million units of new assembly capacity, with comparable increases by parts makers. The industry thus entered the late 1990s with 15 million units of capacity; in 2001 Toyota alone could assemble 1 million more cars inside Japan than it could sell, either at home or through exports. Domestic red ink thus reinforced the trend toward global consolidation. Toyota purchased Hino (2000) and Daihatsu (1998), Ford took over full control of Mazda (1996), Renault acquired Nissan (1999), and GM now controls Isuzu (1998) and has a dominant 20 percent stake

in both Suzuki (2000) and Fuji (1999); only Honda remains outside the fray. A similar consolidation of parts producers is under way, and during the first decade of the twenty-first century the domestic industry will gradually cut employment and shutter factories to deal with excess capacity.

At the same time, Japanese firms have continued to expand overseas. Honda began volume production abroad first, in the United States in 1982. Other firms quickly followed; by 2000 Japanese firms produced 6.3 million units outside Japan, 2.5 million of which were in the United States. Parts suppliers likewise have been building an international presence, with over three hundred firms in the United States, as well as nineteen of the hundred largest global suppliers. Growth has been slower in Europe, but Japanese firms dominate most Asian markets and are expanding in China and Turkey, where they lag behind European firms.

Continental-Sized Producers: China and India

The world's two most populous economies both grew rapidly during the 1990s, driving the market for transport. Neither India nor China had strong indigenous producers. Of three incumbent firms in India, Premier Motors is now defunct, while in 2001 Hindustan Motors still produced the Ambassador, a 1953 British design. China, with protection at the local level, had at least one producer in each province. When foreign ventures were finally allowed, the initial entrants—Suzuki as a partner of Maruti Motors in 1986, and Volkswagen with Shanghai Automotive Works in 1983—quickly dominated the market, and both still account for over half of passenger-car sales.

By the mid-1990s, Volkswagen and Maruti achieved mass-production volumes, with over 200,000 units per year of a single model. Like incumbent firms, however, once in the market neither had an incentive to introduce new models. With new entry and the promise of increased competition as WTO provisions are phased in, both Volkswagen and Maruti scrambled to introduce new models and to lower prices; in 1999–2000 both lost money, though sales recovered thereafter.

In India, Korean firms and Ford have a foothold; in China, GM, Toyota, and several smaller producers now offset Volkswagen. The initial foreign ventures, however, have established supplier networks; Shanghai Auto Works has forty joint ventures in parts production, and additional firms use China (and, increasingly India) as a base for exporting labor-intensive items to their home markets, as well as to supply the million-plus vehicles made in each country.

This combination—at least one firm of large scale, a network of suppliers, a growing domestic market, and an apparent commitment to the WTO process—offers scope for increasing efficiency without the need for exports. Both India and China are likely to remain modest exporters of vehicles but growing exporters of parts, as assemblers are focused on the domestic market. But since entry is outpacing market growth, not all firms will profit, and indeed several ventures must ultimately fail.

Export-Oriented Markets: Turkey and Thailand

As noted above, Turkey and Thailand both turned away from the extreme protectionism that characterized Asia around 1991. In each market several of the dozen-plus incumbent joint ventures responded by modernizing and expanding their plants. They now appear well positioned to export vehicles to supplement sales to the domestic market, allowing an economic scale of operations. Due in part to lower sales taxes on trucks, Thailand is the second-biggest market for full-sized pickups, larger even than Canada; Ford and GM-Isuzu will use production there rather than in the United States to source global exports, while the joint venture Mitsubishi Sittipol exported 63,000 pickups in 2000. Similarly Oyak-Renault, Fiat Tofas, and Ford are producing versions of certain models only in Turkey and will export much of their factories' output to complement the versions they make elsewhere.

The same factors encouraged parts producers to expand or enter, co-locating with potential customers while eyeing exports. The result is an automotive infrastructure that makes it easier for other assemblers to locate in that country. Thailand now has 1.2 million units of assembly capacity, and BMW will add to that; Turkey will soon have over 1 million units, with plants under construction and Toyota planning on entering. This expansion is occurring despite recurring economic crises. Projects that were put on hold in Thailand in 1998, when sales fell to 25 percent of 1996 levels, were restarted by 2000 and are now in operation, while Ford's Ikon project in Turkey progressed despite the 2000 earthquake and 2001 economic crisis. As a result of such dynamics, Turkey and Thailand are the only two new Asian producers to achieve over 100,000 units in exports on a purely commercial basis, levels that assemblers expect to rise as additional unique products enter production. With modest domestic markets and lower import barriers, output will be increasingly centered on these export-oriented plants, while low-volume producers will exit, as GM Opel did in Turkey in 2000.

National Champion Policies: Korea, Malaysia, Indonesia, Iran

Four countries have fostered national favorites, with varying degrees of failure. In Indonesia's case, favored treatment of Timor Putra National, owned by a son of the late president Suharto and tied to Kia of Korea, resulted in Japan's filing a WTO case, which Indonesia lost. The firm was shut down following the 1997 economic crisis, leaving Astra, a joint venture of Toyota, as the dominant force.

In Malaysia President Mahathir supported Proton, producing vehicles under license from Mitsubishi Motors. After fifteen years, output has reached only 200,000 units, too low a volume to support stand-alone operations. Indeed, while in 2001 the Malaysian government trumpeted the development of its own engine, the big global firms are designing engines with target production volumes of at least 750,000 units per year, while investing billions of dollars on hybrid and fuel-cell systems, not the traditional gasoline engine of Proton.

Volumes in fact are limited in part because of the focus on national champions. In theory different countries in ASEAN could specialize in different product niches, an idea backed since 1977 by a series of regional endeavors. ASEAN Industrial Cooperation (AICO), the 1996 successor to the 1988 Brand-to-Brand Complementarity plan, promised 5 percent tariffs and no local content provisions for intra-ASEAN trade by 2003. While parts production under AICO provisions is expanding, for finished vehicles AICO and earlier schemes have all failed, in AICO's case due to Malaysian intransigence. With 300 percent tariffs needed to make Proton viable, Malaysia unilaterally announced it would extend protection through 2005, rather than allow imports from Thailand and Indonesia. This action led to so-far unsuccessful claims for compensation by Thailand (negotiations were still in progress in 2001). Proton clearly faces little near-term pressure to increase efficiency. But it also has limited growth potential; despite its privileged status, it has been unable to quash new entry, including a second national champion, Perodua, producing vehicles for the small-car segment. The willingness of political leaders to postpone liberalization that threatens vested interests keeps the industry inefficient and limited to local markets.

Iran also falls into this pattern, with a national champion, Iran Khodro, which continues to churn out the 1960s-vintage British Hillman Hunter Paykan, benefiting from a 1992 ban on imported vehicles. Nationalized in the 1979 Revolution, the industry is strongly tied to the government, helped by industry employment of 235,000 (and more in parts production). Foreign trade restrictions hamper outside investment; although Iran Khodro will finally introduce a new Peugeot model in 2002, that deal relies on foreign-exchange barter to pay for fees and imported components. High vehicle prices nevertheless have encouraged the French Citroën and Korean Daewoo to attempt ventures with SAIPA, the second-largest producer in Iran. But the tight monopoly seems likely to inhibit growth and investment during the coming decade.

Korea is different in that its industry is competitive in export markets, with calendar-year 2001 sales (including parts exports) likely to surpass $14 billion. Its major firms even have overseas manufacturing operations, especially in India and Eastern Europe; Daewoo is Poland's largest producer. However Daewoo, in bankruptcy in 2001, will likely be bought by GM, while Kia absorbed the truck producer Asia Motors only to encounter financial problems; it was absorbed in turn by the country's leading producer, Hyundai. But DaimlerChrysler now owns 10 percent of Hyundai, which is likely to relinquish autonomy, first in truck production (Renault purchased the rival Ssangyong) and gradually in passenger cars (given its long-standing dependence on Mitsubishi Motors for technology). In the space of four years the domestic industry has been completely restructured, and national champions have lost their autonomy.

Korea prevented vehicle imports, but that will change with WTO-mandated liberalization, inevitably cutting further into domestic sales. The industry will remain dependent on export demand to maintain volume and hence will be vulnerable to the health of overseas small-car markets, especially in the United States, and to any appreciation of the *won*, the Korean currency. International ownership may mitigate this vulnerability, if Korea is used as a global source of small cars. For the time being its existing supplier base—Korea is the only Asian country besides Japan with a parts firm large enough to rank among the top one hundred in the global auto industry—will keep it attractive as a manufacturing locus, helped by a domestic market over four times larger than that of Thailand or Turkey.

Future Prospects

Too small to fund necessary R & D, and with WTO-linked liberalization threatening their viability even at home, independent, locally owned producers have not proved viable. Even in Japan, nine of eleven incumbent firms have lost their autonomy, leaving only Toyota and Honda—and Honda produces and sells more outside than inside Japan. Rather than being shaped by government policy, henceforth the local industry in Asia will depend on each country's historical legacy, as well as geography—the size of domestic and neighboring markets—and economic stability. Not all countries will be known as major producers, but the imperative to build where they sell will result in manufacturers in all of the larger Asian economies. At present, however, with excess capacity in virtually all markets, plant closures are inevitable.

As the first decade of the twenty-first century progresses, the parts sector will fare better, although it too will be dominated by large global players that design and manufacture modules rather than individual components. Its heterogeneous nature, however, makes it less visible politically and in the media, even if this sector is where the greatest gains in employment, exports, and profits are realized.

Mike Smitka

THE ISUZU Z.E.N.

In an effort to combine tradition with modernity, the Japanese carmaker Isuzu unveiled the new Z.E.N. model at the November 2001 Tokyo Motor Show. The car's steering wheel and seats fold away to create a tatami mat floor for tea drinking in a "traditional" setting.

Source: Asia Week (16 November 2001): 14.

Further Reading
Freyssenet, Michel, Andrew Mair, Koichi Shimizu, and Giuseppe Volpato, eds. (1998) *One Best Way? Trajectories and Industrial Models of the World's Automotive Producers.* New York: Oxford University Press.
AutoAsia news service. Retrieved 31 October 2001 from http://www.auto-asia.com.
Crain Publications, Detroit. (weekly) *Automotive News.* Retrieved 31 October 2001, from http://www.automotivenews .com. (Updated daily.)
International Organization of Motor Vehicle Manufacturers. Retrieved 31 October 2001, from http://www.oica.net.
Just-Auto.Com news service. Retrieved 31 October 2001 from http://www.just-auto.com.

AUTONOMOUS REGION OF MUSLIM MINDANAO

Following an agreement in 1976 (known as the Tripoli Agreement) between the Moro National Liberation Front (MNLF) and the Philippine government during the presidency of Ferdinand Marcos, autonomous Muslim governments were set up in Regions IX (Western Mindanao and Sulu) and XII (Central Mindanao). But the autonomy arrangements were never accepted by the MNLF or by the majority of Philippine Muslims. After the People Power Revolution of 1986, a new constitution made specific provision for an Autonomous Region of Muslim Mindanao (ARMM) and a Regional Consultative Commission was appointed to draft the terms of the ARMM. These were eventually set out in Republic Act 6734 of August 1989.

Following the Tripoli Agreement, the scope of the ARMM was defined as the thirteen provinces and nine cities of Mindanao-Sulu-Palawan claimed by the MNLF as traditional Muslim territory. But following a plebiscite in 1989, which was again boycotted by a large number of Philippine Muslims and by the MNLF, only four provinces and no cities voted to join. In 1996 MNLF chairman Nur Misuari returned to the Philippines and became governor of the ARMM. Under the terms of a 1996 peace agreement between the MNLF and the Philippine government, new legislation for an expanded ARMM was to be drafted and submitted to a plebiscite; the mandated plebiscite, however, had still not been held by mid-2001. Meanwhile, there were complaints that the ARMM was underfunded and that its effectiveness had been undermined by inefficiency, nepotism, and favoritism toward MNLF supporters.

The plebiscite was eventually held in August 2001. Predictably, given the present demography of Mindanao, the proposed expansion of the ARMM to include the (now) fifteen provinces and fourteen cities covered by the Tripoli Agreement was supported in the four provinces of the existing ARMM (Lanao del Sur, Maguindanao, Sulu, and Tawi-Tawi) plus the province of Basilan and the city of Marawi but was rejected in all other provinces and cities. This outcome disappointed Muslim autonomy supporters and further undermined the position of Governor Misuari, who subsequently abandoned his office and launched an armed assault on national government forces. Misuari was arrested in Malaysia. In his absence, the national government–supported candidate, Parouk Hussin, was returned as governor in scheduled ARMM elections in November 2001.

Ronald J. May

Further Reading

May, Ronald J. (2001) "Muslim Mindanao: Four Years after the Peace Agreement." In *Southeast Asian Affairs 2001.* Singapore: Institute of Southeast Asian Studies, 263–275.

Stankovitch, Mara, ed. (1999) "Compromising on Autonomy: Mindanao in Transition." *Accord* 6 (April).

Vitug, Marites, and Glenda M. Gloria. (2000) *Under the Crescent Moon: Rebellion in Mindanao.* Quezon City, Philippines: Ateneo Center for Social Policy and Public Affairs, and Institute for Popular Democracy.

AWADH

An historically important province of North India, Awadh was incorporated within the state of Uttar Pradesh after independence (1947). According to legend, it dates back to the days of the epic *Ramayana.* The name *Awadh* is derived from Ayodhya, the capital of the ancient Hindu kingdom of Kosala. Little is known of Ayodhya's history between the seventh and eleventh centuries. Awadh came into prominence under the rule of the Delhi sultans in the twelfth century. Later, it became a province of the Mughal empire after Babur annexed it in 1538. Under Aurangzeb (1658–1707), the capital city, Lucknow, developed as a notable Sunni theological center.

Under the later Mughals, centralized control declined. The governor Sadat Khan (1722–1739) made Awadh practically independent. Subsequently, the English East India Company gained ascendancy over the province. After defeating Nawab Shuja-ud-daulah (1753–1775) at the Battle of Buxar (1764), the company gained the right to free trade in Awadh. During the reign of Wajid Ali Shah (1847–1856), the British government finally annexed Awadh in 1856. Lucknow flourished in the eighteenth century as an important cultural center and rivaled Delhi in its patronage of art, music, and literature.

Sanjukta Das Gupta

Further Reading

Fox, Richard G. (1971) *Kin, Clan, Raja, and Rule: State-Hinterland Relations in Pre-industrial India.* Berkeley and Los Angeles: University of California Press.

Majumdar, R. C., J. N. Chaudhuri, and S. Chaudhuri, eds. (1984) *The Mughal Empire.* Vol. 7 of *The History and Culture of the Indian People.* Bombay, India: Bharatiya Vidya Bhavan.

AWAMI LEAGUE

The Awami League (AL) is the oldest of the major parties in Bangladesh. It was founded in 1949 by Husain Shahid Suhrawardy (1893–1963), who later became prime minister of Pakistan. It was strong only in East Pakistan (present-day

Bangladesh). After Suhrawardy's death, Mujibur Rahman, or Mujib (1921–1975), became de facto leader and led the party to an overwhelming victory in the 1970 elections. In 1966 Mujib put forward a six-point program for provincial autonomy for East Pakistan, which he championed in the 1970 election called by Pakistani president General Agha Muhammad Yahya Khan (1917–1980) as part of his plan to return Pakistan to democracy. Mujib also proclaimed four goals for the AL and for Bangladesh (which he led after the country's independence from Pakistan in 1971): nationalism, secularism, socialism, and democracy. These principles, with the exception of socialism, which has been discarded, still guide the party. Democracy was also discarded when Mujib created a civilian authoritarian state in January 1975, but this lapse was corrected with the return of a freely elected government in 1991. After Mujib's assassination in 1975, the party did not hold power again until Mujib's daughter, Hasina Wajid (b. 1947), became prime minister following the June 1996 election. In the interim, the AL was the principal opposition party, opposing Ziaur Rahman's and Khaleda Zia's Bangladesh

Nationalist Party or BNP (1979–1982 and 1991–1996) and H. M. Ershad's Jatiya Party (1982–1990) both within parliament and, when parliament did not exist, in extraparliamentary activity. During the H. M. Ershad (b. 1930) regime, the AL shared the opposition role with the BNP although the two parties did not cooperate until late 1990, when they caused the downfall of Ershad.

Craig Baxter

Further Reading
Ahmed, Moudud. (1983) *Bangladesh: The Era of Sheikh Mujibur Rahman.* Dhaka, Bangladesh: University Press.

———. (1995) *Democracy and the Challenge of Development: A Study of Politics and Military Intervention in Bangladesh.* New Delhi: Vikas.

Baxter, Craig. (1997) *Bangladesh from a Nation to a State.* Boulder, CO: Westview.

Ziring, Lawerence. (1992) *Bangladesh from Mujib to Ershad: An Interpretative Study.* Karachi, Pakistan: Oxford University Press.

AYUB KHAN (1907–1974), president of Pakistan. General Muhammad Ayub Khan (1907–1974) was president of Pakistan from 1958 to 1969. Born in Rehanna, which was at that time in British India, Ayub Khan rose to power within the Pakistani Army, becoming commander in chief in 1951. He served as minister of defense as well for one year beginning in 1954. In 1958, Ayub Khan was appointed chief martial law administrator by President Iskander Mirza during a time of political turmoil when martial law was declared. Eventually, Ayub Khan took over the role of president, which was confirmed by a referendum in 1960. Five years later, he was reelected. However, he did not complete his term. He started to lose support due to events arising from the war with India in 1965. People believed he was wrong to accept a cease-fire and to agree to the Tashkent Agreement. Political unrest directed at him resulted in his resignation in 1969.

During his presidency, however, Ayub Khan was responsible for several significant reforms and developments. For instance, he was architect of the Regional Cooperation for Development (RCD), an organization devoted to economic cooperation and cultural exchanges among its members—Turkey, Iran, and Pakistan. Although the organization did not reach the status envisioned by its creators, it nonetheless enhanced relations between its member states in a nonthreatening and beneficial manner. After the Iranian revolution, RCD was abandoned in 1979, but it was reestablished as the Economic Cooperation

Awami League supporters in Dhaka protest the results of the 1 October 2001 elections after they were defeated by the Bangladesh Nationalist Party. (AFP/CORBIS)

Ayub Khan with Jacqueline Kennedy at the Kennedy estate in Virginia in September 1962. (BETTMANN/COPRBIS)

Organization (ECO) by Pakistan, Turkey, and Iran in 1985, when the three nations realized the need for a regional organization to promote trade. In 1992, ECO was expanded almost overnight when six former Caspian-region Soviet republics and Afghanistan joined. The expansion of the organization highlighted the necessity of regional cooperation, which was a dream of Ayub Khan.

Houman A. Sadri

Further Reading

Burki, Shahid Javed. (1991) *Historical Dictionary of Pakistan.* Metuchen, NJ: Scarecrow.
Cleveland, William L. (1994) *A History of the Modern Middle East.* Boulder, CO: Westview.
Haynes, Jeff, ed. (1999) *Religion, Globalization, and Political Culture in the Third World.* New York: St. Martin's.

AYUTTHAYA, KINGDOM OF Ayutthaya (1350–1767) politically, economically, and culturally dominated mainland Southeast Asia for four hundred years. Located at the confluence of three major rivers (the Lopburi, Pasak, and Chao Phraya) in the Menam Basin in central Thailand, the distinctive culture that Ayutthaya developed during the reigns of its thirty-three kings has evolved into modern Thai culture and society. UNESCO declared the historical city of Ayutthaya a World Heritage Site in 1991 as a masterpiece of urban planning with a unique cultural heritage.

King Uthong or Ramathibodi I (1314–1369) established Ayutthaya in 1350 when the kingdoms of Sukhothai and Angkor were weakening. The kingdom's location on an island in the middle of the river confluence was strategic defensively since the vicinity was flooded most of the year, protecting the city from attack. The periodic flooding created a fertile alluvial plain capable of sustaining a large population and the development of rice cultivation for export. Ayutthaya's proximity to the sea was advantageous for maritime trade. Ayutthaya controlled access to the kingdoms in the interior and thus became a major communications and trade center. King Uthong's successors expanded the kingdom to occupy present-day central Thailand and the northern section of the Malay peninsula, incorporating the territories of Sukhothai and part of the Angkor empire.

Khmer culture heavily influenced Ayutthaya in its early years. Ayutthayan monarchs adopted the concept of the *devaraja* (god-king) cult, elevating themselves to the status of gods, particularly as the reincarnation of Vishnu. The royalty operated in secrecy, increasing the mystery surrounding the king. The kings rarely made public appearances, and these appearances were often grandiose. The kings integrated Hindu and Mahayana Buddhist religious ceremonies to legitimate and ritualize their rule. Brahman priests presided over these ceremonies, such as the coronation and oath of allegiance, and the Thai monarchy continues this tradition. Sukhothai and Sinhalese cultures also shaped the kingdom beginning in the fifteenth century. The Sukhothai kingdom was previously in control of the region before Ayutthaya overpowered Sukhothai, and Uthong used the laws of Sukhothai as a base for the Ayutthayan code of law. The Buddhist foundation of Sinhalese culture influenced Ayutthaya as it converted to Theravada Buddhism.

The Ayutthayan monarchs created a sophisticated administration and hierarchical social system to control the kingdom's large territory and population. The system comprised a number of ranked and titled officials. Ayutthayan society was stratified into three major classes: royalty, the officials or nobility, and commoners. Persians, Indians, Chinese, Indonesians, Japanese, Europeans, and other foreigners who came to Ayutthaya as merchants were generally excluded from the social strata. Kings such as Trailok or Borommatrailokanat (reigned 1448–1488) also developed an elaborate code of law.

Theravada Buddhism flourished at Ayutthaya, and the Mahayana Buddhist ceremonies that legitimized kingship were incorporated into this other sect of Buddhism, which was adopted throughout mainland Southeast Asia. Ayutthaya was closer to the centers of Theravada Buddhism, Ceylon and Burma, and its central location meant that monks passed through it before traveling to other cities. Ayutthayan monarchs were generous patrons of religion and the religious arts. Kings sent for Sinhalese monks to preside over ceremonies and monasteries and constructed over four hundred monuments and temples, giving the *sangha*, or Buddhist monkhood, wealth and power. Trailok was the first king to be ordained as a monk, and this tradition continues with the Thai monarchy today.

AYUTTHAYA—WORLD HERITAGE SITE

Constructed in 1350, the ancient Kingdom of Siam's second capital remains relatively intact despite its destruction by the Burmese in the eighteenth century. Designated by UNESCO as a World Heritage Site in 1991, Ayutthaya's massive monasteries and sky-scraping spires continue to impress.

Ayutthaya excelled in classical and performing arts, including the fields of literature, painting, classical dance and drama, music, sculpture, architecture, and other art forms. Religious literature flourished, with the adaptation of Indian works such as the *Ramayana* and *Mahabharata*. The *Ramakien*, the Thai version of the *Ramayana*, became the subject of other arts such as painting, dance, and drama. *Khon* was a classical dance form based on this epic, and the use of masks in *khon* began during this period. The masks became the most important part of the *khon* costume, and the use of the masks initiated the narration of the drama since the performers were unable to speak wearing the masks. The courts also entertained with puppetry: *nang yai* (shadow puppets) and *hun* (marionettes). The performances were confined to palace grounds, where they continued for many days accompanied by a *piphat* (orchestra composed of four to eight musicians). Music flourished in Ayutthaya, and compositions and songs from that period continue to be played today.

Numerous poetic forms developed, such as the *chan*, *kaap*, *klawn*, *klong*, and *rai*. The first two forms, *chan* and *kaap*, originated in India, but the poets of the Ayutthayan courts developed their own adaptations of these forms. The Ayutthayan poets borrowed 17 or 18 of the original 109 meters of *chan* and added rhyme schemes and changed the rules concerning syllables. The rules of the poetics forms differed according to tonal, syllable, and rhyme schemes. *Lilit Phra Lo* and *Lilit Yuan Phai* are just two of the epics written during this era. Ayutthayan court artisans developed a distinct painting style and other art forms such as niello ware—in which silver and gold receptacles are decorated with motifs etched onto the receptacle with an alloy metal—and the use of gold leaf on lacquer. The artisans mastered bronze casting and created massive Buddhist icons. Their iconography included the elongation of the lotus flower base and the representation of Buddha in different postures and dressed as a prince.

The images became symbols of the mystic nature of the king.

Religious architecture experienced major transformations. The spire of the Sinhalese *chedi*, or stupa, with its bell-shaped base, was elongated in Ayutthayan style. Temples became massive, imposing structures symbolizing the kingdom's power and indestructibility. The roofs of Ayutthayan temples were very steep and elaborately decorated. Domestic architecture adapted to the amphibious environment of the kingdom. The Siamese elevated house evolved into floating rafts to accommodate flooding and to allow the inhabitants to live near their rice fields.

Ayutthaya as an international trade port became a cosmopolitan city. There were numerous international settlements of Chinese, Japanese, Vietnamese, Persians, Indians, Malays, and even Europeans. The Portuguese established the first European embassy in 1511, and the Dutch, French, and English soon followed suit in order gain trading contracts with the court. The kings also exchanged missions with the French and Chinese courts. Foreign advisers became influential to some kings; an example is Constantine Phaulkon, a Greek, who advised King Narai or Phra Narai (1632–1688). Ayutthaya used the exposure to the different countries to its advantage. The kingdom was able to modernize its military and munitions by using the technological advances of others.

The Burmese sacked Ayutthaya in 1767, destroying temples, palaces, and art works and returning to their own kingdom with booty. The Burmese presence in the kingdom of Chiang Mai since the sixteenth century made Ayutthaya vulnerable to attack from the north. Ayutthaya had enjoyed a century of relative peace, but there was instability around the throne, causing the kingdom to be ill prepared defensively. The Burmese took many of Ayutthaya's inhabitants as war captives. Ayutthaya ceased to be the center of the Siamese world when the new capital, Thonburi (1767–1782), was established further south on the Chao Phraya River by a new ruler. Thonburi was chosen for its strategic location for trade and defense. Another ruling dynasty came into power in 1782 and moved the capital to the other side of the Chao Phraya River to Bangkok in order to increase its defensible position from Burmese attack.

Linda McIntosh

Further Reading
Ayutthaya: The Portraits of Living Legends. (1996) Bangkok, Thailand: Plain Motif.

Breazeale, Kenneth, ed. (1999) *From Japan to Arabia: Ayutthaya's Maritime Relations with Asia.* Bangkok, Thailand: Toyota Thailand Foundation.
Charnvit Kasetsiri. (1976) *The Rise of Ayudhaya: A History of Siam in the Fourteenth and Fifteenth Centuries.* Oxford: Oxford University Press.
Sioris, George A. (1998) *Phaulkon: The Greek First Counsellor at the Court of Siam: An Appraisal.* Bangkok, Thailand: Siam Society.

AZAD, ABU'L-KALAM (1888–1958), president of the Indian National Congress. Born in 1888 in Mecca, Islam's main center of pilgrimage, to a family of Afghan origin, Azad Abu'l Kalam settled with his parents in the Indian city of Calcutta in 1890. Here, his father became famous as spiritual guide and religious scholar *(maulana).* Azad was taught at home, receiving a traditional Islamic education, though he secretly studied English and the writings of the Indian Muslim reformer Sayyid Ahmad Khan (1817–1898). Nevertheless, his religious ideas were traditional, far from Islamic modernism and reformism: God was the supremely authoritative center of the universe, and man's duty was to admire, obey, and worship Him.

Around 1910, he joined the Hindu anti-British revolutionaries of Bengal, in spite of their anti-Muslim attitude. In 1912 he started publishing an Urdu weekly, *Al-Hilal* (The Crescent), which had a wide circulation among the Indian Muslim community. Due to its radical political and religious ideas, the British banned the weekly in 1914. Granted the honorific title of *maulana*, Azad became one of the leading political nationalists, fighting against both the British presence and the partition of India into two different states for Hindus and Muslims. He supported the concept of a confederation of autonomous provinces with their own constitutions, but with strong central ties.

Repeatedly deported and arrested by the British for his ideas, in 1923 he became the youngest president of the Indian National Congress. In 1928 he presided over the Nationalist Muslim Conference. Between 1940 and 1946 he held, for the second time, the position of president of the National Congress. After partition, he served as minister in the Indian government.

Riccardo Redaelli

Further Reading
Azad, Abulkalam. (1978) *India Wins Freedom: An Autobiographical Narrative.* New Delhi: Sangam.
———. (1990) *Selected Speeches and Statements, 1940–47: Maulana Azad.* Edited by P. N. Chopra. New Delhi: Reliance.

Hameed, Syeda Saiyidain. (1998) *Islamic Seal on India's Independence: Abul Kalam Azad: A Fresh Look.* Karachi, Pakistan: Oxford University Press.

Minault, Gail, and Christine W. Troll, eds. (1988) *Abul Kalam Azad: An Intellectual and Religious Biography.* Delhi: Oxford University Press.

AZAD KASHMIR

Azad Kashmir ("Free Kashmir") is the portion of Kashmir controlled by Pakistan, comprising Gilgit, Baltistan, and western Kashmir, an area about 51,200 square kilometers.

Azad Kashmir came about because of convoluted political maneuvering that followed the end of British rule in India in 1947. At that time, all of Kashmir was ruled by Maharaja Hari Singh, whose forefather Maharajah Gulab Singh had bought the province from the British in 1837 for a million pounds sterling.

It was also in 1947 that Punjab and Sind were partitioned and Pakistan created, thus giving Muslims of the subcontinent a homeland.

Hari Singh was not willing to let his land be divided between India and the newly created Pakistan. Instead, he chose to remain independent of the two nations. However, forces larger than he could control erupted in Kashmir. Historically, Kashmir was 60 percent Muslim and 40 percent Hindu and Sikh. The Muslims in Gilgit and Ladakh revolted and by October 1947 they has set up an area that they declared free ("azad") of Hindu and Sikh dominance (rhetoric similar to that used in the creation of Pakistan). Thus was established Azad Kashmir, with its capital at Muzaffarabad. Before long, an army was created, supported and supplied by Pakistan, and many thousands of tribesmen entered Kashmir and headed for Srinagar, the maharaja's capital. Widespread fighting broke out in the region; Hari Singh ceded his kingdom to India and sought refuge in New Delhi.

The Indian army immediately moved to quell the violence. In response, in May 1948, Pakistan sent in troops to defend Azad Kashmir against efforts by the Indian army to overrun the area. The two sides fought each other to a stalemate; in January 1949, they petitioned the United Nations to broker a cease-fire. The U.N. sent in a peacekeeping force and established a cease-fire line, which divided Gilgit, Baltistan, and western Kashmir from the rest of Kashmir. Neither side recognized the cease-fire line as an official border; it was merely a temporary line to keep apart the two warring nations.

Lengthy and fruitless talks followed between India and Pakistan, which did not settle the fate of Kashmir.

Both sides wanted to hold a plebiscite, but could not agree on how it would be managed. Pakistan argues that Hari Singh's cession of his lands to India was not legitimate; therefore, Indian troops must withdraw. Only then can a plebiscite be held. India, on the other hand, claims the maharaja's actions were legitimate and wants all Pakistani troops to withdraw, especially from Azad Kashmir, while Indian troops will stay to keep the peace. And only then can a plebiscite be held. Both sides have fought two wars over Kashmir; in the second war, Pakistan lost 15 percent of its territory, with the creation of Bangladesh.

In 1972, India and Pakistan signed the Simla Accord. According to this agreement, the previous cease-fire line became a permanent line of control, and both nations agreed not to use force to change this boundary. The area remained peaceful until 1989. Unrest has plagued the area ever since, with sporadic violence and buildup of tension. The demands of the last fifty years have not changed, and Kashmir remains a flash point that could send the two nations into another war.

Nirmal Dass

Further Reading
Jha, Prem Shankar. (1996) *Kashmir 1947: Rival Versions of History.* Delhi and New York: Oxford University Press.

Schofield, Victoria. (2000) *Kashmir in Conflict: India, Pakistan, and the Unfinished War.* London; New York: I. B. Tauris.

———. (1996) *Kashmir: In the Crossfire.* London; New York: I. B. Tauris.

Sheikh, Mohammad Naeem. (2001) *The Division of India: How Pakistan Came into Being, and the Lingering Dispute over Kashmir.* Markham, Canada: Commerce Horizons.

AZAHARI, A. M.

(b. 1929–2002), Brunei political leader. Sheikh Ahmad Azahari bin Sheikh Mahmud, known as A. M. Azahari, led the Partai Rakyat Brunei (PRB) in an abortive revolt against the Brunei government in December 1962. Born in Labuan of mixed Arab-Malay parentage, Azahari was mission-educated and studied veterinary science at Bogor, Java, under Japanese sponsorship during the Pacific war (1941–1945). He deserted to join anti-Japanese movements and participated in the Indonesian independence struggle. Azahari became politically active in the early 1950s, agitating for Brunei's independence. Inspired by the left-wing Partai Rakyat Malaya, he formed the PRB in 1955.

Azahari made the resurgence of the ancient empire of Brunei his priority. He supported a "Northern Borneo Federation," mooted by the British (1957), but intended that Brunei would hold the pivotal role and himself the reigns of government. In January 1962 he was nominated to the Brunei Legislative Council and the Brunei-Malaysia Commission (to ascertain public views on the formation of a "Malaysia" federation). Azahari opposed entry into a Malaysia federation on the grounds that it would negate a revival of Brunei hegemony. In April 1962, his motion of resurrecting the "historical sovereignty" of the Sultan of Brunei over Sarawak and British North Borneo was defeated in the council, which resulted in his resignation.

Azahari was in Manila when the revolt broke out. He declared himself prime minister of Negara Kesatuan Kalimantan Utara (NKKU, the Unitary State of North Borneo). But within a week, British forces crushed the rebellion, PRB was proscribed, and Azahari went into exile until his death.

Ooi Keat Gin

Further Reading
Hussainmiya, Haji B. A. (1995) *Sultan Omar Ali Saifuddin III and Britain: The Making of Brunei Darussalam.* Kuala Lumpur, Malaysia: Oxford University Press.
Mohamed Noordin Sopiee. (1974) *From Malayan Union to Singapore Separation.* Kuala Lumpur, Malaysia: University of Malaya Press.
Ongkili, James P. (1967) *The Borneo Response to Malaysia, 1961–1963.* Singapore: Donald Moore.
Ranjit Singh, D. S. (1991) *Brunei 1839–1983: The Problems of Political Survival.* Kuala Lumpur, Malaysia: Oxford University Press.
Sanders, Graham. (1994) *A History of Brunei.* Kuala Lumpur, Malaysia: Oxford University Press.
Zaini Haji Ahmad, ed. (1987) *Partai Rakyat Brunei: The People's Party of Brunei. Selected Documents/Dokumen Terpilih.* Kuala Lumpur, Malaysia: INSAN.

AZERBAIJAN (2002 pop. of Republic 8.1 million), (2002 pop. of East Azerbaijan, Iran, 3.4 million), (2002 pop. of West Azerbaijan, Iran, 2.8 million). Azerbaijan is a mountainous region in West Asia, bounded by the eastern Caucasus, northwestern Zagros range, Talish Mountains, and Caspian Sea and divided between the Republic of Azerbaijan in the north and Iran in the south. The word *Azerbaijan* is derived from the province's ancient name of Media Atropatene and from the Persian satrap Atropates (flourished c. fourth century BCE), who established an independent dynasty there after Alexander of Macedon's death.

Islam was introduced into northern Azerbaijan after the Arab conquest in the seventh century, gradually displacing the Zoroastrianism of the Iranian-

speaking majority. Although Turkic elements had a long presence in ethnically diverse Transcaucasia, most experts agree that Turkification of the region started in the eleventh century, with the massive migration of Oghuz nomads from Central Asia to Asia Minor, under the banner of Seljuk conquest.

Between the eleventh and fifteenth centuries various conquerors incorporated Azerbaijan into vast empires stretching from Asia Minor eastward to the Oxus River. The Safavids (1501–1732), who laid the foundations of modern Persia and made Shi'ism its state religion, came from Azerbaijan. Russia's expansion into the Caucasus in the nineteenth century led to Persian-Russian wars and to the final division of Azerbaijan along the Araks River in 1828.

The Republic of Azerbaijan (area 86,600 square kilometers) is bounded by Iran, Armenia, Georgia, the Russian Federation (Dagestan), and the Caspian Sea. It includes Nakhchevan, separated from the rest of the country by a strip of Armenian territory, and the Karabakh Mountain Area, inhabited mostly by Armenians. A drive for the unification of Karabakh with Armenia in 1988 sparked ethnic violence and led to war between Armenia and Azerbaijan in 1991–1994. In 1922 Azerbaijan, Armenia, and Georgia were incorporated into the Soviet Union. Azerbaijan became a separate Soviet republic in 1936. It declared independence in 1991.

The country has significant oil reserves, exploited intensively since the 1870s, and oil-producing and petrochemical industries centered in its capital, Baku, a Caspian seaport. Azerbaijan oil was critically important for the Soviets during World War II, as were the weapons- and machine-building plants established there. In the twenty-first century Azerbaijan's oil continues to spark Western interests in the country.

BAKU—WORLD HERITAGE SITE

A potpourri of Central Asian and Middle Eastern architectural styles, the walled city of Baku in Azerbaijan allows a unique glimpse at several divergent cultural forms in one place. Baku was designated a UNESCO World Heritage Site in 2000.

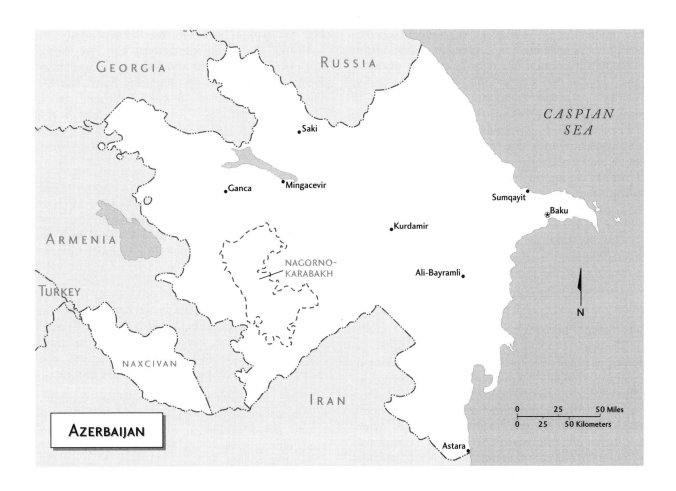

Iranian Azerbaijan includes East Azerbaijan (capital Tabriz), with an area of 65,840 square kilometers, and West Azerbaijan (capital Orumiyeh), with an area of 43,657 square kilometers. Azerbaijan is Iran's most fertile region, producing cereals, tobacco, sugar beets, apricots, and almonds.

Marta Simidchieva

Further Reading

Altstadt, Audrey L. (1992) *The Azerbaijani Turks: Power and Identity under Russian Rule.* Stanford, CA: Hoover Institution Press, Stanford University.

Atabeki, Touraj. (1993) *Azerbaijan: Ethnicity and Autonomy in Twentieth-Century Iran.* London: British Academic Press.

Yarshater, Ehsan, ed. (1989) "Azerbaijan." In *Encyclopaedia Iranica.* Vol. 3. London: Routledge and Kegan Paul, 205–257.

AZERBAIJANIS   The Azerbaijanis are a unique group in the Muslim world: they are mostly Shi'ite Muslims, although ethnically and linguistically they are Turks (Oghuz Turks). The Azerbaijanis (also known as Azeris or Azerbaijani Turks) number 30 to 35 million and live primarily in present-day Iran (20 million), the Republic of Azerbaijan (7.5 million; the nation's independence was reestablished after the fall of the Soviet Union), today's Turkey (1 to 2 million), and Russia (1 million). Under Seljuk (1038–1157) rule, major waves of immigration of Oghuz Turks into Azerbaijan created a clear Turkic majority. Historians debate the ethnic-linguistic composition of the areas north and south of the Araks River and the historical borders of Azerbaijan before the major waves of Turkic immigration there. More Turks came during Mongol Ilkhanid rule from the thirteenth through the fourteenth centuries and during the Qara Qoyunlu and Aq Qoyunlu Turkmen dynasties in the fifteenth century. In the northern part of Azerbaijan, a native Shirvanshah dynasty ruled through the sixteenth century.

Azerbaijani Religions

The Islamization of Azerbaijan took place during the Arab conquest at a date given variably between

639 and 643. Prior to the Islamic conquest, Zoroastrianism was prominent in Azerbaijan and it remains a significant cultural influence among the Azerbaijanis. In the nineteenth and twentieth centuries, Azerbaijanis were among the first proponents of secularism in the Muslim world, advocating study of secular subjects in schools and limitations on the role of clerics in politics. In its constitution of 1996, the Republic of Azerbaijan declared a clear separation between religion and state, and the nation has no official state religion. The majority of the Azerbaijanis in the Republic of Azerbaijan are secular, and Islam is primarily a cultural force in the republic. Among the Azerbaijanis in present-day Iran, a substantial segment is religiously observant, and a large proportion of the clerical elite in Iran is of ethnic Azerbaijani origin.

Azerbaijani Territory

The area that many Azerbaijanis consider their historical territory stretches through much of the Transcaucasus (the south Caucasus) and northwest Iran. The borders in the region of the Republic of Azerbaijan have frequently shifted; the Republic (which is bounded by Russia, the Republic of Georgia, Armenia, Iran, and the Caspian Sea) fills only a small part of the Azerbaijanis' traditional lands. The Azerbaijanis often refer to the part of Azerbaijan north of the Araks River (called Aras in Iran; the river runs through Asiatic Turkey, Armenia, and Azerbaijan) as north Azerbaijan, while the area south of the river in Iran is referred to by them as south Azerbaijan.

For much of its history, Azerbaijani territory has been part of Iran. Iran's capital was frequently in the Azerbaijani provinces, and the rulers of a number of Iranian dynasties (the Safavids, for instance, who ruled from 1501 to 1722 or 1736, depending on which event one chooses to mark their downfall; or the Qajars, who ruled from 1794 to 1925) were predominately ethnic Azerbaijani Turks. In the early nineteenth century, Russia and Iran fought for control of the Caucasus. Iran was defeated in the first military campaign. The sides concluded the Treaty of Gulustan in 1813, and Iran ceded a large part of the Caucasus to Russia. Major confrontation erupted again in 1825, and again Iran was defeated. In February 1828, the Treaty of Turkmenchay was signed, and Iran lost the rest of the Caucasus, including most of the northern part of Azerbaijan. The border was set at the Araks River, thus dividing the Azerbaijanis under two separate empires—Russia and Iran. In the eyes of many Azerbaijanis, this treaty symbolizes the separation of the people.

The Azerbaijani States in the Transcaucasus

During the twentieth century, the Azerbaijanis north of the Araks River have twice established an independent state. The first state, the Azerbaijan Democratic Republic (1918–1920), declared in its constitution equal rights for all citizens regardless of religion, ethnic origin, or gender and granted suffrage to women. Azerbaijan was the first Muslim state to grant women the vote.

The Republic was overrun by Soviet troops in 1920 and incorporated into the USSR. In October 1991, the Republic of Azerbaijan declared its independence from the USSR, and the state was established with the downfall of the Soviet regime in December 1991.

Azerbaijanis in Iran

Iran's three northwesternmost provinces are inhabited predominantly by Azerbaijanis: East Azerbaijan, West Azerbaijan, and Ardabil. Tehran, the capital city, has a large Azerbaijani population as well, estimated at close to 50 percent of the city's residents.

In the twentieth century, Azerbaijani autonomy movements emerged several times in Iran. Whenever central power weakened, Azerbaijani activists and other ethnic groups have exploited the opportunity and articulated ethnic-based demands. This was evident during the 1918–1920 provincial revolts, which precipitated the fall of the Qajar regime, the World War II Allied occupation of Iran (1941–1945/6), and the Islamic Revolution (1979). During 1945–1946, Iranian Azerbaijanis established an independent provincial government in Iran's northwest provinces. This short-lived government was attacked by Tehran's troops, and the rebellion collapsed.

Despite the language and cultural restrictions on ethnic minorities in Iran, distinctive Azerbaijani identity is retained by vast numbers of the Azerbaijanis there. However, most see no contradiction in maintaining both ethnic and Iranian identity and feel ties to both.

Azerbaijani Language and Culture

The language spoken by the Azerbaijanis and that spoken in Turkey are mutually intelligible. Until the twentieth century, Azerbaijanis wrote their language in the Persian-Arabic script. In 1924, the Latin alphabet was officially adopted in Soviet Azerbaijan, predating its adoption by the Republic of Turkey in 1928. In 1940, the Cyrillic alphabet was imposed by the Soviets on the Turkic peoples of the USSR, and thus the Azerbaijanis in the north began writing their publications in this script. This created a gap between the Soviet Azerbaijanis and their co-ethnics in Iran, who have continued to use the Persian-Arabic script. After independence, the Republic of Azerbaijan officially adopted the Latin alphabet, and the use of this script has expanded, especially among the youth, since new textbooks are written in the Latin script. In the Republic of Azerbaijan, the language is referred to officially as Azerbaijani, but on the grassroots level it is often called Turkish.

In Iran, the use of languages other than Persian is restricted (for instance, as of 2000 no schools were allowed to operate in the Azerbaijani language), and only a small segment of the Azerbaijani population is literate in the language, although most ethnic Azerbaijanis frequently speak the language. In their publications, some Iranian Azerbaijani intellectuals have modified the Persian-Arabic script with vowel markers to accommodate their highly vowel-based language. In Iran, the language is often called Azeri or Turki.

Despite the separation of the Azerbaijanis under different empires and regimes since 1828, Azerbaijanis on both sides of the border share many common historical memories, mutual symbols, and family bonds. Throughout most of the Soviet period, when direct ties were severely restricted by both the USSR and Iran, many Azerbaijanis retained connections with their relatives beyond the border, and when the limitations were removed with the Soviet demise, there was an outpouring of family visits and renewal of interchange and cooperation. While many differences have emerged between the Azerbaijanis in the Republic of Azerbaijan and those in Iran since their separation, most tend to view themselves as belonging to the same ethnic group, though not predominantly sharing identification with the same state or political structures.

Family ties are highly valued among Azerbaijanis and have played an important role in preserving the common identity of many Azerbaijanis despite their separation in different states. Most Azerbaijanis in the Republic of Azerbaijan have kinship ties to Azerbaijanis in Iran. The strong extended family network provides assistance and social services to family members

and often fulfills functions that in the West are provided by the state or public organizations. However, these strong family ties often inhibit nationalism and state-building efforts.

In terms of national literature, the Azerbaijanis revere the epic *Dada Qorqut* (twelfth century) and the poetry of Nizami Ganjavi (1369–1404), an ethnic Azerbaijani who wrote primarily in Persian, and of Fizuli (1498–1556), who wrote primarily in a form of Turkish that was common to Azerbaijanis and other Turks in that period, in addition to Persian and Arabic. Azerbaijani folk bards *(ashuq)* continue to recite traditional poetry; Azerbaijanis are known for their love of music and singing.

The writer Mirza Fath Ali Akhundzade (1812–1878) played the most prominent role in the development of modern Azerbaijani literature. Primarily through the plays he wrote, Akhundzade propagated among the Azerbaijanis, and throughout the Turkic and Iranian worlds, the idea of rationalism, anticlericalism, and modern education.

Azerbaijanis are well known for their hand-woven carpets and kilims, especially those from the Tabriz and Kuba-Shirvan regions. Azerbaijani cuisine is highly valued in Iran.

Brenda Shaffer

Further Reading

Alstadt, Audrey. (1992) *The Azerbaijani Turks.* Stanford, CA: Hoover Institute.

Shaffer, Brenda. (2000) "It's Not about Ancient Hatreds, It's about Current Policies: Islam and Stability in the Caucasus." *Caucasian Regional Studies* 5, 1–2.

———. (2000) "The Formation of Azerbaijani Collective Identity in Iran." *Nationalities Papers* 28, 3 (September): 449–477.

———. (2002) *Borders and Brethren: Iran and the Challenge of Azerbaijani Identity.* Cambridge, MA: MIT Press.

Swietochowski, Tadeuz. (1985) *Russian Azerbaijan, 1905–1920: The Shaping of National Identity in a Muslim Community.* Cambridge, U.K.: Cambridge University Press.

———. (1995) *Russia and Azerbaijan: A Borderland in Transition.* New York: Columbia University Press.

BA JIN (b. 1904), popular Chinese writer. Ba Jin (Li Feigan), who has written numerous works in a variety of genres, is one of the most popular Chinese writers of the twentieth century. From the early 1950s until the 1980s, he suffered sometimes vicious political persecution. Although his popularity and prestige were revived in the post-Mao era, the injustices he endured from the 1950s onward seem to have put an end to his creative writing. However, from the late 1920s to the late 1940s, Ba Jin was an extremely prolific writer of fiction, penning more than seventy short stories and twenty novels. These sometimes melodramatic but consistently humanitarian works criticize poverty, war, greed, and other social injustices. His characters confront difficult ethical situations demanding the sacrifice of personal interests for the sake of a larger good.

The best known of these works is his novel *Jia (Family)*, first published in 1931. *Family* chronicles the breakdown of the large and wealthy Gao family between the years 1919 and 1923. In it, Ba Jin represents the traditional Chinese family as a structure that smothers the individual dreams and aspirations of idealistic youth. The novel also depicts the suffering of women in modern China and momentous historical events of the time. *Family* has been canonized as one of the great masterpieces of modern Chinese literature.

Nicholas A. Kaldis

Further Reading

Ba Jin. (1993) *Bajin Xiaoshuo Quanji* (Ba Jin's Collected Fiction). Taipei, Taiwan: Yuanliu.
———. (1989) *Family*. Beijing: Foreign Languages Press.
Lang, Olga. (1967) *Ba Chin and His Writings: Chinese Youth between the Two Revolutions.* Harvard East Asia Series, 28. Cambridge, MA: Harvard University Press.
Mao, Nathan. (1978) *Ba Chin.* Boston: Twayne.

BA TRIEU (Third century CE). Lady Trieu, or Ba Trieu, is also known as Trieu Trinh Nuong or Trieu Thi Trinh. History describes her as a young woman riding an elephant down from the mountains, leading a rebellion against Chinese control over her country in 248 CE. She had a famous mark of distinction: her breasts were so long that she had to throw them over her shoulders while riding into battle. Her insurrection ended in defeat. Two explanations are given for the lack of success. The first is that upon hearing about her, the Chinese commanders ordered their troops to shed all clothes and advanced toward her stark naked. Lady Trieu could not bear the sight of so much exposed flesh, so she turned her elephant around and commanded her troops to retreat. The Chinese pursued them relentlessly until they destroyed all the insurgent forces. The second explanation is less frivolous. After two hundred years of Chinese efforts at assimilating the Vietnamese population, the majority of the local people identified their interests with those of the conquerors so that they no longer supported anti-Chinese movements wholeheartedly as they had done with the Trung sisters, who had led a successful rebellion against the Chinese occupation two hundred years earlier and ruled Vietnam as queens from 40 to 43 CE. Lady Trieu's supporters, indeed, came mainly from the mountains where they had withdrawn to live away from Chinese influence, which became overwhelming after the Trung sisters' rebellion.

Truong Buu Lam

Further Reading

Hodgkin, Thomas. (1981) *Vietnam: The Revolutionary Path.* London: Macmillan.

Taylor, Keith W. (1983) *The Birth of Vietnam.* Berkeley and Los Angeles: University of California Press.

Uy Ban Khoa Hoc Xa Hoi Viet Nam [Committee for the Social Sciences of Vietnam]. (1971) *Lich Su Viet Nam* (trans. *History of Vietnam*). Hanoi, Vietnam: Committee for the Social Sciences Publishing House.

BABA TATSUI (1850–1888), Japanese statesman and political thinker. Baba Tatsui was born in Tosa Province (now Kochi Prefecture) in the area of Kaneko Bridge, Nakanoshima Town, near Kochi Castle. He initially studied at Fukuzawa Yukichi's Keio Gijuku School (now Keio University); later, during the 1870s, he studied English law and politics in England. A champion of the Freedom and People's Rights Movement, he organized the Kokuyukai with the aim of spreading democratic values and became a leader of the Jiyu-to (Liberal Party), Japan's first national political party. Baba later left the party over a disagreement. Critical of Meiji leaders, he was prohibited from writing and speaking in public. In 1885, he was arrested for antigovernment activities, charged for having illegally purchased explosives. Acquitted in 1886, he sought political asylum in the United States where he wrote a long essay in English entitled "The Political Condition of Japan: Showing the Despotism and Incompetence of the Cabinet and the Aims of the Popular Parties" (1888). He died in Philadelphia and was buried there in the Woodlands Cemetery.

William Nelson Ridgeway

Further Reading

Ballhatchet, Helen. (1991) "Baba Tatsui and Victorian Britain." In *Britain and Japan, 1859–1991: Themes and Personalities*, edited by Hugh Cortazzi and Gordon Daniels. New York and London: Routledge.

Soviak, Eugene. (1966) "An Early Meiji Intellectual in Politics: Baba Tatsui and the Jiyuto." In *Modern Japanese Leadership: Transitions and Change*, edited by Harry D. Harootunian and Bernard S. Silberman. Tucson, AZ: University of Arizona Press.

BABIRUSA The babirusa (pig deer, *Babyrousa babyrussa*), a pig-like animal, is distantly related to the hippo and restricted to the Indonesian island of Sulawesi. Babirusa stand 65–80 centimeters high, are often nearly hairless, and range in color from off-white to brown. The upper and lower canine teeth of the male curve toward the forehead, forming four prominent tusks that are used in fights over females and territory. Babirusa are nocturnal and eat fruit, coconuts, and beetles. Babirusa have a complex stomach, like cattle, rather than a simple one like pigs. This observation has given rise to a suggestion that they chew the cud, meaning that their meat might be *halal* (permitted for Muslims), but recent research suggests this is not the case.

Robert Cribb

Further Reading

Whitten, Anthony J., Muslimin Mustafa, and Gregory S. Henderson. (1987) *The Ecology of Sulawesi.* Yogyakarta, Indonesia: Gadjah Mada University Press.

BABISM Babism was founded in 1844 by Sayyid 'Ali Muhammad Shirazi (1819–1850) in Shiraz, Iran. The religion grew out of the Shaykhi school of Twelver Shi'ite Islam, which emphasized Gnostic ideas. Many Shi'ites expected that the Twelfth Imam, a supernatural messiah, would return in 1844 CE. In May of that year, Sayyid 'Ali Muhammad declared to a young Shaykhi leader, Mulla Husayn Bushru'i (c.1814–1849), that he (Sayyid 'Ali Muhammad) had a special relationship to the hidden Twelfth Imam, and so was a "Bab" (Arabic for "door"). He wrote a commentary on the sura of Joseph from the Qu'ran that alluded to these assertions. Mulla Husayn and other young Shaykhi leaders accepted his claims.

The Bab went on pilgrimage to Mecca. On his return to Shiraz he was questioned by the Shi'ite religious authorities about his claims, and found ways to appear to recant them. He was placed under house arrest by the governor of Shiraz, and in 1846, when plague struck Shiraz, he was able to relocate to Isfahan. There he gained the patronage of the governor, Manuchehr Khan. He was summoned by Muhammad Shah (reigned 1834–1848) to Tehran. But the prime minister, fearful that the Bab might gain the royal ear, had him imprisoned in a fortress in Azerbaijan instead.

In 1848 the Bab wrote *Bayan* (Utterance), a book of homilies and laws intended to supersede the Qu'ran, and so made a claim to be a prophet in his own right. He taught that one should try to see God in the faces of others; that interest should be allowed on loans; that unrelated men and women might converse, and that European carpetbaggers should be excluded from some Iranian provinces. By 1849 he was said to have attracted 100,000 Iranians, mostly artisans, merchants, and lower-level clergy, to his religion. Fighting broke out between his partisans and conservative Shi'ites. The state executed the Bab in Tabriz in 1850, and the Babi disturbances were brutally suppressed. In revenge, a cabal of Babis in Tehran attempted unsuccessfully to have Muhammad Shah's successor, Nasir al-Din Shah (1831–1896), assassinated in 1852. In response, Nasir al-Din launched a pogrom against Babis. Altogether, some 5,000 persons perished in Iran during these events. In 1863 one of the Bab's disciples founded the new Baha'i religion, which most Babis accepted.

Juan R. I. Cole

Further Reading
Abbas, Amanat. (1989) *Resurrection and Renewal: The Making of the Babi Movement, 1844–1850.* Ithaca, NY: Cornell University Press.

BABUR (1483–1530), founder of the Mughal empire. Born in Fergana in Central Asia on 14 February 1483, Zahir-ud-din Muhammad—better known as Babur or "the Tiger"—established what became known as the Mughal (or Moghul or Mongol) empire (1526–1857) in India (though he regarded himself as a Timurid Turk). One of the largest centralized empires in the premodern world, the Mughal empire lasted until the British exiled the last emperor in 1858. Babur was an excellent military commander, being a keen archer, horseman, and swimmer, as well as a cultured monarch and a lover of music, nature, gardens, and poetry. He wrote *The Baburnama*, considered to be the first autobiography in Islamic literature, a book that provides us with an official chronicle as well as an intimate personal memoir.

Although most widely associated with India, little about his life was Indian. He was born prince of Fergana in Transoxiana (modern Uzbekistan and Tajikistan), scion of a dynasty that reigned in eastern Iran and Central Asia, and was descended from Amir Temur (c. 1336–1405) on his father's side and Genghis Khan (1167–1227), the famed Mongol ruler, on his mother's. He occupied the throne of Samarqand at twelve, although the following decades were to see him lose and recapture this throne and several other kingdoms, including Kabul, on several occasions. Though a Sunni Muslim, he became, from his thirties, addicted to drink. His political philosophy was dictated by a driving ambition that saw him move due south and east to the Indian subcontinent. Though his forces were vastly outnumbered, Babur was successful through superior military strategy, firearms—matchlock guns and field cannons—and fast cavalry in defeating Ibrahim Lodhi (reigned 1517–1526), the ruler of the Delhi sultanate in North India, in a historic battle at Panipat in April 1526, thereby capturing the throne of Delhi. He spent

The grave of Babur in Kabul, Afghanistan. (PAUL ALMASY/ CORBIS)

1527 and 1528 expanding his empire, principally by defeating the other major power, the Rajput kings of northwestern India. However, he died at Agra, in northern India, on 25 December 1530 at the young age of forty-seven, bequeathing to his son a kingdom—consisting of Central Asian territories, Kabul, the Punjab, Delhi, and part of Bihar to the east and south to Gwalior—that had been conquered but not consolidated. He was later reburied in Kabul.

Chandrika Kaul

Further Reading
Babur, Zahiruddin Muhammad. (1996) *The Baburnama.* Translated and edited by Wheeler M. Thackston. New York: Oxford University Press.
Hasan, Mohibbul. (1985) *Babur: Founder of the Mughal Empire.* Delhi: Manohar.

BAC SON UPRISING The Bac Son uprising took place in a northern province of Vietnam that borders on China. The event happened in late 1940, after the German-sponsored government of Vichy France and Japan, an ally of Germany, had already signed an agreement whereby Japan acknowledged French sovereignty over its Indochinese colony. In exchange, Japan was allowed to use all Indochinese military facilities as well as station a specific number of troops in Indochina. Notwithstanding that accord, on 22 September 1940, the Japanese Canton army attacked and overran a few French outposts along the

Sino-Vietnamese frontier. The operation lasted only three days, but it was sufficient to demonstrate that French Indochinese forces were in no position to resist the Japanese onslaught.

Capitalizing on these circumstances and waiting for the French along their humiliating retreat, Vietnamese anti-French groups—such as members of the Viet Nam Quoc Dan Dang, the local cadres of the Indochinese Communist Party (ICP), and the Tho minority—all took up their arms in an attempt to chase the French military out of the northern provinces of Vietnam, including Bac Son's province of Thai Nguyen. The insurgents succeeded in occupying a couple of French military positions, disarming a number of French and indigenous soldiers, and issuing declarations of independence. Vietnamese historians label this movement the Bac Son uprising, elevating it—as well as the insurgency that occurred two months later in the south, known under the name of the Southern Vietnam uprising—to the same level as many anti-Chinese struggles in the past, such as that of the Trung Sisters in 40 CE, Le Loi in the fifteenth century, or the Tay Son in the late eighteenth century.

The Bac Son uprising naturally ended in disaster within less than a month. In effect, even if the French could not mount an appropriate resistance to Japanese troops, they were ten times better armed and more adequately trained than a few thousand thinly armed and untrained freedom fighters, no matter what degree of determination and enthusiasm the rebels had attained. It has been said that the Bac Son uprising contributed greatly to the military training of the members of the Indochinese Communist Party, for Bac Son constituted that organization's first armed confrontation with colonial forces, and it was also there that the first guerrilla units were set up.

Truong Buu Lam

Further Reading
McAlister, John T. (1969) *Viet Nam: The Origins of Revolution*. New York: Knopf.
Nguyen Khanh Toan, ed. (1989) *Lich su Viet Nam*. Vol. 2. 2d ed. Hanoi, Vietnam: Nha Xuat Ban Khoa Hoc Xa Hoi.

BACHCHAN, AMITABH
(b. 1942), Indian actor. Amitabh Bachchan is the son of the acclaimed Hindi poet Harivansh Rai (b. 1907). He was born in Allahabad, Uttar Pradesh, India on 11 October 1942. After completing his education at Delhi University, Amitabh entered the world of Hindi films (also known as Bollywood) and in the early 1970s had his first string of successful feature films, including *Zanjeer* and *Deewar*. From the 1970s through the mid-1980s, Amitabh continued to dominate India's big screen with films such as *Sholay*, *Silsila*, and *Sharaabi*.

In 1984, he cashed in on his box office stardom and made a successful bid for a seat in the Indian parliament. However, his stint in politics was short-lived, and he soon returned to Bollywood as an actor and CEO of his own entertainment company, Amitabh Bachchan Corporation Limited (ABCL).

To date, Amitabh has appeared in more than 100 Hindi films, and as a testament to his overwhelming worldwide popularity he was selected by the public to be the first Bollywood star immortalized at Madame Toussaud's Wax Museum in London. Amitabh Bachchan lives in Bombay and is married to the famous screen actress Jaya Bhaduri (b. 1948).

Ami P. Shah

Further Reading
Somaaya, Bhawana. (1999) *Amitabh Bachchan: The Legend*. New Delhi: Macmillan India.

BACTRIA
The name of an ancient country in Central Asia, Bactria was the home of Iranian-speaking people from about the eighth century BCE and is thought to have been the birthplace of Zoroaster, the prophet of Persian religion. Bactria lay between the Hindu Kush and the Amu Dar'ya River, in today's Afghanistan, Tajikistan, and Uzbekistan. Its capital city, Bactra, was situated in northern Afghanistan, but since the nineteenth century the site has been no more than a village near the modern city of Mazar-i-Sharif.

Despite its rugged, mountainous, and desert terrain, Bactria was strategically located on the Silk Road linking Europe and China via Western Asia. To control this lucrative trade and to try to subdue the troublesome nomads inhabiting Bactria, Cyrus the Great (c. 585–c. 529 BCE) incorporated Bactria and the nomadic Bactrians into the vast Persian empire that once stretched from Egypt to India. Alexander of Macedon (356–323 BCE), during his conquest of the Persian empire, took Bactria in 328 BCE and ordered the execution of Bessus (d. c. 328 BCE), the ruler of Bactria. A Persian who had been the satrap of Bactria and Sogdia, Bessus fought with the Persians against Alexander's forces but plotted the murder of the last Persian monarch, Darius III (d. 330 BCE), and tried unsuccessfully to usurp the Persian throne.

Alexander left a small Greek garrison in Bactria and installed a Greek governor, before continuing to India on his campaigns. For the next half-century, Bactria was a province of the Seleucid empire, ruled by Alexander's Macedonian Greek successors, but during the reign of the satrap Diodotus I Soter (reigned c. 256–235 BCE), Bactria revolted and became independent.

Bactria remained an island of Greek culture in Central Asia and during its zenith controlled a significant part of what is now Afghanistan, Tajikistan, and Uzbekistan. Around 135 BCE, however, an invasion of Saka nomads from the steppes overran the country. Kushan nomads, from the eastern steppes, in turn conquered the Saka and introduced their Buddhism to Bactria. By around 55 BCE, Bactria had disappeared as an independent political entity and was home to various nomadic groups whose loyalty did not extend beyond the borders of their lands.

The region of Bactria then became known as Balkh; it fell to the Muslims in the seventh century, and thus Islam spread through the area. The violent history of Bactria, however, even today continues to influence the politics of the region.

Rafis Abazov

Further Reading
Holt, Frank Lee. (1999) *Thundering Zeus: The Making of Hellenistic Bactria*. Hellenistic Culture and Society, 32. Berkeley and Los Angeles: University of California Press.
Rawlinson, H. G. ([1909] 1978) *Bactria, from the Earliest Times to the Extinction of Bactrio-Greek Rule in the Punjab*. Reprint ed. Delhi: Bharatiya.
Sarianidi, Viktor Ivanovich. (1985) *The Golden Hoard of Bactria: From the Tillya-Tepe Excavations in Northern Afghanistan*. New York: Abrams.
Tarn W. W. (1997) *The Greeks in Bactria and India*. 3d ed., rev. Chicago: Ares.

BADAKHSHAN Badakhshan is a mountainous region divided between northeastern Afghanistan and the republic of Tajikistan. China borders both units to the north.

Once part of the ancient Greek kingdom of Bactria, the rugged mountain and valley terrain of the Badakhshan Province (2002 pop. 992,000) in northeast Afghanistan covers 43,626 square kilometers between the Hindu Kush Mountains and the Amu Dar'ya River. A panhandle extension juts northward to the Xinjiang region in China, and separates Tajikistan to the north and Pakistan to the south. The extraction of gold and precious stones, such as lapis luzuli, emeralds, amethysts, and rubies, is the chief economic pursuit in the mountains. The fertile river valleys support barley, wheat, opium, and apricots, while animals (cattle, sheep, and goats) graze wherever moisture supports forage. The provincial capital and commercial center is Faizabad (2002 population 149,000 people), on the Kokcha River. The tree-lined streets are in stark contrast to the barren mountains that surround the city. Tajiks comprise the majority ethnic group.

Within Tajikistan, the Gorno-Badakhshan Autonomous Oblast is a poor, sparsely populated, and isolated administrative unit with little political influence. During winter it is an enclosed geographical "dead end" resulting from border closures with neighboring China and Afghanistan and snows that block roads into western Tajikistan and Kyrgyzstan. This multifrontier corner of Central Asia has 44 percent of Tajikistan's land area (165,760 square kilometers) but only 3.3 percent of the population. Khorog (2002 population 29,000) is the capital. The majority Mountain Tajiks share this highland with Kyrgyz nomads, a dwindling number of Russians, and a mixture of Uygars, Kazakhs, and Mountain Tajiks from Afghanistan. The economy revolves around subsistence farming and animal husbandry. Opium smuggling has soared since the 1991 Soviet devolution and subsequent Tajik independence.

Stephen F. Cunha

Further Reading
Eicher, Sharon. (1995) "Tajikistan." In *Environmental Resources and Constraints in the Former Soviet Republics*, edited by P. R. Pryde. Boulder, CO: Westview.

BADAWI, ABDULLAH AHMED (b. 1939), Malaysian politician. Abdullah Ahmed Badawi is Malaysia's deputy prime minister and minister of home affairs and the vice president of the ruling United Malay National Organization (UMNO) party. Born on 26 November 1939 in Pulau Pinang, Badawi graduated from the University of Malaysia in 1964. He was a respected civil servant before running for parliament on the UMNO ticket in 1978. Not always one of Prime Minister Muhammad Mahatir's loyalists, Badawi was one of several politicians who challenged the prime minister in a leadership contest in 1987. But he never left UMNO, and chose to rise through the ranks. He served as minister in the prime minister's office (1981–1984), minister of education (1984–1986), minister of defense (1986–1987), and minister of foreign affairs (1991–1999). Badawi has held key

Deputy Prime Minister Abdullah Ahmad Badawi speaking at the UMNO Party convention in Kuala Lumpur in May 2000. (AFP/CORBIS)

UMNO party posts as well. He was elected party vice president for 1984–1990 and 1996–2000. He was a member of UMNO's thirty-five-person supreme council in 1991 and 1993–1996. Following the sacking and arrest of his longtime political rival, Deputy Prime Minister Anwar Ibrahim, Badawi was promoted to the posts of deputy prime minister, minister of home affairs, and vice president of UMNO, making him the prime minister's heir apparent. Badawi is a pragmatic politician, a pro-business secularist who has supported women's rights and fought against the Islamization of Malaysian politics.

Zachary Abuza

Further Reading
Andaya, Barbara Watson, and Leonard Y. Andaya. (2001) *A History of Malaysia*. 2d ed. Honolulu, HI: University of Hawaii Press.
Crouch, Harold. (1996) *Government and Society in Malaysia*. Ithaca, NY: Cornell University Press.

BAGHDAD (2002 est. pop. 5.6 million). Baghdad, on the Tigris River 150 kilometers from the ancient city of Babylon, was founded by the second Abbasid caliph, al-Mansur, in 762 CE on a site inhabited since the mid-third millennium BCE. The city, which is the capital of modern Iraq, achieved its greatest prominence in the medieval period; it became the capital of the Abbasid empire (749/750–1258) after its foundation and remained the capital until its sack by the Mongols in 1258. In its heyday in the ninth and tenth centuries, Baghdad was probably the largest city in the world, with a population estimated at 1.5 million, covering an area roughly the size of modern Paris inside the outer boulevards.

Named Madinat al-Salam (City of Peace) by its founder, the original eighth-to-tenth-century city was constructed on an immense scale: 100,000 laborers were employed to build a circular inner city some five kilometers in diameter, surrounded by a rampart with 360 towers. Only a few years after its foundation, Baghdad had expanded outside the walls, to the south (Karkh) and to the east bank of the Tigris. The location of the new Abbasid capital reflected the new Eastern orientation of the Islamic *dawla* (state); as was clearly indicated by the rebellion that brought the Abbasids to power, their power base lay in Iraq and western Iran.

Baghdad in Its Heyday
Medieval Arab geographers left detailed descriptions of the city, stressing its magnificence, its huge domed palace (Bab al-Dhahab), and its numerous mosques and extensive markets. Under the Abbasids an elaborate court ritual developed, in which the rulers (descended from the family of the Prophet Muhammad) were segregated from their subjects. They made only ceremonial appearances, in a manner similar to that of the Sasanid monarchs (whose great ruined palace at Ctesiphon lies some forty kilometers south of the medieval city) who had ruled the area from the third to the seventh centuries, and of the Achaemenid rulers who flourished from 559 to 330 BCE.

The city went through many vicissitudes as a result of struggles both between members of the Abbasid family and between the Abbasids and various dynasties that attempted to seize, sometimes successfully, political power during the tenth and eleventh centuries. Despite these conflicts the medieval city was almost unparalleled in its day as a center of law, learning, culture, and commerce. It was the home of the Hanafi and Hanbali schools of Islamic law and of numerous poets, historians, and scholars and had a diverse and international population. Even the Abbasids' rivals (such as the Shi'ite Buyids in the tenth and eleventh

The Saddam City Housing Estate in Baghdad in February 1997. (CAROLINE PENN/CORBIS)

centuries and their Sunni successors, the Seljuks) continued the architectural traditions of the past, with such buildings as the Adudi hospital (982) and the Nizamiyya *madrasah* (Islamic theological college; 1066). Baghdad was also the center of an elaborate and far-reaching banking system, which was crucial in ensuring the city's continuing commercial preeminence. The seventh and ninth Shi'ite imams, Musa al-Kadhim (745–799) and his grandson Muhammad al-Taqi (c. 810–835), are buried at al-Kadhimiya (Kadhimain) just outside Baghdad, and this site remains an important Shi'ite pilgrimage center.

Baghdad's Decline

Baghdad was already in decline in the twelfth century, but major and almost mortal blows were struck by the invasions of the two Mongol conquerors Hulegu (1258) and Timur (Tamerlane; 1393, 1401). Large numbers of the city's inhabitants were killed, and many of its great public buildings destroyed. A period of stagnation and decay followed until the sixteenth and seventeenth centuries, when the city was fought over by the Safavids and the Ottomans, finally passing to the Ottomans in 1638. The Ottoman Evliya Chelebi and other travelers of this period described the city as a prosperous trading center, the main intersection of commerce between Arabia, Anatolia, and Persia. However, little of the splendid medieval architecture survived the Mongol attacks.

The city remained a provincial capital (although under Mamluk governors between 1749 and 1831) for the rest of the Ottoman period, undergoing a brief period of reform and modernization under the energetic Midhat Pasa (1822–1883), governor between 1869 and 1872. Midhat established several modern (secular) schools and introduced a tramway and a printing press, as well as a river steamboat line between Baghdad and Basra. He was also responsible for introducing the body of Ottoman administrative and legal reforms known collectively as the Tanzimat, which had been promulgated elsewhere in the Ottoman empire since the 1830s. The Ottoman *salnameh*s (provincial yearbooks) for 1900–1901 give the male population of the city as 70,000 (57,000 Muslim males, 12,000 Jewish males, and 1,000 Christian males), from which a total population of 120,000–130,000 can be extrapolated.

Baghdad in the Twentieth and Twenty-First Centuries

Southern Iraq was invaded by British troops in 1914, and Baghdad was eventually captured in March 1917. After the war and the collapse of the Ottoman empire, Baghdad became the capital of the new state of Iraq, which remained under British mandate until 1932. The British introduced a monarchy headed by Faisal, son of Sharif Hussein of Mecca, who reigned from 1921 until his death in 1933. In 1958, the monarchy was overthrown in the course of a military coup, and a republic was installed. Baghdad and the rest of Iraq has been ruled by a military-civilian group nominally associated with the Ba'th Party since 1968; in fact, the form of government since 1979 has been a totalitarian dictatorship under the presidency of Saddam Hussein.

The city has grown immensely in recent years. The aggregate of urban communities is mostly populated by Sunni and Shi'ite Muslims, although the Shi'ites are probably more numerous. The Jewish community, a lively presence in the city until mass migration to Israel in the late 1940s and early 1950s, has almost entirely vanished; its commercial role was largely taken over by Shi'ite businesspeople. There are a number of (rather small) communities of Orthodox and Catholic Christians. Baghdad has several universities, as well as the Iraqi Museum, established in the 1920s, which houses unique collections of pre-Islamic antiquities, many marking the beginnings of civilization in the ancient Near East.

Baghdad suffered extensive destruction by aerial bombardment in January–February 1990 during the U.S.-led attack following Iraq's invasion of Kuwait, and the economic sanctions imposed since that time have gravely affected the city's infrastructure. The economy and the urban fabric are unlikely to recover substantially while the present regime remains in power.

Peter Sluglett

Further Reading
Batatu, Hanna. (1978) *The Old Social Classes and the Revolutionary Movements of Iraq: A Study of Iraq's Old Landed and Commercial Classes and of Its Communists, Ba'thists, and Free Officers*. Princeton, NJ: Princeton University Press.

Ibn Hawqal, Abu'l-Qasim Muhammad. (1800) *The Oriental Geography of Ebn Kaukal, an Arabian Traveller of the Tenth Century*. Trans. by William Ouseley. London: Wilson.

Issawi, Charles. (1988) *The Fertile Crescent 1800–1914: A Documentary Economic History*. New York: Oxford University Press.

Lassner, Jacob. (1970) *The Topography of Baghdad in the Early Middle Ages*. Detroit, MI: Wayne State University Press.

Longrigg, Stephen H. (1925) *Four Centuries of Modern Iraq*. Oxford: Clarendon Press.

Wiet, Gaston. (1971) *Baghdad: Metropolis of the Abbasid Caliphate*. Trans. by Seymour Feiler. Norman, OK: University of Oklahoma Press.

BAGONBANTA, FERNANDO (c. late 1500s–c. early 1600s), Ladino poet. Fernando Bagonbanta is credited with writing some of the earliest Tagalog poetry written in the Spanish alphabetic form. These poems appeared in early catechisms and served to teach Filipinos the Spanish language and Catholicism. In 1605, works of Bagonbanta were included in *Memorial de la vida cristiana en lengua tagala* (Guidelines for the Christian Life in the Tagalog Language), published by Francisco Blancas de San José, a Dominican friar, and intended to be an exposition of basic Catholic doctrines in Tagalog. Blancas introduced Bagonbanta as a Ladino, one well versed both in Spanish and Tagalog. Included in *Memorial de la vida cristiana en lengua tagala* is "Salamat nang ualang hanga" (Endless Thanks), a poem translated by Bagonbanta from the Spanish. Little else is known about Bagonbanta's life.

Damon L. Woods

Further Reading
Lumbera, Bienvenido L. (1986) *Poetry 1570–1898: Tradition and Influences in Its Development*. Quezon City, Philippines: Ateneo de Manila University Press.

BAGRAM In 330 BCE, during his military campaigns in Bactria and Central Asia, Alexander of Macedon founded a city fifty miles north of the modern city of Kabul in Afghanistan, at the confluence of the Ghorband and Panjsher Rivers, and named it Alexandria. A few centuries later, due to its position, this military outpost had grown to be a major mercantile emporium on the Silk Road and a Buddhist center, especially under the Kushan dynasty (78–200 CE). The Kushans, a nomadic people, belonged to the Yueh-chih confederation; after having unified all the other Yueh-chih, the Kushans created an empire in present-day north-central Afghanistan and northwestern India. Under the Kushan king Kanisha (c. 78–144 CE), Bactrian Alexandria, now known as Kapisa, became the Kushan summer capital. Rich archaeological discoveries were revealed at the site in the twentieth century.

Probably destroyed in 241 CE by the Iranian Sassanids, Kapisa (modern Bagram; est. pop. 454,000) faced a long period of decline. Deserted by its inhabitants, it became the spring grazing ground for local nomadic tribes. In the 1950s the area, with the Islamic name of Bagram, was selected as a main base for the Afghan air force. Its airport was widely used by the Red Army during the Soviet occupation of Afghanistan (1979–1988). During the subsequent civil war among different Afghan factions, the area was repeatedly conquered and suffered extensive damage. In late 2001 the Bagram airport again became an important base—this time used by U.S. military personnel conducting air strikes against Taliban forces in Afghanistan.

Riccardo Redaelli

Further Reading
Hackin, Joseph. (1954) *Nouvelles recherches archéologiques à Begram, ancienne Kapici, 1939–1940: rencontre de trois civilisations, Inde, Grèce, Chine. Mémoires de la Délégation archéologique française en Afghanistan.* Paris: Impr. Nationale.

BAGUIO (2001 est. pop. 252,386). Baguio (from the Ibaloi word *bigyiw*, a native mosslike green plant), a city in Benguet Province, northwest Luzon, the Philippines, is an important commercial, educational, and cultural center. It was the summer capital of the country until 1976. It is situated 260 kilometers (161 miles) north of Manila, on the pleasant hills of the Cordillera Mountains at about 1,500 meters (4,920 feet) above sea level.

The history of Baguio began in the nineteenth century, when Spanish colonizers began to exploit natural resources, such as copper and gold, in northwest Luzon and established *rancherías* in the fertile valleys of Benguet. After the American occupation of the Philippines in 1898, the governor, William Howard Taft, who later became the president of the United States, suggested building a modern city in Kafagway (later renamed Baguio) to escape the summer heat of Manila. In 1903 Baguio was officially named the summer capital of the Philippines. Between 1904 and 1919 roads and an airport were built to connect Baguio with Manila. However, during World War II the United States was forced to abandon the country, and in 1941 the Japanese Imperial Army occupied the Philippines. During the war a garrison and a concentration camp were established in Baguio. In 1945 the U.S. Army defeated the Japanese occupation forces, and Japanese general Yamashita Tomoyuki was brought to Baguio to sign the capitulation.

After World War II, Baguio grew significantly and became an important commercial, educational, and recreational center for Benguet Province as well for the Cordilleras and Northern Luzon, relying on agriculture, mining (copper and gold), and tourism. It was seriously damaged during an earthquake in 1990 but was quickly rebuilt. It is the home of the Philippine Military Academy, the University of Baguio, St. Louis University, and other universities.

Rafis Abazov

Further Reading
Connaughton, Richard. (2001) *MacArthur and Defeat in the Philippines.* New York: Overlook.
Davis, William G. (1973) *Social Relations in a Philippine Market: Self-Interest and Subjectivity.* Berkeley and Los Angeles: University of California Press.
Rafael, Vicente L. (2000) *White Love and Other Events in Filipino History.* Durham, NC: Duke University Press.
Reed, Robert Ronald. (1976) *City of Pines: The Origins of Baguio as a Colonial Hill Station and Regional Capital.* Berkeley, CA: Center for South and Southeast Asia Studies, University of California.

BAHADUR SHAH (1775–1862), last Mughal emperor of India. Born in Delhi, Bahadur Shah II, second son of Akbar Shah II (reigned 1806–1837), was the last Mughal emperor of India, reigning over a large part of the Indian subcontinent from 1837 to 1857. Although the titular sovereign, Bahadur Shah had no actual power, since the British retained real suzerainty over all the Indian territories they controlled, either directly or indirectly, through the well-known administrative system of "indirect rule." Particularly after the Charter Act of 1833, which expanded British rule over India, his authority extended no further than the walls of his palace.

In 1857, during the so-called Indian Great Mutiny against British colonial rule, the elderly Bahadur Shah became the unwilling leader of the revolt and was used as a figurehead by the mutinous Indian troops. When Delhi was recaptured by the British a few months later, Bahadur Shah was exiled to Rangoon in Burma, and his sons were brutally killed by British soldiers after they had surrendered. Bahadur Shah died in exile.

Bahadur Shah's real interest was not power, but poetry, miniatures, music, and calligraphy. Under the pen name of Zafar, he wrote poems of some note; his lyrics, set to music, were frequently performed in Delhi, while his court became a renowned artistic center.

Riccardo Redaelli

Further Reading
Burke, S. M. (1995) *Bahadur Shah: The Last Mogul Emperor of India.* Lahore, Pakistan: Sang-e-Meel.
Spear, Percival. (1951) *Twilight of the Mughals.* Cambridge, U.K.: Cambridge University Press.

BAHA'I Baha'i is a relatively new world religion that was founded and initially developed in Iran in the 1860s. It emerged from Iranian Shi'a Islam and drew most of its initial adherents from the earlier Babism movement in Iran. Adherents have been at times persecuted as heretics by Muslims in several Islamic nations, including Iran, and as Baha'is sought religious freedom elsewhere, the movement spread to other Asian nations, Europe, and the Americas. In Asia in the twenty-first century, India is the center of the Baha'i religion, while the United States (with a major center in Wilmette, Illinois) and Israel (with world headquarters in Haifa) are also important in the global Baha'i religion. Estimates of the number of Baha'i adherents worldwide are unreliable, ranging from a low of 130,000 to a high of 5,000,000.

Founding and Early Development

The Baha'i faith was founded in Baghdad, Iraq, in 1863 by Mirza Hosayn Ali Nuri (1817–1892), known as Bahaullah (Glory of God). Baha'i grew out of Babism, a messianic movement of Iranian Shi'ite Islam that was suppressed in the 1850s. Mirza Hosayn Ali was a middle son of a high-ranking Iranian official, Mirza Buzurg Nuri (d. 1839). He became a Babi in 1844 and also converted his brother Subh-i Azal. In 1852, in the wake of a Babi attempt on the life of the shah, Bahaullah was imprisoned. Although he was found innocent, he was nevertheless exiled to Ottoman Baghdad. In the 1850s, many claimants, including his brother, arose to Babi leadership. Although he outwardly supported the claim of Azal, Bahaullah attracted a following through his mystical treatises and poetry. Many, including the Ottoman and Iranian governments, acknowledged him as the true leader of the movement.

In spring 1863, the Iranians succeeded in pressuring the Ottomans to move Bahaullah from Baghdad, where he was in constant touch with Iranian pilgrims, to Edirne in European Turkey. Before he left Baghdad, Bahaullah openly declared to a handful of family members and friends that he was the promised one foretold by the Bab. After a brief stay in Istanbul, Bahaullah spent from 1863 to 1868 in Edirne, where he gradually made his claims public. By early 1866, Bahaullah had split with Azal, whose authority as putative pontiff of Babism was shaken. Over time all but a small minority of Babis adopted the new Baha'i faith as followers of Bahaullah.

The dissension between the Babis came to the attention of the Ottomans, who decided to exile the two leaders yet again. Azal was sent to Cyprus. Bahaullah and his followers were sent to the fortress at Akka (now Akko in Israel), along the coast of Ottoman Syria. After two years Bahaullah and his followers were allowed to move into the town of Akka, and he spent the rest of his life in Palestine. In 1872, he finished his *Kitab-*

i Aqdas (Most Holy Book), the book of laws for the new religion he had founded. Bahaullah said he received divine revelations and was a messenger of God, destined to be as influential as Moses, Krishna, Jesus, Zoroaster, and Muhammad. He emphasized that all the great religions had the same divine source, and he preached against religious intolerance. He advocated international peace conferences and an end to war and arms races, sought improved status for women and universal education, opposed royal absolutism and urged parliamentary government, and prescribed local steering committees called houses of justice to administer the affairs of the Baha'is. He ordained a global house of justice as the head of his religion in the future. In the meantime, he advised his followers to look for guidance after his death to his eldest son, 'Abdu'l-Baha 'Abbas (1844–1921). During his own lifetime, Bahaullah's disciple Jamal Effendi spread the Baha'i faith to the Indian subcontinent and Burma, where small communities were established. Bahaullah died in Palestine in 1892.

Baha'i under 'Abdu'l-Baha

Soon after his father's death, 'Abdu'l-Baha faced a schism brought on by the opposition of his younger half-brother Mirza Muhammad 'Ali. 'Abdu'l-Baha responded peacefully, urging his own partisans simply to shun the schismatics, and managed to maintain the unity of the community. In other respects 'Abdu'l-Baha was progressive. He advocated parliamentary democracy and the adoption of modern education and technology in Iran. He condemned the interference of religious authorities in affairs of state, saying that history proved such interference to be a disaster. He was initially wary of the Iranian Constitutional Revolution of 1905–1911 and cautioned the Baha'is against becoming involved in the struggle. However, in 1909, after the success of the Constitution was assured, he urged the Baha'is to support constitutionalism and to attempt to elect Baha'is to the new Iranian parliament. 'Abdu'l-Baha was freed from Ottoman restrictions by the Young Turk Revolution in 1908–1909.

In the 1890s, a Lebanese convert had brought the Baha'i faith to the United States. By 1912, the small American community succeeded in inducing an elderly 'Abdu'l-Baha to speak throughout the country, preaching his father's universalistic teachings and adapting them to a Western audience. He also spoke in Europe. In America, the Baha'i community, although small, survives to this day; the largest American Baha'i center is outside Chicago in Wilmette, Illinois.

'Abdu'l-Baha ordained national houses of justice and established the institution of "the guardian" to serve as the interpreter of scripture after his death. He appointed his grandson Shoghi Effendi Rabbani as the first guardian. The guardians were to be aided by learned Baha'is referred to as "hands of the cause."

Baha'i under Shoghi Effendi Rabbani

In 1921–1957, the Baha'i faith was headed by Shoghi Effendi from Haifa. Shoghi Effendi postponed having the universal house of justice elected; however, he organized the Baha'is into national communities under the close leadership of their national spiritual assemblies, several of which were established in the 1920s, including that of India. Shoghi Effendi accomplished a major reformation of the Baha'i faith, which had previously been somewhat non-creedal, tolerant, and universalistic. Unlike 'Abdu'l-Baha, he forbade the Baha'is to be members of political parties or hold high political office. Whether or not it was Shoghi Effendi's intention, during his ministry Baha'i officials steered the religion toward tight organization, the strict authority of Baha'i institutions over individuals, an emphasis on doctrinal purity, and a more literalist approach to scripture. Shoghi Effendi introduced new sanctions and extended the use of shunning, even to his own parents. He appointed a cadre of hands of the cause to serve as lay bishops. He launched a number of missionary campaigns, which succeeded in spreading the religion thinly around the world. Although the increasingly regimented Iranian Baha'i community probably shrank during his ministry, from perhaps 200,000 to 100,000 committed Baha'is, his emphasis on missionary work in the Third World began to bear fruit toward the end of his life.

The sudden death of Shoghi Effendi without an heir in 1957 bewildered the Baha'is, who had been promised a string of guardians. The hands of the cause took control and worked toward the election of the universal house of justice. This new body, originally envisaged by Bahaullah, was elected in 1963 by the members of national assemblies around the world. One of its first members was Hushmand Fatheazam, a Persian professor and Iranian emigrant to India who was then serving on India's national assembly.

Baha'i after Shoghi Effendi

In 1961, mass conversions to the Baha'i faith had begun in Malwa, India, among scheduled-caste (low-caste) peasants. The Baha'i community of Malwa had originally been small and of largely Parsi ethnic origin. After the conversions, however, India began to emerge as a major Baha'i center. Many of the strict

'ABDU'L-BAHA ON THE EQUALITY OF WOMEN AND MEN:

And among the teachings of Bahaullah is the equality of women and men. The world of humanity has two wings—one is women and the other men. Not until both wings are equally developed can the bird fly. Should one wing remain weak, flight is impossible. Not until the world of women becomes equal to the world of men in the acquisition of virtues and perfections, can success and prosperity be attained as they ought to be.

Source: Selections from the Writings of 'Abdu'l-Baha. Rev. ed. (1982) Haifa: Baha'i World Centre, 302. Quoted at: http://www .bahai.org/article-1-3-4-6.html.

rules that had limited the religion in Iran were relaxed in India, and allowances were made for the syncretism of peasant Hindu converts. The unity of God, unity of religions, and abolition of prejudices were stressed, appealing to low-caste and outcaste converts, although some Indians complained of Iranian Baha'i paternalism toward them. To downplay the Islamic origins of the religion, Baha'i scriptures and prayers were translated into a form of Hindi that is much closer in vocabulary to Sanskrit. By the 1990s there were claims of 2,000,000 Baha'is in India; however, insider estimates were closer to 110,000, and only 5,000 Baha'is were reported in the 1990 Indian census. Similar mass conversions in Vietnam were stopped by the 1975 Communist victory. In the year 2000, there were about 10,000 Baha'is in Thailand and about 25,000 in Pakistan (mostly drawn from the remnant of Hindus in Sind who did not flee from Pakistan to India at partition in 1947). Elsewhere, national communities were quite small, often less than 2,000. The 1979 Islamic revolution brought to power Shi'ite clergymen who had long despised the Baha'i faith as a dangerous heresy. Under Khomeini, around 200 Baha'is were executed, and thousands were imprisoned or expropriated. Many were forced to renounce the faith. The center of the Baha'i religion in Asia thus shifted decisively to India.

Juan R. I. Cole

See also: **Babism; Iran—Human Rights**

Further Reading

Cole, Juan R. I. (1998) *Modernity and the Millennium: The Genesis of the Baha'i Faith in the Nineteenth-Century Middle East.* New York: Columbia University Press.

Garlington, William. (1997) "The Baha'i Faith in India: A Developmental Stage Approach." *Occasional Papers in Shaykhi, Babi, and Baha'i Studies* 1, 2 (June). Retrieved 21 May 2001, from: http://www2.h-net.msu.edu/~bahai/bhpapers/india1.htm.

———. (1999) "The Development of the Baha'i Faith in Malwa: 1941–1974." *Occasional Papers in Shaykhi, Babi, and Baha'i Studies* 3, 1 (February). Retrieved 21 May 2001, from: http://www2.h-net.msu.edu/~bahai/bhpapers/vol3/malwa.htm.

Smith, Peter. (1987) *The Babi and Baha'i Religions.* Cambridge, MA: Cambridge University Press.

BAHASA INDONESIA Modern Indonesian is an Austronesian language, belonging to the same family as Hawaiian, Maori, Tagalog, Cham, and Malagasy. It is based on Malay, the main language of the Malay Peninsula and the eastern coast of Sumatra. Malay's importance derives from its role as the language of a succession of commercial states—notably Srivijaya, Jambi-Melayu, and Melaka—which dominated the lucrative trade routes of the Strait of Malacca from about 500 CE. From the thirteenth century, Malay appears to have spread widely in the coastal regions of the archipelago as a trading lingua franca.

In 1436, Melaka became the first large state in the archipelago to convert to Islam and the city became a major center of Islamic learning and the Malay language, which in turn became the principal language of Islamic conversion and discourse in the region. Arabic script was modified into a form, called *pegon*, suitable for writing Malay. Both Islam and the Malay language were spread further by the Muslim Malay diaspora that followed Melaka's fall to the Portuguese in 1511.

The Dutch East Indies Company (VOC) initially used Malay as a trading language, but found it useful also for administration. Whereas Javanese, the other major language of the archipelago, has elaborate levels of speech which make conversation difficult unless the hierarchical relationship of the speakers is clearly established, "trading Malay" had no such levels and became a conveniently neutral medium of communication. The spread of Malay was also assisted by Dutch ambivalence about promoting use of their own language, preferring to restrict Western education to those whom they felt needed it. Malay was also the main language of urban *peranakan* Chinese—that is, Chinese who retained their broad cultural identity but assimilated much local culture, including language.

In the late nineteenth century, newspapers began to appear in Malay, which gradually became the main indigenous language for engaging with the modern world. In the twentieth century, Malay was extensively used as a literary language by the Balai Pustaka, an official colonial publishing house whose task was to promote literacy. Indonesian nationalists also favored Malay because it was widely known, easy to learn, and lacked the hierarchical rules of Javanese, which they often rejected as "feudal." In 1928, a nationalist youth congress formally adopted Malay as the national language, calling it Indonesian—Bahasa Indonesia— after the independent country to which they aspired. There was no doubt it would be the official language after independence. The transition from Dutch, now rarely used in Indonesia, was hastened by the Japanese occupation (1942–1945), during which the use of Dutch and other European languages was banned. Following independence, Indonesian became the sole language of administration and public life. Regional languages, taught for only a few years in primary school, have been in retreat, though they have been sustained in Christian regions by their use in church services.

Characteristics

The vocabulary of Bahasa Indonesia has been extensively influenced by outside languages, especially Sanskrit, Arabic, Chinese, Dutch, and English, as well as local languages such as Javanese. European influence on syntax has also been considerable. A national language commission has existed since shortly after independence with the dual task of developing Indonesian as a language able to cope with a full range of technical and philosophical topics and of protecting the language against unwanted change, including outside influence. Despite these efforts, however, vocabulary in Indonesian changes rapidly, and urban dialects, incomprehensible to standard speakers, develop and disappear rapidly.

Indonesian has no conjugations or declensions: order rather than inflexion determines the role of words in a sentence. It has, however, an elaborate system of prefixes and suffixes that alter the part of speech of a root word. For instance: the root word *tinggal* (to stay) gives rise to *tinggalnya* (place of residence), *meninggalkan* (to leave behind), *ditinggalkan* (left behind), *ketinggalan* (remainder), *peninggalan* (remains), *sepeninggal* (in the absence of), *tinggalan* (inheritance), and *meninggal* (to die). Other prefixes such as *pasca-* (post-) and *tuna-* (without) are recent developments reflecting Western influences.

Charles Adriaan van Ophuijzen, a colonial education official and later professor of Malay at Leiden

University, developed a spelling system for Malay in 1901, but this system was modified after independence to remove several conventions based on Dutch: in 1947 *oe* became *u* and in 1973, under an Indonesian-Malaysian Language Agreement, *ch* changed to *kh*, *dj* to *j*, *j* to *y*, and *tj* to *c*. Malay also gave rise to the national language *(bahasa kebangsaan)* of independent Malaysia, which differs from Bahasa Indonesia only in accent and some vocabulary.

Robert Cribb

Further Reading

Anwar, Khaidir. (1980) *Indonesian: The Development and Use of a National Language.* Yogyakarta, Indonesia: Gadjah Mada University Press.

Sneddon, J. N. (1996) *Indonesian Reference Grammar.* St. Leonard's, Australia: Allen & Unwin.

BAITURSYNOV, AKHMET (1873–1937),

Kazakh poet, journalist, linguist, educator. Akhmet Baitursynov, born 15 January 1873 in Turgai Oblast, is most noted for his efforts to standardize Kazakh orthography. While Baitursynov was still a child, his father, Baitursyn, was exiled for fifteen years in Siberia for an alleged attack against a czarist official. The family was left destitute, but Baitursynov was able to enroll in 1886 in a Russian-Kazakh secondary school in Turgai. Graduating in 1891, he entered the Orenburg Teachers' School, where he spent the next four years. Both of these institutions were heavily influenced by pedagogic methods established by Ibrahim Altynsarin that stressed teaching in both Kazakh and Russian. Baitursynov graduated in 1895 and held teaching positions at a number of schools in Aqtobe, Kustanai, and Karkaralinsk. That same year he published his first article, "Kirgizskie primety i poslovitsy" (Kazakh Omens and Proverbs), in the regional newspaper, *Turgaiskaia gazeta*. In October 1905 he joined other Kazakhs in the city of Ural and helped create the Kazakh branch of the Constitutional Democrat Party, beginning his active political career. In 1909 he published *Qyryq mysal* (Forty Proverbs), which was influenced by Ivan Krylov's fables but written in a manner that seemed best suited for a Kazakh reader and corresponded to Kazakh culture and nomadic sensibilities. His collection of translations was followed in 1911 by an original collection of poetry entitled *Masa* (Mosquito). Whereas *Qyryq mysal* was pedagogic in nature, *Masa* was much more political and incendiary. In 1913 Baitursynov became the editor of the newspaper *Kazak*, which became the most successful prerevolutionary Kazakh periodical. Following the 1917 Russ-

ian Revolution, he became a leader of the Kazakh political party Alash Orda (The Horde of Alash), which fought for an independent Kazakh state. In 1920 the Bolsheviks consolidated power in Central Asia, and Baitursynov joined them. Throughout the 1920s he was active in educational reforms and helped establish the first Kazakh university. In 1937 he was arrested for harboring bourgeois nationalist sentiments and executed during the Stalinist purges. He was rehabilitated in 1989.

Steven Sabol

Further Reading

Baitursynov, Akhmet. (1989) *Shygharmalary: Olengder, audarmalar, zertteuler* (Collected Works: Verse, Translations, Investigations). Almaty, Kazakhstan: Zhazushy.

———. (1991) *Aq zhol* (The White Road). Almaty, Kazakhstan: Zhalyn.

Syzdyqova, Rabigha. (1990) *Akhmet Baitursynov*. Almaty, Kazakhstan: Bilim.

Winner, Thomas. (1958) *The Oral Art and Literature of the Kazakhs of Central Asia*. Durham, NC: Duke University Press.

BAKHSH, DATA GANJ (d. c. 1072), Sufi master and writer. An honorific title meaning "Master Bestower of Treasure" given to the Sufi master 'Ali b. 'Uthman Jullabi Hujviri, whose shrine in Lahore, Pakistan, is one of the foremost Muslim religious sites in South Asia. Data Ganj Bakhsh was born in Afghanistan and arrived in Lahore in 1039 after an extensive study tour across Arab and Iranian lands in search of religious knowledge. He is best known for his Persian work *Kashf al-mahjub* (The Revelation of the Veiled), an early systematic presentation of Sufism as a distinct Islamic perspective. His mausoleum was constructed soon after his death and has been renovated and expanded numerous times.

In addition to his being revered for his scholarly reputation, Data Ganj Bakhsh has served as the patron saint of the city of Lahore since the twelfth century. His tomb was a major pilgrimage site for kings, Sufi masters, and common people through the medieval period, and its popularity has increased in modern times. Although the shrine is busy year-round with visitors offering prayers and seeking material as well as spiritual benefits, the saint's annual death celebration ('Urs) takes place on the twentieth of Safar (second month of the lunar Islamic calendar) and is now administered by the government of Pakistan. The celebration in 1999 was attended by an estimated 600,000 to 700,000 pilgrims, making it one of the largest gatherings of its kind in the Islamic world. The shrine also regularly hosts concerts of *qawwali* music and performances of *dhamal* dance. The shrine complex is surrounded by both a bazaar and charitable institutions that provide food and medical care to the indigent.

Shahzad Bashir

Further Reading
Hasan, Masudul. (1971) *Hazrat Data Ganj Bakhsh: A Spiritual Biography.* Lahore, Pakistan: Hazrat Data Ganj Bakhsh Academy.
Huda, Qamar-ul. (2000) "Celebrating Death and Engaging in Texts at Data Ganj Bakhsh's *'Urs."* *Muslim World* 90, 3 & 4 (Fall): 377–394.
Hujviri, 'Ali b. 'Uthman. (1976) *The Kashf al-mahjub: The Oldest Persian Treatise on Sufism.* Reprint, translated by Reynold A. Nicholson. Lahore, Pakistan: Islamic Book Foundation.
Latif, Syad Muhammad. (1892) *Lahore: Its History, Architectural Remains, and Antiquities.* Lahore, Pakistan: New Imperial Press.

BAKHTARAN (2002 est. province pop. 2 million; 2002 est. city [Kermanshah] pop. 771,000). Bakhtaran, a province in midwestern Iran formerly called Kermanshah, is both mountainous and endowed with valleys. With an area of approximately 24,500 square kilometers, Bakhtaran is bounded on the north by the province of Kurdistan; on the south by Lorestan and Ilam; on the east by Hamadan; and on the west by Iraq.

The Sasanids founded the city of Kermanshah in the fourth century. The Arabs captured it in the seventh century, and it later became a fortress on the frontier with the Ottoman empire, which managed to occupy it several times, including during World War I.

The economy of Bakhtaran province relies heavily on agriculture. Wheat, oats, barley, corn, clover, beans, oilseeds, rice, and various fruits and vegetables are produced, in addition to animal husbandry and fishing. The main industries in the province are textile manufacturing, food processing, oil refining, carpet making, sugar refining, and production of electrical equipment.

Kurds, Lurs, Arabs, Azeris, and Persians inhabit the province, which is known for its nomadic communities. The official language is Persian, but other languages such as Kurdish, Lori, and Azerbaijani are widely spoken. The major religions are the Shi'a and Sunni branches of Islam. The city of Kermanshah serves as a transition base for Shi'ite Muslims on pilgrimage to Karbala in Iraq, a holy city with the shrine of a grandson of Muhammad, Caliph Hasan, who was

murdered there in 680. Numerous caravansaries serve these pilgrims.

Payam Foroughi and Raissa Muhutdinova-Foroughi

Further Reading
Clark, John Innes, and Brian Drummond Clark. (1969) *Kermanshah: An Iranian Provincial City.* Durham, U.K.: University of Durham, Department of Geography.

BAKHTIARI A nomadic group inhabiting the mountains of Khuzestan, a province in southwestern Iran, the Bakhtiari number almost 900,000. Traditionally, they migrate seasonally with their livestock between summer and winter pastures.

The Bakhtiari are mostly Shi'ite Muslims, but they retain many pre-Islamic customs. They can be divided into two main groups, the Haftlang (fifty-five tribes) and the Charlang (twenty-five tribes). They speak a dialect of Luri, an Iranian language closely related to Kurdish.

Women have an unusually high place in Bakhtiari society; they go about unveiled and can travel freely. The wives of khans or chieftains have been known to act as judges, and women sometimes head a migrating group of other women and children in the summer, after the men depart with the animals to mountainous pastures.

History
Although their origins are obscure, the Bakhtiari are believed to have migrated from Syria in the tenth century CE. They were known as the Great Lurs and retained regional autonomy during the rule of the various empires that dominated the region. In the early twentieth century, oil was discovered in the area they inhabited, and the British courted their khans and paid them to protect the oil wells and pipelines. The Bakhtiari played a pivotal role in the deposition of Ahmad Shah (1898–1930), the last ruler of the Iranian Qajar dynasty (1794–1925), in 1908–1909.

Modern Times
Reza Shah Pahlavi (1878–1944), who was elected shah in 1925, forced many Bakhtiari into settlements in the 1920s and 1930s during his attempts to modernize the country, but the Bakhtiari regained their prominence following his abdication in 1941. His son and successor Muhammad Reza Pahlavi (1919–1980) married Soraya, the daughter of a Bakhtiari khan, and many Bakhtiari returned to their nomadic way of life.

With the Islamic Revolution of 1979, the Bakhtiari became second-class citizens; both their ethnicity and their unorthodox religious practices made them a target of suspicion. Today they make much of their income by weaving and exporting rugs.

Brian M. Gottesman

Further Reading

Mortensen, Inge Demant, and Ida Nicholaisen, eds. (1993) *Nomads of Luristan: History, Material Culture, and Pastoralism in Western Iran.* London: Thames & Hudson.

BALI Bali, one of the islands of Indonesia, begins the archipelago stretching to Timor that is known as the Lesser Sunda Islands. Among these islands, the most densely populated have been Bali and its neighboring island of Lombok. The island of Bali has an area of 5,620 square kilometers. Lying just 8° south of the equator, the island has the even and warm climate of the tropics. These tropical weather conditions, together with the scenic natural beauty of the island, have made it a well-known holiday resort destination.

Bali's volcanic range dominates the landscape and also divides the island in half, since it stretches from east to west. The tallest mountain is the Gunung Agung, or Great Mountain. This was 3,140 meters high before it erupted in 1963. The population density is high, with some 2.5 million people living on the island. The most densely populated areas are the plains of central Bali. These plains produce two crops of rice a year. Large streams that have fanned out southward from the line of active volcanoes have built up a fertile inclined-alluvial plain. This is constantly rejuvenated by water-borne volcanic ash, upon which dense settlements and rice fields have been developed on ingeniously irrigated terraces that extend inland and upward to about 600 meters. The other major crop in terms of acreage covered is maize.

The people of Bali are mostly Hindus. Descended from high-caste Hindu Javanese who were driven eastward by the Islamization of Java, the people have retained an aristocratic society and a strongly communal life that has found expression in an elaborate artistic culture that has reached higher forms on Bali than anywhere else among the island peoples of Indonesia. The temple architecture of Bali is therefore unusually striking and complex. The Balinese also have longstanding traditions of craftsmanship in wood, stone, gold, silver, and weaving. These have export value and also support the considerable tourism industry.

Kog Yue Choong

Further Reading

Black, Star, and David Stuart-Fox. (1980) *Bali.* Hong Kong: Apa.
Dobby, E. G. H. (1958) *Southeast Asia.* London: University of London Press.

Farmers work their terraced rice fields in Bali. (YANN ARTHUS-BERTRAND/CORBIS)

Stuart-Fox, David J. (1992) *Bibliography of Bali: Publications from 1920 to 1990.* Leiden, Netherlands: KITLV (Royal Dutch Institute of Linguistics and Anthropology).

Vickers, Adrian. (1994) *Travelling to Bali: Four Hundred Years of Journeys.* Kuala Lumpur, Malaysia, and New York: Oxford University Press.

BALI BARONG-RANGDA

Barong dances, among the most sacred in Bali, symbolize the intertwining of good and evil and the complex relationship between man and the supernatural. The term *barong* can apply to the dance, the mask, or the character depending on context. The *barong* animal mask represents good, and its types include the tiger, boar, and buffalo; the most characteristic, however, is the *barong kek*, a mythical animal. Two men dance; the one in front carries the *barong* mask, which is sacred and must never touch the ground. Evil is personified by Rangda—literally "widow," but interpreted as a witch associated with spirits of the dead. Several men armed with *keris* (daggers) accompany Rangda when she enters. Under her influence, they go into a trance and stab themselves, but are protected from injury by Barong's presence. Barong's eventual victory is taken to affirm his protection of the village. Both *barong* and *rangda* masks are kept in the village temple between performances. Though interpreted as good versus evil, the two sides are more equivocal, and Barong's victory is never regarded as conclusive.

Tim Byard-Jones

Further Reading

Yousouf, Ghulam-Sarwar. (1994) *Dictionary of Traditional South-East Asian Theatre.* Kuala Lumpur: Oxford University Press.

Eiseman, Fred B., Jr. (1990) *Bali: Sekala and Niskala.* Vol. 1, *Essays on Religion, Ritual, and Art.* Hong Kong: Periplus Editions.

Zoete, B. van, and Walter Spies. (1973) *Dance and Drama in Bali.* Oxford: Oxford University Press.

BALI SUMMIT

The Association of Southeast Asian Nations (ASEAN) was established in 1967 between Indonesia, Malaysia, the Philippines, Singapore, and Thailand. The first leaders' meeting was the Bali Summit of February 1976. ASEAN, officially organized to engage in economic and social cooperation, was actually more concerned with diplomatic and security issues in Southeast Asia. The importance of the Bali Summit was the display of solidarity by the noncommunist nations of Southeast Asia in the aftermath of communist takeovers in Vietnam, Cambodia, and Laos in 1975, and insurgencies elsewhere in the region. The Bali Summit was a milestone for the regional organization, as it established the Declaration of ASEAN Concord, which brought the Zone of Peace, Freedom and Neutrality (ZOPFAN, 1971) formally into the ASEAN ambit, and concluded the Treaty of Amity and Cooperation (TAC). ZOPFAN represents an ASEAN attempt to exclude great power conflicts from the region, while TAC codified an existing understanding that member states respect each others' sovereignty and peacefully resolve disputes. TAC has become the cornerstone of ASEAN cooperation, helping to smooth over a number of intra-ASEAN problems. This has meant solidifying disputed colonial borders, by, for example, mollifying the Philippine claim to Sabah (in East Malaysia), as well as commitments not to interfere in domestic problems, such as secessionist tendencies in Irian Jaya and Aceh (in Indonesia) and among the Muslim population of southern Thailand; at the same time ASEAN also supported Indonesia's controversial annexation of East Timor. Formal defense ties were, however, not included in the Declaration of ASEAN Concord. The Bali Summit also saw the establishment of a secretariat, based in Jakarta, which functions as a coordinating organization for the various ASEAN meetings and a repository of information.

Anthony Smith

Further Reading

Dewi Fortuna Anwar. (1994) *Indonesia in ASEAN: Foreign Policy and Regionalism.* New York and Singapore: St. Martin's Press and the Institute of Southeast Asian Studies.

Palmer, Ronald D., and Thomas J. Reckford. (1987) *Building ASEAN: 20 Years of Southeast Asian Cooperation.* New York: Praeger.

BALINESE

The Balinese are the ethnic and cultural group inhabiting the island of Bali in Indonesia in the Indian Ocean east of Java. Though like other Indonesians they are primarily of Malay ancestry, the Balinese are distinguished by their Hindu religion and culture, dating from before the tenth century. Historically the Balinese were associated with the classical kingdoms of Java. The Majapahit court was the center of the Majapahit empire (thirteenth to sixteenth centuries), the Hindu-Javanese civilization that united much of today's Indonesia. In many respects, today's Balinese culture can be thought of as a fossilized version of Majapahit culture, which had moved to Bali in the fifteenth century. Bali was later divided into several small kingdoms.

The origins of the Balinese are uncertain; the earliest remains of their civilization are stone carvings of the ninth century, but it is thought that the Balinese as an ethnic group are much older. A small group, the Bali Aga (Old Balinese), are thought to be the aboriginal inhabitants of the island.

Balinese society was not significantly influenced by Hindu-Javanese culture. Dutch colonial control over the island was not established until 1908 and had little impact on local culture. The Balinese still retain their distinctive identity in independent Indonesia.

There are about 2.9 million Balinese in Bali. They speak Balinese, an Austronesian language. Balinese has three levels, in reality different languages, depending on the social status of the speaker and listener. Balinese have a strong awareness of space, using the mountains and sea to orient themselves. The position of the mountains and sea, as well as the four cardinal directions, determines the siting of buildings and the direction for sleeping. Balinese believe that their island, and particularly the volcano Gunung Agung, is the center of the world.

Balinese practice their own variation of Hinduism, which pervades all aspects of their culture. Ritual and ceremony are important parts of everyday life. There are many rites of passage, beginning with birth and ending with death; the dead are always cremated. Trances and cockfights are also important social functions. Balinese have a rich artistic tradition stemming from their religious beliefs. Among the most important Balinese arts are batik and ikat textiles, masks and other forms of wood carving, stone sculptures, gamelan music, and a rich literary and dance tradition.

The Balinese are traditionally divided into the four Hindu castes of Brahman (priests and scholars), Kshatriya (warriors and nobles), Weisya (merchants), and Sudra (farmers and laborers), but the caste system in Bali is not as rigid as that of India. More than 90 percent of Balinese belong to the Sudra caste. The family is the basic unit of Balinese life, and a family, or close group of families, lives together in a compound of houses, surrounded by a wall. The *banjar*, or ward, is the next largest social unit. The *desa*, or village, consists of a group of *banjar*s. An additional organization is the *subak*, a farmers' society.

Balinese are primarily an agrarian people, though tourism has become increasingly important as a source of income. Today Bali and the Balinese themselves are objects of tourism. Balinese have adapted well to the presence of tourists, and tourism has in some respects helped to preserve and revive aspects of local culture, while exposing the Balinese to global influences.

Michael Pretes

Further Reading
Barth, Fredrik. (1993) *Balinese Worlds*. Chicago: University of Chicago Press.

Belo, Jane, ed. (1970) *Traditional Balinese Culture*. New York: Columbia University Press.

Covarrubias, Miguel. ([1937] 1974) *Island of Bali*. Reprint ed. New York: Oxford University Press.

Picard, Michel. (1996) *Bali: Cultural Tourism and Touristic Culture*. Trans. by Diana Darling. Singapore: Archipelago.

BALINESE SANGHYANG

Sanghyang is a generic term for Balinese ritual trance dances, accompanied by choral chanting or gamelan gong and often performed to repel evil influences believed to underlie natural disasters and disease. The following general description disregards local variation.

Sanghyang is performed in temples. Dancers are often eight- to ten-year-old girls, "pure" enough to be intermediaries with the spirits. Offerings to the temple goddess and prayers for intercession precede the dance. The trance is induced by prayer, choral chanting, and inhaling incense smoke. In some types of *sanghyang*, gamelan accompaniment starts once trance is achieved. Once dancers are in trance, offerings are made to deities believed to inhabit their bodies. The dancers can be asked to provide healing by recommending herbs to treat sick suppliants. During epidemics, the dancers may be carried through the streets. In the 1930s, *sanghyang* gave rise to the *kecak* form, performed for entertainment and popular with tourists.

Tim Byard-Jones

Further Reading
Belo, J. (1960) *Trance in Bali*. New York: Columbia University Press.

Eiseman, Fred B., Jr. (1990) *Bali: Sekala and Niskala*. Vol. 1: *Essays on Religion, Ritual, and Art*. Hong Kong: Periplus.

Yousouf, Ghulam-Sarwar. (1994) *Dictionary of Traditional South-East Asian Theatre*. Kuala Lumpur, Malaysia: Oxford University Press.

BALISONG

The *balisong* is a Philippine butterfly knife with a blade and two mobile half-handles, which can be opened quickly with one hand. *Balisong* (literally "broken horn"—the handles of the knife were traditionally made from water buffalo horn) comes from the Tagalog *bali*, meaning "broken," and *sungay*, meaning "horn." The *balisong* is also known as the Batangas knife, after the Philippine province where it supposedly originated; Balisong is also the name of a barrio in Batangas, but it is unclear whether the place was named after the knife or the knife after the place. In any event, many *balisong* shops are found in Balisong, as well as in outlying barrios. The normal length of an open *balisong* is 29 centimeters, for which reason it is sometimes referred to as the *vientinueve* ("twenty-nine" in Spanish); however, other lengths are also available. *Balisong* knives were popularized in the West by U.S. soldiers who brought them home to the United States after World War II. As a weapon, the *balisong* belongs to an ancient Malayo-Polynesian fighting system called *kali*, and knife-wielding techniques using the *balisong* are often taught to students of Philippine martial arts. *Balisong* techniques require finger dexterity; some of these are the single flip-up opening and closing, the double flip opening, and the toss and catch opening.

Hishashi Sanada

Further Reading

Kishino Yuzo, et al., eds. (1987) *Encyclopedia of Sports*. Tokyo: Taishukan.

T. Ohbayashi Taryo, et al., eds. (1998) *Encyclopedia of Ethnic Play and Games*. Tokyo: Taishukan.

BALKHASH, LAKE   Lake Balkash is a large lake located in southeast Kazakhstan at 342 meters (1,122 feet) above sea level and covering an area of 17,275 square kilometers (6,670 square miles). The lake is 605 kilometers (376 miles) long, with the western part being 87 kilometers (54 miles) wide and the eastern part only 10 kilometers (6 miles) wide. The two parts are connected by a narrow strait, the Uzynaral, with a depth of only 6 meters (21 feet). These two parts make for hydrological diversity. The water in the western part of the lake is fresh and suitable for consumption, agriculture, and industry, while the water in the eastern part is salty. Overall, the lake is covered with ice between November and April, and the average annual water temperature is about 9° C (48° F).

Several rivers flow into the lake with no outlet. Contributing 80 to 90 percent of the total influx into the lake is the Ili River. However, the volume of water has been reduced by two-thirds due to the installation of the Qapshaghay hydroelectric power station, and the lake's surface has dropped by 2.2 meters (7 feet) between 1970 and 1987. In addition, increased pollution and salinity of the water has limited the fishing industry and diminished the surrounding habitats. So far, no action has been taken to reverse the ecological damage that the lake has suffered.

Daphne Biliouri

BALTAZAR, FRANCISCO   (1788–1862), Filipino poet and playwright. Dubbed the "Prince of Tagalog Poets," Francisco Baltazar is best known for his masterpiece *Florante at Laura*, a staple reading in secondary schools throughout the Philippines. Born Francisco Balagtas on 2 April 1788 in Bulacan province, Baltazar went to Manila to pursue his education when he was eleven years old. He enrolled at Letran College, where he achieved a reputation for eloquence. People commissioned him to write poems and love letters for them, and during these years he also wrote plays.

He met and fell in love with a beautiful young woman named Celia, but his rival, a rich and influential man, had him imprisoned on trumped-up charges. While in prison, he was prompted to write *Florante at Laura*, which he dedicated to Celia. This poem, set in ancient Albania, told the story of two lovers, Florante and Laura, but it also symbolized Filipino suffering under Spanish rule and Filipino struggles for nationhood. Released from prison in 1840, he later moved to Bataan province, where he worked as a government clerk. He married a woman from a rich family in 1842 and settled in the town of Orion.

In 1849 Balagtas changed his surname to Baltazar, consistent with the decree of Governor-General Narciso Claveria, who ordered that every Filipino native adopt a Spanish surname. In 1856, he was imprisoned for shaving the head of a rich man's servant. His wife spent her entire fortune to defray the court expenses. He languished in prison until he was released in 1860, after which he continued writing to support his impoverished family. Baltazar died at Orion, at the age of seventy-four.

Aaron Ronquillo

Further Reading

Agconillo, Teodoro. (1990) *History of the Filipino People*. 8th ed. Quezon City, Philippines: Garotech.

Quirino, Carlos. (1995) "Baltazar, 'Balagtas,' Francisco." In *Who's Who in Philippine History*. Manila, Philippines: Tahanan, 41–42.

Sevilla, Fred. (1997) *Poet of the People, Francisco Balagtas*. Manila, Philippines: Trademark.

BALTISTAN   The most remote region of Pakistan, Baltistan lies in the portion of Jammu and Kashmir that is controlled by Pakistan. It is situated in the Northern Mountains, at Pamir-Nod, where the Hindu Kush, Pamir, Karakorum, and Himalayan Mountains meet, and where the famed K2 and Nanga Parbat

Mountains tower. The Indus River divides Baltistan; in one of the basins created by the river, the old capital city of Skardu is located. Baltistan is commonly known as "Little Tibet." The population of Baltistan is mostly Tibetan-speaking; some of the population have red or blond hair and blue eyes.

Baltistan was once a thriving region, thanks to the extensive trade route that linked China and Kashmir. From earliest times, it was in the cultural sphere of northern India. Alexander of Macedon (356–323 BCE) subdued Baltistan and brought Hellenic influence to the area. Thereafter, Baltistan was part of Gandharan culture and was an important center of Buddhism. It was only in the eighth century CE that Tibetan tribes made inroads into the region and became a dominant part of the population.

In the thirteenth century, during the rule of the Makpon dynasty, Islam came to Baltistan, and the majority of people converted to the new faith. It is often said that only with the Makpon rulers did Baltistan acquire its identity. Their rule lasted until 1840, when the maharajah Ghulab Singh, the Hindu ruler of Jammu and Kashmir, seized the area. When Pakistan was carved out of western India in 1947, the Muslim majority in Kashmir struggled for freedom from the Hindu Dogra regime, which had ties to India. In 1948, Baltistan became a federally governed area of Pakistan.

Nirmal Dass

Further Reading
Afridi, Banat Gul. (1988) *Baltistan in History*. Peshawar, Pakistan: Emjay.

Francke, August Herman. ([1907] 1987) *Baltistan and Ladakh*. Reprint ed. Islamabad, Pakistan: Lok Virsa.

BALUCHI Baluchi is the name of an ethnic group, most of whom inhabit the province of Baluchistan in modern Pakistan. Other Baluchi live in Afghanistan and Iran, and a small number are found in Turkmenistan, Oman, and the coast of East Africa. Their total population numbers around 7.5 to 11 million people.

The Baluchi claim to be descendants of Amir Hamza, the uncle of the Prophet Muhammad, and as a result, most Baluchi follow the Sunni sect of Islam. Some, however, are members of the Zikri sect, followers of a fifteenth-century mahdi (an Islamic messiah) called Nur Pak ("Pure Light"). Zikris are estimated to number more than 750,000; they live mostly in southern Pakistan.

The Baluchi language belongs to the Indo-Iranian family and is thought to be derived from the ancient Median or Parthian language. The Baluchi believe that they originated in the Aleppo region in Syria and then migrated east during the fifth, sixth, and seventh centuries CE until they reached their present homeland, Baluchistan, in the mountainous coastal regions of the Caspian Sea.

For several centuries thereafter, the Baluchi governed themselves through their clan system, except for occasional attempts by Persians, Arabs, and Hindus to conquer them. Not until the twelfth century, under the leadership of Mir Jalal Khan, was there an attempt to unite several Baluchi tribes into a political unit, called the First Baluchi Confederacy. This confederacy did not last due to political rivalries, but it laid the ground for future attempts at political integration and cohesion among the Baluchi. The sixteenth century witnessed the existence of three political Baluchi groups in Baluchistan: the Dodai Confederacy, the Kalat Confederacy, and the Makran State. In the eighteenth century, Mir Adbullah Khan of Kalat managed to unite almost all the Baluchi into one confederacy.

In 1841, British expansion in the region interfered in Baluchi affairs, and the British exerted control over Baluchi territory in an effort to check Russian influence in the area. The British achieved complete administrative control in some areas in 1876 while holding others by military force.

When Pakistan achieved independence in 1947, the Baluchi reacted fiercely against being integrated into this new political entity, and violence between the Baluchi and the Pakistani government erupted. Currently the Baluchi view themselves as an overlooked minority in Pakistan.

The Baluchi are organized into tribes led by a *sardar* (head chief). The tribes are structured through kinship in clans, clan sections, and subsections. Society is patriarchal; a boy's birth is heralded with much fanfare, and ceremonies mark important rites of passage for male children. Seminomadic pastoralism and dry-crop cereal farming are the mainstays of the Baluchi economy, although fishing plays a role in the coastal regions.

Houman A. Sadri

Further Reading
Adamec, Ludwig W. (1996) *Dictionary of Afghan Wars, Revolution, and Insurgencies*. Lanham, MD: Scarecrow.

Cleveland, William L. (1994) *A History of the Modern Middle East*. Boulder, CO: Westview.

Gall, Timothy L., ed. (1998) *Worldmark Encyclopedia of Cultures and Daily Life.* Vol. 3: *Asia and Oceania.* Cleveland, OH: Eastword.

Norton, Augustus Richard, ed. (1996) *Civil Society in the Middle East.* Leiden, Netherlands, and New York: Brill.

BALUCHISTAN

Baluchistan, a mountainous region overlapping Pakistan, Iran, and Afghanistan, consists of Baluchistan Province in southwestern Pakistan (2002 pop. 7.2 million, 344,747 square kilometers; capital Quetta) and Baluchestan va Sistan Province in eastern Iran (2002 pop. 2.1 million, 181,471 square kilometers; capital Zahedan). Baluchistan is an arid plateau descending into narrow coastal plains. Dates, sorghum, barley, and other crops grow in a few well-watered areas (only 4 percent of the land is arable), while pasturing provides sustenance for nomadic and seminomadic peoples in the barren hinterlands.

The Baluchi, most of whom are now Sunni Muslims, migrated here from eastern Persia (eleventh to fifteenth centuries). Various powers overran this rugged buffer between empires dominating the Iranian plateau and the Indian subcontinent—Persians (sixth century BCE), Alexander of Macedon (fourth century BCE), and Arabs (707 CE). The khans of the Kalat region established local rule in the seventeenth century, but in 1876 Britain gained indirect control over Kalat. Eventually the khanate and other Baluchi territories became a province of British India, whose borders with Afghanistan and Persia were settled in 1885 and 1896. Eastern Baluchistan was incorporated into Pakistan in 1947 and granted provincial status in 1970.

Marta Simidchieva

Further Reading

Baloch, Inayatullah. (1987) *The Problem of "Greater Baluchistan": A Study of Baluch Nationalism.* Stuttgart, Germany: Steiner.

Yarshater, Ehsan, ed. (1989) "Baluchistan." In *Encyclopaedia Iranica.* 3d ed. London and New York: Routledge and Kegan Paul, 598–647.

BAMBOO

Bamboo is the generic term for more than one thousand unique subspecies of the grass family that resemble trees. These species are organized into around one hundred families and may be found in tropical and subtropical climates throughout the world, although they are most common in Southeast Asia. Bamboo has thin, oblong, pointed leaves and a strong wooden hollow stem divided into compartments by the joints. It is among the fastest-growing plants in the world, and some species may grow up to 0.5 meter per day. The size of species varies, and the largest bamboo may grow a stem up to 60 meters tall during a lifetime ranging from 12 to 120 years. Bamboo only blossoms and produces seeds after several years of growth, and after blooming, the plant dies. When large areas of bamboo plants blossom simultaneously, it seriously affects the fauna of the area; those animals, like the great panda, that feed on bamboo shoots are forced to migrate and forage elsewhere.

Bamboo is a very strong and flexible material, and it is used for a virtually endless variety of products. In ancient China, strips of bamboo bound together with strings were used as books. Sections of large stems closed by the joint at one end have been used as containers, to hold water or to place writing brushes in. Large stems have also been used as building materials and are widely employed as scaffoldings even when building high-rises. Four to five large stems tied together constitute a small vessel used for fishing on the rivers of southern China. Traditionally, fireworks were made from bamboo, and the stems are also used for furniture, various tools, canes, fencing, fishing poles, musical instruments, papermaking, and pipes of different sorts. Parts of the plant are used in traditional Chinese medicine; the roots are used in treatment of cancer. Both bamboo seeds and shoots are an integral part of Chinese cuisine. The leaves are used to make fodder for animals and fish. In China the bamboo plant has been celebrated for centuries as the symbol of a person's integrity and nobility, and it is an extremely popular motif with painters and poets. Being a fast-growing plant and a high oxygen generator, bamboo has recently been used to revitalize waste-

Bamboo has many uses in Asia. Here, a man climbs on a bamboo construction scaffolding in Hong Kong. (TRAVEL INK/ CORBIS)

THE MANY USES OF BAMBOO

Bamboo is a versatile plant that is widely used throughout East, Southeast, and South Asia. The following excerpt tells how bamboo was used to build houses in rural Burma at the end of the 1800s.

The houses are usually marquee-shaped and consist of one or more rooms with the floor raised on posts seven or eight feet from the ground and another in front much lower and forming a kind of veranda, sometimes open in front. The poorer classes use posts of common wood or even of bamboo and make their walls of mats; the richer use Pyeng-ga-do (*Xylia dolobriformis*) or some other durable and more expensive timber and planked walls. The roof is sometimes composed of small, flat tiles but more generally of thatch; in some places of dhanee leaves soaked in salt water to protect them from the ravages of insects; in others of wa-khat, a kind of flat tile six feet long by two feet broad made of coarse bamboo matting; in others of bamboos split in half longitudinally and, with knots removed, placed side by side and touching each other with the concave side upwards, extending from the ridge to the eaves, over these is placed another series with the concave side downwards so that the roof looks like one of the elongated pan tiles; elsewhere the leaves of the Tsa-loo (*Licuala peltata*) or of the Taw-htan (*Livistona speciosa*): in some of the larger towns shingles are being introduced. The flooring consists of planking in better houses, and of whole bamboos laid side-by-side on bamboo crossbeams and tied with cane in the poorer.

Source: Gazetteer of Burma. (1893) New Delhi: Cultural Publishing House, 408.

land, and it has also become a favorite garden plant in the West.

Bent Nielsen

Further Reading

Farrelly, David. (1995) *The Book of Bamboo: A Comprehensive Guide to This Remarkable Plant, Its Uses, and Its History.* London: Thames & Hudson.

Moulik, Sunanda. (1997) *The Grasses and Bamboos of India.* 2 vols. Jodhpur, India: Scientific Publishers.

Zhu Shilin, Ma Naixun, and Fu Maoyi. (1997) *A Compendium of Chinese Bamboo.* Beijing: China Forestry Publishing House.

BAMIAN (2002 est. city pop 30,000). Bamian refers to a city, a pass, and a valley lying at the foot of the Hindu Kush Mountains in Afghanistan, where, until recently, stood two huge carved statues of the Buddha, designated as world heritage monuments by UNESCO. These sculptures were completed in the second century CE, during the reign of King Kaniska (flourished 78?–103?) of the Kushan dynasty (78–200), whose realm included most of Afghanistan and the northwest portions of Pakistan as well as India.

The statues exhibited a serene blending of Greek and Indian artistic traditions, in the Gandhara style. The larger statue was about fifty-four meters in height, and the smaller about forty meters. Both were carved into the cliff face of the mountains that tower over Bamian. The statues stood in niches shaped like body halos, in Buddhist fashion. Lining the niches were rich frescoes, depicting scenes from the life of the Buddha, as well as of various deities, the most famous of which was the sun god (either Surya or Mithra).

Bamian was an important Buddhist pilgrimage center, and some ten monasteries were built into the surrounding mountains. It also lay at the heart of the Central Asian trade route that linked east and west and north and south; it was especially renowned as a re-export center for gems, pearls, ivory, and spices.

Afghanistan and most of northwest Pakistan remained Buddhist until the arrival of Islam, at which time many of the ancient monasteries and shrines were destroyed. Centuries later, a similar fate befell the Buddhist statues and frescoes at Bamian. On 12 March 2001, both statues were blown to bits on the orders of the Taliban then ruling in Afghanistan. This destruction was part of a massive effort by the Taliban to rid Afghanistan of its non-Muslim past. Despite pleas from art institutions around the world, many Hindu and Buddhist antiquities were destroyed; these were seen as graven images by the devoutly Muslim Taliban and therefore an abomination before the sight of God.

Nirmal Dass

Further Reading
Baker, Piers H. B., and Frank R. Allchin. (1991) *Shahr-i-Zohak and the History of the Bamiyan Valley, Afghanistan.* Oxford, U.K.: B.A.R.
Klimburg-Salter, Deborah E. (1989) *The Kingdom of Bamiyan: Buddhist Art and Culture of the Hindu Kush.* Naples: Istituto universitario orientale, Dipartimento di studi asiatici; Rome; Istituto Italiano per il Medio ed Estremo Oriente.

BAN CHIANG
The village of Ban Chiang, located in Udon Thani Province in northeastern Thailand, is the site of important archaeological excavations. Discovered in 1966, the site has revealed evidence of a prehistoric society dating back to around 3600 BCE. Ban Chiang is one of the largest Bronze Age sites in Thailand, covering approximately 70,000 square meters (753,000 square feet). Excavations have revealed the presence of a highly developed bronze metallurgy, dating back to at least 2000 BCE, and iron metallurgy dating back to around 1000 BCE. Unlike in other Bronze Age discoveries in China, the existence of metallurgical technology in Ban Chiang was not accompanied by the creation of weaponry or ceremonial vessels associated with an advanced political hierarchy. Instead, metal objects were used for personal adornment and hunting, fishing, and woodcraft. Highly decorated ceramic forms found at Ban Chiang provide further evidence of an artistic tradition characterized by sophistication, creativity, and experimentation.

Ban Chiang challenges popular understanding of late prehistory based on Western data and Thai views of prehistory and suggests that the invention of bronze metallurgy occurred more than once at independent locations around the world. Excavations across Thailand have found evidence of prehistoric communities similar to Ban Chiang, namely at Sakon Nakhon, Nakhon Phanom, and Khon Kaen. Ban Chiang was inscribed on the World Heritage List in 1992.

Daniel Oakman

Further Reading
Bhamorabutr, Abha. (1988) *Ban Chiang: The Unexpected Prehistoric Civilization in Thailand.* Bangkok, Thailand: Somsak Rangsiyopas.
Chen, Lufan. (1990) *Whence Came the Thai Race?* Kunming, China: International Cultural Publishing.
Higham, Charles. (1984) *The Ban Chiang Culture in Wider Perspective.* London: British Academy.
White, Joyce. (1982) *Ban Chiang: The Discovery of a Lost Bronze Age.* Philadelphia: University of Pennsylvania Press.

BANDA SEA
Over 200,000 square nautical miles, the Banda is Indonesia's largest and deepest sea. It is located in eastern Indonesia and bounded on the south by a series of small islands and archipelagoes that curve east and north toward the eastern coast of Sulawesi. Banda Sea's convoluted sea floor is mostly four to five kilometers deep. It contains basins—such as the North Banda Basin, South Banda Basin, Weber Deep, and Wetar Trough—as deep as seven kilometers. These act as reservoirs, stabilizing fluctuations in the important water exchange between the South Pacific and Indian Oceans that flows through the Lifamatola Strait at depths below 200 to 300 meters.

The Banda Sea is associated with the fabled spice islands—the Moluccas—the origin of cloves, nutmeg, and mace that attracted Indian, Chinese, Arab, and later European traders. The center of the spice islands is Ambon, capital of Maluku province. The Bandas, southeast of Ambon, are among Indonesia's most interesting island groups.

Wong Poh Poh

Further Reading
Kent, George, and Mark J. Valencia, eds. (1985) *Marine Policy in Southeast Asia.* Berkeley and Los Angeles: University of California Press.
Tomascik, Tomas, Anmarie Janice Mah, Anugerah Nontji, and Mohammad Kasim Moosa. (1997) *The Ecology of the Indonesian Seas, Part One and Part Two.* Hong Kong, China: Periplus.

BANDAR ABBAS (2002 pop. 321,000). Located on the Persian side of the Strait of Hormuz, Bandar Abbas is the major port in southeastern Iran. Its population is mainly a mixture of Arabs and Persians. The fortunes of the early town, known as Jarrun, were closely linked with the nearby island of Hormuz. Attracted by its strategic location at the entrance of the Persian Gulf, the Portuguese captured Hormuz and Jarrun in the early sixteenth century. In 1623, after expelling the Portuguese, the Safavid Shah ʿAbbas I (1571–1629) renamed the port after himself. Determined to make it the preeminent port of his empire, he granted favorable terms to merchants, particularly the English. After a century of unrivaled prosperity Bandar Abbas declined after the Safavid dynasty collapsed in 1722. The establishment of Bushire as Persia's new port further reduced Bandar Abbas's importance, and from 1793 to 1868 it was leased to the ruler of Oman. The modern establishment of road and rail links encouraged some growth, but it was not until the Iran-Iraq War (1980–1988) that important development took place. Its distance from the battlefields led to major investment in infrastructure development. Recently an oil and gas refinery and a shipbuilding yard were added to its existing cotton mill and fish-canning plant.

Thabit Abdullah

BANDAR SERI BEGAWAN (2002 pop. 75,000). Bandar Seri Begawan, capital of Brunei Darussalam, is situated five kilometers upstream from the estuary of the Brunei River. Its existence as a settlement on stilts in reference to the famed present-day Kampong Ayer ("water village") dates back to the sixth century BCE, according to Chinese records. Portuguese descriptions of it during the sixteenth century attested to the glory and prosperity of the ancient empire of Brunei.

Formerly referred to as Brunei Town, Bandar Seri Begawan was named in honor of Sultan Omar Ali Saifuddin III (1914–1986), who abdicated in October 1967 and assumed the title of Seri Begawan Sultan. Perched on the northeastern corner of Brunei, Bandar Seri Begawan is the major urban center of the kingdom, where one-third of the total population of Brunei (276,300 as of 1993) resides. Bandar Seri Begawan functions as the seat of government as well as a commercial center and river port. It is connected by road with major towns such as Seria and Kuala Belait and has an international airport.

During the Japanese occupation (1941–1945), much of the town was destroyed by Allied bombings before the Australian reoccupation. Postwar reconstruction brought about the emergence of new buildings that are juxtaposed with a few remnants of the past.

The landmarks in and around Bandar Seri Begawan include the renowned Kampong Ayer. This floating confederation of more than forty villages, each with its own headman, demonstrates the close affinity of

An aerial view of Begawan and the Brunei River. (MICHAEL S. YAMASHITA/CORBIS)

the local inhabitants to the river and the sea. Rising majestically and overlooking Kampong Ayer is the glittering golden dome and towering minaret of the Omar Ali Saifuddin Mosque, opened in 1958 during the reign of and as a tribute to Sultan Omar Ali Saifuddin III, who was regarded as the "father of modern Brunei." Adjoining the mosque is a reconstruction of a sixteenth-century royal Brunei barge that "floats" in the lagoon, which almost encircles the entire mosque complex. On the outskirts of Bandar Seri Begawan, sprawling one-third of a mile long on a hillock with a view of the Brunei River, is the Istana Nurul Iman ("palace of the light of faith"). Completed in 1984, this magnificent palace combines Western engineering and Eastern architectural designs. With 1,788 rooms, twelve enormous chandeliers, and two golden domes, it is reputedly the world's largest residential palace.

Keat Gin Ooi

Further Reading

Meyers, Sharon, Wendy Moore, and Joseph R. Yogerst. (1993) *The Golden Legacy: Brunei Darussalam.* Bandar Seri Begawan, Brunei: Syabas.
Saunders, Graham. (1994) *A History of Brunei.* Kuala Lumpur, Malaysia: Oxford University Press.

BANDARANAIKE, SIRIMAVO RATWATTE DIAS

(1916–2000), Sri Lankan politician. Sirimavo Bandaranaike dominated the Sri Lankan political scene for four decades, becoming an internationally acclaimed politician. She was born on 16 April 1916 to an influential family. Her parents were Barned Ratwatte Dissawwa and Ratwatte Kumarihamy. In 1940, she married S. W. R. D. Bandaranaike, who became prime minister of Sri Lanka in 1956. He was assassinated three years afterwards. Sirimavo led the Sri Lanka Freedom Party, founded by her husband, and became the world's first female prime minister in 1960. Dominating the politics of the country as prime minister (1960–1965 and 1970–1977) and the leader of the opposition, she changed the name of the country from Ceylon to the ancient Sri Lanka, promulgated a new constitution in 1972, called the Non-Aligned Movement's Conference in 1975, and settled the dispute with India over Kachchative Island.

With adroit political skill and determination, she initiated social welfare programs and nationalization of essential sectors in the economy. Sinhalese was made the official language, resulting in alienation of the Ceylonese Tamils. She was debarred from holding any office after being convicted of abuse of power, but she again made a startling comeback and was ap-

pointed president in 1994 by her own daughter Chandrika Kumaratunge, who was then prime minister. She died on 10 October 2000 from a heart attack.

Patit Paban Mishra

Further Reading

Chandra, Richard de Silva. (1997) *Sri Lanka: A History.* New Delhi: Vikas.
Warnapala, W. A. Wiswa. (1994) *Ethnic Strife and Politics in Sri Lanka.* New Delhi: Navrang.

BANDARANAIKE, SOLOMON WEST RIDGEWAY DIAZ

(1899–1959), Sri Lankan political figure. In British times (since 1776), the Bandaranaikes and the Obeyesekeres were the two richest plantation families in Sri Lanka. Since Portuguese times (c. 1540–1656), this family of originally South Indian origin had occupied important offices and regularly adapted the catholic, protestant, and Anglican religions of the respective colonial rulers. Solomon Bandaranaike's father held the highest position reserved for a "native gentleman" in the British colonial administration, the office of head *mudaliyar*, which dominated and represented the totality of the Singhalese customary village and district office holders. Bandaranaike thus was well prepared to participate in Sri Lankan mass politics as it emerged in the early 1930s.

In 1936, he founded the Sinhala Maha Sabha, a radical pro-Singhalese organization that operated as a faction in the dominant Ceylon National Congress (CNC). When the CNC was transformed into the United National Party (UNP) in 1946, Bandaranaike feared he would be sidelined by the dominant party leaders and after independence (1948) he established in 1951 his own party, the Sri Lanka Freedom Party (SLFP). From the beginning, the SLFP, which advocated an anti-imperialist, anti-minority, and pro-Singhalese program, attempted to mobilize voters that had not been reached by the UNP or that felt alienated by its pro-Western policy and attitudes. In 1956, an election year that coincided with the 2,500-year jubilee of the Buddha's enlightenment, Bandaranaike, under the slogan "Sinhala only," succeeded in integrating diverse Singhalese special interest and social groups in a de facto movement: the ad hoc party alliance, Mahajana Eksath Peramuna (MEP), was comprised of young, low-ranking socialist monks, poorly paid Singhalese school teachers, nurses, ayurvedic (or traditional Indian) doctors, and various classes of village office holders. Based on this network, the SLFP persuaded voters that "Sinhala only" meant the reestablishment of the political, economic, and cultural hegemony of the "Sinhala" people, the "lion race," in addition to the establishment of Sinhala as the exclusive language of state. The SLFP was unable immediately to fulfil these ambitions, and in 1959 Solomon Bandaranaike was shot by a disgruntled Buddhist monk. The participants in, and real motives of, the assassination were never discovered.

From 1959, Bandaranaike's widow, Sirimavo, the daughter of an influential aristocratic family, presided over the party, which won election victories in 1960 and 1970. After seventeen years of political harassment by the UNP, the SLFP, then represented by Sirimavo Bandaranaike, but in effect dominated and reformed by her daughter, Chandrika Kumaratunga, returned to power.

Jakob Roesel

BANDUNG

BANDUNG (2002 est. pop. 2.9 million). Bandung is the capital of West Java and Indonesia's third-largest city. The Sundanese language as spoken in and around Bandung has the highest social status. Bandung was developed by the Dutch after 1810 as a center for the region's plantation industry. It became the capital of West Java in 1864. The city grew rapidly after the building of a railway line to Batavia (Jakarta) in the 1880s. The early twentieth century witnessed a building boom, during which Indonesian architectural motifs were combined with European Art Deco architecture. Its many fine parks and gardens as well as its striking Indo-European buildings earned Bandung the title of the "Paris of Java." The Bandung Institute of Technology was opened in 1920 as the first Dutch-founded university for Indonesians. Here Sukarno, who was to become Indonesia's first president, finished his engineering degree in 1926. The city was proposed as an eventual capital of the Netherlands Indies, and after Indonesia's independence there was speculation (until 1962) that it was to become the capital of Indonesia. In April 1955, Bandung was the site of a grand diplomatic event, the Asian-African Conference (also called the Bandung Conference), in which twenty-nine states participated.

Edwin Wieringa

Further Reading
Murai, Yoshimori. (1983) "Bandung: The Birth and Development of a Priangan Town in West Java." *Southeast Asian Studies* 21, 1:29–46.
Voskuil, R. P. G. A. (1996) *Bandoeng: Beeld van een stad.* Purmerend, Netherlands: Asia Maior.

Wilianto, Herman. (1994) "Life Style and Housing Choice in the City of Bandung, Indonesia." Ph.D. thesis, University of Waterloo, Canada.

BANDUNG CONFERENCE

BANDUNG CONFERENCE The decolonization that characterized the decades following the close of World War II saw a substantial increase in the number of new states throughout Asia. These new nation-states, often called the Third World or the Developing World, eschewed the emerging Cold War between the United States and the Soviet Union. Their leading concerns were remaining nonaligned vis-à-vis superpower conflicts; ending economic dependence on the West; and pursuing ongoing decolonization and economic development.

Indonesia played host to twenty-nine nonaligned nations at an Afro-Asian summit, which was held 18–24 April 1955 in the city of Bandung, Indonesia. This conference marked the emergence of these nations as a third grouping in international politics. The three unofficial leaders of the Third World were present at the Bandung Conference—Indonesia's founding president, Sukarno; China's premier, Zhou En-lai; and India's founding prime minister, Jawaharlal Nehru. At the conference, the People's Republic of China's (PRC) attempted to gain influence in the Third World, and thereafter the PRC pursued a course independent of the Soviet Union. For Indonesia, hosting this conference signaled the emergence of its policy of seeking Third World leadership. The Bandung Conference also led to the formal creation of a nonaligned movement, which, despite the end of the Cold War, has enjoyed an expanding membership, reaching almost one hundred different nations. *(See sidebar overleaf.)*

Anthony Smith

Further Reading
Borthwick, Mark. (1998) *Pacific Century: The Emergence of Modern Pacific Asia.* Oxford: Westview.
Leifer, Michael. (1995) *Dictionary of the Modern Politics of South-East Asia.* London: Routledge.

BANDUNG INSTITUTE OF TECHNOLOGY

BANDUNG INSTITUTE OF TECHNOLOGY The origins of the Bandung Institute of Technology (Institut Teknologi Bandung—ITB) in Bandung, West Java, trace back to 1920 and the founding of the Technische Hogeschool, though the institute in its current form was not officially opened until 2 March 1959. One of Indonesia's most prestigious centers of scientific education and research, ITB offers specializations in science, technology, and fine arts.

UNITY ACROSS THE THIRD WORLD

At the close of the Bandung Conference on 24 April 1955, India's Prime Minister, Jawaharlal Nehru, summarized the sense of unity and growing influence felt by delegates from non-aligned nations.

But, there is yet another spirit of Asia today. As we all know, Asia is no longer passive today; it has been passive enough in the past. It is no more a submissive Asia; it has tolerated submissiveness for so long. Asia of today is dynamic; Asia is full of life. . . . We are great countries in the world who rather like having freedom, if I may say so, without dictation. Well, if there is anything that Asia wants to tell them it is this: No dictation there is going to be in the future; no 'yes-men' in Asia, I hope, or in Africa. We have had enough of that in the past. We value friendship of the great countries and if I am to play my part, I should like to say that we sit with the great countries of the world as brothers, be it in Europe or America. It is not in any spirit of hatred or dislike or aggressiveness with each other in regard to Europe or America, certainly not. We send to them our greetings, all of us here, and we want to be friends with them, to cooperate with them. But we shall only cooperate in the future as equals; there is no friendship when nations are not equal, when one has to obey the other and when one dominates the other. That is why we raise our voice against domination and colonialism from which many of us have suffered so long and that is why we have to be very careful to see that any other form of domination does not come our way. Therefore, we want to be friend with the West and friends with the East and friends with everybody because if there is something that may be called an approach to the minds and spirit of Asia, it is one of toleration and friendship and cooperation, not one of aggressiveness.

I realise, as the Prime Minister of Burma said, that we cannot exercise tremendous influence over the world. Our influence will grow, no doubt. . . . But whether our influence is great or small, it must be exercised in the right direction, in an intelligent direction, in a direction which has integrity of purpose and ideals and objectives as shown in our Resolution. It represents the ideals of Asia, it represents the new dynamism of Asia, because if it does not represent that what are we then? Are we copies of Europeans or Americans or Russians? What are we? We are Asians or Africans. We are none else. If we are camp followers of Russia or America or any other country of Europe, it is, if I may say so, not very creditable to our dignity, our new independence, our new freedom, our new spirit and our new self-reliance.

Source: George M. Kahin. (1955) The Asian-African Conference, Bandung, Indonesia, April, 1955. Ithaca: Cornell University Press, 73–75.

Formerly affiliated with the University of Indonesia, ITB has five faculties and twenty-four departments; its Graduate Studies Program offers twenty-nine degree programs. The faculties are Mathematics and Natural Sciences, Industrial Technology, Civil Engineering and Planning, Earth Sciences and Mineral Technology, and Fine Arts and Design.

ITB also offers nondegree three-year programs providing specific training to civil servants. These include polytechnics for banking, accounting, and computer programming, as well as a photogrammetry and cartography center. Affiliated institutions include schools of railway engineering and telecommunications, and institutions for community research and service.

ITB has two campuses on seventy-seven hectares of land, employs more than one thousand faculty members and has over ten thousand students. The institute has a reputation as a center of student political activism.

Andi Faisal Bakti

Further Reading

ITB: Institut Teknologi Bandung. Retrieved 29 July 2001, from: http://www.itb.ac.id/.

Satuan Tugas Penulisan Kisah Kehidupan Kampus Ganesa. (1995) *Kisah Perjuangan unsur Ganesa 10 dalam kurun waktu 1942–1950* (History of the Bandung Technological Institute during the Japanese Occupation and Struggle for Independence, 1942–1950). Bandung, Indonesia: Penerbit ITB.

BANGALORE (2001 pop. 4.2 million). Bangalore, traditionally known as the garden of India, is now dubbed the Silicon Valley of India and has become the most important center of information-technology software in the nation. The city is the capital of Karnataka State in southern India and is the sixth-largest city in the nation. With one of the highest population-growth rates in India, Bangalore is likely to have a population of nearly 7 million by the year 2011. The city is famous for historical monuments, luscious gardens, and sandalwood and rosewood carvings of statues of gods and goddesses, toys, puppets, historical figures, buildings, and other items that depict social and cultural values of India. Due to the congenial climatic conditions, the Lalbagh Botanical Garden is the main center of attraction for tourists, especially for its centuries-old trees. Another tourist attraction is the Glass House, which is modeled on London's Crystal Palace. It contains a unique collection of tropical and subtropical plants.

Historically, Bangalore is famous for the royal palace of Tipu Sultan (1750–1799, ruler of the erstwhile state of Mysore in Karnataka State), the son of Muslim ruler Haider Ali (1721–1782). Tipu Sultan fought valiantly against the British empire in 1793 and died while fighting the British in the 1799 war to maintain the autonomy of Mysore State against British designs to spread their power and influence by annexing territories in the southern part of India. The British army and the Hyderabad and Maratha rulers had agreed to wage a combined war against Tipu and later distribute among the rulers the conquered territories.

Architecturally, Bangalore is famous for the Bull Temple, which has a tall carved-granite statue of Nandi, a bull on which rode Siva, the creator of the universe according to Indian mythology. There are many beautiful hill resorts in the vicinity of Bangalore. The most famous are Devarayanadurga and Nandi Hills. The waterfalls of Gaganachukki and Bharachukki are the main source of the city's hydroelectric power plant, built in 1905. Bangalore is also known for its Kolar gold mines, the deepest mining pits in the world, with a depth of 10,000 feet beneath the earth's surface. These mines are located 100 to 130 kilometers from Bangalore city.

Bangalore is one of the most modern cities of India and the fastest-growing center of the software industry in the nation. There are approximately one thousand companies in Bangalore in the information-technology sector. This sector contributes one-fifth of the total revenue of Karnataka State. Bangalore is also the center for aircraft manufacturing as well as for defense- and electronic-equipment makers. It is the headquarters of the Indian Space Research Organization. For research and development in silk technology, the city has the only Central Silk Technological Research Institute in the nation.

B. M. Jain

Further Reading

Davies, Philip. (1989) "Bangalore." In *The Penguin Guide to the Monuments of India*. New York: Viking, 531–534.

Hasan, M. Fazul. (1976) *Bangalore through the Centuries*. Bangalore, India: Historical Publications.

BANGKOK (2000 est. pop. 10 million). Bangkok is situated on the Chao Phraya River. It is both the capital and hub of the country; Bangkok's residents establish standards, outlook, dress, and physical comforts that are imitated, in varying degrees, by people in other parts of Thailand. Bangkok is about forty-five

longest roads in Thailand, cuts through inner Bangkok, housing middle-class residences, hotels, and restaurants. The low-lying, unsanitary, and flood-prone inner areas of the city's core are being abandoned to the poor by the rich, who are moving to estates outside the city. By 1990, the city had a million registered motor vehicles and massive traffic congestion was common. The Greater Bangkok Plan gave Bangkok an elevated expressway to connect suburbs and downtown areas; in 1999 a state-of-the-art sky train was launched. A ring road project has also been launched to help motorists avoid the inner city area.

Ooi Giok-ling

Further Reading
Dutt, Ashok K. (1996) *Southeast Asia: A Ten-Nation Region.* Dordrecht, Netherlands: Kluwer.

Waugh, Alec. (1971) *Bangkok: The Story of a City.* Boston: Little, Brown.

Van Beek, Steve. (1999) *Bangkok Then and Now.* Nonthaburi, Thailand: AB Publications.

Hata Tatsuya. (1996) *Bangkok in the Balance.* Bangkok, Thailand: Duang Prateep Foundation.

Sopon Pornchokchai. (1992) *Bangkok Slums: Review and Recommendations.* Bangkok, Thailand: Friedrich-Naumann-Stiftung.

Cars and trucks speed along Sukhumvit Road in Bangkok in 1993. (JAY SYVERSON/CORBIS)

times more populous than Thailand's second-largest city, Chiang Mai. The increasing dominance of the city can be gauged from the 56 percent of the urban population that now live in it, compared with 42 percent in 1947. The metropolis is growing at a rate of 6 percent per year, which is three times the national growth rate. The greater Bangkok area, with only 15 percent of the country's population, generates about half of the gross national product of Thailand and provides about half the number of jobs.

Bangkok used to be a city connected by canals, and was once known as the Venice of the East. Due to population congestion in recent decades, many of the canals have been filled in to serve as roads. The remaining canals are very dirty and polluted, though long boats still serve as taxis on some canals.

One of Bangkok's main business and commercial district lies in Chinatown, which is characterized by bazaar shopping. Ratchadamnoen Avenue is an important artery; formerly many government ministeries were located there, though some are now located in less congested parts of the city. Silom Road is the primary road for financial and banking institutions. A stretch of Sukhumvit Road, which is one of the three

BANGKOK DECLARATION Beset by internal conflicts and divided by ideology, history, religion, and culture, various countries in Southeast Asia came to recognize the need for some sort of cooperative grouping to deal with their unstable environment. Against the backdrop of the Cold War and the conflicts in Laos and Vietnam, on 8 August 1967 Indonesia, Malaysia, the Philippines, Singapore, and Thailand established the Association of Southeast Asian Nations (ASEAN).

The Bangkok Declaration was issued to assert that ASEAN was established first and foremost for the purpose of economic, social, and cultural collaboration and not as a security alliance. To contour the future direction of the region and to promote mutual peace, prosperity, and stability, the Declaration proposed economic partnerships, social relations, and cultural linkages among member countries as a means of accelerating and sustaining peace. Over the years, the Declaration has served as a reference point in dealing with internal squabbles among member countries. The eventual inclusion of all the Southeast Asian countries—Brunei Darussalam in 1984, Vietnam in 1995, Laos and Myanmar (Burma) in 1997, and Cambodia in 1999—is a testimony to the success of the fundamental principles of the Bangkok Declaration.

Geetha Govindasamy

Further Reading

Ganesan, Narayanan. (1999) *Bilateral Tensions in Post–Cold War ASEAN*. Singapore: Regional Strategic and Political Studies Programme, Institute of Southeast Asian Studies.

Gill, Ranjit. (1997) *ASEAN towards the 21st Century: A Thirty-Year Review of the Association of Southeast Asian Nations*. London: ASEAN Academic Press.

Hourn, Kao Kim, and Jeffrey A. Kaplan, eds. (2000) *Asean's Non-Interference Policy: Principles under Pressure?* London: ASEAN Academic Press.

Muhammad Ghazali Shafie, and Tan Sri. (2000) *Malaysia, ASEAN, and the New World Order*. Bangi, Malaysia: Universiti Kebangsaan Malaysia.

Severino, Rodolfo. (1999) *ASEAN Rises to the Challenge*. Jakarta, Indonesia: ASEAN Secretariat.

BANGLADESH—PROFILE

(2001 est. pop. 131.3 million). Bangladesh (officially Gana Prajatantri Bangladesh, or People's Republic of Bangladesh) is a relatively new nation, having become independent in 1971 following a war of independence against Pakistan (it was formerly known as East Pakistan), of which it was previously a part. It is also one of the poorest countries, having been ranked the lowest in Asia in the 2000 Human Development Index prepared by the United Nations Development Program. It was ranked 146 out of 174 countries studied, almost all of those ranked below being from Africa. Per capita gross domestic product is estimated as $1,570 on a purchasing-power basis.

The population density is highest of any country except the city-state of Singapore. Its area is approximately 144,000 square kilometers, about the size of the state of Wisconsin. Bangladesh is bordered in the south by the Bay of Bengal; on the west, north, and much of the east by India; and the southern portion of the east by Myanmar (Burma).

Geography

Bangladesh is a vast delta with few hills. It drains three of the major river systems of South Asia: the Ganges and its tributaries, including the Yamuna (Jumna); the rivers flowing south from Nepal and those flowing north from the Vindhya mountains in India; the Brahmaputra, which rises in Tibet; and the Meghna, which has sources in the Indian state of Meghalaya, portions of which receive the greatest amount of rainfall in the world. Until the sixteenth century, the principal out-let of the Ganges was through the present-day Bhagirathi and Hooghly rivers, passing present-day Calcutta. This route became heavily silted, diverting the main body of the river eastward. The restoration of much of the Ganges flow through its former route is the object of the Farakka barrage just across the border in India. The division of the Ganges waters is a major area of dispute between the two countries.

The rivers are both a blessing and a curse for Bangladesh. They provide transportation, water for irrigation systems, and in flood deposit fertile silt on the riparian areas. Their floods, however, also destroy crops and interrupt road, rail, and water transport systems. In general all over Bangladesh, with the exception of mountainous Chittagong Hill tracts, groundwater is contaminated with arsenic, which has proven difficult to correct. The Chittagong Hill Tracts in the southeast are the only high ground in the country. On the Karnaphuli river, which rises in the Hill Tracts, is the only hydroelectric station.

With the exception of natural gas, Bangladesh has few natural resources other than arable land. There are a few coal deposits that are generally unworkable. No significant petroleum sites have been found. Gas is used for power generation, fertilizer production, and industrial and domestic uses. The quantities that have been discovered and anticipated have made natural gas a potential export, especially to India. Whether or not

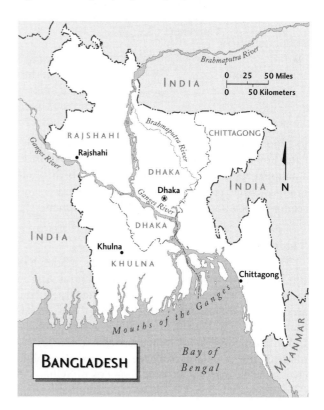

BANGLADESH

Country name: People's Republic of Bangladesh
Area: 144,000 sq km
Population: 131,269,860 (July 2001 est.)
Population growth rate: 1.59% (2001 est.)
Birth rate: 25.3 births/1,000 population (2001 est.)
Death rate: 8.6 deaths/1,000 population (2001 est.)
Net migration rate: -0.76 migrant(s)/1,000 population (2001 est.)
Sex ratio: total population: 1.05 male(s)/female (2001 est.)
Infant mortality rate: 69.85 deaths/1,000 live births (2001 est.)
Life expectancy at birth: total population: 60.54 years, male: 60.74 years, female: 60.33 years (2000 est.)
Major religions: Islam, Hinduism
Major languages: Bangla (official), English
Literacy: total population: 56%, male: 63%, female: 49% (2000 est.)
Government type: parliamentary democracy
Capital: Dhaka
Administrative divisions: 5 divisions
Independence: 16 December 1971 (from West Pakistan)
National holiday: Independence Day, 26 March (1971)
Suffrage: 18 years of age; universal
GDP—real growth rate: 5.3% (2000 est.)
GDP—per capita (purchasing power parity): $1,570 (2000 est.)
Population below poverty line: 35.6% (FY95/96 est.)
Exports: $5.9 billion (2000)
Imports: $8.1 billion (2000)
Currency: taka (Tk)

Source: Central Intelligence Agency. (2001) *The World Factbook* 2001. Retrieved 18 October 2001 from: http://www.cia.gov/cia/publications/factbook.

to export the natural gas has been the subject of debate, however: the government opposes the export of a national resource, but others support exporting natural gas either in its raw form or as electrical power, seeing its as a potential earner of hard currency.

The People

The people of Bangladesh are Bengalis, a branch of the Indo-Aryans who migrated from Central Asia in the second millennium BCE and gradually spread across the northern subcontinent. Bengal was probably inhabited by Dravidians before the arrival of the Indo-Aryans and some Dravidian characteristics remain in the population. There are also Mongoloid characteristics evident in some residents of Sylhet and Chittagong divisions. There also are a number of tribal groups, especially in the Chittagong Hill Tracts (the largest group being the Chakmas), but also in the lowlands, particularly in the north where tribes such as the Garos, who inhabit the hill states of northeastern India, spread into Bangladesh.

The dominant religion is Islam; followers make up about 88 percent of the population. Most of the Muslims are Sunni, with only small numbers of Shi'ites (some of those being Ismailis). Islam began to spread in Bengal early in the second millennium CE, brought mainly by itinerant Muslim preachers, many of whom were Sufis. There seems to be no logical explanation why Islam spread more widely in eastern Bengal than in western areas. The first Muslim ruler of Bengal came in 1202 when a general of the Delhi sultanate conquered Nadia (now in West Bengal) and deposed the Hindu Sena dynasty. From then until the assumption of power by the British in the eighteenth century, the rulers of Bengal were Muslim.

Fundamentalist Islamic political parties have had little electoral impact on the political scene. This is not to say that Islam in not a very important personal matter for Bangladeshis, but the impression given is that it is a personal matter and not one for the state. During the rule of Husain Muhammad Ershad (b. 1930) in the 1980s, however, Islam was made the state religion. Sufism is an important aspect of religious observance for many Bangladeshis, and there are many shrines to *pir*s (honored founders or leaders of Sufi orders).

Most of the remaining Bangladeshis, about 10 percent, are Hindus. Prior to the 1971 war of independence, about 18 percent of the population was Hindu, but many fled to India during the war and did not return. There also was a large exodus of Hindus in the early 1950s following communal riots mainly in Khulna division.

Most of the Hindus remaining in Bangladesh are of the Scheduled Castes, that is, the former untouchables (in India, now called Dalits, or "downtrodden"). Generally, these people are poor and suffer the same disabilities as any who are poverty stricken. Those who are better educated, usually from higher castes, however, do not appear to be discriminated against on the basis of religion. Several have been members of parliament and of the cabinet, and many have held high positions in government service, education, commerce, and industry.

There are small numbers of Christians and Buddhists, often members of tribal groups. Several of the tribes in the Chittagong Hill Tracts are Buddhist, while others are Hindu or animist. Many of the Christians are from lowland tribal groups who live on both sides of the border with India.

Language

Bangladesh is unique in that it is the only unilingual state among the major South Asian states. There are few, if any, persons in Bangladesh who cannot communicate in Bengali *(Bangla)*. Knowledge of English is growing, despite an immediate post-1971 effort to force Bengali even to the extent of forbidding English-language signs.

History

The earliest references to Bengal are in the tablets prepared during the Mauryan empire in the fourth and third centuries BCE. Bengal was either independent (or perhaps semi-independent) or a tributary to various north Indian dynasties, including the Guptas in the fourth and fifth centuries CE.

In 750, Bengal produced a dynasty that came to rule areas outside Bengal itself. This was the Pala dynasty, based at Vikrampur (near Dhaka) in Bengal. As it spread westward, the seat moved to Monghyr (now in Bihar). The Palas were ardent Buddhists. Power gradually declined, and the Palas were overthrown in 1155 by the Senas, an equally ardent Hindu dynasty, which during its short reign worked to revive Brahmanism as the religion of Bengal. This imposition of the caste system after the freedom of casteless Buddhism is thought by some scholars to have made casteless Islam welcome in Bengal.

In 1202, the Sena capital of Nadia (now in West Bengal) fell to a general of the Delhi sultanate and Bengal remained under Muslim rule until the British gained the power of taxation *(diwani)* from the Mughal emperor in 1765, following the British victory in 1757 at Plassey (Pilasi) over the Nawab of Bengal (governor under the Mughal emperor). The capital of Bengal moved from Murshidabad to Calcutta.

The British established Calcutta as the capital of British India as well as the capital of Bengal, and it remained so until the British Indian capital was moved to New Delhi in 1911. Under the British, Bengal included Bihar and Orissa. In 1905, the eastern portion of Bengal was joined with Assam to form a new province of Eastern Bengal and Assam. Muslims welcomed this, as the new province had a Muslim majority. Hindus strongly opposed the loss of the agricultural area that was supplying Calcutta with jute and rice. The partition was revoked in 1911: Bihar and Orissa were split off to form a new province (they became separate provinces in 1937), Assam was separated, and eastern and western Bengal were reunited.

Through acts of parliament, the British granted a measure of local government in 1885 and electoral participation in provincial government through Government of India Acts in 1909, 1919, and 1935. The last of these acts provided "provincial autonomy," under which provincial governments would control most governmental functions. It also continued the system of "separate electorates," under which religious communities would be represented separately with members of each community voting only for candidates from that community. There also were special seats representing interests such as labor, commerce, and industry and, in Bengal, a greatly inflated representation for Europeans. As a result, the majority Muslim community was actually denied a majority in the legislative assembly.

Within the Muslim community, there were two major parties in 1937 (after the 1935 act came into force): the Muslim League, which emphasized national concerns of Muslims throughout British India, and the Krishak Praja Party (KPP, Farmers and Peoples Party), which was concerned primarily with the problems and goals of the Bengal Muslim community. When Pakistan (which included present-day Bangladesh) became independent in 1947, the Muslim League, although in power at that time, began to fade.

Politics

Since its independence, Bangladesh has experienced presidential democracy and civilian and military autocracy. At the beginning of the twenty-first century, it was a parliamentary democracy.

Following the Pakistani surrender on 16 December 1971, the Awami League (a political party formed by former members of the Muslim League) assumed governance of the newly independent state. The Awami League saw a Bangladesh that would be based on the points enunciated by the party's leader, Sheikh Mujibur Rahman (1920–1975): nationalism, secularism, socialism, and democracy. Mujib (as he was often called) returned from jail in Pakistan—where he had been imprisoned during the war for Bangladeshi independence—on 10 January 1972, and accepted the role of prime minister. Before the end of that year, the constitution for a parliamentary system was completed.

The period of reconstruction following the war was marked by increasing corruption and incompetence in government. In January 1975, Bangladesh changed from a parliamentary system to a presidential one, with Mujib as president. In June, Mujib decreed that Bangladesh would become a one-party state, effectively placing all power in his hands. On 15 August 1975, Mujib and many of his family were assassinated by disgruntled army officers. What followed was a period of turmoil, culminating in attempted coups in November.

The military restored order in November but installed a martial law regime in which Major General Ziaur Rahman (known as Zia, 1936–1981) became the dominant figure, assuming the presidency in 1977 and being elected to that office in a contested election in 1978. Parliamentary elections were held in 1979 in which the party established as a vehicle for Zia, the Bangladesh Nationalist Party (BNP), won about two-thirds of the seats. The Awami League came second. Thus, what started as martial law gradually was converted into a presidential system. Zia initiated many

steps toward economic and social development and was the primary mover behind what became the South Asia Association for Regional Cooperation. Zia was assassinated on 30 May 1981.

He was succeeded by Vice President Abdus Sattar (1906–1985), who was then elected to the office of president in November 1981. The Sattar regime was weak, and the way was opened for another general, Husain Muhammad Ershad (b. 1930), to assume power.

Ershad continued many of the policies of Zia but never achieved the same level of popularity. He brought a number of members of the BNP and the Awami League into his cabinet and into his newly formed Jatiya Party (JP, People's Party). Both the BNP, now led by Zia's widow Khaleda Zia (known as Khaleda, b. 1945), and the Awami League, now led by Mujib's daughter, Sheikh Hasina Wajid (known as Hasina, b. 1947) strongly opposed Ershad but also strongly opposed each other. It was not until late 1990 that the two worked together and forced Ershad's resignation in December 1990.

In the election that followed in February 1991, the BNP won a plurality and, with support from the Jamaʿat-e-Islami (a Muslim fundamentalist party), formed a government under Khaleda. The constitution was amended to return to a parliamentary system. The personal dislike between Khaleda and Hasina meant that much energy was spent in this conflict rather than development and governance. Khaleda resigned in November 1995 and called a new election, which the opposition boycotted. New elections took place in June 1996 under a "neutral caretaker government."

The election resulted in a plurality for Hasina's Awami League. It joined in a coalition with Ershad's Jatiya Party to form the government. In a continuing tangle of Bangladeshi politics, the Jatiya Party split, with Ershad's faction supporting the BNP and the other faction remaining in the government. Stability is not the hallmark of politics in Bangladesh.

Economy

The economy of Bangladesh remains based primarily on agriculture, although there has been some growth in industry. The principal agricultural products are rice, jute, and tea, the first for domestic consumption and the latter two largely for export. Bangladesh remains an importer of rice, although production has increased markedly since the late 1970s. Jute, the raw material for burlap, faces a decreasing demand as plastic has overtaken the packaging field. Whether or not natural gas will be exported remains to be decided.

Garments are a growing and important export. Bangladesh has used its low labor costs to great advantage (as have several of its neighboring countries) in the readymade garment sector. There are political and social problems involved with this, especially the issue of child labor. Other industries include the manufacture of nitrogenous fertilizers (using natural gas as the base), the processing of agricultural products, and the assembling of equipment from imported parts.

Farming is almost entirely on small holdings. Land reform laws do not permit the owning of more than thirty-three acres (approximately 13 hectares), but most holdings are much smaller; the average land holding being just under one hectare.

Craig Baxter

Further Reading

Ahmed, Moudud. (1979) *Bangladesh: A Constitutional Quest for Autonomy.* Dhaka, Bangladesh: University Press.

Ali, Muhammad Mohar. (1988) *History of the Muslims of Bengal.* Riyadh, Saudi Arabia: Muhammad ibn Sa'ud Islamic University.

Banu, U. A. B. Razia Akhter. (1992) *Islam in Bangladesh.* Leiden, Netherlands: Brill.

Baxter, Craig. (1997) *Bangladesh: From a Nation to a State.* Boulder, CO: Westview Press.

Baxter, Craig, and Syedur Rahman. (1996) *Historical Dictionary of Bangladesh.* Lanham, MD: Scarecrow Press.

Choudhury, Dilara. (1992) *Bangladesh and the South Asian International System.* Chicago: Kazi Publications.

Eaton, Richard M. (1993) *The Rise of Islam and the Bengal Frontier, 1204–1760.* Berkeley and Los Angeles: University of California Press.

Faaland, Just, and J. R. Parkinson. (1986) *The Political Economy of Development.* New York: St. Martin's.

Islam, Serajul, ed. (1992) *History of Bangladesh, 1704–1972.* Dhaka, Bangladesh: Asiatic Society of Bangladesh.

Jannuzi, F. Tomasson, and James T. Peach. (1980) *The Agrarian Structure of Bangladesh: An Impediment to Development.* Boulder, CO: Westview.

Karim, Nazmul. (1980) *The Dynamics of Bangladesh Society.* New Delhi: Vikas.

Rashid, Haroun. (1979) *An Economic Geography of Bangladesh.* Boulder, CO: Westview.

BANGLADESH—ECONOMIC SYSTEM

After becoming independent from Pakistan in 1971, Bangladesh shifted in the mid-1970s from a socialist to a market-oriented model of development. Despite several economic reforms, however, the country is still far from enjoying an efficient market economy. Bangladesh's economy remains largely agricultural, with a relatively small industrial-manufacturing sector. While agriculture remains dominant in terms of contribution to total gross domestic product (GDP) and employment, the percentage of total agricultural employment nonetheless decreased from 85 percent in 1961 to 63 percent in 1996. The service sector's contribution to total GDP increased sharply from 36 percent in 1970 to around 57 percent in 1998.

Bangladesh has one of the lowest per capita annual incomes in the world ($345 in 1998). Income levels in rural and urban areas differ significantly. In rural areas opportunities for wage employment are limited, and wage rates are low. The level and composition of consumption expenditure also differ in rural and urban areas.

Agriculture

Bangladesh's agriculture is dominated by rice, the staple food crop, which occupies about 75 percent of the total cropped area. Since the early 1980s wheat production has increased significantly and is now around 5 percent of the total cropped area. Potato, chilies, pulses, and oil seeds are complementary noncereal food crops that supplement the staple diet. Besides rice, wheat, and jute, sugarcane and tobacco are major crops. On an experimental basis rubber, coffee, and palm trees are cultivated on a small scale in some areas. Small and medium-sized households produce barely enough food crops to meet their own consumption requirements. Only large farm households can generally sell their surplus cereal products in the market.

Jute is the major cash crop in Bangladesh. Rice and jute are small-scale farming operations in which land, labor, and capital equipment are often interchangeable. The agricultural technology is predominantly traditional and consists mainly of plows, shovels, bullocks, and homemade irrigation implements. Since the early 1970s a considerable number of high-yielding seed varieties (HYV) have been adopted. From 2 percent of the cropped area in 1970, the share of land under HYV cultivation grew to around 30 percent in the 1990s.

Bangladesh agriculture has a very low and declining land-labor ratio. Over time, the average size of farms has become smaller and smaller. For example, in 1960 the average farm size was 1.4 hectares, but in 1984 it was less than one hectare. Along with decreasing farm size came an increasingly unequal distribution of land holdings and increasing landlessness. In the active tenancy market in Bangladesh, around 25 percent of cultivable land is transferred, so that the distribution of cultivated land is less unequal than the distribution of ownership.

Bangladesh has an agricultural economy and the land is both benefited and harmed by flooding. This flooded field is located in the Barisei region. (YANN ARTHUS-BERTRAND/CORBIS)

Industry

Of the various large- and small-scale industries, jute, carpets, paper and newsprint, rayon, sugar, cement, chemicals, fertilizer, and tanneries are the most important. Other notable industries are cotton yarn and textiles, engineering and shipbuilding, iron and steel, oil refining, electric cables and wires, matches, and cigarettes. Of cottage industries, carpet making, shoemaking, bamboo and cane products, earthenware, brass and metal products, small tools and implements, ornaments, and handicrafts are important. In terms of employment, cottage and small-scale industries occupy a significant place. These are for the most part family-oriented enterprises with low capital intensity and traditional technology. Since the late 1980s the ready-to-wear garment industry has rapidly expanded; it now employs more than one million workers (mostly female) and contributes more than 50 percent of total export earnings.

In 1972 the government under Sheikh Mujibur Rahman (1920–1975), popularly known as Sheikh Mujib, nationalized all major industries. While the nationalization decision solved initial political and administrative problems, Sheikh Mujib's government later encountered serious political and economic problems that lasted until he was killed during a military coup in 1975. After political change in 1975, industrial policy was revised to provide a greater role for private enterprise. Since the early 1980s successive regimes further revised industrial policy, but no regime has denationalized the most unprofitable industries, whose losses were caused primarily by disruptions in production, inappropriate and inflexible pricing policy, managerial inefficiency, and above all large-scale corruption.

Bangladesh is a relatively open economy, where the ratio of foreign trade to GDP is around 37 percent and steadily rising. However, its narrow export base is dominated by a few primary commodities (although ready-to-wear garments have become dominant in the export trade in recent years), whereas its essential imports are either basic consumption goods or raw materials and intermediate goods. The narrow base of exports and the noncompressible structure of imports have given rise to a large trade deficit.

Financial System

The financial system of Bangladesh includes an organized or institutionalized financial sector and an unorganized credit market. Dominating the financial sector and accounting for more than 95 percent of its assets is the banking system, composed of the Bangladesh Bank, four nationalized commercial banks, twenty-seven private domestic banks, thirteen foreign banks, and five government-owned specialized banks. The nationalized commercial banks dominate the commercial banking sector, accounting for more than two-thirds of its assets. The foreign banks, with a share of around 10 percent of bank assets, remain active primarily in international transactions relating to foreign trade. Such credit allocation started following the nationalization of domestic banks and financial institutions in 1972. Since then, especially since the 1980s and 1990s, credit has been allocated more by political authorities than by market forces. After meeting the needs of the politically influential sectors, the limited available funds were rationed among economically and politically powerful borrowers. A lack of accountability created incentives for borrowers to default willfully, which led to a culture of loan default as big borrowers treated bank loans as a windfall. As a result during the 1980s and early 1990s, the nationalized banks had to be recapitalized by the government a number of times to keep them operationally solvent. Because the nationalized banks are not subject to competitive pressure or hard-budget constraints, they keep the loan rate of interest high, intending to recover some of the losses caused by the huge "privileged" loans. The indifferent attitude of depositors (and the government) has kept otherwise insolvent banks liquid, but at the cost of financial efficiency.

Future Prospects

Bangladesh remains a test case of economic development. In terms of traditional development economics jargon, Bangladesh has yet to break the "vicious circle of poverty" or "low-level equilibrium trap" to set the economy on the path to self-sustaining growth. How to do this remains controversial. While it is easy to be gloomy, a close examination of the economy reveals some strengths. Remarkably the Bangladesh economy can feed an ever-increasing population from its narrow land base. Food production has increased to near self-sufficiency, with stabilizing food prices. The economy has been gradually deregulated since the early 1980s, and the rate of private saving is rising. Even though foreign investment is not yet forthcoming on a large scale, there are good prospects for the future. As the economic survival of the nation is at stake, Bangladesh cannot afford to fail in its quest for development.

Salim Rashid and Akhtar Hossain

Further Reading

Asian Development Bank (ADB). (1994) *Bangladesh: Stimulating Investment and Growth*, Manila, Philippines: ADB.

Bangladesh Bureau of Statistics (BBS). *Statistical Yearbook of Bangladesh*. Dhaka, Bangladesh: BBS (Various issues).

Hossain, A. (1996) *Macroeconomic Issues and Policies: The Case of Bangladesh*. Delhi: Sage.

BANGLADESH—EDUCATION SYSTEM

The constitution of Bangladesh directs the state to adopt effective measures for extending free and compulsory education for all children "to such stage as may be determined by law." Recent years have recorded some advances in the education sector in Bangladesh. Given the scope of the development problem faced by Bangladesh, however, these improvements are inadequate. After three decades and many education commission reports, Bangladesh has yet to attain the goal of providing free primary education to all children. One reason for this is the failure of politicians and members of the education commissions to commit themselves firmly to the vision of basic education as a fundamental human right and an instrument of social and economic change. Studies have shown that cost recovery as a percentage of unit costs in Bangladesh is higher in primary education than in either secondary or higher education.

Recent Trends and Statistics

Public expenditure on education has been low. The distribution of the overall public-sector budget among the various educational sectors has remained stable in recent years. Primary education has received roughly 47 percent, secondary education 22 percent, and higher education 33 percent of government spending on education over the years. Primary education has gained at the expense of secondary education, while the tertiary sector has maintained its position. Among institutions that teach scientific and technical subjects, only medical colleges have gained in real terms. According to Tan and Mignot's World Bank study, the share of cumulative subsidies accruing to the best-educated 10 percent in a generation in Bangladesh stands at 72 percent, compared with the Asian average of 37 percent (28 percent for Sri Lanka and 31 percent for China). Another measure of inequality, the "education gini coefficient," is a highly unequal 82 for Bangladesh compared with the Asian average of 43 (33 for Sri Lanka and 44 for China; the gini coefficient is a measure of inequality of distribution of education funds. Zero equals complete equality, and one equals complete inequality. The higher the value within this range, the greater the proportion of education funds spent on the few, and the greater the inequality).

Government statistics on educational attainments suggest some optimism. According to the Fifth Five Year Plan (1997–2002), the current literacy rate of 58 percent is increasing at the rate of 7 percent per decade. According to most informed observers, however, these figures are overly optimistic and ignore many problems, not the least that of resources. The

A girl in a school in Dhaka in 1992 draws on her blackboard. (LIBA TAYLOR/CORBIS)

school-age population at the end of the twentieth century expanded at the rate of roughly 1 million each year, putting enormous pressure on the entire school system. Nongovernmental organizations took up the challenge of opening and running primary schools in areas where government schools did not exist. The most famous are those run by the Bangladesh Rural Academy Council, which established some thirty thousand schools not under government auspices in rural areas.

The Structure of the Education System

Ten years of basic schooling culminate in a matriculation exam. For those who do well, this is followed by two years of college. Written public examinations, administered by four regional boards, decide the student's qualifications at each level. These two public examinations are known as the Secondary School Certificate and the Higher Secondary Certificate. The universities and other tertiary institutions have their own entrance examinations. Most public universities follow the British system of a three-year bachelor's (honors) program, although the new private universities have moved to the American model of four-year bachelor's programs. Postgraduate education consists mostly of master's programs, with very few doctoral programs.

Various vocational secondary schools and training centers have developed over the years. Religious education also occupies an important position in the education sector of Bangladesh. The presence of *madrasah*s (Islamic religious schools) is impressive but raises issues of uniform standards.

Primary and Secondary Schooling

Enrollment data in the primary schools show some positive trends, including a rise in female enrollment.

The overall enrollment according to official statistics is 80 percent of the age cohort, although gross enrollment rates are close to 100 percent, because of inclusion of older children in the count. An estimated 20 million students are enrolled in primary schools today. The goal of achieving full enrollment in the six-to-eleven-year age cohort poses major public-policy challenges, due to a shortage of classrooms and teachers in the countryside. The quality of education in the primary sector is low, the overall learning environment poor. Problems include high student-teacher ratios, inadequately trained teachers, and lack of proper books, supplies, and facilities such as laboratories.

The secondary education level also has been severely neglected by policy makers in Bangladesh. According to a survey by the Bangladesh Institute of Development Studies, overcrowding at the secondary level is common. The number of secondary schools has simply not expanded to accommodate all those graduating from primary schools. The enrollment rate has increased to about 30 to 35 percent of the age cohort.

Public and Private Tertiary Education

Public higher education in Bangladesh is nearly free. Since the vast majority of students come from well-to-do households, this may be a luxury the nation cannot afford. Access and equity continue to be major problems in the entire education sector but especially in tertiary education. Until the early 1990s, university education was provided only by public universities (including the highly specialized medical colleges, engineering universities, and polytechnic institutes and colleges). Today, vocational secondary schools, training centers, and on-the-job training opportunities in the private sector are springing up to serve the labor market. The rapid increases in population, urbanization, and incomes have created an enormous demand for good schools at all levels. Parents generally believe that a good education is the ticket to social and economic success. The demand for private tutors is also high. As expected in an environment of weak governance, this has created many opportunities for fraud at all levels in the education sector.

Private universities were first allowed under the Private University Act of 1992. Today, there are seventeen private universities of varying quality operating under this act. The Private University Act requires that at least 5 percent of the student body receive full tuition waivers. This is intended to help poor students take advantage of these institutions. Additionally, the choice of a private university by students from rich families helps create vacancies in the public universities for other students. Proponents of private universities have argued that an expansion of the private universities would improve access to tertiary education for *all* students. After nine years, it seems that, although private universities have increased choice in higher education for many students, the overall impact on equity and access is mixed.

The better private universities have research centers, modern fully networked computing facilities, and air-conditioned classrooms. The full-time faculty and administrators are assisted by a large group of visiting faculty on sabbatical leave from universities all over the world. In their curriculum, books, and faculty training, the private universities have a strong bias toward the U.S. higher education system. The motivation for private universities came from the serious deterioration of education in Dhaka University; the hold of socialistic ideas over academia in general; and the large-scale exodus of local students to foreign institutions, especially to neighboring India. According to one estimate, in 1993 over eighty thousand Bangladeshi students were in Indian colleges, sent there by their parents to get a better education. The loss of foreign exchange entailed by such an import of education from India and the fear of indoctrination by a foreign culture were important concerns for the founders of the private universities. Tuition costs for the entire four years are approximately $10,000 in the best private universities. This is exorbitant compared with the cost of tuition at public universities, but the growth of private universities shows that they clearly met a latent need.

Salim Rashid and Munir Quddus

Further Reading

Ahmad, Muzaffer. (1998) "Education and Governance in Bangladesh." In *Crises in Governance: A Review of Bangladesh's Development 1997.* Dhaka, Bangladesh: UPL, Centre for Policy Dialogue, 317–332.

Quddus, Munir. (1999) "Access to Higher Education in Bangladesh: The Case of Dhaka University." *International Higher Education* (17 November): 15–17.

Quddus, Munir, and Salim Rashid. (2000) "The Worldwide Movement in Private Universities: Revolutionary Growth in Post-Secondary Higher Education." *American Journal of Economics and Sociology* 59, 3 (July): 487–516.

Siddique, Zillur Rahman. (1997) *Visions and Revisions: Higher Education in Bangladesh, 1947–1992.* Dhaka, Bangladesh: University Press.

Tan, J., and A. Mignat. (1991) *Education in Asia: A Comparative Study of Cost and Financing.* Washington, DC: World Bank.

World Bank. (1999) *World Development Report: Knowledge for Development, 1998/1999.* Washington, DC: Oxford University Press.

BANGLADESH—HISTORY

Bangladesh is a relatively new nation but an old region. During British rule, the entire Bengali-speaking region of eastern India was known as Bengal or Bangladesh (land of Bengal). Upon the partition of the Indian subcontinent in 1947, much of that region became East Bengal and then East Pakistan, part of the predominantly Muslim nation of Pakistan. It was separated from the rest of Pakistan by 1,600 kilometers of predominantly Hindu India; language, culture, and lifestyle also separated it from western Pakistan. In 1971, after a civil war, East Pakistan became the independent nation of Bangladesh.

Premodern History

Although only a nation-state since 1971, "Bangladesh" is not a new term. We come across it in an ancient inscription of 1025, which refers to "Vangladesa" as a rainy country. Vanga, or Banga were used to denote Bengal or Bangladesh from 500 BCE to 500 CE. Vanga may derive from the Tibetan word *bans*, meaning "wet." Others take the term Bangla and derive it from an Assamese dialect, in which the original meant "wide plains." The Mughal scholar Abu-l-Fazl (1551–1602) took the original name to be Bang, and took *al* to be a word meaning flood embankments, or dikes, which were common in the region; hence the name Bangal, and eventually Bangladesh, meaning "the country of Bangal" (Bengal). Before the Muslim conquest of Bengal, the different parts of the region had different names, either of the petty dynasties that ruled them or of the subregions ("little Bengals," to paraphrase some scholars). The Muslim conquest led to the integration of the little Bengals into one Great Bengal.

The region is known to have been inhabited by various pre-Aryan peoples around 2500 BCE; by 600 BCE it became part of the Aryan culture, adopting Hinduism and its caste structure. Northern Bengal was part of the Maurya empire (c. 324–c. 200 BCE), and northern Bengal and parts of eastern Bengal also came under the control of the Gupta dynasty (c. 320– c. 500 CE). A period of anarchy followed; then from 750 to 1160 most of eastern and parts of northern Bengal were ruled by the Buddhist Pala dynasty. This period also witnessed the reigns of various petty dynasties throughout the region. In 1160 the Hindu Senas became the hegemons of almost the whole of Bengal; they ruled until their overthow by Turkish Muslim invaders from the north in 1206. The region was

KEY EVENTS IN BANGLADESH HISTORY

2500 BCE Pre-Aryan peoples known to inhabit Bangladesh.

600 BCE Becomes part of the Aryan culture, adopting Hinduism and the caste structure.

1025 CE First mention of Bangladesh, called Vangladesa and described as "rainy country" in an inscription.

c. 324–c. 200 BCE Northern Bengal falls under the Maurya dynasty.

c. 320–c. 500 CE Parts of northern and eastern Bengal fall under Gupta dynasty.

500– 750 CE Period of anarchy.

750–1160 CE Most of eastern and parts of northern Bengal were ruled by the Buddhist Pala dynasty.

1160 Hindu Senas became hegemons of almost all of Bengal.

1206 Senas overthrown by Turkish Muslim invaders from the north. They convert populace to Islam.

14th–17th centuries Converts to Islam settle the riverine delta of eastern Bengal.

17th century–1757 Bangladesh is controlled by Muslim empires (Delhi sultanate and Mughal empire).

1757 British conquest.

1757–1947 Bangladesh ruled by the British as part of India.

1947 Partition of India into India and Pakistan, which was divided into West Pakistan and East Pakistan.

1952 Language riots in East Pakistan when M. A. Jinnah tries to impose Urdu as the national language. Several students are killed, and hope for a united Pakistan fades.

1954 Awami Muslim League party attempts to sustain a democratic government in East Pakistan, but this is shut down by the federal government who accuses the Chief Minister of anti-Pakistani activities.

1956 Framing of the Constitution of 1956, which asserted the dominance of Punjab as the most important Pakistani state.

1958 General Ayub Khan stages a military takeover of Pakistan and installs himself as President of a new "limited" democracy where 40,000 Muslims were selected to vote and delegate money. This alienates the Eastern Pakistanis, deepens the spending gap between West and East Pakistan, and creates incredible grassroots corruption.

1964 Mujib, a leader of the Awami Muslim League party, becomes an outspoken advocate for Bangladeshi autonomy, despite being incarcerated almost continuously between 1959 and 1969.

1965 Ayub Khan attacks India over Jammu and Kashmir. East Pakistanis denounce India and fight bravely.

1966 Mujib announces the famous Six-Point Program, demanding full autonomy for all provinces of Pakistan and special paramilitary troops and separate currency for East Pakistan to stop further flight of capital from East to West Pakistan. Mujib is incarcerated again. The massive press coverage introduces the concept of breaking away from West Pakistan to most Bengalis.

1969 Ayub Khan is forced to resign after signing a peace treaty with India.

1970 Mujib is released and his party wins an absolute majority in the National Assembly for Pakistan elections (162/300 seats). Instead of transferring power to Mujib, General Yahya Khan, the new president of Pakistan, succumbed to the pressure of Zulfikar Ali Bhutto (1928–1979), who won eighty-three seats in West Pakistan. Bhutto wanted power to be transferred to the two "majority leaders" in the two parts of Pakistan.

1971 Bengali masses under student leadership started a movement for total independence; Mujib asks for non-violent civil disobedience. Pakistani troops start indiscriminately killing Bangladeshis, and arrest Majib. Major Ziaur Rahman officially declares independence, and on 10 December, Bangladesh gains its independence.

1972 Mujib is released and becomes Prime Minister.

1975 Mujib and most of his family killed during a coup d'état; the populace celebrated as the inexperienced Mujib and his administration had caused considerable damage to the country. General Zia (the same Major who declared independence) takes power and later is actually elected.

1981 Zia is killed.

1982 Hussain Muhammad Ershad takes power.

1988 Ershad introduces Islam as a state religion.

1990 Corrupt Ershad regime is overthrown.

1991 Neutral caretaker government holds elections, Mujib's daughter Sheikh Hasina contests them after failing to win a majority.

1996 Shiekh Hasina wins election, accepts results.

Islamized under the influence of various Sufi saints, who helped non-Aryan peasant cultivators bring forestland under cultivation. They introduced both the Qur'an and the plow to their new converts, who settled the riverine delta of eastern Bengal from the fourteenth through the seventeenth centuries.

Muslim empires (the Delhi sultanate and the Mughal empire) controlled Bengal for about 200 years, until the British conquest in 1757. Bengal was part of British India until independence and partition in 1947.

East Bengal at the Time of Partition

The genesis of Bangladesh was inherent in the body politic of Pakistan, as the two parts of Pakistan in 1947 had begun on uneven terms. While the western part was already more developed, urban, and industrialized, with a better land-person ratio and communication network than the eastern part, the mass immigration of Hindu business people and professionals to India after the partition further impoverished the eastern part. In contrast to East Bengal, the western part of Pakistan got a generous flow of capital from thousands of rich Muslim emigrants from India who later industrialized the region. Besides the natural advantages of the western part and the inflow of capital from the Muslim Indian emigrants, West Pakistan's discriminatory policy against East Bengal further enriched the west at the cost of the east. It was generally believed that while East Bengal was earning more than 60 percent of Pakistan's total foreign exchange up to the mid-1960s, it received less than 30 percent of the total import and always had a trade deficit with West Pakistan. West Pakistanis held 80 percent or more of the key positions in the civil and military departments in Pakistan. Thus East Bengal practically became a colony of West Pakistan not long after the creation of Pakistan.

Despite their decisive role in the creation of Pakistan and unflinching support for the nation, most East Bengali Muslims were viewed by West Pakistanis as non-martial, inferior, untrustworthy, and lacking the qualities of good Muslims. East Bengalis faced discrimination, contempt, and condescension from West Pakistanis. What started with the arrogance of M. A. Jinnah (1876–1948), the founding father of Pakistan, trying (in 1948) to impose Urdu (the minority language) as the state language of the nation on the majority Bengalis led to the so-called language riots in 1952.

Separatist Movement Begins

In February 1952 Pakistani police killed several unarmed Bengali students at Dhaka for demonstrating in favor of Bengali as one of the state languages of Pak-

istan. The Language Movement organized by Bengali students signaled the beginning of the end of a united Pakistan; afterward Bengalis' estrangement from West Pakistan gradually turned into a separatist movement.

Meanwhile, some Bengali stalwarts of the Muslim League Party, which spearheaded the drive for an independent Muslim Pakistan in the 1940s, organized the People's, or Awami, Muslim League (called the Awami League since 1954) and tried in vain to restore democracy and accountability in Pakistan. In 1954, their attempts to sustain a democratic government in East Bengal failed within a couple of months when the federal government, led by bureaucrats from Punjab, in West Pakistan, unceremoniously dismissed it on the specious charge that the chief minister had engaged in "anti-Pakistani" activities.

The military takeover of Pakistan by General Ayub Khan (1907–1974) in 1958 further alienated many Bengalis from the center, as martial law signaled the completion of the "Punjabization" of Pakistan. Soon Ayub Khan declared himself president of the republic and introduced guided "basic democracy" by disenfranchising all but eighty thousand Pakistanis (forty thousand from each part of the nation), who would elect members of the National Assembly and the president. They were also entrusted with money to spend on development projects in their localities. This bred corruption and vested interests at the grassroots level. Ayub Khan spent the lion's share of the gross national product (GNP) and foreign aid money on development projects, defense, and the new capital at Islamabad. Because the bulk of the money spent during the ten years of Ayub's regime went to West Pakistan, benefiting mostly the Punjabis, most educated Bengalis were resentful.

By 1964 most of the Bengali old guards of the opposition had died, and Sheikh Mujibur Rahman (Mujib) (1920–1975) of the Awami League emerged as the most outspoken Bengali leader, championing the cause of greater autonomy for East Pakistan. With the introduction of the new constitution of Pakistan in 1956, East Bengal became East Pakistan, as the four provinces in the western sector were collectively called West Pakistan. This act, to the chagrin of East Bengalis and people of Sind, Northwestern Frontier, and Baluchistan in the western wing, signaled the ascendancy of West Punjab, the most populous and dominant province in the western wing, as the dominant province of Pakistan. Another demagogue was the not-so-educated, grassroots-based Maulana Bhashani (1880–1976), who in 1957 demanded independence for East Pakistan but in the mid-1960s adopted a compromising attitude toward

Ayub Khan. By then Mujib had emerged among all the prominent leaders of the province as the only champion of an autonomous East Pakistan. Ayub Khan feared Mujib most and kept him behind bars most of the time between 1958 and 1969.

While Mujib and other leaders were in jail, pro-Awami League student leaders organized a secret cell called the Bengal Liberation Front under the leadership of Sirajul Alam Khan (b. 1941). In the late 1960s and up to the emergence of Bangladesh in 1971, they played the most vital role in mobilizing support for an independent country. They coined the radical slogan "Jai Bangla" ("Victory to Bengal") in early 1969, initially to the annoyance of Mujib. They first unfurled the national flag of Bangladesh and persuaded Mujib to hold it in public in March 1971.

Pakistan in the 1960s was going through a difficult time. It annoyed the United States, an old ally and benefactor, by supporting Chinese aggression toward India and afterward by establishing a special friendship with China. At home, Bengalis had been a constant pain in the neck for Islamabad. By 1965, Ayub Khan was convinced that a war with sworn enemy India was winnable. Consequently, he went to war against India with the goal of occupying Indian-occupied Kashmir—a goal that, if achieved, would have given him both legitimacy and lifelong popularity in both parts of Pakistan. During the 1965 India-Pakistan War, East Pakistani Muslims forgot their internal differences with West Pakistan and denounced India, the common "Hindu enemy," as the aggressor. Pakistan, however, did not gain any long-term benefit from the anti-Indian feelings of most Bengalis.

Soon Bengalis realized that the government of Pakistan on the one hand had not made adequate defense arrangements for their province and, on the other hand, did not trust or treat them well, despite Bengali soldiers' heroic performance in the war with India in the disputed Punjab region. Consequently, in February 1966, Mujib announced the famous Six-Point Program, demanding full autonomy for all provinces of Pakistan and special paramilitary troops and separate currency for East Pakistan to stop further flight of capital from East to West Pakistan. Contrary to Ayub Khan's expectations, the Six-Point Program received enormous support from Bengalis. Soon Mujib was incarcerated and implicated in the so-called Agartala Conspiracy to dismember Pakistan with Indian help. The wide media coverage of the Agartala trial proceedings aroused mass enthusiasm in East Pakistan, and the average Bengali no longer abhorred the idea of breaking away from West Pakistan. By early 1969

Ayub Khan had become unpopular even in West Pakistan for signing a peace treaty with India; he was forced to resign in March. Meanwhile, the government had to withdraw the Agartala case and release Mujib and others accused.

After his release, Mujib catapulted to the peak of his popularity. In 1970, his party won 162 out of 300 seats, an absolute majority, in elections for the National Assembly of Pakistan. The Six-Point Program was a crucial factor in winning the election. Instead of transferring power to Mujib, whose party had the absolute majority, General Yahya Khan, the new president of Pakistan, succumbed to the pressure of Zulfikar Ali Bhutto (1928–1979), who won eighty-three seats in West Pakistan. Bhutto wanted power to be transferred to the two "majority leaders" in the two parts of Pakistan. In March 1971, Bengali masses under student leadership started a movement for total independence.

On March 7 Mujib addressed a mammoth public meeting in Dhaka. On the one hand, he asked the Bengalis to start a nonviolent, Gandhian campaign of noncooperation against Islamabad, and on the other hand, he declared that "this time the struggle is for independence." Soon Yahya and Bhutto came to Dhaka, and Mujib had several rounds of talks with them. While people were getting mixed signals about the outcome of the talks, on March 25 Pakistani troops began indiscriminate killing of Bengalis, initially in Dhaka and later everywhere in East Pakistan in the name of preserving the integrity of Pakistan. Before Mujib could react, Pakistani troops arrested him and took him to West Pakistan.

On March 27 a Bengali major, Ziaur Rahman (1936–1981), formally declared independence for Bangladesh over radio at Chittagong, approximately 280 kilometers from Dhaka. Meanwhile, Bengali civilians and members of the armed forces had started the liberation struggle without waiting for any declaration. Ten million Bengalis took refuge in India. Finally, with Indian armed intervention, Bangladesh was liberated on 16 December 1971. In January 1972 Mujib was released and on his return he became prime minister of Bangladesh. However, his tenure of three and a half years proved disastrous for both the nation and his image. In August 1975 some disgruntled young army officers staged a coup d'état and killed him and most of his immediate family. The people who had once admired Mujib as their deliverer from Pakistani misrule, instead of condemning the military takeover and his assassination, celebrated the end of autocracy and one-party dictatorship. The inexperienced Mujib and his associates with similar lower-middle-class and peasant backgrounds had bungled the administration and economy by nationalizing the profit-making privately run industries and financial institutions in the name of socialism and by engaging in corruption, nepotism, and terror.

General Rahman Assumes Power

In November 1975, General Ziaur Rahman (Zia), who first declared the independence of Bangladesh, assumed power in the wake of a mass civil and military upsurge against an attempted pro-Awami League military takeover. He was later elected president and soon emerged as the most popular, honest, and dynamic president of the republic. Whereas the civilian Mujib, known for his love for democracy, had introduced one-party dictatorship, the soldier Zia restored multiparty democracy. He also introduced market economy and shunned "socialism" and "secularism," which had been two of Mujib's Four State Principles along with "nationalism" and "democracy."

Zia's assassination in an abortive military takeover in 1981 by a group of ambitious military officers opposed to Zia's civilianization attempts was followed by a successful military takeover under General Hussain Muhammad Ershad (b. 1930) in 1982. Like Zia, Ershad used Islam to legitimize his regime. Whereas Zia had used Islamic rhetoric, Ershad in 1988 introduced Islam as the state religion by amending the secular constitution. Mujib had failed to understand that although most Bengali Muslims supported Bangladesh, they were less prepared to accept socialism, let alone secularism, as state principles. He should have remembered how they condemned India in support of Pakistan in 1965 during the heyday of Bengalis' struggle for provincial autonomy. Besides the traditional Indophobia or Hinduphobia of East Bengali Muslims, the abysmal failure of Mujib's government to restore law and order and decent living standards for the majority, let alone to attain the promised "Golden Bengal" through socialism and secularism, drew the population to Islamism not long after independence as an alternative to the elusive and counterproductive state ideologies of secularism and socialism. Both Islamic and secular opponents of Mujib exploited the Islamic sentiment of the people to gain legitimacy and political leverage. Globally, poor Muslims in the wake of the Cold War are leaning toward political Islam, and Bangladeshi Muslims are no exceptions.

Since the overthrow of the corrupt military regime of Ershad in 1990, the nation has held three rounds of parliamentary elections under "neutral" caretaker

governments, in 1991 and 1996. Sheikh Hasina (Mujib's daughter; b. 1947) and her Awami League party contested the 1991 elections only to reject the outcome after she failed to get the required majority seats to become prime minister. Finally, in 1996, she succeeded in becoming prime minister after organizing a vitriolic campaign through nationwide general strikes against the democratically elected government of Prime Minister Khaleda Zia (widow of Zia; b. 1945) of the Bangladesh Nationalist Party (BNP). Whereas the former has portrayed the latter as "anti-Liberation" or "pro-Pakistani," the latter, along with other opponents of the Awami League, has portrayed the former as "anti-Islamic" and "pro-India."

The ascendancy of the nouveau riche "vernacular elite" (peasant and lower middle class) as political leaders signals the ascent of clannish, factional, patron-client values at the cost of modern, urban, and middle-class values. Lower-middle-class and peasant leaders of the Awami League, in the name of Bengali nationalism, have displaced dominant Muslim middle and upper classes, who again benefited most by replacing dominant Hindu middle and upper classes that left after the partition of 1947. Meanwhile, due to the corruption and inefficiency of both politicians and bureaucrats, education, political institutions, democratic values, and the economy are degenerating. Political unrest and killing of political opponents and others, at the cost of law and order, education, and stability of the nation, have become the norms. Mutual trust, an essential for democracy, development, and a market economy, is grossly lacking. It is for that reason that parliamentary elections since 1991 have been held under caretaker governments for the sake of transparency—although the losing parties in 1991 and 1996 rejected the election results as rigged and manipulated. Overseas donors prefer to give aid money to nongovernmental organizations (NGOs), which are supposed to represent honest members of society, rather than to "corrupt" politicians and government servants. However, there are allegations about rampant NGO corruption, lack of accountability, and lack of transparency.

In sum, Bangladesh is a Third World nation that had good beginnings and potential to grow after independence but instead stagnated and suffered. The most legitimate question is why, despite the end of West Pakistani exploitation, 50 percent of the population live below the poverty line. The simple explanation would be mismanagement and corruption at every level of administration. There are other unanswered questions regarding the roles of Mujib, Bhutto, and the Pakistani military junta in the creation of Bangladesh. As it appears from *The American Papers*, hitherto classified state papers, Mujib did not want the dismemberment of Pakistan because, he feared, it would lead to a Communist takeover of East Bengal. Other documents suggest that he wanted to become prime minister of Pakistan and end the exploitation and deprivation of East Pakistan by Islamabad. It is curious that for the sake of the integrity of Pakistan, the Pakistani occupation army indiscriminately killed Bengalis, actions that would antagonize even the most ardent supporters of a united Pakistan. It is equally curious that eventually Bhutto and the army abandoned East Pakistan by waging an unwinnable war against India, by which time most Bengalis had already committed to Bangladesh. These premeditated acts suggest that for various reasons, especially fear of the specter of Bengali domination, neither Bhutto nor the military junta was any longer interested in keeping the two parts together.

Taj I. Hashmi

See also: **Bangladesh—Political System; Rahman, Mujibur**

Further Reading
Ahmed, Moudud. (1991) *Bangladesh: Constitutional Quest for Autonomy.* Dhaka, Bangladesh: University Press.
———. (1995) *Democracy and the Challenge of Development: A Study of Politics and Military Interventions in Bangladesh.* Dhaka, Bangladesh: University Press.
Choudhury, G. W. (1998) *The Last Days of United Pakistan.* Dhaka, Bangladesh: Oxford University Press and University Press.
———. (1994) "Islam in Bangladesh Politics." In *Islam, Muslims, and the Modern State,* edited by H. Mutalib and Taj Hashmi. New York: Macmillan and St. Martin's.
———. (2000) *Women and Islam in Bangladesh: Beyond Subjection and Tyranny.* New York: Macmillan and St. Martin's.
Hashmi, Taj I. (1992) *Pakistan as a Peasant Utopia: The Communalization of Class Politics in East Bengal, 1920–1947.* Boulder, CO: Westview.
Islam, Sirajul, ed. (1997) *History of Bangladesh, 1704—1971.* Dhaka, Bangladesh: Asiatic Society of Bangladesh.
Jahan, Rounaq. (1972) *Pakistan: Failure in National Integration.* New York: Columbia University Press.
Jansen, Eric J. (1986) *Rural Bangladesh: Competition for Scarce Resources.* Oslo, Norway: Norwegian University Press.
Khan, Roedad, ed. (1999) *The American Papers: Secret and Confidential India-Pakistan-Bangladesh Documents, 1965–1973.* Karachi, Pakistan: Oxford University Press.
Maniruzzaman, Talukder. (1980) *The Bangladesh Revolution and Its Aftermath.* Dhaka, Bangladesh: Green Book.
Norbye, Ole David Koht, ed. (1990) *Bangladesh Faces the Future.* Oxford: Oxford University Press.
Singh, Sheelendra Kumar, et al., eds. (1971, 1972) *Bangladesh Documents.* Vols. 1 and 2. New Delhi: Ministry of External Affairs.
Sobhan, Rehman. (1993) *Bangladesh: Problems of Governance.* Delhi: Konarak.

BANGLADESH—POLITICAL SYSTEM

Since winning its independence from Pakistan in 1971, Bangladesh has seen periods of presidential and parliamentary democracy and of civilian and military authoritarianism. Until 1947 Bengal was under British imperial rule, and with the partition and independence of India in 1947, the territory that eventually became Bangladesh formed the eastern province of Pakistan. Known as East Bengal until 1955, the province was called East Pakistan from 1955 to 1971.

Colonial Heritage

The Government of India Act, passed by the British Parliament in 1935, provided what it called "provincial autonomy" to the several provinces of British India. The act took effect on 1 April 1937.

The electoral system prescribed in the act contained two elements that affected political development. First, it did not provide universal adult suffrage. To qualify to vote a person had to meet certain educational or taxpaying levels, although the levels were lowered from those stipulated in the previous act of 1919. In Bengal and elsewhere many adults were excluded from the franchise. In Bengal those excluded were most often Muslim peasants in the Muslim majority areas of eastern Bengal. Second, the act continued the system of "separate electorates." Under this system the several religious communities were allotted a specific number of seats in the legislature, and the electors of those seats belonged exclusively to that religious community. In other words, Muslims voted for Muslims, Hindus for Hindus, and so on. As Muslims formed the majority of the population in Bengal, it might be assumed that the Bengal legislative assembly would have a Muslim majority among its members. This, however, was not the case. Of 250 seats, only 119 were designated Muslim, while 80 were designated "general," that is, Hindu, and a substantial number of seats were reserved for special categories, such as labor, commerce and industry, and landholders. There were also a large number of seats for Europeans. The Muslim League governing Pakistan continued the practice of separate electorates, and the 1954 East Bengal provincial election was held under that system.

The careers of three prominent Muslim political leaders of this period had profound effects on politics after Pakistan's independence in 1947. Fazl-ul Haq (1873–1962), a lawyer from the small town of Barisal, was known as "Sher-i-Bangla" (Lion of Bengal). Leading the Krishak Praja Party (KPP, Farmers' People's Party), the vehicle of the eastern Bengal Muslim agriculturists, small traders, and professionals, Fazl-ul Haq served as premier of Bengal from 1937 to 1943. Khwaja Sir Nazimuddin (1894–1964), a member of the landholding Nawab family of Dhaka, was the Bengali leader of the Muslim League and was premier from 1943 to 1945. Husain Shahid Suhrawardy (1893–1963), also then of the Muslim League, was the scion of a prominent political and intellectual family based in Calcutta. He was premier from 1946 to 1947.

Nazimuddin was described as a member of the "national elite," a group that generally addressed national Muslim issues but appeared to neglect the local issues of Bengal. Suhrawardy began to withdraw from the "national elite" during his tenure as prime minister and, as partition approached in 1947, sponsored an unsuccessful plan to create a Bengal dominion separate from India and Pakistan. He also worked to broaden the Muslim League's base of support among Bengali Muslims. After Pakistan's independence, he founded the Awami League (People's League) to expand participation in politics, and he strongly supported joint electorates as opposed to the separate electorates retained by the Muslim League governments of Pakistan. Fazl-ul Haq was the leader of what has been described as the "vernacular elite," based on the use of the Bengali language and concerned first with Bengali interests, not the least of which was the abolition of landlordism. Interestingly the three men are buried in adjacent graves in Dhaka.

The Pakistan Period

The period from 1947 to 1971 in Pakistan saw first a parliamentary form of government in which the parliament was not directly elected. With the early death of the leader of the Pakistan movement and the nation's first governor general, Muhammad Ali Jinnah (1876–1948), followed by the assassination of the first prime minister, Liaquat Ali Khan (1895–1951), the government became unstable. It was unable to enact a constitution until 1956, and the electoral provisions of that constitution eventually ignited East Pakistani anger. The concept of "parity" meant that East and West Pakistan elected the same number of representatives to the legislature even though the population of East Pakistan was greater than that of West Pakistan (the ratio was about 7 to 6 in 1971).

East Pakistanis felt they were shortchanged by the constitutional arrangements, felt poorly represented in the civil and military services, and resented the greater investments made in West Pakistan. As early as 1954 Bengali grievances had been put forward by the United

Front, a combination of the Awami League and Fazl-ul Haq's renamed Krishak Sramik Party (KSP, Farmers' and Workers' Party), which crushed the Muslim League in provincial elections that year.

In 1958 the military coup of Muhammad Ayub Khan (1907–1974) dismissed the elected government and eliminated the East Pakistan Legislative Assembly as a base of protest. In addition Khan curtailed the press and disqualified certain political figures, including Suhrawardy and Fazl-ul Haq.

Mujibur Rahman (1920–1975), who was called "Sheikh Mujib," became de facto leader of the Awami League on the death of Suhrawardy. In 1966 Mujib proposed six points that would, in his view, redress the apparent inequalities between West and East Pakistan. He suggested that (1) the federal parliamentary government provide free and regular elections; (2) the federal government control only defense and foreign

Public political protests are a common feature of politics in Bangladesh. Here, opposition leader Khaleda Zia leads a road march in September 1999 to protest the government's decision to allow Indian goods to be shipped across Bangladesh. (AFP/CORBIS)

PREAMBLE TO THE
CONSTITUTION OF BANGLADESH

(In the name of Allah, the Beneficent, the Merciful)

We, the people of Bangladesh, having proclaimed our Independence on the 26th day of March, 1971 and through [a historic war for national independence], established the independent, sovereign People's Republic of Bangladesh;

[Pledging that the high ideals of absolute trust and faith in the Almighty Allah, nationalism, democracy and socialism meaning economic and social justice, which inspired our heroic people to dedicate themselves to, and our brave martyrs to sacrifice their lives in the war for national independence, shall be fundamental principles of the Constitution;]

Further pledging that it shall be a fundamental aim of the State to realise through the democratic process to socialist society, free from exploitation—a society in which the rule of law, fundamental human rights and freedom, equality and justice, political, economic and social, will be secured for all citizens;

Affirming that it is our sacred duty to safeguard, protect and defend this Constitution and to maintain its supremacy as the embodiment of the will of the people of Bangladesh so that we may prosper in freedom and may make our full contribution towards international peace and co-operation in keeping with the progressive aspirations of mankind;

In our Constituent Assembly, this eighteenth day of Kartick, 1379 B.S corresponding to the fourth day of November, 1972 A.D., do hereby adopt, enact and give to ourselves this Constitution.

Source: Government of Bangladesh. Retrieved 11 April 2002, from: http://www.bangladeshgov.org/pmo/constitution.

affairs; (3) a separate currency or separate fiscal accounts for each province control the movement of capital from east to west; (4) all power of taxation be at the provincial level, with the federal government subsisting on grants from the provinces; (5) each federating unit enter into foreign trade agreements on its own and control the foreign exchange earned; and (6) each unit raise its own militia.

Demand for Autonomy Leads to Independence

Ayub fell in 1969 and was replaced by another general, Muhammad Yahya Khan (1917–1980). Yahya promised an end to martial law, an election, and a new constitution. He proposed an election held on the ba-

sis of population, giving East Pakistan a majority of 162 seats in the constituent assembly of three hundred, and the addition of thirteen seats for women. He kept his promise on the election, which was held in December 1970. Mujib's Awami League won 160 seats, all in East Pakistan, giving it a majority in the assembly, and Mujib insisted on the full inclusion of his six points in the constitution. Yahya objected to the one that would allow only the provincial governments to levy taxes. Zulfiqar Ali Bhutto (1928–1979), whose People's Party had won a majority in West Pakistan, also opposed Mujib's points.

Negotiations failed, and the Pakistani army struck in East Pakistan on 25 March 1971. Mujib was among those arrested. In the subsequent armed conflict, the Bangladeshi Mukti Bahini (Freedom Force) faced the Pakistani forces. India supported Bangladesh and joined the conflict in early December 1971. (This is the date India admits; Pakistan claims the intervention took place in late November.) The conflict ended with the Pakistani surrender on 16 December 1971.

After Independence

Mujib returned to Bangladesh in January 1971, and the Bangladesh Parliament passed a democratic constitution with a parliamentary form of government embodying the basic principals of nationalism, secularism, socialism, and democracy. However, much of the country had been devastated during the conflict, and the people governing it were inexperienced. Poor governance and heightened corruption made the regime increasingly unpopular despite the overwhelming victory of the Awami League in 1973. The victory came amid numerous reports of election rigging.

In January 1975 the parliament supported Mujib's suggestion to change from a parliamentary form to a presidential form of government with Mujib as president. In June he declared Bangladesh a one-party state under the Bangladesh Krishak Sramik Awami League, combining the names of the parties founded by Suhrawardy and Fazl-ul Haq. Mujib was assassinated by disgruntled army officers on 15 August 1975.

A brief civilian government followed, but in November another army uprising was put down. At that point a martial-law government (oddly headed by a civilian) was put in place, supported by the strongman Major General Ziaur Rahman (1936–1981), known as Zia. He assumed the presidency in 1977 and was elected to the office in 1978. Parliamentary elections were held in 1979, and the Bangladesh Nationalist Party (BNP), formed as a vehicle for Zia, won a two-thirds majority. The Awami League was a distant second. Zia initiated a nineteen-point program for the economic and social development of the country that was well under way when he was assassinated in May 1981 in an attempted coup led by a disaffected army officer.

Zia was succeeded by his vice president, Abdus Sattar (1906–1985). Not as strong a leader as Zia, Sattar allowed the BNP to factionalize. Nonetheless, he was elected president in November 1982, defeating an Awami League candidate.

Sattar was ousted from the presidency by a military coup on 24 March 1982 headed by Hussain Muhammad Ershad (b. 1930), and Bangladesh fell into a military dictatorship. General elections in 1986 and 1988 did not change the character of the administration, as Ershad formed the Jatiya Party (JP, another translation of People's Party) as his vehicle and remained the strongman. He adopted Zia's program in effect but did not democratize the system. Opposition was strong, led by Khaleda Zia (b. 1945), Zia's widow, of the BNP and Hasina Wajid (b. 1947), Mujib's daughter, of the Awami League. Although the two women were rivals, they came together in late 1990 to force the resignation of Ershad in December of that year.

In the subsequent election in 1991 Khaleda and the BNP gained a plurality and formed a government with the support of the Jama'at-e-Islami (JI) even though the JI did not join the government. Opposition from the Awami League was intense, making governance difficult. The league demanded new elections under a "neutral caretaker government." Granted this concession, the Awami League was successful in the election in June 1996 and formed a coalition government with the JP. Nevertheless, amid continuing strenuous opposition, good governance has not been the hallmark of the Awami League coalition, as it was not of the BNP government previously.

However, the BNP government managed a notable achievement. The system changed from a presidential democracy to a parliamentary democracy, returning to the original principle of the first independent government. The Awami League completed its term of office in July 2001.

Craig Baxter

See also: **Awami League; Bangladesh Nationalist Party; Bangladesh—Pakistan Relations; British Indian Empire; Jatiya Party; Mughal Empire**

Further Reading
Ahmed, Moudud. (1983) *Bangladesh, Era of Sheikh Mujibur Rahman.* Dhaka, Bangladesh: Vikas.
———. (1995) *Democracy and the Challenge of Development: A Study of Politics and Military Interventions in Bangladesh.* Dhaka, Bangladesh: Vikas.
Baxter, Craig. (1997) *Bangladesh: From a Nation to a State.* Boulder, CO: Westview.
Baxter, Craig, and Syedur Rahman. (1996) *Historical Dictionary of Bangladesh.* 2d ed. Lanham, MD: Scarecrow.
Jahan, Rounaq. (1972) *Pakistan: Failure in National Integration.* New York: Columbia University Press.
Maniruzzaman, Talukder. (1980) *The Bangladesh Revolution and Its Aftermath.* Dhaka, Bangladesh: Bangladesh Books.
Sen, Shila. (1976) *Muslim Politics in Bengal, 1937–1947.* New Delhi: Impex India.
Sobhan, Rehman. (1993) *Bangladesh: Problems of Governance.* Delhi: Konark.

Protestors in Dhaka participate in a 30-hour strike to protest the government's decision to allow India to ship goods across Bangladesh. The protest was led by the Bangladesh Nationalist Party. (AFP/CORBIS)

BANGLADESH NATIONALIST PARTY

The Bangladesh Nationalist Party (BNP) was formed in 1978 under the name JAGODAL (Bengali acronym for People's Party) as a political vehicle to support Bangladesh president Ziaur Rahman (Zia). The titular leader was Abdus Sattar (who succeeded Zia as president when the latter was assassinated in 1981). The party's program is embodied in the nineteen points of Zia that outlined the direction Bangladesh should take in political, economic, and social development. It also strongly emphasizes Bangladeshi nationalism as opposed to a wider Bengali nationhood. The party won more than two-thirds of the parliamentary seats in 1979. The Sattar presidency was weak and was overthrown in 1982 by General Hussain Muhammad Ershad. Looking for stronger leadership, the BNP called upon Khaleda Zia, the widow of Ziaur Rahman, who continued the program and was unstinting in her opposition to Ershad as well as to Awami League leader Hasina Wajid. While the two leaders combined briefly to cause Ershad's resignation in 1990, they have since opposed each other in elections and governance. The BNP won a plurality in the 1991 parliamentary election and formed the government with the support of the Jamaʿat-i-Islami, but it finished second to the Awami League in the 1996 election. The animosity between the BNP and the Awami League has decreased the effectiveness of the government.

Craig Baxter

See also: **Awami League**

Further Reading

Ahamed, Emajuddin. (1988) *Military Rule and the Myth of Democracy*. Dhaka, Bangladesh: University Press.
Baxter, Craig. (1997) *Bangladesh from a Nation to a State*. Boulder CO: Westview.
Hossain, Golam. (1988) *General Ziaur Rahman and the BNP*. Dhaka, Bangladesh: University Press.

BANGLADESH–INDIA RELATIONS

Bangladesh–India relations are peculiar because Bangladesh is bounded by India on three sides—north, east, and west, except for a small portion on the east, where it borders Myanmar (Burma). Bangladesh depends on India for harnessing the resources of the Bay of Bengal, which forms its southern boundary, as well as for providing safe international water routes for trade and commerce. India and Bangladesh share many things due to their geographic proximity: both regions experienced British colonialism, and both have numerous cultural linkages. Both countries lie in the basins of the Ganges and Brahamaputra (known as the Jamuna in Bangladesh) Rivers, on which they both depend.

Early Relations

Bangladesh gained independence from Pakistan in 1971. Bangladesh–India relations began on a positive note when in March 1972 Prime Minister Indira Gandhi (1917–1984) was given a rousing welcome in Bangladesh's capital, Dhaka, by Prime Minister Sheikh Mujibur Rahman (1920–1975), who expressed his country's gratitude for India's role in the creation of Bangladesh. The two signed the twenty-five-year Treaty of Friendship, Cooperation, and Peace on 19 March 1972 in Dhaka. According to the terms of the treaty both governments determined to maintain good neighborly relations in a spirit of peace and friendship. The two leaders resolved to eliminate the vestiges of colonialism, racism, and imperialism. During the regime of Sheikh Mujibur Rahman, New Delhi and Dhaka signed an interim agreement to share the waters of the Ganges River.

Hard-line nationalists and conservative Muslims in Bangladesh accused Sheikh Mujibur Rahman of tilting government policy heavily in favor of India. After his assassination during a coup d'état on 15 August 1975, Bangladesh–India relations grew much more tense. Sheikh Mujibur Rahman's successor, General Ziaur Rahman (1936–1981), ruled Bangladesh from November 1975 to May 1981; unlike his predecessor he was unfavorably disposed toward India.

Tensions started building between the two countries, mainly because of the strong influence of the general's ultra-left and right-wing supporters, who were anti-India. Rahman's fear that India might attempt to destabilize his government impelled him to forge close strategic and security ties with the United States, Pakistan, and China, with a view to containing Indian influence in the subcontinent. Bangladesh also started buying weapons from China, a move that irked India. Border skirmishes in 1976 produced further deterioration in India-Bangladesh relations. The Indian government of Morarji Desai (1896–1995; in power 1977–1979) staunchly opposed cross-border migration and smuggling from Bangladesh, which also strained ties.

Relations in the 1980s

The change in regime in Bangladesh following Rahman's assassination in 1981 and the military coup staged by General H. M. Ershad (b. 1930) in March 1982 contributed more irritants to bilateral relations. Nevertheless, a protocol on inland water transit was signed in 1984 to provide for the development and maintenance of inland waterways. During the Ershad regime, several outstanding unresolved bilateral issues surfaced. These included the repatriation of Bangladeshi Chakama refugees; transfer of the Teen Bigha corridor (a piece of land 85 by 178 meters in area) in the eastern vicinity of West Bengal, and Ganges water sharing on the Farakka barrage, located across the Bhagirathi-Hooghly Rivers in Calcutta.

The Chakama refugees from the Chittagong Hill tracts in southern Bangladesh started pouring into the Indian state of Tripura as early as 1986 in the wake of the looting of their lands and their forced dislocation by dominant Bangladeshi Muslims. The Indian government gave them shelter and humanitarian assistance, a considerable financial burden. India urged Bangladesh to repatriate the refugees, who were creating internal security problems because of their smuggling and drug-trafficking activities in northeastern India and because of the refugees' connections with Indian militant groups in the states of Assam, Tripura, Manipur, and Nagaland. This issue was ultimately resolved in February 1997 at the initiative of the Bangladesh government, which offered a comprehensive package for the resettlement of refugee nationals who returned to their homeland.

Another issue that rocked Dhaka–Delhi relations was related to the transfer of the Teen Bigha corridor to Bangladesh to facilitate access of Bangladeshis to the Angarpota and Dahagram areas. This issue was amicably settled when India transferred the corridor to Bangladesh on a perpetual-lease basis in June 1992. With the removal of this irritant, relations between the two countries improved considerably.

A more complex issue and constant source of friction between Bangladesh and India was the question of distribution of the Ganges's waters after India constructed the Farraka barrage in 1975. An interim agreement on sharing the Farraka waters was signed by the two governments, enabling Bangladesh to use the maximum quantity of water needed for irrigation, except during the dry season. From time to time Bangladesh and India signed memoranda of understanding to work out the use of water, but Bangladesh accused India of not releasing sufficient water. Bangladesh's prime minister, Begum Khalida Zia (served 1991–1996; 2001–present), sought to internationalize this issue by raising it at the U.N. in October 1995, while arguing that unilateral withdrawal of waters by India had created severe problems of desertification, environmental degradation, and unemployment in her country. This issue was later amicably resolved when the Bangladeshi prime minister Sheikh Hasina (served 1996–2001) and her Indian counterpart, H. D. Deve

Gowda, signed a thirty-year treaty on sharing the Ganges Farakka waters in New Delhi on 12 December 1996.

Current Relations

Nevertheless, Bangladesh and India still have a troubled relationship. In India's view the major issue is that the Pakistani Inter Services Intelligence (ISI) carries out anti-Indian activities on the soil of Bangladesh. The Indian government has accused Bangladesh of coordinating its activities with Pakistan's ISI and also of shipping weapons from Bangladesh into the northeastern states of India to supply militant groups such as the United Liberation Front of Assam (ULFA) and the National Socialist Council of Nagaland (NSCN), thus accentuating India's internal security problems. The Indian government urged Bangladesh to help stop such activities in the interest of better bilateral ties. The Hasina government reassured India that Bangladesh was taking measures to stop such activities on her country's soil.

Bangladesh favors reconciliation between India and Pakistan and considers it a crucial factor for regional peace and stability. In view of the nuclear tests carried out by India and Pakistan in May 1998, Bangladesh favors a nonproliferation regime and strongly supports transforming South Asia into a nuclear-weapon-free zone, contrary to the Indian stance. Bangladesh is eager to have the South Asian Association for Regional Cooperation address the common problems of poverty, hunger, unemployment, and economic instability facing the countries of this region. Both Bangladesh and India share similar views on this issue.

Despite the problems between the two countries, India and Bangladesh have an opportunity to work together in economic and trade areas and to harness the natural resources of both countries for their mutual benefit. Together the two must sort out the problem of the demarcation of maritime boundaries through mutual consultation so that their respective economic interests can be protected by judiciously sharing the products and resources of the area. They must come to an understanding on the geostrategic, geopolitical, and security issues they face in order to maintain a positive and friendly relationship.

B. M. Jain

Further Reading

Chakravarty, S. R., ed. (1994) *Foreign Policy of Bangladesh.* Delhi, India: Har-Anand.

Deora, M. S. (1995) *India and the Freedom Struggle of Bangladesh.* New Delhi, India: Discovery.

Dixit, J. N. (1999) *Liberation and Beyond: Indo-Bangladesh Relations.* New Delhi, India: Konark.

BANGLADESH–PAKISTAN RELATIONS

Bangladesh–Pakistan relations make a compelling study for a variety of reasons. The countries share a common history and religion as well as strong fraternal ties. Bangladesh, formerly known as East Pakistan, was part of Pakistan from Pakistan's independence in 1947 until December 1971, when Bangladesh became an independent and sovereign state after a prolonged civil war. East and West Pakistan were geographically separated by a distance of one thousand miles of Indian territory, and, despite their shared history, they had very different cultures and languages. Economically, the plight of the people of East Pakistan was far worse than that of their counterparts in West Pakistan. This led to deepening domestic unrest, as did the neglect that East Pakistan's Bangla Muslims suffered at the hands of Pakistan's ruling elite.

On 7 December 1970, East Pakistan's Sheikh Mujibur Rahman, the head of the Awami League Party, won elections with an overwhelming majority in East Pakistan and a comfortable majority in the Pakistan National Assembly, but Yahya Khan (1917–1980), Pakistan's president, and his military advisers refused to let Sheikh Mujibur Rahman form a government. In March 1971, Pakistan's army was called in to put down a revolt in East Pakistan. Other factors provoking the revolt included West Pakistan's economic exploitation of East Pakistan; the lack of adequate participation by Bengali Muslims in the central administration; and the excessive number of West Pakistanis in top civil and military bureaucratic positions. India offered military support to East Pakistan's Muktibahini (Freedom Fighters), and Pakistan's Lieutenant General A. A. K. Niazi ultimately surrendered to Indian forces. Sheikh Mujibur Rahman became the first prime minister of independent Bangladesh.

Bangladesh-Pakistan relations in the very beginning were marked by mutual apathy and coolness; psychologically, Pakistan was reluctant to accept Bangladesh as a sovereign nation. During the regime of Sheikh Mujibur Rahman (president of Bangladesh from December 1971 to 1972 in absentia; prime minister 1972–1975), relations between the two countries were at the lowest ebb. Although Pakistan's Zulfikar Ali Bhutto (1928–1979) visited Bangladesh in June 1974, he failed to bridge persisting differences on issues such as the repatriation of stranded Bihari Muslims to Pakistan and the division of assets and foreign debt. With the assassination of Sheikh Mujibur Rahman on 15 August 1975, hopes were raised in Pakistan for friendship and cooperation with Bangladesh. The pro-India stance of Mujib (as Sheikh Mujibur Rahman was known) was soon replaced by an anti-India stance under the military regime of President Ziaur Rahman (1936–1981). This change helped patch up Bangladesh's differences with Pakistan.

It was at the initiative of President Ziaur Rahman that the South Asian Association for Regional Cooperation (SAARC) was set up in December 1985; its first summit was held in Dhaka, Bangladesh's capital. At the summit meetings, leaders from seven countries of the South Asian region discussed bilateral and regional issues. They expressed a desire to oppose Indian hegemony in South Asia and shared a common perception of India as a threat to regional peace, security, and stability.

Relations between Bangladesh and Pakistan were also helped by the installation of a democratically elected government in Pakistan in November 1988, under the leadership of Benazir Bhutto (b. 1953). As Pakistan's prime minister, she visited Bangladesh in October 1989 and was accorded a warm welcome by President Hussain Muhammad Ershad (b. 1930). Both leaders agreed to resolve the repatriation issue amicably and to consolidate their fraternal ties for the economic well-being of their peoples. Bhutto underlined the long-term importance of bilateral economic and trade relations. Ershad and Bhutto agreed to set up sugar and cement plants in Bangladesh, and Bangladesh agreed to provide technical assistance to Pakistan in the field of telecommunication and electronics.

Era of Friendship

The early 1990s saw changes in regimes in both Bangladesh and Pakistan. Nawaz Sharif (b. 1949) became Pakistan's prime minister in November 1990, and Begum Khilda Zia (b. 1945) became the prime minister of a democratic government in Bangladesh in March 1991. Friendship and cooperation blossomed between the two countries. Sharif reassured Bangladesh of Pakistan's support in setting up profitable joint ventures. Prime Minister Sharif, during his official visit to Dhaka in May 1991, offered help to the cyclone-affected people of Bangladesh in the form of rice, clothing, medicines, and tents, as well as a check for twenty million rupees. In addition, frequent meetings between Begum Zia and Sharif at the SAARC summit in New Delhi (May 1991), the Harare Commonwealth summit (December 1991), and the Organization of Islamic Conference Summit at Dakar (December 1991) helped consolidate mutual ties and develop a coherent and cooperative approach to re-

gional issues, especially on Kashmir, nuclear nonproliferation, and arms control. Zia made a second visit to Islamabad in August 1992, during which she discussed a wide range of issues with Sharif, including trade, commerce, and social and cultural interaction between common peoples of both countries. They reiterated their firm commitment to the idea of a nuclear-free zone in South Asia.

During the second government of Nawaz Sharif (1997–October 1999), Bangladesh-Pakistan relations were marked by increasing interaction between Sharif and Prime Minister Zia, and then between Sharif and Bangladesh's newly elected prime minister, Sheikh Hasina Wajed (b. 1947). Prime Minister Hasina Wajed visited Islamabad in June 1998, after the May nuclear tests carried out by India and Pakistan. She discussed the nuclear situation in South Asia and appealed to both countries to exercise nuclear restraint and resolve the Kashmir issue amicably through peaceful negotiation.

A Bangladeshi man dressed as Pakistan leader General Pervez Musharraf participates in a protest in Dhaka in September 2000. The Bangladeshis are protesting the atrocities committed by Pakistan army in 1971 during the war that led to Bangladesh's independence. (AFP/CORBIS)

Strained Relations

With the installation of a military regime in Pakistan in October 1999, relations between Dhaka and Islamabad began to deteriorate. Sheikh Hasina's personal dislike for the military regime in Pakistan was apparent when she delivered her speech at the United Nations Millennium Summit in New York, staunchly opposing dictatorial regimes everywhere and advocating the revival of democracy and the safeguarding of human rights globally. General Pervez Musharraf, Pakistan's president, was offended by her comments. Their relations were further strained when sections of the Hamoodur Commission Report, written in Pakistan, on the causes of Pakistan's military defeat in 1971 were made public. The report held that by not transferring power to East Pakistan's duly elected representatives, Yahaya Khan and his top military aides were responsible for the political turmoil created in 1971. Pakistan's deputy high commissioner, Ifranun Rahaman Raza, further inflamed the situation while speaking at a seminar in Dhaka on 27 November 2000, when he made highly controversial remarks about the liberation war in Bangladesh. He said that the atrocities of genocide and rape perpetrated in 1971 in East Pakistan were ignited by Awami League miscreants, not by Pakistani forces, and he discounted any possibility of Pakistan's apologizing to Bangladesh for the actions of the Pakistani army in 1971. In the wake of these remarks, he was declared persona non grata by the government of Bangladesh. The Pakistani government recalled him immediately. Some of the party leaders of the Awami League demanded a boycott of Pakistani goods, but Sheikh Hasina refused to take such a drastic action. Musharraf urged Bangladesh to set aside the tragic past, but Pakistan's military regime revived old misgivings that Pakistan has not yet been reconciled to the reality of Bangladesh as a sovereign and independent nation.

B. M. Jain

See also: **Awami League; India-Pakistan Relations**

Further Reading
Dixit, J. N. (1999) *Liberation and Beyond: Indo-Bangladesh Relations.* New Delhi: Konark.

Huq, Muhammad Shamsul. (1993) *Bangladesh in International Politics: The Dilemmas of Weak States.* Dhaka, Bangladesh: Dhaka University Press.

Niazi, A. A. K. (1998) *The Betrayal of East Pakistan.* New Delhi: Manohar.

BANGSAWAN *Bangsawan* is a form of Malay theater that first came into existence during British colonial rule. It was most popular between 1900 and 1945 but nearly ceased to exist in the 1950s, having failed to compete with other forms of entertainment like films, radio, and television. Today, the Malaysian Ministry of Arts, Culture, and Tourism sponsors the few existing *bangsawan* groups to ensure that *bangsawan* lives as a national heritage and treasure.

Bangsawan is believed to have begun in Penang, Malaya, in the 1870s. It was developed by Wayang Parsi, an Indian theatrical group. It then spread to Singapore, Sumatra in Indonesia, and parts of northern Kalimantan in Borneo, also part of Indonesia. Although *bangsa* means "race" and *wan* means "noble," there is no concrete evidence that *bangsawan* was ever attached to royal courts; there were no court troupes or royal performers. However, *bangsawan* was performed for kings and nobles.

Over the years, *bangsawan* was used as a tool of political propaganda (especially during the Japanese occupation, during which plays produced had to have anti-British sentiments) and also was used for commercial purposes.

Principal *bangsawan* roles included *orang muda* (the hero), *seri panggung* (the prima donna), comedians, the sultan, queen, king of the genies, and ministers and courtiers, hermits, warriors, and female court attendants. *Bangsawan* stories were drawn from local history as well as Middle Eastern, Indian, Chinese, Indonesian, Thai, Islamic, and Western sources. The themes often emphasized adventure, romance, and moral teachings.

Bangsawan had no script. Only the synopsis of the story was given to the cast at the outset. Actors and actresses had to be smart and quick enough to improvise dialogue and action according to the moods of the audience. The success and failure of *bangsawan* relied heavily on the prima donna, who had to be beautiful and able to sing well.

The *bangsawan* stage was much influenced by the Western concept of a closed theater, and it was the first Malay theater form to use a proscenium stage. Wings, borders, and painted backdrops were also used. *Bangsawan's* musical influences came from the Middle East, India, the West, and traditional Malaya (today's Malaysia). The costumes conformed with local settings and cultures.

Nor Faridah Abdul Manaf

Further Reading
Nanney, Nancy K. (1983) "An Analysis of Modern Malaysian Drama." Ph.D. diss. University of Hawaii.

Yousof, Ghulam-Sarwar. (1994) *Dictionary of Traditional South-East Asia Theatre.* Kuala Lumpur, Malaysia: Oxford University Press.

BANKING AND FINANCE INDUSTRY—SINGAPORE

Due to its role as an entrepot for Southeast Asia, Singapore has had a relatively sophisticated financial sector since its colonial period (1819–1959). Trade financing has been the most important activity of the commercial banks, most of which were and are foreign. Recognizing that sustained economic growth (which Singapore has enjoyed) is underpinned by a sound financial system, financial-sector development policy since independence in 1965 has focused on this. An additional objective has been to develop as a major financial center. These objectives have generally been achieved. Singapore's financial system is sound and stable; the country was relatively unscathed by the 1997–1998 Asian financial crisis, and its financial system remained intact.

Singapore is also a financial center of international repute. It pioneered the Asian dollar market in Asia (the counterpart of the Euro dollar market) in 1968 and futures trading in Asia in 1984, with the launching of the Singapore International Monetary Exchange (SIMEX). The country is the fourth-largest foreign exchange trading center in the world, after London, New York, and Tokyo, with an average daily turnover of around $100 billion. The financial sector currently contributes around 12 percent to the gross domestic product, a substantially higher rate than that of most countries, where it averages between 4 and 8 percent. Around 5 percent of the labor force is employed in this sector.

Financial Structure

At the apex of any financial system is the central bank, here the Monetary Authority of Singapore (MAS), established in 1971 and endowed with all central-banking functions except that of currency issue. Through a coordinated policy framework that includes regulation and supervision and infrastructure and human-resource development as well as fiscal incentives, the MAS has contributed to the achievement of sustained economic growth and the development of Singapore as a major financial center.

Table 1 summarizes the present structure of financial institutions in Singapore.

Banking Services

Commercial banks, the largest providers of banking services, are divided into three categories: full, restricted, and offshore. While full-license banks provide the full range of banking services to residents and nonresidents, full-license foreign banks are restricted in terms of their branch and ATM network. The country's four largest banking groups, the Development Bank of Singapore, the Overseas Chinese Banking Corporation, the United Overseas Bank, and the Overseas Union Bank, account for more than 80 percent of local bank assets. Generally, the local banks, with their larger deposit base, are the net lenders in the interbank market, and the foreign banks are the net borrowers. Since 1987, commercial banks have been permitted to engage in the securities business.

The Bank of Hong Kong in Singapore, c. 1900. (UNDERWOOD & UNDERWOOD/CORBIS)

TABLE 1

Financial institutions in Singapore

	End March 1999
Banks	142
Local	9
Foreign	133
Full banks	22
Restricted banks	13
Offshore banks	98
(Banking offices including head and main offices)	(561)
Asian currency units	205
Banks	135
Merchant banks	70
Other	-
Finance companies	15
Merchant banks	70
Insurance companies	159
Direct insurers	59
Professional insurers	49
Captive insurers	51
Representative offices	69
Banks	68
Merchant banks	-
Finance companies	1
Stockbroking companies	78
Investment advisers	148
International money brokers	9
SGX-DT members	
Corporate clearing members	33
Corporate non-clearing members	22
Individual members	520
Commercial associate members	16

SOURCE: MAS (2001: 103).

Restricted and offshore licenses were granted from the 1970s to promote offshore financial services. Their activities are somewhat restricted in the onshore or domestic market to prevent overbanking.

Any bank, with the approval of the MAS, may set up separate accounting units, which are called the Asian Currency Units (ACU), for offshore transactions. This separation is to allow for better monitoring of domestic banking transactions to ensure monetary control. ACUs enjoy preferential tax and regulatory treatment. These and other policies have boosted offshore financial activities. In 1999, ACU deposits reached $448 billion; this compares with deposits of $68 million when the market started in 1968.

Banking services are also provided by finance companies, all of which are local and many of which are bank affiliated. They are restricted to accepting fixed (time) and saving deposits and may, with approval of the MAS, deal in foreign exchange and gold. Their loan portfolio is concentrated in areas generally not taken up by the commercial banks, such as hire purchase (subject to an unsecured lending limit of $5,000), leasing, and factoring. They both compete and complement the

activities of banks. Foreign participation in locally owned finance companies is restricted to 20 percent.

As a group, merchant banks (known as investment banks in some countries) are less homogeneous than commercial banks, because they specialize in one or more areas of corporate finance. In Singapore they are nondepository; they may raise funds from banks, other approved financial institutions, equity holders, and companies controlled by equity holders, and they are permitted to operate ACUs. Their number has expanded rapidly due to the growth of offshore and capital markets.

Contractual Saving Institutions

Singapore's insurance market includes fifty-nine direct insurers and hundred reinsurers and captive insurers, which provide insurance mainly for offshore business. Growth of the market has been rapid since the mid-1990s, fueled by both local and offshore demand. The life-insurance market is fairly concentrated, with the four largest companies accounting for around 90 percent of all premiums. The market for life insurance has been closed for several years to new entrants. This policy was reviewed in 2000. As with banking, there is a desire to develop a few local insurance companies that could effectively compete with foreign companies and in foreign markets.

The other important contractual saving institution is Singapore's compulsory saving scheme, the Central Provident Fund (CPF), established in 1955 to generate savings for retirement. Both employees and employers contribute monthly at prescribed rates, and the savings may be used to purchase approved assets before retirement. Due to its scale and scope, the CPF is an important financial intermediary with significant microeconomic and macroeconomic effects. Because benefits are tied to contributions, it is different from pay-as-you-go social-security systems. Surplus CPF moneys are invested in Singapore government securities, providing a noninflationary source of finance.

Capital Markets

Table 2 shows the funds raised in the capital market during the 1990s. Funds raised expanded significantly from Singapore $9.2 billion in 1991 to reach Singapore $24.4 billion by 1999. More significantly, the shares of equity and debt securities increased from 11.4 to 25.2 percent and 21 to 38 percent, respectively, over the period. Even so, commercial banks remain the main providers of funds, with loans amounting to Singapore $146.5 billion in 1999. There thus is room for capital market expansion.

TABLE 2

Net funds raised in the domestic capital market (S$ Billion)			
	1990	1995	1999
Net funds raised by government	6.2 (67.6%)	10.4 (65.7%)	9.0 (36.8%)
Capital raised by the private sector	1.1 (11.4%)	1.7 (10.6%)	6.1 (25.2%)
Issues of debt securities	1.9 (21.0%)	3.8 (23.7%)	9.3 (38.0%)
Total net funds raised	9.2	15.9	24.4

SOURCE: MAS (2001: 112).

The government-securities market was revamped in 1987 to activate secondary trading. Recent reforms, including the issue of more varied maturities, have increased turnover.

Established in 1973, the Stock Exchange of Singapore (SES) expanded rapidly to become an important regional stock market. It is composed of a Main Board and an over-the-counter market, SESDAQ, a market for the equity needs of small- and medium-sized enterprises.

Financial Reforms

In mid-1997, a Financial Sector Review Group was established to review financial regulations to enable the sector to face the challenges of globalization and to develop Singapore as a premier financial center. The general direction of the reforms is toward opening up financial markets, because prices (interest and exchange rates) were deregulated during the 1970s, and product and practice liberalization is ongoing.

Liberalization of the banking sector will allow foreign banks greater access in the domestic banking sector, partly as a result of international pressure and partly to strengthen local banks. Although foreign ownership of local banks is no longer limited to 40 percent, there are safeguards to protect national interest. To reduce systemic risk, separation of financial and nonfinancial activities of banks is required.

In regard to bank regulation, the MAS has shifted its stance from regulation to supervision, with a view to reviewing the risk management processes, control systems, and asset quality of banks. In line with international best practices, higher standards of corporate governance and transparency are required to reduce information asymmetry and consequently systemic risk.

To make Singapore a leading insurance hub in Asia, the MAS has liberalized entry for direct insurers and insurance brokers. The 49 percent limit on foreign shareholdings of locally owned direct insurers has been abolished to allow mergers and alliances with reputable foreign firms. The enhanced competition should promote efficiency.

In the capital market, the Singapore Exchange was inaugurated in 1999 following the demutualization and merger of the SES with SIMEX. Access will be fully opened from 2002, while commission rates have become fully negotiable. To add breadth and depth to the capital market, restrictions on foreign firms wishing to issue Singapore dollar bonds and transactions in Singapore dollar–denominated securities and derivatives also have been liberalized.

A Financially Strong Singapore

Over the past several decades, Singapore has achieved sustained and rapid economic growth due in part to the efficient mobilization of financial resources. Today, Singapore's fairly diversified and developed financial system not only contributes significantly to output but also reflects its role as a major financial center. Recent and ongoing financial reforms to meet the challenges of globalization are designed to maintain its competitive edge and to reduce systemic risk.

Amina Tyabji

Further Reading

Ariff, Mohamed, Basant Kumar Kapur, and Amina Tyabji. (1996) "Money Market Study: Singapore." In *Money Markets in Asia*, edited by H. Scott and P. Wellons. New York: Oxford University Press.

Khalid, A, and Amina Tyabji. (2001) "Financial Sector Development: Strategies and Challenges." In *The Singapore Economy in the 21st Century: Issues and Strategies*, edited by M. K. Chng, W. T. Hui, A. T. Koh, K. L. Lim, and B. Rao. Singapore: McGraw Hill.

Luckett, D. G., D. L. Schulze, and R. W. Wong. (1994) *Banking, Finance, and Monetary Policy in Singapore*. Singapore: McGraw-Hill.

Monetary Authority of Singapore (MAS). (2001) *Annual Report, 1999–2000*. Singapore: Monetary Authority of Singapore.

Tan, C. H. (1999) *Financial Markets and Institutions in Singapore*. Singapore: Singapore University Press.

World Trade Organization. (1999) *Trade Policy Review Singapore*. Geneva: WTO.

BANTENG The banteng (*Bos javanicus*), also called *banting*, *tsaine*, *sapi-utan*, or *tembadau*, is a bovid species distributed among Assam, Myanmar (Burma), Thailand, Malaysia, Borneo, Java, and Sumatra. It is a shy, often nocturnal, animal found in forested and dry areas. The

A pair of wild banteng oxen at the Doi Inthanon National Park in Thailand in 1994. (GALEN ROWELL/CORBIS)

banteng has been heavily hunted and is now quite rare in the wild. It is still sometimes found in regions where there is good forest cover and little human disturbance. The male is dark brown with a white patch on the rump and white stockings; the female and young are reddish brown. In Myanmar, however, the bulls are also a rufous brown. The banteng has short, rounded olive-green horns and a distinctively pointed head like a deer's. It has a hump behind the neck, but no dewlap, and ranges in height between 150 and 175 centimeters at the withers. In Bali the animal is domesticated and known as the Bali cow, and in some regions a hybrid is bred with zebu.

Paul Hockings

BAO DAI (1913–1997), last of the Nguyen emperors of Vietnam. Bao Dai was born Nguyen Phuc Vinh Thuy. Educated in France, he was crowned emperor on 8 January 1926, took the name Bao Dai ("Protector of Grandeur" or "Keeper or Preserver of Greatness"), and moved back to France at the request of the French. In 1932 the French government allowed him to return to Vietnam, where he attempted a series of reforms in the hope of establishing a modern imperial government and of convincing French officials to allow limited Vietnamese independence under his rule. France rebuffed his attempts, and the emperor settled into a lifestyle characterized by gambling, hunting, and women. During World War II, Bao Dai cooperated with the Japanese and, at their urging, proclaimed the "Empire of Vietnam," independent from France.

When the Communist-led Viet Minh took control during the August Revolution in 1945 after the Japanese withdrawal, Bao Dai abdicated his throne, became known as First Citizen Vinh Thuy, and served in the new Viet Minh legislature. Disillusioned with the Communists, Bao Dai left Vietnam in 1946 and eventually returned to Europe. After signing the Elysée Agreements with French President Vincent Auriol on 8 March 1949, Bao Dai returned to Vietnam as head of state. He ruled Vietnam (within the French Union) through the 1954 Geneva Accords that ended the 1946–1954 war between France and Vietnam and retained his position during the first year of the new Republic of Vietnam (RVN). His administration was marked by the institutionalization of corruption, prostitution, smuggling, racketeering, and drug trafficking through his association with the Binh Xuyen gang in Saigon. After losing an election rigged in favor of Ngo Dinh Diem in 1955, Bao Dai eventually left the country and spent the majority of the rest of his life in France.

Richard B. Verrone

Further Reading

Currey, Cecil B. (1994) "Bao Dai: The Last Emperor." *Viet Nam Generation* 6, 1–2: 199–206.
Jamieson, Neil L. (1993) *Understanding Vietnam*. Berkeley and Los Angeles: University of California Press.

Emperor Bao Dai relaxes in Paris in April 1954. (BETTMANN/CORBIS)

Tucker, Spencer C. (1999) *Vietnam*. Lexington, KY: University Press of Kentucky.

BARAKA

Baraka is an important Islamic concept that describes the magical blessing that flows from a holy man or a holy place. *Baraka (barakat)* does not vanish with the death of the holy man but rather continues. Therefore, shrines of saints are venerated, and the devout can partake of blessing, which is thought to hover like an aura around the holy place. *Baraka* can also be obtained from the relics of a holy man (often his personal effects).

The strongest *baraka* comes from Mecca, the holiest city for the Islamic faith, because it is thought to be the first city created by Adam. The story goes that at Mecca Abraham erected the Kaaba, deemed to be the center of the world, where can be found the Black Stone, a potent source of *baraka*.

People who participate in the annual Hajj (pilgrimage) to Mecca are thought to possess powerful *baraka*, which is said to last a lifetime (and perhaps even beyond). Holy objects obtained in Mecca are also considered a powerful source of blessing. One such object is water from the well of Zamzam. Islamic tradition states that the angel Gabriel dug Zamzam in order to save Hagar and her son Ismail from dying of thirst. Probably this tradition dates from pre-Islamic times.

Nirmal Dass

Further Reading
Farah, Caesar E. (2000) *Islam: Beliefs and Observances*. Hauppauge, NY: Barron's.
Renard, John. (1996) *Seven Doors to Islam: Spirituality and the Religious Life of Muslims*. Berkeley and Los Angeles: University of California Press.
Rippin, Andrew. (2001) *Muslims: Their Religious Beliefs and Practices*. London: Routledge.

BARISAN SOSIALIS

In July 1961, Lim Chin Siong and seven pro-communist People's Action Party (PAP) members of the Legislative Assembly challenged the PAP leadership. When their challenge failed, they were expelled on 26 July 1961 and thirteen PAP assembly members and twenty-two PAP branch officials quit the party to form the Barisan Sosialis (Socialist Front). The new party's officers were Lee Siew Choh, chair; Sandra Woodhull, vice chair; Lim Chin Siong, general secretary; and Ppo Soon Kai, assistant general secretary. They opposed Singapore's merger with Malaysia on the terms proposed by the PAP. In 1963, twenty-four leading members of the

Barisan Sosialis (excluding Lee Siew Choh and the other Barisan assembly members) were detained in a security operation named Cold Store, together with twenty-one trade union leaders, nineteen university graduates and undergraduates (including seventeen from Nanyang University), seven members of rural associations, and five journalists. In the 1963 general election with compulsory voting and a 95 percent turnout, the Barisan won thirteen of the fifty-one seats with 33 percent of the votes.

In 1965 the Barisan Sosialis, having given an unconvincing performance in the Hong Lim by-election of that year, was already a flaccid political force, made weaker by internal fissures. The thirteen Barisan Members of Parliament boycotted Parliament when the Constitution Amendments Bill and the Singapore Independence Bill were passed by a two-thirds majority on 22 December 1965. In 1966, eleven Barisan MPs resigned on the grounds that neither national independence nor parliamentary democracy existed in Singapore. The Barisan decided to take their struggle "against imperialist oppression" to the streets. By 1967, when they called for a general strike, only three trade unions participated and twenty-six declined, and since then Barisan has failed to secure a seat in Parliament.

Kog Yue Choong

Further Reading
Drysdale, John. (1984) *Singapore: Struggle for Success*. Singapore and Kuala Lumpur, Malaysia: Times Books International.

BASEBALL—JAPAN

Baseball, perhaps the most popular sport in Japan, is played by many schoolboys and college students, and millions of spectators view professional games in ballparks and on television. Brought to Japan by Americans teaching in Tokyo in the 1870s, baseball was at first a recreational activity for college students. However, it became a serious and competitive intercollegiate and interscholastic sport by the close of the nineteenth century.

Baseball's Early Years

The first three decades of the twentieth century were the golden age of amateur baseball in Japan, and college and secondary school tournaments became national phenomena. Just as professional baseball began to emerge, government policies aimed at promoting Japanese nationalism placed controls on amateur baseball and played a role in diminishing public support for the professional game. Baseball disappeared during World War II but resumed after the war in schools and colleges.

An expanded professional presence arose in 1948. By the mid-1950s, professional baseball had become the most popular spectator sport in Japan, with two professional leagues, the Central and Pacific Leagues, consisting of six teams each. The 1953 season saw the first televised game, and baseball quickly became a television mainstay.

In a uniquely Japanese feature, almost every team is owned by a major corporation that uses the team for promotional purposes. The most successful and best-known team was the Yomiuri Giants, and the best-known player was that team's home-run hitter, Sadaharu Oh, who played from 1959 to 1980. Even when they were no longer dominant on the field, the Giants remained a symbol of Japanese baseball, just as the New York Yankees have symbolized American baseball for many people.

The Connection with the United States

Throughout the history of Japanese baseball, officials, players, and coaches have maintained contact with the baseball establishment in the United States. Japan was quick to import the latest equipment, techniques, and on a limited basis, American coaches and players. For example, Bobby Valentine, the coach of the New York Mets when that team finished second to the New York Yankees in the 2000 World Series, coached in Japan in 1995, and Charlie Manuel of the Cleveland Indians and Jim Tracy of the Los Angeles Dodgers played there in the 2001 season. The flow of talent in the other direction was slower to develop. Hideo Nomo, who pitched for the Kintetsu Buffaloes, became the first Japanese player in the U.S. major leagues when he joined the Los Angeles Dodgers in 1995. He was followed by several other players, including Ichiro Suzuki of the Seattle Mariners, who was the American League's most valuable player in 2001. American teams employed translators to make the transition easier. In addition, games between American and Japanese teams are now played on a regular basis, and the New York Mets and Chicago Cubs opened their 2000 season in Japan and played their first three games in Tokyo.

Baseball's Popularity in Japan

One of the questions scholars have asked about Japanese baseball is why the sport, which began in the United States, became so popular in Japan. The answer is unclear, but several factors seem to have been involved. First, baseball appeared in Japan along with other Western sports, such as soccer, rugby, and tennis, at a time when Japan was seeking to strengthen ties to the Western world. Second, the physical, mental, and spiritual battle between pitcher and batter was culturally congruent with Japanese values and indigenous sports, such as sumo. Third, the sport was supported by major corporations, who viewed the teams, their uniforms, the stadiums, and media coverage as significant promotional opportunities. Fourth, the sport was amenable to change to fit Japanese culture, such as the hierarchical organization of player rosters. These factors have combined with Japan's continual involvement in sports at the global level to make baseball popular in Japan. Even though baseball remains one of the most popular sports in Japan, global expansion of mass media, particularly television coverage, and talented players' migrations to the United States have greatly affected Japanese baseball today.

Hajime Hirai

Further Reading

Andrews, David L., and Steve J. Jackson, eds. (2001) *Sport Stars: The Cultural Politics of Sporting Celebrity.* London: Routledge.
Cromartie, Warren. (1991) *Slugging It Out in Japan: An American Major Leaguer in the Tokyo Outfield.* New York: Kodansha International.
Oh, Sadaharu. (1984) *Sadaharu Oh: A Zen Way of Baseball.* New York: Times Books.
Whiting, Robert. (1989) *You Gotta Have Wa.* New York: Macmillan.

BASHO (1644–1694), Japanese haiku poet. Matsuo Basho (also known as Kinsaku) is commonly regarded as the greatest haiku poet of Japan and also the one who raised haiku above the level of trivial entertainment, creating an enduring literary form. Basho was born near Osaka of samurai heritage. As a young man he moved to Edo and renounced his samurai status to devote himself to poetry. Recognizing the potential of haiku, Basho's first poem in his new style was written in 1679:

> On a withered branch
> A crow alights
> Autumn evening.

The stark simplicity of the scene and the intersection of the momentary (the crow alighting) and the cosmic (the ending of the year) are characteristic of Basho's style. As Basho was a student of Zen, many of his poems are resonant with Zen philosophy. One of Basho's key aesthetic contributions was the discovery of rustic beauty.

This painting by Yoshitoshi Tsukioka in 1891 shows Basho celebrating the mid-autumn festival with two farmers. (ASIAN ART & ARCHAEOLOGY, INC./CORBIS)

The last decade of Basho's life was devoted chiefly to travel as he recognized that life itself is a journey and sought to embody that metaphor in his own life. In recording his various trips, Basho developed a new literary genre, *haibun*, combining prose narrative and haiku poetry. The finest of his travel diaries, *The Narrow Road to the Deep North*, is a classic of Japanese literature.

The pen name Basho, meaning "banana tree," derives from the plant growing beside his hermitage in Edo where he met disciples and instructed them in poetry. This beloved dwelling was destroyed by fire in 1682, which inspired his decision to spend his final years on the road.

Stephen W. Kohl

Further Reading

Keene, Donald. (1976) "Matsuo Basho." In *World Within Walls*. New York: Holt, Rinehart and Winston, 71–122.

Sato, Hiroaki. (1996) *Basho's Narrow Road*. Berkeley, CA: Stone Bridge Press.

Ueda, Makoto. (1970) *Basho*. Boston: Twayne.

Yasuda, Kenneth. (1957) *The History of Haiku*. Tokyo and Rutland, VT: Charles E. Tuttle.

BASI *Basi* or *su khouan* is an animist ceremony performed at critical points in a person's life to strengthen the soul or spirit in Laos, Thailand, and other nations with a Tai ethnic population. *Basi* is Pali for "ties of thread," and *su khouan* is Lao for "defending the spirit or soul." A group will perform the ceremony to mark a recent or upcoming event such as a birth, marriage, departure for a trip, or arrival from a trip. The group gathers around a centerpiece made from banana leaves on a tray with offerings to the spirit or spirits. The offerings include food, alcohol, incense, candles, and the ties. The master of ceremonies is a male village elder who chants and offers the food and alcohol to the participants' spirits. The participants touch the tray with one hand during the incantation. The master of ceremonies then ties threads around the participants' wrists. Onlookers continue to tie the string around the wrists while wishing good luck. These actions allow the onlookers to receive some of the blessings invoked for the occasion. The objective of the ceremony is to prevent the spirit from wandering from the body during critical moments. The ceremony is a group event that bonds the community together and demonstrates the persistence of animist beliefs in Lao culture.

Linda McIntosh

Further Reading

Evans, Grant. (1998) *The Politics of Ritual and Remembrance: Laos since 1975*. Chiang Mai, Thailand: Silkworm Books.

BASMACHI MOVEMENT

The Basmachi was a Central Asian social and military movement organized in early 1918 to oppose units of the Red Army that, in February 1918, overthrew the Quqon (Kokand) Autonomy—a government established 26 November 1917 in today's eastern Uzbekistan by the fourth Extraordinary Regional Muslim Congress to address the interests of the non-Russian peoples of Central Asia. Those who escaped from the Communist takeover of the Quqon Autonomy, including intellectuals such as Zeki Validov Togan (1890–1969), formed the core of the Basmachi leadership. These intellectuals, some of whom espoused pan-Turkic ideals (holding that the various Turkic peoples of the world should somehow forge closer ties to each other), formed a loose coalition with other local figures, such as religious leaders who sought an Islamic state, nationalists, and the traditional elite from the Bukhara emirate and the Khiva khanate (ancient kingdoms also in today's Uzbekistan), after those entities fell to the Soviet advances and were established as "People's Republics" in 1920.

Though never unified, Basmachi forces were active in the Fergana Valley, parts of which are today in southern Uzbekistan and southeastern Tajikistan, as well as the region around the Aral Sea, from 1918 to 1922. Numbering several thousand (with some estimates as high as 20,000), Basmachi units continually threatened the new Soviet governments in the ancient city of Tashkent (in eastern Uzbekistan) and elsewhere, as well as the Bolshevik-backed regime in Bukhara.

In November 1921, Enver Pasa (1881–1922)—a Turk who was the hero of the Young Turk movement (Ottoman officers who sought to reform what they saw was a corrupt political system in Turkey) and an erstwhile supporter of the Bolshevik regime—defected to the Basmachi side and consolidated many of the forces in eastern Bukhara. However, before he could establish his legitimacy with the other local leaders, Enver Pasa was killed in a battle at Bal'juan (also spelled Balzhuan or Baljuwan; today in western Tajikistan) in August 1922. This effectively ended any effort by Basmachi leaders to present a common front against the ever-growing forces of Mikhail Frunze (1885–1925), the Russian Soviet Army commander.

Small units of the Basmachi fought on during the late 1920s and early 1930s against the collectivization campaign that the Soviets were attempting to institute in Central Asia, which placed both agricultural holdings and pastoral grounds under state ownership. Ibrahim Bek (d. 1932), an ethnic Uzbek, tried to revive the Basmachi movement at the time of the early collectivization campaign. His last attacks, into today's Tajikistan, took place in 1931. His capture that year was the last significant Basmachi event.

During the Soviet period, the term "Basmachi," which can be loosely translated as "bandit" or "brigand," carried a negative connotation. Soviet historiographers stressed the "illegal and backward nature" of the movement and contrasted it with the "positive" character of the Bolsheviks who "liberated" Central Asia. Since 1991, there has been a reevaluation of the Basmachi movement and a resultant positive portrayal of the leaders. Particularly in Uzbekistan, Tajikistan, and Turkmenistan, the heroic efforts of the fighters are highlighted, although the Islamic nature of some of the movement's factions is minimally addressed, given current concerns over Islamic extremism in the region.

Roger D. Kangas

Further Reading

Chokaev, Mustafa. (1928) "The Basmaji Movement in Turkestan." *Asiatic Review* 24, 78 (April): 273–288.

Fraser, Glenda. (1987) "Basmachi: I and II." *Central Asia Survey* 6, 1: 1–73; 6, 2: 7–42.

Paksoy, H. B. (1995) "Basmachi Movement from Within: Account of Zeki Validi Togan." *Nationalities Papers* 23, 2 (June): 373–399.

Ritter, William, S. (1985) "The Final Phase in the Liquidation of Anti-Soviet Resistance in Tadzhikistan: Ibrahim Bek and the Basmachi, 1924–1931." *Soviet Studies* 37 (October): 484–493.

Yimaz, Suhnaz. (1999) "An Ottoman Warrior Abroad: Enver Pasa as an Expatriate." *Middle Eastern Studies* 35, 4 (October): 40–69.

BASRA (2002 est. pop. 1.0 million). Located on the west bank of the Shatt al Arab River 116 kilometers from the Persian Gulf, Basra is Iraq's only outlet to the sea. Most of the population are Shi'ite Muslims originating from the surrounding countryside, while the indigenous inhabitants have remained largely Sunni. The original city, located about 13 kilometers southwest of modern Basra, was founded on the orders of the Caliph 'Umar bin al-Khattab (586?–644) in 638 CE. During its first two centuries Basra was the site of numerous conflicts including the first major in-

In January 2001 an Iraqi woman views the ruins of her house, destroyed by air raids in Basra during the 1991 Gulf War. (REUTERS NEWMEDIA INC./CORBIS)

ter-Muslim battle in 656 CE. Despite this instability Basra was home to some of classical Islam's greatest thinkers, including the theologian Hasan al Basri, the belletrist al-Jahiz, the poet Abu Nuwasand, and the Mu'tazilah school of Islamic interpretation. Basra's fortunes declined with the waning of the Abbasid dynasty (749/750–1258). By the fourteenth century the dwindling population was already relocating to the more secure site of the present city. Throughout the sixteenth and seventeenth centuries Basra vacillated between Persian, Ottoman, and independent tribal control. By the eighteenth century Ottoman control was well established, and for the next two centuries Basra witnessed a rise in commercial activity, particularly through its growing ties with Europe. These ties were further strengthened after British occupation in 1914, when the introduction of modern port facilities allowed Basra to become the world's leading exporter of dates. In 1948 major oil deposits were discovered nearby and Basra was soon transformed into a center for oil refining and export. The Iran-Iraq War (1980–1988) and the 1991 Persian Gulf War caused extensive damage to the city. U.N. sanctions, imposed since 1991, have not allowed the city to rebuild.

Thabit Abdullah

BASSEIN (1999 pop. 150,000). Bassein (Pathein), on the east bank of the Bassein (or Ngawun) River in the Irrawaddy Delta, is the fifth-largest city in Myanmar (Burma). Situated 160 kilometers west of Yangon (Rangoon), it is the capital of Irrawaddy (Ayeyarwady) Division and a principal market and inland seaport for the region, with capacity to develop into a major growth center.

Known to early European travelers as "Cosmin," Bassein has obscure origins. Bassein was part of the old Mon kingdom of Lower Burma until its conquest in the sixteenth century by King Tabinshwehti (1531–1550) and was depopulated in subsequent Mon-Burmese warfare. Following the British annexation of Lower Burma in 1852 and the delta's economic transformation, Bassein became a major rice-milling and rice-export center and an entry point for Indian migrant labor. The population is predominantly Burman but also includes many of Indian descent, as well as Karen (Kayin) and Arakanese (Rakhine).

Bassein is famed for its production of painted parasols and *halawa* confectionary. Its largest and most celebrated temple is the Shwe-mok-daw, which houses a fifteenth-century Buddha image dedicated in the reign of the Mon queen, Shin Sawbu (1453–1472); other

The Lei-kyun-yan-aung Pagoda in Bassein, 1996. (RICHARD BICKEL/ CORBIS)

temples are the Tagaung Mingala-zedi-daw and the Hpaya Ko-Zu, as well as the Mahabodhi Mingala-zedi and Lei-kyun-yan-aung (both extensively renovated in the 1990s).

Patricia M. Herbert

Further Reading
Greenwood, Nicholas. (1995) *Guide to Burma*. 2d ed. Guilford, CT: Globe Pequot Press.

BATAVIA Batavia, currently known as Jakarta, was once the capital city of the Dutch East Indies and was named after the Batavii, prehistoric inhabitants of the Netherlands. In 1610 the Dutch East India Company (VOC) established a trading post in the small port of Jayakarta in northern West Java. The site became the VOC's Asian headquarters in 1619. The settlement quickly overwhelmed Jayakarta, becoming a small Dutch city, complete with canals, walls, and gabled houses, but largely populated by Chinese traders and laborers, who lived within the city under their own laws. In 1740, Dutch fears of a rebellion allegedly planned by Chinese led to the massacre of some of the Chinese residents and the temporary expulsion of the rest.

During the eighteenth century, the city sprawled beyond its walls, and its architecture became more adapted to the tropics. Indonesians, both slave and free, made up an increasing proportion of the population and formed the basis for an evolving mestizo culture. The city retained, however, a reputation as dangerously unhealthy, and there was a high death rate among all population groups.

Batavia's economic role increased with the completion of a modern port at Tanjung Priok in 1886, but it lost some administrative importance in the twentieth century with the movement of government offices to Buitenzorg (Bogor) and Bandung. The city became a municipality in 1903. It was renamed Jakarta by the Japanese occupation forces in 1943.

Robert Cribb

Further Reading
Abeyasekere, Susan. (1984) *Jakarta: A History*. Singapore: Oxford University Press.
Taylor, Jean Gelman. (1983) *The Social World of Batavia: European and Eurasian in Dutch Asia*. Madison, WI: University of Wisconsin Press.

BATIK The word batik is derived from two words: the Javanese word *amba* (to write) and the Malay word *titik* (dot). Thus *ambatik*, shortened to batik, means "to write dots." Patterns are drawn in wax on the cloth by means of a canting, a metal stylus with a reservoir for molten wax, or stamped in wax with blocks carrying patterns. From the initial years of the batik industry (1920s) in the east coast of West Malaysia, the block method "chop" or "stamp" was adopted. The earliest batik made of repeated patterns stamped out using wooden blocks was known as *kain pukul* (stamped cloth). Sometimes the background cloth was dyed while pats of the pattern were painted in by hand. Modern batiks are made by screen printing techniques,

A textile worker creates a batik in Kota Bharu, Malaysia. (EYE UBIQUITOUS/CORBIS)

beginning with one color on white cotton. A later development in this method was to add a layer of wax to obtain the crack lines characteristic of traditional wax-drawn batik. By the 1960s, a Malaysian style of batik emerged. New motifs were tried and a new hand-drawn batik evolved. By the 1970s, the tourist market became a new motivation for batik production. This type of batik goes through very simplified processes, and the patterns are much less complicated. In the early 2000s, batik in Malaysia has come to be defined by certain design styles and sensibilities, and by the high percentage of floral motifs, and not so much with the process used.

Hanizah Idris and Shanthi Thambiah

Further Reading
Adasko, Laura, and Alice Huberman. (1975) *Batik in Many Forms*. New York: William Morrow.
Albrecht, Geraldine. (1969) *Batik*. London: Search Press.
Arny, Sarah. (1987) *Malaysian Batik: Creating New Tradition*. Kuala Lumpur, Malaysia: Kraftangan Malaysia.
Belfer, Nancy. (1972) *Designing in Batik and Tie Dye*. Englewood Cliffs, NJ: Prentice Hall.
Donahue, Leo O. (1981) *Encyclopedia of Batik Designs*. Philadelphia: Art Alliance Press.
Keller, Ira. (1966) *Batik: The Art and Craft*. Rutland, VT: Charles E. Tuttle.
Maxwell, Robyn J. (1987) *Southeast Asian Textiles: The State of the Art*. Clayton, Australia: Monash University.
———. (1990) *Textiles of Southeast Asia: Tradition, Trade and Transformation*. Melbourne, Australia: Oxford University Press.
Peacock, B. A. V. (1977) *Batik, Ikat, Pelangi and Other Traditional Textiles from Malaysia*. Hong Kong: Museum of History.

BATMONKH, JAMBYN (1926–1997), president of Mongolia. Jambyn Batmonkh has the distinction of having been the last president of Mongolia (1984–1990) during the Communist era. He also served as premier of Mongolia from 1974 through 1984. His position as premier ended when then-president Tsedenbal (1916–1991) was removed from the Mongolian People's Revolutionary Party (MPRP, also referred to as the Communist Party of Mongolia), and from state leadership in 1984. Batmonkh became the general-secretary of the MPRP in August 1984 and later the chairman of the presidium of the People's Great Khural (parliament) in December 1984, making him the leader of the country.

After his rise to power, he varied little from the policies of Tsedenbal. Toward the end of the 1980s, Batmonkh faced the pressures of perestroika, forcing his government to follow policies of economic reform that included the restructuring of government. The restructuring of government was inadequate, though, leaving the MPRP bureaucracy in charge of the economic reforms. After the fall of the Berlin Wall and the weakening of the Soviet Union, Batmonkh could no longer rely on Soviet support. Thus, when the people of Mongolia called for an end to Communist rule, Batmonkh's regime floundered and collapsed in March 1990. After that, Batmonkh remained out of the public eye, only rarely appearing in public. He died in Ulaanbaatar in 1997.

Timothy M. May

Further Reading
Sanders, Alan. (1996) *Historical Dictionary of Mongolia.* Lanham, MD: Scarecrow Press.
Dashpurev, D., and S. K Soni. (1992) *Reign of Terror in Mongolia, 1920–1990.* New Delhi: South Asian Publishers.

BAY OF BENGAL The Bay of Bengal occupies the northern part of the Indian Ocean between the Indian subcontinent and mainland Southeast Asia. Shaped like a triangle between the mouth of the Ganges-Brahmaputra Rivers, Sri Lanka, and the Strait of Malacca, the Bay of Bengal roughly covers 1.6 million square kilometers. The waters are usually calm; however, tropical cyclones (originating in the Bay of

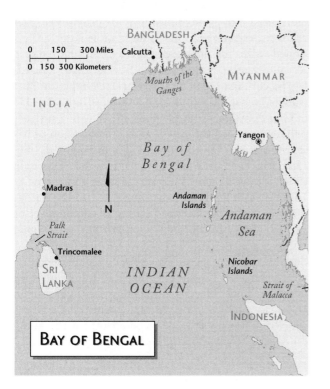

BAY OF BENGAL

KONARAK—WORLD HERITAGE SITE

A monumental temple to the sun god Surya, Konarak was constructed in the thirteenth century as a Brahman sanctuary. The temple Konarak features a lavishly carved, baroque stone chariot with twenty-four wheels and six horses. Overlooking the Bay of Bengal, it was designated in 1984 as a UNESCO World Heritage Site.

Bengal and called "Bengal cyclones") can hit the coastlands and lowlands along the Indian Peninsula and the deltaic Bangladesh. Due to its huge water surface, the Bay of Bengal strikingly influences the monsoon air masses across the mainlands of South and Southeast Asia by diverting the Bay of Bengal branch of the Indian southwest monsoon into one airflow toward the eastern parts of the Indian peninsula and another airstream toward Southeast Asia and by saturating the southwest monsoon and northeast monsoon air masses. Due to the heavy lifting of the landmasses, the Bay of Bengal is surrounded by a rather narrow shelf while the Bay gradually deepens toward the south up to 3,470 meters below sea level.

The eastern part of the Bay of Bengal is traversed by the Andaman and Nicobar Islands, which are built on a submarine tertiary fold ridge between the Arakan mountains (Myanmar) and Sumatra (Indonesia). East of the islands, the Strait of Malacca enters the Andaman Sea from the south, secluding it from the Bay of Bengal. The Mergui archipelago is scattered close to the coast of Southeast Asia, whereas the northernmost part of the Andaman Sea is occupied by the Bay of Martaban. In a submarine depression, the Andaman Sea drops in its central part even to 4,171 meters. The tides are highest along the Myanmar coast with a maximum of seven meters at Rangoon, while elsewhere the mean tides are two to three meters. As most of the streams and rivers of the Indian subcontinent and also some rivers of Southeast Asia flow into the Bay of Bengal, which at the same time experiences heavy monsoon rains (around 3,000 millimeters annually), its waters show a low salt content (mostly below 30 percent). The Bay of Bengal is a secluded part of the Indian Ocean, and it develops its own ocean currents that whirl mostly clockwise, flowing in the Bay of Bengal at a low speed. Along the southern margin of the Bay of Bengal, ancient seafarers found safe passage, which continues for those traveling present-day shipping routes connecting Singapore with Colombo (passing the Strait of Malacca) en route between Europe and East Asia.

Manfred Domores

Further Reading
Singh, G. (1983) *A Geography of India.* 4th ed. Delhi: Atma Ram.

BAYAR, MAHMUT CELAL (1884–1987), president of Turkey. Celal Bayar was cofounder of the Democrat Party and Turkey's third president (1950–1960). Educated in the Bursa French School, Bayar entered a career in banking. Following the 1908 Young Turk Revolution, he served as director of the Izmir chapter of the Committee of Union and Progress. After organizing nationalist forces in Izmir and Bursa in 1919, Bayar joined the nationalist government in Ankara in 1920. In 1924, during the presidency of Mustafa Kemal Ataturk (1881–1938, ruled 1923–1938), Bayar was named director of Is Bankasi (Business Bank); in 1932 he became minister of the economy, and from 1937 to 1939, he served as prime minister. Bayar held a seat in the National Assembly during World War II, but split from the Republican People's Party to form the Democrat Party in 1946, along with Adnan Menderes (1889–1961) and others. When the Democrat Party won the 1950 election, Bayar became the third president of Turkey, and the first president to come from a nonmilitary background. In 1960, the military overthrew the Democrat Party government, and Bayar was removed from office. Tried and convicted of corruption and crimes against the nation, Bayar received a death sentence, which was commuted to life in prison. After serving six years, he was released for health reasons but was forced to retire from active politics.

John M. VanderLippe

Further Reading
Ahmad, Feroz. (1993) *The Making of Modern Turkey.* New York: Routledge.
Keyder, Caglar. (1987) *State and Class in Turkey.* London: Verso.
Zürcher, Erik. (1993) *Turkey: A Modern History.* London: I. B. Tauris.

BAZARGAN, MEHDI (1905–1995), prime minister of Iran. Mehdi Bazargan is probably best known as the first prime minister of revolutionary Iran, since

Ayatollah Khomeini (1900–1989) gave him the job of premier of the provisional government soon after the victory of the revolutionary regime in 1979. Nevertheless, Bazargan's work in the Iranian political sphere was considerably more varied.

Born in 1905 to an affluent trading family in Tabriz, Bazargan started a career in education by teaching engineering at Tehran University after earning a degree in engineering from Paris University. He became politically active by joining the Iran Party, which changed to the National Front when it banded together with two other groups in 1949. When the oil nationalization movement emerged during Dr. Mohammad Mosaddeq's tenure as prime minister, Bazargan was given the position of managing director of the newly nationalized oil industry, which was overseen by the National Iranian Oil Company. However, he returned to teaching when Mosaddeq was overthrown by the 1953 coup.

In May of 1955, he was charged with treason and confined until 1960 after he voiced opposition to some of the shah's policies. Upon release, he joined forces with Ayatollah Mahmud Talequani to establish the Iran Freedom Movement (IFM) political party, which is also known as the Liberation Movement of Iran (LMI). Soon, he was sentenced to ten years in prison for his criticism of the shah's economic and political plan, known as the White Revolution. This time after his release, he stayed out of the political realm until 1977, when he helped found the Human Rights Association.

Then, in 1979, Ayatollah Ruhollah Khomeini designated him prime minister of the provisional government. He resigned just nine months later, disillusioned with his powerlessness against the Islamic Revolutionary Council and the Revolutionary Guards Corps, culminating in his ineffectiveness regarding the student hostage takeover of the American embassy. He did not disappear from the political scene but, instead, publicly opposed the new regime's suppression of basic freedoms and the continuation of the war with Iraq. His party, IFM, was the only legal opposition party in the new government, a move that some considered as largely symbolic. Bazargan was elected to the parliament in 1980, but he was blocked from running for the presidency in the 1984 elections. Often he found his party offices ransacked and was denied facilities for distributing his views. This situation continued beyond Ayatollah Khomeini's death and until his own death in 1995. Nevertheless, many consider Mehdi Bazargan a religiously moderate, progressive, and respected nationalistic leader who advocated the interest of Iran above the interest of Islam.

Houman A. Sadri

Further Reading

Boroujerdi, Mehrzad. (1996) *Iranian Intellectuals and the West: The Tormented Triumph of Nativism.* Syracuse, NY: Syracuse University Press.

Cleveland, William L. (1994) *A History of the Modern Middle East.* Boulder, CO: Westview.

Mawsilili, Ahmad. (1999) *Historical Dictionary of Islamic Fundamentalist Movements in the Arab World, Iran, and Turkey.* Lanham, MD: Scarecrow Press.

BEDAYA In Java, Indonesia, *bedaya* are dancers who perform ritual court dances, including the Bedaya Ketawang sacred dance. *Bedaya* are living embodiments of traditional Javanese high culture, and in addition to dance are expected to be proficient in the Javanese language and literature, as well as able to practice batik and the healing arts. Although many traditional Javanese dances have disappeared, the Bedaya Ketawang of central Java has survived and continues to be performed by *bedaya* once a year.

Bedaya Ketawang emerged in the early seventeenth century in the Javanese state of Mataram and commemorates the coronation of the king of Surakarta, one of the two Mataram divisions. The dance depicts the relationship between Panembahan Senopati, the first ruler of Mataram, and Kanjeng Ratu Kidal, the goddess of the sea and protector of the royal family. The dance is performed by nine *bedaya* wearing the makeup and dress of brides. The dancers prepare for the dance as they would for a marriage ceremony, and the hour-long dance is open only to a select audience who refrain from smoking, drinking, and eating. Some believe that a tenth dancer—the goddess herself—also performs and can be seen by some.

David Levinson

BEDIL *Bedil* is a Malay term meaning a man-made weapon. Technically the term means "small cannon"; it is commonly used in Brunei and Indonesia. In the Malay Peninsula, the term *bedil* is less common than *meriam*, which means the same thing. In addition to a barrel, breech, and firing mechanism, the *bedil* has a hook and some ornaments, which are generally a local variation of Chinese and Muslim motifs. Balls or projectiles are launched by firing gunpowder. The length of the Malay cannon varies from half a meter to more than two meters, and the diameter of the inside muzzle can range from three centimeters to more than ten centimeters.

The origin of firearms, or more specifically cannons, in the Malay archipelago cannot be explained with any certainty. However, when the Portuguese attacked Melaka (Malacca) in 1511, they found quite a large number of cannons in the capital. The cannon can be traced to Muslim and Chinese origins. When, after the fourteenth century, the Muslim rulers in Southeast Asia established closer religious and political relations with their counterparts in the Middle East and South Asia, they also brought home some models of cannons. Intensive diplomatic relations between Muslim rulers in Southeast Asia and the Chinese court from the early fifteenth century could also have provided the Malay rulers in Southeast Asia with access to Chinese cannons.

The use of cannon in the Malay world was not limited to warfare but was also a status symbol. By the fifteenth century Malay rulers began using cannons to provide them with military advantage. Little is known, however, about exactly how the cannon was used at this period. The European expansion to Southeast Asia after 1511 proved the superiority of European can-

Women wearing antique *bedaya* ornaments borrowed from the museum perform the Deoyo dance at the wedding of Sultan Mangkunegara in Java, Indonesia, in 1989. (LINDSAY HEBBERD/CORBIS)

nonry. Subsequently, the Malay *bedil* assumed a new role more as an heirloom than as a weapon. This can be seen in the various titles and names given to the allegedly historical *bedil* used previously in major battles.

Iik A. Mansurnoor

Further Reading
Gardner, G. B. (1936) *Keris and Other Malay Weapons*. Singapore: Progressive Publishing Company.
Gibson-Hill, C. A. (1953) "Notes on the Old Cannon Found in Malaya and Known to Have Been of Dutch Origin." *Journal of Malayan Branch for the Royal Asiatic Society* 26: 145–171.
Reid, Anthony. (1988 and 1993) *Southeast Asia in the Age of Commerce 1450–1680*. 2 vols. New Haven, CT: Yale University Press.
———. (2001) *Charting the Shape of Early Modern Southeast Asia*. Singapore: Institute of Southeast Asian Studies.
Shariffuddin, P. M., and Tom Harrisson. (1969) "Brunei Cannon." *Brunei Museum Journal* 1, 1: 72–118.

BEIJING (2002 est. pop. 7.1 million). Although it did not become the capital of China until the establishment of the Mongol Yuan dynasty (1279–1368), Beijing has long been a politically important northern city. Situated in Hebei Province on the northern edge of the fertile great northern plain and near mountain passes leading from both Manchuria and Mongolia, Beijing is a major junction for road and railroad transportation routes in all directions. Unlike most capitals, Beijing is not located on a major river, although it has been connected to the Grand Canal by means of a smaller canal and the White River (Bai He) since the reign of the Mongol Khubilai Khan (1215–1294). The city's economically and militarily strategic location has led Beijing to serve as regional or national capital for at least two millennia. As the national capital, Beijing served as both a cultural and political center during the imperial era and has acquired, in addition, a greater economic significance since the establishment of the People's Republic of China in 1949.

History

Beijing has been the capital of a unified China during most of the time since the establishment of the Yuan dynasty to the present, but had earlier been capital of the state of Yan under the Liao dynasty (907–1125) and then of northern China under the Jurchen Jin dynasty (1125–1234) from 1153. Known as Yanjing (Capital of Yan) under the Liao, Zhongdu (Middle Capital) during the Jurchen Jin dynasty, and Dadu (Great Capital) during the Yuan, the city was given the name Beijing (Northern Capital) by the third Ming emperor, Yongle (1360–1424), in 1406. The city has been called Beijing ever since, except during the Nationalist era (1927–1949), during which time the national capital was moved to Nanjing, and Beijing was renamed Beiping (Northern Peace).

Bicyclists on a main street in Beijing. Bicycles remain a major form of transportation despite the increasing use of automobiles. (EYE UBIQUITOUS/CORBIS)

BEIJING—THEN AND NOW

"It began, literally, by accident. On the Tuesday after the Knudsen's At Home, when rumors were stilled and all was peace, a party had ridden out under Touchy's auspices to the Marco Polo Bridge, about eight miles from Peking. It was getting late for cross country riding; the spring planting was beginning and there was no galloping slap across the dusty cold fields from landmark to landmark—to a red-walled tomb, a dark patch of wood marking some burial plot. But Touchy, who relieved the monotony of his duties as Commandant of the Legation Guard by the more onerous and exciting ones of Joint Master of the Drag Hunt, knew the county like the inside of his pocket, and led them by devious ways of his own—now along narrow sunk roads, from which only their heads projected as they road along, now across an open sandy patch, still free for an inspiring gallop, till they reached the long high-backed bridge spanning the Hun-ho. It was a hot soft April day—the brilliant light poured over the flat brown landscape, on which the colored walls of temples and tombs, and the dark masses of graveyard trees, detached themselves with great vividness; and all of the way the sharp outline of the Western Hills kept them company on the right, like a bright pink and lavender colored back cloth hung on the sky. They had ridden up on to the arc of the bridge between the Chippendale-looking panels of the carved stone parapets, topped at intervals with those little green effigies of beasts which amused Marco Polo so much as that he counted them in 1263, when he rode across the same bridge into Ch'angtu, or Xanadu, the old Peking. The General handed out this piece of information for the benefit of Judith and Little Annette. 'I expect traffic then looked much as it does now,' he added. 'The road is still the start of the great trade route to Tibet.' Small hooded carts with solid wheels creaked up the slopes of the bridge, drawn by mules or shaggy ponies; strings of donkeys with their laden panniers tripped over the huge steep paving slabs and their neat unshod feet, urged on by men with rough faces and wild clothes; now and then a group of Tibetans, in flapping green and yellow garments, strode past, their wrinkled faces much more than typically Mongolian than the Chinese. Long files of camels were fording the river a little above the bridge, moving with the curious slow rhythm that suggests a waltz in every leg, lifting their strange supercilious heads in a timeless challenge to the distances and deserts."

Source: Ann Bridge. (2000) *Peking Picnic*. London: Rediscoveries, 51–53.

From the Yuan dynasty until the end of the Qing dynasty (1644–1912), Beijing housed both the imperial family and much of China's vast civil-service bureaucracy. The presence in the capital of a Confucian bureaucracy that was staffed through examinations led to Beijing's development as an educational and cultural center. Even as Beijing's political significance declined during the politically tumultuous first half of the twentieth century, the city remained culturally significant with the growth of modern educational institutions. From 1949 to the present, Beijing has resumed its position as national capital and houses the political leadership of the nation. The city also continues to be the educational center of China.

As a municipality, Beijing answers directly to the central government and is autonomous of surrounding Hebei Province. During the decades immediately following the establishment of the People's Republic in 1949, the Beijing municipal government undertook

BEIJING

VENDING MACHINES FOR BEIJING

In order to modernize for tourists and especially for the 2008 Olympics, the government installed 1,400 vending machines in Beijing. The machines provide noodles, soda, tea, and juice and are expected to cut into the business of small food shops. The machines are expected to provide a profit for the vendor, although problems with maintenance, placement, and vandalism have already been reported.

Source: AsiaWeek (2001) "Beijing Touts the Machine Touch," 9 November: 16.

to transform the city into a model socialist city by encouraging the growth of industry, widening many major streets, building new drainage and sewage systems, constructing new government buildings, turning imperial sites into public spaces, and redeveloping parts of the city. In spite of this attempt to reconfigure the city into a new-style Communist capital, however, Beijing retains many of its traditional attributes.

Geography

Beijing as an imperial city was first built by Khubilai Khan in the thirteenth century and later rebuilt by the emperor Yongle in the early fifteenth century. It was constructed according to specifications laid out in the Confucian classics and thus has symbolic as well as political significance. It is situated on a north-south axis with all important buildings facing south, and consists of a series of three concentric walled cities, with the Forbidden City at the center, surrounded by the imperial city and the outer city. The emperor lived in the Forbidden City and performed rituals at important symbolic sites in the outer city, including the Temple of Agriculture and the Temple of Heaven. The massive walls encircling the city were intended to impress as well as protect. Under the Qing dynasty the imperial city was given over to Manchu residents, and Chinese were restricted to the outer city. Qing emperors also built two summer palaces in the western outskirts of Beijing. The first of these, built by the second Qing emperor, Kangxi (1654–1722), was destroyed by Anglo-French forces in 1860. The second

was built by the extravagant Empress Dowager Cixi (1835–1908) in the late nineteenth century.

During the twentieth century, the city limits expanded well beyond the 62 square kilometers encircled by the outer city walls to an area of 16,800 square kilometers. Today's Beijing is both rural and urban, agricultural and industrial. In general, however, the municipality lacks natural resources, including water, and has to import raw materials such as oil and iron that are required by its industries.

Demographics

Beijing's population, which was approximately 800,000 at the beginning of the twentieth century, has now risen to over 13 million in the Beijing administrative district (7.1 million in the city alone), in spite of government efforts during the 1950s and 1960s to keep urban population growth to a minimum. Owing to the city's location and history as a capital city, Beijing's population has historically been racially and ethnically diverse, including Manchus, Mongols, Tibetans, and other groups as well as the majority Han population. By the late twentieth century, however, racial and ethnic minorities had become a tiny percentage of Beijing's population, which is now over 95 percent Han.

Economy

Roughly 20 percent of Beijing's economy is agricultural. Beijing's economy has been dominated by industry since 1949, when the Chinese Communist Party determined to transform Beijing from a center of consumption into a model center of production. Until 1980, the bulk of Beijing's manufacturing sector was engaged in heavy industry, but since then there has been an increasing emphasis on replacing resource-draining and polluting industries with lighter, more environmentally friendly, technology-intensive industries. Nonetheless, Beijing continues to suffer from severe industrial pollution.

As China's population grows and its economy transforms, Beijing's future position in the nation is becoming less certain. Beijing is the political and cultural center of an increasingly fragmented China. An important question for the future is whether both the nation and Beijing's significance within it will remain the same.

J. Megan Greene

Further Reading
Elder, Chris, ed. (1997) *Old Peking: City of the Ruler of the World.* Oxford: Oxford University Press.
Gamble, Sidney D. (1921) *Peking: A Social Survey.* London: Oxford University Press.

Sit, Victor F. S. (1995) *Beijing: The Nature and Planning of a Chinese Capital City.* Chichester, U.K.: John Wiley and Sons.

Strand, David. (1989) *Rickshaw Beijing: City People and Politics in the 1920s.* Berkeley and Los Angeles: University of California Press.

BEIJING OPERA   Widely considered the finest of China's varied opera traditions, Beijing Opera *(jingxi)* combines music, song, speech, mime, dance and acrobatics, exciting spectacle, and subtle beauty. Divided into two basic styles, civil plays mainly concerned with love and martial plays that enact spectacular battle scenes, its subject matter is drawn from historical and mythical tales and classic novels.

Characters depict defined role types such as the clown, the "painted face" warrior, the "flowery" woman, and the martial woman. Each role has its own style of movement, voice, costume, and makeup—the acrobatics of the clown; the platform boots and confident strides of the warrior; the long, flowing "water sleeve" of the "dark-clothed" modest woman. The stage is largely bare, so mime is central to its art.

Music is crucial in the opera; in Chinese they say listen to opera *(tingxi)* not watch. A drummer directs the action on stage and leads a group of gongs and cymbals, which opens the action with a brilliant and earsplitting set. The actors move to the beats of the drum, and each character and type of action is accompanied by a set percussion piece, one for the warrior's entrance, one for riding a horse, and so on. The two-stringed fiddle is the most important melodic instrument, used especially to accompany the singing. Other instruments include a larger fiddle, plucked lutes, flute, and occasionally shawms in the martial plays.

A Beijing Opera singer performs in *Stopping the Horse* in 1981. (DEAN CONGER/CORBIS)

The opera developed comparatively late in nineteenth-century Beijing, but it draws on older forms such as the classical southern *kunqu* opera and regional musical styles—the lively *xipi* and more sedate *erhuang.* Traditionally young boys were sold into the operatic profession and given rigorous training in its exacting arts. These boys, especially those trained in the female roles (women began to perform on stage only in the 1930s), were often prostituted to rich opera enthusiasts. Into the late nineteenth century, families of star performers arose, and the Empress Dowager even had an opera stage constructed in the Forbidden City. However, performers never shook off their dubious societal reputation. After 1949, Beijing Opera was formalized as a national art, and performers were organized into state schools and troupes. During the Cultural Revolution the notorious revolutionary Model Operas were widely promoted, while the traditional plays were banned. Beijing Opera's popularity has waned in modernizing China, but groups of amateur enthusiasts still meet in town parks to sing excerpts from the plays.

Rachel Harris

See also: **Music—China**

Further Reading
Mackerras, Colin. (1997) *Peking Opera.* New York: Oxford University Press.

Wichmann, Elizabeth. (1991) *Listening to Theatre: The Aural Dimensions of Beijing Opera.* Honolulu, HI: University of Hawaii Press.

BELO, BISHOP CARLOS   (b. 1948), Peace advocate and Nobel laureate. Bishop Carlos Filipe Ximenes Belo is known as an outspoken fighter for peace and reconciliation in East Timor. Born on 3 February 1948 near Baucau, East Timor, and educated at missionary schools in Timor, he left for Portugal in 1974 to study theology. During this time he became a member of the Salesian Order. Belo returned to East Timor in 1981 as the director of Fatumaca College, where he developed his famed ties with the Timorese youth. Two years later, the Vatican appointed him as Apostolic Administrator of the Dili Diocese, making him the head of the East Timor church, and in 1988 he was consecrated as bishop.

Bishop Belo's calls for peace and freedom began in 1989, when he wrote to the United Nations secretary-general, condemning the cruelty and abuses of the Indonesian military and denouncing the serious humanitarian situation in his home country. Despite strong pressure from the Indonesian government, he became a focal point for the expression of national aspirations and local culture. His outspokenness on behalf of peace in East Timor was honored in 1996 when he and José Ramos-Horta were jointly awarded the Nobel Peace Prize. The Oslo committee saw him not only as a mediator but also as a representative of hope for a better future. In independent East Timor after 1999, Bishop Belo became an advocate for a society built on compassion and reconciliation.

Frank Feulner

Further Reading

Gunn, Geoffrey C. (1997) *East Timor and the UN: The Case for Intervention.* Lawrenceville, NJ: Red Sea Press.
Kohen, Arnold S. (1999) *From the Place of the Dead: The Epic Struggles of Bishop Belo of East Timor.* New York: St. Martin's Press.
Siagan, Frans S., and Peter Tukan. (1997) *Voice of the Voiceless.* Jakarta, Indonesia: Penerbit Obor.

BENDAHARA The word *bendahara*, related to the Sanskrit word for "treasurer," denoted a job title held by senior officials in Sumatra and Java, whereas in the Malay Peninsula the word denoted the chief minister. Perhaps because of its association with the word *bandar* (a Persian loanword meaning "harbor"), the title could also imply responsibility for the coastal regions; in the *Kaba Cinduo Mato*, an undated Minangkabau text presenting a model of the ideal state, the *bendahara* has responsibility for the coast. In the *Sejarah Melayu* (Malay Annals)—a Malay historiographical text that was probably commissioned by a Malacca *bendahara* and depicts the world of Malacca in the fifteenth and early sixteenth centuries—an ideal picture is presented of powerful *bendahara*s who always play a prominent role and come off better than the other courtiers and even better than most sultans.

Controlled by one lineage, and marrying into Malacca's ruling house, the *bendahara* family came to wield great power, and the *bendahara* frequently acted as kingmaker. Because a Malay ruler tended not to be involved in the day-to-day running of government, the position of *bendahara* offered considerable scope for the exercise of executive power. Sometimes a *bendahara* could assume so much honor and authority that they challenged those of the king. The last Malacca ruler was so convinced that the *bendahara* intended to usurp the throne that he sentenced the *bendahara* to death. Due to the role of the *laksamana* (admiral) as the defender of Johor, Malacca's direct heir, against Acehnese and Portuguese invasions, the *laksamana*

family eclipsed the *bendahara* family in importance by the early seventeenth century. The great offices of state of the former Malacca sultanate became the titles of regional chieftainship in the nineteenth-century Malay states, with the Malacca *bendahara* becoming ruler of Pahang, on the peninsula's east coast.

By 1853 Bendahara Ali (reigned 1806–1857), who already acted as an independent ruler, felt sufficiently confident to declare his autonomy, and in 1881 his son Ahmad assumed the title of sultan. The eighteenth-century Malay state of Perak, however, was a radical deviation from common political practices. In Perak the office of *bendahara* had become a post that the ruler awarded to friends, relatives, or supporters, and finally the title of *bendahara* was regarded as a prerogative of the royal family.

Edwin Wieringa

See also: **Laksamana**

Further Reading

Drakard, Jane. (1999) *A Kingdom of Words: Language and Power in Sumatra.* New York: Oxford University Press.
Gonda, Jan. (1973) *Sanskrit in Indonesia.* New Delhi: International Academy of Indian Culture.
Watson Andaya, Barbara. (1979) *Perak: The Abode of Grace: A Study of an Eighteenth Century Malay State.* Kuala Lumpur, Malaysia: Oxford University Press.
Watson Andaya, Barbara, and Leonard Y. Andaya. (1982) *A History of Malaysia.* London: Macmillan Education.

BENGAL, WEST (2001 pop. 80.2 million). West Bengal is a state in northeastern India, lying to the immediate west of Bangladesh and southeast of Nepal. Its southern boundary is formed by the Bay of Bengal, and its capital city is Calcutta (or Kolkata). The state covers an area of 88,752 square kilometers (the same size as Austria). Both the Ganges and the Brahmaputra Rivers flow through the state, giving it the basis for a rich rice agriculture. The state receives an average of from 160 to 200 centimeters of rain annually, most of it from the northeasterly monsoon.

The state was created in 1947, at the time of Independence, when the Muslim-dominated part the region that had been East Bengal became the eastern wing of Pakistan. The state is divided into sixteen districts and is governed by a 294-seat legislative assembly, which has long been dominated by Marxists. In addition to rice, agricultural products include jute, tea, potatoes, oilseeds, tobacco, wheat, barley, and maize. The numerous manufacturing industries include cars, chemicals, electronics, aluminum, pharmaceuticals,

THE PLEASURES OF COLONIAL LIFE IN WEST BENGAL

"Most Gentlemen and Ladies in *Bengal* live both splendidly and pleasantly, the Fore-noons being dedicated to Business, and after Dinner to Rest, and in the Evening to recreate themselves in Chaises or *Palankins* in the Fields, or the Gardens, or by Water in their *Budgeroes*, which is a convenient Boat, that goes swiftly with the Force of Oars; and, on the River, sometimes there is the Diversion of Fishing or Fowling, or both; and, before Night, they make friendly Visits to one another, when Pride or Contention do not spoil Society, which too often they do among the Ladies, as Discord and Faction do among the Men."

Source: Sir William Foster, ed. ([c. 1706] 1930) *New Account of the East Indies* by Alexander Hamilton. London: Argonaut Press.

ceramics, glass, footwear, steel, railway locomotives, and ships. Coal and china clay are also mined here. The principal language is Bengali, but Hindi and English are widely understood, and the dominant religions are Hinduism and Islam.

Paul Hockings

Further Reading
Majundar, R. C., et al., eds. (1943–1967) *The History of Bengal*. 3 vols. Dhaka, Bangladesh: University of Dhaka.

BENGALI LANGUAGE   Bengali (or Bangla) is spoken by some 230 million people in the Ganges River delta and elsewhere in India, the United Kingdom, and the United States. Distinct dialects of Bengali include those of the Bangladeshi districts Sylhet (Sylhetī) and Chittagong (Chāggāyā) Some consider the latter different enough from Dhaka or Calcutta Standard forms to be a separate language.

A member of the eastern branch of Indo-Aryan, Bengali emerged as a distinct language about a millennium ago, as reflected in a compilation of Buddhist songs, the Caryapada (*Caryāpada*). Middle Bengali literature (1200–1800) consists of religious songs and poetic texts. Modern Bengali has conveyed national(ist)

sentiment since the nineteenth century and is thus both a treasure and an area of struggle. Nineteenth-century Calcutta was a major center of linguistic modernization, where the longer verb endings and Sanskritized lexicon that constituted *Sāddhu bhāśā* ("pedantic language," that is, a literary register originally developed for the sort of Hindu philosophical discourse that flowered in the Bengal Renaissance) shifted to the shortened endings of the *Calit bhasa*, or colloquial Standard, dominant among urban Bengalis today. Literary prose per se emerged along with modern Bengali itself in the nineteenth century colonial context, as did tensions between forms of the language identified with Hinduism and Islam—Sanskritized *Sadhu* versus Persianized *Mussalmani Bangla*. At least in rural areas a mixture of these roots prevailed.

A gap *(diglossia)* not unlike that between *Sadhu* and *Calit* still exists between everyday speech and the forms of writing and speech associated with high culture. Relevant dimensions of variation thus include geographic and religious variants and class-linked diglossic differences. In the United Kingdom, where children of immigrants may need language classes to help them maintain their Bengali heritage, tensions among these variants are manifested in a prejudice against Sylhetī among Bengali-speaking teachers.

Phonology, Sound Symbolism, and Script
Bengali has many of the sounds of Sanskrit, including voiced aspirated stops *bh*, *dh*, and *gh*, though in eastern dialects these merge with *b*, *d*, and *g*. Regional dialects vary markedly in phonology. Nasalization is not phonemic in most eastern dialects. Several consonants in Standard Bengali, like *kh* and *k*, become *h* in eastern dialects.

Spoken Bengali reflects rich sound symbolism, onomatopoetic words that Dimock described as "an unstudied poetry of the spoken language" (Dimock 1989: 55), or even regular associations between individual vowels and feeling-tones (e.g., *æ* associated with unpleasantness). The Nobel laureate poet Sir Rabindranath Tagore (1861–1941) was among the first to write about this phenomenon.

Bengali is written in a script very much like neighboring Assamese, which is derived from the ancient Brahmi. Read from left to right, it hangs below the line. The script is a syllabary, where the characters symbolize syllables; the vowel *ɔ* or *a* rather than *ə* as in Hindi, is implied by consonant symbols.

Syntax, Morphology, and Sociolinguistic Issues
The commonest order of elements in a simple transitive sentence in Bengali is Subject-Object-Verb, and Bengali has postpositions rather than prepositions to

express relations like "for," "under," or "in." But not all sentences need verbs. No linking verb is needed to express such constructions as "He [is] my brother."

Bengali preserves some Sanskrit inflectional morphology. Verbs are marked for aspect, mood, and tense; aspect markers like perfective -*l* or habitual -*t* immediately follow the verb root. (Grammatical forms that signal the frequency, duration, or degree of completion of actions are "aspect" markers.) Nouns and pronouns may be marked for case—nominative, objective, genitive, or locative. Subjects of Bengali sentences may be "experiencers" rather than agents. Such subjects take genitive or accusative case, and subject-verb agreement is suspended. Nouns are not marked for gender. Number marking is optional. There are about a dozen noun classifiers. These include -*ṭā* for countable things, -*khānā* and -*ṭuku* for other things, and -*jon* for persons. Pronouns are marked for number and for either respect or intimacy. Likewise, verbs are marked for the speaker's respect versus intimacy toward the subject, as well as for person (first, second, or third). This presents an ideological problem for some Bengalis who dislike making distinctions among people.

Does one call domestic workers *āpni*, as one would a teacher, *tumi* (an equal), or *tui* (an intimate or a social inferior)? Dil found that Hindu children generally call their parents *tumi* and receive the affectionate *tui* in return, and Muslim children generally call their parents *āpni* and receive *tui* in return. Kin terms and greeting formulas also differ in Muslim and Hindu usage. Yet both communities acknowledge a common poetic-linguistic heritage.

James M. Wilce

Further Reading

Dil, A. (1991) *Two Traditions of the Bengali Language.* Cambridge, U.K.: Islamic Academy.

Dimock, E. C. (1989) *The Sound of Silent Guns and Other Essays.* Delhi: Oxford University Press.

Masica, C. P. (1991) *The Indo-Aryan Languages.* Cambridge, U.K.: Cambridge University Press.

Warner, R. (1992) *Bangladesh Is My Motherland : A Case Study of Bengali and English Language Development and Use among a Group of Bengali Pupils in Britain.* London: Minority Rights Group.

Wilce, J. M. (1998) *Eloquence in Trouble: The Poetics and Politics of Complaint in Rural Bangladesh.* New York: Oxford University Press.

BENGALIS Bengalis are the people of the Bengal region of South Asia, which since 1971 has consisted of the nation of Bangladesh and West Bengal in India. There are also large Bengali populations in the neighboring Indian states of Assam, Bihar, and

A Bengali woman picks tea leaves in what was East Pakistan in 1962. (ROGER WOOD/CORBIS)

Tripura, as well as overseas communities in Great Britain, the United States, and Canada. The worldwide Bengali population is about 150 million in Bangladesh and West Bengal. Bengalis speak Bangla, a language with a long literary tradition. In 1913 Bengali writer Rabindranath Tagore (1861–1941) became the first Asian to receive the Nobel Prize for literature, and many other leading South Asian poets, novelists, filmmakers, and musicians have been Bengalis.

Bengalis are adherents of both Islam and Hinduism, with most Bengalis in India being Hindus and most in Bangladesh being Muslims. There are also small Christian and Buddhist minorities. The Bengalis are mainly a rural people, with about 80 percent of the people in Bangladesh and West Bengal living in small farming villages where wet-rice agriculture is the primary economic activity. A caste-based occupational structure is important in Hindu communities; in Muslim communities it is present but less significant. Villages in both West Bengal and Bangladesh, though part of national and state political systems, are also often governed by councils of elders (*panchayats* in India, *samaj* in Bangladesh), which exert considerable informal control.

David Levinson

Further Reading

Dasgupta, Abhijit. (1998) *Growth with Equity: The New Technology and Agrarian Change in Bengal.* Columbia, MO: South Asia Books.

Davis, Marvin. (1983) *Rank and Rivalry: The Politics of Inequality in Rural West Bengal.* Cambridge, U.K.: Cambridge University Press.

Roy, Manisha. (1992) *Bengali Women.* Chicago: University of Chicago Press.

Talbot, Ian, and Gurharpal Singh, eds. (1999) *Region and Partition: Bengal, Punjab and the Partition of the Subcontinent.* Oxford: Oxford University Press.

BENTINCK, WILLIAM CAVENDISH (1774–1839), British governor general in India.

William Bentinck is best remembered in Indian history for pioneering reforms in Indian society. Born on 14 September 1774 at Bulstrode in England with a silver spoon in his mouth, the second son of the third Duke of Portland was appointed governor of Madras in 1803. He was held responsible for the mutiny in Vellore and was recalled four years afterward. He was elected a member of the British House of Commons in 1815.

Bentinck was appointed governor general of Bengal in 1827 and was successful in turning the annual deficit of about £1.5 million into a surplus of about the same amount. Consequently, the Charter Act of 1833 renewed the government of East India Company, and Bentinck became the governor general of India in 1833. Strongly influenced by the tradition of Utilitarianism—a political school of thought, influenced by Jeremy Bentham and James Mill, which believed in reform through rational administration—he brought about important changes in the administrative structure of India, such as an end to discrimination in public service recruitment, adoption of a liberal attitude toward the press, and the far-reaching measure of making English the official language of India. Although he followed a policy of nonintervention in the day-to-day running of Indian states, he annexed Mysore, Coorg, and central Cachar. He abolished the practice of female infanticide prevalent among some Rajput tribes. Indian reformers such as Raja Rammohan Roy (1772–1833) advocated abolition of the sati system (the custom of burning widows alive with the dead bodies of their husbands). In Regulation of XVII of December 1829, Bentinck declared sati illegal. He also abolished flogging in the Indian Army. In 1835, Bentinck resigned and was replaced by Sir Charles Metcalf; he died four years later in Paris.

Patit Paban Mishra

Further Reading
Ahmed, M. (2000) *Lord William Bentinck.* New Delhi: D.K.

Majumdar, Romesh Chandra, ed. (1989) *The British Paramountcy and Indian Renaissance (1815–1905 A.D.),* Vol. 10, Part 11. Mumbai (Bombay), India: Bharatiya Vidya Bhavan.

Spear, Percival. (1977) *A History of India,* Vol. 2. Harmondsworth, U.K.: Penguin.

BENTO

The origins of the lunchbox style food service *(bento)* are contested. The first *bento* may have been a simple conveyance of foodstuffs for theatergoers during the Tokugawa or Edo Period (1600/1603–1868). It may have begun backstage as a meal to be eaten by actors and stagehands while preparing for a performance. The phrase *maku no uchi bento* designated a style of square box with internal partitions separating rice and the staple food from other pieces of accompanying food such as fish, chicken, pickles, and boiled vegetables. *Maku no uchi* means the space curtained off for parties of outdoor picnickers or the backstage separated by a curtain. Another theory holds that *bento* were used first by travelers on the road, particularly officials journeying between Edo and the provinces. In addition, *bento* may have been used by warriors camping on battlefields or by spectators at sumo wrestling matches.

The chief characteristic of a *bento* is portability. A *bento* is usually individually portioned and prepared for one person; the container may be wood, lacquer, wicker, cardboard, or plastic. In premodern times the foods were salted or dried, convenient for carrying or keeping over time. The main foodstuff is rice, whether wrapped in seaweed, shaped into rice balls, or packed into a compartment in the container. The term "lunchbox" implies a container for a makeshift meal to be eaten as a stopgap while away from home. *Bento* in Japan, however, are often more elaborate preparations.

The preeminent celebration involving the use of *bento* is the spring cherry blossom viewing (*hanami*) on rice matting spread under the cherry trees. Some *bento* for special events are stacked lacquer boxes, fitted out with elaborately prepared foods for sharing. Another version of the stacked box is the *jubako*, the ten-stacked lacquer trays forming a tall *bento*, each containing different types of foods (*osechi ryori*) prepared ahead for the three days of entertainment and celebration at the New Year.

Less elegant, but equally entrenched in Japanese custom, is the *ekibento* (station lunchbox), which was first sold in 1885 for passengers going from Utsunomiya Station to Tokyo's Ueno Station. *Bento* became a significant aspect of travel and stations everywhere have many kiosks selling great varieties of *bento* evoking seasonality and the regions of Japan. Far from being a stopgap meal or fast food, these *bento* have special cachets. Regular travelers know where to buy each variety of *bento* and some stations have to stock up on favorites for the droves of visitors at certain times of year.

The homemade *bento* most people know best is the school lunchbox. Children carry lunchboxes to schools where lunches may not be provided; the "correct" lunches, according to nutritionists and school officials, observe the formula of "something from the mountains and something from the sea," meaning fish, fish paste or seaweed, chicken, pork, beef or egg, and vegetables and grains (usually rice). During wartime when foods were scarce, children's lunchboxes contained sweet potatoes or pumpkin; if the scarce and coveted rice was included, a single red pickled plum *(umeboshi)* embedded in the center of a rectangle of rice would symbolize the Japanese flag *(Hinomaru)*. Hinomaru *bento* was thus supportive of the war effort by encouraging a spartan diet and by visually representing a national icon. School lunches in the early 2000s are often served in classrooms and are more likely to include stews, curries, and breads on metal trays rather than pickles and rice. Still, a home-prepared *bento* is said to emblematize the loving and hardworking mother, just as the wartime box evoked the national struggle.

Merry Isaacs White

See also: **Cuisine—Japan.**

Further Reading

Allison, Anne. (1991) "Japanese Mothers and Obentos: The Lunch-Box as Ideological State Apparatus." *Anthropological Quarterly* 64, 4 (October): 195–208.

Ekuan Kenji. (1998) *The Aesthetics of the Japanese Lunchbox.* Cambridge, MA: MIT Press.

Yoshida Mitsukuni and Sesoko Tsune. (1989) *Naorai: Communion of the Table.* Tokyo: Cosmo Public Relations.

BHAKTI The path of bhakti, the major form of Hindu worship and communal religious practice in India, refers to the devotional love of a deity or deities. The reason for much Indian artistry, bhakti is demonstrated in statues, paintings, temples, and elaborate feasts. The most accepted etymology derives the word from the Sanskrit root *bhaj*, which means "to worship," "to share in," and "to belong to." In the bhakti tradition, love and concern are shared between the god or goddess and the worshiper.

Most forms of Hindu bhakti are monotheistic, emphasizing the worship of a single, personal god, who created the world and cares for its inhabitants. However, some forms also worship a divine couple, a divine family, or a deity and his or her emanations and incarnations. The goals of this worship are to glorify the god or goddess and to gain blessings in life and salvation after death.

Early Developments

Elements of bhakti are found in the earliest Indian religious texts, the Vedas and Upanishads. The worship of the gods Indra and Varuna in the hymns of the Rig Veda contain devotional elements, and the Upanishads speak of a "supreme person" or "inner controller," a view of an ultimate reality or an impersonal Brahman that can be understood as a belief in a personal god. The Katha and Mundaka Upanishads also speak of the ultimate reality bestowing grace on those it chooses. In the *Bhagavad Gita*, a part of the epic story known as the *Mahabharata*, the god Krishna describes in detail the importance of bhakti and declares it superior to other forms of religious belief and practice.

The earliest devotional poetry comes from South India, in hymns to the god Murukan of the third century CE. From the fifth to the ninth centuries CE hymns were written in the Tamil language to the gods Siva and Vishnu, who remain highly popular in India. The bhakti style of worship spread throughout the rest of India in texts such as the Puranas and in the performances of wandering poets, singers, and storytellers.

POEM TO KRISHNA: MIRABAI

My Dark One,
they've placed him off limits—
but I won't live without him.
Delighting in Hari,
coming and going with sadhus,
I wander beyond reach of the world's snare.
Body is wealth
but I give it away—
my head was long ago taken.
Full of rapture,
Mira flees the jabbering townsfolk—
going for refuge
to what cannot perish,
her Dark One.

Source: Andrew Schelling, trans. (1993) *For Love of the Dark One: Songs of Mirabai.* Boston: Shambhala Publications, 53.

BHAKTI

Poem to Kali: Ramprasad Sen

O Mother! my desires are unfulfilled

My hopes are ungratified,

But my life is fast coming to an end.

Let me call You, Mother, for the last time

Come and take me in your arms...

This world knows not how to love;

My heart yearns, O Mother, to go there

Where love reigns supreme.

Source: Jadunath Sinha. (1966) *Rama Prasada's Devotional Songs: The Cult of Shakti.* Calcutta, India: Sinha Publishing House, 7.

The bhakti tradition was appealing because it emphasized the equality of all people in worship. It thus denied India's caste inequities, giving new religious status to low-caste people, to women, and to outcastes. It also emphasized that religious emotion was of greater value than classical knowledge of written texts, so people who were illiterate and uneducated could still be great bhaktas, or devotees.

Bhakti Groups

The Hindu tradition includes three major bhakti groups. The largest group worships the god Vishnu, and its members are called Vaishnavas. Vishnu is most popularly worshiped as Rama and Krishna or Hari, though he has many other forms. The second-largest bhakti group worships the god Siva, and they are known as Saivas or Saivites. The third-largest group worships the goddess as Mother of the Universe, most often as Shakti, Durga, Lakshmi, or Kali. Worshipers of the goddess are called Shaktas. Each of these groups has various subgroups with different understandings of the nature and actions of the deity, different lineages of teachers with their own interpretations of texts and preferred ritual practices, and different regional languages and traditions. Smaller bhakti groups worship other deities.

Bhakti Practices

While some devotees are renouncers, who spend their lives in prayer and service to the god or goddess, most are householders, who worship daily at a home altar and on various holidays and festivals at temples and shrines. The major form of bhakti worship is *puja*, in which the deity, in the form of a statue, picture, or iconic symbol, is presented ritual gifts. The god or goddess is offered flowers, fruit, incense, and other valuable or cherished items, accompanied by prayers and songs. It is believed that the food is accepted by the deity and transformed into *prasad* or sanctified food. This food is eaten by the devotees, who then share in the deity's grace. Sometimes devotees who love the god intensely may have a direct sense of the god's presence, called *darshan*, which involves mutual sight, recognition, and caring between god and devotee. *Puja* may be performed on holidays as a part of traditional yearly worship or at other times to gain special favors. It may be performed to fulfill a promise made to the god or as a form of service to the god and the temple or shrine.

Bhakti rituals also include singing hymns, called *bhajan* or *kirtan*, chanting the god's name or sacred Sanskrit words and phrases, called *mantrajapa*, and reenacting the adventures of the god or goddess in plays and dances. Visualizing the god or goddess and his or her heavens and chanting mantras or sacred words are a part of disciplined bhakti yoga. More ascetic bhakti practices involve difficult pilgrimages to distant holy places, fasting, and extended meditation on the god or goddess.

The goal of bhakti practice is a closer relationship with the god or goddess. The various bhakti groups define this relationship differently, and the most complex literature on the topic derives from writers in the Bengali Vaishnava tradition. Human emotions, *bhavas*, correspond to universal emotional essences or *rasas*, and the goal of bhakti is a full appreciation of these emotions. The most intense emotion is divine erotic love, the passionate love of the god Krishna. He may be loved through five basic relationships: god as master and devotee as servant; god as child and devotee as parent, which is sometimes reversed; god as beloved and devotee as lover; god and devotee as friends; and god and devotee as ultimately one shared spirit, which is the least desirable for Vaishnavas as it lacks passion and drama. Love may be selfish or selfless, but the highest form of love is selfless *prema*, in which the only goal in life is loving and serving the god.

In South Indian Vaishnava bhakti, the most important act is self-surrender *(prapatti)*, the worshiper's total dependence on the god Vishnu. This dependence makes a person a devotee. Morality is important; the devotee must refrain from malice, lying, egotism, and unfriendliness. The god may be loved in his divine or

ENCYCLOPEDIA OF MODERN ASIA

281

heavenly form or in his earthly incarnations, called avatar forms.

The Indian tradition of Saiva-siddhanta includes four stages of love for the god Siva. The devotee follows first the path of the slave, doing temple services such as cleaning, lighting lamps, and growing flowers; then the path of the good son or daughter, meditating on Siva as light and preparing for ritual worship; then the path of the associate, yogic practice; and finally the path of truth, full awareness of Siva. The devotee must have knowledge, ritual action, yogic practice, and a virtuous way of life. When the devotee reaches union with Siva, the sweetness of that state is compared to sugarcane and honey. Love of the god is reflected in the love of all humanity.

The goddess may be worshiped as the single Mother of the Universe; as a couple, with her consort Siva; or in one of her ten manifest forms as the ten Wisdom Goddesses or *dasa mahavidyas*. In Bengali Shaktism the major devotional roles portray the goddess as protective mother and the devotee as child or the goddess as innocent daughter and the devotee as nurturing parent. Worship of the goddess may also be yogic or tantric, in which emotion is less important than detachment and wisdom.

In all these forms of Hindu bhakti, devotion to the god is more important than knowledge, caste and purity rules, and social status. Bhakti is a religious path of love, dedicated to the god or goddess and reflected in compassionate behavior toward humankind, creativity in literature and the arts, and the practice of religious ritual.

June McDaniel

See also: **Caste; Hindu Philosophy; Hindu Values; Hinduism—India; Sanskritization**

Further Reading
Archer, William G. (1960) *The Loves of Krishna in Indian Painting and Poetry*. New York: Grove Press.
Bailly, Constantina Rhodes, trans. (1995) *Meditations on Siva: The Sivastotravali of Utpaladeva*. Albany, NY: State University of New York Press.
Miller, Barbara Stoler, trans. (1991) *The Bhagavad-Gita: Krishna's Counsel in Time of War*. New York: Bantam Books.
Ramanujan, A. K., trans. (1985) *Speaking of Siva*. Harmondsworth, U.K.: Penguin Books.
Schelling, Andrew, trans. (1993) *For Love of the Dark One: Songs of Mirabai*. Boston: Shambhala Publications.
Sinha, Jadunath. (1966) *Rama Prasada's Devotional Songs: The Cult of Shakti*. Calcutta, India: Sinha Publishing House.
Woodroffe, Sir John George, comp. and trans. [Arthur Avalon, pseud.]. (1981) *Hymns to the Goddess and Hymn to Kali*. Twin Lakes, WI: Lotus Press.

BHARATA NATYAM. See **Dance—India.**

BHIL

One of the largest ethnic groups in South Asia (only the Gond in India are slightly more numerous), the Bhils number over 8 million today. The Gond are a Scheduled Tribe inhabiting hills and forests in the western part of central India, primarily the watershed of the Narmada River. Their main concentration, over 2 million, is in Madhya Pradesh state in central India. The term "Bhil," derived from the Dravidian word for "bow," their quintessential weapon, covers many subgroups well known by other names, such as Dubla, Garasia, Patelia, and Vasava.

Bhils are a settled agricultural people, albeit with some brigandage in their past. Those without land work as laborers. The villages have a scattered layout, with less than a hundred huts spread over perhaps three to four square kilometers. Each village is surrounded by fields and communal grazing areas. In the past Bhils exploited the forest by hunting and gathering and also practiced slash-and-burn agriculture until it was made illegal. Farms now grow maize, wheat, millet, wild rice, tobacco, peanuts, and a variety of vegetables. Bhils depend on numerous castes in the area for many basic necessities.

Each village, consisting of two or more extended families, is led by a hereditary headman. The villages are generally exogamous, and marriage is virilocal (married couple living in the husband's family's village). Polygamy is rare. A few Bhils are Christian and Muslim, though many are Hindu, and are animists who worship Wagh deo, the tiger god, Nandervo, the god of agriculture, or Kalika, the earth mother.

Paul Hockings

Further Reading
Koppers, Wilhelm. (1958) *The Bhil in Central India*. New Haven, CT: Human Relations Area Files.
Singh, K. S., ed. (1994) "Bhil." In *The Scheduled Castes* (People of India 3). Delhi: Oxford University Press, 118–143.

BHIT SHAH

Located in Pakistan 200 kilometers from Karachi, the shrine of Bhit Shah is the resting place of Shah Abdul Latif (d. 1752), a noted poet and musician of Sind, a province in modern Pakistan. This Sufi mystic wrote the *Risalo*, a collection of thirty Sindhi poems arranged according to musical nodes, or rhythmic patterns.

The mausoleum and mosque of Shah Abdul Latif were built by Ghulam Shah Kalhoro (d. 1772), the ruler of Sind, in 1765. The ornate buildings (with adjoining graveyard) are covered in blue and white glazed tiles fired in the kilns of nearby Hala. The domed mausoleum has a square plan; the cenotaph of the saint stands beneath the dome, enclosed behind an ornate wooden screen. The mosque has a portico of carved marble columns that seem to spring from blossoming lotus buds. The two buildings, with their compact scale and composite motifs, are beautiful examples of Islamic and Hindu syncretism in the architecture of the Indian subcontinent.

On Thursday evenings local musicians gather around the courtyard of the shrine and recite the Shah's poetry. The *urs* (wedding) ceremony of Shah Abdul Latif is celebrated from the fourteenth until the sixteenth of the month of Safar with a yearly poetry and music festival held in Bhit.

Kishwar Rizvi

Further Reading
Schimmel, Annemarie. (1976) *Pain and Grace: A Study of Two Mystical Writers of Eighteenth-Century Muslim India.* Leiden, Netherlands: Brill.

BHITAI, SHAH ABDUL LATIF (1689–1752),
Sufi poet of Sind. Shah Abdul Latif Bhitai is the most famous Sufi poet of Sind, the region that is now the southeastern corner of Pakistan. Born in the village of Haveli (the present district of Hyderabad), he built nearby the small hamlet of Bhit (Sandhill), where he lived for a large part of his life.

Although not a man of great education, Shah Abdul Latif wrote remarkable lyrics, dialogs, and tales in the Sindhi language. His poems were collected over a century after his death in the famous book, *Shah Jo Risalo.*

In his poems, often based on simple traditional folktales of rural Sind, he emphasized human need for the love, compassion, and wisdom of God. Many of the poems were set to music and sung. His love tales and folk stories, such as *Sassui and Punhun* and *Lilan and Chanesar*, represent the core of popular Sindhi culture. After Shah Abdul Latif's death in 1752, the ruler of Sind, Ghulam Shah Kalhoro built a mausoleum in the poet's honor in Bhit, which is still regularly visited by pilgrims and devotees, and where his poems are continuously recited and sung.

Riccardo Redaelli

Further Reading
Sorley, H. T. (1940) *Shah Abdul Latif of Bhit: His Poetry, Life and Times.* Oxford: Oxford University Press.

BHOPAL (2001 est. pop. 1.4 million). Bhopal, the
capital of Madhya Pradesh State in central India, was founded on the north bank of the Upper Lake in 1723. Cotton, electrical goods, and jewelry are among the city's manufactures, and its major buildings include the Palace of the Nawab, the University of Bhopal, and the still unfinished Taj-il Masjid, which was begun in the late nineteenth century and is said to be the largest mosque in India. In addition the Birla Museum and the State Museum house valuable collections.

In 1984 a large pesticide factory belonging to Union Carbide, an American conglomerate, leaked poisonous isocyanate gas in Bhopal, killing at least 2,500 people and leaving over 100,000 people homeless, the world's worst industrial disaster to that date. The Indian law courts forced the parent company to make financial reparations, but the legal ruling was so complex that even a decade later many of the victims had not received adequate compensation, if any. It seemed that a small army of lawyers and state bureaucrats were the only recipients of the money. Even though the chief executive officer of Union Carbide,

Demonstrators with anti–Union Carbide posters observe a moment of silence to mark the fifteenth anniversary of the disaster on 3 December 1999. (AFP/CORBIS)

an American, was found guilty of homicide, he was never extradited to India.

Paul Hockings

See also: **Air Pollution**

Further Reading
Davies, Philip, and George Michell. (1989) "Bhopal." In *The Penguin Guide to the Monuments of India, Vol. 2: Islamic, Rajput, European.* New York: Viking Penguin; Harmondsworth, U.K.: Penguin Books, 205–206.
Shrivastava, Paul. (1992) *Bhopal: Anatomy of Crisis.* London: Paul Chapman.

BHOSLE, SHIVAJI (1627–1680), Maratha hero. Shivaji, an important figure in Indian history, is remembered for his valor and relentless struggle against the last of the Mughal rulers, Aurangzeb (reigned 1658–1707). Born on 19 February 1627 at Shivaneri, near Junnar in western India, Shivaji's father, Sahaji Bhosle, sent him to the dense jungles of Pune. Under the able guidance of his mother, Jijabai Nimbalkar, and tutor Dadoji Konddev, Shivaji took the vow of driving out the Mughal enemy. He began a career of adventure that captivated many of his and later generations. Beginning as a small fief holder, he carved out the large Maratha kingdom in western and southern India, which included present-day Pune, Raigarh, Ramnagar, Konkan, Kolhapur, and some areas of Karnataka. The killing of Afzal Khan (military commander for the Bijanpur sultanate) in 1659, the attack on Shayiste Khan (Mughal viceroy of Deccan), and the sack of the Mughal port Surat were landmarks in his eventful career. On a visit to Agra, Shivaji was imprisoned by the Mughal emperor. However, he and his son made a dramatic escape in baskets of sweetmeats. Shivaji declared himself sovereign king of Maratha in 1674 in a ceremony at Raigarh, in which he gave himself the title of *Chhatrapati* (sovereign king). Six years later, he died on 3 April 1680 at the age of fifty-three. He bequeathed a well-organized state to his son Sambhaji.

Patit Paban Mishra

Further Reading
Majumdar, R. C., ed. (1984) *The Mughul Empire 1526–1707 ad.* 2d ed. Mumbai (Bombay), India: Bharatiya Vidya Bhavan.
Pagadi, Setumadhavarao S. (1983) *Shivaji.* New Delhi: NBT.
Sarkar, Jadunath. (1972) *Aurangzeb and His Times*, Vol. 4. New Delhi: Orient Longman.

BHUBANESHWAR (2001 est. pop. 647,000). The capital of the Indian state of Orissa since 1948, Bhubaneshwar lies in the district of Puri and is famous for its Hindu temples. Most of the temples of Bhubaneshwar were built between the seventh and thirteenth centuries. The remains of 500 temples still stand around the Bindu Sagar Lake in the Old City. The important temples include the Lingaraja Temple (eleventh through fifteenth centuries), the Parasurameshwara Temple (seventh and eighth centuries), the Mukteshwara Temple (early tenth century) and the Kapileshwara Temple (mid-fifteenth century).

Bhubaneshwar's history dates to the third century BCE. It served as the capital of the Kalinga kingdom in the fourth and fifth centuries CE. The seventh century CE saw the establishment of the Saivite Hindu tradition in the region under the rule of King Sasanka. After Sasanka's death, the Bhauma Kara dynasty came to power, followed by the Soma dynasty. Muslim forces made their presence felt at the end of the sixteenth century. Finally it became British territory in 1757 when Robert Clive defeated the Bengal Nawab Siraj-ud-daula.

Bhubaneshwar today is divided into two sections, the Old City and a modern New City, designed by the architect Otto Koenigsberger, and is an important commercial and political center. Significant industries include cotton textiles and electronics.

Sanjukta Das Gupta

Further Reading
Kalia, Ravi. (1994) *From a Temple Town to a Capital City.* Delhi and Oxford: Oxford University Press.
Mitchell, George. (1989) "Bhubaneshwar." In *The Penguin Guide to the Monuments of India,* edited by George Mitchell. London and New York: Viking, vol. 1: 219–226.

BHUMIPOL ADULYADEJ (b. 1927), Thai monarch. His Majesty King Bhumipol Adulyadej (pronounced Pumipon Adunyadet) is the longest-reigning monarch in the world, having been on the throne since 1946. He is the ninth monarch of the Chakri dynasty, founded in 1782, and celebrated his golden jubilee in 1996. King Bhumipol was born 5 December 1927 in Cambridge, Massachusetts, where his father Prince Mahidol was studying medicine at Harvard. His mother, a nurse, was a commoner, later to become the beloved King's Mother (Somdech Ya).

It was not expected that Prince Bhumipol would become king. However, his father passed away in 1929 and his older brother (Prince Ananda Mahidol), then

The Royal Family of Thailand in 1952. (BETTMANN/CORBIS)

understand the needs of his people. He does not involve himself in partisan politics. However, in 1973 and again in 1992 he intervened to stop political violence and chaos related to confrontations between the military and students and other citizens. Also, on occasion he will speak not as the monarch but as an ordinary Thai citizen to express concerns of the people to the government. In response to the economic crisis of 1997, he proposed his theory of *setakit popieng* (economic self-sufficiency). His power to withhold or grant legitimacy to a government is also an important informal power, which he rarely uses except at the time of a major political crisis.

Gerald W. Fry

Further Reading
Davis, Reginald. (1981) *The Royal Family of Thailand*. London: Nicolas Publications.

Ekachai, Sanitsuda, et al. (1999) *A Visionary Monarch*. Bangkok, Thailand: Post Publishing Company.

Office of the Royal Development Projects Board. (1996) *50 Years of Development Work According to the Initiatives of His Majesty King Bhumibol Adulyadej of Thailand*. Bangkok, Thailand: Office of the Royal Development Projects Board.

Royal Development Project. (1984) *His Majesty King Bhumibol Adulyadej and His Development Work*. Bangkok, Thailand: Royal Development Project.

Samosorn, Amporn. (1996) *The Great King of Thailand*. Bangkok, Thailand: One Asset Management.

a ten-year-old student in Switzerland, was later chosen to become King Rama VIII, following the abdication of King Rama VII. However, in 1946, King Ananda died unexpectedly, resulting in Prince Bhumipol being made the ninth Chakri king at age nineteen. Then a student in Switzerland, he shifted his study from science to political science to prepare for his new leadership role. After his formal coronation in 1950, the king decided to take up residence not at the Grand Palace, but instead at the much more modest Chitlada Villa.

King Bhumipol has many versatile and impressive abilities. His nine major talents and roles (as depicted in Ratchamangkala Hall of the King Rama IX Royal Park) can be briefly summarized as (1) the family man, (2) the artist, (3) the sportsman, (4) the musician, (5) the monarch, (6) the philanthropist, (7) the statesman, (8) the developer, and (9) the innovator of royal projects.

In Thailand's constitutional monarchy, the king is above the normal political arena, though he does sign legislation as a royal formality. Without question, King Bhumipol is the most popular leader anywhere in the world. If an opinion poll were taken in Thailand, he would receive a 99.99 percent approval rating. He is universally admired and respected by the Thai people because of his dedication and commitment to his people. In the years from the mid-1960s to 1994, he never traveled outside Thailand, but instead traveled to all areas and regions of Thailand to

BHUTAN—PROFILE (2001 est. pop. 2 million).
Bhutan is a small, landlocked eastern Himalayan kingdom of 47,000 square kilometers. A natural barrier of mountain ranges separates Bhutan from Tibet in the north, Arunachal Pradesh (India) in the east, and Sikkim in the west. Bhutan's foothills meet the Indian plains of West Bengal and Assam in the south.

While Bhutan shares most of its cultural elements with Tibet, politically the country is part of South Asia, with especially strong links to India by treaty, communications, and recent history. Bhutan's identity is bound up with its Buddhist religion, first introduced by the semi-legendary eighth-century Indian mystic and teacher, Guru Padmasambhava or Guru Rimpoche, the Precious Teacher, who was said to have lived more than one thousand years. Always regarded as different in geography and development from the Tibetan Plateau although the two areas share many cultural features, Bhutan was constituted as a separate state in the seventeenth century and has maintained a distinctive identity ever since.

BHUTAN

Country name: Kingdom of Bhutan

Area: 47,000 sq km

Population: 2,049,412 (July 2001 est.)

Population growth rate: 2.17% (2001 est.)

Birth rate: 35.73 births/1,000 population (2001 est.)

Death rate: 14.03 deaths/1,000 population (2001 est.)

Net migration rate: 0 migrant(s)/1,000 population (2001 est.)

Sex ratio: 1.07 male(s)/female (2001 est.)

Infant mortality rate: 108.89 deaths/1,000 live births (2001 est.)

Life expectancy at birth—total population: 52.79 years, male: 53.16 years, female: 52.41 years (2001 est.)

Major religions: Lamaistic Buddhist 75%, Indian- and Nepalese-influenced Hinduism 25%

Major languages: Dzongkha (official), Bhotes speak various Tibetan dialects, Nepalese speak various Nepalese dialects

Literacy—total population: 42.2%, male: 56.2%, female: 28.1% (1995 est.)

Government type: monarchy; special treaty relationship with India

Capital: Thimphu

Administrative divisions: 18 districts

Independence: 8 August 1949 (from India)

National holiday: National Day (Ugyen Wangchuck became first hereditary king), 17 December (1907)

Suffrage: Each family has one vote in village-level elections

GDP—real growth rate: 6% (2000 est.)

GDP—per capita: (purchasing power parity): $1,100 (2000 est.)

Population below poverty line: not available

Exports: $154 million (f.o.b., 2000 est.)

Imports: $269 million (c.i.f., 2000 est.)

Currency: ngultrum (BTN); Indian rupee (INR)

Source: Central Intelligence Agency. (2001) *The World Factbook* 2001. Retrieved 5 March, 2002 from http://www.cia.gov/cia/publications/factbook

From the eighth to the seventeenth centuries, religious dynasties controlled life in the valleys, and there was no central authority. During this period, Bhutan was regarded as a hidden land, a place of refuge and exile from the troubles of the Tibetan Plateau. One such exile was the great teacher Longchen Rabjampa (1308–1363), who wrote a eulogy of central Bhutan. Another such exile, Shabdrung Ngawang Namgyel (1594–1651?), founded the Bhutanese state.

Physical Characteristics

The country consists of a series of interlocking mountain valleys, running north to south, divided laterally into three belts. The high northern belt is marked by peaks of over seven thousand meters and by major passes; it is sparsely inhabited by yak herders who move to the lower valleys in winter to barter their yak milk and meat.

The middle belt consists of wooded valleys separated by north-south ridges that frame rivers flowing into the Indian plains. These rivers sustain the fertile valleys of the central zone, which lie at altitudes ranging from approximately 1,200 to approximately 2,700 meters. Much of the country's population is concentrated in this area. Rice, maize, and wheat are cultivated in the lower valleys, and barley, buckwheat, and millet are grown higher up. This belt also abounds in dense forests of pine, cypress, fir, maple, oak, and

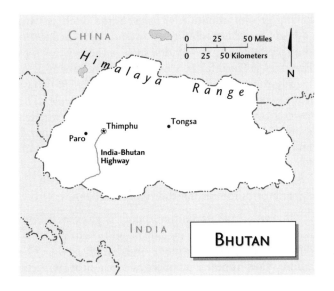

Government

Bhutan is a monarchy. The present ruler, Jigme Singye Wangchuck (b. 1955), is the fourth king in a line founded in 1907. The king and a Council of Ministers, or Lhengye Zhungtshog, constitute the executive authority. They are assisted by the Royal Advisory Council, or Lodoi Tsokde, which has both lay and ecclesiastical members. The king and the Lhengye Zhungtshog are responsible to the National Assembly, which meets twice a year. In 1998, in a major reform initiated by the king, the annually rotating chairman of the Council of Ministers was made the head of the government. The king is head of state. There are no political parties. One national newspaper, *Kuensel*, provides national and international news in English, Dzongkha, and Nepali editions.

At the local level, the village headman is chosen by open voting, as are representatives to the National Assembly. For internal administration, the country is divided into twenty *dzonkhag*s, or regions, so called after the *dzong*s, which combine the function of local government center and monastery. The head of a *dzongkhag* is called a *dzongda*, who is appointed by the central government. Since the late 1980s, devolution of power to the *dzonkhag*s, especially in education, is a government policy.

Politics

Bhutan's overriding aim is to balance development and modernization with maintenance of its traditional culture. Bhutan did not enter the television age until 1999; in the same year that it established Internet capacity. The primacy of Bhutan's traditional culture is emphasized by a policy of *drilam namza* ("discipline and propriety"), which includes the compulsory wearing of national dress and proper ways of behaving in the presence of authority. The king has often stated that his policy is to promote "gross national happiness," rather than a narrowly defined gross national product.

Bhutan's most controversial political issue is the so-called southern problem involving the Nepali-speaking population of the south. Some of the southern population opposed a government census and imposition of *driglam namza*. While an outright rebellion in 1989 was nipped in the bud, demonstrations took place, and the government arrested many implicated in the conspiracy. Supporters of the rebels (called *ngolops*, or antinationals, by the government) subsequently fled to United Nations–run refugee camps in Nepal. The population of these camps is given by the United Nations High Commissioner for Refugees as 100,000, but the Bhutanese government says many are

birch. The county's main road runs west to east through this belt.

The southern belt consists mainly of wooded foothills, rising to 1,500 meters above sea level, with a hot, humid climate. In the twentieth century, this area was settled by Nepali-speaking migrants, whom the government was keen to integrate into the national mainstream, based on the culture and tradition of the historically significant middle belt. The north-south roads to India run through this area.

It is the middle region that is the center of Bhutan's political and historical identity. In the west of this region, the beautiful valley of Paro is the site of Bhutan's holiest shrine, Taksang (the Tiger's Nest), believed to be the place where Guru Padmasambhava arrived on a tiger's back. Tragically, it burned down in 1999. Political power centers on the valley of Thimphu, the capital since 1961. The valley of Bumthang is also full of associations with Guru Rimpoche, while Tongsa is the seat of the present Wangchuck dynasty. The east of the country has its own language and cultural style. It is hotter, drier, and less forested than the west. It is the source of Bhutanese textiles, woven by eastern women working on hand looms.

Three of Bhutan's four major language groups are found in the central belt. Ngalongkha is spoken in the five western valleys that formed the core of political authority in Bhutan. It is from Ngalongkha that the official national language, Dzongkha, was developed.

The second language group is Bumthangkha, which includes dialects spoken in the central valley of Bumthang and its neighboring valleys of Kheng, Kurto, and Mangdelung. The third group is Tsangla, the languages of the Sharchops, who live in the east.

not Bhutanese at all or are illegal immigrants. Leaders of the escapees say that all those in the camps are Bhutanese and were forcibly expelled under a program of ethnic cleansing and suppression of human rights.

Several rounds of minister- and official-level talks between Nepal and Bhutan have established the modalities under which the refugees may be categorized, and there has been a promise from Bhutan to accept the return of all those classified as Bhutanese. Most of those arrested have been freed, including Tek Nath Rizal, regarded as the main leader.

Economy and Way of Life

Bhutan is overwhelmingly agricultural (94 percent of the population), with a superstructure of ecclesiastical and government officers. Government revenues are provided by the sale of electricity, direct subsidies from India, and taxes. In 1961, the government took a leading role in economic planning through a series of five-year plans based on the Indian model. More recently, since the 1980s, an increasing role has been given to the private sector, with transport, postal, and banking services already contracted out. Bhutan's largest single source of revenue is the huge Chukka hydroelectric project. This dam was built by India, which pays Bhutan for the electricity generated and exported to India's northeast. Other electricity projects have been set up, and more are envisaged.

Industrial employers include the Penden Cement Authority, Bhutan Wood Particle Products, Bhutan Carbide and Chemicals Ltd., a fruit-processing plant at Samtse, and distilleries. Tourism and stamps provide foreign-currency income. Commercial ventures include Tashi Commercial and Gaseylu Construction. There are no large-scale industries in Bhutan; royal relatives form corporations in areas such as oil and gas supply (obtained from India), department stores, and construction. Much of the construction work undertaken is paid for by the government or by foreign aid projects, as with the new sewage system for the capital, built with Japanese and Danish government and private aid and employing many local workers.

Land is an important source of wealth, and farmland is passed through the female line. Perhaps uniquely in Asia, there are usually no marriage ceremonies; the groom's moving into the bridal home is generally enough to constitute a marriage. Divorce and second marriage are common. Relative sexual equality and a rather open attitude toward sexuality are also in contrast to Bhutan's southern neighbors.

Bhutanese villages tend to be scattered households surrounded by fields. Towns are a recent phenomenon,

having grown around the *dzong*s. Some, such as Paro or Jakar, have been rebuilt as substantial, planned townships, following fires. Others, such as the new town of Punakha at Kuruthang, are built by government plan. Family houses tend to be substantial affairs of two or more stories with shingle roofs and mud walls. The lower story is mud or stone, and the upper a wooden framed structure, frequently attractively painted. Houses are rebuilt every couple of generations, with the tamping down of the mud walls being the women's job and the erection of the wooden framework of the upper stories the responsibility of a carpenter.

Bhutan's gross domestic product is given as $1,100 per capita, but figures do not do justice to an economy still largely subsistence and barter based. The countryside appears prosperous with neat terraced fields, substantial houses, and people clothed in elegant traditional garments. Unlike much of Asia, there are few urban slums and little begging or unemployment. Rice is a staple but grows only at altitudes below approximately 2,100 meters. Red rice from Paro and Punakha is especially prized. Higher altitudes and poorer soils grow maize or buckwheat and potatoes, a cash crop exchanged for white rice. Chilies are essential to Bhutan's cuisine; the sight of red chilies drying on shingle roofs is a common feature of Bhutanese villages. Cattle grazing is usually carried out in tandem with farming. The herds provide milk for cheese (a hard variety is popular for trekking) and butter but not meat, because of Buddhist precepts about taking life. Average landholdings are between five and thirty acres and are held freehold, but all kinds of arrangements for rent and sharecropping exist.

The government is largely responsible for education and health and has made huge efforts to increase the school-going population and to provide basic health clinics in difficult geographical circumstances. As a result of those efforts, literacy and life expectancy have increased dramatically in the last thirty years.

There is one international airport at Paro; Druk Air is the national carrier. A system of roads has been built and maintained with Indian help, although much of the transport at village level remains on foot and by pony.

Bhutan is very conscious of environmental issues, and official controls on logging are reasonably well enforced. Forests occupy some 60 to 70 percent of land area. Restrictions on hunting and collection of wild plants and animal products, such as musk, are in place.

The government strongly supports traditional arts. Houses must conform to Bhutanese style, and agencies have been set up to promote and preserve traditional crafts. The export of antiques is forbidden, although a series of robberies of religious artifacts, culminating in 2000 with the theft of the country's most sacred relic, a bone of the founder of its main religious sect, carved in the form of the Buddhist deity of Compassion, has revealed a breakdown in traditional respect for religion.

Bhutan has made its policy of preserving its unique culture and identity a top priority. This policy also agrees with the way that much of the world would like to perceive Bhutan and with modern ideas of sustainable development, as well as with the sentiments of the religious-minded and deeply independent people of Bhutan, who have never been colonized. The policy is both successful and timely: Bhutan has taken on many features of modern life while remaining deeply traditional in feeling.

Michael Kowalewski and Sonam Chhoki

Further Reading

Aris, Michael, and Michael Hutt, eds. (1994) *Bhutan: Aspects of Culture and Development.* Gartmore, U.K.: Kiscadale Press.

Dompier, Robert. (1999) *Bhutan.* Boston: Shambhala.

Myers, Diana K., and Susan S. Bean, eds. (1994) *From the Land of the Thunder Dragon: Textile Arts of Bhutan.* Salem, MA: Peabody Essex Museum.

Rose, Leo. (1977) *The Politics of Bhutan.* Ithaca, NY: Cornell University Press.

Rustomji, Nari. (1978) *Bhutan: The Dragon Kingdom in Crisis.* New Delhi: Oxford University Press.

Singh, Nagendra. (1972) *Bhutan: A Kingdom in the Himalayas.* New Delhi: Thomson Press.

Van Strydonck, Guy, F. Pommaret-Imaeda, and Yoshiro Imaeda. (1984) *Bhutan: A Kingdom in the Eastern Himalayas.* London: Serindia.

BHUTAN—HISTORY In Bhutan, history is simultaneously religious and political. For example, the native name of the country, Druk yul, is derived from the name of the Drukpa Buddhist sect. Even now the administrative center (*dzong*) of each district functions as both a monastery and secular governor's seat. The head abbot of the Drukpa sect resides in the main *dzong*, in the capital, which is also the seat of the national government and enjoys parity of esteem with the king.

Bhutan's history was linked to that of Tibet—in which, however, it was never politically included—until the powerful Buddhist Gelug sect of Tibet, founders of the Dalai Lama rulership in the seventeenth century, tried to invade Bhutan several times in the seventeenth and eighteenth centuries. They were repulsed and after a treaty in 1734 Bhutan's focus

turned southward. The Chinese takeover of Tibet and the 1959 flight of the Dalai Lama finally ended official relations with Tibet. Thus while the study of ancient Bhutan is part of Tibetology, contemporary Bhutan belongs to South Asia.

Two of the twelve border-subduing Buddhist temples that the first Tibetan religious king, Songtsen Gampo (d. 649/650) built in the seventh century are in Bhutanese valleys. During the long period in which Tibet was without real central authority (mid-ninth–seventeenth centuries) Bhutan seems to have adopted systems of local rule based on clans and on religious dynasties called *choje* similar to Tibet's, without centralized leadership. The rugged terrain, swift rivers, and thick forests isolated Bhutan's valleys from their neighbors and bolstered the rise of regional powers under elite families or influential local Buddhist centers, before the country's unification in the seventeenth century.

Emergence of Centralized Rule

The Drukpas, a subsect of the Kargyu sect of Mahayana Buddhism, originated in Tibet. Phajo Drukgom Shigpo (1184–1251) carried the sect from Tibet to Bhutan and set up his sons as *choje* in the Thimphu area. The popularity of the Drukpas provided the foundations on which the Bhutanese state was built in 1616 by Shabdrung Ngawang Namgyel (1594–1651?), a Tibetan lama forced to flee Tibet in a succession dispute. In Bhutan he set up a dual system of religious-secular rule, embodied in his seal of the sixteen I's (the sixteen spokes of the wheel, the wheel being highly symbolic in Buddhism and the "I" being the ego). In this seal Shabdrung announced himself as uniting religious and secular power, a concept implicit in Tantric Buddhism, where political power is not distinguished from spiritual mastery. So strong was the impact of Shabdrung that his death was kept secret for sixty years to allow the development of the new state.

To establish its identity as a Drukpa state, Bhutan under Shabdrung and his successors fought five wars with the Tibetan state of the Dalai Lamas and their Mongol allies. The last of these was in 1730 and led to a settlement brokered by the Panchen Lama and Chinese emperor in 1734, establishing a Shabdung reincarnation as the head of Bhutan. Victory in these wars is still celebrated in festivals, especially the annual *Domche* at Punakha.

Real power then devolved to governors, or *desis* (the *deb* rajas of British accounts) after the "retreat" of the Shabdrung in 1651 and continuing throughout the eighteenth century when the Shabdrung incarnations

KEY EVENTS IN BHUTAN HISTORY

1300s The Drukpas, a subsect of the Kargyu sect of Mahayana Buddhism in Tibet, are brought to Bhutan by Phajo Drukgom Shigpo.

1616 A Bhutanese state is established by Shabdrung Ngawang Namgyel.

1734 A series of wars with Tibet and the Mongols end in victory for Bhutan and the establishment of a Shabdrung reincarnation as the head of Bhutan.

1700s The border area with India known as the Duars comes under Bhutanese influence and control.

1800s Life is disrupted by civil wars and conflict with the British in India.

1907 The British recognize Ugyen Wangchuck as king.

1910 The Treaty of Punakha with Britain affords Bhutan full internal sovereignty, while Bhutan agrees to abide by British advice in foreign relations.

1958 Indian premier Jawaharlal Nehru visits Bhutan, and announces a policy of respect for Bhutan's sovereignty while helping its development efforts, a policy still in effect.

1959 The Chinese military occupation of Tibet turns Bhutan more firmly toward India for support.

1960s King Jigme Dorje Wangchuck promotes education and technical development and internal political reform.

1972 Bhutan joins the United Nations.

1990 Ethnic Nepalis who had settled in southern Bhutan begin fleeing the country, claiming organized persecution by the government and lack of human rights.

1998 King Jigme Singye Wangchuck allowes a six-member Council of Ministers approved by the National Assembly to take more control of state affairs.

failed to exercise much power. The regents were the main power till the civil wars of the latter half of the eighteenth and early nineteenth centuries established the local rulers as the main powers, finally leading to the establishment of the monarchy.

In the seventeenth and eighteenth centuries religious authority was centered in the figure determined to be the reincarnation of Shabdrung (called by the British "dharma raja"). The fourth *desi*, Tenzin Rabgay, brought the east of the country into the orbit of the Drukpa state. However the system proved unstable, and local rulers (*pönlops)* became dominant powers in the land, especially in Paro and Tongsa districts, displacing both *desi*s and dharma rajas.

In the eighteenth century the border area with India known as the Duars came under Bhutanese influence and control; Bhutan looked to the Kamrup rajas of Assam for booty, political support, and economic ties—Kamrup rupees circulated in Bhutan as currency.

As the British expanded their rule in India and as Bhutan expanded its interest in the south, Bhutan was brought into the ambit of British Indian policy. Memoirs of successful British expeditions to Bhutan between 1774 and 1783 provide independent accounts of Bhutan at the time. Missions in 1815 and 1838 were less successful, culminating in a disastrous expedition by Ashley Eden in 1863–1864, which led to war in 1864. Bhutan then ceded its Duar territories to Britain in return for annual compensation, then totaling 50,000 rupees.

Hereditary Monarchy

Throughout the eighteenth and nineteenth centuries, Bhutan's civil wars led to the gradual focusing of political power around the governors of Paro and Tongsa. Ultimately the Tongsa governor Ugyen Wangchuck (1862–1926) was successful in uniting the country. He tilted Bhutanese policy toward British India by accompanying the expedition of Francis Edward Younghusband (1863–1942) to Tibet in 1903–1904 as translator and mediator. His role led to his being knighted by Britain. In 1907 the British recognized him as king after he signed a coronation agreement, or *genja*, with lay and ecclesiastical leadership. From then on Bhutan was ruled by a hereditary monarch of the Wangchuck family.

The foundation of the monarchy ended both the period of civil war and conflicts with British India. The British signed the Treaty of Punakha (1910), allowing Bhutan full internal sovereignty, while Bhutan agreed to abide by British advice in foreign relations. Independent India reaffirmed the status quo in the 1949 Indo-Bhutanese Treaty, and this arrangement continues today.

Relations with India were cemented in 1958 when the Indian premier Jawaharlal Nehru (1889–1964) paid a visit to Bhutan, at a time when there were no drivable roads there. Nehru announced a policy of respecting Bhutan's sovereignty while helping its development efforts, a policy still in effect. The Chinese military occupation of Tibet in 1959 meant that Bhutan turned even more firmly toward India and began to look further afield for international support, the lack of which had doomed Tibet.

The memorial in Thimphu to King Jigme Dorje Wangchuck who died in 1972. (DAVID SAMUEL ROBBINS/CORBIS)

Bhutan joined international bodies such as the Colombo Plan (1962); the United Nations (1972); the South Asia Association for Regional Cooperation, of which it was a founding member in 1983; the International Monetary Fund and the World Bank (1981); and the Nonaligned Movement. The United Nations Development Program (UNDP) and Swiss, Danish, Dutch, and Japanese bodies are generous aid donors.

The monarchy has been a modernizing institution in Bhutan. The third king, Jigme Dorje Wangchuck (1928–1972), introduced cooperation with India and with Swiss agencies to promote education and technical development. He also brought about rapid institutional change, setting up a National Assembly and a Royal Advisory Council. He reformed the civil service, making it more modern, and introduced modern secular education in schools not linked to the monastaries. He also granted citizenship to those who had settled in southern Bhutan before 1958. The fourth and present king, Jigme Singye Wangchuck, came to the throne in 1972 and was officially crowned in 1974. In 1998 the king allowed a six-member Council of Ministers approved by the National Assembly to take more control of state affairs, with the head of government being rotated annually among the Cabinet members and the king remaining head of state. He has continued his father's modernization policy. Since 1990 ethnic Nepalis who had settled in southern Bhutan have fled from Bhutan, claiming organized persecution by the government and lack of human rights. About 100,000 have been housed in camps run by the United Nations High Commissioner for Refugees (UNHCR) in eastern Nepal. Another problem is the rise of separatist movements in the neighboring Indian state of Assam. In response to pressure from the Indian government in 1999 and 2000 Bhutan tried to close down the militants' camps. The problems have yet to be resolved.

Michael Kowalewski and Sonam Chhoki

See also: **Bhutanese; Wangchuck, Jigme Singye**

Further Reading

Aris, Michael, and Michael Hutt, eds. (1994) *Bhutan: Aspects of Culture and Development*. Gartmore, U.K.: Kiscadale Press.

Dompier, Robert. (1999) *Bhutan*. Boston: Shambhala.

Olschack, Blanche C. (1979) *Ancient Bhutan: A Study of Early Buddhism in the Himalayas*. Zurich, Switzerland: Swiss Foundation for Alpine Research.

Van Strydonck, Guy, F. Pommaret-Imaeda, and Yoshiro Imaeda. (1984) *Bhutan: A Kingdom in the Eastern Himalayas*. London: Serindia.

BHUTAN—RELIGION

Bhutan's identity is wrapped up in its religion. The country owes its indigenous name (Drukyul) to the Drukpa school of Tibetan Buddhism, which is the official religion of the state. The state founder, Shabdrung Ngawang Namgyel (1594–1651?), was a Buddhist monk of the Drukpa school, and today the king and head abbot of the Drukpa Kargyu sect are held in joint esteem at the peak of the national hierarchy. While the country's religion belongs firmly to the world of Tibetan Buddhism, and its texts are written in classical Tibetan (Chokey), Bhutan selected and developed its own strands of this overarching culture. Of the four main Tibetan sects, the Nyingma and Kargyu are present, with the Drukpa subsect of the Kargyus dominant.

Introduction of Buddhism to Bhutan

Bhutan's initial encounter with Buddhism occurred in the seventh century, when the Tibetan king Songtsen Gampo (d. 649/50) built two of the earliest Tibetan Buddhist temples—Kichu in Paro and Jambay in Bumthang. His temple-building scheme was based on the geomantic (referring to magic based on geographic features) notion that the whole of Tibet was a female demon, which had to be pinned down by the construction of temples. Both temples continue to this day as active religious centers patronized by the royal family.

Bhutanese traditions commonly date the independent introduction of Tibetan Buddhism into Bhutan as a whole to the eighth century, and credit Padmasambhava, popularly called Guru Rimpoche ("Precious Teacher"), a largely mythical figure rumored to have lived from 800 BCE to c. 800 CE. The Nyingma tradition founded by him is characterized by a personal relationship between a guru and his disciples rather than by institutionalized monasticism. Legends of Guru Rimpoche's role as tamer of demons and bringer of culture are popular among other Himalayan Buddhist societies, where he is revered as the second Buddha.

Introduction of the Drukpa Subsect

The Drukpa subsect of the Kargyu sect of Tibetan Buddhism, introduced into Bhutan in the early thirteenth century by Phajo Drukgom Shigpo (1184–1251), came to be particularly identified with Bhutan. It emerged in the seventeenth century as Bhutan's religious-political core under its incarnate head Shabdrung Ngawang Namgyel (1594–1651?), who had sought refuge in Bhutan. The Drukpa theocracy gave the country its name, "Drukyul," and the inhabitants the name of "Drukpas." The predominance of the Drukpa tradition is shown in the invocation of the principal deities of the Drukpa pantheon, such as Palden Lhamo and Yeshey Gonpo, in annual monastic rituals in villages. However the Drukpa Kargyu tradition coexists amicably with the devotion to Guru Rimpoche. Although the state-supported monastic organization is mainly Drukpa Kargyu, some centers are dedicated to the Nyingma tradition. In Bhutan monks are commonly trained in Nyingma tradition to perform Drukpa rituals, and vice versa. Most household prayer-room altars have the statue of the Buddha in the middle flanked by those of Guru Rimpoche on the right and Shabdrung Ngawang Namgyel on the left.

Native Religious Practices

Positioned outside, but coexisting with, the Drukpa monastic tradition is the complex of local ritual specialists called nenjorms (female) or powas (male). This complex is centered on local deities and is oriented toward such material goals as healing and prosperity rather than the spiritual goals of Buddhism. It is an oral tradition, passed from pupil to teacher. A typical rite involves the chanting of verses to summon the practitioner's divinity. The divinity then takes possession of the nenjorm or powa. These rites are performed at household and village levels.

The landscape is full of religious sites—prayer flags flutter in the wind, prayer walls line the paths, temples appear on cliff faces, and water-turned prayer wheels and large and small chortens (structures representing the Buddha's enlightenment) are ubiquitous. Along with mountain hermitages and retreats (gonpas), there are legends of local saints, with rituals and observances associated with them.

Organization of the Official Church

The head of the Bhutanese official church is the head abbot, je khenpo. The national flag displays the yellow and orange colors representing monarchy and religion. The je khenpo is chosen for a three-year period, after which he retires into meditational retreat. Under him are four lopens, or teachers of the monastic body, which numbers about 1,200. The je khenpo has two monastic seats, Punakha in winter and the capital Thimphu in summer. The main monastic body moves annually with him. There are other government-supported monastic communities in the various dzongs, or fortified monasteries, and smaller communities of monks throughout the country with their own lamas and adherents supported by local patrons. Members of these communities outside the main monastic body number about 2,000.

Young Buddhist monks watch a dance performed in honor of the king's birthday in Thimphu, Bhutan. (ALISON WRIGHT/ CORBIS)

Religious Practices among the People

For the ordinary believer in Bhutan, religion begins with the domestic altar or home prayer room. The deities invoked by each household are ancestral. Ritual is overwhelmingly important, and monks are called from the nearest *dzong* to offer rice sculptures called *tormas*. The head practitioner sits in the prayer room to chant the ritual from texts, accompanied by subsidiary practitioners blowing flutes and beating drums facing the altar. Local practitioners, including lapsed monks and nonmonastic religious practitioners called *gomchens*, also provide these services in both towns and villages. In the east, *gomchens* lead ritual performances, scripture recitations, and village-level festivals.

Religious Personalities

Religious faith and identity hinge on the veneration of the powerful personalities who brought Buddhism to what was believed to be an untamed and demon-inhabited area. Many of these were exiles from a foreign land, usually Tibet, who found both refuge and power in the "hidden land" of Bhutan.

Of these personalities Guru Rimpoche is the most important. He is believed to have come to Bhutan flying on a tiger and to have landed at the Tiger's Nest shrine in Paro valley. He also went to Bumthang, where he left his imprints on a rock, now the site of Kurje Temple. A popular legend recounts how he converted the Bumthang king by imparting his teachings through a Bhutanese consort. Each *dzong* celebrates an annual *tsechu* (festival) in his honor, where masked dancers represent the guru in his eight manifestations and his consorts.

Phajo Drukgom Shigpo is also venerated. Chronicles tell of his spreading the word according to prophecy, his battle with opposing sects, and his union with a local woman. The Bridge of Prophecy *(Lungtenzampa)* at the site where he first met her is still the principal bridge into the capital, Thimphu, in the area of his main foundations. His four sons became lineage leaders in various parts of Bhutan.

The most beloved saint and hero of Bhutan is Drukpa Kunley (1455–1529), the mad yogi. Also from Tibet, he found opportunities for his brand of crazy mysticism in Bhutan. His tantric sexual exploits are known to all, and places associated with him became pilgrimage sites. Pilgrims go to Chime Lhakhang at Lobesa to be tapped on the head with the saint's magic *dorje* (thunderbolt of wisdom), which guarantees fertility.

Bhutan is most proud of its native saint, Pema Lingpa (1450–1521). Belonging to the treasure-discoverer tradition of the Nyingma school, he found a series of texts and precious objects and revealed dances, still enacted in Bhutanese monasteries. The Burning Lake *(Membartsho)* where he discovered his most important treasure is a pilgrimage site, and his temple of Tamshing in Bumthang displays a suit of chain mail that he is said to have forged.

The Future

Religious practice has a continuing vitality in Bhutan today as it is wrapped up with feelings of both regional and national identity. People establish their local and family roots by honoring ancestral deities. The state and royal family support the religious work of monasteries, while the people participate fully in religious rites at festivals. Pilgrimages are a regular feature of life. Lay patrons still support monks, rituals, scripture recitations and the building of religious edifices. Initiations by revered gurus are well attended. In 2001, there were plans to set up a university for the study of Buddhism.

Michael Kowaleski and Sonam Chhoki

See also: **Buddhism—Tibet**

Further Reading

Dowman, Keith, trans. (1980) *The Divine Madman: The Sublime Life and Songs of Drukpa Kunley.* London: Rider.

Olschack, Blanche C. (1979) *Ancient Bhutan: A Study of Early Buddhism in the Himalayas.* Zurich, Switzerland: Swiss Foundation for Alpine Research.

Tsewang, Pema, Khenpo Phuntshok Tashi, Chris Butters, and Sigmund K. Saetreng. (1995) *The Treasure Revealer of Bhutan.* Kathmandu, Nepal: Biblioteca Himalayica.

BHUTANESE   "Bhutanese" refers to the people of Bhutan or to one of the languages spoken there. "Bhutan" is the official name of the Himalayan kingdom; the word probably derives from *Bhotanta*—the edge of Tibet—*Bhot* being the Sanskrit version of the Tibetan word for Tibet and *Anta* meaning "end." The term seems to have been picked up by the British from local Indian usage. The Bhutanese themselves call their country Drukyul and themselves Drukpa. The word "Druk" means dragon and refers to the sect of Tibetan Buddhism that became dominant in Bhutan. "Yul" means land, and "pa" is a suffix denoting person. The government promotes a concept of Bhutanese national identity by promoting Bhutanese culture, language, and tradition (*Drilam Namza,* "Code of Conduct and Dress"). Bhutanese dress is compulsory, and government departments are enjoined to use Dzongkha, rather than English, for correspondence.

The Bhutanese are related primarily to the Tibetans in culture, ethnicity, and language. Southern

A Bhutanese man outside a hotel in southwestern Bhutan. (PAPILLIO/CORBIS)

Bhutan is now populated by ethnic Nepalis, but the overall culture of the country remains that of the people of the north and center. Officially "Drukpa" means any citizen of Bhutan, but the term is used loosely to denote the Buddhist peoples in distinction to Nepali-speaking Hindus of the south, although this usage remains unofficial and controversial. The eastern people called Sharchops speak a different language, but share much of their culture with the westerners. The people of the south are referred to officially as Lhotsampas—southerners—under the policy of national unity.

The Himalayas have been less of a barrier to migration than the dense jungles of the southern foothills. Consequently, the southern Himalayas, such as Ladakh, Sikkim, and eastern Nepal, have been populated by waves of migrants from the Tibetan plateau, with which they share cultural, ethnic, and linguistic links. The Drukpa people of Bhutan may be regarded as within this cultural and ethnic band. Historical dates are hard to fix for this process, but the Bhutanese date their identity as Buddhists from the arrival of Guru Rimpoche in the eighth century CE. The ethnic Nepalis came much later, in the twentieth century, as hired workers on projects, as well as small farmers escaping poverty in Nepal.

There are several regional languages in Bhutan. The official language is Dzongkha, "language of the monastery," based on the language spoken in the northwestern valleys. Other Bhutanese languages are Sharchop or Tsangla spoken in the east, Bumthangkha and Mangdep spoken in the center, and Khenkha, a southern language. All these languages belong to the Tibeto-Burman language family. While the northern, western, and central languages are related to the Tibetan family, Sharchop is affiliated with the Tsangla languages, also spoken in the Tawang district of India's Arunachal Pradesh state. Nepali is widely spoken in the south. Most Bhutanese are excellent linguists, fluent in one or more of the local languages as well as Dzongkha, the official language, border Indian languages, Nepali, and, if educated, English.

Michael Kowalewski and Sonam Chhoki

Further Reading

Aris, Michael. (1979) *Bhutan: The Early History of a Himalayan Kingdom.* Warminster, U.K.: Aris & Phillips.
Aris, Michael, and Michael Hutt, eds. (1994) *Bhutan: Aspects of Culture and Development.* Gartmore, U.K.: Kiscadale Press.
Rose, Leo. (1977) *The Politics of Bhutan.* Ithaca, NY: Cornell University Press.

BHUTTO, BENAZIR

BHUTTO, BENAZIR (b. 1953), Prime minister of Pakistan. Benazir Bhutto made history as the first woman to lead a government of an Islamic state on 2 December 1988, when she became prime minister of Pakistan. She served until 1990 and again from 1993 until 1996. She was dismissed from office by two presidents: Ghulam Ishaq Khan (in 1990) and Farooq Leghari (in 1996). Both times she was accused of corruption.

She is the daughter of former Prime Minister Zulfiqar Ali Bhutto, who served from 1971 to 1977. Born in 1953 in Karachi, she completed her early studies in Pakistan. Her higher education was received at Radcliffe College in the United States, where she received a degree in philosophy, politics, and economics. She also attended Oxford University's International Law and Diplomacy program.

Bhutto became politically active by opposing Pakistan's leadership at the time. She became involved with the opposition party, the Pakistan People's Party. This resulted in her being arrested several times, totaling six years of confinement. Her platform focused on the plight of the poor, drawing attention to health, welfare, and education programs.

As prime minister, Bhutto worked hard to heal old wounds and rid society of that which divides, including discrimination between the sexes. She instituted health and education reform throughout Pakistan. Her efforts earned her the Bruno Kreisky Award for Human Rights in 1988. In addition, her alma mater bestowed an honorary Phi Beta Kappa award on her in 1989.

Houman A. Sadri

Further Reading
Cole, Juan R. I., ed. (1992) *Comparing Muslim Societies: Knowledge and the State in a World Civilization.* Ann Arbor, MI: University of Michigan Press.
Haynes, Jeff, ed. (1999) *Religion, Globalization, and Political Culture in the Third World.* New York: St. Martin's Press.

BHUTTO, ZULFIQAR ALI

BHUTTO, ZULFIQAR ALI (1928–1979), Pakistani political figure. As foreign minister of Pakistan from 1963 to 1966, Bhutto established an alliance with China in 1963 and encouraged President Ayub Khan (1907–1974) to wage war against India in 1965. Soon after Ayub Khan's defeat he parted company with him and then started the Pakistan People's Party (PPP) in 1967. His rhetoric was vaguely leftist, and in 1965 he became critical of the American alliance, which had not been of much use to Pakistan. In the elections of 1971, the PPP got a majority of seats in West Pakistan and

Bhutto representing Pakistan at the United Nations in December 1971 during a discussion of a cease-fire with India. (BETT-MANN/CORBIS)

none in East Pakistan. It was thus in Bhutto's interest to hasten the secession of Bangladesh, which he nevertheless publicly deplored. He then became president of Pakistan. In 1972 he signed the Simla Agreement with India, conceding that future conflicts would have to be settled bilaterally. The election of 1977, which he won, was probably rigged. The unrest that followed prompted General Zia ul-Haq to stage a military coup. He deposed and arrested Bhutto, accused him of murder, and had him executed in prison in 1979.

Dietmar Rothermund

BIDYALANKARANA

BIDYALANKARANA (1876–1945), Thai writer and publisher. Prince Bidyalankarana was a man of many talents, occupying high administrative offices, chiefly in financial affairs, while earning a reputation as one of the most accomplished writers of his day, both for his verse and his prose fiction. He was born in Bangkok, the son of Prince Wichaichan, last of the Second Kings. On completing his education at Suan Kulap School, he worked in the Ministry of Public Instruction and then in the Ministry of Finance before accompanying King Chulalongkorn on the king's first state visits to Europe. After a year studying at Cambridge in 1898, he returned to Bangkok and brought out a monthly magazine called *Lak witthaya* (Stealing Knowledge; 1901–1903), a landmark on the Thai literary landscape for bringing to Thai readers translations of Western fiction and providing Thai writers with an outlet to develop a new style of writing, albeit imitative of Western fiction. It was in the pages of *Lak witthaya* that the first translation of a Western novel, Marie Correlli's *Vendetta*, was serialized. Prince

Bidyalankarana was well known as a writer, many of his works appearing under the pen-name "N.M.S." Best known is his *Chotmai Changwang Ram* (Letters of Deputy Ram), a series of seven letters written by a father to his son, which drew its inspiration from George Horace Lorimer's *Letters from a Self-Made Merchant to His Son*. The father's letters offer advice on education, finance, career, friendship, love, marriage, and Buddhism to his son, who is at first studying in England and then returns to resettle in Thailand.

David Smyth

Further Reading
Senanan, Wibha. (1975) *The Genesis of the Novel in Thailand*. Bangkok, Thailand: Thai Wantana Panich.

BIHAR (2001 est. pop. 82.9 million). A state of the Indian Union, Bihar is bordered on the north by Nepal and by the states of West Bengal on the east, Uttar Pradesh on the west, Orissa on the south, and the new state of Jharkhand on the south and southwest. Its capital city is Patna, and the principal language spoken is Hindi. Bihar has a number of rivers flowing through it. The most important is the Ganga (Ganges); others include the Sone, Poonpoon, Falgu, Karmanasa, Durgawati, Damodar, Gandak, Ghaghara, and Kosi.

Bihar always played a significant role in India's history and witnessed the rise and fall of several empires. It finds mention in the Vedas and Puranas. It was here that Siddhartha Gautama (c. 563–c. 483 BCE; the Buddha) and Vardhamana (c. 599–527 BCE; prophet of Jainism) preached their faiths. Great kings of ancient times include Bimbisara, the founder of the Magadhan empire, Udayin who established the city of Pataliputra (modern Patna), and Candragupta Maurya and Asoka of the Maurya dynasty. Then came the Sungas, the Kanvas, and Candragupta Vikramaditya of the Gupta dynasty.

During the medieval period, Bihar was first incorporated within the Delhi sultanate and then became part of the Mughal empire. Taking advantage of the weakness of the later Mughals, the British established their foothold in Bihar with the battle of Plassey in 1757 and consolidated their position through successive battles. Bihar was a part of the Bengal presidency until 12 December 1911, when a separate state of Bihar and Orissa was formed. In 1936 Bihar was separated from Orissa, and in November 2000 Bihar was again bifurcated. The state of Jharkhand was created, consisting of the tribal-dominated districts of south Bihar.

As with most of India, Bihar is predominantly an agricultural state. The principal food grains are paddy rice, wheat, maize, and legumes, and the main cash crops are sugarcane, potatoes, tobacco, oilseeds, onions, chilies, jute, mangoes, and kenaf or *mesta*.

South Bihar was famous for its rich mineral resources, but since the bifurcation of the state in 2000, the industrial and mineral-rich zone has come within the state of Jharkhand. There are however, other important industries located in northern Bihar, including the alumina plant of the Indian Aluminium Company at Muri, the railway-wagon factory of Bharat Wagon Limited at Muzaffarpur and Mokama, and cotton-spinning mills at Siwan, Pandaul, Bhagalpur, Mokama, and Gaya. There are also sugar mills in northcentral Bihar, distilleries, tanning and leather industries in the northern part of the state, and three jute mills at Katihar and Samastipur.

Sanjukta Das Gupta

Further Reading
Das, Arvind N. (1983) *Agrarian Unrest and Socio-Economic Change in Bihar, 1900–1980*. New Delhi: Manohar.
Datta, Kalikinkar. (1967) *The Life and Thought of the People of Bihar*. Calcutta, India: Scientific Book Agency.

BIN LADEN, OSAMA (b. 1957), Islamic militant. Osama bin Laden, an Islamic militant and terrorist, was born in Riyadh, Saudi Arabia, the seventeenth son in a family of over fifty children. His father, Muhammad bin Laden (d. 1968), who came to Saudi Arabia around 1930 from South Yemen, founded the Bin Laden Corporation, one of the largest and richest construction companies in the Arab world.

Osama studied management and economics at Abdul Aziz University in Jeddah, Saudi Arabia, graduating in 1978. The continuing Arab-Israeli conflict, the Iranian Revolution of 1979, and the Soviet invasion of Afghanistan in 1979 contributed to his increasing radicalism and anti-Western views. Osama went to Afghanistan shortly after the Soviet invasion, where he associated himself with the anti-Soviet mujahideen or guerrilla fighters and helped finance their operations. He was especially angered by American involvement in the Gulf War and moved to the Sudan in 1991, where he set up several terrorist training bases.

Osama returned to Afghanistan in 1996, to establish his headquarters, al-Qaeda ("the base"), with the support of Afghanistan's ruling Taliban movement. Osama is the alleged mastermind behind numerous terrorist attacks against Western countries, including the bombings of the U.S. embassies in East Africa in 1998, as well as the attacks on the New York World Trade Center and Pentagon in Washington, D.C., on 11 September 2001. Although thought to be at large or killed in Afghanistan, his whereabouts as of mid-2002 were uncertain.

Michael Pretes

Further Reading
Bodansky, Yossef. (1999) *Bin Laden: The Man Who Declared War on America.* Rocklin, CA: Forum.
Reeve, Simon. (1999) *The New Jackals: Ramzi Yousef, Osama bin Laden, and the Future of Terrorism.* Boston: Northeastern University Press.

BIRCH, JAMES W. W. (1826–1875), First colonial administrator of Malaysia. Born in England on 3 April 1826, James Wheeler Woodford Birch was a midshipman in the Royal Navy, an administrator in Ceylon (1846–1870), and Colonial Secretary at Singapore (1870–1874). But history remembers him as a tragic figure: Within a year of being appointed the first British Resident to Perak, Birch was murdered at Pasir Salak.

According to the terms of the 1874 Pangkor Engagement, the British Residential system was introduced to the hitherto independent western peninsular Malay states of Perak, Selangor, and Sungai Ujong. In theory the British Resident served as an adviser to the Malay ruler; in practice he held executive power. Named British Resident, Birch was a meticulous, energetic, and able administrator. But he was also ignorant of Malay culture and language, impervious to Malay sensitivities, and considered the ruling elite rapacious and incompetent.

His reforms radically and adversely affected Sultan Abdullah and the Malay chiefs. In particular, his reorganization of the revenue system including new taxes and license fees, the abolishment of debt-slavery, and the codification of civil and criminal law earned Birch their fatal enmity. The task of eliminating him was entrusted to the Maharaja Lela. Following the assassination, the British swiftly apprehended the murderers and sentenced them to death. Sultan Abdullah and other chiefs guilty of complicity were banished to the Seychelles. Yusof, the only chieftain untainted by the affair, was appointed regent, and in 1876, became Sultan of Perak.

Ooi Keat Gin

Further Reading
Birch, J. W. W. (1976) *The Journals of J. W. W. Birch, First British Resident of Perak, 1874–1875.* Ed. by P. L. Burns. Kuala Lumpur, Malaysia: Oxford University Press.
Cheah Boon Kheng. (1998) "Malay Politics and the Murder of J. W. W. Birch, British Resident in Perak, in 1875: The Humiliation and Revenge of the Maharaja Lela." *Journal of the Malaysian Branch of the Royal Asiatic Society* 71, 1 (June): 75–106.
Gullick, J. M. (1992) *Rulers and Residents: Influence and Power in the Malay States, 1870–1920.* Kuala Lumpur, Malaysia: Oxford University Press.
Winstedt, R. O., and R. J. Wilkinson. (1974) *A History of Perak.* Kuala Lumpur, Malaysia: Malaysian Branch of the Royal Asiatic Society, Reprint No. 3.

BIRDS AND BIRD CAGES Raising and domesticating birds, as well as the display of birds in finely crafted cages, have played a significant role in Chinese popular culture for at least two thousand years. Today, in such heavily populated urban areas as Hong Kong, Beijing, and Shanghai, birds and bird cages provide an important opportunity for socializing and are a key component of urban China's vital early-morning park culture, particularly among the elderly.

While a visit to a typical Chinese bird market will reveal dozens of varieties of caged birds, among the most popular birds displayed in parks are the *huamei* (babbling thrush, *Garrulax canorus*), the *bailing* (lark, *Alaudidae*), and the *bage* (myna, *Acridotheres cristatellus*). The *huamei* is known for both its singing ability and its fighting ability. The many species of *bailing* are cherished for both their singing and their dancing and are known for their ability to imitate the sounds of other animals. The *bage* is most famous for its ability to imitate human speech. For all species, the price of the bird in the marketplace can fluctuate wildly. While appearance and health are the main factors determining price, the seller's eye for what the customer can or will pay is at least as important.

Most Chinese bird cages continue to be constructed from the traditional building material, bamboo. Bird collectors value bamboo not only for its beauty but also for its strength and lightness, key factors for elderly collectors who may carry several bird cages at one time on daily trips to the park. For stronger or more destructive birds, owners generally prefer metal cages. Wooden cages are generally used only for birds that are breeding. The type of bird is the main factor in determining the shape of the cage. In general, small birds such as the *furong* (lotus bird or canary bird, *Serinus canaria*) are given small, square cages, while *huamei* are given slightly larger, round cages. Other cage shapes include cylindrical, hexagonal, multilevel, and partitioned. Cage shape may also vary according to regional tastes. Cages with special functions include bathing cages, breeding cages, fighting cages, and incubating cages.

The future of raising caged birds as a recreational activity in China appears to be bright. China's economic expansion in recent years has resulted in increased leisure time for the urban working class, and the country's aging population ensures there will be a retired sector in need of hobbies for many years to come. Both these factors have contributed to an ongoing expansion of interest in raising birds.

Adam D. Frank

Further Reading

Chen, Heng. (2000) *Furongniao (jinsiniao) de siyang yu fanzhi* (Raising and Breeding the *Furong* Bird [*Jinsi* Bird]). Beijing: Jin Dun Publishers.

Dai, Guojun, et al. (2000) *Bailing*. Shanghai: Shanghai Science and Technology Publishers.

Qian, Yanwen, et al. (1995) *Zhongguo niaolei tujian* (Illustrated Handbook of Chinese Bird Species). Zhengzhou, China: Henan Science and Technology Publishers.

BIRLA FAMILY Members of the Birla family have been leading industrialists in Rajasthan state, India, for well over a century. Seth Baldevdas Birla (1860–1902), later known as Raja Birla, was a Maheshwari Marwari (trading caste) member who migrated from Calcutta in the 1890s and established his family at Pilani, in the Shekhavati region of Rajasthan. Here he continued to work as a broker and trader until his death, when his sons took over, expanding the family business into areas Indians had not previously been able to exploit. Their industries included jute mills, cotton cloth, coal, and paper. Since independence, the family has been so successful that they have been acknowledged as India's leading industrialists.

G. D. Birla (1894–1983), one of these business magnates, was also one of the sponsors of the first national press agency, the Free Press of India, established in 1927. During the 1929–1931 period, G. D. Birla was a member of the Royal Commission on Labour (also known as the Whitley Commission), which investigated all aspects of labor conditions in British India and made many recommendations In the 1931–1932 period, G. D. Birla, along with Mohandas Gandhi (1869–1948), was one of the delegates to the second session of the Round Table Conference in London. This session was to grapple with the problem of communal representation in general and Muslim representation in particular.

Paul Hockings

Further Reading

Birla, G. D. (1953) *In the Shadow of the Mahatma: A Personal Memoir*. Bombay, India: Orient Longmans.

Timberg, Thomas A. (1978) *The Marwaris: From Traders to Industrialists*. New Delhi: Vikas Publishing House.

BISHKEK (1999 pop. 780,000). Bishkek, the capital of Kyrgyzstan, was named Pishpek until 1926 and Frunze throughout most of the Soviet period. In April 1991, Bishkek acquired its present Kyrgyz name. The city is situated in the valley of the Chu River, north of the Kyrgyz Ala Tau range, at an elevation of 750 meters. Bishkek is on a railway branch connecting the Kyrgyz Republic with Kazakhstan; highway connections with other cities of the republic are complicated by the mountainous topography. There is also an international airport. The population of the city consists mainly of Kyrgyz, Russians, Uzbeks, and Ukrainians.

In the Nestorian Christian cemetery at Bishkek, the oldest tombs date to the Kara-Khitay period (twelfth century). (The Nestorian Christian church separated from the Byzantine church after 431 because of a doctrinal difference.) The khanate of Quqon (Kokand) erected a fortress at Pishpek in the early nineteenth century, which czarist Russian forces destroyed in 1862. The Russian town that arose on the spot was designated a city and district center in the Semirech'e region in 1878. Soviet power was proclaimed at Pishpek on 1 January (or 14 January by the Gregorian calendar), 1918, and the city (renamed Frunze in honor of native son and Red Army commander Mikhail Frunze [1885–1925]) became the capital of the Kirghiz Soviet Socialist Republic from its establishment in 1936.

Major industries in Bishkek include spinning, textile production, and machine building. Today Bishkek is home to government offices, several universities and institutes, the National Academy of Sciences, theaters, orchestras, museums, and parks.

D. Prior

Further Reading

Barthold, Vasilii V. ([1898] 1956) "History of the Semirechyé." In *Four Studies on the History of Central Asia*, trans. by Vladimir Minorsky and Tatiana Minorsky. Reprint ed. Leiden, Netherlands: E. J. Brill, 73–171.

Frunze: Entsiklopediia (Encyclopedia). (1984) Frunze, Kyrgyzstan: Glavnaia redaktsiia Kirgizskoi Sovetskoi Entsiklopedii.

Prior, D. (1994) *Bishkek Handbook: Inside and Out.* Bishkek, Kyrgyzstan: Literary Kyrgyzstan/Far Flung Press.

BITAB, SUFI

BITAB, SUFI (1892–1958), Afghan poet and mystic. Sufi Abdul Bitab, a poet laureate of Afghanistan, also became the leading proponent of mystical thought in his capacity as the master of the Naqshbandi Sufi order. He was born in Kabul and received his initial education from his uncle, Mullah Abdul Ghafur, a prominent Islamic jurist and cleric. For a time, Bitab taught at Kabul's Habibia School and at Kabul University.

His poems are suffused with the Sufi governing principle of love for God and the soul's desire to know and unite with the Divine. Despite the strong mystical tone to his poems, they nevertheless clothe this mysticism in a readily accessible vocabulary of love, desire, and yearning for union. His poems do not show the typical divergence of Sufi thought from orthodox Islam. This is in part due to his training by his devout uncle, and more important to his leadership of the Naqshbandis, who are known for their strict adherence to Sunni Islam. Aside from being a well-known poet, he was also a respected religious scholar and wrote many commentaries on the hadith (a compilation of Islamic traditions). Bitab was made the poet laureate of Afghanistan in 1951. He resided in Kabul all his life and died there.

Nirmal Dass

Further Reading
Dupree, Louis. (1973) *Afghanistan.* Princeton, NJ: Princeton University Press.

Shah, Ikbal Ali, Sirdar. (1982) *Afghanistan of the Afghans.* London: Octagon Press.

BIWA

BIWA The *biwa* is a Japanese plucked lute, usually with a bent neck, four or five strings, and from four to six frets. It is pear-shaped, with a shallow wooden body, three sound holes, and twisted silk strings wound on lateral pegs; it is played with a *bachi* (plectrum). A descendant of the Chinese *pipa*, the *biwa* entered Japan in the late seventh century. *Gakubiwa* denotes the larger type used for *gagaku* (ensemble court music) and solo styles, often mentioned in literary sources. A second category, *mosobiwa* (blind monk's lute), was connected with Tendai Buddhist sutra recitation in Kyushu. *Heikebiwa* arose in the late twelfth century to accompany *heikyoku*, the narration of *The Tale of the Heike* by blind itinerant lay priests known as *biwa hoshi*.

Biwa interludes punctuating sung text were thought to pacify the spirits of dead warriors. *Heikebiwa* guilds influenced *shamisen* styles as well. The *mosobiwa* was the ancestor of more modern instruments and performance styles, such as the *satsumabiwa*; Shimazu Tadayoshi (1492–1568) wrote songs for the *satsumabiwa* to encourage samurai values. Brought to Tokyo in the Meiji period (1868–1912), the orthodox *(seiha) satsumabiwa* school and two offshoots, *kinshinbiwa* and *nishikibiwa*, were extremely popular, especially until the Pacific war's end. Percussive effects, vibrato, and glissandi techniques distinguish *satsumabiwa* styles. A child of the *mosobiwa* of northern Kyushu, *chikuzenbiwa*, begun by Tachibana Kyokuo (1848–1919), appealed to women players with its smaller instrument and style that was suited to lyrical preoccupations. Tsuruta Kinshi (1911–1995) and Takemitsu Toru (1930–1996) brought new attention to the modified *satsumabiwa* with modern compositions.

Linda H. Chance

Further Reading
De Ferranti, Hugh. (2001) "Biwa." In *New Grove Dictionary of Music and Musicians.* Vol. 12. London: Macmillan, 820–824.

———. (1991) "Composition and Improvisation in Satsuma biwa." In *Musica Asiatica.* Vol. 6, edited by Allan Marett. New York: Cambridge University Press, 102–127.

Guignard, Silvain. (1989) "A Japanese Musical Heritage in the Halfshade: The Biwa and Its Narrative Style." *Transactions of the Asiatic Society of Japan* 4: 37–48.

Matisoff, Susan. (1978) *The Legend of Semimaru, Blind Musician of Japan.* New York: Columbia University Press.

Mayeda Akio. (1979) "The Musical Structure of *Heikyoku.*" In *European Studies on Japan*, edited by Charles Dunn and Ian Nish. Tenterden, Kent, U.K.: Paul Norbury Publications, 220–229.

BLACK SEA

BLACK SEA An inland sea located between Southeast Europe and Western Asia, bordering Russia, Ukraine, Romania, Bulgaria, Turkey, and Georgia, the Black Sea is about 4.2 million square kilometers in area. Its average depth is 1,300 meters, reaching 2,245 meters in the central area. The Black Sea is connected with the Mediterranean Sea via the Bosporus, Sea of Marmara, and Dardanelles; the Kerch Strait links it with the Sea of Azov. The rivers that empty into the Black Sea, including the Danube, Dniester, and Dnieper, dump into it 310 square kilometers of fresh water and a sediment load with a considerable amount of pollutants. No marine life exists below 200 meters in the sea, due to a high concentration of hydrogen sulfite.

The total length of the coastline is 3,400 kilometers, with the Crimea being the only peninsula. The Caucasian and Pontic Mountains face the Black Sea in the east and south. The Danube forms an impressive delta on the west.

In summer, the weather is hot and dry, with average July temperatures of 22–24°C, sometimes reaching 30–35°C. Winters are cold, often with rain, snowfall, and severe storms resulting from the intrusion of Arctic air masses. The average January temperatures of 3–8°C may drop to minus 20–30°C in exceptionally cold winters.

The area around the Black Sea was a cradle of various civilizations, including Greece, Rome, Byzantium, Turkey, and Russia. Today, ports and naval bases dot its shores, such as Odessa in the Ukraine, Novorossiysk in Russia, Varna in Bulgaria, and Batumi in Georgia.

Pollution is a major concern of the nations surrounding the Black Sea, who have initiated several cooperative projects aimed at environmental protection. In 1989, eleven countries—Albania, Armenia, Azerbaijan, Bulgaria, Georgia, Greece, Moldova, Romania, Russia, Turkey, and Ukraine—signed the Black Sea Economic Cooperation Pact with a goal of promoting greater democracy, peace, and development in the Black Sea region.

Pavel Dolukhanov

Further Reading

Aybak, Tunc, ed. (2001) *Politics of the Black Sea: Dynamics of Cooperation and Conflict.* London and New York: I. B. Tauris.

Mamaev V. O., D. G. Aubrey, and V. N. Eremeev, eds. (1995) *Bibliography 1974–1994: Black Sea.* Environmental Series N 1. New York: United Nations Publications.

Mavrodiev, Strachimir Chterev. (1999) *Applied Ecology of the Black Sea.* Commack, NY: Nova Science.

BLAVATSKY, HELENA PETROVNA (1831–1891), founder of theosophy.

The granddaughter of a Russian princess, the woman known to the world as Madame Blavatsky was born Helena Petrovna Hahn in Ekaterinoslav (now Dnipropetrovs'k) in the Caucasus. At age fifteen she began to study alchemy. To escape continual family problems, she immersed herself in the occult. At age eighteen she married Nikifor Blavatsky, vice governor in Armenia. Within months she left him and escaped to Istanbul. From there she went to Cairo as a snake charmer, then on to London, Paris, and New York. Inspired by the teachings of a

Helena Petrovna Blavatsky in the 1880s. (BETTMANN/CORBIS)

nonmaterial "master," she developed an understanding of spiritualism.

In 1874 Blavatsky founded the Theosophical Society in association with Colonel Henry Olcott. Leaving New York in 1878, she settled in Madras (now Chennai), India, and established the society's headquarters in Adyar. Membership in the society grew, especially through Blavatsky's successful courting of rich Hindus interested in spiritualism. In 1884 she returned to Europe, where she slowly wrote *The Secret Doctrine* (1888), which influenced W. B. Yeats, George William Russell ("AE"), and Mohandas (Mahatma) Gandhi. Blavatsky returned to London in 1887 and spent her final years there. At her death, the Theosophical Society had close to 100,000 members, including many thousands of Westernized Indians attracted by her promises of a scientific demonstration of spiritual phenomena. Eventually, though, her promises proved empty, as her demonstrations were based more on chicanery than on science.

Paul Hockings

Further Reading

Meade, Marion. (1980) *Madame Blavatsky, The Woman behind the Myth*. New York: G. P. Putnam's Sons.

BOARD GAMES   The oldest board game in Asia, pachisi, is a race game to move pieces from start to goal on the board. Pachisi in ancient India had ninety-six spaces on a cruciform board. Four people play with four pieces, which are moved from outside to inside. The first player who takes all his pieces from start to goal wins. Pachisi and its transformation, *ludo*, spread rapidly to Southeast Asia, the Middle East, Africa, and Europe. In the third century BCE, a combat board game named *shaturanga* (four persons) was invented in India. Four people battled with eight pieces (four pawns, a chariot, a horse, an elephant, and a king). *Shaturanga* is the ancestor of Western chess and Eastern *shogi* (*xiang-chi* in China).

The most popular board games in East Asia are go (*wei ch'i* in China; *baduk* in Korea) and *shogi*. They are played by millions of people in Asia today, especially in China and Japan. Go was invented in China by the sixth century BCE. In the game, two players alternately put black and white stones on the board to surround an area. A stone must be placed on the intersection of the vertical and horizontal lines. There are nineteen horizontal and nineteen vertical lines on the board that forms a grid of 361 points. Whoever has more territory at the end of the game becomes the winner. The oldest Chinese reference (sixth century BCE) said that go was a most elegant game because it was intellectual. Go was introduced into Japan from China or Korea and was spread among priests and aristocrats in Japan.

Shogi is a kind of chess developed from *shaturanga* in India, which was brought to Japan in the eleventh century. In *shogi*, there are nine horizontal and nine vertical lines on the board. *Shogi* is similar to Western chess in that it is played by two players and its object is to checkmate the opponent's king. Checkmate is achieved when the king cannot escape. A game also comes to an end if a player must resign because the king's position is hopeless. In many ways, however, *shogi* is different from chess. The major differences are that the captured pieces may be reused by the capturing player and that each piece becomes stronger when it enters the portion of the board marked as the opponent's area by three horizontal lines. Most *shogi* players feel that this makes *shogi* more profound and interesting than Western chess.

Hisashi Sanada

Further Reading

Kishino Yuzo, Yoshio Kuroda, Yuichi Suzuki, and Takeo Fukugawa, eds. (1987) *Encyclopedia of Sports*. Tokyo: Taishukan.

Obayashi Taryo, Yuzo Kishino, Tsuneo Sogawa, and Shinji Yamashita, eds. (1998) *Encyclopedia of Ethnic Play and Games*. Tokyo: Taishukan.

BOAT PEOPLE   Among the many human tragedies of the conflict in Vietnam was the remarkable odyssey of the Vietnamese "boat people." Throughout the early months of 1975 there was mounting anxiety in South Vietnam over the possible collapse of the government. In anticipation of that event, thousands of South Vietnamese began preparing to flee the country. Motivated by the expected political chaos and fears of persecution, some fled overland to Cambodia, although the majority sought to escape by sea. Thousands of people bought passage on small, rickety, and often unseaworthy wooden boats to flee across the Gulf of Thailand or the South China Sea, giving rise to the term "boat people." More than a million Vietnamese and Hoa (Chinese-Vietnamese) fled their country by boat over the next two decades.

The boat people faced significant challenges right from the start. The typhoon season in Southeast Asia makes travel by sea very dangerous; Thai pirates were a constant threat; gathering supplies was difficult, and most were left with little or no money after paying money for boat passage and bribes to allow them to leave. Many of the boat people initially found asylum in camps in the Philippines, Thailand, Malaysia, and Indonesia. Some even reached Japan and South Korea. The first waves of boat people in 1975 headed for southern Thailand, the nearest landfall. As attacks by Thai pirates increased, their destination shifted to Malaysia, despite the additional mileage and longer time at sea. As conditions in Vietnam worsened in 1976, their numbers rose dramatically, reaching a high of over 21,000 in November alone, a figure larger than the entire total of 15,690 for 1977. When tension between Vietnam and China intensified a year later, ethnic Chinese became a majority of the boat people. During the first seven months of 1979, most of the 66,000 who had reached Hong Kong were ethnic Chinese.

According to the United Nations High Commissioner for Refugees (UNHCR), a total of 214,555 refugees had escaped to Hong Kong after 1975, 160,000 had reached Thailand, 51,722 had arrived in the Philippines, 121,708 in Indonesia, 254,495 in Malaysia, and 1,400 had been granted temporary refuge in South Korea. Many of the boat people who survived these perilous journeys were granted asylum in various Western countries, although a smaller number repatriated to Vietnam. In recent years small numbers of boat people have continued to flee Vietnam. In May of 1999 the last remaining Vietnamese refugee camp at Pillar Point in Hong Kong was formally closed by the government, bringing to an end the long odyssey of the Vietnamese boat people.

James Allan Hafner

Further Reading
Borton, Lady. (1991) *Boat People and Vietnamese Refugees in the United States.* Pittsburgh, PA: Center for Social Studies Education.
Cargill, Mary Terrell, ed. (2000) *Voices of Vietnamese Boat People: Nineteen Narratives of Escape and Survival.* Jefferson, NC: McFarland & Company.
United Nations High Commissioner for Refugees. (Various years) *Refugee Reports.* Geneva, Switzerland: United Nations High Commissioner for Refugees.

BODH GAYA (2001 est. pop. 31,000). A small town in central Bihar state, northeastern India, west of the Phalgu River, Bodh Gaya (also spelled Buddh Gaya) is one of the holiest Buddhist sites. Here, under the *bodhi (bo)* tree, Prince Siddhartha Gautama (c. 566–486 BCE) attained enlightenment after years of penance and became the Buddha. A sapling from the original tree was carried to Anuradhapura in Sri Lanka; that tree flourishes there, and a cutting from it was returned to Bodh Gaya when the original tree died. Adjacent to this descendent tree is the Mahabodhi Temple, a place of pilgrimage for all Buddhists, also sacred to Hindus, who see the Buddha as an incarnation of Vishnu. It is on the site of a temple erected by Asoka in the third century BCE; the current temple (restored in the eleventh century and again in 1882) houses a large gilded image of Buddha.

Bodh Gaya also includes the Shankaracharya Math (a Hindu temple), a Japanese temple, and Burmese, Chinese, Sri Lankan, Bhutanese, Vietnamese, Nepalese, Korean, Taiwanese, and Bangladeshi monasteries. A twenty-five-meter Great Buddha statue in the Japanese Kamakura style was unveiled by the Dalai Lama in 1989. Various monasteries and institutes offer Hinayana and Mahayana meditation courses and retreats.

C. Roger Davis

See also: **Siddhartha Gautama**

Further Reading
Banerjee, Naresh. (1994) *Glimpses of Gaya and Bodh Gaya.* Bodh Gaya, India: Melwani Peace Foundation.

BODRUM (2000 pop. 35,000). In the early twentieth century, Bodrum was a remote fishing village on the Aegean Sea coast in Turkey, but today it is a sophisticated and free-spirited holiday resort. In ancient

The Bodrum harbor on the Aegean Sea. (NIK WHEELER/CORBIS)

times, Bodrum was known as Halicarnassus, a city in the kingdom of Caria and the site of the tomb of the Persian satrap Mausolus. Built around 350 BCE, this monument, which inspired the word "mausoleum," became one of the wonders of the ancient world.

Herodotus, the father of history, was born in Halicarnassus around 484 BCE. He traveled extensively around the known world, even visiting Egypt, before settling in mainland Greece and then Italy, where he died. As well as providing a view of the lands he visited, Herodotus's writings show his methods of gathering and evaluating historical information.

Dominating modern Bodrum is the Castle of Saint Peter, dating from the early fifteenth century CE. It was both a hospice and a sanctuary for the monastic order of the Knights of Saint John, a Christian order of warrior-monks who lived in Bodrum until 1522. Following Turkish independence in 1923, the castle became a prison for over two hundred exiled apolitical Turkish nationals. Today, the castle is a museum, featuring underwater treasures rescued by the Institute of Nautical Archaeology.

Bodrum's latter-day popularity stems from the enthusiastic writings of a legendary intellectual, the so-called Fisherman of Halicarnassus, who was exiled here in 1925. Modern Bodrum is known for sponges, citrus fruits, and boat building. It also draws celebrity vacationers and wealthy part-time residents, including Ahmet Ertegun, the founding partner of Atlantic Records.

Suzanne Swan

Further Reading
Bean, George E. (1971) *Turkey Beyond the Meander*. London: John Murray.

BOGDO KHAN
Bogdo Khan, along with Bogdo Gegeen, is a title for the Living Buddha. Those designated with this title are the "holy enlightened ones," who were high-ranking religious personages considered to be incarnations of the great Mongolian Buddhist scholar and savant Javzandamba (Jebtsumdamba) Hutughtu Zanabazar (1635–1723). They became leaders of Mongolian lamaism (the Mongolian version of the Tantric Buddhism practiced in Tibet) from the seventeenth to the early twentieth centuries.

The eighth and last Bogdo Khan, Agvaanluvsanchoyjindanzanvaanchigbalsambuu (1896–1924), was born into the family of a clerk of the Dalai Lama in Lhasa, Tibet, and taken to Mongolia at four years of age. In 1911, Mongolia proclaimed its independence from Manchu China and created a Tibetan theocracy with the installation of the Bogdo Khan as head of state, a title he retained even after the Communist revolution in 1921. The eighth Bogdo Khan had a mixed reputation during his lifetime because he married and was known to be a sexual profligate and drunkard. After his death, the Communist government disallowed any new incarnations. Since the end of Communism in 1990, the last Bogdo Khan's reputation has been somewhat rehabilitated, but the matter of a new incarnation remains unresolved.

Alicia J. Campi

Further Reading
Bawden, C. R. (1961) *The Jebtsun Damba Khutukhtus of Urga*. Wiesbaden, Germany: O. Harrassowitz.
(2000) *Emperors, Kings, and Heads of State of Mongolia*. Ulaanbaatar, Mongolia: Narantuul Trade Co., Ltd.
Sanders, Alan J. K. (1996) *Historical Dictionary of Mongolia*. Lanham, MD, and London: Scarecrow Press.

BOGOR DECLARATION
The Bogor Declaration was a free-trade manifesto issued by the multinational Asia-Pacific Economic Conference (APEC), which held its annual meeting in Bogor, Indonesia, in 1994. APEC came into being in 1989 with the goal of promoting liberalized trade among various Pacific-area countries. Its member states include some of the world's most robust and rapidly expanding economies, among them the United States and Japan.

Various heads of state attended the Bogor Conference, including Bill Clinton, the U.S. president from 1993 to 2001. Indonesia's President Suharto hosted it. Suharto's human rights record was open to question (he was overthrown a few years later) and some observers felt that the presence of Clinton, and other heads of state, constituted a tacit endorsement of the Indonesian ruler.

The chief result of the conference was an eight-page "Declaration of Common Resolve," which committed APEC's membership to move to "free and open trade and investment" by the year 2010 for industrialized members and by 2020 for developing economies. The members further set as a goal the liberalization of trade with non-APEC countries. The general nature of these commitments and the extended period allowed for their accomplishment caused some to question whether anything substantial was accomplished beyond politically attractive rhetoric.

Robert K. Whalen

Further Reading

Nelan, Bruce W. (1994) "Business First, Freedom Second: Clinton's Indonesia Trip." *Time* (21 November): 78–80.

Post, Tom. (1994) "Traveling Salesman: Clinton Attends APEC in Indonesia." *Newsweek* (21 November) 58–59.

BOKEIKHANOV, ALIKHAN (1866–1937), Kazakh scientist, writer, political activist. Born in 1866 in the province of Karkaralinsk Uezd, Alikhan Bokeikhanov was enrolled in the Muslim school (*madrasa*) in Karkaralinsk, but soon he moved on to the local Russian-Kazakh school, graduating in 1886. Shortly thereafter he enrolled in the elite Omsk Technical School. He graduated in 1890 and enrolled to study in St. Petersburg at the Imperial Forestry Institute. In 1894, he returned to Omsk, where he lived and worked for the next fourteen years. In 1896, he was selected to participate in the so-called Shcherbina Expedition, which was organized by the czarist government not only to assess the natural environment of the steppe region, including land and water resources, but also to research the culture, economy, society, and way of life of the indigenous population. Subsequently, he accepted a position with another government-sponsored mission charged with collecting economic and demographic data in regions that paralleled the Trans-Siberian Railroad from Cheliabinsk to Tomsk in the northern steppe territory. Bokeikhanov's contribution, "Ovtsevodstvo v stepnom krae" (Sheep-Breeding in the Steppe Land), was a thorough analysis of the state of animal husbandry, particularly sheep and goats, in three steppe oblasts (Semipalatinsk, Akmolinsk, and Turgai). During the revolutionary upheaval of 1905, Bokeikhanov became a leading member of a group of Kazakh intellectuals who gravitated politically toward the Constitutional Democrats (Kadets). In 1906, he was elected to the first Russian Duma (Parliament) and after its dissolution by the czar, he fled with other delegates to Vyborg, Finland, to protest the czar's action. In 1910, Bokeikhanov published his major political commentary and best-known work, "Kirgizy" (The Kazakhs), in the Kadet volume on nationalities edited by A. I. Kostelianskii. In 1913, he helped establish the Kazakh-language newspaper *Kazak*, and he published numerous articles there during the next several years. In 1917, he was elected president of the Kazakh political party Alash Orda (The Horde of Alash), which fought unsuccessfully for Kazakh independence from Soviet Russia. In 1920, he joined the Bolshevik party and throughout the 1920s he continued his scientific work. He always remained, however, under a cloud of political suspicion. He was arrested in 1926, in 1928, and again in 1930. He was banished to Moscow where he continued to work, al-beit under closely monitored circumstances. In 1937, he was arrested a final time and executed on 27 November of that year. He was rehabilitated (his reputation was favorably restored) in 1989.

Steven Sabol

Further Reading

Bokeikhanov, Alikhan. (1994) *Shygharmalar* (Collected Works). Almaty, Kazakhstan: Qazaqstan.

———. (1995) *Tangdamaly* (Selected Works). Almaty, Kazakhstan: Qazaq Entsiklopediiasy.

BOKEO (2002 est. pop. 141,000). Bokeo province is located in northern Laos near the intersection of the borders of Thailand, Laos, and Myanmar—commonly known as the "Golden Triangle." It is the smallest province in the nation, and contains 36 towns and more than 400 villages within its provincial borders. The inhabitants of this region represent about thirty-four ethnic groups, making it one of the most ethnically diverse populations in the nation. The makeup of the province changed in 1992 when the districts of Paktha and Pha Oudom were moved to the jurisdiction of Bokeo province.

The city of Huay Xai, which is on the border with Thailand along the Mekong River, is the most populous city in the province. It has been termed "woolly" because it is a boisterous frontier city with a troubled history. It is known for opium trafficking and was a staging point for U.S. troops during that nation's involvement in civil wars in the region starting in the early 1960s.

Linda Dailey Paulson

Further Reading

Gibney, Frank, Jr. (1996) "Muang Xing, Laos: Journey up the Mekong." *Time International* (20 May): 63.

BOLAN PASS Bolan Pass is one of the seven great passes near the western border of Pakistan that have historically linked that land with Afghanistan and Central Asia in conquest and commerce. Being the southernmost pass, it lies in Baluchistan, about 40 kilometers southeast of the city of Quetta, on the great military route leading from the plains of the Indus Valley to the highlands of Sarawan and the Afghan city of Kandahar. At its eastern end the pass commences about 8 kilometers west of Dadur. At this point the elevation is only about 265 meters, whereas at the western outlet it is 2,790 meters. The total length of the pass is 96 kilometers. As one walks westward, the road rises steadily at a rate of about 18 meters every kilometer. The hills on either side of the pass do not seem very high and are mostly less than 125 meters above the road, but they are quite lofty at Bibi-nani, some 42 kilometers from the eastern entrance. At Sir-i-Bolan the passage was so narrow that three horses abreast could hardly pass by the limestone cliffs. At the western end, the pass does not descend again but rather opens out onto the Dasht-i-Bidaulat, a high plain that leads on to Quetta and Khorasan.

Until 1877, when British forces secured the pass, it was subject to brigandage perpetrated by the Marri Baluch. In 1888 the Khan of Kalat ceded control to the British. At the end of the nineteenth century a railroad was built through the pass from Sibi to Quetta and on to the Afghan border at Chaman, as part of British military strategy. The local people are both Brahui (who speak a Dravidian language) and Baluch.

Paul Hockings

Further Reading
Barthorp, Michael. (1982) *The North-West Frontier: British India and Afghanistan, a Pictorial History 1839–1947.* Poole, U.K.: New Orchard Press.

BOLLYWOOD. See **Cinema—India.**

BOLOVENS PLATEAU Located in southern Laos, the Bolovens Plateau is a fertile plain that has historically served as a strategic site in civil and regional warfare. It is located between the Mekong River and the Annamese Cordillera foothills. The basaltic plateau sits at an elevation of 1,100 meters, with its highest peak rising 1,583 meters above sea level. It also gets the heaviest rainfall in the nation—in excess of 406 centimeters annually. This geology and topography contribute to its fertility.

Paksan is the largest city on the plateau, with an estimated population of 25,000. Several ethnic groups reside in the area including the Loven, Nha Huen Sovei, and Sou of the Lao-Theung or Mon-Khmer.

The Bolovens Plateau was a key strategic point in the Indochinese War. The so-called Ho Chi Minh Trail, a conduit for supplies to the North Vietnamese Army, ran from Laos through the area to South Vietnam. The United States Central Intelligence Agency recruited, trained, advised, and paid indigenous personnel in Southern Laos in the late 1960s and early

1970s to combat the North Vietnamese Army. Fighting was reportedly most heavy in 1971 as opposing forces struggled to control the Bolovens Plateau. Many area residents continue to suffer from remaining unexploded ordnance left from the war.

Although much of the plateau remains undeveloped at the turn of the twenty-first century, this is changing. Mining of pagodite, a stone commonly used for carving, is one of the area's industries. Agricultural products—predominantly spices, such as cardamom, and durians—are also important.

The government takes most pride in the regional coffee, which is the nation's primary agricultural export. Of the 4,800 tons of coffee produced in Laos annually, most is grown on the Bolovens Plateau. According to the government of the Lao People's Democratic Republic, "Lao coffee is slowly making a name for itself on the international market as people begin to find out about it and discover that its quality ranks in the front line with Colombian and Brazilian coffees. Lao coffee from the Bolovens Plateau, also called Paksong coffee, has long been famous within Laos for its delicious and strong taste and now that the international community has begun to experience its qualities the future looks fairly bright for this brew."

Land in coffee production has reportedly doubled since 1993; in some instances, coffee has replaced subsistence crops, according to the Centre de coopération internationale en recherché agronomique pour le développement (CIRAD), which is among the international agencies assisting the Laotian Ministry of Agriculture. Issues related to making agricultural improvements in the area have included eliminating monocropping on the Bolovens Plateau and efforts to boost coffee quality.

Linda Dailey Paulson

Further Reading
Kremmer, Christopher. (1998) *Stalking the Elephant Kings: In Search of Laos.* Honolulu, HI: University of Hawaii Press.
Kreutz, Serge. (2001) "Laos/Pakse/The Boloven [*sic*] Plateau." Retrieved 14 January 2002, from: http://www.asiatour.com/laos/e-06paks/el-pak21.htm.
Leary, William M. (1999–2000) "Supporting the 'Secret War': CIA Air Operations in Laos, 1955–1974." *Studies in Intelligence* (Winter). Retrieved 14 January 2002, from: http://www.odci.gov/csi/studies/winter99-00/art7.html.
Penington, Matthew. (1999) "Action Against Hidden Killers Helps Laos." United Nations Development Program, *Choices* (December). Retrieved 14 January 2002, from: http://www.undp.org/dpa/choices/december99/laos.htm.

"THE DANCE OF THE GINGER"

This is a traditional song sung at the Bon festival. Even in the 1930s, it was fading from use and was remembered only by the elderly.

1. In the ginger dance

Beat with the feet, beat with the hands;

If the feet are not in rhythm,

One cannot dance.

2. Shonga old lady

Likes *mezian* cakes

Last night nine, this morning seven (ate she).

Last night's nine

Indigestion did not give.

This morning's seven indigestion gave.

3. In the middle of the ginger field (we made love)

He promised to give me the slipper; I've been fooled.

Now he doesn't even mention the slipper.

Source: John F. Embree. (1979/1939) *Suye Mura: A Japanese Village*. Chicago, IL: The University of Chicago Press, 286.

BON MATSURI Bon Matsuri (Bon Festival), commonly called by its honorific, Obon, is the ancient Buddhist Festival of the Dead, held throughout Japan on 13 to 16 July or August (depending on the region). Solemn rites and observances mark this period when, according to Buddhist belief, the souls of the ancestors are welcomed back to this world for a brief visit. Memorial services are performed, offerings of food, incense, and flowers are made, and graves are visited and cleaned. These actions comfort the souls of the ancestors and thus gain merit for the living.

As the festival approaches, many people travel to their hometown to visit family graves and summon the ancestral spirits. Fires and lanterns are lit in cemeteries and at the entrances to homes to welcome and guide the ancestral spirits, and a sacred branch is erected as a channel to this world. Folk dances (*bon odori*) are performed to distinctive tunes in order to entertain the visiting spirits.

Finally, sending-off fires (*okuribi*) are lit to bid farewell and to guide the spirits safely back to the realms of the dead. Alternatively, lanterns may be floated downstream, carrying the spirits out to sea and back to the shores of the afterworld.

Lucy D. Moss

See also: **Ancestor Worship—East Asia; Buddhism—Japan**

Further Reading
Haga, Hideo (1970) *Japanese Folk Festivals.* Trans. by Hanny Mayer. Tokyo: Miura Printing Company.
Krasno, Rena (2000) *Floating Lanterns and Golden Shrines: Celebrating Japanese Festivals.* Berkeley, CA: Pacific View Press.

BONSAI Bonsai, written in Japanese with two characters meaning "pot" and "to plant," refers to the art of growing miniature plants in containers. Generally bonsai range from five centimeters to one meter in height. Certain techniques, such as pruning, training, and modifying the growing environment, keep the plants small. Some bonsai live longer than fifty years and are cared for by multiple generations.

Bonsai originated in China over one thousand years ago. Japanese envoys returning from China during the Chinese Tang dynasty (618–907 CE) introduced bonsai into Japan. Descriptions of bonsai appear in records from the Japanese Heian period (794–1185), and the art of creating them matured along with the rise of Zen in the fifteenth century. During this time, bonsai appear to have been limited to the world of aristocrats, political figures, scholars, and Buddhist monks, but in the Edo period (1600/1603–1868) bonsai became widespread as a recreation among common people. This trend continued in the late nineteenth and twentieth centuries. Bonsai were first introduced into the West in London in 1902, and subsequently professional bonsai artists have exhibited around the world. Bonsai is practiced as a hobby worldwide, and numerous international bonsai clubs and societies exist.

In Japan, evergreens are the most popular plant for bonsai, though other plants, such as bamboo and plums, are also used. In creating a bonsai, the artist or hobbyist usually tries to re-create miniature versions of the natural, untamed world. But the bonsai might also reflect personal interests, for instance, re-creating the settings of famous plays.

Over thirty recognizable styles of bonsai exist, with the following are the most common. The formal upright style (chokkan) allows a straight plant to grow vertically. The informal upright style (moyogi), in which a plant is encouraged to follow its natural kinks or twists, is popular. In the cascading style (kengai), a plant hangs over the edge of its container, often trailing to the ground like a waterfall. In the windswept style (fukinagashi), the tree trunk and branches are swept to one side

A man prunes a pine tree bonsai to shape at the Saburo Kato nursery in Omiya, Japan. (MICHAEL S. YAMASHITA/CORBIS)

to imitate the shape of a tree buffeted by the wind. In the rock-planting style (ishitsuki), the tree grows from a crack in a rock. The twisting-trunk style (bankan) makes use of a gnarled trunk. In the literati style (bunjin), which imitates the landscape paintings created by literati artists, the trunk grows in an unconventional shape. Bonsai is still widely practiced, not only in Japan but also in many different countries today.

Miyuki Katahira

Further Reading
"Bonsai Daijiten." (1983) *Encyclopedia of Bonsai.* Kyoto, Japan: Dohosha Shuppan.
Chan, Peter. (1985) *Bonsai: The Art of Growing and Keeping Miniature Trees.* London: Tiger Books International.
———. (1987) *Bonsai: Masterclass.* New York: Sterling Publishing.
Stein, Rolf Alfred. (1990) *The World in Miniature: Container Gardens and Dwellings in Far Eastern Religious Thought.* Trans. by Phyllis Brooks. Stanford, CA: Stanford University Press.

BORNEO Borneo is the third largest island in the world after Greenland and New Guinea. Politically, it consists of Kalimantan (the Indonesian portion of the island), Sarawak and Sabah (East Malaysia), and the oil-rich, independent sultanate of Brunei. Well noted for its rich biodiversity, it is a unique place to study natural tropical ecosystems.

Mountain ranges run through the center of the island from north to south. Few peaks exceed 2,000 meters and the highest peak is Mt. Kinabalu (4,101 meters) in Sabah. More than half of the island is under 150 meters in elevation, and tidal water can go up to 100 kilometers inland. Many rivers radiate from the central uplands, the three largest being the Kapuas (1,143 kilometers) flowing to the west, the Barito (900 kilometers) to the south, and the Mahakam (775 kilometers) to the east. They provide an important means of travel as much of the lowland plain, especially in the south, is poorly drained and swampy. Despite the luxuriant vegetation, soils are generally of very poor quality and have high levels of weathering, leaching, and biological activity. The island has a moist, tropical climate. Temperatures are relatively constant throughout the year, 25°C in the lowlands. Rainfall occurs throughout the year, with few months of less than 200 millimeters of rainfall.

Borneo has some of most species-rich habitats on earth. It has an estimated ten to fifteen thousand species of flowering plants, at least three thousand species of trees (including 267 species of dipterocarps,

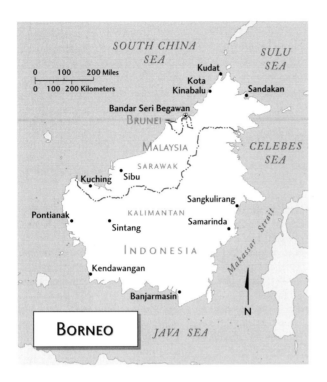

Transformation in Borneo and the Eastern Malay Peninsula. Tokyo: United Nations University Press.

MacKinnon, Kathy, Gusti Hatta, Hakimah Halim, and Arthur Mangalik. (1996) *The Ecology of Kalimantan.* Hong Kong: Periplus Editions.

BORNEO PEOPLES The island of Borneo, the world's third largest, falls under the administration of three modern nations, namely Brunei, Indonesia, and Malaysia. Territories under Malaysia are divided into Sabah and Sarawak, whereas those under Indonesia are known as Kalimantan. Borneo is home for many indigenous groups. Demographically the island is encircled by a ring of Muslim settlements of the Banjarese, Malay, Bugis, Melanau, Bajau, and other smaller language groupings. In almost all major settlements and towns the Chinese can be found as traders, service providers, and businesspeople. The Dayak, Dusun, and Penan and their respective language groupings or ethnic subdivisions predominate in the interior and along the major riverbanks.

The total population of Borneo is estimated around 12.6 million. The Dayak, Dusun, Iban, and Penan and their subgroupings total some 3.2 million or 25 percent of the total population of Borneo. The Land Dayak (Bidayuh), Iban, and Penan and their respective language groupings total around 44 percent of the total population in Sarawak. In central and west Kalimantan, the Dayak form a significant segment of the population. The Dusun in Sabah form some 30 percent of the total population in the state.

The Dusun or Kadazan and their language groupings are found largely near the coastal areas of north Borneo from Kudat to Beaufort and in the interior centering on Tambunan. They traditionally live in longhouses, each accommodating between 150 and 200 inhabitants in two rows of rooms. They form the largest language grouping in Sabah, apart from the Bajau, Malay, Murut, and Chinese. A sizable proportion of the Brunei population also consists of the Dusun, who generally live in the upper parts of the Tutong and Belait rivers.

The Dusun are traditionally known as dry-rice growers. In post-independence Malaysia, the Dusun, like many others, have enjoyed social and political ascendancy. Not only do they hold a national festival of Ka'amatan during the rice harvest season, but they also join diverse modern occupations in the public and private sectors. Most Dusun continue to maintain their traditional way of life and belief system. Several influential chief ministers of Sabah, such as Donald Stephen and Joseph Pairin Kitingan, came from among the Dusun.

the most important group of commercial timber trees in Southeast Asia), two thousand species of orchids, and one thousand species of ferns. It is home to the remarkable carnivorous pitcher plant, occurring in twenty-eight species of the genus *Nepenthes.* Its rich fauna is Asian in origin and characterized by deer, wild cattle, pigs, cats, monkeys, apes (the orangutan being best known), squirrels, and oriental birds.

The island is sparsely populated by 12.5 million people (1990) confined mainly to the coast. But they have far-reaching impacts on the environment, especially in the past twenty years in exploiting the tropical forests, oil and gas resources, and other mineral wealth. Rapid deforestation results from logging, clearing for agriculture, and human settlement schemes. For example, Sabah began exporting timber in early 1960s and by the 1990s all major lowland forests had been logged. Traditional slash-and-burn agriculture is still carried out in Borneo.

There is a strong need for Borneo's development to be planned in a rational way for sustainable use. Its diverse tropical habitats and rich biodiversity are important reservoirs of genetic material for humankind.

Wong Poh Poh

Further Reading
Brookfield, Harold, Lesley Potter, and Yvonne Byron. (1995) *In Place of the Forest: Environmental and Socio-Economic*

A wooden scuplture decorates a Dayak house in Kalimantan, Borneo, Indonesia, c. 1991. (CHARLES & JOSETTE LENARS/CORBIS)

The term "Dayak" in Borneo generally refers to inland or upriver inhabitants. In Kalimantan, the Dayak, known in earlier writings on Borneo as "headhunters," include the major groupings such as the Maloh, Jagoi/Sadong (Bidayuh), and Iban in the Kapuas basin; the Ngaju, Ma'nyan, and Ot Donum in Central Kalimantan; and the Kenyah, Kayan, Bahau, Long Dayeh, Long Bawang, and Modang in east Kalimantan. The Dayak in Kalimantan may be divided into four major groupings: those who live along the Kapuas in the west, along the Barito and other major rivers in the south, along the Mahakam and other major rivers in the east, and at river heads and beyond in the center. In Sarawak, the term "Dayak" has been used to refer to the Bidayuh (Land Dayak) and the Iban (Sea Dayak). The Bidayuh are generally more oriented to the land, whereas the Iban are increasingly found to spread along the rivers and even the seacoast of west Sarawak. By the end of the twentieth century, the Iban had become the most numerous and scattered language grouping in Sarawak. Both the Iban and the Bidayuh in Sarawak claim to have their origins in some part of Kalimantan.

The Dayak traditionally live in longhouses, although, like many other indigenous societies in Borneo, younger couples increasingly live in nuclear families. Dry-rice shifting cultivation continues to be the mainstay of the Dayak subsistence economy. It suits their communal lifestyle, as can be seen in rice harvesting and the annual celebrations of different kinds, including the Gawai Dayak in Sarawak and the Erau in Kalimantan. The Dayak have developed gender-based division of labor: women tend the rice fields and home, whereas men seek extra income outside the home. For example, the latter take up the cultivation of pepper, fishing, hunting, and collection of jungle products. The kinship of Bornean peoples cannot be generalized; however, it may be categorized as parental or dualistic, having elements of both patrilineal and matrilineal categories.

During the days of the Brooke rajas (1842–1946), the Iban were recruited in larger numbers as security forces. In independent Malaysia, the Iban and Dayak in Sarawak, like their counterparts in Sabah, founded their own political parties with some degree of success. Many prominent Dayak in Sarawak have emerged as respected state and national administrators; Jugah Anak Bariang is an example. Due to a particular political climate, the Dayak in Kalimantan never established a successful political party; however, several Dayak leaders such as Tjilik Riwut won national respect in Indonesia.

The Penan form an important segment among the Borneo peoples. First of all, the majority of the Penan maintain a relatively more autonomous jungle lifestyle than any other indigenous group, even though their number is insignificant. Due to their unique lifestyle, they are believed to be remnants of Borneo's oldest inhabitants. They subsist by gathering and hunting, not rarely maintaining surreptitious barter trading with the settled communities within their range of movement. Some of the Penan also participated in the various resettlement schemes launched by the governments. In recent years the Penan have won international attention from the media coverage of their plight. With the encroachment of modern plantation and logging concessions in their territories, the Penan have increasingly found less space for their traditional subsistence and lifeways.

If the coastal population of Borneo have become Muslims and the majority of the Chinese maintain their version of Buddhism or Taoism, the interior and upriver inhabitants, especially the Dusun and the Dayak in general, have opted to accept Christianity or, to a lesser degree, Islam, and many continue to uphold their traditional beliefs, such as Kaharingan in Kalimantan.

The indigenous peoples of Borneo have responded to rapid change in diverse fields. The introduction of modern education and diverse development plans, cash crops, logging concessions, timber, plywood, and mining industries have direct impact on local economies and social arrangements. Many of the youth join the workforce in the newly established factories, industries, offices, and services in bigger towns. Such urbanization has led to the decline, or at least stagnation, of the interior population and thus the decreasing numbers of longhouses in many communities. Politically, the peoples of Borneo have exercised a more assertive voice in the running of local affairs. As Indonesia and Malaysia hold regular general and local elections, the Borneans have increasingly won their wish to administer their own affairs and participated in running the government. More significantly, since movements across national borders in Borneo have been regularized, many language groupings formerly separated by modern national borders now have more opportunities to renew closer ties and establish cooperation.

Iik A. Mansurnoor

Further Reading
Brown, Donald. E. (1970) *Brunei: The Structure and History of a Bornean Malay Sultanate.* Brunei Museum Monograph, no. 2. Bandar, Brunei: Brunei Museum.
Cleary, Mark, and Peter Eaton. (1992) *Borneo: Change and Development.* Singapore: Oxford University Press.
Dove, Michael R. (1985) *Swidden Agriculture in Indonesia.* Amsterdam: Mouton.
Hutton, Wendy, ed. (1997) *East Malaysia and Brunei.* Hong Kong, China: Perilus Editions.
King, Victor T. (1993) *The Peoples of Borneo.* Cambridge, MA: Blackwell Publishers.
Muller, Kal, and David Pickell. (1997) *Borneo: Journey into the Tropical Rainforest.* Lincolnwood, IL: Passport Books.
Padoch, Christine, and Nancy L. Peluso, eds. (1996) *Borneo in Transition: People, Forests, Conservation, and Development.* Kuala Lumpur, Malaysia: Oxford University Press.
Rousseau, Jerome. (1990) *Central Borneo: Ethnic Identity and Social Life in a Stratified Society.* New York: Oxford University Press.
Winzeler, Robert L., ed. (1998) *Indigenous Architecture in Borneo: Traditional Patterns and New Developments.* Williamsburg, VA: Borneo Research Council.

BOROBUDUR Situated in the Borobudur district of central Java, this Buddhist temple is an architectural wonder of the world. Its construction was started in 778 CE by the Sailendra ruler Vishnu and was completed during the reign of his grandson, Samaratunga, in 824 CE. It became the central point in legitimizing Sailendra rule. Borobudur was selected to be the Mount Meru (mythical mountain at the center of the world) of the kingdom and a miniature cosmos was built and dedicated to Buddha. The site was abandoned for centuries and was buried under volcanic ash and vegetation until the beginning of the nineteenth century, when it was cleared. The Dutch began its restoration in 1907.

Representing the nine previous lives of Buddha, nine stone terraces were carved out of a rounded hill. With a height of 42 meters, an area of 15,129 square meters, and 504 Buddha statues, the whole structure resembles the sacred flower of Buddha, the lotus. A large bell-shaped stupa crowns the center. Although Indian in conception, the Borobudur temple reflects the best tradition of Javanese artists carving beautiful Buddha icons and modeling indigenous sculptural patterns. It represents the highest genius of the Sailendra period and is testimony to the Javanese artistic temperament.

Patit Paban Mishra

Further Reading
Coomaraswamy, Anand K. (1972) *History of Indian and Indonesian Art.* New Delhi: Munshiram and Manoharlal.
Gomez, Luis, and Hiram W. Woodward, Jr. (1981) *Borobudur: History and Significance of a Buddhist Monument.* Berkeley and Los Angeles: University of California.

BOSCH, JOHANNES VAN DEN (1780–1844), Dutch colonialist. Johannes van den Bosch was born in Herwijnen, Netherlands. As a young man he served as a military engineer in the Dutch East Indies before returning to senior posts in the Netherlands. In

The ruins of Borobudur Temple with Mt. Merapi in the distance. (EYE UBIQUITOUS/CORBIS)

1829, his proposals for ensuring the profitability of the colony led to his appointment as governor-general (1830–1833). He argued against the liberal ideas that had influenced colonial policy during the preceding two decades, such as allowing market forces to stimulate the planting of tropical crops like coffee and indigo, which were in demand in Europe. Instead he proposed a system of forced cultivation backed by the traditional authority of co-opted indigenous rulers. His so-called Cultivation System (*Cultuurstelsel*) required villages to devote one-fifth of their land and one-fifth of their labor to growing export crops designated by the government, especially indigo, sugar, and coffee. The harvest was then to be delivered to the government at fixed prices and the proceeds were to be offset against land tax (*landrente*). In practice, however, the system varied enormously across Java and was widely seen as oppressive. Van den Bosch argued for restricting the Dutch empire to Java, Sumatra, and tin-rich Bangka, and he reduced the principalities of Yogyakarta and Surakarta in central Java to small enclaves. He was Netherlands minister of colonies from 1834 to 1839.

Robert Cribb

Further Reading
Elson, R. E. (1994) *Village Java under the Cultivation System, 1830–1870.* Sydney: Allen and Unwin.

Fasseur, Cornelis. (1992) *The Politics of Colonial Exploitation: Java, the Dutch, and the Cultivation System.* Ithaca, NY: Cornell University Southeast Asia Program.

BOSE, SUBHAS CHANDRA (1897–1945),
Indian freedom fighter. Subhas Chandra Bose, called "Netaji," has a semimythical status today as an Indian freedom fighter who sided with the Japanese against the British in World War II. Born into a large family in Cuttack, Orissa, on 23 January 1897, Bose studied in Calcutta, where he spent much time in meditation and graduated in philosophy. He then studied for two years at Cambridge, England, and placed fourth in the Indian Civil Service examinations. He soon resigned from the civil service and then met Mohandas Gandhi (1869–1948) in Bombay.

Bose became a Calcutta municipal official but was soon arrested for terrorism and jailed for three years. He was released in 1927 because of continuing ill health. He disagreed with Gandhi over nonviolence but continued on in the Indian National Congress. He was again arrested in 1940 by the British authorities but was soon released after threatening to fast unto death. He was still under house arrest when he disappeared in January 1941.

Bose with British Labour Party politician George Lansbury in London in January 1938. (HULTON-DEUTSCH COLLECTION/ CORBIS)

After walking to Afghanistan, in November 1941 he surfaced in Berlin, broadcasting Nazi propaganda and arguing, "our enemy's enemy is our friend." Bose met Hitler in May 1942, and the latter approved plans for Bose to go to Myanmar (Burma). He left a year later and took command of the Azad Hind Fauj (AHF), or Indian National Army (INA), in fact a rag-tag army made up of deserters from the Indian army and other Indians, mainly Japanese prisoners of war. These men fought near the Indian border against the British but soon became a liability to their imperial Japanese sponsors, who were then retreating in Southeast Asia just as the INA was falling back on Mandalay, then Rangoon (now Yangon), then Bangkok. Bose died in the crash of a Japanese aircraft in Taiwan, in August 1945.

Paul Hockings

Further Reading
Mehra, Parshotam. (1987) "Subhas Chandra Bose (1897–1945)." In *A Dictionary of Modern Indian History 1707–1947*, edited by Parshotam Mehra. Delhi: Oxford University Press, 103–105.
Toye, Hugh. (1959) *Subhash Chandra Bose: The Springing Tiger: A Study of a Revolutionary*. Bombay, India: Jaico Publishing House.

BOSPORUS The Bosporus, the strait separating the Black Sea and the Sea of Marmara, is generally viewed as the boundary between Europe and Asia. About 30 kilometers long, it varies in width from 3,550 to 700 meters and in depth from 37 to 124 meters. It is the only year-round sea outlet for Black Sea countries. The Dardanelles extends for 61 kilometers and links the Sea of Marmara with the Aegean Sea; its average depth is 55 meters, with a maximum of 105. Together the Bosporus and Dardanelles are known as the Turkish Straits.

Heavy pollution in the Black Sea has had adverse effects on the marine life and ecology of the Turkish Straits and the Sea of Marmara, and increasing maritime traffic through the straits has posed safety and pollution concerns for Turkey. The problem is more acute for the Bosporus, as strong currents and narrowness in several parts of the strait make navigation hazardous. At the start of the twenty-first century, an average of 50,000 commercial vessels and 6,500 oil tankers passed through the Bosporus annually; an estimated 15 percent of vessels carry dangerous cargo. Thousands of smaller passenger boats and ferries also use the Bosporus. The strait is four times as busy as the Panama Canal and three times as busy as the Suez Canal. Turkey's largest city, Istanbul, with a population of over 11 million, is situated on both sides of the Bosporus and is vulnerable to the hazards of increasing Black Sea traffic.

Under the 1936 Montreux Treaty, navigation through the Bosporus and Dardanelles is unrestricted for commercial vessels except in wartime. Accidents in the straits and the growing danger of environmental and safety hazards have led Turkey to adopt new rules to enhance the safety of traffic. In 1994 the Turkish government issued regulations governing shipping in the straits, including speed limits for large vessels and the requirement that ships inform Turkish authorities in advance if they carry hazardous cargo. Other regulations require large oil tankers to be accompanied by tugboats in case of breakdown. Not all ships abide by the new regulations: Russia, Greece, and other users of the straits have cited the freedom of passage provided by the Montreux Treaty and questioned Turkey's authority to introduce unilateral measures governing shipping through the straits.

Shipping through the straits has a political dimension as well. In a bid to reduce oil shipping through the straits in the future and with the support of the United States, Turkey strongly backed the construction of a pipeline from the Azerbaijani port of Baku to the Turkish Mediterranean port of Ceyhan. Greece and Bulgaria promoted an alternative oil pipeline plan involving shipping Caspian Sea oil from the Russian port of Novorossiysk to the Bulgarian port of Burgas on the west coast of the Black Sea. This pipeline would link Burgas with the Greek Aegean port of Alexandroupolis, bypassing the Turkish Straits. Whether either pipeline will be constructed is unknown. Although pipelines might relieve the passage of oil through the Bosporus and Dardanelles, Turkey's anxieties about the volume of maritime traffic and ecological damage persist.

Tozun Bahcheli

Further Reading
Guchi, Yucel. (2000) "The Legal Regulation of Passage through the Turkish Straits." *Mediterranean Quarterly* 2, 3 (summer): 87–99.
Ozturk, Bayram, and Nesrin Algan, eds. (2001) *Problems of Regional Seas, 2001: Proceedings of the International Symposium on the Problems of Regional Seas.* Istanbul, Turkey: Turkish Maritime Research Foundation.

BOXER REBELLION The Boxer Rebellion was an antiforeign and antimodern upheaval at the beginning of the twentieth century in north China. It was initiated in the late 1890s by the Chinese martial arts groups known as Yihe Quan ("Boxers United in Righteousness") and reached its climax in 1900 with the support of the central government of the Qing dynasty (1644–1912). Suppressed by a foreign relief army in late 1900, the uprising stands as the strongest and most violent reaction to the escalation of Western aggression in China.

The martial arts tradition had a long history in north China. In the 1890s, some martial arts groups in Shandong province, such as Yihe Quan, Dadaohui ("Big Sword Society") and Shen Quan ("Spirit Boxers"), became especially active and began to be known collectively as Yihe Quan. The belief system of the Boxer movement was loose and inclusive, drawing largely from folklore and popular religion. Although many hold that it was an offshoot of the White Lotus sect, there is not sufficient evidence to establish such a connection. Under the supervision of their masters, the Boxers practiced martial arts by altars or in boxing grounds; they believed their training would render them invulnerable to bullets. Charms and spells were also used to achieve the same purpose. The Boxers were mainly enlisted from peasants, craftsmen, dismissed soldiers, laborers, and jobless drifters. Although the Boxer masters commanded high respect from their followers, no uniform leadership in the Boxer movement existed. Each master could form his own group and create his own tenets.

As the Western powers intensified their imperialist expansion in China after the Sino-Japanese War (1894–1895), the Boxers in Shandong, Zhili, and Shanxi provinces became increasingly antiforeign.

Meanwhile, a series of natural calamities hit north China and deprived many peasants of their livelihood, exacerbating an already tense situation. Believing that the Western presence and the introduction of modern facilities such as railroads and telegraph lines played a role in causing those natural disasters, the Boxers staged a fierce antiforeign upheaval, attacking foreigners and Chinese Christians, and destroying their properties and churches. This brought them into conflict with the Qing local authorities. But some conservative, xenophobic officials sympathized with the Boxers and tried to recruit them for semiofficial local militia. The local officials changed Yihe Quan to Yihe Tuan ("Militia United in Righteousness"), which served as an endorsement for the Boxer movement. The Boxers also changed their slogan from "oppose the Qing and destroy the foreign" *(fan Qing mie yang)* to "support the Qing and destroy the foreign" *(fu Qing mie yang)*.

The Qing central government, headed by the Empress Dowager Cixi (1835–1908), also began to change its policy toward the Boxer movement. Annoyed by the suspicion that the Western powers had attempted to remove her from power, Cixi decided to make use of the antiforeign fanaticism of the Boxers. She ordered the Qing local officials to stop suppressing the Boxers and invited them to Beijing, the capital of the Qing dynasty, to teach martial arts. With the support of the Qing central government, the Boxer movement rapidly spread in the northern and northeastern provinces. Tens of thousands of Boxers entered Beijing from the northern provinces. Their altars mushroomed in Beijing and other northern cities. Women's martial arts organizations, chief among which was

A palace eunuch (L) and and a scholar official being arrested by British forces in Beijing in 1901. (BETTMANN/CORBIS)

Hongdengzhao ("Red Lanterns"), were also formed and joined the Boxers.

In June 1900 Cixi ordered the Boxers and Qing soldiers to attack the foreign legations in Beijing and subsequently declared war on the Western powers. The siege of the foreign legation district lasted for about two months. During the disturbance, hundreds of foreigners, including the German minister Clemens von Ketteler (1853–1900), and thousands of Chinese Christians were killed and numerous churches were destroyed. Qing provincial officials in the south and southeast did not join in the central government's support for the Boxers. Under the excuse of maintaining order, they ensured that the foreigners in their respective jurisdictions were protected and that no antiforeign activity was carried out.

Western powers responded resolutely to the escalation of antiforeign tumult in north China. In June 1900 eight countries (Britain, the United States, Germany, France, Russia, Japan, Italy, and Austria) formed an international relief army (the Allied forces). In July, they attacked and captured Tianjin, a major coastal city in north China. The Allied forces fought the Boxers all the way to Beijing. Refusing to use Western weapons and relying solely on their martial art, the Boxers' resistance soon collapsed. On 14 August 1900 the Allied forces occupied Beijing. Cixi led her court to take refuge in Xi'an, a provincial capital in the northwest. The German general Alfred Waldersee (1832–1904), who was appointed the commander-in-chief of the Allied forces in August, requested reinforcements and continued to suppress the Boxers in the north. Tens of thousands of Boxers, Qing soldiers, and civilians were massacred. By the end of 1900, the Boxer Rebellion had been suppressed.

In December 1900 the Allied forces proposed a truce to the Qing dynasty. In September 1901, the Qing representatives Yikuang (1836–1918) and Li Hongzhang (1823–1901) and those from eleven countries concluded the Boxer Protocol to settle the incident. This treaty stipulated that China pay 450 million taels of silver to the countries that were affected by the Boxer uprising; that the Qing government apologize to those countries and punish the officials who encouraged the antiforeign actions; and that China allow foreign armies to be stationed at strategic points in north China. The Qing dynasty underwent a radical change in policy toward the West after this incident. To mend the damage the Boxer uprising had done to her reputation and to regain endorsement by the Western powers, Cixi launched a radical reform movement starting in 1901, which would eventually

have led China to a constitutional monarchy but which was interrupted by the 1911 Revolution. Having been re-created in literature, art, and folklore, the Boxer Rebellion remains the most terrifying chapter in the relationship between China and the West, and an enduring inspiration for nationalistic agitation in China.

Yingcong Dai

See also: **Qing Dynasty**

Further Reading
Buck, David D. (1987) *Recent Chinese Studies of the Boxer Movement.* Armonk, NY: M. E. Sharpe.
———. (1991) "The 1990 International Symposium on the Boxer Movement and Modern Chinese Society." *Republican China* 16, 2 (April): 113–120.
Cohen, Paul A. (1997) *History in Three Keys: The Boxers as Event, Experience, and Myth.* New York: Columbia University Press.
Esherick, Joseph W. (1987) *The Origins of the Boxer Uprising.* Berkeley and Los Angeles: University of California Press.
Preston, Diana. (2000) *The Boxer Rebellion: the Dramatic Story of China's War on Foreigners That Shook the World in the Summer of 1900.* New York: Walker & Company.

BRAHMAN   Brahman (Brahmin) refers to the priestly category of Hindus. Though only a small minority of the Indian population, Brahmans hold the highest position in the caste system because of their extreme purity and sacerdotal profession. Some also live outside India in Nepal, Sri Lanka, or in small Hindu enclaves in Bali, Lombok, and Thailand. In India there are several hundred Brahman castes, which recognize differences of status among themselves. They constitute a caste-block or *varna*. The various castes are distinguished from one another first in terms of mother tongue (e.g., Tamil Brahmans); then in terms of philosophical sect (e.g., Smarta Brahmans); and finally in terms of a locality that had long been their homeland (e.g., Kongudesa Brahmans, those from the Kongu kingdom in Tamil Nadu).

For at least 2,500 years Brahmans have served as temple priests or family priests *(purohita)*. In modern times they have been teachers, scribes, landowners, or government officials. Because they are disproportionately influential in modern politics, some states have experienced an anti-Brahman backlash.

Brahmans' essential attributes are (1) their supreme level of purity, maintained by a vegetarian diet and by caste endogamy; (2) their literacy in Sanskrit and other

BRAHMAN—WHO ARE THEY?

Thurston's *Castes and Tribes of Southern India* contains a very long section on the Brahman castes of the region. The following text is the opening of the section and indicates just how complex this caste category was and remains in India.

Brahman.—The Brahmans of Southern India are divided into a number of sections, differing in language, manners and customs. As regards to their origin, the current belief is that they sprang from the mouth of the Brahma. In support of thereof, the following verse from the Purusha Suktha (hymn of the primaeval male) of the Rig Veda is quoted:—From the face of Prajapathi (Viratpurusha) came the Brahmans, from the arms of arose the Kshatriyas; from the thighs sprang the Vaisyas; and from the feet the Sudras. Mention of the fourfold division of the Hindu castes is also made in other Vedas, and in the Ithihasas and Puranas.

The Brahmans fall into three groups, following the three Vedas or Sakas, Rig, Yajus and Samam. This threefold division is, however, recognised only for ceremonial purposes. For marriage and social purposes, the divisions based on language and locality are practically more operative. In the matter of the more important religious rites, the Brahmans of Southern India, as elsewhere, closely follow their own Vedas. Every Brahman belongs to one or other of the numerous gotras mentioned in Pravara and Gotra Kandams. All the religious rites are preformed according to the Grihya Sutras (ritual books) pertaining to their Saka or Veda. Of these, there are eight kinds now in vogue, viz.:—

Asvalayana Sutra of the rig Veda}
Apasathamba}
Bharadwaja}
Bhodyana} _____ Sutras of the black Yajus
Sathyashada}
Vaikkanasa}
Kathyayana Sutra of the white Yajuas
Drahyayana Sutra of Sama Veda

All Brahmans claim descent from one or more of the following seven Rishis:—Atri, Bhrigu, Kutsa, Vashista, Gautama, Kasyapa, Angiras. According to some, the Rishis are Agasthya, Angiras, Atri, Bhrigu, Kasyapa, Vashista, and Gautama. Under these Rishis are included eighteen ganams, and under each gnam there are a number of gitras, amounting in all to about 230. Every Brahman is expected to salute his superiors by repeating the Abhivadhanam (salutation) which contains his lineage. As an example, the following may be given:—"I, Krishna by name, of Srivathsa gotra, with the pravara (lineage) of the five Rishis, Bharagava, Chyavana, Apunvana, Aruva, and Jamadagini, following the Apasthamba sutra of the Yajus Saka, am now saluting you." Daily at the close of the Sandhya prayers, this Abhivadhanam formula should be repeated by every Brahman.

Source: Thurston, Edgar & Rangachari, K.(1909) *Castes and Tribes of Southern India*. Madras: Government Press, 267–268.

RITUAL PURITY

This account from a Hindu village in Tamil Nadu, South India, shows the importance of ritual purity and pollution in maintaining the high status of the Brahmans in the Hindu caste system.

Brahmin *jathi* [occupational] groups in the village adhered strictly to the rules of vegetarianism, auspicious time (*raaku kaalam*) and menstrual tabu. The Beri CeTTiar followed the rules more scrupulously than other non-Brahmin *jathi* groups, but all non-Brahmin *jathi* groups indulged in the consumption of meat and fish—foods that were considered to be *kavacci* or polluting. The *jathi* groups who ranked second to the Beri CeTTiar such a Mutaliar, Saliar, Kanakkar, ITaya, Kammaalar and Baljia NaiTu, paid greater attention to the rules than did the next-ranking jathi groups such as Vanniar, NaaTaar, Kusavar, AmbaTTar, Pandaaram, Itayar, NaaTTaar, PaTTanava and Karayaar. Villiar and Harijan *jathi* groups paid the least attention to the rules of ritual abstinence and tabus.

Source: Ebenezer T. Jacob-Pandian (1972) *Dravidianization: A Tamil Revitilization Movement.* Ann Arbor, MI: University Microfilms, 113.

languages; and (3) their knowledge of Hindu liturgy. Their services are still in great demand for weddings and other family ceremonies, and are essential conducting *puja* (worship and offerings) in many temples.

Paul Hockings

Further Reading
Madan, Triloki Nath. (1989) *Family and Kinship: A Study of the Pandits of Rural Kashmir.* 2d ed. Delhi: Oxford University Press.
Nanjundayya, H. V., and L .K. Ananthakrishna Iyer. (1928) "Brahman." In *The Mysore Tribes and Castes.* Vol. 2. Mysore, India: Mysore University, 297–549.

BRAHUI Brahui is the name of a group of tribes that live in Pakistan, eastern Iran, and Afghanistan. Scholars puzzle over their origin because they speak a Dravidian-based language, such as is commonly found in the south of India, despite their northern location.

The largest concentration of Brahui lives in Baluchistan Province in Pakistan. Their numbers are estimated between just under a million to a million and a half.

The Brahui homeland is on the Kalat plateau, in Pakistan. It was in Kalat that the Brahui succeeded in mobilizing and attaining power. In 1666, Mir Ahmed Khan I rose to power as the leader of a group of Brahui tribes. From then on, the khanate of Kalat remained in the hands of Brahui leaders for almost three hundred years. That succession was broken when the British took control of Kalat as part of their expansion efforts in the region. The British retained control until Pakistan achieved its independence in 1948.

The Brahui observe the teachings of Islam, following the Sunni sect. However, some of their traditions originate in India. It is a patriarchal society, where a son's birth is more valued than a daughter's. The societal unit is the tribe, which is governed by a *sadar* (hereditary chief). Blood ties are not the only indicator of membership in a tribe; other factors, such as loyalty and stature, are taken into account as well. In the past, the Brahui were mostly nomadic shepherds. Although some still follow that lifestyle, now others have largely settled into agricultural activities. Their standard of living is low as a result of Pakistan's depressed economic conditions and their own inefficiency in agricultural operations. Government aid has been unable to alter their living conditions. The Brahui are diminishing in numbers as fewer speak Brahui and more become integrated with the Baluchi.

Houman A. Sadri

Further Reading
Gall, Timothy L., ed. (1998). *Asia and Oceania.* Vol 3 of *Worldmark Encyclopedia of Cultures and Daily Life.* Farmington Hills, MI: Gale Group.
Norton, Augustus Richard, ed. (1996) *Civil Society in the Middle East.* Leiden, Netherlands, and New York: Brill.

BRAMAPUTRA RIVER The Bramaputra River, 2,900 kilometers long, is the world's tallest river over sea level. Its source is in the Himalayas, and it flows into the Indian Ocean. The river runs east for 1,800 kilometers through most of southern Tibet (Xizang Autonomous Region), where it is known as the Yarlung Zangbo River, before it suddenly turns south and crosses the Himalayas in 5,000-meter-deep gorges. Reaching India, the Bramaputra (son of Brahma) runs west and south through Assam and Bangladesh, where it merges with the Ganges and forms a huge delta. In Bangladesh, the river is also

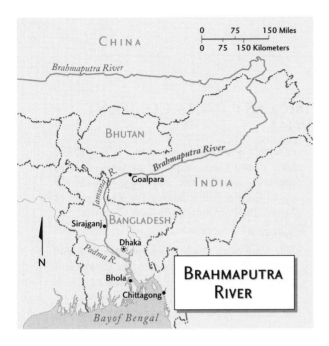

BRAHMAPUTRA
RIVER

known as the Jamuna. The river is navigable for most of its length except for the passage through the Himalayas.

The middle reaches of the riverbed are the agricultural center of Tibet, but heavy flooding and mudslides caused by deforestation are frequent. In Bangladesh, the water level rises four to five meters during the rainy seasons, and almost every year the river breaks its banks or changes course. When onshore storms simultaneously push the seawater into the delta, it results in disastrous floods. At the same time, the inundation and irrigation leave large deposits of fertile soil, so fields in the river valleys are intensively cultivated.

Bent Nielsen

Further Reading
Biswas, Asit K., and Tsuyoshi Hashimoto, eds. (1996) *Asian International Waters: From Ganges-Brahmaputra to Mekong.* Oxford: Oxford University Press.

BRITISH EAST INDIA COMPANY The British East India Company was founded on the last day of 1600 through a royal charter signed by Queen Elizabeth I. In many ways it failed to achieve its initial aim of trade in spices and other items favored by the English people. British subsequent dominance over the Indian subcontinent came only following the Dutch withdrawal for the more lucrative isles of modern Indonesia.

From the beginning there was always tension between the company directors in London and the company officers in the field. The communication technology of the seventeenth and eighteenth centuries was slow; it often took a message two years to travel from London to India and back.

The company made unremarkable small gains until the eighteenth century. The eighteenth century, like the twenty-first, saw an expansion of multinational corporations with the means of enforcing their will. During the early period, factories or trading posts were established through grants from the native rulers in several parts of the subcontinent. To protect these areas, the company employed European and sepoy (*sipahi*, native troops) guards. Slowly, the company gained territory through the employment of military force. In 1757, Sir Robert Clive (1725–1774) won a remarkable victory at Plassey, which solidified British control over the vast territory of Bengal.

Throughout this phase, many of the British who went to India to serve the company were highly corrupt, seeing self-aggrandizement as their main goal. The London company set out to gain greater control over its Asian possessions. Warren Hastings (1732–1818) was commissioned to straighten out the corrupt administration. He is now recognized as the greatest of the governors-general, but he ran afoul of London for political decisions he made. Hastings was sent home to undergo one of the longest and most famous trials of the eighteenth century. After a long legal fight, Hastings was acquitted of the charges. Another famous figure in company history is Arthur Wellesley (1769–1852), later the duke of Wellington of Waterloo fame, who served under his brother, Governor-General Richard Wellesley (1761–1842). Sir Arthur defeated the famous Tipu sultan, acquiring large tracts of territory to the south in 1799.

But the company's history was not all wars and local battles. The permanent settlement of land revenues in 1793, enacted by Lord Cornwallis (1738–1805), brought much hardship to the Bengal peasantry. The last governor-general, Lord Bentinck (1774–1839), was both a social reformer and a builder of infrastructure that would much later set India ahead of other Third World countries after its independence in 1947. Unfortunately, many of his social reforms put the more conservative elements of the subcontinent at odds with the company's rule, leading to the Great Mutiny of 1857–1858.

During the mutiny, the British were barely able to hold on to their great prize. After miraculously winning, the British Crown took over the governance of

TREATY BETWEEN THE BRITISH EAST INDIA COMPANY AND BENGAL

The following text is the first ten articles of a treaty between the British East India Company and the Nawab Shujau-d-daula, of Oudh, and the Nawab Najmu-d-daula, of Benagal set forth in 1765 after the British had established themselves as the rulers of Bengal. The treaty allows British control over trade, a military presence, and also requires Bengal to pay compensation to England for its expenses in the war.

Article 1

A perpetual and universal peace, sincere friendship, and firm union shall be established between His Highness Shujau-d-daula and his heirs, on the one part, and His Excellency Najmu-d-daula and the English East India Company on the other; so that the said contracting powers shall give the greatest attention to maintain between themselves, their dominions and their subjects this reciprocal friendship, without permitting, on either side, any kind of hostilities to be committed, from henceforth, for any cause, or under any pretence whatsoever, and everything shall be carefully avoided which might hereafter prejudice the union now happily established.

Article 2

In case the dominions of His Highness Shujau-d-daula shall at any time hereafter be attacked, His Excellency Najmu-d-daula and the English Company shall assist him with a part or the whole of their forces, according to the exigency of his affairs, and so far as may be consistent with their own security, and if the dominions of His Excellency Najmu-d-daula or the English Company, shall be attacked, His Highness shall be in like manner, assist them with a part of the whole of his forces. In the case of the English Company's forces being employed in His Highness's service, the extraordinary expense of the same is to be defrayed by him.

Article 3

His Highness solemnly engages never to entertain or receive Cossim Ally Khan, the late Soubahadar of Bengal, & C., Sombre, the assassin of the English, nor any of the European deserters, within his dominions, nor to give the least countenance, support, or protection to them. He likewise solemnly engages to deliver up to the English whatever European may in future desert from them into his country.

Article 4

The King Shah Aalum shall remain in full possession of Cora, and such part of the Province of Illiabad [Allahabad] as he now possesses, which are ceded to His Majesty, as a royal demesne, for the support of his dignity and expenses.

Article 5

His Highness Shujau-d-daula engages, in a most solemn manner, to continue Balwant Singh in the zemindaries of Benares, Ghazepore, and all those districts he possessed at the time he came over to the late Nabob Jaffier Ally Khan and the English on condition of his paying the same revenue as heretofore.

Article 6

In consideration of the great expense incurred by the English Company in carrying on the late war, His Highness agrees to pay them (50) fifty *lakhs* of rupees in the following manner; *viz.* (1) twelve *lakhs* in money, and a deposit of jewels to the amount of (8) eight *lakhs* upon the signing of this Treaty, (5) five *lakhs* one month after, and the remaining (25) twenty-five *lakhs* by monthly payments, so as that the whole may be discharged in (13) thirteen months from the date hereof.

Article 8

His Highness shall allow the English Company to carry on a trade, duty free, throughout the whole of his Dominions.

Article 9

All the relations and subjects of His Highness, who in any manner assisted the English during the course of the late war, shall be forgiven, and no ways molested for the same.

Article 10

As soon as this Treaty is executed, the English forces shall be withdrawn from the dominions

CONTINUED ON NEXT PAGE

CONTINUED FROM PREVIOUS PAGE

of His Highness, except such as may be necessary for the garrison of Chunar, or for the defence and protection of the King in the city of Illiabad [Allahabad] if His Majesty shall require a force for that purpose.

Source: A. B. Keith. (1922) *Speeches and Documents on Indian Policy, 1750–1921*. Vol. 1. Oxford: Oxford University Press, 28–30.

India under Queen Victoria's Proclamation of 1 November, 1858, to the Princes and Peoples of India. This executive order was the end of a series of laws that had been limiting the prerogatives of the British East India Company. Although there is an organization today called the East India Company, since 1858 the company has not been a political player on the world's stage. It now sells tea.

Geoffrey Cook

Further Reading
Archer, Mildred, and Graham Parlett. (1992) *Company Paintings of the British Period*. London: Victoria and Albert Museum.
Keay, John, ed. (1994) *The Honourable Company: A History of the East India Company*. New York: Macmillan.
Tuck, Patrick, ed. (1998) *The East India Company, 1600–1858*. New York: Routledge.

BRITISH IN SOUTHEAST ASIA From the early nineteenth century to the early twentieth century, Britain (the United Kingdom) became the world's preeminent naval and trade power. To advance its interests, Britain acquired the largest empire ever known, primarily for purposes of global trade rather than territorial conquest. The extension of British rule into Southeast Asia, including Burma (now Myanmar), Malaya, British Borneo, and Singapore, was primarily to bolster the defense of India, the so-called jewel in the British crown, and to secure the trade routes to China. British rule was largely indirect and accommodating of local power structures—unless British interests were threatened.

The British in the Malay Peninsula and Borneo
Until 1874, British interests in the Malay Peninsula were limited to the three Straits Settlements that facilitated trade through the Strait of Malacca—Singapore, Melaka (Malacca), and Penang—all of which were established in the early nineteenth century by the British East India Company (EIC). The three possessions formed vital links as important seaports to service ships that plied vital trading routes and the naval vessels that protected them. Singapore, for example, was occupied by several hundred indigenous Malays upon its establishment in 1819, but had grown to a population of 85,000 by the 1860s. The British brought in large numbers of Chinese coolie laborers as well as Indians to act as administrators in the Straits Settlements.

By 1873 the British began to drop the policy of noninterference in the affairs of the Malay states because it desired to control the tin, rubber, palm oil, and other resources with which the Malay states were blessed. Tin, mostly from the states of Perak and Selangor, was particularly useful in the manufacture of barrels to store oil and for construction materials. The western states of Perak and Selangor were also notorious for piracy that hampered merchant trade; this provided the British with further reasons for intervention. The murder of the British resident (highest-ranking British official) of Perak, J. W. W. Birch, in November 1875 was a pretext to introduce British-led troops, to enthrone a pliable sultan, and to strengthen British control. The residents acquired vast powers, but by and large the sultans continued to run the daily affairs of those under their rule—notably on issues of custom and religion. Pahang (1888) and Negeri Sembilan (1889) were added and eventually the four states under British rule collectively formed the 1895 Federated Malay States (FMS). Neighboring Siam (now Thailand), under modernizing King Rama IV (Chao Fa Mongkut, reigned 1851–1868), cleverly avoided colonization but was forced to sign the Anglo-Thai agreement of 1855 giving Britain favorable trade access. Thailand also lost the Malay territories of Perlis, Kedah, Kelantan, and Terengganu to British control in the early twentieth century.

On Borneo, James Brooke, adventurer and scion of the Brooke family, independently established himself as the British "white raja" in the mid-nineteenth century. Like Singapore's founder, Sir Stamford Raffles, Brooke wanted to push farther into Southeast Asia than the more cautious British government, which had assumed Borneo to be within the Dutch ambit. Brooke's increasing power in the northern portion of the island, forged largely through alliances with local peoples and the sultan of Brunei, meant that unwittingly "British Borneo" became apart of the empire. The Brooke family dynasty lasted from 1846 until the onset of World War II. In 1963, all of the British territories of maritime Southeast Asia were given independence and merged to form the Federation of Malaysia. Singapore left this federation in 1965 to become an independent nation-state. Unlike the other colonial powers in maritime Southeast Asia, the British had largely preserved the traditional power structures of the Malay Peninsula. The British had also attempted to establish commercial transactions with the Malay people in order to generate a trade market for British goods. This was in direct contrast to the Dutch, who ran more of a tribute system with the Indonesians, whereby produce was exacted as a form of taxation.

The British in Burma

The case of Burma was different in many ways. The British viewed it as an extension of India for reasons of both perceived cultural similarity and strategic value. There was also growing concern that France would try to exercise some influence in the multiethnic region. However the British encountered fierce resistance to their proposed overlordship. Three Anglo-Burmese Wars occurred in 1824–1826, 1852, and 1885, during which Burma was effectively annexed in three phases—Arakan (now Rakhine), Lower Burma, and Upper Burma, respectively. The most serious conflict was the first, with enormous loss of life on both sides. The second conflict arose over disputes over the teak trade and trading routes to southern China. The third and final conflict saw Burma collapse to British authority in fifteen days with the loss of ten men. In February 1886, Burma was officially incorporated into India. However, the Burmese resisted British rule fiercely, and the subsequent occupation was vastly more difficult than Britain's occupation of India or Malaya. After World War II, at Burmese insistence, moves for independence were speeded up and concluded on 4 January 1948. British rule had never been popular in Burma.

The Postwar Era

In the aftermath of World War II, Britain played a crucial role in preparing all its colonies for independence—a move that officials in London saw as the best way to achieve stability in the region in the face of the growing Communist threat. This was in direct contrast to the Netherlands and France, which fought savage wars to return their colonies to the prewar sta-

tus quo. For some years afterward Britain stationed forces in Malaya/Malaysia and Singapore, largely meeting the twin threats of the Communist Emergency (1948–1960) and confrontation with Indonesia (1963–1965). Britain also helped channel considerable aid funds to Southeast Asia through the Colombo Plan, initially to the Commonwealth members but subsequently also to non-Commonwealth nations, forming part of a network of postwar aid relationships designed to create a more stable global environment in the face of potential instability and out of desire to promote affluent trade markets in the long term.

Anthony L. Smith

Further Reading

Rose, Saul. (1962) *Britain and South East Asia*. London: Chatto and Windus.
Tarling, Nicholas. (1975) *Imperial Britain in South-East Asia*. London: Oxford University Press.
———. (1998) *Southeast Asia and the Onset of the Cold War*. Cambridge, U.K.: Cambridge University Press.

BRITISH INDIAN EMPIRE Formally, the British Indian empire existed for ninety years (1858–1947). The empire consisted of large parts of most of the countries in South Asia and briefly included Burma as well. In area and population, British India was the largest colony the world had ever seen. In political and economic importance India was the centerpiece of the British empire. During its time, imperial rule greatly shaped the economy, society, and culture of modern South Asia.

The British Rise to Power

In the eighteenth century Europeans controlled India's maritime trade with Europe. By the end of that century the British East India Company commanded political power in Bengal. The transition from trading to direct rule is explained partly by the needs of trade itself. Indian textiles were the most important items in this trade, paid for by bullion from Europe. The bullion export invited mercantilist criticism in Britain. Local political circumstances that enabled the British to command land revenues in Bengal provided a less-controversial means of payment.

What were these local circumstances? The state system that developed under the Mughal empire (1526–1857) was in disintegration in the eighteenth century, giving rise to a group of successor states that depended on the financial accommodation of Indian merchant-bankers. Pressed to raise more revenues for

This illustration from the *Voyages of Madelslo* published in 1727 shows the first English trading station in India, established at Surat in 1613. (BETTMANN/CORBIS)

the army or for the maintenance of the courts and sometimes in a bid to shake off indebtedness, these states tended to be extortionate on their financiers. The tacit collaboration of these disaffected financiers was crucial in the British rise to power in India. Progressively between 1800 and 1857 the East India Company expanded the area under its direct administration and entered into treaties with the many princely rulers. The treaties promised the states autonomy in return for recognition of British rule outside their territories.

These subsidiary alliances, however, were unequal in a number of senses, and the inequities fed the widespread discontent that exploded in a military mutiny in 1857. The British Crown took over the rule of India after the mutiny was suppressed in 1858.

The Imperial Impact

Crown rule transformed the economy of South Asia. Through trade and investment South Asia and Britain developed close ties, and through Britain, South Asia developed ties with the rest of the world. Trade expanded enormously. India was crucial to Britain as a market for its manufactures, chiefly textiles, machinery, and metals, and as a source of foodstuffs, industrial raw materials, and a few manufactured goods intensive in labor and natural resources. Private property rights and contract laws became well defined,

and imperialism created a powerful centralized state, a modern bureaucracy, and a modern judiciary. Large-scale railway building and the telegraph integrated the region internally, and India was one of the first nations in the world to operate a functioning telegraph line. Export opportunities, well-defined property rights, and the new infrastructure encouraged production of goods for the market instead of for subsistence or local exchange. In turn this commercialization led to a limited form of peasant prosperity and more efficient agriculture in several regions.

Who benefited more from the empire, India or Britain? Classical writings on imperialism, Marxist development scholarship, and major schools of historiography in India argued that the imperial ties and domestic policies conferred more benefits on Britain than on the colonies. If this is the case, economic gains might have continued to provide the impetus for imperialism. In more extreme versions of such views, India was actually impoverished by it. The impoverishment case is weakened, however, by evidence that South Asia experienced positive and significant growth of real income in the last half of the nineteenth century. That Britain received economic gains from its colonies cannot be disputed. Nevertheless, quantitative research suggests that these gains were neither as large as earlier imagined nor crucial to explaining capital accumulation and industrialization in Britain.

BRITISH ENGINEERING IN INDIA

One of the efforts made by the British during their rule of India was the modernization of agriculture. One part of that effort was massive engineering projects to create and re-create irrigation systems like the ones described below.

> One of the first steps which had to be taken by the British irrigation engineer was the restoration, remodelling, and extension of derelict works which suffered from faulty alinement and the absence of a system of distributory canals. Original works were next taken in hand designed on a scale of which India had no previous knowledge. It is not necessary to enter into details of the different systems but some idea may be given of the magnitude of the triumphs which engineering skill achieved. The Grand Anicut, which was built in 1835-6 across the bed of the Cauvery, the first British irrigation work in South India, has a length of over 2 miles. Of the Ganges canal, the first great work in North India, Lord Dalhousie proudly wrote in 1856 that there was not a single canal in Europe of half its magnitude and that it was a work unequalled in its class and character among the efforts of civilized nations. A tunnel over a mile long has been blasted and drilled through the Western Ghats; another, 2 miles long, pierces the Malakand range. The main and distributory canals of the Gadavari system stretch for 2,500 miles; those of the Upper and Lower Ganges canals for nearly 8,000 miles, and they irrigate 2 1/2 million acres. The Chenab canal has a discharge about six times as great as that of the Thames at Teddington; the Sukkur barrage is the largest of its kind in the world; some of the canals in Sind are wider than the Suez Canal. In the Punja alone the area served by State irrigations works is nearly double that irrigated in Egypt. In British India as a whole it is 32 1/2 million acres or one-eighth of the total cultivated area.

> *Source:* Lewis S. S. O'Malley, ed. (1941) *Modern India and the West: A Study of the Interaction of Their Civilizations*. London: Oxford University Press, 244–245.

Furthermore whether or not these gains depended vitally on political subordination is open to debate.

Regardless, imperialism did impose crippling burdens on the South Asian economy. For example, India made a large payment to Britain on the government account for services Britain rendered to the colony. This was a national drain of potential investment funds. To the extent many of these services were overpriced, such as the inflated salaries of British bureaucrats in India, an element of drain indeed existed. However, the true scale of the drain cannot be estimated, for India needed many of the services for which Britain charged

it. A second example is colonial India's large defense spending. The huge Indian army defended the British empire worldwide at the expense of the Indian taxpayer, and the fiscal burden was a heavy one.

The imperial impact had many dimensions. Western learning, Western ideas, and economic exposure together gave rise to a new elite different in mentality from the old landed elite. The new elite consisted of urban middle-class professionals who were more exposed to and deeply impressed by Western science, technology, and the ideas of rationality and humanism. Previously, the principle of equality was practically alien to Indian society, but imperial laws instituted equality, and new schools with a reformist bent propagated the idea of equality. These laws and the new education encouraged social reform movements throughout South Asia. The positions of women, who were severely disadvantaged, and of the lower castes were key themes in this modern discourse on reform, fueled as it was by liberal thinkers and Christian missionaries.

On the other hand, tradition was selectively preserved and perhaps even reinvented as a result of the empire. The British rulers were averse to intervening directly in personal law. Hierarchy was reinforced by the predominance of the Brahmans and the other upper castes in public administration. Hierarchy and the distinctions of caste were also reinforced by the influence of Brahmanical interpretations of Indian society in British administrative ideology. For example, the myth of traditional India as a sedentary, self-sufficient peasant society influenced British policy on landed property.

From Empire to Nation

The journey from empire to nation, or the process of decolonization in India, can be attributed to two types of development: voluntary disengagement of private capital and rising nationalism. Britain's share in Indian trade and investment declined in between the two world wars. Nationalism in South Asia progressed along at least four trajectories: political action to undermine British rule, social reform, religious revivalism, and protests by the laboring or subaltern classes against localized repression. Inevitably, as the idea of equality took deeper root, the desire for freedom grew in intensity. Freedom had different meanings. Freedom from imperial rule was important, but to fight the British effectively required emancipation of the masses from varieties of indigenous repression. Nearly all the major figures in Indian nationalist discourse had to address the problem of how this double mission should be accomplished. Eventually the anti-imperialist struggle took priority over the reformist program. If this nationalism built upon freedom and equality, a different type of nationalism built upon denunciation of European modernity and on illusions about Indian traditions. These illusions were partly a result of British interpretations of traditional India.

The nationalist struggle took shape in the late nineteenth century, and 1930 was a turning point. The mainstream nationalist movement led by the Indian National Congress adopted the idea of total freedom from imperial rule about 1929. After 1930 the world economy and the Indian economy were in mild or deep

ONE ENGLISHMAN'S OPINION

The following poem by a British colonial official summarizes the positives and negatives of life in India.

What varied opinions we constantly hear.
Of our rich, Oriental possessions;
What a jumble of notions, distorted and queer,
Form an Englishman's "Indian impressions"!

First a sun, fierce and glaring, that scorches and bakes;
Palankeens, perspiration, and worry;
Mosquitoes, thugs, cocoanuts, Brahmins, and snakes,
With elephants, tigers and curry.

Then Juggernat, punkahs, tanks, buffaloes, forts,
With bangles, mosques, nautches, and dhingees;
A mixture of temples, Mahometans, ghats,
With scorpions, Hindoos, and Feringhees.

Then jungles, fakeers, dancing-girls, prickly heat,
Shawls idols, durbars, brandy-pawny;
Rupees, clever jugglers, dust-storms, slipper'd feet,
Rainy season, and mulligatawny.

Hot winds, holy monkeys, tall minarets, rice
With crocodiles, ryots, or farmers;
Himalayas, fat baboos, with paunches and pice,
So airily clad in pyjamas.

With Rajahs—But stop, I must really desist,
And let each one enjoy his opinions,
Whilst I show in what style Anglo-Indians exist
In Her Majesty's Eastern dominions.

Source: George F. Atkinson. (1854) *Curry and Rice on Forty Plates or the Ingredients of Social Life at "Our Station" in India.* London: Day & Son, London in 1854.

depression, the commercial significance of India for Britain was becoming steadily more obscure, and the aims of British and Indian economic policies came in sharp and evident conflict. At the end of a decade and a half racked by economic instability, political outburst, and severe repression, freedom became an accomplished fact in South Asia.

But freedom came with fierce Hindu-Muslim violence and a political breakup of the region. The origin of Hindu-Muslim disunity has been a matter of debate. In one school of thought the British cultivated it strategically. In another view it had long been an intrinsic divide. In either case a strong current of religious revivalism had deepened the communal divide, making the accommodation of religious differences increasingly difficult and sharply separating secular politics from the communally sensitive ones.

In the postimperial period the legacy of the empire is evident in the modern economy and infrastructure India retains. In addition the empire's influence shapes the relations between India and Pakistan, the Indian diaspora worldwide, and the seemingly conflicting coexistence of liberal and intolerant political ideologies within both India and Pakistan.

Tirthankar Roy

Further Reading

Bose, Sugata, and Ayesha Jalal. (1998) *Modern South Asia.* New York: Routledge.

Roy, Tirthankar. (2000) *An Economic History of India, 1857-1947.* Delhi: Oxford University Press.

Stein, Burton. (1998) *A History of India.* Malden, MA: Blackwell.

BRITISH MILITARY ADMINISTRATION

British Military Administration (BMA) was imposed on territories in the Southeast Asia theater under the military responsibility of the South East Asia Command (SEAC), under Admiral Lord Louis Mountbatten, Supreme Allied Commander (SAC). SEAC was responsible for the reoccupation and establishment of military administration over vast territories inhabited by more than 160 million people of diverse ethnicity and creed. BMA was established in Burma (present-day Myanmar) from January 1944 to October 1945, in Malaya (present-day peninsular Malaysia) from September 1945 to April 1946, and in British Borneo (now Sarawak, Brunei, and Sabah) from January to July 1946. In Burma, BMA was functioning while military operations against the Japanese continued in earnest. Although no form of BMA was established in Cambodia, Laos, Vietnam, or Indonesia, British military authorities played a major role in maintaining law and order in the period following the capitulation of Japan on 15 August 1945.

Toward the end of 1942, planning had commenced for the establishment of military governments in the Japanese-occupied territories of Southeast Asia. The planning for Burma was in the hands of the government of Burma in exile in Simla, India. The Colonial Office in London undertook this task for Malaya and British Borneo. Both Raja Vyner Brooke of Sarawak, then in Australia, and the Court of Directors of the Chartered Company that administered North Borneo (Sabah) in London agreed to the Colonial Office's handling the planning in consultation with their respective representatives.

BMA's immediate aims were to disarm and remove Japanese troops from the reoccupied territories and to liberate and relieve the hundreds of thousands of prisoners of war and civilian internees. BMA functioned on two levels. At the administrative level, its functions included the provision of transport, equipment, clothing, accommodation and housing, the import of supplies (mainly rice, other foodstuffs, and consumer goods) for the civilian population, and the relief of refugees and displaced individuals. The Civil Affairs Service was responsible for these administrative tasks. At the political level, BMA dealt with local nationalist political groups and militant resistance movements; these often had left-wing elements that vociferously demanded sovereignty and independence. In general, political issues were the responsibility of the Supreme Allied Commander.

BMA confronted two equally acute challenges in the course of its operations, which can be summed up in two words: "rice" and "independence." In the prewar period, Burma, Siam, Cambodia, Laos, and Vietnam were major exporters of rice, the staple food of Southeast and East Asia. Wartime conditions had retarded rice production, as producers reverted to subsistence in the absence of markets, and the cessation of exports during the Japanese occupation had been severely felt. BMA was faced with shortages and the responsibility of distributing the available rice supplies. The task was worsened by widespread lawlessness in the aftermath of the Japanese surrender. Seriously threatening and even forestalling BMA operations were strong nationalist movements—militant and left-wing, fairly organized, well-armed (ironically, with arms supplied by the Allies during the war), and full of self-confidence derived from their wartime experiences.

Burma

SEAC assumed the administration of liberated Burma in January 1944. Subsequently, the Civil Affairs Service (Burma), or CAS (B), established BMA in Burma. Although responsible for restoring law and order, CAS (B) had no authority in political matters; neither did the Supreme Allied Commander. Instead, that authority resided with the exiled Burmese government in India. Furthermore, CAS (B) had to contend with operatives of Force 136, a unit of the Special Operations Executive based in Ceylon (Sri Lanka). Force 136 was charged with fostering guerrilla opposition to the occupying Japanese—an activity fraught with political implications—and in pursuit of its duties it deferred to neither the Supreme Allied Commander nor the Civil Affairs Service.

The task of CAS (B) in Burma was monumental. Apart from Japan itself, Burma suffered the worst destruction of the war: the country had been fought over from south to north in 1942 and again in 1944–1945. In addition to the physical destruction, CAS (B) faced opposition from the nationalist Anti-Fascist People's Freedom League (AFPFL), led by Aung San (1915–1947). In May 1945, a British government White Paper suggested a delay in Burmese self-rule; AFPFL rejected such proposals, demanding nothing less than complete independence from the British Commonwealth.

When the Japanese surrendered, CAS (B) was administering nearly all of Burma except for the area east of the Sittang River. The cessation of hostilities hastened the handover to civilian government. Although the governor of Burma, Sir Reginald Dorman-Smith, assumed office in October 1945, it was another five months before the full transfer of responsibility was effected. During its tenure, CAS (B) had managed to restore the railway and inland water transport system. Acute shortages in consumer goods persisted, however, and prices remained astronomical.

Malaya

Malaya had not been exposed to the same level of Allied bombings as had Burma; hence conditions during the postwar period reflected dilapidation and neglect. Acute shortages of rice and widespread malnutrition were conspicuous problems. The main tasks of the BMA in Malaya were the relief of prisoners of war and internees and the rehabilitation of the country's economy. Both tasks were accomplished, due in great part to advance planning and efficient implementation. Smooth execution of the Key Plan for British Military Administration in Malaya (approved in March 1945) enabled the BMA to be ready to hand over responsibility even before the civilian government was ready to assume control. On the political level, BMA had to contend with the deterioration of relations between Malaya's Malay and Chinese populations, which erupted in armed clashes, food riots, lawlessness and banditry, and several leftist-led industrial strikes. A new political-administrative scheme, the Malayan Union, was in the process of being adopted. The scheme envisaged the union of the nine Malay states and the Straits Settlements of Penang and Melaka; Singapore was to remain a separate British colony. Citizenship under the scheme offered equality of rights to all irrespective of race or creed and also allowed dual citizenship. The Malayan Union came into being on 1 April 1946 and marked the end of BMA in Malaya.

Borneo

Originally, British Borneo came under U.S. command; later, Australia was entrusted with its occupation. After a six-month tenure of military administration under the Australian British Borneo Civil Affairs Unit (BBCAU), British Borneo came under SEAC responsibility. Brigadier C. F. C. Macaskie was in command of the British 50 Civil Affairs Unit and BBCAU. While the former remained behind in Australia, Macaskie and BBCAU established the initial military administration following the Australian Ninth Division landings at Brunei Bay on 10 June 1945. Several British officers served in BBCAU; however, when SEAC assumed responsibility for British Borneo, these officers reverted to 50 Civil Affairs Unit, which then was redesignated the British Military Administration (British Borneo), or BMA (BB). North Borneo and, to a lesser extent, Brunei suffered from Allied bombings that destroyed most urban centers; Sarawak was the least scarred. By the time BMA (BB) commenced operations in January 1946, active hostilities had ceased. BBCAU had performed most of the urgent tasks: containing the spread of disease, clamping down on minor incidents of unrest, relieving prisoners of war and internees, and distributing foodstuffs. It was left to BMA (BB) to continue these tasks and rehabilitate the economy.

Postwar planning in London had decided to convert the British protectorates of Sarawak, Brunei, and North Borneo to crown colonies and to retain the protectorate status of the sultanate of Brunei. Both Raja Vyner Brooke of Sarawak and the Court of Directors of the Chartered Company had agreed to cede their respective domains to Colonial Office administration largely owing to the financially burdensome task of postwar rehabilitation and reconstruction. Accordingly, the new British colonies of Sarawak and North Borneo came into being (1 June 1946 and 15 July 1946, respectively). The case of Sarawak was peculiar. Transfer of authority to the raja's government was made on 15 April 1946. The raja then ceded Sarawak to the British government, and the new colony of Sarawak came into being. The duties of BMA (BB) continued for the sake of distribution of civil supplies until its dissolution on 15 July. On the same date, the handover was effected in North Borneo. Handover in Brunei occurred a week earlier on 6 July 1946.

Ooi Keat Gin

Further Reading
Dennis, Peter. (1987) *Troubled Days of Peace: Mountbatten and South East Asia Command, 1945–46.* Manchester, U.K.: Manchester University Press.

Donnison, Frank Siegfried Vernon. (1956) *British Military Administration in the Far East 1943–46*. London: Her Majesty's Stationery Office.

Reece, Robert Harold William. (1982) *The Name of Brooke: The End of White Rajah Rule in Sarawak*. Kuala Lumpur, Malaysia: Oxford University Press.

Stockwell, Anthony John. (1979) *British Policy and Malay Politics during the Malayan Union Experiment, 1942–1948*. Kuala Lumpur, Malaysia: Malaysian Branch of the Royal Asiatic Society.

Tinker, Hugh, ed. (1984) *Burma: The Struggle for Independence, 1944–48*. London: Her Majesty's Stationery Office.

Tregonning, Kennedy Gordon. (1965) *A History of Modern Sabah (North Borneo 1881–1963)*. Kuala Lumpur, Malaysia: University of Malaya Press.

BRITISH-DUTCH WARS

Although the British and Dutch cooperated to counter Spanish and Portuguese influence, the alliance was uneasy as one tried to take advantage of the other's weakness. Rivalry first emerged over control of the Banda Islands and their nutmeg production. Beginning in 1616, the British settlement on Pulau Run (Run Island) was blockaded for several years, causing the death of expedition leader Captain Nathaniel Courthope. The Dutch governor of the Netherlands East Indies, Jan Pieterszoon Coen, shifted the center of Dutch operations to Batavia (Jakarta) from Bantam after British threats. In 1619, Coen ordered an attack on two British ships, causing the death of Captain John Jourdain. In March 1620, news arrived of a peace agreement signed between Britain and the Netherlands, giving Britain a minority share of the spice trade but granting the Netherlands free rein in the Spice Islands. Coen used the agreement to take full control of the Banda Islands, forcing the British out. The British formally gave up their claim in 1667 with the Peace of Breda following hostilities with the Dutch in the English Channel. The Netherlands emerged dominant in maritime Southeast Asia.

Trouble resurfaced in the late eighteenth century. As the Netherlands was allied to France, Britain took control of some strategic enclaves in the Spice Islands between 1776 and 1801, but it returned these in the 1802 Peace of Amiens treaty. However, in the early nineteenth century the Netherlands came under the sway of Napoleonic France. The arrival of Francophile governor Herman Daendels in 1808 led to British concern over French proxy influence in Southeast Asia. A decision was taken to protect Indian security and Chinese trade by assuming control of Java and its dependencies. In August 1811, a British force of 12,000, led by Lord Minto, easily took Batavia, establishing Stamford Raffles as lieutenant governor of Java. The Dutch had little choice but to cooperate with the new administration.

Raffles's dream of expanding the British Empire into Java and the surrounding islands ended with Napoleon's defeat at Waterloo, as the British wished to reestablish the Netherlands as a strong independent state. Dutch administration was restored to the Dutch East Indies in 1816. Dispute, however, arose over the ownership of Singapore (claimed by the British in 1819) and British presence in western Sumatra. The Anglo-Dutch Treaty of 1824 solidified the boundaries of maritime Southeast Asia, surrendering Sumatra to the Dutch, while granting the British Malacca and Singapore. By this stage the Netherlands had to accept British military and economic dominance and the fact that Dutch colonial rule relied on British guarantees.

Anthony Smith

Further Reading

Bastin, John. (1957) *The Native Policies of Sir Stamford Raffles in Java and Sumatra: An Economic Interpretation*. Oxford: Clarendon Press.

Hall, D. G. E. (1968) *A History of Southeast Asia*. 3d ed. London: The Macmillan Press Ltd.

Raffles, Thomas Stamford. ([1817] 1965). *History of Java*. Reprint. Kuala Lumpur, Malaysia: Oxford University Press.

BROOKE, JAMES

(1803–1868), English adventurer and ruler of Sarawak. Brooke established a dynasty in Sarawak, northwest Borneo, and he and his descendants ruled Sarawak as rajas for a century (1841–1941). Brooke's father was an official of the East India Company (EIC), and Brooke was born in India but educated in England. He joined the EIC and shortly thereafter received a commission as a cavalry officer. A casualty of the Anglo-Burmese War of 1824–1826, Brooke returned to England to recuperate. He resigned from the army and from the EIC. Eager for adventure, he made two voyages to China (1830–1831 and 1834), visiting Penang and Singapore en route.

During the early nineteenth century, Stamford Raffles (1781–1826), who established the British settlement of Singapore in 1819, advocated a greater role for Britain in the Malay Archipelago vis-à-vis the Netherlands. In a prospectus published in 1838, Brooke supported Raffles's vision by arguing that territorial possession should be the basis for developing British trade and commerce instead of the current tentative treaty arrangements.

From his inheritance, Brooke bought the schooner *Royalist* and embarked on a scientific expedition to the Malay Archipelago and New Guinea. Brooke called at Kuching in 1839 to convey to Pangeran Hassim, the regent of Brunei, a letter from the mercantile community of Singapore, thanking him for his aid to shipwrecked British merchant seamen.

Sarawak, then covering the river basins of the Lundu, Sarawak, Samarahan, and Sadong, was a fiefdom of the sultanate of Brunei. The mineral-rich region of Upper Sarawak attracted Hakka Chinese gold miners from Sambas in the early 1820s; in the mid-1820s, Brunei became interested in obtaining antimony from there as well. Owing to ill-treatment from Pangeran Makota, the raja of Sarawak, the local inhabitants of Malays and Bidayuhs (Land Dyaks) staged an anti-Brunei rebellion (1836–1840) that disrupted the antimony trade. Hassim, the regent of Brunei, was sent to Sarawak to end the troubles. Hassim asked Brooke, then en route to Singapore, to quash the uprising and promised to make him raja of Sarawak if he succeeded. Brooke quelled the rebellion, and in 1841 he was proclaimed raja of Sarawak in place of Makota.

Brooke created a regime of enlightened paternal despotism, where the raja ruled in consultation with the Malay *datu* (nonroyal chieftains). He emphasized the development of free trade, protection of native interests, and promotion of their welfare. He opposed the introduction of large-scale European and Chinese capitalist ventures and also eschewed radical changes; changes, if deemed necessary, were to be introduced gradually.

During the 1840s Brooke and the Royal Navy greatly reduced the raiding and plundering activities of the Saribas and Skrang Ibans, which had disrupted trade. Headhunting was suppressed. Brooke survived the Hakka Chinese attack on Kuching of February 1857, defeated Iban resistance led by the warrior Rentap (late 1857), and eliminated a Malay conspiracy aimed at toppling his regime (1860–1861). At the expense of Brunei, Brooke extended the boundaries of Sarawak to the Bintulu River (1861). He was instrumental in establishing the British crown colony of Labuan (1847), with himself as its first governor.

After Brooke died in England in 1868, Sarawak remained relatively unknown to the outside world despite its recognition as an independent state by the United States in 1850 and by Britain in 1863. Brooke's nephew and his nephew's son continued his benevolent practices and ruled as second and third rajas from 1868 until 1941, when Sarawak received a constitution and was ceded to Great Britain. While rudimentary

trade had begun to take root under the Brooke dynasty, the various native inhabitants continued to practice their traditional subsistence-based livelihood.

Ooi Keat Gin

Further Reading
Ooi, Keat Gin. (1997) *Of Free Trade and Native Interests: The Brookes and the Economic Development of Sarawak, 1841–1941*. Kuala Lumpur, Malaysia: Oxford University Press.

Pringle, Robert. (1970) *Rajahs and Rebels: The Ibans of Sarawak under Brooke Rule*. London: Macmillan.

Tarling, Nicholas. (1982) *The Burthen, the Risk, and the Glory: A Biography of Sir James Brooke*. Kuala Lumpur, Malaysia: Oxford University Press.

BROOKE RAJ. See **White Rajas.**

BRUNEI—PROFILE
(2001 pop. 344,000). Negara Brunei Darussalam, the official title assumed by the former British protectorate upon full statehood in 1984, closely resembles a Southeast Asian equivalent of a Middle-Eastern petroleum state. Independent Brunei has taken its place in the world and enjoys multiple political, military, commercial, and cultural links within the region, to the Islamic world with which it identifies, and, not least, with Great Britain, whose protectorate it was from 1888 until its independence. Its capital is Bandar Seri Begawan (formerly Brunei Town). Situated on the northwest coast of the island of Borneo, Brunei shares an ecological niche with the diverse peoples of this huge equatorial island. Ruled by an Islamic dynasty tracing its lineage back to the fourteenth century, modern Brunei comprises but a vestige of its historical territorial sway over the northern half of Borneo island. The combination of small population and sufficient reserves of petroleum and natural gas has propelled this nation of mostly self-sufficient agriculturists and fisher folk to enviable prosperity and even some fame within the course of a single generation.

Physical Geography
Enclosing an area of 5,770 square kilometers, the modern boundaries of Brunei were given definition only in the late nineteenth century. Through a series of cessions and aggressions undertaken by the British and their agents, notably the Brooke dynasty that established its presence in Sarawak in the 1840s, the Sultanate was progressively stripped of its Bornean territories, including large swaths of what today

BRUNEI

Country name: Negara Brunei Darussalam

Area: 5,770 sq km

Population: 343,653 (July 2001 est.)

Population growth rate: 2.11% (2001 est.)

Birth rate: 20.45 births/1,000 population (2001 est.)

Death rate: 3.38 deaths/1,000 population (2001 est.)

Net migration rate: 4.07 migrant(s)/1,000 population (2001 est.)

Sex ratio—total population: 1.1 male(s)/female (2001 est.)

Infant mortality rate: 14.4 deaths/1,000 live births (2001 est.)

Life expectancy at birth—total population: 73.82 years, male: 71.45 years, female: 76.31 years (2001 est.)

Major religions: Islam (official), Buddhism, Christianity, indigenous religions

Major languages: Malay (official), English, Chinese

Literacy—total population: 88.2%, male: 92.6%, female: 83.4% (1995 est.)

Government type: constitutional sultanate

Capital: Bandar Seri Begawan

Administrative divisions: 4 districts

Independence: 1 January 1984 (from UK)

National holiday: National Day, 23 February (1984)

Suffrage: none

GDP—real growth rate: 3% (2000 est.)

GDP—per capita (purchasing power parity): $17,400 (2000 est.)

Population below poverty line: not available

Exports: $2.55 billion (f.o.b., 1999 est.)

Imports: $1.3 billion (c.i.f., 1999 est.)

Currency: Bruneian dollar (BND)

Source: Central Intelligence Agency. (2001) *The World Factbook* 2001. Retrieved 18 October 2001 from: http://www.cia.gov/cia/publications/factbook.

constitutes the East Malaysian states of Sarawak and Sabah, along with the island of Labuan. The cession of the Sarawakan territory of Limbang was long disputed; Limbang physically divides Brunei. Temburong, the portion of Brunei to the east of Limbang, is the least developed district of the nation. It is 1,304 square kilometers in area. The smallest (571 square kilometers) but most populous administrative district of Brunei is Brunei-Muara, named after the river and its estuary. As the historic fount of the Sultanate, the Brunei River is also home to the historic Kampong Ayer, or water village precinct. Today, however, the modern capital, including the landmark Istana, or royal palace, sprawls across the west bank of the river. To the west of Brunei-Muara lies Tutong with an area

of 1,666 square kilometers, while the largest and most westerly district is Belait with an area of 2,724 square kilometers. Besides the nation's capital, other population concentrations are found in Muara, the major deep water port, along with the coastal towns of Tutong, Seria (the center of oil production), and Kuala Belait, commercially oriented toward Sarawak, to which it adjoins.

With a coastline of about 180 kilometers, bisected by four important rivers, the Belait, the Tutong, the Brunei, and the Temburong, Brunei hosts a number of ecological zones, varying according to altitude. From the riverine mangrove forests and freshwater swamps of the lowlands, one ascends hilly terrain covering most of the country to the interior highlands, which rise to

913 meters in Temburong. Some 80 percent of the land remains covered with forest, including extensive strands of primary tropical rain forest in Temburong.

Traditionally, this lush tropical environment fostered a range of economic activities, especially concentrated along the lower reaches of the rivers and their flood plains, such as fishing, hunting, rice farming, and trading, in addition to the gathering or harvesting of exotic forest products, such as the bark of mangroves. It can be said that, prior to the exploitation of Brunei's hydrocarbon resources, subsistence agriculture was the dominant form of production. Aside from small-scale logging, little attempt was made during the Protectorate to exploit or develop Brunei's agricultural and forestry resources. One exception was the establishment of rubber plantations, an industry that faded in the post–World War II period. Coal was exploited at Muara and in Brunei Town during the Protectorate. Reserves of silica sand remain unexploited.

The discovery and exploitation of Brunei's hydrocarbon resources, in line with technological advances, has shaped the man-nature relationship in Brunei and the nation's economic destiny. Oil was first discovered on land near Seria in 1929 by Shell Oil Company, but the focus of oil and gas exploitation has moved in the post–World War II period to offshore fields. While recent attempts have been made to reverse the trend, today a shrinking percentage of the population is engaged in agriculture or fishing activities.

Human Geography

The historical royal center in Brunei was grafted upon a highly heterogeneous indigenous population. Ethnic distinctions, however, have become increasingly blurred since independence. This situation arises not only from homogenizing nation-building strategies of the modern state, but also from conversions as members of the various *puak* (indigenous tribes) embrace Islam and enter the category "Malay" (now defined as totaling 69 percent of the population). Even so, Malay is a catch-all designation embracing not only the dominant Brunei Malay, speakers of a language that is perhaps 80 percent cognate with standard Malay, but also the Dusun (mostly from the Belait district), Tutong, Murut, Kedayan, and Bisayah peoples. One could go further and say that Brunei "Malayness" is problematic. Consider the Kedayan case. An agricultural people whose traditions suggest separate origins from the Malayanized ruling-trading classes, the rustic Kedayan have in recent decades become acculturated to the point where ethnicity no longer becomes a significant cultural marker. The conversion to Islam above all else defines Brunei Malayness.

Standing apart from this privileged category of Brunei "Malays" are the true indigenes, the Iban and Punan, who are animists. Also known as Dyak, the Iban share traditions with their far more numerous ethnic kin in Sarawak and in Indonesian Kalimantan. The Punan minority, a group of hunter-gatherers mostly concentrated in Belait, are also more numerous in Sarawak. Iban and Punan together constitute some 5 percent of the population.

Immigrant groups are dominated by Chinese, whose demographic strength reached 26 percent of the population in the 1960s but has declined to around 15 percent at present. Although many Chinese—speakers of Hakka being most numerous, followed by speakers of Hokkien—can trace their ancestry in Brunei back many generations, most are deemed "stateless," as not having Brunei citizenship. Besides Chinese, whose numbers continue to decline from out-migration, Brunei has attracted a floating population of international expatriates that includes workers in the oil industry, members of the teaching and other professions, and working-class Asians, especially Thai construction workers and domestics from the Philippines.

Governance

Brunei remains a hierarchical and status-riven society in keeping with its feudal origins and absolutist political system. Reigning sultan Hassanal Bolkiah, who has ruled since 1968, is an absolute monarch in whose person are concentrated the powers of prime minister, finance minister, and defense minister. In Sunni Muslim belief, he is also considered by his subjects as head of religion. Paradoxically, certain of the symbols of state reflect the pre-Islamic origins of Southeast Asian monarchy. In appending the term Negara to the official title of the newly independent state, Brunei links its traditions with the *negara* states of the Malay world, whose kingship and court ritual were Hindu in pattern.

While some progress, with British encouragement, had been made toward constitutional monarchy in 1959, the experiment was suspended in 1962 following the unsuccessful armed rebellion by the Indonesian-backed populist Sheikh Azahari. To this day the constitution is but a memorial, parliament remains suspended, elections are unheard of, and political parties lack membership. The only concession to representative government is the creation of village councils.

In Sultan Ali Saifuddin III (reigned 1950–1967) the British secured a staunch ally, and the pro-Western bias continued when Sultan Hassanal Bolkiah replaced his father in 1968. As a profligate prince-playboy in his earlier years, the sultan undoubtedly attracted some of the negative attention now attached to his youngest brother, Prince Jefri. Nevertheless, building upon Islamic and Malay traditions deeply accommodated by his father, the Malaysian- and Sandhurst-educated Sultan Hassanal has gone further in strengthening both his own Islamic credentials and those of the nation. The term *darussalam* ("abode of peace") was contrived at independence to further strengthen the nation's Islamic credentials.

With independence on 1 January 1984, the sultan consolidated family power, with five ministries controlled by four family members. Until stripped of the position in 1999, the Finance Ministry went to Prince Jefri and the Foreign Affairs portfolio to his younger brother Mohamed. Commencing in 1986, the cabinet system was "modernized" with the inclusion of a number of nonroyals. Nevertheless, with key provisions of the constitution suspended, and with the sultan wielding key executive power, the country has been ruled by decree since 1962. A recent example was the declaration of "a state of emergency of the whole state" on 27 June 1998, ostensibly to allow the sultan to make special financial provisions to redress the impact on the budget of a fall in world oil prices. The saving grace for the monarchical system is its perceived ability to provide jobs and welfare.

Economy

In per-capita terms Brunei is one of the richest states in Asia, with an estimated $17,400 per-capita income. Citizens are undoubtedly well provided for in terms of welfare, but poverty is not unknown among certain communities, such as the Iban.

Originally a Shell monopoly, the petroleum industry in Brunei today is dominated by a number of companies belonging to Brunei Shell, a company owned by the royal family, and Shell International. Brunei Shell is responsible for exploration and production of oil and natural gas as well as oil refining. Brunei Liquid Petroleum Gas (LPG) works with Mitsubishi Corporation of Japan in liquefying gas, while another company is concerned with supplying the liquified gas to major clients in Japan, including Tokyo Electric Power Company, the Tokyo Gas Company, and the Osaka Gas Company. In recent years, South Korea has also emerged as a customer for Brunei's natural gas. Also, in recent years a number of new players have entered the oil industry, most notably Elf Aquitaine in a tie-up with royal family interests. Little downstream economic activity is generated by the enclave economy based on hydrocarbon exploitation, nor has Brunei Darussalam been particularly successful in attracting foreign investment along the lines of other growth economies of Southeast Asia. Networks of *bumiputra*, or local businessmen active in such activities as construction, survive on government favors and licenses, but they are highly vulnerable to economic cycles.

Discussions of Brunei's "national" wealth would not be complete without reference to the finances of the royal family, almost a special sector of the economy. The ruling family is arguably the richest family in the world, and there is no distinguishing its fortunes from those of the state. As supreme executive and sovereign, the sultan has the power to dispose of all state assets as he sees fit. The sultan is simply above the law. Even the Brunei government is immune from the process of law, and businessmen in conflict with the government have no recourse to the courts. The net worth of the sultan is the subject of much speculation; he may at one time have been worth between US$40 and US$80 billion, a figure equal to Brunei's reserves. The sultan's international assets include luxury hotels, cattle stations in Australia, and jewelry and art collections. At home the Bolkiah family wealth and presence loom in the shape of sprawling palaces and domains expanding in tandem with the family itself. Family assets include Prince Mohamed's controlling interest in Singapore-registered QAF Holdings and the enormous financial interests of Prince Jefri, including the Sultanate's largest conglomerate, Amedeo Company. It is notable that royal family's economic activity is not reflected in national accounts and falls outside surveys conducted by the government Economic Planning Unit.

The Southeast Asian Games flag is raised to open the 20th Games, held in Brunei in August 1999. (REUTERS NEWMEDIA INC./CORBIS)

One must also consider the link between the Brunei Investment Agency (BIA) and the state, the business elite, and international capital. In theory, it is the BIA, established in 1983 within the Finance Ministry, that is vested with managing the Sultanate's reserves. The directorship of the BIA also passed to Prince Jefri as finance minister. The modus operandi of the BIA has seldom entered public discourse, though its former managing director once revealed that the agency only handled 40 percent of the Sultanate's foreign reserves, with the balance divided among eight foreign banking and investment institutions, or in stocks and shares. But, as exposed in 1998, the BIA's assets, said to be worth US$60 billion before depletion, were depleted of US$16 billion, the amount lost by Prince Jefri in the wake of the collapse of Amedeo Company. Sensationally served a civil suit in the Brunei courts by the sultan, Prince Jefri agreed to an out-of-court settlement as testimony began to cast aspersions upon the wider circles of the royal economy and its close beneficiaries. Only the rebound in oil prices from historic

lows beginning in the latter half of 1999 brought a financial reprieve to Brunei in the wake of the damaging Amedeo scandal.

Major Issues Facing the Nation

In a land without politics the question must eventually be asked, Can the system of dynastic rule be perpetuated forever? The answer from the Middle East is not comforting, as we see in the rise of radical military-led secularist regimes from Libya to Yemen. Examples from the Persian Gulf point up the vulnerability of dynastic monarchies to internal conflict, while the case of Kuwait famously reveals the fragility of resource-rich states in internationally fragile arenas. Political Islam reinvents itself constantly in neighboring Malaysia and Indonesia, and Brunei is not immune to regional currents. Such challenges are real, as even suggested by the environmental crisis visited upon Brunei in the late 1990s by the great Borneo forest fires. The Brunei economy is by definition extroverted and vulnerable because of the way it collects and recycles external rents; it would benefit tremendously from diversification. Modulating the Islamic challenge and meeting the rising economic aspirations of a better-educated population will require skillful and wise leadership, especially on the part of a dynastic successor.

Geoffrey C. Gunn

Further Reading

Bartholomew, James. (1989) *The Richest Man in the World: The Sultan of Brunei*. London: Viking.

Brown, Donald. E. (1970) *Brunei: The Structure and History of a Bornean Malay Sultanate*. Bandar Seri Begawan, Brunei: Brunei Museum Journal.

Cleary, Mark, and Wong Shuang Yann. (1994) *Oil, Economic Development and Diversification in Brunei Darussalam*. London: St. Martin's Press.

Gunn, Geoffrey C. (1993) "Rentier Capitalism in Negara Brunei Darussalam." In *Southeast Asia in the 1990s: Authoritarianism, Democracy and Capitalism*, edited by Kevin Hewison et al. Sydney: Allen & Unwin, 109–132.

———. (1997) *Language, Power and Ideology in Brunei Darussalam*. Athens, OH: Ohio University Center for Asian Studies.

Hussainmiya, B. A. (1995) *Sultan Omar Saifuddin III and Britain: The Making of Brunei Darussalam*. Kuala Lumpur, Malaysia: Oxford University Press.

Kershaw, Roger. (2001) "Perks and Perils of Absolute Rule." In *Monarchy in South-East Asia: The Faces of Tradition in Transition*. London: Routledge.

Leake, David Jr. (1989, 1990) *Brunei: The Modern Southeast-Asian Islamic Sultanate*. Jefferson, NC: McFarland & Co. [1989]; Kuala Lumpur, Malaysia: Forum [1990].

Ranjit Singh, D. S. (1984) *Brunei 1839–1983: The Problems of Political Survival*. Singapore: Oxford University Press.

Saunders, Graham. (1994) *A History of Brunei.* Kuala Lumpur, Malaysia: Oxford University Press.

BRUNEI—POLITICAL SYSTEM

Negara Brunei Darussalam—the name Brunei assumed on full independence from Great Britain on 1 January 1984—retains many features of a Middle Eastern dynastic system despite its Southeast Asian location on the northwest coast of the tropical island of Borneo. One of the few absolute monarchies in the world, Brunei Darussalam projects itself to the world as a peerless Islamic state, albeit imbued with the characteristic features of Malay world kingship and civilization.

Reigning Sultan Hassanal Bolkiah (b. 1946), who came to the throne in 1968, is twenty-ninth in a line that stretches back to a fourteenth-century Malay Muslim ancestor; he holds supreme political power as prime minister, minister of defense, and, since purging his younger brother Jefri in 1999, minister of finance. The sultan's younger brother Mohamed holds the position of minister of foreign affairs. Highly trusted nonroyals also have been permitted to hold office within a limited cabinet system. Power is centered on the prime minister's office, and the sultan is advised by certain key councils.

Brunei was a British protectorate from 1888 and, with the exception of the period of Japanese occupation (1941–1945), was guided by a British Resident installed in 1906. Great Britain retained responsibility for defense and foreign affairs until independence. Although a written constitution and constitutional form of government were forced on the present sultan's father, Sultan Omar Ali Saifuddin III, by the British in 1959, a rebellion staged in 1962 by Sheik Azahari, the republican-leaning and Indonesian-backed leader of the popular Partai Rakyat Brunei (PRB), was crushed by the British. This led to the suspension of important sections of the constitution and the implementation of state-of-emergency legislation, which was still technically in force in 2001. As a result, parliament has not been convened since 1962; important liberties remain circumscribed; and political parties—two of which exist in principle—are largely inoperative, supported by minuscule membership.

Ideological Basis

With independence and the growth of modern media, along with developments in higher education, the state in Brunei has sought to reinforce Malayness, Islam, and Sultanism around the concept "Malay, Islam, Beraja" (Kingship), or MIB. More than a slogan, however, MIB is actively proselytized in the officially controlled media and education system and is taken as an article of faith in official pronouncements.

Brunei supports a heterogeneous population of indigenous peoples such as the Iban, who are also found in the neighboring Malaysian state of Sarawak, along with a significant immigrant Chinese population. It is Brunei-Malay–speaking "Malays," however, who are politically privileged in Brunei. Citizenship remains a restricted category from which most Chinese are excluded. Special privileges are offered to distinguish Brunei-Malay speakers from members of other ethnic groups, such as the Kedayan, Bisayah, Murut, and Belait.

Harking back to a Brunei golden age when the kingdom held sway over large parts of coastal Brunei and traded with the Philippines, the Indonesian archipelago, and even China, modern Brunei exults in its Islamic history, even though archaeological evidence of a Hindu-Buddhistic *negara* (a Malay term for "state") supports the thesis of a flourishing pre-Islamic kingdom astride the Brunei River. Crucial to received models of kingship in Brunei, however, is the historical legacy of borrowing certain key royal insignia, emblems, and symbols, as well as an elaborate code of ranked titles, from the Malacca sultanate. More feudal than Islamic in this Malay setting, the sultan's own title, Yang Di Pertuan ("he who is supreme"), is emblematic of absolutist temporal and religious authority at the apex of a social hierarchy buttressed by a strict code of stratified social relations, in a status-obsessed social-political system.

While MIB is represented as reaching back to a hoary past, the question arises as to just how traditional the current political system actually is. The sultan, a Sandhurst-trained officer, is no stranger to Western ways and, via the British connection, is seen to be a loyal pro-Western ally and client for defense and other contracts. British-derived law, a British-Indian-Malaysian civil-service ethos, and a professional military, along with other imported forms bequeathed to independent Brunei, supply a complete armature of postcolonial controls and censorship necessary to stifle dissent, cripple initiative, and stave off political challenge. Even so, cooptation rather than oppression has been the general modus operandi, with the notable exception of imprisonment of surviving members of the PRB.

Contradictions nevertheless abound. While the trend to Islamicization and even Arabization in religious affairs is increasingly apparent, such as in the increased frequency of the hajj (pilgrimage to Mecca) and the officialized use of Jawi, or Arabic script, in writing Malay, a palpable Westernization is also evi-

The Sultan of Brunei Hassanal Bolkiah inspects the guard of honor during the celebration of his 53rd birthday. (AFP/CORBIS)

dent, not only by way of an expatriate presence but also as a product of economic globalization. To the disdain of many traditionalists, Brunei is increasingly a materialistic society. While Bruneians, the sultan included, revel in the liberalism afforded by overseas study or visits abroad, no such liberalism is tolerated at home. But even where the royal family has been known to indulge in pleasures at home, such extravagances are translated in the language of the *rakyat*, or subjects, as the natural rights of a benign Malay Islamic monarch.

Challenges

Sharing many features with Middle Eastern ruling dynasties, including vulnerability to challenges from would-be reformists and conservatives, it is not surprising that Negara Brunei Darassalum is nonetheless prepared. There is no legal political challenge, as legitimate parties exist only as memorials, and parliament does not convene. Potential military challenge to the person of the sultan is checked by a praetorian guard in the form of a battalion of Gurhka soldiers, while potential disaffection in the armed forces has in part been offset by a move to split it into three distinct services. A potential Islamic challenge to Sunni orthodoxy has in effect been neutralized by the sultan's adroit brokering between modernists and conservatives, with the sultan and his two wives increasingly adopting a more pious public demeanor. Family challenge, doubtless anticipated by the August 1998 nomination of the sultan's eldest son, Al-Muhtadee Billah, as Crown Prince, is always a wild card in dynastic monarchies. Foreign subversion, including a challenge to offshore oil fields or spillover of any war over the Spratley Islands dispute in the South China

Sea, cannot be ruled out. Possible spread of the post-Suharto violence raging in neighboring Indonesia is also a threat. Economic collapse in Brunei Darussalam is unlikely; however, withdrawal of economic legitimacy, such as that triggered by major financial losses, would imperil the closed political system, just as major international exposure of family scandals would damage legitimacy at home.

Geoffrey C. Gunn

See also: **Borneo; Islam—Brunei**

Further Reading
Brown, Donald, E. (1970) *Brunei: The Structure and History of a Bornean Malay Sultanate.* Monograph of the Brunei Museum Journal 2, 2.

Gunn, Geoffrey C. (1997) *Language, Power, and Ideology in Brunei Darussalam.* Ohio University Center for International Studies, Monographs in International Studies, Southeast Asian Series, no. 99. Athens, OH: Ohio University Press.

Hussainmiya, B. A. (1995) *Sultan Omar Ali Saifuddin III and Britain: The Making of Brunei Darussalam.* Kuala Lumpur, Malaysia: Oxford University Press.

BUDDHA. See **Siddhartha Gautama.**

BUDDADASA BHIKKU (1906–1993), Thai Buddhist intellectual and priest. Buddhadasa Bhikku ("servant of the Buddha"; also known as Phra Thepwisutthimethi or Ngu'am) established Suan Mokkhabalarama (now known simply as Wat Suanmokkh, "Garden of the Power of Liberation") as a forest monastery in southern Thailand in 1932. Reflecting Buddhadasa's goal to promote a pure form of Buddhism, Wat Suanmokkh differs dramatically from the vast majority of Buddhist temples in mainland Southeast Asia. There are no gilded Buddhas or the opulent decorative art associated with temples in the region. Monks' *kuti* (small living quarters) are scattered through the forest, and there is a spiritual theater that contains artworks reflecting Buddhist concepts from diverse traditions such as Zen and Tibetan Buddhism.

Buddhadasa was a prolific scholar who wrote hundreds of books and articles about Buddhism. An entire room in the National Library of Thailand is dedicated to his collected works. He emphasized *vipassana*, a deep understanding of the basic principles of the Buddha's teaching, which have practical relevance to everyday life. His work has inspired many Thai intellectuals and activists such as Sulak Sivaraksa, who criticized the growing materialism in modern Thai society and who practiced socially engaged Buddhism. Buddhadasa welcomed dialogue with other religious traditions such as Islam, Christianity, and Hinduism and looked for common bonds among such religions. One of his last acts was to create at Wat Suanmokkh an International Dhamma (doctrine) Heritage to welcome individuals from around the world interested in learning about the core principles of Buddhism.

Gerald W. Fry

Further Reading

Bhikku Buddhadasa. (1986) *Dhammic Socialism*. Ed. and trans. by Donald K. Swearer. Bangkok, Thailand: Thai Inter-Religious Commission for Development.

"Buddhadasa Bhikku." (2001) Retrieved March 2002, from: http://www.suanmokkh.org/tanaj1.htm.

Phra Thepwisutthimethi (Ngu'am). (1989). *Me and Mine: Selected Essays of Bhikku Buddhadasa*. Edited by Donald K. Swearer. Albany, NY: State University of New York Press.

BUDDHISM—CENTRAL ASIA Buddhism reached Central Asia before it reached its second home, China, some time between the third century BCE and the first century CE. The travels of the Buddhists who brought it to Central Asia from India were modeled on the career of Siddhartha Gautama, the Buddha (c. 566–486 BCE). He had spent his career, after his enlightenment, traveling to the courts of various rulers in search of support for his growing community of adherents (the *sangha*), and generations of later Buddhists did the same thing throughout Central Asia. The earliest Indian Buddhist ruler who sent Buddhist missionaries into Central Asia was Asoka (d. 238 BCE).

Central Asia can be defined in various ways; one definition includes most or all of modern Pakistan, Afghanistan, Iran, Uzbekistan, Tajikistan, Kazakhstan, Kyrgyzstan, Turkmenistan, Mongolia, Tibet, southern Siberia, and northwest China. Buddhism spread throughout nearly this entire area from the third century BCE on, and still exists in several area. During this long period, Buddhism encountered many religions, among them Christianity, Zoroastrianism, Manichaeism, Islam, and Taoism, and there were numerous reactions back and forth between these. Several may have influenced important developments in Buddhism.

The peoples of Central Asia who supported Buddhism were diverse; they included dwellers in the city-states that flourished along the trade routes and water sites, residents of small villages, and pastoral nomads. Some were traders who made their living leading car-

avans from one city-state to another, plying the trade routes which connected Europe with South and East Asia and distributed silk, spices, and other goods westward. Central Asia thus presented Buddhism with a variety of natural, social, and religious environments.

Because of all the above factors and others, it would be better to speak of "Buddhisms" in Central Asia, and describe separately each culture's special forms of Buddhism. However, this essay will limit itself to developments common to all or most cultures, because these had the greatest impact not only throughout Central Asia, but also in, for example, China, which obtained its Buddhist teachings largely from Central Asia.

The Historical Record

Knowledge about Buddhism in Central Asia comes from three main sources: texts and inscriptions, archaeological remains, and anecdotal mentions of Buddhism in historical, geographical, and other writings. In general, it may be said that texts tell a lot about what particular Buddhist groups believed (their doctrines), what sacred texts were popular in which areas, what rules were observed in their monastic communities, and something about what rituals were performed. Inscriptions often tell us about how rulers believed in, or used, Buddhism. Archaeological sites show us what monasteries looked like and how temples were arranged. Remains of stupas, which may be either memorials to the Buddha or funerary structures, also tell us about Buddhist worship. Anecdotal literature, which often comes from non-Buddhists, gives us another view of their religious life. In it we can sometimes see the relationship, and conflict, between Buddhism and other religions; we also find details about the spread of Buddhism and the relationship between Buddhism and local societies that Buddhist materials themselves don't mention, and that we sometimes cannot determine from archaeological findings. All these sources must be used to get the fullest picture of what local variations of Buddhism were like in Central Asia.

The Importance of Central Asian Buddhism for China

Of these sources, Buddhist texts in the languages of the area have been the most studied. From these sources it is clear that Hinayana ("Lesser Vehicle") Buddhism was popular for a very long time, especially in western Central Asia. Mahayana ("Great Vehicle") Buddhism was limited, from the period of the second century BCE to perhaps the sixth century CE, mostly to the area around Khotan, in modern Xinjiang, China. This explains why Hinayana Buddhist literature and monastic culture were so important in later forms of Buddhism in Tibet, China, and elsewhere, even though those areas were Mahayana. These texts also help scholars understand better how Hinayana and Mahayana Buddhism developed in general; thus they complement data on Buddhism in India and the many questions that have arisen about its history in India. This appreciation of Buddhism in Central Asia represents a departure from earlier scholarship, which held that Central Asia had no impact on Buddhism as it traveled from India to China. Now we know that the first translators of Buddhist materials into Chinese were Central Asians, and most of the important early translations were made from texts in Central Asian languages, not directly from Sanskrit.

Interaction of Buddhism with Other Religions

Archaeological data reveals instances in which Buddhism interacted with other religions. One drawing, with inscription, seems to suggest the Buddha was equated with Ahura Mazda, the chief Zoroastrian deity, in part of the Iranian world where Zoroastrianism was established. The study of ruins of monasteries may help understand how Buddhist monasticism influenced the development of Christian monasticism. (Texts in Chinese and Sogdian Iranian are also good sources for studying mutual influences between Buddhism and Nestorian Christianity and Buddhism and Manichaeism.)

Perhaps the most overlooked data is the anecdotal. To give just one example, al-Biruni (973–1048), an Arab scholar, stated in about the year 1000 that, prior to the coming of Islam, Buddhism had been established as far as Mosul, present-day southern Iraq. Other Chinese, Persian, and Arabic writings contain much data that should be studied to help us develop a clearer picture of the rich cultures of Buddhism in that vast area.

Michael Walter

Further Reading

Bongard-Levin, Grigorii Maksimovich. (1971) "Central Asia in the Kushan Period." In *Studies in Ancient India and Central Asia*. Calcutta, India: Indian Studies Past & Present.

Emmerick, Ronald E. (1987) "Buddhism in Central Asia." In *Encyclopedia of Religion*, vol. 2, edited by Mircea Eliade. New York: Macmillan, 400–404.

Litvinsky, Boris Anatolevich. (1970) "Outline History of Buddhism in Central Asia." In *Kushan Studies in the U.S.S.R.* Calcutta, India: Indian Studies Past & Present, 53–132.

———. (1979) "Central Asia." In *Encyclopedia of Buddhism*, vol. 4, edited by G. P. Malalasekera et al. Colombo, Sri Lanka: Government Press, 21–52.

Nattier, Jan. (1990) "Church Language and Vernacular Language in Central Asian Buddhism." *Numen* 37: 195–219.

Puri, B. N. (1987) *Buddhism in Central Asia*. Delhi: Motilal Banarsidass.

Sander, Lore. (1979) "Buddhist Literature in Central Asia." In *Encyclopedia of Buddhism*, vol. 4, edited by G. P. Malalasekera et al. Colombo, Sri Lanka: Government Press, 52–75.

Upasak, C. S. (1990) *History of Buddhism in Afghanistan*. Varanasi, India: Central Institute of Higher Tibetan Studies.

BUDDHISM, CHAN Chan (Japanese: Zen) Buddhism is one of the Mahayana Buddhist schools that developed in China. The Chinese term *chan-(na)* is a transliteration of the Sanskrit word *dhyana*, which means meditation. In origin, Chan refers to a Buddhist form of meditation, a religious discipline aimed at mental absorption or trance. Although meditation has always been an essential part of Indian Buddhism, as a Buddhist school Chan is distinctively Chinese. During the course of its development, Chan was closely associated with Chinese literati culture and thought. In addition, Chan also incorporated such indigenous Taoist philosophy into its teachings as nondualism, spontaneity, naturalism, and skepticism toward written and spoken language.

History

Toward the end of the seventh century, certain monks were particularly famous for their engagement in meditation. One monastic community devoted to meditation was the East Mountain School (*Dongshan famen*) on Mount Shuangfeng (Twin Peaks Mountain) in Huangmei (present-day Hubei province) led by Hongren (601–674 CE), who was later known as the Fifth Patriarch of the Chan School in China.

In the eighth century, as Chan came to establish itself as an independent Buddhist school, legends and histories arose that formed a legitimate link between Chinese Chan and the Indian patriarchs. According to classical accounts of the early Chan lineage, Chan was a teaching that descended directly from the Buddha Sakyamuni, who in a sermon made a wordless mind-to-mind transmission (*ixin chuanxin*) to his disciple Mahakasyapa by simply holding a flower while smiling. The line of transmission was carried on through twenty-eight Indian patriarchs and eventually to Bodhidharma (d. 532 CE), an Indian monk who traveled to China and became the First Patriarch of the Chinese Chan School.

From Bodhidharma, the Chan patriarchal lineage allegedly continued through Huike (c. 485–574), Sengzan (d. 606), Daoxin (580–651), and Hongren. At

Hongren, however, the Chan lineage was said to have been split into two main branches: the Northern School led by Shenxiu (605?–706) associated with the teaching of gradual enlightenment (jianwu) and the Southern School led by Huineng (638–713) associated with the teaching of sudden enlightenment (dunwu). Huineng was later recognized as the legitimate Sixth Patriarch of the Chinese Chan School, and his school continued to flourish after the decline of Shenxiu's school. The *Platform Sutra of the Sixth Patriarch (Liuzu Tanjing)* written around 780 is an important text that purports to record Huineng's autobiography, sermons, and dialogues with his disciples.

Following Huineng, the Chan lineage was further divided into the so-called Five Houses (wujia). Of these Chan branches, the School of Linji (Japanese: Rinzai) founded by Liji Ixuan (d. 866) and the School of Caodong (Japanese: Soto) founded by Caoshan Benji (840–901) and Dongshan Liangjia (807–869) gained prominence in the Song dynasty (960–1267). Both schools have flourished in Korea and Japan. Although Chan as a Buddhist school declined in China after the Song, Chan meditation was a common form of Buddhist practice; the joint practice of Chan meditation and the Pure Land *nianfo* (Japanese: *nembutsu*), reciting the Buddha's name, became very popular in late imperial China.

Doctrine and Practice

The vision of Chan as a unique form of Buddhism is epitomized in the following four-part slogan:

A separate transmission apart from the scriptural teachings (jiaowai biechuan);

Not setting up words and letters (buli wenzi);

A direct pointing to the human mind (zhizhi renxin);

Seeing one's self-nature and realizing Buddhahood (jianxing chengfo).

Although individual phrases appeared in the Tang period (618–907 CE), this conception of Chan's identity was formulated during the Song dynasty and attributed retrospectively to Bodhidharma.

Chan's assertion of the universal accessibility of Buddhahood is derived from the ideal of the *tathagatagarbha* (Chinese: *rulai zang*). Meaning literally the embryo of the Tathagata, this doctrine asserts that the Buddha-nature, the absolute reality that is both immanent and empty (Chinese: *kong*; Sanskrit: *sunyata*), is the basis of human existence and perfectibility. Accordingly, every sentient being is endowed with the

Buddha-nature and is inherently enlightened. Enlightenment does not involve a radical transformation of the mind that would entail a long process of cultivation; it is simply the realization of one's innate Buddhahood through one's own effort. Chan rhetorically claims that enlightenment can be attained by anyone regardless of age, gender, and social class.

Many Chan masters of the Tang period were famous for their use of intuitive, iconoclastic devices (shouting, beating, illogical responses, and enigmatic gestures) to enlighten their students. Later in the Song these encounter dialogues (jiyuan wenda) between Chan masters and disciples were recorded and became "public cases" (Chinese: *gong'an*; familiar to Westerners by the name "koan," the Japanese for *gong'an*) used in Chan teaching and training. While the Linji school was particularly associated with *gong'an* meditation, the Caodong school focused on sitting in meditation (Chinese: *zuochan*; Japanese: *zazen*), also known as silent-illumination Chan (*mozhao chan*). Members of Chan monasteries, however, have often practiced both forms of meditation nonexclusively.

Chan and Chinese Literati Culture

The sudden/gradual polarity that characterized the development of Chan became a dominant theme in Chinese poetic criticism, painting theories, and intellectual discourse. Critics and poets frequently discussed poetry in terms of Chan's notion of the relationship between practice and enlightenment. Theorists of painting analyzed artistic expression by analogy to the Northern and Southern Schools. In the realm of Neo-Confucianism, the Chan concept of lineage transmission had significant influence on Zhu Xi's (1130–1200) theory of the orthodox succession of the Dao (daotong). During the Song and Ming (1368–1644) dynasties, Chan's assertion of the inherently enlightened mind also played a crucial role in the Neo-Confucian advocacy of Learning of the Mind (xinxue).

Chan in the Twenty-First Century

While Chan Buddhism as a school declined in China after the thirteenth century, it continues as an important form of Buddhism in present-day Korea and Japan. In addition, Chan doctrine and practice have also attracted a large number of people in the West since the 1960s. There are many Chan meditation centers in America and Europe, and Chan literature is widely translated and read. Known commonly in the West as Zen, Chan has become a popular form of meditation and an intriguing philosophical teaching in the world.

Ding-hwa Hsieh

See also: **Buddhism—China; Buddhism—Japan; Buddhism—Korea**

Further Reading

Buswell, Robert E., Jr. (1989) *The Formation of Ch'an Ideology in China and Korea: The Vajrasamadhi-Sutra, A Buddhist Apocryphon.* Princeton, NJ: Princeton University Press.

Chang, Chung-yuan. (1969) *Original Teachings of Ch'an Buddhism: Selected from the Transmission of the Lamp.* New York: Grove Press, Inc.

Dumoulin, Heinrich. (1988) *Zen Buddhism: A History, India and China.* Trans. by James W. Heisig and Paul Knitter. New York: Macmillan.

Faure, Bernard. (1993) *Chan Insights and Oversights: An Epistemological Critique of the Chan Tradition.* Princeton, NJ: Princeton University Press.

Gregory, Peter N., ed. (1987) *Sudden and Gradual: Approaches to Enlightenment in Chinese Thought.* Studies in East Asian Buddhism, no. 5. Honolulu, HI: University of Hawaii Press.

———, and Daniel A. Getz, Jr., eds. (1999) *Buddhism in the Sung.* Honolulu, HI: University of Hawaii Press.

Heine, Steven, and Dale S. Wright, eds. (2000) *The Koan: Texts and Contexts in Zen Buddhism.* New York: Oxford University Press.

Lai, Whalen, and Lewis R. Lancaster, eds. (1983) *Early Ch'an in China and Tibet.* Berkeley Buddhist Studies Series, no. 5. Berkeley, CA: Asian Humanities Press.

McRae, John R. (1986) *The Northern School and the Formation of Early Ch'an Buddhism.* Studies in East Asian Buddhism, no. 3. Honolulu, HI: University of Hawaii Press.

Miura, Isshu, and Ruth F. Sasaki. (1966) *Zen Dust: The History of the Koan and Koan Study in Rinzai (Lin-chi) Zen.* New York: Harcourt, Brace & World.

Yampolsky, Phillip, trans. (1967) *The Platform Sutra of the Sixth Patriarch.* New York: Columbia University Press.

BUDDHISM—CHINA Buddhism in China underwent a long process of sinicization in which the imported Indian religion was adapted to the indigenous cultural milieu and became an integral part of Chinese life. In the process, Buddhism gained patronage from the ruling elite and support from the common people. It also contributed significantly to the Chinese culture and thought. At the same time, Buddhism was profoundly transformed by Chinese culture, as can be seen in the development of the distinctively Chinese Buddhist schools and the subordination of the Buddhist *sangha* (monastic community) to state control and regulation. Buddhism in China, in short, represents one of the most fascinating cases of acculturation in world history.

Buddhism's Arrival in China

Buddhism arrived in China around the first century CE during the Han dynasty (206 BCE–220 CE). The Silk Road between China and Central Asia was an important route for transmitting this religion. Dunhuang, the frontier town on Han China's northwestern border, became a great Buddhist center; a great number of Buddhist scriptures, sculptures, and wall paintings from that period are preserved. Buddhism also reached central China via Nepal and Tibet, southwest China via Burma, and south China by sea from India.

At the time of Buddhism's arrival, China had already developed a highly advanced culture with sophisticated religious traditions and philosophical systems. Its two main indigenous religious traditions were Confucianism, the teaching of Confucius (551–479 BCE), and Taoism, the teachings of the legendary Yellow Emperor (mid-third millennium BCE) and Laozi (sixth century BCE).

The Han imperial state sponsored Confucianism, which emphasized family values, social responsibility, and the virtues of filial piety and loyalty. Buddhism, with its emphasis on monasticism, celibacy, and withdrawal from society, ran counter to Confucian ethics, and therefore met resistance among the Confucian ruling elite, who saw it as subversive to the Han imperial order.

Although Taoism was not yet constituted as a formal religion, its ideals of longevity and immortality were very popular among the Chinese people. In religious Taoism there were many meditative techniques to help practitioners maintain health, achieve a long life, and even become immortal. It was through its alliance with Taoism that Buddhism was able to take root in China. Many of the Buddhist texts that were translated during this early stage were on the subjects of meditation, and Taoist practitioners helped the foreign monks translate Buddhist scriptures.

The Chinese who converted to Buddhism helped to spread the faith. Some wrote treatises to defend Buddhist teachings against Confucian accusations; others composed apocryphal texts *(weijing or yijing)* in an attempt to increase the acceptance of Buddhism. Indian or Central Asian origins were claimed for these apocryphal texts, but in fact they were produced by native Chinese.

Growth and Expansion

Buddhism offered the people solace during the period of disunity that followed the fall of the Han dynasty. In the north, the non-Chinese rulers were impressed by Buddhist culture and gave Buddhism their full support. In the south, elite members found consolation in Buddhist religious messages, and many of them became interested in Buddhist metaphysics. The "Learning of Mystics" *(xuanxue)* emerged during

TIMELINE—BUDDHISM IN CHINA

1st century CE Buddhism arrives in China during the Han dynasty (206 BCE–220 CE). from Central Asia.

3rd–5th centuries Buddhism offers people solace during the period of disunity that followed the fall of the Han dynasty and is supported by the non-Chinese rulers in the north. The "Learning of Mystics" *(xuanxue)* emerges as a result of the mixture of philosophical Taoism and the Mahayana Buddhist doctrine of emptiness and important religious documents are written.

589 China is unified under the Sui dynasty (581–618). By this time Buddhism has spread across all of China.

618–907 During the Sui and Tang dynasties Buddhism in China enjoys its golden age. Buddhist texts are brought from India and translated into Chinese, new schools of Chinese Buddhism emerge, including Chan and Pure Land, and Buddhism comes under state control.

842–845 The Huichang Suppression takes place during the reign of Emperor Wuzong with empire-wide destruction of temples and shrines, confiscation of temple lands, and laicization of Buddhist clergy.

960–975 Buddhism is revived when Song dynasty Emperor Taizu issues an imperial decree integrating Buddhism into the state's civil order.

972–983 The first Chinese edition of the Tripitaka (the Buddhist canon) is printed in Sichuan. Four other editions are published during the Song.

1280–1368 Tantric Buddhism (a form of Tibetan Buddhism) flourishes under the Mongol Yuan dynasty and later under the Manchu Qing dynasty (1644–1912), but is not adopted by the general Han population.

1535–1615 Ming monk Zhuhong promotes Lay Buddhism, which continues to be popular through the end of the nineteenth century.

1920s A number of Buddhist institutes are established.

1929 The Chinese Buddhist Society is founded.

1953 The Chinese Buddhist Association is founded in Beijing and becomes the national leader of Buddhism after the Cultural Revolution ends.

1966 The Ciji Foundation is founded in Taiwan by the venerable nun master Zhengyan and by the 1990s becomes the largest civic organization in Taiwan.

1966–1969 During the Cultural Revolution Buddhism is repressed with temples closed and monks and nuns sent to work in fields and factories. After the Cultural Revolution, with the aid of government grants, Buddhist monasteries and nunneries are restored, and the damaged Buddhist statues, images, and temples are repaired.

1980s In Taiwan, as authoritarian rule weakens, civic organizations gain more autonomy and many Buddhist communities and organizations become prominent.

this period as a result of the mixture of philosophical Taoism and the Mahayana Buddhist doctrine of emptiness. Important Mahayana scriptures like the Vimalakirti Sutra (Scripture of the Layman Vimalakirti), the Prajna Sutras (Scriptures of the Perfection of Wisdom), and the Saddharmapundarika Sutra (Lotus Sutra) were translated and widely circulated among Chinese intellectuals. Kumarajiva (344–413?), a native of Kucha in Central Asia, was the most important translator of his day.

On the popular level, the Buddhist theory of karma and doctrine of impermanence gained acceptance among the common people. Many Chinese men and women joined Buddhist monastic orders, which offered a welcome haven to those who wanted to escape wars, conscription, and corvée labor. By the time

China was unified in 589 under the Sui dynasty (581–618), Buddhism had pervaded the realm.

The Period of Maturity

The period of the Sui and Tang (618–907) dynasties is often viewed as the golden age of Chinese Buddhism, characterized by intellectual vitality and creativity. The most famous translator was Xuanzang (d. 664), who made a pilgrimage to India and brought back to China hundreds of Buddhist scriptures. He later founded the Faxiang (Mind-Only) School, corresponding to Indian Yogacara Buddhism. The esoteric (Tantric) forms of Buddhism were also introduced to China and flourished briefly. However, the most significant development during this period was the formation of distinctively "sinicized" Buddhist schools: Tiantai, Huayan, Chan, and Pure Land all emerged with great creativity and prominence.

During this period, the state also assumed control over the Buddhist *sangha*. The government took charge of almost all Buddhist activities; it sponsored translation projects, regulated ordination procedures, and controlled the size of the clergy through clerical examinations. Meanwhile, the monasteries were also deeply involved in local community projects, commercial activities, and charitable programs. The "transformation texts" (*bianwen*; marvelous stories drawn from the Buddhist scriptures) and "transformation illustrations" (*bianxiang*) discovered in the Dunhuang area are surviving examples of contemporary efforts to reach the Chinese people on a grassroots level.

In the late Tang, however, the expansion of the Buddhist monasteries, the growth of the clerical population, and the increasing accumulation of tax-free temple lands and wealth eventually prompted the court to suppress Buddhism. The Huichang Suppression (842–845), which occurred during the reign of Emperor Wuzong (reigned 841–846), brought empire-wide destruction of temples and shrines, confiscation of temple lands, and laicization of Buddhist clergy. Although the Huichang Suppression was not the first such incident in Chinese Buddhist history (two earlier incidents occurred in 446 and 574–577), it was the most severe, marking a turning point in the history of Chinese Buddhism. Some argue that Chinese Buddhism entered into an age of decline at this point, while others say that in the following centuries Chinese Buddhism took a new direction to retain its vitality and popularity.

Syncretism

After bringing an end to a century of domination by military warlords, the Song dynasty (960–1267) es-

tablished a new civil order under a centralized government. Emperor Taizu (reigned 960–975) issued an imperial decree integrating Buddhism into the state's civil order, and the first Chinese edition of the Tripitaka (the Buddhist canon) was printed in Sichuan in 972–983. Four other editions were also published during the Song.

Although the Song did not witness the emergence of new Buddhist schools, it was a period marked by doctrinal developments, institutional growth, and a tendency toward syncretism. After a period of decline, Tiantai was revived through the editing of old texts and the composing of new ones. Tiantai also consolidated its institutional foundation by gaining imperial recognition and local support. Huayan, though it ceased to be an independent school, influenced Tiantai and Chan teachings. Pure Land Buddhism was popular among people of all social classes. Chan developed its unique identity and became the dominant form of institutional Buddhism, enjoying prominence both within clerical circles and among the secular elite.

A strong tendency toward syncretism was evident in Chinese religions from Song times onward. It was reflected in the advocacy of harmony among the various Buddhist schools and also in the promotion of "the Unity of the Three Teachings" (in other words, Confucianism, Taoism, and Buddhism). Tantric Buddhism, whose Tibetan form flourished under the Mongol Yuan dynasty (1280–1368) and the Manchu Qing dynasty (1644–1912), held little appeal for the Chinese common people in general. Lay Buddhism, a Buddhist movement that became popular in the Song, rose to prominence under the leadership of the Ming monk Zhuhong (1535–1615) and continued to be active through the end of the nineteenth century.

Chinese Buddhist Schools

Huayan, Tiantai, Pure Land, and Chan were the most significant Buddhist schools in China. While both Chan and Pure Land focused on practice, Huayan and Tiantai were doctrinal schools. Both Tiantai and Huayan built their theories of universal salvation on the doctrine of *tathagatagarbha* (Chinese: *rulai zang*; "embryo of the Tathagata [Buddha]"), or the doctrine of the Buddha-nature. The Tiantai School was named after Mount Tiantai in Zhejiang, southeast China, where its founder Zhiyi (or Zhikai; 538–597) resided. The basic text of the Tiantai School was the Lotus Sutra. Zhiyi's most significant contribution to Chinese Buddhism was his theory of "doctrinal classification" (*panjiao*). He divided the Buddha's divergent and often contradictory teachings into

People lighting prayer candles at Chong Qing, Sichuan, in 1996. (STEPHEN G. DONALDSON PHOTOGRAPHY)

chronological periods based on the Buddha's life in an attempt to integrate them into a complex and coherent scheme. In this way, Zhiyi established an eclectic school that recognized all forms of Buddhist teachings and ranked them in a hierarchical order.

Tiantai emphasizes mutual identification between all things and the absolute on the basis of the Mahayana doctrine of emptiness. The whole universe is present in a grain of sand or a drop of dew, and the wisdom of the Buddha is present in every individual's mind.

The Huayan (garland) School is named after its scripture, the Avatamsaka Sutra (Huayan jing in Chinese). Like Tiantai, Huayan was a purely Chinese product, with no Indian counterpart. Huayan's Third Patriarch, Fazang (643–712), and the Fifth Patriarch, Zongmi (780–841), were the most significant masters. Fazang, who was often considered to be the real founder of the Huayan School, systematized Huayan teachings into a well-coordinated system. Zongmi synthesized Chan and Huayan teachings, and his theory of sudden enlightenment versus gradual enlightenment had significant impact on the development of Chan.

Like Tiantai, Huayan is concerned with the relationship between absolute reality and things in the phenomenal world. The entire universe is seen as a single nexus of conditions in which everything simultaneously depends on and is depended on by everything else.

Buddhism and Chinese Culture

Buddhism introduced many new terms into the Chinese vocabulary and led the Chinese to invent new devices of phonological and grammatical analysis to deal with foreign languages. Buddhism as an organized system of religion stimulated the organization of religious Taoism into an institutional entity with its own canons, doctrinal system, and priesthood. In addition, Buddhism exerted a great impact on Neo-Confucian theories of lineage transmission, mind cultivation and concentration, and attainment of Sagehood. The Buddhist concept of karma and retribution became a dominant theme in Chinese vernacular literature, and images of Buddhist deities and figures such as the bodhisattva Avalokitesvara (Guanyin) and arhats (lohan) were common subjects of artistic expression.

Nonetheless, to assume that Buddhism developed in China as an independent entity is to ignore the long, complex process of acculturation between Buddhism and indigenous elements. The feminization of the bodhisattva Avalokitesvara and the transformation of Maitreya (milo fo), the Future Buddha, into a fat, laughing monk show how Indian deities evolved in the context of Chinese popular religious beliefs and practices.

Buddhism in Contemporary China

In the early twentieth century, the monk Taixu (1889–1947) led a reform movement to organize the Buddhist clergy, promote social engagement and popular education, and propagate Buddhist studies among intellectuals. Under the leadership of Taixu, a number of Buddhist institutes were established in the early 1920s, and the Chinese Buddhist Society was founded in 1929. The movement, however, was hindered by the Sino-Japanese War (1937–1945) and the Civil War between the Communists and Nationalists (1946–1949).

After the Communist victory in 1949, Buddhism suffered from official denunciation and periodic suppression. During the Cultural Revolution (1966–1969), Buddhist temples were closed and monks and nuns were sent to work in fields and factories. After the Cultural Revolution, however, with the aid of government grants, Buddhist monasteries and nunneries have been restored, and the damaged Buddhist statues, images, and temples are being repaired. The government has also helped organize provincial and regional Buddhist associations. The Chinese Buddhist Association in Beijing, which was founded in 1953, has now resumed its national leadership. It sponsors the publication of Buddhist journals, establishes training centers for monks and nuns, and promotes Buddhist studies. The association is eager to extend its network to an international level, and it sends delegates to Buddhist conferences in South Asian countries, the United States, and Europe.

While Buddhism suffered a serious blow under the Communists, it flourished in Taiwan, where the Nationalist government moved after their defeat in 1949. Since the end of martial law in the late 1980s, the government has increasingly granted autonomy to civic organizations, and, as a result, many Buddhist communities and organizations have risen to prominence. Moreover, the lineage of *bhiksuni* (fully ordained nuns) in Taiwan has become the main source of legitimacy for Buddhist women in the world who aspire to receive full ordination. The Ciji Foundation, founded in 1966 by the venerable nun master Zhengyan (b. 1937), is the largest civic organization in Taiwan, claiming 4 million members worldwide in 1994. It has its own medical hospitals, college, and research center. Each year it distributes $20 million to people all over the world suffering from poverty and natural disasters. Under the inspiring influence of Zhengyan and many other Buddhist leaders, Buddhism in Taiwan has moved to a new stage of social engagement.

Ding-hwa Hsieh

See also: **Buddhism, Chan**

Further Reading

Brook, Timothy. (1993) *Praying for Power: Buddhism and the Formation of Gentry Society in Late-Ming China.* Cambridge, MA: Harvard University Press.

Buswell, Robert E., Jr., ed. (1990) *Chinese Buddhist Apocrypha.* Honolulu, HI: University of Hawaii Press.

Ch'en, Kenneth. (1973) *Chinese Transformation of China.* Princeton, NJ: Princeton University Press.

Ching, Julia. (1993) *Chinese Religions.* New York: Orbis Books.

de Bary, Wm. Theodore, et al., eds. (1964) *Sources of Chinese Tradition.* Vol. 1. New York: Columbia University Press, 266–368.

Gernet, Jacques. (1995) *Buddhism in Chinese Society: An Economic History from the Fifth to the Tenth Centuries.* New York: Columbia University Press.

Gimello, Robert M. (1992) "Marga and Culture: Learning, Letters, and Liberation in Northern Sung Ch'an." In *Path to Liberation: The Mârga and Its Transformations in Buddhist Thought,* edited by Robert E. Buswell, Jr., and Robert M. Gimello. Honolulu, HI: University of Hawaii Press, 371–437.

Gregory, Peter N. (1991) *Tsung-mi and the Sinification of Buddhism.* Princeton, NJ: Princeton University Press.

———, and Daniel A. Getz, Jr., eds. (1999) *Buddhism in the Sung.* Studies in East Asian Buddhism, no. 13. Honolulu, HI: University of Hawaii Press.

Hakeda, Yoshito S., trans. (1967) *The Awakening of Faith, Attributed to A'vaghosha.* New York: Columbia University Press.

Huang, Chien-yu Julia, and Robert P. Weller. (1998) "Merit and Mothering: Women and Social Welfare in Taiwanese Buddhism." *The Journal of Asian Studies* 57, 2 (May): 379–396.

Jones, Charles Brewer. (1999) *Buddhism in Taiwan: Religion and the State, 1660–1990.* Honolulu, HI: University of Hawaii Press.

Mair, Victor H. (1989) *T'ang Transformation Texts: A Study of the Buddhist Contribution to the Rise of Vernacular Fiction and Drama in China.* Harvard-Yenching Monograph Series, no. 28. Cambridge, MA: Harvard University Press.

Pao-Ch'ang. (6th century) *Lives of the Nuns: Biographies of Chinese Buddhist Nuns from the Fourth to Sixth Centuries.* Translated by Kathryn Ann Tsai (1994). Honolulu, HI: University of Hawaii Press.

Stockwell, Foster. (1993) *Religion in China Today.* Beijing: New World Press.

Teiser, Stephen F. (1988) *The Ghost Festival in Medieval China.* Princeton, NJ: Princeton University Press.

Weidner, Marsha. (1994) *Latter Days of the Law: Images of Chinese Buddhism 850–1850* Spencer Museum of Art, the University of Kansas in Association with the University of Hawaii Press.

Wright, Arthur F. (1959) *Buddhism in Chinese History.* Stanford, CA: Stanford University Press.

Yu, Chun-fang. *Kuan-yin: The Chinese Transformation of Avalokitesva.* New York: Columbia University Press, 119–148 and 155–175.

BUDDHISM—JAPAN Although Buddhism is not the native faith of Japan, any attempt to understand the culture of the archipelago would be futile unless one considers the Buddhist dimension. One should also examine the development of Buddhism in close association with the history of the land. The teachings of the Buddha came to Japanese shores after being filtered through the immense landmasses of Central Asia, China, and Korea, transmitting in the process not only new religious and philosophical ideas but various other aspects of arts, literature, and ethics. At the same time, the unique character of Japan put its imprint on the foreign faith, reaching, during certain historical periods, a harmonious fusion with the preexisting doctrine of Shinto. The best way, therefore, to approach Japanese Buddhism is to follow its trajectory through the evolution of the history of Japan.

Buddhist–Shinto Synthesis

It is noteworthy that the original faith, Shinto, acquired its particular name only after the introduction of Buddhism in Japan, around 538 CE. It was at that time that the Korean Paekche monarch sent to Japan a small statue of the Buddha and some Buddhist scriptures. This gesture divided the powerful Japanese clans of the times; some showed favor toward the new faith; others were hostile. Buddhism, however, succeeded in penetrating society, especially the aristocracy, mainly due to the support of Prince Shotoku (572–621). Combining administrative talent with scholarly dedication, in addition to having a vision of the importance of Tang China as a cultural model, Prince Shotoku was instrumental in the propagation of Buddhist ideas. The notion that religious and moral systems in Japan can be represented by a tree, where the roots reflect Shinto, the branches and the stem Confucianism, and the flowers Buddhism, is attributed to Prince Shotoku.

Basic Characteristics

In its earliest days in Japan, Buddhism was characterized by elements of both Theravada and Mahayana Buddhism (the two basic "vehicles" into which Buddhism is divided). Later on, Japanese Buddhism almost exclusively followed the Mahayana.

Initially, the movement was from the upper levels of society to the lower, as the aristocracy held most of the power. As power shifted to other classes, however, Buddhism began to expand and flourish among the common people. For a long time, Buddhism was closely associated with the state, as those in power tried both to support and to control it.

Buddhism was also closely associated with family rites, particularly with ceremonies surrounding death, which led to the axiom that while Shinto is connected with the happy moments of life, Buddhism is associated with death and funerals. In addition, Buddhism was associated with ideas and practices of magic.

Finally, Buddhism's ability to avoid falling into the categories that Joseph Kitagawa calls "semi-autonomous pigeonholes of human experience" (Kitagawa 1996: 13)—religion, ethics, and culture—is especially evident in its history in Japan.

Historical Development

In the Nara period (710–794 CE), six major Buddhist schools or sects were influential in religion and government. The words *sects* or *schools* should not be understood in terms of Western dialectics, that is, as mutually antagonistic and polemic. On the contrary, the term meant a kind of friendly and scholarly division among various Buddhist approaches to Truth. Movements of adepts from one school to another were neither uncommon nor blameworthy.

The Six Nara Schools The six schools of Nara Buddhism were Sanron, Hosso, Kegon, Jositsu, Kusha, and Ritsu, and their presence spans roughly the period from 625 to 753. Some scholars have tried to distinguish between those closer to the Theravada and those closer to the Mahayana, but distinctions are not so clear-cut, and a variety of cross-influences can be discerned. The only certainty is that the Ritsu School is the closest to the *vinaya* (moral regulations and monastic rules of discipline) of the original Theravada. It is perhaps the only sect in the Mahayana world that still observes the original rules, which were long forgotten or modified by other sects.

The main characteristic of all six Nara schools is a deep philosophic approach, dealing with the notion of time, matter, reality, suppression of polarity and pursuit of the middle path, and causation. The schools reflect the inclinations of the prevailing Nara aristocracy and seem rather far from the spiritual needs of the common people.

Tendai and Shingon The next phase of Buddhist evolution coincides with the Heian period (794–1185), known for its literary refinement and the cultural influence of Tang China (618–907) The two main Buddhist schools of this period were Tendai and Shingon, which had an enduring influence on Japanese Buddhism. Both Tendai and Shingon were considered esoteric, as the essence of their teachings was transmitted orally from masters to initiates. Their respective founders, Saicho (Dengyo Daishi, 767–822) and Kukai (Kobo Daishi, 774–835), both visited China in search of Buddhist learning and have always been revered in Japan. In fact, legend holds that Kukai did not really die but still sits in deep meditation within the grounds of his monastic center on Mount Koya.

Todai-ji Temple in Nara. (CORBIS)

Tendai's center was on Mount Hiei, at Enryakuji monastery. Saicho's teaching approaches Buddhism from the standpoint of the Five Periods (Time of Wreath, Inducement, Development, Wisdom, and Nirvana) and the Eight Doctrines (Abrupt, Gradual, Mystic, Indeterminate, Hinayana, Mahayana, Distinct, and Perfect). It is firmly based on the Lotus Sutra and in meditative practices. At a later time, around 1100, Tendai monks became militant and periodically descended on the capital to antagonize the government.

Shingon is considered a branch of Tantric Buddhism and is associated with spectacular rites and mystical practices in which mandalas play a powerful role. Apart from visual elements, sounds are also significant: the word *shingon* is a translation of the Sanskrit term *mantra*, the embodiment in sound of a divine power. Kukai himself was greatly influenced by Confucianism, Taoism, Sinhalese Buddhism, and some of the Nara sects. One of his major works, the *Sango-shiiki* (The Ultimate Truth of the Three Teachings) is the first text of comparative philosophy in Japan. It discusses Confucianism, Taoism, and Buddhism in depth.

At this point a parenthesis has to be opened regarding the interesting phenomenon of amalgamation between Buddhism and the native beliefs of Shinto.

This is known by the term Ryobu Shinto, based on the related concept of *honji suijaku* (true-nature manifestation). In essence, the two streams converged harmoniously by an acceptance and adaptation of Shinto divinities into the Buddhist pantheon. This is why, even today, foreign pilgrims in Japan are often puzzled by Buddhist elements in Shinto shrines. This trend survived until the eighteenth century, when a revival of Shinto occurred, to be further substantiated in 1860 when Shinto was reestablished as the main doctrine and separate from Buddhism.

Pure Land Pure Land teachings coincide with the vigorous and militarist Kamakura period (1185–1333), when Buddhism was brought closer to the common people. These were times not only of continuous strife but also of a deeper consciousness of the impermanence of life and of constant fears about the end of the world, corresponding to the Buddhist notion of *mappo shiso* (degeneration of the dharma). Pure Land (Amidism) is centered on the concept of the benevolent Amitabha (Japanese, Amida), who offers hope of salvation in his Western Paradise. Salvation could be attained through faith alone, a doctrine quite at odds with earlier notions of spiritual cultivation on the road to enlightenment. The greatest advocates of this teaching, apart from some earlier precursors, were

Honen (1133–1212) and Shinran (1173–1262). Honen established the Jodo Sect of Pure Land; he stressed the paramount importance of calling the Buddha's name with a sincere and longing heart *(nembutsu)* as a way to guarantee entry into the Western Paradise.

Shinran established the True Pure Land Sect (Jodo Shin Shu) and concentrated veneration on Amida alone, to the exclusion of Sakyamuni (the historical Buddha). He abolished monasticism and accepted the idea of devout lay religious, thereby breaking down the division between clergy and laity that had been a hallmark of Theravada Buddhism.

Nichiren Nichiren is peculiar in the sense that it symbolizes an unusual tendency in Buddhist terms, that of fanaticism and polemics, along with determination and faith. The founder of the sect, Nichiren (1222–1282), based his teaching on the Lotus Sutra, but also created a sort of personal *nembutsu*, the mantra *namu myoho renge-kyo* (reverence to the wonderful Law of the Lotus), focused on the sutra itself rather than on a Buddha. Fearing the era of *mappo*, foreseeing the Mongol invasions, experiencing exile on the remote island of Sado, witnessing constant turbulence and warfare, and mingling with the lowest classes of people, Nichiren developed nationalistic religious ideas. Some Western scholars have called him "the Savonarola of the Orient" because he sought regeneration through adherence to "the true Buddhism." He was an intolerant man, but one with a sense of national mission.

Zen Zen (in Chinese, Chan) represents a specific phase of Buddhist evolution in Japan. Zen originated in India but was deeply marked by its passage through China. It defies any claims at complete analysis, as its very anchor is the axiom that "truth lies outside discussion" and can be grasped only by intuition and through strenuous meditative processes. (Whoever talks about Zen is exterior to Zen.) This discussion will leave aside the great founder, Bodhidharma, who transmitted Zen from India to China in the late fifth century CE, and the illustrious Chinese Patriarchs, and will focus on its adaptation in Japan.

There are three schools of Zen in Japan: Rinzai, represented by its leader Eisai (1141–1215); Soto, represented by Dogen (1200–1253); and Obaku, represented by Ingen (1592–1673). Rinzai and Soto are basic to the tradition; Obaku is a later and minor addition.

The central themes of Japanese Zen are the koan (Zen riddles), satori (instantaneous enlightenment), discipline, total obedience to the master, meditation, and work. Zen influences on Japanese culture are found in the Noh theater, haiku, calligraphy, flower arrangement, painting, gardening, the tea ceremony, and a wide spectrum of Japanese aesthetics.

At its origin, Zen symbolizes the encounter of Chinese with Indian thought; its syncretism can be seen in the Tendai, Shingon, and Tantric ideas expressed in Dogen's *Shobogenzo* (Eye Storehouse of the True Law), a treatise on Zen practice and doctrines.

Tokugawa and Later Times

The Tokugawa period (1600/1603–1868) was marked by the policy of *sakoku* (seclusion), almost total exclusion from contact with the outside world. The separation of Buddhism from Shinto and the policy of *haibutsu kishaku* (exterminate the Buddhas and abandon the scriptures) of the years 1860 and 1871 was a heavy blow to Buddhism. Toward the end of the nineteenth century, there was a revival of Buddhism and new religions were born that were basically Buddhist. Tenrikyo emphasized faith healing. Rissho Kosei Kai (founded in 1938 by Niwano Nikkyo and Naganuma Myoko) and Soka Gakkai (founded in 1930 by Tsunesaburu Makiguchi and for many decades under the dynamic leadership of Ikeda Daisaku) constitute active lay Buddhist movements with numerous international activities in the interests of Buddhism and world peace. Both Rissho Kosei Kai and Soka Gakkai draw on the ideas in the Lotus Sutra.

Buddhism has greatly influenced and in turn been influenced by Japanese tradition and culture. Buddhism contributed to Japanese culture by exposing the archipelago to the intellectual and artistic treasures of China and continental Asia. A new faith, it elevated the spiritual life of a people preoccupied only by "this-worldly" concepts to new heights of "transcendental speculation" and "yearnings for a beyond," in the words of religious scholar Anesaki Masaharu (Anesaki 1995: 7).

Tolerant by definition, and having already peacefully absorbed many ideas and practices through its long route through Central Asia, China, and Korea, Buddhism reached a harmonious coexistence with Shinto. For their part, the Japanese, in adapting Buddhism, showed a unique capacity to selectively draw and transform without blind adherence, a quality they have exhibited in other cultural fields. This has resulted in enduring forms of Buddhist philosophy and practice that are distinctly Japanese.

George A. Sioris

See also: **Buddhism—China; Buddhism—Korea**

Further Reading
Anesaki Masaharu. (1995) *History of Japanese Religion.* London: Kegan Paul.

de Berval, René, ed. (1959) *Présence du Bouddhisme.* Saigon, Vietnam: France-Asie.

Eliot, Sir Charles. (1969) *Japanese Buddhism.* New York: Barnes & Noble.

Hori, I., F. Ikado, T. Wakimoto, and K. Yanagawa, eds. (1981) *Japanese Religion: A Survey by the Agency for Cultural Affairs.* Tokyo: Kondasha International.

Kitagawa, Joseph. (1966) *Religion in Japanese History.* New York: Columbia University Press.

Saunders, E. Dale. (1972) *Buddhism in Japan.* Tokyo: Tuttle.

Sieffert, René. (1968) *Les religions du Japon.* Paris: Presses Universitaires de France.

Suzuki Daisetz. ([1959] 1973) *Zen and Japanese Culture.* Reprint. Princeton, NJ: Princeton University Press.

Tamura Yoshiro. (2000) *Japanese Buddhism, A Cultural History.* Tokyo: Tuttle.

BUDDHISM—KOREA

BUDDHISM—KOREA Buddhism has a sixteen-hundred-year history in Korea. Contemporary Korean Buddhism is distinguished from Chinese Buddhism by the importance it assigns to meditation, and from Japanese Buddhism by its relative lack of strong sectarian divisions.

History

Buddhism first arrived on the peninsula three centuries before the peninsula was brought under the control of one Korean government in 668 CE. Buddhism reached Korea from China and Central Asia and, according to traditional histories, was adopted by the rulers of the northern kingdom of Koguryo in 372 CE, the southwestern kingdom of Paekche in 384 CE, and southeastern kingdom of Shilla in 527 CE.

In the beginning, Buddhism in Korea was a religion for the elite, accepted by government officials as a tool for centralizing authority and as a way to overcome the decentralizing influence of the folk religion of Korea, with its multitude of local deities. By the seventh century, however, various buddhas and bodhisattvas had joined the pantheon of spirits worshiped by peasants, and commoners added temples to the sacred sites they frequented to pray for supernatural intervention in their lives.

Despite the popular appropriation of Buddhist deities and rituals, institutional Buddhism continued to be utilized by governments on the peninsula to reinforce their authority over the general population. When the Shilla kingdom defeated Koguryo and Paekche near the end of the seventh century, it dispatched monks to temples in the countryside to serve as ecclesiastical reminders of Shilla hegemony. The Koryo dynasty, which replaced Shilla early in 936, further institutionalized the role of the Buddhist clergy as an extension of state power by instituting state examinations for monks to parallel the civil service examinations for government officials. Even the Neo-Confucian Choson dynasty (1392–1910), which replaced the Koryo dynasty and demoted Buddhism from its privileged status as the official state religion, assigned warrior monks to state-built temples in strategic locations near the capital and around the country.

In the twentieth century, soon after the Japanese empire absorbed the Choson dynasty in 1910, the Japanese restructured Korean Buddhism, which never formally recognized married Buddhist clergy prior to the twentieth century, by challenging the traditional Korean insistence on clerical celibacy and reserving positions of ecclesiastical authority for married monks. When the Japanese were forced out of Korea in 1945, the anti-Japanese Syngman Rhee government that arose in South Korea reversed the Japanese policy and began expelling married monks from major temples and replacing them with the few monks who had remained celibate and thus faithful to Korean tradition. In North Korea, however, the Japanese tradition of

Buddha Statue at Popchusa Temple in Taejon, South Korea. (CHRIS LISLE/CORBIS)

married monks remained the norm for those few hundred monks who manage the approximately fifty temples that were allowed to remain open to support the claim by the North Korean government that it respects religious freedom.

An Eclectic Nonsectarianism

The dominant Buddhist influence in both North and South Korea is the Mahayana. The same sacred texts and the same sacred personalities that are found in the rest of East Asia are also found in Korea. The Lotus Sutra (the best known Mahayana scripture in East Asia and the main text of the Chinese Tiantai school) has been an important doctrinal guide for Koreans since at least the sixth century, and the Flower Garland Sutra (the main text of the Chinese Huayan school) since the seventh. There is evidence of Pure Land Buddhism and the worship of Amitabha Buddha as well as worship of Maitreya (the future buddha), as early as the first decades of the seventh century. The bodhisattva Avalokitesvara (Guanyin) has also been an important object of devotion in Korea for over a thousand years. Esoteric Buddhism has been on the peninsula so long that the world's oldest printed *dharani* (secret incantations), from the middle of the eighth century, was found in Korea. Meditative Buddhism established its first temples in Korea less than a century later, in the early ninth century.

Korean Buddhism, however, is not an exact copy of Buddhism in China or Japan. Koreans proudly claim that Korean Buddhism is less sectarian than Buddhism in Japan and less dominated by Pure Land rituals than Buddhism in China. Monastic Buddhism in Korea is primarily meditative Buddhism erected on a foundation built from years of doctrinal study and reinforced by Pure Land practices. Korean Buddhists see nothing incongruous in demanding that meditative monks receive rigorous academic training in Buddhist philosophy or in erecting a hall for the recitation of Amitabha Buddha's name within the grounds of a monastery dedicated to the study of doctrine. Koreans trace this eclecticism to the influence of two influential monks, Wonhyo (617–686 CE) of the Shilla dynasty and Chinul (1158–1210), of the Koryo dynasty.

Wonhyo is famous both as a philosopher and as a preacher. He wrote over two hundred works analyzing and harmonizing the arguments of the various competing schools of Buddhist philosophy in China. When he was not writing scholarly treatises, he wandered through the villages of Korea, preaching to illiterate peasants the Pure Land tradition of reciting the name of the Amitabha Buddha. Five centuries later, Chinul bridged the gap between sutra-oriented and meditation-oriented traditions that had divided Koryo Buddhism. Chinul believed that a lengthy and intensive study of the Buddhist sutras was an essential preparation for successful meditative practice. He insisted that monks and nuns had to be well versed in the verbal teachings of Buddhist tradition before they could move beyond them into the nonverbal realm of meditation. Chinul's two-step approach to the pursuit of enlightenment, along with Wonhyo's acceptance of Pure Land chanting, has become the dominant model for Buddhist practice on the peninsula. As the twentieth century drew to a close, nearly 9 million South Koreans, almost one out of five of those living in the Republic of Korea, called themselves Buddhist.

The Twenty-First Century

The Chogye order, the largest denomination in Korea in the twenty-first century, shares with the T'aego order, the second largest, the mutual acceptance of doctrinal, meditative, and Pure Land traditions. The only major difference between the two denominations, which together claim the allegiance of the vast majority of Korean Buddhists is that the T'aego order allows its clerics to marry while the Chogye order insists on celibacy. The Chogye and the T'aego orders, though they are the products of a relatively recent split between the 6,500 clerics who were married in 1945 and the 500 who remained celibate despite Japanese pressure, nevertheless represent continuity with the centuries of nonsectarian Buddhism oriented toward monastic life. Won Buddhism, a third order that was founded in 1916, shares the traditional eclecticism but within a modern, lay-oriented approach. Founded by Pak Chung-bin (1891–1943), Won Buddhism is often identified as a new religion because it replaces Buddhist statues with a simple painted circle, and replaces the traditional sutras with sermons by its founder that reformulate Buddhist doctrines in modern language.

Though at the beginning of the twenty-first century only 9 million Koreans, around one out of five of those living in the South Korea, called themselves Buddhist, most Koreans recognize that Buddhism is an integral part of Korean culture. Over 70 percent of the designated national cultural treasures in South Korea are Buddhist in origin. When Koreans want a break from the hustle and bustle of urban life, they visit Buddhist temples in the mountains. Buddhist images and sounds are often used to provide a traditional backdrop for contemporary movies and television programs. Sixteen hundred years after it was imported from central Asia and China, Buddhism has become Korean.

Don Baker

See also: **Buddhism—China; Buddhism—Japan; Buddhism, Pure Land**

Further Reading
Buswell, Robert E., Jr. (1983) *The Korean Approach to Zen: The Collected Works of Chinul.* Honolulu, HI: University of Hawaii Press.
———. (1992) *The Zen Monastic Experience.* Princeton, NJ: Princeton University Press.
Grayson, James Huntley. (1989) *Korea: A Religious History.* Oxford: Clarendon Press.
Korean Buddhist Research Institute, ed. (1993) *The History and Culture of Buddhism in Korea.* Seoul: Dongguk University Press.
———. (1994) *Buddhist Thought in Korea.* Seoul: Dongguk University Press.
Shim, Jae-ryong. (1999) *Korean Buddhism: Tradition and Transformation.* Seoul: Jimoondang.

BUDDHISM—MONGOLIA

The history of Buddhism in Mongolia is one of sudden starts and stops. From the introduction of Buddhism to the Mongolian nomads (c. 100 BCE) to the early 2000s, there have been years and even centuries where its influence was virtually nonexistent. Yet there were also periods where it was either the state religion or played an important role in almost every aspect of daily life, with lamas serving not only as religious figures, but also as doctors, teachers, and astrologers. Thus, much like the Buddhist belief that history is cyclical, so is the history of Buddhism in Mongolia.

Pre-Mongol Empire

Buddhism first arrived in Mongolia in the 100s BCE with the Hsiung-nu tribes. The religion, however, did not become widespread until much later; indeed, after the decline of the Hsiung-nu, Buddhism was not at all prevalent. In the post-Hsiung-nu period the influence of Buddhism was negligible.

With the ascension of the nomadic tribal confederation of Juan Juan (400–522 CE), Buddhism was revived, although no monasteries were built. Essentially, lamas were able to travel through Mongolia and proselytize, but they still did not have much influence.

The status of Buddhism improved greatly with the rise of the Turks (522–745 CE). It particularly flourished during the reign of the Qaghan T'o-Po (573–581). T'o-Po even commissioned shrines to be built in

Mongolia. Eventually, however, Buddhism went into another decline, though the reasons are uncertain. One reason may have been that the Turkic warrior aristocracy became wary of Buddhism, as it did not promote a warrior spirit. Another reason was the defeat of the ruling royal family in 617. The Turks may have concluded that if the royal family, which had converted to Buddhism, had been defeated then Buddhism was lacking as a spiritual force. A final reason is that Buddhism may have declined because of perpetual wars with the Uighur tribes. Although the Uighurs were initially Buddhists, they converted to Manicheaism in 744 as a reaction against the growing influence of the Buddhism in the first two hundred years of the Tang dynasty (617–906 CE).

Mongolia did not experience another Buddhist revival until the tenth century, although Buddhism increasingly influenced northern China. During the Khitan era (970–1125), Buddhism once again flourished in Mongolia. The Khitans, a Mongol people who conquered part of Mongolia and northern China, established cities on the Kerulen and Orkhon Rivers that became centers of Buddhism. Under the Khitans, Buddhism became a state religion and acted as a counter to Chinese Confucianism, which often permeated the court and bureaucracy of foreign powers that conquered China. It also served as a bond between the people and the new rulers. Although Buddhism flourished in the cities that were built in Mongolia, it did not win many converts among the nomads and few monasteries were established outside of the cities.

Mongol Empire

Buddhism was once again eclipsed after the fall of the Khitans and their defeat by the Jurchen, Tungus tribes from Manchuria. Not until the establishment of the Mongol empire did Buddhism resurface as a force in Mongolia. Even then, its hold was tenuous and dependent on court favor. Although there were many Nestorian Christians in Mongolia, the Mongols as a whole were shamanistic. Buddhism, as well as Islam, only had an impact later. No one is sure which of the Mongol princes invited lamas from Tibet to Mongolia. Some credit Genghis Khan (1165–1227), but it is more likely that either his son Ogodei (c. 1185–1241) or Genghis Khan's grandson Koten, who ruled Koke Nur, established Buddhism once again in Mongolia. Buddhism, however, did not gain many adherents until the reign of Khubilai Khan (1215–1294).

Before his reign as emperor, Khubilai Khan had been involved in a number of religious debates between Taoists, Buddhists, Muslims, and Nestorian Christians. Although he did not convert to any of these

BUDDHISM IN MONGOLIA TIMELINE

100s BCE Buddhism first arrives with the Hsiung-nu tribes, but does not spread for several centuries.

400–522 CE With the ascension of the nomadic tribal confederation of Juan Juan, Buddhism is revived as lamas travel through Mongolia and proselytize.

522–745 The status of Buddhism improves greatly with the rise of the Turks.

573–581 Buddhism flourishes during the reign of the Qaghan T'o-Po. T'o-Po commissions shrines to be built in Mongolia.

617 Buddhism experiences another period of decline, marked by defeat of the ruling royal family who had embraced Buddhism.

970–1125 Buddhism flourishes again during the rule of the Khitans who establish cities on the Kerulen and Orkhon Rivers that become centers of Buddhism and make Buddhism a state religion.

c. 1185–1241 Following another period of decline, Buddhism emerges again under the Mongols, perhaps during the reign of Ogodei or Genghis Khan's grandson Koten.

1235–1280 During the reign of Kubilai Khan Buddhism flourishes again.

1578 Altan Khan converts to Buddhism initiating a Buddhist renaissance, with adherents spread across a broad expanses of inner Asia.

1912—1915 Mongolia becomes an independent nation and then an autonomous part of China. The Mongols establish a Buddhist theocracy.

1924 With Mongolia now under Soviet rule, religion is repressed and the "last" Jebtsum Damba Qutuqtu dies, ending the Mongolian theocracy.

1939 After two decades of Soviet repression, Buddhism effectively disappears as a religion in Mongolia.

1990s Following the end of Soviet rule, Buddhism again flourishes and in 1995 the Dalai Lama locates the ninth Jebtsum Damba Qutuqtu.

religions, Khubilai professed a preference for Buddhism. During his actual reign, Khubilai Khan found the 'Phags pa Lama (1235–1280) of the Sa skya sect a useful political ally. Appointed as state preceptor, 'Phags pa Lama was put in charge of all sects of the Buddhist clergy. As 'Phags pa Lama's political power increased, Khubilai Khan was able to extend his influence in Tibet. The lamas at Khubilai's court also provided the religious sanction he desired for his reign. Furthermore, although Khubilai Khan did not convert to Buddhism, other members of the royal family did.

Post-Mongol Empire

In 1550, several Mongol princes waged a civil war for mastery of Mongolia. In addition, the Oirat Mongols, whose rulers were not descended from Genghis Khan, also competed for power. Altan Khan (1507–1582), descended from Genghis Khan, was the khan of the Tumed Mongols and one of many princes who

sought to unify the Mongol tribes who fragmented into civil war after the fall of the Mongol empire. Despite being a very competent general, Altan Khan could not secure enough support to rise to power. He realized that he needed something to neutralize the influence of Genghis Khan's descendants. At the same time, he also had to counter the Buddhist Red Hat Sect, which flourished in parts of Mongolia and attracted some princes. On one raid, Altan Khan came into contact with a lama and converted to Buddhism. How sincere his conversion was is questionable, but the common people also began to convert.

At the same time, Khutuktu Setsen Khungtaiji, Altan Khan's nephew, entered Tibet after campaigning against the Oirats. He demanded the submission of the Tibetans he encountered, and thus he came into contact with the Yellow Sect lamas. Altan Khan's nephew learned that there were numerous sects in Tibet also struggling for control of Buddhism and the country,

348

and the Yellow Sect was emerging as a dominant power. The nephew reported this intelligence to Altan Khan, who between the years 1567–1576, invited many lamas to his court. In 1578, he invited the chief lama, Sonam Gyatso to personally instruct him in Buddhism. The meetings between Altan Khan and Sonam Gyatso are recorded in the *Altan Tobchi* (Golden Chronicle) and the *Bolor Erike* (The Crystal Rosary).

Sonam Gyatso and Altan Khan agreed that Mongolia should be Buddhist and that Altan Khan would support the conversion. Altan Khan in turn would lend support to Sonam Gyatso in Tibet. Thus they established the *xoyar yusun* ("dual principle"), two prominent men who share religious and political power. In matters of doctrine, the religious figure was absolute; however, in temporal matters the political figure had absolute power. Altan Khan was confirmed in his title Tsadrawar Sechen Khan, or Wise Khan, and he named Sonam Gyatso the Third Dalai Lama.

Altan Khan's power was further secured in the doctrine of reincarnation. The Dalai Lama experienced a revelation that Altan Khan was actually the reincarnation of Khubilai Khan, which gave Altan the power of direct lineage. As Altan Khan was the reincarnation of Khubilai Khan, he was closer to Genghis Khan than the other princes. Later historians even traced his lineage back to the Buddha.

After Altan Khan's conversion in 1578, Mongolia was transformed by a Buddhist renaissance. The religion extended from Tibet into northern and southern Mongolia as well as reaching the Oirats in western Mongolia and eastern Kazakhstan and the Buryats around Lake Baikal located in Russia, just north of present-day Mongolia.

Mongolian Buddhism

The Mongols practiced the Tibetan form of Buddhism, in which the lamas were sheltered in monasteries and were mendicants, that is, dependent upon the population for support. The religious orders promoted clerical celibacy and were only open to males. Under this influence, the numbers of lamas increased dramatically, as often one son from each herdsman family entered the clergy.

The spread of Buddhism in Mongolia had the unintended effect of promoting urbanism. The monasteries became urban centers with nomadic families clustered around them. In return for shelter in times of war, welfare in times of need, or medical and spiritual care, the nomads provided alms and donations of goods. The monasteries also served as banks and commercial centers.

The large monasteries were headed by a figure called a *qubilgan*, or reincarnation. Eventually, the number of *qubilgan*s rose to one hundred thirty, each possessing a monastery and territory. Above the *qubilgan*s were fourteen *qutuqtu*s, or bodhisattvas.

The *qutuqtu*s resided in the thirteen largest monasteries, which were also centers of political power. The Jebtsum Damba Qutuqtu, a *qutuqtu* from one of these monasteries, emerged as the primary lama in Mongolia. Behind the Dalai Lama and the Panchen Lama, the Jebtsum Damba Qutuqtu was considered the third most important leader in Tibetan Buddhism. The first few Jebtsum Damba Qutuqtus were Mongols. In 1740, however, the Manchus or Qing dynasty (1644–1912) mandated that the Jebtsum Damba Qutuqtu's incarnation could only be found in Tibet. By the same mandate, the Dalai Lama was selected from among the Mongols of western China. The monasteries of the *qutuqtu*s were also transformed into major trade centers that accumulated vast amounts of wealth. By the twentieth century the treasuries of the *qutuqtu*s stored almost a quarter of Mongolia's wealth, while approximately one-third of Mongolia's male population served as lamas or were connected in some way to the monasteries. Most of these men were essentially serfs (*shabi-nar*) who were permanently attached to the monastery. The *shabi-nar* maintained the herds of the monasteries and also did work from which the lamas were prohibited, such as slaughtering animals, tanning, and gathering dung for fuel.

During the period when Mongolia was part of the Qing empire, another lama existed within the monasteries of the *qutuqtu*s. This individual was the Da Lama, an administrative figure placed in the monasteries by the Manchus. The Da Lama did not possess any religious function, but simply oversaw what happened in the monastery. In most cases, the Da Lama was not a Mongol but a Manchu. Often he had not received any training as a lama, and possessed a separate staff of bookkeepers and accountants. In this fashion, the Manchus maintained control over the wealth and ensured that the monasteries did not become centers for revolt.

One widely held misconception is that the Ming (1368–1644) and Qing dynasties encouraged the spread of Buddhism in Mongolia, as they believed it would pacify the Mongols and lessen the threat of raids. There is little evidence to substantiate this claim. While Buddhism became an integral part of daily life, the Mongols remained a feared military power until the Khalkha, or Eastern Mongols, fearing the Oirats (who were Buddhist), submitted to the Qing for protection. The Oirats' martial prowess was so great that

Buddhist monks at a temple in Ulaanbaatar, Mongolia, in 1997. (STEPHEN G. DONALDSON PHOTOGRAPHY)

they were not subdued until the mid-eighteenth century. In addition, the Kalmyks of the Volga River in Russia actively served in the armies of Peter the Great and also raided the Muslim tribes of the steppe until the late-eighteenth century, when the majority of them returned to the Qing empire. Buddhism became an integral part of daily life. Lamas were frequently consulted in regard to medical, spiritual, and even herding problems. The Mongols consulted a lama before undertaking any major endeavor during this time.

Twentieth Century

In the early twentieth century, Mongolia and much of the Manchu empire was in a state of tumult. When the empire collapsed in 1912, Mongolia won its independence, although the treaty of 1915 between Imperial Russia, China, and Mongolia relegated it to an autonomous part of China. The Mongols established a theocracy, with the Jebtsum Damba Qutuqtu as head of state. Although he was not Mongolian, the Jebtsum

Damba Qutuqtu remained a unifying figure, and the Buddhist faith was still revered.

In 1921, Chinese suzerainty over Mongolia ended with the invasion of a White Russian army that attempted to establish a base there against the Bolsheviks. Again the Jebtsum Damba Qutuqtu was kept as the nominal head of the government. In late 1921, the Whites were replaced by the Bolsheviks. When the Soviets and the Mongolian revolutionaries took over, they recognized the importance of keeping the Jebtsum Damba Qutuqtu as a figurehead in order to gain popular support. The Mongolian People's Revolutionary Party (MPRP), however, mistrusted the Jebtsum Damba Qutuqtu and forced him to relinquish his secular powers. In 1924, the problem was removed as he was either assassinated or died from a stroke. The MPRP and the Soviets also decreed that the eighth Jebtsum Damba Qutuqtu was to be the last, and they found or forged documents that supported their claim. Thus Mongolian Buddhism lost its titular leader.

The MPRP, following the doctrine of Marx, viewed Buddhism as an "opiate of the people"; however, the majority of the Mongols opposed moving against Buddhism, as both Buddhism and the monasteries were integral to Mongolian life. Several prominent members of the military and government, however, lost their lives when they disagreed with Stalin that Buddhism must be eradicated in Mongolia. It was not until Stalin's puppet Choybalsan (1895–1952) ascended to power that action was taken against the monasteries.

At first, force was attempted and troops were sent against the monasteries. Not only were the monetary assets of the monasteries seized, soldiers also burned the religious texts, and executed the lamas who resisted. Naturally, rebellion occurred in conjunction with attempts to collectivize the nomads.

The MPRP also attacked the monasteries through legal means. New taxation laws were passed. Legislation that prohibited the building of new religious buildings and limited the political activity of the lamas also was enacted. The wealth of the monasteries was drained, and religious instruction to train new monks was prohibited. Moreover, conspiracies were contrived in which many lamas were accused of spying for the Japanese or other countries. The lamas were arrested, tortured into confession, and either imprisoned or executed. By 1939, the population of the monasteries was drastically reduced.

After this period, only a few monasteries remained, and Buddhism as a functioning religion disappeared from Mongolia until the fall of Communism in 1989–1990. During the 1990s, Buddhism once again flourished. In 1995, the Dalai Lama located the ninth Jebtsum Damba Qutuqtu. Although it is unlikely that Buddhism and the monasteries will ever return to their former prominence, there has been a rebirth of interest in the Buddhist religion. Once again, Buddhism has become a vital part of Mongolian life.

Timothy May

See also: **Buddhism—China; Buddhism—Tibet**

Further Reading
Bawden, C. R. (1968) *The Modern History of Mongolia.* New York: Frederick A. Prager.
Jagchid, Sechin. (1988) *Essays in Mongolian Studies.* Provo, UT: David M. Kennedy Center for International Studies.
Heissig, Walther. (1980) *The Religions of Mongolia.* Trans. by Geoffrey Samuel. Berkeley and Los Angeles: University of California Press.
Moses, Larry, and Stephen A. Halkovic Jr. (1985) *Introduction to Mongolian History and Culture.* Bloomington, IN: Indiana University Press.
Moses, Larry. (1977) *The Political Role of Mongolian Buddhism.* Bloomington, IN: Indiana University Press.
Sandag, Shagdariin, and Harry H. Kendall. (2000) *Poisoned Arrows: The Stalin-Choibalsan Mongolian Massacres, 1921–1941.* Boulder, CO: Westview.

BUDDHISM, PURE LAND Pure Land Buddhism is a Mahayana Buddhist tradition originating in India around 100 BCE–100 CE. Although Pure Land is not indigenous to China in terms of its doctrine and scriptures, it became in spirit and character an integral part of Chinese Buddhism. Today it is one of the most prominent forms of Buddhism in China, Korea, and Japan. The term Pure Land or Land of Bliss (Chinese *jingtu*; Japanese *jodo*) derives from the Sanskrit word *sukhavati*, a blissful Western Paradise. The Buddha presiding over the Pure Land is Amitabha (Measureless Light; Chinese *Amito fo*; Japanese *Amida*), also known as Amitayus (Measureless Life). Out of his compassion for all sentient beings, Amitabha vows that anyone who has faith in him will be reborn in his Pure Land.

History

The Chinese Buddhists became interested in Pure Land Buddhism as early as the third century CE. In 402, the monk Huiyuan (334–416 CE) founded the Pure Land Society on Mount Lu (present-day Jiangxi Province), where he and his followers practiced meditation and sought rebirth in Amitabha's Pure Land. Huiyuan was later regarded as the founder and also the first patriarch of Chinese Pure Land Buddhism.

After Huiyuan, the three recognized Pure Land patriarchs were Tanluan (476–542), Daochuo (562–645), and Shandao (613–681), who all made significant contributions to propagating Pure Land Buddhism among the populace. Other important Pure Land masters were Cimin Huiri (680–748) and Fazhao (c. 800), both of whom sought to harmonize Pure Land and Chan teachings and practices.

It is, however, important to note that Pure Land Buddhism did not become a full-fledged school (*zong*), with a clear lineage and system of doctrine, until the Southern Song dynasty (1127–1279), and even then its establishment was due mainly to the efforts of masters of Tiantai Buddhism, another school. Throughout most of Chinese history, Pure Land was mingled with or incorporated into other forms of Buddhism.

Scriptures

The three principal scriptures of Pure Land Buddhism are the Shorter Sukhavativyuha Sutra (the Shorter Scripture Displaying the Pure Land; Chinese *Amito jing*), the Longer Sukhavativyuha Sutra (the Longer Scripture Displaying the Pure Land, Chinese *Wuliangshou jing*), and the Amitayurdhyana Sutra (the Scripture on Contemplating the Buddha of Measureless Life; Chinese *Guan Wuliangshou jing*).

The Shorter Sukhavativyuha Sutra contains a dialogue between the Buddha Sakyamuni and his disciple Sariputra in which the Buddha expounds the nature of faith and devotion for being reborn in Amitabha's Pure Land. The Longer Sukhavativyuha Sutra begins with a dialogue between Sakyamuni and his disciple Ananda about a monk named Dharmakara, who is one of the previous births of Amitabha. Before he attains enlightenment, Dharmakara takes a series of forty-eight vows that express his determination to attain perfect Buddhahood, become a savior of all beings, and establish a Buddha field where people can achieve liberation with ease. After Dharmakara becomes the Buddha Amitabha, he keeps his promise that those who have faith in him, are mindful of his name, or visualize him and his land will be reborn in his paradise.

Both the Shorter and Longer Sutras describe in detail the wondrous qualities of Amitabha's Pure Land. Once one is reborn in the Pure Land, the experience will be blissful because suffering, old age, and death no longer exist. The land is filled with fragrant trees, beautiful flowers, and is decorated with precious gems. Everywhere one goes, one can hear the teachings of the Buddha intoned amid pleasant music and joyful sounds. Gods and humans are spiritually inspired and blessed by Amitabha's power and grace, and they will make easy progress toward nirvana, which is the ultimate outcome of rebirth in Amitabha's Pure Land.

The Longer Sutra (Chinese *Wuliangshou jing*) was translated by Sanghavarman around 252 CE. The Shorter Sutra was translated into Chinese around 402 CE by Kumarajiva (344–413? CE). The Shorter Sutra is the most popularly read Pure Land text, with numerous commentaries produced in many East Asian languages.

The Amitayurdhyana Sutra is a meditation text that details sixteen ways of meditation and the spiritual attainments based on these meditative practices. Aside from meditation through visualizing the Pure Land and the image of Amitabha, the text also teaches a simple path designed for the laity, namely, reciting the phrase "Homage to Amitabha" (Chinese *Nanwu Amito Fo*; Japanese *Nanmu Amida Butsu*). There are no extant Sanskrit versions of this scripture. The Chinese version is titled *Guan Wuliangshou jing*, which is said to have been translated by Kalayasas (n.d.) in the first half of the fifth century. However, many scholars think that it was actually composed in China or Central Asia, not in India.

Doctrine and Practice

Pure Land Buddhism teaches a path of devotion by which one cultivates sufficient faith in the power and grace of the Buddha Amitabha. Because of their weaknesses, however, human beings cannot attain salvation through their own efforts. Some Pure Land masters furthermore teach the doctrine of the "Final Days of the Dharma" (Chinese *mofa*; Japanese *mappo*), an era of spiritual decline when traditional practices for enlightenment taught by the Buddha are no longer effective. Salvation in Pure Land Buddhism, therefore, can only be achieved at another time (in the next rebirth), in another place (the Pure Land), and through another power (Chinese *tali*; Japanese *tariki*), that of Amitabha. Faith and devotion are the essential requirements for one's rebirth in Amitabha's Pure Land.

Rebirth in the Pure Land can be attained through the practices of chanting the Pure Land scriptures, meditating on Amitabha and his Pure Land, worshiping the image of Amitabha, performing meritorious deeds, and reciting Amitabha's name or the phrase "Homage to Amitabha." Of these practices, the recitation of the Buddha Amitabha's name (Chinese *nianfo*; Japanese *nembutsu*) has become the most representative practice of Pure Land Buddhism.

Although Pure Land and Chan held different views about salvation, the Chinese tendency toward harmonization of different forms of Buddhism resulted in a combination of Chan meditation with the Pure Land use of beads to recite the name of Amitabha. Practitioners believed that this joint practice could lead to tranquility and an internal vision of the Pure Land that was identified with one's inherent Buddha-nature.

In addition, it is believed that in order to make his task of salvation more efficient, Amitabha has as his assistant Avalokitesvara (Chinese *guanyin*; Japanese *kannon*), the bodhisattva of compassion. Avalokitesvara is a savior bodhisattva frequently mentioned in Pure Land and other Mahayana Buddhist scriptures. Originally an Indian male deity, Avalokitesvara was transformed into a female in Chinese Buddhism. Her feminine representations began to appear in the Tang dynasty (618–907 CE) and became prevalent in the Song (960–1279). With the wide spread of Pure Land Buddhism, Avalokitesvara has also become the most popular celestial bodhisattva worshipped by East Asian Buddhists.

Pure Land Buddhism represents a good example of how religion has successfully made changes and adjustments to appeal to a wider audience.

Ding-hwa Evelyn Hsieh

See also: **Buddhism, Chan; Buddhism—China**

Further Reading

Chappell, David W. (1977) "Chinese Buddhist Interpretations of the Pure Lands." In *Buddhist and Taoist Studies I*, edited by Michael Saso and David W. Chappell. Honolulu, HI: University of Hawaii Press, 23–53.

Ch'en, Kenneth. (1972) *Buddhism in China: An Historical Survey.* Princeton, NJ: Princeton University Press.

de Bary, William Theodore, et al., eds. (1964) *Sources of Chinese Tradition.* Vol. 1. New York: Columbia University Press.

Ehman, Mark A. (1978) "The Pure Land Sutras." In *Buddhism: A Modern Perspective*, edited by Charles S. Prebish. University Park, PA: The Pennsylvania Press, 118–122.

Getz, Daniel A., Jr. (1999) "Tien-t'ai Pure Land Societies and the Creation of the Pure Land Patriarchate." In *Buddhism in the Sung*, edited by Peter N. Gregory and Daniel A. Getz, Jr. Studies in East Asian Buddhism, no. 13. Honolulu, HI: University of Hawaii Press, 477–523.

Gómez, Luis O., trans. (1996) *The Land of Bliss: The Paradise of the Buddha of Measureless Light.* Honolulu, HI: University of Hawaii Press.

Pas, Julian. (1987) "Dimensions in the Life and Thought of Shan-tao (613–681 CE)." In *Practice in Medieval Chinese Society, Buddhist and Taoist Studies II*, edited by David W. Chappell. Honolulu, HI: University of Hawaii Press, 65–84.

Paul, Diana. (1983) "Kuan-yin: Savior and Savioress in Pure Land Buddhism." In *The Book of the Goddess: Past and Present*, edited by Carl Olsen. New York: Crossroad, 161–175.

Stevenson, Daniel B. (1995) "Pure Land Buddhist Worship and Meditation in China." In *Buddhism in Practice*, edited by Donald S. Lopez, Jr. Princeton, NJ: Princeton University Press, 359–379.

Yu, Chun-fang (2001) *Kuan-yin: The Chinese Transformation of Avalokitesvara*. New York: Columbia University Press.

BUDDHISM—SOUTH ASIA

South Asia, the large geographical region that includes the modern nation-states of India, Bangladesh, Pakistan, Nepal, Bhutan, and Sri Lanka, is the original birthplace and homeland of Buddhism. Over time, however, Buddhism vanished in the heartland of the Indian subcontinent and flourished only at its margins: It is the main religion of Bhutan and Sri Lanka and has a significant presence in Nepal. In the latter decades of the twentieth century, however, Buddhism returned to India, via the migration of Tibetan refugees and the conversion of large numbers of Dalits (formerly called untouchables) and other low-caste Indians.

Origins

Buddhism begins with its founder, Siddhartha Gautama (566–486 BCE). According to traditional biographies of the historical Buddha, however, his career began many, many eons ago when he was a Brahman boy named Sumedha, who worshiped a buddha (the Sanskrit word means "awakened one"). The historical Buddha is regarded as the latest of a long lineage of previous buddhas, including Dipankara. This act of worship was regarded by Dipankara as a sign of the boy's future buddhahood, and he predicted that Sumedha would undertake a long journey, perfecting his character over many lives that would culminate in his birth as Siddhartha Gautama. The tradition tells many of the stories of these former lives in the collection of tales called *jataka*s. In his final birth as Gautama, he was raised a prince in a kingdom in what is now southeastern Nepal and at the age of twenty-nine renounced his royal inheritance and left his parents, young wife, and newborn son in pursuit of religious awakening. After six years of searching, Gautama is said to have attained release from suffering and obtained the title "buddha" at his Awakening.

The Buddha formulated his discovery in terms of four Noble Truths: (1) life in the endless chain of rebirths is inherently dissatisfactory, full of suffering, and mitigated by only fleeting and insubstantial happiness; (2) there is a cause of this suffering; (3) the cessation of suffering is possible; and (4) the path to the cessation of suffering is the Noble Eightfold Path. This path consists of perfecting eight factors of human life:

understanding, thought, speech, action, livelihood, effort, mindfulness, and concentration. The Buddha began to teach what he had discovered to others and founded an order of monks and nuns, who adopted a celibate and peripatetic discipline. The monastic order (*sangha*) was dependent on a larger community of laypeople who earned religious merit by providing monks and nuns with alms.

After the Buddha's death, a council was held to recite and preserve what his disciples recalled of his teachings. Over time these schools codified, in different languages, the Buddha's discourses (sutras) and the monastic code (*vinaya*). A third body of scholastic treatises, called the *abhidharma*, was eventually added to these collections, and collectively the three came to be regarded as the scriptural canon, or Tripitaka. Over the next few centuries, the small community grew in size and split into sectarian divisions, initially primarily over minor differences over monastic discipline but later over scholastic disputes. A second council was held approximately one hundred years after the death of the Buddha, which resulted in a schism between two schools, the Sthaviravada and the Mahasanghika. One early tradition records the presence of as many as eighteen different schools by the third century BCE. As Buddhism spread geographically in India, the various schools preserved their versions of the scriptures in Sanskrit and a variety of linguistic variants of Sanskrit called Prakrits.

By the third century BCE, Buddhism attracted the patronage of the emperor Asoka (d. 238?), who had conquered most of the Indian subcontinent. Asoka brought Buddhism prestige and global aspirations as a religion of the imperial state. He sent Buddhist missions to the far reaches of his empire and beyond,

SANCHI—WORLD HERITAGE SITE

A center of Buddhism in India until the twelfth century CE, the ruins of Sanchi are the oldest surviving Buddhist sanctuary in India. Overlooking a plain 40 kilometers from the city of Bhopal, the remains contain pillars, palaces, monasteries, and temples that date as far back as the second century BCE. Sanchi was designated by UNESCO as a World Heritage Site in 1989.

A SKEPTICAL OBSERVER

The following comments by an early British resident in India indicate just how difficult it was to get an accurate description of Buddhism and other "exotic" practices in South Asia.

The popular account of Buddhism which follows I regard with some distrust, as it reached me through the translations of missionaries, who seem to have falsified, or at least exaggerated, some of the absurdities of the system, in order to obtain a stronger hold over the minds of their proselytes, very few of whom are learned enough to have recourse to their books in the originals for information, and therefore quietly acquiesce in the belief that Buddha and Satan are one and the same person; while their spiritual guides impress on their minds the sinfulness of worshipping the devil. Even the Maha Modeliar, who is a Dutch Protestant, though a man of sense, is so possessed with this idea, that he would fain to have dissuaded us from going into the temple, where there were only some devils, as he called the images of the gods.

Source: Maria Dundas Graham (1812) *Journal of a Residence in India*. London: n.p.

including Gandhara (in Central Asia), Myanmar (Burma), and Sri Lanka. It is not clear what became of all of these missionary efforts, but the Sri Lankan emissary succeeded in establishing Buddhism on the island, where it continued unbroken to the present day. The main school of Buddhism to take hold in Sri Lanka was the Theravada, which preserved its form of the scriptures in the Pali language.

Archaeological evidence from this early period in India depicts a religiosity of merit-making centered on the cult of stupas, that is, constructed monuments often containing bodily relics of the Buddha and his disciples. The *sangha*, which had originally been a community of wandering mendicants, gradually settled in established monasteries. Monks, nuns, and laypeople worshiped relics and made donations for the construction of monasteries and temples located at important sites in the Buddha's life—such as at Lumbini, his birthplace, and Bodh Gaya, the site of his attainment of nirvana (awakening). At Bodh Gaya stands the great pipal tree, which sheltered the Buddha on the night of his awakening and became an object of worship and a site for pilgrimage. Seedlings from this tree were planted throughout the Buddhist world. The largest and oldest sites in India are those at Bharhut and Sanchi, which provide evidence of the worship of objects such as relics, footprints of the Buddha, and the symbolic wheel of the Buddha's teaching. Later, Buddhists would also worship images of the Buddha.

The Emergence of Mahayana Buddhism

In the early years of the Common Era, a new movement gradually emerged in northern India that called itself the Mahayana (the Great Vehicle), in contrast to the earlier eighteen schools that were dubbed the Hinayana (the Lesser Vehicle). The Mahayana provided a broader religious vision for the laity and redefined the religious ideals of Buddhism. It replaced the ideal of the arhat—one who has awakened, following the teachings of a buddha—with that of the bodhisattva—one who has taken a vow to attain awakening. While the arhat is depicted as one who has followed an individualistic path to obtain nirvana, the bodhisattva is a model of compassion, delaying the attainment of nirvana so that he can help others advance spiritually.

Although they did not reject earlier scriptures, the adherents of Mahayana Buddhism declared themselves to be in possession of texts (sutras) that superseded them. These texts were said to be composed by the Buddha but held back from the community until such time as people were ready for them. The sutras articulated Mahayana polemics against the earlier schools, elaborated new doctrines, and celebrated a new pantheon of supernatural buddhas and bodhisattvas who were regarded as saviors. Mahayana Buddhists worshiped figures such as Avalokitesvara, the bodhisattva of compassion; Maitreya, the buddha who is yet to come; and Manjusri, the bodhisattva of wisdom. While Mahayana Buddhism did not abolish the monastic establishment, it did evolve an expanded vision for the laity beyond earning merit by supporting the *sangha* through donations. Theoretically, the aspiration to become a bodhisattva is accessible to anyone, and anyone can be the object of a bodhisattva's compassion.

Theories about the transfer of merit from one person to another had begun to emerge even before the arrival of Mahayana Buddhism, but these theories came to be central to Mahayana ideas about the ability of compassionate beings to act on behalf of others. In its fullest expression, the doctrine of merit-transfer culminated in a school of thinking that suggested that the merit of buddhas and bodhisattvas could be accumulated in a cosmic realm known as the Land of Bliss, where one could be reborn and easily obtain nirvana through the merit of compassionate beings. This notion of rebirth in the Land of Bliss, developed in India in the first century CE, introduced an element of saving grace to Mahayana Buddhism. This and other such ideas also entailed the development of new cosmologies to house the proliferation of various buddha lands and celestial bodhisattvas.

Alongside this increasingly devotional strain of religious practice, Mahayana Buddhism developed and expanded in new directions the earlier traditions of meditation and textual study. Philosophical developments regarding the impermanence and insubstantiality of the human self were expanded to articulate the emptiness of all phenomena, even Buddhist doctrine itself. The Mahayanists built universities and developed sophisticated scholastic and philosophical traditions. One such monastic university was Nalanda in northern India (established since at least the second century CE), the most important center of Buddhist learning for nearly a millennium. Notable philosophers from within the Mahayana tradition over the next few centuries include Nagarjuna (c. 150–250), founder of the Madhyamika school of Buddhist philosophy; the brothers Asanga and Vasubandhu (fourth century), founders of the Yogacara school; and the logicians Dignaga (fifth century) and Dharmakirti (seventh century).

Despite the influence and popularity of Mahayana Buddhism, some Hinayana schools continued to flourish up through the seventh and eighth centuries CE. Their differences were mostly philosophical and geographic. The Pudgalavadins, who articulated a more substantial sense of personhood than other Buddhists were willing to admit, were successful under the patronage of the emperor Harsa (seventh century) of Kanauj. The Sarvastivadins advocated a philosophical realism and flourished in northwestern India and

The façade of the Anuradhapura Stupa in Sri Lanka. (EYE UBIQUITOUS/CORBIS)

THE EARLY BRITISH VIEW OF BUDDHISM

This description from 1908 provides some insight into the British view of the Buddhism they encountered in northern South Asia. Clearly, they were more accepting of what they saw as the original form and critical of Tibetan Buddhism.

It is to the indefatigable researches of Brian Hodgson that we owe the discovery of Buddhism as a living religion in Nepal. While resident in Katmandu he investigated the subject closely, and the results are embodied in a most interesting paper in the second volume of the *Transactions of Royal Asiatic Society*. He showed how the philosophic agnosticism of Buddha gave way to the theory that the Adi Buddha, by his union with the primordial female energy called Pranja, gave birth to five Buddhas, who each produced from himself by *dhyana* (meditation) another being called his Bodi-satwa or son. The chief of these latter was Avalokita, who, with his Sakti, Tara, eventually became the key-stone of Northern Buddhism. Those arose also numerous other Buddhas, demons and deities, all of which were objects of worship; and then came the introduction of the Tantrik mysticism, based on the pantheistic idea of Yoga, or the ecstatic union of the soul with the supreme spirit. At this stage, as in Tantric Hinduism, the Saktis, or female counterparts of the Bodhusatwas, occupied the most prominent position, and the esoteric cult of these female deities became every whit as obscene as that practiced by the Kaula or extreme sect of Sakta Hindus. It was this form of Buddhism which was introduced into Tibet, where it became even more debased by the incorporation of demon worship which preceded it, as has been ably described by Colonel Waddell (*India Census Report*, 1901, paragraph 648).

Source: *Imperial Gazetteer of India: Afghanistan and Nepal*. (1908)
Calcutta: Superintendent of Government Printing, 111.

Central Asia. An offshoot of this school was the Sautrantika, which also had a significant following in the same region. The Vibhajyavadins, who, like the Theravadins, can be traced back to the Sthaviravada branch, could be found in South India. Unfortunately, none of these Indian schools has survived to the present day, and our knowledge of their scriptures and texts comes mostly from Chinese translations of Sanskrit and Prakrit text fragments.

The Theravada in Sri Lanka, although not always fully supported by royal patronage, developed for the most part geographically isolated from many of the vicissitudes in political fortune that helped determine the fate of Indian Buddhist schools. The Theravada was not immune to internal schisms, however, and was for part of its history divided into three fraternities—the Mahavihara, the Jetavana, and the Abhayagiri. The Abhayagiri was less conservative than the other two sects and was receptive to some Mahayana ideas. A critical figure in Theravada history is the scholar-monk Buddhaghosa (fifth century), an Indian who traveled to Sri Lanka to translate into Pali the ancient Sinhala commentaries and to compose new exegeses and texts of his own. Buddhaghosa and his circle are responsible for the codification and interpretation of the main doctrines of Pali Buddhism.

In India, Buddhism flourished during the Gupta period (c. 320–c. 500 CE) and for the next several centuries alongside Hinduism and Jainism, often competing with them for the patronage and support of ruling dynasties. By the eighth century, however, Buddhism was in decline in India, and its great universities were gradually taken over by a new Buddhist movement called Tantra.

The Development of Tantra

As Mahayana Buddhism had critiqued the Buddhist establishment and infused the tradition with new creative energy centuries earlier, the Tantric movement played a similar role in the seventh and eighth centuries. Although undoubtedly dating to much earlier than the seventh century, Tantra refers to esoteric religious teachings that emerged in medieval India in both Hindu and Buddhist contexts. Tantric teachers were wandering saints called *siddha*s, said to be in command of ritual and magical powers. They used *dharani*s (sacred mantras, or incantations), mandalas (circular diagrams of psychological and spiritual achievements as well as meditation aids), and rich symbolic language and ritual practice to bring about radical religious experience and transformation. Some yogic techniques and symbols were antinomian (rejecting established morality) and violated social, sexual, and dietary norms. For this reason, many of the teachings of Tantric Buddhism were secret. Elaborate initiation rituals and careful tutelage under a guru were required for adherents to gain access to them.

Despite its initial esotericism, however, Tantra came to be incorporated into the monastic establishment, and its methods of meditation, its philosophical and literary traditions, and its ritual practice became institutionalized. For some it was regarded as a natural development within Mahayana Buddhism, whereas for others it came to be considered a third vehicle called the Vajrayana (the Diamond or Thunderbolt Vehicle).

For reasons not entirely clear to historians, Buddhism gradually disappeared in India. Some scholars have argued that the Mahayana turn toward devotional styles of worship made Buddhism susceptible to assimilation and absorption by the predominantly Hindu culture, in which devotional worship (bhakti) of deities gained great popularity in the medieval period. Others suggest that laxity and decay in the *sangha*, combined with its failure to elicit broad support from the laity, led to an inherent weakness in Indian Buddhism. In any case, after the sixth century, Buddhism lost widespread state support to Hinduism, although it continued to receive royal patronage in eastern India from the Pala dynasty (c. 750–1150). The great monastic centers and universities were already in decline when the Turks arrived and sacked them in the twelfth and thirteenth centuries. Theravada Buddhism continued to have a presence in South India until the seventeenth century.

GOLDEN TEMPLE OF DAMBULLA— WORLD HERITAGE SITE

Designated a UNESCO World Heritage Site in 1991, this enormous cave-temple complex has been one of the most important pilgrimage spots for Sri Lankans for more than 2,200 years. Covering an extraordinary 2.1 square kilometers underground, Dambulla's intricately painted murals and 157 statues are perfectly preserved.

Remnants and Recent Developments

At the same time as Buddhism was disappearing in India, it was spreading throughout Asia. Theravada Buddhism was established in Sri Lanka from the third century BCE, and it became the dominant religion of the island and the principal source of the expansion of Theravada Buddhism to mainland Southeast Asia. Mahayana Buddhism was exported in the early centuries of the Common Era to China and from there to the rest of East Asia, whereas Vajrayana came to be established in Tibet and Nepal, as well as other regions of the Himalayas, including Bhutan, Sikkim, and Ladakh.

The Newar community of the Kathmandu valley preserves the only forms of Mahayana and Vajrayana Buddhism that have endured in a South Asian cultural environment. This form of Buddhism is closely interwoven with Hinduism, the dominant religion in Nepal. Theravada monasteries have been established in Nepal since the 1950s by monks and nuns from Sri Lanka and Southeast Asia. They have attracted some support and even "conversion" on the part of traditionally Newar Buddhists.

In modern times, Buddhism was reintroduced to India from several different directions. A Sri Lankan monk named Anagarika Dharmapala (1864–1933) founded the Mahabodhi Society in 1891 to reawaken Indian interest in Buddhism and to restore and maintain Buddhist pilgrimage sites in India. These pilgrimage centers, especially Bodh Gaya, witness a steady stream of Buddhist pilgrims from the entire Buddhist world. Among some Vaishnavite Hindus, Buddhism is embraced as one form of Hinduism and as a component of Indian cultural heritage that inspires national pride.

Buddhism also has been enlisted as a religious ideology that could sustain a social movement seeking justice, self-esteem, and emancipation for India's untouchables against the dominant Hindu social order. Bhimrao Ramji Ambedkar (1891–1956) promoted a humanitarian and egalitarian interpretation of Buddhism among the untouchable caste of *mahar*s in Maharashtra. This led to the mass conversions of millions of his followers to Buddhism, some of whom regard Ambedkar as a bodhisattva.

The Chinese occupation of Tibet in 1959 resulted in large numbers of Tibetan refugees fleeing to India. The Dalai Lama and his community in exile currently live in Dharamsala in northern India. The Tibetan refugees have built monasteries and centers of learning and have attracted worldwide attention to their cause.

Buddhism has not remained untouched by colonialism and modernity. In Sri Lanka, reform movements have developed an interpretation of Buddhism that privileges its rational, ethical, and humanitarian aspects over ritual practice and supernaturalism. Meditation practice is now used widely by laypeople as well as monks as a means of coping with the stresses of modern life, in a way unprecedented in premodern times. Western scholarship also has developed its own scholastic history and conventions and prompted a renewed interest in the textual tradition among South Asians.

Maria Heim

See also: **Literature, Sinhalese; Siddhartha Gautama**

Further Reading

Conze, Edward. (1967) *Buddhist Thought in India*. London: Allen and Unwin.

Gelner, David N. (1992) *Monk, Householder, and Tantric Priest: Newar Buddhism and Its Hierarchy of Ritual*. Cambridge, U.K.: Cambridge University Press.

Gombrich, Richard. (1988) *Theravada Buddhism: A Social History from Ancient Benaras to Modern Colombo*. London: Routledge and Kegan Paul.

Harvey, Peter. (1997) *An Introduction to Buddhism*. Cambridge, U.K.: Cambridge University Press.

Lamotte, Etienne. (1988) *History of Indian Buddhism*. Trans. from the French by S. Boin-webb. Louvain, Belgium: Peters Press.

Schopen, Gregory. (1997) *Bones, Stones, and Buddhist Monks: Collected Papers on Archaeology, Epigraphy, and Texts of Monastic Buddhism in India*. Honolulu, HI: University of Hawaii Press.

Strong, John. (1995) *The Experience of Buddhism: Sources and Interpretations*. Belmont, CA: Wadsworth.

Warder, A. K. (1980) *Indian Buddhism*. Delhi: Motilal Banarsidass.

BUDDHISM, THERAVADA—SOUTHEAST ASIA

In orthodox Buddhism, Theravada, "the way of the elders," is a tradition that has sought to preserve and uphold the teachings and practices of the Buddha, Siddhartha Gautama (c. 566–486 BCE), the historical founder of the tradition. The present-day Buddhist communities of the Southeast Asian countries of Myanmar (Burma), Thailand, Laos, and Cambodia are self-consciously Theravadin. While orthodoxy remains a central ideal, the Buddhist world of Southeast Asia is diverse and complex, a variegated landscape of institutions, practices, and beliefs, both historically and phenomenologically.

History of Buddhism in Southeast Asia

A historical overview of Buddhist Southeast Asia can usefully be divided into three broad periods: an early phase of religious diversity; a classical period during which Theravada Buddhism rose to preeminence; and a period of modernization shaped in part by colonial and postcolonial forces.

Early Phase In the earliest stage of development, many forms of Buddhism were present in Southeast Asia. Theravada, Mahayana, and Tantric Buddhist traditions are evident in Sanskrit, Pali, and vernacular inscriptions, as well as in archaeological and artistic remains. Inscriptions from Sriksetra in lower Myanmar, dated to the fifth and sixth centuries CE, attest to the presence of Theravada Buddhism in the region. A century later the Chinese traveler Yijing recorded the presence not only of Theravada, but also of other early Buddhist schools in this region. Mahayana Buddhist traditions were in evidence in the Burman kingdom of Pagan (flourished eleventh–thirteenth centuries), in the Dvaravati-Mon kingdoms that flourished in present-day Myanmar and central Thailand, and the Angkor kingdom in Cambodia.

Brahmanical and Hindu religious traditions were also present throughout Southeast Asia. Hindu gods appeared in the religious pantheon of Southeast Asia, and *dharmasastra*s, or legal traditions, were followed in royal courts. Angkor, a powerful Khmer kingdom founded in the ninth century CE in present-day Cambodia, was a predominantly Hindu kingdom centered around the cult of kings who identified themselves with the great Hindu gods Siva or Vishnu. Indigenous religious practices continued to be widespread throughout Southeast Asia after the introduction of Buddhist and Hindu traditions, which remained elite, courtly traditions until as late as the thirteenth century.

Classical Period The thirteenth century marks a period of significant change in the religious landscape of Southeast Asia. Theravada Buddhism assumed a preeminence through the influence and importation of the Sinhalese Theravada lineage from Sri Lanka beginning in the twelfth century, when Southeast Asian Buddhist monks traveled to Sri Lanka to study with Sinhalese monks. While Mon monks made up the majority of this group according to some sources, a son of the Angkor Buddhist king Jayavarman VII (c. 1120–c.1215) also traveled to Sri Lanka as part of this monastic assembly. Reordained in Sri Lanka, these Southeast Asian monks returned to Myanmar and spread the Sinhalese lineage throughout mainland Southeast Asia, thereby establishing the Theravada as the dominant form of Buddhism in the region. Theravada then became a popular religion for the first time, one that changed and was changed by the still-present indigenous and Hindu traditions that continued to be a part of the total religious landscape of Southeast Asia.

Modern Innovations The eighteenth and nineteenth centuries brought new forces and innovations to the Theravadin world as the ideas and ideals of European modernity interacted with the Theravadin worldviews and the colonial powers entered Myanmar, Cambodia, and Laos. In Thailand, the only Southeast Asian country never colonized by an outside power, Buddhists both resisted Western influences by maintaining traditional thought and practices and modernized some Buddhist practices in response to Western ideas. Most notable was the reform of the Buddhist monastic community during the reigns of the Thai kings Mongkut (1804–1868) and Chulalongkorn (1853–1910), who modernized the educational system and consolidated the Thai *sangha* (monastic community) into a national institution, contributing to the dynasty's rule of the entire country from the capital in Bangkok.

The interaction between Buddhism and the colonial powers elsewhere in Southeast Asia was complex; the transformation and modernization of Buddhism was not solely the result of Western influences but also a result of Buddhist responses and innovations under these historical conditions. In Myanmar the monastic community suffered from the withdrawal of patronage that had been provided by the king and aristocracy, but it also proved resilient under colonial domination. Political monks came to the fore and led movements of resistance to colonial power and cultures.

Southeast Asia and the Buddhist World

Arguably of equal importance to the record of dates, kings, and kingdoms that make up the Buddhist history of Southeast Asia is the conception of historical development present in Buddhist historical sources. Buddhist chronicles display a consciousness of being part of a larger Buddhist world. These chronicles, writ-

POVERTY, WEALTH, AND MERIT

Contemporary Buddhists in Thailand are faced with the task of reconciling ancient beliefs about the virtue of poverty with the modern emphasis on wealth. In the village of Sagatiam in Central Thailand, people reconcile the two through sayings such as the following:

The Lord Buddha taught us to be good, not to be rich or poor.

If we are good, we are apt to be rich later.

If we do good, we shall be richer later. Merit helps us.

Source: Jaspar C. Ingersoll. (1969) *The Priest and the Path: An Analysis of the Priest Role in a Central Thai Village.* Ann Arbor, MI: University Microfilms, 255.

ten in both Pali and vernacular languages, articulate a Buddhist historical vision describing an origin in the birth of the historical Buddha, the development of his religious teachings and order in India, the flourishing of Buddhism in Sri Lanka, and the transmission of Buddhism to Southeast Asia. Southeast Asian Buddhists saw themselves as the preservers and upholders of the Theravada tradition and as the legitimate inheritors of the Buddha's teachings. Southeast Asian chronicles such as the *Jinakalamali*, a sixteenth-century Pali chronicle from northern Thailand, describe both the Buddha's journeys to Southeast Asia during his lifetime and his predictions of the Buddhist kingdoms that would arise in the millennium after his death.

Buddhist Thought and Practice in Southeast Asia: Buddha, *Dhamma*, *Sangha*

The Buddha of the present historical age, Buddha Gautama, stands at the center of the Theravadin worldview, teachings, and devotional practices. According to orthodox Theravadin thought, only one Buddha can be present in the universe at a time, but the Theravadin pantheon is not limited to the Buddha Gautama alone. A lineage of Buddhas arises sequentially in the universe and extends into a limitless past and future. Theravadin literature focuses on twenty-six Buddhas, the twenty-four Buddhas who proceeded the Buddha Gautama and the Buddha Metteyya (in Sanskrit, Maitreya) who follows him.

THE COMPLEXITY OF THAI BUDDHISM

Buddhism as it is expressed in Thailand, as across much of Buddhist Asia, is complex and reflects influences from Hinduism and local religious traditions. The following description from the village of Sagatiam in central Thailand shows how this complexity plays out in the form of the different religious practitioners who serve the local population.

Several observers of village Buddhism have pointed out the elaborate richness of the religious fabric: the diverse threads of the Buddhist and Brahmanic [Hindu] traditions along with the indigenous tradition of worship of spirits and a host of supernatural objects; as well as the complex interweaving of religious, magical and divinatory emphases. In such a rich social-cultural fabric, we naturally find a large inventory of religious roles to be played. These roles vary greatly in the extent to which they are elaborated, in the number of actors who perform them, and in the number of other roles these actors also perform.

The most important religious figure in Thai society is the Buddhist priest (*pra*), whose social status has the most highly elaborated and formalized role expectations in Thai culture... In addition to the general laity, composed of people with greatly varying degrees of piety and of participation in temple affairs, we find also people practicing several types of healing and divination which have religious associations. Some actors performing these healing or divining activities occupy definite statuses with distinct role expectations, while other people similarly engaged do not have positions with very fully patterned expectations. Indeed, some of these activities scarcely lend themselves to neat role classification, since the actors tend to mix the various types of healing and divination practices in different combinations. Also, people may spend as much as full time in one or more of these activities or as little as a few occasions a year.

[. . .]

One main type of occult specialist not particularly associated with the priesthood, who deserves mention here, is the medium or shaman who goes into a trance. The death some years ago of the Sagatiam's head priest's mother removed the last person in the village of Sagatiam who could become possessed by spirits. This woman became possessed by a spirit called Lord of the Place (*jao tii*).

Source: Jaspar C. Ingersoll. (1969) *The Priest and the Path: An Analysis of the Priest Role in a Central Thai Village.* Ann Arbor, MI: University Microfilms, 64–66.

Buddhas permeate the Theravadin world of Southeast Asia. A multiplicity of Buddhas depicted in artistic and narrative representations serve as focuses for devotion and worship. In temples throughout the region, multiple Buddhas are present: altars are filled with statues of Buddhas, and murals depict their life stories. The walls of the central hall of Wat Sutat in Bangkok, Thailand, are painted with murals depicting the lives of the twenty-four Buddhas preceding the Buddha Gautama, who is represented by a magnificent statue.

Throughout Southeast Asia the five Buddhas of the present cosmological age, the *bhadda kappa* (the auspicious eon), are most frequently represented and worshiped. The Shwezigon Pagoda in Yangon (Rangoon), Myanmar, is said to contain bodily relics of not only the Buddha Gautama but also his three direct predecessors, the Buddhas Kakusandha, Konagamana, and Kassapa. The presence of these relics contributes to the power of this sacred place.

Metteyya is the focus of particular devotion in Southeast Asia. Merit accrued in a variety of forms of worship and practices as diverse as making a donation to the monastic community or hearing the preaching of Buddhist texts is dedicated to being reborn in the future when Metteyya will arise in the world, ushering in a utopian era of happiness and well-being. In Myanmar the *weikza*s, practitioners of esoteric meditation and alchemical rituals, attempt to prolong their lives supernaturally so that they may still be alive in the time of Metteyya.

The *dhamma* (in Sanskrit, dharma), the teaching of the Buddha, takes many forms in Southeast Asia. The *dhamma* can be thought of as the collection of teachings in Buddhist texts. For Theravada Buddhism, the most important texts are in the Pali canon; these texts, in orthodox Theravadin thought, contain the original words and teachings of the Buddha. The Pali canon has three divisions: the *vinaya*, or monastic codes; the *sutta*s (in Sanskrit, sutras), discourses of the Buddha; and the *abhidhamma* (in Sanskrit, *abhidharma*), or scholastic treatises. These texts were maintained orally for centuries after the Buddha's death and took written form only during the first century BCE to the first century CE. The presence of the Pali canon is one of the primary unifying features of these Theravadin cultures, but in many ways this canon has a greater value as an idea than it does in actual practice. The Pali canon as a library of texts is not commonly used in monastic centers throughout Southeast Asia.

Particular texts and genres form what Anne Blackburn called a "practical canon" popularly used in teaching and preaching the dharma. Chief among these texts are the *jataka* stories, narratives of the Buddha's previous lifetimes as a bodhisattva, or Buddha-to-be. The *jataka*s are classified among Theravada canonical texts, but literary and artistic traditions based on these stories have continued to evolve in Southeast Asia. Of the over 550 *jataka* stories, the final ten are the most popular and best known in South-

east Asia. This cycle of the Buddha's ten final lifetimes before his rebirth as the Buddha Gautama is told and represented in painted murals. Postcanonical *jataka* stories were composed in Southeast Asia in both Pali and in vernacular languages.

In Southeast Asian Buddhist thought, the *dhamma* has power not only through its meaning but through the very forms of the words themselves; when the *dhamma* is preached, it can effect change. Throughout Southeast Asia and in Sri Lanka as well, Pali texts are chanted as a form of protection. This practice, called *paritta* ("protection"), speaks to the power of the Buddha's *dhamma* and of the monks who chant the texts. Collections of *paritta* text are popular throughout the region in practices focused as much on sound and power as on meaning.

Another primary way of encountering the *dhamma* is through meditative practices. While meditation was traditionally practiced almost exclusively by monks—and by only a small percentage of monks at that—in the second half of the twentieth century, meditation movements grew among the laity as well. Developing originally in Myanmar, lay meditation has become an increasingly important and popular practice for laymen and -women alike. Large meditation movements exist in Thailand as well, where meditation training is directed by both monks and lay meditation masters. One of the most popular movements in Thailand in recent decades is the Dhammakaya movement, where meditation is taught as part of modern Buddhist practice. Training the mind and body through meditation is seen as efficacious for dealing with the complexities of the modern world.

As in all Buddhist cultures, the Buddhist community in Southeast Asia is made up of two primary constituencies: the monastic *sangha* and the laity. Monastic

Buddhist monks in Bangkok, Thailand, receive alms. (EYE UBIQUITOUS/CORBIS)

populations in Myanmar and Thailand are very large, among the largest in the Buddhist world, although the number of monks is constantly in flux. The majority of men who take ordination in the *sangha* do not become monks for life, but rather for a more limited time, from a few months to several years. Some monks remain in the monastic community for their whole lives, but there is neither a requirement that monks ordain for life nor a stigma about leaving the monastic robes to return to a lay life. This is a decidedly different pattern of monastic life from that practiced in other parts of Buddhist Asia. Among Theravada Buddhists in Sri Lanka, men must make the commitment to ordain for the length of their lives; those who leave the monastic life are often seen as disgraced, although this judgment has softened in recent times.

In Southeast Asia on the other hand, ordination as a novice or a monk is part of life-cycle rituals for many Buddhists. Boys or young men may ordain as novices or monks for a limited time as both part of the transition to adult life and a way to earn significant amounts of karmic merit through taking ordination. This merit is often dedicated to the parents or family members who support the ordination rituals by giving the *sangha* their sons, the greatest possible gift. Traditionally ordination was an avenue for education and social mobility. In recent decades, especially in Thailand, other possibilities for advancement are open for young men, but a monastic education is still seen as a valuable resource for later life. As monks, men learn at least basic Pali chanting that can be incorporated into lay rituals at other stages of life. Furthermore, once a man leaves the monastic *sangha*, he often becomes a strong lay supporter of his local wat, or monastic temple, performing duties that are prohibited for monks according to the monastic code, such as dealing with the wat's finances.

The monastic community in Southeast Asia is officially limited to monks. A lineage of nuns was introduced into Myanmar but disappeared after the thirteenth century. There has never been a tradition of fully ordained nuns in the rest of Southeast Asia, but women do lead religious lives apart from the lay world. Taking a set of vows in addition to the ordinary vows that structure the moral and spiritual lives of Buddhist laity, these women dedicate their lives to ethical and spiritual goals similar to those of monks. Wearing robes and shaving their heads, the *maeji* in Thailand and the *thila-shin* in Myanmar construct lives for themselves as renunciants. Support of these female renunciants varies in different parts of Southeast Asia. In Myanmar, where there are large numbers of women living as *thila-shin*, the role of these renunciant women

is visible, and they receive the support of the lay community. This has not always been the case in Thailand, where the *maeji* have fought for recognition and support and face difficult obstacles to pursuing the education and training available to monks and novices. In recent decades a movement has grown throughout the Buddhist world, including the Theravadin countries, to renew the ordination of women. While some members of the Theravadin community support the reintroduction of an official nuns' lineage through still-existent Mahayana nun lineages in East Asia, there is also large-scale opposition in the monastic *sangha*. Some monks argue that it is impossible to reintroduce a legitimate Theravadin ordination lineage for nuns because the ordination ritual requires the presence of nuns fully ordained in a Theravadin lineage.

The Buddhist world of Southeast Asia is endlessly complex and evolving. Ideals of orthodoxy are preserved in dynamic traditions interacting with other religious traditions, influences from other parts of the Buddhist world, as well as the forces of modernity in and outside Asia. While common patterns of belief and practice reveal the connections between the Buddhist traditions of Myanmar, Thailand, Laos, and Cambodia, scholarly attention to the history and living traditions of these Buddhist cultures reveals not only these shared patterns of the Theravadin world but also its diversity.

Karen Derris

Further Reading

Bangchang, Supaphanna. (1988) "A Pali Letter Sent by the Aggamahasenapati of Siam to the Royal Court at Kandy in 1756." *Journal of the Pali Text Society* 12: 185–212.

Barnes, Nancy J. (1996) "Buddhist Women and the Nun's Order in Asia." In *Engaged Buddhism: Buddhist Liberation Movements in Asia*, edited by Christopher Queen and Sallie King. Albany, NY: State University of New York Press, 259–294.

Bartholomeuz, Tessa. (1994) *Women under the Bo Tree: Buddhist Nuns in Sri Lanka*. Cambridge, U.K.: Cambridge University Press.

Bizot, François. (1993) *Le Bouddhisme des Thais* (The Buddhism of the Thais). Bangkok, Thailand: Éditions des Chariers de France.

Blackburn, Anne M. (1999) "Looking for the *Vinaya*: Monastic Discipline in the Practical Canons of the Theravada." *Journal of the International Association of Buddhist Studies* 22, 2: 281–309.

Buannag, Jane. (1973) *Buddhist Monk, Buddhist Layman: A Study of Urban Monastic Organizations in Central Thailand*. Cambridge Studies in Social Anthropology 6. Cambridge, U.K.: Cambridge University Press.

Coedes, George. (1925) "Documents sur l'histoire politique et religieuse de Laos Occidental" (Documents on the Political and Religious History of Western Laos). *Bulletin de l'École Française d'Extreme-Orient* 25: 4–8.

Collins, Steven. (1990) "On the Very Idea of the Pali Canon." *Journal of the Pali Text Society* 15: 89–126.

Davis, Richard. (1994) *Maung Metaphysics: A Study of Northern Thai Myth and Ritual.* Bangkok, Thailand: Pandora.

Evans, Grant. (1998) *The Politics of Ritual and Remembrance: Laos since 1975.* Chiang Mai, Thailand: Silkworm Books.

Gombrich, Richard. (1988) *Theravada Buddhism.* London: Routledge.

Horner, I. B., trans. (1978) *The Clarifier of the Sweet Meaning.* London: Pali Text Society.

———, and Padmanabh S. Jaini, trans. (1985) *Apocryphal Birth Stories: Pannasa-jataka.* London: Pali Text Society.

Houtman, Gustaaf. (1999) *Mental Culture in Burmese Crisis Politics: Aung San Suu Kyi and the National League for Democracy.* Tokyo: Institute for the Study of Languages and Cultures of Asia and Africa, Tokyo University of Foreign Studies.

Jayawickrama, N. A., trans. (1978) *The Epochs of the Conqueror.* London: Pali Text Society.

Keyes, Charles F. (1983) "Merit-Transference in the Kammic Theory of Popular Theravada Buddhism." In *Karma: An Anthropological Inquiry,* edited by C. F. Keyes and E. V. Daniel. Berkeley and Los Angeles: University of California Press.

———. (1995) *The Golden Peninsula: Culture and Adaptation in Mainland Southeast Asia.* Honolulu, HI: University of Hawaii Press.

Reynolds, Frank E., and Mani B. Reynolds. (1982) *Three Worlds According to King Ruang: A Thai Buddhist Cosmology.* Berkeley, CA: Center for South and Southeast Asian Studies.

Schober, Juliane. (1997) *Sacred Biography in the Buddhist Traditions of South and Southeast Asia.* Honolulu, HI: University of Hawaii Press.

Smith, Bardwell L., ed. (1978) *Religion and Legitimation of Power in Thailand, Laos, and Burma.* Chambersburg, PA: Anima Books.

Spiro, Melford E. (1982) *Buddhism and Society: A Great Tradition and Its Burmese Vicissitudes.* Berkeley and Los Angeles: University of California Press.

Strong, John S. (1995) *The Experience of Buddhism: Sources and Interpretations.* Belmont, CA: Wadsworth.

———. (1998) "Les Reliques des cheveux du Bouddha au Shwe Dagon de Rangoon" (Relics of Buddha's hair at Shwezigon in Rangoon). *Aseanie* 2: 70–107.

Swearer, Donald K. (1995) *The Buddhist World of Southeast Asia.* Albany, NY: State University of New York Press.

Tambiah, Stanley J. (1970) *Buddhism and the Spirit Cults of North-east Thailand.* Cambridge, U.K.: Cambridge University Press.

Wales, H. G. Quartich. (1969) *Dvaravati: The Earliest Kingdom of Siam.* New York: Cambridge University Press.

Wyatt, David K. (1984) *Thailand: A Short History.* New Haven, CT: Yale University Press.

———. (1994) *Studies in Thai History.* Chiang Mai, Thailand: Silkworm Books.

BUDDHISM—TIBET

BUDDHISM—TIBET Tibetan Buddhism is the dominant religious system throughout the Tibetan cultural area, which includes not only the central provinces of Tibet (the "Tibet Autonomous Region" of the People's Republic of China) and the eastern and western regions of the Tibetan plateau (divided among several Chinese provinces), but also neighboring areas in northern Nepal and India, the independent states of Bhutan and Mongolia, parts of Russia, and several Central Asian republics that were parts of the former Soviet Union. In recent decades the influence of Tibetan Buddhism has spread beyond this vast geographical area; Tibetan Buddhism is now attracting followers in North America, Europe, and Australia.

History

Buddhism was first formally introduced to Tibet in the seventh century. Traditional Tibetan accounts relate that the history of Buddhism began in the distant past when the buddha sPyan ras gzigs (pronounced Chenrezi) began to prepare the land and its people for the eventual dissemination of Buddhism. This preparation enabled King Srong btsan sgam po (Songtsen Gampo, c. 618–650 CE) to begin the formal establishment of Buddhism in Tibet by marrying two Buddhist women from neighboring countries. Traditional accounts contend that the king and his wives were really emanations of buddhas who assumed their respective identities in order to bring Buddhism to Tibet.

The process of dissemination continued during the reign of King Khri srong De btsan (Trisong Detsen, c. 740–798), who invited the Indian scholar to Tibet. Despite the king's sponsorship, Santaraksita reportedly encountered opposition from both demons and people loyal to the old order (referred to in Buddhist histories as "Bon") and was forced to leave the country. The king subsequently invited Padmasambhava, an Indian master with a reputation for magical powers, who according to traditional accounts defeated the demonic and human forces that had frustrated Santaraksita's mission. Subsequently, the three founded the first monastery in Tibet, bSam yas (Samye), and Tibetans began to enter the Buddhist monastic order.

Buddhism grew rapidly under the sponsorship of the Tibetan kings. This success, however, engendered opposition, and King Ral pa can (Relbachen, reigned 815–836), an ardent supporter of the new religion, was assassinated and replaced by King gLang dar ma (Lang Darma, reigned 838–842), who reportedly persecuted Buddhism. King gLang dar ma in turn was assassinated by a disaffected Buddhist monk, and his death marked the end of the Tibetan royal dynasty.

The following centuries were characterized by a period of interregnum during which no person or group

BUDDHISM IN THE MOUNTAINS OF TIBET

"Tibetan Buddhism incorporates beliefs that reflect that mountainous environment of the region. Given the importance of the mountains, it is not surprising that mountains are associated with the gods.

"The other great divinity, in some ways more central in the Sherpa conception of Mani Rimdu, is a god associated with the sacred mountain of the region, Khumbila. Sacred mountains quite often symbolize repositories of ancestral collective generative power in Tibetan thought. Mount Khumbila is thought to be holy in part because it is shaped like a torma, or ritual offering cake. Since a torma is at once symbolic of a god's body, of food for him and of his body as food, and of a phallus, this mountain and its deity are well suited to play the role of 'father' in a drama of the primal crime.

"According to Jerstad... this god is called the gnassrung, which means 'place protector,' and his name in full is Zur-ra ra-rgyan. He is, furthermore, according to Jerstad's informants, a local manifestation of the meditation god named Rdo-rje-thig-le. Rdo-rje-thig-le is, in turn, one particular manifestation of the great deity Kun-tu-bzang-po (Sherpa Kuntu Zangbu) the principal Sherpa representation of the Adi-Buddha or primordial Buddha."

Source: Robert A. Paul (1982) *The Tibetan Symbolic World: Psychoanalytic Explorations.* Chicago: University of Chicago Press, 116.

was able to consolidate power. Despite the political turmoil, however, Buddhism continued to grow. The dominant tradition of Buddhism was based on a scholastic archetype inherited from the great monastic universities of northern India, from whence Buddhism was disseminated to Tibet.

The most influential early proponent of this model was Atisa (982–1054), one of the four directors of Nalanda Monastic University. His arrival in Tibet in 1042, in response to an invitation from the kings of western Tibet, marks the beginning of what traditional histories refer to as the "second dissemination" *(spyi dar)* of Buddhism. Atisa stressed the importance of intensive study of Buddhist philosophy, practice of meditation, and adherence to monastic discipline. This model became the paradigm of the dGe lugs pa (Gelukpa) order, which continues as the largest order in Tibetan Buddhism.

In addition to the scholastic model advocated by Atisa, other forms of Buddhism enjoyed significant popularity in Tibet. The most influential of these were charismatic and often iconoclastic lineages that mostly came from the Indian regions of Bihar and Bengal.

These lineages emphasized esoteric meditative and ritual practices derived from texts called *tantras*, which focused on the manipulation of subtle energies combined with visualizations. These practices were emphasized in the rNying ma pa (Nyingmapa) and bKa' brgyud pa (Kagyupa) schools, the lineages of which are traced to Indian tantric masters. The other two orders of Tibetan Buddhism, the Sa skya pa and dGe lugs pa, place greater emphasis on the scholastic traditions that were largely derived from Indian monastic universities. It should be noted, however, that all four orders of Tibetan Buddhism have scholastic lineages as well as esoteric tantric practices, and that they combine both traditions in their teachings and meditative training.

In the thirteenth century the Sa skya pa order assumed temporal hegemony in Tibet when Sa skya Pandita (Sakya Pandita, 1182–1251) was appointed regent by the Mongol ruler Godan Khan. This followed Sa skya Pandita's mission to Mongolia, during which he ceded sovereignty of Tibet to the Mongols, but which also led to Godan Khan's conversion to Buddhism. The Khan offered to serve as patron of Bud-

An artist painting a terra cotta religious icon at Jokhang Temple in Lhasa, Tibet, in 1996. (STEPHEN G. DONALDSON PHOTOGRAPHY)

dhism; in turn, Sa skya Pandita and his successors became chaplains in the Mongol court.

Sa skya pa supremacy lasted until the fourteenth century, when Mongol power waned. Various Mongol chieftains continued to exercise considerable influence in Tibet, however, and in the seventeenth century the Fifth Dalai Lama, Ngag dbang blo bzang rgya mtsho (Ngawang Losang Gyatso, 1617–1682), assumed temporal leadership of Tibet with the backing of Mongol troops. Thus began a period of rule by successive Dalai Lamas that continued until the invasion and annexation of Tibet by the People's Republic of China, which began in 1950 and was formalized in 1959.

The Twentieth Century

Following the victory of Mao Zedong (1893–1976), leader of the People's Republic of China, and the Communists in 1947, China set its sights on Tibet. Mao claimed that Tibet had always been a part of China and that its independence (which was formally declared by the Tibetan government in 1911) was an aberration, one that had been engineered by the machinations of "foreign imperialists."

In 1950, Mao dispatched thousands of troops to Tibet with the aim of "liberating" the country and rejoining it to the Chinese "motherland." Initially, Tibetans were told that the invaders only wanted to improve the lot of the peasant masses and that they would not harm traditional Tibetan religion or culture. After solidifying their control, however, Chinese soldiers began to reshape the culture in accordance with Mao's interpretation of Marxism. At the same time, Chinese officials gradually reduced the power and authority of the Dalai Lama and the Tibetan government. Matters came to a crisis in March 1959, when a massive demonstration by Tibetans against Chinese rule led to military actions in which an estimated 80,000 Tibetans were killed.

The Fourteenth Dalai Lama, bsTan 'dsin rgya mtsho (Tenzin Gyatso, b. 1935), fled to India, where he was given asylum and allowed to form a government-in-exile in the hill station town of Dharamsala in Himachal Pradesh. During the Cultural Revolution, communist cadres (both Chinese and Tibetan) went on an orgy of destruction in Tibet, destroying thousands of monasteries, looting countless works of religious art, and ransacking the vast libraries. In addition, thousands of religious leaders were imprisoned, and according to Tibetan government-in-exile estimates, over one million people were killed. Following Mao's dictum that "religion is poison," Chinese Red Guards attempted to eradicate the old religion and culture of Tibet.

Over 100,000 Tibetans followed the Dalai Lama into exile, and the new arrivals were given tracts of land by the Indian government. In the ensuing decades, the exiles built several prosperous farming communities,

BUDDHISM IN TIBET—THE VIEW OF EARLY WESTERN MISSIONARIES

The following text written by two French missionaries in the mid-nineteenth century provides a less than positive view of Buddhism as they enter Lhasa, the capital of Tibet, in search of converts.

After eighteen months' struggle with sufferings and obstacles of infinite number and variety, we were at length arrived at the termination of our journey, though not at the close of our miseries. We had no longer, it is true, to fear death from famine or frost in this inhabited country; but trials and tribulations of a different character were no doubt about to assail us, amidst the infidel populations, to whom we desired to preach Christ crucified for the salvation of mankind. Physical troubles over, we had now to undergo moral sufferings; but we relied, as before, on the infinite goodness of the Lord to aid us in the fight, trusting that He who had protected us against the malice of man, in the very heart and capital of Buddhism.

Source: Huc Evariste-Regis and Joseph Gabet. ([1851] 1987)
Travels in Tartary, Thibet and China, 1844–1846. New York:
Dover Publications, 168.

mostly in southern India, and reestablished many of the monasteries that were destroyed in Tibet.

In Tibet, meanwhile, the numbers of monks allowed by the Chinese government have been severely reduced, and the three great central Tibetan monasteries of dGa' ldan (Ganden), Se ra (Sera), and 'Bras spungs (Drepung)—which formerly housed tens of thousands of monks—today are allowed only several hundred monks each. In addition, monastic activities are strictly monitored by the government because monks and nuns have been at the forefront of anti-Chinese agitations. Chinese secret police are in permanent residence in many Tibetan monasteries, and several army bases have been built near major monastic centers. Monks and nuns are required to spend most of their days studying Marxist dogma in "patriotic reeducation" courses and are actively discouraged from learning the traditional curriculum that was once the foundation of Tibetan Buddhist study and practice.

Despite the repression in the land of its origin, Tibetan Buddhism is popular all over the world. Thousands of Tibetan Buddhist centers operate in the United States, Europe, and Australia, and Tibetan teachers like the Dalai Lama commonly draw large crowds when they lecture. Major events such as the annual Kalacakra initiation given by the Dalai Lama attract people from all over the world, and Tibetan religion and culture are the subjects of major Hollywood films and popular writing. Westerners in the tens of thousands consider themselves to be Tibetan Buddhists, and the popularity of the tradition continues to grow, fueled by the charisma of prominent Tibetan teachers, the enthusiastic support of celebrities, and sympathetic reporting by most of the Western media.

John Powers

See also: **Buddhism—Central Asia; Buddhism—China; Buddhism—Mongolia; Dalai Lama; Potala Palace**

Further Reading
Cozort, Daniel. (1986) *Highest Yoga Tantra*. Ithaca, NY: Snow Lion Press.

Dudjom Rinpoche. (1991) *The Nyingma School of Tibetan Buddhism*. 2 vols. London: Wisdom Press.

Gyaltsen, Khenpo Könchog. (1986) *The Garland of Mahamudra Practices*. Ithaca, NY: Snow Lion Press.

Gyatso, Janet. (1998) *Apparitions of the Self: The Secret Autobiography of A Tibetan Visionary*. Princeton, NJ: Princeton University Press.

Gyatso, Tenzin (Dalai Lama XIV). (1984) *Kindness, Clarity and Insight*. Ithaca, NY: Snow Lion Press.

———. (1991) *Path to Bliss: A Practical Guide to Stages of Meditation*. Ithaca, NY: Snow Lion Press.

Hopkins, Jeffrey. (1983) *Meditation on Emptiness*. London: Wisdom Press.

Jackson, David. (1994) *Enlightenment by a Single Means*. Vienna: Verlag der Österreichiscen Akedemie der Wissenschaften.

Klein, Anne C. (1995) *Meeting the Great Bliss Queen: Buddhists, Feminists, and the Art of the Self*. Boston: Beacon Press.

Powers, John. (1995) *Introduction to Tibetan Buddhism*. Ithaca, NY: Snow Lion Press.

Shakya, Tsering. (1999) *The Dragon in the Land of Snows: A History of Modern Tibet Since 1947*. New York: Columbia University Press.

BUDDHISM—VIETNAM

Buddhism is the main religion in Vietnam, practiced by three-quarters of the population. Unlike its Southeast Asian neighbors, who are largely Theravada Buddhist, Vietnam embraces Mahayana Buddhism, including both Chan (Zen) and Pure Land traditions. (In southern Vietnam, a largely Khmer minority practices Theravada Buddhism.) Although Buddhism entered Vietnam from both India and China, the predominant political, cultural, and religious influences were Chinese. Over the centuries, however, the Vietnamese have created a form of Buddhist religiosity that is distinctively their own.

History

The first few centuries of the first millennium were marked by the expansion of Indian culture and religion into Southeast Asia. Archaeological evidence from Champa, in what is now central Vietnam, yields figures of buddhas and bodhisattvas and Sanskrit inscriptions dating from the second or third century CE. Inscriptions address Hindu gods predominantly, especially Siva, but there are also praises to the Buddha. Later archaeological finds from Dong Duong in central Vietnam indicate the presence of Buddhist temples and statues. Although most of this evidence is suggestive of Mahayana Buddhism, a Hinayana presence is mentioned by the seventh-century Chinese traveler Yi Jing. As for northern Vietnam, in the second and third centuries CE, the Giao Chi province was visited by such prominent figures as the Sogdian monk Kang Seng Hui and the Indian monks Kalyaoaruci and Marajavaka; they propagated the dharma, founded relic mounds (stupas) and temples, and translated Buddhist scriptures from Sanskrit into Chinese.

Chinese Buddhist influence in Vietnam, however, was eventually far more substantial and enduring than Indian Buddhist influence. Vietnam was ruled by China for more than a millennium (111 BCE–939 CE), and Chinese political domination and culture exerted a more direct and profound impression on Vietnam than on any other Southeast Asian culture. The first recorded instance of a Chinese missionary in Vietnam is Mou Po, who propagated Buddhism in northern Vietnam in the second century CE. However, Mahayana Buddhism from China really became dominant and widespread beginning in the fifth century CE. Buddhism in Vietnam, as in China, existed throughout its long history alongside, and sometimes in competition with, Confucianism, Taoism, and ancestor worship.

The most prominent form of Buddhism to take hold in Vietnam was Thien (in Sanskrit, Dhyana; in Chinese, Chan; in Japanese, Zen). Traditional sources record the transmission of three major Thien sects from China, beginning with the arrival of the Indian master Vinataruci in 580 CE, who was trained in China in the lineage begun by Bodhidharma. He came to be regarded as the first Thien patriarch in Vietnam. The founder of the second Vietnamese Thien school was Vo Ngon Thong, a Chinese master who arrived in Vietnam in 820. The founding in the eleventh century of the third Thien tradition, the Thao Duong school, occurred after Vietnam's independence from China. Buddhism attained increasing importance as the state religion for several of the subsequent Vietnamese dynasties. The Thao Duong advocated a unified practice of Thien and Pure Land traditions. Chan meditation practice and Pure Land recitation came to be regarded as compatible methods for attaining enlightenment, and the unification of these two traditions was seen as politically expedient for seeking favor for Buddhism at court.

During the Tran dynasty (1225–1400) the Vietnamese people pressed southward and brought Champa under their rule. At this time an additional school of Buddhism, the Truc Lam, developed. It fused Confucianism, Taoism, and Buddhism in a spirit of national unity against foreign domination, especially against incursions by the Mongols. Truc Lam combined the otherworldly aspirations of Thien insight with the practical humanism of Confucianism. In time, however, the political elite increasingly supported Confucianism at the expense of Buddhism, though a resurgence of Buddhism occurred in the seventeenth century, stimulated by the arrival of Chinese monks of the Linji (in Vietnamese, Lam-Te; in Japanese, Rinzai) tradition. The Lam-Te became the foundation of most of Vietnam's present-day monastic institutions.

During the Nguyen dynasty (1802–1955), the political elite favored Confucianism exclusively, and Buddhist monks withdrew from political activity. Christian

The White Statue of Buddha on Thuy Son Mountain south of Danang in 1993. (STEVE RAYMER/CORBIS)

missionaries started arriving in Vietnam beginning in the sixteenth century, and the increasing influence of Christianity under French colonial rule presented a further challenge to Buddhism.

Buddhism experienced a revival in the twentieth century starting in the 1930s, when it was embraced as a central component in the various nationalist movements that sought independence from the French. Their efforts included an emphasis on the study of Buddhist texts, a new focus on projects of social welfare, and an attempt to abolish what were regarded as superstitious elements. One particularly influential Buddhist movement was the Hoa Hao sect, which taught a heterodox form of Buddhism propounded by its charismatic founder Huynh Phu So (1919–1947). In 1951 the All-Vietnam Buddhist Association was founded, uniting all the previous Buddhist organizations and sects of Buddhism and declaring Buddhism to be Vietnam's national religion. Buddhism was also prominent and visible in the

protest movements in the years of war that followed independence. In the 1960s activist Buddhist monks contributed to the downfall of the Diem regime; in the decades following, they sought alternative systems of economic development and social progress to those provided by Western capitalist and Marxist ideologies.

Beliefs and Practices

Buddhism emphasizes the release of human beings from suffering. The schools most prominent in Vietnam incorporate dual aspects of Mahayana Buddhism, namely, wisdom and compassion, and regard them as compatible and skillful means for attaining liberation from suffering. Thien recommends insight, wisdom, and realization through meditation, while the Pure Land tradition emphasizes compassion, worship, and recitation of the name of the Buddha Amitabha. Adherents of Pure Land Buddhism seek rebirth in the Pure Land, or Western Paradise, through single-minded devotion to Amitabha rather than spiritual awakening through their own meditative achievements. In the Pure Land, enlightenment is easily attained.

The nonsectarian and unified nature of Vietnamese Buddhism is apparent in the temple practices of monks and laypeople. Buddhist temples in Vietnam include images of both Sakyamuni and Amitabha, as well as numerous bodhisattvas. Monastic temples incorporate a daily regimen of meditation, study, and sutra chanting, as well as name recitation. Laypeople practice Buddhism by name recitation, visiting temples to offer flowers, incense, and candles to the Buddha and the monastic community (monks traditionally have been revered not only for their ideals of personal salvation, but also for their supernatural powers and skills in healing and divination), and praying for deceased loved ones.

The popular religion has always been eclectic, and elements of Confucianism, Taoism, ancestor worship, and spirit cults continue to complement Buddhist practices. Veneration of sacred objects, including relics, sutra texts, and amulets, for their protective qualities, is also common. With its long history of change and adaptation, its eclectic syncretism, and tolerance by Vietnam's Marxist government, Buddhism in Vietnam seems likely to enjoy continued popularity in the twenty-first century.

Maria Heim

See also: **Buddhism—China; Buddhism, Chan; Buddhism, Pure Land**

Further Reading

Cleary, J. C. (1991) "Buddhism and Popular Religion in Medieval Vietnam." *Journal of the American Academy of Religion* 59, 1: 93–118.

Finot, Louis. (1931) "Outlines of the History of Buddhism in Indo-China." In *Buddhistic Studies*, edited by Bimala Churn Law. Calcutta, India: Thacker, 749–767.

Keyes, Charles F. (1995) *The Golden Peninsula: Culture and Adaptation in Mainland Southeast Asia.* Honolulu, HI: University of Hawaii Press.

Mai-Tho-Truyen. (1962) *Le Bouddhisme au Vietnam (Buddhism in Vietnam; Phat-Giao Viet-Nam).* Saigon, Vietnam: Pagoda Xa-Loi.

Mus, Paul. (1975) *India Seen from the East: Indian and Indigenous Cults in Champa.* Edited by Ian Mabbett and David Chandler. Trans. by Ian Mabbett. Victoria, Australia: Centre of Southeast Asian Studies, Monash University.

Nhat-Hanh, Thich. (1967) *Vietnam: Lotus in a Sea of Fire.* New York: Hill and Wang.

Taylor, Keith Weller. (1983) *The Birth of Vietnam.* Berkeley and Los Angeles: University of California Press.

Thien-An, Thich. (1975) *Buddhism and Zen in Vietnam in Relationship to the Development of Buddhism in Asia.* Edited by Carol Smith. Los Angeles: College of Oriental Studies, Graduate School.

BUDDHIST LIBERAL DEMOCRATIC PARTY—CAMBODIA

During the 1980s, civil war wracked Cambodia. One faction, the Kampuchean People's National Liberation Front (KPNLF), was headed by Son Sann (1911–2000), onetime prime minister from 1967 to 1968 under Prince Norodom Sihanouk (b. 1922). The KPNLF mobilized its support in Cambodian refugee camps in Thailand.

Since Son Sann lived in Paris, and thus was physically removed from Cambodia, the KPNLF opened a Bangkok office, which was headed by Ieng Mouly (b. 1950). The KPNLF was the only faction favoring a liberal democracy for Cambodia. For the election in 1993, the KPNLF retitled itself the Buddhist Liberal Democratic Party (BLDP), with Son Sann as president. The BLDP won only six seats, but it was included in the ruling coalition along with the two major parties. Ieng Mouly became the Minister of Information.

The BLDP split in May 1995. The government then recognized the BLDP as represented by the faction of Ieng Mouly, who was elected BLDP president in July. In August, Son Sann and his supporters were expelled from the BLDP, whereupon they formed the Son Sann Party. Later, a breakaway BLDP faction formed the Light of Liberty Party. During the 1998 election, none of the three parties won a seat, so they disbanded. Former BLDP members then joined either the Cambodian People's Party or the Sihanoukist Party, which were the two main political parties.

Michael Haas

See also: **Cambodia—History**

Further Reading

Chandler, David P. (1991) *The Tragedy of Cambodia History: Politics, War, and Revolution since 1945.* New Haven, CT: Yale University Press.

Haas, Michael. (1991) *Genocide by Proxy: Cambodian Pawn on a Superpower Chessboard.* New York: Praeger.

BUDI UTOMO

On 20 May 1908, Indonesia's Wahidin Sudira Usada (1852–1917) founded Budi Utomo (Noble Conduct), the first organized movement to create Indonesian nationalism and seek the end of Dutch rule through peaceful means. Wahidin believed that education was the key to reviving national awareness among the *priyayi* (elite). The Javanese princess Raden Adjang Kartini had already stressed the importance of education to awaken the Javanese. Wahidin worked closely with Gunawan Mangunkusumo of the School of Training Physicians in Batavia (now Jakarta) to raise the status of indigenous people through Western knowledge and their own traditional culture. Budi Utomo grew rapidly, and about forty branches were established. Students and bureaucrats joined the organization, and it worked to broaden its scope. Budi Utomo began to emphasize improvements in agriculture and trade. The radical members wanted political activity, which was opposed by the conservatives. With the rise of the political party Sarekat Islam from 1912 to 1916, Budi Utomo was no longer felt to be effective, and its membership went down. In 1935, it was dissolved officially. However, its importance in the early phase of the Indonesian independence movement can be gauged by the fact that 20 May, its date of founding, is commemorated in Indonesia as the Day of National Awakening.

Patit Paban Mishra

Further Reading

Mintz, Jeanne S. (1961) *Indonesia: A Profile.* New York: D. Van Nostrand.

Sardesai, D. R. (1981) *Southeast Asia: Past and Present.* New Delhi: Vikas.

BUFFALO, WATER The Asiatic water buffalo is considered the true buffalo, *Bubalus bubalis*. The African or cape buffalo is *Sycerus caffer*. Buffalo is known as *carabao* in the Philippines, *shui niu* (water buffalo) in China, and *kerbau* in Malaysia.

The size of buffalo varies. Small buffalo in China weigh 250 kilograms. Buffalo in Thailand weigh between 450 and 550 kilograms; those in Laos, up to 500 to 600 kilograms. Some weighing even 1,000 kilograms have been observed. Height varies from 100 to 148 centimeters, depending on age. Similarly, body length ranges from 160 to 215 centimeters.

Buffalo are sensitive to extreme cold and not as adaptable as cattle to very cold climates. They do not do well where the sun is inadequate to ripen crops such as cotton, grapes, or rice. Although the general belief is that the buffalo is a tropical animal, river buffalo have been employed to pull snowplows during the winter in Bulgaria. Buffalo are also found in the former Soviet states of Georgia and Azerbaijan as well as in the cold and mountainous areas of Pakistan, Afghanistan, and Nepal. Sizable herds in Italy and the former Soviet Union range above 40° N latitude.

Likenesses of buffalo have been found on seals made in the Indus Valley in India and Pakistan more than five thousand years ago, and records show that the buffalo was in use in China more than four thousand years ago. Although some evidence suggests that the buffalo was domesticated in the areas that are now India and Pakistan, some experts argue that the buffalo was first domesticated as a work animal in Mesopotamia during the Akkadian dynasty, about 2500 BCE. Archaeological evidence of buffalo as a domesticated animal has been limited to seals and bone findings. Buffalo, however, were brought from Mesopotamia to modern Syria, Israel, and Egypt only in 600 CE. Buffalo migrated eastward and westward from their countries of origin in Mesopotamia, India, and Pakistan. In the last two millennia, such migrations have accounted for colonies of buffalo being established in the Philippines and Indonesia.

Types of Domesticated Buffalo

There are two general types of domesticated water buffalo—swamp buffalo and river buffalo. The distinction is based on habitat. The swamp buffalo is native to swampland and wallows in mud and feeds on coarse marsh grasses and reeds. The river buffalo, on the other hand, prefers to wallow in rivers and ponds. River breeds include all the milking breeds in India and Pakistan, such as the Murrah, Jafarabadi, Mehsana, Surti, and others.

Swamp buffalo are slate gray, droopy necked, and look like oxen with huge backswept horns. They are native to the eastern half of Asia from India to Taiwan. These buffalo are found in China and areas stretching from the Philippines in Southeast Asia to as far west as India. The swamp buffalo has been iden-

A boy riding a water buffalo in Yangon, Mynamar, in 1996. (STEPHEN G. DONALDSON PHOTOGRAPHY)

tified essentially as the China buffalo. Although mostly employed as a work animal, the swamp buffalo is also used for meat but almost hardly ever for milk. But some experts believe that this buffalo has the potential for milk production similar to that of the milch river breeds, with the milk yielding a product rich in butterfat (ghee).

River buffalo are native to the western half of Asia and are found farther west in India, Egypt, and Europe. They are usually either black or dark gray. They have tightly coiled or drooping straight horns and actually prefer to wallow in clean water and ponds. River buffalo produce more milk than swamp buffalo and are used in dairies.

Water buffalo are generally herd animals with an innate attachment to a site or a herd. Their lifespan ranges from twenty to thirty years—two to three times the lifespan of cattle. The gestation period is 270 to 285 days—about a month longer than that of cattle. Poor management and poor nutrition have been blamed for the belief that the buffalo is slow to mature sexually and slow to rebreed after calving. Buffalo estrus is difficult to detect, and the estrus cycle averages about twenty-four days. Matings occur at night.

Buffalo cows normally reach breeding age at about two years and can bear their first calves at three. The bulls generally reach breeding age at about three but are not fully mature until they are about eight years old. The large bulls that have been deemed best for breeding are often selected for draft animals, which are castrated. Others are sent to slaughter. In China, the castration of male calves not required for breeding is done by knife and ligature at around one year of age.

Buffalo and cattle belong to the same family, although genetically buffalo are further removed from cattle than from the American bison, which has been hunted to near extinction. A closer living relative is the European forest bison. The domesticated swamp buffalo is almost identical to the wild arni, whereas the domesticated river buffalo has no wild prototype. Buffalo do not generally interbreed with domestic cattle, although cross-breeding by farmers has been reported but not well documented. Worldwide, the population has been rising, but in many countries in Southeast Asia, there has been a decline.

Ooi Giok-Ling

Further Reading
Cockrill, W. Ross, ed. (1976) *The Buffaloes of China*. Rome: Food and Agriculture Organization.
———. (1974) *The Husbandry and Health of the Domestic Buffalo*. Rome: Food and Agriculture Organization.

Epstein, H. (1969) *Domestic Animals of China*. Farnham Royal, U.K.: Commonwealth Agricultural Bureau.
MacGregor, R. (1941) "The Domestic Buffalo." *Veterinary Records* 53: 441–550.
National Research Council. (1981) *The Water Buffalo: New Prospects for an Underutilized Animal*. Washington, DC: National Academy Press.
Zeuner, F. E. (1963) *A History of Domesticated Animals*. London: Hutchison.

BUH Buh wrestling, along with archery and horseback riding, is considered one of the three "manly" sports of Mongolia. At its highest level of competition, Buh takes place at the annual Nadam (meetings) held by the various nomadic (or formerly nomadic) tribes in Mongolia. These competitions in Inner Mongolia attract some 30,000 spectators annually. Buh is believed to have developed out of Mongolian horse-breaking techniques and perhaps was practiced to develop and maintain these skills. Wrestlers wear riding boots, a belt, and a leather vest called a *zudg*. The goal is to force one's opponent to touch the ground with any part of his body except the soles of his feet or palms of his hands. In its traditional form, there is neither a ring nor a time limit, and it is a test of strength and endurance. Buh wrestling has gained some popularity in Japan, as it similar to Japanese sumo wrestling.

David Levinson

Further Reading
"Boke Wrestling." (2001) Retrieved 24 October 2001, from: http://www.mongolwrestling.f2s.com/bokemongolia.htm.

BUKHARA (1997 est. pop. 237,000). Bukhara is an ancient city in modern Uzbekistan. Long a major center of learning in the eastern Islamic world, Bukhara was also capital of a state of the same name, from the sixteenth century to 1924.

Bukhara was an important trading post on the Silk Route connecting China with the Middle East well before Arab armies conquered the city in 709. After the Arab conquest, the population gradually converted to Islam. In the late ninth century Bukhara became the capital of the Samanid dynasty (892–1005), which presided over the revival of the Persian literary tradition after two centuries of Arabic-language domination. Bukhara remained a major center of Persian language and civilization until the twentieth century.

After the decline of the Samanids, the armies of Ghengis Khan sacked Bukhara in 1220. Although the

The Ark Fortress or Citadel in Bukhara which since the first millennium has served as the home of various rulers of the region. It has also been destroyed and rebuilt numerous times. (DAVID SAMUEL ROBBINS/CORBIS)

city's political eclipse continued until the mid-sixteenth century when it became the capital of Shaybanid dynasty, Bukhara was celebrated as a center of Islamic learning. Imam Ismaiʿil al-Bukhari (d. 869), the great collector of hadith, or the traditions of the Prophet Muhammad, had worked in Bukhara. Baha' al-Din Naqshband (d. 1388) established the influential Naqshbandi Sufi order in Bukhara. After the sixteenth century Bukhara's *madrasa*s (seminaries) attracted students from all Central Asia and from as far away as Tatarstan and India.

Bukhara came under Russian protection in 1868; in 1920 the Soviets, with the help of disaffected Buk-harans, overran the country and established a Bukharan People's Soviet Republic. In 1924 Central Asian state boundaries were redrawn on an ethnonational basis, the Bukharan republic was abolished, and Bukhara was included in Uzbekistan. Bukhara lost its status as a capital city; Uzbek replaced Persian as the official language.

Today Bukhara is a regional city in Uzbekistan, with an economy based on the exploitation of nearby oil and gas resources and the processing of cotton and karakul-sheep wool. Much of the city's architecture dates from the Soviet period, but the old city boasts several architectural monuments, such as the tenth-century mausoleum of the Samanid dynasty and the Kalon minaret, the tallest structure in the world when it was built in 1127.

Adeeb Khalid

BUKHARA—WORLD HERITAGE SITE

The Historic Centre of Bukhara was designated a UNESCO World Heritage Site in 1993 for its architecture and urban environment that have remained intact over many centuries.

Further Reading

Aini, Sadriddin. (1998) *Sands of the Oxus: Boyhood Reminiscences of Sadriddin Aini.* Trans. by John Perry and Rachel Lehr. Malibu, CA: Mazda.

Becker, Seymour. (1968) *Russia's Protectorates in Central Asia: Bukhara and Khiva, 1865–1924.* Cambridge, MA: Harvard University Press.

Carrere d'encausse, Hélène. (1988) *Islam and the Russian Empire.* Berkeley and Los Angeles: University of California Press.

Frye, Richard. (1965). *Bukhara: The Medieval Achievement.* Norman, OK: University of Oklahoma Press.

McChesney, R. D. (1992) *Waqf in Central Asia: Four Hundred Years in the History of a Muslim Shrine.* Princeton, NJ: Princeton University Press.

BUKHARA, KHANATE OF

The Bukhara khanate, so-called after the ancient city of Bukhara (located in the present-day Republic of Uzbekistan), was one of two khanates or kingdoms founded by the successors of Muhammad Shaybani-khan (1451–1510), descended from Shayban, a grandson of Genghis Khan, in 1511. Following in the footsteps of the prolific Timurid dynasty, the Shaybanid empire of Central Asia at its peak included all of Central Asia to the Iranian plateau and the Hindu Kush mountain range. The first khanate at Bukhara and the second at Khwarizm were founded on the ruins of Shaybani-khan's conquests.

Between the 1560s and 1860s, Bukhara was thus the capital of an independent state—the khanate, later the emirate of Bukhara. It was situated at a crucial location on the Silk Route and had embassies and extensive trade arrangements with the Russian czars, the Mughal empire, and parts of Western Europe. Items of export from the khanate included varieties of fruits, rice, cotton, and silk. The city of Bukhara, at the center of the khanate, was an urban center with protective walls, a fortress, several residential and commercial quarters, and numerous religious monuments. In addition, there were numerous elaborate caravansaries (inns for traveling caravans), specialized bazaars, and vaulted galleries, all attesting to the commercial importance of the city in the sixteenth and seventeenth centuries.

The Shaybanid dynasty ended at Bukhara in 1598 and at Khwarizm (later named Khiva) in 1687, adding political disintegration to the already existing economic and cultural decline of this area of Central Asia. The outlying areas of both these khanates, which had previously been loosely bound to the central cities, now broke away to form independent principalities, while the Uzbek tribal aristocracy seized power at the center. Tribal skirmishes continued for control of the two governments, though power was actually wielded by a mayor of the palace (called the *atalik* in Bukhara and the *inak* in Khiva), while dynastic rulers merely served as figureheads. The khanate survived in the region in a reduced form, until its absorption into the Russian empire in the 1880s.

Manu P. Sobti

Further Reading

Becker, Seymour. (1968) *Russia's Protectorates in Central Asia: Bukhara and Khiva, 1865–1924.* Cambridge, MA: Harvard University Press.

Burton, Audrey. (1997) *The Bukharans: A Dynastic, Diplomatic, and Commercial History, 1550–1702.* New York: St. Martin's Press.

Frye, Richard. (1997) *Bukhara: The Medieval Achievement.* Costa Mesa: CA: Mazda.

———. (1998) *The Heritage of Central Asia: From Antiquity to the Turkish Expansion.* Princeton, NJ: Markus Wiener.

Knobloch, Edgar. (1972) *Beyond the Oxus: Archaeology, Art, and Architecture of Central Asia.* Totowa, NJ: Rowman and Littlefield.

BUKHARIAN JEWS

Bukharian Jews, who call themselves *yahudy,* are one of the world's most ancient Jewish communities. Related to Iranian and Afghani Jews, they speak a Bukharian dialect of the Tajik language. The first Jews came to Central Asia after it was conquered by the Persian empire about 520 BCE. Archaeological findings point to several waves of resettlement of Jews from Persia to Central Asia in the fourth century BCE as well as in the first four centuries CE. Major Jewish communities were established in the ancient Central Asian towns of Merv, Termez, and Balkh.

After the Arab conquest of Central Asia in the seventh century, Bukhara and Samarqand become the main centers of Jewish life in the region. As many as 30,000 Jews lived in those cities, according to the great twelfth-century Jewish traveler and explorer Benjamin of Tudela.

The Mongol invasion in the thirteenth century hit the Jews of Central Asia hard: all the communities except the one in Bukhara were destroyed, and subsequently all Jews in Central Asia were known as Bukharian Jews. During the reign of Timur (or Tamerlane, (1370–1405), Jews settled in Samarqand and Shakhrisabz. Beginning in the sixteenth century and for almost three hundred years, Jews live in almost total isolation, confined to their own urban quarters, denied basic rights, and limited to such occupations as silk dyeing, crafts, and minor trade.

By the middle of the nineteenth century, Jews were living in almost every Central Asian town. At this time the Mahallai Yahudien, or Jewish Quarter, was built in Samarqand and still exists today. During the Russian colonization of the region (1853–1872), Jews actively supported the Russians, who gave them Russian citizenship and encouraged their investment in industry and trade. Many Jews were involved in the textile business, processing and trading cotton. As the result, by the beginning of twentieth century, the Jewish community was substantially richer. A national intelligentsia emerged. Contacts with Jews from Russia and other countries spread the idea of Zionism, and emigration to Palestine began. (In 1892 a Bukharian quarter in Jerusalem was established called Sh'hunat Buhori.)

With the establishment of Soviet rule in Central Asia (1917–1922) and the founding of the Soviet Republics of Uzbekistan, Tajikistan, and Turkmenia, Bukharian Jews played a significant role in the region's cultural and socioeconomic development. But due to Communist policies, they had largely assimilated and lost their cultural heritage by the early 1970s. The rise of anti-Semitism and nationalism caused a mass emigration of Bukharian Jews to Israel (about 100,000), the United States (60,000), and other nations. Today, only about 10,000 Bukharian Jews remain in Central Asia, and their communities are on the verge of vanishing.

Mikhail Degtiar

Further Reading
Benyaminov, Meyer R. (1992) *Bukharian Jews.* New York: Gross Brothers.
Encyclopedia Judaica. (1971–1972) New York: Macmillan.
Hopkirk, Peter. (1994) *The Great Game: The Struggle for Empire in Central Asia.* New York: Kodansha.
Sachar, Howard M. (1976) *A History of Israel From the Rise of Zionism to Our Time.* Tel Aviv, Israel: Steimatzky's Agency.

BULGARIANS Descendants of the medieval Bulgars and Slavs, Bulgarians form the ethnic majority in Bulgaria. The Slavs settled in the Balkans in the sixth to seventh century CE, absorbing the indigenous Hellenized Thracians. They lived in tribes and farming communes ruled by a *knyaz* (lord), who presided over the tribal council attended by all men of military age. The Slavs venerated the thunder god Perun, the goddess of love Lada, and other deified forces of nature.

The Bulgars were Turkic nomads originating on the Central Asian steppes. Their society was a military hierarchy headed by a khan (chieftain) from the noble clans. The Bulgars worshiped Tangra, creator of the sky and the earth, and venerated the wolf, dog, horse, and other animals.

Early History
In the early seventh century, khan Kubrat (d. 650?) united the Bulgars between the Black and Caspian Seas in a tribal confederation known as Great Bulgaria. It was overrun by the Khazars shortly after his death. Afterward, Bulgar tribes led by Kubrat's son khan As-

parukh migrated to the Danube delta. They formed an alliance with the Slav tribal confederation of the southern Danubian plains and defeated the army of Constantine IV Pogonatus. In 681, the Byzantine emperor ceded to the Bulgars the lands between the Danube and the Balkan mountains. The first Bulgarian kingdom, founded in that year, was ruled as a khanate until the middle of the ninth century.

In 864, Boris I (852–889) converted to Orthodox Christianity and made it the state religion, also adopting the Byzantine model of government. The new faith augmented the integration of Bulgars and Slavs into one polity. In 866, Boris I adopted the Cyrillic (Slavic) alphabet, created by the Byzantine monks Cyril and Methodius. Slavic Bulgarian became the official language of liturgy and state administration and the basis of Bulgarian national identity.

This sense of identity survived the fall of the state under Byzantine rule in 1018. An uprising in 1185 led to the establishment of the second Bulgarian kingdom, but Tatar incursions from 1273 on, and feudal rivalries, contributed to its decline and culminated in the Ottoman conquest of 1396.

Ottoman Rule
During the early centuries of Ottoman rule, Bulgarian culture was centered in the monasteries; the native aristocracy disappeared, replaced by Ottoman military landholders, and the higher church hierarchy was in the hands of Greek clergy, since all Christian subjects of the sultan were considered a single millet, or religious group. A Bulgarian national revival in the eighteenth and nineteenth centuries was spearheaded by merchants and craftsmen guilds, and the quest for political independence led to a Bulgarian uprising in 1876, which was crushed. The subsequent Russo-Turkish war ended in 1878 with a treaty stipulating an independent Bulgarian state, but European fears of Russian dominance over the area forced the creation of the independent principality of Bulgaria and the autonomous East Roumelia in the Ottoman empire. The prince, elected from one of the minor European dynasties, was to be approved by the great powers. Most potential candidates were from the numerous German principalities. The unification of Roumelia and the principality in 1885 through a militia coup provoked a Serbian offensive against Bulgaria, which was successfully repelled.

Territorial disputes among the successor states of the Ottoman empire led to two Balkan wars (1912–1914) and played a part in Bulgaria's joining the Central Powers in World War I. After the war popular discontent led to political dissension, uprisings, and government retaliation. In 1941, Bulgaria allowed German troops on its territory, becoming a member of the Axis alliance.

World War II and After

In September 1944, with the Soviet Army at the borders and partisans marching into the cities, the Fatherland Front, an alliance of leftist parties, took power and declared war on Germany. The monarchy was abolished in a 1946 referendum and a people's republic proclaimed. The following year a Soviet-type constitution entrenched the Communist Party's sole right to govern and paved the way for the nationalization of industry and cooperation of farmland.

As in most of Eastern Europe, the Communist regime fell in 1989 amid mass demonstrations. Presently, the country is a parliamentary democracy with a National Assembly of 240 members elected by proportional representation. The president, elected by direct vote for not more than two five-year mandates, appoints the prime minister from the majority party.

Marta Simidchieva

Further Reading

Crampton, Richard J. (1997) *A Concise History of Bulgaria*. Cambridge, U.K.: Cambridge University Press.
Pundeff, Marin V. (1994) *Bulgaria in American Perspective: Political and Cultural Issues*. Boulder, CO: East European Monographs.
Tzvetkov, Plamen. (1993) *A History of the Balkans: A Regional Overview from a Bulgarian Perspective*. 2 vols. San Francisco: Edwin Mellen Press.

BULLYING.   See Ijime.

BULOSAN, CARLOS   (1913–1956), Filipino writer and poet. Carlos Bulosan was born in Binalonan, a small village in Pangasinan Province in the central Philippines, on 2 November 1911. In 1930, at the age of seventeen, he left his homeland for the United States, and paid $75 for passage on the Dollar Line to Seattle, Washington. He would never return to the Philippines, nor would he ever become a U.S. citizen. Bulosan lived difficult years of unemployment, illness, and dangerous labor-union activity on the farms of California and fish canneries in Alaska. In 1942 he published a volume of poetry entitled *Letter from America* and in 1943 another book of poems, *Voice of Bataan*, a tribute to those soldiers who died in

that battle. In that same year, President Franklin Delano Roosevelt commissioned Bulosan to write one of the essays, "Freedom from Want," in "The Four Freedoms," a wartime collection that appeared in the *Saturday Evening Post*. He attracted nationwide attention for his *Laughter of My Father* (1944), a collection of short stories serialized in the *New Yorker*. *America Is in the Heart* (1946), considered by many to be his most important work, is a semiautobiographical book describing his boyhood in the Philippines, his journey to America, and the many hardships he encountered as a Filipino and migrant worker in that country.

During the postwar years, he became an outspoken critic of those who exploited workers and the poor. Associated with leftist and socialist causes, Bulosan, along with other labor activists, was blacklisted in the 1950s. He spent his last years in Seattle, poor and in failing health. At the same time McCarthyism was starting to rear its ugly head, Bulosan was being rediscovered in literary circles. Carlos Bulosan died on 11 September 1956. In 1995, a posthumously discovered novel, *The Cry and the Dedication*, about the Huk rebellion against colonization and U.S. domination of the Philippines, was published.

Craig Loomis

Further Reading

Bloom, Harold, ed. (1999) *Asian-American Writers*. Philadelphia: Chelsea House Publishers.
San Juan, E., Jr., ed. (1995) *On Becoming Filipino: Selected Writings of Carlos Bulosan*. Philadelphia: Temple University Press.

BUMIPUTRA   Literally "son of the soil," *bumiputra* is a term used to describe the indigenous Malay population in Malaysia that is constitutionally granted "special rights" in society. During the 1959 negotiations that led to the creation of Malaysia, the leaders of the three ethnic communities reached an understanding that in return for citizenship and full legal and economic rights for the Chinese and Indians, the Malays would dominate the civil service and political leadership. Ostensibly barred from the public sector, the more urbanized ethnic Chinese community went on to dominate Malaysia's private sector, causing a widening socioeconomic gap among the ethnic communities.

In 1965, the Bumiputra Economic Congress was held and, for the first time, economic aspirations were presented in racial terms. As a result, the Bumiputra

BUN BANG FAI

Bank was established to channel capital to Malay-oriented projects and Malay-owned corporations. Yet communal tensions increased, culminating in the 13 May 1969 race riots in which 196 people were killed. After the riots, the government took great steps to strengthen the Malay identity of the state.

From May 1969 to March 1971, democracy was suspended and the National Operations Council ruled by emergency powers. During this period the government implemented the New Economic Policy, a radical affirmative action program that sought to improve the standard of living of the *bumiputras*. The New Economic Policy had two goals: to reduce and eradicate poverty and to eliminate the identification of race with economic function. To achieve the first goal, the government concentrated on developing the countryside where the majority of Malays lived. To achieve the second goal, the government adopted a radical affirmative action program so that jobs and higher-education opportunities reflected the racial composition of the country. In addition to affirmative action, the replacement of English with Malay as the official language and language of instruction by 1982 greatly favored the Malays at the expense of the minority communities.

The government set goals for the share of corporate equity owned by Malays from 2.5 percent in 1970 to 30 percent by 1990. To achieve this, the government discriminated against ethnic Chinese and citizens of other countries in favor of *bumiputras* by giving Malay business special preferences, licenses, contracts, and credits, while putting pressure on Chinese and foreign-owned firms to take on Malay partners. As a Malay middle class and upper class have emerged after three decades of affirmative action, there are now growing calls to end race-based programs and policies—yet they remain supported by the majority of the rural-based *bumiputras*, whose standard of living still remains below the national average.

Zachary Abuza

Further Reading

Andaya, Barbara Watson, and Leonard Y. Andaya. (2001) *A History of Malaysia.* 2d ed. Honolulu, HI: University of Hawaii Press.

Crouch, Harold. (1996) *Government and Society in Malaysia.* Ithaca, NY: Cornell University Press.

Gomez, Edmund Terrence, and K. S. Jomo. (1997) *Malaysia's Political Economy.* New York: Cambridge University Press.

BUN BANG FAI The Bun Bang Fai Festival is one of twelve lowland Lao religious customs and celebrates the oncoming of the rainy season and fertility. The two-day festival is held in lowland Laos and neighboring Thailand during late May or early June. The timing of the festival varies depending on each village. Bun Bang Fai is sometimes celebrated with Visakha Bucha, a Buddhist holiday celebrating the birth, death, and rebirth of the Buddha. The village coordinates with the local temple, which holds a ceremony on the morning of the first day of the festival. After the temple ceremony, the villagers parade around with rockets made from bamboo or plastic tubing filled with gunpowder, charcoal, and sulfur. Carrying phallic images, both male and female participants dance after the rockets. Such displays are meant to provoke the gods into releasing lightning followed by rain. The contest for the best rocket then begins. The rockets are shot into the sky, and the rocket that travels the farthest is the winner. The intention of the explosions is also to startle the gods, causing the release of rain. The celebration continues with folk music performances and other activities. Bun Bang Fai underlines the animist and agricultural foundation of Lao culture with the emphasis on rain to insure a prosperous season for rice, other crops, and ultimately life.

Linda S. McIntosh

Further Reading

Gerson, Ruth. (1996) *Traditional Festivals of Thailand.* Kuala Lumpur, Malaysia; New York: Oxford University Press.

BUNJINGA The Japanese term *bunjinga* refers to a style of painting produced by literati (*bunjin*). *Bunjinga* traces its roots to the paintings of Chinese literati of Song dynasty (960–1267). In Japan, *bunjinga* is also known as *nanga* (Southern pictures) in reference to the theories of the Ming-dynasty connoisseur, critic, and painter Dong Qichang (1555–1636), who categorized Chinese painters as belonging either to the orthodox and academic Northern School or to the creative and expressive Southern School. In Japan, *bunjinga*'s origins may be traced to the philosopher Ogyu Sorai (1666–1728), who believed in the Chinese notion that the true gentleman was well versed in the arts of painting and calligraphy.

Bunjinga painters came from diverse backgrounds and included samurai, *ronin* (masterless samurai), poets, and professional painters. Japanese artists learned about Chinese literati painting from the Zen priest-

376

ENCYCLOPEDIA OF MODERN ASIA

painters who came to Japan in the seventeenth century, Chinese professional and amateur painters in Nagasaki, Chinese woodblock-printed painting manuals, and imported paintings. *Bunjinga* paintings were done with brush and ink, and occasionally also with color. These paintings were often contained by a poem, which demonstrated the artist's calligraphic expertise. *Bunjinga* could take a variety of formats, including hanging scrolls, hand scrolls, small-format album leaves, and folding screens, and their subject matter was diverse, ranging from realistic depictions of birds and flowers to abstracted landscapes.

Of the Japanese *bunjinga* artists, Ike no Taiga (1723–1776) and Yosa Buson (1716–1783) are notable. Taiga's work is characterized by its wittiness and humor as well as its use of dotted and textured brushstrokes accompanied by light and cheery color. In addition, Taiga was an accomplished calligrapher. Buson was a highly praised haiku poet who saw painting as a career that would allow him to earn a living to support his poetry writing. His paintings are light and airy with a playful spirit.

The literati tradition continued into the nineteenth century as artists sought to emulate Chinese ideals more closely than their predecessors. Nineteenth-century *bunjinga* painters came largely from the educated samurai class. Notable among these artists were Okada Beisanjin (1744–1820) and Uragami Gyokudo (1745– 1820). While Beisanjin employed a variety of styles in his paintings, his later works are characterized by forceful brushstrokes that create unusual forms and give texture to his images. Gyokudo's work is more dramatic and somber; he uses layers of brushwork to create feathery mountains and clouds. Whether relying on Chinese style or departing from it, the *bunjinga* tradition allowed the artists of Japan a creative freedom that resulted in the production of some of the culture's finest works of art.

Catherine Pagani

See also: **Painting—Japan; Calligraphy—Japan; Poetry—Japan**

Further Reading

Addiss, Stephen. (1987) *Tall Mountains and Flowing Waters: The Arts of Urgamo Gyokudo.* Honolulu, HI: University of Hawaii Press.

———. (1976) *Zenga and Nanga: Paintings by Japanese Monks and Scholars.* New Orleans, LA: New Orleans Museum of Art.

Cahill, James. (1972) *Scholar Painters of Japan.* New York: Asia Society.

French, Calvin L. (1974) *The Poet-Painters: Buson and his Followers.* Ann Arbor, MI: University of Michigan Press.

Yonezawa Yoshiho and Chu Yoshizawa. (1974) *Japanese Painting in the Literati Style.* New York: Weatherhill.

BUNRAKU   Bunraku, named after the theater manager Uemura Bunrakuken (1737–1810), is the most revered of Japan's many forms of puppet theater (*ningyo shibai*). Three arts are intertwined in a performance: puppet manipulation (*ningyo zukai*), chanting of the dramatic text by a single narrator (*tayu*), and musical accompaniment by a single samisen (a three-stringed lute) player. The musical style is known as *gidayu*, after its creator, the chanter Takemoto Gidayu (1651–1714), or *joruri*, from a sixteenth-century narrative *Joruri junidan* (Twelve Tales of Princess Joruri) that became a popular puppet play. When the theater district in the city of Edo (now Tokyo) burned in 1657, many puppet troupes moved to Osaka, which thereafter became the center for puppet theater in Japan.

History

A sophisticated, professional puppet theater came into existence in the early eighteenth century when two theaters, the Takemoto-za and the Toyotake-za, competed with each other in Osaka's Dotonbori entertainment district. At the Takemoto-za, playwright Chikamatsu Monzaemon (1652–1724), chanter Takemoto Gidayu, and theater manager Takeda Izumo I (d. 1747) produced the first domestic play (*sewamono*) written for the puppets, *Sonezaki shinju* (The Love Suicides at Sonezaki, 1703), and history plays (*jidaimono*) such as *Kokusenya gassen* (The Battles of Coxinga, 1715). Chikamatsu's dramas are known for their beautiful language and psychological depth of characterization. In the 1730s, puppeteers created complex puppets whose eyes, eyebrows, mouth, hands and even fingers moved realistically. Each puppet required a team of three puppeteers responsible for movements of the head and right hand, the left hand, and the feet, respectively. Revolving stages and trap doors created magical special effects. Exciting all-day plays were written to take advantage of the new technical developments. Over a period of three years, Takeda Izumo II (1691–1756), Namiki Senryu (1695–1751), and Miyoshi Shoraku (1696–1775) jointly wrote the "Three Great Masterpieces" of puppet drama for performance at the Takemoto-za: *Sugawara denju tenarai kagami* (The House of Sugawara, 1746), *Yoshitsune senbon zakura* (Yoshitsune and the Thousand Cherry Trees, 1747), and Japan's most famous revenge play, *Kanadehon chushingura* (The Treasury of Loyal Retainers, 1748). At the Toyotake-za, *Ichinotani futaba gunki* (Chronicle of the Battle of Ichinotani, 1751) was so popular with audiences that it ran for twelve

Famous Japanese puppeteer Yoshida Tamao holds a Bunraku puppet, c. 1979. (JACK FIELDS/CORBIS)

months. Kabuki troupes quickly mounted live versions of the plays, retaining the chanted narrative and thus adding *gidayu* music to their other styles. In the mid-eighteenth century, Bunraku's popularity rapidly declined as the scale of competing Kabuki productions became ever more lavish and spectacular. From the middle of the nineteenth century to the present time, a single puppet troupe continued the Bunraku tradition in Osaka.

Characteristics

Bunraku puppet dramas have high literary value and are performed for adult audiences. The team of chanter and accompanying samisen player, which changes at the beginning of each scene, sets the pace and mood of a performance, while puppeteers follow the tempo and emotion of the music. The chanter is so important that chanting without puppets (*sujoruri*) can be staged. Puppeteers spend up to thirty years learning to create natural, human movements with the puppets. The spectator sees, in addition to four or five puppet characters, a dozen or more puppeteers surrounding them and the chanter's facial expressions that powerfully convey anger, laughter, or anguish. In order to infuse the inanimate puppets with life, the chanter uses a richly emotional vocal style that draws audience attention to him. Therefore, the spectator's perception of a "character" in drama is multifaceted, created from all of the components of the performance. In especially important scenes, five or six chanters may be seated onstage, each taking the voice of one character, a technique that was borrowed from the first-person acting of competing Kabuki theaters.

Today, a single Bunraku troupe, subsidized by the Ministry of Education, is housed in the new National Bunraku Theater in Osaka. The troupe performs a repertory of traditional plays in Osaka, Tokyo, and other cities, usually for runs of two or three weeks.

James Brandon

See also: **Drama—Japan**

Further Reading

Adachi, Barbara C. (1985) *Backstage at Bunraku: A Behind the Scenes Look at Japan's Traditional Puppet Theatre.* New York: Weatherhill.

Ando Tsuruo. (1970) *Bunraku: The Puppet Theatre.* Trans. by Don Kenny. New York: Walker/Weatherhill.

Dunn, C. J. (1966) *The Early Japanese Puppet Theatre Drama.* London: Luzac.

Gerstle, Andrew C. (1986) *Circles of Fantasy: Convention in the Plays of Chikamatsu.* Cambridge, MA: Council on East Asian Studies, Harvard University.

Gerstle, Andrew C., Kiyoshi Inobe, and William P. Malm. (1990) *Theater as Music: The Bunraku Play "Mt. Imo and Mt. Se: An Exemplary Tale of Womanly Virtue."* Ann Arbor, MI.: Center for Japanese Studies, the University of Michigan.

Jones, Stanleigh H., Jr., trans. and ed. (1985) *Sugawara and the Secrets of Calligraphy.* New York: Columbia University Press.

———, Jr., trans. (1993) *Yoshitsune and the Thousand Cherry Trees: A Masterpiece of the Eighteenth Century Japanese Puppet Theatre.* New York: Columbia University Press.

Keene, Donald, trans. (1961) *Major Plays of Chikamatsu.* New York: Columbia University Press.

———. (1965) *Bunraku: The Art of the Japanese Puppet Theatre.* Tokyo: Kodansha.

———, trans. (1970) *Chushingura: The Treasury of Loyal Retainers.* New York: Columbia University Press.

Scott, A. C. (1963) *The Puppet Theatre of Japan.* Rutland, VT: Charles E. Tuttle.

Shuzaburo Hironaga. (1976) *The Bunraku Handbook.* Tokyo: Maison Des Arts.

Sziland, Paul. (1966) *Bunraku: The Japanese Puppet Theatre.* New York: Dunetz and Lovett.

BURAKU LIBERATION LEAGUE

The Buraku Liberation League (BLL), or Buraku Kaiho Domei, is the main pressure group of Japan's largest minority, the *burakumin* (hamlet people). For over fifty years, BLL has fought against discrimination and for equality for the *burakumin*, whose ancestors belonged to the outcast group called *eta* or *hinin* during the Edo period (1603–1868). By the end of the 1990s, the BLL counted 200,000 members and 2,200 branches throughout thirty-nine prefectures in Japan.

One of the BLL's predecessors was the Greater Japan Brotherhood Society for Reconciliation (Dainippon Doho Yuwakai), founded in 1903. Its main objective was to urge *buraku* people to improve their social, economic, and educational situation through their own efforts, so as to win acceptance by the rest of Japanese society. However, self-improvement did not lead to any changes in the discriminatory attitudes of non-*burakumin* people. Thus in 1922, another attempt was made with the creation of the National Levelers' Association (Suiheisha), which was the direct antecedent of the BLL. Suiheisha changed its focus from self-improvement to denunciation of those who discriminated against *burakumin (kyudan toso)*, and people were forced to apologize for their discriminatory behavior. Suiheisha achieved considerable success, but with the beginning of World War II the campaign was discouraged and the Suiheisha ultimately dissolved.

In 1946, the fight against *buraku* discrimination was taken up again with the founding of the National Committee for Buraku Liberation, or NCBL (Buraku Kaiho Zenkoku Iinkai), which was renamed the Buraku Liberation League (Buraku Kaiho Domei) at its tenth annual convention in 1955. The committee and later the BLL successfully encouraged the national government to enact laws to improve the living environment of *buraku* areas.

In 1979, the BLL underwent internal struggles, and a breakaway group formed the National Buraku Liberation Alliance (Zenkoku Buraku Kaiho Rengokai), which was closely affiliated with the Communist Party. This group claimed that special measures were no longer necessary and actually reinforced discriminatory practices. BLL, however, remained close to the (former) Socialist Party and campaigned for special measures like the enactment of the Fundamental Law for Buraku Liberation.

Due to the BLL's continuous efforts, the social, economic, and political situation of the *burakumin* improved decisively until the end of the 1990s. Nevertheless, discriminatory attitudes and behaviors seem to prevail, for instance, the secret circulation of lists of *buraku* areas and *buraku* people among businesses. Thus further BLL "enlightenment" initiatives are needed.

Martina H. Timmermann

Further Reading
BLRI. (1998) *Buraku Problem in Japan 2: Buraku Liberation News (No. 51–100) from 1989 to 1998*. Compiled by Buraku Liberation Research Institute. Osaka, Japan: Buraku Liberation and Human Rights Research Institute.
Neary, Ian. (1997) "Burakumin in Contemporary Japan." In *Japan's Minorities: The Illusion of Homogeneity*, edited by Michael Weiner. London and New York: Routledge, 50–78.

BURAKUMIN In Japan at the end of the nineteenth century awareness of family social status was disappearing. It ceased to make a difference which of the four main social groups—samurai, peasant, artisan, or merchant—one had belonged to before 1870; success in the new social and economic circumstances was more important. However, the descendants of the outcaste population, called variously *eta, kawata,* or *hinin*—today's *burakumin* (literally, "hamlet people")—remained in their ghetto-like communities. Mainstream Japanese avoided employing or marrying them. By the middle of the twentieth century, the government estimated that there were over a million *burakumin*, as they came to be called; however, the Buraku Liberation League, the pressure group active on their behalf, suggests that there are over 3 million Japanese who continue to face status discrimination, or would be discriminated against if their status origins were known. Policies adopted since 1960 have improved the social situation of *burakumin*, but in the early 2000s still have failed to completely erase social stigma.

Background
In Tokugawa Japan (1600/1603–1868), residents of communities outside the four main classes performed a variety of functions considered socially unacceptable. Some were tanners or disposed of dead animals; others were beggars or street performers; still others worked in prisons. Some were directly under the control of the daimyo (feudal lord) and policed and maintained the major roads. Many were peasant farmers toiling on the poorest land who also pursued trades such as working leather or bamboo. Some of these occupations, such as working leather, were regarded as ritually polluting in Shinto or Buddhist traditions, but not all were; nevertheless, the status regulations of the premodern period prevented normal social contact between outcastes and their neighbors. All regions of Japan were host to at least one outcaste community, but the largest concentration was found in central and western Japan.

The dismantling of the status structure in the 1870s included the emancipation of former outcastes from strict rules on what they could wear and where they could go, but prejudices about their literal and ritual uncleanness endured. Moreover, in many areas the local bureaucrats made sure that *burakumin* be identified in the newly created family registers, and some continued to work at jobs associated with dead animals such as butchers or shoemakers. Overall, during the late nineteenth century *burakumin* were unable to escape from the margins of society. Often they could find only work that others refused, for example, in match factories or poorly capitalized mines.

Steps toward Improvement

In the 1870s and 1880s a few of the wealthier *burakumin* families joined the liberal protest movement, but this had little impact on public consciousness or government policy. Working class radicalism after 1918, which inspired the formation of an organized labor movement and the development of the early feminist movement, encouraged the creation of a society dedicated to fight for *burakumin* interests—the Suiheisha or Levelers Association. The Suiheisha was founded in 1922 and for twenty years survived government attempts to close it down. It encouraged *burakumin* to oppose the discrimination they encountered in everyday life and demanded changes in government policy and the social structure that, it argued, sustained and re-created prejudice.

After 1945, there was a brief period of optimism that the occupational reforms might have removed the social bases of discrimination. As the economy began to revive and society adapted to new circumstances, it became clear, however, that *burakumin* communities were not benefiting from the rapid economic growth; indeed, their residents were excluded from employment in major companies and still shunned in marriage arrangements. The 1950s and 1960s were a time of mass migration to the cities to fill the growing factories. Some *burakumin* sought individual solutions to their problems in the anonymity of the metropolitan areas, deliberately cutting themselves off from their families and friends. As long as their backgrounds were not investigated too carefully, they passed as mainstream Japanese and found employment and a marriage partner. The other solution was for *burakumin* to organize to improve their own self-esteem and to demand that the government enforce equality of treatment. In 1955, the Buraku Liberation League was formed as a direct successor to the Suiheisha. At first the government did not take its demands seriously and established a committee of enquiry only in 1961. On the basis of the report produced four years later, a ten-year improvement program was launched in 1969. Ten years was not long enough to solve the problem, and the program was extended several times.

In many *burakumin* communities, the living environment was transformed by the provision of high-

rise apartment blocks, new schools, clinics, and community centers. Grants were made available to encourage *burakumin* children to stay in school. Some money was directed into projects aimed at challenging and changing popular attitudes. In the early 2000s there are signs that the vicious circle of poverty, low educational achievement, and poorly paid work may have been weakened if not entirely destroyed. Over 90 percent of *burakumin* children continue in school until they are eighteen. There is evidence, too, of some success in both business and politics.

Nevertheless, private detectives are routinely hired by prospective parents or employers to check out an individual's status background even though local authorities such as the Osaka prefecture have made this procedure illegal. Prejudice and discrimination remain. Severe distress, sometimes leading to suicide, still occurs when parents prevent their children from marrying because of the partner's family background.

During the 1990s, the Japanese government adopted a more robust commitment to human rights protection and promotion that may translate into proactive measures to dispel discrimination and provide redress for those who feel their rights have been violated. However, despite signs that old ideas are weakening, it is clear that discriminatory ideas endure.

Ian Neary

Further Reading

Devos, G., and H. Wagatsuma. (1972) *Japan's Invisible Race.* Berkeley and Los Angeles: University of California Press.

Neary, Ian. (1989) *Political Protest and Social Control in Prewar Japan—The Suiheisha and the Origins of Buraku Liberation.* Manchester, U.K.: Manchester University Press.

Kitaguchi Suehiro. (1999) *An Introduction to the Buraku Issue.* Richmond, UK: Japan Library.

Upham, F. K. (1987) *Law and Social Change in Postwar Japan.* Cambridge, MA: Harvard University Press.

BUREAU OF RELIGIOUS AFFAIRS The Bureau of Religious Affairs, an official government agency within the People's Republic of China (PRC), enforces PRC policies related to religious affairs. It is directly administered by the State Council and was established in 1954.

The bureau's task is to register venues (such as monasteries and churches) for "normal religious activities," to ensure that religious organizations are not subject to any foreign domination and to protect freedom of religious belief. Article 36 of the 1982 constitution defines "normal religious activities" as activities that do not "disrupt public order, impair the health of citizens, or interfere with the educational system of the state." This definition reflects the post-1976 shift away from the fiercely antireligious stance of Mao Zedong (1893–1976).

The PRC claims that the bureau fosters the rule of law and patriotism by linking legitimate religious activities with the maintenance of state order, national unity, and socialist development. The bureau has been instrumental in helping various religious bodies reclaim and restore properties lost or destroyed during the Cultural Revolution (1966–1976). It also has tended to scrutinize or prosecute some religious groups and activities more than others, especially so-called ethnic religions (Buddhism in Tibet and Inner Mongolia, Islam in Xinjiang), small unregistered bodies (charismatic Protestant Christian "house churches"), "superstitions" *(mixin)* such as fortune-telling and faith healing, and politically suspect groups (Falun Gong/Falun Dafa).

Jeffrey L. Richey

Further Reading

Dean, Kenneth. (1997) "Ritual and Space: Civil Society or Popular Religion?" In *Civil Society in China*, edited by Timothy Brook and B. Michael Frolic. Armonk, NY: M. E. Sharpe.

Gladney, Dru C. (1994) "Salman Rushdie in China: Religion, Ethnicity, and State Definition in the People's Republic." In *Asian Visions of Authority: Religion and the Modern States of East and Southeast Asia*, edited by Charles F. Keyes, Laurel Kendall, and Helen Hardacre. Honolulu, HI: University of Hawaii Press.

MacInnis, Donald E. (1989) *Religion in China Today: Policy and Practice.* Maryknoll, NY: Orbis Books.

U.S. Commission on International Religious Freedom. (2000) *Findings on Russia, China, and Sudan; and Religious Persecutions in the World.* Washington, DC: Government Printing Office.

BURMA.   See **Myanmar.**

BURMA INDEPENDENCE ARMY   The

Burma Independence Army (BIA) was the founding armed movement of young Burmese nationalists during World War II and the forerunner of the modern Burma army, or Tatmadaw. The BIA was formally inaugurated in Bangkok, Thailand, on 28 December 1941 by a meeting of the famed "Thirty Comrades," including Aung San (1915–1947) and Ne Win (b. 1911), who had been trained on Hainan Island by Imperial Japan. Shortly afterward, the first BIA troops

entered Burma with the Japanese Fifteenth Army. In the next few months, the BIA expanded to around 23,000 soldiers under arms, fighting one major battle with retreating British forces at Shwedaung near Prome (Pyay). But against the backdrop of war, the BIA was later accused of abuses against Karen civilians and local Muslims. In August 1942, the BIA was replaced by the Burma Defense Army, which in 1943 was superceded by the Burma National Army (BNA). On 27 March 1945, the BNA joined the uprising against the Japanese, and later became the Patriotic Burmese Forces under the interim British administration (1945–1948). It formed a central element of the Burmese army at independence in 1948.

Martin Smith

Further Reading

Ba Than, U. (1962) *The Roots of the Revolution.* Rangoon, Myanmar: Government Printing Press.

Becka, Jan. (1983) *The National Liberation Movement in Burma during the Japanese Occupation Period (1941–1945).* Prague, Czechoslovakia: Czechoslovak Academy of Sciences.

Callahan, Mary P. (1996) "The Origins of Military Rule in Burma." Ph.D. diss. Cornell University.

Izumiya, Tatsuro. (1981) *The Minami Organ.* Rangoon, Myanmar: Universities Press.

This section of the Burma Road in China photographed in June 1944 contains 24 switchbacks. (BETTMANN/CORBIS)

BURMA ROAD   Opened to automobile traffic in 1938, the famous Burma Road, linking northeast Myanmar (Burma) with southwest China, was the country's most strategic road link with the outside world for much of the twentieth century. Starting from the railway terminus at Lashio in northern Shan State, the road winds through mountain terrain for much of its 1,120-kilometer (700-mile) course, crossing the China frontier at Muse en route to Kunming, the Yunnan Province capital.

Built mostly by Chinese workers, the road was of major geopolitical significance, opening the way for trade and modern communications between British Burma and China. As a result, its completion hastened the Japanese invasion of Burma during World War II in an attempt by the Imperial Japanese army to cut off this new supply route to the Nationalist forces of Chiang Kai-shek. However, the grandiose Japanese war aims to occupy both Burma and China ultimately failed. The region became a major theater of conflict, and, for a brief period at the war's end, the Burma Road was linked up by the British with the Ledo Road, enabling direct road connections between India, Burma, and China.

After independence, commercial traffic along the Burma Road steadily declined. During a quarter century of isolationist government by General Ne Win's Burma Socialist Programme Party (BSPP, 1962–1988), much of the territory adjacent to the Burma Road was under insurgent control.

Only after the collapse of both the BSPP and the insurgent Communist Party of Burma during 1988 and 1989 were efforts made to upgrade the road with the support of neighboring China, which began to build closer relations with the new State Law and Order Restoration Council government in Yangon (formerly Rangoon). In the twenty-first century, the Burma Road was again earmarked for major business expansion.

Martin Smith

Further Reading
Anders, Leslie. (1965) *The Ledo Road: General Joseph W. Stilwell's Highway to China*. Norman, OK: University of Oklahama Press.
Kington, Miles. (1989) "The Burma Road." In *Great Journeys*, edited by Philip Jones Griffiths et al. London: BBC Books.
Smith, Nicol. (1940) *Burma Road: The Story of the World's Most Romantic Highway*. New York: Garden City Publishing.
Tan Pei-Ying. (1945) *The Building of the Burma Road*. New York: McGraw-Hill.

BURMA-THAILAND RAILWAY   The Burma-Thailand Railway was built by the Imperial Japanese Army (IJA) between June 1942 and October 1943 using Allied Prisoners of War (POWs) and Asian laborers. The labor force consisted of over 60,000 American, Australian, British, and Dutch POWs and an estimated 270,000 conscripted workers from Burma, Malaya, and Thailand. The Japanese estimated that the 420-kilometer (260-mile) railway line linking Ban Pong, 50 kilometers (31 miles) east of Bangkok and Thanbyuzayat, 60 kilometers (37 miles) south of Moulmein in southwestern Burma, would take between five and six years to complete. Fearing that their positions in Burma were vulnerable to attack, the IJA decided early in 1943 to increase the rate of construction. Working from both ends, they planned to complete the line within sixteen months and launch an attack on India.

The appalling physical conditions endured by those working on the railway were compounded by increasingly heavy workloads and the brutal treatment meted out by prison guards. During the construction, an estimated 80,000 Asian laborers and 13,000 POWs died of malnutrition, disease, overwork, and beatings. The railway was completed on 16 October 1943, but it was used only once before Allied forces bombed the bridge spanning the Kwai River, a tributary of the Mae Klong River in western Thailand. Most of the railway was dismantled after the war, although a small section, including the bridge, is still used.

The Burma-Thailand Railway has come to symbolize the brutality of the IJA during World War II. The events inspired the novel *Bridge on the River Kwai* by the French writer Pierre Boulle, which in turn inspired a film of the same name. Every year the destruction of the Kwai River bridge is symbolically reenacted with a fireworks display in memory of those who died.

Daniel Oakman

Further Reading
Brooke, Micool. (1995) *Captive of the River Kwae*. Bangkok, Thailand: Merman Books.
Clarke, Hugh V. (1986) *A Life for Every Sleeper: A Pictorial Record of the Burma-Thailand Railway*. Sydney: Allen and Unwin.
Ebury, Sue. (1994) *Weary: The Life of Sir Edward Dunlop of the Burma-Thailand Railway*. New York: Viking.
Kinving, Clifford. (1998) *River Kwai Railway: The Story of the Burma-Siam Railroad*. London and Herdon, VA: Brassey's.
McCormack, Gavan, and Nelson, Hank. (1993) *The Burma-Thailand Railway: Memory and History*. Sydney: Allen and Unwin.

Thompson, Kyle. (1994) *A Thousand Cups of Rice: Surviving the Death Railway*. Austin, TX: Eakin Press.

BURMANS

The designation "Burman" (Bama[r] in Burmese) is mostly used to distinguish the ethnicity of the people associated with the kingdom of Myanmar (Burma), which had become dominant in the region from the tenth century, from the ethnicity of the peoples of other Buddhist kingdoms in the area or from other ethnic groups in general. The native language of Burmans is Burmese, also known as Myanma(r), and Burmans make up approximately 68 percent of Myanmar's estimated 47 million people. Though not consistently, "Burman" usually denotes a particular ethnic group, but "Burmese" by contrast has historically referred mostly to citizenship or nationality, including members of all of Myanmar's ethnic groups.

Burman Royal Dynasties

Burmans arrived relatively late in the region from the highlands north of present-day India and from Yunnan in today's China, assimilating or supplanting several indigenous groups. They asserted themselves in Upper Burma at the expense of earlier established and highly sophisticated Pyu and Mon kingdoms, from which they benefited in their writing, arts, and religion. They established the Pagan dynasty (c. 849–1287 CE), which reached its height under King Anawrahta (reigned 1044–1077) and his son Kyanzittha (reigned 1084–1112). Having adopted Theravada Buddhism, they built an impressively large number of pagodas and Buddhist monasteries. However, the kingdom succumbed under Mongol and Shan attacks, after which the Shan dominated Upper Burma and the Mon Lower Burma.

Burmans reasserted control in the Toungoo dynasty (1530–1752). Centered upon Toungoo in Lower Burma, it reached its height under King Bayinnaung (d. 1581). However, the dynasty was weakened by war with the Siamese, war in Manipur, and wars with the Portuguese and was finally ended by a Lower Burma rebellion.

The Konbaung dynasty (1752–1885), the last Burman royal dynasty, was established in Shwebo under Alaungpaya (1714–1760), who defeated the Mon, attacked the British Negrais trading post, and sacked the Siamese capital of Ayutthaya. This dynasty brought Arakan, Manipur, and other areas under Burman control for the first time.

Buddhism is an important element of Burman identity. Here, a Buddhist monk walks through a monastery in Mandalay. (CHARLES & JOSETTE LENARS/CORBIS)

Colonial History

After adventurers came missionaries, traders, and then representatives from foreign governments. After the Portuguese and the Dutch, the British arrived. From neighboring India, the British conquered the country in the course of three Anglo-Burmese Wars between 1824 and 1885 and put an end to the Burman royal dynasties.

The British emphasized trade, for which control over the sea-lanes was vital. After the third war, Mandalay, the old Burman capital in central Burma, decreased in importance relative to Rangoon (now Yangon) in the delta, leaving the British in control of riverine and sea trade involving the ports and considerably weakening Burman royalty. The colonial government made use of many non-Burmans: the civil service, police, military, and commerce involved mostly Indians, Chinese, and some non-Burman ethnic groups. Many people were brought in, especially from India and China, to fulfill this need. Burmans were primarily targeted by the British to help expand agriculture, in particular, rice cultivation.

Under the royal system, the king was the chief patron of Buddhism, and the British policy of separating state and religion meant that the office of the last *sangharaja (thathanabaing)*, the senior monk adviser to the king, was not renewed. Since Burman ethnicity was shaped by and understood in terms of Buddhism as sponsored by the king, these developments contributed to Burmans' feeling marginalized. They asserted themselves in the early decades of the twentieth century primarily through newly founded Buddhist institutions, including the Young Men's Buddhist Association (YMBA), established in 1906. Buddhism became politicized through the "shoe question" (whether Europeans would be allowed to wear shoes in monasteries and pagodas) in 1917. Uncertainty arose over how Burma, until then ruled as part of India, fit into the Montagu-Chelmsford Reforms (proposed in 1918 but implemented in 1919) on the question of India's independence. In the wake of this, the Greater Council for Burmese Associations, an alliance of Buddhist groups, was founded in 1920. It took a more political turn, advocating the boycott of foreign goods. Leadership during this period still came primarily from monks, including U Wisara and U Ottama, who set early parameters for Burman nationalism.

Burman nationalism was strengthened by various factors. The economic downturn of the 1930s indebted Burman farmers, culminating in the 1930 Saya San millenarian rebellion. In the context of this unrest, the nationalist Dobama (or Thakin) movement, founded on narrow Burman ethnic grounds in 1930, most effectively rallied for national independence. This movement recruited students from Rangoon University, including U Nu and Aung San, who eventually became the country's leaders and developed a more inclusive, though no less recognizably Burman form of nationalism.

During the colonial period, other ethnic groups such as the Karen and Indians received what Burmans regarded as favorable treatment from the British. Ethnic groups that during the Konbaung period had been on tributary terms with the king were permitted to keep their traditional chiefdoms, received special employment, and also were deemed more sympathetic to British colonialism and more receptive to "foreign" intervention. Many had converted to Christianity. Where they were Buddhist, many also had a *sangha* (monastic order) independent of networks dominated by Burman nationalists. This contributed to a politicized ethnicity from which it is still difficult to escape today.

Yet to categorize the population of Myanmar predominantly in terms of Burmans versus non-Burmans is unsatisfactory. With no incontrovertible racial or other markers, the category "Burman" has historically been permeable and open to construction: royal dynasties drew on a variety of ethnicities, and there is much variation among those who consider themselves Burmans. Some ethnic minorities, in particular, the Pyu, dominant between the seventh and ninth centuries, are thought to have been completely assimilated into Burman and other ethnic groups, leaving traces only in their writing, archaeology, and Chinese sources. Some individual members of ethnic groups, particularly Mon, Shan, Karen, and also Chinese residents, may identify themselves as Burmans

to various degrees, some to the extent of complete assimilation.

Gustaaf Houtman

Further Reading
Aung Thwin, Michael. (1985) *Pagan: The Origins of Modern Burma.* Honolulu, HI: University of Hawaii Press.

Koenig, W. J. (1990) *The Burmese Polity, 1752–1819: Politics, Administration, and Social Organization in the Early Kon-baung Period.* Center for Southeast Asian Studies, no. 34. Ann Arbor, MI: University of Michigan Press.

Lieberman, Victor. (1984) *Burmese Administrative Cycles: Anarchy and Conquest c. 1580–1760.* Princeton, NJ: Princeton University Press.

Mendelson, E. M. (1975) *Sangha and State in Burma: A Study of Monastic Sectarianism and Leadership.* Edited by John P. Ferguson. London: Cornell University Press.

Mi Mi Hkaing. (1962) *Burmese Family.* Bloomington, IN: Indiana University Press.

Nash, Manning. (1965) *The Golden Road to Modernity: Village Life in Contemporary Burma.* New York: Wiley.

Scott, James George. (1910) *The Burman, His Life and Notions.* London: Macmillan.

Spiro, Melford E. (1970) *Buddhism and Society; A Great Tradition and Its Burmese Vicissitudes.* New York: Harper & Row.

BURMESE Burmese is the national language of Myanmar (Burma) and is the native language of the Burman ethnic majority, who make up approximately two-thirds of Myanmar's population of slightly over 50 million. The rest of the nation's indigenous population is diverse, speaking between sixty and one hundred other languages between them, depending on the criteria used to distinguish languages from one another. In urban centers there are also long-established and substantial communities speaking various South Asian and Chinese languages. Most non-Burmans live in the areas near Myanmar's borders with Thailand, Laos, China, India, and Bangladesh, although many live interspersed with Burmans and with each other and speak Burmese and other languages in addition to their native language. Burmese is little spoken outside Myanmar but is widely dispersed, and fragmented communities of Burmese expatriates may be found around the world.

Burmese belongs to the Tibeto-Burman language family, which comprises approximately 350 languages spoken across a vast territory stretching from the Himalayas to mainland Southeast Asia. Burmese has by far the largest number of speakers of any of the Tibeto-Burman languages, most of which have only a few thousand speakers and many of which may disappear during the twenty-first century.

Most of the other languages spoken in Myanmar also belong to the Tibeto-Burman language family, including some languages, such as Arakanese (Rakhine), Intha, and Danu, which are so similar to Burmese as to be considered by some to be dialects of Burmese rather than separate languages. Other Tibeto-Burman languages of Myanmar include the Loloish languages, such as Lahu, Lisu, and Akha (Hani), spoken in the Golden Triangle area near the borders with Thailand, Laos, and China, and others such as the Karen, Kachin, and Chin groups of languages. The remaining languages belong to the Mon-Khmer family, such as Mon, Wa, and Palaung, and the Tai-Kadai family, to which Thai also belongs, such as Shan and Tai Khun.

Burmese Script

Burmese script is a close cousin of Mon script, which was adapted from a script used in southern India, a descendant of the Brahmi script, which was the ancestor of many Indic scripts found in South and Southeast Asia. The earliest examples of written Burmese are stone inscriptions of the eleventh and twelfth centuries CE. It is widely believed that the square-shaped letters of the stone inscriptions developed into the distinctive round-shaped letters of Burmese today because texts were traditionally written on palm leaves, which would split easily if angled shapes were scratched on them. Whether or not this is true, to this day Burmese handwriting with consistent, even, round shapes is praised.

The writing system evolved between the period of the early inscriptions and the sixteenth century CE, when it assumed a form similar to its present-day form. As in English, the spoken language has changed considerably since that time, with the result that a faithful transliteration of written Burmese, such as the American Library Association-Library of Congress (ALA-AC) system designed for library cataloguing often gives little impression of the way words are pronounced in Burmese today because some combinations of symbols are pronounced differently from the sounds represented by the symbols individually. The phonetic transcription used in this article is the one devised by John Okell (1994) to represent the sound of Burmese words for learners of Burmese who know English. The difference between the ALA-LC transliteration and the phonetic transcription can be seen in the following example: the Burmese word for "television" would be transliterated as *rup´ mraṅ´ saṃ krā´´* but is transcribed here as *youq-myin-than-jà*.

The Indian script from which Burmese script is derived was originally designed for Indo-Aryan languages such as Pali, the language of the Buddhist scriptures. Burmese script has retained certain features and symbols that are needed for writing the many words Burmese has borrowed from Pali. The doubled consonants and retroflex consonants common in Indian languages do not occur in Burmese words. Pali loanwords (words taken from another language and at least partially naturalized) in Burmese, typically specialist and learned vocabulary, are often easily identified by these features. Compare the Pali loanword for "indication," written *lakkhaṇā* (pronounced *leq-khă-na*), with a close Burmese equivalent *ă-c'eq*.

Burmese script is mostly alphabetic and is written from left to right like English. There are separate symbols to represent vowels and consonants, but the symbols are organized in syllabic clusters. Within each cluster, the symbols are not necessarily written in left-to-right order and so are not always arranged in the same order that they are pronounced. For example, to write the syllable *ti* ("worm"), the vowel *i* is placed on top of the consonant *t*, but to write *tu* ("nephew"), the *u* must hang below the *t*.

The literacy rate in Burma has often been said to be high compared to that in other nations in the region, but accurate data are difficult to obtain. One recent source suggests that nearly 80 percent of Burmese people over the age of fifteen are literate, but other sources have put the figure much lower.

Burmese Grammar

Like the vast majority of the languages spoken in mainland East and Southeast Asia, Burmese is a tone language. The tonal contrasts involve not only the usual differences in pitch and vowel length, but also differences in phonation type—whether the voice is breathy or sharp in character. The presence or absence of a glottal stop, written as a final -*q* in the transcription, at the end of the syllable may also be considered to be part of the tonal system.

Some of the sounds used in Burmese are considered unusual because they occur relatively rarely in many of the world's languages. These are the so-called voiceless nasals, which include the sound of air escaping through the nose. The Burmese word for "investment," *yìn-hnì-hmyouq-hnan-hmú*, contains examples of two such sounds, written *hn-* and *hm-* in the transcription.

In Burmese, most morphemes, or single units of meaning, consist of a single syllable. Words and phrases may be formed by combining morphemes in pairs or sometimes longer strings. Four such morphemes, "picture-see-sound-hear," combine to form the word for "television" *youq-myin-than-jà* mentioned earlier.

As in most Tibeto-Burman languages, in Burmese the verb usually comes at the end of the sentence, following its object. Otherwise, the order of words and phrases in the rest of a Burmese sentence can be ordered in many ways to reflect the tone and emphasis of an utterance. The meaning remains unambiguous because grammar words can be attached to words and phrases to show their syntactic relationship with one another, to identify the subject and object, and so on. Thus a typical Burmese sentence consists of a number of phrases marked with grammar words, ending with a verb at the end. For example, the sentence "U Ba came to Mandalay with his mother" would be rendered in Burmese as "U Ba-SUBJECT Mandalay-TO mother-WITH came-verb" *(Ù Bá-gá Mandălè-go ă-me-néh la-deh).*

Pronouns denoting people and things (such as "I," "we," "it") can often be left out of a sentence in Burmese when the context makes the intended meaning clear. One would normally respond to the question "Did he slice the mango?" with just the verb "sliced" *(hlì-deh)* in Burmese because it is clear from the context who had sliced what.

The Burmese language exists in a colloquial style used in spoken, informal contexts and a literary style used in official, formal settings. The main difference between the two is that they have separate sets of grammar words and some other vocabulary. The colloquial-style example sentence used earlier, "U Ba came to Mandalay with his mother," could be rendered in literary style by simply substituting the literary style for the grammar words and the word for "mother," giving *Ù Bá-dhi Mandălè-dhó mí-gin-hnín la-í.*

Justin Watkins

Further Reading

Allott, Anna. (1985) "Language Policy and Language Planning in Burma." In *Papers in Southeast Asian Linguistics: Language Policy, Language Planning and Sociolinguistics in Southeast Asia*, edited by David Bradley. Canberra, Australia: Pacific Linguistics, 131–154.

Myanmar Language Commission. (1993) *Myanmar-English Dictionary.* Yangon, Myanmar: Myanmar Language Commission.

Okell, John. (1984) *Script, Literary Style* and *Spoken Language.* Vols. 1, 2 of *Burmese: An Introduction* . . . DeKalb, IL: Northern Illinois University.

Okell, John, and Anna Allott. (2001) *Burmese/Myanmar: A Dictionary of Grammatical Forms.* Richmond, U.K.: Curzon Press.

Wheatley, Julian. (1990) "Burmese." In *The Major Languages of East and South-East Asia*, edited by Bernard Comrie. London: Routledge, 106–126.

BURMESE ARTS In Myanmar (Burma), no distinction is made between fine arts and applied arts, and the term "arts" encompasses architecture as well as a wealth of traditional arts and crafts. Much of Myanmar's artistic expression is inspired by and devoted to the nation's predominant faith, Buddhism. For centuries, Myanmar's kings and people have supported the building of Buddhist temples and monasteries as meritorious deeds. The scale of temple-building achieved at Pagan (Bagan) from the eleventh to thirteenth century has never been matched, but the tradition survived the ending of royal rule and patronage brought about by British colonial rule (from three territorial annexations in the nineteenth century until 1948) and continues today under state and private patronage. The construction and ornamentation of temples (by wall paintings, stucco relief work, carvings, and sculptures) and of monasteries are a primary focus for Myanmar's artistic expression. Much of Myanmar's cultural life from the village level upward is dominated by Buddhist activities such as communal alms-giving and novitiation ceremonies and by temple and other festivals—all occasions for music, song, and dance. Myanmar's ethnic groups also possess distinctive music and dance traditions and art forms.

Arts and Crafts

Artisans, as skilled producers of artifacts for religious and devotional use as well as for domestic, secular use, are traditionally accorded high respect. Pagan-period inscriptions record the types of crafts that the Burmese people classify as the ten arts *(pan hse myo)*, comprising the artistic creations of: blacksmiths, gold and silversmiths, bronze casters, stone masons, stone sculptors, stucco and plaster workers, woodcarvers, wood turners, painters, and lacquer artists. Other crafts include cloth appliqué hangings *(kalaga)*, textile weaving, pottery, basketry, lapidary, and gold-leaf production. Many art forms show influences from India and China and, most notably, from Mon and Thai (Siamese) traditions, introduced by artisans and musicians who were brought back as captives from conquests of neighboring kingdoms. From the late nineteenth century onward some Western influence is apparent. During the colonial period, many local crafts declined, unable to compete with cheap imports and a decline in patronage, but efforts were also made under government auspices to nurture arts and crafts by establishing schools for weaving, lacquer, and ceramics and by holding exhibitions with prizes for outstanding artists. The Burmese people excelled in producing masterpieces of intricate woodcarving, ornate silverware, and fine lacquerware. From the late 1980s, the opening of the nation to tourism and foreign investment has given fresh impetus to some tra-

Two Burman women in a workshop making lacquerware. (EYE UBIQUITOUS/CORBIS)

ditional arts, particularly lacquerware and cloth hangings, as well as to the reproduction of antiquities.

Performing Arts

Myanmar has a strong performing-arts tradition that preserves many classical forms but that has also been receptive to new elements and influences. The court or classical arts, as practiced for centuries under royal and noble patronage, are still performed at state and public performances. Theatrical performances take various forms, all accompanied by music and with dance, song, dialogue, and poetry recitations.

Puppet Theater Although puppetry is recorded as early as an inscription of 1444, the puppet theater's development and popularization date from the patronage of the eighteenth-century minister for theater, U Thaw. Performances traditionally lasted a whole night, with a full-length drama presented to the audience by a cast of twenty-eight hand-carved stringed puppets. The dramatic themes were taken from previous lives of the Buddha (the *jataka* stories) and from the Burmese chronicles. The puppet theater (*yok-thei thabin*) declined greatly from the 1920s onward and survives only in a truncated form in state cultural performances, tourist shows and, occasionally, pagoda festivals.

Classical Drama Burmese plays or drama shows (*zat pwe*) are musical plays with dancers, and performances can last a whole night. The plays draw their inspiration from the Buddhist *jataka* stories and the lives of

kings and also from the *Ramayana*, introduced as a dance-drama form from Thailand after the conquest of Ayutthaya in 1767. The works of the nineteenth-century court dramatists U Kyin U and U Ponnya have endured. A more lighthearted operetta-type performance is the *anyein*, which has much clowning and repartee as well as all female dancers. Famed twentieth-century dancers and theatrical performers were U Po Sein (d. 1952) and, in the postwar period, Shwe Man Tin Maung (d. 1969). The advent of foreign films and the founding of Myanmar's own motion picture industry in 1918 contributed to the decline of some traditional forms of entertainment but also to the rise of such new forms as modern melodramas and contemporary plays (*pya-zat*).

Music and Song The first historical record of Myanmar's music and dance comes from Chinese accounts describing a mission from the ancient Pyu kingdom in 800–802 CE. Among the instruments mentioned were the boat-shaped harp (*saing-gauk*) and the crocodile zither (*mi-gyaung*), both still played today. The distinctive thirteen-stringed Burmese harp is played as a solo instrument and as an accompaniment to solo song. Another traditional instrument is the bamboo xylophone (*pat-tala*). The Burmese possess a unique musical ensemble known as the *hsaing-waing*, which is used for theatrical performances and religious and festive occasions. It is composed of drums, percussion, and wind instruments, the most important being a circle of drums (*pat-waing*) suspended from a circular

Dancers in traditional costume in a performance of the *Ramayana* in March 2000. (NIK WHEELER/CORBIS)

wooden frame (with the player seated in its center), a gong circle *(kyi waing)*, oboes *(hne)*, bamboo clappers, brass cymbals, and a distinctive large drum *(pat-ma)* suspended from an elaborate gilded and glass-inlaid frame in the form of a composite flying animal *(pyinsarupa)*. Drums are played to announce and accompany processions and entertainments and include the *si-daw* (royal drums), double-headed drums formerly played at court and other ceremonial occasions, and the *do-bat*, a small double-headed drum worn suspended across the player's chest and played at village and religious festivities.

The Burmese possess a repertory of several hundred traditional classical songs *(thachin-gyi)* whose texts have been collected into standard reference anthologies, the *Maha Gita* and the *Gita Withawdani*. Categories of song include the *kyo, bwe,* and *thachingan* (old court songs based on classical literature) and *yodaya* (songs of Thai origin), as well as *nat-chin* (songs associated with the spirits) and *baw-le* and *lun-gyin* (laments).

Preservation and Sponsorship of the Arts

Following independence in 1948, state schools for the fine arts and music and drama were opened in Mandalay and Rangoon (now Yangon) as part of the government's program to promote and revive the nation's cultural heritage, which was perceived as having declined under British colonial rule and the Japanese wartime occupation (1942–1945). The national museum and national library, founded in the 1950s, faced the task of recovering from the wartime loss of treasured collections and research materials. Myanmar's Ministry of Culture consists of the Department of Fine Arts, Department of Cultural Institute, and Department of Archaeology. The Department of Fine Arts is responsible for state entertainments (music, theater, dance programs, and tours) and promoting, through research and preservation, Myanmar's cultural heritage. In the 1990s, a new National Museum and a new National Library as well as a Defense Services Museum were constructed in Yangon, and many museums—including Chin, Kayah, Rakhine (Arakan), and Mon State cultural museums, the Motion Picture Museum, and the new Bagan Archaeological Museum—were opened. The Department of Archaeology is responsible for archaeological excavations at ancient sites, for renovation of ancient temples and buildings, and for the maintenance of newly reconstructed palaces at Mandalay, Pegu, and Shwebo. Some of these government-sponsored works have been criticized for the standard of workmanship and alleged use of forced labor. In 1996, the University of Culture opened, offering courses in music, dramatic arts, painting, and sculpture. Modern art forms and design, cinematography, and musical innovations are increasing as Myanmar becomes more open to outside influences and markets, but artists and performers are still very much subject to state censorship and control.

Patricia M. Herbert

See also: **Literature—Myanmar; Mon; Pagan, Pagodas, Burmese**

Further Reading

Fraser-Lu, Sylvia. (1994) *Burmese Crafts: Past and Present.* Oxford: Oxford University Press.
———. (2000) *Burmese Lacquerware.* Bangkok, Thailand: Orchid Press.
Htin, Aung. ([1939] 1957) *Burmese Drama.* Reprint ed. Oxford: Oxford University Press.
Inglis, Kim, ed. (1998) *Myanmar Style: Art, Architecture, and Design.* Hong Kong: Periplus Editions.
Isaacs, Ralph, and T. Richard Blurton. (2000) *Visions from the Golden Land: Burma and the Art of Lacquer.* London: British Museum Press.

Singer, Noel F. (1992) *Burmese Puppets*. Kuala Lumpur, Malaysia: Oxford University Press.

———. (1995) *Burmese Dance and Theatre*. Kuala Lumpur, Malaysia: Oxford University Press.

Theingi, Ma. (1994) *The Illusion of Life: Burmese Marionettes*. Bangkok, Thailand: White Orchid Press.

Ye, Htut. (1997) *Myanmar Dances*. Yangon, Myanmar: Win Sarpay.

BURSA (2002 pop. 1.2 million). Bursa, capital of the province of Bursa (2002 population 2.2 million), at the foot of Ulu Dag (Great Mountain) near the thermal springs of Cekirge in northwestern Turkey, was founded as Proussa by Prussias I of Bithynia in the second century BCE. In the fourteenth century Osman I (1251–1326), founder of the Ottoman empire, attempted to capture the city by staging a blockade outside its walls. First attempts failed, but in 1326 the besieged city surrendered to Sultan Orhan (reigned 1324–1362), son of Osman. Orhan named the city Bursa. Under Ottoman rule, Bursa was the Muslim city closest to the Christian world. Silk became the city's largest export, and the Ottoman court its greatest consumer. Bursa saw the birth of Ottoman architecture, including the Ulu Mosque, erected in 1399 under Bayezid I (1389–1402). After Timur's troops captured Bursa in 1402 and destroyed most of the city, the Ottoman capital moved to Edirne, although Bursa remained the heart of the Ottoman empire for many years. Even after Mehmed II (1432–1481) conquered Constantinople, Bursa was still the center for campaigns to the east. Today automotive industry has replaced the silk industry, but the early Ottoman mosques and tombs recall Bursa's distinguished past.

T. Isikozlu-E.F. Isikozlu

Further Reading
Statistical Yearbook of Turkey, 1998. (1998) Ankara, Turkey: Devlet Istatistik Enstitusu

BUSTARD, HUBARA The Hubara bustard (also Houbara or Macqueen's; *Chlamydotis undulata*) is one of five species of the Otididae family of game birds found in South Asia. The name "hubara" is derived from Arabic, while "bustard" is a corruption of the Latin *Avis tarda* ("slow bird"). Bustards are three-toed, mostly polygamous birds adapted to running.

The Hubara bustard is a large bird with a thick ruff of black and white feathers down each side of the neck. The lower parts of the body are white, with bluish-gray bars running through the tail. The bird visits South Asia in the winter, during September to March, migrating to the desert and semidesert areas of Pakistan and northwestern India from the Near East. The same species has also been sighted in northwestern Europe. In spite of its protective coloration, Arab elites and others hunting the bustard with falcons have greatly reduced the numbers in recent times. The flesh of this and other bustards has long been esteemed in Europe and Asia.

Of the other four bustard species found in South Asia, the smaller species are called Floricans, while the Great Indian bustard (*Choriotis nigriceps*) is the largest and best known, though extremely rare today. The Great Indian bustard too occurs in Pakistan and northwestern India, can weigh up to 18 kilograms, and can have an overall height of a meter. The recent spread of agriculture into semidesert areas of South Asia threatens all bustards with extinction, as do tourism and the wide use of chemical pesticides.

Paul Hockings

BUTO. See **Dance, Modern—East Asia.**

BUZKASHI *Buzkashi*, a traditional sport of Central Asia, is still played by men in northern Afghanistan and by Afghan refugees in Pakistan. In the past it was played by Turkic peoples in Central Asia and western China. During a violent equestrian contest, riders on horseback compete to grab the carcass of a goat or calf off the ground and ride off with it. The sport probably developed as an offshoot of the riding activities of the nomadic peoples of Central Asia.

Two Afghan teams compete in a *buzkashi* match in Peshawar, Pakistan, in March 2000. (AFP/CORBIS)

Buzkashi is closely related to local power structures in rural Afghanistan. Horses are bred, raised, and trained by local political leaders who hire riders to compete in the tournaments organized by the owners. Tournaments are held in the winter when men are free of agricultural responsibilities and also to mark special occasions such as a marriage. Staging a well-attended and successful tournament raises the status of the sponsor, whereas a poor tournament damages the host's reputation.

Play begins with men riding around a field and charging to the center to fight for the carcass. A rider is victorious when he takes the carcass from the crowd of riders, rides off with it and drops it to the ground. A brief chant of praise is then offered for the rider, horse, and owner, and another round of play begins. The winning rider receives a prize of a carpet, rifle, or money, and the owner of the horse gains the prize of prestige. Disputes are common, over rough play and over who controls the carcass, and, more important, between political rivals whose day-to-day political rivalry is played out on the field by their hired riders.

In the 1950s, the Afghanistan government promoted *buzkashi* as a tourist attraction and a symbol of centralized power and national unity; there were provincial teams and an annual tournament overseen by the king. In 1983, the annual tournament was ended by the Soviet-controlled government. The sport was transferred to Pakistan by Afghan refugees and in the Taliban era was played primarily in the northern provinces.

David Levinson

Further Reading

Azoy, G. Whitney. (1982) *Buzkashi: Game and Power in Afghanistan.* Philadelphia: University of Pennsylvania Press.

Michaud, Roland, and Sabrina Michaud. (1988) *Horsemen of Afghanistan.* London: Thames and Hudson.

BYZANTINES The Byzantine empire is conventionally said to begin in 330 BCE, the year that the Roman empire's eastern capital was transferred to Constantinople. The Byzantines called themselves Romaioi, citizens of Rome, and regarded their ruler as absolute temporal and spiritual head of Rome and all its conquests. The emperors successfully defended the reduced eastern Roman provinces against onslaught from Persian and then Islamic invaders, but the effort left them powerless to protect the western empire, where the last emperor was deposed in 876 CE. Despite betrayal by western Christianity, the Byzantine empire survived as the repository of Greek and Roman civilization for 1,100 years.

History

The history of Byzantium is that of Constantinople—the queen city—and its emperors. Constantine I (c. 272–337 CE) emerged from civil war to found New Rome, named Constantinople, on the site of Byzantium, a colony Miletus built on a strategic peninsula where Asia meets Europe. The empire he bequeathed his sons included Roman provinces from Africa to England, but northern Europe was soon lost to Frankish, Visigoth, and Lombard invaders, and, better to command their armies, the emperors resided in Antioch. Theodosius II (401–450) divided the empire between his two sons; the West was reduced to a remnant before Emperor Justinian (483–565) sent General Belisarius and then Narses to recapture it.

From 600, the eastern flank was under attack; during the reign of Heraclius (575–641), the Persian Sasanid dynasty encroached as far as the Euphrates and disputed the *theme* (regional political unit) of Armenia. In 626, the Sasanids joined Avar invaders from the Balkans to besiege unsuccessfully Constantinople. In 647, Islamic raiders began annually to penetrate the heart of Anatolia, besieging Constantinople in 674 and 717. In 813, the Bulgars camped outside the Theodosian walls; the death of their leader, Krum, saved the city, and his successors were paid to push back the Rus (Russian tribes), who in 860 made a whirlwind naval attack on Constantinople.

Basil I (?–886) founded a dynasty that expanded the empire almost to its former borders, but from 894 the Bulgar attacks resumed; the death of their leader Simeon (927) saved the city again. Final victory went to Basil II (958–1025); in 1014, he blinded 15,000 Bulgar prisoners, and Bulgaria was absorbed into the empire.

In 1025, misrule by various rival factions enabled the Seljuk Turks to expand westward from Baghdad and penetrate central Anatolia; the emperor Romanus IV Diogenes (?–1071) cobbled together an army that met the Turks at Malazgirt (former Manzikert) in 1071. His rival General Andronicus Ducas deserted at a critical moment; the battle was lost, and the emperor captured. Armenia was taken, Cilicia became a separate Armenian kingdom, and the Seljuks parceled out south-central and east Anatolia to their followers, who forcibly converted the population.

In 1204, the Fourth Crusade, supporting the disinherited Alexius V, succeeded in capturing Constantinople, and Count Baldwin of Flanders became the first Latin emperor. Three Byzantine successor states were established at Nicaea, Trebizond, and Epirus.

In 1261, the emperor of Nicaea, Michael VIII Palaeologus, recaptured Constantinople and secured his conquests by dynastic marriages. Succeeding emperors reopened negotiations on unity with the Church of Rome, but their subjects preferred the turban to the miter and repudiated agreements. The Ottoman Turks had deprived the empire of its hinterland, and in 1453, after a siege in which a sea blockade played a decisive part, the city fell to Sultan Mehmed II, surnamed the Conqueror.

The Army and the Law

The Byzantine emperor, a religious, political, and military leader drawn from one of the leading landowning dynasties, was supported by his patriarch, a senate, and a huge civil service. Free bread and entertainment, religious endorsement, and military success kept the emperor in power. A strong emperor could appoint his successor; otherwise the succession fell to aristocratic candidates supported by the army. The blue and green chariot-racing factions represented rival parties, whose conflicts culminated in the Nika riots (532) and the burning of the city. The city's Theodosian walls, completed by Arcadius (c. 377–408), a massive ditch and double wall construction that still totally surrounds the peninsula, kept invaders at bay.

The legal and administrative system, which was recodified by Justinian and described by Constantine VII (907–959), concentrated local power in the hands of the governors of the *themes*, administered by civilian and military governors. Unlike western powers, the empire had to maintain a standing army, consisting of regiments raised from each *theme* and the emperor's personal Varangarian Guards (from 989) as well as a navy. The major defensive weapon was Greek fire, an incendiary mixture that could be shot by bellows from city walls or the deck of a warship. Military tactics originally consisted of leading huge, well-drilled armies on foreign campaigns. Against fast-moving border raiders, Nikephorus II Phokas's (?–969) book *On Skirmishing Warfare* marked a change to staged ambushes of returning bands loaded with booty at passes in the Taurus Mountains.

Religion

Orthodox Christianity became a state-sponsored hierarchic cult intertwined with civil life and culture. At the first Church Council at Nicaea in 325 CE, by presiding himself, Constantine demonstrated that he would cede neither the administration nor the creed to his nominee, the patriarch. Schism after schism sloughed off alternative churches—the Arians (325), Nestorians (431), and, most seriously, Monophysites (Syrian Orthodox Church) and Gregorians (Armenian Church) (451). By failing to contain these two substantial churches in the state system, the empire created potentially rebellious groups on the crucial eastern frontiers. Surprisingly, despite sporadic persecution, there is no evidence that Syrians or Armenians deserted en masse to the Persian or Islamic cause.

From the fourth century, monasticism spread from Egypt; the church, by amassing huge untaxed estates and removing able-bodied men from productive enterprise, became a drain on the economy. As the Islamic advance continued, from the seventh century the patriarchs of Alexandria, Jerusalem, and Antioch fell under foreign domination. The army ascribed the invaders' success to the Islamic embargo on human images, and Emperor Leo III (c. 685–741) banned icon worship. Many monks fled, protecting their treasures both from the invading Muslims and overenthusiastic Iconoclast mobs, but icons were finally restored in 831.

Culture

Constantine decorated his rebuilt capital by plundering art treasures and building materials from Greek and Roman sites as far afield as Egypt. Surrounded by classical models, Byzantine art gradually developed more formal, stylized designs first seen in the churches of Justinian, including Saint Sophia, a magnificent dome-over-transept cathedral of revolutionary design, with four acres of gold tesserae and a jeweled cross set against stars in the dome. Church ceremonial was arranged to display the emperor directly under the dome, a symbol of God and empire. After the barren Iconoclastic period, the ninth century saw new Greek poetry, Photius the Patriarch's encyclopedia of Greek culture, the invention of the telegraph, and a famous golden plane tree with singing birds. Art (mainly religious) continued to flourish until the sack of Constantinople in 1204; looted material is displayed in Venice. The position of the peasants, who, from the time of Diocletian (?–305) had been a repressed and exploited workforce, worsened as the empire shrank.

Legacy

Byzantium produced a ruling class of magnificent simplicity and dedication coupled with individual characteristics of duplicity and pragmatism; the system persisted in the centralized authoritarian organization of the Muslim state. Both European and Turkish neglect of Byzantine history is rapidly being reversed; however, the fate of surviving monuments is far from secure.

Kate Clow

Further Reading

Herrin, Judith. (1987) *The Formation of Christendom*. Princeton, NJ: Princeton University Press.

Norwich, John Julius. (1995) *Byzantium: The Early Centuries, the Apogee, and the Decline*. London: Penguin/Viking.

Runciman, Steven. (1951) *The Crusades*. Cambridge, U.K.: Cambridge University Press.

———. (1965) *The Fall of Constantinople, 1453*. Cambridge, U.K.: Cambridge University Press.

Whittow, Mark. (1996) *The Making of Byzantium, 600–1025*. Berkeley and Los Angeles: University of California Press.

CADRE SYSTEM—CHINA In China, the term "cadre" refers both to all party functionaries and civil servants in administrative institutions, public organizations, and armed forces and to persons in leading positions. It is important to differentiate between party, administrative, and military cadres. As the term covers party and state leaders as well as village officials or policemen, it does not refer to a homogeneous group.

Since 1956 cadres were classified according to twenty-five ranks *(ji)*. Grade twenty-five was the lowest grade. The original classification was dependent on the time a person had attended the revolutionary movement or was admitted into the Communist Party as well as one's contributions to the revolution or "liberation." The early classification was influenced by the Soviet cadre system but also by traditional ranking patterns of the civil service in imperial times.

The cadre system that had been in existence in China since the 1950s was remodeled in 1993 by the Provisional Regulations for Public Service into fifteen grades, starting with the prime minister at grade one and running down to ordinary officials at grades ten through fifteen.

The grading is the same on each level of the party, in the People's Congresses (parliaments), and in the Political Consultative Conferences. This same grading also regulates salaries and privileges. State cadres, that is, civil servants paid by the state, are put on the official schedule by the responsible personnel offices. Organization departments are responsible for party cadres. State cadres are paid out of the official budgets, whereas the other rural cadres have to be paid by extrabudgetary means. Each cadre grade is treated differently, with privileges increasing as grade level rises. "High cadres" (grade five and up) enjoy the greatest privileges as far as salaries, labor conditions, size and standard of accommodation, medical treatment, and pensions are concerned. They also receive more servants paid by the state, a better official car with driver, the right to travel first class in trains and planes on official trips, and last but not least, access to detailed information on China and foreign countries.

This hierarchical system is similar to China's traditional civil-service hierarchy, which was also divided into grades in what was known as the *ji*-hierarchy. There were two main categories: civil and military service. From the Tang dynasty (618–907 CE) onward, each category was divided into nine grades, each grade being divided into two classes, upper *(shang)* and lower *(xia)*, for a total of eighteen ranks. Each grade was characterized by special insignias and salaries. The higher the rank, the greater the attendant privileges and nonmaterial advantages.

Today, as in the past, losing an official position or exclusion from the hierarchy means the loss of all kinds of privileges as well as a significant decrease in standard of living. Success in such a system and the social security it offers make it very attractive to become a member of the party and to join some kind of network that will guarantee advancement in the hierarchy.

Thomas Heberer

Further Reading
Christiansen, Flemming, and Rai Shirin. (1996) *Chinese Politics and Society*. New York: Prentice Hall/Harvester Wheatsheaf.

Heberer, Thomas, and Wolfgang Taubmann. (1998) *Chinas Ländliche Gesellschaft im Umbruch. Urbanisierung und Sozioökonomischer Wandel auf dem Lande.* Opladen, Germany: Westdeutscher Verlag.
Lieberthal, Kenneth. (1995) *Governing China: From Revolution through Reform.* New York: W. W. Norton & Company.
Schurmann, Franz. (1968) *Ideology and Organization in Communist China.* Berkeley and Los Angeles: University of California Press.

CAGAYAN RIVER   The Cagayan River is the longest and largest river in the Philippines. The Cagayan Valley in Luzon is covered by the deep alluvium deposited by the river and its various tributaries, the main ones being the Chico, Ilagan, and Magat Rivers. Sediments of Tertiary and Quaternary origin, mostly limestone sands and clays blanketed the Cayagan Basin to deposits of 3,000 to 4,500 meters. The Cayagan Valley is one of the chief tobacco areas in the Philippines and also produces rice, corn, yams, bananas, and coconut. The river rises at an elevation of approximately 1,524 meters in the Caraballo Mountains of central Luzon, and flows north for some 446 kilometers to its mouth at Bubuyan Channel at the town of Aparri.

The river drops rapidly to 91 meters above sea level some 227 kilometers from the river mouth. Most of the larger tributaries of the Cagayan enter the valley from the cordilleran lands to the west of it. From the point where the river enters the valley, it flows north in broad meanders and acquires the major tributaries of the Magat and the Ilagan.

Both the Cagayan River and all its tributaries are subject to extensive flooding during the heavy rainfall that occurs during the monsoon and also the typhoon seasons. The Cagayan River has not been a major transport artery except for light barges, which can ascend the river for about sixty-five kilometers. Small craft often use the Cagayan.

Kog Yue Choong

Further Reading
Wernstedt, F. L., and J. E. Spencer. (1967) *The Philippine Island World.* Berkeley and Los Angeles: University of California Press.

CALCUTTA   Capital of West Bengal state, former capital (1773–1912) of British India, Calcutta (in Bengali, Kalikata) is India's largest metropolitan area and a major port. Founded in 1690 by Job Charnock, a British merchant, the area included three villages. The British East India Company gained proprietary rights to them in 1698 under the Mughals. By 1727, shipping in Calcutta totaled 10,000 tons: silks and muslins from Dhaka, cotton fabrics from Bengal, saltpeter from Bihar, rice, sesame oil, and sugar all had a ready export market. The population grew from 12,000 in 1710 to 100,000 in 1735.

In 1756, the nabob of Bengal sacked Calcutta and imprisoned British soldiers in what became known, after many prisoners had suffocated, as "the Black Hole of Calcutta." The British recaptured the city in 1757, and the Regulating Act (1773) gave the governor of Bengal the position of governor-general of British-controlled India. During the governorships of Warren Hastings (1773–1785) and Richard Colley Wellesley (1798–1805), the European enclave assumed an elegant look: Lord Wellesley wanted India to be governed from an impressive palace rather than a mercantile office. The Indian town, however, was filled with bazaars and slums.

A "Bengal Renaissance" produced such figures as Rammohan Roy (1772–1833) and Sir Rabindranath Tagore (1861–1941), a Nobel-laureate poet, along with an accent on intellectual freedom, a monotheistic version of Hinduism, and a moral code suited to an educated middle class. A powerful spiritual movement led by Ramakrishna Paramahamsa and Swami Vivekanada in the late nineteenth century, followed by a nationalist upsurge, conferred unique leadership status on the city. Despite Rudyard Kipling's negative focus in *City of Dreadful Night*, many citizens were proud of the British empire's largest city after London.

The 1943 famine, wartime anxieties, the 1946 riots, the partition of Bengal in 1947, the postwar population explosion, and declining industry since the 1960s, along with widespread poverty and chronic labor unrest, have increasingly put the city in crisis. The work of Mother Teresa's Calcutta mission focused worldwide attention on the city's squalor, starvation, and disease. Calcutta continues, however, a major financial, cultural, and educational center, catering to a cosmopolitan population speaking Bengali, English, Hindi, and Urdu. The Calcutta moviemakers produce commercial gems, and Dominique Lapierre's book *City of Joy* may outweigh Kipling's view of the city.

C. Roger Davis

Further Reading
Chaudhuri, Sukanta, ed. (1995) *Calcutta, The Living City.* 2 vols. Oxford, U.K.: Oxford University Press.
Fernandes, Leela. (1997) *Producing Workers: The Politics of Gender, Class, and Culture in the Calcutta Jute Mills.* Philadelphia: University of Pennsylvania Press.

Hutnyk, John. (1996) *The Rumour of Calcutta: Tourism, Charity, and the Poverty of Representation*. London: Zed Books.
Ray, Amalendu. (1990) *Calcutta: An Annotated Bibliography*. Columbia, MO: South Asia Books.

CALENDARS—EAST ASIA

East Asia has a rich tradition of astronomical observation. Until the nineteenth century, the chief calendars in use in the region were derived from the Chinese. To this day, traditional calendars are used to mark religious and traditional festivals and holidays; the Gregorian calendar regulates civic affairs.

The Chinese Calendar

The beginnings of the Chinese calendar are steeped in legend; it is said that the legendary emperor Huangdi created it in 2637 BCE. Evidence for the calendar can be traced back to the fourteenth century BCE. In effect, it is a lunisolar calendar, derived from astronomical observations of the longitude of the sun and the phases of the moon. Therefore, its year matches the tropical year (the period between two successive times that the sun reaches its most northerly point in the sky), and its months concur with the synodic months (the period between two successive full moons or two conjunctions of the sun and moon). In the Chinese calendar as in the Jewish, an ordinary year has twelve months, while a leap year has thirteen months. An ordinary year has 353, 354, or 355 days, and a leap year has 383, 384, or 385 days.

In order to arrive at a Chinese year, the dates of the new moons are determined. A new moon is construed as the completely "black" moon (when the moon is in conjunction with the sun), not the first visible crescent as stipulated in Jewish and Islamic calendars. The date of the new moon is the first day of a new month. Next, the dates when the sun's longitude is a multiple of 30 degrees are calculated. These dates are known as the Principal Terms and are used to calculate the number of each month. Therefore, each month carries the number of the Principal Term that occurs in that month.

All astronomical observations are made for the meridian 120 degrees east of Greenwich, which approximately matches the east coast of China. Unlike other calendars, the Chinese calendar does not count years in an infinite sequence. Instead, years have names that are repeated every sixty years. Within a given sixty-year cycle, each year is assigned a name made up of two parts: the Celestial Stem, whose terms cannot be translated into English, and the Terrestrial Branch, whose terms correspond to animals of the Chinese zodiac. This method of using a sixty-year cycle is ancient; the sixty-year cycles are numbered from 2637 BCE, when the Chinese calendar is said to have started.

The Japanese Calendar

The Japanese calendar is similar to the Chinese, given the many cultural exchanges between the two nations, and is said to date from 660 BCE, from the reign of the emperor Jimmu, the legendary first emperor of Japan. In China and elsewhere, the calendar was used to count the passage of time, but in Japan, the reckoning of time as such had little importance. The Japanese used the Chinese sixty-year cycle for naming days and years, with each day being determined as "good" or "bad." Side by side with this practice, by 807 CE, a seven-day week, with names related to the planets, was also in use, although the need to know "good" or "bad" days continued. By 1007, the seven-day week was common in Japan.

Little attention was paid to the calendar as a means of reckoning time until 1684, when three Japanese astronomers (Harumi Shibukawa, Anbu Yasutomi, and Jinzan Tani) advocated calendrical reform. However, their efforts met with little success, since the ruling elite was more interested in astrology and mystical interpretations of the days of the week than in precise timekeeping. The three reformers labored on in isolation, completely unaware of the advances being made by the Chinese with the aid of Jesuit missionaries. Only in the Meiji period (1868–1912) did Japan finally use a consistent and relatively accurate method for recording time, with the adoption of the Gregorian calendar. However, the old associations intrinsic to Japanese culture remain, such as the determination of festivals, the naming of years after the current emperor, and the significance of astrology and the zodiac.

The Korean Calendar

As with Japan, the source of the Korean calendar is China. The Korean calendar was not merely a method of keeping time, it was also an expression of divine will in that, as in Japan, it was used to determine "good" and "bad" days. It was the responsibility of the king to maintain an annual calendar. The Korean calendar served as an astronomical almanac, predicting the movements of the sun, moon, and five visible planets over the course of the year. These predictions then allowed court astrologers to determine "good" or "bad" days.

One of the first recorded Korean calendars is the Tai Chu calendar, which was created by Hong Loxia during the reign of emperor Wu (156–86 BCE) of the Han dynasty (206 BCE–220 CE), who had incorporated

Korea into China. Given the use of the Chinese ephemeris (a table of locations of heavenly bodies), many errors had crept into the Tai Chu calendar by the time of the Northern Song (960–1126) and the Southern Song (1127–1279). These inaccuracies necessitated calendrical reform during the reign of Khubilai Khan (1215–1294), who reconquered Korea, and again under the first Ming emperor, Hongwu (1328–1398), who also ruled over Korea. Finally, Kim Yuk (1580–1658), a Korean official, strongly advocated calendrical reform using Gregorian calculations. He was following the lead of China, which had adopted the Western methodology under the guidance of Johann Adam Schall von Bell (1591–1666), a German Jesuit missionary and astronomer, at the beginning of the Qing dynasty (1644–1912).

But it would be another century before Korea finally adopted Gregorian principles and established the new Shixian calendar. However, this adoption met fierce resistance in the character of Yi Hangno (1792–1868), a scholar who defended traditional ways against innovations from the West. Yi Hangno argued that although the Western calendar was accurate and precise, it failed to fulfill the traditional role of a calendar in Korean society, namely, the determination of sacrificial rites, rituals for the end of the year, marriage rites, daily tasks, and monthly recitations. In short, the Gregorian calendar destroyed Confucian ritual, ethics, and philosophy. However, once Gregorian principles were established, there was no going back to the old ways.

Nirmal Dass

Further Reading

Ho, Peng Yoke. (1977) *Modern Scholarship on the History of Chinese Astronomy*. Canberra, Australia: Faculty of Asian Studies, Australian National University.

Miller, Lyman. (2000) "Korea's Encounter with the West." Course reading for Stanford University history course 92a, Roots of Modern East Asia. Retrieved 22 April 2002, from: http://www.stanford.edu/class/history92a/readings/ Kencounter.html.

Pannekoek, Anton. (1961) *A History of Astronomy*. London: G. Allen & Unwin.

Reingold, Edward, and Nachum Dershowitz. (2001) *Calendrical Calculations*. New York: Cambridge University Press.

Sugimoto, Masayoshi, and David L. Swain (1978) *Science and Culture in Traditional Japan, A.D. 600–1854*. Cambridge, MA: MIT Press.

CALENDARS—SOUTH ASIA   Differences among calendars arise because a year does not fall into equal units of any sort, and various peoples have used various units to divide the solar year (the time the sun takes to perform a complete revolution around "the heavens," beginning from a certain star and returning to the same), which is 365.2422 days long. The several calendars of South Asia—Hindu, Christian, Islamic—were either solar or solilunar (like the ecclesiastical calendar in Europe)

Indian Calendars

The earliest calendar used in India counted twelve lunar months in a year of 360 days. A lunar month averages 29.53 days, and twelve lunar synodic (relating to the period between two successive conjunctions of a heavenly body) months yield a year of 354 days, 8 hours, 48 minutes, 36 seconds—10.88 days shorter than a solar year. In the oldest-known Sanskrit text, the Rig Veda (of perhaps 1000 BCE), a passage suggests that scholar-priests understood the need for an extra intercalary month every so often; the Atharva Veda mentions this practice as a way of making events fall in their "proper" seasons.

The basic principles of the Vedic calendar of the first millennium BCE are recorded in the *Jyotishavedanga*. Although far from clear, this work seems to acknowledge a year of 366 days, divided into three seasons of four months each. The seasons were important for agricultural as well as ritual reasons. Indians later subdivided their year into six seasons: spring, hot season, rainy season, autumn, winter, frosty season; each contained two months.

Ancient Indian astronomy and calendrical reckoning were no doubt advanced, as compared with the rest of Asia (except for China and Babylonia). However, there were two inadequacies: India had no telescopes before the seventeenth century, and astronomers north of the Narmada River calculated the year as 365 days, 6 hours, 12 minutes, 34 seconds, while those south of that river calculated 365 days, 6 hours, 12 minutes, 30 seconds. (A true astronomical or solar year is 365 days, 5 hours, 48 minutes, 46 seconds.) Ancient Indian astronomers had only two instruments, the gnomon (the pointer on a sundial) and the armillary sphere (a model of the circles of the celestial sphere). From the time of the noted astronomer Aryabhata (c. 476–550 CE), however, they were commonly aware that the earth revolved around the sun. The Indians were concerned with achieving such accuracy in their calendar because of the need to fix the date of various Brahmanic ceremonies to coincide with given moments in the cosmic cycle and thus to ensure their regularity and effectiveness.

Of various early Indian writings on astronomy, the *Surya Siddhanta* has to some extent survived. It makes use of an extraordinary "quadruple period" *(caturyuga)* or Great Year *(mahayuga)* of 4,320,000 solar years, divided into four cosmic years. The synodic month was divided into thirty lunar days *(tithi)*, which were of shorter duration than solar days *(savana)*. The theory explaining the equinoxes maintained that an oscillation occurred, with a velocity of fifty-four *savana* per year.

In a different usage of the term *yuga*, one *yuga* consisted of sixty months plus one intercalary month, to equal 1,830 days. At first in the Brahmanic period (c. 800–600 BCE), an intercalary month of thirty days was added every five years, but later (in the *Satapatha Brahmana*) this was adjusted to a twenty-five- or twenty-six-day month: five years with an intercalary month of thirty days gave a total of 1,830 days; five years with an intercalary month of twenty-six days gave a total of 1,826 days; and five years with an intercalary month of twenty-five days gave a total of 1,825 days. (The actual number of days in five years is 1826.25.)

The passage of time was also measured in terms of politically based Indian eras, some of which are still cited by nationalists. The oldest of these is the Vikrama era, dating from the start of the reign of King Vikramaditya of Ujjain in 58 BCE. More common in modern usage is the Saka era, dating from the beginning of the Saka dynasty in Ujjain in 78 CE. There is also the Gupta era, commemorating the ascent to the throne by Candragupta I in 320 CE. Finally the Harsa era dates from 606 CE, when the influential emperor Harsavardhana of Kanyakubja began his reign.

Christian and Islamic Calendars

Both the Christian and the Islamic calendars have been in widespread use throughout South Asia, the Christian one since the eighteenth century and the Islamic one since the thirteenth century. The Christian calendar dated events from the purported birth of Christ (year 1), and the traditional Christian method of dating events either BC (before Christ) or AD (*anno domini*, "in the year of our Lord") persists to this day. Even the terms CE and BCE (Common Era and Before the Common Era), popularized as a way of avoiding the Christian terminology, are still anchored to the Christian calendar.

The Islamic era dates from Muhammad's hegira *(Hijra)*, or flight to Medina, which is believed to have occurred on Thursday, 15 July 622 (old style; 18 July new style). Year 1 of the era began on the following day. The Islamic year is lunar, with twelve lunar months and no intercalation. This means that the months retrograde throughout the entire year in the course of 32 1/2 solar or astronomical years. (To con-

vert a *Hijra* year to a Gregorian one, multiply 0.970224 by the year, and add 621.5774. After cutting off six decimal places from the product, the sum will be the year of the Common Era.)

Paul Hockings

Further Reading
Filliozat, Jean. (1963) "Ancient Indian Science." In *History of Science: Ancient and Medieval Science from the Beginnings to 1450*. Edited by René Taton. New York: Basic Books, 133–160.

Perinbanayagam, R. S. (1982) *The Karmic Theater: Self, Society, and Astrology in Jaffna*. Amherst, MA: University of Massachusetts Press.

CALENDARS—SOUTHEAST ASIA

The Western calendar is effectively universal in today's globalized world, but parts of Southeast Asia still use their Indian-derived calendars for local and religious purposes. These calendars divide, historically, into three groups: the calendar used in Cambodia and Champa from the seventh century CE, using the era dating from 78 CE, which is called the *saka*; the calendar used in Indonesia, especially Java, from the ninth century, which also uses *saka*; and the calendar used in Burma, Thailand, and Laos from the thirteenth century, using the era of 638 CE, called the *thekkarit* by the Burmese and *chulasakarat* by the others (the term means "little era," whereas the *saka*, which it largely replaced, was called *mahasakarat* ("big era"). European influence in mainland Southeast Asia and Muslim influence in Indonesia eventually weakened these indigenous modes. They are called indigenous despite their Indian origin because each region developed its characteristic way of adopting and amplifying the Indian mode.

Lunar Months

These calendars all use the moon's path to measure the months of the year. The moon's circuit in the sky was divided into twenty-seven sections called *naksatra*, twelve of which gave their names to the lunar months because the moon was in or near that *naksatra* when it was full. A Cambodian variant upon using the Indian (Sanskrit) names of the months was sometimes to use Indian seasonal names instead, whereas the Burmese used their own particular set of names as equivalents, and the Thai used numerals with a complexity typical of this whole subject. Focusing on the conventional first month of the lunar year, Caitra, then in southern Thailand this was month 5, in most of the north it was month 7, and in parts of the north and of Laos it was month

6. One can see the difficulties historians face in making conversions, or in correctly interpreting the data.

Expressing the Year

It is common today to simply say, for example, "It is 2 May 2002." In Asia generally, dates were expressed in a far more elaborate way, each main region having its own distinctive style. A year number usually formed part of the date (given according to the various eras mentioned above, or perhaps in terms of the Buddha Era, dating variously to 544 BCE or 543 BCE), but then various additions were customary, the most familiar of which is known from the Chinese custom of attaching one of twelve animal names to the year: 2001 for instance was the year of the horse. The Thai inherited this custom and added to it by using pairs of words (also of Chinese origin, that have no meaning in Thai) to designate the years on a cycle that in this instance lasted for sixty years, not just twelve. If one year was "rat *kap cai*," the next year would be "ox *dap plao*," and the next rat year—which would come eleven years later— would be "rat *rawai cai*." The cycle would wind on until "rat *kap cai*" eventually came round again. This system has its uses. If a king is said to have come to the throne in an "ox *dap plao*" year, then it should normally to be possible to verify in which block of 60 years the event occurred.

The Burmese, for their part, also adopted a cycle of twelve years, but they took over the names that the Indians and the rest of Southeast Asia applied to the lunar months (Caitra, Vaisakha, Jyestha, Ashadha, Sravana, Bhadrapada, Asvina, Karttika, Margasirsha, Pausa, Magha, and Phalguna).

Moving to Cambodia there is an even more elaborate system, used also in India, known as chronograms. We have five senses and we have two eyes, so we could write "senses-eyes-senses" if we wanted an exotic way to represent the number 525. This is what the Cambodians did. On an inscription we might find, for instance, that the year is not called 561, but (by their mapping of noun to number) "arrows-seasons-face."

The Indonesians, on the other hand, were content merely to give the year in numeric form, as they had very elaborate ways of embroidering the remainder of the date. There could sometimes be fourteen elements in a date, of which five (called the *pancanga*—another Indian inheritance) were in effect obligatory. The first was the day of the month in the lunar calendar; days of the month were known as the *tithi*. Each *tithi* had two halves, called the *karana*; this was the second obligatory element in a date. To these items were added the day of the week (each one consisting of three elements), which was the third obligatory element. The *naksatra* (which defines the moon's position, as mentioned above) was the fourth, and the fifth element was the *yoga*, an arbitrary number derived by finding the positions of the sun and the moon in degrees of celestial longitude, adding the two values together and dividing the result by 13 degrees and 20 arc minutes. (This last step is taken because 13 degrees and 20 arc minutes, if multiplied by 27—the total number of *naksatra*s—equals 360 degrees).

Balancing the Calendar with Extra Days and Months

For the days of the lunar month, everyone used the moon's waxing and waning phases, where one choice—used by the Indians—was to take account of where the moon actually was. Thus, if the moon was still in the same *naksatra* on successive days (moving slowly), that day's number would be repeated, whereas if the moon traversed an entire *naksatra* in one day (moving fast), that day would be suppressed. Both fluctuations often happened in the same month so the succession of days might be . . . 8, 9, 9, 10. . . . 19, 20, 22, 23. . . Here the moon's motion is slow toward the start of the month and fast toward the end. The second choice, used by the Burmese and the Thai, was to have no extra or suppressed days within a month, but to alternate the length of the month, with twenty-nine days in one month and thirty days in the next.

Adjusting the days in a month, however, was not sufficient: it was also necessary to adjust the months themselves in order to keep the calendar in sync. The procedure in mainland Southeast Asia involved on occasion giving a year thirteen lunar months instead of the usual twelve, and even less frequently adding an extra day to a month that would normally have only twenty-nine days. The frequency required was seven extra months in nineteen years (twenty-one months in fifty-seven years) and an additional eleven extra days in fifty-seven years. With alternate months of twenty-nine and thirty days a "normal" lunar year had 354 days in it; the occasional extra day gave the Thai years with 355 days in them, and the extra month gave them years with 384 days in them. This was because if a year had an extra day in it, the Thai did not allow it also to have an extra month. The Burmese, on the other hand, reversed the rule and said only years with an extra month could have an extra day, resulting in lunar years that were variously 354 days, 384 days, and 385 days long. Even these close neighbors had lunar calendars that would often not agree with one another.

Recalling that the Indians dropped or added days to the lunar month as immediately required, it is not surprising to learn that they did the same thing for the months. The Indonesians followed suit, slotting in the extra month as soon as it became due. If the moon was in the same *naksatra* (at dawn) two days running, that day was counted twice. By the same thinking, if the sun was in the same sign of the zodiac for two new moons in a row, that month was counted twice. There was much less need to suppress lunar months: this occurred only rarely and at a point late in the lunar year.

The Days of the Week

For the weekdays, all groups adopted names equivalent to those used in the West, using the Sanskrit equivalents for the sun, the moon, and the five planets of ancient astronomy (Mercury, Venus, Mars, Jupiter, and Saturn). Sun-day (Sunday) is *aditya-vara*, Moon-day (Monday) is *chandra-vara*, and so on. The order in which the weekdays occur has an astrological principle behind it. Assume that each planet in turn governs successive hours of the day through the week. If you make the sun rule the first hour of day one, then by rotation the moon will rule the first hour of day two, and so on round.

This planetary week received two kinds of embellishment: In the north of Thailand it was combined with the cycle of sixty that the Thai also employed for the years. Thus, 1 January 2002 is "snake *ruang sai*" as to the year and "Tuesday *kat sai*" as to the day. In Indonesia two other kinds of week were recognized, one of six days and the other of five days. This gave a cycle of 210 days (5 x 6 x 7 = 210), which was then divided into thirty lots of seven days, called the *wuku*. In this system 1 January 2002 would be labeled *was paniruan anggara* (Tuesday) in the *wuku balamuki*.

Each of the basic ingredients of a date—year, month, day, and weekday—had its own elaboration, which developed differently in different regions. Each of these calendars, therefore, deserves consideration in its own right.

J. C. Eade

Further Reading:
De Casparis, J. G. (1978) *Indonesian Chronology*. Leiden, Netherlands: E. J. Brill.
Eade, J. C. (1995) *The Calendrical Systems of Mainland Southeast Asia*. Leiden, Netherlands: E. J. Brill.
Faraut, F. G. (1910) *Astronomie cambodgienne*. Saigon, Vietnam: F-H. Schneider.
Pethsarath, Prince. (1959) "The Laotian Calendar." In *The Kingdom of Laos*, edited by René de Berval. Saigon, Vietnam: France-Asie.

CALENDARS—WEST ASIA West Asia has a long history of reckoning time, and each important culture in the region has devised a calendar that serves to mark important religious and social events. It was only in the early twentieth century that Asian nations adopted the Gregorian calendar, and traditional calendars continue to retain their importance in the religious and cultural life of the region.

One of the earliest surviving calendars is the Jewish or Hebrew calendar, which was established by the patriarch Hillel II about 359 CE and which retains features that hark back to the calendar used by the Babylonians in the seventh century BCE. These features include the names of the months and the nineteen-year cycle. The Hebrew calendar, as currently in religious use, was fully formulated by the tenth century CE. It is used by Jews all over the world and is the official calendar of Israel.

The Jewish calendar is lunisolar; that is, the years agree with the tropical (solar) year and the months coincide with the synodic (lunar) months. This formulation can lead to complications. Because twelve months are approximately eleven days shorter than the tropical year, a leap month (or an intercalary month) is inserted every third year to keep the calendar synchronized with the seasons. In ancient Israel, religious leaders determined the date for Passover each spring by observing if the roads were dry enough for pilgrims and if the lambs were ready for slaughter. If not, another month would be added. Structurally, an ordinary (or nonleap) year has 353, 354, or 355 days, and a leap year has 383, 384, or 385 days. An ordinary year has twelve months, and a leap year has thirteen months. Every month starts on the day of a new moon. The three lengths of the years are known as "deficient," "regular," and "complete." A complete year is created by adding a day to the month of November (Heshvan); a deficient year results when a day is removed from the month of December (Kislev). New Year's Day can fall on four days: Rosh Hashanah (a celebration of the creation of the world, usually 1 October); Tu B'shevat (the new year for trees, when fruit tithes are to be brought, usually 15 February); New Year for Kings, which starts on 1 April; and New Year for Animal Tithes (a time for taxes, which starts on 1 September). A Jewish day begins not at midnight, but either at sunset or when three medium-sized stars become visible. Sunset marks the start of the twelve hours of night, whereas sunrise marks the start of the twelve hours of day. Thus, night hours may be longer or shorter than day hours, depending on the season. In the Jewish calendar, years are counted from the time of creation of the world, which is said to have taken place in 3761 BCE, which was the start of year 1 am (Anno Mundi, the year of the world).

Islamic Calendar

The Islamic (or Hijri) calendar, on the other hand, is a purely lunar calendar and was introduced about 632 CE by 'Umar ibn al-Khattab (c. 586–644 CE), who was the second caliph and a close companion of Muhammad (c. 570–632), the founder of Islam. The Islamic calendar contains twelve months based upon the motions of the moon. Therefore, the Islamic calendar is consistently shorter than a tropical year, because twelve synodic months equal about 354 days. The calendar is based upon two verses found in the Qur'an.

The originating date of the Islamic calendar is the Hijrah (flight), when Muhammad fled Mecca (after facing persecution for his teachings) and found refuge in Medina. The date of this flight is determined as 16 July 622 CE, which became the year 1 AH (Anno Hegirae, the year of the hegira). To Muslims, the Hijri calendar has great religious and historical significance. Each month starts when the lunar crescent is first seen (by a cleric) after a new moon. Although new moons can be predicted with fair accuracy, the actual visibility of the crescent is more problematic to predict. Factors such as weather, the atmosphere, and the location of the cleric all become crucial factors. This makes it difficult to predict when exactly a new month will start. Most Muslims depend on a local sighting of the moon, but some follow an authoritative declaration made somewhere else in the Muslim world. Both are deemed valid in Islam, although they often lead to different starting days for the months. One consequence of this practice is that a reliable Islamic calendar cannot be printed because only estimates of the visibility of the lunar crescent can be given, and the actual month may start a day earlier or later than what is predicted in the printed calendar. However, since 1999 Saudi Arabia has not relied on a visual sighting of the crescent moon to determine the start of a new month. Rather, the Saudi Islamic calendar is based on a calculated astronomical moon, where the times when the sun and the moon set are compared on the 29th of an Islamic month. If the sun sets before the moon, the next day is the first of a new month; and if the moon sets before the sun, the next day is the last (30th) of the current month. The times for the setting of the sun and the moon are based upon the coordinates of Mecca.

Permutation in Iran

A permutation of the Islamic calendar occurred in Iran during the nineteenth century, when a new religion, Baha'i, was established. The Baha'i faith advocates the oneness of all humanity and the oneness of all religions, and works toward bringing harmony between religion, science, and reason in order to achieve world peace.

Given their strong adherence to reason and science, it is not surprising that the Baha'is sought to rectify the Islamic calendar. Their religious calendar is purely solar, consisting of 365 days. Each year is divided into nineteen months; each month has nineteen days, with four intercalary days (five in a leap year). Baha Allah (1817–1892), the founder of the faith, stipulated that leap days should always precede the nineteenth month because it was during these days that followers were taught to fast, be hospitable, feast, and give gifts in charity. Baha Allah also divided time into cycles of nineteen years (the Vahid). Nineteen such cycles equal one period (Kul-e-Shai). This nineteen-year cycle brings time reckoning in western Asia back to the era of the ancient Babylonians.

Nirmal Dass

Further Reading
Aveni, Anthony F. (1989) *Empires of Time: Calendars, Clocks and Cultures.* New York: Basic Books.
Freeman-Grenville, Greville Stewart Parker. (1995) *The Muslim and Christian Calendars.* Reading, U.K.: Garnet Publishing.
O'Neil, William Matthew. (1975) *Time and the Calendars.* Manchester, U.K.: Manchester University Press.

CALICUT (2001 est. city pop. 437,000). Calicut (or Kozhikode) refers to both the city of Calicut and to the surrounding district. Located on the southwest coast of India on the Arabian Sea, Calicut is a major city of the state of Kerala.

Vasco da Gama landed off Calicut in 1498, assuring it a place in all Western atlases. In the years between 1102 and 1498 CE, Calicut became the most important political power in central and north Kerala under the rule of the Zamorin. The tolerant policies of the Zamorin toward Arab traders and its position as an important port for spice and timber trade contributed to the growth of the city.

Calicut was briefly under Mysorean occupation ending in 1799. Subsequently, the British annexed it. In the colonial period it was the headquarters of the Malabar District. Calicut continued to be an important port engaged in international maritime trade until the 1920s.

Today Calicut city measures 30.61 square kilometers and has a population of 420,000 with 100 percent

CALICUT

This extract is from one of the earliest and one of the best-known travel guides to India. It has been reprinted by several publishers in the 1990s

Can those three of four bungalows, with that stick-like lighthouse between them and the half-dozen tiled and thatched roofs peeping from amongst the trees, compose Calicut—the city of worldwide celebrity, which immortalised herself by giving a name to calico? Yes…We shall meet few Europeans in the street: there are scarcely twenty in this place, including all the varieties of civilians, merchants, missionaries, and officers… Most of the residents inhabit houses built upon an eminence to the north of the town; others live as close as possible to the sea. A dreary life they must lead, one would suppose, especially during the monsoon, when the unhappy expatriated's ears are regaled by no other sounds than but the pelting of the rain, the roaring of the blast, and the creaking of the cocoa trees, whilst a curtain of raging sea, black sky, and watery air, is all that meets his weary ken."

Source: Sir Richard Francis Burton ([1851] 1991) *Goa and the Blue Mountains; Or, Six Months of Sick Leave.* Berkeley and Los Angeles: University of California Press.

literacy. Calicut district has a population of 2.6 million. It is one of the most industrially advanced districts of Kerala. The main commodities exported and imported are pepper and rice respectively. Hinduism, Islam, and Christianity are the chief religions of the district.

R. Gopinath

Further Reading
Menon, A. Sreedhara. (1979) *Social and Cultural History of Kerala.* New Delhi: Sterling Publishers.

CALLIGRAPHY—CHINA
Chinese calligraphy (from the Greek *kalligraphia*, "beautiful writing") is the art of writing that educated Chinese have practiced for millennia. All students of written Chinese practice calligraphy, but becoming a good calligrapher requires practice, self-discipline, and an artistic sense. Chinese calligraphy, therefore, is more than just the mere art of penmanship.

The Chinese Character
Chinese is an ideographic, and in some cases pictographic, language. Thus each Chinese character is a monosyllabic word that conveys an idea. Characters, insofar as they are sometimes pictographic, also provide a visual expression of the ideas that they represent in a way that purely phonetic scripts do not. Characters, each composed of a series of strokes, make up words when written in a particular order. No matter how many strokes a character may be composed of, it must fit perfectly inside an imaginary box that is the same size as those of the characters preceding and following it. A character usually has two components: a radical that indicates meaning in a very broad sense, and a phonetic component that indicates sound, also in a broad sense. These components may be side by side or one on top of the other, inside the imaginary box within which each character is composed. Calligraphy is the art of writing these characters.

History of Writing and Calligraphy
Historically, writing and power have been intimately related in China, and calligraphy has been of much greater importance there than penmanship has been in Western societies. The earliest examples of writing in China appear on oracle bones from the Shang dynasty (1766–1045 BCE). These oracle bones were tortoise shells and scapula of mammals, etched

A Buddhist monk at the Jade Buddha Temple in Shanghai practices calligraphy. (DAVE BARTRUFF/CORBIS)

hensible spoken language, made the written language that much more important.

Over time, education in China's written language became essential to participation in government, and an imperial examination system evolved to test candidates' skill in written expression. From the Tang (618–907) to the Qing dynasty (1644–1912), calligraphy was considered an important criterion for passing all three levels of these civil-service examinations. The quality of one's calligraphy was thought to provide insight into one's moral character. Beautiful calligraphy became a symbol of culture, education, self-discipline, and erudition.

Certain people became known for their calligraphy, and the calligraphy of other people became known because the calligraphers themselves were famous or powerful. Writing on paintings, memorials, and other materials became a way for superiors to impart wisdom, advice, and injunctions to their inferiors. Virtually any literate person recognized the calligraphy of the emperor and the most important government figures of the time.

Calligraphic Styles

A variety of styles of calligraphy, or scripts, evolved over time, each coming to be identified with particular types or styles of writing. The script that became standard during the reign of Qin Shihuangdi is known as small seal (*xiaozhuan*) script. Today, this script is difficult for people to read and is generally used only in works of art. Among other scripts that have evolved, the most common is regular (*kaishu*) script, in which each stroke of a character is clearly written. Because of its clarity, regular script is generally used for printing. The clerical (*lishu*) style was developed during the Han dynasty (206 BCE–220 CE). Today, it is most commonly used in inscriptions on monuments and public buildings. Writers of informal notes or letters probably use the running (*xingshu*) style of script, in which the separate strokes of a given character are often run together. A variation on the running style is the grass (*caoshu*) style, which actually omits strokes and joins separate characters together. The grass style was particularly popular among literati in the late imperial era.

Calligraphy as Art

Chinese calligraphy is ornamental. Its beauty lies in both the concepts expressed and the form of expression. Throughout the Chinese world, people display decorative calligraphy in homes and businesses. Couplets, often written on strips of red paper, hang at the entrances of homes; lucky characters are pasted on the

with questions for the gods and then held over heat until they cracked. Shamans (magicians), who had written the inscriptions in the first place, interpreted the cracks as divine answers to the questions. People with the ability to write in ancient China, therefore, had the power to communicate with heaven and to interpret heaven's will. Early Chinese rulers, eager to empower themselves in every possible way, surrounded themselves by those who could write and help them communicate with heaven.

Although, as the oracle bones show us, writing existed in China at least three thousand years ago, there was not a unified written language in China until the third century BCE. At that time, Qin Shihuangdi (c. 259–210 BCE), the first emperor of the Qin dynasty (221–206 BCE), who was trying to reshape the numerous kingdoms of the Chinese landmass into a unified empire, standardized writing. The creation of a single, unified written language in a nation full of spoken dialects, where there was no universally compre-

walls and windows of shops, restaurants, and homes at the Chinese New Year; and scrolls of calligraphy hang in living rooms.

Perhaps because calligraphy is an art form and a means of self-expression rather than simply a vehicle for conveying meaning, works of art, such as paintings, sculptures, and buildings, are themselves often adorned with calligraphy. In many cases, the inscriptions on paintings and etchings on buildings, monuments, and places of natural beauty are expressions of appreciation, commentaries, or labels appended by later owners or observers (often the emperor). These calligraphic additions are not generally seen as detracting from the original piece, but as adding something to it.

Contemporary Calligraphy

During the twentieth century, China underwent several attempts to simplify the written language. Language reformers, hoping to increase literacy, introduced both phonetic scripts using roman letters and simplified characters, the forms of which, interestingly, are derived in many instances from *caoshu*, or the grass style of calligraphy. Although the phonetic systems have not become especially popular, more than two thousand simplified versions of commonly used characters were introduced by the People's Republic of China (PRC) as the official written form between 1956 and 1964; their use in the PRC has relegated the more complex forms of characters and the art of writing them to the past for most Chinese.

Nonetheless, calligraphy has remained important in post-1949 China, and the calligraphy of famous Communist Party members can be seen on various signs throughout China. The characters for the name of the newspaper called the *People's Daily (renmin ribao)*, for instance, are printed in the calligraphy of Mao Zedong (1893–1976). The presence of Mao's calligraphy on the front page of every edition of the *People's Daily* shows the world that the paper benefited from his patronage. While the forms of characters may have changed during the twentieth century, therefore, the functions of calligraphy have remained essentially the same. Calligraphy is the artistic expression of the power of language by the individual. Both the form and content of calligraphy inform the reader or viewer about the morality, education, and dedication of the calligrapher.

J. Megan Greene

Further Reading

Chiang, Yee. (1973) *Chinese Calligraphy: An Introduction to Its Aesthetic and Technique.* Cambridge, MA: Harvard University Press.

Kraus, Richard Curt. (1991) *Brushes with Power: Modern Politics and the Chinese Art of Calligraphy.* Berkeley and Los Angeles: University of Califonia Press.
Proser, Adriana G. (1995) Moral Characters: Calligraphy and Bureaucracy in Han China (296 B.C.E.–C.E. 220)." Ph.D. diss. Columbia University.

CALLIGRAPHY—JAPAN *Sho* is the modern Japanese term for the art of brush writing, and refers to calligraphy in which Chinese characters or Japanese phonetic writing or both are transformed into objects of artistic expression or works of art. *Shodo* is the traditional term for calligraphy, and means "the way or practice of brush writing." It has been practiced in Japan ever since the introduction of Chinese characters and calligraphy about fifteen hundred years ago. At that time Chinese calligraphy was already one of the oldest and most distinctive art forms in East Asia, so that Japanese calligraphy began as the inheritor of a long and illustrious tradition. Today the terms *sho* and *shodo* are often used interchangeably, but *shodo* is used more for practice that focuses on beautiful writing and artistic expression, whereas *sho* generally refers to artwork by calligraphers with an interest in or commitment to the underlying philosophy, aesthetic principles, and historical tradition.

Calligraphy is one of the most respected art forms in Japan because the brush strokes are able to capture the artist's intentional and unintentional artistic expression as well as every nuance of their character, spirit, and state of mind. The *sho* artist requires a high degree of classical training, and an ability to improvise in the manner of a jazz musician, responding spontaneously to constantly changing conditions. Japan's first modern philosopher, Kitaro Nishida (1870–1945), referred to *sho* as congealed music. The primary tools used in the art of *sho* are called the Four Treasures: *fude* (brushes made of long, flexible animal hair); *sumi* (black ink made by grinding carbon ink sticks on an ink stone); *suzuri* (the ink stone); and *gasen-shi* (a highly absorbent paper that gives the brush strokes a wide range of hues, tones, shading, and diffusion).

Kanji and Kana: Two Traditions of *Sho* in Japan

Japanese calligraphy evolved along two separate paths. The first maintained a fidelity to classical Chinese writing but gradually infused it with a subtle but distinctive Japanese aesthetic, related to form, composition, style, and even subject matter. The second borrowed elements from Chinese characters to develop a Japanese syllabary with original calligraphic principles, aesthetic values, and style.

Kanji is the Japanese name for Chinese characters, and kana is Japanese phonetic writing, which the Japanese devised from kanji gradually, during the eighth and ninth centuries. By the time the art of calligraphy was introduced to Japan at the end of the fifth century CE, China had five main script styles and numerous variations. The three structural scripts were known in Japanese as *tensho* (the ancient seal or primitive style), *reisho* (the scribe or semi-primitive style), and *kaisho* (the standard, formal style). Two more-fluid scripts lent themselves to artistic and emotional expression: *gyosho* (semi-cursive, running style) and *sosho* (cursive, grass style).

Kaisho, gyosho, and *sosho* appealed to Japanese kanji calligraphers, who tended to specialize in using the one that most suited their personality and temperament. They studied by copying the compositions, techniques, and script styles of the Chinese masters, after which they would create original compositions with Chinese poems and prose. In the late twentieth century a number of kanji artists have started actively creating compositions using their own original poetry and prose.

As the Japanese adapted kanji to represent sounds in the language, each of the syllables came to be represented by more than one kanji, with a few hundred in all, many chosen for the similarity of their sounds. This style of writing was called *man'yo-gana,* named after the oldest collection of poems in Japanese, *Man'yoshu,* all of which were written in this style. Gradually, an elegant and fluid form or *man'yo gana* evolved, and all the variations that developed during this process are called *hentai-gana.* Over the next hundred years these became quite abstract, and many no longer resembled the original Chinese characters.

At the same time a second form of writing evolved using one kanji for each syllable. These were gradually simplified by palace women as a practical kind of shorthand. By the tenth century the kanji had been transformed into minimalist letters, each representing a syllable. This syllabary was called *hiragana* and was also known as *onna-dé* or "woman's hand." Although *hiragana* and *hentai-gana* were initially different, these elegant, delicate, and distinctively Japanese forms of calligraphy were often combined. Later on, as the written language developed, kanji characters were combined with *hiragana.* As a result, many kana *sho* artists often combined *hentai-gana, hiragana,* and kanji characters (used for the meaning, not the sound, of the characters) in their calligraphy.

Three special features give kana *sho* its beauty: *ren-men-tai,* the threads of ink that connect the syllables in fluid, continuous streams of writing; *chirashi-gaki,* an organic irregularity in the composition, with variations in the shape and tone of the lines and in the shape of the negative spaces between and around the lines; and the vast selection of letter forms that can be chosen for each syllable. The *katakana* alphabet, which is primarily used for writing words of foreign origin, never developed into a form of *sho.*

Historical Background

The art of calligraphy became established in Japan when a number of Korean monks and artisans immigrated to Japan around the end of the fifth century CE, by which time it had already reached a high artistic level in China. In the mid-sixth century another group of Koreans came to Japan to introduce Buddhism, and this further extended the awareness and practice of *sho.* One of the leading figures in the advancement of *sho* was Prince Shotoku (574–622), who mastered Chinese calligraphy and encouraged the teachings of Buddhism. Under his influence, many great masterpieces of calligraphy were imported from China. In 610, a Korean monk introduced the technology for making ink sticks and paper, and this facilitated the spread of *sho.* During the Chinese Tang dynasty (618–907), many Japanese monks and students were sent to China to study Chinese culture and calligraphy.

When China entered a state of decline at the end of the ninth century, Japan's Emperor Uda (867–931) took the opportunity to suspend trade and diplomatic relations in order to foster a more indigenous Japanese culture. Over the next couple of centuries kana *sho* experienced a golden age of creativity.

During the twelfth century Taira no Kiyomori (1118–1181), the head of what was briefly Japan's most powerful clan, encouraged the reopening of trade with China and the importation of Song-dynasty culture. The Japanese monk Eisai (1141–1215) was sent to China to study Buddhism and returned with the teachings of Chan (in Japanese, Zen). The spirit and philosophy of Zen eventually had a profound impact on Japanese culture, including the practice of kanji *sho,* and after some time, a piece of calligraphic art was displayed as an integral part of tea ceremony *(cha no yu).*

Up to the end of the twelfth century, educated people practiced forms of kana and kanji *sho* that placed considerable value on technical excellence. As the samurai rose to power, they were influenced by the values of naturalness and simplicity in Zen philosophy, which led to a significant shift in artistic taste and moral values. Emphasis was given to the practice of kanji and a writing style that expressed the artist's total being and reflected his state of mind and inner consciousness. Several monks of the period, including Ikkyu (1394–1481) were renowned for *sho* that had a bold, grounded quality and expressed deep spirituality and a sense of freedom.

For a couple of centuries the interest in kana *sho* remained quite low, and the writing styles became formalized by a few schools that preserved this art form. In the latter part of the sixteenth century, three exceptional kana artists helped revive the practice of kana *sho* and it began to recover its position within Japanese culture. The most illustrious calligrapher of the three was Koetsu Hon'ami (1558–1637), who was also a renowned *raku* potter and *makie* lacquerware artist.

The Meiji era (1868–1912) was a period of total transformation, and the influence of foreign, mostly European culture and values was strongly felt in Japan. Tenrai Hidai (1872–1939), the leading *sho* artist of his day, shifted the conceptual emphasis of calligraphy from the practice of self-cultivation and technical proficiency (or both) to one that added the element of artistic merit. Hidai recognized *sho*'s potential as a modern art form and set an example by his own artwork and teaching. Public interest and appreciation in *sho* was increased by advances in printing technology that made it possible to publish many books on calligraphy, and many fine reproductions of well-known Japanese and Chinese calligraphers.

Contemporary *Sho*

After World War II, artists began to embrace self-expression, liberalism, and artistic freedom. In the early 1950s, a group of young kanji artists led by Shiryu Morita created *zen-ei sho*, a new genre of avant-garde calligraphy that had spatial form, energy, and dynamic movement, inspired in part by modern Western abstract art, and in part by Zen philosophy and aesthetics. They often transformed Chinese characters into abstract images, or created large-scale works in which impressionistic single characters swept off the paper. Although their art was not looked on favorably or even accepted by mainstream Japanese *sho* artists, it received international recognition and was widely exhibited in Europe and the United States.

Mainstream traditional *sho* is divided into four categories: kanji, kana, *chowa-tai* (which combines kanji and kana), and *tenkoku* or seal carving. There are also three categories of nontraditional *sho*: *sho-jisu sho*, which is art created with one or two kanji; *kindai-shibun sho*, a contemporary style of kanji and kana used in writing modern poetry; and *zen-ei sho*, with its avant-garde kanji characters.

Today, a small number of brush artists are creating a form of modern abstract expressionist brush art called *boku-sho*, which means ink images. This contemporary lyrical style has an aesthetic that Westerners can relate to quite easily, and the future may well see the influence of this brush art spread beyond Japan's geographic and cultural boundaries.

Mondo Secter and Ari Tomita

See also: **Calligraphy—China; Calligraphy—Korea**

Further Reading

Hirayama Kan'getsu. (1965). *Shin Nihon Shodo-shi* (New Japanese Calligraphy History). Tokyo: Yuhodo.
Hisamatsu, Shin'ichi. (1971) *Zen and the Fine Arts*. New York: Kodansha.
Miyajima Shin'ichi and Yasuhiro Sato. (1985) *Japanese Ink Painting*. Los Angeles, CA: Los Angeles County Museum of Art.
Munsterberg, Hugo. (1957) *The Arts of Japan, an Illustrated History*. Boston: Tuttle.
Nakamura Nihei, ed. (1997) *Gendai-no Sho Gei-jutsu: Boku Sho-no Sekai* (Modern Art of *Sho*: World of *Boku Sho*). Kyoto, Japan: Tanko-sha.
Nakata Yujiro. (1973) *The Art of Japanese Calligraphy*. New York: Weatherhill.
Onoe Saishu. (1954) *Sho no Nagare* (The Flow of *Sho*). Tokyo: Meiji Sho'in.
Westgeest, Helen. (1996) *Zen in the Fifties*. Zwolle, Netherlands: Waanders Uitgevers.

CALLIGRAPHY—KOREA   Calligraphy has been an art form in Korea since at least the fourth century CE. It derives from written Chinese, which was adopted for writing Korean around the second century CE. Even after the first phonetic alphabet was devised for Korean in 1446, writing Chinese characters with artistry and skill was highly valued and a requisite of the Korean nobility.

Korean calligraphy is categorized into five basic writing styles. Block style *(haeso)* consists of square characters such as those used in woodblock printing and modern-day newspaper and book printing. The cursive style *(choso)* or "grass writing" is used by those adept at writing Chinese characters as a daily practice. The style is so named because it joins the abbreviated and simplified strokes of characters into a woven image resembling a blade of grass. The semicursive style *(haengso)*, also commonly used in everyday writing, combines characteristics of both the block and cursive styles. The two most ornate styles are *chonso* and *yeso*. *Chonso* contains long lines of a uniform width and most closely resembles the early form of Chinese characters. *Yeso* is a highly stylized form with origins dating back earlier than those of the block style. There are

At a meeting of North and South Korean leaders in Pyongyang in June 2000, the leaders attend a calligraphy demonstration at the children's palace. (REUTERS NEWMEDIA INC./CORBIS)

subcategories within each of these styles, and accomplished calligraphers develop their own unique styles.

Although it is known that calligraphy was taught at royal academies and state institutions during the Three Kingdoms period (57 BCE–667 CE), few examples from that period remain. Following Chinese practice, the rulers of the Koryo kingdom (918–1392) included the composition of verse and its calligraphic rendering in the recruitment examinations for state officials. Throughout this period and much of the Choson dynasty (1392–1910), calligraphy styles closely followed those of the great Chinese masters. In the nineteenth century, however, Korean calligraphers developed individual, creative styles independent of Chinese models. Most noted of these is the *chusa* style of Kim Chong-hui (1786–1856). Kim was a leader in Korean experimentation with seal-style characters and the simplified square-style calligraphy found on ancient steles. Through this experimentation, Kim's uniquely Korean *chusa* style developed.

Calligraphy using the Korean alphabet began in the late eighteenth century. Stroke formation of Korean alphabet calligraphy closely resembles that of the basic writing styles for Chinese characters. Calligraphy written in both Chinese and Korean characters is taught in elementary schools and in private calligraphy schools. The most influential Korean calligrapher of the twentieth century was Son Che-hyong (1903–1981, artistic name Sojon), who was a master of all five basic calligraphy styles. His organizational efforts led to the inclusion of the popular calligraphy division in the Republic of Korea's National Arts Exhibition.

David E. Shaffer

See also: **Calligraphy—Japan**

Further Reading
Adams, Edward B. (1995) *Korea Guide.* 8th ed. Seoul: Seoul International Publishing House.
Korean National Commission for UNESCO. (1973) *A Study of Traditional Culture in Korea: Its Present Situation and Prospect in 1970s.* Seoul: KNCU.

CAM RANH BAY   Located in Vietnam's Khanh Hoa Province, about 33 kilometers south of Nha Trang, Cam Ranh Bay is a protected natural deep-water harbor that has been an important way station for navigators since the days of Marco Polo. The bay is very large at its widest berth (three to five kilometers) and is surrounded on three sides by land and slight hills. These geographic features enable ships to find safe harbor easily and make the bay easy to protect. Cam Ranh Bay saw its most active usage during the Vietnam War (1954–1975). In the 1960s, as the American military buildup increased, the need for another deep-water port to relieve congestion in Saigon, South Vietnam's only modern port facility, was realized at Cam Ranh Bay. Beginning in May–June 1965, the U.S. Army Corps of Engineers began to construct large cargo-handling facilities, connecting roads, warehouses, fuel tanks, and a large pier that could handle six large vessels simultaneously. In June 1972 the U.S. turned these facilities over to the Republic of Vietnam, which surrendered them to the Democratic Republic of Vietnam in April 1975. Since then the bay and base have been used by both the Socialist Republic of Vietnam and the former Soviet Union as a port and naval facility.

Richard B. Verrone

Further Reading
Cima, Ronald J., ed. (1989) *Vietnam: A Country Study.* Washington, DC: U.S. Government Printing Office.
Dunn, Carroll H. (1972) *Base Development in South Vietnam, 1965–1970.* Washington, DC: U.S. Government Printing Office.
Karnow, Stanley. (1991) *Vietnam: A History.* New York: The Viking Press.

CAMBODIA—PROFILE   (2001 est. 11.4 million). Cambodia occupies 181,040 square kilometers of peninsular Southeast Asia. Modern Cambodia is bordered by Vietnam, Thailand, Laos, and the Gulf of Thailand, which is a part of the South China Sea. It is all that remains of the once-powerful Khmer empire that flourished in the ninth through the twelfth centuries and dominated much of mainland Southeast Asia.

The frequency with which the official name of the country has changed is emblematic of the many polit-

CAMBODIA

Country name: Kingdom of Cambodia
Area: 181,040 sq km
Population: 12,491,501 (2001 est.)
Population growth rate: 2.25% (2001 est.)
Birth rate: 33.16 births/1,000 population (2001 est.)
Death rate: 10.65 deaths/1,000 population (2001 est.)
Net migration rate: 0 migrant(s)/1,000 population (2001 est.)
Sex ratio: 0.94 male(s)/female (2001 est.)
Infant mortality rate: 65.41 deaths/1,000 live births (2001 est.)
Life expectancy at birth—total population: 56.82 years; male: 54.62 years; female: 59.12 years (2001 est.)
Major religion: Theravada Buddhist
Major languages: Khmer (official), French, English
Literacy—total population: 35%; male: 48%, female: 22% (1990 est.)
Government type: multiparty liberal democracy under a constitutional monarchy established in September 1993
Capital: Phnom Penh
Administrative divisions: 20 provinces and 4 municipalities
Independence: 9 November 1953 (from France)
National holiday: Independence Day, 9 November (1953)
Suffrage: 18 years of age; universal
GDP—real growth rate: 4% (2000 est.)
GDP—per capita: (purchasing power parity): $1,300 (2000 est.)
Population below poverty line: 36% (1997 est.)
Exports: $942 million (f.o.b., 2000 est.)
Imports: $1.3 billion (f.o.b., 2000 est.)
Currency: riel (KHR)

Source: Central Intelligence Agency. (2001) *The World Book Factbook* 2001. Retrieved 5 March 2002, from http://www.cia.gov/cia/publications/factbook.

ical and social changes that have characterized modern Cambodia. Cambodia's current official title, the Kingdom of Cambodia, marks a return to name it had in the years immediately following independence, granted by the French in 1953. It has also been known officially as the Khmer Republic (1970–1975), Democratic Kampuchea (1975–1979), the People's Republic of Kampuchea (1979–1989), and the State of Cambodia (1989–1993).

Geography

Cambodia could be compared to a saucepan, or to a bowl. In the center of the country is a lowland plain, which is bordered by the Dangrek Mountains along the Thai border, the Cardamom Mountains to the south, and the Elephant Mountains even further south. There are also mountain ranges in the east. The country's highest peak is Mount Aural, which rises 1,813 meters (5,948 feet) above sea level.

The most significant geographical feature of Cambodia is the Tonle Sap. Tonle Sap is the name given to a river that is a tributary of the Mekong River, which flows through China, Myanmar (Burma), Laos, and Thailand, before running for more than 500 kilometers (more than 300 miles) through Cambodia, into Vietnam, and then to the South China Sea. Tonle Sap is also the name of a lake, into and from which the Tonle Sap River flows.

The Tonle Sap is remarkable because its flow reverses with the seasons. During the dry season (November

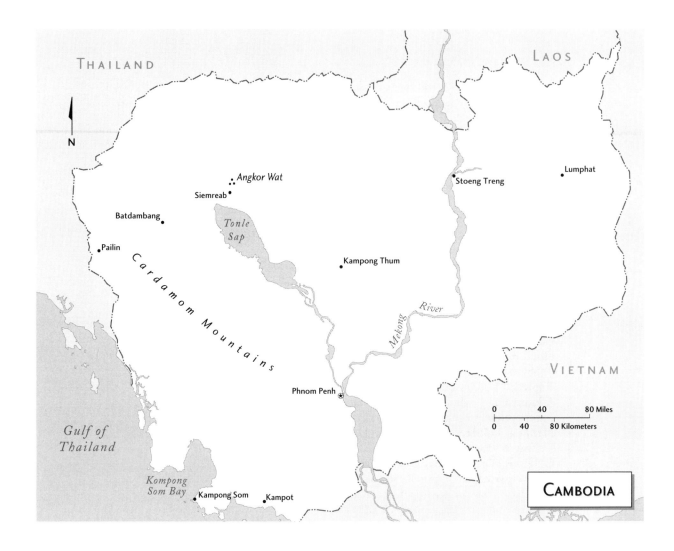

CAMBODIA

to April), the Tonle Sap River flows south from the lake into the Mekong River. During this period, the lake remains narrow and long, covering about 5 percent of Cambodia. During the wet season (May to October), the Mekong River rises, and the Tonle Sap River can no longer flow into it. The Tonle Sap river reverses its direction, flowing north into the Tonle Sap lake. The lake swells and overflows, covering almost 15 percent of the country. When the Tonle Sap flows into the Mekong, it leaves behind a layer of soil rich in nutrients. Rice farmers capitalize on this soil to grow their crops, and in the lake, the nutrients are eaten by fish. Together, fish and rice form the staple of the Cambodian diet.

Politics

Politics in Cambodia reflects the country's turbulent modern history. Having passed through a series of revolutionary changes since independence, the most radical and infamous of which was the rule of the Khmer Rouge between 1975 and 1979, the current system of government is officially a multiparty liberal democracy under a constitutional monarchy. This system was formed after warring factions in Cambodia agreed, in 1991, to conduct national elections under the direct supervision of the United Nations.

In 2001, the head of the government was Prime Minister Hun Sen (b. 1952), a former low-ranking officer of the Khmer Rouge who quickly rose through the ranks of the Khmer Rouge's Vietnamese-backed successor regime, the People's Republic of Kampuchea. Hun Sen was appointed prime minister after national elections conducted in 1998 delivered a majority of seats to his Cambodian People's Party (CPP), which governed in coalition with the royalist FUNCINPEC (Front Uni National pour un Cambodge Indépendant, Neutre, Pacifique, et Coopératif; National United Front for an Independent, Neutral, Peaceful, and Cooperative Cambodia) party, led by Prince Norodom Ranariddh. The prince is a son of Cambodia's King Sihanouk (b. 1922), who remains the country's most enduring political figure.

Economy

More than 75 percent of Cambodia's workforce is employed in agriculture. The primary agricultural crop is rice. Other crops include corn, rubber, sugarcane, and vegetables. Many Cambodians earn a living fishing from the Tonle Sap, while others grow a variety of fruit—among them being bananas, durian, mango, and papaya. Set against the agriculture sector is a steady growth in the industry sector, primarily fueled by the establishment of foreign-owned garment factories, which capitalize on Cambodia's cheap labor. The garment industry employs more than 100,000 people, and accounts for almost $700 million per year in exports.

A major feature of the economic system is its dependence on international assistance. During the 1980s, it was the assistance of Vietnam and the Soviet-led international socialist bloc that prevented the Cambodian economy from collapse. In the last decade of the twentieth century, the international community supported the Cambodian budget, and provided the funds for most capital investment, with China emerging as a major donor to the government. While self-sustainability is a long-term goal of the Cambodian government, this remains elusive.

People

Unlike many of its Southeast Asian neighbors, Cambodia is relatively ethnically homogenous. The dominant ethnic group is the Khmer, whose language (Khmer) is the national language of Cambodia, and whose religion, Theravada Buddhism, is also the national religion. The largest ethnic minority groups in Cambodia are the Chinese and the Vietnamese, many of whom have lived in the country for several generations. While relations between the Khmer and Chinese normally are quite amicable, and often feature intermarriage, relations between the Khmer and Vietnamese are often characterized by suspicion and animosity that are rooted in history and stem from the Khmer perception that the Vietnamese desire to "swallow up" Cambodian territory. The Chams, descendants of the former kingdom of Champa, now central Vietnam, are the third most populous ethnic minority. While the majority of the people of Cambodia are Buddhists, most Chams are Muslim.

In addition to the Khmer and these three dominant ethnic minorities, there are other less populous ethnic groups in Cambodia. Referred to as Khmer Leou (highland Khmer), these ethnic groups live in the mountainous regions of Cambodia. They include the Brao, Kuy, Saoch, and Pear ethnic groups, as well as ethnic Thai and Lao minorities. Each of these groups has its own language and customs.

Boats on the Mekong River at sunset in 2001. (STEVE RAYMER/CORBIS)

Contemporary Cambodia

Cambodia remains one of the poorest countries in the world, and is faced with a raft of significant social and political challenges. Paramount among these is the alleviation of poverty, especially in rural Cambodia, where more than 80 percent of the population lives. Rates of infant mortality are among the highest in Asia, while the access of the majority of the population to education, health care, and a sanitary water supply remains at critically low levels. In recent years, the popular belief that the majority of rural Cambodians owned the land they lived on has been undermined, and rural landlessness has emerged as a major factor in explaining the incidence of poverty. This problem has been exacerbated by land-grabbing by government officials and high-ranking members of the armed forces, who are able to take advantage of a poorly developed legal system and a culture of impunity among those exercising political power.

Apart from poverty, another challenge facing contemporary Cambodia is how the country will reconcile calls for more vibrant democracy and a more active role for civil society with a hierarchical political culture firmly grounded in centuries of tradition. A proliferation of local nongovernmental organizations and the establishment of a fledgling trade union movement provide evidence of an emerging civil society. Drawing on the traditions of a hierarchical political culture that inhibits popular participation and a dialogue over the formulation of policy, the government continues to struggle with how it should integrate these new democratic institutions into the broader political system.

David M. Ayres

Further Reading
Chandler, David. (1991) *The Tragedy of Cambodian History: Politics, War, and Revolution since 1945.* Bangkok, Thailand: Silkworm Press.
Chandler, David. (1993) *A History of Cambodia.* Sydney: Allen and Unwin.
Hoskin, John. (1992) *Cambodia: A Portrait.* Hong Kong, China: Elsworth Books.
Kamm, Henry. (1998) *Cambodia: Report from a Stricken Land.* New York: Arcade Publishing.
Mabbett, Ian, and David Chandler. (1995). *The Khmers.* Oxford: Blackwell Publishers.

CAMBODIA—CIVIL WAR OF 1970–1975

On 18 March 1970, while Cambodia's leader, Prince Norodom Sihanouk (b. 1922), was on an official visit to the Soviet Union, he was deposed by his country's national assembly. Leading the coup against Sihanouk were his erstwhile ally, Lon Nol (1913–1985), and his cousin, Prince Sisowath Sirikmatak. Within days, as political chaos enveloped Cambodia, a civil war erupted. For the next five years, before the Khmer Rouge assumed control of the country and began its nearly four-year reign of terror, the once relatively peaceful Cambodian countryside served as a battlefield for the warring factions. It was a period of stark divisions: between rural and urban Cambodians, between politicians and their constituents, between the beneficiaries of massive corruption and its victims, and between the richest and poorest members of Cambodian society.

The Coup

The 1970 coup in Cambodia had been brewing since at least 1966, when Norodom Sihanouk lost control of the National Assembly, which had been his rubber stamp since the elections of September 1955. The elections had proved a disaster for the Cambodian left, which eventually claimed only five of eighty-two assembly seats, and they provided a resounding victory for the conservatives, many of whom harbored anti-Sihanouk tendencies. Capitalizing on the poor employment prospects of urban youths, surging anger over corruption, and blatant mismanagement of public utilities, the right-wing assembly—led by Lon Nol and ably encouraged by the charismatic Sirikmatak—sought to overturn much of Sihanouk's socialist economic agenda. The prince's opponents finally moved against him while he was out of the country, using the National Assembly to withdraw confidence in him as chief of state.

While the coup has become synonymous with Lon Nol, he was an unlikely conspirator against his leader. Lon Nol had loyally served Norodom Sihanouk since before Cambodia achieved independence in 1953. He had been the flamboyant Sihanouk's unassuming minister of defense as well as his prime minister. Sihanouk's ouster pitted the two contrasting figures against each other. In Phnom Penh, Lon Nol and the other leaders of the coup set about dismantling the 1,900-year-old Cambodian monarchy and establishing a Khmer republic. Sihanouk responded to the coup against him by aligning himself with his sworn enemies in the Khmer Rouge movement, which, for much of the previous decade, he had sought to eliminate. The prince gave the Khmer Rouge the air of legitimacy they had for so long lacked. In turn, the Khmer Rouge submerged their own revolutionary agenda beneath a rhetoric that centered on calls for the prince's return to power.

International Dimensions

The conflict that ensued had such complex international dimensions that it may be inappropriate, at least in its early days, to label what actually transpired as a civil war. In Moscow at the time he was informed of his ouster, Sihanouk flew on to Beijing, where he met with North Vietnam's premier Pham Van Dong, who offered him the support of Cambodia's Khmer Rouge, the North Vietnamese Army, and the National Liberation Front (Viet Cong). Sihanouk used Radio Beijing to issue a call to arms and soon after announced the establishment of the Royal Government of National Union, more commonly known by its French acronym, GRUNK.

Opposing Sihanouk's unlikely alliance with the Khmer Rouge was the republican regime of Lon Nol. Vehemently opposed to the Vietnamese Communists, and especially to their use of Cambodian territory to aid their war effort against the United States and the South Vietnamese government, the republican regime enjoyed both U.S. and South Vietnamese support. Cambodia effectively became what has been eloquently referred to by the author William Shawcross as a "sideshow" to the conflict in Vietnam.

On the Battlefield

Any assessment of what happened on the battlefield in the civil war is overshadowed by the fact that the war was won, convincingly in the end, by the Khmer Rouge and Sihanouk. In the first months of the civil war, with Sihanouk's GRUNK supported by five fully equipped North Vietnamese Army units, the republican army suffered massive territorial losses. It lost control of almost all of the provinces of Svay Rieng, Rattanakiri, and Mondolkiri, and more than a half of Kompong Cham, Prey Veng, Takeo, and Kampot. While it is plausible to argue that the GRUNK victories were the result of massive Vietnamese assistance, it is equally plausible to argue they were the result of the totally inept leadership of their opponents.

The foot soldiers of the Khmer Republic were as brave and as skilled as were their Khmer Rouge opponents. Benefiting from the fruits of U.S. assistance, they were also in many cases much better equipped than their rivals. They ultimately failed, not because of their own deficiencies, but because those who led them were incompetent and oftentimes corrupt and because they rarely demonstrated any genuine concern for those they commanded. Many of the republican generals conducted the war effort from Phnom Penh, where they became regular patrons of popular nightspots and cafés, and from where they could speculate on Phnom Penh real estate with the money they had siphoned from the coffers of American assistance. Commanding officers frequently sent understrength units into battle, as they had enlisted nonexistent "phantom soldiers" on their payrolls so that they could pocket their salaries. These same officers, and their superiors, frequently sold arms and supplies to their opponents.

As the battles raged on, the Khmer Rouge were able to assume increasing control of the war effort. Capitalizing on Sihanouk's popularity in the countryside, their forces swelled from approximately 15,000 early in 1970 to more than 200,000 by the end of 1972. Many also joined the Khmer Rouge ranks after witnessing the destruction wrought by U.S. B-52 bombers and Cambodian T-28 fighter planes. Between February and August 1973, the United States dropped more than 250,000 tons of bombs on Cambodia.

The Final Siege

It was arguably the massive U.S. aerial bombardment campaign that prolonged the life of the war and that slowed down what seemed an inevitable result. By late 1974 the Khmer Republic could be defined almost in terms of the city limits of Phnom Penh and Battambang, Cambodia's second city. Overflowing with displaced persons who had fled from the strife-ridden countryside, the cities became hotbeds of dissatisfaction with the inept Lon Nol regime. As the Khmer Rouge tightened its grip over the country, Phnom Penh's survival became dependent on a U.S.-sponsored airlift of rice and other basic commodities. Travel through the city became increasingly dangerous, while measures for fuel and electricity rationing were tightened.

The Khmer Rouge began their final assault on Phnom Penh on 1 January 1975. Republican politicians who had not already fled overseas tried to maintain a sense of normalcy. A few sought to stitch together a last-ditch compromise with Sihanouk and his allies, but their efforts were to no avail. Having ringed the city and cut off essential supplies, the Sihanoukists and Khmer Rouge had little motivation to compromise. With victory in sight, they continued to tighten the screws. On the morning of 17 April 1975 Khmer Rouge troops began to march victoriously into Phnom Penh. Former ministers and high-ranking officials of the republic were asked to report to the ministry of information, where they were arrested and later executed.

Lon Nol had already fled to Hawaii, where he would remain until his death. Sirikmatak, taking refuge in the French embassy, surrendered to Khmer Rouge forces on 20 April. He was taken to the French sports club, the Cercle Sportif, where he was executed.

The Khmer Rouge ruled Cambodia for the next three years, eight months, and twenty days.

David M. Ayres

See also: **Khmer Rouge; Killing Fields; Lon Nol; Phnom Penh; Phnom Penh Evacuation; Sihanouk, Norodom**

Further Reading
Chandler, David. (1991) *The Tragedy of Cambodian History: Politics, War and Revolution since 1945.* Bangkok, Thailand: Silkworm Press.
Corfield, Justin. (1994) *Khmer Stand Up! A History of the Cambodian Government, 1970–1975.* Clayton, Australia: Monash University Centre of Southeast Asian Studies.
Deac, Wilfred. (1997) *Road to the Killing Fields: The Cambodian War of 1970–1975.* College Station, TX: Texas A&M University Press.
Isaacs, Arnold. (1984) *Without Honor: Defeat in Vietnam and Cambodia.* Baltimore, MD: Johns Hopkins University Press.
Kiernan, Ben. (1985) *How Pol Pot Came to Power: A History of Communism in Kampuchea, 1930–1975.* London: Verso.
Shawcross, William. (1986) *Sideshow: Kissinger, Nixon and the Destruction of Cambodia.* London: Hogarth Press.

CAMBODIA—ECONOMIC SYSTEM The nature of Cambodia's economic system reflects the deep complexity of Cambodian society. On one hand, it has witnessed great changes, having ebbed and flowed with the shifting ideological convictions of the country's ruling regimes and with their shifting international and political alliances. On the other hand, it has been characterized by the continuity of the seasons of planting and harvesting that have molded social and religious life in Cambodia for centuries. Cambodia's economic system, like the society it supports, has been shaped by the country's agricultural heritage and orientation. This article provides an overview of this economic system, tracing its evolution and structure, and describing how it functions on the outer fringes of the global economy.

Evolution of the Economic System
Following substantial destruction and disruption to Cambodia's economic infrastructure and economic management apparatuses during the 1970–1975 civil war, the Khmer Rouge effectively overturned economic life in Cambodia. It is this period (1975–1979) that is central to understanding the economic system of Cambodia today. Intent on rebuilding the country from the ground up, the Khmer Rouge regime was responsible for implementing massive changes in the nature of the Cambodian economic system. First, the regime ruthlessly dismantled the formal economic structures of the regimes they had succeeded. Cambodia's currency, the riel, was abolished; the national bank was literally blown up; and the systems of taxation and fiscal and monetary regulation were ignored. Second, the regime overturned the informal agricultural economic sector by collectivizing village-centered economic activities. The legacy of these collectivization measures continues to hamper agricultural productivity in some parts of Cambodia today, with the massive but poorly planned dikes and irrigation works of the Khmer Rouge upsetting the natural irrigation flows.

The regime that succeeded the Khmer Rouge in January 1979, the People's Republic of Kampuchea (PRK), was confronted with the enduring legacy of its predecessor. With many of the country's brightest technicians dead, and with economic infrastructure in ruins, the PRK was supported by Vietnam and by the Soviet-led international socialist bloc in rehabilitating economic life in Cambodia. The result of their endeavors was a centrally planned economy, heavily reliant on Vietnamese and Soviet technical assistance, that traded almost exclusively with Council for Mutual Economic Assistance (CMEA) countries. Economic activity was concentrated on a slowly reemerging agricultural sector, with very little industrial activity and a services sector that did little more than support agricultural development and the activities of the Communist government.

When the Soviet Union began to collapse, so too did Vietnamese and Soviet economic support to Cambodia. The Cambodian government responded to what was a critical economic crisis by introducing measures to liberalize the local economy. Private property rights, which had been partially restored by the regime in 1985, were fully restored in 1989; private enterprise and investment were encouraged, price control mechanisms dismantled, and national bank activities reformed. The pace of economic liberalization accelerated after the peace agreements were signed by Cambodia's warring factions at Paris in 1991. Gross domestic product (GDP) grew at an annual average of 5.9 percent (in real terms) between 1990 and 1995. Fueled by the arrival of the United Nations personnel who had been sent to Cambodia to supervise the elections that were at the core of the Paris agreements, much of the growth was concentrated in the industry and services sectors. Agricultural performance during this critical period, especially in rice production, was poor.

The Economic System since UNTAC
The Cambodian economic system since the UNTAC (United Nations Transitional Authority in Cam-

Women prune and weed bean plants on the Banteay Dek Commune in Kandal Province, Cambodia, in 1996. (KEVIN R. MORRIS/CORBIS)

bodia) period, when the United Nations launched its most expensive single peacekeeping operation in order to create an environment where free and fair elections could be conducted in Cambodia, has been characterized by a number of features. First, there has been continued growth in the industry sector, led by a proliferation of new garment factories. Nonexistent before the UNTAC period, the garment industry has expanded so rapidly in recent years (more than 60 percent since 1998) that it now accounts for almost $700 million a year in exports, approximately 70 percent of which are exported to the United States. The industry employs more than 100,000 Cambodians, the majority of them young women. In recent times, it has become the focus of a fledgling trade-union movement.

A second feature of the economic system has been the effect of the violence that enveloped Cambodia's political environment in July 1997. When Hun Sen ousted his political rival and co-prime minister, Prince Norodom Ranariddh, many of Cambodia's foreign investors and international aid donors scaled back or canceled their involvement in the country. Coupled with the effects of the Asian economic crisis that was dominating the region at the time, the events of July 1997 caused Cambodia's economic growth to fall from 7 percent in 1996 to 1 percent in 1997 and 1998. It also had a dramatic effect on the tourism industry. Tourist arrivals in the second half of 1997 were down more than 50 percent compared with arrivals in the

second half of 1996, hotel vacancies increased, and investment in tourism-related infrastructure stagnated. Following the 1998 national elections, international aid donors slowly returned to the country, and the local tourism industry also rebounded strongly.

A third feature of the economic system has been the gradual decline in external investment. The events of July 1997 and the Asian economic crisis precipitated a fall in investment in Cambodia from which the country has not yet recovered. Foreign investment in the first quarter of 2000, for example, was down 79 percent on investment figures for the first quarter of 1999. A number of factors have accounted for the declining investment, including perceptions about lack of government stability and competence in Cambodia, concerns about the level of corruption in the government, and the decline in intraregional investment in Southeast Asia—an obvious consequence of the Asian economic crisis.

A fourth feature of the economic system has been its dependence on external support. An important outcome of the Paris agreements was Cambodia's return to the fold of development assistance from the wider international community, including both multilateral and bilateral development agencies. These agencies have played significant roles in providing the government with the advice and technical assistance it has needed to shift from the command economy of the

1980s to its current free-market orientation. They have also been instrumental in reconstructing, rehabilitating, and developing the infrastructure and productive capacity of Cambodia's economic system. The downside of the massive influx of development assistance has been increased dependency on that aid. Development assistance has accounted for approximately 20 percent of Cambodia's GDP since the signing of the Paris agreements, with development aid per capita among the highest in the region.

Massive reform initiatives, often driven by foreign donors, have been a fifth feature of the contemporary economic system. With inflation during the period immediately prior to the 1993 elections running at more than 120 percent, a poor revenue base, low levels of investment, and state industries often recording massive losses, Cambodia's economic system was in dire need of reform. The government embraced a reform agenda oriented toward developing a market economy with a flourishing private sector. Measures have been adopted to attract investment, control inflation, and increase revenues from taxation. These measures aside, the reform agenda has often stumbled, with concerns about generous tax concessions given to foreign investors, poorly developed measures for tax collection, the diversion of revenues from logging operations, and the activities of corrupt officials at all levels of government.

The final feature of the economic system has been the continued division between the formal and informal economies. While the government, with the support of international agencies, has been particularly concerned with economic reform in Cambodia as well as with the country's integration into the regional and global economies, the majority of Cambodians have minimal interaction with this formal economy. Most Cambodians live in rural areas, so few pay income taxes, and few produce goods that are sold to regional and international markets. Instead, they participate in essentially local economies, selling their labor or surplus to purchase what they do not produce themselves. Increased consumerism, fueled by demand for Western consumer products, will inevitably result in a greater interaction between rural Cambodians and the formal economy.

Money and Banking

Cambodia's currency and banking systems were abolished by the Khmer Rouge regime between 1975 and 1979. The systems that were reestablished by the PRK regime in 1980 followed the central-planning models of Cambodia's Communist benefactors, Vietnam and the Soviet Union. Currency was controlled by a national bank, which merely printed money to match the government's liquidity needs. Commercial banking functions, undertaken through a meager branch network, were also the sole domain of the national bank. Economic liberalization measures adopted in 1988–1989 resulted in the establishment of a two-tier banking system in which national bank and commercial banking functions were separated. The government actively encouraged the opening of foreign and domestic private commercial banks, while the national bank was encouraged to take a more independent approach to monetary policy.

Since then, it would seem that the liberalization measures have had mixed and limited successes. While there has been an official separation between national bank functions and the activities of the government, the bank has been guilty, on several occasions, of printing money to meet the government's spending requirements. The number of players in the private banking sector has proliferated since the 1993 elections. Although this indicates that the government's market-oriented ideology has had some success, there are concerns about the activities of some commercial banks, with several critics suggesting that they have been established in conjunction with elaborate money laundering schemes and with a burgeoning narcotics industry.

An additional concern is the practice of substituting foreign currencies for the Cambodian currency, the riel. In Phnom Penh, and throughout much of the remainder of Cambodia, U.S. dollars are frequently substituted for the riel, especially in larger transactions. Prices in many stores are quoted and advertised in U.S. dollars, while many employers pay their workers in the American currency. The baht of neighboring Thailand is the primary substitution currency in many regions of Cambodia's west. The major problem with currency substitution is that the government's control of monetary policy is reduced. Plans were set in place in the mid-1990s that were intended to lead to the "dedollarization" of the economy, but there is little evidence that this has occurred.

External Trade

Since the breakdown of the Soviet bloc, with which Cambodia conducted most of its external trade through the 1980s, measures have been taken to liberalize the country's international trade. These measures have included the streamlining of many tariffs as well as the abolition of quantity restrictions on a broad range of goods. Stimulated by these measures by high levels of economic growth among neighboring countries and by the growth of the domestic economy, Cambodia's foreign trade expanded rapidly through the 1990s. The downside to this improvement is that Cambodia ran current account deficits through the 1990s that on occasions reached almost 16 percent of GDP.

Cambodia's export trade is concentrated in two areas: natural resources and light manufacturing. Together, exports in these areas have accounted for almost two-thirds of Cambodia's total exports through the 1990s. The export of Cambodia's natural-resources is a source of considerable concern, as raw timber has been felled (with and without the approval of the authorities) at a rate that even the government concedes is unsustainable. Light manufacturing exports are almost all from the garment industry, the remarkable growth of which is largely attributable to the Cambodian government's attractive foreign investment incentives and the country's relatively low labor costs. The nature of Cambodia's exports reflects the economy's weak productive capacity, with few manufactured goods (excluding garments) or consumable items figuring in total export patterns.

In stark contrast to export patterns, Cambodia's imports have consistently reflected a demand for petroleum products, transport vehicles and machinery, and basic manufactured goods. While the majority of these products are imported to provide the industry and services sectors with essential capital goods, others (such as televisions, stereos, and motor scooters) reflect increased consumerism among the Cambodian people, especially among those living in urban areas. The current account deficit and the export and import patterns discussed above are of concern to the government, which aims to put in place long-term policies that will ensure that Cambodia is able to produce or finance what it consumes.

Cambodia's major trading partners are its Southeast Asian neighbors. Singapore is by far the largest source of imports, as the island state is a major source of transshipment of goods from other countries with final destinations in Asia. After Singapore, Cambodia's nearest neighbors—Thailand and Vietnam—are its largest sources of imports. Together, these three countries accounted for approximately 70 percent of Cambodia's imports through the 1990s. Cambodia's exports follow a similar pattern, with Thailand and Singapore being the dominant export destinations. Cambodia's recent admission to the Association of Southeast Asian Nations (ASEAN), delayed because of the events of July 1997, will in all likelihood reinforce these trading patterns, with ASEAN countries continuing to dominate Cambodian exports and imports.

With an infrastructure that continues to struggle to overcome the devastating legacies of the past, poor productive economic capacity, an unskilled labor force, and relatively inexpensive labor, Cambodia will continue to hold its position on the outer edges of the global economy. The capacity of the country's economic system to deliver greater prosperity to the Cambodian people will continue to be dependent on significant changes and policy reforms. There remains an urgent need to address the many inappropriate relationships that exist between the government and big business, ad hoc taxation arrangements, corrupt officials, and knee-jerk politically motivated policy changes if Cambodia's economic system is to develop to the benefit of the Cambodian people.

David M. Ayres

Further Reading
Chan Sophal, et al. (1998) "Cambodia: Challenges and Options of Regional Economic Orientation." Conference Papers. Phnom Penh, Cambodia: Cambodia Development Resource Institute.

Chan Sophal, et al. (1999) *Impact of the Asian Financial Crisis on the SEATEs: The Cambodian Perspective*. Phnom Penh, Cambodia: Cambodia Development Resource Institute.

Keat Chhon, and Aun Porn Moniroth. (1999) *Cambodia's Economic Development: Policies, Strategies and Implementation*. London: ASEAN Academic Press.

Mysliweic, Eva. (1988) *Punishing the Poor: The International Isolation of Kampuchea*. Oxford, U.K.: Oxfam.

Royal Government of Cambodia. (1995) *First Five-Year Socioeconomic Development Plan*. Phnom Penh, Cambodia: Ministry of Planning.

Vickery, Michael. (1986) *Kampuchea: Politics, Economics and Society*. London: Pinter.

———. (1990) "Notes on the Political Economy of the People's Republic of Kampuchea." *Journal of Contemporary Asia* 20: 435–65.

CAMBODIA—EDUCATION SYSTEM

Cambodia's education system holds a very important place in the country's plans for integrating itself into the regional and international economies and for reducing the poverty of its people. The Cambodian government, and the many international and nongovernmental organizations that provide it with development assistance, regard education as the key to developing the human resources and skills that will allow Cambodia to take its place in these economies. The country's education system, once the envy of many countries in Southeast Asia, was almost totally destroyed during the 1970s, and it has had to contend with the legacy of this destruction in the years since.

Students in their uniforms on the playground of Sisowath School in Phnom Penh in 1996. (KEVIN R. MORRIS/CORBIS)

Structure of the Education System

The formal educational structure consists of six years of primary school (grades 1–6), three years of lower secondary school (grades 7–9), and three years of upper secondary school (grades 10–12). Before 1996 the structure was 5:3:3, and before 1985 it was 4:3:3. In prerevolutionary Cambodia, the educational structure was 6:4:3. Therefore, while educational provision has increased in recent years, it has not yet reached the level of the period prior to the rule of the Khmer Rouge. Higher education is available at the Royal University of Phnom Penh, the Royal Agricultural University, the Royal University of Fine Arts, the Faculty of Medicine, the Faculty of Law and Economics, the Faculty of Business (National Institute of Management), the Institute of Technology of Cambodia (formerly the Higher Technical Institute of Khmer-Soviet Friendship), and the Maharishi Vedic University (an Australian-funded institution in rural Prey Veng Province). Private education exists at all levels of the education system. In primary and secondary education, private schools have been opened by ethnic minority communities as well as for the children of the relatively small wealthy expatriate community residing in Cambodia. Private higher education is available at Norton University and at a number of other institutions, such as Regent College. Also, there is a flourishing industry, especially in Phnom Penh, in unregulated private schools that offer students instruction in foreign languages and computer skills.

The current structure of Cambodia's education system stems from the chaos that enveloped the country in the aftermath of the destruction caused by the Khmer Rouge. The Ministry of Education, while operational since 1979, was officially formed by a Council of Ministers subdecree in 1980. Although the ministry's departments were restructured in August 1998, there is still no legislation in place to regulate the new arrangements. Provincial authorities, with meager funding from the Ministry of Economy and Finance, continue to bear the burden of responsibility for local education budgets, while several government higher-education institutions remain outside the authority of the Ministry of Education. The result is that educational management and systems for educational planning and administration remain highly fragmented and often largely ineffective.

Historical Development of the Education System

A system of education has been in place in Cambodia since at least the thirteenth century. This traditional education system was centered on local temples and involved teaching students about the foundations of religion, basic literacy, and skills such as carpentry that were relevant to the rural life of most Cambodians. While this nonformal system endured after the arrival of the French in Cambodia, it was gradually replaced by a Westernized educational model. The French authorities did not pursue this modern education system with any great enthusiasm and seemed reluctant to devote the educational resources that were needed to meet local demand. The educational legacy of the colonial period in Cambodia was the importation of the Western idea of a formal school system and the gradual undermining of its traditional counterpart. The colonial era introduced to Cambodians the idea that education could lead to upward social mobility. It was a realization that led to unprecedented demand for access to education in the years that immediately followed independence.

Contrary to popular perceptions that the postindependence period was a golden era of development in Cambodia, the education system was characterized by chronic crisis. Policies focused on getting as many students as possible enrolled at all levels of the education system were often unaffordable, and were concentrated on the very small modern sector of the economy (to the detriment of rural needs). While Cambodia's educational enrollment statistics were often the envy of many other countries in the region, they hid the reality of an education system that was largely irrelevant, had too many underqualified teachers, and possessed poorly equipped classrooms.

In 1970, with the outbreak of civil war, Cambodia's educational problems went from bad to worse. Many schools were leveled by bombs, while others were used by the warring parties as barracks, munitions warehouses, and prisons. Teachers fled their posts, moving to the city, joining the army, or attempting to move abroad. The victory of the Khmer Rouge only compounded the destruction. Cambodia's new rulers swiftly cast aside the education system of the old regime. Classrooms were abandoned, books were left to rot or were used to roll cigarettes, and former schoolteachers, professors, and higher-education students were targeted as class enemies and were often singled out for execution. The Khmer Rouge regime did have a ministry of education, and even produced a couple of school textbooks. By 1979, however, very few children in Cambodia were receiving any form of instruction. The education system was effectively ruined: infrastructure had degenerated significantly, books and teaching materials no longer existed, and many of the nation's teachers were dead.

The regime that succeeded the Khmer Rouge was staffed by its survivors. Confronted with unparalleled destruction, it valiantly struggled to overcome educational chaos. By the end of the 1980s, educational enrollment levels (especially in primary schools) had largely overcome the legacy of the Khmer Rouge period. While this was an impressive achievement, other problems remained.

Education in the 1990s and Beyond

After the peace agreements were signed by Cambodia's warring factions in 1991, the reconstruction and development of the education system was considered to be of critical importance. Marked improvements to educational infrastructure over the 1990s are evident. The quality, relevance, and availability of school textbooks have also improved. Beyond these improvements, which have been largely driven and financed by foreign aid donors, the education system remains incapable of delivering to Cambodia a skilled workforce.

The country's teachers, who are grossly underpaid, have resorted to charging their students unofficial fees. Many are spending less time in the classroom as they seek additional employment elsewhere. Almost 20 percent of students in urban areas, and 26 percent in rural areas, have repeated at least one grade at school. From every one thousand students who begin primary school, only twenty-seven will graduate from upper secondary school. Girls, students from remote areas, and the poor are all grossly underrepresented in education statistics. With these significant problems as a backdrop, and the school-age population continuing to grow, the Cambodian government still denies the education sector the funding it needs to realize its important role in Cambodian society.

David M. Ayres

See also: **Royal University of Phnom Penh**

Further Reading
Asian Development Bank. (1996) "Cambodia Education Sector Study." Manila, Philippines: Asian Development Bank.
Ayres, David. (2000) *Anatomy of a Crisis: Education, Development, and the State in Cambodia, 1953–1998.* Honolulu, HI: University of Hawaii Press.
———. (1999) "The Khmer Rouge and Education: Beyond the Discourse of Destruction." *History of Education* 28: 205–18.
Sloper, David, ed. (2000) *Higher Education in Cambodia: The Social and Educational Context for Reconstruction.* Bangkok, Thailand: UNESCO Principal Regional Office for Asia and the Pacific.

CAMBODIA—HISTORY The origins of the earliest inhabitants of Cambodia are unknown. Scholars are uncertain whether they came from China, India, or insular Southeast Asia. Sources indicate that as far back as 4000 BCE a mix of prehistoric and Khmer people lived in the area that is now Cambodia. Although a language related to present-day Khmer was

KEY EVENTS IN CAMBODIAN HISTORY

c. 4000 BCE   Khmer and other peoples are living in the region.

1st century CE   A language related to Khmer is spoken in the region. The Funan state, influenced by India, rules the region.

6th century   The Funan state is displaced by the Chenla state from the north.

9th–14th centuries   The Angkor empire flourishes across much of mainland southeast Asia.

12th century   The Hindu Angkor empire converts to Buddhism.

1353   Angkor falls to the Siamese and over the next five centuries loses territory to neighboring states.

1863–1941   Cambodia is a French protectorate.

1941–1945   Cambodia is occupied by the Japanese.

1942   The monks' rebellion marks the beginning of Cambodian nationalism.

1945   The French resume control.

1953   Cambodia becomes an independent nation with the end of French rule.

1955   In elections marked by corruption, Sangkum, the party of Norodom Sihanouk, comes to power.

1970   Sihanouk is deposed and replaced by Lon Nol. The nation is renamed Khmer Republic.

1970–1975   The period of civil war.

1975–1979   Cambodia is ruled by the Khmer Rouge.

1978–1988   Vietnam attacks and occupies Cambodia. Cambodia is renamed the People's Republic of Kampuchea.

1989   The name is changed again to the State of Cambodia.

1991   The Paris Peace Agreement is signed creating a large U.N. peacekeeping effort in Cambodia.

1993   An election is held under U.N. direction but the results are set aside and a power-sharing government is created.

1996–1998   The power-sharing government fails.

1998   Following elections a coalition government is formed.

---

spoken in the region in the first century CE, the earliest recorded sources are Chinese records from the first century. These refer to Funan, the first Indianized state in the region and a precursor to the Khmer empire. Indianized influences included Hinduism and Sanskrit and may have been introduced from Java. The importance of Funan declined during the sixth century, when Chenla, a neighboring political entity to the north, became dominant.

The Angkorian Empire

The Angkorian empire flourished between the ninth and fourteenth centuries, at its height incorporating not only present-day Cambodia, but also much of Laos, Thailand, and Vietnam. Originally a Hindu kingdom, it became Mahayana Buddhist during the twelfth century. The empire established sophisticated administrative structures; a system of roads connecting government outposts, towns, and cities; and the temple complex known today as Angkor Wat.

The first Angkorian king, Jayavarman II (c. 770–850), was consecrated in a ceremony at Phnom Kulen in 802. The ceremony, recorded in Khmer and Sanskrit inscriptions, marked the beginning of Angkorian civilization. It is not known precisely where Jayavarman II came from, possibly the island of Java or a kingdom in Sumatra. He established a royal Brahmanic cult based on worship of a specific *lingam* (a stylized phallic symbol) representing Siva. The *lingam* bestowed Jayavarman II and future Angkorian kings with sacred legitimacy, establishing the religious basis of the Angkorian monarchy. From this, the notion of the universal monarch emerged. The association of Phnom Kulen with the source of Khmer identity continues into the present day.

The art and architecture of Angkor evolved over time, expressing the political and religious course of Angkorian civilization. The next important monarch, Indravarman (reigned 877–889), created a reservoir for the irrigation system that inextricably linked agrarian and urban development. While allowing for irrigation during the dry season, the reservoir symbolically embodied the oceans surrounding Mt. Meru—home of the gods—and, by implication, further affirmed the association of the king with the gods. During the reign of Suryavarman II (d. 1150), the kingdom expanded through wars against the Chams in the east and the Mons in the west. It was during this reign that the Angkor Wat temple was built.

Angkor was sacked by the Chams in 1177, and hydrological projects were abandoned. The next Angkorian king, Jayavarman VII (c. 1120–c.1218), defeated the Chams in battle, scenes of which are depicted in bas-relief at Angkor Thom. The last of the great Angkorian kings, Jayavarman VII represented a departure from previous notions of kingship. A Buddhist, he transformed Angkor into a Mahayana Buddhist kingdom and sought to deliver himself and his people from suffering. His reign was characterized by great public works projects, including roads, temples, rest houses, reservoirs, and hospitals. Under his authority, Angkor reached the height of its political and territorial power.

The Middle Period

After the death of Jayavarman VII, the Angkorian empire declined. This has been attributed to internal rebellions, the introduction of Theravada Buddhism, and the rise of Siam (Thailand). Angkor fell to the Siamese first in 1353 and then again in the mid-fifteenth century, when it was abandoned as a political center. The capital moved south, first to Udong, and eventually to Phnom Penh.

From the fall of Angkor until the mid-nineteenth century, Cambodia lost territory to its more populous neighbors, Siam and Vietnam. With external threats on either side, Cambodia's kings appealed to either one side or the other for protection. This led to continuing loss of territory and fear of obliteration. By the 1830s, much of eastern Cambodia was a satellite of Vietnam, and two provinces in the northwest were under Siam. Cambodia was approximately its present size when it became a French protectorate in 1863.

French Colonialism

During the period of the French protectorate (1863–1941), there were many international interventions in Cambodia. Although the French claimed they saved Cambodia from further territorial losses to Siam and Vietnam, some say the creation of French Indochina furthered Vietnamese hegemonic designs on Cambodia. The French used Cambodia as a buffer between their investments in Vietnam and the Thai and British presence to the west. While the French focused on Vietnam as the center of capitalism, infrastructure, and education in the colony, Cambodia was preserved as a quaint romantic backwater. Education was not a priority. Stereotyping the Khmer as childlike, seductive, and lazy, the French placed the Vietnamese in civil service positions throughout Indochina. A large influx of Vietnamese settlers into Cambodia at this time reinforced the notion that Cambodia was a portion of Indochina first and Cambodia second. Thus the French, whether intentionally or not, fostered animosity between the Cambodians and the Vietnamese that would remain a strong undercurrent.

Three incidents of resistance during colonial times show that Cambodia was not simply the sleepy backwater the French imagined. The first was the Affair of 1916, when large delegations of peasants traveled from

The Silver Pagoda at the Royal Palace in Phnom Penh which was built by King Norodom in 1892. The floor is covered by 5,000 silver tiles. (BRIAN A. VIKANDER/CORBIS)

the provinces to Phnom Penh to petition the king to lower taxes. The second was the killing of a French tax collector, Bardez, who was beaten to death while on duty. And the third was the monks' rebellion in 1942, which marked the emergence of Cambodian nationalism. Although none of these incidents had significant repercussions in shaping colonial rule, they are important for showing the gulf that existed between Cambodian and French perceptions.

Nationalism and Independence

Nationalism emerged late in colonial Cambodia. Before World War II, there was little organized activity. Nor did the Japanese, who occupied Cambodia from 1941 to 1945, promote anticolonial sentiment there as they did in other places. During the Japanese occupation, the French remained in administrative positions, placing Prince Norodom Sihanouk (b. 1922) on the throne in 1941. In 1945 the French were removed from office and were interned by the Japanese; Sihanouk declared Cambodia free from the French protectorate. After the war, the French returned with the compliance of Sihanouk and against the wishes of the nationalists.

After the return of the French, Cambodian nationalism was supported by Thai and Vietnamese interests anxious to have the French leave for their own purposes. The Khmer Issarak (Free Khmer), an opposition political group, was prominent in rural areas, while the Democrat Party dominated urban politics. Both groups criticized Sihanouk for seemingly acquiescing to the French. Sihanouk, meanwhile, negotiated for independence on his own, and the French, who were preoccupied with their problems in Vietnam, granted it in 1953.

In the years following independence, Sihanouk became the prominent figure in Cambodian politics. He abdicated the throne and created the national organization Sangkum Reastr Niyum, effectively eclipsing his opposition. In the election of 1955, which was marked by widespread corruption and violence, the Sangkum won all the seats in parliament. In the following years, while Sihanouk portrayed himself as a benevolent father figure presiding over an island of peace, his opponents criticized his violent suppression of political opponents.

Sihanouk pursued a policy of isolation and neutrality that became increasingly difficult during the Vietnam War. It also exacerbated Cambodia's disconnection from the economic, cultural, and political changes of the time. In 1963 Sihanouk refused U.S. aid, and when U.S. troops entered the war in 1965, he broke off diplomatic ties with the United States. In 1970, a coup supported by the United States deposed Sihanouk and installed his defense minister, Lon Nol (1913–1985). The country was renamed the Khmer Republic and the monarchy was abolished. As a result, Cambodian Communist movement, the Khmer Rouge, which opposed the American-backed Lon Nol government, gained increasing support. Support came from Chinese and Vietnamese Communist organizations and from Sihanouk. Students, teachers, and intellectuals joined, and the Khmer Rouge significantly increased its base. From 1970 to 1975, Cambodia was plunged into civil war, and the eastern provinces were bombed by the United States in the secret mission Operation Breakfast. This created massive displacement and famine.

Khmer Rouge

The Khmer Rouge ruled Cambodia from April 1975 to January 1979. At the time they took over and renamed the country Democratic Kampuchea, no one could foresee the violence that would follow. No single explanation for what happened can suffice. Rather it was the convergence of particular events, in a particular place and juncture in history, that allowed the situation to unfold. The factors are subject to scholarly debate. They include the experience of the Khmer Communists in the Indochina Communist Party, the isolation of the Khmer Rouge in the jungle since 1962, the experience of the Khmer Rouge leadership in France when the French Communists were in their most Stalinist period, the association with Sihanouk, the displacement of the population during the war, the absence of any foreign presence, and the severe lack of food and infrastructure in Cambodia in 1975.

On 17 April 1975 the Khmer Rouge entered Phnom Penh, declared victory, and ordered the evacuation of the city. The Khmer Rouge was a Maoist-inspired group who believed that the Cambodian revolution was unique in the history of the world. After a visit to China, where Chinese premier Chou En-lai (1898–1976) counseled them to move slowly in order to avoid the mistakes China had made in the Great Leap Forward, they proclaimed, "Our country's place in history will be assured. We will be the first nation to create a completely communist society without wasting time on intermediate steps."

The Khmer Rouge embarked on a massive social reengineering project, which was implemented with Stalinist terror. Criticizing the corrupting power of modernization, the Khmer Rouge emptied the cities, forced the population into agricultural collectives, closed the country to outside influences, and outlawed money, private property, and organized religion. Cambodia was turned into a massive agricultural work camp laboring under the rulers' obsessive compulsion for self-reliance, which drove them to demand two rice crops a year.

The Khmer Rouge coveted secrecy. Its authority was *angka*, the organization. *Angka* produced few written documents. The identity of the leaders was unknown for some time. Eventually it became clear that Pol Pot (c. 1925–1998) was Brother Number 1. A pseudonym for Saloth Sar, Pol Pot was a former teacher who had been educated in France. His brother-in-law, Ieng Sary, was Brother Number 2, Son Sen was minister of defense, and Khieu Samphan was president. The Khmer Rouge became increasingly paranoid over time and purged many of its own inner circle. An estimated 1 to 3 million people perished from starvation, disease, and state-sponsored killings during the Khmer Rouge period.

The People's Republic of Kampuchea

The Khmer Rouge period ended almost as abruptly as it began. On 25 December 1978, responding to Khmer Rouge attacks inside Vietnamese territory, Vietnamese forces entered Cambodia, pushed the Khmer Rouge to the Thai border, and began their ten-year armed occupation of the country. Three days later, they announced the formation of the People's Republic of Kampuchea (PRK), a government based on a Vietnamese Communist model, and named as president Heng Samrin, a former Khmer Rouge officer who had fled to Vietnam.

The PRK did not receive widespread legitimacy in Cambodia or in the international community. It was not seated at the United Nations, was refused U.N. aid, and was boycotted by the United States. A three-part resistance movement was formed on the Thai border, which was composed of the Khmer Rouge, FUNCINPEC (the royalist resistance group organized by Sihanouk), and the Khmer People's National Liberation Front (KPNLF), organized by former Prime Minister Son Sann. More than 300,000 refugees lived in refugee camps on the Thai-Cambodia border. In 1985 internal power shifted within the PRK, and Hun Sen, another former low-level Khmer Rouge officer, became prime minister. In 1989, the PRK changed its name to the State of Cambodia (SOC).

The Paris Peace Talks and UNTAC

In the early 1990s, the Cambodian conflict was perceived as a leftover remnant of the Cold War. The Paris Peace Agreement was signed on 23 October

1991. It was a compromise solution worked out by foreigners to end international assistance to the warring factions and to transform the military conflict into a civil one. This was to be accomplished through an election—a peaceful transition of power.

The United Nations Transitional Authority in Cambodia (UNTAC) was the largest and most expensive peacekeeping mission the U.N. had ever undertaken. Its mandate was to create a neutral political environment by disarming the four factions—FUNCINPEC, DK, KPNLF, and SOC. This did not happen. The SOC refused to relinquish control to UNTAC, and the Khmer Rouge pulled out of the process. They refused to disarm, stopped cooperating with UNTAC, and boycotted the election. This meant that none of the factions could be demobilized, a fact that ultimately strengthened the existing SOC structure. The SOC maintained control of the bureaucracy, army, police, media, and judicial system. UNTAC's successes were limited to repatriating the 300,000 refugees from the Thai border, promoting human-rights awareness and voter education, and organizing the election.

The election was held on schedule in May 1993, despite the flawed political environment. Ignoring threats to their personal safety, over 90 percent of the registered voters voted. FUNCINPEC won a plurality of votes, and the SOC's Cambodian People's Party (CPP) came in second. Hun Sen refused to acknowledge the results, however, and threatened to resume civil war. After some confusion, and contrary to the U.N. mandate, Sihanouk brokered a power-sharing agreement whereby FUNCINPEC's Prince Norodom Ranariddh became first prime minister, and Hun Sen became second prime minister. This created parallel structures throughout all levels of government, based on previous hierarchical patterns of patron-client networks. FUNCINPEC and CPP operated as factions more than as political parties, each maintaining their own army and police force. The CPP remained, as it had during UNTAC time, in control of the system.

Cambodia to the End of the 1990s

The coalition, never workable, unraveled in the mid-1990s. Rural commune elections scheduled for 1997, and parliamentary elections scheduled for 1998, loomed as potential sources of conflict. In spring 1997 Hun Sen provoked a rift within FUNCINPEC. In March his bodyguards were implicated when nineteen people were killed in a grenade attack on a peaceful demonstration led by opposition leader Sam Rainsy outside the National Assembly. In July he ousted the first prime minister in a violent confrontation.

Paralleling the disintegration of the coalition was the disintegration of the Khmer Rouge. The two were not unrelated. In August 1996, Ieng Sary, who controlled the northwest city of Pailin, had defected, bringing ten thousand Khmer Rouge troops into the government forces. In return, Ieng Sary had been granted amnesty and allowed to maintain control of Pailin. From then, the two prime ministers began to compete for the remaining Khmer Rouge. Both framed their appeal under the guise of national reconciliation. In spring 1997, in response to reports that Khmer Rouge soldiers were negotiating with Ranariddh, Pol Pot ordered the killing of Son Sen (Pol Pot's former defense minister), his wife, and twelve other members of his family. In July, on the pretext that Ranariddh was illegally negotiating with the Khmer Rouge, Hun Sen staged his ouster.

The confrontation exploded in two days of street fighting in Phnom Penh. Over a hundred people were killed, many having been tortured and executed. Ranariddh and other opposition leaders were forced into exile. As a result, Cambodia lost its seat at the U.N. and its entrance into the Association of Southeast Asian Nations (ASEAN) was delayed.

In the spring of 1998, under pressure from the international community and wanting to legitimize his rule, Hun Sen agreed to let the opposition return and participate in the election of August 1998. The results of that election were contested by both FUNCINPEC and the Sam Rainsy organization. The CPP won a plurality but not enough votes to form a government without a coalition. Initially the opposition parties refused to join and protesters filled the streets of Phnom Penh. After negotiations with the king, FUNCINPEC eventually agreed to enter a coalition and a government was formed in November 1998.

Jeanne Morel

See also: **Angkor Wat; Cambodia—Political System; Cambodia—Profile; Hun Sen; Khmer Rouge; Phnom Penh; Ranariddh, Norodom; Sihanouk, Norodom; United Nations Transitional Authority in Cambodia**

Further Reading

Ang, Choulean, Eric Prenowitz, and Ashley Thompson. (1996) *Angkor: Past, Present, and Future.* Phnom Penh, Cambodia: Apsara.

Chandler, David. (1996) *A History of Cambodia.* 2d ed. Boulder, CO: Westview Press.

Hedler, Steven, and Judy Legerwood. (1996) "Politics of Violence: An Introduction." In *Propaganda, Politics, and Violence in Cambodia, Democratic Transition under United Nations Peace-Keeping.* New York: M. E. Sharpe.

Hendrickson, Dylan, ed. (1998) *Accord: An International Review of Peace Initiatives* 5. London: Conciliation Resources.

Jackson, Karl D. (1989) *Cambodia 1975—1978 Rendezvous with Death.* Princeton, NJ: Princeton University Press.

Osborne, Milton. (1994) *Sihanouk: Prince of Light, Prince of Darkness.* Honolulu, HI, University of Hawaii Press.

CAMBODIA—POLITICAL SYSTEM

Cambodia's political system is a product both of the country's troubled and oftentimes turbulent modern history and of factors rooted deeply in its premodern development. This article examines the political and governmental units that constitute Cambodia's political system and explores the political system in terms of its current structures and its historical development.

Structure of the Contemporary Political System

Cambodia's system of government officially is a multiparty liberal democracy under a constitutional monarchy. This system was established and adopted in September 1993, after the conclusion of a process of political reconstruction sponsored and overseen by the United Nations. King Norodom Sihanouk, who had first assumed the throne in 1941, before abdicating in favor of his father in 1954, returned as chief of state after the conclusion of that process. Under the framework established by the constitution, the king serves as the head of state for life. Possibly in response to the very active and often controversial roles Sihanouk has played in the political process in Cambodia since independence, the constitutional framework also clearly articulates that the king reigns but does not govern and is to serve as the symbol of the unity and continuity of the nation. The head of government, elected in 1998, is Prime Minister Hun Sen, whose appointment was officially made by the monarch after a vote of confidence by the National Assembly.

The National Assembly constitutes the first of the two legislative branches of the system of government. Its 122 members are elected by popular vote to serve five-year terms in parliament. The July 1998 elections resulted in a victory by Hun Sen's Cambodian People's Party (CPP), which secured 41 percent of the vote, and therefore 64 seats in the assembly. The CPP's major opponents were the royalist FUNCINPEC (Front Uni National pour un Cambodge Indépendant, Neutre, Pacifique, et Coopératif; National United Front for an Independent, Neutral, Peaceful, and Cooperative Cambodia) party (32 percent of the vote and 43 seats) and the Sam Rainsy Party (14 percent of the vote and 15 seats). The second legislative branch of the government is the Senate. It was formed following the November 1998 coalition agreement signed between

THE PREAMBLE TO
THE CONSTITUTION OF CAMBODIA

Adopted 21 September 1993

We, the People of Cambodia

Accustomed to having been an outstanding civilization, a prosperous, large, flourishing and glorious nation, with high prestige radiating like a diamond

Having declined grievously during the past two decades, having gone through suffering and destruction, and having been weakened terribly,

Having awakened and resolutely rallied and determined to unite for the consolidation of national unity, the preservation and defense of Cambodia's territory and precious sovereignty and the fine Angkor civilization, and the restoration of Cambodia into an "Island of Peace" based on multi-party liberal democratic responsibility for the nation's future destiny of moving toward perpetual progress, development, prosperity, and glory,

With This Resolute Will

We inscribe the following as the Constitution of the Kingdom of Cambodia:

Source: Cambodia Information Center. Retrieved 8 March 2002, from: http://www.cambodia.org/facts/constitution.html#Preamble.

the CPP and FUNCINPEC, which settled an impasse over FUNCINPEC allegations of electoral discrepancies in the July elections. The Senate currently has 61 members, whose appointments are officially made by the king, who also nominates two of its members. Of these appointments, CPP recommended 31 members, FUNCINPEC 21 members, and the Sam Rainsy Party 7 members.

The system of government also provides for an independent judiciary. At the head of the judiciary is the Supreme Council of the Magistracy, which was provided for in the 1993 constitution, and which was eventually formed in December 1997. Judicial authority is exercised through a supreme court and lower provincial courts.

Development of the Cambodian Political System

Examining Cambodia's political system only in terms of the formal structures that were adopted as a part of the United Nations–sponsored peace process would lead to a substantially skewed understanding of the system. An appreciation for Cambodia's historical development is essential to understand the nature of the country's political system completely. In particular, we need to account for the development of the political culture that has dominated Cambodia since the Angkor era (eighth to thirteenth centuries CE), when the Khmer ruled the most powerful state in Southeast Asia. We also need to account for the destructive legacies of Cambodia's more recent past, which left the local political scene fractured and factionalized.

Cambodia's political culture has been established upon a complex system of patron-client relations. The roots of this system are grounded in the Angkor era, which began with the consecration of a united Khmer state under King Jayavarman II. In 802 CE Jayavarman participated in a religious ritual that celebrated the cult of the God-King (*devaraja*), and in which he became a universal monarch (*chakravartin*). These events provided the foundations of a political culture in which

Two Cambodian women in Phnom Penh with voter registration forms in 1992. (CATHERINE KARNOW/CORBIS)

leaders are distanced from their subjects, and that does not recognize an obligation for those with power to serve the interests of those over whom that power is exercised. The legacy of the political culture is that power, in the Cambodian political environment, has become an end in itself—those with authority seeking to become more powerful without regard for the lives of those over whom they exercise that power.

That attitude, which for centuries has facilitated the rise of leaders with no sense of accountability to those they lead, was institutionalized in modern Cambodia with the political rise of Norodom Sihanouk. Selected by Cambodia's French colonial masters to assume the throne because of a perception he would be easily manipulated, Sihanouk soon turned on the French and was credited with achieving independence for Cambodia in 1953. Over the next several years, especially after he had abdicated the throne but retained his royal credentials, Sihanouk established a political system that placed him firmly at its center and that gave him almost absolute control over the levers of power. While the veneer of democracy was maintained with a National Assembly and national congresses, through which the people could take their grievances directly to Sihanouk, power was effectively concentrated in the hands of one person, who seemed able to do as he pleased without responding to voices of his constituents.

The political system revealed its inherent weakness when Sihanouk was eventually deposed by the National Assembly in 1970. Without the apparatuses, institutions, or historical precedents to facilitate reasoned debate, or even to tolerate opposing voices and figures of opposition, the political system was cast aside in favor of armed conflict. While the regime that deposed Sihanouk tried to reorient the political system, dispensing with the monarchy and embracing re-

publicanism, its fundamental tenets remained unchanged. Cambodia's new ruler, Lon Nol, adopted an authoritarian approach to ruling Cambodia and ignored many of the new democratic political institutions he had established.

Sihanouk was cast outside Lon Nol's political system and aligned himself with the communist Khmer Rouge, who assumed power in 1975. Maintaining the authoritarianism of their predecessors, the Communists continued to see no relationship between rulers and ruled and established participatory institutions in name only. When the Khmer Rouge was ousted in 1979, Cambodia's new Vietnamese-sponsored rulers again refused to allow those with alternative political ideas to participate in their system. Instead, opposition groups camped on the Thai-Cambodian border and waged war with the ruling regime for more than a decade.

The Paris Peace Agreements, signed on 23 October 1991, were intended to lay the groundwork for the establishment of a political system based on a pluralistic democracy. The peace agreements provided for the conduct of national elections, through which a constituent assembly could be elected and a new constitution could be promulgated. While the new constitution that eventually was adopted provided the framework for governance discussed above, it failed to account for the authoritarian political culture that has evolved in Cambodia for more than a millennium. The result is that many of the institutions and processes established by the 1993 constitution have been ignored by Cambodia's post-1993 political leaders. The National Assembly rarely debates issues of pressing national concern, the Senate is largely inactive, few commentators would attest that the judiciary is independent, and political violence—directed especially at opposition political figures—remains endemic.

David M. Ayres

See also: **Buddhist Liberal Democratic Party; Cambodia—Civil War of 1970–1975; Cambodian People's Party; FUNCINPEC; Heng Samrin; Hun Sen; Khmer Rouge; Killing Fields; Lon Nol; Phnom Penh Evacuation; Pol Pot; Ranariddh, Norodom; Sam Rainsy; Samphan, Khieu; Sihanouk, Norodom; United Nations Transitional Authority in Cambodia**

Further Reading

Brown, Macalister, and Joseph Zasloff. (1998) *Cambodia Confounds the Peacemakers, 1979–1998.* Ithaca, NY: Cornell University Press.

Chandler, David. (1991) *The Tragedy of Cambodian History: Politics, War, and Revolution since 1945.* Bangkok, Thailand: Silkworm Press.

International Crisis Group. (2000) *Cambodia: The Elusive Peace Dividend*. Phnom Penh, Cambodia: ICG.

Lizée, Pierre. (2000) *Peace, Power, and Resistance in Cambodia: Global Governance and the Failure of International Conflict Resolution*. London: Macmillan.

CAMBODIA-LAOS RELATIONS

As neighboring nations, Laos and Cambodia have passed through many difficult phases in their relations. Territorial acquisition in the historical period, a shared 535-kilometer border, and similar experiences at the hands of the French and the United States have affected relations between the two nations. Ethnic Lao are found in Rotanak Kiri, Preah Vihear, and Banteay Meanchey Provinces in Cambodia, and Khmer live in Champassak and Attapeu Provinces in Laos.

Interaction Prior to the Twentieth Century

The political and cultural interactions between the two countries were shaped by expanding kingdoms in ancient and medieval times, as the Khmer ruins at Wat Pho and in southern Laos suggest. Cambodian kingdoms such as Funan, Chenla, and Angkor controlled parts of Laos, and some Khmer Brahmanical and Buddhist elements penetrated into Laos. The Indianized state of Funan began to disintegrate in the middle of the sixth century. Chenla, its vassal state, had its capital at Sresthapura in southern Laos. The central and upper regions of Laos were occupied by Chenla ruler Jayavarman I (reigned 657–681). Jayavarman II (c. 770–850), the ruler of Angkor, even had built a hospital at Sai Fong.

Laos was unified after the Lao prince Fa Ngum rose to power in 1353. He established the state of Lan Xang (million elephants) in 1353 with the help of Angkor king Jayavarman Paramesvara, and his kingdom extended from Sipsong Panna in the upper Mekong to northern Cambodia. Fa Ngum's queen, Jayavarman's daughter, was responsible for converting the people to Theravada Buddhism, and Fa Ngum received from his father-in-law a gold statue of the Buddha, Pali scriptures, and a mission of monks under Phra Mahapasaman. The statue, called Prabang, was installed at Fa Ngum's capital, which was renamed Luang Prabang.

The Colonial Period

The next important stage in Lao-Cambodian relations was set when the three Indochinese nations (Cambodia, Laos, and Vietnam) came under French colonial rule. Laos became a French protectorate in 1893, the Indochinese Union was created in 1907, and the fates of the Indochinese nations were linked as a French colony. Vietnam, the most powerful of the three, held the dominant position. Outsiders such as the French, Chinese, and even Vietnamese exercised control over the two other countries' administration and economy, and the concept of an Indochinese federation was frequently raised. At the Treaty of Versailles at the end of World War I, Ho Chi Minh (1890–1969), the Vietnamese revolutionary, pleaded for self-determination for the Indochinese people.

Strains of nationalism developed in the three countries, with different intensity and ideologies, but a Communist-led nationalism was common to all. The French reestablished control of Indochina after World War II, leading to the First Indochina War (1946–1954), in which Vietnam's Viet Minh, Cambodia's Khmer Issarak, and Laos's Pathet Lao fought against the French. On 1 March 1951, a Viet-Khmer-Lao alliance was formed with the goal of defeating the colonial masters and achieving real independence.

The Vietnam War Era

After the Geneva Conference of 1954, Laos and Cambodia went their separate ways, but their destinies again became closely intertwined in 1960s. Cambodia was a party to the Geneva Accords of 1962, which dealt with the fate of Laos. Cambodia's Prince Norodom Sihanouk (b.1922) was in favor of a neutral Laos and made efforts to end its civil war.

With the escalation of the conflict between the United States and North Vietnam, Laos and Cambodia became increasingly involved in the Vietnam War. The Ho Chi Minh Trail—a supply route from North to South Vietnam that the United States wanted to cut—passed through both countries. Hanoi's primary aim was unification of both Vietnams.

In Cambodia, the coup by General Lon Nol (1913–1985) on 18 March 1970 added a new dimension to the turmoil. On April 21, the United Indochinese Front was established. The summit conference was attended by Pham Van Dong representing North Vietnam, Norodom Sihanouk as head of the National United Front of Cambodia, Souphanouvong (1909–1995) from the Pathet Lao, and Nguyen Huu Tho, representing the provisional government of South Vietnam. The delegates pleaded for solidarity among peoples of Indochina.

The Communists strengthened their position in the border regions of Laos, South Vietnam, and Cambodia while at the same time there was increasing cooperation between General Lon Nol and the rightist leaders in Laos. It was even suggested that a defensive alliance of South Vietnam, Cambodia, Thailand, and

Laos be created to combat the Communists. The Communist Pathet Lao and Khmer Rouge were increasing their hold on Laos and Cambodia, respectively, however, and with the departure of the last American troops from Vietnam and the fall of Saigon in 1975, the whole of Indochina became Communist.

Fallen Comrades: Battlefield to Marketplace, 1975–Present

Peace in Indochina proved elusive, however, and the former comrades soon went to war again. Vietnam invaded Cambodia in December 1977 to overthrow the brutal regime of Pol Pot, who rejected Souphanouvong's peace initiative. Laos signed a friendship treaty with Vietnam in July 1977, but relations between Cambodia and Vietnam were deteriorating. The Vietnamese attack on Cambodia in December 1978 and the Chinese attack on Vietnam in February 1979 changed the scenario, and Laos and Cambodia's relations cooled. Laos dispatched a token number of troops to Cambodia to help the Vietnamese. After the installation of the Heng Samrin regime in Cambodia, the two countries again became close and signed a cooperation agreement in March 1979. The Indochinese Federation and United Resistance (1979–1984) targeted China as the main enemy, and Vietnam's hegemony over Indochina was again established.

The Indochinese states have been moving towards reconciliation and greater regional cooperation, with "market economy" as their new mantra. Laos and Cambodia have begun multilateral cooperation through the Association of Southeast Asian Nations (ASEAN) and the Mekong River Commission. They are also cooperating in tourism, fisheries, wildlife, national biodiversity conservation, and the preservation of historic sites. As a sign of this improved relationship, a boundary demarcation project was launched in February 2001, and Laos and Cambodia can again look to the future with renewed hope.

Patit Paban Mishra

Further Reading
Mishra, Patit Paban. (1999) *A Contemporary History of Laos.* New Delhi: National Book Organization.
Stuart-Fox, Martin. (1997) *A History of Laos.* Cambridge, U.K.: Cambridge University Press.

CAMBODIA-VIETNAM RELATIONS
Formal contacts between Vietnam and Cambodia date back to the early seventeenth century, when Cambodia was the stronger of the two countries. Prior to the seventeenth century the two countries did not share a common border since the kingdom of Champa still existed in central Vietnam. As Vietnam gradually absorbed Champa and expanded southward, contacts with Cambodia were established and increased. The second half of that century saw a shift in strength and the first two Vietnamese military interventions in Cambodia. Both interventions followed requests by members of the Cambodian royal family for military support in succession struggles. Vietnam's first formal annexation of Cambodian territory took place in 1698, and by the end of the eighteenth century Vietnam had expanded southwards to the shores of the Gulf of Thailand.

During the first half of the nineteenth century, Vietnam's influence over Cambodia increased, leading to de facto administrative control over the central and eastern parts of the country in the 1830s and early 1840s. During this period Vietnam temporarily gained the upper hand over Thailand in the competition for influence in Cambodia. However, Thailand never completely lost its influence as the western and northwestern parts of Cambodia remained under Thai control or influence up to the arrival of the French in the 1860s.

Since the end of the French colonial era in the mid-1950s, relations between Cambodia and Vietnam have been complex and characterized by periods of open hostility and warfare. Cambodia was dragged into the expanding Vietnam War in the late 1960s and early 1970s. After the end of the wars in both countries in 1975, relations between Cambodia and Vietnam were tense; they deteriorated sharply in 1977 and 1978, leading to full warfare. The Vietnamese military intervention on 25 December 1978 resulted in the overthrow of the existing government in Cambodia and a Vietnamese presence that would last for over a decade. Following the Vietnamese withdrawal in 1989, relations have been manageable but with recurring differences relating to two main issues: the situation of the ethnic Vietnamese minority in Cambodia and the disputed border between the two countries.

Relations from the 1950s until 1975
Following the end of the French Indochina War in the mid-1950s, independent Cambodia experienced good relations with the Democratic Republic of Vietnam (North Vietnam) but less amicable relations with the Republic of Vietnam (South Vietnam). During the 1960s relations between Cambodia and the National Liberation Front (NLF) in South Vietnam were good, and this led to increased tension between Cambodia and the South Vietnamese government. Following the

overthrow of Prince Norodom Sihanouk in early 1970, relations between Cambodia and South Vietnam improved, but Cambodia's relations with North Vietnam and the NLF deteriorated sharply because the leadership of Cambodia's new regime was opposed to the foreign policy of the overthrown government. Cambodia was also directly drawn into the expanding Vietnam War. The political changes in Cambodia were followed by a wave of attacks on ethnic Vietnamese in Cambodia. The ethnic Vietnamese in Cambodia were caught in an upsurge of officially mandated anti-Vietnamese sentiments that linked them to the military presence of North Vietnam and NLF armed forces in Cambodia. Large numbers of Vietnamese fled Cambodia for South Vietnam. In the early 1970s, the exiled Prince Sihanouk and the Cambodia Communist Party (also known as the Khmer Rouge or Red Khmers) formed an alliance, which was supported by North Vietnam.

Relations from 1975 to 1978

Following the end of the wars in both Cambodia and Vietnam in April 1975, relations between the two countries, now both ruled by Communists, were expected to be good, but this was not the case. Most of Cambodia's remaining ethnic Vietnamese were driven out, and military clashes occurred along the border in May and June 1975. During the second half of 1975 and throughout 1976 the situation along the border remained stable. Then, in early 1977, Cambodia gradually increased activity, escalating to military attacks, to emphasize its claims to certain areas that were under Vietnamese control. Eventually Vietnam responded by attacking Cambodia, and by the end of 1977 the two countries were in a de facto state of war. On 25 December, Vietnam launched an intervention that resulted in its takeover of Phnom Penh on 7 January 1978.

Relations from 1979 to 1991

Vietnam's military intervention brought down the Cambodian government, but the overthrown leadership was not captured. In early January 1979, a new government was formed in Phnom Penh by Cambodians who had earlier taken refuge in Vietnam and who opposed the former government. The new administration, with Vietnamese support, gained control of the major populated areas, but the deposed government remained militarily active in rural areas, particularly along the Thai border. This situation prevailed for most of the 1980s. Vietnam gradually withdrew from Cambodia, its last troops leaving in September 1989.

During the 1980s, people who had sought refuge in Vietnam in the 1975–1978 period began to return to Cambodia. Those returning included not only ethnic Khmers but also ethnic Vietnamese, leading to the reemergence of a Vietnamese minority in Cambodia. The official policy of the Cambodian authorities was to regulate Vietnamese migration to Cambodia but not to prevent it.

Relations since 1991

Following the Paris Agreements of 23 October 1991, which officially ended the Cambodian conflict, the United Nations carried out an ambitious peace-keeping operation, leading up to general elections in May 1993. During this period relations with Vietnam came to focus mainly on the repeated attacks on the ethnic Vietnamese in Cambodia. Most of the attacks were attributed to the Party of Democratic Kampuchea (PDK); some, however, may have been carried out by ordinary Cambodians encouraged by the anti-Vietnamese rhetoric of the PDK and other parties. Such violence has continued to be an issue of concern between the Cambodian coalition governments and Vietnam and has been broadened to include the Cambodian government's policies towards the Vietnamese minority.

Another issue in bilateral relations has been how to manage the disputed borders—both on land and at sea. Overall the two countries desire to resolve the disputed issues, and they have initiated talks both on border issues and on the issue of violence toward ethnic Vietnamese.

Ramses Amer

See also: **United Nations Transitional Authority in Cambodia**

Further Reading

Amer, Ramses. (1997) "The Border Conflicts Between Cambodia and Vietnam." *Boundary and Security Bulletin* 5, 2 (Summer): 80–91.

———. (1994) "The Ethnic Vietnamese in Cambodia—A Minority at Risk?" *Contemporary Southeast Asia* 16, 2 (September): 210–238.

Evans, Grant, and Kelvin Rowley.(1984) *Red Brotherhood at War: Indochina Since the Fall of Saigon.* London: Verso Editions.

CAMBODIAN PEOPLE'S PARTY The Cambodian People's Party (CPP) was founded in 1951, when the Khmer People's Revolutionary Party (KPRP) was formed. The party maintained its historical continuity from that date, distancing itself from the Party of Democratic Kampuchea (Khmer Rouge), which was formed at a KPRP congress in 1960. When the Khmer Rouge regime was ousted in 1979, the KPRP assumed state power in Cambodia and ruled the country until 1991. In October 1991, as Cambodia prepared for national elections under the supervision of the United Nations, the CPP officially abandoned its Marxist-Leninist roots and embraced the free market.

The CPP lost the 1993 elections to the royalist FUNCINPEC party (National United Front for an Independent, Neutral, Peaceful, and Cooperative Cambodia). With control of much of the army, security forces, and local administration, the CPP forced itself into a coalition government, with its leader, Hun Sen, named second prime minister. In 1997 Hun Sen led a coup against FUNCINPEC first prime minister Norodom Ranariddh. While a FUNCINPEC official, Ung Huot, maintained the position of first prime minister, Hun Sen's rule over the country was virtually unopposed. The CPP won the majority of seats at the July 1998 elections, with Hun Sen assuming the role of the sole prime minister of Cambodia.

David M. Ayres

Further Reading

Brown, Macalister, and Joseph Zasloff. (1998) *Cambodia Confounds the Peacemakers, 1979–1998*. Ithaca, NY: Cornell University Press.
Vickery, Michael. (1994) "The Cambodian People's Party: Where Has It Come from, Where Is It Going?" *Southeast Asian Affairs*: 102–17.

CAMEL, ARVANA DROMEDARY

The dromedary, or one-humped camel (*Camelus dromedarius*), is considered a semidomesticated animal, freely ranging but under the herder's control. The Arvana breed developed in Turkmenistan in antiquity and may have been domesticated there 5,000 to 6,000 years ago (separately from the Arabian dromedary). Rock drawings of dromedaries dated 3000–1500 BCE occur in northern Turkmenistan. The Seljuks probably introduced camels to Turkey, Iran, and Afghanistan during their conquests in the twelfth century. For Turkmen tribes in the Kara-Kum Desert, Arvana camels supply milk, meat, wool, and transportation (as pack and riding animals). Of all dromedary breeds, Arvana camels have the highest milk yield (averaging fifteen kilograms a day), with 4 percent fat. They are reared all over Turkmenistan and in Kazakstan, Uzbekistan, and Azerbaijan. Females are bred when

they are three years old. The average gestation lasts 385 days; females give birth about every two years. The wool (two to three kilograms in an average clipping) is widely used to produce yarn for knitted wear. As beasts of burden, dromedaries are unsurpassed in their ability to cross deserts. In an eight- to ten-hour day Arvana camels can carry packs weighing up to three hundred kilograms for a distance of up to thirty-five kilometers. Males are used for pack service from four to five until fifteen to sixteen years of age.

Victor Fet

Further Reading

Dmitriev, N. G., and L. K. Ernst. (1989) *Animal Genetic Resources of the USSR*. Rome: Animal Production and Health Paper FAO.
Gauthier-Pilthers, H., and A. Dagg. (1981) *The Camel: Its Evolution, Ecology, Behavior, and Relationship to Man*. Chicago: University of Chicago Press.

CAMEL, BACTRIAN

The two-humped Bactrian camel (*Camelus bactrianus*) of Afghanistan, northern China, Mongolia, and the former Soviet Union is valued for its resistance to dry conditions, its ability to travel for long periods with little water or food, and its hardiness to cold weather. While Mongols place great importance on the horse, they often prefer the camel for long-distance movement, across the Gobi Desert, for example. The camel was also the preferred beast on the Silk Road.

The camel was the favorite mount of the Turkish founders of the Seljuk empire (1038–1157), as illustrated by the fact that the Mongolian word for a gelded horse referred to a gelded camel among the Seljuks. Rashid al-Din (c. 1247–1318), the Persian historian,

A man rides a Bactrian camel on the sand dunes near Dunhuang, China. (WOLFGANG KAEHLER/CORBIS)

ENCYCLOPEDIA OF MODERN ASIA

noted that the Turks first invaded Iran and other points in the Middle East because the area provided good grazing land for camels, that is, dry with limited but good grass.

Although camels generally are not considered a food source, some Asians eat camel meat, and *shubat*, fermented camel milk, is a Turkish favorite. Among the Kazakhs, who rank it second only to koumiss from mares in desirability, *shubat* is considered healthful, particularly for tuberculosis prevention and treatment. Kazakhs and other Asians find uses for camel leather as well.

In addition to its economic significance, the camel holds a special position in regional folklore. Camels are considered cantankerous, obstinate, and willful. Genghis Khan's mother compared him to a "randy camel bull snapping at the heels of its young" (Ligeti 1971: 47) after he killed his younger brother during a dispute. Despite its bad reputation, the camel is also considered spirited, and today the "white orphan camel colt" of the popular Mongolian folk song, abandoned by all, pulling up the rear with the heaviest load, has become the very symbol of Mongolia as it tries to catch up to the modern world despite its limitations.

Paul D. Buell

Further Reading
Hare, John. (1998) *The Lost Camels of Tartary : A Quest into Forbidden China*. London: Little, Brown.
Ligeti, Louis, ed. (1971) *Histoire Secrète des Mongols*. Monumenta Linguae Mongolicae Collecta, no. 1. Budapest, Hungary: Akadémiai Kiadó.
Schafer, Edward. (1950) "The Camel in China Down to the Mongol Dynasty." *Sinologica* 2: 65–193.
Seitov, Z. S., K. I. Duysembayev, A. N. Khasenov, V. P. Cherepanova, and V. T. Velokobylenko. (1979) *Kumys shubat* (Kumiss and Camel Kumiss). 3d ed., edited by A. Ye. Orlovskaya. Almaty, Kazakhstan: Kaynar.

CAMERON HIGHLANDS
Cameron Highlands, an area of about 670 square kilometers (260 square miles), is located in peninsular Malaysia, in the northwest corner of the state of Pahang. Its name is strongly associated with tea, farming, and tourism. The tea plantations, begun in the 1920s, are on the steeper slopes and are a mainstay of the Malaysian tea industry. Vegetable farming is carried out by ethnic Chinese farmers mainly in the valleys nearer to the main road leading to the highlands. Per year, intensive farming yields three to four crops, which are exported to Kuala Lumpur, Ipoh, and Singapore. Some slash-and-burn cultivation is also carried out by the

Orang Asli, the indigenous minority peoples of peninsular Malaysia.

With its cooler temperatures (18°–22°C) and a reduced seasonal effect from the monsoons, Cameron Highlands was used as a "change-of-air" station for British officers during the colonial period. Later, it developed into a significant tourism center, with economic activities centered around three townships: Ringlet, Tanah Rata, and Brinchang. Bungalows and hotels, the first of which was constructed in 1934, are available for short- and long-term rentals.

Wong Poh Poh

Further Reading
Clarkson, James D. (1968) *The Cultural Ecology of a Chinese Village: Cameron Highlands, Malaysia*. Chicago: University of Chicago Press.
Shirasaka, S. (1988) "The Agricultural Development of Hill Stations in Tropical Asia: A Case Study in the Cameron Highlands, Malaysia." *Geographical Review of Japan*, 61B, 2: 191–211.

CANDI OF JAVA *Candi* are archaeological treasures from past civilizations in Java. Many originally served as religious monuments, while a number of them also used to be related to the courts of various Javanese kingdoms. There are hundreds of *candi*, large and small, that have been excavated so far. Only a few of them have undergone restoration. The most dense population of *candi* can be found in the interior heartland of Java, as well as in the eastern part of the island. A few *candi*, albeit not as numerous and elaborate in their structure as the *candi* of Java, can also be found in West Java and some parts of Sumatra.

The builders of the *candi* of Java were the various Buddhist and Hindu dynasties ruling Java from the eighth century through the fifteenth century CE. The Hindu kingdom of Mataram was credited with building many of them. The oldest of these excavated *candi* is a complex of *candi* found in the Dieng plateau in central Java. They were built in the late eighth to early ninth centuries.

While most *candi* are Hindu, a number of them were built by Buddhist dynasties. The largest of the *candi* of Java, the Borobudur, was in fact built by the Buddhist dynasty of Sailendra in the ninth century. Covering an area of 15,129 square meters and standing 42 meters high, the Borobudur is one of largest ancient monuments in the world. The most elaborate of the Hindu *candi*, the Prambanan group, was built around half a century after Borobudur was completed.

Built by the Hindu Mataram kingdom, the Prambanan consists of 3 large *candi* surrounded by 224 minor ones. It was built as a commemoration of the return of Hindu rule in Java after the demise of the Buddhist Sailendra. It is also believed that Prambanan was meant as a Hindu's answer to the grandeur of Borobudur.

With the shift of power to the east at the turn of the second millennium, *candi* construction also moved eastward. The major east Java kingdoms, such as Kediri, Singasari, and Majapahit, are credited with building *candi* in this area. While serving in functions similar to those of central Java's *candi*, the east Java variants are rather distinct in their construction material and layout. For instance, while the central Java *candi* are invariably built with andesite, many in east Java, especially from later period (thirteenth to fifteenth centuries under Majapahit), used red bricks. While most of the *candi* in central Java are facing to the east, the east Java ones face to the west.

Irman G. Lanti

Further Reading
Dumarçay, Jacques. (1986) *The Temples of Java*. Translated and edited by Michael Smithies. Singapore: Oxford University Press.
Provincial Government of Central Java, Indonesia. (1982) *Candi in Central Java, Indonesia*. Jakarta, Indonesia: Jayakarta Agung Offset.
Ariswara. (1982) *Temples of Java*. Jakarta, Indonesia: Intermasa.

CANNING, CHARLES JOHN (1812–1862),
Governor-General of the British East India Company. Viscount Charles John Canning of Kilbrahan, County Kilkenny, Ireland, was educated at Eton College and Christ Church in Oxford, England, where he graduated in classics and mathematics in 1832. Entering Parliament in 1836, he became undersecretary of state for foreign affairs in 1841. In 1855, the government of Lord Palmerston (1784–1865), then prime minister, appointed him governor-general of the East India Company's possessions in India, and he assumed office in February 1856.

Canning's career is indelibly associated with the suppression of the first large-scale Indian revolt against British rule (1857–1858), known variously as the Indian Mutiny, the Great Indian Rebellion, or the First War of Indian Independence. He became the first viceroy of British India after the takeover of the territory by the British in 1858. He combined fairness with firmness in his handling of the mutiny and its aftermath, earning the respectful title "Clemency Canning."

He believed that undue harshness and racially motivated punishments of Indians would damage prospects for the reestablishment of peaceful government.

Canning was raised to an earldom in 1859. He initiated major reforms in the armed forces and the finances of the government of India, introducing, for instance, the income tax. The Indian Councils Act of 1861 greatly improved the administrative basis of the empire. Canning retired in March 1862, broken in health and spirit by the death of his beloved wife in 1861. He died in London on 17 June 1862.

Chandika Kaul

Further Reading
Maclagan, Michael. (1962) *"Clemency" Canning*. London: Macmillan.

CANTONESE. See Yue.

CAO DAI
Cao Daism (also called *Dai Dao Tam Ky Pho Do*, Third Revelation of the Great Way) is an indigenous Vietnamese religion centered in Tay Ninh Province in southern Vietnam that was officially founded and first propagated by Ngo Van Chieu (1878–1926), an administrative official in the French colonial administration that ruled Vietnam from the second half of the nineteenth century until 1945. Chieu claimed to have a series of revelations in 1926 that stated that all religions were one. Cao Dai is an amalgam of different beliefs that borrow from Buddhism, Christianity, Confucianism, Taoism, and Western nineteenth-century romanticism and grew under the leadership of its first Supreme Chief, Le Van Trung.

Tenets
Cao Dai (literally "High Palace") is the name of God to the religion's followers, who believe that the history of religion is divided into three major periods of revelation, as told by Chieu's revelations: the Era of Creation (or Era of Innocence), the Era of Progress (or Era of Wars, or Era of Self-Destruction), and the Era of Annihilation (or Era of Preservation). In the first two, individuals chosen by God were given the mission to serve humanity by founding the Great Way and its five branches, Geniism (a Vietnamese indigenous religion), Christianity, Taoism, Confucianism, and Buddhism, each based on the customs of the the people who embraced them.

These religions and their truths, as revealed by their messengers, were to represent all human spirituality.

But the people of the world, through inherent weakness and the multiplicity of those religions, brought about conflict instead of love and peace. In the third period, God gave the world a final liberation, uniting those religions into one religion to bring about ultimate unity.

Cao Daists believe that God created the universe, the plants and animals, and mankind, and to each he gave a part of his spirit. All human beings are brothers and sisters and come from the same God, the father of all. God himself is worshiped in the form of a single eye shining over a pantheon of saints, Buddhas, genies, and immortals that together represent a universal consciousness of which mankind is a part. From a moral standpoint, Cao Daism stresses to people their duties toward themselves, their family, their society, nature, and humanity (the universal family). Philosophically Cao Daists renounce wealth and riches as paths to true spiritual fulfillment and emphasize the control of greed, anger, and desires. Spiritually, Cao Daism endorses reincarnation and teaches meditation and self-cultivation as the way to spiritual elevation and fulfillment. Followers venerate such figures as Sun Yat-sen, Joan of Arc, Vietnamese prophet Tranh Trinh, Julius Caesar, Buddha, Confucius, and Victor Hugo.

Organization

Cao Dai has an elaborate organizational structure. It has a governing body called the Cuu Trung Dai (College of Men) with one *giao tong* (pope) who leads the Cuu Trung Dai. There are three *chuong phap* (legistlative cardinals), one belonging to each of the three legislative branches: the *Nho* (Confucianist), the *Thich* (Buddhist), and the *Dao* (Taoist). There are three *dau su* (cardinals), one for each branch. The *chuong phap* decide on religious laws and the *dau su* have the right to direct, both spiritually and temporally, the so-called Disciples of God or lay faithful, and also have the right to enact laws, which must be submitted for the approval of the pope. Next in line of power are the thirty-six *phoi su* (archbishops), twelve for each branch, with three *chanh phoi su* (principal archbishops). There are seventy-two *giao su* (bishops), twenty-four for each branch, who are responsible for the education of the disciples. The three thousand *giao huu* (priests) are also split evenly among the branches, presiding over ritual ceremonies in the province temples. The *giao huu* are in charge of propagating the religion. There are an unlimited number of *le sanh* (student priests), who are drawn from the most virtuous of the subdignitaries, or *pho tri su*. The *chanh tri su* (minor office-bearers) look after the adepts in the villages. There are also *pho tri su* (subdignitaries) and *thong su*

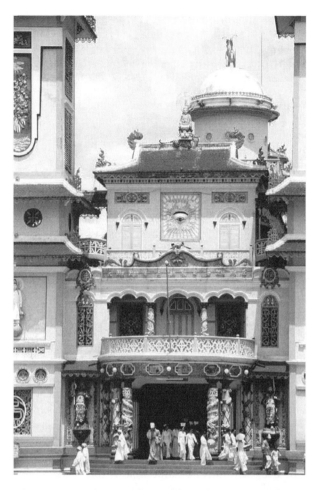

The Cao Dai Holy See and Grand Temple in Tay Ninh, Vietnam, in 1993. The temple was built in 1927. (STEVE RAYMER/ CORBIS)

(religious village administrators). Finally, there are an unlimited number of *tin do* (adepts), or followers, of Cao Dai. Female dignitaries may reach the rank of cardinal only.

In the 1950s the Cao Dai joined the forces opposed to Ngo Dinh rule in the Republic of South Vietnam (RVN). They formed a Cao Dai army and joined a military alliance with the Binh Xuyen gang and the Hoa Hao religious sect that also fought against Diem's forces. The coalition was eventually defeated and a fragile coexistence between the RVN government and the three groups was recognized.

Before the fall of the RVN in 1975, the Cao Dai claimed between 1 and 2 million adherents. The Socialist Republic of Vietnam officially recognized Cao Daism in 1986, and the movement still has its world headquarters in Tay Ninh Province. Today there are perhaps 6 million Cao Daists around the world.

Richard B. Verrone

Further Reading

Cima, Ronald J., ed. (1989) *Vietnam: A Country Study*. Washington, D.C.: U.S. Government Printing Office.

Do, Merdeka Thien-Ly Huong. (1994) *Cao Daiism: An Introduction*. Washington, D.C.: Cao Dai Temple Overseas Center for Dai Dao Studies.

Wallace, Anthony F. C. (1966) *Religion: An Anthropological View*. New York: Random House.

CAO XUEQIN (1715–1763), Chinese author. Cao Xueqin (Ts'ao Hsueh-ch'in) was born in Nanjing into a powerful and wealthy family. Shortly after Cao's birth, the family became involved in political intrigues, falling into disgrace and financial ruin. From 1742, Cao lived in poverty in the western suburbs of Beijing, making a little money selling his own paintings. It was here he wrote *Shitou ji* (The Story of the Stone). Although the manuscript was left unfinished when he died in 1763, hand-written copies with eighty chapters began to appear before long. In 1792, the novel was printed with an additional forty chapters, usually attributed to Gao E, under the title *Honglou meng* (The Dream of the Red Chamber). It is one of the most celebrated novels in the history of Chinese literature. The novel, which has some strong autobiographical elements, focuses on the downfall of the Jia family. The principal characters are Baoyu, who is born from a stone into the Jia family, and Daiyu, who is deeply but unhappily in love with Baoyu. The decline of the Jia family follows the death of one of the daughters who was an imperial consort, but in the end the imperial favors are restored, and Baoyu passes the imperial examinations. The novel has been translated into English several times.

Bent Nielsen

Further Reading

Cao Xueqin. (1973–1986; 1979–1987) *The Story of the Stone: A Chinese Novel in Five Volumes*. Trans. by David Hawkes and John Minford. Harmondsworth, U.K.: Penguin Books; Bloomington, IN: Indiana University Press.

CAPPADOCIA Cappadocia, which used to be known as Katpatuka (Land of Beautiful Horses) in old Persian, is a region in central Anatolia, 300 kilometers southeast of Ankara, the capital city of modern-day Turkey.

Cappadocia is known for its unusual landscape, the result of the violent eruption of volcanoes, Mount Erciyes (3,917 meters) and Mount Hasan (3,268 meters), some 3 million years ago. Lava and volcanic dust and ashes covered the region, which eventually hardened

CAPPADOCIA—WORLD HERITAGE SITE

A UNESCO World Heritage Site since 1985 and a backdrop for *Indiana Jones and the Last Crusade*, Cappadocia is world-renowned for its Byzantine sanctuaries and fourth-century underground towns actually chiseled into its rock face.

into a thick layer of tuff. Over the years, water and wind eroded the soft and brittle volcanic surface, creating deep valleys and many different types of strange rock formations, such as rock cones and fairy chimneys.

Archaeological evidence shows that Cappadocia was inhabited as early as the Paleolithic period (c. 2.5 million BCE –10,000 BCE), and continued to serve as home to the peoples of many different civilizations, including the Hittites, Greeks, and the Romans. Dwellings were dug into the rocks and provided shelter from the environment, defense against foreign invasions, and refuge from religious persecution. These dwellings interconnect, forming some two hundred to three hundred underground cities, equipped with elaborate air ventilation systems, water storage units, and in some cases, even stables and wineries. One of the most famous and well excavated is Kaymakli, where Christians hid from the pagan Roman invaders during the seventh century.

Parts of the underground cities are still used by Cappadocia's present-day inhabitants. For example, underground canals are used to regulate water in the nearby farmland, and local produce, such as potatoes and citrus fruits, is stored in subterranean storage units. People still live in above-ground rock structures, some of which are even used as hotels and inns. Cappadocia is a popular tourist destination, with over a million foreign visitors in 1997.

Junhee Kim

Further Reading

Demir, Omer. (1995) *Cradle of Civilization Cappadocia*. Chennai, India: International Society of the Investigation of Ancient Civilizations.

CARABALLO MOUNTAINS Formed by the merging of the Cordillera Central and the Sierra Madre mountain ranges in north central Luzon Island, the Caraballo Mountains lie in the center of Luzon, the largest island in the Philippines archipelago. The mountains' highest elevation is around 1,680 meters.

The Caraballo Mountains remain one of the few heavily forested areas in the Philippines, and the timber resources of the region are much exploited. The mountainous areas also include watersheds: the Cagayan River, the longest river in the country, begins in the Caraballo Mountains. The river flows northward, providing irrigation water for several provinces.

Some of the least populated areas in the Philippines are located in the Caraballo Mountains. The climate in this area is relatively mild, with a dry season from November to February and a wet season from May to October. The area is situated outside the direct path of typhoons.

The Caraballo Mountains witnessed heavy battles at the end of the Second World War. After U.S. troops recaptured Manila in early 1945, General Yamashita Tomoyuki, the Japanese commander of the occupation troops in the Philippines, retreated with around 120,000 soldiers to the Caraballo Mountains and the Cordillera Central. This densely forested area with its numerous mountain passes and caves formed a natural defense line for the Japanese. Intensive fighting continued for several weeks, leading to losses on both sides. With the help of Filipino guides, U.S. troops managed to outmaneuver the Japanese, forcing them to surrender.

Several ethnic groups inhabit the Caraballo and Cordillera Mountains. One tribe, the Ikalahan, controls almost 15,000 hectares of tribal lands in the mountains and is preserving them from agricultural development while protecting the forests and watersheds. Using wild fruits growing in the forests, the Ikalahan produce fruit products, which they sell in urban markets, and are planning to do the same with orchids, truffles, and mushrooms.

Rafis Abazov

Further Reading

Kummer, David. (1992) *Deforestation in the Postwar Philippines.* Geography Research Papers, no. 234. Chicago, IL: University of Chicago Press.

Sides, Hampton. (2001) *Ghost Soldiers: The Forgotten Epic Story of World War II's Most Dramatic Mission.* New York: Doubleday.

Steinberg, David J. (1994) *The Philippines.* 3d ed. Boulder, CO: Westview Press.

CARAVANS The English word "caravan" comes from the Persian word *karwan*, used throughout Cen-

tral Asia to signify an organized, traveling column of animals, people, and cargo. Before the advent of motorized transport, a caravan following the Silk Road between China and the Middle East might consist of a thousand or more Bactrian (two-humped) camels each carrying several hundred pounds of goods or passengers, slung in panniers on the camel's back. Depending on caravan size and cargo, a caravan chief's staff might consist of a guide, accountant, supervisor of food and campsite, and security detail for defense against bandits, as well as scores of camel drivers, one for every twenty or thirty camels. The convoy might also include horses, a few dromedary camels for riding, guard dogs, and sheep.

Commercial caravans were best suited to carry compact, valuable, imperishable goods. Silks, spices, jade, brass, coral, and rhubarb roots once figured in the east-west trade; in the twenty-first century illegal narcotics have met the criteria for caravan transport in remote areas of Central Asia.

The normal pace of Bactrian camels, between two and three miles an hour or roughly thirty miles a day, determined a caravan's speed; wells could be fifty or even a hundred miles apart. Camels could go without water for three days, perhaps four if travel was by night, as it often was in East Turkistan's Taklimakan Desert.

A caravansary or caravan inn, with sleeping alcoves in tiers around a courtyard, usually lay at the end of each day's stage. At a prosperous oasis city such as Samarqand, caravansaries clustered around a city gate. Sometimes a day's stage ended in the countryside at a fortified caravansary or *rabat*, which resembled a small town with a market, café, bath *(hammam)*, latrines, and perhaps a small mosque.

SAFRONBOLU—WORLD HERITAGE SITE

Safronbolu was an important stop for trade caravans en route to Europe or Asia; the architecture in this Turkish city became the model for urban development in the Ottoman empire. Designated a UNESCO World Heritage Site in 1994, the city contains classic wood and stone dwellings.

The ruins of Rabat-i-Sangbast, twenty-four miles south of Mashhad in modern Iran, lie at the intersection of three historic caravan routes, one from the Mediterranean via Hamadan and Neyshabur, another from India via Herat, and a third from China via Samarqand and Mary (former Merv).

David Nalle

Further Reading
Bugnon, Didier. (1707) *Rélations exacte concernant les Caravanes ou cortèges des Marchands d'Asie* (Exact Accounts of the Caravans or Corteges of Asian Merchants). Nancy, France (no publisher). Rare Book Collection, Library of Congress.

Grant, C. P. (1937) *The Syrian Desert: Caravans, Travel, and Exploration.* London: A. C. Black.

Lattimore, Owen. (1995) *The Desert Road to Turkestan.* Tokyo and New York: Kodansha International.

O'Kane, Bernard. (1987) *Timurid Architecture in Khurasan.* Costa Mesa, CA: Mazda.

Pope, Arthur Upham. (1969) *Persian Architecture.* London: Oxford University Press.

Sauvaget, Jean. (1939–1940) "Caravansérails syrien du moyen age" (Syrian Medieval Caravansaries). *Ars Islamica* 1, 2.

Thaxton, Wheeler, trans. (1989) *A Century of Princes (Report on a Timurid Delegation, 1419).* Cambridge, MA: Agha Khan Program for Islamic Architecture.

Wellard, James. (1977) *Samarkand and Beyond: A History of Desert Caravans.* London: Constable.

CARDAMON MOUNTAINS

The Chuor Phnom Kravanh (Cardamon Mountains) in southwest Cambodia derive their title from the spice of the same name. Generally oriented on a northwest-southeast axis, this range of high hills extends somewhat discontinuously for approximately 160 kilometers west from the Chuor Phnom Damrei (Elephant Range) to the Thailand border. Dense tropical forests cover the western slopes, where annual rainfall averages 3,800–5,000 millimeters, while the eastern slopes along the interior plain rarely exceed 1,500 millimeters. The highest mountain in Cambodia, Phnom Aural (1,813 meters), is located near Pouthisat, between Kompong Chang and Kompong Speu provinces, while farther west, the elevation reaches 1,563 meters.

Sparsely populated by Dravidian peoples who commercially grew cardamoms and pepper until 1975, the Cardamon Mountains were a stronghold for soldiers of the Khmer Rouge (Cambodian Reds) as recently as 1998. The area retains a high degree of biodiversity, and several species once presumed extinct have recently been discovered alive in the mountainous interior. In support, the national government, with the assistance of World Wide Fund for Nature (WWF) and the United Nations Development Program, has designated a number of protected reserves in the area. Increasing in-migration by both Khmer and Khmer Islam (or Cham) from nearby provinces, including Kampot, Kompong Speu, and Kompong Cham—some of whom are returning to their home province after years of displacement by the Pol Pot regime, while newcomers come to buy land on which to settle and farm—and environmental pressure from extensive gem mining and logging—both legal and illegal—present serious challenges to the mountainous ecosystem, however.

Greg Ringer

Further Reading
Ringer, Greg. (2000) "Tourism in Cambodia, Laos and Myanmar: From Terrorism to Tourism?" In *Tourism in South and Southeast Asia: Issues and Cases,* edited by C. Michael Hall and Stephen Page. Oxford: Butterworth-Heinemann, 178–194.

World Commission on Protected Areas. (1998) *Mountain Protected Areas Update.* Geneva: International Union for the Conservation of Nature.

CARPETS—CENTRAL ASIA

In Central Asia, remnants of fine handmade wool carpets preserved in graves as old as the fifth century BCE imply that the tradition of carpet weaving dates to still earlier times, although these ancient rugs were not necessarily locally woven. Central Asian rugs today are traditionally wool pile on a wool foundation. In older rugs, cotton was used in the pile or to supplement the foundation, but cotton warps are a late introduction. Some few Central Asian carpets use silk, but these are rare, compared with those of wool. (Kilims are rugs or covers made by Turks of Central Asia of flat-woven material.)

With the exception of sixteenth-century court carpets and some later Uzbek city carpets, Central Asian carpets are primarily village-woven wool rugs, bags, horse trappings, and other small pieces. The traditional color of Central Asian rugs is madder-dyed red (from the madder herb), with indigo blue the usual secondary color, along with small amounts of brown, yellow, and other colors. Until the second half of the nineteenth century, only natural dyes were used, which explains the deep brilliant reds still preserved today on nineteenth-century examples. A common design is a repeated geometric motif known as a gul (Persian for rose), an octagon-shaped pattern sometimes called an elephant foot. Little is known about the history of Central Asian rugs, aside from those pieces made in royal courts; some village-made rugs have been dated as early as 1650.

Turkmen Rugs

The best-known and most highly prized Central Asian rugs are those made by Turkmen, primarily in Turkmenistan, northeast Iran, northern Afghanistan, and Uzbekistan. The oldest Turkmen confederation is the Ersari (Azeri), and until recently the elite clan of the Ersari was the Saltuq (Seljuk). The Ersari, who lived in the old emirate of Bukhara, in the southern Amu Dar'ya region of Uzbekistan, and in northern Afghanistan, included many groups, each of which had distinctive rug patterns, such as the Chub Bash, Kizil Ajak, and Sullayman (sixteenth–late nineteenth century). Ersari rugs tend to be more coarsely woven than other Turkmen rugs and have the most archaic patterns.

In Turkmenistan proper, there were two main weaving divisions in the Turkmen social order, the Salor confederation and the Yomut. The Salor, the dominant confederation in the West, split, with first the Saryk (early eighteenth century) and then the Tekke (eighteenth century) usurping power in southern Turkmenistan. Rug collectors prize Salor, Saryk, and Tekke weavings, and antique Salor and Tekke rugs generally bring high prices at auctions.

The Yomut are in the Caspian area and in northern Turkmenistan. By allying themselves with the Uzbek khans of Khiva, they gained power (1600–1873) and dominated several other groups whose weaving are lumped with theirs into a homogenous Yomut group that to this point has not been differentiated. Yomut rugs have more variations in design than do other Turkmen weavings, no doubt because they were made by various groups dominated by the Yomut. Another distinct weaving group, the Chaudor, produces the darkest and least attractive Turkmen rugs overall. They are also the least likely to depend on red and blue, featuring colors such as brown, often with an olive-green cast.

Uzbek Rugs

One of the most prolific non-Turkmen weaving groups is that of the Uzbek people. Because they frequently copy the rugs of their Turkmen neighbors, it is difficult to distinguish Uzbek rugs, and for many years, most Uzbek rugs were sold as Turkmen. In the 1990s, experts began to attribute many of the so-called Afghan Turkmen rugs to the Uzbek, particularly those with less evenly spaced patterns. Yet even today significant numbers of rugs described as Turkmen, particularly those coming from Afghanistan, are actually Uzbek. Complicating this is the fact that Uzbek carpets include some made by Tajik weavers, and it is unclear how to tell one from the other.

Not all Uzbek carpets are village-made. Carpet workshops in Bukhara and other cities wove excellent large carpets (c. fifteenth to twentieth century). Some Uzbek formal-workshop carpets that date to the sixteenth century are much like the best Persian rugs of the Safavid dynasty (1501–1722/1736) in quality, differing only in colors and designs. These masterpieces are referred to as Salting carpets (1588–1598), after a magnificent carpet in the Victoria and Albert Museum in London. Based on color, artistic style, and writing (lines of poetry woven into the borders), some were probably produced in the Uzbek courts at Herat and Bukhara around 1590.

Rugs of Other Central Asian Peoples

A number of Turkic weaving groups produce small numbers of wool pile rugs primarily for domestic use: the Karakalpaks, Kazakhs, Kyrgyz, and Mongols. Because these groups were never encouraged to produce rugs for export, they stayed truer to the old traditions. The Turkmen and Uzbek, on the other hand, wove the majority of their rugs for sale. The designs reacted first to Russian and then to Western market forces. The noncommercial weaving groups tended to weave objects suited to their lifestyle, such as bags, door covers, yurt or *gur* wrappings, horse trappings, and odd-shaped small rugs.

J. Barry O'Connell, Jr.

Further Reading

Hoffmeister, Peter. (1980) *Turkoman Carpets in Franconia.* Ed. with notes by A. S. B. Crosby. Edinburgh, Scotland: Crosby Press.

Jourdan, Uwe. (1989) *Oriental Rugs*, Vol. 5: *Turkoman.* Woodbridge, Suffolk, U.K., and Augsberg, Germany: Oriental Textile Press, distributed by Antique Collectors' Club.

Mackie, Louise W., and Jon Thompson, eds. (1980) *Turkmen: Tribal Carpets and Traditions.* Washington, DC: Textile Museum.

Moshkova, Valentina Georgievna. (1996) *Carpets of the People of Central Asia of the Late XIX and XX Centuries.* Ed. and trans. by George W. O'Bannon and Ovadan K. Amanova-Olsen. Tucson, AZ: G. W. O'Bannon.

Pinner, Robert, and Murray L. Eiland Jr. (1999) *Between the Black Desert and the Red: Turkmen Carpets from the Wiedersperg Collection.* San Francisco: Fine Arts Museums of San Francisco.

Thacher, Amos Bateman. (1977) *Turkoman Rugs: An Illustrated Monograph on the Rugs Woven by the Turkoman Tribes of Central Asia.* London: Holland Press.

Vanshing Jewels: Central Asian Tribal Weavings: Catalog of an Exhibition by the Rochester Museum & Science Center. (1990) Essays by George O'Bannon et al. Rochester, NY: Rochester Museum & Science Center.

CASHMERE INDUSTRY

Cashmere hair from varieties of cashmere goats is a major agricultural product of China and Mongolia. Cashmere is the down hair shed by goats living in the high, dry altitudes of Eurasia. Cashmere lies beneath the coarse outer hair and provides insulation from the cold. This rare precious natural fiber has been known since Roman times for its lightness, warmth, and softness. For hundreds of years, it was used exclusively in luxury fabrics that only royalty could afford. Napoleon gave cashmere shawls to his empress, Eugenie, and Queen Victoria prized the fabric. In the 1920s, it was developed into fashionable clothing by the Parisian designers Coco Chanel and Jean Patou.

China is the world's largest producer of cashmere, generating around 10,000 tons per year, over 60 percent of the world market of 16,500 tons. Mongolia is the second-largest producer with about 3,000 tons annually; the cashmere industry has been a major component of the Mongolian economy. Other cashmere-producing countries are New Zealand, Nepal, Iran, Afghanistan, Australia, and the United States.

Originally the cashmere-manufacturing industry developed in Scotland, which was noted for its specialized-weave knit techniques in underwear. In the second half of the twentieth century, cashmere processing and manufacturing increasingly moved to the countries of fiber origin, especially China, although Scotland still produces very high quality cashmere clothing.

It takes a Kashmir goat four years to produce enough hair for one sweater. To collect the hair, the herders comb the goats by hand every spring, and the hair is sold in bales. The cashmere industry is divided into three distinct sectors: raw (greasy) cashmere gathered by herders; processed (dehaired) cashmere, the product of a refined combing, cleaning, and sorting process; and finished (manufactured) cashmere products, including yarns and clothing, usually knit on hand-operated machines. Two kilograms of raw cashmere yield one kilogram of dehaired cashmere.

The Cashmere Industry in China

Cashmere-down hair in China comes from goats grazing on the plains of Inner Mongolia, Xinjiang, and the Himalayan Mountain highlands leading to the Tibetan Plateau—regions surrounding the Gobi Desert.

The fibers are locally combed, cleaned, dyed, and spun before being knitted into fabric in North Chinese mills or before being exported. In 1997, China produced 9,742 tons of raw cashmere and imported 827 tons of raw cashmere, exporting no raw greasy cashmere. A sum of 5,285 tons was processed; half was used in the domestic market, and half was exported. The half that remained in China was made into finished goods, about a quarter of which went into domestic sales, while the rest was exported.

The Cashmere Industry in Mongolia

Cashmere is the second-largest hard-currency-earning export of Mongolia. In 1997, Mongolia produced 2,558 tons of raw cashmere. A total of 1,731 tons remained in the domestic market, while 827 tons were exported to China. Some 866 tons were processed in the country, and 603 tons were exported. Mongolia manufactured 263 tons of cashmere finished goods, exporting all but 38 tons of it.

At the end of 1997, Mongolia had over 10 million cashmere goats, double the herd size of 1990, grazing mainly in the eight Gobi provinces. The number of goats has been increasing from 12.3 percent to 18.5 percent annually in the past decade. If such increases continue, the U.S. Agency for International Development postulates that by 2014 goat numbers will increase to 14 million head and will supply 4,200 tons of raw cashmere.

Cashmere Trade and Future Prospects

During Mongolia's socialist era (1921–1990), cashmere was exported mainly to Europe. Exports shifted dramatically to China in the democratic era since 1990, with the prime beneficiaries being the Mongolian *arat* (nomadic herder) producer and the Chinese manufacturing establishment. With the rapid growth of cashmere loans from the Western banking system, Mongolian customers were unable to buy the nomads' raw cashmere, so that the nomads increasingly turned to Chinese traders who came to them in the Gobi Desert. With a change of government from Communist Party rule to a coalition of democratic parties in 1996, the Mongolian authorities were convinced to lift their mid-1990s ban on the export of raw cashmere and replace it with a 30 percent export tax on raw cashmere. The tax was poorly implemented, as corrupt senior officials realized that they could make fortunes by selling raw cashmere tax free to Chinese factories. It is estimated that at least 50 percent of Mongolian raw cashmere is smuggled to China with no duties paid on either side. This has enabled China to capture the

Mongolian raw cashmere-export market, depress the Mongolian manufacturing sector, and take control of the world cashmere market.

The Chinese now mix the longer Mongolian hair fibers with shorter Chinese fibers to increase yarn strength. In the 1990s, Chinese dominance of the world's cashmere market and rapid expansion of Mongolian goat herds led to what most experts agree was an oversupply of low-quality cashmere. World prices of raw cashmere dropped from about $60 per kilogram in 1989 to $15 per kilogram in 1998. Mongolia's lower-quality fibers come from its older goats. Diseases and the collapse of the Russian goat-meat market in the 1990s reduced Mongolia's goat slaughter. The older goats produced thicker, lower-quality fibers, which added to the Chinese hair resulted in a less luxurious and less expensive product. This accounts for the flood of finished cashmere goods at greatly reduced prices, which became available on the world market in the 1990s. However, two successive disastrous winters in 1999–2001 in Mongolia and Inner Mongolia killed off millions of goats, which will improve fiber quality in the short term. It is expected that breeding-improvement-programs are needed to improve quality in the long run.

Alicia J. Campi

Further Reading
Mongolian Statistical Yearbook. (1997) "Agriculture in Mongolia, 1971–1996: A Statistical Profile." Ulaanbaatar, Mongolia: Mongol Ulsyn Undesnii Statistikiin Gazar.

U.S. Department of Agriculture, Economic Research Service. (1992) *Agricultural Statistics of the People's Republic of China.* Compiled by Hunter Colby. Washington, DC: U.S. Department of Agriculture, Economic Research Service.

CASPIAN SEA The Caspian Sea divides the Eurasian landmass, separating the mountainous Caucasus region to the west from the deserts of Central Asia to the east. At 372,000 square kilometers in area, the peanut-shaped Caspian Sea is the world's largest inland lake, enclosed by Azerbaijan, Iran, Kazakhstan, Russia, and Turkmenistan. The Caspian basin is twenty-eight meters below sea level and is fed mainly by the Volga River, which flows southeast from Russia. The salty lake plunges to a depth of about one thousand meters in the south, but is only somewhat over three meters deep in the northern waters. The Caspian is a seasonal habitat for birds migrating from Europe and Asia, including flamingos and the rare white-tailed eagle. Baku, Astrakhan, Aqtau, Atyrau, and Makhachkala are the most important ports.

Oil and Natural Gas
The Caspian Sea contains some of the world's largest deposits of oil and natural gas. Hydrocarbon exploitation in the Caspian Sea was limited during the Soviet era, but since the dissolution of the Soviet Union in 1991, the Caspian basin's huge, undeveloped natural resources have been the source of much international attention. Previously, the sea's legal status was governed by 1921 and 1940 treaties between the Soviet Union and Iran, but since Azerbaijan, Kazakhstan, and Turkmenistan received their independence, the Caspian littoral states have been unable to agree on a new legal regime governing the use of the surface, water, and subsea hydrocarbon resources. Despite the absence of a multilateral agreement, several countries already have begun oil and natural gas exploration in the Caspian. International energy consortiums, such as the Azerbaijan International Operating Company, have invested billions of dollars in developing infrastructure to develop and export the oil and natural gas.

Caviar
The Caspian Sea is also the source of about 90 percent of the world's caviar. However, the lack of an international agreement safeguarding the sea's environment has led to overfishing and poaching of sturgeon, the fish whose roe or eggs are used to make the delicacy, resulting in dwindling fish stocks. Environmentalists have warned that poaching of beluga, the largest and rarest sturgeon, is threatening to push the species into extinction. Legal trade in Caspian caviar is estimated to be worth $100 million per year, but the illegal catch in the four former Soviet republics is believed to be ten to twelve times higher. In spring 2001, the United Nations Convention on International Trade in Endangered Species (CITES) banned exports of caviar from Azerbaijan, Kazakhstan, Russia, and Turkmenistan. Despite opposition from environmentalists in March 2002, CITES lifted the export ban on the former Soviet republics, citing improved management of their sturgeon stocks.

Andrew D. Neff

Further Reading
Ebel, Robert E., and Rajan Menon, eds. (2000) *Energy and Conflict in Central Asia and the Caucasus.* Lanham, MD: Rowman & Littlefield.

Gokay, Bulent, ed. (2001) *The Politics of Caspian Oil.* New York: St. Martin's Press.

CASTE "Caste" refers to a rigid system of ranked social inequality with significant barriers to mobility or to intimate associations between different strata. The word also refers to one of the ranked strata or subgroups that make up such a system. Traditional India is considered the classic example of a caste system, but the concept has also been used to describe extreme forms of racial, ethnic, and class segregation in other societies. "Caste" comes from the Portuguese *casta*, meaning lineage, breed, race, or category (first attested used in English in 1613).

Caste in Traditional India

Hindus usually describe the caste system with one or both of two ancient concepts: *varna* and *jati*. *Varna* (color) refers to the categories that are described in the early Indian religious texts such as the Rig Veda (origins 1500–1200 BCE; present form c. 200 BCE) and the *Laws of Manu* (c. 200 BCE–100 CE). These texts describe four ranked categories: priests (Brahmans), warriors (Kshatriyas), farmers and merchants (Vaisyas), and laborers and servants (Sudras). The first three categories are considered "twice-born" (*dvija*s) and are allowed to study the sacred scriptures. A fifth category of outcasts is referred to in *The Laws of Manu* as *chandala*. They are supposedly outside Hindu society, but historically are an integral part of it. Westerners have referred to this group as untouchables. They were usually associated with activities considered to be polluting, such as removing feces or dead animals. In contemporary India, the government refers to these groups as Scheduled Castes. Mohandas (Mahatma) Gandhi (1869–1948) called them *Harijan*s (children of God). Many of them have adopted the name *Dalit*s (the oppressed).

The actual social structure in India has long varied from the *varna* scheme described in the sacred texts. Society has been differentiated into several thousand named social categories usually referred to as *jati*s (lineage, species, race). Scholars do not know whether *jati*s developed from *varna*s. It is clear that the *varna* scheme has long served as a simplified indigenous model of the caste system, whose legitimacy was advocated primarily by Brahmans and other high-caste groups. The description of the *jati* system that follows attempts to summarize the information developed during the period that Britain ruled India (1848–1947 CE) and the views of social scientists in the first quarter-century after Indian independence.

Most *jati*s were associated with a particular traditional occupation or ritual activity, such as barber, drummer, cow herder, priest, and so forth. These categories were ranked in a rough hierarchy based to a

significant degree on their supposed ritual purity, with Brahmans at the top and untouchables at the bottom. Ritual purity was partly an attribute of birth, and partly due to the fastidiousness with which individuals and castes conformed to certain lifestyle norms. Bathing before meals, purification of cooking areas, being a vegetarian, minimizing associations with those of low caste, keeping women relatively secluded, not allowing widows to remarry, and avoiding manual work in the fields were a few of the behaviors usually associated with ritual purity. The status of a caste was also affected by the members' wealth, political power, and the *varna* category with which they were associated. For example, Rajputs, who are common in much of northern India, are usually classified as Kshatryas and hence claim a higher status than the Vaisya or Sudra castes in their region.

These *jati* categories were divided into—or more accurately composed of—numerous regional subcastes, ranging from a few hundred families to tens of thousands. Subcastes were usually endogamous, (composed of families who intermarried with one another and refused to marry others). Because of endogamy, many members of a subcaste were kin by birth or marriage. Most castes also practiced commensality; that is, they ate only with members of their own or a higher caste.

Most castes participated in agricultural production or modern occupations. In only a few artisan and service castes, such as clothes washers, barbers, and goldsmiths, did most members earn their living by carrying out their traditional occupation. Many castes, however, performed their traditional functions on specific occasions. For example, drummer castes in south India serve as drummers for certain festivals or rituals. The great majority of castes were classified as Sudras, though their ritual status varied from quite high to very low. Some of the most common Sudra castes were barbers, carpenters, blacksmiths, goldsmiths, oilseed pressers, farmers, potters, cow herders, shepherds, flower growers, vegetable gardeners, grain parchers, sweetmeat makers, tailors, weavers, clothes washers, and bangle makers. The three higher *varna*s, as well as the category of untouchables or Scheduled Castes, each contained a number of distinct castes.

A typical village might include members of from five to twenty-five castes. There were nearly always some type of Brahman and an array of Sudra castes in a local area. In some places, there were castes that claimed to be Kshatriyas or Vaisyas, but in many areas of the South, those *varna*s were not represented. Typically, a dominant caste or coalition controlled most local political and economic resources—especially land and the labor needed to work it. While caste rank was associ-

CASTE

Edgar Thurston's *Castes and Tribes of Southern India* is an attempt to provide a full accounting of all the castes of the region. Although incomplete, it remains the most comprehensive list. The following is a sample of the listings.

Baita Kammara.—The name, meaning outside blacksmiths, applied to Kamsala blacksmiths, who occupy a lowly position, and work in the open air or outside a village.

Bajantri.—A synonym of Mangala, indicating their occupation as professional musicians.

Bakuda.—A sub-division of Holeya.

Balanollu.—Balanollu and Badranollu are names of gotras of Ganigas, the members of which may not cut *Erythoxylon monogynum*.

Balasantosha.— The Balansantosha or Balasanta vandlu (those who are children) are described in the Kurnool Manual as "ballad reciters, whose chief stories are the Bobbili katha, or the story of the siege of the fort of Bobbili in Vizagapatam by Bussy"; the Kurnool settled in the Tamil district of Madura.

Bovi.—The name of the palanquin-bearing section of the Mogers of South Canara. Some Besthas from Mysore, who have settled in this district, are also called Bovi, which is a form of Boyi (bearer).

Boya (see Bedar).—Boya has also been recorded as a sub-division of Malam, a name for Ekari.

Source: Edgar Thurston and K. Rangachari. (1909) *Castes and Tribes of Southern India.* Madra, India: Government Press, 266–267.

ated with economic and political power, the correlation was very imperfect. In most areas, the controllers of land and labor were not Brahmans; frequently they were higher-status Sudra castes. The dominant caste was often able to mobilize considerable physical force to protect its interests. Members of this dominant group typically served as patrons (*jajmans*) for whom Brahman priests performed religious rites in return for gifts and fees. The dominant caste was also the patron of a variety of specialist castes—barbers, blacksmiths, sweepers, and so forth—who provided various goods and services. In return for their services, these clients were given a portion of the patron's grain at harvest time. Where the integration of the division of labor at a village level was accomplished by patron-client (*jajmani*) relationships, markets and extreme forms of coercion (for example, slavery or serfdom) may have been less prevalent. Scholars disagree about how extensive this system was.

In contrast to a caste, which was a category of people of similar rank and characteristics, a subcaste was an actual social group or network. Families were linked to members of their subcaste in other villages in the region. In many areas, daughters had to marry men from other villages, creating intervillage networks of kin and in-laws. Many subcastes had a council of respected leaders (*panchayat*) who settled disputes and disciplined errant members. These regional subcastes were usually endogamous; that is, husbands and wives had to be from the same subcaste. In turn, their children were members of this subcaste. Endogamy was the primary determinant of subcaste boundaries. The exception was a number of castes in north India and a few in south India who practiced what anthropologists refer to as hypergamy. That is, males could marry women from a caste of slightly lower rank. In all castes, parents arranged most marriages. While a local *jati* or subcaste was a circle of peers, there were important variations in the status of the families in a subcaste. These differences were related to wealth, influence over other families, and lifestyle, especially ritual purity. A family's status could be increased if it arranged marriages with higher-status families.

Typically, a local caste category was segmented into several endogamous subcastes. For example, there was often more than one subcaste of cow herders in a given area or even in the same village. From the perspective of others, the cow herders belonged to the same caste; from their perspective, enough differences existed so that they neither intermarried nor ate with one another. Most people in a village knew the broad caste category of everyone else, though they often did not know their subcaste.

In principle, individuals and groups could not change their caste, but in practice there was considerable social mobility—usually involving small shifts in rankings. This typically occurred when a subcaste or lineage increased in wealth or political power. It then emulated the lifestyles of higher castes, adopted a new name, or claimed that it belonged to a higher *varna*. In a local area, the exact ranking of groups was subject to dispute and debate. Most disagreement was over whether a caste was just above or just below another local caste.

Most religious minorities in India, including Muslims, Christians, and Sikhs (who together make up about 15 percent of the population), also had caste-like divisions. Marriages were usually within these caste subgroups, and various forms of deference were shown to high-ranking strata. Non-Hindus are, however, usually less concerned about purity and pollution and commensality. The representation of these groups in any given area is, however, enormously variable. For example, in some areas of the Punjab, Sikhs constitute the overwhelming bulk of the population, while the same is true for Christians in a few areas of south India.

There have long been protests against the caste system, including those by the historical Buddha (563–483 BCE), the bhakti (devotional movements; 800–1800), and the anti-Brahman movement in south India (c. 1916–1940).

Theories of Caste

Scholars have proposed various explanations for this system of inequality. Louis Dumont has argued that the patterns found in Hindu India are due to its unique ideology, which values hierarchy based on distinctions of ritual purity and pollution. This notion contrasts with Western ideology, which places a high value on equality and individualism. McKim Marriott has emphasized even more strongly the distinctive nature of the Hindu caste system. In contrast to the Western dualistic understanding of biology and morality, Hindus, according to Marriott, have a monistic concept; there is no clear line between biol-

ogy and morality. The substances that make up the body are inherited from parents. They affect not only one's physical capacities, but shape one's moral capacities. Conversely, the morality of an individual's behavior eventually affects the quality of the substances that make up the body. Both Dumont and Marriott have been criticized for overemphasizing the role and ideas of Brahmans and for neglecting the resistance of lower castes, alternative indigenous ideologies, and the frequent deviation of actual behavior from these largely Brahmanical ideals. Moreover, their theories provide little insight into the changes that are occurring in contemporary India.

Beginning with A. M. Hocart, another scholarly tradition sees those with significant political and economic power (kings, lesser rulers, and dominant castes) as the creators and sustainers of the caste system. Specialized groups of subordinates provide rulers and dominant castes with services, and eventually these groups develop into castes. Kings and local rulers enforce this division of labor and the related status distinctions. An obvious criticism of this theory is that while most agrarian societies have had kings and local rulers, only India developed an elaborate caste system. Gerald Berreman has suggested that castes emerged as tribal and ethnic groups were incorporated into larger state structures. Nicholas Dirks has argued that the extreme elaboration and rigidity of the caste system did not fully emerge until the *pax Britannia* of the early nineteenth century. The colonial regime gave upper castes nearly unqualified control of property and prevented lower castes from using force to resist upper caste domination and ideology. The government census attempted to record officially the ranking of castes, which made the system more rigid than it had been.

Murray Milner, Jr., argues that in traditional India, status was a crucial form of power and, relative to most societies, independent of economic and political power. Hence, castes are best understood as an extreme form of status group. Milner proposes a theory of status relationships based on four characteristics of status. Status is not expansible; hence, if some move up, others must move down; therefore, mobility tends to be restricted. Status is inalienable; property and wealth can be stolen or taken by force, but status is dependent on the opinion of others and cannot simply be appropriated. Hence, once status systems are institutionalized, they are relatively stable; some form of the caste system has existed in India for three thousand years. Status is acquired through conformity to the norms of the group; hence, those with high status tend to elaborate and complicate the norms to make conformity difficult. The extensive norms governing

ENDING CASTE DISCRIMINATION

The founders of modern India believed that discrimination and the lack of opportunity for many Indians associated with the caste system was a serious hurdle to modernization and political stability. Caste discrimination was banned and "affirmative action" as a remedy was accepted in India's first Constitution, adopted on 26 January 1950.

Prohibition of discrimination on grounds of religion, race, caste, sex or place of birth.

(1) The State shall not discriminate against any citizen on grounds only of religion, race, caste, sex, place of birth or any of them.

(2) No citizen shall, on grounds only of religion, race, caste, sex, place of birth or any of them, be subject to any disability, liability, restriction or condition with regard to—

(a) access to shops, public restaurants, hotels and places of public entertainment; or

(b) the use of wells, tanks, bathing *ghats*, roads and places of public resort maintained wholly or partly out of State funds or dedicated to the use of the general public.

(3) Nothing in this article shall prevent the State from making any special provision for women and children.

(4) Nothing in this Article or in Clause (2) of Article 29 shall prevent the State from making any special provision for the advancement of any socially and educationally backward classes of citizens or for the Scheduled Castes and the Scheduled Tribes.

Source: Ministry of Information and Broadcasting. (1957) *India's Constitution.* Delhi: The Ministry.

purity and pollution are an obvious example of this process. Status is acquired through associations: associating with superiors increases your status; associating with inferiors decreases it. This is especially so for intimate associations. Eating and sex are symbols of intimacy in all societies: hence the strong emphasis on dining with and marrying those of similar status. (As the theory suggests, these behaviors are found in other caste-like systems such as aristocracies, racially segregated societies, and adolescent cliques.)

Feminist scholars have elucidated the role of women and gender differences in the understanding and significance of caste and the centrality of gender inequality and male dominance in the caste system. Male dominance may be a necessary but not sufficient condition of the caste system.

Caste in Contemporary India

The Constitution of 1949 outlawed untouchability and government discrimination based on caste. Places in Parliament, universities, and government jobs were specifically reserved for the Scheduled Castes, or former untouchables. In 1990, the government expanded the number of government jobs and university admissions reserved for disadvantaged castes from 22.5 percent to 49 percent. In addition to Scheduled Castes, positions were reserved for Other Backward Classes (OBC), which includes mainly lower- and middle-status Sudra castes. The openings available to upper-caste members were significantly reduced—in a job market where there was already high unemployment. This action led to violent protests in many parts of India and to increased emigration of professional

Villagers view the victims of a massacre in India on 22 April 1999. The low caste villagers were killed by the Ranvir Sena militia in retaliation for the earlier killing of 35 upper caste famers by Communist rebels. (AFP/CORBIS)

families to developed countries. The reservations program was upheld by the Indian Supreme Court, but it has accentuated the mobilization of castes as political entities.

In 1996, a coalition of parties called the United Front and dominated by OBC gained control of the government of India; the cabinet contained only one Brahman—an indication of the increased influence of lower castes. Political parties dominated by upper castes mobilized in the name of Hindu nationalism *(Hindutva)*, and in March 1998 they gained control of the government. The emergence of Hindu nationalism was associated with the sometimes violent persecution of Muslims, Christians, and lower-caste groups. Similar caste-linked political struggles and conflict took place for control of many of the state governments. Hindu nationalist parties and organizations have recruited some lower-caste members into leadership positions. Of course, many factors (in addition to caste) shaped political coalitions and outcomes.

With greater urbanization and industrialization, it has become impractical for people to be overly concerned about who is sitting next to them in public restaurants or factory lunchrooms. Hence, the norms of commensality have been greatly weakened. Even in arranging marriages, wider categories of people are considered appropriate as potential spouses, and increased attention is paid to their education and financial resources rather than to their subcaste. Public statements about the superiority or inferiority of castes are now unusual and considered inappropriate, though in private they are still expressed and taken into account in arranging marriages. Subcaste councils *(pan-chayats)* have few effective sanctions for deviant members, though more inclusive caste associations *(shabas)* are increasingly active in pressing the economic and political interests of their members. These changes are occurring in villages too, though their intensity varies by region and caste. Muslims and other minorities are even more likely to reject the legitimacy or presence of castes within their communities, claiming that it is a Hindu institution. Just as Westerners differ greatly on the meaning of class or race, the very meaning of caste for Indians has become more variable and ambiguous.

Murray Milner, Jr.

Further Reading
Berreman, Gerald D., ed. (1981) *Social Inequality: Comparative Developmental Approaches.* New York: Academic Press.
Béteille, André. (1965) *Class, Caste, and Power: Changing Patterns of Stratification in a Tanjore Village.* Berkeley and Los Angeles: University of California Press.
Dirks, Nicholas. (1987) *The Hollow Crown: Ethnohistory of an Indian Kingdom.* New York: Cambridge University Press.
Dumont, Louis. (1980) *Homo Hierarchicus: The Caste System and Its Implications.* Chicago: University of Chicago Press.
Fuller, Christopher J., ed. (1996) *Caste Today.* Delhi, India: Oxford Press.
Hocart, A. M. (1950) *Caste.* New York: Russell and Russell.
Jeffery, Patricia, and Roger Jeffery. (1996) *Don't Marry Me to a Plowman! Women's Everyday Lives in Rural North India.* Boulder, CO: Westview.
Liddle, Joanna, and Rama Joshi. (1986) *Daughters of Independence: Gender, Caste, and Class in India.* London: Zed.
Mandelbaum, David. (1970) *Society in India.* Berkeley and Los Angeles: University of California Press.
Marriott, McKim. (1976) "Hindu Transactions: Diversity without Dualism." In *Transaction and Meaning,* edited by Bruce Kapferer. Philadelphia, PA: ISHI.
Milner, Murray, Jr. (1994) *Status and Sacredness: A General Theory of Status Relations and an Analysis of Indian Culture.* New York: Oxford University Press.
Mukhopadhyay, Carol Chapnick, and Susan Seymour. (1994) *Women, Education, and Family Structure in India.* Boulder, CO: Westview.
Parry, Jonathan P. (1979) *Caste and Kinship in Kangra.* London: Routledge and Kegan Paul.
Raheja, Gloria Goodwin. (1988) *The Poison in the Gift: Ritual, Prestation, and the Dominant Caste in a North Indian Village.* Chicago: University of Chicago Press.
Srinivas, M. N. (1976) *The Remembered Village.* Delhi: Oxford University Press.
Weber, Max. (1958) *The Religion of India: The Sociology of Hinduism and Buddhism.* Translated and edited by Hans H. Gerth and Don Martindale. New York: Free Press.

CATHAYA TREE The cathaya tree (*Cathaya argyrophylla*) belongs to the pine family (*Pinaceae*). The only two living species of the cathaya are found in southwest China in the southeastern parts of Sichuan, the northeastern parts of Guizhou, the southwestern parts of Hunan, the northeastern parts of Guangxi, and in the Kunming area of Yunnan. The cathaya is an evergreen tree bearing cones and grows to about twenty meters. It was only in the 1950s that this species

was discovered, and the extent of the cathaya, as far as can be ascertained, is limited to some three thousand trees. It has therefore been considered an endangered species, and cathaya seedlings are being raised by Chinese conservation organizations. One fossil species of the cathaya has been found in Germany.

Bent Nielsen

Further Reading
Vidakovic, Mirko. (1991) *Conifers: Morphology and Variation.* Trans. By Maja Soljan. Croatia: Graficki Zavod Hrvatske.

CATHOLICISM, ROMAN—PHILIPPINES
The Philippines is the only Christian nation in Asia. Although more than 80 percent of Filipinos are said to be Roman Catholic, many fewer are genuine Catholics. There is a wide gap between professing Catholics and orthodox Catholics. Most people believe in a Christianized Bathalism (from the name Bathala, or God), and the traditional indigenous religions and respect for nature have profoundly shaped religious beliefs and practices in the Philippines.

Introduction of Catholicism
The Roman Catholic faith was introduced by the Portuguese navigator Ferdinand Magellan (c. 1480–1521) in 1521, but the expedition led by the Spanish explorer Miguel Lopez de Legazpi (c. 1510–1572) brought a permanent presence. As was the case in Latin America, the mendicant orders (orders combining both cloistered and community work) were responsible for bringing and spreading the Catholic religion among the local inhabitants.

BAROQUE PHILIPPINE CHURCHES—WORLD HERITAGE SITE

For representing a unique interpretation of sixteenth-century Spanish Baroque by traditional Filipino and Chinese craftsmen, the churches of Manila, Santa Maria, Paoay, and Miag-ao were designated World Heritage Sites by UNESCO in 1993.

CATHOLICISM, ROMAN—PHILIPPINES

THE CONVERSION OF
FILIPINOS TO CATHOLICISM

Perhaps the most enduring of Spain's influences on the Philippines is Roman Catholicism. In 2001, nearly five centuries after Spanish arrival, a majority of Filipinos are Catholics and the Philippines is the only Christian nation in Asia. The following is the account of the first baptism of Filipinos by Magellan's companion Antonio Pigafetta on 7 April 1521.

After dinner the priest and some of the others went ashore to baptize the queen, who came with forty women. We conducted her to the platform and she was made to sit down upon a cushion, and the other women near her, until the priest was ready. She was shown an image of our Lady, a very beautiful wooden Child Jesus, and a cross. Thereupon she was overcome with contrition and asked for baptism amid her tears. We named her Johanna after the emperor's mother; her daughter, the wife of the prince, Catherina, the queen of Mazaua, Lisabeta, and the others each their (distinctive) name. Counting men, women and children, were baptized eight hundred souls. The queen was young and beautiful, and was entirely covered with a white and black cloth. Her mouth and nails were very red, while on her head she wore a large hat of palm leaves in the manner of a parasol, with a crown about it of the same leaves, like the tiara of the pope; and she never goes any place without an attendant. She asked us to give her the little Child Jesus to keep in place of her idols; and then she went away. In the afternoon the king and queen, accompanied by numerous persons came to the shore. Thereupon, the captain had many trombs of fire and large mortars discharged, by which they were most highly delighted. The captain and the king called one another brothers. That king's name was Raia Humabon. Before that week had gone, all the persons of that island, and some from the other islands were baptized. We burned one hamlet which was located in a neighboring village because it refused to obey the king or us. We set up the cross there for those people were heathens. Had they been Moros, we could have erected a column there as a token of greater hardness, for the Moros are much harder to convert than the heathen.

Source: Emma H. Blair and James Robertson, eds. (1903–1909) *The Philippine Islands.* Cleveland, OH: Arthur H. Clark, I: 97.

In addition to the six Augustinian friars who accompanied Legazpi's expedition, twelve Franciscans came in 1577, and Dominicans and Jesuits arrived in 1581; all carried on programs of evangelism and indoctrination. Financially supported by the Spanish crown, the friars represented a political as well as a religious presence. The Spanish friar was often the figure of authority outside Manila.

The early optimism that had characterized Spanish missionary work was later replaced by a disillusionment partly caused by the realization that the Filipinos were not passive recipients of this new religion. Catholicism in the Philippines was to a certain extent unique because the Filipinos added aspects of their traditional religion to it.

Nature of Filipino Catholicism

Catholicism provided a world of metaphors that Filipinos continue to use, particularly in times of crisis. Their enthusiasm for certain aspects of Catholi-

444

ENCYCLOPEDIA OF MODERN ASIA

St. Williams Cathedral and the Ten Commandments at Laoag, Ilocos Norte, in 1998. (STEPHEN G. DONALDSON PHOTOGRAPHY)

cism should not, however, be mistaken for total acceptance of it. For example, in Philippine culture, where women had been equal to men and had often been in positions of power as priestesses, the Virgin Mary became the symbol of the new faith. In addition, where childhood had been idealized, the Santo Niño, or Holy Child, was venerated.

The foreignness of Catholicism was demonstrated in at least two areas: education and the clergy. Although the Spaniards established a number of schools and colleges (for example, the University of Santo Tomas in 1611), these were closed to Filipinos. The religious orders were also closed to Filipinos because of the Spanish concept of purity of blood—the requirement that the applicant prove that his or her family had been Christians for four generations. It was not until the eighteenth century that Filipinos were trained to be priests, and even then they became only "lay" priests and were not allowed to become friars (members of mendicant orders) or regulars. Regulars are those who belong to a *regula*, or order, such as Augustinian or Dominican.

During the Spanish domination of the Philippines, the various orders (with the exception of the Franciscans) amassed large tracts of land, often as the result of donations or by direct purchase. Prior to the Philippine Revolution in 1896, the orders owned 25 percent of the farming land in the provinces surrounding Manila. Thus, the church became a major economic force, in addition to its religious and political importance, and this fact had social consequences. Those who worked with and for the friars in managing their haciendas became an emerging elite at the beginning of the nineteenth century.

The conflict between the Philippines and Spain that culminated in the Philippine Revolution was in part an extension of the ongoing hostilities between secular Filipino priests and Spanish friars and as such can be viewed in religious as well as political terms. The execution of three Filipino priests, Mariano Gomes, José A. Burgos, and Jacinto Zamora, on 17 February 1872 illustrated the lengths to which the friars would go. The three were falsely accused of participating in the Cavite Mutiny in January 1872 and were put to death.

After independence was declared on 12 June 1898, the new constitution included a provision for the separation of church and state, and this policy continued with the arrival of the United States.

Philippine Catholicism in Recent Times

Vatican II (1962) and the declaration of martial law (1972) resulted in significant changes in the role of the Roman Catholic Church in the Philippines. The cause of social justice was taken up by priests and nuns, often at the risk of their lives.

The imagery or metaphors of Catholicism were sometimes associated with those opposing the regime of Ferdinand Marcos (1917–1998) and the martial law imposed at that time. For example, Al Santos used the *sinakulo*, a dramatic presentation of the Easter story, to illustrate the condition of those living in the slums of Manila, who are presented as suffering Christs, oppressed by those in power. Other uses of Catholic metaphors were unintentional. The political martyr Benigno Aquino, Jr. (1932–1983), came to be viewed as the slain savior, and his widow Corazon Aquino (b. 1933) as the suffering Mary Magdalene. She spoke of her husband's death as the country's resurrection.

Yet, despite the changes introduced in recent years, Catholicism in the Philippines has remained much the same as it had been from the beginning. The ancient animistic deities have been transformed into Christian figures, and ancient beliefs have continued to permeate religious beliefs and practices.

Damon L. Woods

See also: **Iglesia Ni Christo; Philippine Independent Church**

Further Reading
Enriquez, Virgilio G. (1994) *From Colonial to Liberation Psychology: The Philippine Experience.* Manila, Philippines: De La Salle University Press.
Maggay, Melba Padilla. (1987) *The Gospel in Filipino Context.* Mandaluyong, Metro Manila, Philippines: OMF Literature.
Phelan, John Leddy. (1959) *The Hispanization of the Philippines: Spanish Aims and Filipino Responses, 1565–1700.* Madison, WI: University of Wisconsin Press.

CATHOLICISM, ROMAN—VIETNAM

Although an estimated 80 percent of Vietnam's population practice Buddhism to some extent, there are an estimated 3 million Roman Catholics in Vietnam, approximately 3.75 percent of the nation's population. Catholicism first reached Vietnam in the sixteenth century with the arrival of Portuguese missionaries. By the early seventeenth century, Catholic priests from Portugal and France had established several missions in Vietnam. In 1624 there were an estimated twenty-one Jesuits in the nation. At first the Portuguese priests were dominant in numbers and in influence. In fact, the Vietnamese referred to Catholicism as the "Portuguese religion," and they tended to view all Europeans as Portuguese.

Alexandre de Rhodes

Despite the early predominance of Portuguese Jesuits, the most influential missionary in Vietnam in the seventeenth century was Father Alexandre de Rhodes (1591–1660), a Frenchman. De Rhodes, born in Avignon, possessed an unusual gift for learning and for understanding languages, and his major contribution to Vietnamese history was the development of *quoc ngu*, the romanized script of the Vietnamese language. This process of alphabetizing the Vietnamese vernacular had been undertaken earlier by a Portuguese missionary, but de Rhodes pursued the work further, believing that the development of *quoc ngu* would help the spread of Catholicism in Vietnam. *Quoc ngu* is now the official writing system of Vietnam. De Rhodes also codified the Vietnamese language and produced a number of written works, including the famous *Dictionarium Annamiticum* and a Vietnamese language catechism. In addition, de Rhodes wrote several memoirs and a history of Tonkin.

While in Vietnam, on and off between 1627 and 1645, de Rhodes did not limit himself to academic pursuits. He is said to have trained Vietnamese catechists and to have baptized an estimated nine thousand Vietnamese.

Persecution

Throughout the seventeenth and eighteenth centuries, missionaries continued to attempt to spread Catholicism throughout Vietnam. Several Catholic orders, such as the Jesuits and the Dominicans, were present. In addition, there were also orders of Catholic nuns who established convents in various parts of the country. At times, the missionaries were tolerated by the Vietnamese government, but more often than not they were persecuted. Some missionaries, Alexandre de Rhodes among them, were simply expelled from Vietnam; others were executed. These persecutions were more pronounced during the eighteenth century, and they tended to follow the political climate in Vietnam. Persecution of Catholics tended to occur when the Vietnamese government needed to consolidate its power or assert its authority. At such times, Catholicism's doctrine was the principal problem. The facts that Catholicism is monotheistic and that its claims to spirituality are exclusive brought it into conflict with the traditional, Confucian order of things in Vietnam. In spite of this, by the early nineteenth century, there were hundreds of thousands of Vietnamese Catholic converts.

Catholics and the Colonial Government

Following the creation of the Société des Missions Etrangères (the Society of Foreign Missions) in 1664, French missionaries became the most active and the most numerous in Vietnam. The Société's principal aim was the spread of Catholicism in Asia, and it received not only the support of the papacy, but also of the French monarchy. Often dependent on merchant ships to transport them to Vietnam, French missionaries developed close ties with French merchants. As a result, in the eyes of many Vietnamese officials, there was little difference between French missionaries and French merchants. French interests in missionary activity in Vietnam followed the political situation in France itself—waning during the French Revolution, but waxing again on the eve of French consolidation of power in Vietnam in 1885 when Emperor Ham Nghi was forced to flee the capital. By the time France had colonized Vietnam, Laos, and Cambodia in the late nineteenth century, there were an estimated 2 million Vietnamese Catholic converts. In fact, repression of Catholic missionaries and Catholic converts provided a rationale for bringing French troops in to Vietnam to protect them.

Despite the strong anticlerical sentiments of many French administrators, French colonial authorities were not averse to missionary activity since it was hoped that Catholicism would foster Vietnamese acceptance of the French colonial government. In addition, some Catholic missions in Vietnam served a useful purpose in the eyes of the French administration, since many offered Catholic schooling to Vietnamese children at little, if any, cost to the French colonial government. French colonial administrators appreciated these schools both for their cost efficiency and for the fact that they helped inculcate Vietnamese children with French cultural and social values. Among the most famous of these schools was the Collège d'Adran, founded in 1861. There were also a number of girls' schools established by orders such as the Sisters of St. Paul de Chartres.

Because of their close ties with the French administration, Vietnamese Catholics tended to dominate in the fields of business and education. Vietnamese Catholics were more likely to hold civil-service positions within the colonial administration, and their higher levels of education meant that they were also more likely to become professionals. As a result, Vietnamese Catholics tended to be wealthier than their non-Catholic compatriots. In spite of the fact that the majority of Vietnamese Catholics, particularly in the northern area of the country, were peasants, the influence of the educated Catholics was significant.

During the Franco–Viet Minh War (1946–1954), many Vietnamese Catholics favored independence from France, but most were wary of the Viet Minh leadership's Marxist leanings. As a result, they supported, in 1949, the institution of the Bao Dai government, which the French supported. Following

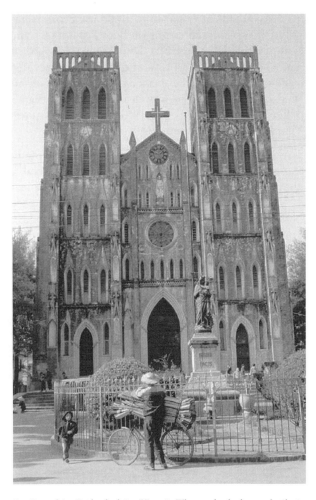

St. Joseph's Cathedral in Hanoi. The cathedral was built in 1886. (CHRISTOPHE LOVINY/CORBIS)

France's defeat at Dien Bien Phu and the Geneva accords of 1954 that established a demilitarized zone at the seventeenth parallel, an estimated 600,000 to 700,000 Vietnamese Catholics from northern Vietnam made their way to the south of the country in order to support the government of Ngo Dinh Diem (1901–1963), himself a Catholic. This influx of Vietnamese Catholics in southern Vietnam raised their numbers from approximately 450,000 to 1.1 million. This Catholic community in the south became the backbone of Ngo Dinh Diem's government. They were to become a formidable presence thanks to Diem's patronage. Diem's government gave key positions in the military and in the government to Vietnamese Catholics. Diem's brother, Ngo Dinh Thuc, was archbishop of Hue.

Catholics in the Vietnamese Government

The favored position of the Vietnamese Catholic minority in southern Vietnam created conflict with the majority Buddhist population. Buddhist protests resulted in severe repression of Buddhist monks and communities during the Ngo Dinh Diem government. The tension and the repression of Buddhists subsided somewhat following the assassination of Diem and his brother Ngo Dinh Nhu, who headed South Vietnam's police and security forces, in 1963 and during Nguyen Van Thieu's government (1965–1975).

Following the end of the war with the United States and reunification of Vietnam in 1975, a considerable number of Vietnamese Catholics left Vietnam for fear of reprisals and persecution for having supported the Ngo Dinh Diem government and the government of South Vietnam. Many have made their way to the United States and to France. In Vietnam today, Catholicism is protected by the Vietnamese constitution. In spite of such safeguards, Catholicism has been monitored closely by the Vietnamese government and Catholic activities have been significantly curtailed. There are presently an estimated 3 million Catholics in Vietnam.

Micheline R. Lessard

Further Reading
Héduy, Philippe. (1998) *Histoire de l'Indochine* (History of Indochina). Paris: Albin Michel.
Hertz, Solange, trans. (1966) *Rhodes of Vietnam: In China and Other Kingdoms of the Orient.* Westminster, MD: Newman.
Phan, Peter. (1998) "Alexandre de Rhodes' Mission in Vietnam: Catechesis and Inculturation." *Vietnamologica* 3: 3–32.
Tuck, Patrick. (1987) *French Catholic Missionaries and the Politics of Imperialism in Vietnam, 1857–1914.* Liverpool, U.K.: Liverpool University Press.

CAUCASIA   Caucasia is an isthmus bounded by the Black and Caspian Seas and by the steppes of the southern tier of the Russian federation and Iran. The region is dominated by the Caucasus Mountains. Historical Caucasia encompasses not only the central region of Georgia and the southern region of Armenia but also Caucasian Albania and Azerbaijan in the east and the diverse peoples of northern Caucasus. The preeminent communication and commercial arteries are rivers, especially the Terek in the north, the Kura in Georgia and Azerbaijan, and the Araks in Armenia. Caucasia's historical importance rests upon its central position in Eurasia and the endurance of local cultures in the face of tremendous imperial pressures.

To medieval Arab geographers, Caucasia (al-Kabk) was "the mountain of languages." Although Armenian belongs to the Indo-European linguistic group and Georgian anchors the separate Caucasian linguistic family, both languages show evidence of intimate contact with Persian and with one another. Connections between Georgian and Sumerian and between Georgian and Basque (ancient Greek writers referred to both ancient Spain and Georgia as "Iberia") have been hypothesized but remain unproven. Many of the languages of northern Caucasia—including Chechen, Ingush, Avar, Lak, Lezgian, and Udi—belong to the northeast subgroup of the Caucasian family.

Caucasia has long been an arena for Eurasian cross-cultural encounters. Some investigators have situated the Garden of Eden in the area, a notion seemingly reinforced by the Judeo-Christian tradition that the ark of Noah came to rest on Mount Ararat in present-day Turkey. Historically, Caucasia was affected by five of the great periods of Eurasian integration: the period when the ancient Silk Road flourished, the period of the Hellenistic civilization of Alexander of Macedon, the period of Islamic expansion, the period of the Mongol empire, and the period of the Russian empire and the Soviet Union.

Caucasia and the Persian Sphere
For much of its early history Caucasia was the northern limit of Persian (Iranian) civilization. The Scythians, Sarmatians, and other nomads of ancient northern Caucasia were Persianized. The sedentary Georgian and Armenian peoples, too, were members of the expansive Persian commonwealth. Scholars have exposed many links between Caucasian and Persian civilizations, including linguistic parallels, the sharing of Persian proper names, Zoroastrianism, long-distance trade, conceptions of kingship (including *farnah*, or divine radiance), and legendary and historical traditions—particularly the Persian epic tradition crystallized in the eleventh-century CE *Shahnameh* by the Persian poet Firdawsi. Achaemenid and Sasanid inscriptions demonstrate that the Persians were cognizant of the social and cultural bonds with their Caucasian neighbors.

Greco-Roman influence already had penetrated Caucasus by the time of the Greek city-states, as is symbolized by Jason and the Argonauts, who reputedly journeyed to Colchis in western Georgia. However, classical influence was limited mostly to coastal regions. Although Greek was adopted by some of the local elites as their written language, Aramaic—the scribal language of Achaemenid Persia—seems to have been more widespread. More important, classical civilization did not displace the Caucasians' traditional orientation toward Persian-dominated western Asia.

The Effect of Christianity

Georgian and Armenian, along with Caucasian Albanian, became written languages only with the conversion of local dynasts to Christianity in the first half of the fourth century. In some respects Christianization was truly revolutionary. Armenian and Georgian developed into literary languages, and distinctive written historical traditions were created. Conversion also enabled a possible future alliance with Christian Byzantium. With the destruction of Zoroastrian Persia by the Muslims in the seventh century, the sedentary peoples of Caucasia increasingly came to identify themselves with Christian Byzantium.

Sasanid Persia's campaigns to restore Georgia and Armenia to the Persian political and religious sphere were unsuccessful. They did, however, nudge Georgia and Armenia into the Byzantine orbit. Beginning in 387 CE, Armenia was often partitioned between the Byzantines and the Persians. In 428, the Sasanid "King of Kings" managed to disband the Armenian Arsacid monarchy; a similar fate met its eastern Georgian counterpart by the year 580. Georgian political elites subsequently associated themselves with Constantinople in the seventh century. A result of this association was their acceptance of the Council of Chalcedon (in 451) definition of Christ as both divine and human in nature, and this, in turn, sparked lasting tensions between the Georgians and the Armenians, who leaned toward Monophysitism—the doctrine that Christ's nature was purely divine.

Rise of the Bagratids

The destruction of Sasanid Persia in 651 and the subsequent occupation of much of Caucasia by the Muslims upset the noble hierarchy of central and southern Caucasia. The Armenian Bagratid family took advantage of the tumultuous situation and established itself throughout the Armenian districts, also seizing power in neighboring Georgia. The Bagratids, who were Christian, then assumed the charge against the Muslims. Simultaneously, its Georgian branch established itself along the Byzantine-Georgian frontier and entertained close relations with Constantinople.

From the late ninth to the eleventh century, the Bagratids carved Armenia into a number of kingdoms and principalities, although one realm, Vaspurakan, was ruled by the rival Artsruni family. Pressures from the Seljuk Turks and the Byzantines and the rivalries among the Bagratids themselves led to the Byzantine annexation of the Armenian kingdoms in the mid-eleventh century. As a result, some Armenian elites migrated to southeastern Asia Minor and established the independent Armenian Cilician kingdom.

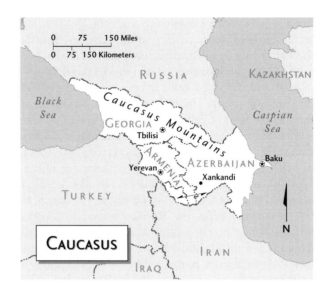

It was the Georgian branch of the Bagratid family that was to have lasting success in Caucasia itself. These Bagratids gathered the disparate Georgian territories, creating the first politically unified Georgian enterprise in the early eleventh century. They subsequently annexed much of Caucasian Armenia. Although the Muslim Seljuks were the chief adversary, the Georgian monarchs minted Islamic-type coins, patronized Sufis (Islamic mystics), and sponsored epic literature at their court written along Persian lines, such as the thirteenth-century *Knight in the Panther's Skin* by Shota Rustaveli. In many respects, Caucasia was still oriented toward the Near East.

The Georgian pan-Caucasian empire fell into disarray with inept rule early in the thirteenth century and was dismantled shortly thereafter by the Mongols. At this time, several autonomous principalities and kingdoms appeared in Caucasia. Following a number of particularly destructive invasions led by Timur (Tamerlane) in the late fourteenth century, the Christian princes of Caucasia lost one of their most important allies when Constantinople fell to the Ottomans in 1453. In the following century, Caucasia again became the arena of imperial competition with the Ottomans and Safavids of Persia vying for control. One historian considered the period from the fall of Armenian Cilicia in 1375 until the reign of Shah Abbas in the early seventeenth century to be the dark ages of Armenian history.

The Rise of Russian Influence

In the sixteenth century, the Persians and Ottomans waged a bloody competition for control of Armenia. At the same time, the Russians were expanding southward. In 1554, the Russians captured the city of Astrakhan, giving them dominance over the Volga River and a foothold in the vicinity of the Caspian. Shortly thereafter a series of Russian embassies was dispatched to the Georgian kingdoms. This marked the first substantial and sustained contact between Caucasia and the Russian empire. Indeed, after the dissolution of Byzantium, many Caucasian Christians looked to Orthodox Russia as a potential savior. The eastern Georgian realm voluntarily became a protectorate of Russia in 1783. In 1801, the Russian czar, Alexander I, unilaterally annexed eastern Georgia. In the ensuing decades, much of Caucasia—*Zakavkazia* (*Trans*caucasia), a concept reflecting Russian imperialism—was brought under czarist authority. However, not all of Armenia fell under Russian rule. A large part of historical Armenia was controlled by the Ottoman government and remains part of Turkey today. The genocide unleashed upon the Armenians in 1915 is a lasting memory of this division.

Although Russian occupation halted indigenous political autonomy, it also brought unprecedented stability to Transcaucasia. Standardized written languages, educational systems, infrastructure, and unprecedented national consciousnesses for the Georgians, Armenians, and Azeris were created during Russian rule. Through Russia, Caucasian elites acquired access to European intellectual ideas, including socialism, Marxism, and nationalism.

When Nicholas II was removed from power in February 1917, political authority in Transcaucasia fragmented. In November 1917, the Transcaucasian Commissariat was formed to govern the entire region. By the following January, the Democratic Federative Republic of Transcaucasia was established. The federation was short lived, however. After a month, it dissolved into three independent republics: Georgia, Armenia, and Azerbaijan. All were crushed by Bolshevik troops in 1920–1921. They were reunited in the Federal Union of Soviet Socialist Republics of Transcaucasia in 1922, and then each emerged as an independent constituent republic of the USSR in 1936. The three retained this status until the collapse of the Gorbachev revolution in the early 1990s. By the end of 1991, Armenia, Azerbaijan, and Georgia emerged from the turmoil as independent nations.

Stephen H. Rapp, Jr.

Further Reading

Allen, W. E. D. ([1932] 1971) *A History of the Georgian People, from the Beginning down to the Russian Conquest in the Nineteenth Century.* Reprint ed. London: Routledge and Kegan Paul.

Burney, Charles, and David Marshall Lang. (1972) *The Peoples of the Hills: Ancient Ararat and Caucasus.* New York: Praeger.

Hovannisian, Richard G., ed. (1997) *The Armenian People: From Ancient to Modern Times.* 2 vols. New York: St. Martin's.

Suny, Ronald Grigor. (1994) *The Making of the Georgian Nation.* Rev. ed. Bloomington, IN: Indiana University Press and Hoover Institution Press.

———, ed. (1996) *Transcaucasia, Nationalism, and Social Change: Essays in the History of Armenia, Azerbaijan, and Georgia.* Rev. ed. Ann Arbor, MI: University of Michigan Press.

Toumanoff, Cyril. (1963) *Studies in Christian Caucasian History.* Washington, DC: Georgetown University Press.

———. (1966) "Armenia and Georgia." In *The Cambridge Medieval History.* Vol. 4. Cambridge, U.K.: Cambridge University Press, 593–637, 983–1009.

CEBU (2000 est. island pop. 2.4 million; est. city pop. 718,000), City and island in the Philippines. The oldest city in the Philippines, Cebu City (the capital of Cebu province, on the east coast of Cebu Island) is the third-largest metropolis in the country and the major city in the southern Philippines. Cebu Island lies in the central Philippine archipelago, surrounded by the Bohol Strait in the southeast, the Tanon Strait in the west, the Visayan Sea in the north, and the Camotes Sea in the east. The island is approximately 196 kilometers long and 32 kilometers wide, with a land area of 4,422 square kilometers. Overpopulated, the island suffers from environmental degradation because of the dense population.

According to historical records, the island hosted the first European settlements in the Philippine archipelago. Ferdinand Magellan (c. 1480–1521), the Portuguese explorer, landed on Cebu on 7 April 1521 in the course of discovering the Philippines (he was later killed at nearby Mactan Island). An Italian traveling with Magellan, Antonio Pigafetta (1491–1534?), in an account of his experiences on the voyage, wrote that he saw ships from Siam, China, and Arabia at Cebu when the Portuguese sailed into the port; thus the city was already an important settlement before the Europeans arrived.

Miguel López de Legazpi (c. 1510–1570) founded the first Spanish settlement and Catholic mission on the island on 27 April 1565. Cebu City remained the capital of the Spanish possessions in the Philippines until 1571, when Manila on Luzon Island became the main administrative center. In Cebu City are the oldest church in the Philippines, the Basilica Minor del Santo Nino, in front of which is the cross that Magellan erected for the first Mass celebrated in the Philippines; the oldest school—San Carlos, founded in 1595; and the oldest street—Colon.

Today, Cebu City is an important economic center not only for Cebu Island but for the Visaya Islands and Mindanao as well. Cebu Island's economy includes agriculture, mining (coal, copper, limestone, silver), and small-scale manufacturing, such as food processing, textile, footwear, and furniture. Cebu City is also the educational center of the southern Philippines, with several major universities and colleges. The city has an international airport, and the port has maintained its international importance through the centuries.

Rafis Abazov

Further Reading
Fenner, Bruce Leonard. (1985) *Cebu under the Spanish Flag, 1521–1896: An Economic-Social History.* Cebu City, Philippines: San Carlos Publications, University of San Carlos.
Steinberg, David J. (1994) *The Philippines.* 3d ed. Boulder, CO: Westview.

CELEBES SEA
The Celebes Sea (Sulawesi Sea) is a roughly triangular section of the western edge of the Pacific Ocean, located just north of the equator between the east cost of Borneo, the south coast of Mindanao Island (Philippines), and the northern reaches of Sulawesi. It occupies a total area of around 427,000 square kilometers (165,000 square miles), stretching approximately 675 kilometers (420 miles) north-south and 837 kilometers (520 miles) east-west. The Sulu archipelago and Mindanao Island form the northern borders of the sea; the Sangi Islands lie to the east; Sulawesi (Celebes) Island borders the south; and Borneo is on the west. The Celebes Sea opens on to the Philippine Sea in the east and is connected to the Java Sea through the Makassar Strait in the southwest.

The deepest area is around 6,220 meters (20,406 feet). In the area close to the major islands and archipelagos, however, the sea is warm and not very deep. There are numerous seamounts, many of them volcanic, rising from the sea floor and capped with corals. The warm tropical water (annual average 26° C) makes the Celebes Sea an abundant fishing ground. Many areas around the numerous beautiful islands are suitable for diving and attract foreign tourists, contributing scarce hard currency to the Indonesian and Philippines economies.

Rafis Abazov

Further Reading
Severns, Mike. (1994) *Sulawesi Seas: A Photographer's Journey in Indonesia.* Concord, CA: Staples-Ecenbarger.

Joint Intelligence Study Publishing Board. (1944) *Joint-Army-Navy Intelligence Study of Celebes Sea Area.* Washington, DC: Joint Intelligence Study Publishing Board.

CENTRAL ASIA—EARLY MEDIEVAL PERIOD
The history of early medieval Central Asia is distinguished from that of other regions by the transition from a primarily Iranian population to a Turkic population. This region, particularly the part of Central Asia between the Syr Dar'ya and Amu Dar'ya Rivers, was traditionally home to nomads as well as a sedentary population located around cities and oases. The inhabitants were originally composed of Iranian stock, mixed with other groups. However, as the ancient period ended in the sixth century CE, a new dominant group entered Central Asia. Originating from Mongolia, the nomadic Turks began as overlords of a more sedentary Iranian population but eventually supplanted the Iranians as the majority population by the thirteenth and fourteenth centuries, as nomadic migrations brought more Turkic groups to the region.

The Turkic Empire
The Turks originated in present-day Mongolia, in or around the Altay Mountains. Ethnically and linguistically heterogeneous, the Turks are thought to have been a subgroup of the Juan-Juan people. Under the leadership of Tumen, the Turks became independent in 552 CE.

Unsatisfied with only independence, Tumen then led the Turks against the Juan-Juan and defeated them, which allowed Tumen to carve out a new empire. Although much of their new Turkic empire centered on the former Juan-Juan lands in Mongolia, Turkic forces marched west into the areas of modern-day Kazakhstan, Xinjiang, and other regions of Central Asia in pursuit of the fleeing Juan-Juan. Tumen remained in Mongolia, ruling the eastern Turks as the *qaghan* (emperor); he died in 552, while his brother Ishtemi ruled Central Asia as the *yabghu* (prince). By 558, Ishtemi (reigned 552–576) had extended Turkic rule to the Volga River.

Although the eastern Turks had been in contact with major sedentary powers since the rise of Tumen, the western Turks had limited contact with sedentary powers until they crossed the Syr Dar'ya River. In 557, Ishtemi allied with the Sasanid dynasty (224/228–651) of Persia against the Hepthalite empire that occupied much of Mawarannahr (the territory between the Amu Dar'ya and Syr Dar'ya Rivers) and present-day Khurasan and Afghanistan. By 565, the Hepthalite empire had fallen, and the Amu Dar'ya served as the border between the nomadic Turks and the sedentary Sasanids. The Turks, however, continued to expand their power westward through the steppes, eventually reaching the Black Sea.

At this time, the Turkic empire remained heterogeneous not only in ethnic and linguistic terms but also in terms of its religions. Zoroastrianism had existed in the region for hundreds of years, and Nestorian Christianity had made inroads, as had Buddhism from India, although most of the Turks remained pagans.

Under the Turkic regime, trade grew steadily. The trade routes, particularly the famous Silk Road, fell under the protection of the Turkic qaghans. Furthermore, Central Asia served as a key intermediate region for the exchange of goods from China for those of Persia, Siberia, and even present-day Europe. The result of international trade in the region was a growing cross-cultural influence in Central Asia due to the stability of the Turkic empire.

The importance of trade came to the forefront when war broke out between the Turks and the Sasanids in 569 over trade issues. Although the Turks crossed the Amu Dar'ya and invaded the region of Khurasan, their efforts were fruitless because they could not overcome the fortification systems and the resilience of the Sasanid army. War erupted again in 588–589 between the two powers, again with negligible results.

The Turkic empire was fairly short lived, however. Due to a severe famine and a resurgence in Chinese power under the Sui dynasty (581–618) and later the Tang dynasty (618–907), combined with a succession crisis, the eastern Turkic empire collapsed. The western Turks, fairly distant from China, continued, but also underwent a period of civil war. The eventual winner of this war was T'ung Yabghu (reigned 618–630). Again, trade began to flourish, but with his assassination in 630, civil war again erupted, effectively disrupting not only the empire but also trade. For almost a hundred years, Central Asia was in a state of civil war fought between a number of factions for mastery of the former western Turkic empire.

A second empire formed under Su-Lu (reigned 717–738), who accepted the suzerainty or overlordship of China. Essentially this amounted to sending a mission to China to offer tribute: China's authority was only nominal. In addition, Su-Lu maintained close ties with the Sasanids, who were under attack by a rapidly rising Arab empire with a new religion. Under Su-Lu, the Turks successfully foiled the invasions of the Arabs, defeating them in 737, shortly before Su-Lu's death. After his death, however, a central figure

failed to emerge among the Turks, and the armies of Islam conquered the rest of Mawarannahr.

Muslim Conquest of Central Asia

After the decline of the Turks, numerous local dynasties of Turkic and Sogdian origin arose in the cities and trade centers. (The Sogdians were the Iranian population dwelling in much of Central Asia before the arrival of the Turks; during the time of Alexander of Macedon, much of the region was known as Sogdia.) Little unity existed among these dynasties, although they soon would have reason to establish a common cause.

The collapse of the Sasanid dynasty in Iran under the attacks of the armies of Islam brought the Arabs to the Amu Dar'ya River. In 655, Muslim troops crossed the river to raid rather than conquer. The true invasion did not occur until 682, the delay being due to the first Arab civil war, which lasted from 656 to 661. Another civil war in 680–692 also delayed the penetration of Islam in Central Asia because it shifted considerable forces from Mawarannahr to the Middle East.

The first Muslim governor of Mawarannahr did not take power until 705, when Qutayba ibn Muslim (reigned 705–715) arrived. He settled soldiers in the towns, which helped maintain Muslim control over the conquered lands. Furthermore, to increase his troop strength, Qutayba also demanded troops from the conquered dynasts. Relying more on brutality than diplomacy, Qutayba expanded his province while destroying much of the pre-Islamic culture. His tenure of office ended abruptly in 715 when he was killed. His death led to the defeat of the Muslim armies; thus much of the territory that Qutayba had conquered was lost.

The Abbasid caliphate replaced the Umayyad caliphate after a brief war lasting from 744 to 750. The Abbasids, who found most of their support in Khurasan, bordering Central Asia, established a new caliphate. Due to their Khurasanian origins, the Abbasids evidenced Iranian and Central Asian influences. During this period, Central Asia truly became part of the Islamic world.

Two other powers also had designs on Central Asia. The Tang dynasty reestablished Chinese presence in eastern Turkistan (the region of present-day Central Asia and Afghanistan). At the same time, an emerging Tibetan empire also expanded into Central Asia. The Tang armies, however, defeated the Tibetan armies. By 749, the Tang armies reached the Fergana Valley. In 751, at the Talas River in present-day Kyrgyzstan, however, the Tang efforts fell short as Zayid ibn Salih, an Arab general in command of the Umayyad caliphate forces in Central Asia, defeated their armies. With the defeat of the Tang and Tibetan empires, combined with the decline of the Turks, the Abbasid caliphate began to assert its control firmly over Central Asia.

Despite these conquests, Islam as a religion penetrated more slowly as it competed with well-established religions such as Buddhism, Zoroastrianism, Nestorian Christianity, and even Judaism. Despite the population's slow conversion to Islam, a new culture emerged in Central Asia combining elements of Islam and nomadic, Persian, and traditional sedentary cultures.

Although Islam triumphed, unity was not guaranteed. Eventually, the local dynasties that had remained in power either through submission or conversion to Islam, as well as new dynasties, began to assert themselves against the Abbasid caliphate. The dynasty that came to the fore in the ninth century became known as the Samanids (864–999).

In 738, Saman-Khudah, the Persian ruler of Balkh, a region in modern Afghanistan, converted to Islam. His grandsons all became governors of Mawarannahr in the ninth century, but the true founder of the dynasty was Isma'il ibn Ahmed (892–907), who became governor in 893 and ruled until his death in 907. Under his leadership, the Samanids defeated the Karluk Turks north of the Syr Dar'ya as well as the emerging Saffarid dynasty (873–900) in Iran. Isma'il maintained his allegiance to the caliph, although he effectively acted as an independent ruler. With the defeat of the Saffarids, the Samanids added the province of Khurasan to their domains.

Isma'il and the Samanids ruled a confederation of tribes and cities in which regional dynasts ruled the provinces. The key to the Samanids' success came through their army, the core of which was based on the *ghulam* (slave) system. Slaves, usually Turks, were purchased and then trained as warriors or administrators. This gave rise to a professional army and civil service or bureaucracy. In turn, the role of the nobility, who had formerly occupied border fortresses, was reduced. They then moved into the cities, making a transition from involvement in a military elite to involvement in local affairs. Despite their normal loyalty to their master, the *ghulam*s, like all professional soldiers, could overthrow the ruler and place one who better represented their interests on the throne.

Certain conditions promoted prosperity. First, the rulers ensured security for the growth of trade and agriculture. Second, the ruling powers had an interest in their subjects' welfare. This was usually demonstrated by taxing fairly rather than taxing for exploitative gain. The Samanids carried out both of these

conditions, which resulted in urban growth and maintenance of the irrigation system that was central to the regional agriculture. Furthermore, under the Samanids, trade expanded in all directions.

A cultural renaissance also occurred. The Samanids, as well as the nobles who now lived near the cities, became patrons of knowledge and the arts. With the spread of Islam, Arabic, as the language of Islam, also spread. Persian, however, remained the vernacular. The Samanids also attracted many of the great scholars of the Islamic world, such as Ibn Sina (Avicenna) (980–1037) and Firdawsi (940–1020).

Despite the Iranian origins of the Samanids, Central Asia slowly became Turkicized through the importation of Turkic *ghulam*s. Turkification became more rapid, however, as more Turkic tribes entered Samanid territory. By 1000, Turks had overrun the Samanid realm, and local governments asserted their own authority in the ensuing chaos. Two Turkic governments replaced the last Iranian rulers of Central Asia, yet they maintained strong ties to the system of government used by the Samanids.

Ghaznavids and Karakhanids

The Ghaznavid dynasty (977–1187) arose from *ghulam*s who established their own state in Khurasan, Afghanistan, and northern India. Sebuk Tegin (reigned 977–997), the governor of the city of Ghazni in eastern Afghanistan, established the Ghaznavid empire in 977. His son, Mahmud (reigned 998–1030), became its most renowned ruler after gaining control of the empire in a civil war. Mahmud also established the empire's independence from the Samanids by renouncing Samanid suzerainty. Furthermore, he sought and secured the recognition of the Abbasid caliph. The Ghaznavids, particularly under Mahmud, fought as *ghazi*s (frontier soldiers, often religious fighters along the frontiers of the Islamic world) and expanded the influence of Islam into India. Despite an impressive army, the Ghaznavid empire was eventually eclipsed by the Seljuks, who settled in Khurasan.

The Karakhanid dynasty (999–1212) ruled Mawarannahr, East Turkistan, and the lands north of the Syr Dar'ya. It is thought that the Karakhanids originated from Karluk Turks around Kashi in modern Xinjiang Uygur in western China, who converted to Islam through the influence of Sufi Muslims. Under Sufi influence, Islam continued to find converts in Central Asia, particularly among the Turks beyond the Syr Dar'ya. The emergence of the Karakhanids marked the shift to the Turkification of the region as well.

Initially, the Karakhanids fought the Samanids and slowly conquered Mawarannahr, achieving final victory in 999 with Nasr Ilis's (d. 1012) conquest of Bukhara. In 1001, Nasr Ilis and Mahmud of Ghazni completed a treaty that drew the Amu Dar'ya as the border between their respective states. With the Karakhanid domination of Central Asia, the Turkic language replaced Iranian as the primary language and even emerged as a medium for literature with the publication in 1069 of *The Wisdom of Royal Glory*, which was a mirror for princes on how to rule, based on Turk, Muslim, and Sufi traditions. In addition, the Karakhanids maintained the Samanid administrative apparatus but ruled from the steppe. Unlike the Samanids and Ghaznavids, the Karakhanids relied on conscription of nomadic cavalry rather than professional armies of *ghulam*s. Still, these two empires were eventually supplanted by another group of Turks.

The Seljuks

The Seljuks (1038–1157) were part of the Oghuz Turkic tribes and were named after their khan, or ruler, Seljuk. In 985, Seljuk converted to Islam, like the Karakhanids, through the influence of Sufis. Seljuk and his tribespeople first served as mercenaries for the Samanids and the Karakhanids but eventually crossed the Amu Dar'ya and were allowed to settle in Khwarazm, the region from the lower Amu Dar'ya River valley west to the Caspian Sea and east to Bukhara.

After Mahmud of Ghazni conquered Khwarazm, he realized the growing power of the Seljuks and defeated them. The Seljuks, however, persevered, and soon more entered the region during the reign of Masud (b. Mahmud; reigned 1031–1041). At first the Seljuks wished to settle in the region in return for their military services. Masud, however, also feared their growing numbers and engaged them in war.

The Seljuks defeated Masud and eventually brought most of the Ghaznavid empire under their dominion. By 1055, their armies had reached Baghdad and defeated the Shi'ite Buyid dynasty (c. 945–1055). As a reward, the caliph named Toghril (founder of the Seljuk dynasty; reigned 1038–1063) sultan, thus effectively making Toghril the secular leader of Islam.

Using armies of nomadic tribesmen and *ghulam*s, the Seljuks expanded their empire from Central Asia into Anatolia. Alp Arslan (reigned 1063–1072) led the onslaught into Anatolia by defeating the Byzantines at Manzikirt in 1071. In Central Asia, Alp Arslan's successor, Sultan Malikshah (reigned 1072–1092), conquered Mawarannahr in 1074 and captured the cities of Bukhara and Samarqand. Like the Ghaznavids and

Karakhanids, the Seljuks maintained the Samanid system of government by governing through local dynasties and were heavily influenced by the great *wazir* (vizier) Nizam al-Mulk. As the leaders of the Islamic world, the Seljuks spread Sunni Islam.

The decline of Seljuk power began with the death of Malikshah in 1092, followed shortly by the assassination of Nizam al-Mulk. This period also marked the end of the great conquests, resulting in less plunder for nomadic groups and a slow ascension of several local dynasties. Sultan Sanjar (reigned 1118–1157) attempted to maintain order, but his authority declined after his defeat by the Kara Kitai in 1141. In 1155, Oghuz tribesmen captured and killed Sanjar, effectively ending a unified empire. Although local Seljuk dynasties continued to rule in parts of Iran, Anatolia, and the Arab lands, Central Asia fell to the Kara Kitai.

Kara Kitai

The Kara Kitai initially ruled northern China and part of Mongolia as the Liao dynasty (907–1125). The Kara Kitans, a Mongolian people, were however driven out of China in 1124/5 by a Manchurian group, the Jurchen. A group of Kara Kitans fled west under the command of Yeh-lu Ta-Shi (reigned 1124–1143). Although the ruling corps was made up of predominately Kara Kitans, other ethnic groups joined them.

In 1129, the Kara Kitans conquered Kashi and Hotan, also in western Xinjiang Uygur. Choosing the city of Balasaghun in the Chu Valley in southeast Kazakhstan as their capital, Yeh-lu Ta-Shi ruled as the Gur Khan. In 1137, his armies entered Mawarannahr and began its conquest, ending with the defeat of Sanjar at the Qatwan steppe in 1141.

Like previous conquerors, the Kara Kitans left the local dynasties as their governors but maintained their dominion through the use of fast-moving nomadic armies. Kara Kitai was a very diverse state. The majority of the subjects were Muslim, but the ruling elite were Buddhists and of non-Iranian or Turkic heritage. Although order was maintained, the arrival of Kuchluq, prince of the Turkic Naimans and a rival of Genghis Khan, ignited underlying emotions as he persecuted Muslims and deposed the Gur Khan to set up his own short-lived kingdom, which lasted from 1211 to 1218.

As the Seljuks declined, the province of Khwarazm steadily increased in power. It had benefited greatly from Ghaznavid rule, and even during the rule of the Seljuks, Khwarazm remained fairly independent. Its rise to the height of its power began in 1097 with the appointment of Muhammad ibn Anushtegin (a vassal of the Seljuk sultan; reigned 1097–1127) as governor. He received the title of Khwarazmshah and accepted Seljuk suzerainty.

Muhammad's son Atsiz (reigned 1127–1156) followed his father's example for much of his reign. However, with the defeat of Sanjar in 1141, Atsiz shifted his tribute to the Kara Kitai and rejected the Seljuks as his overlords. The caliph also recognized Atsiz as an independent sultan, boosting the legitimacy of his rule. Atsiz, no longer fettered by the Seljuks, then expanded northward by conquering land on the Syr Dar'ya and Mangishlai on the Caspian Sea.

After the death of Atsiz in 1156, Atsiz's son Il-Arslan (reigned 1156–1172) continued to build the kingdom into a powerful state that controlled the trade routes from the Kipchak steppe (stretching from the Black Sea through modern Kazakhstan), the Middle East, China, the Russian principalities, and Siberia. Although he continued to pay tribute to Kara Kitai, the Khwarazmshah was fairly independent. Khwarazmian expansion continued under the next ruler, Tekesh (1172–1200), who conquered Khurasan.

Tekesh's successor, 'Ala al-Din Muhammad II (1200–1220), brought the empire to its apogee and also caused its destruction. With the aid of Kuchluq, Muhammad II defeated the Kara Kitan armies near Talas. While Kuchluq received the territories north and east of the Syr Dar'ya, Muhammad II received Mawarannahr. The vainglorious Muhammad II soon considered himself to be the second Alexander of Macedon. Because his empire stretched from the Syr Dar'ya to Iraq, it was difficult to refute his claims.

Despite his military success, his empire was fragile. Muhammad II suffered from poor relations with the Abbasid caliphate, which he failed to conquer in 1217. Furthermore, his power base rested on Kipchak tribesmen, whose primary loyalty rested with his mother, the daughter of a Kipchak khan. Muhammad II also alienated the local nobility by breaking with Samanid tradition. Instead of relying on the local dynasties, he appointed numerous family members as governors and local rulers.

Muhammad II's downfall began when a caravan arrived in Otrar on the Syr Dar'ya River (in present-day Kazakhstan) from Mongolia. Merchants, sponsored by Genghis Khan and his newly created empire, had come to trade. In addition they wished to establish friendly diplomatic relations with the Khwarazmshah on behalf of the great Mongol ruler. Muhammad II, whether through ego, greed, or other motives, allowed Inalchuq, the governor of the city of Otrar, to massacre the merchants and offended Mongolian ambas-

sadors who sought reparation before hostilities escalated. The ambassadors returned to Genghis Khan highly insulted, thus setting the Mongol armies in motion and resulting in the complete collapse of the Khwarazmian empire.

Timothy May

Further Reading
Barthold, Vasili. (1977) *Turkestan Down to the Mongol Invasions.* Philadelphia: Porcupine.

Christian, David. (1998) *A History of Russia, Central Asia, and Mongolia.* Malden, MA: Blackwell.

Golden, Peter B. (1992) *An Introduction to the History of the Turkic Peoples.* Wiesbaden, Germany: O. Harrassowitz.

Grousset, René. (1970) *The Empire of the Steppes: A History of Central Asia.* New Brunswick, NJ: Rutgers University Press.

Sinor, Denis, ed. (1990) *The Cambridge History of Early Inner Asia.* Cambridge, U.K.: Cambridge University Press.

Soucek, Svat. (2000) *A History of Inner Asia.* Oxford, U.K.: Oxford University Press.

CENTRAL ASIA—HUMAN RIGHTS The five republics of Central Asia (Kazakhstan, Kyrgyzstan, Tajikistan, Turkmenistan, and Uzbekistan), which emerged after the collapse of the Soviet Union in 1991, began their existence as independent countries with a common Soviet heritage in regards to human rights. For both governments and citizens, economic and social rights are now at least on a par with freedom of expression, association, religion, and other traditional measures of human rights. None of the states has a particularly good record in implementing internationally recognized human-rights standards, though all insist that they respect those standards and aspire to put them into practice. Some Central Asian officials point to their Asian as well as their Soviet heritage to justify the problematic human-rights records of their countries. The Central Asian republics have subscribed to the standards laid out in the Universal Declaration of Human Rights.

While each Central Asian state has a distinctive record in the observance of human rights, some shortcomings are common to all. Human-rights problems most frequently cited by citizens of the Central Asian countries include law enforcement that has failed to abandon the Soviet-era belief that it is more important to have a high rate of success in "solving" crimes than it is to catch the actual perpetrator, with resultant police brutality directed at extracting confessions; lack of an independent judiciary, with the result that those in power misuse the courts for political purposes, and there is little opportunity to challenge arbitrary actions of officials or to seek redress for human-rights violations; pervasive corruption, leading to a host of perceived human-rights violations; and poor prison conditions.

Kazakhstan

When Kazakhstan began its existence as an independent state, it had the beginnings of a civil society, in the form of numerous grassroots public organizations, some of which were engaged in human-rights monitoring. A large number of independent print and broadcast media developed throughout the country and began reporting abuses by officials. The national parliament actively opposed some actions of the executive branch. In view of these developments as well as the Kazakstani leadership's commitment to privatization and a rapid transition to a market economy, the country gained the reputation in the international community of making a respectable start on the road to democracy.

But postindependence elections have been consistently criticized, by domestic monitors and by foreign observers, for falling short of international standards. After complaining that the national parliament was hampering his plans for the economy, President Nursultan Nazarbaev in 1995 dissolved the legislature and for a time ruled by decree. He obtained additional powers for himself under a new constitution that also limited the powers of parliament, thereby weakening the system of checks and balances that had begun to develop.

In 1999, two opposition politicians were refused registration as presidential candidates on grounds of previous minor legal infractions (in one case, having taken part in an unauthorized public meeting), and opposition parliamentary candidates were harassed by the authorities. In at least four cases, government complicity was alleged in physical assaults on candidates.

The problems of government opponents did not end with the elections. Former Prime Minister Akezhan Kazhegeldin, one of the disqualified presidential candidates, fled the country to avoid prosecution on charges of embezzlement, which he insisted were invented by the government. Official attempts to have him detained abroad and to have his foreign bank account frozen were unsuccessful until July 2000, when he was arrested in Italy on an Interpol warrant. An Italian court promptly freed him.

Despite progressive encroachments on political rights, in the opinion of many of the country's citizens, Kazakhstan's most serious human-rights violations occur in the socioeconomic field, where living standards have declined, salaries and pensions have frequently been in arrears for months if not years, and unemployment has spread. Corruption has remained pervasive. Strikes and unauthorized public protests over living conditions have often led to arrests and beatings; in a major strike in southern Kazakhstan in 1998, demonstrators beat police.

In the early years after independence, several nongovernmental organizations developed specifically to monitor the observance of human rights. Among the most active on the national level were the Kazakhstan International Bureau for Human Rights and the Rule of Law and the Kazakhstan Helsinki Federation, but many more, including the independent trade unions, were involved in human-rights monitoring and reporting. A human-rights commission was set up in 1996 to report to the president, but its findings were never made public. The commission's initial advisory board included leaders of two human-rights monitoring groups who almost immediately became involved in a dispute with the executive secretary, after the latter publicly attacked all nongovernmental organizations as a threat to the state. The commission was subsequently weakened, in the view of independent human-rights monitors, by the appointment of members unfamiliar with human-rights concepts.

After 1995, the media were subject to increasing government restrictions and sometimes to outright harassment. The government used its ownership of all printing facilities to exert control over the print media. In 1997, a redistribution of broadcast frequencies took place; the government took the opportunity to close down a number of critical private television and radio stations by rejecting their bids for frequencies. In 1999, the government closed some independent newspapers and pressured the media to limit coverage of opposition presidential and parliamentary candidates.

Although Kazakhstan's leadership is officially committed to maintaining ethnic balance, and stirring up ethnic enmity is a serious criminal charge, policies favoring ethnic Kazakhs have become more and more prevalent. A law requiring half of all broadcasting to be in Kazakh, which has the status of a state language, has been resented not only by non-Kazakhs but also by ethnic Kazakhs whose first language is Russian. Nongovernmental groups representing the interests of the Slavic community have been regularly harassed by the authorities. Groups representing Cossack interests were not allowed to function legally until several years after independence.

Kyrgyzstan

Kyrgyzstan acquired an international reputation as the Central Asian state farthest advanced on the road to democracy. But the promise of its early postindependence years has been unfulfilled, as the government of President Askar Akaev has become more authoritarian and gains in implementation of human rights have been eroded. The sharpest decline occurred in 2000, when the Kyrgyz leadership harassed and even imprisoned opposition politicians and human-rights activists to limit their success in parliamentary and presidential elections.

More than in any other Central Asian state, Kyrgyzstan's parliament has acted as an active check on the power of the executive branch. Political parties, ranging from the Communists to liberal democratic groups, have played a considerable role in the life of the country and have ensured a healthy opposition, though they were subjected to increasing harassment by the authorities in 1999 and 2000. Pressure on the opposition culminated in 2000 with the disqualification and subsequent arrests of several well-known opposition candidates for the parliamentary election; some candidates were disqualified between the first and second rounds of voting. Felix Kulov, the most credible opponent of President Akaev in the presidential election of October 2000, was arrested during the parliamentary election. Although Kulov was freed after an international outcry, the sentence was later reconfirmed by a higher court, and he remains in prison, facing additional charges. The parliamentary election was judged by international observers to have fallen short of international standards.

In the immediate postindependence period, Kyrgyzstan developed relatively liberal conditions for the information media. Attacking government officials for corruption and abuse of office became a favorite theme, especially in the print media. Some officials retaliated by charging journalists and editors with libel, which remained a criminal offense despite the efforts of the president to persuade the parliament to change the law. Several prominent journalists spent time in jail or faced heavy fines as a result of such charges; the independent media regarded these cases as government intimidation.

A broad spectrum of grassroots nongovernmental organizations has formed in Kyrgyzstan, where the concept of civil society seems to have become well rooted. Several groups monitor human rights, including social and economic rights. Some groups have clashed with the police during unauthorized demonstrations in support of pensioners and others who have suffered severe declines in their living standards. In 1998, the government deregistered the most prominent of the human-rights monitoring groups, the Kyrgyz Committee for Human Rights. It was later reregistered, but experienced constant harassment by the authorities, culminating in 2000 with an attempt to arrest the group's chairperson, who sought refuge with the International Helsinki Federation in Vienna.

Although attempts have been made to reform the judiciary and free it from government influence, many citizens consider that the strong role of the state prosecutor, who is seen as a guardian of the government's interests, ensures that courts do not protect the interests of ordinary people.

A human-rights commission was established under the president's office in 1997. Human-rights activists have complained that though a well-known opposition politician was appointed to head the commission, none of its members has any experience in the field of human rights. As of 2000, Kyrgyzstan was in the process of creating an ombudsman's office with help from international organizations.

Tajikistan

Tajikistan's existence as an independent state has been overshadowed by the civil war that began in mid-1992. A peace accord was signed in 1997 between the two main combatants, the government in Dushanbe, representing primarily former Communist elements from the southern region of Kulyab, and the Islamic and democratic opposition. Large segments of the political spectrum in the country were excluded from the peace agreement, which resulted in sporadic fighting and armed attacks on individuals.

During the civil war, scant regard was given to human rights, though this situation began to change as active fighting wound down and the thousands of refugees who had fled to Afghanistan and other neighboring countries returned to their homes. International organizations, in particular the United Nations High Commissioner for Refugees and the Organization for Security and Cooperation in Europe, assisted in the resettlement and reintegration of the refugees to ensure that their basic human rights were respected. Reports indicate that this process has been largely successful.

National and local officials, journalists, businesspeople, and others continued to be assassination targets well into 2000. Some killings have been attributed to rival government factions. Attempts to disarm former opposition fighters were not completely effective, and large numbers of weapons remain in circulation, making it easy for small independent groups to arm themselves. In addition to assaults by political rivals on one another, the government's security forces have attacked civilians, sometimes holding individuals for ransom. The country as a whole was reported to have serious problems with the kidnapping and rape of women. The inability of the government to establish control throughout the country has meant that law enforcement remains ineffective and unable to protect citizens' rights. In 1996 the Tajik government promised to establish the post of human rights ombudsman, but nothing came of it.

Once opposition political parties were legitimized as part of the peace process, some of them began to publish their own newspapers. The government has closed or harassed these and other independent publications. A number of independent television stations obtained licenses but also experienced government harassment.

President Imomali Rakhmonov, a former Communist official, has repeatedly described Islam as a political threat, but bowed in 1998 to international pressure and persuaded the parliament to drop a ban on political parties with a religious orientation. Despite the participation of officials of the Islamic Revival Party in the government, the Muslim community is still overseen by the State Committee on Religious Affairs, and private religious instruction is restricted.

Turkmenistan

Turkmenistan is considered by many in the international human-rights community to have the poorest human-rights record of any state in Central Asia. Political and economic reform has hardly begun, and some of the gains of the late Soviet era in freedom of speech, association, and religion have been undone. The country's leader, President Saparmurat Niyazov, has not only surrounded himself with a personality cult outdoing that of Stalin, but is in the process of creating a state ideology focusing on the president as the omnipotent father figure of the nation, so that there is no need for civil society. In any case, an independent entity, whether a nongovernmental institution or a genuinely private enterprise, is regarded with great suspicion by the authorities.

Opposition political groups were always small and weak in Turkmenistan; by 2000, the few individuals who actively opposed government policies were either in prison or under close supervision of the National Security Committee, and their influence was nonexistent. Several grassroots environmental organizations were able to register in the early 1990s and enjoyed some degree of cooperation with the Ministry of Nature Protection because environmental protection was perceived by the authorities as apolitical. At least two of these groups later drew governmental ire when they began monitoring human-rights problems. There

were no groups engaged specifically in human-rights monitoring, but a number of unregistered nongovernment organizations tried to deal with specific human-rights issues, such as the rights of the handicapped, hospital patients, and refugees. Few nongovernmental organizations could register with the Ministry of Justice after 1995.

In 1999 and 2000, thousands of prisoners were released under a series of amnesties. This may have been in reaction to international criticism of prison conditions in which many prisoners died of disease and extreme heat. At the end of 1999, the People's Assembly formally abolished the death penalty.

The information media have been under tight government control. Both print and broadcast media were used by the state as propaganda devices rather than as providers of information. Foreign, including Russian, newspapers were available by subscription but were too expensive for most citizens. Satellite antennas could be purchased and installed, but few outside the cities could afford them. In the years after independence, a number of private Internet providers appeared in Turkmenistan; they were closed down in May 2000.

In Ashgabat, thousands of people were displaced from their homes as part of the grandiose presidential scheme to reconstruct the capital. Some were offered apartments in poor-quality Soviet-era housing developments, but many received neither compensation nor other living quarters. Under a presidential decree issued in 2000, the police were prohibited from searching private homes. The government cited this as an example of state concern for human rights, but oversight for implementation of the decree was handed to the very agencies (the Ministry of Internal Affairs, the State Prosecutor's Office, and the security service) that had most abused citizens' privacy.

Uzbekistan

Since 1992, the leadership of Uzbekistan has used the threat of Islamic extremism to justify its authoritarianism and disregard for human rights. Socially conservative pious Muslims have been a particular target of government harassment, especially after the Tajik civil war broke out in 1992, and again in 1998 when the murder of a policeman in the conservative Fergana Valley town of Namangan was the pretext for the arrests of thousands of Muslims. In February 2000, a series of bombs was detonated in Tashkent. President Islam Karimov announced that he was the intended target and unleashed another round of arrests of "Muslim extremists," which swept up a number of human-rights activists. Some were incarcerated in a new prison that had become notorious for the number of deaths of inmates, from both police brutality and disease.

Genuine political opposition is not tolerated, though a number of political parties exist. Opposition groups (the mildly nationalist Birlik Movement and the Erk Democratic Party) that were allowed not only to exist but to publish their own newspapers until a few months after independence were stripped of their registration in 1993. The few people who later considered themselves members of these groups were harassed by the authorities; many of those who did not leave the country were jailed in 1999–2000. Some members of opposition groups formed organizations to monitor human rights. The government used this as an excuse to refuse registration to all but one human-rights nongovernmental organization, claiming that the other groups were merely fronts for banned political organizations.

An ombudsman's office was set up under the parliament in 1997 to deal specifically with human-rights problems. In her annual reports, the ombudsman noted that the majority of cases brought to the office involved problems with the law enforcement and judicial systems. The office's success rate in dealing with these problems was low.

As is the case elsewhere in Central Asia, law enforcement officials in Uzbekistan are notorious for beating detainees. They are also reported to plant evidence, usually small amounts of narcotics, a few bullets, or weapons, on persons arrested for political reasons. Independent media exist in Uzbekistan, but they function under fairly strict government scrutiny. Criticism of the government is not tolerated.

Bess Brown

Further Reading

Amnesty International (2000) "Annual Reports." Retrieved 1 August 2000, from: http://www.amnesty.org.

Human Rights Watch. "Europe/Central Asia." Retrieved 1 August 2000, from: http://www.hrw.org/europe/index.php.

U.S. Department of State. "Human Rights/Country Reports." Retrieved 3 August 2000, from: http://www.usis.usemb.se/human.

CENTRAL ASIA—LATE MEDIEVAL AND EARLY MODERN Central Asia entered modernity in the wake of Russian conquest in the last quarter of the nineteenth century. Russian penetration into

the Kazakh steppe from western Siberia began in the seventeenth and eighteenth centuries and was completed in the 1840s with the suppression of the Kazakh hordes. In 1864, Russian resumed its conquest, finishing in 1884 with the capture of the last Turkmen oasis of Merv. The imposition of Russian rule in Central Asia resulted in the distortion of "native" capitalism in the area, which was subsequently turned into a major supplier of raw materials, predominately cotton, to Russian industries.

The Kazakh Steppe and the Start of Russian Conquest

At the beginning of the eighteenth century, the Kazakh ethnic groups, who lacked political unity, coalesced into three confederations. These were Uly Juz (the Greater Horde), occupying the Jetysu (Seven Rivers) district in the southeast portion of present-day Kazakhstan; Orta Juz (the Middle Horde) in the central part; and Kishi Juz (the Lesser Horde) between the Aral Sea and the Ural River in the west. The division was the result of varying conditions for cattle rearing, which prevailed on the Kazakh steppe.

Each horde, composed of a number of ethnic groups, was ruled by a khan with a group of subordinate sultans, who claimed to have descended from Genghis Khan. The Genghisid descent was also a central factor in the peculiar vertical division of Kazakh society into two groups—the Aq Suyek (White Bone) people, of high status, and the Qara Suyek (Black Bone) people, who were commoners.

Islam, which began penetrating into the southeastern Kazakh steppe after a battle at the Taras River in 751, had very little effect on the social structure of Kazakh society, although descent from eminent Muslim ancestors could also entitle some individuals, called *qoja*s, to prestigious White Bone status. The main effect of Islam on the Kazakhs was in culture, that is, education and literature, and even here its impact was limited due to their nomadic lifestyle.

Kazakh justice was to a large extent based on the principle of *qun* (retribution), which varied from the death penalty to fines, depending on the offense. Kazakh customary law had three sources: custom, practice in the court of the *bii*s (the nobles), and resolutions taken at regular meetings of the *bii*s.

The social and political structure of Kazakh society was highly codified in what is known as *Jeti Jargby* (Seven Verdicts) during the reign of the Middle Horde's khan Tauke (1680–1718), who succeeded in briefly reuniting the three Kazakh hordes.

The eighteenth-century Kazakh economy was based on cattle breeding, although the encroachment of the Kazakh ethnic groups on the regions south of the steppe in the sixteenth century had resulted in some urban and agricultural development and trade with the settled population. To the north and west, commercial relations with the Russians had also begun.

The Russian advance into the Kazakh steppe was a gradual process, the actual beginning of which is usually associated with the request by Khan Abulkhair (Abilay; 1693–1748) to Russia to be a suzerain (overlord) of the Lesser Horde. The request was granted in 1731. Nevertheless, the founding dates of such Russian towns as Uralsk (now Oral), Guryev (now Atyrau; 1645), and Ust-Kamenogorsk, or Oskemen (1720) indicate that the actual Russian encroachment into the western and northeastern steppes started long before.

A bloody invasion by the Jungars (a subdivision of the Mongols) in 1723 and threats constantly emanating from the east forced the khans of the Middle and Greater Hordes also to accept Russian suzerainty in 1740 and 1742, respectively.

While signing an oath of allegiance, the Kazakh khans pledged to protect adjacent Russian borders, to defend Russian trade caravans, to provide troops when needed, and to pay tribute to Russia. Until the end of the eighteenth century, the political picture of the area remained unchanged, because during that period Russia was engaged in subduing the Caucasus.

Beginning in the early nineteenth century, Russia initiated a more aggressive policy toward the Kazakh hordes in an effort to annex their territories. New strategic goals led Russia to abolish the Middle Horde in 1822, the Lesser Horde in 1824, Bukey's (Bukeevskaia) Horde (formed c. 1800 to the west of the Lesser Horde) in 1845, and the Greater Horde in 1848. With the suppression of the Kazakh hordes, the first stage of Russia's conquest of Central Asia was completed.

Transoxiana in the Eighteenth Century

By the start of the eighteenth century, Transoxiana, the territory between the Amu Dar'ya and Syr Dar'ya Rivers, was dominated by three principalities—the Bukhara emirate, the Quqon khanate, and the Khiva khanate.

The Bukhara emirate, the most populous (3 million people in the nineteenth century) and influential of the three, was situated in the basin of the Zeravshan River. It was ruled by the Uzbek dynasty of Mangyt, who rose to power in the early eighteenth century as *ataliq* (majordomo) under the Astrakhanid (Janid) dynasty (1598–1785), which was of Genghisid origin.

The first Mangyt *ataliq* was Khudoyar Bi, who began his service in 1714 and made the position hereditary. In 1722, he was succeeded by his son Muhammad Hakim Bi, whose term (1722–1740) was marked by fighting with the Kazakh hordes who were escaping from the conquests of the Jungar Mongols from Xinjiang in western China. The next Mangyt *ataliq*, Muhammad Rahim Bi (reigned 1740–1758), further consolidated his power, although the throne was nominally occupied by the Janids until 1785.

The actual start of the Mangyt dynasty is associated with the accession of Shah Murad (reigned 1785–1800), who assumed the title of emir, which was most probably derived from *amir-al-muminin* ("commander of the believers"). The shift to an emirate was a significant step, aimed at stressing an Islamic, rather than tribal, legacy and consolidating Bukhara's leading position in Transoxiana.

Administratively, the emirate was divided into *vilayat*s (*viloyat, velayat*: provinces), ruled by *hokim*s (heads of provincial administration). The *vilayat*s were subdivided into *tuman*s (districts) and finally into *kent*s (settlements). The principal function of *hokim*s was collection of taxes and distribution of water. There were two types of taxes—*zakyat*, a tax on merchandise, movable property, and cattle; and *tanap*, a tax on land property. The land tax constituted the bulk of the emir's revenues, and it was generally paid in cash, although calculated as a percentage of the harvest. In the Bukhara emirate, the land, being the most valuable commodity, was of several types: *waqf* (possessions of religious institutions), *mulk* (freehold), and *tankhwah* (gift-lands handed over, usually to the military, by the emir, largely exempt of taxation).

The system of justice was based on Islamic *shari'a* (canon) and *adat* (customary) laws. The chief judicial official was the *kazi* (judge), assisted by the *aglian* (barristers). The muftis (jurists) were the exponents of the law; the chief mufti was the emir's chief counselor.

The Bukhara economy was based on irrigated agriculture and trade. The main trade items were cotton and textiles, and the main trading partner was Russia. Among other exports were silk, dyes, and fruits, whereas from Russia Bukhara imported pottery, metal products, sugar, paper, tin, fur, mercury, candles, textiles, and other manufactured goods. Although other towns also conducted trade directly with foreign countries, Bukhara was the emirate's most important commercial center. It was also the center of silk production and astrakhan-cloth trade. Domestic trade developed as well, serving as a unifying factor.

For the eastern part of Transoxiana, the Fergana Valley, the eighteenth century was marked by the rise to power of the Ming dynasty of Uzbek origin (distinct from the Chinese Ming). It eventually led to the establishment of the Quqon khanate, with a population of a million people, in 1798. Quqon rulers Irdana Biy (reigned 1740–1769) and Narbuta Biy (reigned 1769–1788) succeeded in consolidating the state.

Starting from the nineteenth century, the Quqon khans fought to expand their territories in the north and northwest into the steppe along the north bank of the Syr Dar'ya River. In 1803–1809, they conquered the cities of Tashkent, Shymkent (Chimkent), and Sayram. Akmeshit (now Kyzyl Orda) was founded in 1820. A stronghold was built in Pishpek (now Bishkek, capital of Kyrgyzstan) in 1846. Quqon's military campaigns led to a series of wars with Bukhara and the Kazakh and Kyrgyz ethnic groups during the first half of the nineteenth century. The Kyrgyz accepted Russian suzerainty in 1855–1876.

The Quqon khanate reached the zenith of its might during the rule of Madali Khan (reigned 1822–1842). The khanate then consisted of modern-day southern Kazakhstan, northern Uzbekistan, the Pamir regions of Tajikistan, and almost the whole of Kyrgyzstan.

The administrative system of Quqon was virtually the same as that of Bukhara, except that the subdivisions of the *vilayat*s were known as *beklik* instead of *tuman*. Quqon's economy was also based on irrigated agriculture, trade, and silk production. The Quqon khans were known for their patronage of the arts.

During the eighteenth century, the khanate of Khiva (500,000 people), situated on the lower Amu Dar'ya River, was ruled by the Uzbek Yadigarid dynasty (1603–1804) and was subsequently replaced by the Kungrat (Inakid) dynasty (1804–1920). In 1804, Iltuzer, an Uzbek noble holding the hereditary position of *inak* (prime minister), proclaimed himself khan of Khiva and established a new dynasty.

Unlike Bukhara and Quqon, Khiva had no subdivisions, and its towns enjoyed more autonomy. The majority of land was in the possession of the khan and of Muslim institutions. Extensive irrigation canals, fed by the Amu Dar'ya, were maintained by forced labor, usually made up of one male from each family. About 75 percent of the population was settled and carried on irrigated cultivation of wheat, millet, cotton, and fruit. Both internal and external trade evolved but to a lesser extent than in Bukhara and Quqon. Khiva's

foreign-trade partners were Afghanistan, Persia, and Russia. The Amu Dar'ya was extensively used for the conveyance of goods.

The Karakalpaks, another Turkic people living around the Amu Dar'ya delta, frequently revolted. Khiva's north and southwest borders were raided by Kazakh and Turkmen groups. The latter were the principal supplier of Persian slaves to the Khiva and Bukhara markets. The nomad Turkmen, lacking political unity, consisted of a number of separate ethnic groups, the most remarkable of which were Tekke, Tomud, and Ersary, occupying the territories immediately south of the Khiva khanate and the southern portion between the Caspian and Aral Seas.

At the middle of the nineteenth century, the ruling and living standards in Central Asia were much lower than those in medieval Europe, where large-scale foreign invasions, pillage, and devastation had ended some two hundred years earlier than they did in Central Asia. This situation, along with the absence of agreement between the three principalities, made them vulnerable to Russian conquest.

The Second Stage of Russian Conquest (1864–1884)

Russia's engagement in the Crimean War (1853–1856) and the pacifying of Sheikh Shamil's mutiny in the Caucasus (1843–1859) resulted in an interval of relative calm for several years between the suppression of the Kazakh hordes (1848) and the start of the final stage of Russian conquest (1864). Yet during this period, the Quqon strongholds of Ak Mechet and Pishpek were seized in 1853 and 1862, respectively. In addition, in 1854 Russians founded Fort Vernoe (now Almaty) in order to have access to Transoxiana across the Syr Dar'ya. The Russians resumed their conquest in 1864 with the seizure of the Quqon towns of Shymkent and Aulie Ata (now Zhambyl) in what is now southern Kazakhstan. Tashkent was routed in 1865. In 1868, after losing several battles to Russia, the emir of Bukhara, Muzaffar al-din Bakhadur Khan (reigned 1860–1885), signed a peace treaty. Under the treaty, Bukhara became a Russian protectorate and lost a considerable portion of its territories, including Samarqand.

In 1869, Russian troops reached the eastern shore of the Caspian Sea from the Caucasus and established the harbor of Krasnovodsk (now Turkmenbashy), a stronghold for future advances into Khiva and the Turkmen lands. In 1873, Khiva became a Russian protectorate, lost its western lands, and pledged to pay tribute. In 1876, the Quqon khanate was abolished.

In 1879, Russian troops moved against the Turkmen ethnic groups but were defeated at Geok-Tepe. In 1881, after the second attempt, Geok-Tepe fell. With the seizure of the last Turkmen stronghold of Merv in 1884, Russia's military conquest of Central Asia was completed. From Merv, Russia brought its troops farther to the south, close to the Afghan border, which caused a brief military clash (the Kushka Incident) between Russia and Afghanistan in 1885.

In the early 1890s, Russia pushed farther from Fergana to the Pamirs, close to British India. To avoid further confrontation, in 1895 Russia and Great Britain reached an agreement on their mutual respecting of zones of interest. This agreement was confirmed by the Anglo-Russian Convention of 1907.

As a result of the Russian conquest, new administrative divisions were introduced in Central Asia. The territories acquired in Transoxiana were united into the governorate-general of Turkistan, with headquarters in Tashkent. The governorate-general was divided into five oblasts (districts), namely Syrdarya (with the capital in Tashkent), Semirechie (Vernyi), Fergana (Skobelev), Samarqand, and Zakaspiyskaia (Ashkhabad). The emirate of Bukhara and the khanate of Khiva became Russian protectorates.

The western part of the Kazakh steppe was converted into the Uralsk oblast (center Uralsk), the central part into the Turgai and Akmolinsk oblasts. The Akmolinsk oblast was united with the eastern Semipalatinsk oblast to form the governorate-general of the steppe.

The Russian conquest of Central Asia was overwhelmingly motivated by economics. After the establishment of Russian rule, the area became a valuable market for Russian industrial goods and a source of raw materials, primarily cotton. By 1914, more than 50 percent of the cotton used by Russian light industry was supplied from Central Asia. The region's industrial development centered on cotton. Two-thirds of the local labor force was employed in cotton-processing and textile enterprises. At the same time, Central Asia was heavily dependent on Russia's grain imports. The construction of railroads and a telegraph network, crucial for exercising control over the new territories, also aided the region's development.

The other major consequence of Russian conquest was colonization by agricultural settlers, mainly Russians and Ukrainians. In 1895, a special Russian mission was sent to the Kazakh steppe to establish a land fund for newcomers. The nomads' grazing lands in the northern, eastern, and western steppes were expropriated.

The Russians did not interfere with the natives' general way of life, although they did abolish slavery.

Education continued to be based on the Qur'an and on Arabic-Persian tradition. At the same time, the Russians opened a number of schools for natives where Russian was the language of instruction. Jadidism, the Muslim progressive movement for cultural reforms that arose in Central Asia in the early twentieth century, was to a large extent catalyzed as a result of the introduction of Western cultural achievements in the wake of Russian colonization.

Thus, in the eighteenth and first half of the nineteenth century, Central Asia was distinctly divided into the nomad Kazakh steppe to the north and the three Transoxianan principalities to the south. The Kazakh hordes, who had failed to produce any efficient political unity by that time, felt insecure in the face of the constant invasions of Jungars from the east, and this insecurity caused their submission to Russian suzerainty. Russia's subsequent penetration into the area, followed by a military conquest (1864–1884), was firmly consolidated by the end of the nineteenth century. By imposing its rule in Central Asia, Russia sought to meet economic and geopolitical goals. For Central Asia proper, the capitalization of its agriculture and the acceleration of segmental industrialization had little impact on the traditional way of life and left feudal socioeconomic structures to a great extent intact.

Natalya Yu. Khan

Further Reading

Allworth, Edward, ed. (1994) *Central Asia: 130 Years of Russian Dominance, a Historical Overview.* 3d ed. Durham, NC: Duke University Press.

Bacon, Elizabeth E. (1966) *Central Asians under Russian Rule: A Study in Culture Change.* Ithaca, NY: Cornell University Press.

Bartold, Vasilii Vladimirovich. (1962) *Four Studies on the History of Central Asia.* Trans. by V. Minorsky and T. Minorsky. Leiden, Netherlands: Brill.

Brower, Daniel R., and Edward J. Lazzerini, eds. (1997) *Russia's Orient: Imperial Borderlands and Peoples, 1700–1917.* Indianapolis, IN: Indiana University Press.

Hopkirk, Peter. (1990) *The Great Game: The Struggle for Empire in Central Asia.* New York: Kodansha.

Meyer, Karl Ernest, and Shareen Blair Brysac. (1999) *Tournament of Shadows: The Great Game and the Race for Empire in Central Asia.* Washington, DC: Cornelia and Michael Bessie.

Roy, Olivier. (2000) *The New Central Asia.* New York: New York University Press.

Rywkin, Michael. (1963) *Russia in Central Asia.* New York: Collier.

Sahni, Kalpana. (1997) *Crucifying the Orient: Russian Orientalism and the Colonization of the Caucasus and Central Asia.* Bangkok, Thailand: White Orchid Press; Oslo, Norway: Institute for Comparative Research in Human Culture.

Soucek, Svat. (2000) *A History of Inner Asia.* Cambridge, U.K.: Cambridge University Press.

Wheeler, Geoffrey. (1964) *The Modern History of Soviet Central Asia.* London: Weidenfeld and Nicolson.

CENTRAL ASIA—MODERN

The modern era of Central Asian history begins with the Russian empire's conquest of the region. Russian expansion toward Central Asia was facilitated by the absence of any physical obstacles; having consolidated their hold over the steppe lands inhabited by Kazakh nomads, Russian armies moved rapidly southward between 1853 and 1873, winning easy battles against each of the three states in the region—Ququon, Bukhara, and Khiva, all in modern Uzbekistan. Russian armies annexed parts of their territory and reduced the remaining parts to vassal status. Ququon was fully annexed in 1878, but Bukhara and Khiva continued as protectorates until 1920. The annexed territories were formed into the Russian province of Turkestan, with the capital at Tashkent. The Kazakh lands became the Steppe province.

The Colonial Order

Although Central Asia was physically contiguous with European Russia, its relationship to the center was typical of the high age of European imperialism. Russians saw little in common between themselves and the indigenous population and built new "European" cities there for themselves.

In northern Central Asia the nomadic lands (both in the Steppe province and in northern Turkestan) became targets for planned settlement by Russian peasants from European Russia and the Ukraine. The floodgates opened with the creation of the Resettlement Administration as an organ of the imperial Russian government. This resettlement was intended to ease the pressure on Russia's agricultural regions by settling allegedly "excess" land not used by the nomads.

Southern Central Asia, already densely populated, saw little Russian settlement except in the cities. Here the colonial relationship was based on the production of cotton, which fed Russia's textile industry and freed it from dependence on imported cotton. The introduction of long-fiber American varieties in the 1880s started a boom that continued until World War I and transformed local Central Asian society and economy, as older elites suffered a loss of status, while new groups rose to prominence. Among the successful were merchants, who benefited from the new economic situation, and urban intellectuals. At the same time, the region became increasingly dependent on European Russia for its food supply, as more and more land was devoted to cotton cultivation.

The new Central Asian intellectuals, called the Jadids ("proponents of the new method," from the new, phonetic method of teaching the Arabic alphabet that they advocated), sought to articulate a new vision of the future for their society. Intensely aware of their lack of political power, they argued that only through education and the acquisition of modern knowledge could they take their rightful place in the world. They favored thorough cultural reform, beginning with elementary school education. In advocating social and cultural reform, the Jadids also introduced new visions of identity based on the idea of the nation, replacing the dynastic and tribal identities of the past. Their conception of the nation was rooted primarily in the common Muslim faith of Central Asia, but they gradually came to emphasize the people's Turkic ethnic roots as well. The Jadids faced opposition from both conservative elites in their own society and from the Russian state, always suspicious of unauthorized political activity. The rural population, however, remained outside these debates.

The Crisis of the Colonial Order

Peace ended in Central Asia in 1916, when, after two years of debilitating losses in World War I, the Russian government revoked Central Asians' exemption from military service and mobilized them for work behind the lines. The announcement heightened existing tensions, especially among nomads who had recently lost their land to Russian settlers. The result was a massive uprising of the local population in which government bureaucrats and Russian settlers were attacked. Official vengeance was swift and brutal. The government confiscated large amounts of the nomads' land, forcing thousands of families to flee to Chinese territory. In some districts as much as 20 percent of the nomadic population died.

The crisis was heightened by the fall of the Russian monarchy in March 1917, but the Russian Revolution brought great hope to Central Asians. The Jadids saw the revolution as an opportunity for inclusion in the mainstream of a liberal democratic Russia. For the rural population, however, concerns were much more immediate. The grain harvest was poor in 1917, and with Central Asia's dependence on imported food, a full-fledged famine raged in the region by the end of the year.

The famine, far more than any empirewide trends, defined the political struggle in Central Asia during the course of the Russian Revolution and the civil war that followed. The Russian community in Central Asia

MODERN CENTRAL ASIA TIMELINE

1853–1873 The Russian empire consolidates control of the region through a series of military conquests. Varieties of long-fiber American cotton are introduced and start a boom that continues until World War I and transforms Central Asian society and economy.

1880s The Jadids, a new intellectual movement, articulate a new vision of the future for Central Asian society based on education and the acquisition of modern knowledge.

1916 The Russian government, which had previously exempted Central Asians from military service, conscripts them for work behind-the-lines in World War I. Massive uprisings by Central Asians are severely repressed by the Russians.

1917–1920 The Russian Revolution ends the rule of the Russian empire. Central Asian efforts to achieve political independence are crushed by the Soviets. In 1917 the region experiences a serious famine.

1920s–1930s Islam is repressed by Soviet authorities with Islamic schools replaced with public education, mosques closed, clerics persecuted, and Arabic writing replaced with Latin script and then Cyrillic in 1940.

1924–1925 The Soviets bring their policy of creating "ethnic-based" republics to Central Asia and the Soviet Socialist republics of Uzbekistan and Turkmenistan are created.

1929 Agriculture is collectivized and nomadic pastoralism repressed.

1929 Tajikistan is established as an autonomous republic in the Soviet Union.

1936 Kyrgyzstan and Kazkhstan are established as autonomous republics in the Soviet Union.

1953–1982 A period of relative political stability in the region, with national and local leaders loyal to the Communist leadership in Moscow.

1986 Nationalist riots erupt in Almaty, the capital of Kazakhstan when the Soviet leadership replaces the Kazakh Communist leader.

1991 The Soviet Union dissolves and the five Central Asian republics become independent nations and join the post-Soviet Commonwealth of Independent States.

1991–2001 The nations seek to establish economic and political stability, establish relations with Western nations, and control internal unrest tied to political corruption and the emergence of Islamic nationalism.

sought to maintain its privileged access to food during the political crisis. In Tashkent, Russians seized power in the name of the Soviets in October 1917, even before the Bolshevik Revolution had taken place in Petrograd, and sought to exclude the Muslim population from the new institutions of power. The violence against the Kazakh nomads that began in 1916 never abated, and indeed it intensified under a new revolutionary guise. An autonomous government proclaimed by the Jadids in Quqon on November 1917 as an alternative to the Tashkent Soviet regime was destroyed by military force in February 1918.

In this chaos emerged the Basmachi, armed bands, locally organized and owing allegiance to individual commanders, who provided basic protection to Muslim peasants and attempted some alleviation of the terrible famine. Although they have been both reviled as counterrevolutionary bandits and celebrated as heroes of national liberation, their goals were local. They did not have a well-articulated political program but instead reacted to the situation as it developed. Because of the famine, the struggle in Central Asia became one between the cities and the countryside; the cities ultimately triumphed, thanks to the might of the Red Army. The Basmachi were won over by what turned out to be temporary political and economic concessions. Many Basmachi leaders fled to Afghanistan; others were captured and tried.

The Soviet Order

When Moscow finally acquired control over Central Asia in 1920 with the Red Army's victory in the civil war, it set out actively to recruit Central Asians in the new institutions of power. Among the Central Asians entering the new institutions were many Jadids, who saw in the new order an opportunity to transform their society. There was indeed a great deal in common between the programs of change espoused by the Jadids and those of the Bolsheviks in the early years of the Soviet period. The Bolshevik agenda included universal literacy and elementary education, improving the position of women, and transforming cultural conceptions of hygiene and public health. Much of this coincided with the program of change the Jadids had articulated.

Bukhara provided the best example of the community of interests between the Jadids and the Bolsheviks. The Russian Revolution of 1917 gave Bukharan Jadids hope that the emir, or local ruler, might proclaim reforms, but the hope was dashed and the Jadids were brutally suppressed. They escaped to Turkestan, where they organized openly under the name of the Young Bukharans. Desperation radicalized their political stance, while the Bolsheviks provided a clear example of what was possible. The Young Bukharans drew closer to the Bolsheviks, who helped them overthrow the emir by armed force in September 1920. The emir escaped into the mountains of present-day Tajikistan, and the Young Bukharans proclaimed a Bukharan People's Soviet Republic (BNSR). Broadly similar events led to the installation of a people's republic in Khiva, now renamed Khorazm.

The BNSR had a short and traumatic life. Throughout its existence it faced insurgency in the mountainous eastern area of the country. The Soviet government recognized its independence, but was not inclined to let its leaders choose policies entirely independently. It pushed the BNSR government to adopt radical social and economic policies and to tie its economy more closely to that of the Soviet Union. Frustrated by this pressure, some Young Bukharans went over to the insurgency in 1921, while others continued to seek compromise.

The Soviets were committed to the process of national self-determination for the many nationalities inhabiting the vast country, and to the creation of territorial entities in which this self-determination could be exercised. This countrywide process arrived in Central Asia in 1924 and, among other things, spelled the end of the BNSR. Turkestan, Bukhara, and Khorazm were all entities whose boundaries bore no resemblance to the ethnic composition of their populations; such disregard for ethnic boundaries had been common in the premodern world. By 1924 central authorities in Moscow had decided that this abnormal situation could not be allowed to continue. The territory of Central Asia was divided so that each "national" group had its own republic. During 1924 and 1925 the demarcation was completed with the full participation of local party and state officials, and the three existing republics were replaced by the Soviet Socialist republics (SSRs) of Uzbekistan and Turkmenistan. Uzbekistan included in it the autonomous republics of Tajikistan and Kyrgyzstan, which were upgraded to SSR status in 1929 and 1936, respectively. At the same time, certain areas of Turkestan were ceded to the Russian Federation, where they were combined with other Kazakh-inhabited areas to form the autonomous republic of Kazakhstan, which in turn became an SSR in 1936.

This political organization in Central Asia was based on a radically new principle of national identity, and the division into five republics presumed a clearcut division that did not always exist in fact. Nevertheless, over the next several decades, these new national identities were endowed with great power through state-sponsored cultivation of individual national languages, literature, arts, and education.

What the regime brought about was nothing short of a cultural revolution: rapid modernization and forced secularization of society and culture. The traditional system of Muslim education, of which Bukhara was especially a major center, was dismantled through economic pressure in the 1920s and overt repression in the 1930s. In its place appeared a widespread system of modern schools. The literary languages were reformed and brought closer to the vernacular. In 1928 the Arabic script universally used in Central Asia was replaced by the Latin and in 1939–1940 by the Cyrillic. State funding also allowed for books and newspapers to be printed in unprecedented quantities.

The Jadids were enthusiastic participants in this revolution, although they had no control over its direction or scope, and indeed it went much further than they had envisaged. This was especially the case with the campaign against Islam that the Soviets pursued from the mid-1920s on. As a result Islamic education was pushed underground, and religious observance decreased greatly. Mosques were closed by the thousands, and Muslim scholars arrested, exiled, or executed in great numbers.

Central Soviet policies also called for the "nativization" (korenizatsiia) of the state apparatus in the non-Russian parts of the Soviet Union. Members of

JOINT STATEMENT OF THE MEMBER STATES OF THE UNITED NATIONS SPECIAL PROGRAMME FOR THE ECONOMIES OF CENTRAL ASIA (SPECA), U.N. ECE, AND ESCAP AT THE PRESENTATION OF SPECA

Following the demise of the Soviet Union and establishment of independent nations in Central Asia, these nations faced major economic problems. In March 1998 at Tashkent, agreement was reached on programs to develop the economic infrastructure and those programs were supported by a statement issued in Akmaty, Kazakhstan, in April 2000.

New Stage of Implementation of the United Nations Special Programme for the Economies of Central Asia (SPECA)

The Republic of Kazakhstan, the Kyrgyz Republic, the Republic of Tajikistan, the Republic of Uzbekistan, United Nations Economic Commission for Europe (ECE) and Economic and Social Commission for Asia and Pacific (ESCAP) actively develop international cooperation aimed at accelerating economic development of all the states of Central Asia. We do appreciate that further strengthening of economic ties among the Central Asian states and their economic integration with Europe and Asia will contribute in a positive way to the process of their transition to a market economy.

It was for this purpose that in March 1998 our States have adopted the Tashkent Declaration on the United Nations Special Programme for the Economies of Central Asia (SPECA). Since that time, a serious progress has been registered at some priority areas of the Programme. SPECA Project Working Groups on Rational and Efficient Use of Energy and Water Resources in Central Asia, on Transport Infrastructure and Border Crossing Facilitation and on International Economic Conference on Tajikistan in the Regional Context of Central Asia have started their work. These inter-state groups have agreed their Programmes of Work and have come close to the stage of developing and implementing concrete projects of regional importance. We have finished with organisational issues of SPECA and have improved environment for the implementation of the Programme by adopting the Concept of the Programme.

Today we reconfirm our dedication to the aims and purposes of the SPECA Programme and officially announce the beginning of a new stage in its implementation. We shall join our forces in order to progress in solving priority tasks of the Programme for the benefit of the peoples of our states. We appeal to the world community to share with us both the difficult tasks of implementing the Programme and the benefits of developing regional cooperation.

Source: Documents about Special UN Programmes for the Economies of Central Asia. Retrieved 5 December 2001, from: http://missions.inu.int.

local populations were to be inducted into positions of authority to overcome the imperial past that the new regime had inherited. In Central Asia nativization never went far enough to completely eliminate Russian influence, but nevertheless, it was a resounding success in terms of creating a new political class completely at home in the Soviet order. During the 1920s this class edged out older intellectuals from positions of power.

In 1929 the state decreed the collectivization of agriculture. This campaign was conducted with great violence, especially in nomadic areas, where it also entailed the sedentarization of the nomads. In Kazakhstan the dislocation of the nomadic economy created a tragedy that assumed genocidal proportions. Although no indisputable figures exist, perhaps as many as 1.5 million Kazakhs died in the 1930s. Between 1928 and 1932 alone, 80 percent of herd animals were destroyed. Along with collectivization came a centrally planned economy, which concentrated decision making in Moscow, as well as a purge of public figures in which two generations of local political and cultural leadership were destroyed in Central Asia. Thousands were executed, and many times that number sent off to prison camps. Leadership passed to a new generation.

The centrally planned economy in Central Asia meant, above all, the predominance of cotton. The Soviet Union pursued a policy of "cotton independence" for its textile industry, and Central Asia was assigned the task of ensuring this independence. Central Asia was turned into a massive cotton plantation, so that at the end of the Soviet period, Uzbekistan alone was producing more cotton than the United States. The ecological consequences were devastating. Relentless irrigation led to the shrinking of the Aral Sea, while reckless use of pesticides and fertilizers produced lethal levels of pollution.

Nevertheless, in the peaceful years after Khrushchev (who led the Soviet Union from 1953 to 1964), cotton also provided a way for Central Asian political elites to reclaim some local autonomy. As stability became the most important virtue in Soviet political life under Brezhnev (who led the country from 1964 to 1982), party elites in the republics were largely left to their own devices as long as they fulfilled centrally imposed economic obligations and did not rock the boat politically. During this period all five republics were headed by long-serving Communist Party leaders who headed largely autonomous political machines serving, on the one hand, to deliver cotton to the center and, on the other, to distribute political influence locally. While these leaders enjoyed all the benefits of power

in the Soviet order, they also emerged as *national* leaders. These political arrangements, built on informal ties among a cohort of politicians, are only now being understood by historians.

Post–Soviet Central Asia

These political arrangements were questioned by Brezhnev's successors, Yuri Andropov (1982–1984) and Mikhail Gorbachev (1985–1991), in their attempts to root out corruption in Soviet life. A federal investigative commission found massive corruption in Uzbekistan. Numerous high-ranking officials were dismissed and disgraced. But such measures, which were seen as attacking the autonomy of Central Asian republics, produced national resentment. In December 1986, when Moscow summarily dismissed Dinmuhamed Kunaev, the long-serving Kazakh Party secretary, and replaced him with a Russian functionary sent from Moscow, nationalist riots erupted in Almaty, the capital of Kazakhstan. Nevertheless in the following years, as the Soviet order weakened for reasons having little to do with Central Asia, the republics of Central Asia remained the most stable parts of the Soviet Union and supported the USSR's continued existence to the very end. The economies of Central Asian republics were much too tightly tied to the rest of the Soviet Union to make independence an attractive option.

Events in 1991, however, left the countries of Central Asia no choice. As the Soviet Union dissolved, they emerged on the international stage as sovereign states. Their leaderships, still rooted in the political machines that had crystallized in the 1960s, appealed to strong national identities forged in the Soviet years to provide legitimacy to the new states. At the same time there has been a strong impetus to rediscover aspects of national history and culture that were taboo under the Soviet regime. The region has witnessed a substantial re-Islamization, as people have sought to rediscover their spiritual heritage. The collapse of the centralized Soviet economy has generated massive crises, leaving the newly independent countries to overcome their dependence on cotton and to attempt to enter a global marketplace to which they had little exposure in the previous century.

The complex heritage of modern Central Asia defies easy categorizations. The period of Russian and Soviet rule saw the merciless exploitation of the natural resources of the region. It witnessed two terrible famines, a civil war, and a prolonged period of political bloodletting in which the flower of two generations perished. The same period, however, saw the elimination of illiteracy, the establishment of modern state forms, and the creation of national identities that undergird the regimes of the post-Soviet period. Central Asia today embodies the contradictions inherited from the twentieth century.

Adeeb Khalid

See also: **Communism—Central Asia; Energy Central Asia; Ethnic Conflict—Central Asia; Islam—Central Asia; Jadidism; Media—Central Asia; Nationalist Movement in Central Asia; Perestroika; Post–Communism; Radioactive Waste and Contamination; Russification and Sovietization; Westernization—Central Asia**

Further Reading
Allworth, Edward, ed. (1994) *Central Asia: 130 Years of Russian Dominance, a Historical Overview.* Durham, NC: Duke University Press.

Becker, Seymour. (1968) *Russia's Protectorates in Central Asia: Bukhara and Khiva, 1865–1924.* Cambridge, MA: Harvard University Press.

Buttino, Marco. (1993) "Politics and Social Conflict during a Famine: Turkestan Immediately after the Revolution." In *In a Collapsing Empire: Underdevelopment, Ethnic Conflicts, and Nationalisms in the Soviet Union*, edited by Marco Buttino. Milan, Italy: Fondazione Giangiacomo Feltrinelli.

Carrère d'Encausse, Hélène. (1988) *Islam and the Russian Empire.* Berkeley and Los Angeles: University of California Press.

Khalid, Adeeb. (1998) *The Politics of Muslim Cultural Reform: Jadidism in Central Asia.* Berkeley and Los Angeles: University of California Press.

Levin, Theodore. (1997) *A Hundred Thousand Fools of God: Musical Travels in Central Asia (and Queens, New York).* Bloomington, IN: Indiana University Press.

Roy, Olivier. (2000) *The New Central Asia.* London: I. B. Tauris.

CENTRAL ASIA—CHINA RELATIONS
Following the collapse of the Soviet Union in 1991, China faced the challenge of managing bilateral relations with the newly independent Central Asian states. The independence of these states exacerbated long-smoldering ethnic unrest in China's Xinjiang Autonomous Region, which borders several of the Central Asian states. After establishing relations with the Central Asian republics in early 1992, China signed more than twenty agreements on boundaries and economic and cultural cooperation with these nations within a short period.

Boundary Settlements
The China–Central Asian boundary was originally established by "unequal" treaties—the 1860 Treaty of Beijing, the 1864 Protocol on the Northwest Boundary, the 1881 Sino-Russian Treaty of Ili, and the 1884 Sino-Russian Treaty of Kashgar. According to the Chinese, by these treaties, Czarist Russia gained 440,000 square kilometers of territory at the expense of China. After the independence of the Central Asian states, China was willing to accept the unequal treaties as the basis for new boundary agreements.

Following several years of negotiations, on 4 July 1996, China concluded a boundary agreement with Kyrgyzstan. China and Kyrgyzstan have since concluded agreements to open new border crossings and construct a rail line linking the two countries. On 4 July 1998, leaders signed a Sino-Kazakhstan boundary treaty. This marked the comprehensive settlement of questions unresolved by history concerning the unsettled 1,700-kilometer Sino-Kazakh boundary.

Beijing has not concluded an agreement resolving the historically complicated Sino-Tajik boundary dispute. China has consistently asserted that Russia violated the 1884 Sino-Russian Kashgar Boundary Treaty in 1892 and occupied more than 20,000 square kilometers of Chinese territory in the Pamir Mountains and that the boundary remains undelimited. Nevertheless, the leaders of the two nations have negotiated many agreements, including an agreement to open a road connecting China and Tajikistan to ease border trade.

Regional Strategic Concerns
The Central Asian states see China as a potential economic and demographic threat. One concern is China's dramatic population growth. With its large territory and abundant natural resources, Central Asia is logically a place for China to covet. More than 300,000 Chinese have settled in Central Asia, and this may grow to 500,000 over the next few years. Kazakh officials believe that if the flood of Chinese coming to Kazakhstan continues, Chinese will overwhelm Kazakhstan in ten to fifteen years. Chinese traders have purchased considerable amounts of real estate in Kyrgyzstan.

China is also very apprehensive about instability along the border. Following a Shanghai summit, on 26 April 1996, Russia, Kazakhstan, Kyrgyzstan, and Tajikistan signed an agreement with China on confidence-building measures along the border. On 24 April 1997 they agreed to withdraw military forces 100 kilometers along the 3,500-kilometers boundary. A third agreement of 3 July 1998 emphasized cooperation to dampen ethnic unrest in the region. Each government pledged to take steps to fight against arms smuggling and not to allow its territory to be used for activities undermining the national sovereignty, security, and social order of any of the five countries.

Ethnic Unrest

Since the independence of the Central Asian states in 1991, ethnic unrest in Xinjiang has been a major concern for Beijing. A continuing source of tension in China–Central Asian relations are the sensitive issues of pan-Turkic nationalism and the Xinjiang separatist movement. Historically, China has struggled to maintain central government control over the region. Russian and Soviet intrigue and local independence movements have been recent issues. An Eastern Turkestan Republic was briefly established in 1944, in what is now Xinjiang; it had a national anthem and a national flag—a white crescent and star against a blue background. Led by Islamic scholars, the Uighurs of Xinjiang wanted a homeland free of Chinese influence. In 1962 China crushed a revolt by tens of thousands of Kazakhs who then fled across the border to Soviet Kazakhstan. Chinese now feel that the smoldering independence movements in Xinjiang are the main threat to stability in western China.

A central issue in most all communiqués and agreements between China and other Central Asian states is a commitment not to support any separatist movements. Both Kazakhstan and Kyrgyzstan, with 200,000 and 80,000 Uighurs respectively, have agreed to suppress such movements. Several separatist movements have moved from Kazakhstan to Turkey, and Kyrgyzstan has prevented organization of an ethnic Uighur political party. The Uighur nationalist organizations that continue to operate from within the Central Asian states remain a major cause of tension in Central Asian relations with China.

Countries with fundamentalist Islamic orientations are a factor in promoting ethnic unrest in the region. The Jama'at-e-Islami, based in Pakistan, has encouraged Islamic activism in Xinjiang, as have other Islamist movements, such as the Taliban (when it was in power in Afghanistan). Uighurs do receive religious training in Pakistan, and Afghan and Islamic militants have smuggled arms into China. The number of Islamic schools in China has grown rapidly; in 1997 the government closed down as many as three hundred "illegal" schools. Many small neighborhood mosques have become the focal point of anti-Chinese activities. The Chinese have clamped down on what it considers "illegal religious activities" and has closed many mosques.

The rise in ethnic unrest and pro-independence demonstrations and other activities in the 1990s have deep historical and religious roots and will persist for the foreseeable future. Many leaders are not simply religious fanatics, but are Pan-Turkic nationalists. The support for the movement comes from neighboring Turkic-speaking countries. Despite the pledge by the governments of Kazakhstan and Kyrgyzstan not to support the Xinjiang separatist movement, supporters of the movement openly operate from these countries. Uighurs living in Turkey also support the movement. Pan-Turkic nationalism and anti-Chinese colonialism are important causes of the unrest. Uighurs are trying to preserve their cultural identity and to resist the mass influx of Chinese settlers into their region.

Economic Interests

In the 1990s Central Asia quickly became an important center of China's economic attention. Border trade is an important part of the growing economic ties. In 1989 Xinjiang's trade with Soviet Central Asia amounted to only $118.5 million. Trade has continued to grow and now accounts for 60 percent of the region's foreign trade. In 1995 total trade between China and Central Asia was an estimated $718 million, of which $500 million was accounted for by border trade. Since 1991, China has emerged as the second-largest trading partner for the Central Asian countries, significantly displacing Russian influence in the region. China is now Kazakhstan's major trading partner, and 25 percent of Kyrgyzstan's foreign trade is with China.

The development of oil and gas is an area of important strategic economic cooperation. In 1994 China signed an agreement with Turkmenistan to construct a Turkmenistan-China-Japan gas pipeline. In 1997 China won the bid to develop Kazakhstan's Uzen oil field and construct a 3,000-kilometer oil pipeline from Kazakhstan's Caspian oilfields at Tengiz to Xinjiang and then to China's eastern coast. Additionally, China signed agreements with Kazakhstan to develop the Aktyubinsk oil fields along the Russian-Kazakh border. Total Chinese investment in developing oil resources in Kazakhstan is estimated at $9.7 billion, equivalent to 50 percent of Kazakhstan's gross national product. These agreements are a clear indication that China and Central Asia are developing an important economic and strategic link. China not only is seeking to ensure its energy security for the future, but also is attempting to shift the focus of Central Asia's global vision toward China and away from Russia and Turkey.

Eric Hyer

Further Reading
Benson, Linda. (1990) *The Ili Rebellion: The Moslem Challenge to Chinese Authority in Xinjiang.* Armonk, NY: M. E. Sharpe.
Burles, Mark. (1999) *Chinese Policy toward Russia and the Central Asian Republics.* Santa Monica, CA: RAND.

Christian, David. (1998) *A History of Russia, Central Asia, and Mongolia.* Malden, MA: Blackwell.

Christoffersen, Gaye. (1998) *China's Intentions for Russian and Central Asian Oil and Gas.* NBR Analysis Series, vol. 9, no. 2.

Hopkirk, Peter. (1994) *The Great Game: The Struggle for Empire in Central Asia.* New York: Kodansha.

Mandelbaum, Michael, ed. (1994) *Central Asia and the World.* New York: Council on Foreign Relations.

Olcott, Martha Brill. (2000) *Central Asia and China.* London: Royal Institute of International Affairs.

Snyder, Jed C., ed. (1995) *After Empire: The Emerging Geopolitics of Central Asia.* Washington, DC: National Defense University Press.

CENTRAL ASIA—RUSSIA RELATIONS

Political, cultural, and military clashes have strongly affected Central Asia–Russia relations. In the nineteenth century, Russia tried to put the territories of today's Central Asian states under its control in order to benefit from the region's natural resources and fertile agricultural lands. Russia also hoped thereby to play an active role in the Middle East and South Asia. The Central Asian states strongly opposed Russian policies and fought to preserve their national identities and economic and political autonomy.

The Czarist Period

Until the 1860s, czarist Russia occupied the entire Kyrgyz Steppe (in present-day central Kazakhstan). Turkistan was under the political control of three Turkish khanates, Bukhara, Khiva, and Quqon (Kokand). These khanates had simple social, military, and administrative organizations, and they were often in conflict with one another. To gain a commercial advantage by controlling the historic Silk Road, at that time the main commercial link between Europe and Asia, the Russians attacked the Quqon khanate. In 1865, they occupied the city of Tashkent in the Bukhara khanate and then created a separate Turkistan province, whose area included today's Kazakhstan and parts of Uzbekistan and Kyrgyzstan. The emir of Bukhara asked the Russians to leave Tashkent, but the Russians defeated the Bukharans and seized the cities of Khojend (present-day Khudzhand) and Uroteppa.

In January 1868, General K. P. von Kaufman, the first governor-general of Turkistan, signed a peace treaty with Quqon that made the latter a vassal of Russia. In June 1868, the emir of Bukhara was forced to sign a similar treaty, which made his khanate part of Russia. In 1873, General Kaufman organized a military operation to Khiva and forced the khan to accept the Russian protectorate. Thus all three khanates became vassals of Russia, and much of their territory was absorbed into Turkistan province.

After building a strategic railroad from the Caspian Sea to Turkistan, Russia defeated the Turkmen in 1881 and created the Transcaspian province. In 1884, the Turkmen were forced to recognize Russian authority. By 1886, Russia had divided the Turkistan governorship-general into three parts: Syr Dar'ya province, Fergana province, and Zeraushan district.

Although czarist Russia tried to solidify its dominance over Central Asia, three problems emerged. First, Russia encouraged an increased production of cotton in the region, which created a grain deficit that led to a famine. Second, because Russians were encouraged to colonize Turkistan, the native Turkic inhabitants were forced to move to less fertile lands. Third, the Russian settlers began to dominate commercial activities. Thus the Turkic communities in Central Asia came to resent Russian domination and hoped to put an end to Russian colonization and settlement.

After the 1905 Revolution by Russian workers and military officials in Central Asia against the czarist regime, Muslim nationalists, known as Jadids, began to surface in the Kyrgyz Steppe and Turkistan. In 1909, the Jadids established their first political organization in Bukhara and advocated setting up schools that taught both religion and such secular subjects as Tatar, Arabic, and Russian languages and literatures; history; philosophy of history; history of Islam; sociology; arithmetic; geography; agriculture; physics; and chemistry. They supported the unification of Turkistan under the Russian empire, but their opinion ultimately failed to carry the day.

The October 1917 Revolution

Leftist groups—the Bolsheviks, Mensheviks, and members of the Social Revolutionary Party—had begun to appear in Turkistan in 1917. On 7 April, the three leftist groups set up the Turkistan Committee of the Provisional Government, which then arrested General Aleksey Nikolayevich Kuropatkin (1848–1921), the czarist governor-general of Turkistan. A soviet (council) of workers and soldiers was also established in the city of Tashkent. The Turkish communities, however, did not involve themselves in the conflict between the czarist regime and the leftists. At a May 1916 congress of the Muslims in Russia, delegates elected a Central Muslim Council, dominated by the Jadids. At congresses in May and September 1917, the Turkish inhabitants of Central Asia demanded the creation of an autonomous federated republic of Turkistan in the new Russia.

At the same time, the leftist groups in the Tashkent soviet had diverging views of the new regime in Russia. On 19 November 1917, the Bolsheviks of Tashkent created their own government, the Council of People's Commissars. In turn, another All-Muslim Congress met in Quqon on 26–27 November 1917 and set up the Muslim Provisional Government of Autonomous Turkistan. But because this government lacked military power, it decided to join an anti-Communist organization called the Southeastern Union of Cossacks, Mountain Caucasians, and Peoples of the Steppe. Upon the military suppression of the Tashkent soviet by the Moscow Bolsheviks, the emir of Bukhara signed an agreement with the Tashkent administration of the Bolshevik government in Moscow, in which the latter recognized the independence of Bukhara.

In 1919, at the Third Congress of the Communist Party of Turkistan in Tashkent, a struggle between the Muslims and the Russian settlers emerged at the governmental level. The Fourth Red Army drove the Russian anti-Communist forces out of Turkistan in July. In September, the Eighth Congress of Soviets and the Fourth Congress of the Communist Party of Turkistan met in Tashkent. During the sessions, the Russian settlers rejected direct participation of native people in local governmental organs. But when the Soviet troops of the Fourth Red Army returned to Tashkent to suppress the growing uprising there (encouraged by British forces, which desired to control Iran and the Transcaspian region), the political situation altered in favor of the Muslims. To solve the problem in Tashkent, the Moscow government authorized the Fourth Red Army to investigate the situation. The Fourth Red Army Party Conference overruled the previous decision concerning the nonparticipation of Muslims in local Soviet organizations.

Near the end of the civil war (1918–1920) in Russia, the Soviets decided to reorganize Khiva. On 25 December 1919, Soviet troops from Russia crossed the Khivan borders, and a pro-Soviet Revolutionary Committee was set up. On 4 April 1920, Khiva became the People's Republic of Khorezm. The Soviet government in Moscow used similar tactics with Bukhara, when the Russian workers and the small revolutionary Young Bukharan group staged a revolt there. In September 1920, with the assistance of Russian troops, the People's Republic of Bukhara was established.

Formation of Soviet Central Asia

In the Declaration of the Rights of the Peoples of Russia, Vladimir Lenin (1870–1924), the founder of the Soviet Union, declared all people in Russia to be equal and sovereign. Everyone had a right to self-determination, and during the civil war people were allowed to freely develop their native cultures, a measure enacted to obtain the support of local Muslims in Central Asia for the Bolshevik regime in Moscow. But in 1918, when the Bolsheviks began to consolidate their power in Moscow, they discussed the right of self-determination within the framework of debate on the future structure of the Soviet regime. Two conflicting proposals appeared. The first was a loose political arrangement in which socialist states would remain sovereign entities, thus rejecting the founding of an integral Soviet federation. The second was a proposal put forward by Joseph Stalin (1879–1953) for autonomization, which meant withdrawing state sovereignty from independent socialist republics and providing them with only limited autonomous status. Lenin chose the middle way. The socialist republics would have a right to self-determination, but only the workers could participate in this decision.

The Turkic communities were disappointed with this new policy. Some nationalist groups rebelled against Soviet authority, but they were ultimately forced to become part of the Soviet federation. At Lenin's request, Stalin prepared a new policy for non-Russian nationalities, which promoted a process of nation building. At the same time, independent socialist republics would have only limited autonomous status.

In December 1922, the Communist Party granted the larger non-Russian nationality groups the status of republics in the Soviet Union. In October 1923, the Fourth Congress modified the Soviet Union's constitution, and on 29 September 1924, the Fifth Congress decided to change the name from People's Republic to Socialist Republic. In October 1924, the Central Executive Committee of the Soviet Union voted to establish two socialist republics in Central Asia (Uzbekistan and Turkmenistan), as well as two autonomous republics (Tajikistan and Kazakhstan). (A socialist republic was a sovereign Soviet state that had united with other Soviet republics in the USSR, exercising independent authority in its territory and having its own constitution; an autonomous republic was a constituent part of a socialist republic.) On 5 December 1929, Tajikistan became a republic of the Soviet Union, and on 5 December 1936, the same status was granted to Kyrgyzstan and Kazakhstan. These republics together made up Soviet Central Asia.

The Cold War Period

Under the Soviet regime, Russian dominance over Central Asia reached its highest level. In the political arena, the Communist Party of the Soviet Union put all regional and local organizations under its control. The decisions of the republics had to conform with the policies of the central authority in Moscow.

Although in each republic the first secretary of the republic's Communist Party was a native inhabitant, the second-secretary, who was a Russian, controlled and managed all administrative, economic, and governmental affairs. Thus the native people were absent from the policy-making process of the Soviet Union.

In the economic field, Moscow planned and regulated the economic policies of each republic of the Soviet Union. The Soviet regime encouraged Russian specialists and workers to migrate into the non-Russian republics.

In the cultural field, the Soviet regime tried to create a unified Soviet nationality; thus non-Russians were subjected to a Russification policy. In the 1930s, the number of Russian schools in the non-Russian republics was increased. The Russian language was promoted as the first language of all the Soviet peoples. Finally, Russian became the official language of the republics and had to be used in all official communications.

The Central Asian republics were sensitive about their traditions and national identities and reacted against Russian dominance, particularly the nationality policy. Despite Moscow's policies, native inhabitants tried to preserve their identities and objected to the Russians' view of themselves as civilizers of primitive people.

Collapse of the Soviet Union

Mikhail Gorbachev (b. 1931), the last secretary-general of the USSR, proposed that the Soviet Union preserve its powerful position while granting more autonomy to the various republics. The president of the Russian Federation, Boris Yeltsin (b. 1931), wanted to retain some form of union among the Soviet republics, and this was the view of the Central Asian states as well. On 23 April 1991, Gorbachev and the leaders of Russia, Ukraine, Belarus, and the five Central Asian members signed an agreement for a new treaty that provided for a union of sovereign states to replace the Soviet Union. The Communist Party of the Soviet Union and officials of the Red Army and KGB attempted a coup against Mikhail Gorbachev's administration in Moscow (19–21 August 1991) in the name of restoring order and law in the USSR, but they failed to overthrow the government.

But the August coup intensified the nationalistic feelings of the Soviet republics and their desire for independence. During the election campaign Boris Yeltsin had maintained that Russia should become independent in order to solve domestic economic and social problems. Ukraine and Belarus had the same idea. After the aborted August coup, Yeltsin became

more popular and powerful. Ukraine became concerned that implementation of the new union treaty was not possible, and therefore held a referendum in which voters opted for independence. Russia for its part realized that without Ukraine, the new union treaty would be meaningless. As a result, on 8 December 1991, without consulting with the Central Asian states, Russia, Ukraine, and Belarus signed a formal agreement announcing the formation of the Commonwealth of Independent States (CIS).

This agreement angered the Central Asian states, because it destroyed their hopes of retaining a strong center. The Central Asian states held a meeting on 12 December 1991 in Ashkabad, the capital of Turkmenistan, and discussed the establishment of a Turkistan federation. At the request of Nursultan Nazarbaev (b. 1940), the president of Kazakhstan, the other members accepted the idea, and joined as cofounders. After the Slavic republics (Russia, Belarus, and Ukraine) accepted the proposal, the CIS recognized the independence and the existing borders of its eleven cofounders: Armenia, Azerbaijan, Belarus, Kazakhstan, Kyrgyzstan, Moldavia, Russia, Tajikistan, Turkmenistan, Ukraine, and Uzbekistan. The agreement created only a loose federation, because its governing bodies, a council of heads of states and a council of heads of governments, lacked authority to impose decisions on any member. The council was to be assisted by committees that focused on areas such as foreign affairs, defense, and economics. The agreement did not settle questions about a common military policy and nuclear-weapons control.

Post–Cold War Era

From 1991 to 1993, the Russian authorities viewed any close relations with the Central Asian states as destructive to their economic and democratic reforms—in their eyes, the Central Asian leaders had failed to establish democratic regimes, maintaining instead authoritarian regimes that violated human rights. For that reason, the Russians refused any form of union with the Central Asian states. Russia introduced economic reforms without consulting the Central Asian states, stopped financial assistance to Central Asia, and followed protectionist economic policies that created difficulties for Central Asia. In short, Russia's economic and monetary policies prevented the Central Asian states from conducting independent economic, budgetary, and financial policies. As a result, the Central Asian states introduced national currencies and limited their relations with Russia. They attempted to gain direct access to world markets. In 1993, they even decided to create a Central Asia Regional Council, excluding Russia. Under the influence of ultranationalist and Communist groups, Russia changed its policy toward Central Asia in 1993, attempted to create a CIS customs union, and increased its financial assistance to these states.

In December 1991, at the first summit of heads of CIS member states in Minsk, the CIS decided that each state should be free to create its own national army. On 15 May 1992, Armenia, Kazakhstan, Kyrgyzstan, Russia, Tajikistan, and Uzbekistan signed the Treaty on Collective Security during the summit of heads of CIS member states in Tashkent. The treaty established a collective security council consisting of heads of member states and commanders of CIS joint armed forces. In addition, the member states were to refrain from the use of force or threat of force in their relations with one another. They were to abstain from entering into blocs hostile to one another, and they agreed to conduct consultations on security issues and coordinate their defense policies.

In October 1992, the CIS reached an agreement on military security in Bishkek, Kyrgyzstan. The CIS decided on the establishment of collective observer and peacekeeping forces to end armed conflicts in the CIS. But the attitudes of Russia and other member states jeopardized the agreements regarding collective security. Central Asian members were concerned that such agreements might be dominated by Russia. During the CIS summit in February 1995 in Almaty, Kazakhstan, Russia proposed a common defense of CIS frontiers, including airspace. This proposal was rejected.

On the question of Russians living in the region, the Central Asian states tried to avoid any confrontation with Russia. They were concerned that Russia might use these Russians as an excuse to intervene militarily in their domestic affairs. Nevertheless, despite Russia's demands, the Central Asian states (except Turkmenistan) refused to grant dual citizenship.

In the case of transportation of oil and gas reserves of the Caspian Sea region, the Central Asian states prefer to follow a multiple pipeline-network policy. They do not want to see Russian dominance over their regional resources. There is still a debate among the Central Asian states on the nature of Russia's involvement, its percentage share, and the transportation routes.

Present-Day Relations

The Central Asian states today completely oppose any continuation of Russian dominance over the region; they prefer to develop alternative economic, political, and security relations with other major countries, such the United States and the European Union,

while preserving their relations with Russia. The Central Asian states want to preserve their independence and territorial integrity and intend to become members of the international community.

In military affairs, the Central Asian states see Russia as a potential ally in their struggle against domestic opposition, radical Islam, and ethnic and territorial conflicts in the region. They welcome the Russian presence to balance the power of neighbors such as China, Iran, and Afghanistan.

Ertan Efegil

Further Reading

Allison, Roy, ed. (1996) *Challenges for the Former Soviet South.* Washington, DC: Brookings Institution Press.

Allworth, Edward, ed. (1994) *Central Asia: 130 Years of Russian Dominance: A Historical Overview.* 3d ed. Durham, NC: Duke University Press.

Barner-Barry, Carol, and Cynthia A. Hody. (1995) *The Politics of Change: The Transformation of the Former Soviet Union.* New York: St. Martin's.

Dawisha, Karen, and Bruce Parrott. (1994) *Russia and the New States of Eurasia: The Politics of Upheaval.* Cambridge, U.K.: Cambridge University Press.

Goldman, Minton F. (1996) *The Eurasian Republics, and Central/Eastern Europe.* 6th ed. Guilford, CT: Dushkin/McGraw-Hill.

Hayit, Baymirza. (1987) *Sovyetler Birligi'ndeki Turklugun ve Islamin Bazi Meseleleri* (Some Problems of Islam and the Turkish Community in the Soviet Union). Istanbul, Turkey: Turk Dunyasi Arastirmalari Vakfi.

Hunter, Shireen T. (1996) *Central Asia since Independence.* Washington, DC: Center for Strategic and International Studies.

Medish, Vadim. (1987) *The Soviet Union.* 3d ed. Englewood Cliffs, NJ: Prentice-Hall.

Melvin, Neil. (1995) *Regional Foreign Policies in the Russian Federation.* London: Royal Institute of International Affairs.

Nogee, Joseph L., and R. Judson Mitchell. (1997) *Russian Politics: The Struggle for a New Order.* Boston: Allyn and Bacon.

Rywkin, Michael. (1982) *Moscow's Muslim Challenge: Soviet Central Asia.* New York: M. E. Sharpe.

Smith, Graham, ed. (1996) *The Nationalities Question in the Post-Soviet States.* New York: Longman.

Taylor, Trevor. (1994) *European Security and the Former Soviet Union: Dangers, Opportunities, and Gambles.* London: Royal Institute of International Affairs.

Zhang, Yongjin, and Rouben Azizian, eds. (1998) *Ethnic Challenges beyond Borders: Chinese and Russian Perspectives of the Central Asian Conundrum.* Oxford: Macmillan.

CENTRAL ASIAN LANGUAGES An enormous number of languages are spoken by the various ethnic groups that inhabit Central Asia. Turkic languages, which belong to the Altaic family of world languages, are the most frequently spoken in Central Asia, followed by the Iranian (mainly Tajik) and Slavic languages (Russian and Ukrainian), which belong to the Indo-European family. The numerous languages of Central Asia reflect the various peoples who moved into and through the region and demonstrate the significance of this area not only for its natural resources but also for its strategic role as a major crossroad in Asia.

The Russian language has been an important influence in Central Asian education, administration, and interethnic communication since the time of imperial Russia and during the Soviet regime. Each ethnic language used in the area was given its own Cyrillic alphabet by the Soviet regime during the 1940s. In post-Soviet Central Asia, however, the independent states changed their language policies, declaring the language of the ethnic majority as the state language. Uzbekistan and Turkmenistan have also changed their alphabets from Cyrillic to Latin. Central Asian states use their state languages increasingly in education, although they are having difficulties in finding course materials in these languages. There is a growing demand for courses in English as a foreign language, rather than Russian, because there is a desire to integrate with the international community.

Languages of Kazakhstan

The official language of Kazakhstan is Kazakh, a Turkic language, although Russian is also commonly used and is the language of interethnic communication. Most of the population is bilingual in Russian as well as their own ethnic languages. The languages spoken in Kazakhstan are Kazakh, Russian, Ukrainian, German, Uzbek, Tatar, and "other", a category that includes languages as diverse as Armenian, Bashkir, Korean, Polish, and Romanian.

Languages of Kyrgyzstan

The official language of Kyrgyzstan is Kyrgyz, a Turkic language. Russian is used as the interethnic language of communication. Seventy percent of the populationcan speak Kyrgyz. One-third of the Kyrgyz and many of the minorities speak Russian fluently. The most commonly used languages are Kyrgyz, Russian, Uzbek, Dungan, Ukrainian, Uighur, Crimean Tatar and Tatar, Meskhetian Turkish, Kazakh, Tajik, German, and Korean. As in Kazakhstan, a large number of other languages are also present in small numbers.

Languages of Tajikistan

The official language of Tajikistan is Tajik, an Iranian language. Russian is used as the interethnic language of communication. Major languages used are Tajik, Uzbek, Russian, Tatar, Kyrgyz, and "other."

Languages of Turkmenistan

The official language of Turkmenistan is Turkmen, a Turkic language, spoken by 77 percent of the population. Other major languages are Uzbek, Russian, Kazakh, and "other."

Languages of Uzbekistan

The official language of Uzbekistan is Uzbek, a Turkic language. It is spoken by 74.3 percent of the population, of which ethnic Uzbeks make up 80 percent. Russian is the other main language. Although Russian may act as the interethnic language of communication, the minorities are increasingly learning Uzbek. Other languages spoken in Uzbekistan include Tajik, Kazakh, Karakalpak, Tatar, and "other."

Turkic Languages of Central Asia

Although almost all Turkic languages are represented in Central Asia, the Turkic languages with the most speakers in the area are Bashkir, Crimean Tatar, Karakalpak, Kazakh, Kyrgyz, Volga Tatar, Turkmen, Uighur, and Uzbek. Most of the Turkic languages are closely related, and it is sometimes difficult to draw the distinction between languages and dialects. Spoken forms are generally mutually intelligible, with intelligibility decreasing the greater the distance separating two languages. The imperial Russians and later the Soviets classified and named the Turkic languages to fit their own political aims, sometimes naming dialects as separate languages and giving them their own alphabets. Because of population movements—voluntary or forced migrations (such as those initiated by Stalin during the 1940s)—Turkic-speaking groups have been mixed. The influence of Islam can be seen in the Arabic and Persian words in the lexicons of the Turkic languages. The influence of Iranian languages is greater in some languages, such as Uzbek, because of the speakers' geographical proximity to and history shared with speakers of Iranian languages. The influence of Russian, which was the main language of administration and education during both imperial Russian and Soviet periods, is felt especially in the lexicons of individual languages and in the sound systems. Since the early 1990s, Uzbeks and Turkmen have worked to eliminate Russian and other foreign words. The Turkic languages spoken in Central Asia were written in Arabic script before the 1920s. During the late 1920s, there was a common Latin alphabet for all Turkic languages, but around 1940 the Soviets decided to give the Turkic languages and dialects their own

Cyrillic alphabets. After 1990, Uzbekistan and Turkmenistan adopted Latin alphabets. Kazakhstan, Kyrgyzstan, and Tajikistan still use their versions of the Cyrillic alphabet.

Similarities between the Turkic languages start with vowel harmony, which is the main aspect of their sound systems. Vowel harmony is the agreement of vowels in a word according to where they are produced in the mouth; that is, whether they are pronounced in the front or the back of the mouth, or whether the lips are rounded or not, and so forth. The main feature of the syntactic system of Turkic languages is agglutination through a rich system of inflectional and derivational suffixes. For example, the verbs carry time and aspect suffixes as well as personal endings, along with suffixes for negation and question; therefore it is possible to have very long words rather than the sentences typical of other languages. Nouns can be made into verbs and into other nouns; verbs can be changed into nouns and into other verbs through adding suffixes. Adjectives and genitives always precede the noun, and the position before the verb is reserved for the new information that is the focus of the sentence. The normal word order is subject-object-verb; thus the subject occurs at the beginning of the sentence, and the direct object immediately precedes the verb. Instead of prepositions, Turkic has postpositions, and the nouns take dative, accusative, ablative, locative, genitive, and possessive suffixes.

Bashkir Bashkir belongs to the Kipchak (Uralian Kipchak) branch of the Turkic languages. It is spoken in Russia as well as in Central Asia. It is close to Tatar. Its dialects are Kuvakan, Yurmaty, and Burzhan. It was given its own Cyrillic alphabet by the Soviets.

Crimean Tatar Crimean Tatar belongs to the Kipchak (Ponto-Caspian, or Southern) branch of the Turkic languages. It was written in Arabic script until 1928, but between 1928 and 1938 the Latin alphabet was used; this was followed by Cyrillic, and after 1990 the Latin alphabet was adopted. The standard language is based on the Central dialect, but there are also Northern and Southern dialects. It is spoken in Central Asia due to forced migrations from the Crimea in the 1940s.

Karakalpak Karakalpak belongs to the Kipchak (Central) branch of the Turkic languages. It has two main dialects, Northeast and Southeast. It is spoken in the Karakalpak region of Uzbekistan, as well as in Afghanistan, Kazakhstan, Kyrgyzstan, and Turkmenistan. It is very close to Kazakh, although the region where it is spoken is part of Uzbekistan.

Kazakh Kazakh belongs to the Kipchak (Central) branch of the Turkic languages. Its dialects are Northeastern Kazakh, Southern Kazakh, and Western Kazakh. It is the official language of Kazakhstan; outside Central Asia it is spoken in China, Mongolia, Iran, and Afghanistan, as well as by small groups in Turkey and Germany. Kazakh and Karakalpak are closely related; the latter can be regarded as almost a dialect of Kazakh.

Kyrgyz Kyrgyz belongs to the Northern branch of the Turkic languages. It has Northern and Southern dialects. Outside Central Asia, it is spoken in Afghanistan and China, where the Kyrgyz are an official nationality and use an Arabic script. It is also used in Turkey by Kyrgyz immigrants.

Tatar Tatar belongs to the Kipchak (Uralian Kipchak) branch of the Turkic languages. It has three main dialects, which are sometimes referred to as languages: Volga Tatar (also known as Middle Tatar or Kazan Tatar), Western Tatar (also known as Misher), and Eastern Tatar (Siberian Tatar). Tatar is spoken in the Republic of Tatarstan in Russia and in a number of districts in Bashkortostan, Mari, El, Udmurtia, Mordvina, and many other regions of European Russia, as well as in Uzbekistan, Kazakhstan, Azerbaijan, Kyrgyzstan, Tajikstan, and Turkmenistan. The oldest surviving Tatar texts date to the thirteenth century. The modern literary language has developed under the influence of spoken Tatar since the nineteenth century. The writing system was based on Arabic script until 1927, when a Latin alphabet came into use; it was replaced in 1939 by a Cyrillic script. Recently a decision to switch to the Latin alphabet was made.

Turkmen Turkmen belongs to the Southwest (Oghuz) branch of the Turkic languages. Its major dialects are Yomut, Teke, Salir, Sarik, Goldeng, Arsar, and Chowdr. The standard, based on the Yomut and Teke dialects, was developed in the 1920s. As a literary language, Turkmen appeared during the eighteenth century in Arabic script. A Latin alphabet was introduced in 1929 and was replaced by a Cyrillic alphabet in 1940. In 1993, a new Turkmen alphabet in Latin script was adopted.

Uighur Uighur (Eastern Turki) belongs to the Eastern branch of the Turkic languages. It is the official language of the region of Xinjiang Uygur (along with Standard Mandarin) in northwest China and the native language of ethnic Uighurs. In Kazakhstan the Taranci dialect and in Uzbekistan the Kashgar-Yarkand dialects of Uighur are used. Soviet Standard Uighur was written in the Latin alphabet, and later a

Cyrillic alphabet was introduced. In China, Cyrillic was introduced during the 1950s, followed by Latin in the 1960s, and in 1983 an Arabic alphabet was reinstated.

Uzbek   Uzbek belongs to the Eastern branch of the Turkic languages. It has been the official language of Uzbekistan since 1989. It is used also in Afghanistan and China as well as in the states of the former Soviet Union. Written standard Uzbek is based on the form of the language spoken in Tashkent and the Fergana valley, areas under the influence of Iranian languages, namely Tajik. Its major dialects are Qarlug, Kipchak, and Oghuz. Uzbek is known as the direct descendant of Chagatay, a medieval literary language commonly used in Central Asia. After being written in various forms of the Arabic alphabet until the late 1920s, a Latin alphabet was used until the 1940s, when a Cyrillic alphabet was given to the Uzbeks by the Soviet administration. In 1993, after independence, Uzbekistan adopted a Latin alphabet and started a language-cleansing project to get rid of borrowed Russian words.

Indo-Iranian Languages in Central Asia

The Iranian branch of this group is common in Central Asia, mainly in Tajikistan, where it is known as Tajik, a dialect descended from Middle Persian.

In the Iranian languages, the nouns are inflected for case, number, gender, and definiteness or indefiniteness. There are prepositions and postpositions (which mark belonging or definiteness). Another typical feature of these languages is the distinction between absolute and oblique cases. The absolute case is used for the predicate nominative, and the oblique case is the marker of indirect, postpositional, or prepositional objects. The verb system is complex, with conjugations and suffixes. The basic word order is subject-object-verb. Relative clauses follow the noun they describe, and most adjectives follow rather than precede the noun.

Tajik   Tajik belongs to a subgroup of the West Iranian languages that includes Farsi and Dari, the languages spoken in Iran and Afghanistan, respectively. Because of intense contact with Turkic-language speakers and a high rate of bilingualism with Uzbek and Kyrgyz, Tajik has been influenced by the Turkic languages. Its lexicon also has many terms from Russian. The main dialect division in Tajik is between the Northwestern and Southwestern groups. The Northwestern dialects, which are the basis of Standard Tajik, are also spoken in southern Uzbekistan. The most northern Northwestern dialects have the most Turkicized structure. The language has no grammatical gender or articles, but person and number distinctions are

maintained. Nouns are marked for specificity: one marker in the singular and two in the plural. Objects of transitive verbs are marked by a suffix. Verbs are formed using one of two basic stems, present and past; aspect is as important as tense. Verbs agree with the subject in person and number. Tajik verbs are normally compounds consisting of a noun and a verb. Word order is subject-object-verb.

Tajik was written in Arabic script until the early 1900s. A Latin alphabet was introduced in 1928 and was used until replaced by the Cyrillic alphabet in 1940. A modified Cyrillic alphabet is in use, but recently the government has attempted to return to the Latin alphabet.

Cigdem Balim-Harding

Further Reading
Akiner, Sirin. (1986) *Islamic Peoples of the Soviet Union.* New York: KPI.
Bennigsen, Alexander, and Samuel Enders Wimbush. (1986) *Muslims of the Soviet Empire: A Guide.* Bloomington, IN: Indiana University Press.
Campbell, George L. (2000) *Compendium of the World's Languages.* 2d ed. 2 vols. London: Routledge.
Comrie, Bernard. (1981) *The Languages of the Soviet Union.* New York: Cambridge University Press.
———. (1990) *The World's Major Languages.* Oxford, U.K.: Oxford University Press.
Fierman, William. (1991) *Language Planning and National Development: The Uzbek Experience.* Contributions to the Sociology of Language 60. Berlin and New York: Mouton de Gruyter.
Johanson, Lars, and Eva Csato, eds. (1998) *The Turkic Languages.* London: Routledge.
Landau, Jacob M., and Barbara Kellner-Heinkele. (2000) *Politics of Language in the ex-Soviet Muslim States.* London: Hurst.

CENTRAL ASIAN REGIONALISM   Central Asian regionalism is a somewhat abstract notion that suggests cohesion among the Central Asian states of Kazakhstan, Kyrgyzstan, Tajikistan, Turkmenistan, and Uzbekistan based on common circumstances of geography, ethnicity, language, culture, history, and religion.

Geography and History

Geographic proximity is the main influence in shaping regional understandings, and Central Asia is no exception. Located at the crossroads of the old Silk Road, the Central Asian states have historically shared the same fate when confronted by expansionist powers—conquest. Invaders came from all sides; the geography of Central Asia (Russia and the open steppes to the north, mountains to the south and east and the Caspian Sea to the west) lent itself to the strategic pursuit of power and wealth. The ancient cities of Bukhara, Samarqand, Osh, Merv, and Almaty served not only as trade centers for the settled urban populations of the region, but also as trophies for foreign invaders.

Dating back to the Scythian conquest of the Cimmerian state between 750 and 700 BCE, the peoples of Central Asia have suffered a long succession of foreign invasions. Invading peoples have included the Greeks, the Mongols, the Huns, the Avars, the Khazars, the Turks, the Arabs, the Russians and the Soviets. As a result of these conquests there were great infusions of language, culture, and religion that worked to shape the region by blending foreign and local customs. In this fashion many of the more distinctive features of Uzbek and Kazak society, for example, became diluted in favor of a more homogenous "Central Asian" identity.

Ethnicity

The interplay between ethnicity and identity in Central Asia is a major contributor to the notion of Central Asian regionalism. As waves of conquerors moved through the region the indigenous Central Asia peoples mixed with ethnically similar and dissimilar peoples. Over time, whole ethnic groups were moved in and out of the region in order to create a more manageable political situation for the invading armies. Accordingly, ethnic identity became relatively fluid, as past influences, such as a sedentary or nomadic lifestyle and "traditional" geographic homelands and bloodlines became intertwined or even eliminated. Today, tribes and clans are most commonly described as the institutions that exercise localized control of politics and economics. Historically they are perpetuated through family bloodlines, geography, and past allegiances. Regional power groupings maintain local bases of support, while national offices preserve regional and local connections. Today government ministries are often dominated by members of a single clan, as is the case in Uzbekistan and Turkmenistan.

To complicate matters, however, the term *clan* is employed differently across Central Asia. In Kazakhstan, Kyrgyzstan, and Turkmenistan the clans are based on lines of descent, emanating originally from the Kazakh Greater, Lesser, and Golden Hordes. Their respective political and social structures are based on kinship, which was traced patriarchally. Their territories are named after the inhabiting groups (Turkmen in Turkmenistan, Kazakhs in Kazakhstan, Kyrgyz in Kyrgyzstan, and Karakalpaks in Karakalpakstan). This nomadic model of clan identification con-

trasts with the sedentary model of clan organization and identification in Uzbekistan and Tajikistan, where clans are based on regional networks of patron-client relations, themselves based on the political and administrative institutions of their respective states. As a consequence of this structure, clan names are a derivative of their geographic locale, most often an oasis city, rather than blood lines. Uzbek examples include the Samarqand, Bukhara, and Tashkent clans. Examples from Tajikistan include the Khujandi and Kulabi clans. As is the case in Afghanistan, Central Asia's southern neighbor, the institutions of tribes and clans and their direct connection to ethnicity and identity can produce social, political, and economic instability on a grand scale. And yet it is these same institutions that provide the fundamental logic for the assertion of Central Asian regionalism.

Language

A common Turkic linguistic heritage, except in Tajikistan, where the dialect is a derivation of the Persian Farsi, and the accompanying cultural markers, such as festivals and customs, underscores the ethnicity and identity elements of regionalism. It is important to note that while each of the Central Asian states has experienced a cultural renaissance since their independence, most notably expressed by the official adoption of the titular languages, Russian remains the lingua franca of the region. This holdover from the colonial past serves as a unifying factor across the region for the conduct of business, science, and other cooperative affairs.

Religion

Finally, the prevalence of Islam across the region is yet another factor that contributes to the construction of Central Asia as a single collective unit. The ability of Islam to cross ethnic, linguistic, social, political, or territorial boundaries makes it both a great force for consolidation and peace and a force for instability and violence. After the terrorist attacks of 11 September 2001, Islam in Central Asia is seen as a threat to the Western powers, and as such something that needs to be contained. To date the leaders of the Central Asian republics have been all too happy to oblige the West in its attempts to suppress "radical" or "fundamentalist" Islamic movements. Religious-based political parties, or popular fronts, as they are better know in the region, are outlawed in all five of the Central Asian states. No other factor, including the independence of the region from the former Soviet Union, is considered more important as a defining factor for the future of the region.

Regionalism in Central Asia will continue to evolve as the leaders and populations of those republics seek to define and establish their place within an increasingly integrated world.

Anthony Bichel

Further Reading
Allworth, Edward, ed. (1994) *Central Asia, 130 Years of Russian Dominance, A Historical Overview*. Durham, NC: Duke University.
Gleason, Gregory. (1997) *The Central Asian States: Discovering Independence*. Boulder, CO: Westview Press.
Grousset, Rene. (1970) *The Empire of the Steppes: A History of Central Asia*. Trans. by Naomi Walford. New Brunswick, NJ: Rutgers University Press.

CENTRAL HIGHLANDS OF VIETNAM

(1990 pop. 2.9 million). The central highlands of Vietnam comprise three provinces—Gia Lai–Kon Tum, Dac Lac, and Lam Dong. They include 55,569 square kilometers or 16.6 percent of the country's total area but only 4.1 percent of its total population. The population density of the central highlands is 52 persons per square kilometer, compared to 215 for the country and more than 1,000 in the Red River Delta. While the Kinh-Vietnamese are the dominant ethnic group in the low coastal areas, the central highlands are the home of indigenous peoples such as the Xo-dang, Ba-na, Gio-rai, E-de, Mo-nong, and Ma. These Austroasiatic and Austronesian groups arrived from southern China and settled in the highlands around 2500–1500 BCE because of the fertile soils, rich fauna, and favorable climate. Some groups are still practicing swidden (slash-and-burn) agriculture and living in longhouses.

In the sixteenth century CE, the Kinh-Vietnamese conquered the eastern lowlands, and traders bartered salt, fabrics, and ironware for bush products without endangering the indigenous cultural patterns. In the middle of the nineteenth century, a few French priests moved near the city of Kon Tum in order to evangelize the hill tribes. From 1888 onward, the French administration encouraged Kinh settlements in the central highlands to relieve the overcrowded Red River Delta and, at the same time, to procure labor for the new plantation sector. By 1954, French colonists had extended the tea, rubber, and coffee plantations to about 110,000 hectares, and the number of Kinh working there had risen to at least 150,000 people. One-half to two-thirds of the Khin in the central highlands, as well as some ethnic Chinese people, lived in towns associated with the plantations, such as Kon Tum, Pleiku, and Buan Me Thuot.

During the Vietnam War (1954–1975), the peoples of the central highlands were suspected of disloyalty by both the Communist Viet Minh and the South Vietnamese government, and they suffered ill-treatment from both sides. Defoliation programs during the war caused large areas to become toxic. Altogether, between 200,000 and 220,000 people died. In the postwar period about 2 million Kinh were sent to "new economic zones" in the highlands, greatly affecting the cultural patterns of the hill tribes, who now comprise less than a quarter of the population of the central highlands.

G. R. Zimmermann

Further Reading
Cao Van Luong. (1966) "Le lutte des minorités nationales du Tây Nguyen." *Études Vietnamiennes* 8: 115–137.
Condominas, Georges. (1994) *We Have Eaten the Forest: The Story of a Montagnard Village in the Central Highlands of Vietnam*. New York: Kodansha.
Zimmermann, Gerd R. (1998) "Indigenous Tribes and Kinh-Vietnamese Infiltration in the Tây Nguyen Highlands of South Central Vietnam." *Internationales Asienforum/International Quarterly for Asian Studies* 29, 3–4: 337–351.

CERAMICS—JAPAN

The radical changes that Japan has undergone over the last hundred years to become a major world economic power have not resulted in the loss of the country's rich and diverse ceramic tradition. In the early 2000s, Japan's ceramic artists and craftspeople are among the most numerous of any country in the world.

The art of the tea ceremony (*chado*) is connected to the history of ceramics in Japan. The old imperial capital city of Kyoto is one of many localities known for its ceramics, particularly the low-fired *raku* pots that are associated with the tea ceremony's founding tea master, Sen no Rikyu. *Raku* means "leisure," but it is also the family name of the Kyoto potters who made tea bowls using what is now generically called the *raku* process, in which a highly porous, partly fired clay pot is glazed, fired to maturity, and cooled quickly. The red-hot pot is removed from a small kiln and quickly placed in leaves or other material that smokes and creates accidental effects through the uneven removal of oxygen from the glaze, carbon deposits on parts of the pot, and sometimes crackles in certain glazes. These tea bowls epitomize the aesthetic sense of *shibui*—quiet, simple beauty.

Kaiseki, the food served to guests at a tea ceremony, also required special ceramics. *Kaiseki* originally consisted of a combination of simply prepared foods presented in an elegant way that incorporated ceramics as an important element. The appropriate foods must look well in a dish, and both dish and food must fit the season and be compatible with the space in which the meal takes place. Even prior to the development of *kaiseki*, Japanese party food was served in small individual and separate dishes, because mixing items on one plate or bowl compromised the purity of the unique flavors of each item. This preference is expressed in the proliferation of various shapes, sizes, glazes (or lack of glazes), colors, and textures used in ceramic plates, bowls, and teapots that are part of the same feast. The ware used must also fit the type of food or drink: coffee or English tea requires special European-style cups with saucers, while Japanese tea and rice wine (sake) require their own ware.

Other traditional arts that utilize ceramics have contributed to the development and appreciation of pottery: the tiny water bottles used with ink stones in calligraphy, clay incense holders for altar offerings, vases for ikebana (flower arrangement), and pots for miniature tree cultivation (bonsai). Motifs from ceramic decorations appear in other forms, for example, on kimono silks, fans, and wrapping paper. Ceramic objects are a ubiquitous part of Japan's consumer culture, which, in turn, has ensured the vitality of ceramics as an artistic as well as commercial enterprise.

Origins

The people who inhabited Japan during the Jomon period (10,000–300 BCE) were named after the traces they left in clay—rope impressions made when cords of fiber were pressed onto soft, moist clay. Jomon culture evolved into the more complex Yayoi culture (300 BCE–300 CE), during which time Japan partook of the spread of Chinese influence and the economic transformation introduced by rice cultivation.

Japanese ceramics, like other aspects of Japanese culture, were affected by the recurring waves of contact with China and Korea. Along with the introduction of new technology and techniques for kiln building, firing, glazing, and forming, Buddhist and Confucian ideas affected the way in which potters and their patrons and clients approached the craft.

Arita, Imari, and Porcelains

In the early sixteenth century, a Japanese is said to have returned from a five-year visit to China, where he learned porcelain manufacture with blue-and-white decoration *(some-tsuke)*. He introduced to Japan the technique of using cobalt salts to paint designs on pots formed of the white clay brought from China, which

were then glazed and fired. Production was not to last, however, since this type of clay was not available in Japan until the early seventeenth century, when abundant China clay (porcelain) deposits were discovered in the Arita region of Kyushu. In the mid-seventeenth century, the Dutch East India Company began to import Japanese porcelain made by potters using the cobalt salts technique in Arita. A large-scale export industry developed, and because the porcelain ware was shipped from Imari port in Arita, the export ware was called Imari ware by Europeans.

Arita designs were originally influenced by Korea and China, but in time Chinese and European potteries began in turn to copy Japanese Imari designs. Arita is also known for two other types of porcelain, Nabeshima and Kakiemon, which had styles distinct from the export porcelains. Both are highly valued by Japanese collectors and have ornate designs that reflect the tastes of the Tokugawa period (1600/1603–1868). Arita continues to be a major pottery region in Japan.

Another major ceramic-producing locality is Seto, located near Nagoya City; Seto has a variety of different potteries, some small and some with automated

A Bizen ware sake bottle, c. 1392-1573. (SAKAMOTO PHOTO RESEARCH LABORATORY/CORBIS)

BIZEN WARE

Glazes are not applied to Bizen ware before firing, instead the unique characteristics spring from the firing process. The chemical oxidation and reduction of the iron rich clay found in the Bizen region during the firing, plus flying ash from the pine wood used as fuel, create the delightful effects that are prized.

Pots touching each other protect the clay surface from some of the effects caused by the kiln atmosphere to create interesting "shadows" that contrast with the surrounding surface. Ash flying about in certain parts of the kiln reacts with the superheated clay surface of pots to create rough textured glaze spots called *goma* (sesame seeds). A blue-black hue (*ao-Bizen*) is produced when the oxygen content of the kiln's atmosphere is reduced, causing iron oxide and metallic iron to appear on the clay body. Cords of straw soaked in brine and wrapped around pots create *hidasuke* (fire-cord markings) during the firing: the straw burns away, allowing sodium from the salt to react with the clay to form bright red glaze streaks on the neutral background of the pot's surface. All of these effects and their variations (pots coming from the same kiln vary), give Bizen its distinctiveness. Bizen's spontaneity, directness, and simplicity evoke its subtle aesthetic.

Victor N. Kobayashi

Sources: Frederick Baekeland and Robert Moes. (1993) *Modern Japanese Ceramics in American Collections.* New York: Japan Society. Herbert H. Sanders. (1967) *The World of Japanese Ceramics.* Tokyo: Kodansha International.

production-line methods of turning out huge numbers of pots. Seto, like many pottery-producing areas of Japan, dates back to feudal times and is an area that has good supplies of natural clay.

Scattered throughout Japan are numerous active kiln sites, many of which trace their histories to the Momoyama period (1573–1600), when Korean craftspeople were brought (often forcibly) to Japan to produce various wares. The six old kiln sites that have survived from these times are Tamba, Bizen, Shigaraki, Echizen, Seto, and Tokoname. Many potters had been supported by feudal lords, but with the Meiji Restoration in 1868, the fief system was abolished, and clan potteries went into decline. Some of the craftspeople active today in these areas, however, are considered direct descendants of the founding potters.

Western Influences

The most important Western influences on ceramics came after the opening of Japan to the West in 1853. Beginning in the late 1800s, new techniques, including mass production, rapidly entered Japan with the Meiji government's efforts to destroy feudal institutions and to industrialize and modernize the nation. The German chemist and engineer Gottfried Wagener (1831–1897) was hired as a government adviser, and through his work in Arita, potters and manufacturers were introduced to plaster molds, new glazes and pigments, use of coal for firing kilns, and other Western approaches to pottery making. Trade schools were established to train workers for modern industries, including ceramics.

The mass production of ceramic ware created a new industry, but some traditional potteries continued. Revitalization of traditional methods began primarily after World War II. For example, Toyo Kaneshige (1896–1967), a seventy-eighth-generation potter in Bizen in Okayama prefecture, noting the decline in quality of Bizen ceramics over the generations, revived interest in the high artistic standards set by the tea bowls of the medieval period and began experimenting with the firing methods (such as using no kiln furniture to stack the pots) of his ancestors, creating spectacular examples of Bizen ware. In recognition of Kaneshige's contributions, the national government designated him a Living National Treasure.

Over the years, ancient kiln sites that had fallen into disuse and near oblivion were in many cases later reestablished by potters attempting to revive and reproduce the ceramic traditions of the site, while claiming that the new pottery had authentic connections with the distant past. Thus there is a certain myth-making aspect to the history of ceramics in Japan that smoothes over discontinuities by implying an unbroken tradition.

Japan also was influenced by the European reaction against mass-produced ware. This revolt was articulated in Victorian England by William Morris (1834–1898), who called for the recognition and appreciation of the beauty of traditional arts and crafts in the industrial age. In Japan, Soetsu Yanagi (1869–1961), with the celebrated potters Shoji Hamada (1894–1978) and Kanjiro Kawai (1890–1966), started the *mingei* ("people's crafts") movement and founded the Japan Folk Art Association. Yanagi wrote essays on the philosophy of *mingei*, and his work *The Unknown Craftsman* represents a fusion of Buddhist philosophy and the ideals of the Arts and Crafts Movement. Yanagi was concerned about the decline of traditional village potteries and worked to create an appreciation of the ceramic works produced in villages. He was also especially interested in the revival of the folk arts of Korea (which Japan ruled from 1910 until the end of World War II) and Okinawa. At the same time, he helped the formation of an aesthetic mystique of the anonymous crafts-artist who works intensely, but is not driven by individualistic ego, which continues to inspire Japanese and Western craftspeople. The English potter Bernard Leach (1887–1979) was a strong supporter of the Japanese *mingei* movement and formed close friendships with Yanagi, Hamada, and Kawai.

Hamada, originally from Tokyo, established himself in the pottery village of Mashiko, where he lived the life of a *mingei* potter, not signing his pots in the belief that the collective tradition was the author.

Proliferation of Styles

Some potteries have been established more recently, born of the fact that ceramic styles proliferate depending on the market. Many potters adopt the style that is in fashion, while others work in the same style for several generations.

The variety of ceramic ware found in Japan is partly due to local conditions—clays vary widely depending on the site, and potters enjoy treating unique characteristics of the clay body as elements in the design of a pot. For example, tiny stones found in the clay in the old city of Hagi (Yamaguchi prefecture) can burst through the clay during firing, forming various subtly colored effects that make some Hagi ware highly prized.

The variety is also due to the periods of influence from abroad—Chinese and Korean cultures have greatly affected Japanese ceramics, just as they did other arts. As mentioned earlier, a major influence occurred in the Momoyama period, when the warlord Hideyoshi brought Korean master potters to Japan.

Some potters in villages today are direct descendants of the original potters from Korea, and Karatsu ware (named after its locale, a castle town on the coast of the Sea of Japan) is a notable example of Korean influences. One type of Karatsu ware uses a suspension of iron oxide in water, which is painted onto a glazed ware before it is fired. After the iron oxide painting of a tree or other design dries, a thin overglaze is applied, and when the pot has been fired, the effect is that of an elegant brush painting on the teacup or dish. Another type of Karatsu ware utilizes impressed patterns on the moist clay that is covered with a white slip (a creamy mixture of clay and water), which is carefully scraped off so that the white slip remains in the impressions. This inlay technique is called *mishima* (named after a shrine in Japan's Mishima city) by international potters, though the technique actually originated with the captured Korean potters brought to Japan. In Korea, the *mishima* technique was taken to elegant heights in the gray-green celadon porcelain ware of the Koryo dynasty (918–1392). Much of the signature work of the potter Tatsuzo Shimaoka (b. 1919) uses this technique in a unique way: impressions made by cords (reminiscent of ancient Jomon earthenware patterns) are inlaid with white slip and high fired using a transparent glaze.

Toward Modern Expression

The ceramic artist Kenkichi Tomimoto (1886–1963) freed the art of pottery from its traditional constraints, including *mingei*. Along with Bernard Leach, Torimoto used the potter's wheel, rather than having workers make the pots that the potter then glazed. Tomimoto also excelled in creating original works and in 1949 started the first ceramic arts department in a college in Japan: the Kyoto Municipal College of Fine Arts. Since Tomimoto, Japan has seen a growth of studio ceramists who create contemporary expressions in clay, some inspired by artists such as America's revolutionary Peter Voulkos

(b. 1924), who treated ceramics primarily as an expressive medium, breaking out of the constraints of its utilitarian functions. Two examples of this opening of Japan to the international contemporary movement in ceramics are Mutsuo Yanagihara (b. 1934), who studied under Tomimoto, and Kimpei Nakamura (b. 1935), whose father Banzan makes tea bowls in the traditional manner.

Victor Kobayashi

See also: **Ceramics—Korea**

Further Reading
Baekeland, Frederick, and Robert Moes. (1993) *Modern Japanese Ceramics in American Collections*. New York: Japan Society.

Cardozo, Sidney B., and Hirano Masaaki. (1987) *Uncommon Clay: The Life and Pottery of Rosanji*. Tokyo: Kodansha.

Moeran, Brian. (1997) *Folk Art Potters of Japan: Beyond an Anthropology of Aesthetics*. Honolulu, HI: University of Hawaii Press.

Sanders, Herbert H. (1967) *The World of Japanese Ceramics*. Tokyo: Kodansha.

Yanagi Soetsu. (1972) *The Unknown Craftsman: A Japanese Insight into Beauty*. Tokyo: Kodansha.

CERAMICS—KOREA Korea has a long history of pottery making, dating back to the prehistoric era, and for the last two millennia it has been a leader in ceramic arts. A sizable portion of the ceramics work in the world today owes its genesis to techniques developed by Korean craftspeople. Early Korean pottery was highly influenced by that of neighboring China, but truly indigenous ceramic ware appeared in Shilla early in the Three Kingdoms period (220–265 CE). High-fired stoneware first appeared in the fourth century, and ceramics took the form of jars, pots, cups, urns, figurines, and roof tiles. The pottery of this period came to be identified by the kingdom in which it was produced. Koguryo and Paekche ceramics were noted for their brown and green glazes, while Shilla ceramics were recognized by more random color in the glazes.

Koryo Celadons

Ceramics reached their zenith in the twelfth century during the Koryo kingdom (918–1392). This period is most noted for its exquisite greenish celadons (glazes). Early Koryo plain celadons were influenced by Song China, but later works show a unique and distinct style. Some celadons were painted with white or black slips or iron oxide, while others were inlaid using an ingenious Korean technique. The pattern was incised and filled with white or black slip. The work was then fired, covered with celadon glaze, and refired. With the Mongol invasions in the thirteenth century, slight changes in firing methods and simplification of techniques led to degradation in designs, decorative patterns, and color quality.

Choson Porcelain

The decline of Koryo celadon gave rise to an unusual type of pottery known as *punchong* ware, which was the only pottery allowed for use by commoners in the first two centuries of the Choson dynasty (1392–1910). Although the glazing was similar to that of Koryo celadon, the decorative technique was different. The most typical type of *punchong* decoration was the stamping-and-inlaying technique. It consisted of stamped-on designs with white slip brushed on. After the set slip was scraped off, the stamped designs remained filled with white clay. During the Japanese invasions of 1592–1598, exquisite pieces of celadon and *punchong* ware were seized and kilns were destroyed, bringing an end to the production and use of *punchong* ware.

After the Japanese invasions, Choson white porcelain developed under royal patronage. The Confucian state required a more simple style than the elaborate designs of Koryo. Choson white porcelain was first characterized by an opaque whiteness, later by cobalt-blue decorations, and later still by folkloric designs. In the twentieth century, Koryo kilns in the far southwest were excavated by South Korea in an at-

A Longquan ware celedon jar with lotus petal lid created c. 1279-1368. (ASIAN ART & ARCHAEOLOGY, INC./CORBIS)

tempt to research the techniques used and duplicate these fine ceramics.

David E. Shaffer

See also: **Ceramics—Japan**

Further Reading
Adams, Edward B. (1995) *Korea Guide.* Rev. ed. Seoul: Seoul International Publishing House.
———. (1987) *Korean Folk Art and Crafts.* Seoul: Seoul International Publishing House.
———. (1986) *Korea's Pottery Heritage.* 2 vols. Seoul: Seoul International Publishing House.
Covell, Jon. (1986) *The World of Korean Ceramics.* Honolulu, HI: Dae-Won-Sa; Seoul: Si-sa-yong-o-sa.

CHAEBOL   A *chaebol* is a type of Korean conglomerate, similar to the prewar *zaibatsu* of Japan, which has multiplied in the Republic of Korea (South Korea) since the 1960s. A *chaebol* may be defined as "a diversified business group which is exclusively owned and controlled by a person and that person's family" (Kang 1997: 31). Its two major characteristics are that it is a business group that is owned and governed by the dominant shareholder and his family (a divergence from the legal definition of a *chaebol*—according to the Fair Trade Law of Korea—as a large-scale business group), and that it is a diversified business group with coverage extending from manufacturing to services, and from small retailers to multinational corporations.

The fact that it is family-owned, however, constitutes a major difference between the Korean *chaebol* and the prewar Japanese *zaibatsu*. The Japanese *zaibatsu* "family" was not always made up of blood relatives. An excellent manager could belong to the "family" in Japan, but not in Korea. The ownership of currently existing corporate groups in Japan has been diversified to their affiliates, main banks, and the public. To make another comparison, in the United States in the 1960s, conglomerates were diversified in business and assets, but not necessarily owned by dominant families.

Thirty *chaebol* are famous: their names are announced officially as the thirty largest business groups on the first of April every year. In 1998 they accounted for 46 percent of total sales in the manufacturing sector, 24.1 percent of value added (comprised of wages, cost of borrowing, rent, depreciation, and net profit before corporate tax), and 12.9 percent of employment in the same manufacturing sector.

Chaebol have been the leading force in Korean economic development. At the same time, however, they are the target of strong and widespread criticism. That is, the *chaebol* are successful but are not necessarily fair competitors.

The Development of the *Chaebol*
Historically, the *chaebol* have grown under a government-led development strategy. The South Korean government selected as "national champions" certain companies in the major industries during the first Five Year Economic Development Plan in the early 1960s, and subsidized them through financial aid, tax exemptions, suppression of the labor movement, and so forth. The firms singled out by the government received enormous economic benefits and were able to rise to a level of international competitiveness.

With their information-gathering and lobbying power, the *chaebol* leadership could influence government officials to approve policy loans, which were obtained by forcing the banks to follow government policy. The *chaebol* thus were able to borrow continuously under favorable conditions, based not on the soundness of

Daewoo Group chief Kim Woo-Choong in July 1999. After promising major reforms, the organization, the second largest chaebol in South Korea, collapsed in August 1999. In 2001, Kim was reported by Korean officials to be hiding in Europe to escape prosecution (AFP/CORBIS)

their operations but on their lobbying power. In addition, the *chaebol* got special tax exemptions.

This unhealthy development policy eventually drove the Korean economy to the financial crisis of 1997. In November 1997, bad loans held by Korean banks comprised about 15 percent (32.2 trillion won) of their total loans, while the corresponding figure for advanced countries is generally less than 1 percent. Most of these nonperforming loans had been granted to the thirty largest *chaebol*.

The Korean *chaebol* have diversified through various related and unrelated fields of business including electronics, the automotive sector, heavy industry, textiles and garments, petrochemicals, banking, information, and telecommunications. Often depicted as an octopus, the typical *chaebol* has grown many different business legs in order to diversify its operations and thereby minimize its risks so as to secure financing at low interest rates.

Two strategies were used by the *chaebol* to facilitate their rapid expansion: mutual loan guarantees between related companies within the same *chaebol*, and cross investments between the affiliated companies of one *chaebol*. These strategies allowed the *chaebol* to increase their leverage while maintaining the unity of their corporate governance.

Negative Impact of *Chaebol* on Korea

While the *chaebol* have helped Korea attain rapid economic growth and are the manufacturers of world-renowned brand names, they have also become an obstacle to further economic development. First, the *chaebol* have hindered and distorted efficient market development through their wielding of both market and nonmarket power. This has allowed them to block the normal development of small and medium-sized industries, due to unfair distribution of resources and entry barriers. Second, they hinder smooth industrial development in this time of transition from traditional to information- and communication-based industries. The problem is that the *chaebol* still operate via traditional mass-production systems for standardized products, using unskilled or semi-skilled laborers. Third, the development of the financial industry itself has been stunted because capital from the financial institutions is concentrated in *chaebol* loans—as shown by the large number of nonperforming loans. Fourth, the *chaebol* have distorted the distribution of income and assets.

Reforms

In response to the 1997 financial crisis, the Korean government has carried out reforms of banks and corporations. The *chaebol* reforms include enhancing transparent business management through the early introduction of consolidated financial statements, banning the system of cross guarantees between individual subsidiaries of a business group, defining core sectors and cooperation with small and medium-sized firms, making majority shareholders and management more accountable for their actions, banning *chaebol* dominance of nonbanking financial institutions, prohibiting mutual investments between subsidiaries, and banning illegal hereditary transfer of *chaebol* ownership.

Some of the reforms have shown good results, but others have yet to bear fruit. By the end of 1999, the *chaebol* had eliminated almost all mutual loan guarantees between affiliates—loans which for the top thirty business groups amounted to four times their own capital in 1997. The average debt/equity ratio of the top five groups, excluding Daewoo, fell from 386 percent in 1998 to less than 200 percent by the end of 1999. By June 1999, the top thirty *chaebol* had spun off 484 firms; this has helped them focus on their core competencies and has enhanced their competitiveness.

Reform of the corporate governance structure is still incomplete. Until transparent corporate governance systems are set up, *chaebol* reform cannot be termed a success. Until recently, the corporate governance structure of a *chaebol* was centered in the owner and the *chaebol* subsidiaries, whose average combined shareholdings reached 50.5 percent in 1999 but declined to 44 percent in 2000. The *chaebol* head dominated decision making, a practice that is criticized because of the consequent lack of surveillance, supervision, and accountability.

Since the foreign exchange crisis of 1997, the Korean *chaebol* have begun to change their corporate structures (e.g., by establishing protections for minor shareholders and by allowing directors from outside the firm) including their governance, though management is still dominated by the owner-manager head.

In the twenty-first century, the new model for corporate governance ought to ensure proper surveillance from both inside and outside the firm. The decision-making power should be shifted from the dominant family to a board of directors that represents the greater number of shareholders. A 1999 law required that companies whose assets are more than two trillion Korean won must nominate directors from outside the firm for more than half the total board members. In addition, the group-suit system will be legalized in 2002. Along with these reforms bank management should be allowed to be independent from government manipulation. One important reform will be to shift the *chaebol*'s traditional group management system to an independent management system, as the group system is contrary to fair market competition.

Korea will probably choose to replace its rent-seeking model with the market-based corporate governance model that is popular in Western countries such as the United States and the United Kingdom, where household and institutional investors are the main shareholders: they empower the board of directors, which in turn supervises management and hires and fires the CEO. This is the desirable and expected direction of *chaebol* reform in the twenty-first century.

Chul-Kyu Kang

Further Reading
Kang, Chul-Kyu. (1997) "Diversification Process and the Ownership Structure of Samsung Chaebol." In *Beyond The Firm*, edited by Takao Shiba and Masahiro Shimotani. New York: Oxford University Press.
———. (1999) *Chaebol gaehyuk ui kyongjehak* (The Economics of Chaebol Reform). Seoul: Dasan.
Kang, Chul-Kyu, Chi-Sang Chang, and Jong-Pyo Choi. (1991) *Chaebol: seongjang ui juyeok in ga tamyok ui hwasin inga?* (Chaebol: The Leading Actors of Growth or the Incarnation of Avarice?). Seoul: Bibong.
Kim, Dae-Hwan, and Kyun Kim, eds. (1999) *Hanhuk chaebol gaehyuk ron* (Studies of Korean Chaebol Reform). Seoul: Nanam.
Kim, Seok Ki. (1987) "Business Concentration and Government Policy: A Study of the Phenomenon of Business Groups in Korea, 1945–85." D.B.A. diss. Harvard University.

CHAGANG PROVINCE

(2002 pop. 1.5 million). Chagang province (Chagangdo) is located inland along the northern border of North Korea. The Amnok (Yalu) River, which flows between Korea and China, marks the province's border. North Korea created Chagang province in 1949 from portions of North P'yongan and South Hamgyong provinces. Since then, Chagang has been reconfigured four times and currently has an area of 16,764 square kilometers, divided into 15 counties (*kun*). The provincial capital is at Kanggye, and the other two cities are Manp'o and Hich'on.

The Nangnim mountain range accounts for the province's high average elevation. The province also has many rivers because of the numerous tributaries of the Amnok River. Abundant waterways and fertile soil support a robust agriculture, whose key products are rice and grains, beans, fruits, and vegetables. Nearly a thousand species of trees and plants thrive throughout the province. Lead, zinc, gold, copper, lime, and coal are mined, among other minerals.

Jennifer Jung-Kim

Further Reading
Cho, Chung-Kyung, Phyllis Haffner, and Fredric M. Kaplan. (1991) *The Korea Guidebook*. 5th ed. Boston: Houghton Mifflin.

CHAGATAY

Chagatay, also known as Chaghatay, Chagatai or Jagataic, was the Turkic literary language of Central Asia in the fifteenth to early twentieth centuries, written in the Arabic or (in a few early manuscripts) the Uighur script. Some of the greatest works of Islamic literature were written in Chagatay, including the autobiography of the emperor Babur (1483–1530) and the poems of Nava'i (1441–1501). Chagatay was also the language of the Khivan tradition of historiography, which spanned four centuries, and was the official chancery language of the khanate of Khiva (1804–1873).

The present name of the language is ultimately identified with the Mongol prince Chagatai (d. 1242), one of the sons of Genghis Khan, whose name in subsequent centuries came to be applied to the state centered on his original *ulus*, or portion of the Mongol Empire, including the Central Asian oasis region of Transoxania. Having outlasted the end of the Chagatai state and the rise of the Timurids (fifteenth century), the term Chagatai denoted the nomadic Turkic population of this territory, and later to some extent the Turkic literary language of the region, though Turki or *Turk tili* (Turk language) remained the usual native name for this language down to the first decades of the twentieth century. The designations Chagatay and Eastern Turkish were popularized in the nineteenth century by European Orientalists, some of whom restricted Chagatay to mean the classical language of the fifteenth and early sixteenth centuries. Soviet scholars have used the term *Starouzbekskii iazyk* (Old Uzbek language) to denote a group of spoken and written forms including Chagatay.

Over its entire history Chagatay could claim to unite, in a developed and flexible idiom, a widespread and diverse literate population from Khorasan to Kashgaria, and from European Russia beyond the Aral Sea to the steppes of Kazakhstan. Besides numerous works of poetry and fiction, writings in Chagatay include histories, biographies, religious literature and hagiographies, genealogies, geographical works, travels, various treatises (*risalah*), and a wide variety of documents and correspondence.

The Language

Chagatay is classified as a Central Asian Turkic language, with some linguistic traits related to Kipchak and Oghuz Turkic. Chagatay followed the Karakhanid (eleventh–thirteenth centuries) and Khorezmian (thirteenth–fourteenth centuries) literary languages in the Eastern Middle Turkic period. Its vocabulary was considerably enriched by borrowings from Persian and Arabic. The position of Chagatay as a precursor of the modern literary Uzbek and Uighur languages is assumed but has not been fully investigated.

Throughout the period of its use Chagatay coexisted with literary Persian. There were many bilingual writers, and most Chagatay authors adopted Persian and Arabic expressions extensively. Nevertheless, the language contributed to a distinctive Turkic ethnic consciousness in Central Asia. The fifteenth-century poet Nava'i devoted his last composition, *Muhakamat al-Lughatayn* (Judgment of Two Languages, 1499), to a vigorous argument on the superiority of Turki (Chagatay) over Persian.

The Literature

With few exceptions, poetry in Chagatay was modeled closely upon Persian examples. The oldest surviving works of Chagatay belles lettres belong to the early fifteenth century. During this period, Sakkaki and Ata'i wrote panegyrics and other court poetry for Timurid royal patrons, including Ulugh Beg (1394–1449). Some poems in the single *divan* (collection) of Ata'i record Turkic proverbs, adages, and folk meters. Lutfi (1370?–1460?) was a master of the *tuyugh*, a difficult native Turkic quatrain form with an *aaba* rhyme scheme in which the rhyming words must all be homonyms. Mir 'Ali Shir Nava'i, or Nava'i, wrote in both Chagatay and Persian, though his Chagatay works earned greater renown. Nava'i brought the Chagatay language to its full development as a mode of literary expression and presided over its classical era. Among his numerous works in all genres are four *divans*, a five-part cycle of verse tales *(mathnavi)* entitled *Khamsah*, a translation from Persian of a Sufi hagiographic work by his friend the poet Jami (1414–1492), and *Muhakamat al-Lughatayn*. One of the most important sources on Timurid society is Nava'i's biographical compendium in Chagatay, *Majalis an-Nafa'is* (Assemblies of Refined Men, 1490/1), which gives biographies and literary samples from over four hundred men of letters, many of whom Nava'i knew. It is virtually the only source of information on the lives of the forerunners of Nava'i in Chagatay literature. The emperor Zahir ud-Din Muhammad Babur, founder of the Mughal dynasty in India, was also a celebrated author. His memoir, the *Babunameh* (Book of Babur), is treasured as a work of biography for its lucid depiction of events in the life of a compelling historical personality. Babur also wrote excellent poetry. His *divan* contains all types of the poetic art characteristic of his times, including examples of the virtuosic *tuyugh* quatrain. Chagatay poetry continued to be composed down through the era of the nineteenth-century khanates of Khiva and Quqon, though the artistic ideal was generally imitative.

Perhaps the most popular and influential work of religious literature in Chagatay was a *divan* of prayers and hymns supposed to be the work of the famous twelfth-century Sufi Hoja Ahmad Yasavi, though the collection is known only from much later manuscripts. The genre of Islamic hagiography (stories of the lives, works, and lineages of holy men) also produced several original works in Chagatay.

The oldest histories in Chagatay were produced for the early Shaybanid Uzbek rulers, whose invasions from the steppes drove the Timurids from power at the beginning of the sixteenth century. The *Zubdat al-Athar* (Cream of Annals, after 1525) by 'Abdallah Nasrallahi was the first example in Chagatay of the Islamic general history. Subsequently, Chagatay historiography was written mostly in Khiva, and to a lesser extent Quqon. The Khivan king and historian Abu'l Ghazi Bahadur Khan (1603–1663) wrote his general history, *Shajarah-i Turk* (Genealogy of the Turks), by himself because, he said, he could find no one else in his realm who was qualified to do so. This book was one of the first Central Asian historical works to become known in Europe. In the nineteenth century, Khivan historians beginning with Shir Muhammad Munis (1778–1829) wrote an uninterrupted series of original works that chronicled the rulers of the country, the Qongrat dynasty (eighteenth century–1873). One of the last works in late Chagatay was Muhammad Yusuf Bek Bayani's *Khwarizm Tarikhi* (History of Kwarizm [Khiva], 1921), which, though written in medieval manuscript form, featured the innovated use of punctuation, apparently in imitation of Russian writing.

In the 1920s, the Soviet government's intensive efforts to construct and promulgate an Uzbek literary language finally supplanted Chagatay, and the latter disappeared from use. The Chagatay documents in the archives of the khanate of Khiva (preserved in Saint Petersburg, Russia) remain a valuable and largely untouched body of source material on the history of medieval Central Asia.

D. Prior

Further Reading

Aboul-Ghazi Behadour Khan. (1871–1874, 1970) *Histoire des Mongols et des Tatares.* Trans. by Petr I. Desmaisons. St. Leonards, U.K.: Ad Orientem and Amsterdam: Philo Press.

Babur, Zahiru'd-din Muhammad, Padshah Ghazi. (1922) *The Babur-nama in English.* Trans. by Annette S. Beveridge. London: Luzac.

Bodrogligeti, András J. E. (2001) *A Grammar of Chagatay.* Languages of the World/Materials, no. 155. Munich: Lincom Europa.

Browne, Edward G. (1920, 1928, 1964) *A Literary History of Persia.* Vol. 3, *The Tartar Dominion (1265–1502).* Cambridge, U.K.: Cambridge University Press.

Eckmann, János. (1965) "Die tschaghataische Literatur (Chagatay Literature)." In *Philologiae Turcicae Fundamenta* (*Fundamentals of Turkic Philology*) 2, edited by Louis Bazin, et al. Wiesbaden, Germany: Franz Steiner Verlag, 304–402.

———. (1966) *Chagatay Manual* Indiana University Uralic and Altaic Series, no. 60. Bloomington, IN: Indiana University Press

Hofman, Henry F. (1969) *Turkish Literature: A Biobibliographical Survey.* Section 3. *Moslem Central Asian Turkish Literature, Being in the Main a List of 'Chaghatayan' Authors and Works in 'Chaghatay' as Registered in Professor M. F. Koprulu's Article: 'Cagatay edebiyati', IA.* Vol. 3. *With Some Additions (Nava'iana, However, Excepted).* Utrecht, Netherlands: University of Utrecht/Royal Asiatic Society.

Menges, Karl H. (1995) *The Turkic Languages and Peoples: An Introduction to Turkic Studies.* 2d ed. Wiesbaden, Germany: Harrassowitz Verlag.

Mir Ali Shir. (1966) *The Muhakamat al-Lughatai* (Judgment of Two Languages). Trans. by Robert Devereux. Leiden, Netherlands: E. J. Brill.

Munis, Shir Muhammad Mirab and Muhammad Riza Mirab Agahi. (1999) *Firdaws al-Iqbal: History of Khorezm.* Trans. by Yuri Bregel. Leiden, Netherlands: E. J. Brill.

Pavet de Courteille, Abel. ([1870] 1972). *Dictionnaire Turk-Oriental: Destinée principalement à faciliter la lecture des ouvrages de Bâber, d'Aboul-Gâzi, de Mir Ali-Chir Nevâï, et d'autres ouvrages en langues touraniennes* (Eastern Turkish Dictionary: Intended Primarily to Facilitate the Reading of the Works of Babur, Abu'l Ghazi, Mir 'Ali Shir Nava'i, and Other Works in Turanian Languages). Amsterdam: Philo Press.

CHAGOS ARCHIPELAGO

The Chagos Archipelago (formerly called the Oil Islands) is a cluster of islands in the central Indian Ocean, administered by the United Kingdom, and having a total land area of 197square kilometers. They are actually a group of atolls arranged in a circle around the Chagos Bank and lie 500 kilometers due south of the most southerly island in the Maldive Republic. The only product is coconut oil.

In 1971 the Chagos inhabitants, who are mainly French Creole in origin, were ordered to leave by the British government and most were resettled in Mauri-tius, where the archipelago had been administered. This move was mandated so that the large island of Diego Garcia, where most of the people lived, could be leased to the United States as an intercontinental air base. However, in 2000 the British High Court ruled that the inhabitants had been illegally evicted, and ordered that those who wanted to return there from Mauritius be allowed to do so. Most of the returnees would resettle Peros Banhos or Salomon, but not Diego Garcia 150 kilometers to the south of those islands.

Paul Hockings

CHAJON NORI

Nori means "play" or "game" in Korean. Chajon Nori is one of the traditional massive battle games in Korea. This game dates from about 1000 CE, during the latter Three Kingdoms period. The game commemorates victory in battle; nowadays, it celebrates the harvest.

This battle game, also known as the "War of Moving Bodies," is held around the fifteenth day of the first month of the lunar calendar. It is played in most parts of Korea. Villagers make chariots with oak trees after supplicating the Mountain God for his approval. The villagers are divided into two teams, the East and the West, on the festival day. Everyone has his own part to play in this game. The players in the lead, with their arms crossed, push their opponents with their shoulders, or mount an attack against the opponent, pulling down the opponent commander. The game comes to an end when the chariot of either team is pulled down to the ground or the commander falls to the ground. It sometimes lasts until midnight. The players on the winning team celebrate their victory by throwing their straw sandals high up into the air, or throwing away the parts of the enemy chariot. Winning is supposed to portend a good harvest.

Hisashi Sanada

Further Reading

Kishino, Yuzo, Yoshio Kuroda, Yuichi Suzuki, and Takeo Fukagawa, eds. (1987) *Encyclopedia of Sports.* Tokyo: Taishukan.

Obayashi, Taryo, Yuzo Kishino, Tsuneo Sogawa, Shinji Yamashita, eds. (1998) *Encyclopedia of Ethnic Play and Games.* Tokyo: Taishukan.

CHANDIGARH

(2001 est pop. 808,000). Chandigarh became the capital of the Punjab and Haryana states in northwestern India in the 1950s. After partition in 1947, when Punjab's principal city Lahore was claimed by Pakistan, the new state needed a capital. Premier Jawaharlal Nehru (1889–1964) seized the opportunity to realize his vision of a city symbolic of the future of India. The originally chosen architect, Matthew Nowicki, was killed in a 1950 airplane crash. Swiss-French modernist architect Charles-Édouard Jeanneret (called Le Corbusier; 1887–1965) produced the master plan. Chandigarh is orderly and regulated, with modern concrete buildings, broad boulevards, and open parks; it has an air of prosperity and is considered the cleanest and healthiest city in India. Yet it has been controversial ever since it was completed in the 1960s. Detractors complain that its design was flawed, self-indulgent, and "un-Indian," with provision for fast-flowing traffic, unnecessarily large parking lots, and buildings requiring expensive air conditioning. The premier attraction of Chandigarh is the Rock Garden, a series of interconnected rocky grottoes, walkways, and landscaped waterfalls, including more than five thousand animal and humanoid figures fashioned from discarded materials. Also of interest are the Museum and Art Gallery, the Science Museum, and a large Rose Garden containing over a thousand varieties of roses.

C. Roger Davis

Further Reading

Kalia, Ravi. (2000) *Chandigarh: The Making of an Indian City.* Oxford: Oxford University Press.

CHANG FEE MING (b. 1959), Malaysian artist. Chang Fee Ming is known for large watercolor paintings depicting traditional Asian arts and ways of life in a photo-realist style. A native of Dungun in Terengganu in northeastern Malaysia, Chang is a self-taught artist with a background in commercial design. As he developed his distinctively detailed and colorful style, Chang was inspired during travels in Bali and became committed to recording vanishing arts and preindustrial scenes in his work. Evoking an atmosphere of timeless, sun-drenched calm, Chang's paintings are often detailed depictions of traditional arts, such as intricately woven and decorated fabrics.

Chang's work was shown at "The Road to Mandalay," an exhibition and sale held in Jakarta in 1995, to which only patrons of his work were invited. Traveling for several months every year to make sketches for the exacting paintings executed in his studio in Terengganu, Chang has journeyed to India, Nepal, and Thailand as well as to Myanmar (Burma), in addition to frequent excursions within Malaysia and to Bali. As his reputation grows, collectors in distant cities have sought to acquire Chang's paintings, a few of which are available in the form of prints.

E. M. Hill

Further Reading
Ooi Kok Chuen. (1995) *The World of Chang Fee Ming.* Terenganu, Malaysia: Chang Fee Ming.
Simmonds, Nigel. (1996) "A Realistic View." *Regent Magazine* 63: 48–53.

CHANG RIVER   Called the Changjiang (Long River) in Chinese, the Chang (Yangtze) at 3,900 miles is the third-longest river in the world and the longest one in Asia. It originates in the Tanggulashan on the border of Tibet and Qinghai Province and then runs south until it empties into the East China Sea near Shanghai. The river derives its name from the ancient kingdom of Yang, which settled regions along it.

The Chang originates in the Kunlun Mountains and then runs south through the high mountain valleys in Qinghai, Tibet, and Yunnan Provinces before turning northeast at Shiigu. From there, the Chang flows through Sichuan Province before entering the famous Three Gorges. It then crosses central China through Hubei, Hunan, Jiangxi, Anhui, and Jiangsu Provinces before emptying into the East China Sea at Chongming Island, ten miles north of Shanghai. Stretching the length of the country, the Chang has served as the unofficial boundary between north and south China—no bridge was built over the eastern section of the Chang until 1969, when the Changjiang Daqiao Bridge was built at Nanjing.

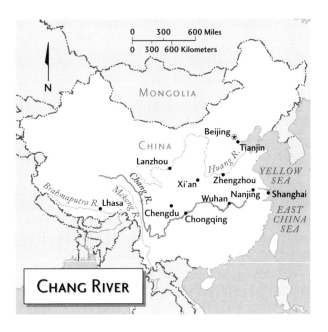

CHANG RIVER

ENCYCLOPEDIA OF MODERN ASIA

THE YANGTZE

Writer and editor Simon Winchester had the rare opportunity to travel the length of the Chang (Yangtze) River. In the excerpt below, he reflects at the end of his journey.

I reached into my pocket for the little prayer block that the monk had given back in Dêgê—I had hoped, I think, that I might imprint a few good thoughts on the waters and send them scurrying down to sea level. But it was not there: I had left it behind, carelessly. It was back in the army base. In any case, I told myself, for me to do such a thing was more than a little out of character: I was no Buddhist, I had no real idea what sentiments had been inscribed on the wood, and would feel plagued that I had performed some disingenuous act, just for the symbolic sake of it.

So instead I got out a cigar. A friend had given it to me in Hong Kong. The Mandarin Hotel had imported a Cuban maestro from Cohiba in Havana, and had set him to work hand-rolling cigars in a corner of the hotel lobby. My friend had bought two for me, for some exorbitant sum. One, he said, was to be smoked at the start of the Yangtze journey, and the second was to be savored in the mood victorious if, and only if, I reached the headwaters. This battered and somewhat stale object that I pulled from my jacket pocket was the very one.

I straightened it as best I could and listened to it: there was the slightest crackle of a few stale leaves, but not too much—it seemed to have kept most of its supple softness, and it might not be too bad. So I tilted my head out of the breeze and lit it slowly and carefully, then blew a cloud of pure blue smoke out into the chilly air.

Once, a few weeks back, this had been a grand cigar; now, old and tired from its journey, it had just a hint of its glory: in any restaurant it would have been sent right back. Out here, though, it was the best smoke I could ever, ever imagine. And so I sat there in a state of utter contentment, listening to the gurgling of the stream, listening to the lone Tibetan behind me marshaling the yaks from a herd that had been scattered in the storm, and listening to the soughing winds. They began to pick up again, and they started to scatter the grass and riffle the calm surface of the river waters once more.

Source: Simon Winchester. (1996) *The River at the Center of the World: A Journey up the Yangtze and Back in Chinese Time.* New York: Holt, 393–394.

Throughout Chinese history, the Chang has featured prominently in the development of culture and trade. As far back as the Neolithic period, settlements have been found along the lower Chang. Qin dynasty founder Qin Shi Huangdi built waterways and canals to allow trade from Yangzhou to Guangzhou, a distance of 1,200 miles. Since then, the Chang has been the main transportation artery across central China as it passes through many of its economic and industrial centers. Since the Tang era, the Chang delta has become a center for growing and shipping rice.

About 1,800 miles of the Chang is navigable year-round. In the early 1990s, the Chang and its major tributaries drained an area of 1.8 million square kilometers—a quarter of China's total cultivated land—in which 386 million people live. The network of rivers and associated canals carries some 85 percent of China's domestic waterborne traffic. It passes through many of its major cities, including Kunmin, Chengdu, Chongqing, Wuhan, Shanghai, and Nanjing. The gross value of industrial product of the areas along the Chang makes up about 40 percent of China's total.

Keith Leitich

Further Reading
Huang, Philip C. (1990) *The Peasant Family and Rural Development in the Yangzi Delta, 1350–1988.* Stanford, CA: Stanford University Press.
Van Slyke, Lyman P. (1988) *Yangtze: Nature, History, and the River.* Reading, MA: Addison-Wesley.

CHAO ANOU (1767–1829), Lao monarch. Chao Anou, or Anuvong, was the last ruler of the Lao kingdom of Viang Chan (present-day Vientiane, capital of Lao People's Democratic Republic) and a significant patron of Lao Buddhism. Born in Viang Chan, Chao Anou ascended the throne in 1805 and initiated construction of many temples, including Vat Si Saket. He also undertook repairs to the Phathat Luang temple complex and added the cloister surrounding the stupa, a dome-shaped structure that serves as a Buddhist shrine.

Chao Anou improved relations with the reigning Nguyen dynasty of Vietnam and united the central and southern kingdoms of Laos by placing his son on the throne of Champasak, the southern Lao kingdom. In 1826, Chao led an unsuccessful attempt to win independence from Siam, Viang Chan's suzerain, and recover lost territory on the Khorat plateau. The Siamese retaliated, destroying Viang Chan, except Vat Si Saket and Phathat Luang. The Siamese troops took tens of thousands of the people in Viang Chan and its vicinity captive and relocated the prisoners of war to Siam. Chao Anou fled to Vietnam but returned in 1828 to find his capital in ruins. The Siamese eventually captured Chao Anou, who died cruelly in a Bangkok prison a year later. Chao Anou is considered a national hero for his attempts to unify the Lao kingdom and gain independence from Siam and for his contributions to Lao Buddhism.

Linda McIntosh

Further Reading
Ngaosyvath, Mayoury, and Pheuiphathn Ngaosyvath. (1998) *Path to Conflagration: Fifty Years of Diplomacy and Warfare in Laos, Thailand, and Vietnam 1778–1828.* Ithaca, NY: Cornell University Press and SEAP.

CHAO PHRAYA RIVER AND DELTA The Chao Phraya River is the primary river in Thailand, formed by the confluence of the Ping and Nan Rivers. The headwaters meet near the city of Nakhon Sawan in western central Thailand. The river is more than 230 kilometers in length and flows south to the Gulf of Thailand. It is key to the region's transportation and economy.

The river drains one-third of the nation, including the central plains and lowlands. Its numerous tributaries are part of the delta, which serves as the watershed for western Thailand.

The Chao Phraya River is entirely navigable by watercraft and continues to be important to the Thai economy. The river valley is the nation's most productive agricultural region. The World Bank helped finance irrigation of the river basin beginning in the 1960s. Its waters continue to irrigate various crops, primarily rice. Thailand is consistently one of the world's leading rice exporters (usually ranked first or second). The delta's tributaries are interconnected by a series of canals, also used for transportation.

Linda Dailey Paulson

Further Reading
Takaya, Yoshikazu. (1987) *Agricultural Development of a Tropical Delta: A Study of the Chao Phraya Delta.* Honolulu, HI: University of Hawaii Press.
Van Beek, Stephen. (1995) *The Chao Phraya: River in Transition.* Oxford: Oxford University Press.

CHART THAI Chart Thai is one of Thailand's major political parties, founded in the 1970s by General Chatichai Choonhavan (1922–1999). In the July 1988 election, Chart Thai and its political allies won a majority, giving it the right to form the coalition government. Chatichai was credited with restoring democracy as he became the first prime minister in twelve years to have been elected following a string of appointed prime ministers, though appointment was constitutionally legal and Chatichai himself did not do anything to restore democratic rule. He rose to power on the urban middle-class support that had grown substantially during the 1980s, and enjoyed a high degree of legitimacy owing to the restoration of democracy and rapid economic growth. Chart Thai had a probusiness platform and oversaw significant deregulation of the Thai economy between 1988 and 1991. But Chart Thai politicians were hampered by constant allegations of corruption, and in the 1990 election, Chart Thai was accused of spending $120 million in votebuying. Rampant corruption on the part of Chatichai and his government was the military's justification for the February 1991 coup d'état, led by Generals Suchinda Kraprayoon and Sunthorn Kongsompong, though in reality the military's fear of losing power to powerful business interests was the prime motivation of the coup and Chatichai's arrest.

In the March 1992 election, the Chart Thai finished second with 73 seats and joined the military-led coalition government. Throughout the 1990s Chart Thai served as an opposition or minor coalition partner, but, tarnished by corruption scandals, it has been unable to regain its popularity. Chart Thai joined the Democrat Party–led coalition government in November 1997 and the Thai Rak Thai–led coalition government in February 2001. Chart Thai is the party most associated with vote-buying and money politics and has been unable to broaden its base of support.

Zachary Abuza

Further Reading
Pasuk Phongpaichit and Chris Baker. (1995) *Thailand: Economy and Politics*. New York: Oxford University Press.

CHATTERJEE, BANKIM CHANDRA
(1838–1894), Indian writer. Born to a high-caste Brahman family in Kantalpara, Bengal, British India, Chatterjee, or Bankim, as he is known to Bengalis was a noted scholar of Bengali, English, and Sanskrit as a student. He was in the first group of students to pass the Entrance (1857) and the Bachelor of Arts examinations of the Calcutta University. In 1869, he obtained a Bachelor of Law degree.

Bankim joined the Provincial Executive Service in 1858 and served at various places as deputy collector and deputy magistrate (the highest ranks achievable by Indians at that time). He was greatly respected for his judicial wisdom and for his impartial and effective management of areas under his jurisdiction. However, his independent spirit often caused trouble with his British superiors, most of whom did not have his erudition.

Bankim was a prolific author in Bengali, writing poems, prose, and drama. He was the first major Bengali

author and set the style followed and modified by subsequent authors, especially in prose. He also was an acclaimed journalist, the founder of and frequent contributor to *Bangadarshan* (Review of Bengal), a successful periodical. His prose works included romances, historical fiction, and essays, which in the guise of humor examined and criticized the many absurdities, wrongdoings, and injustices of the British and the Indians of the times. While his poems were not of as high a standard as his prose, one, *Vandemataram* (Hymn to Mother), became a rallying cry for the seekers of Indian independence.

Bankim vehemently protested demeaning articles on Hinduism by a British missionary. He went to write extensively on Hinduism, going back to the original texts, and played an important part in the movement that some have called neo-Hinduism. Apart from many articles, his opus consists of thirty-three books (and collections) in Bengali and one in English. Many of his Bengali books were translated into English in his lifetime. Since then they have also been translated into Swedish and German.

Ranès C. Chakravorty

Further Reading
Banerjee, Brojendranath, and Sajani Kanta Das. (1940–1942) *The Complete Works of Bankimchandra Chatterjee* (9 volumes) Calcutta, India: Bangiya Sahitya Parishat.
Das, Sisir Kumar. (1984) *The Artist in Chains: The Life of Bankimchandra Chatterji*. New Delhi: New Statesman.

CHAUDHURI, NIRAD CHANDRA (1897–1999), Indian critic and writer. Nirad Chaudhuri, who for the first half of his life was a civil servant, was one of India's foremost critics and writers who opposed the withdrawal of the British empire from the Subcontinent. He was born in Kishorganj, a small town in East Bengal, and moved to Calcutta at the time of Indian independence. He then rose to prominence with the first of two autobiographical books, *The Autobiography of an Unknown Indian* (1951). The second, written toward the end of an extremely long life, was *Thy Hand, Great Anarch! India 1921–1952* (1987), in which he showed himself as a "scholar gypsy" living only for literature. In between these two masterly volumes, there were several others, all of which received the acclaim of Western critics. Most notable—although controversial for many Indian critics—were his overviews of Indian society entitled *The Continent of Circe: Being an Essay on the Peoples of India* (1965) and *Hinduism, a Religion to Live By* (1979). From 1953 to 1965, he was attached as a

writer to the French Embassy in New Delhi, but late in his life he moved to Oxford where he died in 1999.

Paul Hockings

Further Reading
Chaudhuri, Nirad C. (1951) *The Autobiography of an Unknown Indian*. London: Macmillan.

CHAVALIT, YONGCHAIYUDH (b. 1932),
Thai general and politician. Chavalit Yongchaiyudh was a career military officer, graduating from the Royal Military Academy in 1953 and from the Command and General Staff College in the United States in 1964. He served as army commander in chief in 1986 before his appointment as Supreme Commander of the Armed Forces, the position he held from 1987 to 1990. Chavalit was a member of a group of politically oriented soldiers who sought to address social injustices and alleviate rural poverty while ensuring the military's dominant role in Thai politics. Under Chavalit's command, the military also became involved in business ventures.

He resigned from the army in 1990, having achieved the rank of general, and entered politics. He was appointed by Prime Minister Chatichai Choonhaven to be deputy prime minister and minister of defense in March 1990, positions he only held for ten weeks before the coalition lost a no-confidence vote. Chavalit went on to form the New Aspiration Party (NAP), which has been a coalition member in several governments since 1992. Chavalit served in a number of cabinet positions: minister of interior (September 1992– December 1994), minister of labor (September 1993– January 1994), deputy prime minister (July 1994–October 1994), and deputy prime minister and minister of defense (July 1995–November 1996). Following the vote of no confidence that forced Prime Minister Banharn Silpa-Archa from office, the NAP won the November 1996 election and Chavalit became prime minister, a position he held from November 1996 to November 1997. But his government was unable to effectively respond to the 1997 Asian economic crisis. Following the vote of no confidence that forced Prime Minister Banharn Silpa-Archa from office, the NAP won the November 1996 election and Chavalit became prime minister, a position he held from November 1996 to November 1997. He was initially thought of as a reformer, and he advocated drafting a new constitution that he hoped would codify the military's leading role in politics. Chavalit's political support came from the rural northeast where he engaged in rampant vote buying, at the expense of the urban middle class. Yet, as the economy fell into recession, he was unable to support rural development projects. As the economy worsened, Chavalit's varied policy responses led to a deepening crisis. Fiscal mismanagement, a growing debt crisis, and the protection of several major financial corporations led to the collapse of the baht. Chavalit contended that only by centralizing power further could the economy be restored, and he tried to block the passage of a new constitution in 1997 that shifted political and fiscal control to the provinces. Both the military and his rural constituency, however, supported the new constitution, and he was forced to accept it.

He called for emergency powers so that he could restore political and economic order, but the military withdrew their support for him. Under intense pressure from the king and the military, Chavalit was forced to resign and call early elections in November 1997, based on the new constitution approved that October, which was the most democratic constitution in Thai history. He reentered the government in February 2001 as minister of defense and deputy prime minister in a coalition government headed by Prime Minister Thaksin Shinawatra.

Zachary Abuza

Further Reading
Phongpaichit, Pasuk, and Christ Baker. (1995) *Thailand: Economy and Politics*. New York: Oxford University Press.
———. (2000) *Thailand's Crisis*. Bangkok, Thailand: Silkworm.

CHEJU PROVINCE (2000 pop. 543,000). Cheju
Island is the largest island in and a province of South Korea, located about 140 kilometers south of Mokp'o in the East China Sea (Namhae, or South Sea, in Korean). The product of Mount Halla, the tallest mountain in South Korea at 1,950 meters, the rugged island is composed of unique volcanic rock formations and maintains a subtropical climate. Originally known as the isolated island kingdom of T'amna, it first came under the control of the Koryo kingdom (918–1392) in 938 and was later conquered by the Mongols and used to raise cattle and horses during the fourteenth century. The island was governed as part of Cholla province from the thirteenth to the twentieth centuries. In 1925, it fell under Japanese colonial rule. Finally, after the withdrawal of Japanese forces from Korea, it was declared a province in 1946.

The people of Cheju have developed a distinct dialect and lifestyle, focused on two major cities: Cheju on the north side of the island and Sogwip'o on the south. Agriculture, fishing, and tourism are the main industries. Besides ancient guardians made from volcanic rocks called "stone grandfathers" (tol harubang), Cheju is famous for its subtropical fruits, such as tangerines, pineapples, and bananas. Successful demonstrations by the islanders have kept modern industrial factories from being built, which has contributed to the preservation of many beautiful beaches.

Richard D. McBride II

Further Reading

Austin, Audrey. (1989) "Cheju-do: Korea's Island of Rocks, Wind, and Women." *Korean Culture* 10, 4 (Winter): 34–40.

Marcou, David. (1996) "Korea's Island Paradise: The Sites and Culture of Cheju Island." *Korean Culture* 17, 2 (Summer): 30–36.

CHEN DUXIU (1879–1942), Chinese politician. Born on 8 October 1879 in Anqing, Anhui, Chen Duxiu was famous for his role in the iconoclastic intellectual and revolutionary political movements in China. Chen's experience in studying for and passing the lowest level of the traditional imperial examination (*xiucai*) convinced him that the dynastic government of China was corrupt and disastrous for the Chinese people. In 1901 he studied in Japan and began his lifelong commitment to political organizing, founding the reformist *Chinese Youth Society*. From 1903 to 1907, he established and wrote for revolutionary journals in Shanghai and Anhui. In 1907 he fled in exile to Japan.

After the 1911 revolution, Chen held a minor government position and then took up teaching. During the 1913 "Second Revolution" he fled again to Japan. These early life experiences and defeats influenced him to become a critic of Chinese civilization and society. In 1915 Chen founded *Youth* magazine. This magazine, which changed its name a year later to *New Youth*, became the most important liberal and revolutionary magazine in China. It was a forum to propagate science and human rights under the famous slogan "Support Mr. Science and Mr. Democracy." Chen was influenced by the reformist ideas in Japan and the political philosophies of eighteenth-century France and nineteenth-century America. He layered his political criticism of China's feudalism with a scathing attack on Confucianism. He blamed Chinese culture for destroying human dignity, oppressing women, and suppressing individuality and creativity. His withering attacks provided a generation with the ammunition to criticize Chinese tradition.

In 1917 Chen was named dean of Beijing University's School of Letters. In this capacity he befriended Chinese student leaders and intellectuals. He formed study groups and journals that discussed the cause of China's deterioration. In 1919 he resigned his deanship to join the students who were protesting the Beijing government's domestic and foreign policies, and became a leader in the May 4th movement of that year. Initiated in Beijing, violence, massive protests, and arrests became nationwide. Chen, too, was a prisoner for three months. Upon his release from jail, he became a Marxist, and within two years, in 1921, he was established as Secretary General of the Chinese Communist Party. He held this post until 1927.

Chen's leadership of the Communist Party is still highly debated. He favored a traditional Marxist revolutionary program that relied on the working class, established an independent political organization, placed social reform as a priority before military uprisings, and sought equality with Moscow in determining the world revolutionary movement. Chen was accused of deviating from the party line in all these areas. He opposed Mao Zedong's strategy of placing the rural areas in command and of relying on armed force; he criticized Moscow's plan to ally with the Guomindang; and he failed to respect Stalin's leadership. In 1928 he refused a summons to travel to Moscow for an evaluation of his failures. The following year he became attracted to the writings of Stalin's major rival, Leon Trotsky. As a result, Chen was expelled from the party. His negative experience in the party was further exacerbated by the execution of his two sons by the Nationalist Chinese in 1927 and 1928.

Chen led the Chinese Trotskyist Party from 1930 until his arrest by the Nationalists in 1932. In 1933 he was sentenced to thirteen years in prison but was released in 1937. He began to organize against the Japanese invasion of China. The Communists, however, attacked him for his Trotskyist position and accused him of being a spy for the Japanese. He retreated into private life and wrote his autobiography, along with letters to friends expressing his faith in democracy and science. Some claim he was still a socialist in the Trotskyist tradition, and others claim he returned to his old May 4th views, but without the denunciation of Confucianism and Chinese culture. He died of a heart attack on 27 May 1942 in Jiangjin, a remote area of Sichuan Province.

After decades of abuse, the Chinese government allowed Chen to be reburied in his home town, and, beginning in the late 1980s, allowed for extensive and objective research of his life and political views. Independent societies were established for the study of Chen Duxiu. His influence as a democrat, socialist, iconoclast, and promoter of human rights was gradually recognized.

Richard Kagan

Further Reading

Benton, Gregor, ed. and trans. (1998) *Chen Duxiu's Last Articles and Letters, 1937–1942.* Surrey, U.K.: Curzon.
Feigon, Lee. (1983) *Chen Duxiu, Founder of the Chinese Communist Party.* Princeton, NJ: Princeton University Press.

CHEN KAIGE (b. 1952), Chinese film director. With his film *Yellow Earth* (1984), Chen Kaige was the first member of the acclaimed Fifth Generation of Chinese film directors to achieve international success. The Fifth Generation, who were graduates of the first class of the reopened Beijing Film Academy following the Cultural Revolution (1966–1976), came of age after the death of Mao Zedong (1893–1976) and reacted against the melodrama and didacticism of the Chinese film tradition. *Yellow Earth* contains gorgeous visuals similar to Chinese paintings. Deceptively simple with minimal dialogue and action, it is a multilayered examination of the impact of China's feudal culture and modern revolution on the peasants. Chen's next film to make a big international splash was *Farewell My Concubine* (1993), a lavish production set in the Beijing Opera of the twentieth century and dealing with the betrayal of art and love. It garnered the Palm d'Or prize at the Cannes Film Festival and other prizes. Chen's most recent film, *The Emperor and the Assassin* (1999), is a historical epic about Qin Shi Huangdi or Ying Zheng, the emperor who unified China in the third century BCE.

With the collapse of the state film industry in the 1990s, Chen and other filmmakers had to seek overseas financing for their projects. Domestic critics have accused them of pandering to Western taste and distorting Chinese realities. Chen, however, is an intensely personal artist who believes that the redemption of China lies in its cultural tradition.

Robert Y. Eng

Further Reading

Chen Kaige. (1990) "Breaking the Circle: The Cinema and Cultural Change in China." *Cineaste* 18, 3: 28–32.
Zha, Jianying. (1995) *China Pop.* New York: New Press.

CHEN SHUI-BIAN (b. 1951), president of the Republic of China. Chen Shui-bian became the president of the Republic of China (Taiwan) on 20 May 2000 in only the second direct popular presidential election held in that country. He ran as an opposition pro–Taiwan independence candidate against Lien Chan, the Guomindang (Nationalist) candidate and James Soong, the Independent candidate. His accession to the presidency was heavily criticized by the officials in Beijing, because they feared he would declare Taiwan an independent and sovereign state.

Chen was born on 18 February 1951 in a poor Taiwanese family in Tainan county in southern Taiwan. In June 1969 he attained the highest possible score on the university entrance examination and entered the prestigious National Taiwan University, where he majored in commercial law. In law school, Chen met his wife, Wu Shu-jen, a woman with a strong sense of Taiwanese nationalism. Soon after graduation, Chen joined the Formosan International Marine and Commercial Law Office, where he worked until 1989, rising to the position of chief lawyer. This position gave him the financial independence to engage in politics.

In 1980, encouraged by his wife and his loyalties to his friends, Chen became a defense lawyer for the leaders of the Tang-wai (Opposition) Party, who had been charged with sedition in the famous "Kaohsiung" incident of 1979. His participation in this lengthy trial aroused him to enter politics on a mission of promoting human rights, democracy, and social justice. During the 1990s, he served on the Taipei City Council and in the Legislative Yuan. He became a leading figure in the opposition party, renamed the Democratic Progressive Party in 1987. His popularity made him and his family the focus of political attacks. His wife was crippled when a truck ran her over in a clearly politically motivated accident. Chen himself served six months in jail on the charge of libel.

In 1994 Chen ran successfully for Taipei mayor. In this position, he attacked corruption, lowered the crime rate, and opened relationships with other countries by establishing sister city programs and hosting international conferences. His improvements earned Taipei a place in *Asiaweek*'s top five best cities in Asia.

Richard C. Kagan

Further Reading

Kagan, Richard C. (1998) *Mayor Chen Shui-bian. Taipei, Taiwan: Building a Community and a Nation.* Taipei, Taiwan: Asia-Pacific Academic Exchange Foundation.
Wachtman, Alan. (1994) *Taiwan: Identity and Democratization.* New York: M. E. Sharpe.

CHEN YUN

CHEN YUN (1905–1995), Chinese political figure. Chen Yun was noteworthy for his continuous place in the inner group of Chinese leaders and long service on the Central Committee and Politburo of the Chinese Communist Party (CCP), yet was never a contender for top leader from the 1930s until his death in 1995. Born in Qingpu near Shanghai 13 June 1905, he worked as a typesetter in Shanghai before joining the CCP in 1925. He later served as a union organizer, guerrilla soldier, and secret agent. He participated in the Long March and emerged as a key party economic thinker and ideological theorist, especially during the 1942 Rectification Campaign. In 1949, he became the head economic planner, responsible for stabilization and reconstruction.

Close to Zhou Enlai (1898–1976) and Deng Xiaoping (1904–1997) in outlook, Chen agreed with Zhou on the need for incentives to spur agricultural production. At the critical Lushan conference to review the results of the Great Leap Forward in 1959, he remained silent and did not criticize Mao Zedong (1893–1976). Following the Great Leap, he toured the countryside to assess its failures, and later supported the moderate policies of Deng and Liu Shaoqi. Nonetheless, his efforts to reduce the costs of grain shipments to urban areas laid the ground for the later internal deportation of youth. "Set aside" but not punished for his moderation during the Cultural Revolution (1966–1976), Chen began to formulate many of the ideas that later formed the core of the Deng era reforms. He disagreed with Deng only over timing of the early reforms, but from the mid-1980s criticized the reform process for going too far.

Chen supported Deng's second return to power in 1977, and was rewarded with chairmanship of the Central Disciplinary Inspection Committee in 1978. As Deng's reforms got underway, Chen described them as a caged bird, that is, the economy could fly freely, but within the limits of state planning. Chen held no high positions during the 1980s, except for his membership on the Central Committee; due to his prestige and influence, however, he was considered fifth in the hierarchy. Though he resigned from the Central Committee in 1987, Chen was a crucial supporter of Deng's hard line during the Tiananmen Incident of 1989. Nevertheless, he aided efforts to sideline Deng after 1989, and fought Deng's last reform campaign in 1992. He died on 10 April 1995.

Joel R. Campbell

Further Reading
Becker, Jasper. (2000) *The Chinese*. New York: The Free Press.

Evans, Richard. (1995) *Deng Xiaoping and the Making of Modern China*. London: Penguin.
Fairbank, John King. (1986) *The Great Chinese Revolution, 1800–1985*. New York: Harper & Row.
Roberts, J. A. G. (1999) *A Concise History of China*. Cambridge, MA: Harvard University Press.
Salisbury, Harrison. (1992) *The New Emperors: China in the Era of Mao and Deng*. Boston: Little, Brown & Co.
Spence, Jonathan. (1990) *The Search for Modern China*. New York: W. W. Norton.

CHENAB RIVER

CHENAB RIVER The Chenab River, one of the five great rivers that give Punjab its name (in Persian *panj* means "five" and *ab* means "river"), has a total length of 1,087 kilometers. It rises in Lahul, Kashmir, south of Ladakh, and then flows through Kashmir, and south into Pakistan. In the upper reaches it is called the Chandra. After leaving the mountains it follows a southwesterly course, and becomes navigable at Aknur. It joins with the Jhelum near Jhang Maghiana, and here the Emerson (or Trimmu) Barrage has been built. Further downstream to the west of Bahawalpur the Chenab joins with the Sutlej River at the Panjnad Barrage, the two then forming the Panjnad River. This soon joins with the Indus River to the northeast of Chachran. Ancient names for the Chenab were Asikni and Chandrabhaga. Classical Greek writers rendered these names as Akesines, and Sandabaga or Sandabal.

The Chenab Canal, opened in 1887, is the largest canal in Pakistan. It irrigates extensive lands lying just to the south of the Chenab River. In 1892 the Chenab Colony was formed, an irrigated tract of land that quickly became a rich and thickly populated agricultural area of over a million hectares.

Paul Hockings

Further Reading
Eglar, Zekiye. (1960). *A Punjabi Village in Pakistan*. New York: Columbia University Press.

CHENGDE

CHENGDE (2002 pop. 166,000). Chengde is a middle-size city in northern Hebei Province, China. It developed around the hill station of Bishu Shanzhuang (Mountain Hamlet to Flee Summer Heat), where the Qing court used to stay several months a year between 1703 and 1820. Designed in 1703 by the Kangxi emperor (reigned 1662–1722) and enlarged by his grandson, the Qianlong emperor (reigned 1736–1795), the summer residence of Chengde forms a unique ensemble of mighty hills, natural parks, artificial lakes, and palatial complexes that provides refer-

The Temple of Universal Peace in Chengde. (PIERRE COLOMBEL/CORBIS)

ences to the architectural landmarks of the Qing dynasty (1644–1912). The landscape of the hill station was indeed conceived to represent a microcosm of China and Central Asia. The Waiba Miao monasteries, a series of Buddhist temples with a Tibetan appearance, surround Bishu Shanzhuang on two sides. The Potala Temple and the Sumeru Temple are the best-known samples of Sino-Tibetan architecture. The residence's most prominent temple is the Taoist Jinshan pagoda at the center of the garden district. The temples, palaces, and forests suffered extensive damage from the warlords of the republican period (1912–1949) and the Red Guards of the Cultural Revolution (1966–1976). Restored during the 1980s, Bishu Shanzhuang and Waiba Miao are now on the UNESCO World Heritage List.

Philippe Forêt

Further Reading
Foret, Philippe. (2000) *Mapping Chengde: The Qing Landscape Enterprise.* Honolulu, HI: University of Hawaii Press.

CHENGDU (2002 est. pop. 1.9 million). Chengdu is the capital of China's Sichuan Province and is situated in the center of the province on a fertile but dry plain. Chengdu was founded in the third century BCE by the ancient state of Qin, and benefited from one of the oldest and best Chinese irrigation systems, con-

structed in the same century with water from the Min River, which is still in effective use today. It has remained a prosperous city through the centuries and gained a position as one of the most important trade centers of the empire; traders in Chengdu were the first to use paper money, in the tenth century. Chengdu also became the center of the silk brocade manufacturing industry. The 1937–1945 Japanese occupation of eastern China gave Chengdu an unexpected boost, because the Chinese Nationalist Party (Guomindang) established its capital in Sichuan and moved important industries to the city.

Chengdu has a wide variety of industries. Heavy machinery, aluminum plants, chemical plants, and electronics are important. In addition to that, the textile industry, manufacturing cotton, wool, silk, and satin products, is a major part of the economy. The city has a number of universities and other higher education institutions, including a college of traditional Chinese medicine.

Bent Nielsen

Further Reading
Stapleton, Kristin Eileen. (2000) *Civilizing Chengdu: Chinese Urban Reform, 1895–1937.* Cambridge, MA: Harvard University Press.
Bruun, Ole. (1988) *The Reappearance of the Family as the Economic Unit: A Sample Survey of Individual Households in Workshop Production and Crafts.* Chengdu, China: Uni-

Mao statue and Western brand-name billboards in Chengdu in June 1996. (STEPHEN G. DONALDSON PHOTOGRAPHY)

versity of Copenhagen, Center for East and Southeast Asian Studies.

———. (1993) *Business and Bureaucracy in a Chinese City: An Ethnography of Private Business Households in Contemporary China.* Berkeley, CA: University of California, Center for Chinese Studies.

CHENNAI. See **Madras.**

CHERA   Chera (or Kerala) is the name of a Tamil dynasty that for over eleven centuries ruled most of the area of the modern state of Kerala as well as western districts of what is now the state of Tamil Nadu in southern India. During that era the Tamilagam or Tamil-speaking territory extended to the west coast of India, and a separate Malayalam language had not yet developed. The Chera capital was originally Vanji, on the Periyar River near Cochin; later Tiru-vanjikkalam near the mouth of that river became the capital. The kings were said to be of the Vanavar tribe and were Tamil speakers.

Around the beginning of the Common Era the Chera king Nedunjeraladan went to war with Perunarkilli, king of the neighboring Chola dynasty, and both perished. Subsequent generations of the two royal families fought with each other, but in the second century CE the two dynasties were united by a marriage. When the Chola capital of Puhar was destroyed by floods, its king was aided by the Chera king Cenguttuvan, a grandson of the Chola king Karikkal. Under him the Cheras were the dominant power in the south. For a while there seem to have been two royal lines among the Cheras. However Karikkal's successor Cey was conquered by the neighboring Pandya dynasty, which assumed the ascendancy until it was overcome in turn by the Pallava dynasty. Nonetheless the royal line lingered on until Chera rule finally disintegrated in the twelfth century CE. As late as the eighteenth and nineteenth centuries the rajas of Cochin claimed descent from the Chera line.

Chera history is known mostly from epic poetry. In addition an Alexandrian Greek mariner's handbook, *The Periplus of the Erythraean Sea,* mentions five thriving seaports on the Kerala coast in the first century CE. In later centuries Jews and Christians moved to this coast from the Middle East. Roman and Alexandrian traders came here, and an as yet undiscovered temple of Augustus was reported to exist in the city of Kuranganur. Today the modern population in the area of the former Chera kingdom is probably ethnically similar to the ancient inhabitants, and the Dravidian languages of Tamil and Malayalam are spoken in the region.

Paul Hockings

Further Reading

Nilakanta Sastri, K. A. (1966) *A History of South India from Prehistoric Times to the Fall of Vijayanagar.* 3d ed. London and Madras, India: Oxford University Press.

Woodcock, George. (1967) "The Age of the Cheras." In George Woodcock, *Kerala, a Portrait of the Malabar Coast.* London: Faber and Faber, 73–97.

CHHATTISGARH (2001 pop. of new state 20.8 million). Chhattisgarh, a region of central India with an area of 97,612 square kilometers, is noted for its distinct tribal populations. It has also been called Gondavana, "the land of the Gonds," who form the largest tribal entity. Other important groups include the Baiga, Birhor, Kamar, Kanwar, Oraon, and Saura. In very early times the region was known as South Kosala; the name "Chhattisgarh" is scarcely two centuries old. The region was ruled by the Kalchuries of Ratanpur until the mid-1800s and then occupied by the Bhonsales of Nagpur. After the fall of the Delhi sultanate in 1857, the region came under British rule, and with the British administration came railways and substantial population growth. The region was known as the Chhattisgarh division in a greater administrative unit known as the Central Provinces.

Chhattisgarh today is also the name of a new state created in 2000 from the eastern third of the state of Madhya Pradesh; it lies exactly in the Chhattisgarh region and has an area of 169,452 square kilometers. This state consists of sixteen districts taken from the older Madhya Pradesh state, with Raipur as the capital. Totally landlocked, Chhattisgarh is surrounded by the states of Jharkhand, Orissa, Andhra Pradesh, Maharashtra, Madhya Pradesh, and Uttar Pradesh. Probably India's richest state in terms of its natural and mineral resources, in 1998–1999 Chhattisgarh's net domestic product was nevertheless in the range of only $210–$299.

Paul Hockings

Further Reading

Fuchs, Stephen. (1960) *The Gond and Bhumia of Eastern Mandla.* Bombay, India: Asia Publishing House.

CHIANG KAI-SHEK (1887–1975), Chinese Nationalist general and president. A major twentieth-century Chinese leader, Chiang Kai-shek headed China's first modern government after 1928 and led the country against Japan in World War II. Chiang Kai-shek (in pinyin romanization, Jiang Jieshi) came from a gentry family in Fenghua county in Zejiang province. He studied at military academies in China and Japan in preparation for a military career.

In Japan, Chiang joined Sun Yat-sen's revolutionary society, the Tongmenghui, which later evolved into the Guomindang, or Nationalist Party. Chiang returned to China in 1911 and participated in various campaigns with Nationalist units against the Manchu Qing dynasty, which had ruled China since 1644. The last Qing emperor abdicated in 1912, and the Nationalists took control of China. In 1922 Sun summoned Chiang to Canton to work for his reorganized Nationalist party. Chiang traveled to the Soviet Union in 1923 to observe the Red Army and became chief of staff of the Nationalist army and commandant of its military academy (called the Whampoa Military Academy, later the Central Military Academy).

In July 1926 Chiang was appointed commander-in-chief of the National Revolutionary Army and launched the Northern Expedition to unify China (the north at that time being under the control of various warlords). Rapid successes against larger warlord forces resulted in intense competition between the left wing of the Nationalist party and its allies (the Soviet Union and the Chinese Communists) and the anti-Communist forces led by Chiang. He ended the coalition with the Soviet Union and purged the Chinese Communists from the Nationalist party. The Northern Expedition completed the nominal unification of China in 1928 and established its capital at Nanjing.

Chiang led the Nationalist government and its military forces during the Nanjing decade (1928–1937), defeating rivals within the party and making many reforms. But his government was trapped between Japan's rising imperialism, which sought to conquer China before it could modernize and truly unite, and the Chinese Communists, with their vision of a Marxist China. Japanese aggression culminated in the July 1937 Marco Polo Bridge Incident. The result was an eight-year Sino-Japanese war, which merged to become part of World War II in Asia in 1941.

China emerged as one of the victorious Big Four allied powers in 1945, but the war had shattered China's economy and the morale of the Nationalists. Mao Zedong won the ensuing civil war and established the Communist People's Republic of China in 1949. Chiang's defeated Nationalists retreated to Taiwan. Elected president of the Republic of China in 1948, Chiang continued to serve on Taiwan until his death in 1975.

The United States, which withdrew its support for the Nationalists in the civil war, resumed its alliance with Chiang's government after the outbreak of the Korean War in 1950. U.S. military and economic aid and reforms instituted by the Nationalist government turned Taiwan into an economic powerhouse, and later a democratic nation.

Jiu-Hwa Lo Upshur

Further Reading
Chiang Kai-shek. (1957) *Soviet Russia in China: A Summing Up at Seventy.* New York: Farrar, Straus and Cudahy.
Furuya, Keiji. (1981) *Chiang Kai-shek: His Life and Times.* Abridged English version by Chun-ming Chang. New York: St. John's University.
Wu, Tien-wei. (1976) *The Sian Incident: A Pivotal Point in Modern Chinese History,* Ann Arbor, MI: University of Michigan Press.

CHIANG MAI (2000 est. pop. 170,000). Chiang Mai is Thailand's second biggest city, located approximately 700 kilometers (440 miles) northwest of the capital Bangkok. Chiang Mai is roughly twenty times smaller than Bangkok, but in many ways it rivals the capital as Thailand's cultural and historic heart. Chiang Mai is an ancient city dating back to the thirteenth century (in 1996, it celebrated its 700th birthday), when it served as the capital of Lan Na ("a million rice fields")—one of the Tai peoples' earliest kingdoms.

Chiang Mai is also a province, the fifth largest in Thailand, with a population of approximately 1.5 million (1999). Thailand's administrative system is organized by province, not by region. Therefore, Chiang Mai, known as the "Rose of the North," is the provincial capital.

Built within a series of moats, the old city of Chiang Mai covers only about 4 square kilometers (2.5 square miles) yet is packed with markets, temples, and narrow streets. More modern development and construction, prohibited in the old city, has focused on the growing suburbs. The result is a city that represents Thailand's colorful and rich past, while at the same time providing the best that a modern metropolis can offer.

With over three hundred temples—nearly as many as Bangkok—Chiang Mai is one of the most important religious centers in Thailand. The oldest temple in the area, the spectacular Wat Prathat, is situated near the summit of Doi Suthep mountain, around which Chiang Mai was built. The temple, which contains relics of the Lord Buddha, attracts Buddhist pilgrims from all over the world.

Alongside this history, Chiang Mai is also rapidly modernizing and developing into a major commercial center. Tourists use the city as a base for jungle trekking in Northern Thailand, and to visit the re-

gion's various hill tribes. Chiang Mai offers a wide array of tour operators and business services for those wanting to explore the more remote parts of the north. Renowned for its night bazaar, Chiang Mai is a vital hub for silks, lacquerware, teak, silver, stoneware, and jewelry. Craft shops can be found throughout the city and local area. Less flattering, Chiang Mai has also become a base for narcotics, as well as the government's war on the drug trade. Located close to the infamous "Golden Triangle" border region between Thailand, Laos, and Myanmar (Burma), the city is considered by some to be the unofficial capital of the opium trade's distribution. At the end of the twentieth century, the Thai government had some success in reducing opium production in the north of Thailand.

Chiang Mai is widely considered to be more "relaxed" than Bangkok and other cities in Thailand. Life generally has a slower pace there, and the residents are famous for their easygoing attitude and good sense of humor. With a unique combination of old and new, Chiang Mai is one of the more fascinating cities in Asia.

Arne Kislenko

Further Reading
Moore, Elizabeth, Philip Stott, and Suriyavudh Sukhasvasti. (1996) *Ancient Capitals of Thailand.* Bangkok, Thailand: Asia Books.
Parahomwichit, Paitoon, ed. (1996) *Chiang Mai: Wannii na bii thi 700* (Chiang Mai: Today at the 700th Year). Chiang Mai, Thailand: Witin Books.

CHIBA (2000 est. pop. 5.9 million). Chiba Prefecture is situated in the central region of Japan's island of Honshu. A residential and industrial satellite of Tokyo, Chiba occupies an area of 5,150 square kilometers, with its population mostly concentrated in the northwest. Its main geographical features are the Kanto Plain in the north, which meets the hilly Boso Peninsula in the south. The main rivers are the Tonegawa and the Edogawa. The prefecture is bordered by the Pacific Ocean and Tokyo Bay and by Tokyo, Saitama, and Ibaraki Prefectures. In earlier centuries the prefecture comprised Shimosa, Kazusa, and Awa provinces. It assumed its present name and borders in 1875.

The capital of the prefecture is Chiba City, some 34 kilometers southeast of Tokyo. A military base during World War II, the city later was reconstructed to make it a core of the Keiyo industrial region with its thermal power and steel plants. Chiba is one of Japan's main international ports. It is home to Chiba University, and land reclaimed from Tokyo Bay provides housing for Tokyo commuters. In feudal times, as a castle town it was ruled by the Chiba family, and in the Edo period (1600/1603–1868) it was a post station for several highways. The other important cities of the prefecture are Funabashi, Ichikawa, Matsudo, and Choshi.

Industrial pollution ended fishing in Tokyo Bay. In prewar days, weaving and soy sauce production were traditional occupations. The northwest is the site of heavy industry, such as petrochemical processing, electrical and steel industries, and shipbuilding. Elsewhere are intensive rice growing and dairy farming. Narita is the site of the new Tokyo International Airport and thus the center of the nation's air transport. The cultural and recreational amenities include Narita's Buddhist temple Shinshoji, excellent ocean beaches in the Kujukurihama area, the national parks in Suigo-Tsukuba and southern Boso, and Tokyo Disneyland, which opened in 1983.

E. L. S. Weber

CHICKEN According to ancient Chinese texts, the chicken or common fowl came to China around 1400 BCE; it is one of the first domesticated animals mentioned in writing. Most geneticists think that the ancestor of domestic chickens (*Gallus gallus*), the red jungle fowl (also *Gallus gallus*), was first domesticated in South Asia, in present-day Vietnam and Thailand, perhaps as early as the sixth millennium BCE. Red jungle fowl still flourish in the wild in southern Asia from Kashmir east to Sumatra, living in the teak forests and in the Himalayas as high as 2,000 meters; thus they are a rare example of a domesticated animal's wild ancestor still being alive today. Red jungle fowl are about 65 centimeters long and are often seen feeding in forest clearings, usually one cock with several hens; each hen may have five to six chicks.

In Southeast Asia, domestic chickens are valued not only for their flesh and eggs, but for the fighting proclivities of cocks. In Indonesia and nearby lands, fighting cocks provide a major sport for the inhabitants.

Chickens were probably not seen in Greece until around 600 BCE; nowadays, the animals are common around the world. In Roman religion, the bird was sacred to Mars, the god of war, and to many ancient peoples cocks symbolized courage. In Christianity, the cock's crow signifies the resurrection of Christ.

Paul Hockings

CHILDREN'S DAY—JAPAN Children's Day (*kodomo no hi*) is a national holiday in Japan, celebrated on the fifth of May. The day was formerly named *tango no sekku* (Boys' Day) and honored only boys, and it retains a strong male emphasis. Girls participate in various group activities to mark the day, but they do not have special rituals of their own.

Boys are reminded of the virtues of strength, courage, and perseverance, and wishes are made that they will grow up healthy, strong, and successful. The carp fish, admired for its strength and determination in swimming upstream against powerful currents, is a favorite symbol, and huge carp flags (*koi nobori*) fly from house rooftops in honor of each of a family's sons. Boys display their collections of miniature suits of armor, helmets, weapons and traditional warrior and hero dolls (*musha ningyo*). Popular characters include Shoki (a celebrated general) and Kintaro (a Herculean boy). Boys invite their friends and relatives to share sweet rice cakes wrapped in bamboo, and iris or oak leaves, which symbolize strength and the overcoming of obstacles. Long sword-shaped iris leaves are considered particularly auspicious, for their Japanese name *shobu* has the same pronunciation as the word meaning striving for success. Iris leaves are added to hot baths on this day as a charm against illness and bad luck. In many areas children give public performances and events highlighting children are held.

Lucy D. Moss

Further Reading
Krasno, Rena (2000) *Floating Lanterns and Golden Shrines: Celebrating Japanese Festivals.* Berkeley, CA: Pacific View Press.

CHILDREN'S DAY—TURKEY In 1935, Mustafa Kemal Ataturk, founder of the Turkish Republic, dedicated National Sovereignty and Children's Day to Turkey's children. This holiday is celebrated in Turkey each year on 23 April. During Turkey's Independence War, the provisional Grand National Assembly met in Ankara for the first time on 23 April 1920 and laid down the foundations for the national republic that replaced the Ottoman empire. This event became Turkey's National Sovereignty Day and remained the only official holiday—besides religious holidays—until 1925, when the anniversary of the republic's 1923 establishment became another holiday. In 1929, the Association for the Protection of Children sought to establish a special state holiday devoted to making less fortunate children happy and joyful. The government thus declared the last week of every April to be Children's Week and 23 April to be Children's Day. The association encouraged holding a nationwide series of celebrations for children, and in subsequent years Children's Day was incorporated into National Sovereignty Day celebrations. In 1935, the two holidays were combined and named National Sovereignty and Children's Day.

During celebrations children perform on the fields of most stadiums throughout the country, with many spectators in attendance. As part of their activities, children send representatives to substitute for high governmental officials, including the president, prime minister, governors, and mayors. Children also replace deputies in the Grand National Assembly and hold a session to discuss children's issues. For the past several decades, Turkish officials have sought ways to internationalize Children's Day. As part of these efforts in 1986, the Turkish National Assembly decided to invite children of other nations to celebrate this holiday. Each year groups of children from other nations travel to Turkey to join the festivities held for them and to stay with Turkish families. Foreign children's groups also participate in the special session of the Grand National Assembly and pledge to foster world peace. UNICEF thus recognized Children's Day as International Children's Day.

Emine Ö. Evered

Further Reading
Lewis, Bernard. (1968) *The Emergence of Modern Turkey*. Oxford: Oxford University Press.
Shaw, S., and E. K. Shaw. (1976) *History of the Ottoman Empire and Modern Turkey*. Cambridge, U.K.: Cambridge University Press.

CHILUNG Chilung (Keelung, Jilong) is situated on the northeast coast of Taiwan and is the seaport of the capital Taibei, 27 kilometers to the southwest. Chilung is built at a natural harbor sheltered by mountains. The harbor is not located near the mouth of a river, so there is no problem with silting. A fort was built during the Spanish occupation in 1626. Later, the harbor came under Dutch occupation, but the town was not founded until 1723 when Chinese settlers brought it under Chinese jurisdiction. In 1862, Chilung became one of the treaty ports, and during the Japanese occupation of Taiwan (1895– 1945), the harbor was enlarged and developed. When the Japanese retreated, the harbor was totally devastated and clogged with more than 150 sunk vessels.

The harbor has been renovated and connected with the city by a highway and railway tunnel, and it is one of the most important deep-water harbors in the region. Chilung has a large modern fleet of fishing boats and a substantial fishing industry. Important industries are shipyards, manufacture of fertilizers and cement, and computer hardware and accessories.

Bent Nielsen

Further Reading
Hsieh, Chiao-min. (1964) *Taiwan-ilha Formosa: A Geography in Perspective*. London: Butterworths.
Zhang, Chantal. *Les Européens aux portes de la Chine: L'Exemple de Formose au XIXe siècle*. Aix-en-Provence, France: Publications de l'Université de Provence.

CHIN The Chin are a Tibeto-Burmese people who predominate in the great range of hills that run up western Myanmar (Burma) from the Arakan Yoma into Mizoram in northeast India. More than forty different subgroups have been categorized among the Chin inhabitants of Myanmar, including the Kuki, Chinbok, Tashon, and Asho. There are also related subgroups in neighboring India, but, in general, the Chin of Myanmar are known by the collective name of *Zomi*, whereas their ethnic cousins in India are known as *Mizo*.

There are few records of early Chin history. Chin settlers are believed to have lived in the lowlands of central Myanmar from around the middle of the first millennium CE, but Chin communities were gradually forced westward into the mountains by ethnic Burmans and other migrants during the next thousand years. Several Chin subgroups maintain the traditional custom of wearing facial tattoos, which is believed to date back to these times since, according to folklore, it prevented slave-raiding by Burman men or other incomers who found Chin women attractive.

In modern times, the socioeconomic development of the Chin peoples has been held back by the rugged terrain, which has made communications difficult. Of all the ethnic minority regions in Myanmar, the Chin hills have always been the most dependent on lowland areas for food and supplies.

The development of modern Chin political movements has also lagged behind, partly due to the diversity of subgroups. Like the Karens and Kachins, many Chins converted to Christianity under British rule and also served in the British colonial army. But under the colonial system of administration there was little advancement of Chin peoples in national representation or government.

After Burmese independence in 1948, although a special division was created from the former Chin hills territory under the British, the Chin region continued to be characterized by its isolation, with many villagers continuing to pursue traditional methods of swidden (slash-and-burn) cultivation in the hills. Many young Chin men also joined the Burmese armed forces as a way to escape the continuing poverty.

Eventually, a Chin state was refashioned in 1974 from the special division. However, many Chin people also live in the adjoining Rakhine State, as well as Sagaing, Magwe (Magway), and Pegu (Bago) divisions. As a result, during the twentieth century Chin nationalists advocated creating a "pan-Chin" state to combine all these populations (estimated at more than 1 million), with some leaders even wanting to include their Mizo cousins in India. This was an idea that the British also briefly considered before their departure from the two countries in 1947–1948, but any substantial restructuring of boundaries is likely to remain a pipe dream.

Nevertheless, during the 1990s Chin nationalism appeared to be on the rise, with an insurgent Chin National Front movement active in the Indian borderlands and Chin representatives winning seats in the 1990 election. Christian evangelism was also resurgent, leading to restrictions by local Burmese army commanders who, it was alleged, gave preference to the Buddhist faith.

Martin Smith

Further Reading

Lebar, Frank, Gerald Hickey, and John Musgrave. (1964) *Ethnic Groups of Mainland Southeast Asia*. New Haven, CT: Human Relations Area Files.

Lehman, Frederick K. (1963) *The Structure of Chin Society*. Urbana, IL: University of Illinois Press.

Smith, Martin. (1999) *Burma: Insurgency and the Politics of Ethnicity*. 2d ed. London: Zed Books.

Vum Ko Hau. (1963) *Profile of a Burma Frontier Man*. Bandung, Indonesia: Kilatmadju.

Vumson. (1986) *Zo History*. Aizawl, India: N. T. Thawnga.

CH'IN DYNASTY.   See **Qin Dynasty.**

CHIN STATE   (2000 pop. 532,000). The Chin State in northwestern Myanmar (Burma) comprises some of the least developed hill regions in the country. Formerly governed under the British Frontier Areas Administration, a Chin Special Division was created from these mostly forested highlands at independence (1948). In 1974 the division was politically upgraded into a Chin State, measuring 36,019 square kilometers (13,907 square miles) in area. Consisting of 9 townships and 505 wards or village-tracts, the capital is located at Haka in the northern part of the state. Other towns include Falam, Tiddim, and Paletwa.

With an estimated population of only 410,000 people (1990), Chin State's population density is one of the lowest in Myanmar. Most of the inhabitants are ethnic Chins, although there are ten thousand Rakhines, who mainly inhabit the Kaladan River valley in the west of the state. Other ethnic groups include Nagas and Burmans.

The difficult geography of the state historically has played a dominating role in political and economic life. Many communities live at subsistence level. Despite its borderland location, there are few road or communication links with either central Myanmar or its international neighbors. To the west lies Bangladesh, to the north the Mizoram and Manipur states of India, to the east the Sagaing and Magwe (Magway) Divisions, while to the south is the modern-day Rakhine State. The highest peak is Mount Victoria (3,053 meters [10,200 feet]), which is situated in the southeast near the Magwe (Magway) Division border.

Timber—teak, cane, pine, and other woods—is the state's most valuable natural resource. Economic modernization, however, has largely bypassed the territory. Farming, including swidden (slash-and-burn) cultivation, is the main economic activity for most inhabitants. The principal crops are rice, maize, and millet, as well as local planting of wheat, chilies, groundnuts, cotton, sugarcane, apples, oranges, and other garden fruits. During the twentieth century, attempts were made to increase agricultural production through methods such as irrigation, terraced farming, and the use of fertilizers and insecticides, but the total acreage under cultivation remained low.

In the first decades after independence from Britain in 1948, the Chin State was infrequently disrupted by insurgencies. From the late 1980s, however, ethnic discontent increased, manifested by the formation in 1987 of the Chin National Front—which carried out guerrilla strikes in the Indo-Bangladesh border region—as well as the victory of Chin opposition candidates in the 1990 general election. Demands included calls for greater autonomy as well as the right to develop closer economic and cultural linkages with Chin communities living outside the state's borders.

Martin Smith

Further Reading

Images Asia, Karen Human Rights Group, and the Open Society Institute's Burma Project. (1998) *All Quiet on the*

Western Front?: The Situation in Chin State and Sagaing Division, Burma. Chiang Mai, Thailand: Images Asia.

Lehman, Frederick K. (1963) *The Structure of Chin Society.* Urbana, IL: University of Illinois Press.

Smith, Martin. (1999) *Burma: Insurgency and the Politics of Ethnicity.* 2d ed. London: Zed Books.

Vumson. (1986) *Zo History.* Aizawl, India: N.T. Thawnga.

CHINA—PROFILE (2001 est. pop. 1.3 billion). China is a complex civilization with a history spanning several millennia. Since the success of a Communist-led revolution in 1949, China has been known as the People's Republic of China (PRC). For the most part, its borders have been unchanged since then. However, there is some disputed territory on the high Himalayan borders between Tibet, which is under PRC control, and India. In a remarkably peaceful transition, Hong Kong (a port on China's southern coast) returned to PRC sovereignty from British colonial control in 1997, and nearby Macao from Portuguese colonial control in 1999. The thriving island economy of Taiwan, off the coast of the China mainland, is populated by Chinese people; whether or not it is a part of China is in dispute.

CHINA—PROFILE

Country name: People's Republic of China

Area: 9,596,960 sq km

Population: 1,273,111,290 (July 2001 est.)

Population growth rate: 0.88% (2001 est.)

Birth rate: 15.95 births/1,000 population (2001 est.)

Death rate: 6.74 deaths/1,000 population (2001 est.)

Net migration rate: -0.39 migrant(s)/1,000 population (2001 est.)

Sex ratio—total population: 1.09 male(s)/female

Infant mortality rate: 28.08 deaths/1,000 live births (2001 est.)

Life expectancy at birth—total population 71.62 years, male: 69.81 years, female: 73.59 years (2001 est.)

Major religions: Daoist (Taoist), Buddhist (officially atheist)

Major languages: Standard Chinese or Mandarin (Putonghua, based on the Beijing dialect), Yue (Cantonese), Wu (Shanghaiese), Minbei (Fuzhou), Minnan (Hokkien-Taiwanese), Xiang, Gan, Hakka dialects

Literacy—total population: 81.5%, male: 89.9%, female: 72.7% (1995 est.)

Government type: Communist state

Capital: Beijing

Administrative divisions: 23 provinces, 5 autonomous regions, and 4 municipalities

Independence: Unification under the Qin dynasty 221 BCE ; Qing dynasty replaced by the Republic on 12 February 1912; People's Republic established 1 October 1949)

National holiday: Founding of the People's Republic of China, 1 October (1949)

Suffrage: 18 years of age; universal

GDP—real growth rate: 8% (2000 est.)

GDP—per capita (purchasing power parity): $3,600 (2000 est.)

Population below poverty line: 10% (1999 est.)

Exports: $232 billion (f.o.b., 2000)

Imports: $197 billion (f.o.b., 2000)

Currency: yuan (CNY)

Source: Central Intelligence Agency. (2001) *The World Factbook* 2001. Retrieved 18 October 2001, from: http://www.cia.gov/cia/publications/factbook.

At the start of the twenty-first century, China, with 21 percent of the total global population, is the world's most populous nation. Its vast territory covers an extreme range of altitudes, climates, landforms, and natural resources. The PRC is a poor country that is developing rapidly. Its economy is one of the fastest growing on earth. Its government is one of the world's few remaining Communist regimes. The political system is struggling to remain viable by transforming China from a command economy to a successful socialist market economy. The social transformation of China's people is also breathtaking. To understand what is going on in Asia during the early twenty-first century, it is essential to comprehend the rapid changes taking place in China.

Geography

China is similar in size and latitude to the lower forty-eight states of the United States. It is mostly in the temperate zone of the northern hemisphere, with its southernmost areas in the subtropical zone. Most of China experiences strong annual extremes in temperature and rainfall because of its location on the huge Eurasian continental landmass. On the east and south, China is bordered by seas that facilitate ocean commerce. Moving from east to west, China rises from sea level to high plateaus and mountains, including the Himalayas, the world's highest mountains, in Tibet. Therefore, most of China's major rivers flow from west to east.

Where people live in China is determined largely by climate and topography. The half of China's territory that is located in the west, northwest, and north is mostly deserts, arid grasslands, high plateaus, and mountains. About 6 percent of the population lives there. In contrast, 94 percent of the population lives in the half of China's land area that includes the warm, moist, southern, southeastern, and central provinces, the densely populated eastern and coastal provinces, and the northeast.

Politics

During the PRC's first twenty-seven years, during which the nation was led by Chairman Mao Zedong (1893–1976), China's totalitarian government established and maintained tight control of the population, right down into families. A U.S.-led embargo isolated China starting in the early 1950s; at the same time, China closed off its borders and defended itself from any perceived colonial or imperialist threats. Especially from the late 1950s through the subsequent decade, China heightened its own isolation, suppressing most information about what was happening in the country and focusing inward. The Communist government attempted to overcome the past and transform the beliefs and ideas of China's people, using a succession of disruptive and even catastrophic ideological movements, including the Great Leap Forward from 1958 to 1961 and the Cultural Revolution of the late 1960s and the 1970s. Arbitrary imprisonment, murder, maiming, and other forms of political harassment and physical harm were commonplace during the Maoist decades.

After Mao's death in 1976, his successors Deng Xiaoping (1904–1997) and then Jiang Zemin (b. 1926) instituted some political changes. As a result, the Communist Party greatly reduced its intrusion into people's personal and family lives. Other improvements include experiments with local village elections and attempts to establish and strengthen a legal system to replace arbitrary rule. But the whole political and economic system is riddled with corruption. Political rights in China are still very limited and human rights are frequently violated. Since troops massacred demonstrators in and around Beijing's Tiananmen Square in 1989, the government has cracked down on democratic movements and unofficial religious groups. Because capitalist and democratic ideas from abroad have eroded the perceived legitimacy of the Communist government in the eyes of the people, the government is now using nationalism to rally its citizens. By Western and advanced Asian standards, the people of China today do not yet have a free press or independent media, freedom of association, freedom of religion, or free speech.

Population

China's first modern census in 1953 counted 583 million people, a far larger number than expected. In the 1950s, the government equalized access to food-growing land in its rural land reform and widely introduced public health measures to improve health and reduce mortality. By 1957, in comparison to the late 1940s, the country's death rate had been approximately halved. However, Mao Zedong's ill-conceived Great Leap Forward brought about agricultural disasters and famine, causing 30 million excess deaths in the period 1958–1961. Thereafter, the government moderated its rural policies and the death rate dropped again. Mortality has remained low ever since. China's low death rate, combined with continuing high birth rates, caused rapid population growth from the 1950s into the 1970s. China's compulsory family-planning program was implemented in rural areas in the 1970s, reducing the birth rate and population growth rate to low levels beginning in the late 1970s. China's population is growing at one percent per year, which is low for a developing country. By the year 2000, China's population had reached approximately 1.3 billion, well over twice the 1953 count.

Economy

In 1949, almost the entire Chinese population was engaged in subsistence agriculture. Only 11 percent of the people lived in urban areas. Modern industry had been brought in by foreign colonial powers only to the coastal city of Shanghai and the northeast provinces (Manchuria). China's Communist government used the Soviet Union as its model of economic development: Starting in the mid-1950s, China's leadership collectivized agricultural land and siphoned off surplus rural production for investment in heavy industry in the cities. This system successfully promoted China's rapid heavy industrialization, but the distortions it introduced into the economy were serious and long-lasting. For example, laborers were prevented from leaving the countryside even if they could be more productive in a town or city. Further, the rural and urban structures of compensation were remarkably flat, and incomes were kept extremely low. The minimal or nonexistent rewards for educational attainment, efficiency, creativity, or work effectiveness in urban and rural areas suppressed incentives to work hard and to excel.

By the 1970s, it was clear to many of China's leaders that certain parts of the economy were not succeeding. Collective agriculture was barely able to keep grain production ahead of China's rapid population growth, and per capita production of other essential foods had declined since the 1950s. In 1978, Deng Xiaoping launched the economic reform period, which began with the abandonment of collectivized agriculture and the return of agricultural land-use rights to each rural family. The government also raised the official purchase prices of grain and other agricultural commodities, and greatly increased the supply of chemical fertilizer. In response, agricultural production increased rapidly in the early 1980s. Simultaneously, the government began to allow rural industries (called "township and village enterprises," or TVEs), light industries, provision of services, village and street markets, and private companies. With this partial introduction of a market economy, growth of the gross domestic product has averaged 8 percent a year since 1978. On the whole, the piecemeal dismantling of China's command economy and gradual introduction of market forces has been a success.

One factor in this success has been the invigoration of rural and urban work incentives in a liberalized policy environment. Another element has been China's opening to the outside world during the economic reform. The booming economy has been based partly on export-led growth, as foreign investors have set up companies and joint ventures in the coastal provinces to make light industrial products for the global market. A third element has been a belated and ongoing shift of laborers from agriculture to industry and services, accompanied by a policy change allowing some migration out of rural areas for work in towns, cities, and other parts of the country. Surplus rural laborers can now more easily go where their work is in greater demand.

Education and Human Capital

Part of China's economic success is traceable to the fact that the human capital embodied in China's working-age population increased dramatically in the second half of the twentieth century. The PRC began with a huge population that was very poor and agrarian, illiterate and uneducated, frequently ill, and traumatized by civil war, Japanese invasion, and high mortality. In contrast, by the 1990s the average life expectancy was around seventy years. Most diseases that plagued the people in the mid-twentieth century were gone or controlled fifty years later.

China's government promotes universal literacy and attainment of at least a primary education. Of the working-age population (arbitrarily defined as between ages fifteen and sixty-five for international comparison) at the beginning of the twenty-first century, only 6 percent of men and 17 percent of women are illiterate. Success in achieving basic literacy is more pronounced in urban areas than rural, and in eastern and coastal provinces compared to most of the provinces in the western half of China.

Environment

China has an unusual variety in its ecological systems and a rich natural resource base, but its enor-mous population places huge demands on its environment. Continuing population growth and rapidly rising living standards are combining to pollute China's air, water, and soil, and to strain the country's food-growing capacity, deplete forests, and exacerbate water scarcity in north and west China. Amidst great natural diversity of animals and plants, many species are threatened or have become extinct. In arid regions, the deserts are expanding, taking over existing grasslands and arable land. China's national government is aware of environmental problems and pollution, and is implementing some policies to reverse or slow ecological deterioration. However, a high priority of China's leaders is the fastest possible economic development. When economic goals and environmental goals conflict, the economy tends to take precedence.

Peoples and Ethnicity

China has a largely homogeneous population based on its officially designated ethnic categories. The Han Chinese nationality comprises 92 percent of the population, though there are some intragroup differences among the category defined as Han Chinese. The fifty-five minority nationalities are unevenly distributed throughout the country. In most of China's populous provinces, only from 1 to 2 percent of the population is non-Han. In general, each minority group is concentrated in one province or several contiguous ones. In only two provinces are Han Chinese in the minority: Tibet in the west and Xinjiang in the northwest. Most of China's land border regions are inhabited by minority nationalities with ethnic kin across the border, which, from the government's perspective, causes major security problems.

Most of China's minority nationalities have been strongly influenced by the Chinese language, historical Chinese culture, and powerful intrusions during the Communist period. Many of the minority groups are highly assimilated. Others remain distinctive in their religion, clothing, housing, language, food, lifestyle, economic life, arts, or customs. Most of the minorities appear to have adapted to overwhelming Han numerical dominance, but some members of certain minority nationalities (Tibetans, along with Uighurs and some other Muslim minorities) are particularly restive. Policies toward the minorities have varied over time. At the beginning of the twenty-first century, some of the minority groups are allowed to have one (or more than one) additional child per couple above the quota for Han Chinese. Other preferential policies are financial subsidies, health and economic assistance, and some affirmative action programs to give the minorities political representation or educational advantages. At the same time, China's government suppresses minority individuals or groups campaigning for freedom of expression and religion, genuine autonomy within the PRC, or independence.

Culture and Language

China has a rich ancient culture. For more than a century, Chinese thinkers and leaders have struggled to determine what aspects of that culture should be preserved and which aspects should be discarded so that China may become a modern, developed, great power. Mao's Cultural Revolution (1966–1976), during which traditional culture came under attack for its perceived elitism, represented an extreme of intentional destruction, but even today the government attempts to discredit cultural forms that it feels do not sit well with its Communist ideology. Much of China's cultural heritage has also been lost or destroyed through invasion from abroad, civil war, neglect, and globalization. Elements of Chinese traditional culture that remain today are near-universal marriage, close family life, Chinese cuisines and special foods, Chinese traditional medicine, intensive agricultural production, traditional walled-courtyard housing, great respect for education, patrilineal family structure, son preference, male dominance in the workplace, a China-centered perspective, disdain for most other cultures, deference to individuals of higher status, ability to function in hierarchical systems, traditional arts and handicrafts, spoken Chinese dialects, and China's written language.

Society

For a century, the experiences of each new generation in China have differed vastly from the experiences of the previous generation. A series of cataclysmic events—collapse of the last dynasty, civil war, the Japanese invasion, Communist social transformation, attacks on certain social groups, famine, the Cultural Revolution—traumatized tens or hundreds of millions of people at vulnerable stages in their life cycle. At the same time, Chinese society was permanently transformed in many positive ways as well. China's brutal traditional custom of binding and breaking the feet of girls and women completely ceased in the twentieth century, saving hundreds of millions of girls from this crippling disfiguration. The social position of China's girls and women rose sharply in that century, a wrenching cultural shift in any society. There has been vast, generally positive change in male-female relationships. Quality of life for almost all China's people has improved to a stunning degree, especially with regard to survival and health, quantity and variety of food, education, and living standards.

Though China remains primarily rural, the urban proportion of the population increased from 11 percent in 1949 to 36 percent at the end of the twentieth century. Communist policies have set up an economic, political, and social structure that gives extreme advantages to the urban population at the expense of rural people. The World Bank reports that rural incomes are less than one-third of urban incomes, a difference much higher than in most countries. Barriers to geographic and social mobility instituted or strengthened in the Maoist period continue to hold down rural incomes. However, the economic reform period has lifted the great majority of the population out of absolute poverty; remaining pockets of poverty tend to be in mountainous and remote areas.

China in the Twenty-First Century

At the beginning of the twenty-first century, China's people and government wish for the nation to take its rightful place of leadership in global affairs. In many ways, the PRC does function as a responsible, sometimes forward-looking international leading nation. It is an active member of most United Nations organizations, the World Bank system, and many Asian regional organizations. Other Asian nations tend to treat China with caution and respect, in part because of its huge population and territory and rising economic clout, and in part out of fear of possible Chinese aggression. For example, China claims vast reaches of the South China Sea and East China Sea in areas much closer to other countries and claimed by them also. China's unilateral occupation of islands in the disputed regions has raised widespread concern.

Compared with most other developing countries and with other countries in transition from command economies to market or capitalist economies, the PRC is succeeding extraordinarily well. China's biggest economic problem today is employment. The age structure is greatly concentrated in the working-age groups, and the population of working age is still increasing rapidly. As a legacy of China's traditional economy and of Maoist economics, China has one or two hundred million surplus laborers in agriculture, plus tens of millions of surplus workers in industry and government. About one-third of the state-owned enterprises are reported to be losing money, including many of the larger ones. The banking system that has been propping them up is crippled by nonperforming loans to the state sector. Transforming the economy to increase efficiency and productivity means at least temporarily laying off surplus rural and urban workers. The biggest economic challenge is to generate new employment opportunities for those adults who are unemployed, laid off, underemployed, or looking for more productive employment.

China's government is trying to prove that a Communist one-party political system is still viable in the modern world, even though most such governments have now collapsed. The pervasiveness of corruption at all levels weakens the government's claims to popular legitimacy. The government is trying to confront the corruption problem and shrink the bloated bureaucracy, but the perceived necessity of keeping the Communist Party in power at all costs continues to mean denying democratic freedom to China's people, imprisoning those who speak out against autocracy, arresting and suppressing journalists, preventing people from forming nongovernmental organizations, and biasing the content of education. As China's people become wealthier, more educated, and in greater contact with international norms, the PRC political system becomes less viable over time.

Chinese society and culture have been weakened and transformed in myriad ways both by the Communist government from within and by foreign influences from without. Change has been so fast and confusing that many Chinese people are experiencing a spiritual and cultural vacuum. One of China's big issues in the twenty-first century is to build a modern, stable society that satisfies the needs of China's own people as they perceive them.

China's historic demographic transition from traditional high death and birth rates to modern low death and birth rates is nearly complete. The process occurred very quickly. This implies that in the coming decades, China will experience rapid and extreme aging of its population structure. Elderly dependency will place great burdens on China's families and on society because of the escalating needs of the aged for health care, personal care, and financial support.

The cumulative harm to China's environment caused by population growth, rising affluence, industrialization, and the low priority given to addressing this environmental destruction is another concern. Annual economic losses from pollution, deforestation, erosion, desertification, and other ecological disasters are estimated to equal 5–10 percent of China's gross domestic product. Many of China's leaders would like to postpone cleaning up China's environmental problems until China is a rich country more easily able to afford the cost, but others argue that the losses are too massive and the country must reverse the deterioration immediately.

The Future

China has just experienced a century of instability and rapid change in most aspects of life. Almost every part of Chinese society is still in flux. Economic transformation continues unabated. Living standards are rising and lifestyles are changing fast. Politics is shifting more slowly. China may follow the pattern already seen in many other Asian societies, in which economic development has preceded political development, with democratization lagging a decade or two behind the achievement of fairly high incomes and educational attainment. The achievement of full equality between males and females will take decades more. Continuing urbanization will tilt the balance away from conservative rural customs and attitudes. As China continues to modernize, it may come to resemble more closely Taiwan or Hong Kong, places where Chinese culture has adapted to the interconnected global system without losing its distinctive characteristics. Nevertheless China, by virtue of its huge geographic and population size, will remain unique in many respects.

Judith Banister

Further Reading
Antic, Tamar Manuelyan. (1997) *Sharing Rising Incomes: Disparities in China.* Washington, DC: World Bank.
Economy, Elizabeth, and Michel Oksenberg, eds. (1999) *China Joins the World: Progress and Prospects.* New York: Council on Foreign Relations Press.
Kim, Samuel S. (1998) *China and the World: Chinese Foreign Policy Faces the New Millennium.* 4th ed. Boulder, CO.: Westview Press.
Lieberthal, Kenneth. (1995) *Governing China: From Revolution through Reform.* New York: W. W. Norton.
Starr, John Bryan. (1999) *Understanding China.* London: Profile Books.

CHINA—ECONOMIC SYSTEM In the last two decades of the twentieth century, the Chinese economic system changed from a command economy, which dated from shortly after the Communists took control in 1949, to a mixed economy.

The Command Economy before Reform

A command economy is an economic system in which the means of production are publicly owned and economic activity is controlled by a central authority that assigns quantitative production targets and allots raw materials to production units. It involves comprehensive economic planning on the basis of targets and balancing of materials.

China's command economy was first established in 1950–1951 and was followed by the introduction of a Soviet-style five-year plan, the First Five-Year Plan, for the period of 1953 to 1957. The Soviet model was ideologically sound in that it was supported by Marxist theory, but more important, it seemed to the Chinese a necessity when they had to face the deterioration of the economy following a century of wars and turmoil. With the ability to mobilize resources quickly on a national scale, this administrative approach was effective in its initial phase.

From the early 1950s, the Chinese central industrial ministries and administrative regions were required to assign production targets to the enterprises under their jurisdiction. Each group of enterprises was then required to formulate annual production, cost, and labor plans and to submit them to the higher echelons—that is, the industrial ministries or bureaus—for approval. During the same period, procedures for making annual plans "from the bottom to the top" and "from the top to the bottom" were introduced and standardized. There were frequent consultations and exchanges of information at various levels of the hierarchy. Moreover, a centralized system of supplying raw materials was established.

The central bureaucracy played a predominant role in the economy. In the industrial sector, for example, the state owned outright enterprises that produced more than 60 percent of the gross value of industrial output, and all but a small portion of the remainder was owned collectively. In the urban sector, the government not only prescribed output targets and allocated energy resources, it also set the prices for key commodities, determined the level and general distribution of investment funds, set wage levels and employment targets, ran the wholesale and retail networks, and controlled financial policy and the banking system. The foreign-trade system became a government monopoly in the early 1950s as well. Similarly, in the countryside, from the mid-1950s, the government prescribed cropping patterns, set the level of prices, and fixed output targets for all major crops. Most rural commercial transactions were carried out by the Supply and Marketing Cooperatives—nominally an organization of farming cooperatives but in fact a heavily bureaucratized organization that functioned as the rural wing of the Ministry of Commerce.

In order to run the command economy, the chief organ of planning, the State Planning Commission, was established in 1952 and placed under the State Council when the latter was made supreme executive body by the 1954 constitution. At the same time, the State Construction Commission was organized to oversee capital investment under the five-year plans in 1956; the State Economic Commission was established to take over short-term—up to annual—plan responsibilities, leaving the State Planning Commission to concentrate on long-term and perspective planning. Also

FIVE LARGEST COMPANIES IN CHINA

According to *Asia Week*, the five largest companies in China are as follows.

Company	Sector	Sales ($ millions)	Rank in Asia
State Power	Energy	42,587.7	19
China Petroleum and Chem.	Chemicals	39,729.5	21
Petrochina	Petroleum	29,231.4	28
China Telecom	Telecommunications	20,812.9	44
Sinochem	Chemicals Trading	18,035.5	58

Source: Asia Week. 2001 (9 November): 111.

created in 1956 were the General Bureau for Supply of Raw Materials, to handle material allocation, and the State Technological Commission, to plan long-term technical development. The State Statistical Bureau was established in 1952, its provincial and municipal statistical departments in 1953, and below them administrative and special district officers in 1954.

Centralization and Decentralization The organization of planning grew more centralized, reaching a peak in 1955–1956. China had nearly 200,000 separate enterprises, operating with widely varying technologies, product assortments, and levels of efficiency, even within the same industry. Yet, the data gathered, transmitted, and processed for central planning were irregular, sometimes incomplete, and often overestimated. As both the number of commodities and the number of enterprises for which the central planning bodies assumed responsibility grew rapidly, the maintenance of such a high degree of centralization of both planning and management became increasingly cumbersome. In 1957 and 1958, the government adopted a series of decentralization measures to shift some responsibilities onto the localities, increase the scope for local initiative, and strengthen central control of the most important plan targets and enterprises.

In this round of decentralization, most planning tasks were transferred to officials closer to the scene of production in an effort to shorten lines of communication and reduce absentee management. This took place when the ministries passed most of the enterprises they had controlled to regional authorities, which gained more rights to allocate scarce resources. Most planning tasks then fell on the shoulders of regional and local authorities. This move was also a regionalization of planning, in which several industrial ministries were abolished after losing a majority of their enterprises. Subsequently, the sixty thousand communes received an administrative and planning role in rural areas. They replaced the *xiang*, or township governments, in 1958. In principle, only the most important enterprises remained under direct ministerial control. Even many of these were supposed to come under dual subordination to ministries and regional authorities, although in practice ministerial control came to dominate. The 1957–1958 decentralization was never entirely reversed.

The Chinese command economy traditionally operated with a strong centralized monopoly over commerce. Monopoly purchase of grain actually preceded agricultural collectivization in China, and even during the Cultural Revolution (1966–1976), when much of the industrial management system was being decentralized, central control of agricultural procurement and distribution of key consumer goods continued. Although there were around thirty thousand rural and suburban periodic markets (that is, markets that opened periodically), they were tightly controlled, and it was forbidden to transact goods such as grain and cotton, over which the Ministry of Commerce had a monopoly.

Shortages in China's Command Economy All command economies have followed development strategies that stress high levels of investment in, and give priority to, heavy industry. China was no exception. As might be expected, the focus on heavy industry was

A major development in the Chinese economy in the last half of the twentieth century was increasing industrialization. Here, workers on an assembly line assemble electronic boards in a factory in Dong Guna, Guangdong Province. (BOHEMIAN NOMAD PICTUREMAKERS/CORBIS)

accompanied by severe shortages of consumer goods as well as, ironically, producer goods.

The shortages seemed to arise from three sources. First, the government simply channeled so many resources into investment and heavy industry that there was little left for households. Second, shortages resulted from the soft budget constraints of enterprises. Most enterprises were quite profitable, and they faced no risk of bankruptcy. As a result, enterprises pursued unrestrained growth and had an almost unlimited desire for investment. Typically, each planning unit of an enterprise tried to make sure it would have the inputs it needed to fulfill its plan targets, plus a margin for insurance. Each therefore tended to overstate its needs and to treat the requirements of other planning jurisdictions as residual. Third, and related to the second, when managers were promoted based on their ability to fulfill the state-set output volume, their demand for inputs tended to expand until total demand ran up against the total available supply of resources. The overdemand for production inputs, without much concern about efficiency or quality of output, resulted in constant shortage of the supply of resources. Command economies have thus a built-in tendency to become "shortage economies."

Other Features of China's Command Economy In addition to the characteristics mentioned above, China's command economy adopted an urban-biased social-welfare policy to encourage industrial development. The policy provided not only lifetime full employment but also virtually free housing, free health care, and free retirement benefits. Excluded were nonurban residents, however, and the government controlled obtaining permits for urban residence.

The government also controlled internal migration and job assignment in the urban sector through a house-registration system, which largely replaced the free labor market after 1957, although the post-Mao reforms have attempted to revive it.

The Post-Mao Economic Reforms and a Mixed Economy

Since the death of Mao Zedong in 1976, China has been trying to reform its economy, with gradual but somewhat parallel changes in the rural and urban sectors. The reforms of Deng Xiaoping (1904–1997) have been accompanied by a flurry of complaints about the inefficiency of Soviet-style central planning and, in particular, about China's unwieldy, overlapping, and inefficient administrative bureaucracy, along with the excessive dependence of enterprises on their planning apparatus. To end the latter, post-Mao leaders have sought to institute a system of managerial and production responsibility, under which producers become more responsible for marketing their output, procuring supplies, operating in a cost-effective manner, and financing their investments from their own earnings or repayable bank loans. In these post-Mao reforms, the government has emphasized raising personal income and consumption and introducing new management systems to help increase productivity. It has also focused on foreign trade as a major vehicle for economic growth.

In the late 1970s, China started to pursue agricultural reforms, dismantling the commune system and introducing the household-responsibility system, which gave peasants greater decision making in agricultural activities. The development of the household-responsibility system itself can be roughly divided into three phases: the work-quota contract phase, the output-quota contract phase, and the responsibility contract phase. In the work-quota contract phase, the household was responsible for the hours of work contracted on the collective land with the production input from the collective. In the output-quota contract phase, the household was responsible for the quantity of output contracted given the production input from the collective. In the responsibility contract phase, the household was responsible for everything from input to output. The government has also encouraged nonagricultural activities, such as township and village enterprises, in rural areas. Agriculture thus has been decollectivized, small-scale private trade and workshops have been legalized, and the role of market forces has been substantially increased.

In the urban sector, the goal of enterprise reform grows ever loftier. Its original goal was to solve the problem of low incentive and inefficiency in state enterprises. As the reform has progressed, the goal has become changing the managerial mechanism to make state enterprises competitive in the market.

The Four Phases of China's Economic Reform Reform of China's state-owned enterprises has gone through four phases. The first phase (1979–1984) focused on giving a certain amount of autonomy to enterprises in exchange for their improved efficiency. The second phase (1984–1986) focused on ways to enhance the vitality of state enterprises. The third phase (1987–1996) focused on the reconstruction of state enterprises' managerial mechanisms. The fourth phase, beginning in 1997, has tried to get rid of money-losing enterprises, hence starting a period of much-delayed privatization.

As in other socialist countries, Chinese reformers have followed a dual approach. In addition to the state sector, they have allowed the more marketized sector—consisting mainly of small- to mid-sized private and collective firms—to expand explosively in both rural and urban areas. In some cases, the enterprise capital is still state owned, but the facilities are leased to individuals or groups that operate them on a profit-or-loss basis. Since the mid-1990s, stock and bond markets have also sprung up, and over 400,000 enterprises have incorporated themselves.

Within the planning network, many large enterprises still have a primary obligation to meet plan targets, but the latter are supposed to be set low enough to allow a margin of overfulfillment. Production that is beyond state targets or not covered by targets is to be sold in competitive markets, and enterprises that do this successfully are supposed to be able to keep part of the resulting profit for bonuses and investment under their control. Prices have also been gradually deregulated and are now largely free of controls for output not subject to mandatory planning, although subsidies and production quotas in agriculture still hold down grain prices.

CAN CHINA'S ECONOMIC INDICATORS BE TRUSTED?

Some experts argue that some of basic economic indicators published by the Chinese government are less than accurate. Among these are an economic growth rate of an average of nearly 10% per year from 1980 to 1999, which some experts believe is at least 2% too high and suspect figures about the amount of cultivated land in China. China once claimed only 95 million hectares of cultivated land and then claimed 130 million hectares in 2000. Experts believe that 150 million hectares is more accurate. The difference has important policy implications as China can feed itself on 150 million but not on 95 million and with more difficulty on 130 million.

Source: Vaclav Smil. (2001) "It Doesn't Add Up." *Asia Week* (30 November): 24.

FOR CHINA'S BANKING SECTOR, SMALL MAY BE BETTER

China's banking sector is dominated by the four large state-owned banks: The Industrial and Commercial Bank of China, Bank of China, Agricultural Bank of China, and China Construction of China. Experts agree that all are badly in need of reform to end chronic problems caused by mismanagement, ties to the government bureaucracy, and poorly performing loans. One source of overall reform might be the over 100 smaller banks that have emerged across China since 1996 when new policies allowed their formation. Many of these semi-independent, cooperatively owned banks have been more successful than the larger banks over the last five years. Their success is based on better customer service, more modern facilities, better management of loans, and a profit orientation. It is expected that they will also prove more able to compete in the global banking marketplace as China joins the World Trade Organization.

Source: Allen T. Cheng. (2000) "The Advantage of Being Small." *Asia Week* (16 November): 35.

Historically, price ceilings for consumer goods were supported by formal rationing of some staple foodstuffs and other daily necessities, as well as of a number of consumer durables. This system has been virtually replaced by market allocation, together with far higher prices, although housing may still be purchased through work units at a much lower price.

In recent years, a dual market for urban housing has sprung up, in which some apartments of relatively high quality are leased through the market at some of the world's highest rents. Shanghai, for example, has rents much higher than those in New York City and nearly as high as those in Tokyo.

Reform of Large-Scale Industry Although larger-scale industry has remained subject to central planning controls, similar market-type reforms have long been implemented. Reformers have worked to expand market links within the state-planning network while reducing control by government agencies. In 1982, the number of ministries and commissions directly under the State Council was cut from ninety-eight to fifty-two and subsequently to forty-one, and their total staff was reduced from 49,000 to 32,000. As their decision-making rights grow, enterprises are supposed to become more profit oriented in order to be stimulated to reduce waste, raise quality and labor productivity, better tailor their products to user needs, and upgrade production. They are to move away from the one-sided emphasis on output volume—a hallmark of a command economy. In addition, provincial governments and over nine hundred enterprises now have rights to conduct foreign trade on their own.

By the late 1980s, the economy had become overheated with increasing rates of inflation. China's economy regained momentum in the early 1990s, after Deng Xiaoping's Chinese New Year's visit to southern China in 1992 gave economic reforms new impetus. The Fourteenth Party Congress later in the year backed up Deng's renewed push for market reforms, stating that China's key task in the 1990s was to create a "socialist market economy," an economy that would accommodate a variety of forms of ownership and permit coexistence of government planning and market mechanisms. Continuity in the political system but bolder reforms in the economic system were announced as the hallmarks of the ten-year development plan for the 1990s.

Challenges for the Twenty-First Century

Despite China's impressive economic development during the past two decades, reforming the state-enterprises sector, modernizing the banking system, and creating a social-welfare system remain major hurdles. Many small loss-making enterprises have now been closed or sold, but larger losing enterprises are usually merged with viable state enterprises or simply continue to be subsidized. Most discharged workers have continued to receive minimum compensation, including early retirement and opportunities to go into business for themselves. However, the rising unemployment rates are expected to be further pumped up after China joins the World Trade Organization.

There are three types of economic activities in China: those stipulated by mandatory planning, those done according to indicative planning (in which central planning of economic outcomes is indirectly implemented), and those governed by market forces. The second and third types have grown at the expense of the first, but goods of national importance and almost all large-scale construction come under the mandatory planning system. Operational supervision over economic projects has devolved primarily to provincial, municipal, and county governments. The market economy generally involves small-scale or highly perishable items that circulate within local market areas only. In addition, enterprises themselves are gaining increased independence in a range of activities. Almost every year brings additional changes in the lists of goods that fall under each of the three types of planning. Overall, the Chinese economic system contains a complex mixture of relationships: state ownership, shareholding, collective ownership, private ownership, foreign direct investment, and public ownership through shareholding. Indeed, the nonstate investment in fixed assets in China at the beginning of the twenty-first century reached 47 percent of its total, and it has continued to grow. The search continues for an optimal balance between plan and market, although the Communist Party reserves the right to make broad decisions on economic priorities and policies.

Xiaobo Hu

See also: **Development Zones—China; Shenzhen Special Economic Zone**

Further Reading

Huang Yasheng. (1999) *Inflation & Investment Controls in China: The Political Economy of Central-Local Relations during the Reform Era.* Cambridge, U.K.: Cambridge University Press.

Lin, Justin Yifu, Fang Cai, and Zhou Li. (1996) *The China Miracle: Development Strategy and Economic Reform.* Hong Kong: Chinese University Press.

Naughton, Barry. (1995) *Growing out of the Plan: Chinese Economic Reform, 1978–1993.* Cambridge, U.K.: Cambridge University Press.

Perkins, Dwight H. (1966) *Market Control & Planning in Communist China.* Cambridge, MA: Harvard University Press.

CHINA—EDUCATION SYSTEM
China's education system, the world's largest, serves over 200 million primary and secondary school pupils. It achieved remarkable gains from 1949 to 2000 despite political upheaval and low levels of funding. When the People's Republic was founded in 1949, 20 percent of school-age children attended primary school. Fifty years later the net enrollment ratio was 99 percent, and the proportion of China's population that was illiterate had dropped from 80 to 14 percent.

The Cultural and Political Economy of Schooling

China's massive educational project is anchored by her citizens' belief in the power of schooling. Surveys indicate that educational expenses get first priority in family budgets, followed by health and housing. Education reforms throughout the 1990s have resulted in a shift of financial responsibility from the central government to local communities. Funding comes from all levels of government, from enterprise taxes, from surcharges on rural households, and from tuition, fees, and private contributions. The government decreased its funding of education from 84.5 percent in 1991 to 68.9 in 1998, while tuition as a source of funding for education rose from 4.42 to 12.5 percent. Decrease in national funding has forced schools to generate income from school businesses, services, and fee-paying students, exacerbating educational disparities between rich and poor counties.

Such disparities hinder China's education "action plan," which calls for universal senior secondary schooling, a 15 percent matriculation rate to higher education, national systems of lifelong learning and knowledge innovation, and the elimination of illiteracy by the year 2010. However, the government's own officers criticize its disproportionately low investments in education. In 1999 China ranked 145th out of 153 nations in terms of per-capita education spending. Although national policy prescribes government educational expenditures of 4 percent of GDP, the current figure is 2.5 percent, virtually unchanged since the 1950s.

Beyond Access to Quality Primary Education

A majority of urban children have attended preschool since the 1980s, reflecting the mobilization of women outside the household and the one-child family policy. By the early 2000s, the government hopes to achieve a gross preschool enrollment rate of 45 percent for three- to five-year-olds, and 60 percent for children in their last year of kindergarten.

Nearly all children attend and graduate from primary school. In 1997 net enrollment rates of 98.9 percent and promotion rates of 93.7 percent represented an impressive increase over 1980 figures of 93 and 75.9 percent respectively. In 1999 China's 582,300 primary schools enrolled 134.7 million pupils. As China's baby-boom echo generation matriculates into secondary school, declining primary-school enrollments in cities like Shanghai and Nanjing have allowed officials to close poor schools, reduce class size, and raise teaching standards. Changed standards for the primary school curriculum, implemented on a trial basis in 2001, are designed to facilitate well-rounded training in language arts, social studies, mathematics and sciences, physical education, and art and music. English-language and information-technology instruction begin in grade three in schools with adequate resources.

Continuous media attention on funding irregularities and student workload indicates how competition for educational resources extends to the lowest levels of schooling. Shanghai's regulations on tuition and fees are typical in prohibiting donations linked to entrance, mid-year tuition increases, and extra fees for supplementary courses for all students. The Ministry of Education has made lightening the oppressive workload of school children its urgent educational goal for the new millennium. Yet, measures promoting that end (including restrictions on homework) can prove unpopular with parents who fear jeopardizing their children's educational future.

Universalizing and Diversifying Secondary Schooling

China's gross enrollment rate for pupils in junior secondary school (grades 7–9), part of the compulsory education system since 1985, was 88.6 percent in 1998. Coastal cities that have universalized junior secondary schooling have abolished selective entrance examinations in favor of neighborhood schooling. Nationally, junior secondary schools enrolled approximately 77 million pupils in 2000 and will operate for several more years under the strain of increased enrollments, with class sizes regularly exceeding fifty-five pupils.

Graduation from junior secondary school marks the transition of adolescents to stratified senior secondary schools, work, or unemployment. While junior secondary school dropout rates, 3.23 percent in 1998, remain a concern, promotion rates to senior secondary school increased from 40.6 to 57.5 percent between 1990 and 1997. Senior secondary schooling is nearly universalized in metropolitan areas like Shanghai, where 95 percent of junior secondary graduates continued their education in 2000.

Senior secondary-school reforms have included the introduction of new textbooks, elective courses, credit systems, information technology, and an approach to moral education that emphasizes community participation, discovery learning, and "healthy leisure." New curricular standards implemented in 2001 give individual schools more flexibility in deciding how their teachers can best engage students in a well-rounded course of study in Chinese, English, mathematics, computer sciences, social studies, biology, chemistry, physics, geography, music, arts, and physical sciences. College preparatory courses, criticized as too difficult, have been streamlined to offer students time for co-curricular pursuits. Systems of accreditation are being developed for advanced teachers and private schools, and increased educational qualifications and in-service training are mandated for teachers and principals.

The content, structure, and guidelines for competency and matriculation examinations are also changing to conform to changing curricular standards. Many cities and provinces have adopted a college entrance examination system that requires examinations in Chinese, English, and mathematics, plus one or two optional subjects, usually chosen from politics, history, physics, and chemistry. High-achieving students are sometimes exempted from exams. Expanding college enrollment fuels such reforms. The chances for students in metropolitan centers to enter college have never been greater (and college has never cost more). Of Beijing senior secondary graduates, 70 percent entered higher education in 2000. Living in educational centers drastically improves a student's opportunity for higher education; those areas have more resources to spend on education and consequently have more seats available in high schools, colleges, and universities. China's first Spring College Entrance Examination was held in 2000. Only 1,100 examinees sat for Beijing's 1,755 college places. In contrast, 35,000 examinees in Anhui province vied for 6,190 places, making it harder for qualified students to advance to the upper levels of schooling.

Expanding and "Commercializing" Tertiary Education

Relative to other developing countries, the base of China's educational pyramid is very broad while the top is very narrow. In 1990, 3 percent of Chinese eighteen- through twenty-two-year-olds were studying in tertiary institutions, compared to 8 percent in India, and fewer than one out of every 100 citizens was a college graduate. Since China's integration into the global economy, higher education has entered a period of unprecedented expansion. In 1999, enrollment in nearly 1,100 regular tertiary institutions was 4.13 million, an increase in one year of 770,000 students. Enrollment in adult higher education was 3.05 million, an increase of almost 250,000. In the first decade of the twenty-first century, the proportion of eighteen- through twenty-two-year-olds in higher education is expected to expand from 9 to 15 percent.

Reforms in higher education are directed toward decentralized funding, ending state-supported higher education, institutional accountability, and quality. Generally, institutions are increasing in size due to expanded recruitment and consolidation. Disciplines and majors are being redefined. Some universities allow early graduation for qualified students. At the same time, housing, education, and health services for university staff and faculty have been cut as universities contract out services. While the number of university students more than tripled from 1992 to 1999, the number of support staff fell 35.3 percent.

Student services and financial aid are at the forefront of change. National, provincial, city, and institutional measures to help students afford college have accompanied dramatic increases in tuition, which in Beijing ranged in 2000 from 4,200 *yuan* for ordinary majors at second tier institutions to 6,000 *yuan* for medical and foreign language courses at premier institutions. Universities offer teaching and research assistantships, and the banking industry along with the Ministries of Education and Finance are supporting national student loan programs.

Raising Teaching Standards in the Face of Teacher Shortages

Efforts are underway to require primary and secondary school teachers to have four-year college degrees, and a national continuing education mandate requires extensive in-service training of between 240 and 520 hours every five years. Coupled with expansion in secondary and tertiary education, efforts to raise standards have created a shortfall of qualified teachers. The teacher-student ratio in universities increased sharply in 1999; at the same time, a record number of faculty are on the verge of retirement. Universities are now compelled to attract faculty by increasing pay and opportunities for travel abroad. Competition has also developed among universities in the training of teachers. Comprehensive universities are encouraged to establish teacher-training programs, and normal universities are responding with more specialized and flexible training options.

Enhancing the quality and stability of the teaching force is urgent in rural areas where primary school teachers are not state employees but rather hired by local communities as *minban* (community managed) teachers. *Minban* teachers work in public and community schools but are paid by subsidies and nonbudgetary allocations from villages and townships. Because these teachers receive no regular salary from the government, it has been difficult for them to maintain an adequate standard of living. In response, several ministries recently issued a joint announcement to recognize qualified *minban* teachers as state employees. Regional variation in the quality of the teaching force has also inspired distance education programs for female and ethnic minority teachers in impoverished counties in rural and western China.

Private Schooling: Filling the Gap in Capacity and Funding

Private schooling reemerged at all levels of the system in the 1990s. In 2000 there were over 50,000 non-

state educational institutions, reflecting a diversity of programs and administrative and fiscal autonomy. Nonstate preschools and kindergartens made up 20 percent of the total. In addition, there were over 2000 nonstate primary and secondary schools, 37 nationally accredited nonstate colleges, and over 300 pilot nonstate colleges offering diploma courses.

Lack of state funding, rigidity in the public sector, and restricted entrance to public schools are among the reasons for the rise of private schools. The state's policy of actively encouraging, supporting, and guiding and effectively administering private schools is also designed to boost the economy by prompting families to use their savings on the one "commodity" they consistently desire—education for their children.

Private education has become a major force in reform. Many private schools are short-term or proprietary institutions; others provide a forum for experimentation in teaching and community-government relations. Private girls' schools, for example, experiment with a wide array of curricula—in music, drawing, driver's training, martial arts, information technology, and psychology—designed to meet the "special" needs of healthy female development. They fill educational gaps left by a state unable or unwilling to provide sufficient schooling to meet public demand. Because private schools face opposition from local authorities protective of scarce funds, many are embroiled in community-level conflicts.

Educating China's Margins

Disparities in access to quality education are a product of complex patterns of historical regional, ethnic, and gender discrimination. China's best and worst educated regions reflect the economic inequities that exist between the coastal and interior regions. Census data from 1993 indicate that Beijing and Shanghai are China's educational centers, with 5.5 and 3.2 university graduates and 14.3 and 15.3 senior secondary school graduates per 100 residents. By contrast, Shandong province and the Guangxi-Zhuang autonomous region counted only .3 university graduates and 5.7 and 5.3 senior secondary school graduates per 100 residents.

China has been a high-profile player in international initiatives to end illiteracy and exploitative child labor and to universalize basic schooling. External aid from organizations like the World Bank and the United Nations, and domestic support from programs like Project Hope, the China Youth Development Foundation's social welfare program, have been directed toward these ends, especially in regions inhabited by the poorest 20 percent of China's population. Efforts in the 1990s have targeted the two-thirds of illiterates and school dropouts who are poor, minority, rural, females. China has reintroduced all-girls' schools and classrooms in rural and urban communities.

Females make up an increasing proportion of non-compulsory schooling. However, their location within the system (disproportionately weighted in the humanities, foreign languages, and teacher education) is still heavily determined by gender. Nationally as of 1997, 37.32 percent of students in regular higher education institutions were female. Female full-time college teachers made up 35.21 of the teaching staff, 38.16 and 48.28 percent of the general secondary and primary staff respectively, and 94.57 percent of kindergarten teachers. Female enrollment accounted for 63.17 percent of students in secondary technical schools, 45.56 percent of students in general secondary schools, 48.53 percent of students in vocational schools, 47.63 percent of students in primary school, 46.58 percent of students in kindergarten, and 36.2 percent of students in special education programs.

The push to universalize basic education has also thrown a spotlight on the ethnic minority regions, which span 60 percent of China's territory and generally lag behind on economic and education indicators. Although minority students on average attend primary schools at Han Chinese levels, literacy rates for 28 of the 55 minority groups are below that of the Han majority, and minority students are significantly underrepresented in secondary and higher education. A widespread system of two-track schools that teach in either Mandarin or the local minority language perpetuates discrimination. Originally designed to protect minority cultures, the system places minority students at a disadvantage in competing for jobs in government and business, which require Chinese-language skills.

Arguably, China's disabled population is the group most marginalized by the structures and practices of formal and nonformal education. In 1990 the government adopted legislation to protect the rights of China's 60 million disabled citizens, one-quarter of whom live in extreme poverty. The same year, the Ministry of Education signed a Special Education Project Task Agreement with 21 provinces to universalize compulsory education among disabled children. At that time 358,372 disabled children were enrolled in all types of schools, almost exclusively outside the mainstream system. The agreement provides for building and reconstructing special-education schools and training thousands of new special education teachers.

Chinese Education and Globalization

In 1999 China's State Council endorsed an "Action Plan for Vitalizing Education for the Twenty-First Century." The plan outlines the challenges facing Chinese education, including improving quality; enhancing teacher, vocational, moral, distance, and adult education; simultaneously expanding and improving tertiary education; and rationalizing educational law. China's leaders hope these initiatives will make high-quality, student-centered education more widely accessible, that they will encourage lifelong learning, and, ultimately, revitalize China.

How China handles its education challenges matters well beyond its national boundaries. Scholars and teachers worldwide look to China's educational system for inspiration. Students emerging from Chinese schools are shaping global patterns of the production of knowledge, especially in science and technology. Finally, collaborative scholarly networks, enhanced as increasing numbers of Chinese intellectuals participate in international scholarly and professional organizations, have lead to an explosion of research on Chinese education. These trends indicate that China will be a leader in educational reform in the twenty-first century.

Heidi A. Ross

Further Reading

Education for All: The Year 2000 Assessment Final Country Report of China. (2000) Beijing: Chinese National Commission for UNESCO.

Hannum, Emily. (1999) "Political Change and the Urban-Rural Gap in Education in China, 1949–1990." *Comparative Education Review* 43, 2: 192–211.

Lin, Jing, and Heidi Ross. 1998. "The Potentials and Problems of Diversity in Chinese Education." *McGill Journal of Education* 33, 1: 31–49.

Lin, Jing. (1999) *Social Transformation and Private Education in China.* Westport, CT: Praeger.

Liu, Judith, Heidi Ross, and Donald Kelly, eds. (2000) *The Ethnographic Eye: An Interpretive Study of Education in China.* New York: Falmer Press.

Postiglione, Gerard A., ed. (1999) *China's National Minority Education: Culture, Schooling, and Development.* New York: Falmer Press.

CHINA—HISTORY. See **Cultural Revolution; Han Dynasty; Jurchen Jin Dynasty; Long March; Ming Dynasty; Qin Dynasty; Qing Dynasty; Republican China; Shang Dynasty; Sino-Japanese War; Sino-Japanese Conflict, Second; Sui Dynasty; Tang Dynasty; Warring States Period—China; Xia Dynasty; Yuan Dynasty; Zhou Dynasty.**

CHINA—HUMAN RIGHTS
The history of human rights in China divides into three parts: the rallying cries of human rights activists, the political and academic arguments of the government and foreign scholars, and Beijing's suppression of human rights. The activists do not concern themselves with the intellectual or historical origins of human rights, or with their "Western" relationship to China. They are engaged in the application, not in the historical legitimacy of the rights. The cultural theorists argue whether China is exceptional and thus not part of the universal code of human rights, or whether China has a historical background that fostered human rights ideas. Beijing's actions have created a vast response of critics both inside and outside China.

Political Leaders and Movements
The earliest known discussions of human rights in China's context began in the late 1890s. Since the Chinese terminology was not standardized for several decades, the terms "natural law" (*tianfu*) and "human rights" (*renquan*) were used arbitrarily, just as they were in the West when Tom Paine introduced the term in 1791 in *The Rights of Man*. Revolutionaries such as Zou Jung (1885–1905) used a call to human rights to drive out the Manchu rulers and bring political freedom to the Chinese. Others changed their name to announce their new allegiance: Feng Zi-you means Freedom Feng; Liu Yazi, a lifelong advocate of human and women's rights and constitutionalism, became so infatuated with Rousseau's views that he changed his name to Liu Jenquan, or Human Rights Liu, when he was only sixteen in 1902.

The acceptance of human rights for China was not universal. Radicals and reformers like Liang Qichao (1873–1927) adopted a Darwinian and Spenserian view that denied the existence of human rights because all rights were considered to be created by the powerful. From this point of view, only the strongest survived. It was necessary for the state to become strong in order to protect the people, even if the people's rights were denied. What is significant in the criticism of human rights doctrine is that the argument is not based on Chinese values, but on Western criticism of human rights theory. The debate within China about human rights was a pragmatic one—would they strengthen or weaken China; not whether they were foreign or domestic.

The collapse of the Qing dynasty in 1911 ushered in a period of domestic and international chaos: warlords, Japanese intervention, the rise of nationalist reformers, and Communist revolutionaries. Sun Yat-sen, the founder of the Guomindang, disparaged the concept of human rights. All rights and power came from the political party or the state. People's rights were valid as long as they supported the state. Citizens who opposed the state lost their rights. These ideas were shared by the leaders of both the Nationalist government under Chiang Kai-shek, and the current Communist leadership.

Conversely, many early Nationalists and Communists supported the rights of the individual. Gao Yihan (1885–1968), a GMD leader, advocated for political and civil rights—freedom of speech, freedom of conscience, freedom of assembly, and rule by law. Chen Duxiu (1879–1942), one of the founders of the Communist Party, initially argued for civil and political rights in the tradition of the American and French revolutions. Li Dazhao (1888–1927), another founder of the Communist Party, stressed the socialist rights of economic and labor rights over the civil and political rights of the individual. But he did not renounce the traditional nineteenth-century definition of individual rights. His stress on people's rights (*min ben*) was related more to the ideas of socialism than to the Confucian stress on the people's livelihood.

During and after the May Fourth Movement of 1919, many journals debated the nature and the pros and cons of human rights. The most vigorous debates were published in *New Youth*, *New Tide*, and *Human Rights*. Freedom of thought and of publication clearly and naturally dominated the concerns of these editors. Human rights were not only necessary to protect the individual from the state, but even more important, were also necessary to provide for the dignity of the individual. Without rights, people would lose their human dignity and collapse into a state of slavery. It was the duty of both the citizen and the state to provide for the common good of all people.

The trend toward social utility was reinforced by the visits of John Dewey (1859–1952) and Bertrand Russell (1872–1970) to China and the writings of English idealists such as T. H. Green (1836–1882) and David George Ritchie (1853–1903), social liberals such as L. T. Hobhouse (1864–1929), and socialists such as Harold Laski (1893–1950). The popularization of terms such as freedom, democracy, and human rights made them part of the rhetorical framework of the 1920s. They were not always defined in academic terms because they were familiar and considered to be norms that were applicable to China's crisis.

The May Fourth Movement was not monolithic in its analysis of why human rights did not exist in China. The *New Tide* group felt that the tradition of Confucianism had caused the Chinese to repress their feelings

THE AMERICAN VIEW ON HUMAN RIGHTS IN CHINA

Criticism of Chinese human rights policies and practices by the United States is a continuing source of conflict in relations between the two nations. U.S. criticism is provided each year in the Country Reports on Human Rights published by the Bureau of Democracy, Human Rights, and Labor of the U.S. Department of State. The extract below is from the 1999 report on China released on 25 February 2000.

Section 2. Respect for Civil Liberties, Including:

a. Freedom of Speech and Press

The Constitution states that freedom of speech and of the press are fundamental rights to be enjoyed by all citizens; however, the Government restricts these rights in practice. The Government interprets the Communist Party's "leading role," as mandated in the preamble to the Constitution, as circumscribing these rights. The Government does not permit citizens to publish or broadcast criticisms of senior leaders or opinions that directly challenge Communist Party rule. The Party and Government continue to control many—and, on occasion, all—print and broadcast media tightly and use them to propagate the current ideological line. There are more than 10,000 openly distributed publications, including 2,500 newspapers. All media employees are under explicit, public orders to follow CCP directives, and "guide public opinion" as directed by political authorities. Both formal and informal guidelines continue to require journalists to avoid coverage of many politically sensitive topics. Journalists also must not divulge "state secrets" in accordance with the State Security Law. These public orders, guidelines, and statutes greatly restrict the freedom of broadcast journalists and newspapers to report the news and lead to a high degree of self-censorship. Overall, during the year press freedom deteriorated further. During the early part of the year, newspaper closures or suspensions increased; efforts by the authorities to block the reception of foreign news also increased during the year, particularly prior to sensitive anniversaries.

More than in recent years, the press was exploited by the Government as an effective propaganda tool to disseminate an official line. For example, in its press coverage of NATO's action against Serbia, NATO was depicted as bent on using the conflict in Kosovo as an excuse to expand its influence. Casualties caused by NATO attacks on Serb forces received prominent coverage, but there was almost no mention of the plight of ethnic Albanian Kosovars. The Government's manipulation of the press to mold public opinion had violent results when demonstrators targeted foreign diplomatic facilities in Beijing after NATO's mistaken bombing of the Chinese embassy in Belgrade.

Journalists were given explicit instructions during the year to minimize coverage of negative issues and emphasize positive achievement in preparation for the October 1 celebration of the 50th anniversary of the founding of the PRC. The general worsening of the political atmosphere greatly increased the tendency of journalists, writers, and publishers to censor themselves.

Source: Bureau of Democracy, Human Rights, and Labor, U.S. Department of State. (2000) "China." In *1999 Country Reports on Human Rights Practices* (25 February). Retrieved 12 October 2001 from: http://www.state.gov/www/global/human_rights/1999_hrp_report/china.html.

and their sense of dignity. The *New Youth* writers, Chen Duxiu, Li Dazhao, and Gao Yihan blamed the government and the warlords for violating what they claimed were their rights of freedom of thought, assembly, and representation in government.

During the Nanjing Decade, 1927–1937, and the war against Japan, 1937–1945, many of these debates became moot. The commitment to national salvation against the Japanese and the civil war between the Nationalists and Communists created a military campaign mentality. The debate transformed to questions of dictatorship versus democracy. Nonetheless, liberals and scholars such as Hu Shi (1891–1962), Luo Longji (c. 1898–1965), Zhang Junmai (1886–1969), and Zhang Pengqun (1892–1957), also known as P. C. Chang, and organizations such as the *Xinyue* Group, the China League for Civil Rights, and the China Democratic League vigorously argued for the adoption of human rights, though from very different, and often contradictory, perspectives. Hu Shi argued for both civil and economic rights. For him, human rights were universal and were to be established in the legal and constitutional system of the Republic of China, a stance that created a backlash in the GMD, which attacked him for his views and passed laws that were even more authoritarian.

Luo's views were directly related to Harold Laski's argument that human rights were historical and contextual. Rights and laws reflected the needs of the social and economic system. They should be used functionally to create a safer and more wholesome society. At times, the individual's freedom may need to be curtailed. Zhang Junmai attempted to synthesize the humanism of neo-Confucianism with the philosophical perspective of human rights. He believed that China's traditional ethics, which were based on conscious and promoted human dignity, were not only the best approach to legitimizing human rights and democracy, but that, in fact, China may also have been the real source for the West's views of human rights.

P. C. Chang was China's chief representative to the Commission on Human Rights, which created the Universal Declaration of Human Rights. He is given credit for Article 1, which refused to claim that rights were based on natural law or divine inspiration. Faintly, echoing Zhang Zhunmai, Chang stressed the innateness of dignity and conscience.

Human Rights with Chinese Characteristics

The establishment of the People's Republic of China in 1949 resulted in a total rejection of the legitimacy of human rights arguments. Human rights were a product of the bourgeoisie and were thus used to maintain the rule of the capitalist and imperialist class. With a few but startling exceptions in 1957 and 1978, any mention of human rights was taboo and resulted in imprisonment.

However, just before and after the massacre of pro-democracy students in Tiananmen Square (4 June 1989), the Communist authorities began to engage in the human rights debate to justify their authority and their rule. In 1991 a white paper on human rights declaimed that: "Since the very day of its founding, the Communist Party of China has been holding high the banner of democracy and human rights." This stunning declaration was followed up with academic conferences on human rights and the creation of several institutes especially devoted to human rights, such as the China Society for Study on Human Rights. From 1995 to 1998 the Confucius Foundation in Beijing sponsored a series of international forums with the purpose of discussing Confucius and Human Rights. By the late 1990s, Beijing signed the two covenants on economic, social, and cultural rights.

The study of human rights in China is initiated and managed by the Communist Party and the government. It has not included meetings with Chinese citizens or with local nongovernmental organizations active in human rights. The official position is that China has developed a socialist system of human rights with Chinese characteristics. Stages of economic and industrial development determine the scope and quality of human rights. Liu Huaqiu, head of the Chinese delegation at the Vienna World Conference on Human rights in 1993 defined the Chinese view succinctly:

> The concept of human rights is a product of historical development. It is closely associated with specific social, political and economic conditions and the specific history, culture and values of a particular country. Different historical development stages have different human rights requirements. Countries at different development stages or with different historical traditions and cultural backgrounds also have different understanding and practice of human rights.

From this point of view, the most basic rights are those of subsistence and shelter. These "economic" rights are considered superior to, and of greater priority than, political and civil rights.

There is more to the definition than a mere enunciation of domestic policy. China argues that America and the West use the invasive argument that human rights are universal to force China to peacefully evolve into a colony of Western economic and political control. Beijing does not argue that Chinese cultural (e.g., Confucianism) values prevent it from accepting Westernization. Rather, it is China's anti-imperialist stand and its desire to create its own national identity in the twenty-first century that makes it refuse to accept standards that serve the interests of Washington, D.C.

Beijing's Repression of Human Rights

The Chinese government has maintained that its sovereignty excludes foreign powers from interfering in its affairs. It has adamantly refused to allow independent agencies to investigate openly and report on its alleged human rights abuses. According to its critics, China has engaged in massive abuse of human rights. With regard to political and civil rights, it has tortured and executed prisoners of conscience, repressed religious organizations, prohibited democratic organizations and meetings, arrested and detained people without trial, and engaged in widespread abuse and repression of women, the unemployed, minorities, and the poor. The Chinese leadership has been accused of long-term genocidal practices against the Tibetan people. Contrary to the Beijing's claim that it favors economic and social rights, it has been accused of destroying the environment, censoring the educational system, exploiting workers, and engaging in organized official corruption.

The Tiananmen Square Massacre resulted in a massive amount of attention to human rights conditions in China. The call for human rights became widespread, though underground, in China, and was openly publicized by Chinese groups abroad. Wang Dan, Wuer Kaixi, and other leaders of the student movement found exile in America and Europe, where they organized resistance groups and published journals such as *China Spring*. American human rights organizations joined forces: Amnesty International and Asia Watch were joined by online sources—Tibet On Line Resource Gathering, and Asia Observer. The U.S. government's pressure on China to adhere to human rights standards was most visible in the arguments surrounding the congressional review of China's Most-Favored-Nation status and the arguments over entry to the World Trade Organization. The most sensational and informative moment for the Chinese citizenry came on 30 June 1998, when President Bill Clinton spoke on the "Shanghai Radio 990" call-in show. Broadcasting to China's largest city, the president declared, "whatever differences of opinion we have about what human rights policy ought to be . . . we still have a lot in common . . . . I believe that the forces of history will bring about more convergence in our societies going forward."

Beijing's response to these overtures has been negative. A diatribe entitled *The China That Can Say No* best expresses the voluminous official reactions to the human rights movement. It counters the arguments by exposing America's human rights abuses and the hypocrisy of the leadership. In the United Nations Commission on Human Rights, Beijing's diplomats claim their right of sovereignty and denounce what they depict as fallaciousness of the attacks on their integrity. Human rights activities in China are considered to be antigovernment in nature and result in harsh punishment. China also considers America's campaigns and support of human rights to be an extension of America's imperialistic attitudes. Thus, the creation and development of human rights remains primarily a political, not a cultural, response to repressive regimes. In the early twenty-first century, the struggle for human rights continues.

Richard C. Kagan

Further Reading
de Bary, William Theodore, and Tu Weiming, eds. (1998) *Confucianism and Human Rights.* New York: Columbia University Press.
Edwards, R. Randle, Louis Henkins, and Andrew J. Nathan, eds. (1986) *Human Rights in Contemporary China.* New York: Columbia University Press.
Kelly, David, and Anthony Reid, eds. (1998) *Asian Freedoms: The Idea of Freedom in East and Southeast Asia.* Cambridge, U.K.: Cambridge University Press.
Ness, Peter Van, ed. (1999) *Debating Human Rights: Critical Essays from the United States and Asia.* New York: Routledge.
Svensson, Marina. (1997) *The Chinese Conception of Human Rights in China, 1898–1949.* Lund, Sweden: University of Lund. (Will be republished by University of California Press.)

CHINA—INTERNAL MIGRATION From the 1950s to late 1978, strict controls limited population mobility in China. Even by the time of the 1982 census, China still had a very low level of migration to urban areas for a country at its level of development.

Pre-Reform Migration
In the early 1950s, rural migrants moved to the cities in large numbers. Estimates suggest that from 1949 to 1953 the urban population grew by twenty million, 70 percent of which was attributable to migration. To combat the growing pressure on housing, transportation, education, and health facilities, a system designed to monitor population movement was introduced in 1951. Through a series of regulations culminating in the "Regulations of Household Registration in the People's Republic of China" issued in 1958, the Chinese government developed perhaps the strictest set of controls over the movement of population in the modern world. The basis of control was the *hukou*, or household registration system. Deriving from China's traditional household registration system, it also incorporated elements of the labor registration system of the Soviet Union. Under the system

each household possessed a registration book listing its members and categorizing the household as "agricultural" or "nonagricultural." This division has become a fundamental social divide in China, producing what has been called "a castelike system of social stratification" that keeps the peasants on the land and reinforces a spatial hierarchy in which Beijing, Shanghai, and the other big cities are considered the most desirable places to live and therefore the most difficult to move to.

Under the planned economy with overwhelming state control, people were supposed to reside and work only where they had their *hukou*; any stay in other places over three days needed to be registered at the police station. Transfer of *hukou* was granted only under such circumstances as an assignment to a job in another area or a marriage across administrative boundaries. The *hukou* was the passport to employment and the rations that were issued only locally.

Despite the severe restrictions, considerable rural-to-urban migration still existed. According to official estimates, between 25 and 30 million people obtained *hukou* transfers from one province to another between 1949 and 1978. This figure does not include *hukou* migration within provinces, which would have been of a greater magnitude, or unsanctioned, non-*hukou* migration.

The government organized both economic and political oriented migrations during this period. Economic migrations primarily involved skilled workers in large-scale development projects and students pursuing higher education. In the 1950s peasants were officially recruited into the urban labor force and given nonagricultural status. Later they would be recruited as contract workers for the urban labor force. At the same time, more than 1 million people were moved from heavily populated areas of Shangdong Province to open up sparsely populated areas elsewhere between 1955 and 1960, while in January 1959 it was announced that Zhejing Province was to send 300,000 young people to help develop Ningxia Province. Large public-works projects also forced significant migrations; by the mid-1980s, more than 5 million people had been moved to make way for reservoir construction.

Political migrations included job assignments to frontier areas such as Xinjiang, Inner Mongolia, and Tibet; punishment or political exile; and conscription. Punishment and political exile produced some of the most substantial urban-to-rural migration of the period. It is estimated that between 400,000 and 700,000 rightists were exiled to the rural areas in 1957, where some were to stay for more than twenty years. During the Cultural Revolution urban areas sustained a net loss of almost five million people to rural exile. Individuals who had been politically disgraced were sent for particularly long periods, but ordinary intellectuals and cadres were also sent to the countryside to undergo months or even years of labor reform. In the early 1970s, some 20 million Red Guards were directed to go to the villages for reeducation.

Apart from those organized migrations, spontaneous permanent migrations are estimated to have involved at least 10 million people from 1949 to the mid-1980s. Most spontaneous migrants were peasants continuing migration patterns established before restrictions were imposed. However, before the economic reforms of the late 1970s institutional barriers to migration imposed by the government made movement from a village to an urban area as difficult as movement across national borders elsewhere in the world.

Internal Migration since 1978

The scale of internal migration in China increased enormously with the advent of economic reforms. Figures commonly given for the migrant population vary from 40 to as high as 100 million. Migrants are generally divided into three categories: those who have crossed an administrative border with official permission (*qianyi renkou*), the floating population (*liudong renkou*) or "blind migrants" (*mangliu*) without official permission, and temporary contractual laborers from the rural areas (*mingong*). The floating population in the biggest cities is estimated to form between one-fifth and one-third of their total population. Big cities everywhere have attracted very large numbers, but migrants also go to rapidly industrializing areas such as the Pearl River Delta in Guangdong Province and the towns of southern Jiangsu.

The majority of migrations in China are within the same province. According to the 1990 census, between 1985 and 1990 there were more than 23 million movements within provinces, compared to more than 11 million between provinces. Available data indicate that approximately one-third of migration was interprovincial in 1990, representing rapid change from 1988, when less than one-fifth of migration had been interprovincial. Migrants from the eastern region tend to stay closer to their native areas, whereas migrants from the less developed central and western regions are more likely to travel to the more developed seaboard provinces, especially those of southeastern China.

Four major reasons have been commonly identified in migration during the reform era: urban-rural disparity, rural surplus labor, development of township and village enterprises (TVEs) and urbanization of rural towns, and business opportunities. Indeed, rapid economic development has offered tremendous job opportunities to migrant workers.

Although it became much easier to move from one area to another after 1978, household registration has remained extremely difficult to change. In 1985 the Ministry of Public Security issued a new regulation on temporary residence certificates for the urban areas. Migrant workers who have obtained these are allowed to live in the urban areas but do not enjoy the social benefits to which permanent urban residents are entitled.

The impact of migration is varied. It has given some people the chance to lift themselves out of poverty and to acquire new skills. At the same time, the influx of rural migrants has caused the urban infrastructure considerable strain. Many migrants lead difficult lives in overcrowded and unsanitary conditions. While migrant earnings have brought new wealth to the countryside, some fear that the departure of so many young, educated residents will be to the detriment of rural society. However, there is no doubt that by providing cheap labor and filling in economic vacuums, migrants have made major contributions to China's economic success.

Xiaobo Hu

See also: **China—Population Resettlement; Rural Workers, Surplus—China**

Further Reading
Davin, Delia. (1999) *Internal Migration in Contemporary China*. New York: St. Martin's Press.
Day, Lincoln H., and Ma Xia, eds. (1994) *Migration and Urbanization in China*. Armonk, NY: M. E. Sharpe.
Solinger, Dorothy. (1993) "Chinese Transients and the State: A Form of Civil Society?" *Politics and Society* 21, 1: 91–122.

CHINA—POLITICAL SYSTEM
China lags far behind other world powers in official government interest in democracy. This curious state of affairs cannot be fully explained historically. After all, every contemporary democracy has a nondemocratic past. But in China the past weighs unusually heavily.

A Tradition That Scorned Politics
Since before 500 BCE, politics in China were more social than institutional. In the past, various philosophical schools had contended, and something of a feudal structure had been evident, with healthy competition among aristocratic clans, emperor, and officialdom. But long before the People's Republic of China (PRC) was

founded in 1949, Confucianism overwhelmed other schools of thought, aristocracy faded, and emperor and officialdom fused into a unitary, though decentralized, overwhelmingly Confucian state. Ideas of popular sovereignty, rule of law, separation of powers, federalism, and checks and balances never blossomed under this stiflingly rigid tradition. Rather than favoring limited government achieved through fragmenting authority, the ideal was to achieve good government through a state with a virtuous ruler, resembling a family with a benevolent, protective father.

New Politics That Scorned Tradition
Twentieth-century Chinese political movements felt the need to look abroad for fresh ideas. European Marxism appealed more than European democracy, probably because although it was "modern" it differed less dramatically from traditional Chinese notions of power. Chinese tradition mixed with Marxism to create a hybrid ideology known as the political thought of Mao Zedong (1893–1976), which seemed to fit social revolution, a new intellectual orthodoxy, and a new centralized and unitary state better than did chaotic competitive democracy. Political-reform debates still turn on how global standards of democracy, human rights, markets, and private property with Chinese characteristics might be adopted. The weakness of old forms is criticized more sharply than the old forms themselves, inviting revivalist themes. Today, one official view (no longer limited to Mao's thought), one core leader, a single pyramid of state power, and a single Communist Party remain stronger ideals than do institutions that might divide and restrain state power.

From Scorn to Halting Reform
Having rejected almost every state form at one time or another, the PRC today faces the problem of what form to accept. China has rejected democracy in favor of Marxism, Marxism in favor of Mao's thought, and Mao's thought in favor of a less coherent "practical" approach to orthodoxy. China has rejected a constitutional state in favor of a Stalinist state, the familiar Stalin model in favor of a mobilizational Maoist variant (emphasizing ideological themes, political education meetings, mass rallies to demonstrate loyalty), and the Maoist variant in favor of a state more insulated from its ruling party. China has rejected liberal political parties in favor of a Leninist Communist party and now is deeply ambivalent about that move. In fact, even while strongly rejecting the idea of private factions, China has rejected any firm institutional direction in favor of more personal rule by factional elders. China today is more certain of what it does not want

than of what it does want. After several disruptive, occasionally violent spasms of experimentation, political change at the PRC's half-century mark proceeds cautiously, incrementally, and practically.

China's political system, far from a static structure, has evolved through a sequence of momentous cycles and continues to evolve, if less tumultuously. Each phase has added to the accomplishments of the previous one.

1949–1954

The phase from 1949 to 1954 opened with the Communist takeover of China and with land redistribution, party building, and struggle against U.N. intervention in Korea. It ended with the proclamation of a new state constitution. Characteristically, the new constitution was not a vigorously bargained popular grant of authority. Rather, as China's leader put it, "This Draft Constitution of ours is chiefly a summing-up of our experience in revolution and construction, but at the same time it is a synthesis of domestic and international experience" (Mao Zedong 1954: 141–147).

The PRC's first five years witnessed China's assertion of autonomy. China was no longer a territory occupied by a foreign army, a semicolony with its commerce dominated by foreign companies, or a divided society with a weak center—the one that served tea at meetings of international powers. The strong appeal of the new order was that a new China had stood up. Chinese abroad yearned to return and contribute to the glorious national project of building the new China.

The party-army that finally mounted a victorious military campaign after twenty years of rural guerrilla warfare abruptly faced the task of governing. And surprisingly quickly, images of wide-eyed peasants marching into cosmopolitan Shanghai were replaced with images of confidence. The Communists' patriotic credentials, hard won during years of resistance to Japanese occupation, were enhanced as they sent foreigners packing, confiscated foreign property, closed foreign missions, and within a year were fighting U.N. and American troops to a standstill in Korea.

In urban areas, with demonstrative political campaigns and draconian tactics, the Chinese Communist Party (CCP) took charge of seaports, swiftly clamped down on coastal smuggling, opium dens, and prostitution rings, and established effective control of banking, national security, and foreign policy. Not only was the party patriotic, it was also strong. Elites of the old regime were assured that patriotic service to the new

CHAIRMAN MAO ON THE BASIS OF THE CHINESE POLITICAL SYSTEM

"Wherever our comrades go, they must build good relations with the masses, be concerned for them and help them overcome their difficulties. We must unite with the masses; the more of the masses we unite with, the better."

Source: Mao Zedong (1976). *Quotations from Chairman Mao Tsetung.* Beijing: Foreign Language Press, 154.

order would be welcome. In rural areas, where the party presence was thinner, mobile work teams led sometimes-violent public rebuke of landlords and redistribution of property. For the first time in over a century, the nation was not embroiled in civil or foreign war. The new regime's standing would never be higher.

Nonetheless, after five years, despite political successes and despite aggressive party building, the first national census, a formal state constitution, and borrowed Soviet-style enterprises and civilian and military bureaucracies, the shape of the new political system had yet to be drawn.

1955–1961

The phase from 1955 to 1961 opened with a stepped-up pace of agricultural collectivization and early moves by Chairman Mao to stem loss of personal power to party leaders with factional networks. It passed through a bizarre attempt to reorganize rural China into radical "people's communes." It ended with Mao recovering from the visible failure of his "Great Leap Forward" experiment.

Yearning to perpetuate the politics that allowed his movement to rise to power, Mao felt he had to motivate succeeding generations to carry on the spirit of revolution. He maneuvered to establish a "correct" view of the political world, encourage universal study of it, and mobilize popular support directly without having to filter his message through channels controlled by CCP factions and bureaucracies.

An early battleground was rural property. Concerned that small landholders could not go it alone and that a controlling landlord class might revive, Mao

PREAMBLE TO THE CONSTITUTION OF CHINA

Adopted on 4 Dec 1982

China is a country with one of the longest histories in the world. The people of all of China's nationalities have jointly created a culture of grandeur and have a glorious revolutionary tradition.

After 1840, feudal China was gradually turned into a semi-colonial and semi-feudal country. The Chinese people waged many successive heroic struggles for national independence and liberation and for democracy and freedom.

Great and earthshaking historical changes have taken place in China in the 20th century.

The Revolution of 1911, led by Dr. Sun Yat-sen, abolished the feudal monarchy and gave birth to the Republic of China. But the historic mission of the Chinese people to overthrow imperialism and feudalism remained unaccomplished.

After waging protracted and arduous struggles, armed and otherwise, along a zigzag course, the Chinese people of all nationalities led by the Communist Party of China with Chairman Mao Zedong as its leader ultimately, in 1949, overthrew the rule of imperialism, feudalism and bureaucrat-capitalism, won a great victory in the New-Democratic Revolution and founded the People's Republic of China. Since then the Chinese people have taken control of state power and become masters of the country.

After founding the People's Republic, China gradually achieved its transition from a New-Democratic to a socialist society. The socialist transformation of the private ownership of the means of production has been completed, the system of exploitation of man by man abolished and the socialist system established. The people's democratic dictatorship held by the working class and based on the alliance of workers and peasants, which is in essence the dictatorship of the proletariat, has been consolidated and developed. The Chinese people and the Chinese People's Liberation Army have defeated imperialist and hegemonist aggression, sabotage and armed provocations and have thereby safeguarded China's national independence and security and strengthened its national defense. Major successes have been achieved in economic development. An independent and relatively comprehensive socialist system of industry has basically been established. There has been a marked increase in agricultural production. Significant advances have been made in educational, scientific and cultural undertakings, while education in socialist ideology has produced noteworthy results. The life of the people has improved considerably.

Both the victory in China's New-Democratic Revolution and the successes in its socialist cause have been achieved by the Chinese people of all nationalities, under the leadership of the Communist Party of China and the guidance of Marxism and Leninism and Mao Zedong Thought, by upholding truth, correcting errors and surmounting numerous difficulties and hardships. The basic task of the nation in the years to come is to concentrate its effort on socialist modernization. Under the leadership of the Communist Party of China and the guidance of Marxism-Leninism and Mao Zedong Thought, the Chinese people of all nationalities will continue to adhere to the people's democratic dictatorship and the socialist road, steadily improve socialist institutions, develop socialist democracy, improve the socialist legal system, and work hard and self-reliantly to modernize the country's industry, agriculture, national defense and science and technology step by step to turn China into a socialist country with a high level of culture and democracy.

The exploiting classes as such have been abolished in our country. However, class struggle will continue to exist within certain bounds for a long time to come. The Chinese people must fight against those forces and elements, both at home and abroad, that are hostile to China's socialist system and try to undermine it.

Taiwan is part of the sacred territory of the People's Republic of China. It is the inviolable duty of all Chinese people, including our com-

CONTINUED ON NEXT PAGE

CONTINUED FROM PREVIOUS PAGE

patriots in Taiwan, to accomplish the great task of reunifying the motherland.

In building socialism it is essential to rely on workers, peasants and intellectuals and to unite all forces that can be united. In the long years of revolution and construction, there has been formed under the leadership of the Communist Party of China a broad patriotic united front which is composed of the democratic parties and people's organizations and which embraces all socialist working people, all patriots who support socialism and all patriots who stand for the reunification of the motherland. This united front will continue to be consolidated and developed. The Chinese People's Political Consultative Conference, a broadly based representative organization of the united front which has played a significant historical role, will play a still more important role in the country's political and social life, in promoting friendship with other countries and in the struggle for socialist modernization and for the reunification and unity of the country.

The People's Republic of China is a unitary multi-national state created jointly by the people of all its nationalities. Socialist relations of equality, unity and mutual assistance have been established among the nationalities and will continue to be strengthened. In the struggle to safeguard the unity of the nationalities, it is necessary to combat big-nation chauvinism, mainly Han chauvinism, and to combat local national chauvinism. The state will do its utmost to promote the common prosperity of all the nationalities.

China's achievements in revolution and construction are inseparable from the support of the people of the world. The future of China is closely linked to the future of the world. China consistently carries out an independent foreign policy and adheres to the five principles of mutual respect for sovereignty and territorial integrity, mutual non-aggression, non-interference in each other's internal affairs, equality and mutual benefit, and peaceful coexistence in developing diplomatic relations and economic and cultural exchanges with other countries. China consistently opposes imperialism, hegemonism and colonialism, works to strengthen unity with people of other countries, supports the oppressed nations and the developing countries in their just struggle to win and preserve national independence and develop national economies, and strives to safeguard world peace and promote the cause of human progress.

This Constitution, in legal form, affirms the achievements of the struggles of the Chinese people of all nationalities and defines the basic system and basic tasks of the state; it is the fundamental law of the state and has supreme legal authority. The people of all nationalities, all state organs, the armed forces, all political parties and public organizations and all enterprises and institutions in the country must take the Constitution as the basic standard of conduct, and they have the duty to uphold the dignity of the Constitution and ensure its implementation.

Source: International Court Network. Retrieved 8 March 8, 2002, from: http://www.uni-wuerzburg.de/law/ch00000_.html.

advocated collective ownership. He pressed against mounting opposition for higher and higher levels of collectivization, from small Mutual Aid Teams to various forms of collective farm and finally giant People's Communes, some embracing thousands of families. At their zenith, the communes were a vehicle for Mao's Great Leap Forward (1958–1960), which assumed that peasants with proper political motivation could sharply raise production of everything from food to steel. Twenty-five thousand communes were hastily organized in four months. Approaching truly communist social organization, this experiment was the biggest, most radical in history.

The political system changed dramatically, to put the leader in direct communication with the public, bypassing established organizations. When Mao's opponents tried to use his failed Great Leap Forward program against him, he parried with renewed radicalism. Considering the CCP unsympathetic now, he promoted a political style designed to weaken the CCP in favor of dominance by the chairman. He began a campaign to emulate ideological study as practiced in the army, tighter censorship (by a central office not run by the party), purges of commune leaders (by central work teams not controlled by the party), and an open break with "revisionist" (no longer really Marxist) Moscow. Cumulatively these initiatives weakened institution building in favor of personal leadership.

1962–1969

The phase from 1962 to 1969 opened with the unfolding of Mao's counterattack, passed through the first three chaotic and often-violent years of the Great Proletarian Cultural Revolution (1966–1969), during which the party actually ceased to function, and ended with the party's first National Congress in thirteen years. None of the specific political innovations of those three years lasted. Rather, their extremes afterward made possible a lurch in the opposite direction.

In contrast to the Great Leap Forward, the Cultural Revolution—especially during its first three years—was urban more than rural and was aimed at political organization more than economics. While party, army, and government were told to stand by passively, student and worker groups with militant names formed, arrested Mao's opponents, humiliated them with public parades and trials, and even commandeered weapons from army barracks to fight opposing groups in the streets. China recalled its foreign diplomats, withdrew from foreign trade, and shut out foreign culture. In addition to being ideological, the Cultural Revolution was strongly nativist.

Mao was seventy-five and suffering from Parkinson's disease when the CCP revived in 1969. At the end, his stature and reputation were as important as his program and strategic maneuvers. The political system almost froze as the chairman of thirty-five years withdrew from day-to-day leadership, but his authority remained uncontested. The pendulum swung left for the last time.

1970–1978

The 1970s continued the tumult with an attempt on Mao's life, followed by reopening of diplomatic relations with the United States. It progressed through Mao's last moves to keep his revolutionary vision alive, his death in 1976, and a two-year "moment" of controlled succession under Chairman Hua Guofeng. It ended with the rise of a leading target of the Cultural Revolution, Deng Xiaoping, in 1978. So heavily personal was Mao's regime that it could not survive him for more than two years.

Under Deng and his supporters, the pendulum swung dramatically to the right. But while locking arms to reject Mao's legacy, Deng and his supporters differed on what to put in its place. Some advocated a return to the Stalinist 1950s before the Great Leap Forward. Others advocated forward-looking experiments with markets and democracy. Popular sentiments reinforced each side. Many people, fearing unemployment and chaos, yearned for effective government, whatever its form. Many others, fearing old-style corruption and privilege, favored legal, market, and democratic reforms. Underneath it all was spreading economic and social complexity that would gradually tilt the balance toward government with expanding individual and associational autonomy.

1979–1989

The 1980s opened with a multipronged reform program to undo Mao's style. Out went ideological study, political campaigns, communes, and party control of every organization (except the army, a hierarchy of its own). In came a private sector, foreign investment, Chinese study abroad, and private hiring of labor (Marx's bedrock objection to capitalism because it treated people as commodities). Only politics were slow to change. Limited proposals for more democracy, freedom, and rule of law were voiced but stifled. A two-month occupation of Tiananmen Square in Beijing, outside the top leaders' compound, by student demonstrators campaigning for these proposals ended violently. The shooting of hundreds of demonstrators near the square on 4 June 1989 silenced the immediate protest but made reform of such authority a virtual necessity for the next generation.

1990–2002

At the twentieth century's end, China's political system was pushed by necessity more than it was pulled by design. Although the leaders remained unchallenged for office, their hold on power was in danger of eroding. China's authoritarian state had entered a period of gridlock and reactive evolution. The possibility of decisive restructuring toward any form of democracy seemed remote.

Today elite figures who prefer the pre–Great Leap Forward era are a voice for control, order, and planning. They have succeeded at that style of politics, trust it, and feel secure as long as it prevails. Their public is unemployed, economically insecure, or simply most comfortable with socialism and a paternalistic state.

Elite figures who prefer more law, markets, and democracy are a voice for reform. They mostly want China to grow strong and prosperous, and they observe the strongest and most prosperous nations to be capitalist democracies. Their public finds opportunity in the expanding private sector and a more narrowly defined role for government.

Lifting prospects of the reform side are trends that naturally make Chinese society more complex and hence less amenable to political interference. Markets rely on one another and on private banking, insurance, and law. Foreign investors expect internationally agreed commercial rules to apply. China's thriving private firms far outperform state-owned firms; a government wary of high unemployment and attendant crime and social unrest badly needs these private contributions. Young Chinese educated abroad introduce competitive innovations that their elders only dimly comprehend. Satellite communications and the Internet, both mushrooming all over China, bring information that no official censor can delete.

Eerily like the empire of old, authoritarian one-party rule in China may continue only insofar as it learns to live with these irrepressible social developments. If it tries to stifle them, most likely it will be discarded.

Institutions: Shrinking Scope, Growing Importance

The Chinese political system still has a leader, although he is less dominant than previously. The CCP continues to dominate, although a challenging party probably is not far away, given China's growing freedom. A few senior factional leaders still control the dominant party. The system remains hierarchical and formally centralized, although it is losing some control to increasingly active provinces. Actual federalism, though, as with other limits on central authority, remains elusive. State ideology is all but dead. The formerly rubber-stamp National People's Congress is beginning to assert a more standard, autonomous legislative role. And leaders are beginning to accept constitutional term limits.

The People's Liberation Army (PLA)—embracing air, land, naval, and strategic forces totaling at least 2.5 million, the world's largest military—seems destined to fall into line, although it remains unusually free of civilian authority and even has its own stake in the new economy. The leadership has made it a priority to ease the PLA out of the civilian economy. The stage is set for younger leaders to replace retiring senior generals by 2003. And public discussion of military doctrine is increasingly focused on high-tech modernization. Reining in the military may prove to be the most enduring legacy of Jiang Zemin—general secretary of the CCP (1992–2002), president (1993–2003), and chairman of the Central Military Commission (1992–present). How China evolves is actually part of a much larger story that matches relative political values deriving from various national cultures'

own historical experiences against political values stemming from the universal philosophical appeal of democracy.

Gordon A. Bennett

See also: **Communism—China; Confucianism—China; Cultural Revolution—China; Deng Xiaoping; Great Leap Forward; Jiang Zemin; Mao Zedong**

Further Reading
Davis, Deborah. (1995) *Urban Spaces in Contemporary China: The Potential for Community in Post-Mao China.* New York: Cambridge University Press.
Fewsmith, Joseph. (2000) *Elite Politics in Contemporary China.* Armonk, NY: M. E. Sharpe.
Macfarquhar, Roderick, ed. (1997) *The Politics of China: The Eras of Mao and Deng.* New York: Cambridge University Press.
Mao Zedong. (1954) "On the Draft Constitution of the People's Republic of China." In *Selected Works.* Beijing: Foreign Language Press, 5: 141–147.
Schell, Orville, and David Shambaugh. (1999) *The China Reader: The Reform Era.* New York: Random House.
Shambaugh, David, ed. (2000) *The Modern Chinese State.* New York: Cambridge University Press.
Terrill, Ross. (1999) *Mao: A Biography.* Rev. ed. Stanford, CA: Stanford University Press.
Yang, Dali. (1997) *Beyond Beijing: Liberalization and the Regions in China.* New York: Routledge.

CHINA—POPULATION RESETTLEMENT
Compared with Westerners, the Chinese are relatively immobile. China's 1990 census and sample surveys during the 1990s estimated that on average less than 1 percent of the Chinese population move to another city or county each year. Even after taking into account migrants missed by the criteria used in these sources, the mobility of the Chinese is still far lower than that in Western societies. Until the 1980s, China was an overwhelmingly agricultural nation whose sedentary, family-centered production system discouraged mobility; when large-scale population movements did occur, they were usually caused by natural disasters or wars. The varieties, processes, and outcomes of population relocations that have occurred since the 1980s are useful lenses through which one can gauge the tremendous political, social, and economic transformations China has experienced.

Historical Population Relocations
For thousands of years the dominant form of population movement in China was that of peasants searching for new arable land. As they left the middle region and delta of the Yellow River—the cradles and

origins of Chinese civilization—they shifted the nation's political and economic center of gravity toward the south. During the Han dynasty (202 BCE–220 CE), the vast majority of the Chinese population resided north of the Chang (Yangtze) River. By the Tang dynasty (618–907 CE), the Chang River Delta and Sichuan (in western China) had emerged as new centers of settlement; by the Ming dynasty (1368–1644) the Chang River Delta had become the most densely populated area in.

The southward movements of population were further accelerated by political turmoil and invasions from the north. Invasions by the Xiongnu and other "barbarians" during the Wei, Jin, and Northern and Southern dynasties (220–581), rebellions at the end of the Tang dynasty, and invasions by the Jin at the end of the Northern Song dynasty (960–1126), for example, all triggered large-scale population relocations toward southern China.

Government-Initiated Population Relocations Since 1949

The government of the People's Republic of China that was founded in 1949 has repeatedly initiated "planned" population relocations to achieve specific policy objectives. In the early 1950s, the government sent troops, farmers, and youths to northwestern and northeastern border areas such as Xinjiang and Heilongjiang, where they were to reclaim so-called wastelands and set up state farms. That would achieve the dual objectives of consolidating ethnic Han Chinese control over border areas and accelerating the economic development of those regions. Similarly, national security concerns motivated the government to relocate industries and personnel to "Third Front" inland regions during the 1950s and 1960s, driven by the rationale that coastal areas were too vulnerable during times of war.

Between the late 1960s and mid-1970s millions of educated youths were forced to leave urban areas and go "up to the mountains and down to the countryside" (xiangshan xiaxiang) to be reeducated by farmers. This rustication movement was a product of the Cultural Revolution; the young people were joined out in the countryside by the the politically persecuted and counterrevolutionaries. After the end of the Cultural Revolution in 1976, however, the majority of these victims of forced relocation were able to return to where they had come from.

Government-initiated relocations since the 1980s have been mainly oriented toward economic development objectives. For example, poverty-alleviation programs have relocated hundreds of thousands of people from resource-poor areas to locations in more favorable environments. In addition, the construction of the Three Gorges Dam that began in the late 1990s necessitates the relocation of over a million people, mostly to newly constructed towns and communities near their original homes.

Household Registration, Mobility Control, and Self-Initiated Migrations

A hallmark of the Chinese centrally planned economy is the household registration (hukou) system, established in the late 1950s and still functioning as a means of state control in the late 1990s. Every person in China has a hukou that indicates where he/she legitimately dwells. During the 1960s and 1970s, hukou entitled individuals to rationed food and clothing. Three decades later, a local hukou is still essential for obtaining subsidized benefits such as housing, schooling, and health care. It is extremely difficult for peasants to obtain urban hukou or to transfer their hukou to urban areas, thus making their survival in urban areas almost impossible. For decades, then, the hukou system served as an effective damper on self-initiated, rural-urban migrations and divided China into two separate entities, one rural and one urban. At the same time, until the 1990s the government was the main agent of labor allocation, via job assignments to graduates and job transfers for state employees. Government-sponsored work-related relocations are typically accompanied by hukou transfers that legitimize the migrants' residence in the new location.

From the 1980s, strong push forces in the countryside and new pull forces in urban areas have compelled the government to relax migration control. The mammoth rural labor surplus, estimated as up to one-sixth of the population, urgently needed to be absorbed outside of agriculture. At the same time, economic reforms induced foreign investment and encouraged urban consumption and services, both demanding cheap labor. In response, the government invented a variety of new permits and hukou statuses to facilitate the temporary migration of peasants, unleashing a floating population estimated to be anywhere between 20 million and 100 million by the mid-1990s. Marketization, decollectivization, and decentralization further undermined the state's role in labor allocation and engendered the emergence of labor markets in China. But the labor market is highly gendered and segmented. Young single peasant women are sought after, but upon marriage and childbirth most women stay in the villages to farm while their husbands may continue to engage in migrant work. In urban areas, peasant migrants are relegated to the bottom rungs and are generally blocked from prestigious and high-paying jobs.

Unlike the first three decades of the People's Republic, post-Mao China is marked by population relocations primarily from inland to coastal regions, high rates of rural-urban migration, increasing prominence of self-initiated moves that rely heavily on social networks, and in general a greater heterogeneity of migration types. But rural-rural migration continues to be important, especially since marriage migration remains the leading reason for female migration in China. The enormity of the population relocations, in conjunction with the legacies of social institutions such as the *hukou* system, have fostered new thoughts and debates on the social and economic implications of migration. Topics under discussion include the emergence of new social classes in Chinese cities, segmentation of the labor market, the impact of migrants on urban services, gendered division of labor in peasant households, and the feminization of agriculture.

C. Cindy Fan

Further Reading

Chan, Kam Wing, and Li Zhang. (1999) "The *Hukou* System and Rural-Urban Migration in China: Processes and Changes." *China Quarterly* 160: 818–55.

Chen, Cheng-Siang. (1980) *A Geographical Atlas of China.* Hong Kong: Cosmos Books.

Davin, Delia. (1999) *Internal Migration in Contemporary China.* London: Macmillan.

Fan, C. Cindy. (1999) "Migration in a Socialist Transitional Economy: Heterogeneity, Socioeconomic and Spatial Characteristics of Migrants in China and Guangdong Province." *International Migration Review* 33(4): 950–983.

———. (2000) "Migration and Gender in China." In *China Review 2000*, edited by Chung-Ming Lau and Jianfa Shen. Hong Kong: Chinese University Press.

———, and Youqin Huang. (1998) "Waves of Rural Brides: Female Marriage Migration in China." *Annals of the Association of American Geographers* 88(2): 227–251.

Solinger, Dorothy J. (1999) *Contesting Citizenship in Urban China: Peasant Migrants, the State, and the Logic of the Market.* Berkeley and Los Angeles: University of California Press.

Wang, Gabe T. (1999) *China's Population: Problems, Thoughts and Policies.* Aldershot, U.K.: Ashgate.

Yang, Yunyan. (1994) *Zhongguo Renkou Qianyi Yu Fanzhan Di Chanqi Zhanlue?* (Long-Term Strategies of Population Migration and Development in China). Wuhan, China: Wuhan Chubanshe.

BELARUS

UKRAINE

MOLDOVA

ROMANIA

BULGARIA

Black Sea

Istanbul

GREECE

Ankara

TURKEY

Adana

GEORGIA

Caucasus Mts.

T'bilisi

ARMENIA

Yerevan

AZERBAIJAN

Baku

Caspian Sea

KAZAKHSTAN

Astana

Aral Sea

Syr Dar'ya

Amu Dar'ya

Kara Kum

Lake Balkash

Almaty

Bishkek

Tashkent

UZBEKISTAN

Fergana Valley

KYRGYZSTAN

Tian Sh

Taklimaka Desert

TURKMENISTAN

Ashgabat

Dushanbe

TAJIKISTAN

Pamirs

Tehran

IRAN

Nicosia

CYPRUS

SYRIA

LEBANON

ISRAEL

JORDAN

Tigris

Euphrates

Baghdad

IRAQ

Zagros Mountains

KUWAIT

Persian Gulf

EGYPT

SAUDI ARABIA

QATAR

UNITED ARAB EMIRATES

OMAN

Red Sea

ERITREA

SUDAN

YEMEN

DJIBOUTI

SOMALIA

ETHIOPIA

UGANDA

KENYA

RWANDA

BURUNDI

DEMOCRATIC

REPUBLIC

OF THE CONGO

TANZANIA

ZAMBIA

ZIMBABWE

MOZAMBIQUE

MADAGASCAR

AFGHANISTAN

Kabul

Peshawar

Islamabad

Lahore

PAKISTAN

New Delhi

Karachi

Jammu and Kashmir

Indus River

Himalaya

NEPA

Kathm

Ganges River

INDIA

Mumbai

Arabian Sea

Madras

SRI LANK

Colombo

Lakshadweep

MALDIVES

Male

N

MAURITIUS

Port Louis

Réunion

INDIAN

R

0	500	1000 Miles
0	500	1000 Kilometers

60°E

MAP 2 5 2004